GONGDIRMG - GINGER

MOCODAM - MOCODAMIA

Oxford Colour French Dictionary Plus

Second Edition

FRENCH–ENGLISH
ENGLISH–FRENCH

FRANÇAIS–ANGLAIS
ANGLAIS–FRANÇAIS

OXFORD
UNIVERSITY PRESS

Great Clarendon Street, Oxford OX2 6DP

Oxford University Press is a department of the University of Oxford.
It furthers the University's objective of excellence in research, scholarship, and education by publishing worldwide in

Oxford New York

Auckland Bangkok Buenos Aires Cape Town Chennai
Dar es Salaam Delhi Hong Kong Istanbul Karachi Kolkata
Kuala Lumpur Madrid Melbourne Mexico City Mumbai Nairobi
São Paulo Shanghai Taipei Tokyo Toronto

Oxford is a registered trade mark of Oxford University Press in the UK and in certain other countries

Published in the United States
by Oxford University Press Inc., New York

First published 1995 as The Oxford Colour French Dictionary
Revised edition published 1998
Second edition published 2001

British Library Cataloguing in Publication Data

Data available

Library of Congress Cataloging in Publication Data

Data available

ISBN 0–19–864560–0
ISBN 0–19–864564–3 (US edition)

10 9 8 7 6 5 4

Typeset by Tradespools Ltd
Printed in Spain by Book Print S. L.

Contents

Preface

The *Oxford Colour French Dictionary Plus* is a dictionary designed primarily for students of French. The clear presentation and colour headwords make it easily accessible. It contains completely new sections, not found in the *Oxford Colour French Dictionary*, on French life and culture, letter-writing, and French grammar, making it even more useful for students up to intermediate level.

List of contributors

Second Edition

Editors:

Marianne Chalmers
Rosalind Combley
Catherine Roux
Laura Wedgeworth

Supplementary Material:

Marianne Chalmers
Martine Pierquin
Glynnis Chantrell
Valerie Grundy
Natalie Pomier

Proof-reading:

Andrew Hodgson

First Edition

Editors:

Michael Janes
Dora Latiri-Carpenter
Edwin Carpenter

Introduction

This dictionary is designed as an effective and practical reference tool for the student, adult learner, traveller, and business professional. It provides user-friendly treatment of core vocabulary across a broad spectrum of written and spoken language.

Enhanced coverage

The wordlist of the previous edition has been comprehensively revised to reflect recent additions to both languages and to cover such topics as **computing** and the **Internet**.

A further new feature of the dictionary is the special status given to more complex grammatical words which provide the basic structure of both languages. These ***function words*** are given a special layout to make them instantly accessible and offer clearly presented translation options and examples, with **short usage notes** to warn of possible pitfalls.

Coverage of verbs has been significantly extended so that all **French verbs** in the text are cross-referenced to the appropriate section of the expanded verb tables. Examples of the three main French verb groups, as well as *avoir* and *être*, are conjugated in the most commonly used tenses. A quick **reference guide** giving the English translation of an example verb in the principal tenses has been included, followed by exemplified guidance on **how to conjugate a reflexive verb**.

Easy reference

The dictionary layout has been designed to be **clear**, streamlined, and easy to consult. The wordlist has been fully **alphabetized**, with all English compounds and French hyphenated compounds in their correct alphabetical positions. **Bullet points** separate each new part of speech within an entry, making it easy to scan. Nuances of sense or usage are pinpointed by semantic indicators (in condensed type in round brackets) or by typical collocates (*in italics in round brackets*) with which the word frequently occurs, quickly guiding the user to the appropriate translation. Extra help is given in the form of **symbols** to mark the register of language unambiguously. An exclamation mark ! indicates colloquial language and a cross ✱ indicates slang.

Each headword is followed by its **phonetic transcription** between slashes, except in the case of English compound headwords where the pronunciation can be derived from that of each of the component parts. The symbols used for the pronunciation are those of the International Phonetic Alphabet. Any unpredictable plural forms or irregular English conjugations, comparative and superlative forms are also given in brackets.

This dictionary is designed to present essential information in an accessible format, providing the user with a fast track to **clear and effective communication**.

Proprietary terms

The pronunciation of French

Vowels

a	*as in*	patte	/pat/	ɑ	*as in*	pâte	/pɑt/
ɑ̃		clan	/klɑ̃/	e		dé	/de/
ɛ		belle	/bɛl/	ɛ̃		lin	/lɛ̃/
ə		demain	/dəmɛ̃/	i		gris	/gʀi/
o		gros	/gʀo/	ɔ		corps	/kɔʀ/
ɔ̃		long	/lɔ̃/	œ		leur	/lœʀ/
œ̃		brun	/bʀœ̃/	ø		deux	/dø/
u		fou	/fu/	y		pur	/pyʀ/

Semi-Vowels

j	*as in*	fille	/fij/
ɥ		huit	/ɥit/
w		oui	/wi/

Consonants

Aspiration of 'h'

Where it is impossible to make a liason this is indicated by /'/ immediately after the slash e.g. *haine* /'ɛn/.

b	*as in*	bal	/bal/	ŋ	*as in*	camping	/kɑ̃piŋ/
d		dent	/dɑ̃/	p		porte	/pɔʀt/
f		foire	/fwar/	ʀ		rire	/ʀiʀ/
g		gomme	/gɔm/	s		sang	/sɑ̃/
k		clé	/kle/	ʃ		chien	/ʃjɛ̃/
l		lien	/ljɛ̃/	t		train	/tʀɛ̃/
m		mer	/mɛʀ/	v		voile	/vwal/
n		nage	/naʒ/	z		zèbre	/zɛbʀ/
ɲ		gnon	/ɲɔ̃/	ʒ		jeune	/ʒœn/

Glossary of grammatical terms

Abbreviation A shortened form of a word or phrase made by leaving out some letters or by using only the initial letter of each word: **etc., DNA**

Active In the active form the subject of the verb performs the action: **she whistled = elle a sifflé**

Adjective A word describing a noun: **a *red* pencil = un crayon *rouge***

Adverb A word that describes or changes the meaning of a verb, an adjective, or another adverb: **he drives *fast* = il conduit *vite*; *fairly* often = *assez* souvent**

Article The definite article, **the = le, la, l', les**, and indefinite article, **a/an = un, une**, are used in front of a noun

Attributive An adjective or noun is attributive when it is used directly before a noun: **the *big* dog = le *grand* chien; *birthday* card = carte d'anniversaire**

Auxiliary verb One of the verbs used to form the perfect, pluperfect, and future perfect tenses. In French the auxiliary verbs are **avoir** and **être**: **I have read the letter = j'*ai* lu la lettre; he had already gone = il *était* déjà parti**

Cardinal number A whole number representing a quantity: **one, two, three = un/une, deux, trois**

Clause A self-contained section of a sentence that contains a subject and a verb

Collective noun A noun that is singular in form but refers to a group of persons or things, e.g. **royalty, grain**

Collocate A word that regularly occurs with another; in French **livre** is a typical collocate of the verb **lire**

Comparative The form of an adjective or adverb for comparing two or more nouns or pronouns, often using **more**, **less** or **as (plus, moins, aussi)**: **smaller = plus petit; more frequently = plus fréquemment; as intelligent = aussi intelligent**

Compound adjective An adjective formed from two separate words : **tout-puissant = all-powerful; nord-américain = North American**

Compound noun A noun formed from two or more separate words: **porte-clés = keyring**

Conditional tense A tense of a verb that expresses what would happen if something else occurred: **I would invite them = je les inviterais**

Conjugation Variation of the form of a verb to show tense, person, mood, etc.

Conjunction A word used to link clauses: **and = et, because = parce que**

Definite article: **the = le, la, l', les**

Demonstrative pronoun A pronoun indicating the person or thing referred to: ***this one* is cheaper = *celui-ci* est moins cher**

Determiner A word that comes before a noun to show how it is being used: **the = le, la, l', les; some = du/de l'/de la/des; my = mon/ma/mes**

Direct object the noun or pronoun directly affected by the verb: **she ate *the apple* = elle a mangé *la pomme***

Direct speech A speaker's actual words or the use of these in writing

Ending Letters added to the stem of verbs, as well as to nouns and adjectives, according to tense, number, gender

Exclamation A sound, word, or remark expressing a strong feeling such as anger, fear, or joy: **ouch! = aïe!**

Feminine One of the two noun genders in French: **la femme = the woman; la carte = the card**

Future tense The tense of a verb that refers to something that will happen in the future: **I will go = j'irai**

Gender One of the two groups of nouns in French: masculine and feminine

Imperative A form of a verb that expresses a command: **hurry up! = dépêche-toi!**

Imperfect tense The tense of a verb that refers to an uncompleted or a habitual action in the past: **I went there every day = j'y allais tous les jours**

Impersonal verb A verb used in English only with **'it'** and in French only with **'il': it is raining = il pleut**

Indefinite article: a/an = un, une

Indefinite pronoun A pronoun that does not identify a specific person or object: **one = on; something = quelque chose**

Indicative form The form of a verb used when making a statement of fact or asking questions of fact: **we like animals = nous aimons les animaux**

Indirect object The noun or pronoun indirectly affected by the verb, at which the direct object is aimed: **she gave *him* the key = elle *lui* a donné la clé**

Indirect speech A report of what someone has said which does not reproduce the exact words

Infinitive The basic part of a verb: **to play = jouer**

Inflect To change the ending or form of a word to show its tense or its grammatical relation to other words: **donne** and **donnez** are inflected forms of the verb **donner**

Interrogative pronoun A pronoun that asks a question: **who? = qui?**

Intransitive verb A verb that does not have a direct object: **he died yesterday = il est mort hier**

Invariable adjective An adjective that has the same form in the feminine as the masculine, as French **ivoire, transmanche**

Invariable noun A noun that has the same form in the plural as the singular as. English **sheep, species,** French **précis, rabais**

Irregular verb A verb that does not follow one of the set patterns and has its own individual forms, e.g. English **to be**, French **être**

Masculine One of the two noun genders in French: **le garçon = the boy; le livre = the book**

Modal verb A verb that is used with another verb to express permission, obligation, possibility, such as **might, should.** The French modal verbs are **devoir, pouvoir, savoir, vouloir, falloir**

Negative Expressing refusal or denial: **there aren't any = il n'y en a pas; he won't go = il ne veut pas partir**

Noun A word that names a person or thing

Number The state of being either singular or plural

Object The word or group of words which is immediately affected by the action indicated by the verb, as **livre** in **il a lu le livre,** or **voiture** in **elle lave la voiture**

Ordinal number A number that shows the position of a person or thing in a series: **the *third* time = la *troisième* fois, the *fourth* door on the left = la *quatrième* porte à gauche**

Part of speech A grammatical term for the function of a word; noun, verb, adjective, etc., are parts of speech

Passive In the passive form the subject of the verb experiences the action rather than performs it: **he was punished = il a été puni**

Past participle The part of a verb used to form past tenses: **she had *gone* = elle était *partie***

Perfect tense The tense of a verb that refers to an action that has taken place in a period of time that includes the present: **I have already eaten = j'ai déjà mangé; my bike has been stolen = on m'a volé mon vélo**

Person Any of the three groups of personal pronouns and forms taken by verbs. In the singular the **first person** (e.g. **I/je**) refers to the person speaking; **the second person** (e.g. **you/tu**) refers to the person spoken to; the **third person** (e.g. **he, she, it/il, elle**) refers to the person spoken about. The corresponding plural forms are **we/nous, you/vous, they/ils, elles**

Personal pronoun A pronoun that refers to a person or thing

Phrasal verb A verb in English combined with a preposition or an adverb to have a particular meaning: **run away = se sauver**

Phrase A self-contained section of a sentence that does not contain a full verb

Pluperfect tense The tense of a verb that refers to something that happened before a particular point in the past: **when I arrived, he *had* already *left* = quand je suis arrivé, il *était* déjà *parti***

Plural Of nouns, etc., referring to more than one: **the children = les enfants**

Possessive adjective An adjective that shows possession, belonging to someone or something: **my = mon/ma/mes**

Possessive pronoun a pronoun that shows possession, belonging to someone or something: **mine = le mien/la mienne/les miens/les miennes**

Predicative An adjective is predicative when it comes after a verb such as **be** or **become** in English, or after **être** or **devenir** in French: **she is beautiful = elle est belle**

Prefix A group of letters added to the beginning of a word to change its meaning, e.g. **anti-, ultra-, non-**

Preposition A word that stands in front of a noun or pronoun, usually indicating movement, position or time: ***on* the chair = *sur* la chaise; *towards* the car = *vers* la voiture**

Present participle The part of a verb in English that ends in **-ing**; the corresponding ending in French is **-ant**

Present tense The tense of a verb that refers to something happening now: **I make = je fais**

Pronoun A word that stands instead of a noun: **he = il, she = elle, mine = le mien/la mienne/ les miens/les miennes**

Proper noun A name of a person, place, institution etc. written with a capital letter at the start; **France, the Alps, Madeleine, l'Europe** are all proper nouns

Reflexive pronoun A pronoun that goes with a reflexive verb: in French **me, te, se, nous, vous, se**

Reflexive verb a verb whose object is the same as its subject. In French it is used with a reflexive pronoun and conjugated with **être**: **you should wash yourself = tu devrais te laver**

Regular verb A verb that follows a set pattern in its different forms

Relative pronoun A pronoun that introduces a subordinate clause, relating to a person or thing mentioned in the main clause: **the book *which* I chose = le livre *que* j'ai choisi**

Reported speech Another name for **Indirect speech**

Sentence A sequence of words, with a subject and a verb, that can stand on their own to make a statement, ask a question, or give a command

Singular Of nouns, etc., referring to just one: **the tree = l'arbre**

Stem The part of a verb to which endings are added; **donn-** is the stem of **donner**

Subject In a clause or sentence, the noun or pronoun that causes the action of the verb: ***he* caught the ball = *il* a attrapé le ballon**

Subjunctive A verb form that is used to express doubt or uncertainty in English. It is more widely used in French, particularly after certain conjunctions and with verbs of wishing, fearing, ordering, forbidding followed by **que**: **I want you to be good = je veux que tu sois sage; you may be right = il est possible que tu aies raison**

Subordinate clause A clause which adds information to the main clause of a sentence, but cannot function as a sentence by itself, e.g. **when it rang** in **she answered the phone when it rang**

Suffix A group of letters joined to the end of a word to form another word, as **-eur** in **grandeur** or **-able** in **véritable**

Superlative The form of an adjective or adverb that makes it the 'most' or 'least': **the *biggest* house = *la plus grande* maison; the *cheapest* CD = le CD *le moins cher***

Tense The form of a verb that tells when the action takes place: present, future, imperfect, perfect, pluperfect are all tenses

Transitive verb A verb that is used with a direct object: **I wrote the letter = j'ai écrit la lettre**

Verb A word or group of words that describes an action: **the children are playing = les enfants jouent**

Abbreviations/Abréviations

adjective	*a*	adjectif
abbreviation	*abbr, abrév*	abréviation
adverb	*adv*	adverbe
anatomy	*Anat*	anatomie
archeology	*Archeol, Archéol*	archéologie
architecture	*Archit*	architecture
motoring	*Auto*	automobile
auxiliary	*aux*	auxiliaire
aviation	*Aviat*	aviation
botany	*Bot*	botanique
commerce	*Comm*	commerce
computing	*Comput*	informatique
conjunction	*conj*	conjonction
cookery	*Culin*	culinaire
determiner	*det, dét*	déterminant
electricity	*Electr, Électr*	électricité
figurative	*fig*	sens figuré
geography	*Geog, Géog*	géographie
geology	*Geol, Géol*	géologie
grammar	*Gram*	grammaire
humorous	*hum*	humoristique
interjection	*interj*	interjection
invariable	*inv*	invariable
law	*Jur*	droit
linguistics	*Ling*	linguistique
literal	*lit*	littéral
phrase	*loc*	locution
medicine	*Med, Méd*	médecine
military	*Mil*	armée
music	*Mus*	musique
noun	*n*	nom
nautical	*Naut*	nautisme
feminine noun	*nf*	nom féminin
masculine noun	*nm*	nom masculin
masculine and feminine noun	*nm,f* or *nmf* or *nm/f*	nom masculin et féminin
computing	*Ordinat*	informatique

pejorative	*pej, péj*	péjoratif
philosophy	*Phil*	philosophie
photography	*Photo*	photographie
plural	*pl*	pluriel
politics	*Pol*	politique
possessive	*poss*	possessif
past participle	*pp*	participe passé
prefix	*pref, préf*	préfixe
preposition	*prep, prép*	préposition
present participle	*pres p*	participe présent
pronoun	*pron*	pronom
psychology	*Psych*	psychologie
past	*pt*	prétérit
something	*qch*	quelque chose
somebody	*qn*	quelqu'un
railway	*Rail*	chemin de fer
relative pronoun	*rel pron, pron rel*	pronom relatif
religion	*Relig*	religion
somebody	*sb*	quelqu'un
school	*School, Scol*	scolaire
sport	*Sport*	sport
something	*sth*	quelque chose
technology	*Tech*	technologie
theatre	*Theat, Théât*	théâtre
television	*TV*	télévision
university	*Univ*	université
American English	*US*	anglais américain
auxiliary verb	*v aux*	verbe auxiliaire
intransitive verb	*vi*	verbe intransitif
reflexive verb	*vpr*	verbe pronominal
transitive verb	*vt*	verbe transitif
transitive and intransitive verb	*vt/i*	verbe transitif et intransitif
translation equivalent	≈	équivalent approximatif
trademark	®	marque déposée
colloquial	[!]	familier
slang	[✖]	argot

a /a/ ⇒AVOIR [5].

à /a/ *préposition*

à+le = au
à+les = aux

....➤ (avec verbe de mouvement) to.

....➤ (pour indiquer où l'on se trouve) ~ **la maison** at home; ~ **Nice** in Nice.

....➤ (âge, date, heure) ~ **l'âge de...** at the age of...; **au XIXe siècle** in the 19th century; ~ **deux heures** at two o'clock.

....➤ (description) with; **aux yeux verts** with green eyes.

....➤ (appartenance) ~ **qui est ce stylo?** whose pen is this?; **c'est ~ vous?** is this yours?

....➤ (avec nombre) ~ **90 km/h** at 90 km per hour; ~ **10 minutes d'ici** 10 minutes from here; **des tomates ~ 3 francs le kilo** tomatoes at 3 francs a kilo; **un timbre ~ 3 francs** a 3-franc stamp; **nous avons fait le travail ~ deux** two of us did the work; **mener 5 ~ 4** to lead 5 (to) 4.

....➤ (avec être) **c'est ~ moi** it's my turn; **je suis ~ vous tout de suite** I'll be with you in a minute; **c'est ~ toi de décider** it's up to you to decide.

....➤ (hypothèse) ~ **ce qu'il paraît** apparently; ~ **t'entendre** to hear you talk.

....➤ (exclamatif) ~ **ta santé!** cheers!; ~ **demain/bientôt!** see you tomorrow/soon!

....➤ (moyen) ~ **la main** by hand; ~ **vélo** by bike; ~ **pied** on foot; **chauffage au gaz** gas heating.

abaissement /abɛsmɑ̃/ *nm* (de taux, de prix) cut; (de seuil) lowering.

abaisser /abese/ [1] *vt* lower; (*levier*) pull *ou* push down; (fig) humiliate. □ **s'~** *vpr* go down, drop; (fig) demean oneself; **s'~ à** stoop to.

abandon /abɑ̃dɔ̃/ *nm* abandonment; (de personne) desertion; (de course) withdrawal; (naturel) abandon; **à l'~** in a state of neglect.

abandonner /abɑ̃dɔne/ [1] *vt* abandon; (*épouse, cause*) desert; (renoncer à) give up, abandon; (céder) give (**à** to); (*course*) withdraw from; (Ordinat) abort. □ **s'~ à** *vpr* give oneself up to.

abasourdir /abazuʀdiʀ/ [2] *vt* stun.

abat-jour /abaʒuʀ/ *nm inv* lampshade.

abats /aba/ *nmpl* offal.

abattement /abatmɑ̃/ *nm* dejection; (faiblesse) exhaustion; (Comm) reduction; ~ **fiscal** tax allowance.

abattre /abatʀ/ [11] *vt* knock down; (*arbre*) cut down; (*animal*) slaughter; (*avion*) shoot down; (affaiblir) weaken; (démoraliser) demoralize. **ne pas se laisser ~** not let things get one down. □ **s'~** *vpr* come down, fall (down).

abbaye /abei/ *nf* abbey.

abbé /abe/ *nm* priest; (supérieur d'une abbaye) abbot.

abcès /apsɛ/ *nm* abscess.

abdiquer /abdike/ [1] *vt/i* abdicate.

abdomen /abdɔmɛn/ *nm* abdomen.

abdominal (*pl* **-aux**) /abdɔminal/ *a* abdominal. **abdominaux** *nmpl* (Sport) stomach exercises.

abeille /abɛj/ *nf* bee.

aberrant, **~e** /abɛʀɑ̃, -t/ *a* absurd.

abêtir /abetiʀ/ [2] *vt* turn into a moron.

abîme /abim/ *nm* abyss.

abîmer /abime/ [1] *vt* damage, spoil. □ **s'~** *vpr* get damaged *ou* spoilt.

ablation /ablasjɔ̃/ *nf* removal.

aboiement /abwamɑ̃/ *nm* bark, barking; **~s** barking.

abolir /abɔliʀ/ [2] *vt* abolish.

abondance /abɔ̃dɑ̃s/ *nf* abundance; (prospérité) affluence. **abondant**, **~e** *a* abundant, plentiful.

abonder /abɔ̃de/ [1] *vi* abound (en in); **~ dans le sens de qn** agree wholeheartedly with sb.

abonné, **~e** /abɔne/ *nm,f* (lecteur) subscriber; (voyageur, spectateur) season-ticket holder.

abonnement /abɔnmɑ̃/ *nm* (à un journal) subscription; (de bus, Théât) season-ticket; (au gaz) standing charge.

abonner (**s'**) /(s)abɔne/ [1] *vpr* subscribe (**à** to).

abord /abɔʀ/ *nm* access; **~s** surroundings; **d'~** first.

abordable /abɔʀdabl/ *a* (*prix*) affordable; (*personne*) approachable; (*texte*) accessible.

aborder /abɔʀde/ [1] *vt* approach; (*lieu*) reach; (*problème*) tackle. ● *vi* reach land.

aborigène /abɔʀiʒɛn/ *nm* aborigine.

aboutir /abutiʀ/ [2] *vi* succeed, achieve a result; **~ à** end (up) in, lead to; **n'~ à rien** come to nothing.

aboutissement /abutismɑ̃/ *nm* outcome; (de carrière, d'évolution) culmination.

aboyer /abwaje/ [31] *vi* bark.

abrégé /abʀeʒe/ *nm* summary.

abréger /abʀeʒe/ [14] [40] *vt* (*texte*) shorten, abridge; (*mot*) abbreviate, shorten; (*visite*) cut short.

abreuver /abʀœve/ [1] *vt* water; (fig) overwhelm (**de** with). □ **s'~** *vpr* drink.

abréviation /abʀevjasjɔ̃/ *nf* abbreviation.

abri /abʀi/ *nm* shelter; **à l'~** under cover; (en lieu sûr) safe; **à l'~ de** sheltered from; **se mettre à l'~** take shelter.

abricot /abʀiko/ *nm* apricot.

abriter /abʀite/ [1] *vt* shelter; (recevoir) house. □ **s'~** *vpr* (take) shelter.

abrupt, **~e** /abʀypt/ *a* steep, sheer; (fig) abrupt.

abruti, **~e** /abʀyti/ *nm,f* ⊡ idiot.

absence /apsɑ̃s/ *nf* absence; **il a des ~s** sometimes his mind goes blank.

absent, **~e** /apsɑ̃, -t/ *a* (*personne*) absent, away; (*chose*) missing; **il est toujours ~** he's still away; **d'un air ~** absently. ● *nm,f* absentee.

absenter (**s'**) /(s)apsɑ̃te/ [1] *vpr* go *ou* be away; (sortir) go out, leave.

absolu, **~e** /apsɔly/ *a* absolute.

absorbant, **~e** /apsɔʀbɑ̃, -t/ *a* (*travail*) absorbing; (*matière*) absorbent.

absorber /apsɔʀbe/ [1] *vt* absorb;

être absorbé par qch be engrossed in sth.

abstenir (s') /(s)apstəniʀ/ [58] *vpr* abstain; **s'~ de** refrain from.

abstrait, ~e /apstʀɛ, -t/ *a & nm* abstract.

absurde /apsyʀd/ *a* absurd.

abus /aby/ *nm* abuse, misuse; (injustice) abuse; **~ de confiance** breach of trust.

abuser /abyze/ [1] *vt* deceive. ● *vi* go too far; **~ de** abuse, misuse; (profiter de) take advantage of; (*alcool*) overindulge in. □ **s'~** *vpr* be mistaken.

abusif, -ive /abyzif, -v/ *a* excessive; (impropre) wrong; (injuste) unfair.

académie /akademi/ *nf* academy; (circonscription) local education authority.

acajou /akaʒu/ *nm* mahogany.

accablant, ~e /akablɑ̃, -t/ *a* (*chaleur*) oppressive; (*fait, témoignage*) damning.

accabler /akable/ [1] *vt* overwhelm; **~ d'impôts** burden with taxes; **~ d'injures** heap insults upon.

accéder /aksede/ [14] *vi* **~ à** (*lieu*) reach; (*pouvoir, trône*) accede to; (*requête*) grant; (Ordinat) access; **~ à la propriété** become a homeowner.

accélérateur /akseleʀatœʀ/ *nm* accelerator.

accélérer /akseleʀe/ [14] *vt/i* accelerate. □ **s'~** *vpr* speed up.

accent /aksɑ̃/ *nm* accent; (sur une syllabe) stress, accent; **mettre l'~ sur** stress; **~ aigu/grave/circonflexe** acute/grave/circumflex accent.

accentuer /aksɑ̃tɥe/ [1] *vt* (*lettre, syllabe*) accent; (fig) emphasize, accentuate. □ **s'~** *vpr* become more pronounced, increase.

accepter /aksɛpte/ [1] *vt* accept; **~ de faire** agree to do.

accès /aksɛ/ *nm* access; (porte) entrance; (de fièvre) bout; (de colère) fit; (d'enthousiasme) burst; (Ordinat) access; **les ~ de** (voies) the approaches to; **facile d'~** easy to get to.

accessoire /akseswaʀ/ *a* secondary, incidental. ● *nm* accessory; (Théât) prop.

accident /aksidɑ̃/ *nm* accident; **~ de train/d'avion** train/plane crash; **par ~** by accident.

accidenté, ~e *a* (*personne*) injured (in an accident); (*voiture*) damaged; (*terrain*) uneven, hilly.

accidentel, ~le *a* accidental.

acclamer /aklame/ [1] *vt* cheer, acclaim.

accommoder /akɔmɔde/ [1] *vt* adapt (**à** to); (cuisiner) prepare; (assaisonner) flavour. □ **s'~ de** *vpr* make the best of.

accompagnateur, -trice /akɔ̃paɲatœʀ, -tʀis/ *nm, f* (Mus) accompanist; (guide) guide; **~ d'enfants** accompanying adult.

accompagner /akɔ̃paɲe/ [1] *vt* accompany. □ **s'~ de** *vpr* be accompanied by.

accomplir /akɔ̃pliʀ/ [2] *vt* carry out, fulfil. □ **s'~** *vpr* take place, happen; (*vœu*) be fulfilled.

accord /akɔʀ/ *nm* agreement; (harmonie) harmony; (Mus) chord; **être d'~** agree (**pour** to); **se mettre d'~** come to an agreement, agree; **d'~!** all right!, OK!

accorder /akɔʀde/ [1] *vt* grant; (*couleurs*) match; (Mus) tune; (attribuer) (*valeur, importance*) assign. □ **s'~** *vpr* (se mettre d'accord) agree; (s'octroyer) allow oneself; **s'~ avec** (s'entendre avec) get on with.

accotement /akɔtmɑ̃/ *nm* verge; **~ non stabilisé** soft verge.

accouchement /akuʃmɑ̃/ *nm* childbirth; (travail) labour.

accoucher /akuʃe/ [1] *vi* give birth (**de** to); (être en travail) be in labour. ● *vt* deliver. **accoucheur** *nm* **médecin ∼** obstetrician.

accoudoir /akudwaʀ/ *nm* arm-rest.

accoupler /akuple/ [1] *vt* (Tech) couple. □ **s'∼** *vpr* mate.

accourir /akuʀiʀ/ [20] *vi* run up.

accoutumance /akutymɑ̃s/ *nf* familiarization; (Méd) addiction.

accoutumer /akutyme/ [1] *vt* accustom. □ **s'∼** *vpr* get accustomed.

accro /akʀo/ *nmf* ⊡ (drogué) addict; (amateur) fan.

accroc /akʀo/ *nm* tear, rip; (fig) hitch.

accrochage /akʀɔʃaʒ/ *nm* hanging; hooking; (Auto) collision; (dispute) clash; (Mil) encounter.

accrocher /akʀɔʃe/ [1] *vt* (suspendre) hang up; (attacher) hook, hitch; (déchirer) catch; (heurter) hit; (attirer) attract. □ **s'∼** *vpr* cling, hang on (**à** to); (se disputer) clash.

accroissement /akʀwasmɑ̃/ *nm* increase (**de** in).

accroître /akʀwɑtʀ/ [24] *vt* increase. □ **s'∼** *vpr* increase.

accroupir (s') /(s)akʀupiʀ/ [2] *vpr* squat.

accru, ∼e /akʀy/ *a* increased, greater.

accueil /akœj/ *nm* reception, welcome.

accueillant, ∼e /akœjɑ̃, -t/ *a* friendly, welcoming.

accueillir /akœjiʀ/ [25] *vt* receive, welcome; (*film, livre*) receive; (prendre en charge) (*réfugiés, patients*) take care of, cater for.

accumuler /akymyle/ [1] *vt* (*énergie*) store up; (*capital*) accumulate. □ **s'∼** *vpr* (*neige, ordures*) pile up; (*dettes*) accrue.

accusation /akyzasjɔ̃/ *nf* accusation; (Jur) charge; **l'∼** (magistrat) the prosecution.

accusé, ∼e /akyze/ *a* marked. ● *nm, f* defendant, accused.

accuser /akyze/ [1] *vt* accuse (**de** of); (blâmer) blame (**de** for); (Jur) charge (**de** with); (fig) emphasize; **∼ réception de** acknowledge receipt of.

acharné, ∼e /aʃaʀne/ *a* relentless, ferocious. **acharnement** *nm* (énergie) furious energy; (ténacité) determination.

acharner (s') /(s)aʃaʀne/ [1] *vpr* persevere; **s'∼ sur** set upon; (poursuivre) hound; **s'∼ à faire** (s'évertuer) try desperately; (s'obstiner) keep on doing.

achat /aʃa/ *nm* purchase; **∼s** shopping; **faire l'∼ de** buy; **faire des ∼s** do some shopping.

acheminer /aʃ(ə)mine/ [1] *vt* dispatch, convey; (*courrier*) handle. □ **s'∼ vers** *vpr* head for.

acheter /aʃ(ə)te/ [6] *vt* buy; **∼ qch à qn** (pour lui) buy sth for sb; (chez lui) buy sth from sb. **acheteur, -euse** *nm, f* buyer; (client de magasin) shopper.

achèvement /aʃɛvmɑ̃/ *nm* completion.

achever /aʃ(ə)ve/ [6] *vt* finish (off). □ **s'∼** *vpr* end.

acide /asid/ *a* acid, sharp. ● *nm* acid.

acier /asje/ *nm* steel.

acné /akne/ *nf* acne.

acompte /akɔ̃t/ *nm* deposit, part-payment.

à-côté (*pl* **∼s**) /akote/ *nm* side issue; **∼s** (argent) extras.

acoustique /akustik/ *nf* acoustics (+ *sg*). ● *a* acoustic.

acquéreur /akeʀœʀ/ *nm* purchaser, buyer.

acquérir /akeʀiʀ/ [7] *vt* acquire, gain; (*biens*) purchase, acquire.

acquis, ~e /aki, -z/ *a* acquired; (*fait*) established; **tenir qch pour ~** take sth for granted. ●*nm* experience. **acquisition** *nf* acquisition; purchase.

acquitter /akite/ [1] *vt* acquit; (*dette*) settle. □ **s'~ de** *vpr* (*promesse*) fulfil; (*devoir*) discharge.

âcre /ɑkʀ/ *a* acrid.

acrobatie /akʀɔbasi/ *nf* acrobatics (+ *pl*); **~ aérienne** aerobatics (+ *pl*).

acte /akt/ *nm* act, action, deed; (Théât) act; (Jur) deed; **~ de naissance/mariage** birth/marriage certificate; **~s** (compte rendu) proceedings; **prendre ~ de** note.

acteur /aktœʀ/ *nm* actor.

actif, -ive /aktif, -v/ *a* active; (*population*) working. ●*nm* (Comm) assets; **avoir à son ~** have to one's credit *ou* name.

action /aksjɔ̃/ *nf* action; (Comm) share; (Jur) action; (effet) effect; (initiative) initiative. **actionnaire** *nmf* shareholder.

activer /aktive/ [1] *vt* speed up; (*feu*) boost. □ **s'~** *vpr* hurry up; (s'affairer) be very busy.

activité /aktivite/ *nf* activity; **en ~** (*volcan*) active; (*fonctionnaire*) working; (*usine*) in operation.

actrice /aktʀis/ *nf* actress.

actualité /aktɥalite/ *nf* topicality; **l'~** current affairs; **les ~s** news; **d'~** topical.

actuel, ~le /aktɥɛl/ *a* current, present; (d'actualité) topical. **actuellement** *adv* currently, at the present time.

acupuncture /akypɔ̃ktyʀ/ *nf* acupuncture.

adaptateur /adaptatœʀ/ *nm* (Électr) adapter.

adapter /adapte/ [1] *vt* adapt; (fixer) fit. □ **s'~** *vpr* adapt (oneself); (Tech) fit.

additif /aditif/ *nm* (note) rider; (substance) additive.

addition /adisjɔ̃/ *nf* addition; (au café) bill; (US) check. **additionner** [1] *vt* add; (totaliser) add (up).

adepte /adɛpt/ *nmf* follower; (d'activité) enthusiast.

adéquat, ~e /adekwa, -t/ *a* suitable; (suffisant) adequate.

adhérent, ~e /adeʀɑ̃, -t/ *nm, f* member.

adhérer /adeʀe/ [14] *vi* adhere, stick (**à** to); **~ à** (*club*) be a member of; (s'inscrire à) join.

adhésif, -ive /adezif, -v/ *a* adhesive; **ruban ~** sticky tape.

adhésion /adezjɔ̃/ *nf* membership; (soutien) support.

adieu (*pl* **~x**) /adjø/ *interj & nm* goodbye, farewell.

adjectif /adʒɛktif/ *nm* adjective.

adjoint, ~e /adʒwɛ̃, -t/ *nm, f* assistant; **~ au maire** deputy mayor. ●*a* assistant.

adjuger /adʒyʒe/ [40] *vt* award; (aux enchères) auction. □ **s'~** *vpr* take (for oneself).

admettre /admɛtʀ/ [42] *vt* let in, admit; (tolérer) allow; (reconnaître) admit, acknowledge; (*candidat*) pass.

administrateur, -trice /administʀatœʀ, -tʀis/ *nm, f* administrator, director; (Jur) trustee; **~ de site Internet** Webmaster.

administratif, -ive /administʀatif, -v/ *a* administrative; (*document*) official. **administration** *nf* administration; (gestion) management; **l'A~** Civil Service.

administrer /administʀe/ [1] *vt* run, manage; (*justice, biens, antidote*) administer.

admirateur, -trice /admiʀatœʀ, -tʀis/ *nm,f* admirer.

admiration /admiʀasjɔ̃/ *nf* admiration.

admirer /admiʀe/ [1] *vt* admire.

admission /admisjɔ̃/ *nf* admission.

ADN *abrév m* (**acide désoxyribonucléique**) DNA.

adolescence /adɔlesɑ̃s/ *nf* adolescence. **adolescent, ~e** *nm,f* adolescent, teenager.

adopter /adɔpte/ [1] *vt* adopt. **adoptif, -ive** *a* (*enfant*) adopted; (*parents*) adoptive.

adorer /adɔʀe/ [1] *vt* love; (plus fort) adore; (Relig) worship, adore.

adosser /adɔse/ [1] *vt* lean (**à, contre** against). □ **s'~** *vpr* lean back (**à, contre** against).

adoucir /adusiʀ/ [2] *vt* soften; (*boisson*) sweeten; (*chagrin*) ease. □ **s'~** *vpr* soften; (*chagrin*) ease; (*temps*) become milder. **adoucissant** *nm* (fabric) softener.

adresse /adʀɛs/ *nf* address; (habileté) skill; **~ électronique** e-mail address.

adresser /adʀese/ [1] *vt* send; (écrire l'adresse sur) address; (*remarque*) address; **~ la parole à** speak to. □ **s'~ à** *vpr* address; (aller voir) (*personne*) go and ask *ou* see; (*bureau*) enquire at; (viser, intéresser) be directed at.

adroit, ~e /adʀwa, -t/ *a* skilful, clever.

adulte /adylt/ *nmf* adult. ● *a* adult; (*plante, animal*) fully-grown.

adultère /adyltɛʀ/ *a* adulterous. ● *nm* adultery.

adverbe /advɛʀb/ *nm* adverb.

adversaire /advɛʀsɛʀ/ *nmf* opponent, adversary.

aérer /aeʀe/ [1] *vt* air; (*texte*) space out. □ **s'~** *vpr* get some air.

aérien, ~ne /aeʀjɛ̃, -jɛn/ *a* air; (*photo*) aerial; (*câble*) overhead.

aérobic /aeʀɔbik/ *nm* aerobics (+ *sg*).

aérogare /aeʀɔgaʀ/ *nf* air terminal.

aéroglisseur /aeʀɔglisœʀ/ *nm* hovercraft.

aérogramme /aeʀɔgʀam/ *nm* airmail letter; (US) aerogram.

aéronautique /aeʀɔnotik/ *a* aeronautical. ● *nf* aeronautics (+ *sg*).

aéroport /aeʀɔpɔʀ/ *nm* airport.

aérospatial, ~e (*mpl* **-iaux**) /aeʀɔspasjal, -jo/ *a* aerospace.

affaiblir /afebliʀ/ [2] *vt* weaken. □ **s'~** *vpr* get weaker.

affaire /afɛʀ/ *nf* affair, matter; (Jur) case; (histoire, aventure) affair; (occasion) bargain; (entreprise) business; (transaction) deal; (question, problème) matter; **~s** (Comm) business; (Pol) affairs; (problèmes personnels) business; (effets personnels) things; **c'est mon ~** that's my business; **avoir ~ à** deal with; **ça fera l'~** that will do the job; **ça fera leur ~** that's just what they need; **tirer qn d'~** help sb out of a tight spot; **se tirer d'~** get out of trouble.

affairé, ~e /afeʀe/ *a* busy.

affaisser (s') /(s)afese/ [1] *vpr* (*terrain, route*) sink, subside; (*poutre*) sag; (*personne*) collapse.

affamé, ~e /afame/ *a* starving.

affectation /afɛktasjɔ̃/ *nf* (nomination) (à une fonction) appointment; (dans un lieu) posting; (de matériel, d'argent) allocation; (comportement) affectation.

affecter /afɛkte/ [1] *vt* (feindre) affect; (toucher, affliger) affect; (destiner) assign; (nommer) appoint, post.

affectif, -ive /afɛktif, -v/ *a* emotional.

A

affection /afɛksjɔ̃/ *nf* affection; (maladie) complaint.

affectueux, -euse /afɛktɥø, -z/ *a* affectionate.

affichage /afiʃaʒ/ *nm* billposting; (électronique) display.

affiche /afiʃ/ *nf* (public) notice; (publicité) poster; (Théât) bill; **être à l'~** (*film*) be showing; (*pièce*) be on.

afficher /afiʃe/ [1] *vt* (*annonce*) put up; (*événement*) announce; (*sentiment*) display; (Ordinat) display.

affirmatif, -ive /afiʀmatif, -v/ *a* affirmative. **affirmation** *nf* assertion.

affirmer /afiʀme/ [1] *vt* assert; (soutenir) maintain.

affligé, ~e /afliʒe/ *a* distressed; **~ de** afflicted with.

affluer /aflye/ [1] *vi* flood in; (*sang*) rush.

affolant, ~e /afɔlɑ̃, -t/ *a* alarming.

affoler /afɔle/ [1] *vt* throw into a panic. □ **s'~** *vpr* panic.

affranchir /afʀɑ̃ʃiʀ/ [2] *vt* stamp; (à la machine) frank; (*esclave*) emancipate; (fig) free. **affranchissement** *nm* (tarif) postage.

affreux, -euse /afʀø, -z/ *a* (laid) hideous; (mauvais) awful.

affrontement /afʀɔ̃tmɑ̃/ *nm* confrontation.

affronter /afʀɔ̃te/ [1] *vt* confront. □ **s'~** *vpr* confront each other.

affûter /afyte/ [1] *vt* sharpen.

afin /afɛ̃/ *prép & conj* **~ de faire** in order to do; **~ que** so that.

africain, ~e /afʀikɛ̃, -ɛn/ *a* African. **A~, ~e** *nm, f* African.

Afrique /afʀik/ *nf* Africa; **~ du Sud** South Africa.

agacer /agase/ [10] *vt* irritate, annoy.

âge /ɑʒ/ *nm* age; (vieillesse) (old) age; **quel ~ avez-vous?** how old are you?; **~ adulte** adulthood; **~ mûr** maturity; **d'un certain ~** middle-aged.

âgé, ~e /ɑʒe/ *a* elderly; **~ de cinq ans** five years old.

agence /aʒɑ̃s/ *nf* agency, bureau, office; (succursale) branch; **~ d'interim** employment agency; **~ de voyages** travel agency; **~ publicitaire** advertising agency.

agenda /aʒɛ̃da/ *nm* diary; **~ électronique** electronic organizer.

agent /aʒɑ̃/ *nm* agent; (fonctionnaire) official; **~ (de police)** policeman; **~ de change** stockbroker; **~ commercial** sales representative.

agglomération /aglɔmeʀasjɔ̃/ *nf* town, built-up area.

aggraver /agʀave/ [1] *vt* aggravate, make worse. □ **s'~** *vpr* get worse.

agile /aʒil/ *a* agile, nimble.

agir /aʒiʀ/ [2] *vi* act; (se comporter) behave; (avoir un effet) work, take effect. □ **s'~ de** *vpr* (être nécessaire) **il s'agit de faire** we/you *etc.* must do; (être question de) **il s'agit de faire** it is a matter of doing; **dans ce livre il s'agit de** this book is about; **dont il s'agit** in question; **il s'agit de ton fils** it's about your son; **de quoi s'agit-il?** what is it about?

agitation /aʒitasjɔ̃/ *nf* bustle; (trouble) agitation; (malaise social) unrest.

agité, ~e /aʒite/ *a* restless, fidgety; (troublé) agitated; (*mer*) rough.

agiter /aʒite/ [1] *vt* (*bras, mouchoir*) wave; (*liquide, boîte*) shake; (troubler) agitate; (discuter) debate. □ **s'~** *vpr* bustle about; (*enfant*) fidget; (*foule, pensées*) stir.

agneau (*pl* **~x**) /aɲo/ *nm* lamb.

agrafe /agʀaf/ *nf* hook; (pour

papiers) staple. **agrafeuse** *nf* stapler.

agrandir /agʀɑ̃diʀ/ [2] *vt* enlarge; (*maison*) extend. □ **s'∼** *vpr* expand, grow. **agrandissement** *nm* extension; (de photo) enlargement.

agréable /agʀeabl/ *a* pleasant.

agréé, **∼e** /agʀee/ *a* (*agence*) authorized; (*nourrice, médecin*) registered; (*matériel*) approved.

agréer /agʀee/ [15] *vt* accept; **∼ à** please; **veuillez ∼, Monsieur, mes salutations distinguées** (personne non nommée) yours faithfully; (personne nommée) yours sincerely.

agrégation /agʀegasjɔ̃/ *nf highest examination for recruitment of teachers*. **agrégé, ∼e** *nm, f* teacher (*who has passed the agrégation*).

agrément /agʀemɑ̃/ *nm* charm; (plaisir) pleasure; (accord) assent.

agresser /agʀese/ [1] *vt* attack; (pour voler) mug.

agressif, **-ive** /agʀesif, -v/ *a* aggressive. **agression** *nf* attack; (pour voler) mugging; (Mil) aggression.

agricole /agʀikɔl/ *a* agricultural; (*ouvrier, produit*) farm. **agriculteur** *nm* farmer. **agriculture** *nf* agriculture, farming.

agripper /agʀipe/ [1] *vt* grab. □ **s'∼** *vpr* cling (**à** to).

agroalimentaire /agʀɔalimɑ̃tɛʀ/ *nm* food industry.

agrumes /agʀym/ *nmpl* citrus fruit(s).

ai /e/ ⇒**avoir** [5].

aide /ɛd/ *nf* help, assistance; (en argent) aid; **à l'∼ de** with the help of; **venir en ∼ à** help; **∼ à domicile** home help; **∼ familiale** mother's help; **∼ sociale** social security; (US) welfare. ●*nmf* assistant.

aide-mémoire *nm inv* handbook of key facts.

aider /ede/ [1] *vt/i* help, assist; (subventionner) aid, give aid to; **∼ à faire** help to do. □ **s' ∼ de** *vpr* use.

aïeul, **∼e** /ajœl/ *nm, f* grandparent.

aigle /ɛgl/ *nm* eagle.

aigre /ɛgʀ/ *a* sour, sharp; (fig) sharp.

aigrir /egʀiʀ/ [2] *vt* embitter. □ **s'∼** *vpr* turn sour; (*personne*) become embittered.

aigu, **∼ë** /egy/ *a* (*douleur, problème*) acute; (*objet*) sharp; (*voix*) shrill; (Mus) high(-pitched); (*accent*) acute.

aiguille /egɥij/ *nf* needle; (de montre) hand; (de balance) pointer; **∼ à tricoter** knitting needle.

aiguilleur /egɥijœʀ/ *nm* pointsman; **∼ du ciel** air traffic controller.

aiguiser /eg(ɥ)ize/ [1] *vt* sharpen; (fig) stimulate.

ail (*pl* **∼s** *ou* **aulx**) /aj, o/ *nm* garlic.

aile /ɛl/ *nf* wing.

ailier /elje/ *nm* winger; (US) end.

aille /aj/ ⇒ALLER [8].

ailleurs /ajœʀ/ *adv* elsewhere, somewhere else; **d'∼** besides, moreover; **nulle part ∼** nowhere else; **par ∼** moreover, furthermore; **partout ∼** everywhere else.

aimable /ɛmabl/ *a* kind.

aimant /ɛmɑ̃/ *nm* magnet.

aimer /eme/ [1] *vt* like; (d'amour) love; **j'aimerais faire** I'd like to do; **∼ bien** quite like; **∼ mieux** *ou* **autant** prefer.

aîné, **∼e** /ene/ *a* eldest; (de deux) elder. ●*nm, f* eldest (child); (premier de deux) elder (child); **∼s** elders; **il est mon ∼** he is older than me *ou* my senior.

A

ainsi /ɛ̃si/ *adv* like this, thus; (donc) so; **et ~ de suite** and so on; **pour ~ dire** so to speak, as it were; **~ que** as well as; (comme) as.

air /ɛʀ/ *nm* air; (mine) look, air; (mélodie) tune; **~ conditionné** air-conditioning; **avoir l'~** look, appear; **avoir l'~ de** look like; **avoir l'~ de faire** appear to be doing; **en l'~** (up) in the air; (*promesses*) empty; **prendre l'~** get some fresh air.

aire /ɛʀ/ *nf* area; **~ d'atterrissage** landing-strip; **~ de pique-nique** picnic area; **~ de repas** rest area; **~ de services** (motorway) services.

aisance /ɛzɑ̃s/ *nf* ease; (richesse) affluence.

aise /ɛz/ *nf* joy; **à l'~** (sur un siège) comfortable; (pas gêné) at ease; (fortuné) comfortably off; **mal à l'~** uncomfortable; ill at ease; **aimer ses ~s** like one's creature comforts; **mettre qn à l'~** put sb at ease; **se mettre à l'~** make oneself comfortable.

aisé, ~e /eze/ *a* easy; (fortuné) well-off.

aisselle /ɛsɛl/ *nf* armpit.

ait /ɛ/ ⇒AVOIR [5].

ajourner /aʒuʀne/ [1] *vt* postpone; (*débat, procès*) adjourn.

ajout /aʒu/ *nm* addition.

ajouter /aʒute/ [1] *vt* add (**à** to); **~ foi à** lend credence to. □ **s'~** *vpr* be added.

ajuster /aʒyste/ [1] *vt* adjust; (*cible*) aim at; (adapter) fit; **~ son coup** adjust one's aim.

alarme /alaʀm/ *nf* alarm; **donner l'~** raise the alarm.

alarmer /alaʀme/ [1] *vt* alarm. □ **s'~** *vpr* become alarmed (**de** at).

Albanie /albani/ *nf* Albania.

alcool /alkɔl/ *nm* alcohol; (eau de vie) brandy; **~ à brûler** methylated spirit. **alcoolique** *a & nmf* alcoholic. **alcoolisé, ~e** *a* (*boisson*) alcoholic. **alcoolisme** *nm* alcoholism.

alcootest /alkɔtɛst/ *nm* breath test; (appareil) Breathalyser®.

aléa /alea/ *nm* hazard. **aléatoire** *a* unpredictable, uncertain; (Ordinat) random.

alentours /alɑ̃tuʀ/ *nmpl* surroundings; **aux ~ de** (de lieu) around; (de chiffre, date) about, around.

alerte /alɛʀt/ *a* (*personne*) alert; (vif) lively. ● *nf* alert; **~ à la bombe** bomb scare. **alerter** [1] *vt* alert.

algèbre /alʒɛbʀ/ *nf* algebra.

Algérie /alʒeʀi/ *nf* Algeria.

algue /alg/ *nf* seaweed; **les ~s** (Bot) algae.

aliéné, ~e /aljene/ *nm, f* insane person.

aliéner /aljene/ [14] *vt* alienate; (céder) give up. □ **s'~** *vpr* alienate.

aligner /aliɲe/ [1] *vt* (*objets*) line up, make lines of; (*chiffres*) string together; **~ sur** bring into line with. □ **s'~** *vpr* line up; **s'~ sur** align oneself on.

aliment /alimɑ̃/ *nm* food.

alimentaire /alimɑ̃tɛʀ/ *a* (*industrie*) food; (*habitudes*) dietary; **produits ~s** foodstuffs.

alimentation /alimɑ̃tasjɔ̃/ *nf* feeding, supply(ing); (régime) diet; (aliments) food; **magasin d'~** grocery shop *ou* store.

alimenter /alimɑ̃te/ [1] *vt* feed; (fournir) supply; (fig) sustain. □ **s'~** *vpr* eat.

allaiter /alete/ [1] *vt* (*bébé*) breast-feed; (US) nurse; (*animal*) suckle.

allée /ale/ *nf* path, lane; (menant à une maison) drive(way); (dans un cinéma, magasin) aisle; (rue) road; **~s et venues** comings and goings.

allégé, **~e** /aleʒe/ *a* diet; (*beurre, yaourt*) low-fat.

alléger /aleʒe/ [14] [40] *vt* make lighter; (*fardeau, chargement*) lighten; (fig) (*souffrance*) alleviate.

allégresse /alegʀɛs/ *nf* gaiety, joy.

alléguer /alege/ [14] *vt* (*exemple*) invoke; (prétexter) allege.

Allemagne /almaɲ/ *nf* Germany.

allemand, **~e** /almɑ̃, -d/ *a* German. ● *nm* (Ling) German. **A~**, **~e** *nm, f* German.

aller /ale/ [8]

● *verbe auxiliaire*

····➤ **je vais l'appeler** I'm going to call him; **j'allais partir** I was about to leave; **va savoir!** who knows?; **~ en s'améliorant** be improving.

● *verbe intransitif*

····➤ (se déplacer) go; **allons-y!** let's go!; **allez!** come on!

····➤ (se porter) **comment allez-vous?, comment ça va?** how are you?; **ça va** (**bien**) I'm fine; **qu'est-ce qui ne va pas?** what's the matter?; **ça ne va pas la tête?** [!] are you mad? [!].

····➤ (mettre en valeur) **~ à qn** suit sb; **ça te va bien** it really suits you.

····➤ (convenir) **ça va ma coiffure?** is my hair OK?; **ça ne va pas du tout** that's no good at all.

□ **s'en aller** *verbe pronominal*

····➤ go; **va-t'en!** go away!; **ça ne s'en va pas** (*tache*) it won't come out.

● *nom masculin*

····➤ outward journey; **~ (simple)** single (ticket); (US) one-way (ticket); **~ retour** return (ticket); (US) round trip (ticket); **à l'~** on the way out.

allergie /alɛʀʒi/ *nf* allergy. **allergique** *a* allergic (**à** to).

alliance /aljɑ̃s/ *nf* alliance; (bague) wedding-ring; (mariage) marriage.

allier /alje/ [45] *vt* combine; (Pol) ally. □ **s'~** *vpr* combine; (Pol) form an alliance; (*famille*) become related (**à** to).

allô /alo/ *interj* hallo, hello.

allocation /alɔkasjɔ̃/ *nf* allowance; **~ chômage** unemployment benefit; **~s familiales** family allowance.

allonger /alɔ̃ʒe/ [40] *vt* lengthen; (*bras, jambe*) stretch (out); (coucher) lay down. □ **s'~** *vpr* get longer; (s'étendre) lie down; (s'étirer) stretch (oneself) out.

allouer /alwe/ [1] *vt* allocate; (*prêt*) grant.

allumer /alyme/ [1] *vt* (*bougie, gaz*) light; (*lampe, appareil*) turn on; (*pièce*) switch the light(s) on in; (fig) arouse. □ **s'~** *vpr* (*lumière, appareil*) come on.

allumette /alymɛt/ *nf* match.

allure /alyʀ/ *nf* speed, pace; (démarche) walk; (apparence) appearance; **à toute ~** at full speed; **avoir de l'~** have style; **avoir des ~s de** look like; **avoir une drôle d'~** be funny-looking.

allusion /alyzjɔ̃/ *nf* allusion (**à** to); (implicite) hint (**à** at); **faire ~ à** allude to; hint at.

alors /alɔʀ/ *adv* (à ce moment-là) then; (de ce fait) so; (dans ce cas-là) then; **ça ~!** well!; **et ~?** so what? ● *conj* **~ que** (pendant que) while; (tandis que) when, whereas.

alouette /alwɛt/ *nf* lark.

alourdir /aluʀdiʀ/ [2] *vt* weigh down; (rendre plus important) increase.

A

aloyau (*pl* **~x**) /alwajo/ *nm* sirloin.

Alpes /alp/ *nfpl* **les ~** the Alps.

alphabet /alfabɛ/ *nm* alphabet. **alphabétique** *a* alphabetical.

alphabétiser /alfabetize/ [1] *vt* teach to read and write.

alpinist /alpinist/ *nmf* mountaineer.

altérer /alteʀe/ [14] *vt* (*fait, texte*) distort; (abîmer) spoil; (donner soif à) make thirsty. □ **s'~** *vpr* deteriorate.

alternance /altɛʀnɑ̃s/ *nf* alternation; **en ~** alternately.

altitude /altityd/ *nf* altitude, height.

amabilité /amabilite/ *nf* kindness.

amaigrir /amegʀiʀ/ [2] *vt* make thin(ner).

amande /amɑ̃d/ *nf* almond; (d'un fruit à noyau) kernel.

amant /amɑ̃/ *nm* lover.

amarre /amaʀ/ *nf* (mooring) rope; **~s** moorings.

amas /amɑ/ *nm* heap, pile.

amasser /amɑse/ [1] *vt* amass, gather; (empiler) pile up. □ **s'~** *vpr* pile up; (*gens*) gather.

amateur /amatœʀ/ *nm* amateur; **~ de** lover of; **d'~** amateur; (péj) amateurish.

ambassade /ɑ̃basad/ *nf* embassy. **ambassadeur, -drice** *nm,f* ambassador.

ambiance /ɑ̃bjɑ̃s/ *nf* atmosphere. **ambiant, ~e** *a* surrounding.

ambigu, ~ë /ɑ̃bigy/ *a* ambiguous.

ambitieux, -ieuse /ɑ̃bisjø, -z/ *a* ambitious. **ambition** *nf* ambition.

ambulance /ɑ̃bylɑ̃s/ *nf* ambulance.

ambulant, ~e /ɑ̃bylɑ̃, -t/ *a* itinerant, travelling.

âme /ɑm/ *nf* soul; **~ sœur** soul mate.

amélioration /ameljɔʀasjɔ̃/ *nf* improvement.

améliorer /ameljɔʀe/ [1] *vt* improve. □ **s'~** *vpr* improve.

aménagement /amenaʒmɑ̃/ *nm* (de magasin) fitting out; (de grenier) conversion; (de territoire) development; (de cuisine) equipping.

aménager /amenaʒe/ [40] *vt* (*magasin*) fit out; (transformer) convert; (*territoire*) develop; (*cuisine*) equip.

amende /amɑ̃d/ *nf* fine; **faire ~ honorable** make amends.

amener /am(ə)ne/ [6] *vt* bring; (causer) bring about; **~ qn à faire** cause sb to do. □ **s'~** *vpr* [!] turn up.

amer, -ère /amɛʀ/ *a* bitter.

américain, ~e /ameʀikɛ̃, -ɛn/ *a* American. **A~, ~e** *nm,f* American.

Amérique /ameʀik/ *nf* America; **~ centrale/latine** Central/Latin America; **~ du Nord/Sud** North/South America.

amertume /amɛʀtym/ *nf* bitterness.

ami, ~e /ami/ *nm,f* friend; (amateur) lover; **un ~ des bêtes** an animal lover. ● *a* friendly.

amiable /amjabl/ *a* amicable; **à l'~** (*divorcer*) by mutual consent; (*se séparer*) on friendly terms; (*séparation*) amicable.

amical, ~e (*mpl* **-aux**) /amikal, -o/ *a* friendly.

amiral (*pl* **-aux**) /amiʀal, -o/ *nm* admiral.

amitié /amitje/ *nf* friendship; **~s** (en fin de lettre) kind regards; **prendre qn en ~** take a liking to sb.

amnistie /amnisti/ *nf* amnesty.

amoindrir /amwɛ̃dRiR/ [2] *vt* reduce.
amont: **en ~** /ɑ̃namɔ̃/ *loc* upstream.
amorcer /amɔRse/ [10] *vt* start; (*hameçon*) bait; (*pompe*) prime; (*arme à feu*) arm.
amortir /amɔRtiR/ [2] *vt* (*choc*) cushion; (*bruit*) deaden; (*dette*) pay off; **~ un achat** make a purchase pay for itself.
amortisseur /amɔRtisœR/ *nm* shock absorber.
amour /amuR/ *nm* love; **pour l'~ de** for the sake of.
amoureux, **-euse** /amuRø, -z/ *a* (*personne*) in love; (*relation, regard*) loving; (*vie*) love; **~ de qn** in love with sb. ● *nm, f* lover.
amour-propre /amuRpRɔpR/ *nm* self-esteem.
amphithéâtre /ɑ̃fiteɑtR/ *nm* amphitheatre; (d'université) lecture hall.
ampleur /ɑ̃plœR/ *nf* extent, size; (de vêtement) fullness; **prendre de l'~** spread, grow.
amplifier /ɑ̃plifje/ [45] *vt* amplify; (fig) expand, develop. □ **s'~** *vpr* (*son*) grow; (*scandale*) intensify.
ampoule /ɑ̃pul/ *nf* (électrique) bulb; (sur la peau) blister; (Méd) phial, ampoule.
amusant, **~e** /amyzɑ̃, -t/ *a* (*blague*) funny; (*soirée*) enjoyable, entertaining.
amuse-gueule /amyzgœl/ *nm inv* cocktail snack.
amusement /amyzmɑ̃/ *nm* amusement; (passe-temps) entertainment.
amuser /amyze/ [1] *vt* amuse; (détourner l'attention de) distract. □ **s'~** *vpr* enjoy oneself; (jouer) play.
amygdale /amidal/ *nf* tonsil.
an /ɑ̃/ *nm* year; **avoir dix ~s** be ten years old; **un garçon de deux ~s** a two-year-old boy; **à soixante ~s** at the age of sixty; **les moins de dix-huit ~s** under eighteens.
analogie /analɔʒi/ *nf* analogy.
analogue /analɔg/ *a* similar, analogous (**à** to).
analphabète /analfabɛt/ *a & nmf* illiterate.
analyse /analiz/ *nf* analysis; (Méd) test. **analyser** [1] *vt* analyse; (Méd) test.
ananas /anana(s)/ *nm* pineapple.
anarchie /anaRʃi/ *nf* anarchy.
anatomie /anatɔmi/ *nf* anatomy.
ancêtre /ɑ̃sɛtR/ *nm* ancestor.
anchois /ɑ̃ʃwa/ *nm* anchovy.
ancien, **~ne** /ɑ̃sjɛ̃, -jɛn/ *a* old; (de jadis) ancient; (*meuble*) antique; (précédent) former, ex-, old; (dans une fonction) senior; **~ combattant** veteran. ● *nm, f* senior; (par l'âge) elder. **anciennement** *adv* formerly. **ancienneté** *nf* age, seniority.
ancre /ɑ̃kR/ *nf* anchor; **jeter/lever l'~** cast/weigh anchor.
andouille /ɑ̃duj/ *nf* sausage (*filled with chitterlings*); (idiot ◻) fool; **faire l'~** fool around.
âne /ɑn/ *nm* donkey, ass; (imbécile ◻) dimwit ◻.
anéantir /aneɑ̃tiR/ [2] *vt* destroy; (exterminer) annihilate; (accabler) overwhelm.
anémie /anemi/ *nf* anaemia.
ânerie /ɑnRi/ *nf* stupid remark.
anesthésie /anɛstezi/ *nf* (opération) anaesthetic.
ange /ɑ̃ʒ/ *nm* angel; **aux ~s** in seventh heaven.
angine /ɑ̃ʒin/ *nf* throat infection.
anglais, **~e** /ɑ̃glɛ, -z/ *a* English. ● *nm* (Ling) English. **A~**, **~e** *nm, f* Englishman, Englishwoman.
angle /ɑ̃gl/ *nm* angle; (coin) corner.
Angleterre /ɑ̃glətɛR/ *nf* England.

A

anglophone /ɑ̃glɔfɔn/ *a* English-speaking. ● *nmf* English speaker.

angoissant, ~e /ɑ̃gwasɑ̃, -t/ *a* alarming; (effrayant) harrowing.

angoisse /ɑ̃gwas/ *nf* anxiety. **angoissé, ~e** *a* anxious. **angoisser** [1] *vi* worry.

animal (*pl* **-aux**) /animal, -o/ *nm* animal; **~ familier, ~ de compagnie** pet. ● *a* (*mpl* **-aux**) animal.

animateur, -trice /animatœʀ, -tʀis/ *nm, f* organizer, leader; (TV) host, hostess.

animation /animasjɔ̃/ *nf* liveliness; (affairement) activity; (au cinéma) animation; (activité dirigée) organized activity.

animé, ~e /anime/ *a* lively; (affairé) busy; (*être*) animate.

animer /anime/ [1] *vt* liven up; (*débat, atelier*) lead; (*spectacle*) host; (pousser) drive; (encourager) spur on. □ **s'~** *vpr* liven up.

anis /ani(s)/ *nm* (Culin) aniseed; (Bot) anise.

anneau (*pl* **~x**) /ano/ *nm* ring; (de chaîne) link.

année /ane/ *nf* year; **~ bissextile** leap year; **~ civile** calendar year.

annexe /anɛks/ *a* (*document*) attached; (*question*) related; (*bâtiment*) adjoining. ● *nf* (bâtiment) annexe; (US) annex; (document) appendix; (électronique) attachment. **annexer** [1] *vt* annex; (*document*) attach.

anniversaire /anivɛʀsɛʀ/ *nm* birthday; (d'un événement) anniversary. ● *a* anniversary.

annonce /anɔ̃s/ *nf* announcement; (publicitaire) advertisement; (indice) sign.

annoncer /anɔ̃se/ [10] *vt* announce; (prédire) forecast; (être l'indice de) herald. □ **s'~** *vpr* (*crise, tempête*) be brewing; **s'~ bien/mal** look good/bad. **annonceur** *nm* advertiser.

annuaire /anɥɛʀ/ *nm* year-book; **~ (téléphonique)** (telephone) directory.

annuel, ~le /anɥɛl/ *a* annual, yearly.

annulation /anylasjɔ̃/ *nf* cancellation; (de sanction, loi) repeal; (de mesure) abolition.

annuler /anyle/ [1] *vt* cancel; (*contrat*) nullify; (*jugement*) quash; (*loi*) repeal. □ **s'~** *vpr* cancel each other out.

anodin, ~e /anɔdɛ̃, -in/ *a* insignificant; (sans risques) harmless, safe.

anonymat /anɔnima/ *nm* anonymity; **garder l'~** remain anonymous. **anonyme** *a* anonymous.

anorexie /anɔʀɛksi/ *nf* anorexia.

anormal, ~e (*mpl* **-aux**) /anɔʀmal, -o/ *a* abnormal.

anse /ɑ̃s/ *nf* handle; (baie) cove.

Antarctique /ɑ̃taʀktik/ *nm* Antarctic.

antenne /ɑ̃tɛn/ *nf* aerial; (US) antenna; (d'insecte) antenna; (succursale) agency; (Mil) outpost; **à l'~** on the air; **~ chirurgicale** mobile emergency unit; **~ parabolique** satellite dish.

antérieur, ~e /ɑ̃teʀjœʀ/ *a* previous, earlier; (placé devant) front; **~ à** prior to.

antiaérien, ~ne /ɑ̃tiaeʀjɛ̃, -ɛn/ *a* anti-aircraft; **abri ~** air-raid shelter.

antiatomique /ɑ̃tiatɔmik/ *a* **abri ~** nuclear fall-out shelter.

antibiotique /ɑ̃tibjɔtik/ *nm* antibiotic.

anticipation /ɑ̃tisipasjɔ̃/ *nf* **d'~** (*livre, film*) science fiction; **par ~** in advance.

anticiper /ɑ̃tisipe/ [1] *vt* **~ (sur)**

anticipate; (effectuer à l'avance) bring forward.

anticorps /ɑ̃tikɔʀ/ *nm* antibody.

antidater /ɑ̃tidate/ [1] *vt* backdate, antedate.

antigel /ɑ̃tiʒɛl/ *nm* antifreeze.

Antilles /ɑ̃tij/ *nfpl* **les ~** the West Indies.

antipathique /ɑ̃tipatik/ *a* unpleasant.

antiquaire /ɑ̃tikɛʀ/ *nmf* antique dealer.

antiquité /ɑ̃tikite/ *nf* (objet) antique; **l'A~** antiquity.

antisémite /ɑ̃tisemit/ *a* anti-Semitic.

antiseptique /ɑ̃tisɛptik/ *a & nm* antiseptic.

antivol /ɑ̃tivɔl/ *nm* anti-theft device; (Auto) steering lock.

anxiété /ɑ̃ksjete/ *nf* anxiety.

anxieux, **-ieuse** /ɑ̃ksjø, -z/ *a* anxious. ● *nm, f* worrier.

août /u(t)/ *nm* August.

apaiser /apeze/ [1] *vt* calm down; (*colère, militant*) appease; (*douleur*) soothe; (*faim*) satisfy. □ **s'~** *vpr* (*tempête*) die down.

apathie /apati/ *nf* apathy. **apathique** *a* apathetic.

apercevoir /apɛʀsəvwaʀ/ [52] *vt* see. □ **s'~ de** *vpr* notice; **s'~ que** notice *ou* realize that.

aperçu /apɛʀsy/ *nm* (échantillon) glimpse, taste; (intuition) insight.

apéritif /apeʀitif/ *nm* aperitif, drink.

aphte /aft/ *nm* mouth ulcer.

apitoyer /apitwaje/ [31] *vt* move (to pity). □ **s'~** *vpr* **s'~ sur (le sort de) qn** feel sorry for sb.

aplanir /aplaniʀ/ [2] *vt* level; (fig) iron out.

aplatir /aplatiʀ/ [2] *vt* flatten (out). □ **s'~** *vpr* (s'immobiliser) flatten oneself.

aplomb /aplɔ̃/ *nm* balance; (fig) self-confidence; **d'~** (en équilibre) steady; **je ne suis pas bien d'~** [!] I don't feel very well.

apogée /apɔʒe/ *nm* peak.

apologie /apɔlɔʒi/ *nf* panegyric.

apostrophe /apɔstʀɔf/ *nf* apostrophe; (remarque) remark.

apothéose /apɔteoz/ *nf* high point; (d'événement) grand finale.

apparaître /apaʀɛtʀ/ [18] *vi* appear; **il apparaît que** it appears that.

appareil /apaʀɛj/ *nm* device; (électrique) appliance; (Anat) system; (téléphone) phone; (avion) plane; (Culin) mixture; (système administratif) apparatus; **~ (dentaire)** brace; (dentier) dentures; **~ (photo)** camera; **c'est Gabriel à l'~** it's Gabriel on the phone; **~ auditif** hearing aid; **~ électroménager** household electrical appliance.

appareiller /apaʀeje/ [1] *vi* (*navire*) cast off, put to sea.

apparemment /apaʀamɑ̃/ *adv* apparently.

apparence /apaʀɑ̃s/ *nf* appearance; **en ~** outwardly; (apparemment) apparently.

apparent, **~e** /apaʀɑ̃, -t/ *a* apparent; (visible) conspicuous.

apparenté, **~e** /apaʀɑ̃te/ *a* related; (semblable) similar.

apparition /apaʀisjɔ̃/ *nf* appearance; (spectre) apparition.

appartement /apaʀtəmɑ̃/ *nm* flat; (US) apartment.

appartenir /apaʀtəniʀ/ [58] *vi* belong (**à** to); **il lui appartient de** it is up to him to.

appât /apɑ/ *nm* bait; (fig) lure.

appauvrir /apovʀiʀ/ [2] *vt* impoverish. □ **s'~** *vpr* become impoverished.

appel /apɛl/ *nm* call; (Jur) appeal; (supplique) appeal, plea; (Mil) call-up; (US) draft; **faire ~** appeal; **faire ~ à** (recourir à) call on; (invoquer) appeal to; (évoquer) call up; (exiger) call for; **faire l'~** (Scol) call the register; (Mil) take a roll-call; **~ d'offres** (Comm) invitation to tender; **faire un ~ de phares** flash one's headlights.

appeler /aple/ [38] *vt* call; (téléphoner) phone, call; (nécessiter) call for; **en ~ à** appeal to; **appelé à** (destiné) destined for. □ **s'~** *vpr* be called; **il s'appelle Tim** his name is Tim *ou* he is called Tim.

appellation /apelasjɔ̃/ *nf* name, designation.

appendice /apɛ̃dis/ *nm* appendix. **appendicite** *nf* appendicitis.

appesantir /apəzɑtiʀ/ [2] *vt* weigh down. □ **s'~** *vpr* grow heavier; **s'~ sur** dwell upon.

appétissant, **~e** /apetisɑ̃, -t/ *a* appetizing.

appétit /apeti/ *nm* appetite; **bon ~!** enjoy your meal!

applaudir /aplodiʀ/ [2] *vt/i* applaud. **applaudissements** *nmpl* applause.

application /aplikasjɔ̃/ *nf* (soin) care; (de loi) (respect) application; (mise en œuvre) implementation; (Ordinat) application program.

appliqué, **~e** /aplike/ *a* (*travail*) painstaking; (*sciences*) applied; (*élève*) hard-working.

appliquer /aplike/ [1] *vt* apply; (*loi*) enforce. □ **s'~** *vpr* apply oneself (**à** to), take great care (**à faire** to do); **s'~ à** (concerner) apply to.

appoint /apwɛ̃/ *nm* support; **d'~** extra; **faire l'~** give the correct money.

apport /apɔʀ/ *nm* contribution.

apporter /apɔʀte/ [1] *vt* bring; (*aide, précision*) give; (causer) bring about.

appréciation /apʀesjasjɔ̃/ *nf* estimate, evaluation; (de monnaie) appreciation; (*jugement*) assessment.

apprécier /apʀesje/ [45] *vt* appreciate; (évaluer) assess; (*objet*) value, appraise.

appréhender /apʀeɑ̃de/ [1] *vt* dread, fear; (arrêter) apprehend.

apprendre /apʀɑ̃dʀ/ [50] *vt* learn; (être informé de) hear, learn; (de façon indirecte) hear of; **~ qch à qn** teach sb sth; (informer) tell sb sth; **~ à faire** learn to do; **~ à qn à faire** teach sb to do; **~ que** learn that; (être informé) hear that.

apprenti, **~e** /apʀɑ̃ti/ *nm,f* apprentice. **apprentissage** *nm* apprenticeship; (d'un sujet) learning.

apprêter /apʀete/ [1] *vt* prepare; (*bois*) prime; (*mur*) size. □ **s'~ à** *vpr* prepare to.

apprivoiser /apʀivwaze/ [1] *vt* tame.

approbation /apʀɔbasjɔ̃/ *nf* approval.

approchant, **~e** /apʀɔʃɑ̃, -t/ *a* close, similar.

approcher /apʀɔʃe/ [1] *vt* (*objet*) move near(er) (**de** to); (*personne*) approach; **~ de** get nearer *ou* closer to. ● *vi* approach. □ **s'~ de** *vpr* approach, move near(er) to.

approfondir /apʀɔfɔ̃diʀ/ [2] *vt* deepen; (fig) (*sujet*) go into sth in depth; (*connaissances*) improve.

approprié, **~e** /apʀɔpʀije/ *a* appropriate.

approprier (**s'**) /(s)apʀɔpʀije/ [45] *vpr* appropriate.

approuver /apʀuve/ [1] *vt* approve; (trouver louable) approve of; (soutenir) agree with.

approvisionner /apʀɔvizjɔne/ [1] *vt* supply (**en** with); (*compte en banque*) pay money into. □ **s'~** *vpr* stock up.

approximatif, **-ive** /apʀɔksimatif, -v/ *a* approximate.

appui /apɥi/ *nm* support; (de fenêtre) sill; (pour objet) rest; **à l'~ de** in support of; **prendre ~ sur** lean on.

appui-tête (*pl* **appuis-tête**) /apɥitɛt/ *nm* headrest.

appuyer /apɥije/ [31] *vt* lean, rest; (presser) press; (soutenir) support, back. ● *vi* **~ sur** press (on); (fig) stress. ▫ **s'~ sur** *vpr* lean on; (compter sur) rely on.

après /apʀɛ/ *prép* after; (au-delà de) after, beyond; **~ avoir fait** after doing; **~ tout** after all; **~ coup** after the event; **d'~** (selon) according to; (en imitant) from; (adapté de) based on. ● *adv* after (wards); (plus tard) later; **le bus d'~** the next bus. ● *conj* **~ qu'il est parti** after he left. **après-demain** *adv* the day after tomorrow. **après-guerre** (*pl* **~s**) *nm ou f* postwar period. **après-midi** *nm ou f inv* afternoon. **après-rasage** (*pl* **~s**) *nm* aftershave. **après-ski** *nm inv* moonboot. **après-vente** *a inv* after-sales.

a priori /apʀijɔʀi/ *adv* (à première vue) offhand, on the face of it; (sans réfléchir) out of hand. ● *nm* preconception.

à-propos /apʀɔpo/ *nm* timing, timeliness; (fig) presence of mind.

apte /apt/ *a* capable (**à** of); (ayant les qualités requises) suitable (**à** for); (en état) fit (**à** for).

aptitude /aptityd/ *nf* aptitude, ability.

aquarelle /akwaʀɛl/ *nf* watercolour.

aquatique /akwatik/ *a* aquatic; (Sport) water.

arabe /aʀab/ *a* Arab; (Ling) Arabic; (*désert*) Arabian. ● *nm* (Ling) Arabic. **A~** *nmf* Arab.

Arabie /aʀabi/ *nf* **~ Saoudite** Saudi Arabia.

arachide /aʀaʃid/ *nf* groundnut; **huile d'~** groundnut oil.

araignée /aʀeɲe/ *nf* spider.

arbitraire /aʀbitʀɛʀ/ *a* arbitrary.

arbitre /aʀbitʀ/ *nm* referee; (au cricket, tennis) umpire; (expert) arbiter; (Jur) arbitrator. **arbitrer** [1] *vt* (*match*) referee, umpire; (Jur) arbitrate in.

arbre /aʀbʀ/ *nm* tree; (Tech) shaft.

arbuste /aʀbyst/ *nm* shrub.

arc /aʀk/ *nm* (arme) bow; (courbe) curve; (voûte) arch; **~ de cercle** arc of a circle.

arc-en-ciel (*pl* **arcs-en-ciel**) /aʀkɑ̃sjɛl/ *nm* rainbow.

arche /aʀʃ/ *nf* arch; **~ de Noé** Noah's ark.

archéologie /aʀkeɔlɔʒi/ *nf* archaeology.

archevêque /aʀʃəvɛk/ *nm* archbishop.

architecte /aʀʃitɛkt/ *nmf* architect. **architecture** *nf* architecture.

Arctique /aʀktik/ *nm* Arctic.

ardent, ~e /aʀdɑ̃, -t/ *a* burning; (passionné) ardent; (*foi*) fervent. **ardeur** *nf* ardour; (chaleur) heat.

ardoise /aʀdwaz/ *nf* slate; **~ électronique** notepad computer.

arène /aʀɛn/ *nf* arena; **~s** amphitheatre; (pour corridas) bullring.

arête /aʀɛt/ *nf* (de poisson) bone; (bord) ridge.

argent /aʀʒɑ̃/ *nm* money; (métal) silver; **~ comptant** cash; **prendre pour ~ comptant** take at face value; **~ de poche** pocket money.

argenté, ~e /aʀʒɑ̃te/ *a* silver(y); (*métal*) (silver-)plated.

argenterie /aʀʒɑ̃tʀi/ *nf* silverware.

Argentine /aʀʒɑ̃tin/ *nf* Argentina.

argile /aʀʒil/ *nf* clay.

argot /aʀgo/ *nm* slang.

argument /aʀgymɑ̃/ *nm* argument; ~ **de vente** selling point. **argumenter** [1] *vi* argue.

aristocratie /aʀistɔkʀasi/ *nf* aristocracy.

arithmétique /aʀitmetik/ *nf* arithmetic. ● *a* arithmetical.

armature /aʀmatyʀ/ *nf* framework; (de tente) frame.

arme /aʀm/ *nf* arm, weapon; ~ **à feu** firearm; ~**s** (blason) coat of arms.

armée /aʀme/ *nf* army; ~ **de l'air** Air Force; ~ **de terre** Army.

armer /aʀme/ [1] *vt* arm; (*fusil*) cock; (*navire*) equip; (renforcer) reinforce; (Photo) wind on; ~ **de** (garnir de) fit with. □ **s'**~ **de** *vpr* arm oneself with.

armoire /aʀmwaʀ/ *nf* cupboard; (penderie) wardrobe; (US) closet; ~ **à pharmacie** medicine cabinet.

armure /aʀmyʀ/ *nf* armour.

arnaque /aʀnak/ *nf* ⓘ swindling; **c'est de l'**~ it's a swindle *ou* con ⓘ.

aromate /aʀɔmat/ *nm* herb, spice.

aromatisé, ~**e** /aʀɔmatize/ *a* flavoured.

arôme /aʀom/ *nm* aroma; (additif) flavouring.

arpenter /aʀpɑ̃te/ [1] *vt* pace up and down; (*terrain*) survey.

arqué, ~**e** /aʀke/ *a* arched; (*jambes*) bandy.

arrache-pied: **d'**~ /daʀaʃpje/ *loc* relentlessly.

arracher /aʀaʃe/ [1] *vt* pull out *ou* off; (*plante*) pull *ou* dig up; (*cheveux, page*) tear *ou* pull out; (par une explosion) blow off; ~ **à** (enlever à) snatch from; (fig) force *ou* wrest from. □ **s'**~ **qch** *vpr* fight over sth.

arranger /aʀɑ̃ʒe/ [40] *vt* arrange, fix up; (réparer) put right; (régler) sort out; (convenir à) suit. □ **s'**~ *vpr* (se mettre d'accord) come to an arrangement; (se débrouiller) manage (**pour** to).

arrestation /aʀɛstasjɔ̃/ *nf* arrest.

arrêt /aʀɛ/ *nm* stopping, (de combats) cessation; (de production) halt; (lieu) stop; (pause) pause; (Jur) ruling; **aux** ~**s** (Mil) under arrest; **à l'**~ (*véhicule*) stationary; (*machine*) idle; **faire un** ~ (make a) stop; **sans** ~ (sans escale) nonstop; (sans interruption) constantly; ~ **maladie** sick leave; ~ **de travail** (grève) stoppage; (Méd) sick leave.

arrêté /aʀete/ *nm* order; ~ **municipal** bylaw.

arrêter /aʀete/ [1] *vt* stop; (*date*) fix; (*appareil*) turn off; (renoncer à) give up; (appréhender) arrest. ● *vi* stop. □ **s'**~ *vpr* stop; **s'**~ **de faire** stop doing.

arrhes /aʀ/ *nfpl* deposit; **verser des** ~ pay a deposit.

arrière /aʀjɛʀ/ *a inv* back, rear. ● *nm* back, rear; (football) back; **à l'**~ in *ou* at the back; **en** ~ behind; (*marcher, tomber*) backwards; **en** ~ **de** behind.

arrière-boutique (*pl* ~**s**) *nf* back room (of the shop). **arrière-garde** (*pl* ~**s**) *nf* rearguard. **arrière-goût** (*pl* ~**s**) *nm* after-taste. **arrière-grand-mère** (*pl* **arrière-grands-mères**) *nf* great-grandmother. **arrière-grand-père** (*pl* **arrière-grands-pères**) *nm* great-grandfather. **arrière-pays** *nm inv* backcountry. **arrière-pensée** (*pl* ~**s**) *nf* ulterior motive. **arrière-plan** *nm* (*pl* ~**s**) background.

arrimer /aʀime/ [1] *vt* secure; (*cargaison*) stow.

arrivage /aʀivaʒ/ *nm* consignment.

arrivée /aʀive/ *nf* arrival; (Sport) finish.

arriver /aʀive/ [1] *vi* (*aux être*)

arrive, come; (réussir) succeed; (se produire) happen; **~ à** (atteindre) reach; **~ à faire** manage to do; **je n'arrive pas à faire** I can't do; **en ~ à faire** get to the stage of doing; **il arrive que** it happens that; **il lui arrive de faire** he (sometimes) does.

arriviste /aʀivist/ *nmf* go-getter, self-seeker.

arrondir /aʀɔ̃diʀ/ [2] *vt* (make) round; (*somme*) round off. □ **s'~** *vpr* become round(ed).

arrondissement /aʀɔ̃dismɑ̃/ *nm* district.

arroser /aʀoze/ [1] *vt* water; (*repas*) wash down (with a drink); (*rôti*) baste; (*victoire*) drink to. **arrosoir** *nm* watering-can.

art /aʀ/ *nm* art; (don) knack (**de faire** of doing); **~s et métiers** arts and crafts; **~s ménagers** home economics (+ *sg*).

artère /aʀtɛʀ/ *nf* artery; (**grande**) **~** main road.

arthrite /aʀtʀit/ *nf* arthritis.

arthrose /aʀtʀoz/ *nf* osteoarthritis.

artichaut /aʀtiʃo/ *nm* artichoke.

article /aʀtikl/ *nm* article; (Comm) item, article; **à l'~ de la mort** at death's door; **~ de fond** feature (article); **~s de voyage** travel goods.

articulation /aʀtikylasjɔ̃/ *nf* articulation; (Anat) joint.

articuler /aʀtikyle/ [1] *vt* articulate; (structurer) structure; (assembler) connect (**sur** to).

artificiel, **~le** /aʀtifisjɛl/ *a* artificial.

artisan /aʀtizɑ̃/ *nm* artisan, craftsman; **l'~ de** (fig) the architect of.

artisanal, **~e** (*mpl* **~aux**) /aʀtizanal/ *a* craft; (*méthode*) traditional; (amateur) home-made; **de fabrication ~e** hand-made, hand-crafted.

artiste /aʀtist/ *nmf* artist. **artistique** *a* artistic.

as¹ /a/ ⇒AVOIR [5].

as² /ɑs/ *nm* ace.

ascenseur /asɑ̃sœʀ/ *nm* lift; (US) elevator.

ascension /asɑ̃sjɔ̃/ *nf* ascent; **l'A~** Ascension.

aseptiser /asɛptize/ [1] *vt* disinfect; (stériliser) sterilize; **aseptisé** (péj) sanitized.

asiatique /azjatik/ *a* Asian. **A~** *nmf* Asian.

Asie /azi/ *nf* Asia.

asile /azil/ *nm* refuge; (Pol) asylum; (pour malades, vieillards) home; **~ de nuit** night shelter.

aspect /aspɛ/ *nm* appearance; (facettes) aspect; (perspective) side; **à l'~ de** at the sight of.

asperge /aspɛʀʒ/ *nf* asparagus.

asperger /aspɛʀʒe/ [40] *vt* spray.

asphyxier /asfiksje/ [45] *vt* (*personne*) asphyxiate; (*entreprise, réseau*) paralyse. □ **s'~** *vpr* suffocate; gas oneself; (*entreprise, réseau*) become paralysed.

aspirateur /aspiʀatœʀ/ *nm* vacuum cleaner.

aspirer /aspiʀe/ [1] *vt* inhale; (*liquide*) suck up. ● *vi* **~ à** aspire to.

aspirine® /aspiʀin/ *nf* aspirin.

assainir /asenɪʀ/ [2] *vt* clean up.

assaisonnement /asɛzɔnmɑ̃/ *nm* seasoning.

assassin /asasɛ̃/ *nm* murderer; (Pol) assassin. **assassiner** [1] *vt* murder; (Pol) assassinate.

assaut /aso/ *nm* assault, onslaught; **donner l'~ à, prendre d'~** storm.

assemblage /asɑ̃blaʒ/ *nm* assembly; (combinaison) collection; (Tech) joint.

assemblée /asɑ̃ble/ *nf* meeting; (gens réunis) gathering; (Pol) assembly.

assembler /asɑ̃ble/ [1] *vt* assemble, put together; (réunir) gather. □ **s'∼** *vpr* gather, assemble.

asseoir /aswaʀ/ [9] *vt* sit (down), seat; (*bébé, malade*) sit up; (affermir) establish; (baser) base. □ **s'∼** *vpr* sit (down).

assermenté, ∼e /asɛʀmɑ̃te/ *a* sworn.

assez /ase/ *adv* (suffisamment) enough; (plutôt) quite, fairly; **∼ grand/rapide** big/fast enough (**pour** to); **∼ de** enough; **j'en ai ∼** (**de**) I've had enough (of).

assidu, ∼e /asidy/ *a* (zélé) assiduous; (régulier) regular; **∼ auprès de** attentive to. **assiduité** *nf* assiduousness, regularity.

assiéger /asjeʒe/ [14] [40] *vt* besiege.

assiette /asjɛt/ *nf* plate; (équilibre) seat; **∼ anglaise** assorted cold meats; **∼ creuse/plate** soup-/dinner-plate; **ne pas être dans son ∼** feel out of sorts.

assigner /asiɲe/ [1] *vt* assign; (*limite*) fix.

assimilation /asimilasjɔ̃/ *nf* assimilation; (comparaison) likening, comparison.

assimiler /asimile/ [1] *vt* **∼ à** liken to; (classer) class as. □ **s'∼** *vpr* assimilate; (être comparable) be comparable (**à** to).

assis, ∼e /asi, -z/ *a* sitting (down), seated. ● ⇒ASSEOIR [9].

assise /asiz/ *nf* (base) foundation; **∼s** (tribunal) assizes; (congrès) conference, congress.

assistance /asistɑ̃s/ *nf* audience; (aide) assistance; **l'A∼** (**publique**) welfare services.

assistant, ∼e /asistɑ̃, -t/ *nm,f* assistant; (Scol) foreign language assistant; **∼s** (spectateurs) members of the audience; **∼e sociale** social worker.

assister /asiste/ [1] *vt* assist; **∼ à** attend, be (present) at; (*accident*) witness; **assisté par ordinateur** computer-assisted.

association /asɔsjasjɔ̃/ *nf* association.

associé, ∼e /asɔsje/ *nm,f* partner, associate. ● *a* associate.

associer /asɔsje/ [45] *vt* associate; (mêler) combine (**à** with); **∼ qn à** (*projet*) involve sb in; (*bénéfices*) give sb a share of. □ **s'∼** *vpr* (*sociétés, personnes*) become associated, join forces (**à** with); (s'harmoniser) combine (**à** with); **s'∼ à** (*joie, opinion de qn*) share; (*projet*) take part in.

assommer /asɔme/ [1] *vt* knock out; (*animal*) stun; (fig) overwhelm; (ennuyer Ⓘ) bore.

Assomption /asɔ̃psjɔ̃/ *nf* Assumption.

assortiment /asɔʀtimɑ̃/ *nm* assortment.

assortir /asɔʀtiʀ/ [2] *vt* match (**à** with, to); **∼ de** accompany with. □ **s'∼** *vpr* match; **s'∼ à qch** match sth.

assoupir (**s'**) /(s)asupiʀ/ [2] *vpr* doze off; (s'apaiser) subside.

assouplir /asupliʀ/ [2] *vt* make supple; (fig) make flexible.

assourdir /asuʀdiʀ/ [2] *vt* (*personne*) deafen; (*bruit*) muffle.

assouvir /asuviʀ/ [2] *vt* satisfy.

assujettir /asyʒetiʀ/ [2] *vt* subjugate, subdue; **∼ à** subject to.

assumer /asyme/ [1] *vt* assume; (*coût*) meet; (accepter) come to terms with, accept.

assurance /asyʀɑ̃s/ *nf* (self-)assurance; (garantie) assurance; (contrat) insurance; **∼s sociales**

social insurance; **~ automobile/ maladie** car/health insurance.

assuré, **~e** /asyʀe/ *a* certain, assured; (sûr de soi) confident, assured. ● *nm, f* insured party.

assurer /asyʀe/ [1] *vt* ensure; (fournir) provide; (exécuter) carry out; (Comm) insure; (stabiliser) steady; (*frontières*) make secure; **~ à qn que** assure sb that; **~ qn de** assure sb of; **~ la gestion/ défense de** manage/defend. □ **s'~** *vpr* take out insurance; **s'~ de/ que** make sure of/that; **s'~ qch** (se procurer) secure sth. **assureur** *nm* insurer.

astérisque /asteʀisk/ *nm* asterisk.

asthmatique /asmatik/ *a & nmf* asthmatic.

asthme /asm/ *nm* asthma.

asticot /astiko/ *nm* maggot.

astreindre /astʀɛ̃dʀ/ [22] *vt* **~ qn à qch** force sth on sb; **~ qn à faire** force sb to do.

astrologie /astʀɔlɔʒi/ *nf* astrology. **astrologue** *nmf* astrologer.

astronaute /astʀɔnot/ *nmf* astronaut.

astronomie /astʀɔnɔmi/ *nf* astronomy.

astuce /astys/ *nf* smartness; (truc) trick; (plaisanterie) wisecrack.

astucieux, **-ieuse** /astysjø, -z/ *a* smart, clever.

atelier /atəlje/ *nm* (local) workshop; (de peintre) studio; (séance de travail) workshop.

athée /ate/ *nmf* atheist. ● *a* atheistic.

athlète /atlɛt/ *nmf* athlete. **athlétisme** *nm* athletics.

Atlantique /atlɑ̃tik/ *nm* Atlantic (Ocean).

atmosphère /atmɔsfɛʀ/ *nf* atmosphere.

atomique /atɔmik/ *a* atomic; (*énergie, centrale*) nuclear.

atomiseur /atɔmizœʀ/ *nm* spray.

atout /atu/ *nm* trump (card); (avantage) asset.

atroce /atʀɔs/ *a* atrocious.

attabler (s') /(s)atable/ [1] *vpr* sit down at table.

attachant, **~e** /ataʃɑ̃, -t/ *a* charming.

attache /ataʃ/ *nf* (agrafe) fastener; (lien) tie.

attaché, **~e** /ataʃe/ *a* **être ~ à** (aimer) be attached to. ● *nm, f* (Pol) attaché.

attacher /ataʃe/ [1] *vt* tie (up); (*ceinture, robe*) fasten; (*bicyclette*) lock; **~ à** (attribuer à) attach to. ● *vi* (Culin) stick. □ **s'~** *vpr* fasten, do up; **s'~ à** (se lier à) become attached to; (se consacrer à) apply oneself to.

attaquant, **~e** /atakɑ̃, -t/ *nm, f* attacker; (au football) striker; (au football américain) forward.

attaque /atak/ *nf* attack; **~ (cérébrale)** stroke; **il va en faire une ~** he'll have a fit; **~ à main armée** armed attack.

attaquer /atake/ [1] *vt* attack; (*banque*) raid. ● *vi* attack. □ **s'~ à** *vpr* attack; (*problème, sujet*) tackle.

attardé, **~e** /ataʀde/ *a* backward; (*idées*) outdated; (en retard) late.

attarder (s') /(s)ataʀde/ [1] *vpr* linger.

atteindre /atɛ̃dʀ/ [22] *vt* reach; (blesser) hit; (affecter) affect.

atteint, **~e** /atɛ̃, -t/ *a* **~ de** suffering from.

atteinte /atɛ̃t/ *nf* attack (**à** on); **porter ~ à** attack; (*droit*) infringe.

atteler /atle/ [38] *vt* (*cheval*) harness; (*remorque*) couple. □ **s'~ à** *vpr* get down to.

attelle /atɛl/ *nf* splint.

attenant, **~e** /atnɑ̃, -t/ *a* **~ (à)** adjoining.

attendant: **en ~** /ɑ̃natɑ̃dɑ̃/ *loc* meanwhile.

attendre /atɑ̃dʀ/ [3] *vt* wait for; (*bébé*) expect; (être le sort de) await; (escompter) expect; **~ que qn fasse** wait for sb to do. ● *vi* wait; (au téléphone) hold. □ **s'~ à** *vpr* expect.

attendrir /atɑ̃dʀiʀ/ [2] *vt* move (to pity). □ **s'~** *vpr* be moved to pity.

attendu¹ /atɑ̃dy/ *prép* given, considering; **~ que** considering that.

attendu², **~e** /atɑ̃dy/ *a* (escompté) expected; (espéré) long-awaited.

attentat /atɑ̃ta/ *nm* assassination attempt; **~ (à la bombe)** (bomb) attack.

attente /atɑ̃t/ *nf* wait(ing); (espoir) expectations (+ *pl*).

attenter /atɑ̃te/ [1] *vi* **~ à** make an attempt on; (fig) violate.

attentif, **-ive** /atɑ̃tif, -v/ *a* attentive; (scrupuleux) careful; **~ à** mindful of; (soucieux) careful of.

attention /atɑ̃sjɔ̃/ *nf* attention; (soin) care; **~ (à)!** watch out (for)!; **faire ~ à** (écouter) pay attention to; (prendre garde à) watch out for; (prendre soin de) take care of; **faire ~ à faire** be careful to do. **attentionné**, **~e** *a* considerate.

attentisme /atɑ̃tism/ *nm* wait-and-see policy.

atténuer /atenɥe/ [1] *vt* (*violence*) reduce; (*critique*) tone down; (*douleur*) ease; (*faute*) mitigate. □ **s'~** *vpr* subside.

atterrir /ateʀiʀ/ [2] *vi* land. **atterrissage** *nm* landing.

attestation /atɛstasjɔ̃/ *nf* certificate.

attester /atɛste/ [1] *vt* testify to; **~ que** testify that.

attirant, **~e** /atiʀɑ̃, -t/ *a* attractive.

attirer /atiʀe/ [1] *vt* draw, attract; (causer) bring. □ **s'~** *vpr* bring upon oneself; (*amis*) win.

attiser /atize/ [1] *vt* (*feu*) poke; (*sentiment*) stir up.

attitré, **~e** /atitʀe/ *a* accredited; (habituel) usual, regular.

attitude /atityd/ *nf* attitude; (maintien) bearing.

attraction /atʀaksjɔ̃/ *nf* attraction.

attrait /atʀɛ/ *nm* attraction.

attraper /atʀape/ [1] *vt* catch; (*corde, main*) catch hold of; (*habitude, accent*) pick up; (*maladie*) catch; **se faire ~** [I] get told off.

attrayant, **~e** /atʀɛjɑ̃, -t/ *a* attractive.

attribuer /atʀibɥe/ [1] *vt* allocate; (*prix*) award; (imputer) attribute. □ **s'~** *vpr* claim (for oneself). **attribution** *nf* awarding, allocation.

attrouper (s') /(s)atʀupe/ [1] *vpr* gather.

au /o/ ⇒À.

aubaine /obɛn/ *nf* godsend, opportunity.

aube /ob/ *nf* dawn, daybreak.

auberge /obɛʀʒ/ *nf* inn; **~ de jeunesse** youth hostel.

aubergine /obɛʀʒin/ *nf* aubergine; (US) eggplant.

aucun, **~e** /okœ̃, okyn/ *a* (dans une phrase négative) no, not any; (positif) any. ● *pron* (dans une phrase négative) none, not any; (positif) any; **~ des deux** neither of the two; **d'~s** some. **aucunement** *adv* not at all, in no way.

audace /odas/ *nf* daring; (impudence) audacity.

audacieux, **-ieuse** /odasjø, -z/ *a* daring.

au-delà /od(ə)la/ *adv* beyond. ● *prép* **~ de** beyond.

au-dessous /od(ə)su/ *adv* below.

●*prép* ~ **de** below; (couvert par) under.
au-dessus /od(ə)sy/ *adv* above. ●*prép* ~ **de** above.
au-devant /od(ə)vɑ̃/ *prép* **aller ~ de qn** go to meet sb; **aller ~ des désirs de qn** anticipate sb's wishes.
audience /odjɑ̃s/ *nf* audience; (d'un tribunal) hearing; (succès, attention) success.
audimat® /odimat/ *nm* **l'~** the TV ratings.
audiovisuel, **~le** /odjɔvizɥɛl/ *a* audio-visual.
auditeur, **-trice** /oditœʀ, -tʀis/ *nm, f* listener.
audition /odisjɔ̃/ *nf* hearing; (Théât, Mus) audition.
auditoire /oditwaʀ/ *nm* audience.
augmentation /ogmɑ̃tasjɔ̃/ *nf* increase; **~ (de salaire)** (pay) rise; (US) raise.
augmenter /ogmɑ̃te/ [1] *vt/i* increase; (*employé*) give a pay rise *ou* raise to.
augure /ogyʀ/ *nm* (devin) oracle; **être de bon/mauvais ~** be a good/bad sign.
aujourd'hui /oʒuʀdɥi/ *adv* today.
auparavant /opaʀavɑ̃/ *adv* (avant) before; (précédemment) previously; (en premier lieu) beforehand.
auprès /opʀɛ/ *prép* **~ de** (à côté de) beside, next to; (comparé à) compared with; **s'excuser/se plaindre ~ de** apologize/complain to.
auquel /okɛl/ ⇒LEQUEL.
aura, **aurait** /oʀa, oʀɛ/ ⇒AVOIR [5].
aurore /oʀɔʀ/ *nf* dawn.
aussi /osi/ *adv* (également) too, also, as well; (dans une comparaison) as; (si, tellement) so; **~ bien que** as well as. ●*conj* (donc) so, consequently.
aussitôt /osito/ *adv* immediately; **~ que** as soon as, the moment; **~ arrivé** as soon as he arrived.
austère /ostɛʀ/ *a* austere.
Australie /ɔstʀali/ *nf* Australia.
australien, **~ne** /ostʀaljɛ̃, -ɛn/ *a* Australian. **A~**, **~ne** *nm, f* Australian.
autant /otɑ̃/ *adv* (*travailler, manger*) as much (**que** as); **~ (de)** (quantité) as much (**que** as); (nombre) as many (**que** as); (tant) so much, so many; **~ faire** one had better do; **d'~ plus que** all the more than; **en faire ~** do the same; **pour ~** for all that.
autel /otɛl/ *nm* altar.
auteur /otœʀ/ *nm* author; **l'~ du crime** the perpetrator of the crime.
authentifier /otɑ̃tifje/ [45] *vt* authenticate.
authentique /otɑ̃tik/ *a* authentic.
auto /oto/ *nf* car; **~ tamponneuse** dodgem, bumper car.
autobus /otɔbys/ *nm* bus.
autocar /otɔkaʀ/ *nm* coach.
autochtone /otɔktɔn/ *nmf* native.
autocollant, **~e** /otɔkɔlɑ̃, -t/ *a* self-adhesive. ●*nm* sticker.
autodidacte /otɔdidakt/ *nmf* self-taught person.
auto-école (*pl* **~s**) /otɔekɔl/ *nf* driving school.
automate /otɔmat/ *nm* automaton, robot.
automatique /otɔmatik/ *a* automatic.
automatisation /otɔmatizasjɔ̃/ *nf* automation.
automne /otɔn/ *nm* autumn; (US) fall.
automobile /otɔmɔbil/ *a* motor, car; (US) automobile. ●*nf* (motor) car; **l'~** the motor industry; (Sport)

motoring. **automobiliste** *nmf* motorist.

autonome /otɔnɔm/ *a* autonomous; (Ordinat) stand-alone.

autoradio /otɔʀadjo/ *nm* car radio.

autorisation /otɔʀizasjɔ̃/ *nf* permission, authorization; (permis) permit.

autorisé, **~e** /otɔʀize/ *a* (*opinions*) authoritative; (approuvé) authorized.

autoriser /otɔʀize/ [1] *vt* authorize, permit; (rendre possible) allow (of); (donner un droit) **~ qn à faire** entitle sb to do.

autoritaire /otɔʀitɛʀ/ *a* authoritarian.

autorité /otɔʀite/ *nf* authority; **faire ~** be authoritative.

autoroute /otɔʀut/ *nf* motorway; (US) highway; **~ de l'information** (Ordinat) information superhighway.

auto-stop /otostɔp/ *nm* hitch-hiking; **faire de l'~** hitch-hike; **prendre qn en ~** give a lift to sb.

autour /otuʀ/ *adv* around; **tout ~** all around. ● *prép* **~ de** around.

autre /otʀ/ *a* other; **un ~ jour/livre** another day/book; **~ chose/part** something/somewhere else; **quelqu'un/rien d'~** somebody/nothing else; **quoi d'~?** what else?; **d'~ part** on the other hand; (de plus) moreover, besides; **vous ~s Anglais** you English. ● *pron* **un ~, une ~** another (one); **l'~** the other (one); **les ~s** the others; (autrui) others; **d'~s** (some) others; **l'un l'~** each other; **l'un et l'~** both of them. **d'un jour à l'~** (bientôt) any day now; **entre ~s** among other things.

autrefois /otʀəfwa/ *adv* in the past; (précédemment) formerly.

autrement /otʀəmɑ̃/ *adv* differently; (sinon) otherwise; (plus ◻) far more; **~ dit** in other words.

Autriche /otʀiʃ/ *nf* Austria.

autrichien, **~ne** /otʀiʃjɛ̃, -jɛn/ *a* Austrian. **A~**, **~ne** *nm,f* Austrian.

autruche /otʀyʃ/ *nf* ostrich.

autrui /otʀɥi/ *pron* others, other people.

aux /o/ ⇨À.

auxiliaire /oksiljɛʀ/ *a* auxiliary. ● *nmf* (assistant) auxiliary. ● *nm* (Gram) auxiliary.

auxquels, **-quelles** /okɛl/ ⇨LEQUEL.

aval: **en ~** /ɑ̃naval/ *loc* downstream.

avaler /avale/ [1] *vt* swallow.

avance /avɑ̃s/ *nf* advance; (sur un concurrent) lead; **~ (de fonds)** advance; **à l'~** in advance; **d'~** already; **en ~** early; (*montre*) fast; **en ~ (sur)** (menant) ahead (of).

avancement /avɑ̃smɑ̃/ *nm* promotion.

avancé, **~e** /avɑ̃se/ *a* advanced.

avancer /avɑ̃se/ [10] *vi* move forward, advance; (*travail*) make progress; (*montre*) be fast; (faire saillie) jut out. ● *vt* move forward; (dans le temps) bring forward; (*argent*) advance; (*montre*) put forward. ◻ **s'~** *vpr* move forward, advance; (se hasarder) commit oneself.

avant /avɑ̃/ *nm* front; (Sport) forward. ● *a inv* front. ● *prép* before; **~ de faire** before doing; **en ~ de** in front of; **~ peu** shortly; **~ tout** above all. ● *adv* (dans le temps) before, beforehand; (d'abord) first; **en ~** (dans l'espace) forward(s); (dans le temps) ahead; **le bus d'~** the previous bus. ● *conj* **~ que** before; **~ qu'il (ne) fasse** before he does.

avantage /avɑ̃taʒ/ *nm* advantage; (Comm) benefit.

avantager /avɑ̃taʒe/ [40] *vt* favour; (embellir) show off to advantage.

avantageux, -euse /avɑ̃taʒø, -z/ *a* advantageous, favourable; (*prix*) attractive.

avant-bras /avɑ̃bʀa/ *nm inv* forearm.

avant-centre (*pl* **avants-centres**) /avɑ̃sɑ̃tʀ/ *nm* centre forward.

avant-coureur (*pl* **~s**) /avɑ̃kuʀœʀ/ *a* precursory, foreshadowing.

avant-dernier, -ière (*pl* **~s**) /avɑ̃dɛʀnje, -jɛʀ/ *a & nm,f* last but one.

avant-goût (*pl* **~s**) /avɑ̃gu/ *nm* foretaste.

avant-hier /avɑ̃tjɛʀ/ *adv* the day before yesterday.

avant-poste (*pl* **~s**) /avɑ̃pɔst/ *nm* outpost.

avant-première (*pl* **~s**) /avɑ̃pʀəmjɛʀ/ *nf* preview.

avant-propos /avɑ̃pʀɔpo/ *nm inv* foreword.

avare /avaʀ/ *a* miserly; **~ de** sparing with. ● *nmf* miser.

avarié, ~e /avaʀje/ *a* (*aliment*) spoiled.

avatar /avataʀ/ *nm* misfortune.

avec /avɛk/ *prép* with. ● *adv* [!] with it *ou* them.

avènement /avɛnmɑ̃/ *nm* advent; (d'un roi) accession.

avenir /avniʀ/ *nm* future; **à l'~** in future; **d'~** with (future) prospects.

aventure /avɑ̃tyʀ/ *nf* adventure; (sentimentale) affair. **aventureux, -euse** *a* adventurous; (hasardeux) risky.

avérer (s') /(s)aveʀe/ [14] *vpr* prove (to be).

averse /avɛʀs/ *nf* shower.

avertir /avɛʀtiʀ/ [2] *vt* inform; (mettre en garde, menacer) warn. **avertissement** *nm* warning.

avertisseur /avɛʀtisœʀ/ *nm* alarm; (Auto) horn; **~ d'incendie** fire-alarm; **~ lumineux** warning light.

aveu (*pl* **~x**) /avø/ *nm* confession; **de l'~ de** by the admission of.

aveugle /avœgl/ *a* blind. ● *nmf* blind man, blind woman.

aviateur, -trice /avjatœʀ, -tʀis/ *nm,f* aviator.

aviation /avjasjɔ̃/ *nf* flying; (industrie) aviation; (Mil) air force.

avide /avid/ *a* greedy (**de** for); (anxieux) eager (**de** for); **~ de faire** eager to do.

avion /avjɔ̃/ *nm* plane, aeroplane, aircraft; (US) airplane; **~ à réaction** jet.

aviron /aviʀɔ̃/ *nm* oar; **l'~** (Sport) rowing.

avis /avi/ *nm* opinion; (conseil) advice; (renseignement) notification; (Comm) advice; **à mon ~** in my opinion; **changer d'~** change one's mind; **être d'~ que** be of the opinion that; **~ au lecteur** foreword.

avisé, ~e /avize/ *a* sensible; **être bien/mal ~ de** be well-/ill-advised to.

aviser /avize/ [1] *vt* advise, notify. ● *vi* decide what to do. □ **s'~ de** *vpr* suddenly realize; **s'~ de faire** take it into one's head to do.

avocat, ~e /avɔka, -t/ *nm,f* barrister; (US) attorney; (fig) advocate; **~ de la défense** counsel for the defence. ● *nm* (fruit) avocado (pear).

avoine /avwan/ *nf* oats (+ *pl*).

avoir /avwaʀ/ [5]

●*verbe auxiliaire*

····➤ have; **il nous a appelés hier** he called us yesterday.

●*verbe transitif*

····➤ (possession) have (got).

····➤ (obtenir) get; (au téléphone) get through to.

····➤ (duper) 🄸 have; **on m'a eu!** I've been had!

····➤ ~ **chaud/faim** be hot/hungry.

····➤ ~ **dix ans** be ten years old.

●**avoir à** *verbe + préposition*

····➤ to have to; **j'ai beaucoup à faire** I have a lot to do; **tu n'as qu'à leur écrire** all you have to do is write to them.

●**en avoir pour** *verbe + préposition*

····➤ **j'en ai pour une minute** I will only be a minute; **j'en ai eu pour 100 francs** it cost me 100 francs.

●**il y a** *verbe impersonnel*

····➤ there is; (pluriel) there are; **qu'est-ce qu'il y a?** what's the matter?; **il est venu il y a cinq ans** he came here five years ago; **il y a au moins 5 km jusqu'à la gare** it's at least 5 km to the station.

●*nom masculin*

····➤ (dans un magasin) credit note.

····➤ (biens) asset (+ *pl*).

avortement /avɔʀtəmɑ̃/ *nm* (Méd) abortion.

avorter /avɔʀte/ [1] *vi* (*projet*) abort; (**se faire**) ~ have an abortion.

avoué, ~**e** /avwe/ *a* avowed. ● *nm* solicitor; (US) attorney.

avouer /avwe/ [1] *vt* (*amour, ignorance*) confess; (*crime*) confess to, admit. ● *vi* confess.

avril /avʀil/ *nm* April.

axe /aks/ *nm* axis; (essieu) axle; (d'une politique) main line(s), basis; ~ (**routier**) main road.

ayant /ɛjɑ̃/ ⇒AVOIR [5].

azote /azɔt/ *nm* nitrogen.

azur /azyʀ/ *nm* sky-blue.

baba /baba/ *nm* ~ (**au rhum**) (rum) baba; **en rester** ~ 🄸 be flabbergasted.

babillard /babijaʀ/ *nm* ~ **électronique** (Internet) bulletin board system, BBS.

babines /babin/ *nfpl* **se lécher les** ~ lick one's chops.

babiole /babjɔl/ *nf* trinket.

bâbord /bɑbɔʀ/ *nm* port (side).

baby-foot /babifut/ *nm inv* table football.

bac /bak/ *nm* (Scol) ⇒BACCALAURÉAT; (bateau) ferry; (récipient) tub; (plus petit) tray.

baccalauréat /bakalɔʀea/ *nm* school leaving certificate.

bâche /bɑʃ/ *nf* tarpaulin.

bachelier, **-ière** /baʃəlje, -jɛʀ/ *nm, f* holder of the *baccalauréat*.

bachoter /baʃɔte/ [1] *vi* cram (for an exam).

bâcler /bɑkle/ [1] *vt* botch (up).

bactérie /bakteʀi/ *nf* bacterium; ~**s** bacteria.

badaud, ~**e** /bado, -d/ *nm, f* onlooker.

badigeonner /badiʒɔne/ [1] *vt* whitewash; (barbouiller) daub.

badiner /badine/ [1] *vi* banter.

baffe /baf/ *nf* 🄸 slap.

baffle /bafl/ *nm* speaker.

bafouiller /bafuje/ [1] *vt/i* stammer.

bagage /bagaʒ/ *nm* bag; (connaissances) knowledge; **~s** luggage; **~ à main** hand luggage.

bagarre /bagaʀ/ *nf* fight.

bagatelle /bagatɛl/ *nf* trifle; (somme) trifling amount.

bagnard /baɲaʀ/ *nm* convict.

bagnole /baɲɔl/ *nf* ▣ car.

bague /bag/ *nf* (bijou) ring.

baguette /bagɛt/ *nf* stick; (de chef d'orchestre) baton; (chinoise) chopstick; (pain) baguette; **~ magique** magic wand; **~ de tambour** drumstick.

baie /bɛ/ *nf* (Géog) bay; (fruit) berry; **~ (vitrée)** picture window; (Ordinat) bay.

baignade /bɛɲad/ *nf* swimming.

baigner /beɲe/ [1] *vt* bathe; (*enfant*) bath. ● *vi* **~ dans l'huile** swim in grease. □ **se ~** *vpr* have a swim. **baigneur, -euse** *nm,f* swimmer.

baignoire /bɛɲwaʀ/ *nf* bath(tub).

bail (*pl* **baux**) /baj, bo/ *nm* lease.

bâiller /baje/ [1] *vi* yawn; (être ouvert) gape.

bailleur /bajœʀ/ *nm* **~ de fonds** (Comm) sleeping partner.

bain /bɛ̃/ *nm* bath; (baignade) swim; **prendre un ~ de soleil** sunbathe; **~ de bouche** mouthwash; **être dans le ~** (fig) be in the swing of things; **se remettre dans le ~** get back into the swing of things; **prendre un ~ de foule** mingle with the crowd.

bain-marie (*pl* **bains-marie**) /bɛ̃maʀi/ *nm* double boiler.

baiser /beze/ [1] *vt* (*main*) kiss; ▣ screw ▣. ● *nm* kiss.

baisse /bɛs/ *nf* fall, drop; **être en ~** be going down.

baisser /bese/ [1] *vt* lower; (*radio, lampe*) turn down. ● *vi* (*niveau*) go down, fall; (*santé, forces*) fail. □ **se ~** *vpr* bend down.

bal (*pl* **~s**) /bal/ *nm* dance; (habillé) ball; (lieu) dance-hall; **~ costumé** fancy-dress ball.

balade /balad/ *nf* stroll; (en auto) drive.

balader /balade/ [1] *vt* take for a stroll. □ **se ~** *vpr* (à pied) (go for a) stroll; (en voiture) go for a drive; (voyager) travel.

baladeur /baladœʀ/ *nm* personal stereo.

balafre /balafʀ/ *nf* gash; (cicatrice) scar.

balai /balɛ/ *nm* broom.

balance /balɑ̃s/ *nf* scales (+ *pl*); **la B~** Libra.

balancer /balɑ̃se/ [10] *vt* swing; (doucement) sway; (lancer ▣) chuck ▣; (se débarrasser de ▣) chuck out ▣. ● *vi* sway. □ **se ~** *vpr* swing; sway; **s'en ~** ▣ not to give a damn ▣.

balancier /balɑ̃sje/ *nm* (d'horloge) pendulum; (d'équilibriste) pole.

balançoire /balɑ̃swaʀ/ *nf* swing.

balayage /balejaʒ/ *nm* sweeping; (cheveux) highlights.

balayer /baleje/ [31] *vt* sweep (up); (*vent*) sweep away; (se débarrasser de) sweep aside.

balbutiement /balbysimɑ̃/ *nm* stammering; **les ~s** (fig) the first steps.

balcon /balkɔ̃/ *nm* balcony; (Théât) dress circle.

baleine /balɛn/ *nf* whale.

balise /baliz/ *nf* beacon; (bouée) buoy; (Auto) (road) sign. **baliser** [1] *vt* mark out (with beacons); (*route*) signpost; (*sentier*) mark out.

balivernes /balivɛʀn/ *nfpl* nonsense.

ballant, ~e /balɑ̃, -t/ *a* dangling.

balle /bal/ *nf* (projectile) bullet; (Sport) ball; (paquet) bale.

ballerine /balʀin/ *nf* (danseuse) ballerina; (chaussure) ballet pump.

ballet /balɛ/ *nm* ballet.

ballon /balɔ̃/ *nm* (Sport) ball; **~** (**de baudruche**) balloon; **~ de football** football.

ballonne, **~e** /balɔne/ *a* bloated.

balnéaire /balneɛʀ/ *a* seaside.

balourd, **~e** /baluʀ, -d/ *nm,f* oaf. ● *a* uncouth.

balustrade /balystʀad/ *nf* railing.

ban /bɑ̃/ *nm* round of applause; **~s** (de mariage) banns; **mettre au ~ de** cast out from.

banal, **~e** (*mpl* **~s**) /banal/ *a* commonplace, banal.

banane /banan/ *nf* banana.

banc /bɑ̃/ *nm* bench; (de poissons) shoal; **~ des accusés** dock; **~ d'essai** (test) testing ground.

bancaire /bɑ̃kɛʀ/ *a* (*secteur*) banking; (*chèque*) bank.

bancal, **~e** (*mpl* **~s**) /bɑ̃kal/ *a* wobbly; (*solution*) shaky.

bande /bɑ̃d/ *nf* (groupe) gang; (de papier) strip; (rayure) stripe; (de film) reel; (pansement) bandage; **~ dessinée** comic strip; **~** (**magnétique**) tape; **~ sonore** sound-track.

bande-annonce (*pl* **bandes-annonces**) /bɑ̃danɔ̃s/ *nf* trailer.

bandeau (*pl* **~x**) /bɑ̃do/ *nm* headband; (sur les yeux) blindfold.

bander /bɑ̃de/ [1] *vt* bandage; (*arc*) bend; (*muscle*) tense; **~ les yeux à** blindfold.

banderole /bɑ̃dʀɔl/ *nf* banner.

bandit /bɑ̃di/ *nm* bandit. **banditisme** *nm* crime.

bandoulière: **en ~** /ɑ̃bɑ̃duljɛʀ/ *loc* across one's shoulder.

banlieue /bɑ̃ljø/ *nf* suburbs; **de ~** suburban. **banlieusard**, **~e** *nm,f* (suburban) commuter.

bannir /baniʀ/ [2] *vt* banish.

banque /bɑ̃k/ *nf* bank; (activité) banking; **~ de données** databank.

banqueroute /bɑ̃kʀut/ *nf* bankruptcy.

banquet /bɑ̃kɛ/ *nm* banquet.

banquette /bɑ̃kɛt/ *nf* seat.

banquier, **-ière** /bɑ̃kje, -jɛʀ/ *nm,f* banker.

baptême /batɛm/ *nm* baptism, christening. **baptiser** [1] *vt* baptize, christen; (nommer) call.

bar /baʀ/ *nm* (lieu) bar.

baragouiner /baʀagwine/ [1] *vt/i* gabble; (*langue*) speak a few words of.

baraque /baʀak/ *nf* hut, shed; (maison 🅘) house.

baratin /baʀatɛ̃/ *nm* 🅘 sweet *ou* smooth talk.

barbare /baʀbaʀ/ *a* barbaric. ● *nmf* barbarian.

barbe /baʀb/ *nf* beard; **~ à papa** candy-floss; (US) cotton candy; **quelle ~!** 🅘 what a drag! 🅘.

barbelé /baʀbəle/ *a* **fil ~** barbed wire.

barber /baʀbe/ [1] *vt* 🅘 bore.

barboter /baʀbɔte/ [1] *vi* (dans l'eau) paddle, splash. ● *vt* (voler 🅘) pinch.

barbouiller /baʀbuje/ [1] *vt* (souiller) smear (**de** with); **tu es tout barbouillé** your face is all dirty; **être barbouillé** feel queazy.

barbu, **~e** /baʀby/ *a* bearded.

barème /baʀɛm/ *nm* list, table; (échelle) scale.

baril /baʀil/ *nm* barrel; (de poudre) keg.

bariolé, **~e** /baʀjɔle/ *a* multicoloured.

baromètre /baʀɔmɛtʀ/ *nm* barometer.

baron, **~ne** /baʀɔ̃, -ɔn/ *nm,f* baron, baroness.

barque /baʀk/ *nf* (small) boat.

barrage /baʀaʒ/ *nm* dam; (sur route) roadblock.

barre /baʀ/ *nf* bar; (trait) line, stroke; (Naut) helm; **~ de boutons** (Ordinat) toolbar.

barreau (*pl* **~x**) /baʀo/ *nm* bar; (d'échelle) rung; **le ~** (Jur) the bar.

barrer /baʀe/ [1] *vt* block; (*porte*) bar; (rayer) cross out; (Naut) steer. ▫ **se ~** *vpr* Ⓘ leave.

barrette /baʀɛt/ *nf* (hair) slide.

barrière /baʀjɛʀ/ *nf* (porte) gate; (clôture) fence; (obstacle) barrier.

bar-tabac (*pl* **bars-tabac**) /baʀtaba/ *nm* café (*selling stamps and cigarettes*).

bas, **basse** /bɑ, bɑs/ *a* (*niveau, table*) low; (*action*) base; **au ~ mot** at the lowest estimate; **en ~ âge** young; **~ morceaux** (viande) cheap cuts. ● *nm* bottom; (chaussette) stocking; **~ de laine** (fig) nest-egg. ● *adv* low; **en ~** down below; (dans une maison) downstairs; **en ~ de la page** at the bottom of the page; **plus ~** further *ou* lower down; **mettre ~** give birth (to). **bas de casse** *nm inv* lower case. **bas-côté** (*pl* **~s**) *nm* (de route) verge; (US) shoulder.

bascule /baskyl/ *nf* (balance) scales (+ *pl*); **cheval/fauteuil à ~** rocking-horse/-chair.

basculer /baskyle/ [1] *vi* topple over; (*benne*) tip up.

base /bɑz/ *nf* base; (fondement) basis; (Pol) rank and file; **de ~** basic. **base de données** *nf* database.

baser /bɑze/ [1] *vt* base. ▫ **se ~ sur** *vpr* go by.

bas-fonds /bɑfɔ̃/ *nmpl* (eau) shallows; (fig) dregs.

basilic /bazilik/ *nm* basil.

basilique /bazilik/ *nf* basilica.

basque /bask/ *a* Basque. **B~** *nmf* Basque.

basse /bɑs/ ⇒BAS.

basse-cour (*pl* **basses-cours**) /bɑskuʀ/ *nf* farmyard.

bassesse /bɑsɛs/ *nf* baseness; (action) base act.

bassin /basɛ̃/ *nm* (pièce d'eau) pond; (de piscine) pool; (Géog) basin; (Anat) pelvis; (plat) bowl; **~ houiller** coalfield.

bassine /basin/ *nf* bowl.

basson /bɑsɔ̃/ *nm* bassoon.

bas-ventre (*pl* **~s**) /bɑvɑ̃tʀ/ *nm* lower abdomen.

bat /ba/ ⇒BATTRE [11].

bataille /batɑj/ *nf* battle; (fig) fight.

bâtard, **~e** /bɑtaʀ, -d/ *a* (*solution*) hybrid. ● *nm, f* bastard.

bateau (*pl* **~x**) /bato/ *nm* boat; **~ pneumatique** rubber dinghy. **bateau-mouche** (*pl* **bateaux-mouches**) *nm* sightseeing boat.

bâti,**~e** /bɑti/ *a* **bien ~** well-built.

bâtiment /bɑtimɑ̃/ *nm* building; (industrie) building trade; (navire) vessel.

bâtir /bɑtiʀ/ [2] *vt* build.

bâton /bɑtɔ̃/ *nm* stick; **conversation à ~s rompus** rambling conversation; **~ de rouge** lipstick.

battant /batɑ̃/ *nm* (vantail) flap; **porte à deux ~s** double door.

battement /batmɑ̃/ *nm* (de cœur) beat(ing); (temps) interval; (Mus) beat.

batterie /batʀi/ *nf* (Mil, Électr) battery; (Mus) drums; **~ de cuisine** pots and pans.

batteur /batœʀ/ *nm* (Mus) drummer; (Culin) whisk.

battre /batʀ/ [11] *vt/i* beat; (*cartes*) shuffle; (Culin) whisk; (l'emporter sur) beat; **~ des ailes** flap its wings; **~ des mains** clap; **~ des paupières** blink; **~ en retraite** beat a retreat; **~ la semelle** stamp one's feet; **~ son plein** be in full swing. ▫ **se ~** *vpr* fight.

baume /bom/ *nm* balm.

bavard, **~e** /bavaʀ, -d/ *a* talkative. ● *nm, f* chatterbox.

bavardage /bavaʀdaʒ/ *nm* chatter, gossip. **bavarder** [1] *vi* chat; (jacasser) chatter, gossip.

bave /bav/ *nf* dribble, slobber, (de limace) slime. **baver** [1] *vi* dribble, slobber. **baveux**, **-euse** *a* dribbling; (*omelette*) runny.

bavoir /bavwaʀ/ *nm* bib.

bavure /bavyʀ/ *nf* smudge; (erreur) blunder; **~ policière** police blunder.

bazar /bazaʀ/ *nm* bazaar; (objets [!]) clutter.

BCBG *abrév mf* (**bon chic bon genre**) posh.

BD *abrév f* (**bande dessinée**) comic strip.

béant, **~e** /beɑ̃, -t/ *a* gaping.

béat, **~e** /bea, -t/ *a* (hum) blissful; **~ d'admiration** wide-eyed with admiration.

beau (**bel** *before vowel or mute h*), **belle** (*mpl* **~x**) /bo, bɛl/ *a* beautiful; (*femme*) beautiful; (*homme*) handsome; (*temps*) fine, nice. ● *nm* beauty. ● *adv* **il fait ~** the weather is nice; **au ~ milieu** right in the middle; **bel et bien** well and truly; **de plus belle** more than ever; **faire le ~** sit up and beg; **on a ~ essayer/insister** however much one tries/insists.

beaucoup /boku/ *adv* a lot, very much; **~ de** (nombre) many; (quantité) a lot of; **pas ~ (de)** not many; (quantité) not much; **~ plus/mieux** much more/better; **~ trop** far too much; **de ~** by far.

beau-fils (*pl* **beaux-fils**) /bofis/ *nm* (remariage) stepson.

beau-frère (*pl* **beaux-frères**) /bofʀɛʀ/ *nm* brother-in-law.

beau-père (*pl* **beaux-pères**) /bopɛʀ/ *nm* father-in-law; (remariage) stepfather.

beauté /bote/ *nf* beauty; **finir en ~** end magnificently.

beaux-arts /bozaʀ/ *nmpl* fine arts.

beaux-parents /bopaʀɑ̃/ *nmpl* parents-in-law.

bébé /bebe/ *nm* baby. **bébé-éprouvette** (*pl* **bébés-éprouvette**) *nm* test tube baby.

bec /bɛk/ *nm* beak; (de théière) spout; (de casserole) lip; (bouche [!]) mouth; **~ de gaz** gas street-lamp.

bécane /bekan/ *nf* [!] bike.

bêche /bɛʃ/ *nf* spade.

bégayer /begeje/ [31] *vt/i* stammer.

bègue /bɛg/ *nmf* stammerer. ● *a* **être ~** stammer.

bégueule /begœl/ *a* prudish.

beige /bɛʒ/ *a & nm* beige.

beignet /bɛɲɛ/ *nm* fritter.

bel /bɛl/ ⇒BEAU.

bêler /bele/ [1] *vi* bleat.

belette /bəlɛt/ *nf* weasel.

belge /bɛlʒ/ *a* Belgian. **B~** *nmf* Belgian.

Belgique /bɛlʒik/ *nf* Belgium.

bélier /belje/ *nm* ram; **le B~** Aries.

belle /bɛl/ ⇒BEAU.

belle-fille (*pl* **belles-filles**) /bɛlfij/ *nf* daughter-in-law; (remariage) stepdaughter.

belle-mère (*pl* **belles-mères**) /bɛlmɛʀ/ *nf* mother-in-law; (remariage) stepmother.

belle-sœur (*pl* **belles-sœurs**) /bɛlsœʀ/ *nf* sister-in-law.

belliqueux, **-euse** /belikø, -z/ *a* warlike.

bémol /bemol/ *nm* (Mus) flat.

bénédiction /benediksjɔ̃/ *nf* blessing.

bénéfice /benefis/ *nm* (gain) profit; (avantage) benefit.

bénéficiaire /benefisjɛʀ/ *nmf* beneficiary.

bénéficier /benefisje/ [45] *vi* ~ **de** benefit from; (jouir de) enjoy, have.

bénéfique /benefik/ *a* beneficial.

Bénélux /benelyks/ *nm* Benelux.

bénévole /benevɔl/ *a* voluntary.

bénin, -igne /benɛ̃, -iɲ/ *a* minor; (*tumeur*) benign.

bénir /beniʀ/ [2] *vt* bless. **bénit, ~e** *a* (*eau*) holy; (*pain*) consecrated.

benjamin, ~e /bɛ̃ʒamɛ̃, -in/ *nm, f* youngest child.

benne /bɛn/ *nf* (de grue) scoop; ~ **à ordures** (camion) waste disposal truck; (conteneur) skip; ~ (**basculante**) dump truck.

béquille /bekij/ *nf* crutch; (de moto) stand.

berceau (*pl* ~**x**) /bɛʀso/ *nm* (de bébé, civilisation) cradle.

bercer /bɛʀse/ [10] *vt* (balancer) rock; (apaiser) lull; (leurrer) delude.

béret /beʀɛ/ *nm* beret.

berge /bɛʀʒ/ *nf* (bord) bank.

berger, -ère /bɛʀʒe, -ɛʀ/ *nm, f* shepherd, shepherdess.

berne: **en** ~ /ɑ̃bɛʀn/ *loc* at half-mast.

berner /bɛʀne/ [1] *vt* fool.

besogne /bəzɔɲ/ *nf* task, job.

besoin /bəzwɛ̃/ *nm* need; **avoir** ~ **de** need; **au** ~ if need be; **dans le** ~ in need.

bestiole /bɛstjɔl/ *nf* [!] bug.

bétail /betaj/ *nm* livestock.

bête /bɛt/ *a* stupid. ● *nf* animal; ~ **noire** pet hate; ~ **sauvage** wild beast; **chercher la petite** ~ be overfussy.

bêtise /betiz/ *nf* stupidity; (action) stupid thing.

béton /betɔ̃/ *nm* concrete; ~ **armé** reinforced concrete; **en** ~ (*mur*) concrete; (*argument* [!]) watertight. **bétonnière** *nf* concrete mixer.

betterave /bɛtʀav/ *nf* beet; ~ **rouge** beetroot.

beugler /bøgle/ [1] *vi* bellow; (*radio*) blare out.

beur /bœʀ/ *nmf & a* [!] second-generation North African living in France.

beurre /bœʀ/ *nm* butter. **beurré, ~e** *a* buttered; [!] drunk. **beurrier** *nm* butter-dish.

bévue /bevy/ *nf* blunder.

biais /bjɛ/ *nm* (moyen) way; **par le** ~ **de** by means of; **de** ~, **en** ~ at an angle; **regarder qn de** ~ look sideways at sb.

bibelot /biblo/ *nm* ornament.

biberon /bibʀɔ̃/ *nm* (feeding) bottle; **nourrir au** ~ bottle-feed.

bible /bibl/ *nf* bible; **la B**~ the Bible.

bibliographie /biblijɔgʀafi/ *nf* bibliography.

bibliothécaire /biblijɔtekɛʀ/ *nmf* librarian.

bibliothèque /biblijɔtɛk/ *nf* library; (meuble) bookcase.

bic® /bik/ *nm* biro®.

bicarbonate /bikaʀbɔnat/ *nm* ~ (**de soude**) bicarbonate (of soda).

biceps /bisɛps/ *nm* biceps.

biche /biʃ/ *nf* doe; **ma** ~ darling.

bichonner /biʃɔne/ [1] *vt* pamper.

bicyclette /bisiklɛt/ *nf* bicycle.

bide /bid/ *nm* (ventre [!]) paunch; (échec [!]) flop.

bidet /bidɛ/ *nm* bidet.

bidon /bidɔ̃/ *nm* can; (plus grand) drum; (ventre [!]) belly; **c'est du** ~ [!] it's a load of hogwash [!]. ● *a inv* [!] phoney.

bidonville /bidɔ̃vil/ *nf* shanty town.

bidule /bidyl/ *nm* [!] thing.

Biélorussie /bjelɔʀysi/ *nf* Byelorussia.

bien /bjɛ̃/ *adv* well; (très) quite, very; ~ **des** (nombre) many; **tu as**

~ **de la chance** you are very lucky; **j'aimerais ~** I would like to; **ce n'est pas ~ de** it is not nice to; **~ sûr** of course. ● *nm* good; (patrimoine) possession; **~s de consommation** consumer goods. ● *a inv* good; (passable) all right; (en forme) well; (à l'aise) comfortable; (beau) attractive; (respectable) nice, respectable. ● *conj* **~ que** (al-) though; **~ que ce soit** although it is. **bien-aimé, ~e** *a & nm,f* beloved. **bien-être** *nm* well-being.

bienfaisance /bjɛ̃fəzɑ̃s/ *nf* charity; **fête de ~** charity event. **bienfaisant, ~e** *a* beneficial.

bienfait /bjɛ̃fɛ/ *nm* (kind) favour; (avantage) beneficial effect. **bienfaiteur, -trice** *nm,f* benefactor.

bien-pensant, ~e /bjɛ̃pɑ̃sɑ̃, -t/ *a* right-thinking.

bienséance /bjɛ̃seɑ̃s/ *nf* propriety.

bientôt /bjɛ̃to/ *adv* soon; **à ~** see you soon.

bienveillance /bjɛ̃vɛjɑ̃s/ *nf* kind-(li)ness.

bienvenu, ~e /bjɛ̃vny/ *a* welcome. ● *nm,f* **être le ~, être la ~e** be welcome.

bienvenue /bjɛ̃vny/ *nf* welcome; **souhaiter la ~ à** welcome.

bière /bjɛʀ/ *nf* beer; (cercueil) coffin; **~ blonde** lager; **~ brune** ≈ stout; **~ pression** draught beer.

bifteck /biftɛk/ *nm* steak.

bifurquer /bifyʀke/ [1] *vi* branch off, fork.

bigarré, ~e /bigaʀe/ *a* motley.

bigoudi /bigudi/ *nm* curler.

bijou (*pl* **~x**) /biʒu/ *nm* jewel; **~x en or** gold jewellery. **bijouterie** *nf* (boutique) jewellery shop; (Comm) jewellery. **bijoutier, -ière** *nm,f* jeweller.

bilan /bilɑ̃/ *nm* outcome; (d'une catastrophe) (casualty) toll; (Comm) balance sheet; **faire le ~ de** assess; **~ de santé** check-up.

bile /bil/ *nf* bile; **se faire de la ~** [!] worry.

bilingue /bilɛ̃g/ *a* bilingual.

billard /bijaʀ/ *nm* billiards (+ *pl*); (table) billiard-table.

bille /bij/ *nf* (d'enfant) marble; (de billard) billiard-ball.

billet /bijɛ/ *nm* ticket; (lettre) note; (article) column; **~ (de banque)** (bank) note; **~ de 50 francs** 50-franc note.

billetterie /bijɛtʀi/ *nf* cash dispenser.

billion /biljɔ̃/ *nm* billion; (US) trillion.

bimensuel, ~e /bimɑ̃sɥɛl/ *a* fortnightly, bimonthly. ● *nm* fortnightly magazine.

binette /binɛt/ *nf* hoe; (visage) face; (Internet) smiley.

biochimie /bjɔʃimi/ *nf* biochemistry.

biodégradable /bjɔdegʀadabl/ *a* biodegradable.

biographie /bjɔgʀafi/ *nf* biography.

biologie /bjɔlɔʒi/ *nf* biology. **biologique** *a* biological; (*produit*) organic.

bis /bis/ *nm & interj* encore.

biscornu, ~e /biskɔʀny/ *a* crooked; (bizarre) cranky [!].

biscotte /biskɔt/ *nf* continental toast.

biscuit /biskɥi/ *nm* biscuit; (US) cookie; **~ salé** cracker; **~ de Savoie** sponge-cake.

bise /biz/ *nf* [!] kiss; (vent) north wind.

bison /bizɔ̃/ *nm* buffalo.

bisou /bizu/ *nm* [!] kiss.

bistro(t) /bistʀo/ *nm* [!] café, bar.

bit /bit/ *nm* (Ordinat) bit.

bitume /bitym/ *nm* asphalt.

bizarre /bizaʀ/ *a* odd, strange. **bizzarerie** *nf* peculiarity.

blafard, **~e** /blafaʀ, -d/ *a* pale.

blague /blag/ *nf* 🅸 joke; **sans ~!** no kidding! 🅸.

blaguer /blage/ [1] 🅸 *vi* joke.

blaireau (*pl* **~x**) /blɛʀo/ *nm* shaving-brush; (animal) badger.

blâmer /blame/ [1] *vt* criticize.

blanc, **blanche** /blɑ̃, blɑ̃ʃ/ *a* white; (*papier, page*) blank. ● *nm* white; (espace) blank; **~ d'œuf** egg white; **~ de poireau** white part of the leek; **~** (**de poulet**) chicken breast; **le ~** (linge) whites; **laisser en ~** leave blank. **B~**, **Blanche** *nm, f* white man, white woman. **blanche** *nf* (Mus) minim.

blanchiment /blɑ̃ʃimɑ̃/ *nm* (d'argent) laundering.

blanchir /blɑ̃ʃiʀ/ [2] *vt* whiten; (*personne*: fig) clear; (*argent*) launder; (Culin) blanch; **~** (**à la chaux**) whitewash. ● *vi* turn white.

blanchisserie /blɑ̃ʃisʀi/ *nf* laundry.

blason /blazɔ̃/ *nm* coat of arms.

blasphème /blasfɛm/ *nm* blasphemy.

blé /ble/ *nm* wheat.

blême /blɛm/ *a* pallid.

blessant, **~e** /blesɑ̃, -t/ *a* hurtful.

blessé, **~e** /blese/ *nm, f* casualty, injured person.

blesser /blese/ [1] *vt* injure, hurt; (par balle) wound; (offenser) hurt. □ **se ~** *vpr* injure *ou* hurt oneself. **blessure** *nf* wound.

bleu, **~e** /blø/ *a* blue; (Culin) very rare; **~ marine/turquoise** navy blue/turquoise; **avoir une peur ~e** be scared stiff. ● *nm* blue; (contusion) bruise; **~** (**de travail**) overalls (+ *pl*).

bleuet /bløɛ/ *nm* cornflower.

blindé, **~e** /blɛ̃de/ *a* armoured; (fig) immune (**contre** to); **porte ~e** security car. ● *nm* armoured car, tank.

blinder /blɛ̃de/ [1] *vt* armour; (fig) harden.

bloc /blɔk/ *nm* block; (de papier) pad; **serrer à ~** tighten hard; **en ~** (matériau) in a block; (nier) outright.

blocage /blɔkaʒ/ *nm* (des prix) freeze, freezing; (des roues) locking; (Psych) block.

bloc-notes (*pl* **blocs-notes**) /blɔknɔt/ *nm* note-pad.

blocus /blɔkys/ *nm* blockade.

blond, **~e** /blɔ̃, -d/ *a* fair, blond. ● *nm, f* fair-haired man, fair-haired woman.

bloquer /blɔke/ [1] *vt* block; (*porte, machine*) jam; (*roues*) lock; (*prix, crédits*) freeze. □ **se ~** *vpr* jam; (*roues*) lock; (*freins*) jam; (*ordinateur*) crash; **bloqué par la neige** snowbound.

blottir (**se**) /(sə)blɔtiʀ/ [2] *vpr* snuggle, huddle (**contre** against).

blouse /bluz/ *nf* overall. **blouse blanche** *nf* white coat.

blouson /bluzɔ̃/ *nm* jacket, blouson.

bluffer /blœfe/ [1] *vt/i* bluff.

bobine /bɔbin/ *nf* (de fil, film) reel; (Électr) coil.

bobo /bobo/ *nm* 🅸 sore, cut; **avoir ~** have a pain.

bocal (*pl* **-aux**) /bɔkal, -o/ *nm* jar.

bœuf (*pl* **~s**) /bœf, bø/ *nm* bullock; (US) steer; (viande) beef; **~s** oxen.

bogue /bɔg/ *nm* (Ordinat) bug.

bohème /bɔɛm/ *a & nmf* bohemian.

boire /bwaʀ/ [12] *vt/i* (*personne, plante*) drink; (*argile*) soak up; **~ un coup** 🅸 have a drink.

bois /bwa/ ⇨BOIRE [12]. ● *nm*

(matériau, forêt) wood; **de ~, en ~** wooden. ● *nmpl* (de cerf) antlers.

boiseries /bwazʀi/ *nfpl* panelling.

boisson /bwasɔ̃/ *nf* drink.

boit /bwa/ ⇒BOIRE [12].

boîte /bwat/ *nf* box; (de conserves) tin, can; (entreprise ⊡) firm; **en ~** tinned, canned; **~ à gants** glove compartment; **~ aux lettres** letter-box; **~ aux lettres électronique, blé** mailbox; **~ de nuit** night-club; **~ postale** post-office box; **~ de vitesses** gear box.

boiter /bwate/ [1] *vi* limp. **boiteux, -euse** *a* lame; (*raisonnement*) shaky.

boîtier /bwatje/ *nm* case.

bol /bɔl/ *nm* bowl; **~ d'air** a breath of fresh air; **avoir du ~** ⊡ be lucky.

bolide /bɔlid/ *nm* racing car.

Bolivie /bɔlivi/ *nf* Bolivia.

bombardement /bɔ̃baʀdəmɑ̃/ *nm* bombing; shelling.

bombarder /bɔ̃baʀde/ [1] *vt* bomb; (par obus) shell; **~ qn de** (fig) bombard sb with. **bombardier** *nm* (Aviat) bomber.

bombe /bɔ̃b/ *nf* bomb; (atomiseur) spray, aerosol.

bombé, ~e /bɔ̃be/ *a* rounded; (*route*) cambered.

bon, bonne /bɔ̃, bɔn/ *a* good; (qui convient) right; **~ à/pour** (approprié) fit to/for; **bonne année** happy New Year; **~ anniversaire** happy birthday; **~ appétit/voyage** enjoy your meal/trip; **bonne chance/nuit** good luck/night; **~ sens** common sense; **bonne femme** (péj) woman; **de bonne heure** early; **à quoi ~?** what's the point? ● *adv* **sentir ~** smell nice; **tenir ~** stand firm; **il fait ~** the weather is mild. ● *interj* right, well. ● *nm* (billet) voucher, coupon; **~ de commande** order form; **pour de ~** for good. **bonne** *nf* (domestique) maid.

bonbon /bɔ̃bɔ̃/ *nm* sweet; (US) candy.

bonbonne /bɔ̃bɔn/ *nf* demijohn; (de gaz) cylinder.

bond /bɔ̃/ *nm* leap; **faire un ~** (de surprise) jump.

bonde /bɔ̃d/ *nf* plug; (trou) plughole.

bondé, ~e /bɔ̃de/ *a* packed.

bondir /bɔ̃diʀ/ [2] *vi* leap; (de surprise) jump.

bonheur /bɔnœʀ/ *nm* happiness; (chance) (good) luck; **au petit ~** haphazardly; **par ~** luckily.

bonhomme (*pl* **bonshommes**) /bɔnɔm, bɔ̃zɔm/ *nm* fellow; **~ de neige** snowman. ● *a inv* good-hearted.

bonifier (se) /(sə)bɔnifje/ [45] *vpr* improve.

bonjour /bɔ̃ʒuʀ/ *nm & interj* hallo, hello, good morning *ou* afternoon.

bon marché /bɔ̃maʀʃe/ *a inv* cheap. ● *adv* cheap(ly).

bonne /bɔn/ ⇒BON.

bonne-maman (*pl* **bonnes-mamans**) /bɔnmamɑ̃/ *nf* ⊡ granny.

bonnement /bɔnmɑ̃/ *adv* **tout ~** quite simply.

bonnet /bɔnɛ/ *nm* hat; (de soutien-gorge) cup; **~ de bain** swimming cap. **bonneterie** *nf* hosiery.

bonsoir /bɔ̃swaʀ/ *nm* good evening; (en se couchant) good night.

bonté /bɔ̃te/ *nf* kindness.

bonus /bɔnys/ *nm* (Auto) no-claims bonus.

boots /buts/ *nmpl* ankle boots.

bord /bɔʀ/ *nm* edge; (rive) bank; **à ~ (de)** on board; **au ~ de la mer** at the seaside; **au ~ des larmes** on the verge of tears; **~ de la route** roadside.

B

bordeaux /bɔʀdo/ *a inv* maroon. ● *nm inv* Bordeaux.

bordel /bɔʀdɛl/ *nm* brothel; (désordre 🅘) shambles.

border /bɔʀde/ [1] *vt* line, border; (*tissu*) edge; (*personne, lit*) tuck in.

bordereau (*pl* **~x**) /bɔʀdəʀo/ *nm* (document) slip.

bordure /bɔʀdyʀ/ *nf* border; **en ~ de** on the edge of.

borgne /bɔʀɲ/ *a* one-eyed.

borne /bɔʀn/ *nf* boundary marker; (pour barrer le passage) bollard; **~ (kilométrique)** ≈ milestone; **~s** limits.

borné, ~e /bɔʀne/ *a* (*esprit*) narrow; (*personne*) narrow-minded.

borner (se) /(sə)bɔʀne/ [1] *vpr* confine oneself (**à** to).

bosniaque /bɔsnjak/ *a* Bosnian. **B~** *nmf* Bosnian.

Bosnie /bɔsni/ *nf* Bosnia.

bosse /bɔs/ *nf* bump; (de chameau) hump; **avoir la ~ de** 🅘 have a gift for; **avoir roulé sa ~** have been around. **bosselé, ~e** *a* dented; (*terrain*) bumpy.

bosser /bɔse/ [1] *vi* 🅘 work (hard).

bossu, ~e /bɔsy/ *a* hunchbacked. ● *nm, f* hunchback.

botanique /bɔtanik/ *nf* botany. ● *a* botanical.

botte /bɔt/ *nf* boot; (de fleurs, légumes) bunch; (de paille) bundle, bale; **~s de caoutchouc** wellingtons.

botter /bɔte/ [1] *vt* 🅘 **ça me botte** I like the idea.

bottin® /bɔtɛ̃/ *nm* phone book.

bouc /buk/ *nm* (billy-)goat; (barbe) goatee; **~ émissaire** scapegoat.

boucan /bukɑ̃/ *nm* 🅘 din.

bouche /buʃ/ *nf* mouth; (lèvres) lips; **~ bée** open-mouthed; **~ d'égout** manhole; **~ d'incendie** (fire) hydrant; **~ de métro** entrance to the underground *ou* subway (US). **bouche-à-bouche** *nm inv* mouth-to-mouth resuscitation. **bouche-à-oreille** *nm inv* word of mouth.

bouché, ~e /buʃe/ *a* (*profession, avenir*) oversubscribed; (stupide: péj) stupid.

bouchée /buʃe/ *nf* mouthful.

boucher¹ /buʃe/ [1] *vt* block; (*bouteille*) cork. ◻ **se ~** *vpr* get blocked; **se ~ le nez** hold one's nose.

boucher², -ère /buʃe, -ɛʀ/ *nm, f* butcher. **boucherie** *nf* butcher's (shop); (carnage) butchery.

bouchon /buʃɔ̃/ *nm* stopper; (en liège) cork; (de stylo, tube) cap; (de pêcheur) float; (embouteillage) traffic jam; **~ de cérumen** plug of earwax.

boucle /bukl/ *nf* (de ceinture) buckle; (de cheveux) curl; (forme) loop; **~ d'oreille** earring. **bouclé, ~e** *a* (*cheveux*) curly.

boucler /bukle/ [1] *vt* fasten; (enfermer 🅘) shut up; (encercler) seal off; (*budget*) balance; (terminer) finish off. ● *vi* curl.

bouclier /buklije/ *nm* shield.

bouddhiste /budist/ *a & nmf* Buddhist.

bouder /bude/ [1] *vi* sulk. ● *vt* stay away from.

boudin /budɛ̃/ *nm* black pudding.

boue /bu/ *nf* mud.

bouée /bwe/ *nf* buoy; **~ de sauvetage** lifebuoy.

boueux, -euse /buø, -z/ *a* muddy.

bouffe /buf/ *nf* 🅘 food, grub.

bouffée /bufe/ *nf* puff, whiff; (d'orgueil) fit; **~ de chaleur** (Méd) hot flush.

bouffi, ~e /bufi/ *a* bloated.

bouffon, ~ne /bufɔ̃, -ɔn/ *a* farcical. ● *nm* buffoon.

bougeoir /buʒwaʀ/ *nm* candlestick.

bougeotte /buʒɔt/ *nf* **avoir la ~** ⊡ have the fidgets.

bouger /buʒe/ [40] *vt/i* move. □ **se ~** *vpr* ⊡ move.

bougie /buʒi/ *nf* candle; (Auto) spark(ing)-plug.

bouillant, ~e /bujɑ̃, -t/ *a* boiling; (très chaud) boiling hot.

bouillie /buji/ *nf* (pour bébé) baby cereal; (péj) mush; **en ~** crushed, mushy.

bouillir /bujiʀ/ [13] *vi* boil; (fig) seethe; **faire ~** boil.

bouilloire /bujwaʀ/ *nf* kettle.

bouillon /bujɔ̃/ *nm* (de cuisson) stock; (potage) broth.

bouillonner /bujɔne/ [1] *vi* bubble.

bouillotte /bujɔt/ *nf* hot-water bottle.

boulanger, -ère /bulɑ̃ʒe, -ɛʀ/ *nm, f* baker. **boulangerie** *nf* bakery. **boulangerie-pâtisserie** *nf* bakery (*selling cakes and pastries*).

boule /bul/ *nf* ball; **~s** (jeu) boules; **jouer aux ~s** play boules; **une ~ dans la gorge** a lump in one's throat; **~ de neige** snowball.

bouleau (*pl* **~x**) /bulo/ *nm* (silver) birch.

boulet /bulɛ/ *nm* (de forçat) ball and chain; **~ (de canon)** canonball; **~ de charbon** coal nut.

boulette /bulɛt/ *nf* (de pain, papier) pellet; (bévue) blunder; **~ de viande** meat ball.

boulevard /bulvaʀ/ *nm* boulevard.

bouleversant, ~e /bulvɛʀsɑ̃, -t/ *a* deeply moving. **bouleversement** *nm* upheaval. **bouleverser** [1] *vt* turn upside down; (*pays, plans*) disrupt; (émouvoir) upset.

boulimie /bulimi/ *nf* bulimia.

boulon /bulɔ̃/ *nm* bolt.

boulot, ~te /bulo, -ɔt/ *a* (rond ⊡) dumpy. ● *nm* (travail ⊡) work.

boum /bum/ *nm & interj* bang. ● *nf* (fête ⊡) party.

bouquet /bukɛ/ *nm* (de fleurs) bunch, bouquet; (d'arbres) clump; **c'est le ~!** ⊡ that's the last straw!

bouquin /bukɛ̃/ *nm* ⊡ book. **bouquiner** [1] *vt/i* ⊡ read. **bouquiniste** *nmf* second-hand bookseller.

bourbier /buʀbje/ *nm* mire; (fig) tangle.

bourde /buʀd/ *nf* blunder.

bourdon /buʀdɔ̃/ *nm* bumble-bee. **bourdonnement** *nm* buzzing.

bourg /buʀ/ *nm* (market) town (centre), village centre.

bourgeois, ~e /buʀʒwa, -z/ *a & nm,f* middle-class (person), (péj) bourgeois. **bourgeoisie** *nf* middle class(es).

bourgeon /buʀʒɔ̃/ *nm* bud.

bourgogne /buʀgɔɲ/ *nm* Burgundy.

bourlinguer /buʀlɛ̃ge/ [1] *vi* ⊡ travel about.

bourrage /buʀaʒ/ *nm* **~ de crâne** brainwashing.

bourratif, -ive /buʀatif, -v/ *a* stodgy.

bourreau (*pl* **~x**) /buʀo/ *nm* executioner; **~ de travail** (fig) workaholic.

bourrelet /buʀlɛ/ *nm* weather-strip, draught excluder; (de chair) roll of fat.

bourrer /buʀe/ [1] *vt* cram (**de** with); (*pipe*) fill; **~ de** (*nourriture*) stuff with; **~ de coups** thrash; **~ le crâne à qn** brainwash sb.

bourrique /buʀik/ *nf* donkey; ⊡ pig-headed person.

bourru, ~e /buʀy/ *a* gruff.

bourse /buʀs/ *nf* purse;

B

(subvention) grant; **la B~** the Stock Exchange.

boursier, -ière /buRsje, -jɛR/ *a* (*valeurs*) Stock Exchange. ● *nm, f* grant holder.

boursoufler /buRsufle/ [1] *vt* (visage) cause to swell; (peinture) blister.

bousculade /buskylad/ *nf* crush; (précipitation) rush. **bousculer** [1] *vt* (pousser) jostle; (presser) rush; (renverser) knock over.

bousiller /buzije/ [1] *vt* ▣ wreck.

boussole /busɔl/ *nf* compass.

bout /bu/ *nm* end; (de langue, bâton) piece; (morceau) bit; **à ~** exhausted; **à ~ de souffle** out of breath; **à ~ portant** point-blank; **au ~ de** (après) after; **venir à ~ de** (finir) manage to finish; **d'un ~ à l'autre** throughout; **au ~ du compte** in the end; **~ filtre** filter-tip.

bouteille /butɛj/ *nf* bottle; **~ d'oxygène** oxygen cylinder.

boutique /butik/ *nf* shop; (de mode) boutique.

bouton /butɔ̃/ *nm* button; (sur la peau) spot, pimple; (pousse) bud; (de porte, radio) knob; **~ de manchette** cuff-link. **boutonner** [1] *vt* button (up). **boutonnière** *nf* buttonhole. **bouton-pression** (*pl* **boutons-pression**) *nm* press-stud; (US) snap.

bouture /butyR/ *nf* cutting.

bovin, ~e /bɔvɛ̃, -in/ *a* bovine. **bovins** *nmpl* cattle (*pl*).

box (*pl* **~** *ou* **boxes**) /bɔks/ *nm* lock-up garage; (de dortoir) cubicle; (d'écurie) (loose) box; (Jur) dock.

boxe /bɔks/ *nf* boxing.

boyau (*pl* **~x**) /bwajo/ *nm* gut; (corde) catgut; (galerie) gallery; (de bicyclette) tyre; (US) tire.

boycotter /bɔjkɔte/ [1] *vt* boycott.

BP *abrév f* (**boîte postale**) PO Box.

bracelet /bRaslɛ/ *nm* bracelet; (de montre) watchstrap.

braconnier /bRakɔnje/ *nm* poacher.

brader /bRade/ [1] *vt* sell off. **braderie** *nf* clearance sale.

braguette /bRagɛt/ *nf* fly.

braille /bRaj/ *nm & a* Braille.

brailler /bRɑje/ [1] *vt/i* bawl.

braise /bRɛz/ *nf* embers (+ *pl*).

braiser /bReze/ [1] *vt* (Culin) braise.

brancard /bRɑ̃kaR/ *nm* stretcher; (de charrette) shaft.

branche /bRɑ̃ʃ/ *nf* branch.

branché, ~e /bRɑ̃ʃe/ *a* ▣ trendy.

branchement /bRɑ̃ʃmɑ̃/ *nm* connection. **brancher** [1] *vt* (*prise*) plug in; (à un réseau) connect.

brandir /bRɑ̃diR/ [2] *vt* brandish.

branler /bRɑ̃le/ [1] *vi* be shaky.

braquer /bRake/ [1] *vt* (*arme*) aim; (*regard*) fix; (*roue*) turn; (*banque*: ▣) hold up; **~ qn contre** turn sb against. ● *vi* (Auto) turn (the wheel). ▫ **se ~** *vpr* dig one's heels in.

bras /bRa/ *nm* arm; (de rivière) branch; (Tech) arm; **~ dessus ~ dessous** arm in arm; **~ droit** (fig) right hand man; **~ de mer** sound; **en ~ de chemise** in one's shirtsleeves. ● *nmpl* (fig) labour, hands.

brasier /bRɑzje/ *nm* blaze.

brassard /bRasaR/ *nm* armband.

brasse /bRas/ *nf* breast-stroke; **~ papillon** butterfly (stroke).

brasser /bRase/ [1] *vt* mix; (*bière*) brew; (*affaires*) handle a lot of. **brasserie** *nf* brewery; (café) brasserie.

brave /bRav/ *a* (bon) good; (valeureux) brave. **braver** [1] *vt* defy.

bravo /bRavo/ *interj* bravo. ● *nm* cheer.
bravoure /bRavuR/ *nf* bravery.
break /bRɛk/ *nm* estate car; (US) station-wagon.
brebis /bRəbi/ *nf* ewe.
brèche /bRɛʃ/ *nf* gap, breach; **être sur la ~** be on the go.
bredouille /bRəduj/ *a* empty-handed.
bredouiller /bRəduje/ [1] *vt/i* mumble.
bref, brève /bRɛf, -v/ *a* short, brief. ● *adv* in short; **en ~** in short.
Brésil /bRezil/ *nm* Brazil.
Bretagne /bRətaɲ/ *nf* Brittany.
bretelle /bRətɛl/ *nf* (de sac, maillot) strap; (d'autoroute) access road; **~s** (pour pantalon) braces; (US) suspenders.
breton, ~ne /bRətɔ̃, -ɔn/ *a & nm* (Ling) Breton. **B~, ~ne** *nm,f* Breton.
breuvage /bRœvaʒ/ *nm* beverage.
brève /bRɛv/ ⇒BREF.
brevet /bRəvɛ/ *nm* **~ (d'invention)** patent; (diplôme) diploma.
breveté, ~e /bRəvte/ *a* patented.
bribes /bRib/ *nfpl* scraps.
bricolage /bRikɔlaʒ/ *nm* do-it-yourself (jobs).
bricole /bRikɔl/ *nf* trifle.
bricoler /bRikɔle/ [1] *vi* do DIY; (US) fix things, tinker with.
bricoleur, -euse /bRikɔlœR, -øz/ *nm,f* handyman, handywoman.
bride /bRid/ *nf* bridle.
bridé, ~e /bRide/ *a* **yeux ~s** slanting eyes.
brider /bRide/ [1] *vt* (*cheval*) bridle; (fig) keep in check.
brièvement /bRijɛvmɑ̃/ *adv* briefly.
brigade /bRigad/ *nf* (de police) squad; (Mil) brigade; (fig) team.
brigadier *nm* (de gendarmerie) sergeant.
brigand /bRigɑ̃/ *nm* robber.
brillant, ~e /bRijɑ̃, -t/ *a* (*couleur*) bright; (luisant) shiny; (remarquable) brilliant. ● *nm* (éclat) shine; (diamant) diamond.
briller /bRije/ [1] *vi* shine.
brimade /bRimad/ *nf* vexation.
brimer [1] *vt* bully, harass, **se sentir brimé** feel put down.
brin /bRɛ̃/ *nm* (de muguet) sprig; (d'herbe) blade; (de paille) wisp; **un ~ de** (un peu) a bit of.
brindille /bRɛ̃dij/ *nf* twig.
brioche /bRijɔʃ/ *nf* brioche, sweet bun; (ventre ▣) paunch.
brique /bRik/ *nf* brick.
briquet /bRikɛ/ *nm* (cigarette-) lighter.
brise /bRiz/ *nf* breeze.
briser /bRize/ [1] *vt* break. □ **se ~** *vpr* break.
britannique /bRitanik/ *a* British. **B~** *nmf* Briton; **les B~s** the British.
brocante /bRɔkɑ̃t/ *nf* bric-à-brac trade; (marché) flea market.
broche /bRɔʃ/ *nf* brooch; (Culin) spit; **à la ~** spit-roasted.
broché, ~e /bRɔʃe/ *a* paperback.
brochet /bRɔʃɛ/ *nm* pike.
brochette /bRɔʃɛt/ *nf* skewer.
brochure /bRɔʃyR/ *nf* brochure, booklet.
broder /bRɔde/ [1] *vt/i* embroider.
broderie *nf* embroidery.
broncher /bRɔ̃ʃe/ [1] *vi* **sans ~** without turning a hair.
bronchite /bRɔ̃ʃit/ *nf* bronchitis.
bronze /bRɔ̃z/ *nm* bronze.
bronzé, ~e /bRɔ̃ze/ *a* (sun-) tanned.
bronzer /bRɔ̃ze/ [1] *vi* (*personne*) get a (sun-)tan.
brosse /bRɔs/ *nf* brush; **~ à dents** toothbrush; **~ à habits** clothes

brush; **en ~** (*coiffure*) in a crew cut.

brosser /bʀɔse/ [1] *vt* brush; (fig) paint. □ **se ~** *vpr* **se ~ les dents/les cheveux** brush one's teeth/hair.

brouette /bʀuɛt/ *nf* wheelbarrow.

brouhaha /bʀuaa/ *nm* hubbub.

brouillard /bʀujaʀ/ *nm* fog.

brouille /bʀuj/ *nf* quarrel.

brouiller /bʀuje/ [1] *vt* (*vue*) blur; (*œufs*) scramble; (*amis*) set at odds; **~ les pistes** cloud the issue. □ **se ~** *vpr* (*ciel*) cloud over; (*amis*) fall out.

brouillon, ~ne /bʀujɔ̃, -ɔn/ *a* untidy. ● *nm* (rough) draft.

brousse /bʀus/ *nf* **la ~** the bush.

brouter /bʀute/ [1] *vt/i* graze.

broyer /bʀwaje/ [31] *vt* crush; (moudre) grind.

bru /bʀy/ *nf* daughter-in-law.

bruine /bʀɥin/ *nf* drizzle.

bruissement /bʀɥismɑ̃/ *nm* rustling.

bruit /bʀɥi/ *nm* noise; **~ de couloir** (fig) rumour.

bruitage /bʀɥitaʒ/ *nm* sound effects.

brûlant, ~e /bʀylɑ̃, -t/ *a* burning (hot); (*sujet*) red-hot; (*passion*) fiery.

brûlé /bʀyle/ *nm* burning; **ça sent le ~** I can smell something burning. ● ⇒BRÛLER [1].

brûler /bʀyle/ [1] *vt/i* burn; (*essence*) use (up); (*cierge*) light (à to); **~ un feu (rouge)** jump the lights; **~ d'envie de faire** be longing to do. □ **se ~** *vpr* burn oneself.

brûlure /bʀylyʀ/ *nf* burn; **~s d'estomac** heartburn.

brume /bʀym/ *nf* mist. **brumeux, -euse** *a* misty; (*esprit*) hazy.

brun, ~e /bʀœ̃, -yn/ *a* brown, dark. ● *nm* brown. ● *nm, f* dark-haired person. **brunir** [2] *vi* turn brown; (bronzer) get a tan.

brushing /bʀœʃiŋ/ *nm* blow-dry.

brusque /bʀysk/ *a* (*personne*) abrupt; (*geste*) violent; (soudain) sudden.

brusquer /bʀyske/ [1] *vt* be abrupt with; (précipiter) rush.

brut, ~e /bʀyt/ *a* (*diamant*) rough; (*champagne*) dry; (*pétrole*) crude; (Comm) gross.

brutal, ~e (*mpl* **-aux**) /bʀytal, -o/ *a* brutal. **brutalité** *nf* brutality.

brute /bʀyt/ *nf* brute.

Bruxelles /bʀysɛl/ *npr* Brussels.

bruyant, ~e /bʀɥijɑ̃, -t/ *a* noisy.

bruyère /bʀyjɛʀ/ *nf* heather.

bu /by/ ⇒BOIRE [12].

bûche /byʃ/ *nf* log; **~ de Noël** Christmas log; **ramasser une ~** [!] fall.

bûcher /byʃe/ [1] *vt/i* [!] slog away (at) [!]. ● *nm* (supplice) stake.

bûcheron /byʃʀɔ̃/ *nm* lumberjack.

budget /bydʒɛ/ *nm* budget. **budgétaire** *a* budgetary.

buée /bɥe/ *nf* condensation.

buffet /byfɛ/ *nm* sideboard; (table garnie) buffet.

buffle /byfl/ *nm* buffalo.

buisson /bɥisɔ̃/ *nm* bush.

buissonnière /bɥisɔnjɛʀ/ *af* **faire l'école ~** play truant.

bulbe /bylb/ *nm* bulb.

bulgare /bylgaʀ/ *a & nm* Bulgarian. **B~** *nmf* Bulgarian.

Bulgarie /bylgaʀi/ *nf* Bulgaria.

bulldozer /byldozɛʀ/ *nm* bulldozer.

bulle /byl/ *nf* bubble.

bulletin /byltɛ̃/ *nm* bulletin, report; (Scol) report; **~ d'information** news bulletin; **~ météorologique** weather report; **~ (de vote)** ballot-paper; **~ de salaire** pay-slip.

buraliste /byʀalist/ *nmf* tobacconist.

bureau (*pl* **~x**) /byʀo/ *nm* office; (meuble) desk; (comité) board; **~ d'études** design office; **~ de poste** post office; **~ de tabac** tobacconist's (shop); **~ de vote** polling station.

bureaucrate /byʀokʀat/ *nmf* bureaucrat. **bureaucratie** *nf* bureaucracy. **bureaucratique** *a* bureaucratic.

bureautique /byʀotik/ *nf* office automation.

burlesque /byʀlɛsk/ *a* (*histoire*) ludicrous; (*film*) farcical.

bus /bys/ *nm* bus.

buste /byst/ *nm* bust.

but /by(t)/ *nm* target; (dessein) aim, goal; (football) goal; **avoir pour ~ de** aim to; **de ~ en blanc** point-blank; **dans le ~ de** with the intention of; **aller droit au ~** go straight to the point.

butane /bytan/ *nm* butane, Calor gas®.

buté, ~e /byte/ *a* obstinate.

buter /byte/ [1] *vi* **~ contre** knock against; (*problème*) come up against. ● *vt* antagonize. □ **se ~** *vpr* (s'entêter) become obstinate.

buteur /bytœʀ/ *nm* (au football) striker.

butin /bytɛ̃/ *nm* booty, loot.

butte /byt/ *nf* mound; **en ~ à** exposed to.

buvard /byvaʀ/ *nm* blotting-paper.

buvette /byvɛt/ *nf* (refreshment) bar.

buveur, -euse /byvœʀ, -øz/ *nm, f* drinker.

c' /s/ ⇒CE.

ça /sa/

● *pronom démonstratif*

····➤ (sujet) it; that; **~ flotte** it floats; **~ suffit!** that's enough!; **~ y est!** that's it!; **~ sent le brûlé** there's a smell of burning; **~ va?** how are things?

····➤ (objet) (proche) this; (plus éloigné) that; **c'est ~** that's right.

····➤ (dans expressions) **où ~?** where?; **quand ~?** when?; **et avec ~?** anything else?

çà /sa/ *adv* **~ et là** here and there.

cabane /kaban/ *nf* hut; (à outils) shed.

cabaret /kabaʀɛ/ *nm* cabaret.

cabillaud /kabijo/ *nm* cod.

cabine /kabin/ *nf* (à la piscine) cubicle; (de bateau) cabin; (de camion) cab; (d'ascenseur) cage; **~ d'essayage** fitting room; **~ de pilotage** cockpit; **~ de plage** beach hut; **~ (téléphonique)** phone booth, phone box.

cabinet /kabinɛ/ *nm* (de médecin) surgery; (US) office; (d'avocat) office; (clientèle) practice; (cabinet collectif) firm; (Pol) Cabinet; (pièce) room; **~s** (toilettes) toilet; (US) bathroom; **~ de toilette** bathroom.

câble /kɑbl / *nm* cable; (corde) rope; (TV) cable TV. **câbler** *vt* [1] cable; (TV) install cable television in.

cabosser /kabɔse/ [1] *vt* dent.
cabotage /kabɔtaʒ/ *nm* coastal navigation.
cabrer (se) /(sə)kabʀe/ [1] *vpr* (*cheval*) rear; **se ~ contre** rebel against.
cabriole /kabʀijɔl/ *nf* **faire des ~s** caper about.
cacahuète /kakawɛt/ *nf* peanut.
cacao /kakao/ *nm* cocoa.
cachalot /kaʃalo/ *nm* sperm whale.
cache /kaʃ/ *nm* mask. ● *nf* hiding place; **~ d'armes** arms cache.
cache-cache /kaʃkaʃ/ *nm inv* hide-and-seek.
cache-nez /kaʃne/ *nm inv* scarf.
cacher /kaʃe/ [1] *vt* hide, conceal (à from). ◻ **se ~** *vpr* hide; (se trouver caché) be hidden.
cachet /kaʃɛ/ *nm* (de cire) seal; (à l'encre) stamp; (de la poste) postmark; (comprimé) tablet; (d'artiste) fee; (chic) style, cachet.
cachette /kaʃɛt/ *nf* hiding-place; **en ~** in secret.
cachot /kaʃo/ *nm* dungeon.
cachottier, -ière /kaʃɔtjɛ, -jɛʀ/ *a* secretive.
cacophonie /kakɔfɔni/ *nf* cacophony.
cactus /kaktys/ *nm* cactus.
cadavérique /kadaveʀik/ *a* (*teint*) deathly pale.
cadavre /kadavʀ/ *nm* corpse; (de victime) body.
caddie /kadi/ *nm* (de supermarché)® trolley; (au golf) caddie.
cadeau (*pl* **~x**) /kado/ *nm* present, gift; **faire un ~ à qn** give sb a present.
cadenas /kadna/ *nm* padlock.
cadence /kadɑ̃s/ *nf* rhythm, cadence; (de travail) rate; **en ~** in time; (*marcher*) in step.
cadet, ~te /kadɛ, -t/ *a* youngest; (entre deux) younger. ● *nm, f* youngest (child); younger (child).
cadran /kadʀɑ̃/ *nm* dial; **~ solaire** sundial.
cadre /kɑdʀ/ *nm* frame; (lieu) setting; (milieu) surroundings; (limites) scope; (contexte) framework; **dans le ~ de** (à l'occasion de) on the occasion of; (dans le contexte de) in the framework of. ● *nm* (personne) executive; **les ~s** the managerial staff.
cadrer /kadʀe/ [1] *vi* **~ avec** tally with. ● *vt* (*photo*) centre.
cafard /kafaʀ/ *nm* (insecte) cockroach; **avoir le ~** [!] be down in the dumps.
café /kafe/ *nm* coffee; (bar) café; **~ crème** espresso with milk; **~ en grains** coffee beans; **~ au lait** white coffee.
cafetière /kaftjɛʀ/ *nf* coffee-pot; **~ électrique** coffee machine.
cage /kaʒ/ *nf* cage; **~ d'ascenseur** lift shaft; **~ d'escalier** stairwell; **~ thoracique** rib cage.
cageot /kaʒo/ *nm* crate.
cagibi /kaʒibi/ *nm* storage room.
cagneux, -euse /kaɲø, -z/ *a* **avoir les genoux ~** be knock-kneed.
cagnotte /kaɲɔt/ *nf* kitty.
cagoule /kagul/ *nf* hood; (passe-montagne) balaclava.
cahier /kaje/ *nm* notebook; (Scol) exercise book; **~ de textes** homework notebook; **~ des charges** (Tech) specifications (+ *pl*).
cahot /kao/ *nm* bump, jolt.
cahoteux, -euse *a* bumpy.
caïd /kaid/ *nm* [!] big shot.
caille /kɑj/ *nf* quail.
cailler /kɑje/ [1] *vi* curdle; **ça caille** [!] it's freezing. ◻ **se ~** *vpr* (*sang*) clot; (*lait*) curdle. **caillot** *nm* (blood) clot.

caillou (*pl* **~x**) /kaju/ *nm* stone; (galet) pebble.

caisse /kɛs/ *nf* crate, case; (tiroir, machine) till; (guichet) cash desk; (au supermarché) check-out; (bureau) office; (Mus) drum; **~ enregistreuse** cash register; **~ d'épargne** savings bank; **~ de retraite** pension fund. **caissier, -ière** *nm,f* cashier.

cajoler /kaʒɔle/ [1] *vt* coax.

calcaire /kalkɛʀ/ *a* (*sol*) chalky; (*eau*) hard.

calciné, ~e /kalsine/ *a* charred.

calcul /kalkyl/ *nm* calculation; (Scol) arithmetic; (différentiel) calculus; **~ biliaire** gallstone.

calculatrice /kalkylatʀis/ *nf* calculator. **calculer** [1] *vt* calculate. **calculette** *nf* (pocket) calculator.

cale /kal/ *nf* wedge; (pour roue) chock; (de navire) hold; **~ sèche** dry dock.

calé, ~e /kale/ *a* ⓘ clever.

caleçon /kalsɔ̃/ *nm* boxer shorts (+ *pl*); underpants (+ *pl*); (de femme) leggings.

calembour /kalɑ̃buʀ/ *nm* pun.

calendrier /kalɑ̃dʀije/ *nm* calendar; (fig) schedule, timetable.

calepin /kalpɛ̃/ *nm* notebook.

caler /kale/ [1] *vt* wedge. ● *vi* stall; (abandonner ⓘ) give up.

calfeutrer /kalføtʀe/ [1] *vt* (*fissure*) stop up; (*porte*) draught proof.

calibre /kalibʀ/ *nm* calibre; (d'un œuf, fruit) grade.

calice /kalis/ *nm* (Relig) chalice; (Bot) calyx.

califourchon: **à ~** /akalifuʀʃɔ̃/ *loc* astride.

câlin, ~e /kɑlɛ̃, -in/ *a* (*regard, ton*) affectionate; (*personne*) cuddly.

calmant /kalmɑ̃/ *nm* sedative.

calme /kalm/ *a* calm. ● *nm* peace; calm; (maîtrise de soi) composure; **du ~!** calm down!

calmer /kalme/ [1] *vt* (*personne*) calm down; (*situation*) defuse; (*douleur*) ease; (*soif*) quench. □ **se ~** *vpr* (*personne, situation*) calm down; (*agitation, tempête*) die down; (*douleur*) ease.

calomnie /kalɔmni/ *nf* (*orale*) slander; (écrite) libel. **calomnier** [45] *vt* slander; libel. **calomnieux, -ieuse** *a* slanderous; libellous.

calorie /kalɔʀi/ *nf* calorie.

calque /kalk/ *nm* tracing; (**papier**) **~** tracing paper; (fig) exact copy.

calquer /kalke/ [1] *vt* trace; (fig) copy; **~ qch sur** model sth on.

calvaire /kalvɛʀ/ *nm* (croix) Calvary; (fig) suffering.

calvitie /kalvisi/ *nf* baldness.

camarade /kamaʀad/ *nmf* friend; (Pol) comrade; **~ de jeu** playmate. **camaraderie** *nf* friendship.

cambouis /kɑ̃bwi/ *nm* dirty oil.

cambrer /kɑ̃bʀe/ [1] *vt* arch. □ **se ~** *vpr* arch one's back.

cambriolage /kɑ̃bʀijɔlaʒ/ *nm* burglary. **cambrioler** [1] *vt* burgle. **cambrioleur, -euse** *nm,f* burglar.

camelot /kamlo/ *nm* ⓘ street vendor.

camelote /kamlɔt/ *nf* ⓘ junk.

caméra /kameʀa/ *nf* (cinéma, télévision) camera.

caméscope® /kameskɔp/ *nm* camcorder.

camion /kamjɔ̃/ *nm* lorry, truck. **camion-citerne** (*pl* **camions-citernes**) *nm* tanker. **camionnage** *nm* haulage. **camionnette** *nf* van. **camionneur** *nm* lorry *ou* truck driver; (entrepreneur) haulage contractor.

camisole /kamizɔl/ *nf* ~ (**de force**) straitjacket.

camoufler /kamufle/ [1] *vt* camouflage.

camp /kɑ̃/ *nm* camp; (Sport, Pol) side.

campagnard, ~**e** /kɑ̃paɲaʀ, -d/ *a* country. ● *nm, f* countryman, countrywoman.

campagne /kɑ̃paɲ/ *nf* country; countryside; (Mil, Pol) campaign.

campement /kɑ̃pmɑ̃/ *nm* camp, encampment.

camper /kɑ̃pe/ [1] *vi* camp. ● *vt* (esquisser) sketch. □ **se** ~ *vpr* plant oneself. **campeur, -euse** *nm, f* camper.

camping /kɑ̃piŋ/ *nm* camping; **faire du** ~ go camping; (**terrain de**) ~ campsite. **camping-car** (*pl* ~**s**) *nm* camper-van; (US) motorhome. **camping-gaz**® *nm inv* (réchaud) camping stove.

Canada /kanada/ *nm* Canada.

canadien, ~**ne** /kanadjɛ̃, -ɛn/ *a* Canadian. **C**~, ~**ne** *nm, f* Canadian. **canadienne** *nf* (veste) fur-lined jacket; (tente) ridge tent.

canaille /kanɑj/ *nf* rogue.

canal (*pl* **-aux**) /kanal, -o/ *nm* (artificiel) canal; (bras de mer) channel; (Tech, TV) channel; (moyen) channel; **par le** ~ **de** through. **canalisation** *nf* (tuyaux) mains (+ *pl*). **canaliser** [1] *vt* (*eau*) canalize; (fig) channel.

canapé /kanape/ *nm* sofa.

canard /kanaʀ/ *nm* duck; (journal [!]) rag.

canari /kanaʀi/ *nm* canary.

cancans /kɑ̃kɑ̃/ *nmpl* [!] gossip.

cancer /kɑ̃sɛʀ/ *nm* cancer; **le C**~ Cancer. **cancéreux, -euse** *a* cancerous. **cancérigène** *a* carcinogenic.

cancre /kɑ̃kʀ/ *nm* dunce.

candeur /kɑ̃dœʀ/ *nf* ingenuousness.

candidat, ~**e** /kɑ̃dida, -t/ *nm, f* (à un examen, Pol) candidate; (à un poste) applicant, candidate (**à** for).

candidature /kɑ̃didatyʀ/ *nf* application; (Pol) candidacy; **poser sa** ~ **à un poste** apply for a job.

candide /kɑ̃did/ *a* ingenuous.

cane /kan/ *nf* (female) duck. **caneton** *nm* duckling.

canette /kanɛt/ *nf* (bouteille) bottle; (boîte) can.

canevas /kanva/ *nm* canvas; (ouvrage) tapestry; (plan) framework, outline.

caniche /kaniʃ/ *nm* poodle.

canicule /kanikyl/ *nf* scorching heat; (vague de chaleur) heatwave.

canif /kanif/ *nm* penknife.

canine /kanin/ *nf* canine (tooth).

caniveau (*pl* ~**x**) /kanivo/ *nm* gutter.

cannabis /kanabis/ *nm* cannabis.

canne /kan/ *nf* (walking) stick; ~ **à pêche** fishing rod; ~ **à sucre** sugar cane.

cannelle /kanɛl/ *nf* cinnamon.

cannibale /kanibal/ *a & nmf* cannibal.

canoë /kanɔe/ *nm* canoe; (Sport) canoeing.

canon /kanɔ̃/ *nm* (big) gun; (ancien) cannon; (d'une arme) barrel; (principe, règle) canon.

canot /kano/ *nm* dinghy, (small) boat; ~ **de sauvetage** lifeboat; ~ **pneumatique** rubber dinghy. **canotier** *nm* boater.

cantatrice /kɑ̃tatʀis/ *nf* opera singer.

cantine /kɑ̃tin/ *nf* canteen.

cantique /kɑ̃tik/ *nm* hymn.

cantonner /kɑ̃tɔne/ [1] *vt* (Mil) billet. □ **se** ~ **dans** *vpr* confine oneself to.

cantonnier /kɑ̃tɔnje/ *nm* road mender.

canular /kanylaʀ/ *nm* hoax.

caoutchouc /kautʃu/ *nm*

rubber; (élastique) rubber band; ~ **mousse** foam rubber.

cap /kap/ *nm* cape, headland; (direction) course; (obstacle) hurdle; **franchir le ~ de la cinquantaine** pass the fifty mark; **mettre le ~ sur** steer a course for.

capable /kapabl/ *a* capable (**de** of); **~ de faire** able to do, capable of doing.

capacité /kapasite/ *nf* ability; (contenance, potentiel) capacity.

cape /kap/ *nf* cape; **rire sous ~** laugh up one's sleeve.

capillaire /kapilɛʀ/ *a* (*lotion, soins*) hair; (**vaisseau**) ~ capillary.

capitaine /kapitɛn/ *nm* captain.

capital, **~e** (*mpl* **-aux**) /kapital, -o/ *a* key, crucial, fundamental; (*peine, lettre*) capital. ● *nm* (*pl* **-aux**) (Comm) capital; (fig) stock; **capitaux** (Comm) capital. **capitale** *nf* (ville, lettre) capital.

capitalisme /kapitalism/ *nm* capitalism.

capitonné, **~e** /kapitɔne/ *a* padded.

capituler /kapityle/ [1] *vi* capitulate.

caporal (*pl* **-aux**) /kapɔʀal, -o/ *nm* corporal.

capot /kapo/ *nm* (Auto) bonnet; (US) hood.

capote /kapɔt/ *nf* (Auto) hood; (US) top; (préservatif ⓘ) condom.

capoter /kapɔte/ [1] *vi* overturn; (fig) collapse.

câpre /kɑpʀ/ *nf* (Culin) caper.

caprice /kapʀis/ *nm* whim; (colère) tantrum; **faire un ~** throw a tantrum. **capricieux**, **-ieuse** *a* capricious; (*appareil*) temperamental.

Capricorne /kapʀikɔʀn/ *nm* **le ~** Capricorn.

capsule /kapsyl/ *nf* capsule; (de bouteille) cap.

capter /kapte/ [1] *vt* (*eau*) collect; (*émission*) get; (*signal*) pick up; (fig) win, capture.

captif, **-ive** /kaptif, -v/ *a & nm,f* captive.

captiver /kaptive/ [1] *vt* captivate.

capturer /kaptyʀe/ [1] *vt* capture.

capuche /kapyʃ/ *nf* hood. **capuchon** *nm* hood; (de stylo) cap.

car /kaʀ/ *conj* because, for. ● *nm* coach; (US) bus.

carabine /kaʀabin/ *nf* rifle.

caractère /kaʀaktɛʀ/ *nm* (lettre) character; (nature) nature; **~s d'imprimerie** block letters; **avoir bon/mauvais ~** be good-natured/ bad-tempered; **avoir du ~** have character.

caractériel, **~le** /kaʀakteʀjɛl/ *a* (*trait*) character; (*enfant*) disturbed.

caractériser /kaʀakteʀize/ [1] *vt* characterize. □ **se ~ par** *vpr* be characterized by. **caractéristique** *a & nf* characteristic.

carafe /kaʀaf/ *nf* carafe.

Caraïbes /kaʀaib/ *nfpl* **les ~** the Caribbean.

carambolage /kaʀɑ̃bɔlaʒ/ *nm* pile-up.

caramel /kaʀamɛl/ *nm* caramel; (bonbon) toffee.

carapace /kaʀapas/ *nf* shell.

caravane /kaʀavan/ *nf* (Auto) caravan; (US) trailer; (convoi) caravan.

carbone /kaʀbɔn/ *nm* carbon; (**papier**) ~ carbon (paper). **carboniser** [1] *vt* burn (to ashes).

carburant /kaʀbyʀɑ̃/ *nm* (motor) fuel.

carburateur /kaʀbyʀatœʀ/ *nm* carburettor; (US) carburetor.

carcan /kaʀkɑ̃/ *nm* constraints (+ *pl*).

carcasse /kaʀkas/ *nf* (squelette) carcass; (armature) frame; (de voiture) shell.

cardiaque /kaʀdjak/ *a* heart. ● *nmf* heart patient.

cardinal, **~e** (*mpl* **-aux**) /kaʀdinal, -o/ *a & nm* cardinal.

Carême /kaʀɛm/ *nm* **le ~** Lent.

carence /kaʀɑ̃s/ *nf* shortcomings (+ *pl*); inadequacy; (Méd) deficiency; (absence) lack.

caresse /kaʀɛs/ *nf* caress; (à un animal) stroke. **caresser** [1] *vt* caress, stroke; (*espoir*) cherish.

cargaison /kaʀgɛzɔ̃/ *nf* cargo.

cargo /kaʀgo/ *nm* cargo boat.

caricature /kaʀikatyʀ/ *nf* caricature.

carie /kaʀi/ *nf* (trou) cavity; **la ~ (dentaire)** tooth decay.

carillon /kaʀijɔ̃/ *nm* chimes (+ *pl*); (horloge) chiming clock.

caritatif, **-ive** /kaʀitatif, -v/ *a* **association caritative** charity.

carnage /kaʀnaʒ/ *nm* carnage.

carnassier, **-ière** /kaʀnasje, -jɛʀ/ *a* carnivorous.

carnaval (*pl* **~s**) /kaʀnaval/ *nm* carnival.

carnet /kaʀnɛ/ *nm* notebook; (de tickets, timbres) book; **~ d'adresses** address book; **~ de chèques** chequebook.

carotte /kaʀɔt/ *nf* carrot.

carpe /kaʀp/ *nf* carp.

carré, **~e** /kaʀe/ *a* (forme, mesure) square; (fig) straightforward; **un mètre ~** one square metre. ● *nm* square; (de terrain) patch.

carreau (*pl* **~x**) /kaʀo/ *nm* (window) pane; (par terre, au mur) tile; (dessin) check; (aux cartes) diamonds (+ *pl*); **à ~x** (*tissu*) check(ed); (*papier*) squared.

carrefour /kaʀfuʀ/ *nm* crossroads (+ *sg*).

carrelage /kaʀlaʒ/ *nm* tiling; (sol) tiles.

carrément /kaʀemɑ̃/ *adv* (complètement) completely; (*stupide, dangereux*) downright; (*dire*) straight out; **elle a ~ démissionné** she went straight ahead and resigned.

carrière /kaʀjɛʀ/ *nf* career; (terrain) quarry.

carrossable /kaʀɔsabl/ *a* suitable for vehicles.

carrosse /kaʀɔs/ *nm* (horse-drawn) coach.

carrosserie /kaʀɔsʀi/ *nf* (Auto) body(work).

carrure /kaʀyʀ/ *nf* shoulders; (fig) necessary qualities, calibre.

cartable /kaʀtabl/ *nm* satchel.

carte /kaʀt/ *nf* card; (Géog) map; (Naut) chart; (au restaurant) menu; **~s** (jeu) cards; **à la ~** (*manger*) à la carte; (*horaire*) personalized; **donner ~ blanche à** give a free hand to; **~ de crédit** credit card; **~ grise** (car) registration document; **~ d'identité** identity card; **~ magnétique** swipe card; **~ de paiement** debit card; **~ postale** postcard; **~ à puce** smart card; **~ de séjour** resident's permit; **~ des vins** wine list; **~ de visite** (business) card.

cartilage /kaʀtilaʒ/ *nm* cartilage.

carton /kaʀtɔ̃/ *nm* cardboard; (boîte) (cardboard) box; **~ à dessin** portfolio; **faire un ~** [!] do well.

cartonné, **~e** /kaʀtɔne/ *a* **livre ~** hardback.

cartouche /kaʀtuʃ/ *nf* cartridge; (de cigarettes) carton. **cartouchière** *nf* cartridge-belt.

cas /kɑ/ *nm* case; **au ~ où** in case; **~ urgent** emergency; **en aucun ~** on no account; **en ~ de** in the event of, in case of; **en tout ~** in any case; (du moins) at least; **faire ~ de** set great store by; **~ de conscience** moral dilemma.

casanier, -ière /kazanje, -jɛʀ/ *a* home-loving.

cascade /kaskad/ *nf* waterfall; (au cinéma) stunt; (fig) spate, series (+ *sg*).

cascadeur, -euse /kaskadœʀ, -øz/ *nm, f* stuntman, stuntwoman.

case /kɑz/ *nf* hut; (de damier) square; (compartiment) pigeon-hole; (sur un formulaire) box.

caser /kaze/ [1] *vt* [I] (mettre) put; (loger) put up; (dans un travail) find a job for; (marier: péj) marry off.

caserne /kazɛʀn/ *nf* barracks; **~ de sapeurs-pompiers** fire station.

casier /kɑzje/ *nm* pigeon-hole, compartment; (à bouteilles, chaussures) rack; **~ judiciaire** criminal record.

casque /kask/ *nm* (de motard) crash helmet; (de cycliste) cycle helmet; (chez le coiffeur) (hair-) drier; **~ (à écouteurs)** headphones; **~ anti-bruit** ear defenders; **~ de protection** safety helmet.

casquette /kaskɛt/ *nf* cap.

cassant, ~e /kɑsɑ̃, -t/ *a* brittle; (brusque) curt.

cassation /kɑsasjɔ̃/ *nf* **cour de ~** appeal court.

casse /kɑs/ *nf* (objets) breakages; (lieu) breaker's yard; **mettre à la ~** scrap.

casse-cou /kɑsku/ *nmf inv* daredevil.

casse-croûte /kɑskʀut/ *nm inv* snack.

casse-noix /kɑsnwa/ *nm inv* nutcrackers (+ *pl*).

casse-pieds /kɑspje/ *nmf inv* [I] pain (in the neck) [!].

casser /kɑse/ [1] *vt* break; (annuler) annul; **~ les pieds à qn** [I] annoy sb. ● *vi* break. □ **se ~** *vpr* break; (partir [I]) be off [I].

casserole /kasʀɔl/ *nf* saucepan.

casse-tête /kɑstɛt/ *nm inv* (problème) headache; (jeu) brain teaser.

cassette /kasɛt/ *nf* casket; (de magnétophone) cassette, tape; (de vidéo) video tape; **~ audionumérique** digital audio tape.

cassis /kasi(s)/ *nm inv* blackcurrant.

cassure /kɑsyʀ/ *nf* break.

castor /kastɔʀ/ *nm* beaver.

castration /kastʀasjɔ̃/ *nf* castration.

catalogue /katalɔg/ *nm* catalogue.

catalyseur /katalizœʀ/ *nm* catalyst; (Auto) catalytic convertor.

catastrophe /katastʀɔf/ *nf* disaster, catastrophe.
catastrophique *a* catastrophic.

catch /katʃ/ *nm* (all-in) wrestling.

catéchisme /kateʃism/ *nm* catechism.

catégorie /kategɔʀi/ *nf* category.
catégorique *a* categorical.

cathédrale /katedʀal/ *nf* cathedral.

catholique /katɔlik/ *a* Catholic; **pas très ~** a bit fishy.

catimini: en ~ /ɑ̃katimini/ *loc* on the sly.

cauchemar /koʃmaʀ/ *nm* nightmare.

cause /koz/ *nf* cause; (raison) reason; (Jur) case; **à ~ de** because of; **en ~** (en jeu, concerné) involved; **pour ~ de** on account of; **mettre en ~** implicate; **remettre en ~** call into question.

causer /koze/ [1] *vt* cause; (discuter de [I]) **~ travail** talk shop; **~ de** talk about. ● *vi* chat. **causerie** *nf* talk.

causette /kozɛt/ *nf* **faire la ~** have a chat.

caution /kosjɔ̃/ *nf* surety; (Jur) bail; (appui) backing; (garantie) deposit; **libéré sous ~** released on bail. **cautionner** [1] *vt* guarantee; (soutenir) back.

cavalcade /kavalkad/ *nf* stampede, rush.

cavalier, -ière /kavalje, -jɛʀ/ *a* offhand; **allée cavalière** bridle path. ● *nm, f* rider; (pour danser) partner. ● *nm* (aux échecs) knight.

cave /kav/ *nf* cellar. ● *a* sunken.

caveau (*pl* **~x**) /kavo/ *nm* vault.

caverne /kavɛʀn/ *nf* cave.

CCP *abrév m* (**compte chèque postal**) post office account.

CD *abrév m* (**compact disc**) CD.

CD-ROM *abrév m inv* (**compact disc read only memory**) CD-ROM.

ce, c', cet, cette (*pl* **ces**) /sə, s, sɛt, se/

c' before e. **cet** before vowel or mute h.

●**ce, cet, cette** (*pl* **ces**) *adjectif démonstratif*

····➤ this; (plus éloigné) that; **ces** these; (plus éloigné) those; **cette nuit** (passée) last night; (à venir) tonight.

●**ce, c'** *pronom démonstratif*

····➤ **c'est** it's *ou* it is; **c'est un policier** he's a policeman; **~ sont eux qui l'ont fait** THEY did it; **qui est-~?** who is it?

····➤ **ce que/qui** what; **~ que je ne comprends pas** what I don't understand; **elle est venue, ~ qui est étonnant** she came, which is surprising; **~ que tu as de la chance!** how lucky you are!; **tout ~ que je sais** all I know; **tout ~ qu'elle trouve/peut** everything she finds/can.

CE *abrév f* (**Communauté européenne**) EC.

ceci /səsi/ *pron* this.

cécité /sesite/ *nf* blindness.

céder /sede/ [14] *vt* give up; **~ le passage** give way; (vendre) sell. ● *vi* (se rompre) give way; (se soumettre) give in.

cédérom /sedeʀɔm/ *nm* CD-ROM.

cédille /sedij/ *nf* cedilla.

cèdre /sɛdʀ/ *nm* cedar.

CEI *abrév f* (**Communauté des États indépendants**) CIS.

ceinture /sɛ̃tyʀ/ *nf* belt; (taille) waist; **~ de sauvetage** lifebelt; **~ de sécurité** seatbelt.

cela /səla/ *pron* it, that; (pour désigner) that; **~ va de soi** it is obvious; **~ dit/fait** having said/done that.

célèbre /selɛbʀ/ *a* famous. **célébrer** [14] *vt* celebrate. **célébrité** *nf* fame; (personne) celebrity.

céleri /sɛlʀi/ *nm* (en branches) celery. **céleri-rave** (*pl* **céleris-raves**) *nm* celeriac.

célibat /seliba/ *nm* celibacy; (état) single status.

célibataire /selibatɛʀ/ *a* single. ● *nm* bachelor. ● *nf* single woman.

celle, celles /sɛl/ ⇒CELUI.

cellier /selje/ *nm* wine cellar.

cellulaire /selylɛʀ/ *a* cell; **emprisonnement ~** solitary confinement; **fourgon** *ou* **voiture ~** prison van; **téléphone ~** cellular phone.

cellule /selyl/ *nf* cell.

celui, celle (*pl* **ceux, celles**) /səlɥi, sɛl, sø/ *pron* the one; **~ de mon ami** my friend's; **~-ci** this (one); **~-là** that (one); **ceux-ci** these (ones); **ceux-là** those (ones).

cendre /sɑ̃dʀ/ *nf* ash.

cendrier /sɑ̃dʀije/ *nm* ashtray.

censé, ~e /sɑ̃se/ *a* **être ~ faire** be supposed to do.

censeur /sɑ̃sœʀ/ *nm* censor; (Scol) administrator in charge of discipline.

censure /sɑ̃syʀ/ *nf* censorship. **censurer** [1] *vt* censor; (critiquer) censure.

cent /sɑ̃/ *a & nm* (a) hundred; **~ un** a hundred and one; **20 pour ~** 20 per cent.

centaine /sɑ̃tɛn/ *nf* hundred; **une ~ (de)** (about) a hundred.

centenaire /sɑ̃tnɛʀ/ *nm* (anniversaire) centenary.

centième /sɑ̃tjɛm/ *a & nmf* hundredth.

centimètre /sɑ̃timɛtʀ/ *nm* centimetre; (ruban) tape-measure.

central, **~e** (*mpl* **-aux**) /sɑ̃tʀal, -o/ *a* central. ● *nm* (*pl* **-aux**) **~ (téléphonique)** (telephone) exchange. **centrale** *nf* power-station.

centre /sɑ̃tʀ/ *nm* centre; **~ commercial** shopping centre; (US) mall; **~ de formation** training centre; **~ hospitalier** hospital. **centrer** [1] *vt* centre. **centre-ville** (*pl* **centres-villes**) *nm* town centre.

centuple /sɑ̃typl/ *nm* **le ~ de** a hundred times; **au ~** a hundredfold.

cep /sɛp/ *nm* vine stock.

cépage /sepaʒ/ *nm* grape variety.

cèpe /sɛp/ *nm* cep.

cependant /səpɑ̃dɑ̃/ *adv* however.

céramique /seʀamik/ *nf* ceramic; (art) ceramics (+ *sg*).

cercle /sɛʀkl/ *nm* circle; (cerceau) hoop; (association) society, club; **~ vicieux** vicious circle.

cercueil /sɛʀkœj/ *nm* coffin.

céréale /seʀeal/ *nf* cereal; **~s** (Culin) (breakfast) cereal.

cérébral, **~e** (*mpl* **-aux**) /seʀebʀal, -o/ *a* cerebral; (*travail*) intellectual.

cérémonie /seʀemɔni/ *nf* ceremony; **sans ~s** (*repas*) informal; (*recevoir*) informally.

cerf /sɛʀ/ *nm* stag.

cerfeuil /sɛʀfœj/ *nm* chervil.

cerf-volant (*pl* **cerfs-volants**) /sɛʀvɔlɑ̃/ *nm* kite.

cerise /s(ə)ʀiz/ *nf* cherry. **cerisier** *nm* cherry tree.

cerne /sɛʀn/ *nm* ring.

cerner /sɛʀne/ [1] *vt* surround; (*question*) define; **avoir les yeux cernés** have rings under one's eyes.

certain, **~e** /sɛʀtɛ̃, -ɛn/ *a* certain; (sûr) certain, sure (**de** of; **que** that); **d'un ~ âge** no longer young; **un ~ temps** some time. **certainement** *adv* (probablement) most probably; (avec certitude) certainly. **certains**, **-es** *pron* some people.

certes /sɛʀt/ *adv* (sans doute) admittedly; (bien sûr) of course.

certificat /sɛʀtifika/ *nm* certificate.

certifier /sɛʀtifje/ [45] *vt* certify; **~ qch à qn** assure sb of sth; **copie certifiée conforme** certified true copy.

certitude /sɛʀtityd/ *nf* certainty.

cerveau (*pl* **~x**) /sɛʀvo/ *nm* brain.

cervelle /sɛʀvɛl/ *nf* (Anat) brain; (Culin) brains.

ces /se/ ⇒CE.

césarienne /sezaʀjɛn/ *nf* Caesarean (section).

cesse /sɛs/ *nf* **n'avoir de ~ que** have no rest until; **sans ~** constantly, incessantly.

cesser /sese/ [1] *vt* stop; **~ de faire** stop doing. ● *vi* cease; **faire ~** put an end to.

cessez-le-feu /seselfø/ *nm inv* ceasefire.

cession /sɛsjɔ̃/ *nf* transfer.

C

c'est-à-dire /setadiʀ/ *conj* that is (to say).

cet, **cette** /sɛt/ ⇒CE.

ceux /sø/ ⇒CELUI.

chacun, **~e** /ʃakœ̃, -yn/ *pron* each (one), every one; (tout le monde) everyone; **~ d'entre nous** each (one) of us.

chagrin /ʃagʀɛ̃/ *nm* sorrow; **avoir du ~** be sad.

chahut /ʃay/ *nm* row, din.

chahuter /ʃayte/ [1] *vi* make a row. ● *vt* (*enseignant*) be rowdy with; (*orateur*) heckle.

chaîne /ʃɛn/ *nf* chain; (de télévision) channel; **~ (d'assemblage)** assembly line; **~s** (Auto) snow chains; **~ de montagnes** mountain range; **~ de montage/fabrication** assembly/production line; **~ hi-fi** hi-fi system; **~ laser** CD player; **en ~** (*accidents*) multiple; (*réaction*) chain. **chaînette** *nf* (small) chain. **chaînon** *nm* link.

chair /ʃɛʀ/ *nf* flesh; **bien en ~** plump; **en ~ et en os** in the flesh; **~ à saucisses** sausage meat; **la ~ de poule** goose pimples. ● *a inv* (**couleur**) **~** flesh-coloured.

chaire /ʃɛʀ/ *nf* (d'église) pulpit; (Univ) chair.

chaise /ʃɛz/ *nf* chair; **~ longue** deckchair.

châle /ʃɑl/ *nm* shawl.

chaleur /ʃalœʀ/ *nf* heat; (moins intense) warmth; (d'un accueil, d'une couleur) warmth. **chaleureux, -euse** *a* warm.

chalumeau (*pl* **~x**) /ʃalymo/ *nm* blowtorch.

chalutier /ʃalytje/ *nm* trawler.

chamailler (se) /(sə)ʃamɑje/ [1] *vpr* squabble.

chambre /ʃɑ̃bʀ/ *nf* (bed)room; (Pol, Jur) chamber; **faire ~ à part** sleep in separate rooms; **~ à air** inner tube; **~ d'amis** spare *ou* guest room; **~ de commerce (et d'industrie)** Chamber of Commerce; **~ à coucher** bedroom; **~ à un lit/deux lits** single/twin room; **~ pour deux personnes** double room; **~ forte** strong-room; **~ d'hôte** bed and breakfast, B and B. **chambrer** [1] *vt* (*vin*) bring to room temperature.

chameau (*pl* **~x**) /ʃamo/ *nm* camel.

chamois /ʃamwa/ *nm* chamois.

champ /ʃɑ̃/ *nm* field; **~ de bataille** battlefield; **~ de courses** racecourse; **~ de tir** firing range.

champêtre /ʃɑ̃pɛtʀ/ *a* rural.

champignon /ʃɑ̃piɲɔ̃/ *nm* mushroom; (moisissure) fungus; **~ de Paris** button mushroom.

champion, **~ne** /ʃɑ̃pjɔ̃, -ɔn/ *nm, f* champion. **championnat** *nm* championship.

chance /ʃɑ̃s/ *nf* (good) luck; (possibilité) chance; **avoir de la ~** be lucky; **quelle ~!** what luck!

chanceler /ʃɑ̃sle/ [38] *vi* stagger; (fig) falter, waver.

chancelier /ʃɑ̃səlje/ *nm* chancellor.

chanceux, **-euse** /ʃɑ̃sø, -z/ *a* lucky.

chandail /ʃɑ̃daj/ *nm* sweater.

chandelier /ʃɑ̃dəlje/ *nm* candlestick.

chandelle /ʃɑ̃dɛl/ *nf* candle; **dîner aux ~s** candlelight dinner.

change /ʃɑ̃ʒ/ *nm* (foreign) exchange; (taux) exchange rate.

changement /ʃɑ̃ʒmɑ̃/ *nm* change; **~ de vitesse** (dispositif) gears.

changer /ʃɑ̃ʒe/ [40] *vt* change; **~ qch de place** move sth; (échanger) change (**pour**, **contre** for); **~ de nom/voiture** change one's name/car; **~ de place/train** change places/trains; **~ de direction**

change direction; **~ d'avis** *ou* **d'idée** change one's mind; **~ de vitesse** change gear. □ **se ~** *vpr* change, get changed.

chanson /ʃɑ̃sɔ̃/ *nf* song.

chant /ʃɑ̃/ *nm* singing; (chanson) song; (Relig) hymn.

chantage /ʃɑ̃taʒ/ *nm* blackmail.

chanter /ʃɑ̃te/ [1] *vt* sing; **si cela vous chante** [!] if you feel like it. ● *vi* sing; **faire ~** (délit) blackmail.

chanteur, **-euse** *nm, f* singer.

chantier /ʃɑ̃tje/ *nm* building site; **~ naval** shipyard; **mettre en ~** get under way, start.

chaos /kao/ *nm* chaos.

chaparder /ʃapaʀde/ [1] *vt* [!] pinch [!], filch.

chapeau (*pl* **~x**) /ʃapo/ *nm* hat; **~!** well done!

chapelet /ʃaplɛ/ *nm* rosary; (fig) string.

chapelle /ʃapɛl/ *nf* chapel.

chapelure /ʃaplyʀ/ *nf* (Culin) breadcrumbs.

chaperonner /ʃapʀɔne/ [1] *vt* chaperone.

chapiteau (*pl* **~x**) /ʃapito/ *nm* marquee; (de cirque) big top; (de colonne) capital.

chapitre /ʃapitʀ/ *nm* chapter; (fig) subject.

chaque /ʃak/ *a* every, each.

char /ʃaʀ/ *nm* (Mil) tank; (de carnaval) float; (charrette) cart; (dans l'antiquité) chariot.

charabia /ʃaʀabja/ *nm* [!] gibberish.

charade /ʃaʀad/ *nf* riddle.

charbon /ʃaʀbɔ̃/ *nm* coal; **~ de bois** charcoal.

charcuterie /ʃaʀkytʀi/ *nf* pork butcher's shop; (aliments) (cooked) pork meats. **charcutier**, **-ière** *nm, f* pork butcher.

chardon /ʃaʀdɔ̃/ *nm* thistle.

charge /ʃaʀʒ/ *nf* load, burden; (Mil, Électr, Jur) charge; (responsabilité) responsibility; **avoir qn à ~** be responsible for; **~s** expenses; (de locataire) service charges; **être à la ~ de** (*personne*) be the responsibility of; (*frais*) be payable by; **~s sociales** social security contributions; **prendre en ~** take charge of.

chargé, **~e** /ʃaʀʒe/ *a* (*véhicule*) loaded; (*journée, emploi du temps*) busy; (*langue*) coated. ● *nm, f* **~ de mission** head of mission; **~ d'affaires** chargé d'affaires, **~ de cours** lecturer.

chargement /ʃaʀʒəmɑ̃/ *nm* loading; (objets) load.

charger /ʃaʀʒe/ [40] *vt* load; (Ordinat, Photo) load; (attaquer) charge; (*batterie*) charge; **~ qn de** (*fardeau*) weigh sb down with; (*tâche*) entrust sb with; **~ qn de faire** make sb responsible for doing. ● *vi* (attaquer) charge. □ **se ~ de** *vpr* take charge *ou* care of.

chariot /ʃaʀjo/ *nm* (à roulettes) trolley; (US) cart; (charrette) cart.

charitable /ʃaʀitabl/ *a* charitable.

charité /ʃaʀite/ *nf* charity; **faire la ~ à** give (money) to.

charlatan /ʃaʀlatɑ̃/ *nm* charlatan.

charmant, **~e** /ʃaʀmɑ̃, -t/ *a* charming.

charme /ʃaʀm/ *nm* charm; (qui envoûte) spell. **charmer** [1] *vt* charm. **charmeur**, **-euse** *nm, f* charmer.

charnel, **~le** /ʃaʀnɛl/ *a* carnal.

charnière /ʃaʀnjɛʀ/ *nf* hinge; **à la ~ de** at the meeting point between.

charnu, **~e** /ʃaʀny/ *a* plump, fleshy.

charpente /ʃaʀpɑ̃t/ *nf* framework; (carrure) build.

charpentier /ʃaʀpɑ̃tje/ *nm* carpenter.

charpie /ʃaʀpi/ *nf* **en ~** in shreds.

charrette /ʃaʀɛt/ *nf* cart.

charrue /ʃaʀy/ *nf* plough.

chasse /ʃas/ *nf* hunting; (au fusil) shooting; (poursuite) chase; (recherche) hunt(ing); **~ (d'eau)** (toilet) flush; **~ sous-marine** harpoon fishing.

chasse-neige /ʃasnɛʒ/ *nm inv* snowplough.

chasser /ʃase/ [1] *vt* hunt; (au fusil) shoot; (faire partir) chase away; (*odeur, employé*) get rid of. ● *vi* go hunting; (au fusil) go shooting.

chasseur, -euse /ʃasœʀ, -øz/ *nm, f* hunter. ● *nm* bellboy; (US) bellhop; (avion) fighter plane.

châssis /ʃɑsi/ *nm* frame; (Auto) chassis.

chasteté /ʃastəte/ *nf* chastity.

chat /ʃa/ *nm* cat; (mâle) tomcat.

châtaigne /ʃɑtɛɲ/ *nf* chestnut. **châtaignier** *nm* chestnut tree. **châtain** *a inv* chestnut (brown).

château (*pl* **~x**) /ʃɑto/ *nm* castle; (manoir) manor; **~ d'eau** water tower; **~ fort** fortified castle.

châtiment /ʃɑtimɑ̃/ *nm* punishment.

chaton /ʃatɔ̃/ *nm* (chat) kitten.

chatouillement /ʃatujmɑ̃/ *nm* tickling. **chatouiller** [1] *vt* tickle. **chatouilleux, -euse** *a* ticklish; (susceptible) touchy.

châtrer /ʃɑtʀe/ [1] *vt* castrate; (*chat*) neuter.

chatte /ʃat/ *nf* female cat.

chaud, ~e /ʃo, -d/ *a* warm; (brûlant) hot; (vif: fig) warm. ● *nm* heat; **au ~** in the warm(th); **avoir ~** be warm; be hot; **il fait ~** it is warm; it is hot; **pour te tenir ~** to keep you warm. **chaudement** *adv* warmly; (*disputé*) hotly.

chaudière /ʃodjɛʀ/ *nf* boiler.

chaudron /ʃodʀɔ̃/ *nm* cauldron.

chauffage /ʃofaʒ/ *nm* heating; **~ central** central heating.

chauffard /ʃofaʀ/ *nm* (péj) reckless driver.

chauffer /ʃofe/ [1] *vt/i* heat (up); (*moteur, appareil*) overheat. □ **se ~** *vpr* warm oneself (up).

chauffeur /ʃofœʀ/ *nm* driver; (aux gages de qn) chauffeur.

chaume /ʃom/ *nm* (de toit) thatch.

chaussée /ʃose/ *nf* road(way).

chausse-pied (*pl* **~s**) /ʃospje/ *nm* shoehorn.

chausser /ʃose/ [1] *vt* (*chaussures*) put on; (*enfant*) put shoes on (to). ● *vi* **~ bien** (aller) fit well; **~ du 35** take a size 35 shoe. □ **se ~** *vpr* put one's shoes on.

chaussette /ʃosɛt/ *nf* sock.

chausson /ʃosɔ̃/ *nm* slipper; (de bébé) bootee; **~ de danse** ballet shoe; **~ aux pommes** apple turnover.

chaussure /ʃosyʀ/ *nf* shoe; **~ de ski** ski boot; **~ de marche** hiking boot.

chauve /ʃov/ *a* bald.

chauve-souris (*pl* **chauves-souris**) /ʃovsuʀi/ *nf* bat.

chauvin, ~e /ʃovɛ̃, -in/ *a* chauvinistic. ● *nm, f* chauvinist.

chavirer /ʃaviʀe/ [1] *vt* (*bateau*) capsize; (*objets*) tip over.

chef /ʃɛf/ *nm* leader, head; (supérieur) boss, superior; (Culin) chef; (de tribu) chief; **architecte en ~** chief *ou* head architect; **~ d'accusation** (Jur) charge; **~ d'équipe** foreman; (Sport) captain; **~ d'État** head of State; **~ de famille** head of the family; **~ de file** (Pol) leader; **~ de gare** stationmaster; **~ d'orchestre** conductor; **~ de service**

department head; **~ de train** guard; (US) conductor.

chef-d'œuvre (*pl* **chefs-d'œuvre**) /ʃɛdœvʀ/ *nm* masterpiece.

chef-lieu (*pl* **chefs-lieux**) /ʃɛfljø/ *nm* county town, administrative centre.

chemin /ʃəmɛ̃/ *nm* road; (étroit) lane; (de terre) track; (pour piétons) path; (passage) way; (direction, trajet) way; **avoir du ~ à faire** have a long way to go; **~ de fer** railway; **par ~ de fer** by rail; **~ de halage** towpath; **~ vicinal** country lane.

cheminée /ʃəmine/ *nf* chimney; (intérieure) fireplace; (encadrement) mantelpiece; (de bateau) funnel.

cheminot /ʃəmino/ *nm* railwayman; (US) railroad man.

chemise /ʃəmiz/ *nf* shirt; (dossier) folder; (de livre) jacket; **~ de nuit** nightdress. **chemisette** *nf* short-sleeved shirt. **chemisier** *nm* blouse.

chêne /ʃɛn/ *nm* oak.

chenil /ʃəni(l)/ *nm* (pension) kennels (+ *sg*).

chenille /ʃənij/ *nf* caterpillar; **véhicule à ~s** tracked vehicle.

cheptel /ʃɛptɛl/ *nm* livestock.

chèque /ʃɛk/ *nm* cheque; **~ sans provision** bad cheque; **~ de voyage** traveller's cheque. **chéquier** *nm* chequebook.

cher, chère /ʃɛʀ/ *a* (coûteux) dear, expensive; (aimé) dear; (dans la correspondance) dear. ● *adv* (*coûter, payer*) a lot (of money); (en importance) dearly. ● *nm,f* **mon ~, ma chère** my dear.

chercher /ʃɛʀʃe/ [1] *vt* look for; (*aide, paix, gloire*) seek; **aller ~** go and get *ou* fetch, go for; **~ à faire** attempt to do; **~ la petite bête** be finicky.

chercheur, -euse /ʃɛʀʃœʀ, -øz/ *nm,f* research worker.

chèrement /ʃɛʀmɑ̃/ *adv* dearly.

chéri, ~e /ʃeʀi/ *a* beloved. ● *nm,f* darling.

chérir /ʃeʀiʀ/ [2] *vt* cherish.

chétif, -ive /ʃetif, -v/ *a* puny.

cheval (*pl* **-aux**) /ʃəval, -o/ *nm* horse; **à ~** on horseback; **à ~ sur** astride, straddling; **faire du ~** ride, go horse-riding.

chevalerie /ʃəvalʀi/ *nf* chivalry.

chevalet /ʃəvalɛ/ *nm* easel; (de menuisier) trestle.

chevalier /ʃəvalje/ *nm* knight.

chevalière /ʃəvaljɛʀ/ *nf* signet ring.

cheval-vapeur (*pl* **chevaux-vapeur**) /ʃəvalvapœʀ/ *nm* horsepower.

chevaucher /ʃəvoʃe/ [1] *vt* sit astride. □ **se ~** *vpr* overlap.

chevelu, ~e /ʃəvly/ *a* (péj) long-haired; (Bot) hairy.

chevelure /ʃəvlyʀ/ *nf* hair.

chevet /ʃəvɛ/ *nm* **au ~ de** at the bedside of; **livre de ~** bedside book.

cheveu (*pl* **~x**) /ʃəvø/ *nm* (poil) hair; **~x** (chevelure) hair; **avoir les ~x longs** have long hair.

cheville /ʃəvij/ *nf* ankle; (fiche) peg, pin; (pour mur) (wall) plug.

chèvre /ʃɛvʀ/ *nf* goat.

chevreuil /ʃəvʀœj/ *nm* roe (deer); (Culin) venison.

chevron /ʃəvʀɔ̃/ *nm* (poutre) rafter; **à ~s** herringbone.

chez /ʃe/ *prép* (au domicile de) at the house of; (parmi) among; (dans le caractère ou l'œuvre de) in; **aller ~ qn** go to sb's house; **~ le boucher** at *ou* to the butcher's; **~ soi** at home; **rentrer ~ soi** go home. **chez-soi** *nm inv* home.

chic /ʃik/ *a inv* smart; (gentil) kind. ● *nm* style; **avoir le ~ pour** have a knack for; **~ (alors)!** great!

chicane /ʃikan/ *nf* double bend;

chercher ~ à qn pick a quarrel with sb.

chiche /ʃiʃ/ *a* mean (**de** with); **~ que je le fais!** ▣ I bet you I can do it.

chichis /ʃiʃi/ *nmpl* ▣ fuss.

chicorée /ʃikɔʀe/ *nf* (frisée) endive; (à café) chicory.

chien /ʃjɛ̃/ *nm* dog; **~ d'aveugle** guide dog; **~ de garde** watch-dog. **chienne** *nf* dog, bitch.

chiffon /ʃifɔ̃/ *nm* rag; (pour nettoyer) duster; **~ humide** damp cloth. **chiffonner** [1] *vt* crumple; (préoccuper ▣) bother.

chiffre /ʃifʀ/ *nm* figure; (numéro) number; (code) code; **~s arabes/romains** Arabic/Roman numerals; **~s (statistiques)** statistics; **~ d'affaires** turnover.

chiffrer /ʃifʀe/ [1] *vt* put a figure on, assess; (*texte*) encode. ▫ **se ~ à** *vpr* come to.

chignon /ʃiɲɔ̃/ *nm* bun, chignon.

Chili /ʃili/ *nm* Chile.

chimère /ʃimɛʀ/ *nf* fantasy.

chimie /ʃimi/ *nf* chemistry. **chimique** *a* chemical. **chimiste** *nmf* chemist.

chimpanzé /ʃɛ̃pɑ̃ze/ *nm* chimpanzee.

Chine /ʃin/ *nf* China.

chinois, ~e /ʃinwa, -z/ *a* Chinese. ● *nm* (Ling) Chinese. **C~, ~e** *nm, f* Chinese.

chiot /ʃjo/ *nm* pup(py).

chipoter /ʃipɔte/ [1] *vi* (manger) pick at one's food; (discuter) quibble.

chips /ʃips/ *nf inv* crisp; (US) chip.

chirurgie /ʃiʀyʀʒi/ *nf* surgery; **~ esthétique** plastic surgery. **chirurgien** *nm* surgeon.

chlore /klɔʀ/ *nm* chlorine.

choc /ʃɔk/ *nm* (heurt) impact, shock; (émotion) shock; (collision) crash; (affrontement) clash; (Méd) shock; **sous le ~** in shock.

chocolat /ʃɔkɔla/ *nm* chocolate; (à boire) drinking chocolate; **~ au lait** milk chocolate; **~ chaud** hot chocolate; **~ noir** plain *ou* dark chocolate.

chœur /kœʀ/ *nm* (antique) chorus; (chanteurs, nef) choir; **en ~** in chorus.

choisir /ʃwaziʀ/ [2] *vt* choose, select.

choix /ʃwa/ *nm* choice, selection; **fromage ou dessert au ~** a choice of cheese or dessert; **de ~** choice; **de premier ~** top quality.

chômage /ʃomaʒ/ *nm* unemployment; **au ~, en ~** unemployed; **mettre en ~ technique** lay off.

chômeur, -euse /ʃomœʀ, -øz/ *nm, f* unemployed person; **les ~s** the unemployed.

choquer /ʃɔke/ [1] *vt* shock; (commotionner) shake.

choral, ~e (*mpl* **~s**) /kɔʀal/ *a* choral. **chorale** *nf* choir, choral society.

chorégraphie /kɔʀegʀafi/ *nf* choreography.

choriste /kɔʀist/ *nmf* (à l'église) chorister; (à l'opéra) member of the chorus *ou* choir.

chose /ʃoz/ *nf* thing; (**très**) **peu de ~** nothing much; **pas grand ~** not much.

chou (*pl* **~x**) /ʃu/ *nm* cabbage; **~ (à la crème)** cream puff; **~ de Bruxelles** Brussels sprout; **mon petit ~** ▣ my dear.

chouchou, ~te /ʃuʃu, -t/ *nm, f* (de professeur) pet; (du public) darling.

choucroute /ʃukʀut/ *nf* sauerkraut.

chouette /ʃwɛt/ *nf* owl. ● *a* ▣ super.

chou-fleur (*pl* **choux-fleurs**) /ʃuflœʀ/ *nm* cauliflower.

choyer /ʃwaje/ [31] *vt* pamper.

chrétien, **~ne** /kʀetjɛ̃, -jɛn/ *a & nm,f* Christian.

Christ /kʀist/ *nm* **le** ~ Christ.

chrome /kʀom/ *nm* chromium, chrome.

chromosome /kʀɔmozom/ *nm* chromosome.

chronique /kʀɔnik/ *a* chronic. ● *nf* (rubrique) column; (nouvelles) news; (annales) chronicle.

chronologique /kʀɔnɔlɔʒik/ *a* chronological.

chronomètre /kʀɔnɔmɛtʀ/ *nm* stopwatch. **chronométrer** [14] *vt* time.

chrysanthème /kʀizɑ̃tɛm/ *nm* chrysanthemum.

chuchoter /ʃyʃɔte/ [1] *vt/i* whisper.

chut /ʃyt/ *interj* shh, hush.

chute /ʃyt/ *nf* fall; (déchet) offcut; ~ (**d'eau**) waterfall; ~ **de pluie** rainfall; ~ **des cheveux** hair loss; ~ **des ventes** drop in sales; ~ **de 5%** 5% drop. **chuter** [1] *vi* fall.

Chypre /ʃipʀ/ *nf* Cyprus.

ci /si/ *adv* here; **~-gît** here lies; **cet homme-~** this man; **ces maisons-~** these houses.

ci-après /siapʀɛ/ *adv* below.

cible /sibl/ *nf* target.

ciboulette /sibulɛt/ *nf* (Culin) chives (+ *pl*).

cicatrice /sikatʀis/ *nf* scar.

cicatriser /sikatʀize/ [1] *vt* heal. □ **se** ~ *vpr* heal.

ci-dessous /sidəsu/ *adv* below.

ci-dessus /sidəsy/ *adv* above.

cidre /sidʀ/ *nm* cider.

ciel (*pl* **cieux**, **ciels**) /sjɛl, sjø/ *nm* sky; (Relig) heaven; **cieux** (Relig) heaven.

cierge /sjɛʀʒ/ *nm* (church) candle.

cigale /sigal/ *nf* cicada.

cigare /sigaʀ/ *nm* cigar.

cigarette /sigaʀɛt/ *nf* cigarette.

cigogne /sigɔɲ/ *nf* stork.

ci-joint /sijwɛ̃/ *adv* enclosed.

cil /sil/ *nm* eyelash.

cime /sim/ *nf* peak, tip.

ciment /simɑ̃/ *nm* cement.

cimetière /simtjɛʀ/ *nm* cemetery, graveyard; ~ **de voitures** breaker's yard.

cinéaste /sineast/ *nmf* film-maker.

cinéma /sinema/ *nm* cinema; (US) movie theater.
cinémathèque *nf* film archive; (salle) film theatre.
cinématographique *a* cinema.

cinéphile /sinefil/ *nmf* film lover.

cinglant, **~e** /sɛ̃glɑ̃, -t/ *a* (*vent*) biting; (*remarque*) scathing.

cinglé, **~e** /sɛ̃gle/ *a* [F] crazy.

cinq /sɛ̃k/ *a & nm* five.

cinquante /sɛ̃kɑ̃t/ *a & nm* fifty.

cinquième /sɛ̃kjɛm/ *a & nmf* fifth.

cintre /sɛ̃tʀ/ *nm* coat-hanger; (Archit) curve.

cirage /siʀaʒ/ *nm* polish.

circoncision /siʀkɔ̃sizjɔ̃/ *nf* circumcision.

circonflexe /siʀkɔ̃flɛks/ *a* circumflex.

circonscription /siʀkɔ̃skʀipsjɔ̃/ *nf* district; ~ **électorale** constituency; (US) district; (de conseiller, maire) ward.

circonscrire /siʀkɔ̃skʀiʀ/ [30] *vt* (*incendie, épidémie*) contain; (*sujet*) define.

circonspect, **~e** /siʀkɔ̃spɛkt/ *a* circumspect.

circonstance /siʀkɔ̃stɑ̃s/ *nf* circumstance; (situation) situation; (occasion) occasion; **~s atténuantes** mitigating circumstances.

circuit /siʀkɥi/ *nm* circuit; (trajet) tour, trip.
circulaire /siʀkylɛʀ/ *a & nf* circular.
circulation /siʀkylasjɔ̃/ *nf* circulation; (de véhicules) traffic.
circuler /siʀkyle/ [1] *vi* (se répandre, être distribué) circulate; (aller d'un lieu à un autre) get around; (en voiture) travel; (*piéton*) walk; (être en service) (*bus, train*) run; **faire ~** (*badauds*) move on; (*rumeur*) spread.
cire /siʀ/ *nf* wax.
ciré /siʀe/ *nm* oilskin.
cirer /siʀe/ [1] *vt* polish.
cirque /siʀk/ *nm* circus; (arène) amphitheatre; (désordre: fig) chaos; **faire le ~** [!] make a racket [!].
ciseau (*pl* **~x**) /sizo/ *nm* chisel; **~x** scissors.
ciseler /sizle/ [6] *vt* chisel.
citadelle /sitadɛl/ *nf* citadel.
citadin, **~e** /sitadɛ̃, -in/ *nm, f* city-dweller. ● *a* city.
citation /sitasjɔ̃/ *nf* quotation; (Jur) summons.
cité /site/ *nf* city; (logements) housing estate; **~ universitaire** (university) halls of residence.
citer /site/ [1] *vt* quote, cite; (Jur) summon.
citerne /sitɛʀn/ *nf* tank.
citoyen, **~ne** /sitwajɛ̃, -ɛn/ *nm, f* citizen.
citron /sitʀɔ̃/ *nm* lemon; **~ vert** lime. **citronnade** *nf* lemon squash, (still) lemonade.
citrouille /sitʀuj/ *nf* pumpkin.
civet /sivɛ/ *nm* stew; **~ de lièvre** jugged hare.
civière /sivjɛʀ/ *nf* stretcher.
civil, **~e** /sivil/ *a* civil; (non militaire) civilian; (poli) civil. ● *nm* civilian; **dans le ~** in civilian life; **en ~** in plain clothes.
civilisation /sivilizasjɔ̃/ *nf* civilization.
civiliser /sivilize/ [1] *vt* civilize. □ **se ~** *vpr* become civilized.
civique /sivik/ *a* civic.
clair, **~e** /klɛʀ/ *a* clear; (éclairé) light, bright; (*couleur*) light; **le plus ~ de** most of. ● *adv* clearly; **il faisait ~** it was already light. ● *nm* **~ de lune** moonlight; **tirer une histoire au ~** get to the bottom of things. **clairement** *adv* clearly.
clairière /klɛʀjɛʀ/ *nf* clearing.
clairsemé, **~e** /klɛʀsəme/ *a* sparse.
clamer /klame/ [1] *vt* proclaim.
clameur /klamœʀ/ *nf* clamour.
clan /klɑ̃/ *nm* clan.
clandestin, **~e** /klɑ̃dɛstɛ̃, -in/ *a* secret; (*journal*) underground; (*immigration, travail*) illegal; **passager ~** stowaway.
clapier /klapje/ *nm* (rabbit) hutch.
clapoter /klapɔte/ [1] *vi* lap.
claquage /klakaʒ/ *nm* strained muscle; **se faire un ~** pull a muscle.
claque /klak/ *nf* slap; **en avoir sa ~ (de)** [!] be fed up (with) [!].
claquer /klake/ [1] *vi* bang; (*porte*) slam, bang; (*fouet*) crack; (se casser [!]) conk out; (mourir [!]) snuff it [!]; **~ des doigts** snap one's fingers; **~ des mains** clap one's hands; **il claque des dents** his teeth are chattering. ● *vt* (*porte*) slam, bang; (dépenser [!]) blow; (fatiguer [!]) tire out.
claquettes /klakɛt/ *nfpl* tap dancing.
clarifier /klaʀifje/ [45] *vt* clarify.
clarinette /klaʀinɛt/ *nf* clarinet.
clarté /klaʀte/ *nf* light, brightness; (netteté) clarity.
classe /klas/ *nf* class; (salle: Scol) classroom; (cours) class, lesson; **aller en ~** go to school; **faire la ~**

teach; ~ **ouvrière/moyenne** working/middle class.

classement /klasmɑ̃/ *nm* classification; (d'élèves) grading; (de documents) filing; (rang) place, grade; (de coureur) placing.

classer /klase/ [1] *vt* classify; (par mérite) grade; (*papiers*) file; (Jur) (*affaire*) close. □ **se** ~ *vpr* rank.

classeur /klasœʀ/ *nm* (meuble) filing cabinet; (chemise) file; (à anneaux) ring binder.

classification /klasifikasjɔ̃/ *nf* classification.

classique /klasik/ *a* classical; (de qualité) classic; (habituel) classic, standard. ● *nm* classic; (auteur) classical author.

clavecin /klavsɛ̃/ *nm* harpsichord.

clavicule /klavikyl/ *nf* collarbone.

clavier /klavje/ *nm* keyboard; ~ **numérique** keypad.

clé, **clef** /kle/ *nf* key; (outil) spanner; (Mus) clef; ~ **anglaise** (monkey-)wrench; ~ **de contact** ignition key; ~ **à molette** adjustable spanner; ~ **de voûte** keystone; **prix** ~**s en main** (de voiture) on-the-road price. ● *a inv* key.

clémence /klemɑ̃s/ *nf* (de climat) mildness; (indulgence) leniency.

clergé /klɛʀʒe/ *nm* clergy.

clérical, ~**e** (*mpl* **-aux**) /kleʀikal, -o/ *a* clerical.

cliché /kliʃe/ *nm* cliché; (Photo) negative.

client, ~**e** /klijɑ̃, -t/ *nm,f* customer; (d'un avocat) client; (d'un médecin) patient; (d'hôtel) guest; (de taxi) passenger.

clientèle /klijɑ̃tɛl/ *nf* customers, clientele; (d'un avocat) clients, practice; (d'un médecin) patients, practice; (soutien) custom.

cligner /kliɲe/ [1] *vi* ~ **des yeux** blink; ~ **de l'œil** wink.

clignotant /kliɲɔtɑ̃/ *nm* (Auto) indicator, turn.

clignoter /kliɲɔte/ [1] *vi* blink; (*lumière*) flicker; (comme signal) flash.

climat /klima/ *nm* climate.

climatisation /klimatizasjɔ̃/ *nf* air-conditioning.

clin d'œil /klɛ̃dœj/ *nm* wink; **en un** ~ in a flash.

clinique /klinik/ *a* clinical. ● *nf* (private) clinic.

clinquant, ~**e** /klɛ̃kɑ̃, -t/ *a* showy.

clip /klip/ *nm* video.

cliquer /klike/ [1] *vi* (Ordinat) click (**sur** on).

cliqueter /klikte/ [38] *vi* (*couverts*) clink; (*clés, monnaie*) jingle, (*ferraille*) rattle. **cliquetis** *nm* clink(ing), jingle, rattle.

clivage /klivaʒ/ *nm* divide.

clochard, ~**e** /klɔʃaʀ, -d/ *nm,f* tramp.

cloche /klɔʃ/ *nf* bell; (imbécile [!]) idiot; ~ **à fromage** cheese-cover.

cloche-pied: **à** ~ /aklɔʃpje/ *loc* **sauter à** ~ hop on one leg.

clocher /klɔʃe/ *nm* bell-tower; (pointu) steeple; **de** ~ parochial.

cloison /klwazɔ̃/ *nf* partition; (fig) barrier.

cloître /klwatʀ/ *nm* cloister. **cloîtrer (se)** [1] *vpr* shut oneself away.

cloque /klɔk/ *nf* blister.

clos, ~**e** /klo, -z/ *a* closed.

clôture /klotyʀ/ *nf* fence; (fermeture) closure; (de magasin, bureau) closing; (de débat, liste) close; (en Bourse) close of trading. **clôturer** [1] *vt* enclose, fence in; (*festival, séance*) close.

clou /klu/ *nm* nail; (furoncle) boil; (de spectacle) star attraction; **les** ~**s**

(passage) pedestrian crossing; (US) crosswalk.

clouer /klue/ [1] *vt* nail down; (fig) pin down; **être cloué au lit** be confined to one's bed; **~ le bec à qn** shut sb up.

clouté, **~e** /klute/ *a* studded; **passage ~** pedestrian crossing; (US) crosswalk.

coaliser (se) /(sə)kɔalize/ [1] *vpr* join forces.

coalition /kɔalisjɔ̃/ *nf* coalition.

cobaye /kɔbaj/ *nm* guinea-pig.

cocaïne /kɔkain/ *nf* cocaine.

cocasse /kɔkas/ *a* comical.

coccinelle /kɔksinɛl/ *nf* ladybird; (US) ladybug.

cocher /kɔʃe/ [1] *vt* tick (off), check. ● *nm* coachman.

cochon, **~ne** /kɔʃɔ̃, -ɔn/ *nm,f* (personne Ⓘ) pig. ● *a* Ⓘ filthy. ● *nm* pig. **cochonnerie** *nf* (saleté Ⓘ) filth; (marchandise Ⓘ) rubbish, junk.

cocon /kɔkɔ̃/ *nm* cocoon.

cocorico /kɔkɔʀikɔ/ *nm* cock-a-doodle-doo.

cocotier /kɔkɔtje/ *nm* coconut palm.

cocotte /kɔkɔt/ *nf* (marmite) casserole; **~ minute®** pressure-cooker; **ma ~** Ⓘ my dear.

cocu, **~e** /kɔky/ *nm,f* Ⓘ deceived husband, deceived wife.

code /kɔd/ *nm* code; **~s** dipped headlights; **se mettre en ~s** dip one's headlights; **~ (à) barres** bar code; **~ confidentiel (d'identification)** PIN number; **~ postal** post code; (US) zip code; **~ de la route** Highway Code. **coder** [1] *vt* code, encode.

coéquipier, **-ière** /kɔekipje, -jɛʀ/ *nm,f* team mate.

cœur /kœʀ/ *nm* heart; (aux cartes) hearts (+ *pl*); **~ d'artichaut** artichoke heart; **~ de palmier** palm heart; **à ~ ouvert** (*opération*) open-heart; (*parler*) freely; **avoir bon ~** be kind-hearted; **de bon ~** willingly; (*rire*) heartily; **par ~** by heart; **avoir mal au ~** feel sick *ou* nauseous; **je veux en avoir le ~ net** I want to be clear in my own mind (about it).

coffre /kɔfʀ/ *nm* chest; (pour argent) safe; (Auto) boot; (US) trunk. **coffre-fort** (*pl* **coffres-forts**) *nm* safe.

coffret /kɔfʀɛ/ *nm* casket, box; (de livres, cassettes) boxed set.

cogner /kɔɲe/ [1] *vt/i* knock. □ **se ~** *vpr* knock oneself; **se ~ la tête** bump one's head.

cohabitater /kɔabite/ [1] *vi* live together.

cohérent, **~e** /kɔeʀɑ̃, -t/ *a* coherent; (homogène) consistent.

cohue /kɔy/ *nf* crowd.

coi, **~te** /kwa, -t/ *a* silent.

coiffe /kwaf/ *nf* headgear.

coiffer /kwafe/ [1] *vt* do the hair of; (*chapeau*) put on; (surmonter) cap; **~ qn d'un chapeau** put a hat on sb; **coiffé de** wearing; **être bien/mal coiffé** have tidy/untidy hair. □ **se ~** *vpr* do one's hair.

coiffeur, **-euse** /kwafœʀ, -øz/ *nm,f* hairdresser. **coiffeuse** *nf* dressing-table.

coiffure /kwafyʀ/ *nf* hairstyle; (métier) hairdressing; (chapeau) hat.

coin /kwɛ̃/ *nm* corner; (endroit) spot; (cale) wedge; **au ~ du feu** by the fireside; **dans le ~** locally; **du ~** local.

coincer /kwɛ̃se/ [10] *vt* jam; (caler) wedge; (attraper Ⓘ) catch. □ **se ~** *vpr* get jammed.

coïncidence /kɔɛ̃sidɑ̃s/ *nf* coincidence.

coing /kwɛ̃/ *nm* quince.

coït /kɔit/ *nm* intercourse.

col /kɔl/ *nm* collar; (de bouteille) neck; (de montagne) pass; **~ blanc** white-collar worker; **~ roulé**

polo-neck; (US) turtle-neck; **~ de l'utérus** cervix; **se casser le ~ du fémur** break one's hip.

colère /kɔlɛʀ/ *nf* anger; (accès) fit of anger; **en ~** angry; **se mettre en ~** lose one's temper; **faire une ~** throw a tantrum.

coléreux, -euse /kɔleʀø, -z/ *a* quick-tempered.

colin /kɔlɛ̃/ *nm* (merlu) hake; (lieu noir) coley.

colique /kɔlik/ *nf* diarrhoea; (Méd) colic.

colis /kɔli/ *nm* parcel.

collaborateur, -trice /kɔlabɔʀatœʀ, -tʀis/ *nm,f* collaborator; (journaliste) contributor; (collègue) colleague.

collaboration /kɔlabɔʀasjɔ̃/ *nf* collaboration (**à** on); (à ouvrage, projet) contribution (**à** to).

collaborer /kɔlabɔʀe/ [1] *vi* collaborate (**à** on); **~ à** (*journal*) contribute to.

collant, ~e /kɔlɑ̃, -t/ *a* (moulant) skin-tight; (poisseux) sticky. ● *nm* (bas) tights; (US) panty hose.

colle /kɔl/ *nf* glue; (en pâte) paste; (problème 🄸) poser; (Scol 🄸) detention.

collecter /kɔlɛkte/ [1] *vt* collect.

collectif, -ive /kɔlɛktif, -v/ *a* collective; (*billet, voyage*) group.

collection /kɔlɛksjɔ̃/ *nf* collection; (ouvrages) series (+ *sg*); (du même auteur) set. **collectionner** [1] *vt* collect. **collectionneur, -euse** *nm,f* collector.

collectivité /kɔlɛktivite/ *nf* community; **~ locale** local authority.

collège /kɔlɛʒ/ *nm* secondary school (*up to age 15*); (US) junior high school; (assemblée) college. **collégien, ~ne** *nm,f* schoolboy, schoolgirl.

collègue /kɔlɛg/ *nmf* colleague.

coller /kɔle/ [1] *vt* stick; (avec colle liquide) glue; (*affiche*) stick up; (mettre 🄸) stick; (par une question 🄸) stump; (Scol 🄸) **se faire ~** get a detention; **je me suis fait ~ en maths** I failed *ou* flunked maths. ● *vi* stick (**à** to); (être collant) be sticky; **~ à** (convenir à) fit, correspond to.

collet /kɔlɛ/ *nm* (piège) snare; **~ monté** prim and proper; **mettre la main au ~ de qn** collar sb.

collier /kɔlje/ *nm* necklace; (de chien) collar.

colline /kɔlin/ *nf* hill.

collision /kɔlizjɔ̃/ *nf* (choc) collision; (lutte) clash; **entrer en ~ (avec)** collide (with).

collyre /kɔliʀ/ *nm* eye drops (+ *pl*).

colmater /kɔlmate/ [1] *vt* plug, seal.

colombe /kɔlɔ̃b/ *nf* dove.

Colombie /kɔlɔ̃bi/ *nf* Colombia.

colon /kɔlɔ̃/ *nm* settler.

colonel /kɔlɔnɛl/ *nm* colonel.

colonie /kɔlɔni/ *nf* colony; **~ de vacances** children's holiday camp.

colonne /kɔlɔn/ *nf* column; **~ vertébrale** spine; **en ~ par deux** in double file.

colorant /kɔlɔʀɑ̃/ *nm* colouring.

colorier /kɔlɔʀje/ [45] *vt* colour (in).

colosse /kɔlɔs/ *nm* giant.

colza /kɔlza/ *nm* rape(-seed).

coma /kɔma/ *nm* coma; **dans le ~** in a coma.

combat /kɔ̃ba/ *nm* fight; (Sport) match; **~s** fighting. **combatif, -ive** *a* eager to fight; (*esprit*) fighting.

combattre /kɔ̃batʀ/ [11] *vt/i* fight.

combien /kɔ̃bjɛ̃/ *adv* **~ (de)** (quantité) how much; (nombre) how many; (temps) how long; **~ il a changé!** (comme) how he has changed!; **~ y a-t-il d'ici à ...?** how

C

far is it to ...?; **on est le ~ aujourd'hui?** what's the date today?

combinaison /kɔ̃binɛzɔ̃/ *nf* combination; (de femme) slip; (bleu de travail) boiler suit; (US) overalls; **~ d'aviateur** flying-suit; **~ de plongée** wetsuit.

combine /kɔ̃bin/ *nf* trick; (fraude) fiddle; (intrigue) scheme.

combiné /kɔ̃bine/ *nm* (de téléphone) receiver, handset.

combiner /kɔ̃bine/ [1] *vt* (réunir) combine; (calculer) devise; **~ de faire** plan to do.

comble /kɔ̃bl/ *a* packed. ● *nm* height; **~s** (mansarde) attic, loft; **c'est le ~!** that's the (absolute) limit!

combler /kɔ̃ble/ [1] *vt* fill; (*perte, déficit*) make good; (*désir*) fulfil; **~ qn de cadeaux** lavish gifts on sb.

combustible /kɔ̃bystibl/ *nm* fuel.

comédie /kɔmedi/ *nf* comedy; (histoire [I]) fuss; **~ musicale** musical; **jouer la ~** put on an act. **comédien**, **~ne** *nm, f* actor, actress.

comestible /kɔmɛstibl/ *a* edible.

comète /kɔmɛt/ *nf* comet.

comique /kɔmik/ *a* comical, funny; (*genre*) comic. ● *nm* (acteur) comic; (comédie) comedy; (côté drôle) comical aspect.

commandant /kɔmɑ̃dɑ̃/ *nm* commander; (dans l'armée de terre) major; **~** (**de bord**) captain; **~ en chef** Commander-in-Chief.

commande /kɔmɑ̃d/ *nf* (Comm) order; (Tech) control; **~s** (d'avion) controls.

commandement /kɔmɑ̃dmɑ̃/ *nm* command; (Relig) commandment.

commander /kɔmɑ̃de/ [1] *vt* command; (acheter) order; (*étude, œuvre d'art*) commission; **~ à** (maîtriser) control; **~ à qn de** command sb to. ● *vi* be in command.

comme /kɔm/ *adv* **~ c'est bon!** it's so good!; **~ il est mignon!** isn't he sweet! ● *conj* (dans une comparaison) as; (dans une équivalence, illustration) like; (en tant que) as; (puisque) as, since; (au moment où) as; **vif ~ l'éclair** as quick as a flash; **travailler ~ sage-femme** work as a midwife; **~ ci ~ ça** so-so; **~ il faut** properly; **~ pour faire** as if to do; **jolie ~ tout** as pretty as anything; **qu'est-ce qu'il y a ~ légumes?** what is there in the way of vegetables?

commencer /kɔmɑ̃se/ [10] *vt/i* begin, start; **~ à faire** begin *ou* start to do.

comment /kɔmɑ̃/ *adv* how; **~?** (répétition) pardon?; (surprise) what?; **~ est-il?** what is he like?; **le ~ et le pourquoi** the whys and wherefores.

commentaire /kɔmɑ̃tɛʀ/ *nm* comment; (d'un texte, événement) commentary. **commentateur**, **-trice** *nm, f* commentator.

commenter /kɔmɑ̃te/ [1] *vt* comment on; (*film, visite*) provide a commentary for; (radio, TV) commentate.

commérages /kɔmeʀaʒ/ *nmpl* gossip.

commerçant, **~e** /kɔmɛʀsɑ̃, -t/ *a* (*rue*) shopping; (*personne*) business-minded. ● *nm, f* shopkeeper.

commerce /kɔmɛʀs/ *nm* trade, commerce; (magasin) business; **faire du ~** be in business.

commercial, **~e** (*mpl* **-iaux**) /kɔmɛʀsjal, -jo/ *a* commercial. **commercialiser** [1] *vt* market.

commettre /kɔmɛtʀ/ [42] *vt* commit.

commis /kɔmi/ *nm* (de magasin) assistant; (de bureau) clerk.

commissaire /kɔmisɛʀ/ *nm* commissioner; (Sport) steward; **~ (de police)** (police) superintendent. **commissaire-priseur** (*pl* **commissaires-priseurs**) *nm* auctioneer.

commissariat /kɔmisaʀja/ *nm* **~ (de police)** police station.

commission /kɔmisjɔ̃/ *nf* commission; (course) errand; (message) message; **~s** shopping.

commode /kɔmɔd/ *a* handy, convenient; (facile) easy; **il n'est pas ~** he's a difficult customer. ● *nf* chest (of drawers). **commodité** *nf* convenience.

commotion /kɔmosjɔ̃/ *nf* **~ (cérébrale)** concussion.

commun, ~e /kɔmœ̃, -yn/ *a* common; (*effort, action*) joint; (*frais, pièce*) shared; **en ~** jointly; **avoir** *ou* **mettre en ~** share; **le ~ des mortels** ordinary mortals. **communal, ~e** (*mpl* **-aux**) *a* of the commune, local.

communauté /kɔmynote/ *nf* community; **~ de biens** joint ownership.

commune /kɔmyn/ *nf* (circonscription, collectivité) commune.

communicatif, -ive /kɔmynikatif, -v/ *a* (*personne*) talkative; (*gaieté*) infectious.

communication /kɔmynikasjɔ̃/ *nf* communication; (téléphonique) call; **~s** (relations) communications (+ *pl*); **voies** *ou* **moyens de ~** communications (+ *pl*).

communier /kɔmynje/ [45] *vi* (Relig) receive communion; (fig) commune.

communiqué /kɔmynike/ *nm* statement; (de presse) communiqué.

communiquer /kɔmynike/ [1] *vt* pass on, communicate; (*date, décision*) announce. ● *vi* communicate. □ **se ~ à** *vpr* spread to.

communiste /kɔmynist/ *a & nmf* communist.

commutateur /kɔmytatœʀ/ *nm* (Électr) switch.

compagne /kɔ̃paɲ/ *nf* companion.

compagnie /kɔ̃paɲi/ *nf* company; **tenir ~ à** keep company; **en ~ de** together with; **~ aérienne** airline.

compagnon /kɔ̃paɲɔ̃/ *nm* companion.

comparable /kɔ̃paʀabl/ *a* comparable (**à** to). **comparaison** *nf* comparison; (littéraire) simile.

comparaître /kɔ̃paʀɛtʀ/ [18] *vi* (Jur) appear (**devant** before).

comparatif, -ive /kɔ̃paʀatif, -v/ *a & nm* comparative.

comparer /kɔ̃paʀe/ [1] *vt* compare (**à** with). □ **se ~** *vpr* compare oneself; (être comparable) be comparable.

compartiment /kɔ̃paʀtimɑ̃/ *nm* compartment.

comparution /kɔ̃paʀysjɔ̃/ *nf* (Jur) appearance.

compas /kɔ̃pa/ *nm* (pair of) compasses; (boussole) compass.

compassion /kɔ̃pasjɔ̃/ *nf* compassion.

compatible /kɔ̃patibl/ *a* compatible.

compatir /kɔ̃patiʀ/ [2] *vi* sympathize; **~ à** share in.

compatriote /kɔ̃patʀijɔt/ *nmf* compatriot.

compensation /kɔ̃pɑ̃sasjɔ̃/ *nf* compensation. **compenser** [1] *vt* compensate for, make up for.

compère /kɔ̃pɛʀ/ *nm* accomplice.

compétence /kɔpetɑ̃s/ *nf* competence; (fonction) domain, sphere; **entrer dans les ~s de qn** be in sb's domain. **compétent, ~e** *a* competent.

compétition /kɔ̃petisjɔ̃/ *nf* competition; (sportive) event; **de ~** competitive.

complaire (se) /(sə)kɔ̃plɛʀ/ [47] *vpr* **se ~ dans** delight in.

complaisance /kɔ̃plɛzɑ̃s/ *nf* kindness; (indulgence) indulgence.

complément /kɔ̃plemɑ̃/ *nm* supplement; (Gram) complement; **~ (d'objet)** (Gram) object; **~ d'information** further information. **complémentaire** *a* complementary; (*renseignements*) supplementary.

complet, -ète /kɔ̃plɛ, -t/ *a* complete; (*train, hôtel*) full. ● *nm* suit.

compléter /kɔ̃plete/ [14] *vt* complete; (agrémenter) complement. □ **se ~** *vpr* complement each other.

complexe /kɔ̃plɛks/ *a* complex. ● *nm* (sentiment, bâtiments) complex.

complexé, ~e /kɔ̃plekse/ *a* **être ~** have a lot of hang-ups.

complice /kɔ̃plis/ *nm* accomplice.

compliment /kɔ̃plimɑ̃/ *nm* compliment; **~s** (félicitations) compliments, congratulations.

compliquer /kɔ̃plike/ [1] *vt* complicate. □ **se ~** *vpr* become complicated.

complot /kɔ̃plo/ *nm* plot.

comportement /kɔ̃pɔʀtəmɑ̃/ *nm* behaviour; (de joueur, voiture) performance.

comporter /kɔ̃pɔʀte/ [1] *vt* (être composé de) comprise; (inclure) include; (*risque*) entail. □ **se ~** *vpr* behave; (*joueur, voiture*) perform.

composant /kɔ̃pozɑ̃/ *nm* component.

composé, ~e /kɔ̃poze/ *a* composite; (*salade*) mixed; (guindé) affected. ● *nm* compound.

composer /kɔ̃poze/ [1] *vt* make up, compose; (*chanson, visage*) compose; (*numéro*) dial; (*page*) typeset. ● *vi* (transiger) compromise. □ **se ~ de** *vpr* be made up *ou* composed of. **compositeur, -trice** *nm, f* (Mus) composer.

composter /kɔ̃pɔste/ [1] *vt* (*billet*) punch.

compote /kɔ̃pɔt/ *nf* stewed fruit; **~ de pommes** stewed apples.

compréhensible /kɔ̃pʀeɑ̃sibl/ *a* understandable; (intelligible) comprehensible.

compréhensif, -ive /kɔ̃pʀeɑ̃sif, -v/ *a* understanding.

compréhension /kɔ̃pʀeɑ̃sjɔ̃/ *nf* understanding, comprehension.

comprendre /kɔ̃pʀɑ̃dʀ/ [50] *vt* understand; (comporter) comprise, be made up of. □ **se ~** *vpr* (*personnes*) understand each other; **ça se comprend** that is understandable.

compresse /kɔ̃pʀɛs/ *nf* compress.

comprimé /kɔ̃pʀime/ *nm* tablet.

comprimer /kɔ̃pʀime/ [1] *vt* compress; (réduire) reduce.

compris, ~e /kɔ̃pʀi, -z/ *a* included; (d'accord) agreed; **~ entre** (contained) between; **service (non) ~** service (not) included; **tout ~** (all) inclusive; **y ~** including.

compromettre /kɔ̃pʀɔmɛtʀ/ [42] *vt* compromise. **compromis** *nm* compromise.

comptabilité /kɔ̃patibilite/ *nf* accountancy; (comptes) accounts; (service) accounts department.

comptable /kɔ̃tabl/ *a* accounting. ● *nmf* accountant.

comptant /kɔ̃tɑ̃/ *adv* (*payer*) (in) cash; (*acheter*) for cash.

compte /kɔ̃t/ *nm* count; (facture,

comptabilité) account; (nombre exact) right number; ~ **bancaire**, ~ **en banque** bank account; **prendre qch en** ~, **tenir** ~ **de qch** take sth into account; **se rendre** ~ **de** realize; **demander/rendre des** ~**s** ask for/ give an explanation; **à bon** ~ cheaply; **s'en tirer à bon** ~ get off lightly; **travailler à son** ~ be self-employed; **faire le** ~ **de** count; **pour le** ~ **de** on behalf of; **sur le** ~ **de** about; **au bout du** ~ all things considered; ~ **à rebours** countdown.

compte-gouttes /kɔ̃tgut/ *nm inv* (Méd) dropper; **au** ~ (fig) in dribs and drabs.

compter /kɔ̃te/ [1] *vt* count; (prévoir) allow, reckon on; (facturer) charge for; (avoir) have; (classer) consider; ~ **faire** intend to do. ● *vi* (calculer, importer) count; ~ **avec** reckon with; ~ **parmi** (figurer) be considered among; ~ **sur** rely on, count on.

compte(-)rendu /kɔ̃tʀɑ̃dy/ *nm* report; (de film, livre) review.

compteur /kɔ̃tœʀ/ *nm* meter; ~ **de vitesse** speedometer.

comptine /kɔ̃tin/ *nf* nursery rhyme.

comptoir /kɔ̃twaʀ/ *nm* counter; (de café) bar.

comte /kɔ̃t/ *nm* count.

comté /kɔ̃te/ *nm* county.

comtesse /kɔ̃tɛs/ *nf* countess.

con, ~**ne** /kɔ̃, kɔn/ *a* ⊠ bloody stupid ⊠. ● *nm, f* ⊠ bloody fool ⊠.

concentrer /kɔ̃sɑ̃tʀe/ [1] *vt* concentrate. ▫ **se** ~ *vpr* be concentrated.

concept /kɔ̃sɛpt/ *nm* concept.

concerner /kɔ̃sɛʀne/ [1] *vt* concern; **en ce qui me concerne** as far as I am concerned.

concert /kɔ̃sɛʀ/ *nm* concert; **de** ~ in unison.

concerter /kɔ̃sɛʀte/ [1] *vt* organize, prepare. ▫ **se** ~ *vpr* confer.

concession /kɔ̃sesjɔ̃/ *nf* concession; (terrain) plot.

concevoir /kɔ̃svwaʀ/ [52] *vt* (imaginer, engendrer) conceive; (comprendre) understand; (élaborer) design.

concierge /kɔ̃sjɛʀʒ/ *nmf* caretaker.

concilier /kɔ̃silje/ [45] *vt* reconcile. ▫ **se** ~ *vpr* (s'attirer) win (over).

concis, ~**e** /kɔ̃si, -z/ *a* concise.

conclure /kɔ̃klyʀ/ [16] *vt* conclude; ~ **à** conclude in favour of. ● *vi* ~ **en faveur de/contre** find in favour of/against. **conclusion** *nf* conclusion.

concombre /kɔ̃kɔ̃bʀ/ *nm* cucumber.

concordance /kɔ̃kɔʀdɑ̃s/ *nf* agreement.

concourir /kɔ̃kuʀiʀ/ [20] *vi* compete. ● *vt* ~ **à** contribute towards.

concours /kɔ̃kuʀ/ *nm* competition; (examen) competitive examination; (aide) help; (de circonstances) combination.

concret, **-ète** /kɔ̃kʀɛ, -t/ *a* concrete.

concrétiser /kɔ̃kʀetize/ [1] *vt* give concrete form to. ▫ **se** ~ *vpr* materialize.

conçu, ~**e** /kɔ̃sy/ *a* **bien/mal** ~ well/badly designed.

concubinage /kɔ̃kybinaʒ/ *nm* cohabitation; **vivre en** ~ live together, cohabit.

concurrence /kɔ̃kyʀɑ̃s/ *nf* competition; **faire** ~ **à** compete with; **jusqu'à** ~ **de** up to a limit of.

concurrencer /kɔ̃kyʀɑ̃se/ [10] *vt* compete with.

concurrent, ~**e** /kɔ̃kyʀɑ̃, -t/

C

nm, f competitor; (Scol) candidate. ● *a* rival.

condamnation /kɔ̃danasjɔ̃/ *nf* condemnation; (peine) sentence; **~ centralisée des portières** central locking. **condamné, ~e** *nm, f* condemned man, condemned woman. **condamner** [1] *vt* (censurer, obliger) condemn; (Jur) sentence; (*porte*) block up.

condition /kɔ̃disjɔ̃/ *nf* condition; **~s** (prix) terms; **à ~ de** *ou* **que** provided (that); **sans ~** unconditional(ly); **sous ~** conditionally.

conditionnel, ~le /kɔ̃disjɔnɛl/ *a* conditional. ● *nm* conditional (tense).

conditionnement /kɔ̃disjɔnmɑ̃/ *nm* conditioning; (emballage) packaging.

condoléances /kɔ̃dɔleɑ̃s/ *nfpl* condolences.

conducteur, -trice /kɔ̃dyktœʀ, -tʀis/ *nm, f* driver.

conduire /kɔ̃dɥiʀ/ [17] *vt* take (**à** to); (guider) lead; (Auto) drive; (*affaire*) conduct; **~ à** (faire aboutir) lead to. ● *vi* drive. ▫ **se ~** *vpr* behave.

conduit /kɔ̃dɥi/ *nm* duct.

conduite /kɔ̃dɥit/ *nf* conduct, behaviour; (Auto) driving; (tuyau) pipe; **voiture avec ~ à droite** right-hand drive car.

confection /kɔ̃fɛksjɔ̃/ *nf* making; **de ~** ready-made; **la ~** the clothing industry.

conférence /kɔ̃feʀɑ̃s/ *nf* conference; (exposé) lecture; **~ au sommet** summit meeting. **conférencier, -ière** *nm, f* lecturer.

confesser /kɔ̃fese/ [1] *vt* confess. ▫ **se ~** *vpr* go to confession.

confiance /kɔ̃fjɑ̃s/ *nf* trust; **avoir ~ en** trust.

confiant, ~e /kɔ̃fjɑ̃, -t/ *a* (assuré) confident; (sans défiance) trusting.

confidence /kɔ̃fidɑ̃s/ *nf* confidence.

confidentiel, ~le /kɔ̃fidɑ̃sjɛl/ *a* confidential.

confier /kɔ̃fje/ [45] *vt* **~ à qn** entrust sb with; **~ un secret à qn** tell sb a secret. ▫ **se ~ à** *vpr* confide in.

confiner /kɔ̃fine/ [1] *vt* confine; **~ à** border on. ▫ **se ~** *vpr* confine oneself (**à, dans** to).

confirmation /kɔ̃fiʀmasjɔ̃/ *nf* confirmation. **confirmer** [1] *vt* confirm.

confiserie /kɔ̃fizʀi/ *nf* sweet shop; **~s** confectionery.

confisquer /kɔ̃fiske/ [1] *vt* confiscate.

confit, ~e /kɔ̃fi, -t/ *a* candied; (*fruits*) crystallized. ● *nm* **~ de canard** confit of duck.

confiture /kɔ̃fityʀ/ *nf* jam.

conflit /kɔ̃fli/ *nm* conflict.

confondre /kɔ̃fɔ̃dʀ/ [3] *vt* confuse, mix up; (étonner) confound. ▫ **se ~** *vpr* merge; **se ~ en excuses** apologize profusely.

conforme /kɔ̃fɔʀm/ *a* **être ~ à** comply with; (être en accord) be in keeping with.

conformer /kɔ̃fɔʀme/ [1] *vt* adapt. ▫ **se ~ à** *vpr* conform to.

conformité /kɔ̃fɔʀmite/ *nf* compliance, conformity; **agir en ~ avec** act in accordance with.

confort /kɔ̃fɔʀ/ *nm* comfort; **tout ~** with all mod cons. **confortable** *a* comfortable.

confrère /kɔ̃fʀɛʀ/ *nm* colleague.

confronter /kɔ̃fʀɔ̃te/ [1] *vt* confront; (*textes*) compare. ▫ **se ~ à** *vpr* be confronted with.

confus, ~e /kɔ̃fy, -z/ *a* confused; (gêné) embarrassed.

congé /kɔ̃ʒe/ *nm* holiday; (arrêt momentané) time off, leave; (avis de départ) notice; **en ~** on holiday *ou* leave; **~ de maladie/maternité** sick/ maternity leave; **jour de ~** day off; **prendre ~ de** take one's leave of.

congédier /kɔ̃ʒedje/ [45] *vt* dismiss.

congélateur /kɔ̃ʒelatœʀ/ *nm* freezer.

congeler /kɔ̃ʒle/ [6] *vt* freeze.

congère /kɔ̃ʒɛʀ/ *nf* snowdrift.

congrès /kɔ̃gʀɛ/ *nm* conference; (Pol) congress.

conjoint, ~e /kɔ̃ʒwɛ̃, -t/ *nm,f* spouse. ● *a* joint.

conjonctivite /kɔ̃ʒɔ̃ktivit/ *nf* conjunctivitis.

conjoncture /kɔ̃ʒɔ̃ktyʀ/ *nf* situation; (économique) economic climate.

conjugaison /kɔ̃ʒygɛzɔ̃/ *nf* conjugation.

conjugal, ~e (*mpl* **-aux**) /kɔ̃ʒygal, -o/ *a* conjugal, married.

conjuguer /kɔ̃ʒyge/ [1] *vt* (Gram) conjugate; (*efforts*) combine. □ **se ~** *vpr* (Gram) be conjugated; (*facteurs*) be combined.

conjurer /kɔ̃ʒyʀe/ [1] *vt* (éviter) avert; (implorer) beg.

connaissance /kɔnɛsɑ̃s/ *nf* knowledge; (personne) acquaintance; **~s** (science) knowledge; **faire la ~ de** meet; (apprécier une personne) get to know; **perdre/reprendre ~** lose/regain consciousness; **sans ~** unconscious.

connaisseur /kɔnɛsœʀ/ *nm* expert, connoisseur.

connaître /kɔnɛtʀ/ [18] *vt* know; (*difficultés, faim, succès*) experience; **faire ~** make known. □ **se ~** *vpr* (se rencontrer) meet; **s'y ~ en** know (all) about.

connecter /kɔnɛkte/ [1] *vt* connect; **être/ne pas être connecté** be on-/off-line. □ **se ~ à** *vpr* (Ordinat) log on to.

connerie /kɔnʀi/ *nf* ⊠ **faire une ~** do something stupid; **dire des ~s** talk rubbish.

connu, ~e /kɔny/ *a* well-known.

conquérant, ~e /kɔ̃keʀɑ̃, -t/ *nm,f* conqueror.

conquête /kɔ̃kɛt/ *nf* conquest.

consacrer /kɔ̃sakʀe/ [1] *vt* devote; (Relig) consecrate; (sanctionner) sanction. □ **se ~ à** *vpr* devote oneself to.

conscience /kɔ̃sjɑ̃s/ *nf* conscience; (perception) awareness; (de collectivité) consciousness; **avoir/ prendre ~ de** be/become aware of; **perdre/reprendre ~** lose/regain consciousness; **avoir bonne/ mauvaise ~** have a clear/guilty conscience.

conscient, ~e /kɔ̃sjɑ̃, -t/ *a* conscious; **~ de** aware *ou* conscious of.

conseil /kɔ̃sɛj/ *nm* (piece of) advice; (assemblée) council, committee; (séance) meeting; (personne) consultant; **~ d'administration** board of directors; **~ en gestion** management consultant; **~ des ministres** Cabinet; **~ municipal** town council.

conseiller[1] /kɔ̃seje/ [1] *vt* advise; **~ à qn de** advise sb to; **~ qch à qn** recommend sth to sb.

conseiller[2]**, -ère** /kɔ̃seje, -jɛʀ/ *nm,f* adviser, counsellor; **~ municipal** town councillor; **~ d'orientation** careers adviser.

consentement /kɔ̃sɑ̃tmɑ̃/ *nm* consent.

conséquence /kɔ̃sekɑ̃s/ *nf* consequence; **en ~** (comme il convient) accordingly; **en ~ (de quoi)** as a result of which.

conséquent, ~e /kɔ̃sekɑ̃, -t/ *a* consistent, logical; (important) substantial; **par ~** consequently, therefore.

conservateur, **-trice** /kõsɛʀvatœʀ, -tʀis/ *a* conservative. ● *nm,f* (Pol) conservative; (de musée) curator. ● *nm* preservative.

conservation /kõsɛʀvasjõ/ *nf* preservation; (d'espèce, patrimoine) conservation.

conservatoire /kõsɛʀvatwaʀ/ *nm* academy.

conserve /kõsɛʀv/ *nf* tinned *ou* canned food; **en ~** tinned, canned; **boîte de ~** tin, can.

conserver /kõsɛʀve/ [1] *vt* keep; (en bon état) preserve; (Culin) preserve. ◻ **se ~** *vpr* (Culin) keep.

considérer /kõsideʀe/ [14] *vt* consider; (respecter) esteem; **~ comme** consider to be.

consigne /kõsiɲ/ *nf* (de gare) left-luggage office; (US) baggage checkroom; (somme) deposit; (ordres) orders; **~ automatique** left-luggage lockers; (US) baggage lockers.

consistance /kõsistɑ̃s/ *nf* consistency; (fig) substance, weight. **consistant**, **~e** *a* solid; (épais) thick.

consister /kõsiste/ [1] *vi* **~ en/dans** consist of/in; **~ à faire** consist in doing.

consoler /kõsɔle/ [1] *vt* console. ◻ **se ~** *vpr* find consolation; **se ~ de qch** get over sth.

consolider /kõsɔlide/ [1] *vt* strengthen; (fig) consolidate.

consommateur, **-trice** /kõsɔmatœʀ, -tʀis/ *nm,f* (Comm) consumer; (dans un café) customer.

consommation /kõsɔmasjõ/ *nf* consumption; (accomplissement) consummation; (boisson) drink; **de ~** (Comm) consumer.

consommer /kõsɔme/ [1] *vt* consume, use; (manger) eat; (boire) drink; (*mariage*) consummate. ◻ **se ~** *vpr* (être mangé) be eaten; (être utilisé) be used.

consonne /kõsɔn/ *nf* consonant.

constat /kõsta/ *nm* (official) report; **~ (à l')amiable** accident report drawn up by those involved.

constatation /kõstatasjõ/ *nf* observation, statement of fact. **constater** [1] *vt* note, notice; (certifier) certify.

consternation /kõstɛʀnasjõ/ *nf* dismay.

constipé, **~e** /kõstipe/ *a* constipated; (fig) uptight.

constituer /kõstitɥe/ [1] *vt* (composer) make up, constitute; (organiser) form; (être) constitute; **constitué de** made up of. ◻ **se ~** *vpr* **se ~ prisonnier** give oneself up.

constitution /kõstitysjõ/ *nf* formation, setting up; (Pol, Méd) constitution.

constructeur /kõstʀyktœʀ/ *nm* manufacturer, builder.

construction /kõstʀyksjõ/ *nf* building; (structure, secteur) construction; (fabrication) manufacture.

construire /kõstʀɥiʀ/ [17] *vt* build; (*système, phrase*) construct.

consulat /kõsyla/ *nm* consulate.

consultation /kõsyltasjõ/ *nf* consultation; (réception: Méd) surgery; (US) office; **heures de ~** surgery *ou* office (US) hours.

consulter /kõsylte/ [1] *vt* consult. ● *vi* (*médecin*) hold surgery, see patients. ◻ **se ~** *vpr* consult together.

contact /kõtakt/ *nm* contact; (toucher) touch; **au ~ de** on contact with; (*personne*) by contact with, by seeing; **mettre/couper le ~** (Auto) switch on/off the ignition;

prendre ~ avec get in touch with. **contacter** [1] *vt* contact.

contagieux, -ieuse /kɔ̃taʒjø, -z/ *a* contagious.

conte /kɔ̃t/ *nm* tale; **~ de fées** fairy tale.

contempler /kɔ̃tɑ̃ple/ [1] *vt* contemplate.

contemporain, ~e /kɔ̃tɑ̃pɔʀɛ̃, -ɛn/ *a & nm,f* contemporary.

contenance /kɔ̃t(ə)nɑ̃s/ *nf* (volume) capacity; (allure) bearing; **perdre ~** lose one's composure.

contenir /kɔ̃t(ə)niʀ/ [58] *vt* contain; (avoir une capacité de) hold. ▫ **se ~** *vpr* contain oneself.

content, ~e /kɔ̃tɑ̃, -t/ *a* pleased, happy (**de** with); **~ de faire** pleased *ou* happy to do.

contenter /kɔ̃tɑ̃te/ [1] *vt* satisfy. ▫ **se ~ de** *vpr* content oneself with.

contenu /kɔ̃t(ə)ny/ *nm* (de récipient) contents (+ *pl*); (de texte) content.

conter /kɔ̃te/ [1] *vt* tell, relate.

contestation /kɔ̃tɛstasjɔ̃/ *nf* dispute; (opposition) protest.

contester /kɔ̃tɛste/ [1] *vt* question, dispute; (s'opposer) protest against. ● *vi* protest.

conteur, -euse /kɔ̃tœʀ, -øz/ *nm,f* storyteller.

contigu, ~ë /kɔ̃tigy/ *a* adjacent (**à** to).

continent /kɔ̃tinɑ̃/ *nm* continent.

continu, ~e /kɔ̃tiny/ *a* continuous.

continuer /kɔ̃tinɥe/ [1] *vt* continue. ● *vi* continue, go on; **~ à** *ou* **de faire** carry on *ou* go on *ou* continue doing.

contorsionner (se) /(sə)kɔ̃tɔʀsjɔne/ [1] *vpr* wriggle.

contour /kɔ̃tuʀ/ *nm* outline, contour; **~s** (d'une route) twists and turns, bends.

contourner /kɔ̃tuʀne/ [1] *vt* go round, by-pass; (*difficulté*) get round.

contraceptif, -ive /kɔ̃tʀasɛptif, -v/ *a* contraceptive. ● *nm* contraceptive. **contraception** *nf* contraception.

contracter /kɔ̃tʀakte/ [1] *vt* (*maladie*) contract; (*dette*) incur; (*muscle*) tense; (*assurance*) take out. ▫ **se ~** *vpr* contract.

contractuel, ~le /kɔ̃tʀaktɥɛl/ *nm,f* (agent) traffic warden.

contradictoire /kɔ̃tʀadiktwaʀ/ *a* contradictory; (*débat*) open.

contraignant, ~e /kɔ̃tʀɛɲɑ̃, -t/ *a* restricting.

contraindre /kɔ̃tʀɛ̃dʀ/ [22] *vt* force, compel (**à faire** to do).

contrainte /kɔ̃tʀɛ̃t/ *nf* constraint.

contraire /kɔ̃tʀɛʀ/ *a* opposite; **~ à** contrary to. ● *nm* opposite; **au ~** on the contrary; **au ~ de** unlike.

contrarier /kɔ̃tʀaʀje/ [45] *vt* annoy; (*projet, volonté*) frustrate; (chagriner) upset.

contraste /kɔ̃tʀast/ *nm* contrast.

contrat /kɔ̃tʀa/ *nm* contract.

contravention /kɔ̃tʀavɑ̃sjɔ̃/ *nf* (parking) ticket; **en ~** in breach (**à** of).

contre /kɔ̃tʀ(ə)/ *prép* against; (en échange de) for; **par ~** on the other hand; **tout ~** close by. **contre-attaque** (*pl* **~s**) *nf* counter-attack. **contre-attaquer** [1] *vt* counter-attack. **contre-balancer** [10] *vt* counterbalance.

contrebande /kɔ̃tʀəbɑ̃d/ *nf* contraband; **faire la ~ de** smuggle.

contrebas: en ~ /ɑ̃kɔ̃tʀəbɑ/ *loc* below.

contrebasse /kɔ̃tʀəbɑs/ *nf* double bass.

contrecœur: à ~ /akɔ̃tʀəkœʀ/ *loc* reluctantly.

contrecoup /kɔ̃tʀəku/ *nm* effects, repercussions.

contredire /kɔ̃tʀədiʀ/ [37] *vt* contradict. ▫ **se ~** *vpr* contradict oneself.

contrée /kɔ̃tʀe/ *nf* region; (pays) land.

contrefaçon /kɔ̃tʀəfasɔ̃/ *nf* (objet imité, action) forgery.

contre-indiqué, **~e** /kɔ̃tʀɛ̃dike/ *a* (Méd) contra-indicated; (déconseillé) not recommended.

contre-jour: **à ~** /akɔ̃tʀəʒuʀ/ *loc* against the light.

contrepartie /kɔ̃tʀəpaʀti/ *nf* compensation; **en ~** in exchange, in return.

contreplaqué /kɔ̃tʀəplake/ *nm* plywood.

contresens /kɔ̃tʀəsɑ̃s/ *nm* misinterpretation; (absurdité) nonsense; **à ~** the wrong way.

contretemps /kɔ̃tʀətɑ̃/ *nm* hitch; **à ~** (fig) at the wrong time.

contribuable /kɔ̃tʀibɥabl/ *nmf* taxpayer.

contribuer /kɔ̃tʀibɥe/ [1] *vt* contribute (**à** to, towards).

contrôle /kɔ̃tʀol/ *nm* (maîtrise) control; (vérification) check; (des prix) control; (poinçon) hallmark; (Scol) test; **~ continu** continuous assessment; **~ des changes** exchange control; **~ des naissances** birth control; **~ de soi-même** self-control; **~ technique (des véhicules)** MOT (test).

contrôler /kɔ̃tʀole/ [1] *vt* (vérifier) check; (surveiller, maîtriser) control. ▫ **se ~** *vpr* control oneself.

contrôleur, **-euse** /kɔ̃tʀolœʀ, -øz/ *nm, f* inspector.

convaincre /kɔ̃vɛ̃kʀ/ [59] *vt* convince; **~ qn de faire** persuade sb to do.

convalescence /kɔ̃valesɑ̃s/ *nf* convalescence; **être en ~** be convalescing.

convenable /kɔ̃vnabl/ *a* (correct) decent, proper; (approprié) suitable; (acceptable) reasonable, acceptable.

convenance /kɔ̃vnɑ̃s/ *nf* **à ma ~** to my satisfaction; **les ~s** convention.

convenir /kɔ̃vniʀ/ [58] *vt/i* be suitable; **~ à** suit; **~ que** admit that; **~ de qch** (avouer) admit sth; (s'accorder sur) agree on sth; **~ de faire** agree to do; **il convient de** it is advisable to; (selon les bienséances) it would be right to.

convention /kɔ̃vɑ̃sjɔ̃/ *nf* agreement, convention; (clause) article, clause; **~s** (convenances) convention; **de ~** conventional; **~ collective** industrial agreement.

convenu, **~e** /kɔ̃vny/ *a* agreed.

conversation /kɔ̃vɛʀsasjɔ̃/ *nf* conversation.

convertir /kɔ̃vɛʀtiʀ/ [2] *vt* convert (**à** to; **en** into). ▫ **se ~** *vpr* be converted, convert.

conviction /kɔ̃viksjɔ̃/ *nf* conviction; **avoir la ~ que** be convinced that.

convivial, **~e** (*mpl* **-iaux**) /kɔ̃vivjal, -jo/ *a* convivial; (Ordinat) user-friendly.

convocation /kɔ̃vɔkasjɔ̃/ *nf* (Jur) summons; (d'une assemblée) convening; (document) notification to attend.

convoi /kɔ̃vwa/ *nm* convoy; (train) train; **~ (funèbre)** funeral procession.

convoquer /kɔ̃vɔke/ [1] *vt* (*assemblée*) convene; (*personne*) summon; **être convoqué pour un entretien** be called for interview.

coopération /koɔpeʀasjɔ̃/ *nf* cooperation; (Mil) civilian national service abroad.

coordination /koɔʀdinasjɔ̃/ *nf* coordination. **coordonnées** *nfpl* coordinates; (adresse) address and telephone number.

copain /kɔpɛ̃/ *nm* friend; (petit ami) boyfriend.
copie /kɔpi/ *nf* copy; (Scol) paper; **~ d'examen** exam paper *ou* script; **~ de sauvegarde** back-up copy.
copier /kɔpje/ [45] *vt/i* copy; **~ sur** (Scol) copy *ou* crib from.
copieux, -ieuse /kɔpjø, -z/ *a* copious.
copine /kɔpin/ *nf* friend; (petite amie) girlfriend.
coq /kɔk/ *nm* cockerel.
coque /kɔk/ *nf* shell; (de bateau) hull.
coquelicot /kɔkliko/ *nm* poppy.
coqueluche /kɔklyʃ/ *nf* whooping cough.
coquet, ~te /kɔkɛ, -t/ *a* flirtatious; (élégant) pretty; (*somme* ⊡) tidy.
coquetier /kɔktje/ *nm* eggcup.
coquillage /kɔkijaʒ/ *nm* shellfish; (coquille) shell.
coquille /kɔkij/ *nf* shell; (faute) misprint; **~ Saint-Jacques** scallop.
coquin, ~e /kɔkɛ̃, -in/ *a* mischievous. ● *nm, f* rascal.
cor /kɔʀ/ *nm* (Mus) horn; (au pied) corn.
corail (*pl* **-aux**) /kɔʀaj, -o/ *nm* coral.
corbeau (*pl* **~x**) /kɔʀbo/ *nm* (oiseau) crow.
corbeille /kɔʀbɛj/ *nf* basket; **~ à papier** waste-paper basket.
corbillard /kɔʀbijaʀ/ *nm* hearse.
cordage /kɔʀdaʒ/ *nm* rope; **~s** (Naut) rigging.
corde /kɔʀd/ *nf* rope; (d'arc, de violon) string; **~ à linge** washing line; **~ à sauter** skipping-rope; **~ raide** tightrope; **~s vocales** vocal cords.
cordon /kɔʀdɔ̃/ *nm* string, cord; **~ de police** police cordon.
cordonnier /kɔʀdɔnje/ *nm* cobbler.
Corée /kɔʀe/ *nf* Korea.
coriace /kɔʀjas/ *a* tough.
corne /kɔʀn/ *nf* horn.
corneille /kɔʀnɛj/ *nf* crow.
cornemuse /kɔʀnəmyz/ *nf* bagpipes (+ *pl*).
corner /kɔʀne/ [1] *vt* (*page*) turn down the corner of; **page cornée** dog-eared page. ● *vi* (Auto) hoot, honk.
cornet /kɔʀnɛ/ *nm* (paper) cone; (crème glacée) cornet, cone.
corniche /kɔʀniʃ/ *nf* cornice; (*route*) cliff road.
cornichon /kɔʀniʃɔ̃/ *nm* gherkin.
corporel, ~le /kɔʀpɔʀɛl/ *a* bodily; (*châtiment*) corporal.
corps /kɔʀ/ *nm* body; (Mil) corps; **combat ~ à ~** hand-to-hand combat; **~ électoral** electorate; **~ enseignant** teaching profession.
correct, ~e /kɔʀɛkt/ *a* proper, correct; (exact) correct.
correcteur, -trice /kɔʀɛktœʀ, -tʀis/ *nm, f* (d'épreuves) proofreader; (Scol) examiner; **~ liquide** correction fluid; **~ d'orthographe** spell-checker.
correction /kɔʀɛksjɔ̃/ *nf* correction; (d'examen) marking, grading; (punition) beating.
correspondance /kɔʀɛspɔ̃dɑ̃s/ *nf* correspondence; (de train, d'autobus) connection; **vente par ~** mail order; **faire des études par ~** do a correspondence course.
correspondant, ~e /kɔʀɛspɔ̃dɑ̃, -t/ *a* corresponding. ● *nm, f* correspondent; penfriend; (au téléphone) **votre ~** the person you are calling.
correspondre /kɔʀɛspɔ̃dʀ/ [3] *vi* (s'accorder, écrire) correspond; (*chambres*) communicate. ● *v + prép* **~ à** (être approprié à) match, suit; (équivaloir à) correspond to. □ **se ~** *vpr* correspond.
corrida /kɔʀida/ *nf* bullfight.

corriger /kɔʀiʒe/ [40] *vt* correct; (*devoir*) mark, grade, correct; (punir) beat; (guérir) cure.

corsage /kɔʀsaʒ/ *nm* bodice; (chemisier) blouse.

corsaire /kɔʀsɛʀ/ *nm* pirate.

Corse /kɔʀs/ *nf* Corsica. ● *nmf* Corsican. **corse** *a* Corsican.

corsé, **~e** /kɔʀse/ *a* (*vin*) full-bodied; (*café*) strong; (scabreux) racy; (*problème*) tough.

cortège /kɔʀtɛʒ/ *nm* procession; **~ funèbre** funeral procession.

corvée /kɔʀve/ *nf* chore.

cosmonaute /kɔsmɔnot/ *nmf* cosmonaut.

cosmopolite /kɔsmɔpɔlit/ *a* cosmopolitan.

cosse /kɔs/ *nf* (de pois) pod.

cossu, **~e** /kɔsy/ *a* (*gens*) well-to-do; (*demeure*) opulent.

costaud, **~e** /kɔsto, -d/ ! *a* strong. ● *nm* strong man.

costume /kɔstym/ *nm* suit; (Théât) costume.

cote /kɔt/ *nf* (classification) mark; (en Bourse) quotation; (de cheval) odds (**de** on); (de candidat, acteur) rating; **~ d'alerte** danger level; **avoir la ~** be popular.

côte /kot/ *nf* (littoral) coast; (pente) hill; (Anat) rib; (Culin) chop; **~ à ~** side by side; **la C~ d'Azur** the (French) Riviera.

côté /kote/ *nm* side; (direction) way; **à ~** nearby; **voisin d'à ~** next-door neighbour; **à ~ de** next to; (comparé à) compared to; **à ~ de la cible** wide of the target; **aux ~s de** by the side of; **de ~** (regarder) sideways; (*sauter*) to one side; **mettre de ~** put aside; **de ce ~** this way; **de chaque ~** on each side; **de tous les ~s** on every side; (partout) everywhere; **du ~ de** (vers) towards; (dans les environs de) near.

côtelette /kotlɛt/ *nf* chop.

coter /kɔte/ [1] *vt* (Comm) quote; **coté en Bourse** listed on the Stock Exchange; **très coté** highly rated.

cotiser /kɔtize/ [1] *vi* pay one's contributions (**à** to); (à un club) pay one's subscription. □ **se ~** *vpr* club together.

coton /kɔtɔ̃/ *nm* cotton; **~ hydrophile** cotton wool.

cou /ku/ *nm* neck.

couchant /kuʃɑ̃/ *nm* sunset.

couche /kuʃ/ *nf* layer; (de peinture) coat; (de bébé) nappy; (US) diaper; **~s** (Méd) childbirth; **~s sociales** social strata.

coucher /kuʃe/ [1] *vt* put to bed; (loger) put up; (étendre) lay down; **~ (par écrit)** set down. ● *vi* sleep. □ **se ~** *vpr* go to bed; (s'étendre) lie down; (*soleil*) set. ● *nm* **~ (de soleil)** sunset; **au ~ du soleil** at sunset.

couchette /kuʃɛt/ *nf* (de train) couchette; (Naut) berth.

coude /kud/ *nm* elbow; (de rivière, chemin) bend; **~ à ~** side by side.

cou-de-pied (*pl* **cous-de-pied**) /kudpje/ *nm* instep.

coudre /kudʀ/ [19] *vt/i* sew.

couette /kwɛt/ *nf* duvet, continental quilt.

couler /kule/ [1] *vi* flow, run; (*fromage, nez*) run; (*fuir*) leak; (*bateau*) sink; (*entreprise*) go under; **faire ~ un bain** run a bath. ● *vt* (*bateau*) sink; (*sculpture, métal*) cast. □ **se ~** *vpr* slip (**dans** into).

couleur /kulœʀ/ *nf* colour; (peinture) paint; (aux cartes) suit; **~s** (teint) colour; **de ~** (*homme, femme*) coloured; **en ~s** (*télévision, film*) colour.

couleuvre /kulœvʀ/ *nf* grass snake.

coulisse /kulis/ *nf* (de tiroir) runner; **à ~** (*porte, fenêtre*) sliding;

~s (Théât) wings; **dans les ~s** (fig) behind the scenes.

couloir /kulwaʀ/ *nm* corridor; (Sport) lane; **~ de bus** bus lane.

coup /ku/ *nm* blow; (choc) knock; (Sport) stroke; (de crayon, chance, cloche) stroke; (de fusil, pistolet) shot; (fois) time; (aux échecs) move; **donner un ~ de pied/poing à** kick/punch; **à ~ sûr** definitely; **après ~** after the event; **boire un ~** [I] have a drink; **~ sur ~** in rapid succession; **du ~** as a result; **d'un seul ~** in one go; **du premier ~** first go; **sale ~** dirty trick; **sous le ~ de la fatigue/colère** out of tiredness/anger; **sur le ~** instantly; **tenir le ~** hold out; **manquer son ~** [I] blow it [I]; **~ de chiffon** wipe (with a rag); **~ de coude** nudge; **~ de couteau** stab; **~ d'envoi** kick-off; **~ d'État** (Pol) coup; **~ de feu** shot; **~ de fil** [I] phone call; **~ de filet** haul, (fig) police raid; **~ de foudre** love at first sight; **~ franc** free kick; **~ de frein** sudden braking; **~ de grâce** coup de grâce; **~ de main** helping hand; **~ d'œil** glance; **~ de pied** kick; **~ de poing** punch; **~ de soleil** sunburn; **~ de sonnette** ring (on a bell); **~ de téléphone** (tele-) phone call; **~ de tête** wild impulse; **~ de théâtre** dramatic event; **~ de tonnerre** thunderclap; **~ de vent** gust of wind.

coupable /kupabl/ *a* guilty. ● *nmf* culprit.

coupe /kup/ *nf* cup; (de champagne) goblet; (à fruits) dish; (de vêtement) cut; (dessin) section; **~ de cheveux** haircut.

couper /kupe/ [1] *vt* cut; (*arbre*) cut down; (arrêter) cut off; (*voyage*) break up; (*appétit*) take away; (*vin*) water down; **~ par** take a short cut via; **~ la parole à qn** cut sb short. ● *vi* cut. □ **se ~** *vpr* cut oneself; **se ~ le doigt** cut one's finger; (*routes*) intersect; **se ~ de** cut oneself off from.

couple /kupl/ *nm* couple; (d'animaux) pair.

coupure /kupyʀ/ *nf* cut; (billet de banque) note; (de presse) cutting; (pause, rupture) break; **~ (de courant)** power cut.

cour /kuʀ/ *nf* (court)yard; (du roi) court; (tribunal) court; **~ (de récréation)** playground; **~ martiale** court-martial; **faire la ~ à** court.

courageux, -euse /kuʀaʒø, -z/ *a* courageous.

couramment /kuʀamɑ̃/ *adv* frequently; (*parler*) fluently.

courant, ~e /kuʀɑ̃, -t/ *a* standard, ordinary; (en cours) current. ● *nm* current; (de mode, d'idées) trend; **~ d'air** draught; **dans le ~ de** in the course of; **être/mettre au ~ de** know/tell about; (à jour) be/bring up to date on.

courbature /kuʀbatyʀ/ *nf* ache; **avoir des ~s** be stiff, ache.

courber /kuʀbe/ [1] *vt* bend.

coureur, -euse /kuʀœʀ, -øz/ *nm, f* (Sport) runner; **~ automobile** racing driver; **~ cycliste** racing cyclist. ● *nm* womanizer.

courgette /kuʀʒɛt/ *nf* courgette; (US) zucchini.

courir /kuʀiʀ/ [20] *vi* run; (se hâter) rush; (*nouvelles*) go round; **~ après qn/qch** chase after sb/sth. ● *vt* (*risque*) run; (*danger*) face; (*épreuve sportive*) run *ou* compete in; (fréquenter) do the rounds of; (*filles*) chase (after).

couronne /kuʀɔn/ *nf* crown; (de fleurs) wreath.

couronnement /kuʀɔnmɑ̃/ *nm* coronation, crowning; (fig) crowning achievement.

courrier /kuʀje/ *nm* post, mail; (à écrire) letters; **~ du cœur** problem page; **~ électronique** e-mail.

cours /kuʀ/ *nm* (leçon) class; (série de leçons) course; (prix) price; (cote) (de valeur, denrée) price; (de devises) exchange rate; (déroulement, d'une rivière) course; (allée) avenue; **au ~ de** in the course of; **avoir ~** (*monnaie*) be legal tender; (fig) be current; (Scol) have a lesson; **~ d'eau** river, stream; **~ du soir** evening class; **~ particulier** private lesson; **~ magistral** (Univ) lecture; **en ~** current; (*travail*) in progress; **en ~ de route** along the way.

course /kuʀs/ *nf* running; (épreuve de vitesse) race; (activité) racing; (entre rivaux: fig) race; (de projectile) flight; (voyage) journey; (commission) errand; **~s** (achats) shopping; (de chevaux) races; **faire la ~ avec qn** race sb.

coursier, -ière /kuʀsje, -jɛʀ/ *nm,f* messenger.

court, ~e /kuʀ, -t/ *a* short. ● *adv* short; **à ~ de** short of; **pris de ~** caught unawares. ● *nm* **~ (de tennis)** (tennis) court.

courtier, -ière /kuʀtje, -jɛʀ/ *nm,f* broker.

courtiser /kuʀtize/ [1] *vt* woo, court.

courtois, ~e /kuʀtwa, -z/ *a* courteous. **courtoisie** *nf* courtesy.

cousin, ~e /kuzɛ̃, -in/ *nm,f* cousin; **~ germain** first cousin.

coussin /kusɛ̃/ *nm* cushion.

coût /ku/ *nm* cost; **le ~ de la vie** the cost of living.

couteau (*pl* **~x**) /kuto/ *nm* knife; **~ à cran d'arrêt** flick knife.

coûter /kute/ [1] *vt/i* cost; **coûte que coûte** at all costs; **au prix coûtant** at cost (price).

coutume /kutym/ *nf* custom.

couture /kutyʀ/ *nf* sewing; (métier) dressmaking; (points) seam.

couturier *nm* fashion designer. **couturière** *nf* dressmaker.

couvée /kuve/ *nf* brood.

couvent /kuvɑ̃/ *nm* convent.

couver /kuve/ [1] *vt* (*œufs*) hatch; (*personne*) overprotect, pamper; (*maladie*) be coming down with, be sickening for. ● *vi* (*feu*) smoulder; (*mal*) be brewing.

couvercle /kuvɛʀkl/ *nm* (de marmite, boîte) lid; (qui se visse) screwtop.

couvert, ~e /kuvɛʀ, -t/ *a* covered (**de** with); (habillé) covered up; (*ciel*) overcast. ● *nm* (à table) place setting; (prix) cover charge; **~s** (couteaux etc.) cutlery; **mettre le ~** lay the table; (abri) cover; **à ~** (Mil) under cover; **à ~ de** (fig) safe from.

couverture /kuvɛʀtyʀ/ *nf* cover; (de lit) blanket; (toit) roofing; (dans la presse) coverage; **~ chauffante** electric blanket.

couvre-feu (*pl* **~x**) /kuvʀəfø/ *nm* curfew.

couvre-lit (*pl* **~s**) /kuvʀəli/ *nm* bedspread.

couvrir /kuvʀiʀ/ [21] *vt* cover. □ **se ~** *vpr* (s'habiller) wrap up; (se coiffer) put one's hat on; (*ciel*) become overcast.

covoiturage /kɔvwatyʀaʒ/ *nm* car sharing.

cracher /kʀaʃe/ [1] *vi* spit; (*radio*) crackle. ● *vt* spit (out); (*fumée*) belch out.

crachin /kʀaʃɛ̃/ *nm* drizzle.

craie /kʀɛ/ *nf* chalk.

craindre /kʀɛ̃dʀ/ [22] *vt* be afraid of, fear; (être sensible à) be easily damaged by.

crainte /kʀɛ̃t/ *nf* fear (**pour** for); **de ~ de**/**que** for fear of/that. **craintif, -ive** *a* timid.

crampon /kʀɑ̃pɔ̃/ *nm* (de chaussure) stud.

cramponner (se) /(sə)kʀɑ̃pɔne/ [1] *vpr* **se ~ à** cling to.

cran /kʀɑ̃/ *nm* (entaille) notch; (trou) hole; (courage ⊡) guts ⊡, courage; **~ de sûreté** safety catch.

crâne /kʀɑn/ *nm* skull.

crapaud /kʀapo/ *nm* toad.

craquer /kʀake/ [1] *vi* crack, snap; (*plancher*) creak; (*couture*) split; (fig) (*personne*) break down; (céder) give in. ● *vt* (*allumette*) strike; (*vêtement*) split.

crasse /kʀas/ *nf* grime.

cravache /kʀavaʃ/ *nf* (horse) whip.

cravate /kʀavat/ *nf* tie.

crayon /kʀɛjɔ̃/ *nm* pencil; **~ de couleur** coloured pencil; **~ à bille** ballpoint pen; **~ optique** light pen.

créateur, -trice /kʀeatœʀ, -tʀis/ *a* creative. ● *nm, f* creator, designer.

crèche /kʀɛʃ/ *nf* day nursery, crèche; (Relig) crib.

crédit /kʀedi/ *nm* credit; (somme allouée) funds; **à ~** on credit; **faire ~** give credit (**à** to).

créer /kʀee/ [15] *vt* create; (*produit*) design; (*société*) set up.

crémaillère /kʀemajɛʀ/ *nf* **pendre la ~** have a house-warming party.

crème /kʀɛm/ *a inv* cream. ● *nm* (**café**) **~** espresso with milk. ● *nf* cream; (dessert) cream dessert; **~ anglaise** egg custard; **~ fouettée** whipped cream; **~ pâtissière** confectioner's custard. **crémerie** *nf* dairy. **crémeux, -euse** *a* creamy. **crémier, -ière** *nm, f* dairyman, dairywoman.

créneau (*pl* **~x**) /kʀeno/ *nm* (trou, moment) slot, window; (dans le marché) gap; **faire un ~** parallel-park.

crêpe /kʀɛp/ *nf* (galette) pancake. ● *nm* (tissu) crêpe; (matière) crêpe (rubber).

crépitement /kʀepitmɑ̃/ *nm* crackling; (d'huile) sizzling.

crépuscule /kʀepyskyl/ *nm* twilight, dusk.

cresson /kʀəsɔ̃/ *nm* (water)cress.

crête /kʀɛt/ *nf* crest; (de coq) comb.

crétin, ~e /kʀetɛ̃, -in/ *nm, f* ⊡ moron ⊡.

creuser /kʀøze/ [1] *vt* dig; (évider) hollow out; (fig) go into in depth. □ **se ~** *vpr* (*écart*) widen; **se ~ (la cervelle)** ⊡ rack one's brains.

creux, -euse /kʀø, -z/ *a* hollow; (*heures*) off-peak. ● *nm* hollow; (de l'estomac) pit; **dans le ~ de la main** in the palm of the hand.

crevaison /kʀəvɛzɔ̃/ *nf* puncture.

crevasse /kʀəvas/ *nf* crack; (de glacier) crevasse; (de la peau) chap.

crevé, ~e /kʀəve/ *a* ⊡ worn out.

crever /kʀəve/ [1] *vt* burst; (*pneu*) puncture, burst; (exténuer ⊡) exhaust; (œil) put out. ● *vi* (*pneu, sac*) burst; (mourir ⊡) die.

crevette /kʀəvɛt/ *nf* **~ grise** shrimp; **~ rose** prawn.

cri /kʀi/ *nm* cry; (de douleur) scream, cry; **pousser un ~** cry out, scream.

criard, ~e /kʀijaʀ, -d/ *a* (*couleur*) garish; (*voix*) shrill.

crier /kʀije/ [45] *vi* (fort) shout, cry (out); (de douleur) scream; (grincer) creak. ● *vt* (*ordre*) shout (out).

crime /kʀim/ *nm* crime; (meurtre) murder.

criminel, ~le /kʀiminɛl/ *a* criminal. ● *nm, f* criminal; (assassin) murderer.

crinière /kʀinjɛʀ/ *nf* mane.

crise /kʀiz/ *nf* crisis; (Méd) attack; (de colère) fit; **~ cardiaque** heart attack; **~ de foie** bilious attack; **~ de nerfs** hysterics (+ *pl*).

crisper /kʀispe/ [1] *vt* tense; (énerver [!]) irritate. □ **se ~** *vpr* tense; (*mains*) clench.

critère /kʀitɛʀ/ *nm* criterion.

critique /kʀitik/ *a* critical. ●*nf* criticism; (article) review; (*commentateur*) critic; **la ~** (personnes) the critics. **critiquer** [1] *vt* criticize.

Croate /kʀɔat/ *a* Croatian. **C~** *nmf* Croatian.

Croatie /kʀɔasi/ *nf* Croatia.

croche /kʀɔʃ/ *nf* quaver.

croche-pied (*pl* **~s**) /kʀɔʃpje/ *nm* [!] **faire un ~ à** trip up.

crochet /kʀɔʃɛ/ *nm* hook; (détour) detour; (signe) (square) bracket; (tricot) crochet; **faire au ~** crochet.

crochu, **~e** /kʀɔʃy/ *a* hooked.

crocodile /kʀɔkɔdil/ *nm* crocodile.

croire /kʀwaʀ/ [23] *vt* believe (**à, en** in); (estimer) think, believe (**que** that). ●*vi* believe.

croisade /kʀwazad/ *nf* crusade.

croisement /kʀwazmɑ̃/ *nm* crossing; (fait de passer à côté de) passing; (carrefour) crossroads.

croiser /kʀwaze/ [1] *vi* (*bateau*) cruise. ●*vt* cross; (*passant, véhicule*) pass; **~ les bras** fold one's arms; **~ les jambes** cross one's legs; (*animaux*) crossbreed. □ **se ~** *vpr* (*véhicules, piétons*) pass each other; (*lignes*) cross. **croisière** *nf* cruise.

croissance /kʀwasɑ̃s/ *nf* growth.

croissant, **~e** /kʀwasɑ̃, -t/ *a* growing. ●*nm* crescent; (pâtisserie) croissant.

croix /kʀwa/ *nf* cross; **~ gammée** swastika; **C~-Rouge** Red Cross.

croquant, **~e** /kʀɔkɑ̃, -t/ *a* crunchy.

croque-monsieur /kʀɔkməsjø/ *nm inv* toasted ham and cheese sandwich.

croque-mort (*pl* **~s**) /kʀɔkmɔʀ/ *nm* [!] undertaker.

croquer /kʀɔke/ [1] *vt* crunch; (dessiner) sketch; **chocolat à ~** plain chocolate. ●*vi* be crunchy.

croquis /kʀɔki/ *nm* sketch.

crotte /kʀɔt/ *nf* dropping.

crotté, **~e** /kʀɔte/ *a* muddy.

crottin /kʀɔtɛ̃/ *nm* (horse) dropping.

croupir /kʀupiʀ/ [2] *vi* stagnate.

croustillant, **~e** /kʀustijɑ̃, -t/ *a* crispy; (*pain*) crusty; (fig) spicy.

croûte /kʀut/ *nf* crust; (de fromage) rind; (de plaie) scab; **en ~** (Culin) in pastry.

croûton /kʀutɔ̃/ *nm* (bout de pain) crust; (avec potage) croûton.

CRS *abrév m* (**Compagnie républicaine de sécurité**) French riot police; **un ~** *a member of the French riot police*.

cru¹ /kʀy/ ⇒CROIRE [23].

cru², **~e** /kʀy/ *a* raw; (*lumière*) harsh; (*propos*) crude. ●*nm* vineyard; (vin) vintage wine.

crû /kʀy/ ⇒CROÎTRE [24].

cruauté /kʀyote/ *nf* cruelty.

cruche /kʀyʃ/ *nf* jug, pitcher.

crucial, **~e** (*mpl* **-iaux**) /kʀysjal, -jo/ *a* crucial.

crudité /kʀydite/ *nf* (de langage) crudeness; **~s** (Culin) raw vegetables.

crue /kʀy/ *nf* rise in water level; **en ~** in spate.

crustacé /kʀystase/ *nm* shellfish.

cube /kyb/ *nm* cube. ●*a* (*mètre*) cubic.

cueillir /kœjiʀ/ [25] *vt* pick, gather; (*personne* [!]) pick up.

cuiller, **cuillère** /kɥijɛʀ/ *nf* spoon; **~ à soupe** soup spoon; (mesure) tablespoonful.

cuir /kɥiʀ/ *nm* leather; **~ chevelu** scalp.

cuire /kɥiʀ/ [17] *vt* cook; **~ (au**

four) bake. ● *vi* cook; **faire ~** cook.

cuisine /kɥizin/ *nf* kitchen; (art) cookery, cooking; (aliments) food; **faire la ~** cook.

cuisiner /kɥizine/ [1] *vt* cook; (interroger [!]) grill. ● *vi* cook.

cuisinier, **-ière** /kɥizinje, -jɛʀ/ *nm, f* cook. **cuisinière** *nf* (appareil) cooker, stove.

cuisse /kɥis/ *nf* thigh; (de poulet) thigh; (de grenouille) leg.

cuisson /kɥisɔ̃/ *nf* cooking.

cuit, **~e** /kɥi, -t/ *a* cooked; **bien ~** well done *ou* cooked; **trop ~** overdone.

cuivre /kɥivʀ/ *nm* copper; **~** (**jaune**) brass; **~s** (Mus) brass.

cul /ky/ *nm* (derrière [*]) backside, bottom, arse [*].

culbuter /kylbyte/ [1] *vi* (*personne*) tumble; (*objet*) topple (over). ● *vt* knock over.

culminer /kylmine/ [1] *vi* reach its highest point *ou* peak.

culot /kylo/ *nm* (audace [!]) nerve, cheek; (Tech) base.

culotte /kylɔt/ *nf* (de femme) pants (+ *pl*), knickers (+ *pl*); (US) panties (+ *pl*); **~ de cheval** riding breeches; **en ~ courte** in short trousers.

culpabilité /kylpabilite/ *nf* guilt.

culte /kylt/ *nm* cult, worship; (religion) religion; (office protestant) service.

cultivateur, **-trice** /kyltivatœʀ, -tʀis/ *nm, f* farmer.

cultiver /kyltive/ [1] *vt* cultivate; (*plantes*) grow.

culture /kyltyʀ/ *nf* cultivation; (de plantes) growing; (agriculture) farming; (education) culture; (connaissances) knowledge; **~s** (terrains) lands under cultivation; **~ physique** physical training.

culturel, **~le** /kyltyʀɛl/ *a* cultural.

cumuler /kymyle/ [1] *vt* accumulate; (*fonctions*) hold concurrently.

cure /kyʀ/ *nf* (course of) treatment.

curé /kyʀe/ *nm* (parish) priest.

cure-dent (*pl* **~s**) /kyʀdɑ̃/ *nm* toothpick.

curer /kyʀe/ [1] *vt* clean. □ **se** [illegible] **les dents/ongles** clean one's teeth/nails.

curieux, **-ieuse** /kyʀjø, -z/ *a* curious. ● *nm, f* (badaud) onlooker.

curiosité /kyʀjozite/ *nf* curiosity; (objet) curio; (spectacle) unusual sight.

curriculum vitae /kyʀikylɔm vite/ *nm inv* curriculum vitae; (US) résumé.

curseur /kyʀsœʀ/ *nm* cursor.

cutané, **~e** /kytane/ *a* skin.

cuve /kyv/ *nf* vat; (à mazout, eau) tank.

cuvée /kyve/ *nf* (de vin) vintage.

cuvette /kyvɛt/ *nf* bowl; (de lavabo) (wash)basin; (des cabinets) pan, bowl.

CV *abrév m* (**curriculum vitae**) CV.

cyberbranché, **~e** /sibɛʀbʀɑ̃ʃe/ *a* cyberwired.

cybercafé /sibɛʀkafe/ *nm* cybercafe.

cyberespace /sibɛʀsɛpas/ *nm* cyberspace.

cybernaute /sibɛʀnot/ *nmf* Netsurfer.

cybernétique /sibɛʀnetik/ *nf* cybernetics (+ *pl*).

cyclisme /siklism/ *nm* cycling.

cycliste /siklist/ *nmf* cyclist. ● *nm* cycling shorts. ● *a* cycle.

cyclone /siklon/ *nm* cyclone.

cygne /siɲ/ *nm* swan.

cynique /sinik/ *a* cynical. ● *nm* cynic.

C

d'/d/ ⇒DE.

d'abord /dabɔʀ/ *adv* first; (au début) at first.

dactylo /daktilo/ *nf* typist. **dactylographier** [45] *vt* type.

dada /dada/ *nm* hobby-horse.

daim /dɛ̃/ *nm* (fallow) deer; (cuir) suede.

dallage /dalaʒ/ *nm* paving. **dalle** *nf* slab.

daltonien, ~ne /daltɔnjɛ̃, -ɛn/ *a* colour-blind.

dame /dam/ *nf* lady; (cartes, échecs) queen; **~s** (jeu) draughts; (US) checkers.

damier /damje/ *nm* draught-board; (US) checker-board; **à ~** chequered.

damner /dane/ [1] *vt* damn.

dandiner (se) /(sə)dɑ̃dine/ [1] *vpr* waddle.

Danemark /danmaʀk/ *nm* Denmark.

danger /dɑ̃ʒe/ *nm* danger; **en ~** in danger; **mettre en ~** endanger.

dangereux, -euse /dɑ̃ʒ(ə)ʀø, -z/ *a* dangerous.

danois, ~e /danwa, -z/ *a* Danish. ● *nm* (Ling) Danish. **D~, ~e** *nm, f* Dane.

dans /dɑ̃/ *prép* in; (mouvement) into; (à l'intérieur de) inside, in; **être ~ un avion** be on a plane; **~ dix jours** in ten days' time; **boire ~ un verre** drink out of a glass; **~ les 10 francs** about 10 francs.

danse /dɑ̃s/ *nf* dance; (art) dancing.

danser /dɑ̃se/ [1] *vt/i* dance. **danseur, -euse** *nm, f* dancer.

darne /daʀn/ *nf* steak (of fish).

date /dat/ *nf* date; **~ limite** deadline; **~ limite de vente** sell-by date; **~ de péremption** use-by date.

dater /date/ [1] *vt/i* date; **à ~ de** as from.

datte /dat/ *nf* (fruit) date.

daube /dob/ *nf* casserole.

dauphin /dofɛ̃/ *nm* (animal) dolphin.

davantage /davɑ̃taʒ/ *adv* more; (plus longtemps) longer; **~ de** more; **je n'en sais pas ~** that's as much as I know.

de, d' /də, d/

d' before vowel or mute h.

● *préposition*

····➤ of; **le livre ~ mon ami** my friend's book; **un pont ~ fer** an iron bridge.

····➤ (provenance) from.

····➤ (temporel) from; **~ 8 heures à 10 heures** from 8 till 10.

····➤ (mesure, manière) **dix mètres ~ haut** ten metres high; **pleurer ~ rage** cry with rage.

····➤ (agent) by; **un livre ~ Marcel Aymé** a book by Marcel Aymé.

● **de, de l', de la, du,** (*pl* **des**) *déterminant*

····➤ some; **du pain** (some) bread; **des fleurs** (some) flowers; **je ne bois jamais ~ vin** I never drink wine.

de + le = du
de + les = des

dé /de/ *nm* (à jouer) dice; (à coudre) thimble; **~s** (jeu) dice.

débâcle /debɑkl/ *nf* (Géog) breaking up; (Mil) rout.

déballer /debale/ [1] *vt* unpack; (révéler) spill out.
débarbouiller /debaʀbuje/ *vt* wash the face of. □ **se ~** *vpr* wash one's face.
débarcadère /debaʀkadɛʀ/ *nm* landing-stage.
débardeur /debaʀdœʀ/ *nm* (vêtement) tank top.
débarquement /debaʀkəmɑ̃/ *nm* disembarkation. **débarquer** [1] *vt/i* disembark, land; (arriver ⓘ) turn up.
débarras /debaʀa/ *nm* junk room; **bon ~!** good riddance!
débarrasser /debaʀase/ [1] *vt* clear (**de** of); **~ qn de** relieve sb of; (*défaut, ennemi*) rid sb of. □ **se ~ de** *vpr* get rid of.
débat /deba/ *nm* debate.
débattre /debatʀ/ [11] *vt* debate. ● *vi* **~ de** discuss. □ **se ~** *vpr* struggle (to get free).
débauche /deboʃ/ *nf* debauchery; (fig) profusion.
débaucher /deboʃe/ [1] *vt* (licencier) lay off; (distraire) tempt away.
débile /debil/ *a* weak; ⓘ stupid. ● *nmf* moron ⓘ.
débit /debi/ *nm* (rate of) flow; (élocution) delivery; (de compte) debit; **~ de tabac** tobacconist's shop; **~ de boissons** bar.
débiter /debite/ [1] *vt* (*compte*) debit; (fournir) produce; (vendre) sell; (dire: péj) spout; (couper) cut up.
débiteur, -trice /debitœʀ, -tʀis/ *nm,f* debtor. ● *a* (*compte*) in debit.
déblayer /debleje/ [31] *vt* clear.
déblocage /deblɔkaʒ/ *nm* (de prix) deregulating. **débloquer** [1] *vt* (*prix, salaires*) unfreeze.
déboiser /debwaze/ [1] *vt* clear (of trees).
déboîter /debwate/ [1] *vi* (*véhicule*) pull out. ● *vt* (*membre*) dislocate.
débordement /debɔʀdəmɑ̃/ *nm* (de joie) excess.
déborder /debɔʀde/ [1] *vi* overflow. ● *vt* (dépasser) extend beyond; **~ de** (*joie etc.*) be brimming over with.
débouché /debuʃe/ *nm* opening; (carrière) prospect; (Comm) outlet; (sortie) end, exit.
déboucher /debuʃe/ [1] *vt* (*bouteille*) uncork; (*évier*) unblock. ● *vi* come out (**de** from); **~ sur** (*rue*) lead into.
débourser /debuʀse/ [1] *vt* pay out.
debout /dəbu/ *adv* standing; (levé, éveillé) up; **être ~, se tenir ~** be standing, stand; **se mettre ~** stand up.
déboutonner /debutɔne/ [1] *vt* unbutton. □ **se ~** *vpr* unbutton oneself; (*vêtement*) come undone.
débrancher /debʀɑ̃ʃe/ [1] *vt* (*prise*) unplug; (*système*) disconnect.
débrayer /debʀeje/ [31] *vi* (Auto) declutch; (faire grève) stop work.
débris /debʀi/ *nmpl* fragments; (détritus) rubbish (+ *sg*); debris.
débrouillard, ~e /debʀujaʀ, -d/ *a* ⓘ resourceful.
débrouiller /debʀuje/ [1] *vt* disentangle; (*problème*) solve. □ **se ~** *vpr* manage.
début /deby/ *nm* beginning; **faire ses ~s** (en public) make one's début; **à mes ~s** when I started out. **débutant, ~e** *nm,f* beginner. **débuter** [1] *vi* begin; (dans un métier etc.) start out.
déca /deka/ *nm* ⓘ decaf.
deçà: **en ~** /ɑ̃dəsa/ *loc* this side. ● *prép* **en ~ de** this side of.
décacheter /dekaʃte/ [6] *vt* open.

décade /dekad/ *nf* ten days; (décennie) decade.

décadent, **~e** /dekadɑ̃, -t/ *a* decadent.

décalage /dekalaʒ/ *nm* (écart) gap; **~ horaire** time difference. **décaler** [1] *vt* shift.

décalquer /dekalke/ [1] *vt* trace.

décamper /dekɑ̃pe/ [1] *vi* clear off.

décanter /dekɑ̃te/ *vt* allow to settle. ▫ **se ~** *vpr* settle.

décapant /dekapɑ̃/ *nm* chemical agent; (pour peinture) paint stripper. ● *a* (*humour*) caustic.

décapotable /dekapɔtabl/ *a* convertible.

décapsuleur /dekapsylœʀ/ *nm* bottle-opener.

décédé, **~e** /desede/ *a* deceased. **décéder** [14] *vi* die.

déceler /desle/ [6] *vt* detect; (démontrer) reveal.

décembre /desɑ̃bʀ/ *nm* December.

décemment /desamɑ̃/ *adv* decently. **décence** *nf* decency. **décent**, **~e** *a* decent.

décennie /deseni/ *nf* decade.

décentralisation /desɑ̃tʀalizasjɔ̃/ *nf* decentralization. **décentraliser** [1] *vt* decentralize.

déception /desɛpsjɔ̃/ *nf* disappointment.

décerner /desɛʀne/ [1] *vt* award.

décès /desɛ/ *nm* death.

décevant, **~e** /des(ə)vɑ̃, -t/ *a* disappointing. **décevoir** [52] *vt* disappoint.

déchaîner /deʃene/ [1] *vt* (*enthousiasme*) rouse. ▫ **se ~** *vpr* go wild.

décharge /deʃaʀʒ/ *nf* (de fusil) discharge; **~ électrique** electric shock; **~ publique** municipal dump.

décharger /deʃaʀʒe/ [40] *vt* unload; **~ qn de** relieve sb from. ▫ **se ~** *vpr* (*batterie, pile*) go flat.

déchausser (se) /(sə)deʃose/ [1] *vpr* take off one's shoes; (*dent*) work loose.

dèche /dɛʃ/ *nf* ⊡ **dans la ~** broke.

déchéance /deʃeɑ̃s/ *nf* decay.

déchet /deʃɛ/ *nm* (reste) scrap; (perte) waste; **~s** (ordures) refuse.

déchiffrer /deʃifʀe/ [1] *vt* decipher.

déchiqueter /deʃikte/ [38] *vt* tear to shreds.

déchirement /deʃiʀmɑ̃/ *nm* heartbreak; (conflit) split.

déchirer /deʃiʀe/ [1] *vt* (par accident) tear; (lacérer) tear up; (arracher) tear off *ou* out; (diviser) tear apart. ▫ **se ~** *vpr* tear. **déchirure** *nf* tear.

décibel /desibɛl/ *nm* decibel.

décidément /desidemɑ̃/ *adv* really.

décider /deside/ [1] *vt* decide on; (persuader) persuade; **~ que/de** decide that/to; **~ de qch** decide on sth. ▫ **se ~** *vpr* make up one's mind (**à** to).

décimal, **~e** (*mpl* **~aux**) /desimal, -o/ *a & nf* decimal.

décisif, **-ive** /desizif, -v/ *a* decisive.

décision /desizjɔ̃/ *nf* decision.

déclaration /deklaʀasjɔ̃/ *nf* declaration; (commentaire politique) statement; **~ d'impôts** tax return.

déclarer /deklaʀe/ [1] *vt* declare; (*naissance*) register; **déclaré coupable** found guilty; **~ forfait** (Sport) withdraw. ▫ **se ~** *vpr* (*feu*) break out.

déclencher /deklɑ̃ʃe/ [1] *vt* (Tech) set off; (*conflit*) spark off; (*avalanche*) start; (*rire*) provoke. ▫ **se ~** *vpr* (Tech) go off. **déclencheur** *nm* (Photo) shutter release.

déclic /deklik/ *nm* click.

déclin /deklɛ̃/ *nm* decline.

déclinaison /deklinɛzɔ̃/ *nf* (Ling) declension.

décliner /dekline/ [1] *vt* (refuser) decline; (dire) state; (Ling) decline.

décocher /dekɔʃe/ [1] *vt* (*coup*) fling; (*regard*) shoot.

décollage /dekɔlaʒ/ *nm* take-off.

décoller /dekɔle/ [1] *vt* unstick. ● *vi* (*avion*) take off. □ **se ~** *vpr* come off.

décolleté, **~e** /dekɔlte/ *a* low-cut. ● *nm* low neckline.

décolorer /dekɔlɔʀe/ [1] *vt* fade; (*cheveux*) bleach. □ **se ~** *vpr* fade.

décombres /dekɔ̃bʀ/ *nmpl* rubble.

décommander /dekɔmɑ̃de/ [1] *vt* cancel.

décomposer /dekɔ̃poze/ [1] *vt* break up; (*substance*) decompose. □ **se ~** *vpr* (pourrir) decompose.

décompte /dekɔ̃t/ *nm* deduction; (détail) breakdown.

décongeler /dekɔ̃ʒle/ [6] *vt* thaw.

déconseillé, **~e** /dekɔ̃sɛje/ *a* not recommended, inadvisable.

déconseiller /dekɔ̃sɛje/ [1] *vt* **~ qch à qn** advise sb against sth.

décontracté, **~e** /dekɔ̃tʀakte/ *a* relaxed.

déconvenue /dekɔ̃vny/ *nf* disappointment.

décor /dekɔʀ/ *nm* (paysage) scenery; (de cinéma, théâtre) set; (cadre) setting; (de maison) décor.

décoratif, **-ive** /dekɔʀatif, -v/ *a* decorative.

décorateur, **-trice** /dekɔʀatœʀ, -tʀis/ *nm, f* (de cinéma) set designer. **décoration** *nf* decoration. **décorer** [1] *vt* decorate.

décortiquer /dekɔʀtike/ [1] *vt* shell; (fig) dissect.

découdre (se) /(sə)dekudʀ/ [19] *vpr* come unstitched.

découler /dekule/ [1] *vi* **~ de** follow from.

découper /dekupe/ [1] *vt* cut up; (*viande*) carve; (détacher) cut out.

découragement /dekuʀaʒmɑ̃/ *nm* discouragement.

décourager /dekuʀaʒe/ [40] *vt* discourage. □ **se ~** *vpr* become discouraged.

décousu, **~e** /dekuzy/ *a* (*vêtement*) which has come unstitched; (*idées*) disjointed.

découvert, **~e** /dekuvɛʀ, -t/ *a* (*tête*) bare; (*terrain*) open. ● *nm* (de compte) overdraft; **à ~** exposed; (fig) openly.

découverte /dekuvɛʀt/ *nf* discovery; **à la ~ de** in search of.

découvrir /dekuvʀiʀ/ [21] *vt* discover; (voir) see; (montrer) reveal. □ **se ~** *vpr* (se décoiffer) take one's hat off; (*ciel*) clear.

décrasser /dekʀase/ [1] *vt* clean.

décrépit, **~e** /dekʀepi, -t/ *a* decrepit. **décrépitude** *nf* decay.

décret /dekʀɛ/ *nm* decree. **décréter** [14] *vt* order; (dire) declare.

décrié, **~e** /dekʀije/ *a* criticized.

décrire /dekʀiʀ/ [30] *vt* describe.

décroché, **~e** /dekʀɔʃe/ *a* (*téléphone*) off the hook.

décrocher /dekʀɔʃe/ [1] *vt* unhook; (obtenir Ⓘ) get. ● *vi* (abandonner Ⓘ) give up; **~ (le téléphone)** pick up the phone.

décroître /dekʀwatʀ/ [24] *vi* decrease.

déçu, **~e** /desy/ *a* disappointed.

décupler /dekyple/ [1] *vt/i* increase tenfold.

dédaigner /dedeɲe/ [1] *vt* scorn.

dédain /dedɛ̃/ *nm* scorn.

dédale /dedal/ *nm* maze.

dedans /dədɑ̃/ *adv & nm* inside; **en ~** on the inside.

D

dédicacer /dedikase/ [10] *vt* dedicate; (signer) sign.

dédier /dedje/ [45] *vt* dedicate.

dédommagement /dedɔmaʒmɑ̃/ *nm* compensation. **dédommager** [40] *vt* compensate (**de** for).

déduction /dedyksjɔ̃/ *nf* deduction; ~ **d'impôts** tax deduction.

déduire /dedɥiʀ/ [17] *vt* deduct; (conclure) deduce.

déesse /deɛs/ *nf* goddess.

défaillance /defajɑ̃s/ *nf* (panne) failure; (évanouissement) blackout. **défaillant**, ~**e** *a* (*système*) faulty; (*personne*) faint.

défaire /defɛʀ/ [33] *vt* undo; (*valise*) unpack; (démonter) take down. □ **se** ~ *vpr* come undone; **se** ~ **de** rid oneself of.

défait, ~**e** /defɛ, -t/ *a* (*cheveux*) ruffled; (*visage*) haggard; (*nœud*) undone. **défaite** *nf* defeat.

défaitiste /defetist/ *a & nmf* defeatist.

défalquer /defalke/ [1] *vt* (*somme*) deduct.

défaut /defo/ *nm* fault, defect; (d'un verre, diamant, etc.) flaw; (pénurie) shortage; **à** ~ **de** for lack of; **pris en** ~ caught out; **faire** ~ (*argent etc.*) be lacking; **par** ~ (Jur) in one's absence; ~ **de paiement** non-payment.

défavorable /defavɔʀabl/ *a* unfavourable.

défavoriser /defavɔʀize/ [1] *vt* discriminate against.

défectueux, **-euse** /defɛktɥø, -z/ *a* faulty, defective.

défendre /defɑ̃dʀ/ [3] *vt* defend; (interdire) forbid; ~ **à qn de** forbid sb to. □ **se** ~ *vpr* defend oneself; (se protéger) protect oneself; (se débrouiller) manage; **se** ~ **de** (refuser) refrain from.

défense /defɑ̃s/ *nf* defence; ~ **de fumer** no smoking; (d'éléphant) tusk.

défenseur *nm* defender.

défensif, **-ive** *a* defensive.

déferler /defɛʀle/ [1] *vi* (*vagues*) break; (*violence*) erupt.

défi /defi/ *nm* challenge; (provocation) defiance; **mettre au** ~ challenge.

déficience /defisjɑ̃s/ *nf* deficiency. **déficient**, ~**e** *a* deficient.

déficit /defisit/ *nm* deficit. **déficitaire** *a* in deficit.

défier /defje/ [45] *vt* challenge; (braver) defy.

défilé /defile/ *nm* procession; (Mil) parade; (fig) (continual) stream; (Géog) gorge; ~ **de mode** fashion parade.

défiler /defile/ [1] *vi* march; (*visiteurs*) stream; (*images*) flash by; (*chiffres, minutes*) add up. □ **se** ~ *vpr* [!] sneak off.

défini, ~**e** /defini/ *a* (Ling) definite.

définir /definiʀ/ [2] *vt* define.

définitif, **-ive** /definitif, -v/ *a* final, definitive; **en définitive** in the end.

définition /definisjɔ̃/ *nf* definition; (de mots croisés) clue.

définitivement /definitivmɑ̃/ *adv* definitively, permanently.

déflagration /deflagʀasjɔ̃/ *nf* explosion.

déflation /deflasjɔ̃/ *nf* deflation. **déflationniste** *a* deflationary.

défoncé, ~**e** /defɔ̃se/ *a* (*terrain*) full of potholes; (*siège*) broken; (*drogué*: [!]) high.

défoncer /defɔ̃se/ [10] *vt* (*porte*) break down; (*mâchoire*) break. □ **se** ~ *vpr* [!] to give one's all.

déformation /defɔʀmasjɔ̃/ *nf* distortion. **déformer** [1] *vt* put out of shape; (*faits, pensée*) distort.

défouler (se) /(sə)defule/ [1] *vpr* let off steam.

défrayer /defʀeje/ [31] *vt* (payer) pay the expenses of; **~ la chronique** be the talk of the town.
défricher /defʀiʃe/ [1] *vt* clear.
défroisser /defʀwase/ [1] *vt* smooth out
défunt, **~e** /defœ̃, -t/ *a* (mort) late. ● *nm, f* deceased.
dégagé, **~e** /degaʒe/ *a* (*ciel*) clear; (*front*) bare. **d'un ton ~** casually.
dégagement /degaʒmɑ̃/ *nm* clearing; (football) clearance.
dégager /degaʒe/ [40] *vt* (exhaler) give off; (désencombrer) clear; (faire ressortir) bring out; (*ballon*) clear. □ **se ~** *vpr* free oneself; (*ciel, rue*) clear; (*odeur*) emanate.
dégarnir (se) /(sə)degaʀniʀ/ [2] *vpr* clear, empty; (*personne*) be going bald.
dégâts /degɑ/ *nmpl* damage (+ *sg*).
dégel /deʒɛl/ *nm* thaw. **dégeler** [6] *vi* thaw (out).
dégénéré, **~e** /deʒeneʀe/ *a & nm, f* degenerate.
dégivrer /deʒivʀe/ [1] *vt* (Auto) de-ice; (*réfrigérateur*) defrost.
déglinguer /deglɛ̃ge/ ⊡ [1] *vt* bust. □ **se ~** *vpr* break down.
dégonflé, **~e** /degɔ̃fle/ *a* (*pneu*) flat; (lâche ⊡) yellow ⊡.
dégonfler /degɔ̃fle/ [1] *vt* deflate. ● *vi* (*blessure*) go down. □ **se ~** *vpr* ⊡ chicken out.
dégouliner /deguline/ [1] *vi* trickle.
dégourdi, **~e** /deguʀdi/ *a* smart.
dégourdir /deguʀdiʀ/ [2] *vt* (*membre, liquide*) warm up. □ **se ~** *vpr* **se ~ les jambes** stretch one's legs.
dégoût /degu/ *nm* disgust.
dégoûtant, **~e** /degutɑ̃, -t/ *a* disgusting.
dégoûter /degute/ [1] *vt* disgust; **~ qn de qch** put sb off sth.
dégradant, **~e** /degʀadɑ̃, -t/ *a* degrading.
dégradation /degʀadasjɔ̃/ *nf* damage; **commettre des ~s** cause damage.
dégrader /degʀade/ [1] *vt* (abîmer) damage. □ **se ~** *vpr* (se détériorer) deteriorate.
dégrafer /degʀafe/ [1] *vt* unhook.
degré /dəgʀe/ *nm* degree; (d'escalier) step.
dégressif, **-ive** /degʀesif, -v/ *a* graded; **tarif ~** tapering charge.
dégrèvement /degʀɛvmɑ̃/ *nm* **~ fiscal** *ou* **d'impôts** tax reduction.
dégringolade /degʀɛ̃gɔlad/ *nf* tumble.
dégrossir /degʀɔsiʀ/ [2] *vt* (*bois*) trim; (*projet*) rough out.
déguerpir /degɛʀpiʀ/ [2] *vi* clear off.
dégueulasse /degœlas/ *a* ⊠ disgusting, lousy.
dégueuler /degœle/ [1] *vt* ⊠ throw up.
déguisement /degizmɑ̃/ *nm* (de carnaval) fancy dress; (pour duper) disguise.
déguiser /degize/ [1] *vt* dress up; (pour duper) disguise. □ **se ~** *vpr* (au carnaval etc.) dress up; (pour duper) disguise oneself.
déguster /degyste/ [1] *vt* taste, sample; (savourer) enjoy.
dehors /dəɔʀ/ *adv* **en ~ de** outside; (hormis) apart from; **jeter/mettre ~** throw/put out. ● *nm* outside. ● *nmpl* (aspect de qn) exterior.
déjà /deʒa/ *adv* already; (avant) before, already.
déjeuner /deʒœne/ [1] *vi* have lunch; (le matin) have breakfast. ● *nm* lunch; **petit ~** breakfast.
delà /dəla/ *adv & prép* **au ~ (de)**, **par ~** beyond.
délai /delɛ/ *nm* time-limit; (attente) wait; (sursis) extension (of time);

sans ~ immediately; **dans un ~ de 2 jours** within 2 days; **finir dans les ~s** finish within the deadline; **dans les plus brefs ~s** as soon as possible.

délaisser /delese/ [1] *vt* (négliger) neglect.

délassement /delasmɑ̃/ *nm* relaxation.

délation /delasjɔ̃/ *nf* informing.

délavé, **~e** /delave/ *a* faded.

délayer /deleje/ [31] *vt* mix (with liquid); (*idée*) drag out.

délecter (se) /(sə)delɛkte/ [1] *vpr* **se ~ de** delight in.

délégué, **~e** /delege/ *nm, f* delegate.

délibéré, **~e** /delibeʀe/ *a* deliberate; (résolu) determined.

délicat, **~e** /delika, -t/ *a* delicate; (plein de tact) tactful. **délicatesse** *nf* delicacy; (tact) tact. **délicatesses** *nfpl* (kind) attentions.

délice /delis/ *nm* delight. **délicieux**, **-ieuse** *a* (au goût) delicious; (charmant) delightful.

délier /delje/ [45] *vt* untie; (délivrer) free. ◻ **se ~** *vpr* come untied.

délimiter /delimite/ [1] *vt* determine, demarcate.

délinquance /delɛ̃kɑ̃s/ *nf* delinquency. **délinquant**, **~e** *a & nm, f* delinquent.

délirant, **~e** /deliʀɑ̃, -t/ *a* delirious; (frénétique) frenzied; ⓘ wild.

délire /deliʀ/ *nm* delirium; (fig) frenzy. **délirer** [1] *vi* be delirious (**de** with); ⓘ be off one's rocker ⓘ.

délit /deli/ *nm* offence.

délivrance /delivʀɑ̃s/ *nf* release; (soulagement) relief; (remise) issue. **délivrer** [1] *vt* free, release; (*pays*) liberate; (remettre) issue.

déloyal, **~e** (*mpl* **-aux**) /delwajal, -jo/ *a* disloyal; (*procédé*) unfair.

deltaplane /dɛltaplan/ *nm* hang-glider.

déluge /delyʒ/ *nm* downpour; **le D~** the Flood.

démagogie /demagɔʒi/ *nm* demagogy. **démagogue** *nmf* demagogue.

demain /dəmɛ̃/ *adv* tomorrow.

demande /dəmɑ̃d/ *nf* request; **~ d'emploi** job application; **~ en mariage** marriage proposal.

demander /dəmɑ̃de/ [1] *vt* ask for; (*chemin, heure*) ask; (nécessiter) require; **~ que/si** ask that/if; **~ qch à qn** ask sb sth; **~ à qn de** ask sb to; **~ en mariage** propose to. ◻ **se ~** *vpr* **se ~ si/où** wonder if/where.

demandeur, **-euse** /dəmɑ̃dœʀ, -øz/ *nm, f* **~ d'emploi** job seeker; **~ d'asile** asylum-seeker.

démangeaison /demɑ̃ʒezɔ̃/ *nf* itch(ing).

démanteler /demɑ̃tle/ [6] *vt* break up.

démaquillant /demakijɑ̃/ *nm* make-up remover. **démaquiller (se)** [1] *vpr* remove one's make-up.

démarchage /demaʀʃaʒ/ *nm* door-to-door selling.

démarche /demaʀʃ/ *nf* walk, gait; (procédé) step.

démarcheur, **-euse** /demaʀʃœʀ, -øz/ *nm, f* (door-to-door) canvasser.

démarrage /demaʀaʒ/ *nm* start.

démarrer /demaʀe/ [1] *vi* (*moteur*) start (up); (partir) move off; (fig) get moving. ● *vt* ⓘ get moving.

démarreur /demaʀœʀ/ *nm* starter.

démêlant /demelɑ̃/ *nm*

conditioner. **démêler** [1] *vt* disentangle.

déménagement /demenaʒmɑ̃/ *nm* move; (transport) removal.

déménager /demenaʒe/ [40] *vi* move (house). ● *vt* (*meubles*) remove.

déménageur /demenaʒœʀ/ *nm* removal man.

démence /demɑ̃s/ *nf* insanity.

démener (se) /(sə)demne/ [6] *vpr* move about wildly; (fig) put oneself out.

dément, ~e /demɑ̃, -t/ *a* insane. ● *nm, f* lunatic.

démenti /demɑ̃ti/ *nm* denial.

démentir /demɑ̃tiʀ/ [46] *vt* deny; (contredire) refute; **~ que** deny that.

démerder (se) /(sə)demɛʀde/ [1] *vpr* ⊠ manage.

démettre /demɛtʀ/ [42] *vt* (*poignet etc.*) dislocate; **~ qn de** relieve sb of. □ **se ~** *vpr* resign (**de** from).

demeure /dəmœʀ/ *nf* residence. **mettre en ~ de** order to.

demeurer /dəmœʀe/ [1] *vi* live; (rester) remain.

demi, ~e /dəmi/ *a* half(-). ● *nm, f* half. ● *nm* (bière) (half-pint) glass of beer; (football) half-back. ● *adv* **à ~** half; (*ouvrir, fermer*) half-way; **à la ~e** at half past; **une heure et ~e** an hour and a half; (à l'horloge) half past one; **une ~-journée/-livre** half a day/pound. **demi-cercle** (*pl* **~s**) *nm* semicircle. **demi-finale** (*pl* **~s**) *nf* semifinal. **demi-frère** (*pl* **~s**) *nm* half-brother, stepbrother. **demi-heure** (*pl* **~s**) *nf* half-hour, half an hour. **demi-litre** (*pl* **~s**) *nm* half a litre. **demi-mesure** (*pl* **~s**) *nf* half-measure. **à demi-mot** *adv* without having to express every word. **demi-pension** *nf* half-board. **demi-queue** *nm* boudoir grand piano. **demi-sel** *a inv* slightly salted. **demi-sœur** (*pl* **~s**) *nf* half-sister, stepsister.

démission /demisjɔ̃/ *nf* resignation.

demi-tarif (*pl* **~s**) /dəmitaʀif/ *nm* half-fare.

demi-tour (*pl* **~s**) /dəmituʀ/ *nm* about turn; (Auto) U-turn; **faire ~** turn back.

démocrate /demɔkʀat/ *nmf* democrat. ● *a* democratic. **démocratie** *nf* democracy.

démodé, ~e /demɔde/ *a* old-fashioned.

demoiselle /dəmwazɛl/ *nf* young lady; (célibataire) single lady; **~ d'honneur** bridesmaid.

démolir /demɔliʀ/ [2] *vt* demolish.

démon /demɔ̃/ *nm* demon. **le D~** the Devil. **démoniaque** *a* fiendish.

démonstration /demɔ̃stʀasjɔ̃/ *nf* demonstration; (de force) show.

démonter /demɔ̃te/ [1] *vt* take apart, dismantle; (*installation*) take down; (fig) disconcert. □ **se ~** *vpr* come apart.

démontrer /demɔ̃tʀe/ [1] *vt* demonstrate; (indiquer) show.

démoraliser /demɔʀalize/ [1] *vt* demoralize.

démuni, ~e /demyni/ *a* impoverished; **~ de** without.

démunir /demyniʀ/ [2] *vt* **~ de** deprive of. □ **se ~ de** *vpr* part with.

dénaturer /denatyʀe/ [1] *vt* (*faits*) distort.

dénigrement /denigʀəmɑ̃/ *nm* denigration.

dénivellation /denivɛlasjɔ̃/ *nf* (pente) slope.

dénombrer /denɔ̃bʀe/ [1] *vt* count.

dénomination /denɔminasjɔ̃/ *nf* designation.

dénommé, **~e** /denɔme/ *nm,f* **le ~ X** the said X.

dénoncer /denɔ̃se/ [10] *vt* denounce. ▫ **se ~** *vpr* give oneself up. **dénonciateur, -trice** *nm,f* informer.

dénouement /denumɑ̃/ *nm* outcome; (Théât) dénouement.

dénouer /denwe/ [1] *vt* undo. ▫ **se ~** *vpr* (*nœud*) come undone.

dénoyauter /denwajote/ [1] *vt* stone.

denrée /dɑ̃ʀe/ *nf* **~ alimentaire** foodstuff.

dense /dɑ̃s/ *a* dense. **densité** *nf* density.

dent /dɑ̃/ *nf* tooth; **faire ses ~s** teethe; **~ de lait** milk tooth; **~ de sagesse** wisdom tooth; (de roue) cog. **dentaire** *a* dental.

denté, **~e** /dɑ̃te/ *a* (*roue*) toothed

dentelé, **~e** /dɑ̃tle/ *a* jagged.

dentelle /dɑ̃tɛl/ *nf* lace.

dentier /dɑ̃tje/ *nm* dentures (+ *pl*), false teeth (+ *pl*).

dentifrice /dɑ̃tifʀis/ *nm* toothpaste.

dentiste /dɑ̃tist/ *nmf* dentist.

dentition /dɑ̃tisjɔ̃/ *nf* teeth, dentition.

dénudé, **~e** /denyde/ *a* bare.

dénué, **~e** /denɥe/ *a* **~ de** devoid of.

dénuement /denymɑ̃/ *nm* destitution.

déodorant /deɔdɔʀɑ̃/ *nm* deodorant.

dépannage /depanaʒ/ *nm* repair; (Ordinat) troubleshooting. **dépanner** [1] *vt* repair; (fig) help out. **dépanneuse** *nf* breakdown lorry.

dépareillé, **~e** /depaʀeje/ *a* odd, not matching.

départ /depaʀ/ *nm* departure; (Sport) start; **au ~ de Nice** from Nice; **au ~** (d'abord) at first.

département /depaʀtəmɑ̃/ *nm* department.

dépassé, **~e** /depɑse/ *a* outdated.

dépasser /depɑse/ [1] *vt* go past, pass; (*véhicule*) overtake; (excéder) exceed; (*rival*) surpass; **ça me dépasse** Ⓘ it's beyond me. ● *vi* stick out.

dépaysement /depeizmɑ̃/ *nm* change of scenery; (désagréable) disorientation.

dépêche /depɛʃ/ *nf* dispatch.

dépêcher /depɛʃe/ [1] *vt* dispatch. ▫ **se ~** *vpr* hurry (up).

dépendance /depɑ̃dɑ̃s/ *nf* dependence; (à une drogue) dependency; (bâtiment) outbuilding.

dépendre /depɑ̃dʀ/ [3] *vt* take down. ● *vi* depend (**de** on); **~ de** (appartenir à) belong to.

dépens /depɑ̃/ *nmpl* **aux ~ de** at the expense of.

dépense /depɑ̃s/ *nf* expense; expenditure.

dépenser /depɑse/ [1] *vt/i* spend; (*énergie etc.*) use up. ▫ **se ~** *vpr* get some exercise.

dépérir /depeʀiʀ/ [2] *vi* wither.

dépêtrer (se) /(sə)depetʀe/ [1] *vpr* get oneself out (**de** of).

dépeupler /depœple/ [1] *vt* depopulate. ▫ **se ~** *vpr* become depopulated.

déphasé, **~e** /defɑze/ *a* Ⓘ out of step.

dépilatoire /depilatwaʀ/ *a & nm* depilatory.

dépistage /depistaʒ/ *nm* screening. **dépister** [1] *vt* detect; (*criminel*) track down.

dépit /depi/ *nm* resentment; **par ~** out of pique; **en ~ de** despite; **en ~ du bon sens** in a very illogical way. **dépité**, **~e** *a* vexed.

déplacé, **~e** /deplase/ *a* (*remarque*) uncalled for.

déplacement /deplasmɑ̃/ *nm* (voyage) trip.

déplacer /deplase/ [10] *vt* move. □ **se ~** *vpr* move; (voyager) travel.

déplaire /deplɛʀ/ [47] *vi* **~ à** (irriter) displease; **ça me déplaît** I don't like it.

déplaisant, **~e** /deplɛzɑ̃, -t/ *a* unpleasant, disagreeable.

dépliant /deplijɑ̃/ *nm* leaflet.

déplier /deplije/ [45] *vt* unfold.

déploiement /deplwamɑ̃/ *nm* (démonstration) display; (militaire) deployment.

déplorable /deplɔʀabl/ *a* deplorable. **déplorer** [1] *vt* (trouver regrettable) deplore; (*mort*) lament.

déployer /deplwaje/ [31] *vt* (*ailes, carte*) spread; (*courage*) display; (*armée*) deploy.

déportation /depɔʀtasjɔ̃/ *nf* (en 1940) internment in a concentration camp.

déposer /depoze/ [1] *vt* put down; (laisser) leave; (*passager*) drop; (*argent*) deposit; (*plainte*) lodge; (*armes*) lay down. ● *vi* (Jur) testify. □ **se ~** *vpr* settle.

dépositaire /depozitɛʀ/ *nmf* (Comm) agent.

déposition /depozisjɔ̃/ *nf* (Jur) statement.

dépôt /depo/ *nm* (entrepôt) warehouse; (d'autobus) depot; (particules) deposit; (garantie) deposit; **laisser en ~** give for safe keeping; **~ légal** formal deposit of a publication with an institution.

dépouille /depuj/ *nf* skin, hide; **~ (mortelle)** mortal remains.

dépouiller /depuje/ [1] *vt* (*courrier*) open; (*scrutin*) count; (écorcher) skin; **~ qn de** strip sb of.

dépourvu, **~e** /depuʀvy/ *a* **~ de** devoid of; **prendre au ~** catch unawares.

déprécier /depʀesje/ [45] *vt* depreciate. □ **se ~** *vpr* depreciate.

déprédations /depʀedasjɔ̃/ *nfpl* damage (+ *sg*).

dépression /depʀesjɔ̃/ *nf* depression; **~ nerveuse** nervous breakdown.

déprimer /depʀime/ [1] *vt* depress.

depuis /dəpɥi/

● *préposition*

····➤ (point de départ) since; **~ quand attendez-vous?** how long have you been waiting?

····➤ (durée) for; **~ toujours** always; **~ peu** recently.

● *adverbe*

····➤ since; **il a eu une attaque le mois dernier, ~ nous sommes inquiets** he had a stroke last month and we've been worried ever since.

● **depuis que** *conjonction*

····➤ since, ever since; **Sophie a beaucoup changé depuis que Camille est née** Sophie has changed a lot since Camille was born.

député /depyte/ *nm* ≈ Member of Parliament.

déraciné, **-e** /deʀasine/ *nm, f* rootless person.

déraillement /deʀajmɑ̃/ *nm* derailment.

dérailler /deʀaje/ [1] *vi* be derailed; (fig ⓘ) be talking nonsense; **faire ~** derail. **dérailleur** *nm* (de vélo) derailleur.

déraisonnable /deʀɛzɔnabl/ *a* unreasonable.

dérangement /deʀɑ̃ʒmɑ̃/ *nm*

bother; (désordre) disorder, upset; **en ~** out of order; **les ~s** the fault reporting service.

déranger /deʀɑ̃ʒe/ [40] *vt* (gêner) bother, disturb; (dérégler) upset, disrupt. ◻ **se ~** *vpr* (aller) go; (fig) put oneself out; **ça te dérangerait de...?** would you mind...?

dérapage /deʀapaʒ/ *nm* skid. **déraper** [1] *vi* skid; (fig) (*prix*) get out of control.

déréglé, **~e** /deʀegle/ *a* (*vie*) dissolute; (*estomac*) upset; (*mécanisme*) (that is) not running properly.

dérégler /deʀegle/ [14] *vt* make go wrong. ◻ **se ~** *vpr* go wrong.

dérision /deʀizjɔ̃/ *nf* mockery; **tourner en ~** ridicule.

dérive /deʀiv/ *nf* **aller à la ~** drift.

dérivé /deʀive/ *nm* by-product.

dériver /deʀive/ [1] *vi* (*bateau*) drift; **~ de** stem from.

dermatologie /dɛʀmatɔlɔʒi/ *nf* dermatology.

dernier, **-ière** /dɛʀnje, -jɛʀ/ *a* last; (*nouvelles, mode*) latest; (*étage*) top. ● *nm, f* last (one); **ce ~** the latter; **le ~ de mes soucis** the least of my worries.

dernièrement /dɛʀnjɛʀmɑ̃/ *adv* recently.

dérober /deʀɔbe/ [1] *vt* steal. ◻ **se ~** *vpr* slip away; **se ~ à** (*obligation*) shy away from.

dérogation /deʀɔgasjɔ̃/ *nf* special authorization.

déroger /deʀɔʒe/ [40] *vi* **~ à** depart from.

déroulement /deʀulmɑ̃/ *nm* (d'une action) development.

dérouler /deʀule/ [1] *vt* (*fil etc.*) unwind. ◻ **se ~** *vpr* unwind; (avoir lieu) take place; (*récit, paysage*) unfold.

déroute /deʀut/ *nf* (Mil) rout.

dérouter /deʀute/ [1] *vt* disconcert.

derrière /dɛʀjɛʀ/ *prép & adv* behind. ● *nm* back, rear; (postérieur Ⓘ) behind Ⓘ; **de ~** (*fenêtre*) back, rear; (*pattes*) hind.

des /de/ ⇒DE.

dès /dɛ/ *prép* (right) from; **~ lors** from then on; **~ que** as soon as.

désabusé, **~e** /dezabyze/ *a* disillusioned.

désaccord /dezakɔʀ/ *nm* disagreement.

désaffecté, **~e** /dezafɛkte/ *a* disused.

désagréable /dezagʀeabl/ *a* unpleasant.

désagrément /dezagʀemɑ̃/ *nm* annoyance, inconvenience.

désaltérer (**se**) /(sə)dezalteʀe/ [14] *vpr* quench one's thirst.

désamorcer /dezamɔʀse/ [10] *vt* (*situation, obus*) defuse.

désapprobation /dezapʀɔbasjɔ̃/ *nf* disapproval. **désapprouver** [1] *vt* disapprove of.

désarçonner /dezaʀsɔne/ [1] *vt* throw.

désarmement /dezaʀməmɑ̃/ *nm* (Pol) disarmament.

désarroi /dezaʀwa/ *nm* distress.

désastre /dezastʀ/ *nm* disaster. **désastreux**, **-euse** *a* disastrous.

désavantage /dezavɑ̃taʒ/ *nm* disadvantage. **désavantager** [40] *vt* put at a disadvantage.

désaveu (*pl* **~x**) /dezavø/ *nm* denial. **désavouer** [1] *vt* deny.

descendance /dɛsɑ̃dɑ̃s/ *nf* descent; (enfants) descendants (+ *pl*). **descendant**, **~e** *nm, f* descendant.

descendre /desɑ̃dʀ/ [3] *vi* (*aux être*) go down; (venir) come down; (*passager*) get off *ou* out; (*nuit*) fall; **~ à pied** walk down; **~ par l'ascenseur** take the lift down; **~ de** (être issu de) be descended from; **~ à l'hôtel** go to a hotel; **~ dans la rue** (Pol) take to the streets. ● *vt* (*aux avoir*) (*escalier etc.*) go *ou* come down; (*objet*) take down; (abattre ⓘ) shoot down.

descente /desɑ̃t/ *nf* descent; (à ski) downhill; (raid) raid; **dans la ~** going downhill; **~ de lit** bedside rug.

descriptif, -ive /dɛskʀiptif, -v/ *a* descriptive. **description** *nf* description.

désemparé, ~e /dezɑ̃paʀe/ *a* distraught.

désendettement /dezɑ̃dɛtmɑ̃/ *nm* reduction of the debt.

déséquilibré, ~e /dezekilibʀe/ *a* unbalanced; ⓘ crazy. ● *nm, f* lunatic. **déséquilibrer** [1] *vt* throw off balance.

désert, ~e /dezɛʀ, -t/ *a* deserted. ● *nm* desert.

déserter /dezɛʀte/ [1] *vt/i* desert. **déserteur** *nm* deserter.

désertique /dezɛʀtik/ *a* desert.

désespérant, ~e /dezɛspeʀɑ̃, -t/ *a* utterly disheartening.

désespéré, ~e /dezɛspeʀe/ *a* in despair; (*état, cas*) hopeless; (*effort*) desperate.

désespérer /dezɛspeʀe/ [14] *vt* drive to despair. ● *vi* despair, lose hope; **~ de** despair of. □ **se ~** *vpr* despair.

désespoir /dezɛspwaʀ/ *nm* despair; **en ~ de cause** as a last resort.

déshabillé, ~e /dezabije/ *a* undressed. ● *nm* négligee.

déshabiller /dezabije/ [1] *vt* undress. □ **se ~** *vpr* get undressed.

désherbant /dezɛʀbɑ̃/ *nm* weed-killer.

déshérité, ~e /dezeʀite/ *a* (*région*) deprived; (*personne*) the underprivileged.

déshériter /dezeʀite/ [1] *vt* disinherit.

déshonneur /dezɔnœʀ/ *nm* disgrace.

déshonorer /dezɔnɔʀe/ [1] *vt* dishonour.

déshydrater /dezidʀate/ [1] *vt* dehydrate. □ **se ~** *vpr* get dehydrated.

désigner /deziɲe/ [1] *vt* (montrer) point to *ou* out; (élire) appoint; (signifier) designate.

désillusion /dezilyzjɔ̃/ *nf* disillusionment.

désinence /dezinɑ̃s/ *nf* (Gram) ending.

désinfectant /dezɛ̃fɛktɑ̃/ *nm* disinfectant. **désinfecter** [1] *vt* disinfect.

désintéressé, ~e /dezɛ̃teʀese/ *a* (*personne, acte*) selfless.

désintéresser (se) /(sə)dezɛ̃teʀese/ [1] *vpr* **se ~ de** lose interest in.

désintoxiquer /dezɛ̃tɔksike/ [1] *vt* detoxify; **se faire ~** to undergo detoxification.

désinvolte /dezɛ̃vɔlt/ *a* casual. **désinvolture** *nf* casualness.

désir /deziʀ/ *nm* wish, desire; (convoitise) desire.

désirer /deziʀe/ [1] *vt* want; (sexuellement) desire; **vous désirez?** what would you like?

désireux, -euse /deziʀø, -z/ *a* **~ de faire** anxious to do.

désistement /dezistəmɑ̃/ *nm* withdrawal.

désobéir /dezɔbeiʀ/ [2] *vi* **~ (à)** disobey. **désobéissant, ~e** *a* disobedient.

désobligeant, ~e /dezɔbliʒɑ̃, -t/ *a* disagreeable, unkind.

désodorisant /dezɔdɔʀizɑ̃/ *nm* air freshener.

désodoriser /dezɔdɔʀize/ [1] *vt* freshen up.

désœuvré, ~e /dezœvʀe/ *a* at a loose end. **désœuvrement** *nm* lack of anything to do.

D

désolation /dezɔlasjɔ̃/ *nf* distress.

désolé, **~e** /dezɔle/ *a* (au regret) sorry; (*région*) desolate.

désoler /dezɔlɛ̃/ [1] *vt* distress. □ **se ~** *vpr* be upset (**de qch** about sth).

désopilant, **~e** /dezɔpilɑ̃, -t/ *a* hilarious.

désordonné, **~e** /dezɔʀdɔne/ *a* untidy; (*mouvements*) uncoordinated.

désordre /dezɔʀdʀ/ *nm* untidiness; (Pol) disorder; **en ~** untidy.

désorganiser /dezɔʀganize/ [1] *vt* disorganize.

désorienter /dezɔʀjɑ̃te/ [1] *vt* disorient.

désormais /dezɔʀmɛ/ *adv* from now on.

desquels, **desquelles** /dekɛl/ ⇨LEQUEL.

dessécher /deseʃe/ [1] *vt* dry out. □ **se ~** *vpr* dry out, become dry; (*plante*) wither.

dessein /desɛ̃/ *nm* intention; **à ~** intentionally.

desserrer /deseʀe/ [1] *vt* loosen; **il n'a pas desserré les dents** he never once opened his mouth. □ **se ~** *vpr* come loose.

dessert /desɛʀ/ *nm* dessert; **en ~** for dessert.

desservir /desɛʀviʀ/ [46] *vt/i* (débarrasser) clear away; (*autobus*) serve.

dessin /desɛ̃/ *nm* drawing; (motif) design; (discipline) art; (contour) outline; **professeur de ~** art teacher; **~ animé** (cinéma) cartoon; **~ humoristique** cartoon.

dessinateur, **-trice** /desinatœʀ, -tʀis/ *nm,f* artist; (industriel) draughtsman.

dessiner /desine/ [1] *vt/i* draw; (fig) outline. □ **se ~** *vpr* appear, take shape.

dessoûler /desule/ [1] *vt/i* sober up.

dessous /dəsu/ *adv* underneath. ● *nm* underside, underneath. ● *nmpl* underwear; **les ~ d'une histoire** what is behind a story; **du ~** bottom; (*voisins*) downstairs; **en ~**, **par-~** underneath. **dessous-de-plat** *nm inv* (heat-resistant) table-mat. **dessous-de-table** *nm inv* backhander. **dessous-de-verre** *nm inv* coaster.

dessus /dəsy/ *adv* on top (of it), on it. ● *nm* top; **du ~** top; (*voisins*) upstairs; **avoir le ~** get the upper hand. **dessus-de-lit** *nm inv* bedspread.

destabiliser /destabilize/ [1] *vt* destabilize, unsettle.

destin /dɛstɛ̃/ *nm* (sort) fate; (avenir) destiny.

destinataire /dɛstinatɛʀ/ *nmf* addressee.

destination /dɛstinasjɔ̃/ *nf* destination; (fonction) purpose; **vol à ~ de** flight to.

destinée /dɛstine/ *nf* destiny.

destiner /dɛstine/ [1] *vt* **~ à** intend for; (vouer) destine for; **le commentaire m'est destiné** this comment is aimed at me; **être destiné à faire** be intended to do; (obligé) be destined to do. □ **se ~ à** *vpr* (*carrière*) intend to take up.

destituer /dɛstitɥe/ [1] *vt* discharge.

destructeur, **-trice** /dɛstʀyktœʀ, -tʀis/ *a* destructive. **destruction** *nf* destruction.

désuet, **-ète** /dezɥɛ, -t/ *a* outdated.

détachant /detaʃɑ̃/ *nm* stain remover.

détacher /detaʃe/ [1] *vt* untie; (ôter) remove, detach; (déléguer) second. □ **se ~** *vpr* come off,

break away; (*nœud etc.*) come undone; (ressortir) stand out.
détail /detaj/ *nm* detail; (de compte) breakdown; (Comm) retail; **au ~** (*vendre etc.*) retail; **de ~** (*prix etc.*) retail; **en ~** in detail; **entrer dans les ~s** go into detail.
détaillant, **~e** /detajɑ̃, -t/ *nm, f* retailer.
détaillé, **~e** /detaje/ *a* detailed.
détailler /detaje/ [1] *vt* (*rapport*) detail; **~ ce que qn fait** scrutinize what sb does.
détaler /detale/ [1] *vi* ⓘ bolt.
détartrant /detaʀtʀɑ̃/ *nm* descaler.
détecter /detɛkte/ [1] *vt* detect. **détecteur** *nm* detector.
détective /detɛktiv/ *nm* detective.
déteindre /detɛ̃dʀ/ [22] *vi* (dans l'eau) run (**sur** on to); (au soleil) fade; **~ sur** (fig) rub off on.
détendre /detɑ̃dʀ/ [3] *vt* slacken; (*ressort*) release; (*personne*) relax. ◻ **se ~** *vpr* (*ressort*) slacken; (*personne*) relax. **détendu**, **~e** *a* (calme) relaxed.
détenir /det(ə)niʀ/ [58] *vt* hold; (*secret, fortune*) possess.
détente /detɑ̃t/ *nf* relaxation; (Pol) détente; (saut) spring; (gâchette) trigger; **être lent à la ~** ⓘ be slow on the uptake.
détenteur, **-trice** /detɑ̃tœʀ, -tʀis/ *nm, f* holder.
détention /detɑ̃sjɔ̃/ *nf* detention; **~ provisoire** custody.
détenu, **~e** /detny/ *nm, f* prisoner.
détergent /detɛʀʒɑ̃/ *nm* detergent.
détérioration /deteʀjɔʀasjɔ̃/ *nf* deterioration; (dégât) damage.
détériorer /deteʀjɔʀe/ [1] *vt* damage. ◻ **se ~** *vpr* deteriorate.
détermination /deteʀminasjɔ̃/ *nf* determination. **déterminé**, **~e** *a* (résolu) determined; (précis) definite. **déterminer** [1] *vt* determine.
déterrer /deteʀe/ [1] *vt* dig up.
détestable /detɛstabl/ *a* (*caractère, temps*) foul.
détester /detɛste/ [1] *vt* hate. ◻ **se ~** *vpr* hate each other.
détonation /detɔnasjɔ̃/ *nf* explosion, detonation.
détour /detuʀ/ *nm* (crochet) detour; (fig) roundabout means; (virage) bend.
détournement /detuʀnəmɑ̃/ *nm* hijack(ing); (de fonds) embezzlement.
détourner /detuʀne/ [1] *vt* (*attention*) divert; (*tête, yeux*) turn away; (*avion*) hijack; (*argent*) embezzle. ◻ **se ~ de** *vpr* stray from.
détraquer /detʀake/ [1] *vt* make go wrong; (*estomac*) upset. ◻ **se ~** *vpr* (*machine*) go wrong.
détresse /detʀɛs/ *nf* distress; **dans la ~, en ~** in distress.
détritus /detʀity(s)/ *nmpl* rubbish (+ *sg*).
détroit /detʀwa/ *nm* strait.
détromper /detʀɔ̃pe/ [1] *vt* set straight. ◻ **se ~** *vpr* **détrompe-toi!** you'd better think again!
détruire /detʀɥiʀ/ [17] *vt* destroy.
dette /dɛt/ *nf* debt.
deuil /dœj/ *nm* (période) mourning; (décès) bereavement; **porter le ~** be in mourning; **faire son ~ de qch** give sth up as lost.
deux /dø/ *a & nm* two; **~ fois** twice; **tous (les) ~** both. **deuxième** *a & nmf* second. **deux-pièces** *nm inv* (maillot de bain) two-piece; (logement) two-room flat. **deux-points** *nm inv* (Gram) colon. **deux-roues** *nm inv* two-wheeled vehicle.

dévaliser /devalize/ [1] *vt* rob, clean out.

dévalorisant, **~e** /devalɔʀizɑ̃, -t/ *a* demeaning.

dévaloriser /devalɔʀize/ [1] *vt* (*monnaie*) devalue. ▫ **se ~** *vpr* (*personne*) put oneself down.

dévaluation /devalɥasjɔ̃/ *nf* devaluation.

dévaluer /devalɥe/ [1] *vt* devalue. ▫ **se ~** *vpr* devalue.

devancer /dəvɑ̃se/ [10] *vt* be *ou* go ahead of; (arriver) arrive ahead of; (prévenir) anticipate.

devant /d(ə)vɑ̃/ *prép* in front of; (distance) ahead of; (avec mouvement) past; (en présence de) in front of; (face à) in the face of; **avoir du temps ~ soi** have plenty of time. ● *adv* in front; (à distance) ahead; **de ~** front. ● *nm* front; **prendre les ~s** take the initiative.

devanture /dəvɑ̃tyʀ/ *nf* shop front; (vitrine) shop window.

développement /devlɔpmɑ̃/ *nm* development; (de photos) developing.

développer /devlɔpe/ [1] *vt* develop. ▫ **se ~** *vpr* (*corps, talent*) develop; (*entreprise*) grow, expand.

devenir /dəvniʀ/ [58] *vi* (*aux être*) become; **qu'est-il devenu?** what has become of him?

dévergondé, **~e** /devɛʀgɔ̃de/ *a & nm,f* shameless (person).

déverser /devɛʀse/ [1] *vt* (*liquide*) pour; (*ordures, pétrole*) dump. ▫ **se ~** *vpr* (*rivière*) flow; (*égout, foule*) pour.

dévêtir /devetiʀ/ [61] *vt* undress. ▫ **se ~** *vpr* get undressed.

déviation /devjasjɔ̃/ *nf* diversion.

dévier /devje/ [45] *vt* divert; (*coup*) deflect. ● *vi* (*ballon, balle*) veer; (*personne*) deviate.

devin /dəvɛ̃/ *nm* soothsayer.

deviner /dəvine/ [1] *vt* guess; (apercevoir) distinguish.

devinette /dəvinɛt/ *nf* riddle.

devis /dəvi/ *nm* estimate, quote.

dévisager /devizaʒe/ [40] *vt* stare at.

devise /dəviz/ *nf* motto; **~s** (monnaie) (foreign) currency.

dévisser /devise/ [1] *vt* unscrew.

dévitaliser /devitalize/ [1] *vt* (*dent*) carry out root canal treatment on.

dévoiler /devwale/ [1] *vt* reveal.

devoir /dəvwaʀ/ [26]

● *verbe auxiliaire*

····➤ **~ faire** (obligation, hypothèse) must do; (nécessité) have got to do; **je dois dire que...** I have to say that...; **il a dû partir** (nécessité) he had to leave; (hypothèse) he must have left.

····➤ (prévision) **je devais lui dire** I was to tell her; **elle doit rentrer bientôt** she's due back soon.

····➤ (conseil) **tu devrais** you should.

● *verbe transitif*

····➤ (*argent, excuses*) owe; **combien je vous dois?** (en achetant) how much is it?

▫ **se devoir** *verbe pronominal*

····➤ **je me dois de le faire** it's my duty to do it.

● *nom masculin*

····➤ duty; **faire son ~** do one's duty.

····➤ (Scol) **~** (**surveillé**) test; **les ~s** homework (+ *sg*); **faire ses ~s** do one's homework.

dévorer /devɔʀe/ [1] *vt* devour.

dévot, **~e** /devo, -ɔt/ *a* devout.

dévoué, **~e** /devwe/ *a* devoted. **dévouement** *nm* devotion.

dévouer (se) /(sə)devwe/ [1] *vpr*

devote oneself (**à** to); (se sacrifier) sacrifice oneself.

dextérité /dɛksteʀite/ *nf* skill.

diabète /djabɛt/ *nm* diabetes. **diabétique** *a & nmf* diabetic.

diable /djɑbl/ *nm* devil.

diagnostic /djagnɔstik/ *nm* diagnosis. **diagnostiquer** [1] *vt* diagnose.

diagonal, **~e** (*mpl* **-aux**) /djagɔnal, -o/ *a* diagonal. **diagonale** *nf* diagonal; **en ~e** diagonally.

diagramme /djagʀam/ *nm* diagram; (graphique) graph.

dialecte /djalɛkt/ *nm* dialect.

dialogue /djalɔg/ *nm* dialogue. **dialoguer** [1] *vi* have talks, enter into a dialogue.

diamant /djamɑ̃/ *nm* diamond.

diamètre /djamɛtʀ/ *nm* diameter.

diapositive /djapozitiv/ *nf* slide.

diarrhée /djaʀe/ *nf* diarrhoea.

dictateur /diktatœʀ/ *nm* dictator.

dicter /dikte/ [1] *vt* dictate. **dictée** *nf* dictation.

dictionnaire /diksjɔnɛʀ/ *nm* dictionary.

dicton /diktɔ̃/ *nm* saying.

dièse /djɛz/ *nm* (Mus) sharp.

diesel /djezɛl/ *nm & a inv* diesel.

diète /djɛt/ *nf* restricted diet.

diététicien, **~ne** /djetetisjɛ̃, -ɛn/ *nm,f* dietician.

diététique /djetetik/ *nf* dietetics. ● *a* **produit** *ou* **aliment ~** dietary product; **magasin ~** health food shop *ou* store.

dieu (*pl* **~x**) /djø/ *nm* god; **D~** God.

diffamation /difamasjɔ̃/ *nf* slander; (par écrit) libel. **diffamer** [1] *vt* slander; (par écrit) libel.

différé: **en ~** /ɑ̃difeʀe/ *loc* (*émission*) pre-recorded.

différemment /difeʀamɑ̃/ *adv* differently.

différence /difeʀɑ̃s/ *nf* difference; **à la ~ de** unlike.

différencier /difeʀɑ̃sje/ [45] *vt* differentiate. □ **se ~** *vpr* differentiate oneself; **se ~ de** (différer de) differ from.

différend /difeʀɑ̃/ *nm* difference (of opinion).

différent, **~e** /difeʀɑ̃, -t/ *a* different (**de** from).

différer /difeʀe/ [14] *vt* postpone. ● *vi* differ (**de** from).

difficile /difisil/ *a* difficult; (exigeant) fussy. **difficilement** *adv* with difficulty.

difficulté /difikylte/ *nf* difficulty; **faire des ~s** raise objections.

diffus, **~e** /dify, -z/ *a* diffuse.

diffuser /difyze/ [1] *vt* (*émission*) broadcast; (*nouvelle*) spread; (*lumière, chaleur*) diffuse; (Comm) distribute. **diffusion** *nf* broadcasting; diffusion; distribution.

digérer /diʒeʀe/ [14] *vt* digest; (endurer 🅘) stomach. **digeste** *a* digestible.

digestif, **-ive** /diʒɛstif, -v/ *a* digestive. ● *nm* after-dinner liqueur.

digital, **~e** (*mpl* **-aux**) /diʒital, -o/ *a* digital.

digne /diɲ/ *a* (noble) dignified; (approprié) worthy; **~ de** worthy of; **~ de foi** trustworthy.

digue /dig/ *nf* dyke; (US) dike.

dilater /dilate/ [1] *vt* dilate. □ **se ~** *vpr* dilate; (*estomac*) distend.

dilemme /dilɛm/ *nm* dilemma.

dilettante /diletɑ̃t/ *nmf* amateur.

diluant /dilɥɑ̃/ *nm* thinner.

diluer /dilɥe/ [1] *vt* dilute.

dimanche /dimɑ̃ʃ/ *nm* Sunday.

dimension /dimɑ̃sjɔ̃/ *nf* (taille) size; (mesure) dimension; (aspect) dimension.

diminuer /diminɥe/ [1] *vt* reduce, decrease; (*plaisir,*

D

courage) dampen; (dénigrer) diminish. ● *vi* (se réduire) decrease; (faiblir) (*bruit, flamme*) die down; (*ardeur*) cool. **diminutif** *nm* diminutive; (surnom) pet name. **diminution** *nf* decrease (**de** in); (réduction) reduction; (affaiblissement) diminishing.

dinde /dɛ̃d/ *nf* turkey.

dîner /dine/ [1] *vi* have dinner. ● *nm* dinner.

dingue /dɛ̃g/ *a* ⓘ crazy.

dinosaure /dinozɔʀ/ *nm* dinosaur.

diphtongue /diftɔ̃g/ *nf* diphthong.

diplomate /diplɔmat/ *nmf* diplomat. ● *a* diplomatic. **diplomatique** *a* diplomatic.

diplôme /diplom/ *nm* certificate, diploma; (Univ) degree. **diplômé, ~e** *a* qualified.

dire /diʀ/ [27] *vt* say; (*secret, vérité, heure*) tell; (penser) think; **~ que** say that; **~ à qn que** tell sb that; **~ à qn de** tell sb to; **ça me dit de faire** I feel like doing; **on dirait que** it would seem that, it seems that; **dis/dites donc!** hey! ▫ **se ~** *vpr* (*mot*) be said; (penser) tell oneself; (se prétendre) claim to be. ● *nm* **au ~ de, selon les ~s de** according to.

direct, ~e /diʀɛkt/ *a* direct. ● *nm* (train) express train; **en ~** (*émission*) live.

directeur, -trice /diʀɛktœʀ, -tʀis/ *nm, f* director; (chef de service) manager, manageress; (de journal) editor; (d'école) headteacher; (US) principal; **~ de banque** bank manager; **~ commercial** sales manager; **~ des ressources humaines** human resources manager.

direction /diʀɛksjɔ̃/ *nf* (sens) direction; (de société) management; (Auto) steering; **en ~ de** (going) to.

dirigeant, ~e /diʀiʒɑ̃, -t/ *nm, f* (Pol) leader; (Comm) manager. ● *a* (*classe*) ruling.

diriger /diʀiʒe/ [40] *vt* (*service, école, parti, pays*) run; (*entreprise, usine*) manage; (*travaux*) supervise; (*véhicule*) steer; (*orchestre*) conduct; (braquer) aim; (tourner) turn. ▫ **se ~** *vpr* (s'orienter) find one's way; **se ~ vers** head for, make for.

dis /di/ ⇒DIRE [27].

discernement /disɛʀnəmɑ̃/ *nm* discernment.

disciplinaire *a* disciplinary. **discipline** *nf* discipline.

discontinu, ~e /diskɔ̃tiny/ *a* intermittent.

discordant, ~e /diskɔʀdɑ̃, -t/ *a* discordant.

discothèque /diskɔtɛk/ *nf* record library; (boîte de nuit) disco(thèque).

discours /diskuʀ/ *nm* speech; (propos) views.

discret, -ète /diskʀɛ, -t/ *a* discreet.

discrétion /diskʀesjɔ̃/ *nf* discretion; **à ~** (*vin*) unlimited; (*manger, boire*) as much as one desires.

discrimination /diskʀiminasjɔ̃/ *nf* discrimination. **discriminatoire** *a* discriminatory.

disculper /diskylpe/ [1] *vt* exonerate. ▫ **se ~** *vpr* vindicate oneself.

discussion /diskysjɔ̃/ *nf* discussion; (querelle) argument.

discutable /diskytabl/ *a* debatable; (critiquable) questionable.

discuter /diskyte/ [1] *vt* discuss; (contester) question. ● *vi* (parler) talk; (répliquer) argue; **~ de** discuss.

disette /dizɛt/ *nf* food shortage.

disgrâce /disgʀɑs/ *nf* disgrace.
disgracieux, -ieuse /disgʀasjø, -z/ *a* ugly, unsightly.
disjoindre /disʒwɛ̃dʀ/ [22] *vt* take apart. □ **se ~** *vpr* come apart.
disloquer /dislɔke/ [1] *vt* (*membre*) dislocate; (*machine*) break (apart). □ **se ~** *vpr* (*parti, cortège*) break up; (*meuble*) come apart.
disparaître /disparɛtʀ/ [18] *vi* disappear; (mourir) die; **faire ~** get rid of. **disparition** *nf* disappearance; (mort) death.
disparate /disparat/ *a* ill-assorted.
disparu, ~e /dispary/ *a* missing. ● *nm, f* missing person; (mort) dead person.
dispensaire /dispɑ̃sɛʀ/ *nm* clinic.
dispense /dispɑ̃s/ *nf* exemption.
dispenser /dispɑ̃se/ [1] *vt* exempt (**de** from). □ **se ~ de** *vpr* avoid.
disperser /dispɛʀse/ [1] *vt* (éparpiller) scatter; (répartir) disperse. □ **se ~** *vpr* disperse.
disponibilité /disponibilite/ *nf* availability. **disponible** *a* available.
dispos, ~e /dispo, -z/ *a* **frais et ~** fresh and alert.
disposé, ~e /dispoze/ *a* **bien/mal ~** in a good/bad mood; **~ à** prepared to; **~ envers** disposed towards.
disposer /dispoze/ [1] *vt* arrange; **~ à** (engager à) incline to. ● *vi* **~ de** have at one's disposal. □ **se ~ à** *vpr* prepare to.
dispositif /dispozitif/ *nm* device; (ensemble de mesures) operation.
disposition /dispozisjɔ̃/ *nf* arrangement, layout; (tendance) tendency; **~s** (humeur) mood; (préparatifs) arrangements; (mesures) measures; (aptitude) aptitude; **mettre à la ~ de** place *ou* put at the disposal of.
disproportionné, ~e /dispʀopɔʀsjɔne/ *a* disproportionate; **~ à** out of proportion with.
dispute /dispyt/ *nf* quarrel.
disputer /dispyte/ [1] *vt* (*match*) play; (*course*) run in; (*prix*) fight for; (gronder ⊡) tell off. □ **se ~** *vpr* quarrel; (se battre pour) fight over; (*match*) be played.
disquaire /diskɛʀ/ *nmf* record dealer.
disque /disk/ *nm* (Mus) record; (Sport) discus; (cercle) disc, disk; (Ordinat) disk; **~ compact** compact disc; **~ dur** hard disk; **~ optique compact** CD-ROM; **~ souple** floppy disk.
disquette /diskɛt/ *nf* floppy disk, diskette; **~ de sauvegarde** back-up disk.
disséminer /disemine/ [1] *vt* spread, scatter.
dissertation /disɛʀtasjɔ̃/ *nf* essay, paper.
disserter /disɛʀte/ [1] *vi* **~ sur** speak about; (par écrit) write about.
dissident, ~e /disidɑ̃, -t/ *a & nm, f* dissident.
dissimulation /disimylasjɔ̃/ *nf* concealment; (fig) deceit.
dissimuler /disimyle/ [1] *vt* conceal (**à** from). □ **se ~** *vpr* conceal oneself.
dissipé, ~e /disipe/ *a* (*élève*) unruly.
dissiper /disipe/ [1] *vt* (*fumée, crainte*) dispel; (*fortune*) squander; (*personne*) distract. □ **se ~** *vpr* disappear; (*élève*) grow restless.
dissolvant /disɔlvɑ̃/ *nm* solvent; (pour ongles) nail polish remover.
dissoudre /disudʀ/ [53] *vt* dissolve. □ **se ~** *vpr* dissolve.

dissuader /disɥade/ [1] *vt* dissuade (**de** from).
dissuasion /disɥazjɔ̃/ *nf* dissuasion; **force de ~** deterrent force.
distance /distɑ̃s/ *nf* distance; (écart) gap; **à ~** at *ou* from a distance.
distancer /distɑ̃se/ [10] *vt* outdistance.
distendre /distɑ̃dʀ/ [3] *vt* (*estomac*) distend; (*corde*) stretch.
distinct, **~e** /distɛ̃(kt), -ɛ̃kt/ *a* distinct.
distinctif, **-ive** /distɛ̃ktif, -v/ *a* (*trait*) distinctive; (*signe, caractère*) distinguishing.
distinction /distɛ̃ksjɔ̃/ *nf* distinction; (récompense) honour.
distinguer /distɛ̃ge/ [1] *vt* distinguish.
distraction /distʀaksjɔ̃/ *nf* absent-mindedness; (passe-temps) entertainment, leisure; (détente) recreation.
distraire /distʀɛʀ/ [29] *vt* amuse; (rendre inattentif) distract; **~ qn de qch** take sb's mind off sth. ▫ **se ~** *vpr* amuse oneself.
distrait, **~e** /distʀɛ, -t/ *a* absent-minded; (*élève*) inattentive.
distrayant, **~e** /distʀɛjɑ̃, -t/ *a* entertaining.
distribuer /distʀibɥe/ [1] *vt* hand out, distribute; (répartir) distribute; (*tâches, rôles*) allocate; (*cartes*) deal; (*courrier*) deliver.
distributeur /distʀibytœʀ/ *nm* (Auto, Comm) distributor; **~** (**automatique**) vending-machine; **~ de billets** (**de banque**) cash dispenser. **distribution** *nf* distribution; (du courrier) delivery; (acteurs) cast; (secteur) retailing.
district /distʀikt/ *nm* district.
dit[1], **dites** /di, dit/ ⇒DIRE [27].
dit[2], **~e** /di, dit/ *a* (décidé) agreed; (surnommé) known as.
diurne /djyʀn/ *a* diurnal; (*activité*) daytime.
divagations /divagasjɔ̃/ *nfpl* ravings.
divergence /divɛʀʒɑ̃s/ *nf* divergence. **divergent**, **~e** *a* divergent. **diverger** [40] *vi* diverge.
divers, **~e** /divɛʀ, -s/ *a* (varié) diverse; (différent) various; (*frais*) miscellaneous; **dépenses ~es** sundries. **diversifier** [45] *vt* diversify.
diversité /divɛʀsite/ *nf* diversity, variety.
divertir /divɛʀtiʀ/ [2] *vt* amuse, entertain. ▫ **se ~** *vpr* amuse oneself; (passer du bon temps) enjoy oneself. **divertissement** *nm* amusement, entertainment.
dividende /dividɑ̃d/ *nm* dividend.
divin, **~e** /divɛ̃, -in/ *a* divine. **divinité** *nf* divinity.
diviser /divize/ [1] *vt* divide. ▫ **se ~** *vpr* become divided; **se ~ par sept** be divisible by seven. **division** *nf* division.
divorce /divɔʀs/ *nm* divorce.
divorcé, **~e** /divɔʀse/ *a* divorced. ● *nm, f* divorcee.
divorcer /divɔʀse/ [10] *vi* **~** (**d'avec**) divorce.
dix /dis/ (/di/ *before consonant,* /diz/ *before vowel*) *a & nm* ten.
dix-huit /dizɥit/ *a & nm* eighteen.
dixième /dizjɛm/ *a & nmf* tenth.
dix-neuf /diznœf/ *a & nm* nineteen.
dix-sept /disɛt/ *a & nm* seventeen.
docile /dɔsil/ *a* docile.
docteur /dɔktœʀ/ *nm* doctor.
doctorat /dɔktɔʀa/ *nm* doctorate, PhD.
document /dɔkymɑ̃/ *nm* document. **documentaire** *a & nm* documentary.

documentaliste /dɔkymɑ̃talist/ *nmf* information officer; (Scol) librarian.

documentation /dɔkymɑ̃tasjɔ̃/ *nf* information, literature; **centre de ~** resource centre.

documenté, ~e /dɔkymɑ̃te/ *a* well-documented.

documenter /dɔkymɑ̃te/ [1] *vt* provide with information. □ **se ~** *vpr* collect information

dodo /dodo/ *nm* **faire ~** (langage enfantin) sleep.

dodu, ~e /dɔdy/ *a* plump.

dogmatique /dɔgmatik/ *a* dogmatic. **dogme** *nm* dogma.

doigt /dwa/ *nm* finger; **un ~ de** a drop of; **montrer qch du ~** point at sth; **à deux ~s de** a hair's breadth away from; **~ de pied** toe. **doigté** *nm* (Mus) fingering, touch; (diplomatie) tact.

dois, doit /dwa/ ⇒DEVOIR [26].

doléances /dɔleɑ̃s/ *nfpl* grievances.

dollar /dɔlaʀ/ *nm* dollar.

domaine /dɔmɛn/ *nm* estate, domain; (fig) domain, field.

domestique /dɔmɛstik/ *a* domestic. ● *nmf* servant. **domestiquer** [1] *vt* domesticate.

domicile /dɔmisil/ *nm* home; **à ~** at home; (*livrer*) to the home.

domicilié, ~e /dɔmisilje/ *a* resident; **être ~ à Paris** live *ou* be resident in Paris.

dominant, ~e /dɔminɑ̃, -t/ *a* dominant. **dominante** *nf* dominant feature.

dominer /dɔmine/ [1] *vt* dominate; (surplomber) tower over, dominate; (*sujet*) master; (*peur*) overcome. ● *vi* dominate; (*équipe*) be in the lead; (prévaloir) stand out.

domino /dɔmino/ *nm* domino.

dommage /dɔmaʒ/ *nm* (tort) harm; **~(s)** (dégâts) damage; **c'est ~** it's a pity *ou* shame; **quel ~** what a pity *ou* shame. **dommages-intérêts** *nmpl* (Jur) damages.

dompter /dɔ̃te/ [1] *vt* tame. **dompteur, -euse** *nm, f* tamer.

DOM-TOM /dɔmtɔm/ *abrév mpl* (**départements et territoires d'outre-mer**) French overseas departments and territories.

don /dɔ̃/ *nm* (cadeau, aptitude) gift. **donateur, -trice** *nm, f* donor. **donation** *nf* donation.

donc /dɔ̃k/ *conj* so, then; (par conséquent) so, therefore; **quoi ~?** what did you say?; **tiens ~!** fancy that!

donjon /dɔ̃ʒɔ̃/ *nm* (tour) keep.

donné, ~e /dɔne/ *a* (fixé) given; (pas cher Ⓘ) dirt cheap; **étant ~ que** given that.

donnée /dɔne/ *nf* (élément d'information) fact; **~s** data.

donner /dɔne/ [1] *vt* give; (*vieilles affaires*) give away; (distribuer) give out; (*fruits, résultats*) produce; (*film*) show; (*pièce*) put on; **ça donne soif/faim** it makes one thirsty/hungry; **~ qch à réparer** take sth to be repaired; **~ lieu à** give rise to. ● *vi* **~ sur** look out on to; **~ dans** tend towards. □ **se ~ à** *vpr* devote oneself to; **se ~ du mal** go to a lot of trouble (**pour faire** to do).

dont /dɔ̃/

● *pronom*

⋯➤ (personne) **la fille ~ je te parlais** the girl I was telling you about; **l'homme ~ la fille a dit...** the man whose daughter said...

⋯➤ (chose) which, **l'affaire ~ il parle** the matter which he is referring to; **la manière ~ elle parle** the way she speaks; **ce ~ il parle** what he's talking about.

····➤ (provenance) from which.

····➤ (parmi lesquels) **deux personnes ~ toi** two people, one of whom is you; **plusieurs thèmes ~ l'identité et le racisme** several topics including identity and racism.

dopage /dɔpaʒ/ *nm* (de cheval) doping; (d'athlète) illegal drug-use.

doper /dɔpe/ [1] *vt* dope. □ **se ~** *vpr* take drugs.

doré, ~e /dɔʀe/ *a* (couleur d'or) golden; (qui rappelle de l'or) gold; (avec de l'or) gilt; **la jeunesse ~e** gilded youth.

dorénavant /dɔʀenavɑ̃/ *adv* henceforth.

dorer /dɔʀe/ [1] *vt* gild; (Culin) brown.

dormir /dɔʀmiʀ/ [46] *vi* sleep; (être endormi) be asleep; **~ debout** be asleep on one's feet; **une histoire à ~ debout** a cock-and-bull story.

dortoir /dɔʀtwaʀ/ *nm* dormitory.

dorure /dɔʀyʀ/ *nf* gilding.

dos /do/ *nm* back; (de livre) spine; **à ~ de** riding on; **au ~ de** (*chèque*) on the back of; **de ~** from behind; **~ crawlé** backstroke.

dosage /dozaʒ/ *nm* (mélange) mixture; (quantité) amount, proportions. **dose** *nf* dose. **doser** [1] *vt* measure out; (contrôler) use in a controlled way.

dossier /dɔsje/ *nm* (documents) file; (Jur) case; (de chaise) back; (TV, presse) special feature.

dot /dɔt/ *nf* dowry.

douane /dwan/ *nf* customs.

douanier, -ière /dwanje, -jɛʀ/ *a* customs. ● *nm* customs officer.

double /dubl/ *a & adv* double. ● *nm* (copie) duplicate; (sosie) double; **le ~ (de)** twice as much *ou* as many (as); **le ~ messieurs** the men's doubles.

doubler /duble/ [1] *vt* double; (dépasser) overtake; (*vêtement*) line; (*film*) dub; (*classe*) repeat; (*cap*) round. ● *vi* double.

doublure /dublyʀ/ *nf* (étoffe) lining; (acteur) understudy.

douce /dus/ ⇒DOUX.

doucement /dusmɑ̃/ *adv* gently; (sans bruit) quietly; (lentement) slowly.

douceur /dusœʀ/ *nf* (mollesse) softness; (de climat) mildness; (de personne) gentleness; (friandise) sweet; (US) candy; **en ~** smoothly.

douche /duʃ/ *nf* shower.

doucher /duʃe/ [1] *vt* give a shower to. □ **se ~** *vpr* have *ou* take a shower.

doudoune /dudun/ *nf* [!] down jacket.

doué, ~e /dwe/ *a* gifted; **~ de** endowed with.

douille /duj/ *nf* (Électr) socket.

douillet, ~te /dujɛ, -t/ *a* cosy, comfortable; (*personne*: péj) soft.

douleur /dulœʀ/ *nf* pain; (chagrin) sorrow, grief. **douloureux, -euse** *a* painful.

doute /dut/ *nm* doubt; **sans ~** no doubt; **sans aucun ~** without doubt.

douter /dute/ [1] *vt* **~ de** doubt; **~ que** doubt that. ● *vi* doubt. □ **se ~ de** *vpr* suspect; **je m'en doutais** I thought so.

douteux, -euse /dutø, -z/ *a* dubious, doubtful.

Douvres /duvʀ/ *npr* Dover.

doux, douce /du, dus/ *a* (moelleux) soft; (sucré) sweet; (clément, pas fort) mild; (pas brusque, bienveillant) gentle.

douzaine /duzɛn/ *nf* about twelve; (douze) dozen; **une ~ d'œufs** a dozen eggs.

douze /duz/ *a & nm* twelve. **douzième** *a & nmf* twelfth.

doyen, **∼ne** /dwajɛ̃, -ɛn/ *nm, f* dean; (en âge) most senior person.

dragée /dʀaʒe/ *nf* sugared almond.

draguer /dʀage/ [1] *vt* (*rivière*) dredge; (*filles* ①) chat up, try to pick up.

drainer /dʀene/ [1] *vt* drain.

dramatique /dʀamatik/ *a* dramatic; (tragique) tragic. ● *nf* (television) drama.

dramatiser /dʀamatize/ [1] *vt* dramatize.

dramaturge /dʀamatyʀʒ/ *nmf* dramatist.

drame /dʀam/ *nm* (genre) drama; (pièce) play; (événement tragique) tragedy.

drap /dʀa/ *nm* sheet; (tissu) (woollen) cloth.

drapeau (*pl* **∼x**) /dʀapo/ *nm* flag.

drap-housse (*pl* **draps-housses**) /dʀaus/ *nm* fitted sheet.

dressage /dʀɛsaʒ/ *nm* training; (compétition équestre) dressage.

dresser /dʀese/ [1] *vt* put up, erect; (*tête*) raise; (*animal*) train; (*liste, plan*) draw up; **∼ l'oreille** prick up one's ears. ▫ **se ∼** *vpr* (*bâtiment*) stand; (*personne*) draw oneself up. **dresseur**, **-euse** *nm, f* trainer.

dribbler /dʀible/ [1] *vi* (Sport) dribble.

drive /dʀajv/ *nm* (Ordinat) drive.

drogue /dʀɔg/ *nf* drug; **la ∼** drugs.

drogué, **∼e** /dʀɔge/ *nm, f* drug addict.

droguer /dʀɔge/ [1] *vt* (*malade*) drug heavily; (*victime*) drug. ▫ **se ∼** *vpr* take drugs.

droguerie /dʀɔgʀi/ *nf* hardware shop. **droguiste** *nmf* owner of a hardware shop.

droit, **∼e** /dʀwa, -t/ *a* (contraire de gauche) right; (non courbe) straight; (loyal) upright; **angle ∼** right angle. ● *adv* straight. ● *nm* right; **∼(s)** (taxe) duty; **le ∼** (Jur) law; **avoir ∼ à** be entitled to; **avoir le ∼ de** be allowed to; **être dans son ∼** be in the right; **∼ d'auteur** copyright; **∼ d'inscription** registration fee; **∼s d'auteur** royalties.

droite /dʀwat/ *nf* (contraire de gauche) right; **à ∼** on the right; (direction) (to the) right; **la ∼** the right (side); (Pol) the right (wing); (*ligne*) straight line. **droitier**, **-ière** *a* right-handed.

drôle /dʀol/ *a* (amusant) funny; (bizarre) funny, odd. **drôlement** *adv* funnily; (très ①) really.

dru, **∼e** /dʀy/ *a* thick; **tomber ∼** fall thick and fast.

drugstore /dʀœgstɔʀ/ *nm* drugstore.

du /dy/ ⇒DE.

dû, **due** /dy/ *a* due. ● *nm* due; (argent) dues; **∼ à** due to. ● ⇒DEVOIR [26].

duc, **duchesse** /dyk, dyʃɛs/ *nm, f* duke, duchess.

duo /dɥo/ *nm* (Mus) duet; (fig) duo.

dupe /dyp/ *nf* dupe.

duplex /dyplɛks/ *nm* split-level apartment; (US) duplex; (émission) link-up.

duplicata /dyplikata/ *nm inv* duplicate.

duquel /dykɛl/ ⇒LEQUEL.

dur, **∼e** /dyʀ/ *a* hard; (sévère) harsh, hard; (*viande*) tough; (*col, brosse*) stiff; **∼ d'oreille** hard of hearing. ● *adv* hard. ● *nm, f* tough nut ①; (Pol) hardliner.

durable /dyʀabl/ *a* lasting.

durant /dyʀɑ̃/ *prép* (au cours de) during; (avec mesure de temps) for;

D

~ **des heures** for hours; **des heures** ~ for hours and hours.

durcir /dyʀsiʀ/ [2] *vt* harden. ● *vi* (*terre*) harden; (*ciment*) set; (*pain*) go hard. ▫ **se** ~ *vpr* harden.

durée /dyʀe/ *nf* length; (période) duration; **de courte** ~ short-lived; **pile longue** ~ long-life battery.

durer /dyʀe/ [1] *vi* last.

dureté /dyʀte/ *nf* hardness; (sévérité) harshness.

duvet /dyvɛ/ *nm* down; (sac) sleeping-bag.

dynamique /dinamik/ *a* dynamic.

dynamite /dinamit/ *nf* dynamite.

dynamo /dinamo/ *nf* dynamo.

eau (*pl* ~**x**) /o/ *nf* water; ~ **courante** running water; ~ **de mer** seawater; ~ **de source** spring water; ~ **douce**/**salée** fresh/salt water; ~ **de pluie** rainwater; ~ **potable** drinking water; ~ **de Javel** bleach; ~ **minérale** mineral water; ~ **gazeuse** sparkling water; ~ **plate** still water; ~ **de toilette** eau de toilette; ~**x usées** dirty water; ~**x et forêts** forestry commission (+ *sg*); **tomber à l'**~ (fig) fall through; **prendre l'**~ take in water. **eau-de-vie** (*pl* **eaux-de-vie**) *nf* brandy.

ébahi, ~**e** /ebai/ *a* dumbfounded.

ébauche /eboʃ/ *nf* (dessin) sketch; (fig) attempt.

ébéniste /ebenist/ *nm* cabinet-maker.

éblouir /ebluiʀ/ [2] *vt* dazzle.

éboueur /ebwœʀ/ *nm* dustman.

ébouillanter /ebujɑ̃te/ [1] *vt* scald.

éboulement /ebulmɑ̃/ *nm* landslide.

ébouriffé, ~**e** /ebuʀife/ *a* dishevelled.

ébrécher /ebʀeʃe/ [14] *vt* chip.

ébruiter /ebʀɥite/ [1] *vt* spread about. ▫ **s'**~ *vpr* get out.

ébullition /ebylisjɔ̃/ *nf* boiling; **en** ~ boiling.

écaille /ekaj/ *nf* (de poisson) scale; (de peinture, roc) flake; (matière) tortoiseshell.

écarlate /ekaʀlat/ *a* scarlet.

écarquiller /ekaʀkije/ [1] *vt* ~ **les yeux** open one's eyes wide.

écart /ekaʀ/ *nm* gap; (de prix) difference; (embardée) swerve; ~ **de conduite** lapse in behaviour; **être à l'**~ be isolated; **se tenir à l'**~ **de** stand apart from; (fig) keep out of the way of.

écarté, ~**e** /ekaʀte/ *a* (*lieu*) remote; **les jambes** ~**es** (with) legs apart; **les bras** ~**s** with one's arms out.

écarter /ekaʀte/ [1] *vt* (séparer) move apart; (*membres*) spread; (*branches*) part; (éliminer) dismiss; ~ **qch de** move sth away from; ~ **qn de** keep sb away from. ▫ **s'**~ *vpr* (s'éloigner) move away; (quitter son chemin) move aside; **s'**~ **de** stray from.

ecchymose /ekimoz/ *nf* bruise.

écervelé, ~**e** /esɛʀvəle/ *a* scatterbrained. ● *nm, f* scatterbrain.

échafaudage /eʃafodaʒ/ *nm* scaffolding; (amas) heap.

échalote /eʃalɔt/ *nf* shallot.

échancré, ~**e** /eʃɑ̃kʀe/ *a* low-cut.

échange /eʃɑ̃ʒ/ *nm* exchange; **en** ~ **(de)** in exchange (for).

échanger [40] *vt* exchange (**contre** for).

échangeur /eʃɑ̃ʒœʀ/ *nm* (Auto) interchange.

échantillon /eʃɑ̃tijɔ̃/ *nm* sample.

échappatoire /eʃapatwaʀ/ *nf* way out.

échappement /eʃapmɑ̃/ *nm* exhaust.

échapper /eʃape/ [1] *vi* **~ à** escape; (en fuyant) escape (from); **~ des mains de** slip out of the hands of; **ça m'a échappé** (fig) it just slipped out; **l'~ belle** have a narrow *ou* lucky escape. □ **s'~** *vpr* escape.

écharde /eʃaʀd/ *nf* splinter.

écharpe /eʃaʀp/ *nf* scarf; (de maire) sash; **en ~** (*bras*) in a sling.

échasse /eʃɑs/ *nf* stilt.

échauffement /eʃofmɑ̃/ *nm* (Sport) warm-up.

échauffer /eʃofe/ [1] *vt* heat; (fig) excite. □ **s'~** *vpr* warm up.

échéance /eʃeɑ̃s/ *nf* due date (for payment); (délai) deadline; (obligation) (financial) commitment.

échéant: **le cas ~** /ləkazeʃeɑ̃/ *loc* if need be.

échec /eʃɛk/ *nm* failure; **~s** (jeu) chess; **~ et mat** checkmate; **tenir en ~** hold in check.

échelle /eʃɛl/ *nf* ladder; (dimension) scale.

échelon /eʃlɔ̃/ *nm* rung; (hiérarchique) grade; (niveau) level.

échevelé, **~e** /eʃəvle/ *a* dishevelled.

écho /eko/ *nm* echo; **~s** (dans la presse) gossip.

échographie /ekɔgʀafi/ *nf* (ultrasound) scan.

échouer /eʃwe/ [1] *vi* (*bateau*) run aground; (ne pas réussir) fail; **~ à un examen** fail an exam. ● *vt* (*bateau*) ground. □ **s'~** *vpr* run aground.

échu, **~e** /eʃy/ *a* (*délai*) expired.

éclabousser /eklabuse/ [1] *vt* splash.

éclair /eklɛʀ/ *nm* (flash of) lightning; (fig) flash; (gâteau) éclair. ● *a inv* (*visite*) brief.

éclairage /eklɛʀaʒ/ *nm* lighting.

éclaircie /eklɛʀsi/ *nf* sunny interval.

éclaircir /eklɛʀsiʀ/ [2] *vt* lighten; (*mystère*) clear up. □ **s'~** *vpr* (*ciel*) clear; (*mystère*) become clearer. **éclaircissement** *nm* clarification.

éclairer /ekleʀe/ [1] *vt* light (up); (*personne*) (fig) enlighten; (*situation*) throw light on. ● *vi* give light. □ **s'~** *vpr* become clearer; **s'~ à la bougie** use candle-light.

éclaireur, **-euse** /eklɛʀœʀ, -øz/ *nm, f* (boy) scout, (girl) guide. ● *nm* (Mil) scout.

éclat /ekla/ *nm* fragment; (de lumière) brightness; (splendeur) brilliance; **~ de rire** burst of laughter.

éclatant, **~e** /eklatɑ̃, -t/ *a* brilliant; (*soleil*) dazzling.

éclater /eklate/ [1] *vi* burst; (exploser) go off; (*verre*) shatter; (*guerre*) break out; (*groupe*) split up; **~ de rire** burst out laughing.

éclipse /eklips/ *nf* eclipse.

éclosion /eklozjɔ̃/ *nf* hatching, opening.

écluse /eklyz/ *nf* (de canal) lock.

écœurant, **~e** /ekœʀɑ̃, -t/ *a* (*gâteau*) sickly; (fig) disgusting. **écœurer** [1] *vt* sicken.

école /ekɔl/ *nf* school; **~ maternelle/primaire/secondaire** nursery/primary/secondary school; **~ normale** teachers' training college. **écolier**, **-ière** *nm, f* schoolboy, schoolgirl.

écologie /ekɔlɔʒi/ *nf* ecology. **écologique** *a* ecological, green. **écologiste** *nmf* (chercheur)

E

ecologist; (dans l'âme) environmentalist; (Pol) Green.

économie /ekɔnɔmi/ *nf* economy; (discipline) economics; **~s** (argent) savings; **une ~ de** (gain) a saving of. **économique** *a* (Pol) economic; (bon marché) economical.

économiser /ekɔnɔmize/ [1] *vt/i* save.

écorce /ekɔʀs/ *nf* bark; (de fruit) peel.

écorcher /ekɔʀʃe/ [1] *vt* (*genou*) graze; (*animal*) skin. □ **s'~** *vpr* graze oneself. **écorchure** *nf* graze.

écossais, **~e** /ekɔsɛ, -z/ *a* Scottish. **É~**, **~e** *nm, f* Scot.

Écosse /ekɔs/ *nf* Scotland.

écoulement /ekulmɑ̃/ *nm* flow.

écouler /ekule/ [1] *vt* dispose of, sell. □ **s'~** *vpr* (*liquide*) flow; (*temps*) pass.

écourter /ekuʀte/ [1] *vt* shorten.

écoute /ekut/ *nf* listening; **à l'~** (**de**) listening in (to); **heures de grande ~** prime time; **~s téléphoniques** phone tapping.

écouter /ekute/ [1] *vt* listen to. ● *vi* listen; **~ aux portes** eavesdrop. **écouteur** *nm* earphones (+ *pl*); (de téléphone) receiver.

écran /ekʀɑ̃/ *nm* screen; **~ total** sun-block.

écraser /ekʀɑze/ [1] *vt* crush; (*piéton*) run over; (*cigarette*) stub out. □ **s'~** *vpr* crash (**contre** into).

écrémé, **~e** /ekʀeme/ *a* skimmed; **demi-~** semi-skimmed.

écrevisse /ekʀəvis/ *nf* crayfish.

écrier (**s'**) /(s)ekʀije/ [45] *vpr* exclaim.

écrin /ekʀɛ̃/ *nm* case.

écrire /ekʀiʀ/ [30] *vt/i* write; (orthographier) spell. □ **s'~** *vpr* (*mot*) be spelt.

écrit /ekʀi/ *nm* document; (examen) written paper; **par ~** in writing.

écriteau (*pl* **~x**) /ekʀito/ *nm* notice.

écriture /ekʀityʀ/ *nf* writing; **~s** (Comm) accounts.

écrivain /ekʀivɛ̃/ *nm* writer.

écrou /ekʀu/ *nm* (Tech) nut.

écrouler (**s'**) /(s)ekʀule/ [1] *vpr* collapse.

écru, **~e** /ekʀy/ *a* (*couleur*) natural; (*tissu*) raw.

écueil /ekœj/ *nm* reef; (fig) danger.

éculé, **~e** /ekyle/ *a* (*soulier*) worn at the heel; (fig) well-worn.

écume /ekym/ *nf* foam; (Culin) scum.

écumer /ekyme/ [1] *vt* skim. ● *vi* foam.

écureuil /ekyʀœj/ *nm* squirrel.

écurie /ekyʀi/ *nf* stable.

écuyer, **-ère** /ekɥije, -jɛʀ/ *nm, f* (horse) rider.

eczéma /ɛgzema/ *nm* eczema.

EDF *abrév f* (**Électricité de France**) *French electricity board.*

édifice /edifis/ *nm* building.

édifier /edifje/ [45] *vt* construct; (porter à la vertu) edify.

Édimbourg /edɛ̃buʀ/ *npr* Edinburgh.

édit /edi/ *nm* edict.

éditer /edite/ [1] *vt* publish; (annoter) edit. **éditeur**, **-trice** *nm, f* publisher; (réviseur) editor.

édition /edisjɔ̃/ *nf* (activité) publishing; (livre, disque) edition.

éditique /editik/ *nf* electronic publishing.

éditorial, **~e** (*pl* **-iaux**) /editɔʀjal, -jo/ *a & nm* editorial.

édredon /edʀədɔ̃/ *nm* eiderdown.

éducateur, **-trice** /edykatœʀ, -tʀis/ *nm, f* youth worker.

éducatif, **-ive** /edykatif, -v/ *a* educational.

éducation /edykasjɔ̃/ *nf* (façon d'élever) upbringing; (enseignement) education; (manières) manners; **~ physique** physical education.

éduquer /edyke/ [1] *vt* (élever) bring up; (former) educate.

effacé, **~e** /efase/ *a* (modeste) unassuming.

effacer /efase/ [10] *vt* (gommer) rub out; (à l'écran) delete; (*souvenir*) erase. ▫ **s'~** *vpr* fade; (s'écarter) step aside.

effarer /efaʀe/ [1] *vt* alarm; **être effaré** be astounded.

effaroucher /efaʀuʃe/ [1] *vt* scare away.

effectif, **-ive** /efɛktif, -v/ *a* effective. ● *nm* (d'école) number of pupils; **~s** numbers. **effectivement** *adv* effectively; (en effet) indeed.

effectuer /efɛktɥe/ [1] *vt* carry out, make.

efféminé, **~e** /efemine/ *a* effeminate.

effervescent, **~e** /efɛʀvesɑ̃, -t/ *a* **comprimé ~** effervescent tablet.

effet /efɛ/ *nm* effect; (impression) impression; **~s** (habits) clothes, things; **sous l'~ d'une drogue** under the influence of drugs; **en ~** indeed; **faire de l'~** have an effect, be effective; **faire bon/mauvais ~** make a good/bad impression; **ça fait un drôle d'~** it feels strange.

efficace /efikas/ *a* effective; (*personne*) efficient. **efficacité** *nf* effectiveness; (de personne) efficiency.

effleurer /eflœʀe/ [1] *vt* touch lightly; (*sujet*) touch on; **ça ne m'a pas effleuré** it did not cross my mind.

effondrement /efɔ̃dʀəmɑ̃/ *nm* collapse. **effondrer (s')** [1] *vpr* collapse.

efforcer (s') /(s)efɔʀse/ [10] *vpr* try (hard) (**de** to).

effort /efɔʀ/ *nm* effort.

effraction /efʀaksjɔ̃/ *nf* **entrer par ~** break in.

effrayant, **~e** /efʀejɑ̃, -t/ *a* frightening; (fig) frightful.

effrayer /efʀeje/ [31] *vt* frighten; (décourager) put off. ▫ **s'~** *vpr* be frightened.

effréné, **~e** /efʀene/ *a* wild.

effriter (s') /(s)efʀite/ [1] *vpr* crumble.

effroi /efʀwa/ *nm* dread.

effronté, **~e** /efʀɔ̃te/ *a* cheeky. ● *nm, f* cheeky boy, cheeky girl.

effroyable /efʀwajabl/ *a* dreadful.

égal, **~e** (*mpl* **-aux**) /egal, -o/ *a* equal; (*surface, vitesse*) even. ● *nm, f* equal; **ça m'est/lui est ~** it is all the same to me/him; **sans ~** matchless; **d'~ à ~** between equals. **également** *adv* equally; (aussi) as well. **égaler** [1] *vt* equal.

égaliser /egalize/ [1] *vt/i* (Sport) equalize; (niveler) level out; (*cheveux*) trim.

égalitaire /egalitɛʀ/ *a* egalitarian.

égalité /egalite/ *nf* equality; (de surface) evenness; **être à ~** be level.

égard /egaʀ/ *nm* consideration; **~s** respect (+ *sg*); **par ~ pour** out of consideration for; **à cet ~** in this respect; **à l'~ de** with regard to; (envers) towards.

égarer /egaʀe/ [1] *vt* mislay; (tromper) lead astray. ▫ **s'~** *vpr* get lost; (se tromper) go astray.

égayer /egeje/ [31] *vt* (*personne*) cheer up; (*pièce*) brighten up.

église /egliz/ *nf* church.

E

égoïsme /egɔism/ *nm* selfishness, egoism.
égoïste /egɔist/ *a* selfish. ● *nmf* egoist.
égorger /egɔʀʒe/ [40] *vt* slit the throat of.
égout /egu/ *nm* sewer.
égoutter /egute/ [1] *vt* drain. □ **s'~** *vpr* (*vaisselle*) drain; (*lessive*) drip dry. **égouttoir** *nm* draining-board.
égratigner /egʀatiɲe/ [1] *vt* scratch. **égratignure** *nf* scratch.
Égypte /eʒipt/ *nf* Egypt.
éjecter /eʒɛkte/ [1] *vt* eject.
élaboration /elabɔʀasjɔ̃/ *nf* elaboration. **élaborer** [1] *vt* elaborate.
élan /elɑ̃/ *nm* (animal) moose; (Sport) run-up; (vitesse) momentum; (fig) surge.
élancé, ~e /elɑ̃se/ *a* slender.
élancement /elɑ̃smɑ̃/ *nm* twinge.
élancer (s') /(s)elɑ̃se/ [10] *vpr* leap forward, dash; (*arbre, édifice*) soar.
élargir /elaʀʒiʀ/ [2] *vt* (*route*) widen; (*connaissances*) broaden. □ **s'~** *vpr* (*famille*) expand; (*route*) widen; (*écart*) increase; (*vêtement*) stretch.
élastique /elastik/ *a* elastic. ● *nm* elastic band; (tissu) elastic.
électeur, -trice /elɛktœʀ, -tʀis/ *nm, f* voter. **élection** *nf* election. **électoral, ~e** (*mpl* **-aux**) *a* (*réunion*) election. **électorat** *nm* electorate, voters (+ *pl*).
électricien, ~ne /elɛktʀisjɛ̃, ɛn/ *nm, f* electrician. **électricité** *nf* electricity.
électrifier /elɛktʀifje/ [45] *vt* electrify.
électrique /elɛktʀik/ *a* electric; (*installation*) electrical.
électrocuter /elɛktʀɔkyte/ [1] *vt* electrocute.
électroménager /elɛktʀɔmenaʒe/ *nm* **l'~** household appliances (+ *pl*).
électron /elɛktʀɔ̃/ *nm* electron. **électronicien, ~ne** *nm, f* electronics engineer.
électronique /elɛktʀɔnik/ *a* electronic. ● *nf* electronics.
élégance /elegɑ̃s/ *nf* elegance. **élégant, ~e** *a* elegant.
élément /elemɑ̃/ *nm* element; (meuble) unit. **élémentaire** *a* elementary.
éléphant /elefɑ̃/ *nm* elephant.
élevage /ɛlvaʒ/ *nm* (stock-) breeding.
élévation /elevasjɔ̃/ *nf* rise; (hausse) rise; (plan) elevation; **~ de terrain** rise in the ground.
élève /elɛv/ *nmf* pupil.
élevé, ~e /ɛlve/ *a* high; (noble) elevated; **bien ~** well-mannered.
élever /ɛlve/ [6] *vt* (lever) raise; (*enfants*) bring up, raise; (*animal*) breed. □ **s'~** *vpr* rise; (dans le ciel) soar up; **s'~ à** amount to. **éleveur, -euse** *nm, f* (stock-) breeder.
éligible /eliʒibl/ *a* eligible.
élimination /eliminasjɔ̃/ *nf* elimination.
éliminatoire /eliminatwaʀ/ *a* qualifying. ● *nf* (Sport) heat.
éliminer /elimine/ [1] *vt* eliminate.
élire /eliʀ/ [39] *vt* elect.
elle /ɛl/ *pron* she; (complément) her; (chose) it. **elle-même** *pron* herself; itself. **elles** *pron* they; (complément) them. **elles-mêmes** *pron* themselves.
élocution /elɔkysjɔ̃/ *nf* diction.
éloge /elɔʒ/ *nm* praise; **faire l'~ de** praise; **~s** praise (+ *sg*).
éloigné, ~e /elwaɲe/ *a* distant; **~ de** far away from; **parent ~** distant relative.
éloigner /elwaɲe/ [1] *vt* take

away *ou* remove (**de** from); (*danger*) ward off; (*visite*) put off. □ **s'~** *vpr* go *ou* move away (**de** from); (affectivement) become estranged (**de** from).

élongation /elɔ̃gasjɔ̃/ *nf* strained muscle.

éloquent, ~e /elɔkɑ̃, -t/ *a* eloquent.

élu, ~e /ely/ *a* elected. ● *nm,f* (Pol) elected representative.

élucider /elyside/ [1] *vt* elucidate.

éluder /elyde/ [1] *vt* evade.

émacié, ~e /emasje/ *a* emaciated.

émail (*pl* **-aux**) /emaj, -o/ *nm* enamel.

émanciper /emɑ̃sipe/ [1] *vt* emancipate. □ **s'~** *vpr* become emancipated.

émaner /emane/ [1] *vi* emanate.

emballage /ɑ̃balaʒ/ *nm* (dur) packaging; (souple) wrapping.

emballer /ɑ̃bale/ [1] *vt* pack; (en papier) wrap; **ça ne m'emballe pas** [!] I'm not really taken by it. □ **s'~** *vpr* (*moteur*) race; (*cheval*) bolt; (*personne*) get carried away; (*prices*) shoot up.

embarcadère /ɑ̃barkadɛr/ *nm* landing-stage.

embarcation /ɑ̃barkasjɔ̃/ *nf* boat.

embardée /ɑ̃barde/ *nf* swerve.

embarquement /ɑ̃barkəmɑ̃/ *nm* (de passagers) boarding; (de fret) loading.

embarquer /ɑ̃barke/ [1] *vt* take on board; (*frêt*) load; (emporter [!]) cart off. ● *vi* board. □ **s'~** *vpr* board; **s'~ dans** embark upon.

embarras /ɑ̃bara/ *nm* (gêne) embarrassment; (difficulté) difficulty.

embarrasser /ɑ̃barase/ [1] *vt* (encombrer) clutter (up); (fig) embarrass. □ **s'~ de** *vpr* burden oneself with.

embauche /ɑ̃boʃ/ *nf* hiring.

embaucher [1] *vt* hire, take on.

embaumer /ɑ̃bome/ [1] *vt* (*pièce*) fill; (*cadavre*) embalm. ● *vi* be fragrant.

embellir /ɑ̃belir/ [2] *vt* make more attractive; (*récit*) embellish.

embêtant, ~e /ɑ̃bɛtɑ̃, -t/ *a* [!] annoying.

embêter /ɑ̃bete/ [1] *vt* bother. □ **s'~** *vpr* be bored.

emblée: d'~ /dɑ̃ble/ *loc* right away.

emblème /ɑ̃blɛm/ *nm* emblem.

emboîter /ɑ̃bwate/ [1] *vt* fit together; **~ le pas à qn** (imiter) follow suit. □ **s'~** *vpr* fit together; **(s')~ dans** fit into.

embonpoint /ɑ̃bɔ̃pwɛ̃/ *nm* stoutness.

embouchure /ɑ̃buʃyr/ *nf* (de fleuve) mouth; (Mus) mouthpiece.

embourber (s') /(s)ɑ̃burbe/ [1] *vpr* get stuck in the mud; (fig) get bogged down.

embouteillage /ɑ̃butɛjaʒ/ *nm* traffic jam.

emboutir /ɑ̃butir/ [2] *vt* (Auto) crash into.

embraser (s') /(s)ɑ̃braze/ [1] *vpr* catch fire.

embrasser /ɑ̃brase/ [1] *vt* kiss; (adopter, contenir) embrace. □ **s'~** *vpr* kiss.

embrayage /ɑ̃brɛjaʒ/ *nm* clutch.

embrayer [31] *vi* engage the clutch.

embrouiller /ɑ̃bruje/ [1] *vt* confuse; (*fils*) tangle. □ **s'~** *vpr* become confused.

embryon /ɑ̃brijɔ̃/ *nm* embryo.

embûches /ɑ̃byʃ/ *nfpl* traps.

embuer (s') /(s)ɑ̃bɥe/ [1] *vpr* mist up.

embuscade /ɑ̃byskad/ *nf* ambush.

émeraude /ɛmRod/ *nf* emerald.
émerger /emɛRʒe/ [40] *vi* emerge; (fig) stand out.
émeri /ɛmRi/ *nm* emery.
émerveillement /emɛRvɛjmɑ̃/ *nm* amazement, wonder.
émerveiller /emɛRveje/ [1] *vt* fill with wonder. ▫ **s'~** *vpr* marvel at.
émetteur /emɛtœR/ *nm* transmitter.
émettre /emɛtR/ [42] *vt* (*son*) produce; (*message*) send out; (*timbre, billet*) issue; (*opinion*) express.
émeute /emøt/ *nf* riot.
émietter /emjete/ [1] *vt* crumble. ▫ **s'~** *vpr* crumble.
émigrant, **~e** /emigRɑ̃, -t/ *nm,f* emigrant. **émigration** *nf* emigration. **émigrer** [1] *vi* emigrate.
émincer /emɛ̃se/ [10] *vt* cut into thin slices.
éminent, **~e**/eminɑ̃, -t/ *a* eminent.
émissaire /emisɛR/ *nm* emissary.
émission /emisjɔ̃/ *nf* (programme) programme; (de chaleur, gaz) emission; (de timbre) issue.
emmagasiner /ɑ̃magazine/ [1] *vt* store.
emmanchure /ɑ̃mɑ̃ʃyR/ *nf* armhole.
emmêler /ɑ̃mele/ [1] *vt* tangle. ▫ **s'~** *vpr* get mixed up.
emménager /ɑ̃menaʒe/ [40] *vi* move in; **~ dans** move into.
emmener /ɑ̃mne/ [6] *vt* take; (comme prisonnier) take away.
emmerder /ɑ̃mɛRde/ [1] ⊠ *vt* **~ qn** get on sb's nerves. ▫ **s'~** *vpr* be bored.
emmitoufler /ɑ̃mitufle/ [1] *vt* wrap up warmly. ▫ **s'~** *vpr* wrap oneself up warmly.
émoi /emwa/ *nm* turmoil; (plaisir) excitement.
émotif, **-ive** /emɔtif, -v/ *a* emotional. **émotion** *nf* emotion; (peur) fright. **émotionnel**, **~le** *a* emotional.
émousser /emuse/ [1] *vt* blunt.
émouvant, **~e** /emuvɑ̃, -t/ *a* moving.
empailler /ɑ̃paje/ [1] *vt* stuff.
empaqueter /ɑ̃pakte/ [38] *vt* package.
emparer (**s'**) /(s)ɑ̃paRe/ [1] *vpr* **s'~ de** get hold of.
empêchement /ɑ̃pɛʃmɑ̃/ *nm* **avoir un ~** to be held up.
empêcher /ɑ̃peʃe/ [1] *vt* prevent; **~ de faire** prevent *ou* stop (from) doing; (il) **n'empêche que** still. ▫ **s'~** *vpr* **il ne peut pas s'en ~** he cannot help it.
empereur /ɑ̃pRœR/ *nm* emperor.
empester /ɑ̃pɛste/ [1] *vt* stink out; (*essence*) stink of. ● *vi* stink.
empêtrer (**s'**) /(s)ɑ̃petRe/ [1] *vpr* become entangled.
empiéter /ɑ̃pjete/ [14] *vi* **~ sur** encroach upon.
empiffrer (**s'**) /(s)ɑ̃pifRe/ [1] *vpr* ⊡ stuff oneself.
empiler /ɑ̃pile/ [1] *vt* pile up. ▫ **s'~** *vpr* pile up.
empire /ɑ̃piR/ *nm* empire.
emplacement /ɑ̃plasmɑ̃/ *nm* site.
emplâtre /ɑ̃plɑtR/ *nm* (Méd) plaster.
emploi /ɑ̃plwa/ *nm* (travail) job; (embauche) employment; (utilisation) use; **un ~ de chauffeur** a job as a driver; **~ du temps** timetable. **employé**, **~e** *nm,f* employee.
employer /ɑ̃plwaje/ [31] *vt* (*personne*) employ; (utiliser) use. ▫ **s'~** *vpr* be used; **s'~ à** devote oneself to. **employeur**, **-euse** *nm,f* employer.
empoigner /ɑ̃pwaɲe/ [1] *vt* grab. ▫ **s'~** *vpr* come to blows.

empoisonnement /ɑ̃pwazɔnmɑ̃/ *nm* poisoning.

empoisonner /ɑ̃pwazɔne/ [1] *vt* poison; (embêter ⓘ) annoy. ▫ **s'~** *vpr* to poison oneself.

emporter /ɑ̃pɔʀte/ [1] *vt* take (away); (entraîner) sweep away; (arracher) tear off. ▫ **s'~** *vpr* lose one's temper; **l'~** get the upper hand (**sur** of); **plat à ~** take-away.

empoté, **~e** /ɑ̃pɔte/ *a* clumsy.

empreinte /ɑ̃pʀɛ̃t/ *nf* mark; **~** (**digitale**) fingerprint; **~ de pas** footprint.

empressé, **~e** /ɑ̃pʀese/ *a* eager, attentive.

empresser (**s'**) /(s)ɑ̃pʀese/ [1] *vpr* **s'~ de** hasten to; **s'~ auprès de** be attentive to.

emprise /ɑ̃pʀiz/ *nf* influence.

emprisonnement /ɑ̃pʀizɔnmɑ̃/ *nm* imprisonment. **emprisonner** [1] *vt* imprison.

emprunt /ɑ̃pʀœ̃/ *nm* loan; **faire un ~** take out a loan.

emprunté, **~e** /ɑ̃pʀœ̃te/ *a* awkward.

emprunter /ɑ̃pʀœ̃te/ [1] *vt* borrow (**à** from); (*route*) take; (fig) assume. **emprunteur**, **-euse** *nm, f* borrower.

ému, **~e** /emy/ *a* moved; (intimidé) nervous.

émule /emyl/ *nmf* imitator.

---

en /ɑ̃/

⇨ Pour les expressions comme **en principe**, **en train de**, **s'en aller**, etc. ⇒**principe**, **train**, **aller**, etc.

● *préposition*

····➤ (lieu) in.

····➤ (avec mouvement) to.

····➤ (temps) in.

····➤ (manière, état) in; **~ faisant** by *ou* while doing; **je t'appelle ~ rentrant** I will call you when I get back.

····➤ (en qualité de) as.

····➤ (transport) by.

····➤ (composition) made of; **table ~ bois** wooden table.

● *pronom*

····➤ **~ avoir/vouloir** have/want some; **ne pas ~ avoir/vouloir** not have/want any; **j'~ ai deux** I've got two; **prends-~ plusieurs** take several; **il m'~ reste un** I have one left; **j'~ suis content** I am pleased with him/her/it/them; **je m'~ souviens** I remember it.

····➤ **~ êtes-vous sûr?** are you sure?

---

encadrement /ɑ̃kadʀəmɑ̃/ *nm* framing; (de porte) frame. **encadrer** [1] *vt* frame; (entourer d'un trait) circle; (superviser) supervise.

encaisser /ɑ̃kese/ [1] *vt* (*argent*) collect; (*chèque*) cash; (*coups* ⓘ) take.

encart /ɑ̃kaʀ/ *nm* **~ publicitaire** (advertising) insert.

en-cas /ɑ̃kɑ/ *nm* (stand-by) snack.

encastré, **~e** /ɑ̃kastʀe/ *a* built-in.

encaustique /ɑ̃kɔstik/ *nf* wax polish.

enceinte /ɑ̃sɛ̃t/ *af* pregnant; **~ de 3 mois** 3 months pregnant. ● *nf* enclosure; **~** (**acoustique**) speaker.

encens /ɑ̃sɑ̃/ *nm* incense.

encercler /ɑ̃sɛʀkle/ [1] *vt* surround.

enchaînement /ɑ̃ʃɛnmɑ̃/ *nm* (suite) chain; (d'idées) sequence.

enchaîner /ɑ̃ʃene/ [1] *vt* chain (up); (*phrases*) link (up). ● *vi* continue. ▫ **s'~** *vpr* follow on.

enchanté, **~e** /ɑ̃ʃɑ̃te/ *a* (ravi) delighted. **enchanter** [1] *vt* delight; (ensorceler) enchant.

E

enchère /ɑ̃ʃɛʀ/ *nf* bid; **mettre** *ou* **vendre aux ~s** sell by auction.
enchevêtrer /ɑ̃ʃəvetʀe/ [1] *vt* tangle. □ **s'~** *vpr* become tangled.
enclave /ɑ̃klav/ *nf* enclave.
enclencher /ɑ̃klɑ̃ʃe/ [1] *vt* engage.
enclin, **~e** /ɑ̃klɛ̃, -in/ *a* **~ à** inclined to.
enclos /ɑ̃klo/ *nm* enclosure.
enclume /ɑ̃klym/ *nf* anvil.
encoche /ɑ̃kɔʃ/ *nf* notch.
encolure /ɑ̃kɔlyʀ/ *nf* neck.
encombrant, **~e** /ɑ̃kɔ̃bʀɑ̃, -t/ *a* cumbersome.
encombre /ɑ̃kɔ̃bʀ/ *nm* **sans ~** without any problems.
encombrement /ɑ̃kɔ̃bʀəmɑ̃/ *nm* (Auto) traffic congestion; (volume) bulk.
encombrer /ɑ̃kɔ̃bʀe/ [1] *vt* clutter (up); (obstruer) obstruct. □ **s'~ de** *vpr* burden oneself with.
encontre: **à l'~ de** /alɑ̃kɔ̃tʀədə/ *loc* against.
encore /ɑ̃kɔʀ/ *adv* (toujours) still; (de nouveau) again; (de plus) more; (aussi) also; **~ plus grand** even larger; **~ un café** another coffee; **pas ~** not yet; **si ~** if only; **et puis quoi ~?** ⊡ what next?
encouragement /ɑ̃kuʀaʒmɑ̃/ *nm* encouragement. **encourager** [40] *vt* encourage.
encourir /ɑ̃kuʀiʀ/ [20] *vt* incur.
encrasser /ɑ̃kʀase/ [1] *vt* clog up (with dirt).
encre /ɑ̃kʀ/ *nf* ink. **encrier** *nm* ink-well.
encyclopédie /ɑ̃siklɔpedi/ *nf* encyclopaedia.
endettement /ɑ̃dɛtmɑ̃/ *nm* debt.
endetter /ɑ̃dɛte/ [1] *vt* put into debt. □ **s'~** *vpr* get into debt.
endiguer /ɑ̃dige/ [1] *vt* dam; (fig) curb.
endimanché, **~e** /ɑ̃dimɑ̃ʃe/ *a* in one's Sunday best.
endive /ɑ̃div/ *nf* chicory.
endoctriner /ɑ̃dɔktʀine/ [1] *vt* indoctrinate.
endommager /ɑ̃dɔmaʒe/ [40] *vt* damage.
endormi, **~e** /ɑ̃dɔʀmi/ *a* asleep; (apathique) sleepy.
endormir /ɑ̃dɔʀmiʀ/ [46] *vt* send to sleep; (médicalement) put to sleep; (duper) dupe (**avec** with). □ **s'~** *vpr* fall asleep.
endosser /ɑ̃dose/ [1] *vt* (*vêtement*) put on; (assumer) take on; (Comm) endorse.
endroit /ɑ̃dʀwa/ *nm* place; (de tissu) right side; **à l'~** the right way round; **par ~s** in places.
enduire /ɑ̃dɥiʀ/ [17] *vt* coat. **enduit** *nm* coating.
endurance /ɑ̃dyʀɑ̃s/ *nf* endurance. **endurant**, **~e** *a* tough.
endurcir /ɑ̃dyʀsiʀ/ [2] *vt* strengthen. □ **s'~** *vpr* become hard(ened).
endurer /ɑ̃dyʀe/ [1] *vt* endure.
énergétique /enɛʀʒetik/ *a* energy; (*food*) high-calorie. **énergie** *nf* energy; (Tech) power. **énergique** *a* energetic.
énervant, **~e** /enɛʀvɑ̃, -t/ *a* irritating, annoying.
énerver /enɛʀve/ [1] *vt* irritate. □ **s'~** *vpr* get worked up.
enfance /ɑ̃fɑ̃s/ *nf* childhood; **la petite ~** infancy.
enfant /ɑ̃fɑ̃/ *nmf* child. **enfantillage** *nm* childishness. **enfantin**, **~e** *a* simple, easy; (puéril) childish; (*jeu, langage*) children's.
enfer /ɑ̃fɛʀ/ *nm* (Relig) Hell; (fig) hell.
enfermer /ɑ̃fɛʀme/ [1] *vt* shut up. □ **s'~** *vpr* shut oneself up.
enfiler /ɑ̃file/ [1] *vt* (*aiguille*)

thread; (*vêtement*) slip on; (*rue*) take.

enfin /ɑ̃fɛ̃/ *adv* (de soulagement) at last; (en dernier lieu) finally; (résignation, conclusion) well; **~ presque** well nearly.

enflammé, **~e** /ɑ̃flame/ *a* (Méd) inflamed; (*discours*) fiery; (*lettre*) passionate.

enflammer /ɑ̃flame/ [1] *vt* set fire to. □ **s'~** *vpr* catch fire.

enfler /ɑ̃fle/ [1] *vt* (*histoire*) exaggerate. ● *vi* (*partie du corps*) swell (up); (*mer*) swell; (*rumeur, colère*) spread. □ **s'~** *vpr* (*colère*) mount; (*rumeur*) grow.

enfoncer /ɑ̃fɔ̃se/ [10] *vt* (*épingle*) push *ou* drive in; (*chapeau*) push down; (*porte*) break down. ● *vi* sink. □ **s'~** *vpr* sink (**dans** into).

enfouir /ɑ̃fwiʀ/ [2] *vt* bury.

enfourcher /ɑ̃fuʀʃe/ [1] *vt* mount.

enfreindre /ɑ̃fʀɛ̃dʀ/ [22] *vt* infringe, break.

enfuir (s') /(s)ɑ̃fɥiʀ/ [35] *vpr* run away.

enfumé, **~e** /ɑ̃fyme/ *a* filled with smoke.

engagé, **~e** /ɑ̃gaʒe/ *a* committed.

engagement /ɑ̃gaʒmɑ̃/ *nm* (promesse) promise; (Pol, Comm) commitment.

engager /ɑ̃gaʒe/ [40] *vt* (lier) bind, commit; (embaucher) take on; (commencer) start; (introduire) insert; (investir) invest. □ **s'~** *vpr* (promettre) commit oneself; (commencer) start; (*soldat*) enlist; (*concurrent*) enter; **s'~ à faire** undertake to do; **s'~ dans** (*voie*) enter.

engelure /ɑ̃ʒlyʀ/ *nf* chilblain.

engendrer /ɑ̃ʒɑ̃dʀe/ [1] *vt* (causer) generate.

engin /ɑ̃ʒɛ̃/ *nm* device; (véhicule) vehicle; (missile) missile.

engloutir /ɑ̃glutiʀ/ [2] *vt* swallow (up).

engouement /ɑ̃gumɑ̃/ *nm* passion.

engouffrer /ɑ̃gufʀe/ [1] *vt* ! gobble up. □ **s'~ dans** *vpr* rush in.

engourdir /ɑ̃guʀdiʀ/ [2] *vt* numb. □ **s'~** *vpr* go numb.

engrais /ɑ̃gʀɛ/ *nm* manure; (chimique) fertilizer.

engrenage /ɑ̃gʀənaʒ/ *nm* gears (+ *pl*); (fig) spiral.

engueuler /ɑ̃gœle/ [1] ✖ *vt* shout at. □ **s'~** *vpr* have a row.

enhardir (s') /(s)ɑ̃aʀdiʀ/ [2] *vpr* become bolder.

énième /ɛnjɛm/ *a* umpteenth.

énigmatique /enigmatik/ *a* enigmatic. **énigme** *nf* enigma; (devinette) riddle.

enivrer /ɑ̃nivʀe/ [1] *vt* intoxicate. □ **s'~** *vpr* get intoxicated.

enjambée /ɑ̃ʒɑ̃be/ *nf* stride. **enjamber** [1] *vt* step over; (*pont*) span.

enjeu (*pl* **~x**) /ɑ̃ʒø/ *nm* stake.

enjoué, **~e** /ɑ̃ʒwe/ *a* cheerful.

enlacer /ɑ̃lase/ [10] *vt* entwine.

enlèvement /ɑ̃lɛvmɑ̃/ *nm* (de colis) removal; (d'ordures) collection; (rapt) kidnapping.

enlever /ɑ̃lve/ [6] *vt* remove (**à** from); (*vêtement*) take off; (*tache, organe*) take out, remove; (kidnapper) kidnap; (gagner) win.

enliser (s') /(s)ɑ̃lize/ [1] *vpr* get bogged down.

enneigé, **~e** /ɑ̃neʒe/ *a* snow-covered.

ennemi, **~e** /ɛnmi/ *a & nm* enemy; **~ de** (fig) hostile to.

ennui /ɑ̃nɥi/ *nm* problem; (tracas) boredom; **s'attirer des ~s** run into trouble.

ennuyer /ɑ̃nɥije/ [31] *vt* bore; (irriter) annoy; (préoccuper) worry; **si**

cela ne t'ennuie pas if you don't mind. □ **s'~** *vpr* get bored.

ennuyeux, **-euse** /ɑ̃nɥijø, -z/ *a* boring; (fâcheux) annoying.

énoncé /enɔ̃se/ *nm* wording, text; (Gram) utterance.

énoncer /enɔ̃se/ [10] *vt* express, state.

enorgueillir (**s'**) /(s)ɑ̃nɔʀgœjiʀ/ [2] *vpr* **s'~ de** pride oneself on.

énorme /enɔʀm/ *a* enormous.

enquête /ɑ̃kɛt/ *nf* (Jur) investigation, inquiry; (sondage) survey; **mener l'~** lead the inquiry. **enquêter** [1] *vi* **~** (**sur**) investigate. **enquêteur**, **-euse** *nm, f* investigator.

enquiquinant, **~e** /ɑ̃kikinɑ̃, -t/ *a* 🅸 irritating.

enraciné, **~e** /ɑ̃ʀasine/ *a* deep-rooted.

enragé, **~e** /ɑ̃ʀaʒe/ *a* furious; (*chien*) rabid; (fig) fanatical.

enrager /ɑ̃ʀaʒe/ [40] *vi* be furious; **faire ~ qn** annoy sb.

enregistrement /ɑ̃ʀ(ə)ʒistʀəmɑ̃/ *nm* recording; (des bagages) check-in. **enregistrer** [1] *vt* (Mus, TV) record; (mémoriser) take in; (*bagages*) check in.

enrhumer (**s'**) /(s)ɑ̃ʀyme/ [1] *vpr* catch a cold.

enrichir /ɑ̃ʀiʃiʀ/ [2] *vt* enrich. □ **s'~** *vpr* grow rich(er). **enrichissant**, **~e** *a* (*expérience*) rewarding.

enrober /ɑ̃ʀɔbe/ [1] *vt* coat (**de** with).

enrôler /ɑ̃ʀole/ [1] *vt* recruit. □ **s'~** *vpr* enlist, enrol.

enroué, **~e** /ɑ̃ʀwe/ *a* hoarse.

enrouler /ɑ̃ʀule/ [1] *vt* wind, wrap. □ **s'~** *vpr* wind; **s'~ dans une couverture** roll oneself up in a blanket.

ensanglanté, **~e** /ɑ̃sɑ̃glɑ̃te/ *a* bloodstained.

enseignant, **~e** /ɑ̃sɛɲɑ̃, -t/ *nm, f* teacher. ● *a* teaching.

enseigne /ɑ̃sɛɲ/ *nf* sign.

enseignement /ɑ̃sɛɲəmɑ̃/ *nm* (profession) teaching; (instruction) education.

enseigner /ɑ̃seɲe/ [1] *vt/i* teach; **~ qch à qn** teach sb sth.

ensemble /ɑ̃sɑ̃bl/ *adv* together. ● *nm* group; (Mus) ensemble; (vêtements) outfit; (cohésion) unity; (maths) set; **dans l'~** on the whole; **d'~** (idée) general; **l'~ de** (totalité) all of, the whole of.

ensevelir /ɑ̃səvliʀ/ [2] *vt* bury.

ensoleillé, **~e** /ɑ̃sɔleje/ *a* sunny.

ensorceler /ɑ̃sɔʀsəle/ [38] *vt* bewitch.

ensuite /ɑ̃sɥit/ *adv* next, then; (plus tard) later.

ensuivre (**s'**) /(s)ɑ̃sɥivʀ/ [57] *vpr* follow; **et tout ce qui s'ensuit** and all the rest of it.

entaille /ɑ̃taj/ *nf* cut; (profonde) gash; (encoche) notch.

entamer /ɑ̃tame/ [1] *vt* start; (inciser) cut into; (ébranler) shake.

entasser /ɑ̃tɑse/ [1] *vt* (*livres*) pile; (*argent*) hoard; (*personnes*) cram (**dans** into). □ **s'~** *vpr* (*objets*) pile up (**dans** into); (*personnes*) squeeze (**dans** into).

entendement /ɑ̃tɑ̃dmɑ̃/ *nm* understanding; **ça dépasse l'~** it's beyond belief.

entendre /ɑ̃tɑ̃dʀ/ [3] *vt* hear; (comprendre) understand; (vouloir dire) mean; **~ parler de** hear of; **~ dire que** hear that. □ **s'~** *vpr* (être d'accord) agree; **s'~** (**bien**) get on (**avec** with); **cela s'entend** of course.

entendu, **~e** /ɑ̃tɑ̃dy/ *a* (convenu) agreed; (*sourire, air*) knowing; **bien ~** of course; (**c'est**) **~!** all right!

entente /ɑ̃tɑ̃t/ *nf* understanding; **bonne ~** good relationship.

enterrement /ãtɛʀmã/ *nm* funeral.
enterrer /ãteʀe/ [1] *vt* bury.
en-tête /ãtɛt/ *nm* heading; **à ~** headed.
entêté, **~e** /ãtete/ *a* stubborn. **entêtement** *nm* stubbornness. **entêter** (**s'**) [1] *vpr* persist (**à**, **dans** in).
enthousiasme /ãtuzjasm/ *nm* enthusiasm. **enthousiasmer** [1] *vt* fill with enthusiasm. **enthousiaste** *a* enthusiastic.
enticher (**s'**) /(s)ãtiʃe/ [1] *vpr* **s'~ de** become infatuated with.
entier, **-ière** /ãtje, -jɛʀ/ *a* whole; (absolu) absolute; (entêté) unyielding. ● *nm* whole; **en ~** entirely.
entonnoir /ãtɔnwaʀ/ *nm* funnel; (trou) crater.
entorse /ãtɔʀs/ *nf* sprain; (fig) **~ à** (*loi*) infringement of.
entortiller /ãtɔʀtije/ [1] *vt* wind, wrap (**autour** around); (duper ⊡) get round.
entourage /ãtuʀaʒ/ *nm* circle of family and friends; (bordure) surround.
entouré, **~e** /ãtuʀe/ *a* (*personne*) supported.
entourer /ãtuʀe/ [1] *vt* surround (**de** with); (réconforter) rally round; **~ qch de mystère** shroud sth in mystery.
entracte /ãtʀakt/ *nm* interval.
entraide /ãtʀɛd/ *nf* mutual aid. **entraider** (**s'**) [1] *vpr* help each other.
entrain /ãtʀɛ̃/ *nm* zest, spirit.
entraînement /ãtʀɛnmã/ *nm* (Sport) training.
entraîner /ãtʀene/ [1] *vt* (emporter) carry away; (provoquer) lead to; (Sport) train; (actionner) drive. □ **s'~** *vpr* train. **entraîneur** *nm* trainer.
entrave /ãtʀav/ *nf* hindrance. **entraver** [1] *vt* hinder.
entre /ãtʀ(ə)/ *prép* between; (parmi) among(st); **~ autres** among other things; **l'un d'~ nous/eux** one of us/them.
entrebâillé, **~e** /ãtʀəbaje/ *a* ajar, half-open.
entrechoquer (**s'**) /(s)ãtʀəʃɔke/ [1] *vpr* knock against each other.
entrecôte /ãtʀəkot/ *nf* rib steak.
entrecouper /ãtʀəkupe/ [1] *vt* **~ de** intersperse with.
entrecroiser (**s'**) /(s)ãtʀəkʀwaze/ [1] *vpr* (routes) intertwine.
entrée /ãtʀe/ *nf* entrance; (vestibule) hall; (accès) admission, entry; (billet) ticket; (Culin) starter; (Ordinat) **tapez sur E~** press Enter; **'~ interdite'** 'no entry'.
entrejambes /ãtʀəʒãb/ *nm* crotch.
entremets /ãtʀəmɛ/ *nm* dessert.
entremise /ãtʀəmiz/ *nf* intervention; **par l'~ de** through.
entreposer /ãtʀəpoze/ [1] *vt* store.
entrepôt /ãtʀəpo/ *nm* warehouse.
entreprenant, **~e** /ãtʀəpʀənã, -t/ *a* (actif) enterprising; (séducteur) forward.
entreprendre /ãtʀəpʀãdʀ/ [50] *vt* start on, undertake; (*personne*) buttonhole; **~ de faire** undertake to do.
entrepreneur /ãtʀəpʀənœʀ/ *nm* (de bâtiment) contractor; (chef d'entreprise) firm manager.
entreprise /ãtʀəpʀiz/ *nf* (projet) undertaking; (société) firm, business, company.
entrer /ãtʀe/ [1] *vi* (*aux être*) go in, enter; (venir) come in, enter; **~ dans** go *ou* come into, enter; (*club*) join; **~ en collision** collide (**avec** with); **faire ~** (*personne*) show in; **laisser ~** let in; **~ en guerre** go to war. ● *vt* (*données*) enter.

E

entre-temps /ɑ̃tʀətɑ̃/ *adv* meanwhile.

entretenir /ɑ̃tʀət(ə)niʀ/ [58] *vt* (*appareil*) maintain; (*vêtement*) look after; (alimenter) (*feu*) keep going; (*amitié*) keep alive; **~ qn de** converse with sb about. □ **s'~** *vpr* speak (**de** about; **avec** to). **entretien** *nm* maintenance; (discussion) talk; (pour un emploi) interview.

entrevoir /ɑ̃tʀəvwaʀ/ [63] *vt* make out; (brièvement) glimpse.

entrevue /ɑ̃tʀəvy/ *nf* meeting.

entrouvert, ~e /ɑ̃tʀuvɛʀ, -t/ *a* ajar, half-open.

énumération /enymeʀasjɔ̃/ *nf* enumeration. **énumérer** [14] *vt* enumerate.

envahir /ɑ̃vaiʀ/ [2] *vt* invade, overrun; (*douleur, peur*) overcome.

enveloppe /ɑ̃vlɔp/ *nf* envelope; (emballage) wrapping; **~ budgétaire** budget. **envelopper** [1] *vt* wrap (up); (fig) envelop.

envergure /ɑ̃vɛʀgyʀ/ *nf* wingspan; (importance) scope; (qualité) calibre.

envers /ɑ̃vɛʀ/ *prép* toward(s), to. ● *nm* (de tissu) wrong side; **à l'~** (*tableau*) upside down; (devant derrière) back to front; (*chaussette*) inside out.

envie /ɑ̃vi/ *nf* urge; (jalousie) envy; **avoir ~ de qch** feel like sth; **avoir ~ de faire** want to do; (moins urgent) feel like doing; **faire ~ à qn** make sb envious.

envier /ɑ̃vje/ [45] *vt* envy. **envieux, -ieuse** *a* envious.

environ /ɑ̃viʀɔ̃/ *adv* about.

environnant, ~e /ɑ̃viʀɔnɑ̃, -t/ *a* surrounding.

environnement /ɑ̃viʀɔnmɑ̃/ *nm* environment.

environs /ɑ̃viʀɔ̃/ *nmpl* vicinity; **aux ~ de** (*lieu*) in the vicinity of; (*heure*) round about.

envisager /ɑ̃vizaʒe/ [40] *vt* consider; (imaginer) envisage; **~ de faire** consider doing.

envoi /ɑ̃vwa/ *nm* dispatch; (paquet) consignment; **faire un ~** send; **coup d'~** (Sport) kick-off.

envoler (s') /(s)ɑ̃vɔle/ [1] *vpr* fly away; (*avion*) take off; (*papiers*) blow away.

envoyé, ~e /ɑ̃vwaje/ *nm, f* envoy; **~ spécial** special correspondent.

envoyer /ɑ̃vwaje/ [32] *vt* send; (lancer) throw; **~ promener qn** Ⓘ send sb packing Ⓘ.

épais, ~se /epɛ, -s/ *a* thick. **épaisseur** *nf* thickness.

épaissir /epesiʀ/ [2] *vt/i* thicken. □ **s'~** *vpr* thicken; (*mystère*) deepen.

épanoui, ~e /epanwi/ *a* (*personne*) beaming, radiant.

épanouir (s') /(s)epanwiʀ/ [2] *vpr* (*fleur*) open out; (*visage*) beam; (*personne*) blossom. **épanouissement** *nm* (éclat) blossoming, full bloom.

épargne /epaʀɲ/ *nf* savings.

épargner /epaʀɲe/ [1] *vt/i* save; (ne pas tuer) spare; **~ qch à qn** spare sb sth.

éparpiller /epaʀpije/ [1] *vt* scatter. □ **s'~** *vpr* scatter; (*fig*) dissipate one's efforts.

épars, ~e /epaʀ, -s/ *a* scattered.

épatant, ~e /epatɑ̃, -t/ *a* Ⓘ amazing.

épaule /epol/ *nf* shoulder.

épave /epav/ *nf* wreck.

épée /epe/ *nf* sword.

épeler /ɛple/ [6] *vt* spell.

éperdu, ~e /epɛʀdy/ *a* wild, frantic.

éperon /epʀɔ̃/ *nm* spur.

éphémère /efemɛʀ/ *a* ephemeral.

épi /epi/ *nm* (de blé) ear; (mèche) tuft of hair; **~ de maïs** corn cob.

épice /epis/ *nf* spice. **épicé, ~e** *a* spicy.

épicerie /episʀi/ *nf* grocery shop; (produits) groceries. **épicier, -ière** *nm, f* grocer.

épidémie /epidemi/ *nf* epidemic.

épiderme /epidɛʀm/ *nm* skin.

épier /epje/ [45] *vt* spy on.

épilepsie /epilɛpsi/ *nf* epilepsy. **épileptique** *a & nmf* epileptic.

épiler /epile/ [1] *vt* remove unwanted hair from; (*sourcils*) pluck.

épilogue /epilɔg/ *nm* epilogue; (fig) outcome.

épinard /epinaʀ/ *nm* **~s** spinach (+ *sg*).

épine /epin/ *nf* thorn, prickle; (d'animal) prickle, spine; **~ dorsale** backbone. **épineux, -euse** *a* thorny.

épingle /epɛ̃gl/ *nf* pin; **~ de nourrice, ~ de sûreté** safety-pin.

épisode /epizɔd/ *nm* episode; **à ~s** serialized.

épitaphe /epitaf/ *nf* epitaph.

éplucheé-légumes /eplyʃlegym/ *nm inv* (potato) peeler.

éplucher /eplyʃe/ [1] *vt* peel; (examiner: fig) scrutinize.

épluchure /eplyʃyʀ/ *nf* **~s** peelings.

éponge /epɔ̃ʒ/ *nf* sponge. **éponger** [40] *vt* (*liquide*) mop up; (*surface, front*) mop; (fig) (*dettes*) wipe out.

épopée /epɔpe/ *nf* epic.

époque /epɔk/ *nf* time, period; **à l'~** at the time; **d'~** period.

épouse /epuz/ *nf* wife.

épouser /epuze/ [1] *vt* marry; (*forme, idée*) adopt.

épousseter /epuste/ [38] *vt* dust.

épouvantable /epuvɑ̃tabl/ *a* appalling.

épouvantail /epuvɑ̃taj/ *nm* scarecrow.

épouvante /epuvɑ̃t/ *nf* terror. **épouvanter** [1] *vt* terrify.

époux /epu/ *nm* husband; **les ~** the married couple.

éprendre (s') /(s)epʀɑ̃dʀ/ [50] *vpr* **s'~ de** fall in love with.

épreuve /epʀœv/ *nf* test; (Sport) event; (malheur) ordeal; (Photo, d'imprimerie) proof; **mettre à l'~** put to the test.

éprouver /epʀuve/ [1] *vt* (ressentir) experience; (affliger) distress; (tester) test.

éprouvette /epʀuvɛt/ *nf* test-tube.

EPS *abrév f* (**éducation physique et sportive**) PE.

épuisé, ~e /epɥize/ *a* exhausted; (*livre*) out of print. **épuisement** *nm* exhaustion.

épuiser /epɥize/ [1] *vt* (fatiguer, user) exhaust. ▫ **s'~** *vpr* become exhausted.

épuration /epyʀasjɔ̃/ *nf* purification; (Pol) purge. **épurer** [1] *vt* purify; (Pol) purge.

équateur /ekwatœʀ/ *nm* equator.

équilibre /ekilibʀ/ *nm* balance; **être** *ou* **se tenir en ~** (*personne*) balance; (*objet*) be balanced. **équilibré, ~e** *a* well-balanced.

équilibrer /ekilibʀe/ [1] *vt* balance. ▫ **s'~** *vpr* balance each other.

équilibriste /ekilibʀist/ *nmf* acrobat.

équipage /ekipaʒ/ *nm* crew.

équipe /ekip/ *nf* team; **~ de nuit/jour** night/day shift.

équipé, ~e /ekipe/ *a* equipped; **cuisine ~e** fitted kitchen.

équipement /ekipmɑ̃/ *nm* equipment; **~s** (installations) amenities, facilities.

équiper /ekipe/ [1] *vt* equip (**de** with). ▫ **s'~** *vpr* equip oneself.

E

équipier, **-ière** /ekipje, -jɛʀ/ *nm,f* team member.

équitable /ekitabl/ *a* fair.

équitation /ekitasjɔ̃/ *nf* (horse-) riding.

équivalence /ekivalɑ̃s/ *nf* equivalence. **équivalent**, **~e** *a* equivalent.

équivaloir /ekivalwaʀ/ [60] *vi* **~ à** be equivalent to.

équivoque /ekivɔk/ *a* equivocal; (louche) questionable. ● *nf* ambiguity.

érable /eʀabl/ *nm* maple.

érafler /eʀafle/ [1] *vt* scratch. **éraflure** *nf* scratch.

éraillé, **~e** /eʀɑje/ *a* (*voix*) raucous.

ère /ɛʀ/ *nf* era.

éreintant, **~e** /eʀɛ̃tɑ̃, -t/ *a* exhausting. **éreinter** (**s'**) [1] *vpr* wear oneself out.

ériger /eʀiʒe/ [40] *vt* erect. □ **s'~ en** *vpr* set (oneself) up as.

éroder /eʀɔde/ [1] *vt* erode. **érosion** *nf* erosion.

errer /ɛʀe/ [1] *vi* wander.

erreur /ɛʀœʀ/ *nf* mistake, error; **dans l'~** mistaken; **par ~** by mistake; **~ judiciaire** miscarriage of justice.

erroné, **~e** /ɛʀɔne/ *a* erroneous.

érudit, **~e** /eʀydi, -t/ *a* scholarly. ● *nm,f* scholar.

éruption /eʀypsjɔ̃/ *nf* eruption; (Méd) rash.

es /ɛ/ ⇒ÊTRE [4].

escabeau (*pl* **~x**) /ɛskabo/ *nm* step-ladder.

escadron /ɛskadʀɔ̃/ *nm* (Mil) company.

escalade /ɛskalad/ *nf* climbing; (Pol, Comm) escalation. **escalader** [1] *vt* climb.

escale /ɛskal/ *nf* (d'avion) stopover; (port) port of call; **faire ~ à** (*avion, passager*) stop over at; (*navire, passager*) put in at.

escalier /ɛskalje/ *nm* stairs (+ *pl*); **~ mécanique** *ou* **roulant** escalator.

escalope /ɛskalɔp/ *nf* escalope.

escargot /ɛskaʀgo/ *nm* snail.

escarpé, **~e** /ɛskaʀpe/ *a* steep.

escarpin /ɛskaʀpɛ̃/ *nm* court shoe; (US) pump.

escient: **à bon ~** /abɔnesjɑ̃/ *loc* wisely.

esclandre /ɛsklɑ̃dʀ/ *nm* scene.

esclavage /ɛsklavaʒ/ *nm* slavery. **esclave** *nmf* slave.

escompte /ɛskɔ̃t/ *nm* discount. **escompter** [1] *vt* expect; (Comm) discount.

escorte /ɛskɔʀt/ *nf* escort.

escrime /ɛskʀim/ *nf* fencing.

escroc /ɛskʀo/ *nm* swindler.

escroquer /ɛskʀɔke/ [1] *vt* swindle; **~ qch à qn** swindle sb out of sth. **escroquerie** *nf* swindle.

espace /ɛspas/ *nm* space; **~s verts** gardens and parks.

espacer /ɛspase/ [10] *vt* space out. □ **s'~** *vpr* become less frequent.

espadrille /ɛspadʀij/ *nf* rope sandal.

Espagne /ɛspaɲ/ *nf* Spain.

espagnol, **~e** /ɛspaɲɔl/ *a* Spanish. ● *nm* (Ling) Spanish. **E~, ~e** *nm,f* Spaniard.

espèce /ɛspɛs/ *nf* kind, sort; (race) species; **en ~s** (*argent*) in cash; **~ d'idiot!** [!] you idiot! [!].

espérance /ɛspeʀɑ̃s/ *nf* hope.

espérer /ɛspeʀe/ [14] *vt* hope for; **~ faire/que** hope to do/that. ● *vi* hope.

espiègle /ɛspjɛgl/ *a* mischievous.

espion, **~ne** /ɛspjɔ̃, -ɔn/ *nm,f* spy. **espionnage** *nm* espionage, spying. **espionner** [1] *vt* spy (on).

espoir /ɛspwaʀ/ *nm* hope; **reprendre ~** feel hopeful again.

esprit /ɛspʀi/ *nm* (intellect) mind; (humour) wit; (fantôme) spirit; (ambiance) atmosphere; **perdre l'~** lose one's mind; **reprendre ses ~s** come to; **faire de l'~** try to be witty.

esquimau, ~de (*mpl* **~x**) /ɛskimo, -d/ *nm, f* Eskimo.

esquinter /ɛskɛ̃te/ [1] *vt* ▣ ruin.

esquisse /ɛskis/ *nf* sketch; (fig) outline.

esquiver /ɛskive/ [1] *vt* dodge. □ **s'~** *vpr* slip away.

essai /esɛ/ *nm* (épreuve) test, trial; (tentative) try; (article) essay; (au rugby) try; **~s** (Auto) qualifying round (+ *sg*); **à l'~** on trial.

essaim /esɛ̃/ *nm* swarm.

essayage /esɛjaʒ/ *nm* fitting; **salon d'~** fitting room.

essayer /eseje/ [31] *vt/i* try; (*vêtement*) try (on); (*voiture*) try (out); **~ de faire** try to do.

essence /esɑ̃s/ *nf* (carburant) petrol; (nature, extrait) essence; **~ sans plomb** unleaded petrol.

essentiel, ~le /esɑ̃sjɛl/ *a* essential. ● *nm* **l'~** the main thing; (quantité) the main part.

essieu (*pl* **~x**) /esjø/ *nm* axle.

essor /esɔʀ/ *nm* expansion; **prendre son ~** expand.

essorage /esɔʀaʒ/ *nm* spin-drying. **essorer** [1] *vt* (*linge*) spin-dry; (en tordant) wring.

essoreuse /esɔʀøz/ *nf* spin-drier; **~ à salade** salad spinner.

essoufflé, ~e /esufle/ *a* out of breath.

essuie-glace /esɥiglas/ *nm inv* windscreen wiper.

essuie-mains /esɥimɛ̃/ *nm inv* hand-towel.

essuie-tout /esɥitu/ *nm inv* kitchen paper.

essuyer /esɥije/ [31] *vt* wipe; (subir) suffer. □ **s'~** *vpr* dry *ou* wipe oneself.

est¹ /ɛ/ ⇒ÊTRE [4].

est² /ɛst/ *nm* east. ● *a inv* east; (partie) eastern; (direction) easterly.

estampe /ɛstɑ̃p/ *nf* print.

esthète /ɛstɛt/ *nmf* aesthete.

esthéticienne /ɛstetisjɛn/ *nf* beautician.

esthétique /ɛstetik/ *a* aesthetic.

estimation /ɛstimasjɔ̃/ *nf* (de coûts) estimate; (valeur) valuation.

estime /ɛstim/ *nf* esteem.

estimer /ɛstime/ [1] *vt* (*tableau*) value; (calculer) estimate; (respecter) esteem; (considérer) consider (**que** that).

estival, ~e (*mpl* **-aux**) /ɛstival, -o/ *a* summer. **estivant, ~e** *nm, f* summer visitor.

estomac /ɛstɔma/ *nm* stomach.

estomaqué, ~e /ɛstɔmake/ *a* ▣ stunned.

Estonie /ɛstɔni/ *nf* Estonia.

estrade /ɛstʀad/ *nf* platform.

estragon /ɛstʀagɔ̃/ *nm* tarragon.

estropié, ~e /ɛstʀɔpje/ *nm, f* cripple. ● *a* crippled.

estuaire /ɛstɥɛʀ/ *nm* estuary.

et /e/ *conj* and; **~ moi?** what about me?; **~ alors?** so what?

étable /etabl/ *nf* cow-shed.

établi, ~e /etabli/ *a* established; **un fait bien ~** a well-established fact. ● *nm* work-bench.

établir /etabliʀ/ [2] *vt* establish; (*liste, facture*) draw up; (*personne, camp, record*) set up. □ **s'~** *vpr* (*personne*) settle; **s'~ à son compte** set up on one's own.

établissement /etablismɑ̃/ *nm* (entreprise) organization; (institution) establishment; **~ scolaire** school.

étage /etaʒ/ *nm* floor, storey; (de fusée) stage; **à l'~** upstairs; **au premier ~** on the first floor.

étagère /etaʒɛʀ/ *nf* shelf; (meuble) shelving unit.

étain /etɛ̃/ *nm* pewter.

E

étais, **était** /etɛ/ ⇒ÊTRE [4].

étalage /etalaʒ/ *nm* display; (vitrine) shop-window; **faire ~ de** flaunt. **étalagiste** *nmf* window-dresser.

étaler /etale/ [1] *vt* spread; (*journal*) spread (out); (*pâte*) roll out; (exposer) display; (*richesse*) flaunt. ◻ **s'~** *vpr* (prendre de la place) spread out; (tomber ⓘ) fall flat; **s'~ sur** (*paiement*) be spread over.

étalon /etalɔ̃/ *nm* (cheval) stallion; (modèle) standard.

étanche /etɑ̃ʃ/ *a* watertight; (*montre*) waterproof.

étancher /etɑ̃ʃe/ [1] *vt* (*soif*) quench.

étang /etɑ̃/ *nm* pond.

étant /etɑ̃/ ⇒ÊTRE [4].

étape /etap/ *nf* stage; (lieu d'arrêt) stopover; (fig) stage.

état /eta/ *nm* state; (liste) statement; (métier) profession; **en bon/mauvais ~** in good/bad condition; **en ~ de** in a position to; **en ~ de marche** in working order; **faire ~ de** (citer) mention; **être dans tous ses ~s** be in a state; **~ civil** civil status; **~ des lieux** inventory of fixtures. **État** *nm* State.

état-major (*pl* **états-majors**) /etamaʒɔʀ/ *nm* (officiers) staff (+ *pl*).

États-Unis /etazyni/ *nmpl* **~ (d'Amérique)** United States (of America).

étau (*pl* **~x**) /eto/ *nm* vice.

étayer /eteje/ [31] *vt* prop up.

été[1] /ete/ ⇒ÊTRE [4].

été[2] /ete/ *nm* summer.

éteindre /etɛ̃dʀ/ [22] *vt* (*feu*) put out; (*lumière, radio*) turn off. ◻ **s'~** *vpr* (*feu, lumière*) go out; (*appareil*) go off; (mourir) die. **éteint**, **~e** *a* (*feu*) out; (*volcan*) extinct.

étendard /etɑ̃daʀ/ *nm* standard.

étendre /etɑ̃dʀ/ [3] *vt* (*nappe*) spread (out); (*bras, jambes*) stretch (out); (*linge*) hang out; (agrandir) extend. ◻ **s'~** *vpr* (s'allonger) lie down; (se propager) spread; (*plaine*) stretch; **s'~ sur** (*sujet*) dwell on.

étendu, **~e** /etɑ̃dy/ *a* extensive. **étendue** *nf* area; (d'eau) stretch; (importance) extent.

éternel, **~le** /etɛʀnɛl/ *a* (*vie*) eternal; (fig) endless.

éterniser (s') /(s)etɛʀnize/ [1] *vpr* (durer) drag on.

éternité /etɛʀnite/ *nf* eternity.

éternuement /etɛʀnymɑ̃/ *nm* sneeze. **éternuer** [1] *vi* sneeze.

êtes /ɛt/ ⇒ÊTRE [4].

éthique /etik/ *a* ethical. ● *nf* ethics (+ *sg*).

ethnie /ɛtni/ *nf* ethnic group. **ethnique** *a* ethnic.

étincelant, **~e** /etɛ̃slɑ̃, -t/ *a* sparkling. **étinceler** [38] *vi* sparkle. **étincelle** *nf* spark.

étiqueter /etikte/ [38] *vt* label. **étiquette** *nf* label; (protocole) etiquette.

étirer /etiʀe/ [1] *vt* stretch. ◻ **s'~** *vpr* stretch.

étoffe /etɔf/ *nf* fabric.

étoffer /etɔfe/ [1] *vt* expand. ◻ **s'~** *vpr* fill out.

étoile /etwal/ *nf* star; **à la belle ~** in the open; **~ filante** shooting star; **~ de mer** starfish.

étonnant, **~e** /etɔnɑ̃, -t/ *a* (curieux) surprising; (formidable) amazing. **étonnement** *nm* surprise; (plus fort) amazement.

étonner /etɔne/ [1] *vt* amaze. ◻ **s'~** *vpr* be amazed (**de** at).

étouffant, **~e** /etufɑ̃, -t/ *a* stifling.

étouffer /etufe/ [1] *vt/i* suffocate; (*sentiment, révolte*) stifle; (*feu*) smother; (*bruit*) muffle; **on étouffe**

it is stifling. ◻ **s'~** *vpr* suffocate; (en mangeant) choke.

étourderie /etuʀdəʀi/ *nf* thoughtlessness; (acte) careless mistake.

étourdi, **~e** /etuʀdi/ *a* absent-minded. ● *nm,f* scatterbrain.

étourdir /etuʀdiʀ/ [2] *vt* stun; (fatiguer) make sb's head spin. **étourdissant**, **~e** *a* stunning.

étourneau (*pl* **~x**) /etuʀno/ *nm* starling.

étrange /etʀɑ̃ʒ/ *a* strange.

étranger, **-ère** /etʀɑ̃ʒe, -ɛʀ/ *a* (inconnu) strange, unfamiliar; (d'un autre pays) foreign. ● *nm,f* foreigner; (inconnu) stranger; **à l'~** abroad; **de l'~** from abroad.

étrangler /etʀɑ̃gle/ [1] *vt* strangle; (*col*) throttle. ◻ **s'~** *vpr* choke.

être /ɛtʀ/ [4]

● *verbe auxiliaire*

····➤ (du passé) have; **elle est partie/venue hier** she left/came yesterday.

····➤ (de la voix passive) be.

● *verbe intransitif* (*aux avoir*)

····➤ be; **~ médecin** be a doctor; **je suis à vous** I'm all yours; **j'en suis à me demander si...** I'm beginning to wonder whether...; **qu'en est-il de...?** what's the news about...?

····➤ (appartenance) be, belong to.

····➤ (heure, date) be; **nous sommes le 3 mars** it's March 3.

····➤ (aller) be; **je n'y ai jamais été** I've never been; **il a été le voir** he went to see him.

····➤ **c'est** it is *or* it's; **c'est moi qui l'ai fait** I did it; **est-ce que tu veux du thé?** do you want some tea?

● *nom masculin*

····➤ being; **~ humain** human being.

····➤ (personne) person; **un ~ cher** a loved one.

étreindre /etʀɛ̃dʀ/ [22] *vt* embrace. **étreinte** *nf* embrace.

étrennes /etʀɛn/ *nfpl* (New Year's) gift (+ *sg*); (argent) money.

étrier /etʀije/ *nm* stirrup.

étriqué, **~e** /etʀike/ *a* tight.

étroit, **~e** /etʀwa, -t/ *a* narrow; (*vêtement*) tight; (*liens, surveillance*) close; **à l'~** cramped. **étroitement** *adv* closely. **étroitesse** *nf* narrowness.

étude /etyd/ *nf* study; (enquête) survey; (bureau) office; (**salle d'**)**~** (Scol) prep room; **à l'~** under consideration; **faire des ~s** (**de**) study; **il n'a pas fait d'~s** he didn't go to university; **~ de marché** market research.

étudiant, **~e** /etydjɑ̃, -t/ *nm,f* student.

étudier /etydje/ [45] *vt/i* study.

étui /etɥi/ *nm* case.

étuve /etyv/ *nf* steam room.

eu, **~e** /y/ ⇒AVOIR [5].

euro /øʀo/ *nm* euro.

Europe /øʀɔp/ *nf* Europe.

européen, **~ne** /øʀɔpeɛ̃, -eɛn/ *a* European. **E~**, **~ne** *nm,f* European.

euthanasie /øtanazi/ *nf* euthanasia.

eux /ø/ *pron* they; (complément) them. **eux-mêmes** *pron* themselves.

évacuation /evakɥasjɔ̃/ *nf* evacuation; (d'eaux usées) discharge. **évacuer** [1] *vt* evacuate.

évadé, **~e** /evade/ *a* escaped. ● *nm,f* escaped prisoner. **évader** (**s'**) [1] *vpr* escape.

évaluation /evalɥasjɔ̃/ *nf*

assessment. **évaluer** [1] *vt* assess.

évangile /evɑ̃ʒil/ *nm* gospel; **l'É~** the Gospel.

évanouir (s') /(s)evanwiʀ/ [2] *vpr* faint; (disparaître) vanish.

évaporation /evapɔʀasjɔ̃/ *nf* evaporation. **évaporer (s')** [1] *vpr* evaporate.

évasif, -ive /evazif, -v/ *a* evasive.

évasion /evazjɔ̃/ *nf* escape.

éveil /evɛj/ *nm* awakening; **en ~** alert.

éveillé, ~e /eveje/ *a* awake; (intelligent) alert.

éveiller /eveje/ [1] *vt* awake(n); (susciter) arouse. □ **s'~** *vpr* awake.

événement /evɛnmɑ̃/ *nm* event.

éventail /evɑ̃taj/ *nm* fan; (gamme) range.

éventrer /evɑ̃tʀe/ [1] *vt* (*sac*) rip open.

éventualité /evɑ̃tɥalite/ *nf* possibility; **dans cette ~** in that event.

éventuel, ~le /evɑ̃tɥɛl/ *a* possible. **éventuellement** *adv* possibly.

évêque /evɛk/ *nm* bishop.

évertuer (s') /(s)evɛʀtɥe/ [1] *vpr* **s'~ à** struggle hard to.

éviction /eviksjɔ̃/ *nf* eviction.

évidemment /evidamɑ̃/ *adv* obviously; (bien sûr) of course.

évidence /evidɑ̃s/ *nf* obviousness; (fait) obvious fact; **être en ~** be conspicuous; **mettre en ~** (fait) highlight. **évident, ~e** *a* obvious, evident.

évier /evje/ *nm* sink.

évincer /evɛ̃se/ [10] *vt* oust.

éviter /evite/ [1] *vt* avoid (**de faire** doing); **~ qch à qn** (*dérangement*) save sb sth.

évocateur, -trice /evɔkatœʀ, -tʀis/ *a* evocative. **évocation** *nf* evocation.

évolué, ~e /evɔlɥe/ *a* highly developed.

évoluer /evɔlɥe/ [1] *vi* evolve; (*situation*) develop; (se déplacer) glide. **évolution** *nf* evolution; (d'une situation) development.

évoquer /evɔke/ [1] *vt* call to mind, evoke.

exacerber /ɛgzasɛʀbe/ [1] *vt* exacerbate.

exact, ~e /ɛgza(kt), -akt/ *a* (précis) exact, accurate; (juste) correct; (*personne*) punctual. **exactement** *adv* exactly. **exactitude** *nf* exactness; punctuality.

ex æquo /ɛgzeko/ *adv* **être ~** tie (**avec qn** with sb).

exagération /ɛgzaʒeʀasjɔ̃/ *nf* exaggeration. **exagéré, ~e** *a* excessive.

exagérer /ɛgzaʒeʀe/ [14] *vt/i* exaggerate; (abuser) go too far.

exalté, ~e /ɛgzalte/ *nm, f* fanatic. **exalter** [1] *vt* excite; (glorifier) exalt.

examen /ɛgzamɛ̃/ *nm* examination; (Scol) exam. **examinateur, -trice** *nm, f* examiner. **examiner** [1] *vt* examine.

exaspération /ɛgxaspeʀasjɔ̃/ *nf* exasperation. **exaspérer** [14] *vt* exasperate.

exaucer /ɛgzose/ [10] *vt* grant; (*personne*) grant the wish(es) of.

excédent /ɛksedɑ̃/ *nm* surplus; **~ de bagages** excess luggage; **~ de la balance commerciale** trade surplus. **excédentaire** *a* excess, surplus.

excéder /ɛksede/ [14] *vt* (dépasser) exceed; (agacer) irritate.

excellence /ɛksɛlɑ̃s/ *nf* excellence. **excellent, ~e** *a* excellent. **exceller** [1] *vi* excel (**dans** in).

excentricité /ɛksɑ̃tʀisite/ *nf*

eccentricity. **excentrique** *a & nmf* eccentric.

excepté, **~e** /ɛksɛpte/ *a & prép* except.

excepter /ɛksɛpte/ [1] *vt* except.

exception /ɛksɛpsjɔ̃/ *nf* exception; **à l'~ de** except for; **d'~** exceptional; **faire ~** be an exception. **exceptionnel**, **~le** *a* exceptional. **exceptionnellement** *adv* exceptionally.

excès /ɛksɛ/ *nm* excess; **~ de vitesse** speeding.

excessif, **-ive** /ɛksesif, -v/ *a* excessive.

excitant, **~e** /ɛksitɑ̃, -t/ *a* stimulating; (palpitant) exciting. ● *nm* stimulant.

exciter /ɛksite/ [1] *vt* excite; (irriter) get excited. □ **s'~** *vpr* get excited.

exclamer **(s')** /(s)ɛksklame/ [1] *vpr* exclaim.

exclure /ɛksklyʀ/ [16] *vt* exclude; (expulser) expel; (empêcher) preclude.

exclusif, **-ive** /ɛksklyzif, -v/ *a* exclusive.

exclusion /ɛksklyzjɔ̃/ *nf* exclusion.

exclusivité /ɛkslyzivite/ *nf* (Comm) exclusive rights (+ *pl*); **projeter en ~** show exclusively.

excursion /ɛkskyʀsjɔ̃/ *nf* excursion; (à pied) hike.

excuse /ɛkskyz/ *nf* excuse; **~s** apology (+ *sg*); **faire des ~s** apologize.

excuser /ɛkskyze/ [1] *vt* excuse; **excusez-moi** excuse me. □ **s'~** *vpr* apologize (**de** for).

exécrable /ɛgzekʀabl/ *a* dreadful. **exécrer** [14] *vt* loathe.

exécuter /ɛgzekyte/ [1] *vt* carry out, execute; (Mus) perform; (tuer) execute.

exécutif, **-ive** /ɛgzekytif, -v/ *a & nm* (Pol) executive.

exécution /egzekysjɔ̃/ *nf* execution; (Mus) performance.

exemplaire /ɛgzɑ̃plɛʀ/ *a* exemplary. ● *nm* copy.

exemple /ɛgzɑ̃pl/ *nm* example; **par ~** for example; **donner l'~** set an example.

exempt, **~e** /ɛgzɑ̃, -t/ *a* **~ de** exempt (**de** from).

exempter /ɛgzɑ̃te/ [1] *vt* exempt (**de** from). **exemption** *nf* exemption.

exercer /ɛgzɛʀse/ [10] *vt* exercise; (*influence, contrôle*) exert; (former) train, exercise; **~ un métier** have a job; **~ le métier de...** work as a... □ **s'~** *vpr* practise.

exercice /ɛgzɛʀsis/ *nm* exercise; (de métier) practice; **en ~** in office; (*médecin*) in practice.

exhaler /ɛgzale/ [1] *vt* emit.

exhaustif, **-ive** /ɛgzostif, -v/ *a* exhaustive.

exhiber /ɛgzibe/ [1] *vt* exhibit.

exhorter /ɛgzɔʀte/ [1] *vt* exhort (**à** to).

exigeant, **~e** /ɛgziʒɑ̃, -t/ *a* demanding; **être ~ avec qn** demand a lot of sb. **exigence** *nf* demand. **exiger** [40] *vt* demand.

exigu, **~ë** /ɛgzigy/ *a* tiny.

exil /ɛgzil/ *nm* exile. **exilé**, **~e** *nm, f* exile.

exiler /ɛgzile/ [1] *vt* exile. □ **s'~** *vpr* go into exile.

existence /ɛgzistɑ̃s/ *nf* existence. **exister** [1] *vi* exist.

exode /ɛgzɔd/ *nm* exodus.

exonérer /egzɔneʀe/ [14] *vt* exempt (**de** from).

exorbitant, **~e** /ɛgzɔʀbitɑ̃, -t/ *a* exorbitant.

exorciser /ɛgzɔʀsize/ [1] *vt* exorcize.

exotique /ɛgzɔtik/ *a* exotic.

E

expansé, **~e** /ɛkspɑ̃se/ *a* (Tech) expanded.

expansif, **-ive** /ɛkspɑ̃sif, -v/ *a* expansive. **expansion** *nf* expansion.

expatrié, **~e** /ɛkspatʀije/ *nm, f* expatriate.

expectative /ɛkspɛktativ/ *nf* **être dans l'~** wait and see.

expédient /ɛkspedjɑ̃/ *nm* expedient; **vivre d'~s** live by one's wits; **user d'~s** resort to expedients.

expédier /ɛkspedje/ [45] *vt* send, dispatch; (*tâche* ⊡) polish off. **expéditeur**, **-trice** *nm, f* sender.

expéditif, **-ive** /ɛkspeditif, -v/ *a* quick.

expédition /ɛkspedisjɔ̃/ *nf* (envoi) dispatching; (voyage) expedition.

expérience /ɛkspeʀjɑ̃s/ *nf* experience; (scientifique) experiment.

expérimental, **~e** (*mpl* **-aux**) /ɛkspeʀimɑ̃tal, o/ *a* experimental. **expérimentation** *nf* experimentation. **expérimenté**, **~e** *a* experienced. **expérimenter** [1] *vt* test, experiment with.

expert, **~e** /ɛkspɛʀ, -t/ *a* expert. ● *nm* expert; (d'assurances) adjuster. **expert-comptable** (*pl* **experts-comptables**) *nm* accountant.

expertise /ɛkspɛʀtiz/ *nf* valuation; (de dégâts) assessment. **expertiser** [1] *vt* value; (*dégâts*) assess.

expier /ɛkspje/ [45] *vt* atone for.

expiration /ɛkspiʀasjɔ̃/ *nf* expiry.

expirer /ɛkspiʀe/ [1] *vi* breathe out; (finir, mourir) expire.

explicatif, **-ive** /ɛksplikatif, -v/ *a* explanatory.

explication /ɛksplikasjɔ̃/ *nf* explanation; (fig) discussion; **~ de texte** (Scol) literary commentary.

explicite /ɛksplisit/ *a* explicit.

expliquer /ɛksplike/ [1] *vt* explain. □ **s'~** *vpr* explain oneself; (discuter) discuss things; (être explicable) be understandable.

exploit /ɛksplwa/ *nm* exploit.

exploitant, **~e** /ɛksplwatɑ̃, -t/ *nm, f* **~ (agricole)** farmer.

exploitation /ɛksplwatasjɔ̃/ *nf* exploitation; (d'entreprise) running; (ferme) farm.

exploiter /ɛksplwate/ [1] *vt* exploit; (*ferme*) run; (*mine*) work.

explorateur, **-trice** /ɛksplɔʀatœʀ, -tʀis/ *nm, f* explorer. **exploration** *nf* exploration. **explorer** [1] *vt* explore.

exploser /ɛksploze/ [1] *vi* explode; **faire ~** explode; (*bâtiment*) blow up.

explosif, **-ive** /ɛksplozif, -v/ *a & nm* explosive. **explosion** *nf* explosion.

exportateur, **-trice** /ɛkspɔʀtatœʀ, -tʀis/ *nm, f* exporter. ● *a* exporting. **exportation** *nf* export. **exporter** [1] *vt* export.

exposant, **~e** /ɛkspozɑ̃, -t/ *nm, f* exhibitor.

exposé, **~e** /ɛkspoze/ *nm* talk (**sur** on); (d'une action) account; **faire l'~ de la situation** give an account of the situation. ● *a* **~ au nord** facing north.

exposer /ɛkspoze/ [1] *vt* display, show; (expliquer) explain; (soumettre, mettre en danger) expose (**à** to); (*vie*) endanger. □ **s'~ à** *vpr* expose oneself to.

exposition /ɛkspozisjɔ̃/ *nf* (d'art) exhibition; (de faits) exposition; (géographique) aspect.

exprès[1] /ɛkspʀɛ/ *adv* specially; (délibérément) on purpose.

exprès², **-esse** /ɛkspʀɛs/ *a* express.

express /ɛkspʀɛs/ *a & nm inv* (**café**) ~ espresso; (**train**) ~ fast train.

expressif, **-ive** /ɛkspʀesif, -v/ *a* expressive. **expression** *nf* expression.

exprimer /ɛkspʀime/ [1] *vt* express. □ **s'~** *vpr* express oneself.

expulser /ɛkspylse/ [1] *vt* expel; (*locataire*) evict; (*joueur*) send off. **expulsion** *nf* (d'élève) expulsion; (de locataire) eviction; (d'immigré) deportation.

exquis, **~e** /ɛkski, -z/ *a* exquisite.

extase /ɛkstɑz/ *nf* ecstasy.

extasier (**s'**) /(s)ɛkstɑzje/ [45] *vpr* **s'~ sur** be ecstatic about.

extensible /ɛkstɑ̃sibl/ *a* (*tissu*) stretch.

extension /ɛkstɑ̃sjɔ̃/ *nf* extension; (expansion) expansion.

exténuer /ɛkstenɥe/ [1] *vt* exhaust.

extérieur, **~e** /ɛksteʀjœʀ/ *a* outside; (*signe, gaieté*) outward; (*politique*) foreign. ● *nm* outside, exterior; (de personne) exterior; **à l'~** (**de**) outside. **extérioriser** [1] *vt* show, externalize.

extermination /ɛkstɛʀminasjɔ̃/ *nf* extermination. **exterminer** [1] *vt* exterminate.

externe /ɛkstɛʀn/ *a* external. ● *nmf* (Scol) day pupil.

extincteur /ɛkstɛ̃ktœʀ/ *nm* fire extinguisher.

extinction /ɛkstɛ̃ksjɔ̃/ *nf* extinction; **avoir une ~ de voix** have lost one's voice.

extorquer /ɛkstɔʀke/ [1] *vt* extort.

extra /ɛkstʀa/ *a inv* first-rate. ● *nm inv* (repas) (special) treat.

extraction /ɛkstʀaksjɔ̃/ *nf* extraction.

extrader /ɛkstʀade/ [1] *vt* extradite.

extraire /ɛkstʀɛʀ/ [29] *vt* extract. **extrait** *nm* extract.

extraordinaire /ɛkstʀaɔʀdinɛʀ/ *a* extraordinary.

extravagance /ɛkstʀavagɑ̃s/ *nf* extravagance. **extravagant**, **~e** *a* extravagant.

extraverti, **~e** /ɛkstʀavɛʀti/ *nm,f* extrovert.

extrême /ɛkstʀɛm/ *a & nm* extreme. **extrêmement** *adv* extremely.

Extrême-Orient /ɛkstʀɛmɔʀjɑ̃/ *nm* Far East.

extrémiste /ɛkstʀemist/ *nmf* extremist.

extrémité /ɛkstʀemite/ *nf* end; (mains, pieds) extremity.

exubérance /ɛgzybeʀɑ̃s/ *nf* exuberance. **exubérant**, **~e** *a* exuberant.

F

F *abrév f* (**franc, francs**) franc, francs.

fabricant, **~e** /fabʀikɑ̃, -t/ *nm,f* manufacturer. **fabrication** *nf* making; manufacture.

fabrique /fabʀik/ *nf* factory. **fabriquer** [1] *vt* make; (industriellement) manufacture; (fig) make up.

fabuler /fabyle/ [1] *vi* fantasize.

fabuleux, **-euse** /fabylø, -z/ *a* fabulous.

fac /fak/ *nf* [!] university.

façade /fasad/ *nf* front; (fig) façade.

face /fas/ *nf* face; (d'un objet) side; **en ~ (de), d'en ~** opposite; **en ~ de** (fig) faced with; **~ à** facing; (fig) faced with; **faire ~ à** face. **face-à-face** *nm inv* (débat) one-to-one debate.

fâcher /fɑʃe/ [1] *vt* anger; **fâché** angry; (désolé) sorry. □ **se ~** *vpr* get angry; (se brouiller) fall out.

facile /fasil/ *a* easy; (*caractère*) easygoing.

facilité /fasilite/ *nf* easiness; (aisance) ease; (aptitude) ability; **~s** (possibilités) facilities, opportunities; **~s d'importation** import opportunities; **~s de paiement** easy terms.

faciliter /fasilite/ [1] *vt* facilitate, make easier.

façon /fasɔ̃/ *nf* way; (de vêtement) cut; **de cette ~** in this way; **de ~ à** so as to; **de toute ~** anyway; **~s** (chichis) fuss; **faire des ~s** stand on ceremony; **sans ~s** (*repas*) informal; (*personne*) unpretentious. **façonner** [1] *vt* shape; (faire) make.

fac-similé (*pl* **~s**) /faksimile/ *nm* facsimile.

facteur, -trice /faktœʀ, -tʀis/ *nm, f* postman, postwoman. ● *nm* (élément) factor.

facture /faktyʀ/ *nf* bill; (Comm) invoice; **~ détaillée** itemized bill. **facturer** [1] *vt* invoice. **facturette** *nf* credit card slip.

facultatif, -ive /fakyltatif, -v/ *a* optional.

faculté /fakylte/ *nf* faculty; (possibilité) power; (Univ) faculty.

fade /fad/ *a* insipid.

faible /fɛbl/ *a* weak; (*espoir, quantité, écart*) slight; (*revenu, intensité*) low; **~ d'esprit** feeble-minded. ● *nm* (personne) weakling; (penchant) weakness. **faiblesse** *nf* weakness. **faiblir** [2] *vi* weaken.

faïence /fajɑ̃s/ *nf* earthenware.

faillir /fajiʀ/ [2] *vi* **j'ai failli acheter** I almost bought.

faillite /fajit/ *nf* bankruptcy; (fig) collapse.

faim /fɛ̃/ *nf* hunger; **avoir ~** be hungry; **rester sur sa ~** (fig) be left wanting more.

fainéant, ~e /feneɑ̃, -t/ *a* idle. ● *nm, f* idler.

faire /fɛʀ/ [33]

⇨ Pour les expressions comme **faire attention, faire la cuisine**, etc. ⇒**attention, cuisine**, etc.

● *verbe transitif*

····➤ (préparer, créer) make; **~ une tarte/une erreur** make a tart/a mistake.

····➤ (se livrer à une activité) do; **~ du droit** do law; **~ du foot/du violon** play football/the violin; **qu'est-ce qu'elle fait?** (dans la vie) what does she do?; (en ce moment précis) what is she doing?

····➤ (dans les calculs, mesures, etc.) **10 et 10 font 20** 10 and 10 make 20; **ça fait 25 francs** that's 25 francs; **~ 60 kilos** weigh 60 kilos; **il fait 1,75 m** he's 1.75 m tall.

····➤ (dans les expressions de temps) **ça fait une heure que j'attends** I have been waiting for an hour.

····➤ (imiter) **~ le clown** act the clown; **faire le malade** pretend to be ill.

····➤ (parcourir) **~ 10 km** do *ou* cover 10 km; **~ les musées** go round the museums.

····➤ (entraîner, causer) **ça ne fait rien** it doesn't matter; **l'accident a fait 8 morts** 8 people died in the accident.

····➤ (dire) say; **'excusez-moi', fit-elle** 'excuse me', she said.

● *verbe auxiliaire*

····➤ **(faire** + infinitif + qn) make; **~ pleurer qn** make sb cry.

····➤ **(faire** + infinitif + qch) have, get; **~ réparer sa voiture** have *ou* get one's car mended.

····➤ **(ne faire que** + infinitif) (continuellement) **ne ~ que pleurer** do nothing but cry; (seulement) **je ne fais qu'obéir** I'm only following orders.

● *verbe intransitif*

····➤ (agir) do, act; **~ vite** act quickly; **fais comme tu veux** do as you please; **fais comme chez toi** make yourself at home.

····➤ (paraître) look; **~ joli** look pretty; **ça fait cher** it's expensive.

····➤ (en parlant du temps) **il fait chaud/gris** it's hot/overcast.

□ **se faire** *verbe pronominal*

····➤ (obtenir, confectionner) make; **se ~ des amis** make friends; **se ~ un thé** make (oneself) a cup of tea.

····➤ **(se faire** + infinitif) **se ~ gronder** be scolded; **se ~ couper les cheveux** have one's hair cut.

····➤ (devenir) **il se fait tard** it's getting late.

····➤ (être d'usage) **ça ne se fait pas** it's not the done thing.

····➤ (emploi impersonnel) **comment se fait-il que tu sois ici?** how come you're here?

····➤ □ **se faire à** get used to; **je ne m'y fais pas** I can't get used to it.

····➤ □ **s'en faire** worry; **ne t'en fais pas** don't worry.

! Lorsque **faire** remplace un verbe plus précis, on traduira quelquefois par ce dernier: **faire une visite** *pay a visit*, **faire un nid** *build a nest.*

faire-part /fɛʀpaʀ/ *nm inv* announcement.

fais /fɛ/ ⇒FAIRE [33].

faisan /fəzɑ̃/ *nm* pheasant.

faisceau (*pl* **~x**) /fɛso/ *nm* (rayon) beam; (fagot) bundle.

fait, **~e** /fɛ, fɛt/ *a* done; (*fromage*) ripe; **~ pour** made for; **tout ~** ready made; **c'est bien ~ pour toi** it serves you right. ● *nm* fact; (événement) event; **au ~ (de)** informed (of); **de ce ~** therefore; **du ~ de** on account of; **~ divers** (trivial) news item; **~ nouveau** new development; **prendre qn sur le ~** catch sb in the act. ● ⇒FAIRE [33].

faîte /fɛt/ *nm* top; (fig) peak.

faites /fɛt/ ⇒FAIRE [33].

falaise /falɛz/ *nf* cliff.

falloir /falwaʀ/ [34] *vi* **il faut qch/qn** we/you *etc.* need sth/so; **il lui faut du pain** he needs bread; **il faut rester** we/you *etc.* have to *ou* must stay; **il faut que j'y aille** I have to *ou* must go; **il faudrait que tu partes** you should leave; **il aurait fallu le faire** we/you *etc.* should have done it; **comme il faut** (*manger, se tenir*) properly; (*personne*) respectable, proper. □ **s'en ~** *vpr* **il s'en est fallu de peu qu'il gagne** he nearly won; **il s'en faut de beaucoup que je sois** I am far from being.

falsifier /falsifje/ [45] *vt* falsify; (*signature, monnaie*) forge.

famé, **~e** /fame/ *a* **mal ~** disreputable, seedy.

fameux, **-euse** /famø, -z/ *a* famous; (excellent [!]) first-rate.

familial, **~e** (*mpl* **-iaux**) /familjal, -jo/ *a* family.

familiale /familjal/ *nf* estate car; (US) station wagon.

F

familiariser /familjaʀize/ [1] *vt* familiarize (**avec** with). □ **se ~** *vpr* familiarize oneself.

familier, **-ière** /familje, -jɛʀ/ *a* familiar; (amical) informal.

famille /famij/ *nf* family; **en ~** with one's family.

famine /famin/ *nf* famine.

fanatique /fanatik/ *a* fanatical. ● *nmf* fanatic.

fanfare /fɑ̃faʀ/ *nf* brass band; (musique) fanfare.

fantaisie /fɑ̃tezi/ *nf* imagination, fantasy; (caprice) whim; (**de**) ~ (*boutons etc.*) fancy. **fantaisiste** *a* unorthodox; (*personne*) eccentric.

fantasme /fɑ̃tasm/ *nm* fantasy.

fantastique /fɑ̃tastik/ *a* fantastic.

fantôme /fɑ̃tom/ *nm* ghost; **cabinet(-)~** (Pol) shadow cabinet.

faon /fɑ̃/ *nm* fawn.

FAQ *abrév f* (**Foire aux questions**) (Internet) FAQ, Frequently Asked Questions.

farce /faʀs/ *nf* (practical) joke; (Théât) farce; (hachis) stuffing.

farcir /faʀsiʀ/ [2] *vt* stuff.

fard /faʀ/ *nm* make-up; **~ à paupières** eye-shadow; **piquer un ~** blush.

fardeau (*pl* **~x**) /faʀdo/ *nm* burden.

farfelu, **~e** /faʀfəly/ *a & nm,f* eccentric.

farine /faʀin/ *nf* flour. **farineux**, **-euse** *a* floury. **farineux** *nmpl* starchy food.

farouche /faʀuʃ/ *a* shy; (peu sociable) unsociable; (violent) fierce.

fascicule /fasikyl/ *nm* (brochure) booklet; (partie d'un ouvrage) fascicule.

fasciner /fasine/ [1] *vt* fascinate.

fascisme /faʃism/ *nm* fascism.

fasse /fas/ ⇒FAIRE [33].

fast-food /fastfud/ *nm* fast-food place.

fastidieux, **-ieuse** /fastidjø, -z/ *a* tedious.

fatal, **~e** (*mpl* **~s**) /fatal/ *a* inevitable; (mortel) fatal. **fatalité** *nf* (destin) fate.

fatigant, **~e** /fatigɑ̃, -t/ *a* tiring; (ennuyeux) tiresome.

fatigue /fatig/ *nf* fatigue, tiredness.

fatigué, **~e** /fatige/ *a* tired.

fatiguer /fatige/ [1] *vt* tire; (*yeux, moteur*) strain. ● *vi* (*moteur*) labour. □ **se ~** *vpr* get tired, tire (**de** of).

faubourg /fobuʀ/ *nm* suburb.

faucher /foʃe/ [1] *vt* (*herbe*) mow; (voler 🄸) pinch; **~ qn** (*véhicule, tir*) mow sb down.

faucon /fokɔ̃/ *nm* falcon, hawk.

faudra, **faudrait** /fodʀa, fodʀɛ/ ⇒FALLOIR [34].

faufiler (se) /(sə)fofile/ [1] *vpr* edge one's way, squeeze.

faune /fon/ *nf* wildlife, fauna.

faussaire /fosɛʀ/ *nmf* forger.

fausse /fos/ ⇒FAUX[2].

fausser /fose/ [1] *vt* buckle; (fig) distort; **~ compagnie à qn** give sb the slip.

faut /fo/ ⇒FALLOIR [34].

faute /fot/ *nf* mistake; (responsabilité) fault; (délit) offence; (péché) sin; **en ~** at fault; **~ de** for want of; **~ de quoi** failing which; **sans ~** without fail; **~ de frappe** typing error; **~ de goût** bad taste; **~ professionnelle** professional misconduct.

fauteuil /fotœj/ *nm* armchair; (de président) chair; (Théât) seat; **~ roulant** wheelchair.

fautif, **-ive** /fotif, -v/ *a* guilty; (faux) faulty. ● *nm, f* guilty party.

fauve /fov/ *a* (couleur) fawn, tawny. ● *nm* wild cat.

faux[1] /fo/ *nf* scythe.

faux², **fausse** /fo, fos/ *a* false; (falsifié) fake, forged; (*numéro, calcul*) wrong; (*voix*) out of tune; **c'est ~!** that is wrong!; **~ témoignage** perjury; **faire ~ bond à qn** stand sb up; **fausse couche** miscarriage; **~ frais** incidental expenses. ●*adv* (*chanter*) out of tune. ●*nm* forgery. **faux-filet** (*pl* **~s**) *nm* sirloin.

faveur /favœʀ/ *nf* favour; **de ~** (*régime*) preferential; **en ~ de** in favour of.

favorable /favɔʀabl/ *a* favourable.

favori, **~te** /favɔʀi, -t/ *a & nm,f* favourite. **favoriser** [1] *vt* favour.

fax /faks/ *nm* fax. **faxer** [1] *vt* fax.

fébrile /febʀil/ *a* feverish.

fécond, **~e** /fekɔ̃, -d/ *a* fertile. **féconder** [1] *vt* fertilize. **fécondité** *nf* fertility.

fédéral, **~e** (*mpl* **-aux**) /fedeʀal, -o/ *a* federal. **fédération** *nf* federation.

fée /fe/ *nf* fairy. **féerie** *nf* magical spectacle. **féerique** *a* magical.

feindre /fɛ̃dʀ/ [22] *vt* feign; **~ de** pretend to.

fêler /fele/ [1] *vt* crack. □ **se ~** *vpr* crack.

félicitations /felisitasjɔ̃/ *nfpl* congratulations (**pour** on). **féliciter** [1] *vt* congratulate (**de** on).

félin, **~e** /felɛ̃, -in/ *a & nm* feline.

femelle /fəmɛl/ *a & nf* female.

féminin, **~e** /feminɛ̃, -in/ *a* feminine; (*sexe*) female; (*mode, équipe*) women's. ●*nm* feminine. **féministe** *nmf* feminist.

femme /fam/ *nf* woman; (épouse) wife; **~ au foyer** housewife; **~ de chambre** chambermaid; **~ de ménage** cleaning lady.

fémur /femyʀ/ *nm* thigh-bone.

fendre /fɑ̃dʀ/ [3] *vt* (couper) split; (fissurer) crack. □ **se ~** *vpr* crack.

fenêtre /fənɛtʀ/ *nf* window.

fenouil /fənuj/ *nm* fennel.

fente /fɑ̃t/ *nf* (ouverture) slit, slot; (fissure) crack.

féodal, **~e** (*mpl* **-aux**) /feɔdal, -o/ *a* feudal.

fer /fɛʀ/ *nm* iron; **~ (à repasser)** iron; **~ à cheval** horseshoe; **~ de lance** spearhead; **~ forgé** wrought iron.

fera, **ferait** /fəʀa, fəʀɛ/ ⇒FAIRE [33].

férié, **~e** /feʀje/ *a* **jour ~** public holiday.

ferme /fɛʀm/ *nf* farm; (maison) farm(house). ●*a* firm. ●*adv* (*travailler*) hard.

fermé, **~e** /fɛʀme/ *a* closed; (*gaz, radio*) off.

fermenter /fɛʀmɑ̃te/ [1] *vi* ferment.

fermer /fɛʀme/ [1] *vt/i* close, shut; (cesser d'exploiter) close *ou* shut down; (*gaz, robinet*) turn off. □ **se ~** *vpr* close, shut.

fermeté /fɛʀməte/ *nf* firmness.

fermeture /fɛʀmətyʀ/ *nf* closing; (dispositif) catch; **~ annuelle** annual closure; **~ éclair®** zip(-fastener); (US) zipper.

fermier, **-ière** /fɛʀmje, -jɛʀ/ *a* farm. ●*nm* farmer. **fermière** *nf* farmer's wife.

féroce /feʀɔs/ *a* ferocious.

ferraille /fɛʀɑj/ *nf* scrap-iron.

ferrer /feʀe/ [1] *vt* (*cheval*) shoe.

ferroviaire /fɛʀɔvjɛʀ/ *a* rail(way).

ferry /fɛʀi/ *nm* ferry.

fertile /fɛʀtil/ *a* fertile; **~ en** (fig) rich in. **fertiliser** [1] *vt* fertilize. **fertilité** *nf* fertility.

fervent, **~e** /fɛʀvɑ̃, -t/ *a* fervent. ●*nm,f* enthusiast (**de** of).

fesse /fɛs/ *nf* buttock. **fessée** *nf* spanking, smack.

festin /fɛstɛ̃/ *nm* feast.

festival (*pl* **~s**) /fɛstival/ *nm* festival.

fêtard, **∼e** /fɛtaʀ, -d/ *nm, f* [!] party animal.

fête /fɛt/ *nf* holiday; (religieuse) feast; (du nom) name-day; (réception) party; (en famille) celebration; (foire) fair; (folklorique) festival; **∼ des Mères** Mother's Day; **∼ foraine** fun-fair; **faire la ∼** live it up; **les ∼s (de fin d'année)** the Christmas season. **fêter** [1] *vt* celebrate; (*personne*) give a celebration for.

fétiche /fetiʃ/ *nm* fetish; (fig) mascot.

feu¹ (*pl* **∼x**) /fø/ *nm* fire; (lumière) light; (de réchaud) burner; **à ∼ doux/vif** on a low/high heat; **∼ rouge/vert/orange** red/green/amber light; **aux ∼x, tournez à droite** turn right at the traffic lights; **avez-vous du ∼?** (pour cigarette) have you got a light?; **au ∼!** fire!; **mettre le ∼ à** set fire to; **prendre ∼** catch fire; **jouer avec le ∼** play with fire; **ne pas faire long ∼** not last; **∼ d'artifice** firework display; **∼ de joie** bonfire; **∼ de position** sidelight.

feu² /fø/ *a inv* (mort) late.

feuillage /fœjaʒ/ *nm* foliage.

feuille /fœj/ *nf* leaf; (de papier) sheet; (formulaire) form; **∼ d'impôts** tax return; **∼ de paie** payslip.

feuilleté, **∼e** /fœjte/ *a* **pâte ∼e** puff pastry. ● *nm* savoury pasty.

feuilleter /fœjte/ [1] *vt* leaf through.

feuilleton /fœjtɔ̃/ *nm* (à suivre) serial; (histoire complète) series.

feutre /føtʀ/ *nm* felt; (chapeau) felt hat; (crayon) felt-tip (pen).

fève /fɛv/ *nf* broad bean.

février /fevʀije/ *nm* February.

fiable /fjabl/ *a* reliable.

fiançailles /fjɑ̃saj/ *nfpl* engagement.

fiancé, **∼e** /fjɑ̃se/ *a* engaged. ● *nm* fiancé. **fiancée** *nf* fiancée.

fiancer (se) [10] *vpr* become engaged (**avec** to).

fibre /fibʀ/ *nf* fibre; **∼ de verre** fibreglass.

ficeler /fisle/ [38] *vt* tie up.

ficelle /fisɛl/ *nf* string.

fiche /fiʃ/ *nf* (index) card; (formulaire) form, slip; (Électr) plug.

ficher¹ /fiʃe/ [1] *vt* (enfoncer) drive (**dans** into).

ficher² /fiʃe/ [1] [!] *vt* (faire) do; (donner) give; (mettre) put; **∼ le camp** clear off. □ **se ∼ de** *vpr* make fun of; **il s'en fiche** he couldn't care less.

fichier /fiʃje/ *nm* file.

fichu, **∼e** /fiʃy/ *a* [!] (mauvais) rotten; (raté) done for; **mal ∼** terrible.

fictif, **-ive** /fiktif, -v/ *a* fictitious. **fiction** *nf* fiction.

fidèle /fidɛl/ *a* faithful. ● *nmf* (client) regular; (Relig) believer; **∼s** (à l'église) congregation. **fidélité** *nf* fidelity.

fier¹, **fière** /fjɛʀ/ *a* proud (**de** of).

fier² (se) /(sə)fje/ [45] *vpr* **se ∼ à** trust.

fierté /fjɛʀte/ *nf* pride.

fièvre /fjɛvʀ/ *nf* fever; **avoir de la ∼** have a temperature. **fiévreux**, **-euse** *a* feverish.

figer /fiʒe/ [40] *vi* (*graisse*) congeal; (*sang*) clot; **figé sur place** frozen to the spot. □ **se ∼** *vpr* (*personne, sourire*) freeze; (*graisse*) congeal; (*sang*) clot.

figue /fig/ *nf* fig.

figurant, **∼e** /figyʀɑ̃, -t/ *nm, f* (au cinéma) extra.

figure /figyʀ/ *nf* face; (forme, personnage) figure; (illustration) picture.

figuré, **∼e** /figyʀe/ *a* (*sens*) figurative.

figurer /figyʀe/ [1] *vi* appear. ● *vt* represent. □ **se ∼** *vpr* imagine.

fil /fil/ *nm* thread; (métallique,

électrique) wire; (de couteau) edge; (à coudre) cotton; **au ~ de** with the passing of; **au ~ de l'eau** with the current; **~ de fer** wire; **au bout du ~** ▣ on the phone.

file /fil/ *nf* line; (voie: Auto) lane; **~ (d'attente)** queue; (US) line; **en ~ indienne** in single file.

filer /file/ [1] *vt* spin; (suivre) shadow; **~ qch à qn** ▣ slip sb sth. ● *vi* (*bas*) ladder, run; (*liquide*) run; (aller vite ▣) speed along, fly by; (partir ▣) dash off; (disparaître ▣) **~ entre les mains** slip through one's fingers; **~ doux** do as one's told; **~ à l'anglaise** take French leave.

filet /filɛ/ *nm* net; (d'eau) trickle; (de viande) fillet; **~ (à bagages)** (luggage) rack; **~ à provisions** string bag (*for shopping*).

filiale /filjal/ *nf* subsidiary (company).

filière /filjɛʀ/ *nf* (official) channels; (de trafiquants) network; **passer par** *ou* **suivre la ~** (*employé*) work one's way up.

fille /fij/ *nf* girl; (opposé à fils) daughter. **fillette** *nf* little girl.

filleul /fijœl/ *nm* godson.

filleule /fijœl/ *nf* god-daughter.

film /film/ *nm* film; **~ d'épouvante/muet/parlant** horror/ silent/talking film; **~ dramatique** drama. **filmer** [1] *vt* film.

filon /filɔ̃/ *nm* (Géol) seam; (travail lucratif ▣) money spinner; **avoir trouvé le bon ~** be onto a good thing.

fils /fis/ *nm* son.

filtre /filtʀ/ *nm* filter. **filtrer** [1] *vt/i* filter; (*personne*) screen.

fin[1] /fɛ̃/ *nf* end; **à la ~** finally; **en ~ de compte** all things considered; **~ de semaine** weekend; **mettre ~ à** put an end to; **prendre ~** come to an end.

fin[2], **~e** /fɛ̃, in/ *a* fine; (*tranche, couche*) thin; (*taille*) slim; (*plat*) exquisite; (*esprit, vue*) sharp; **~es herbes** mixed herbs. ● *adv* (*couper*) finely.

final, **~e** (*mpl* **-aux**) /final, -o/ *a* final.

finale /final/ *nm* (Mus) finale. ● *nf* (Sport) final; (Gram) final syllable. **finalement** *adv* finally; (somme toute) after all. **finaliste** *nmf* finalist.

finance /finɑ̃s/ *nf* finance.

financer [10] *vt* finance.

financier, **-ière** /finɑ̃sje, -jɛʀ/ *a* financial. ● *nm* financier.

finesse /finɛs/ *nf* fineness; (de taille) slimness; (acuité) sharpness; **~s** (de langue) niceties.

finir /finiʀ/ [2] *vt/i* finish, end; (arrêter) stop; (manger) finish (up); **en ~ avec** have done with; **~ par faire** end up doing; **ça va mal ~** it will turn out badly.

finlandais, **~e** /fɛ̃lɑ̃dɛ, -z/ *a* Finnish. **F~**, **~e** *nm, f* Finn.

Finlande /fɛ̃lɑ̃d/ *nf* Finland.

finnois, **~e** /finwa/ *a* Finnish. ● *nm* (Ling) Finnish.

firme /fiʀm/ *nf* firm.

fisc /fisk/ *nm* tax authorities. **fiscal**, **~e** (*mpl* **-aux**) *a* tax, fiscal. **fiscalité** *nf* tax system.

fissure /fisyʀ/ *nf* crack.

fixe /fiks/ *a* fixed; (stable) steady; **à heure ~** at a set time; **menu à prix ~** set menu. ● *nm* basic pay.

fixer /fikse/ [1] *vt* fix; **~ (du regard)** stare at; **être fixé** (*personne*) have made up one's mind. □ **se ~** *vpr* (s'attacher) be attached, (s'installer) settle down.

flacon /flakɔ̃/ *nm* bottle.

flagrant, **~e** /flagʀɑ̃, -t/ *a* flagrant, blatant; **en ~ délit** in the act.

flair /flɛʀ/ *nm* (sense of) smell; (fig) intuition.

flamand, **~e** /flamɑ̃, -d/ *a*

F

Flemish. ● *nm* (Ling) Flemish. **F∼, ∼e** *nm, f* Fleming.

flamant /flamɑ̃/ *nm* flamingo.

flambeau (*pl* **∼x**) /flɑ̃bo/ *nm* torch.

flambée /flɑ̃be/ *nf* blaze; (fig) explosion.

flamber /flɑ̃be/ [1] *vi* blaze; (*prix*) shoot up. ● *vt* (*aiguille*) sterilize; (*volaille*) singe.

flamme /flam/ *nf* flame; (fig) ardour; **en ∼s** ablaze.

flan /flɑ̃/ *nm* custard tart.

flanc /flɑ̃/ *nm* side; (d'animal, d'armée) flank.

flâner /flɑne/ [1] *vi* stroll. **flânerie** *nf* stroll.

flanquer /flɑ̃ke/ [1] *vt* flank; (jeter [!]) chuck; (donner [!]) give; **∼ à la porte** kick out.

flaque /flak/ *nf* (d'eau) puddle; (de sang) pool.

flash (*pl* **∼es**) /flaʃ/ *nm* (Photo) flash; (information) news flash; **∼ publicitaire** commercial.

flatter /flate/ [1] *vt* flatter. □ **se ∼ de** *vpr* pride oneself on.

flatteur, -euse /flatœʀ, -øz/ *a* flattering. ● *nm, f* flatterer.

fléau (*pl* **∼x**) /fleo/ *nm* (désastre) scourge; (personne) pest.

flèche /flɛʃ/ *nf* arrow; (de clocher) spire; **monter en ∼** spiral; **partir en ∼** shoot off.

flécher /fleʃe/ [14] *vt* mark *ou* signpost (with arrows). **fléchette** *nf* dart.

fléchir /fleʃiʀ/ [2] *vt* bend; (*personne*) move, sway. ● *vi* (faiblir) weaken; (*prix*) fall; (*poutre*) sag, bend.

flemme /flɛm/ *nf* [!] laziness; **j'ai la ∼ de faire** I can't be bothered doing.

flétrir (se) /(sə)fletʀiʀ/ [2] *vpr* (*plante*) wither; (*fruit*) shrivel; (*beauté*) fade.

fleur /flœʀ/ *nf* flower; **à ∼ de terre/d'eau** just above the ground/ water; **à ∼s** flowery; **∼ de l'âge** prime of life; **en ∼s** in flower.

fleurir /flœʀiʀ/ [2] *vi* flower; (*arbre*) blossom; (fig) flourish. ● *vt* decorate with flowers. **fleuriste** *nmf* florist.

fleuve /flœv/ *nm* river.

flic /flik/ *nm* [!] cop.

flipper /flipœʀ/ *nm* pinball (machine).

flirter /flœʀte/ [1] *vi* flirt.

flocon /flɔkɔ̃/ *nm* flake.

flore /flɔʀ/ *nf* flora.

florissant, ∼e /flɔʀisɑ̃, -t/ *a* flourishing.

flot /flo/ *nm* flood, stream; **être à ∼** be afloat; **les ∼s** the waves.

flottant, ∼e /flɔtɑ̃, -t/ *a* (*vêtement*) loose; (indécis) indecisive.

flotte /flɔt/ *nf* fleet; (pluie [!]) rain; (eau [!]) water.

flottement /flɔtmɑ̃/ *nm* (incertitude) indecision.

flotter /flɔte/ [1] *vi* float; (*drapeau*) flutter; (*nuage, parfum, pensées*) drift; (pleuvoir [!]) rain. **flotteur** *nm* float.

flou, ∼e /flu/ *a* out of focus; (fig) vague.

fluctuer /flyktɥe/ [1] *vi* fluctuate.

fluet, ∼te /flyɛ, -t/ *a* thin.

fluide /flɥid/ *a & nm* fluid.

fluor /flyɔʀ/ *nm* (pour les dents) fluoride.

fluorescent, ∼e /flyɔʀɛsɑ̃, -t/ *a* fluorescent.

flûte /flyt/ *nf* flute; (verre) champagne glass.

fluvial, ∼e (*mpl* **-iaux**) /flyvjal, -jo/ *a* river.

flux /fly/ *nm* flow; **∼ et reflux** ebb and flow.

FM *abrév f* **(frequency modulation)** FM.

fœtus /fetys/ *nm* foetus.

foi /fwa/ *nf* faith; **être de bonne/mauvaise ~** be acting in good/bad faith; **ma ~!** well (indeed)!

foie /fwa/ *nm* liver.

foin /fwɛ̃/ *nm* hay.

foire /fwaʀ/ *nf* fair; **faire la ~** [!] live it up.

fois /fwa/ *nf* time; **une ~** once; **deux ~** twice; **à la ~** at the same time; **des ~** (parfois) sometimes; **une ~ pour toutes** once and for all.

fol /fɔl/ ⇒FOU.

folie /fɔli/ *nf* madness; (bêtise) foolish thing, folly; **faire une ~, faire des ~s** be extravagant.

folklore /fɔlklɔʀ/ *nm* folklore. **folklorique** *a* folk; [!] eccentric.

folle /fɔl/ ⇒FOU.

foncé, ~e /fɔ̃se/ *a* dark.

foncer /fɔ̃se/ [10] *vt* darken. ●*vi* (s'assombrir) darken; (aller vite [!]) dash along; **~ sur** [!] charge at.

foncier, -ière /fɔ̃sje, -jɛʀ/ *a* fundamental; (Comm) real estate.

fonction /fɔ̃ksjɔ̃/ *nf* function; (emploi) position; **~s** (obligations) duties; **en ~ de** according to; **~ publique** civil service; **voiture de ~** company car. **fonctionnaire** *nmf* civil servant. **fonctionnement** *nm* working.

fonctionner /fɔ̃ksjɔne/ [1] *vi* work; **faire ~** work.

fond /fɔ̃/ *nm* bottom; (de salle, magasin, etc.) back; (essentiel) basis; (contenu) content; (plan) background; (Sport) long-distance running; **à ~** thoroughly; **au ~** basically; **de ~** (*bruit*) background; **de ~ en comble** from top to bottom; **au** *ou* **dans le ~** really; **~ de teint** foundation, make-up base.

fondamental, ~e (*mpl* **-aux**) /fɔ̃damɑ̃tal, -o/ *a* fundamental.

fondateur, -trice /fɔ̃datœʀ, -tʀis/ *nm,f* founder. **fondation** *nf* foundation.

fonder /fɔ̃de/ [1] *vt* found; (baser) base (**sur** on); (**bien**) **fondé** well-founded. □ **se ~ sur** *vpr* be guided by, be based on.

fonderie /fɔ̃dʀi/ *nf* foundry.

fondre /fɔ̃dʀ/ [3] *vt/i* melt; (dans l'eau) dissolve; (mélanger) merge; **faire ~** melt; dissolve; **~ en larmes** burst into tears; **~ sur** swoop on. □ **se ~** *vpr* merge.

fonds /fɔ̃/ *nm* fund; **~ de commerce** business. ●*nmpl* (capitaux) funds.

fondu, ~e /fɔ̃dy/ *a* melted; (métal) molten.

font /fɔ̃/ ⇒FAIRE [33].

fontaine /fɔ̃tɛn/ *nf* fountain; (source) spring.

fonte /fɔ̃t/ *nf* melting; (fer) cast iron; **~ des neiges** thaw.

foot /fut/ *nm* [!] football.

football /futbol/ *nm* football.

footing /futiŋ/ *nm* jogging.

forain /fɔʀɛ̃/ *nm* fairground entertainer; **marchand ~** stall-holder.

forçat /fɔʀsa/ *nm* convict.

force /fɔʀs/ *nf* force; (physique) strength; (hydraulique etc.) power; **~s** (physiques) strength; **à ~ de** by sheer force of; **de ~, par la ~** by force; **~ de dissuasion** deterrent; **~ de frappe** strike force, deterrent; **~ de l'âge** prime of life; **~s de l'ordre** police (force); **~s de marché** market forces.

forcé, ~e /fɔʀse/ *a* forced; (inévitable) inevitable; **c'est ~ qu'il fasse** [!] he's bound to do. **forcément** *adv* necessarily; (évidemment) obviously.

forcené, ~e /fɔʀsəne/ *a* frenzied. ●*nm,f* maniac.

forcer /fɔʀse/ [10] *vt* force (**à faire** to do); (*voix*) strain; **~ la dose** [!] overdo it. ●*vi* force; (exagérer) overdo it. ▫ **se ~** *vpr* force oneself.

forer /fɔʀe/ [1] *vt* drill.

forestier, -ière /fɔʀɛstje, -jɛʀ/ *a* forest. ● *nm, f* forestry worker.

forêt /fɔʀɛ/ *nf* forest.

forfait /fɔʀfɛ/ *nm* (Comm) (prix fixe) fixed price; (offre promotionnelle) package. **forfaitaire** *a* (*prix*) fixed.

forger /fɔʀʒe/ [40] *vt* forge; (inventer) make up.

forgeron /fɔʀʒəʀɔ̃/ *nm* blacksmith.

formaliser (se) /(sə)fɔʀmalize/ [1] *vpr* take offence (**de** at).

formalité /fɔʀmalite/ *nf* formality.

format /fɔʀma/ *nm* format. **formater** [1] *vt* (Ordinat) format.

formation /fɔʀmasjɔ̃/ *nf* formation; (professionnelle) training; (culture) education; **~ permanente** *ou* **continue** continuing education.

forme /fɔʀm/ *nf* form; (contour) shape, form; **~s** (de femme) figure; **être en ~** be in good shape, be on form; **en ~ de** in the shape of; **en bonne et due ~** in due form.

formel, ~le /fɔʀmɛl/ *a* formal; (catégorique) positive.

former /fɔʀme/ [1] *vt* form; (instruire) train. ▫ **se ~** *vpr* form.

formidable /fɔʀmidabl/ *a* fantastic.

formulaire /fɔʀmylɛʀ/ *nm* form.

formule /fɔʀmyl/ *nf* formula; (expression) expression; (feuille) form; **~ de politesse** polite phrase, letter ending. **formuler** [1] *vt* formulate.

fort, ~e /fɔʀ, -t/ *a* strong; (grand) big; (*pluie*) heavy; (*bruit*) loud; (*pente*) steep; (*élève*) clever; **au plus ~ de** at the height of; **c'est une ~e tête** she/he's headstrong. ● *adv* (*frapper*) hard; (*parler*) loud; (très) very; (beaucoup) very much. ● *nm* (atout) strong point; (Mil) fort.

fortifiant /fɔʀtifjɑ̃/ *nm* tonic. **fortifier** [45] *vt* fortify.

fortune /fɔʀtyn/ *nf* fortune; **de ~** (improvisé) makeshift; **faire ~** make one's fortune.

forum /fɔʀɔm/ *nm* forum; **~ de discussion** (Internet) newsgroup.

fosse /fos/ *nf* pit; (tombe) grave; **~ d'orchestre** orchestra pit; **~ septique** septic tank.

fossé /fose/ *nm* ditch; (fig) gulf.

fossette /fosɛt/ *nf* dimple.

fossile /fosil/ *nm* fossil.

fou (**fol** *before vowel or mute h*), **folle** /fu, fɔl/ *a* mad; (*course, regard*) wild; (énorme ▣) tremendous; **~ de** crazy about; **le ~ rire** the giggles. ● *nm* madman; (bouffon) jester. **folle** *nf* madwoman.

foudre /fudʀ/ *nf* lightning.

foudroyant, ~e /fudʀwajɑ̃, -t/ *a* (*mort, maladie*) violent.

foudroyer /fudʀwaje/ [31] *vt* (*orage*) strike; (*maladie etc.*) strike down; **~ qn du regard** look daggers at sb.

fouet /fwɛ/ *nm* whip; (Culin) whisk.

fougère /fuʒɛʀ/ *nf* fern.

fougue /fug/ *nf* ardour. **fougueux, -euse** *a* ardent.

fouille /fuj/ *nf* search; (Archéol) excavation.

fouiller /fuje/ [1] *vt/i* search; (creuser) dig; **~ dans** (*tiroir*) rummage through.

fouillis /fuji/ *nm* jumble.

foulard /fulaʀ/ *nm* scarf.

foule /ful/ *nf* crowd; **une ~ de** (fig) a mass of.

foulée /fule/ *nf* stride; **il l'a fait dans la ~** he did it while he was at *ou* about it.

fouler /fule/ [1] *vt* (*raisin*) press; (*sol*) set foot on; **~ qch aux pieds**

trample sth underfoot; (fig) ride roughshod over sth. □ **se ~** *vpr* **se ~ le poignet/le pied** sprain one's wrist/foot; **ne pas se ~** [!] not strain oneself.

four /fuʀ/ *nm* oven; (de potier) kiln; (Théât) flop; **~ à micro-ondes** microwave oven; **~ crématoire** crematorium.

fourbe /fuʀb/ *a* deceitful.

fourche /fuʀʃ/ *nf* fork; (à foin) pitchfork. **fourchette** *nf* fork; (Comm) bracket, range.

fourgon /fuʀgɔ̃/ *nm* van; (wagon) wagon; **~ mortuaire** hearse.

fourmi /fuʀmi/ *nf* ant; **avoir des ~s** have pins and needles.

fourmiller /fuʀmije/ [1] *vi* swarm (**de** with).

fourneau (*pl* **~x**) /fuʀno/ *nm* stove.

fourni, **~e** /fuʀni/ *a* (épais) thick.

fournir /fuʀniʀ/ [2] *vt* supply, provide; (*client*) supply; (*effort*) put in; **~ à qn** supply sb with. □ **se ~ chez** *vpr* shop at.

fournisseur /fuʀnisœʀ/ *nm* supplier; **~ d'accès à l'Internet** Internet service provider.

fourniture /fuʀnityʀ/ *nf* supply.

fourrage /fuʀaʒ/ *nm* fodder.

fourré, **~e** /fuʀe/ *a* (*vêtement*) fur-lined; (*gâteau etc.*) filled (*with jam, cream, etc.*). ● *nm* thicket.

fourre-tout /fuʀtu/ *nm inv* (sac) holdall.

fourreur /fuʀœʀ/ *nm* furrier.

fourrière /fuʀjɛʀ/ *nf* (lieu) pound.

fourrure /fuʀyʀ/ *nf* fur.

foutre /futʀ/ [3] *vt* [✱] = **ficher²** [1].

foutu, **~e** /futy/ *a* [✱] = **fichu**.

foyer /fwaje/ *nm* home; (âtre) hearth; (club) club; (d'étudiants) hostel; (Théât) foyer; (Photo) focus; (centre) centre.

fracas /fʀaka/ *nm* din; (de train) roar; (d'objet qui tombe) crash.

fracassant, **~e** *a* (bruyant) deafening; (violent) shattering.

fraction /fʀaksjɔ̃/ *nf* fraction.

fracture /fʀaktyʀ/ *nf* fracture; **~ du poignet** fractured wrist.

fragile /fʀaʒil/ *a* fragile; (*peau*) sensitive; (*cœur*) weak. **fragilité** *nf* fragility.

fragment /fʀagmɑ̃/ *nm* bit, fragment. **fragmenter** [1] *vt* split, fragment.

fraîchement /fʀɛʃmɑ̃/ *adv* (récemment) freshly; (avec froideur) coolly. **fraîcheur** *nf* coolness; (nouveauté) freshness. **fraîchir** [2] *vi* freshen, become colder.

frais¹, **fraîche** /fʀɛ, -ʃ/ *a* fresh; (*temps, accueil*) cool; (*peinture*) wet; **~ et dispos** fresh; **il fait ~** it is cool. ● *adv* (récemment) newly, freshly. ● *nm* **mettre au ~** put in a cool place; **prendre le ~** get some fresh air.

frais² /fʀɛ/ *nmpl* expenses; (droits) fees; **aux ~ de** at the expense of; **faire des ~** spend a lot of money; **~ généraux** (Comm) overheads, running expenses; **~ de scolarité** school fees.

fraise /fʀɛz/ *nf* strawberry. **fraisier** *nm* strawberry plant; (gâteau) strawberry gateau.

framboise /fʀɑ̃bwaz/ *nf* raspberry. **framboisier** *nm* raspberry bush.

franc, **franche** /fʀɑ̃, -ʃ/ *a* frank; (*regard*) frank, candid; (*cassure*) clean; (net) clear; (libre) free; (véritable) downright. ● *nm* franc.

français, **~e** /fʀɑ̃sɛ, -z/ *a* French. ● *nm* (Ling) French. **F~**, **~e** *nm, f* Frenchman, Frenchwoman.

France /fʀɑ̃s/ *nf* France.

franchement /fʀɑ̃ʃmɑ̃/ *adv* frankly; (nettement) clearly; (tout à fait) really.

franchir /fʀɑ̃ʃiʀ/ [2] *vt* (*obstacle*)

get over; (*distance*) cover; (*limite*) exceed; (traverser) cross.
franchise /fʀɑ̃ʃiz/ *nf* (qualité) frankness; (Comm) franchise; (exemption) exemption; ~ **douanière** exemption from duties.
franc-maçon (*pl* **francs-maçons**) /fʀɑ̃masɔ̃/ *nm* Freemason. **franc-maçonnerie** *nf* Freemasonry.
franco /fʀɑ̃ko/ *adv* postage paid.
francophone /fʀɑ̃kɔfɔn/ *a* French-speaking. ●*nmf* French speaker.
franc-parler /fʀɑ̃paʀle/ *nm inv* outspokenness.
frange /fʀɑ̃ʒ/ *nf* fringe.
frappe /fʀap/ *nf* (de texte) typing.
frappé, ~**e** /fʀape/ *a* chilled.
frapper /fʀape/ [1] *vt/i* strike; (battre) hit, strike; (*monnaie*) mint; (à la porte) knock, bang; **frappé de panique** panic-stricken.
fraternel, ~**le** /fʀatɛʀnɛl/ *a* brotherly. **fraternité** *nf* brotherhood.
fraude /fʀod/ *nf* fraud; (à un examen) cheating; **passer qch en** ~ smuggle sth in. **frauder** [1] *vt/i* cheat. **frauduleux**, **-euse** *a* fraudulent.
frayer /fʀeje/ [31] *vt* open up. ▫ **se** ~ *vpr* **se** ~ **un passage** force one's way (**à travers, dans** through).
frayeur /fʀɛjœʀ/ *nf* fright.
fredonner /fʀədɔne/ [1] *vt* hum.
free-lance /fʀilɑ̃s/ *a & nmf* freelance.
freezer /fʀizœʀ/ *nm* freezer.
frein /fʀɛ̃/ *nm* brake; **mettre un** ~ **à** curb; ~ **à main** hand brake.
freiner /fʀene/ [1] *vt* slow down; (modérer, enrayer) curb. ●*vi* (Auto) brake.
frêle /fʀɛl/ *a* frail.
frelon /fʀəlɔ̃/ *nm* hornet.
frémir /fʀemiʀ/ [2] *vi* shudder, shake; (*feuille, eau*) quiver.
frêne /fʀɛn/ *nm* ash.
frénésie /fʀenezi/ *nf* frenzy. **frénétique** *a* frenzied.
fréquemment /fʀekamɑ̃/ *adv* frequently. **fréquence** *nf* frequency. **fréquent**, ~**e** *a* frequent. **fréquentation** *nf* frequenting.
fréquentations /fʀekɑ̃tasjɔ̃/ *nfpl* acquaintances; **avoir de mauvaises** ~ keep bad company.
fréquenter /fʀekɑ̃te/ [1] *vt* frequent; (*école*) attend; (*personne*) see.
frère /fʀɛʀ/ *nm* brother.
fret /fʀɛt/ *nm* freight.
friand, ~**e** /fʀijɑ̃, -d/ *a* ~ **de** very fond of.
friandise /fʀijɑ̃diz/ *nf* sweet; (US) candy; (gâteau) cake.
fric /fʀik/ *nm* ▣ money.
friction /fʀiksjɔ̃/ *nf* friction; (massage) rub-down.
frigidaire® /fʀiʒidɛʀ/ *nm* refrigerator.
frigo /fʀigo/ *nm* ▣ fridge. **frigorifique** *a* (*vitrine etc.*) refrigerated.
frileux, **-euse** /fʀilø, -z/ *a* sensitive to cold.
frime /fʀim/ *nf* ▣ **c'est de la** ~ it's all pretence; **pour la** ~ for show.
frimousse /fʀimus/ *nf* face.
fringale /fʀɛ̃gal/ *nf* ▣ ravenous appetite.
fringant, ~**e** /fʀɛ̃gɑ̃, -t/ *a* dashing.
fringues /fʀɛ̃g/ *nfpl* ▣ gear.
friper /fʀipe/ [1] *vt* crumple, crease. ▫ **se** ~ *vpr* crumple, crease.
fripon, ~**ne** /fʀipɔ̃, -ɔn/ *nm,f* rascal. ●*a* mischievous.
fripouille /fʀipuj/ *nf* rogue.
frire /fʀiʀ/ [56] *vt/i* fry; **faire** ~ fry.

frise /fʀiz/ *nf* frieze.

friser /fʀize/ [1] *vt/i* (*cheveux*) curl; (*personne*) curl the hair of; **frisé** curly.

frisson /fʀisɔ̃/ *nm* (de froid) shiver; (de peur) shudder. **frissonner** [1] *vi* shiver; shudder.

frit, **~e** /fʀi, -t/ *a* fried.

frite /fʀit/ *nf* chip; **avoir la ~** ▣ feel good.

friteuse /fʀitøz/ *nf* chip pan; (électrique) (deep) fryer.

friture /fʀityʀ/ *nf* fried fish; (huile) (frying) oil *ou* fat.

frivole /fʀivɔl/ *a* frivolous.

froid, **~e** /fʀwa, -d/ *a & nm* cold; **avoir/prendre ~** be/catch cold; **il fait ~** it is cold. **froidement** *adv* coldly; (*calculer*) coolly. **froideur** *nf* coldness.

froisser /fʀwase/ [1] *vt* crumple; (fig) offend. □ **se ~** *vpr* crumple; (fig) take offence; **se ~ un muscle** strain a muscle.

frôler /fʀole/ [1] *vt* brush against, skim; (fig) come close to.

fromage /fʀɔmaʒ/ *nm* cheese.

fromager, **-ère** /fʀɔmaʒe, -ɛʀ/ *a* cheese. ● *nm, f* (fabricant) cheese-maker; (marchand) cheesemonger.

froment /fʀɔmɑ̃/ *nm* wheat.

froncer /fʀɔ̃se/ [10] *vt* gather; **~ les sourcils** frown.

front /fʀɔ̃/ *nm* forehead; (Mil, Pol) front; **de ~** at the same time; (de face) head-on; (côte à côte) abreast; **faire ~ à** face up to. **frontal**, **~e** (*mpl* **-aux**) *a* frontal; (Ordinat) front-end.

frontalier, **-ière** /fʀɔ̃talje, -jɛʀ/ *a* border; **travailleur ~** commuter from across the border.

frontière /fʀɔ̃tjɛʀ/ *nf* border, frontier.

frottement /fʀɔtmɑ̃/ *nm* rubbing; (Tech) friction. **frotter** [1] *vt/i* rub; (*allumette*) strike.

frottis /fʀɔti/ *nm* **~ vaginal** cervical smear.

frousse /fʀus/ *nf* ▣ fear; **avoir la ~** ▣ be scared.

fructifier /fʀyktifje/ [45] *vi* **faire ~** put to work.

fructueux, **-euse** /fʀyktɥø, -z/ *a* fruitful.

frugal, **~e** (*mpl* **-aux**) /fʀygal, -o/ *a* frugal.

fruit /fʀɥi/ *nm* fruit; **des ~s** (some) fruit; **~s de mer** seafood. **fruité**, **~e** *a* fruity.

frustrant, **~e** /fʀystʀɑ̃, -t / *a* frustrating. **frustrer** [1] *vt* frustrate.

fuel /fjul/ *nm* fuel oil.

fugitif, **-ive** /fyʒitif, -v/ *a* (*passager*) fleeting. ● *nm, f* fugitive.

fugue /fyg/ *nf* (Mus) fugue; **faire une ~** run away.

fuir /fɥiʀ/ [35] *vi* flee, run away; (*eau, robinet, etc.*) leak. ● *vt* (quitter) flee; (éviter) shun.

fuite /fɥit/ *nf* flight; (de liquide, d'une nouvelle) leak; **en ~** on the run; **mettre en ~** put to flight; **prendre la ~** take flight.

fulgurant, **~e** /fylgyʀɑ̃, -t/ *a* (*vitesse*) lightning.

fumé, **~e** /fyme/ *a* (*poisson, verre*) smoked.

fumée /fyme/ *nf* smoke; (vapeur) steam.

fumer /fyme/ [1] *vt/i* smoke.

fumeur, **-euse** /fymœʀ, -øz/ *nm, f* smoker; **zone non-~s** no smoking area.

fumier /fymje/ *nm* manure.

funambule /fynɑ̃byl/ *nmf* tightrope walker.

funèbre /fynɛbʀ/ *a* funeral; (fig) gloomy.

funérailles /fyneʀɑj/ *nfpl* funeral.

funéraire /fyneʀɛʀ/ *a* funeral.

funeste /fynɛst/ *a* fatal.

fur: **au ~ et à mesure** /ofyRea-məzyR/ *loc* as one goes along, progressively; **au ~ et à mesure que** as.

furet /fyRɛ/ *nm* ferret.

fureur /fyRœR/ *nf* fury; (passion) passion; **avec ~** furiously; passionately; **mettre en ~** infuriate; **faire ~** be all the rage.

furieux, **-ieuse** /fyRjø, -z/ *a* furious.

furoncle /fyRɔ̃kl/ *nm* boil.

furtif, **-ive** /fyRtif, -v/ *a* furtive.

fuseau (*pl* **~x**) /fyzo/ *nm* ski trousers; (pour filer) spindle; **~ horaire** time zone.

fusée /fyze/ *nf* rocket.

fusible /fyzibl/ *nm* fuse.

fusil /fyzi/ *nm* rifle, gun; (de chasse) shotgun; **~ mitrailleur** machine-gun.

fusion /fyzjɔ̃/ *nf* fusion; (Comm) merger. **fusionner** [1] *vt/i* merge.

fut /fy/ ⇒ÊTRE [5].

fût /fy/ *nm* (tonneau) barrel; (d'arbre) trunk.

futé, **~e** /fyte/ *a* cunning.

futile /fytil/ *a* futile.

futur, **~e** /fytyR/ *a* future; **~e femme/maman** wife-/ mother-to-be. ● *nm* future.

fuyant, **~e** /fɥijɑ̃, -t/ *a* (*front, ligne*) receding; (*personne*) evasive.

fuyard, **~e** /fɥijaR, -d/ *nm, f* runaway.

gabardine /gabaRdin/ *nf* raincoat.

gabarit /gabaRi/ *nm* size; (patron) template; (fig) calibre.

gâcher /gɑʃe/ [1] *vt* (gâter) spoil; (gaspiller) waste.

gâchette /gɑʃɛt/ *nf* trigger.

gâchis /gɑʃi/ *nm* waste.

gaffe /gaf/ *nf* Ⓘ blunder; **faire ~** be careful (**à** of).

gage /gaʒ/ *nm* security; (de bonne foi) pledge; (de jeu) forfeit; **~s** (salaire) wages; **en ~ de** as a token of; **mettre en ~** pawn; **tueur à ~s** hired killer.

gageure /gaʒyR/ *nf* challenge.

gagnant, **~e** /gaɲɑ̃, -t/ *a* winning. ● *nm, f* winner.

gagne-pain /gaɲpɛ̃/ *nm inv* job.

gagner /gaɲe/ [1] *vt* (*match, prix*) win; (*argent, pain*) earn; (*terrain*) gain; (*temps*) save; (atteindre) reach; (convaincre) win over; **~ sa vie** earn one's living. ● *vi* win; (fig) gain.

gai, **~e** /ge/ *a* cheerful; (ivre) merry. **gaiement** *adv* cheerfully. **gaieté** *nf* cheerfulness.

gain /gɛ̃/ *nm* (salaire) earnings; (avantage) gain; (économie) saving; **~s** (Comm) profits; (au jeu) winnings.

gaine /gɛn/ *nf* (corset) girdle; (étui) sheath.

galant, **~e** /galɑ̃, -t/ *a* courteous; (amoureux) romantic.

galaxie /galaksi/ *nf* galaxy.

gale /gal/ *nf* (de chat etc.) mange.

galère /galɛʀ/ *nf* (navire) galley; **c'est la ~!** [!] what an ordeal!

galérer /galeʀe/ [14] *vi* [!] (peiner) have a hard time.

galerie /galʀi/ *nf* gallery; (Théât) circle; (de voiture) roof-rack; **~ marchande** shopping arcade.

galet /galɛ/ *nm* pebble.

galette /galɛt/ *nf* flat cake; **~ des Rois** Twelfth Night cake.

Galles /gal/ *nfpl* **le pays de ~** Wales.

gallois, **~e** /galwa, -z/ *a* Welsh. ● *nm* (Ling) Welsh. **G~**, **~e** *nm,f* Welshman, Welshwoman.

galon /galɔ̃/ *nm* braid; (Mil) stripe; **prendre du ~** be promoted.

galop /galo/ *nm* canter; **aller au ~** canter; **grand ~** gallop; **~ d'essai** trial run. **galoper** [1] *vi* (*cheval*) canter; (au grand galop) gallop; (*personne*) run.

galopin /galɔpɛ̃/ *nm* [!] rascal.

gambader /gɑ̃bade/ [1] *vi* leap about.

gamelle /gamɛl/ *nf* (de soldat) mess kit; (d'ouvrier) lunch-box.

gamin, **~e** /gamɛ̃, -in/ *a* childish; (*air*) youthful. ● *nm,f* [!] kid.

gamme /gam/ *nf* (Mus) scale; (série) range; **haut de ~** up-market, top of the range; **bas de ~** down-market, bottom of the range.

gang /gɑ̃g/ *nm* [!] gang.

ganglion /gɑ̃glijɔ̃/ *nm* ganglion.

gangster /gɑ̃gstɛʀ/ *nm* gangster; (escroc) crook.

gant /gɑ̃/ *nm* glove; **~ de ménage** rubber glove; **~ de toilette** face-flannel, face-cloth.

garage /gaʀaʒ/ *nm* garage. **garagiste** *nmf* garage owner; (employé) car mechanic.

garant, **~e** /gaʀɑ̃, -t/ *nm,f* guarantor. ● *a* **se porter ~ de** vouch for.

garanti, **~e** /gaʀɑ̃ti/ *a* guaranteed.

garantie /gaʀɑ̃ti/ *nf* guarantee; **~s** (de police d'assurance) cover.

garantir [2] *vt* guarantee; (protéger) protect (**de** from).

garçon /gaʀsɔ̃/ *nm* boy; (jeune homme) young man; (célibataire) bachelor; **~** (**de café**) waiter; **~ d'honneur** best man. **garçonnière** *nf* bachelor flat.

garde¹ /gaʀd/ *nf* guard; (d'enfants, de bagages) care; (service) guard (duty); (infirmière) nurse; **de ~** on duty; **~ à vue** (police) custody; **mettre en ~** warn; **prendre ~** be careful (**à** of); (**droit de**) **~** custody (**de** of).

garde² /gaʀd/ *nm* guard; (de propriété, parc) warden; **~ champêtre** village policeman; **~ du corps** bodyguard.

garde-à-vous /gaʀdavu/ *nm inv* (Mil) **se mettre au ~** stand to attention.

garde-chasse (*pl* **~s**) /gaʀdəʃas/ *nm* gamekeeper.

garde-manger /gaʀdmɑ̃ʒe/ *nm inv* meat safe; (placard) larder.

garder /gaʀde/ [1] *vt* (conserver, maintenir) keep; (*vêtement*) keep on; (surveiller) look after; (défendre) guard; **~ le lit** stay in bed. □ **se ~** *vpr* (*denrée*) keep; **se ~ de faire** be careful not to do.

garderie /gaʀdəʀi/ *nf* day nursery.

garde-robe (*pl* **~s**) /gaʀdəʀɔb/ *nf* wardrobe.

gardien, **~ne** /gaʀdjɛ̃, -ɛn/ *nm,f* (de locaux) security guard; (de prison, réserve) warden; (d'immeuble) caretaker; (de musée) attendant; (de zoo) keeper; (de traditions) guardian; **~ de but** goalkeeper; **~ de la paix** policeman; **~ de nuit** night watchman; **gardienne d'enfants** childminder.

G

gare /gaʀ/ *nf* (Rail) station; **~ routière** coach station; (US) bus station. ● *interj* **~** (**à toi**) watch out!

garer /gaʀe/ [1] *vt* park. □ **se ~** *vpr* park; (s'écarter) move out of the way.

gargouille /gaʀguj/ *nf* water-spout; (sculptée) gargoyle. **gargouiller** [1] *vi* gurgle; (*stomach*) rumble.

garni, **~e** /gaʀni/ *a* (*plat*) served with vegetables; **bien ~** (rempli) well-filled.

garnir /gaʀniʀ/ [2] *vt* (remplir) fill; (décorer) decorate; (couvrir) cover; (doubler) line; (Culin) garnish. **garniture** *nf* (légumes) vegetables; (ornement) trimming; (de voiture) trim.

gars /gɑ/ *nm* 🅘 lad; (adulte) guy, bloke.

gas-oil /gɑzwal/ *nm* diesel (oil).

gaspillage /gaspijaʒ/ *nm* waste. **gaspiller** [1] *vt* waste.

gastrique /gastʀik/ *a* gastric.

gastronome /gastʀɔnɔm/ *nmf* gourmet.

gâteau (*pl* **~x**) /gɑto/ *nm* cake; **~ sec** biscuit; (US) cookie; **un papa ~** a doting dad.

gâter /gɑte/ [1] *vt* spoil. □ **se ~** *vpr* (*viande*) go bad; (*dent*) rot; (*temps*) get worse.

gâterie /gɑtʀi/ *nf* little treat.

gâteux, **-euse** /gɑtø, -z/ *a* senile.

gauche /goʃ/ *a* left; (maladroit) awkward. ● *nf* left; **à ~** on the left; (direction) (to the) left; **la ~** the left (side); (Pol) the left (wing).

gaucher, **-ère** /goʃe, -ɛʀ/ *a* left-handed.

gaufre /gofʀ/ *nf* waffle. **gaufrette** *nf* wafer.

gaulois, **~e** /golwa, -z/ *a* Gallic; (fig) bawdy. **G~**, **~e** *nm,f* Gaul.

gaver /gave/ [1] *vt* force-feed; (fig) cram. □ **se ~ de** *vpr* gorge oneself with; (fig) devour.

gaz /gɑz/ *nm inv* gas; **~ d'échappement** exhaust fumes; **~ lacrymogène** tear-gas.

gaze /gɑz/ *nf* gauze.

gazer /gɑze/ [1] *vi* 🅘 **ça gaze?** how's things?

gazette /gazɛt/ *nf* newspaper.

gazeux, **-euse** /gɑzø, -z/ *a* (boisson) fizzy; (*eau*) sparkling.

gazoduc /gaʒɔdyk/ *nm* gas pipeline.

gazon /gɑzɔ̃/ *nm* lawn, grass.

gazouiller /gazuje/ [1] *vi* (*oiseau*) chirp; (*bébé*) babble.

GDF *abrév m* (**Gaz de France**) *French gas board.*

géant, **~e** /ʒeɑ̃, -t/ *a* giant. ● *nm* giant. **géante** *nf* giantess.

geindre /ʒɛ̃dʀ/ [22] *vi* groan, moan.

gel /ʒɛl/ *nm* frost; (produit) gel; (Comm) freeze; **~ coiffant** hair gel.

gelée /ʒ(ə)le/ *nf* frost; (Culin) jelly; **~ blanche** hoarfrost.

geler /ʒəle/ [6] *vt*/*i* freeze; **on gèle** (on a froid) it's freezing; **il** *ou* **ça gèle** (il fait froid) it's freezing.

gélule /ʒelyl/ *nf* (Méd) capsule.

Gémeaux /ʒemo/ *nmpl* Gemini.

gémir /ʒemiʀ/ [2] *vi* groan.

gênant, **~e** /ʒɛnɑ̃, -t/ *a* embarrassing; (irritant) annoying; (incommode) cumbersome.

gencive /ʒɑ̃siv/ *nf* gum.

gendarme /ʒɑ̃daʀm/ *nm* policeman, gendarme. **gendarmerie** *nf* police force; (local) police station.

gendre /ʒɑ̃dʀ/ *nm* son-in-law.

gène /ʒɛn/ *nm* gene.

gêne /ʒɛn/ *nf* discomfort; (confusion) embarrassment; (dérangement) trouble, inconvenience; (pauvreté) poverty.

gêné, **~e** /ʒene/ *a* embarrassed; (désargenté) short of money.

généalogie /ʒenealɔʒi/ *nf* genealogy.

gêner /ʒene/ [1] *vt* bother, disturb; (troubler) embarrass; (entraver) block; (faire mal) hurt.

général, **~e** (*mpl* **-aux**) /ʒeneʀal, -o/ *a* general; **en ~** in general. ●*nm* (*pl* **-aux**) general.

généralement /ʒeneʀalmɑ̃/ *adv* generally.

généraliser /ʒeneʀalize/ [1] *vt* make general. ●*vi* generalize. □ **se ~** *vpr* become widespread *ou* general.

généraliste /ʒeneʀalist/ *nmf* general practitioner, GP.

généralité /ʒeneʀalite/ *nf* general point.

génération /ʒeneʀasjɔ̃/ *nf* generation.

généreux, **~euse** /ʒeneʀø, -z/ *a* generous.

générique /ʒeneʀik/ *nm* (au cinéma) credits. ●*a* generic.

générosité /ʒeneʀozite/ *nf* generosity.

génétique /ʒenetik/ *a* genetic. ●*nf* genetics.

Genève /ʒənɛv/ *npr* Geneva.

génial, **~e** (*mpl* **-iaux**) /ʒenjal, -jo/ *a* brilliant; (fantastique [!]) fantastic.

génie /ʒeni/ *nm* genius; **~ civil** civil engineering.

génital, **~e** (*mpl* **-aux**) /ʒenital, -o/ *a* genital.

génocide /ʒenɔsid/ *nm* genocide.

génoise /ʒenwaz/ *nf* sponge (cake).

génothèque /ʒenɔtɛk/ *nf* gene bank.

genou (*pl* **~x**) /ʒənu/ *nm* knee; **être à ~x** be kneeling.

genre /ʒɑ̃ʀ/ *nm* sort, kind; (Gram) gender; (allure) **avoir bon/mauvais ~** to look nice/disreputable; (comportement) **c'est bien son ~** it's just like him/her; **~ de vie** lifestyle.

gens /ʒɑ̃/ *nmpl* people.

gentil, **~le** /ʒɑ̃ti, -j/ *a* kind, nice; (sage) good. **gentillesse** *nf* kindness. **gentiment** *adv* kindly.

géographie /ʒeɔgʀafi/ *nf* geography.

geôlier, **-ière** /ʒolje, -jɛʀ/ *nm,f* gaoler, jailer.

géologie /ʒeɔlɔʒi/ *nf* geology.

géomètre /ʒeɔmɛtʀ/ *nm* surveyor.

géométrie /ʒeɔmetʀi/ *nf* geometry. **géométrique** *a* geometric.

gérance /ʒeʀɑ̃s/ *nf* management.

gérant, **~e** /ʒeʀɑ̃, -t/ *nm,f* manager, manageress; **~ d'immeuble** landlord's agent.

gerbe /ʒɛʀb/ *nf* (de fleurs) bunch, bouquet; (d'eau) spray; (de blé) sheaf.

gercer /ʒɛʀse/ [10] *vt* chap; **avoir les lèvres gercées** have chapped lips. ●*vi* become chapped. **gerçure** *nf* crack, chap.

gérer /ʒeʀe/ [14] *vt* manage, run; (traiter: fig) (*crise, situation*) handle.

germe /ʒɛʀm/ *nm* germ; **~s de soja** bean sprouts.

germer /ʒɛʀme/ [1] *vi* germinate.

gestation /ʒɛstasjɔ̃/ *nf* gestation.

geste /ʒɛst/ *nm* gesture.

gesticuler /ʒɛstikyle/ [1] *vi* gesticulate.

gestion /ʒɛstjɔ̃/ *nf* management. **gestionnaire** *nmf* administrator.

ghetto /gɛto/ *nm* ghetto.

gibier /ʒibje/ *nm* (animaux) game.

giboulée /ʒibule/ *nf* shower.

gicler /ʒikle/ [1] *vi* squirt; **faire ~** squirt.

gifle /ʒifl/ *nf* slap in the face. **gifler** [1] *vt* slap.

gigantesque /ʒigɑ̃tɛsk/ *a* gigantic.

G

gigot /ʒigo/ *nm* leg (of lamb).
gigoter /ʒigɔte/ [1] *vi* wriggle; (nerveusement) fidget.
gilet /ʒilɛ/ *nm* waistcoat; (cardigan) cardigan; **~ de sauvetage** life-jacket.
gingembre /ʒɛ̃ʒɑ̃bʀ/ *nm* ginger.
girafe /ʒiʀaf/ *nf* giraffe.
giratoire /ʒiʀatwaʀ/ *a* **sens ~** roundabout.
girofle /ʒiʀɔfl/ *nm* **clou de ~** clove.
girouette /ʒiʀwɛt/ *nf* weathercock, weathervane.
gisement /ʒizmɑ̃/ *nm* deposit.
gitan, **~e** /ʒitɑ̃, -an/ *nm, f* gypsy.
gîte /ʒit/ *nm* (maison) home; (abri) shelter; **~ rural** holiday cottage.
givre /ʒivʀ/ *nm* frost; (sur pare-brise) ice.
givré, **~e** /ʒivʀe/ *a* ⊡ crazy.
glace /glas/ *nf* ice; (crème) ice-cream; (vitre) window; (miroir) mirror; (verre) glass.
glacé, **~e** /glase/ *a* (*vent, accueil*) icy; (*hands*) frozen; (*gâteau*) iced.
glacer /glase/ [10] *vt* freeze; (*gâteau, boisson*) chill; (pétrifier) chill. ▫ **se ~** *vpr* freeze.
glacier /glasje/ *nm* (Géog) glacier; (vendeur) ice-cream seller. **glacière** *nf* coolbox. **glaçon** *nm* ice-cube.
glaïeul /glajœl/ *nm* gladiolus.
glaise /glɛz/ *nf* clay.
gland /glɑ̃/ *nm* acorn; (ornement) tassel.
glande /glɑ̃d/ *nf* gland.
glander /glɑ̃de/ [1] *vi* ⊡ laze around.
glaner /glane/ [1] *vt* glean.
glauque /glok/ *a* (fig) murky; (*street*) squalid.
glissade /glisad/ *nf* (jeu) slide; (dérapage) skid.
glissant, **~e** /glisɑ̃, -t/ *a* slippery.
glissement /glismɑ̃/ *nm* sliding; gliding; (fig) shift; **~ de terrain** landslide.
glisser /glise/ [1] *vi* slide; (être glissant) be slippery; (sur l'eau) glide; (déraper) slip; (*véhicule*) skid. ● *vt* (*objet*) slip (**dans** into); (*remarque*) slip in. ▫ **se ~** *vpr* slip (**dans** into).
glissière /glisjɛʀ/ *nf* slide; **porte à ~** sliding door; **~ de sécurité** (Auto) crash-barrier; **fermeture à ~** zip.
global, **~e** (*mpl* **-aux**) /glɔbal, -o/ *a* (entier, général) overall. **globalement** *adv* as a whole.
globe /glɔb/ *nm* globe; **~ oculaire** eyeball; **~ terrestre** globe.
globule /glɔbyl/ *nm* (du sang) corpuscle.
gloire /glwaʀ/ *nf* glory, fame. **glorieux**, **-ieuse** *a* glorious. **glorifier** [45] *vt* glorify.
glose /gloz/ *nf* gloss.
glossaire /glɔsɛʀ/ *nm* glossary.
gloussement /glusmɑ̃/ *nm* chuckle; (de poule) cluck.
glouton, **~ne** /glutɔ̃, -ɔn/ *a* gluttonous. ● *nm, f* glutton.
gluant, **~e** /glyɑ̃, -t/ *a* sticky.
glucose /glykoz/ *nm* glucose.
glycérine /gliseʀin/ *nf* glycerin(e).
GO *abrév fpl* (**grandes ondes**) long wave.
goal /gol/ *nm* ⊡ goalkeeper.
gobelet /gɔblɛ/ *nm* cup; (en verre) tumbler.
gober /gɔbe/ [1] *vt* swallow (whole); **je ne peux pas le ~** ⊡ I can't stand him.
goéland /gɔelɑ̃/ *nm* (sea)gull.
gogo: **à ~** /agɔgo/ *loc* ⊡ galore, in abundance.
goinfre /gwɛ̃fʀ/ *nm* (glouton ⊡) pig. **goinfrer (se)** [1] *vpr* ⊡ stuff oneself (**de** with).

golf /gɔlf/ *nm* golf; (terrain) golf course.

golfe /gɔlf/ *nm* gulf.

gomme /gɔm/ *nf* rubber; (US) eraser; (résine) gum. **gommer** [1] *vt* rub out.

gond /gɔ̃/ *nm* hinge; **sortir de ses ∼s** Ⓘ go mad.

gondoler (se) /(sə)gɔ̃dɔle/ [1] *vpr* (*bois*) warp; (*métal*) buckle.

gonflé, ∼e /gɔ̃fle/ *a* swollen; **il est ∼** Ⓘ he's got a nerve.

gonflement /gɔ̃fləmɑ̃/ *nm* swelling.

gonfler /gɔ̃fle/ [1] *vt* (*ballon, pneu*) pump up, blow up; (augmenter) increase; (exagérer) inflate. ● *vi* swell.

gorge /gɔʀʒ/ *nf* throat; (poitrine) breast; (vallée) gorge.

gorgée /gɔʀʒe/ *nf* sip, gulp.

gorger /gɔʀʒe/ [40] *vt* fill (**de** with); **gorgé de** full of. □ **se ∼** *vpr* gorge oneself (**de** with).

gorille /gɔʀij/ *nm* gorilla; (garde Ⓘ) bodyguard.

gosier /gozje/ *nm* throat.

gosse /gɔs/ *nmf* Ⓘ kid.

gothique /gɔtik/ *a* Gothic.

goudron /gudʀɔ̃/ *nm* tar. **goudronner** [1] *vt* tarmac.

gouffre /gufʀ/ *nm* abyss, gulf.

goujat /guʒa/ *nm* lout, boor.

goulot /gulo/ *nm* neck; **boire au ∼** drink from the bottle.

goulu, ∼e /guly/ *a* gluttonous. ● *nm, f* glutton.

gourde /guʀd/ *nf* (à eau) flask; (idiot Ⓘ) fool.

gourer (se) /(sə)guʀe/ [1] *vpr* Ⓘ make a mistake.

gourmand, ∼e /guʀmɑ̃, -d/ *a* greedy. ● *nm, f* glutton.

gourmandise /guʀmɑ̃diz/ *nf* greed; **∼s** sweets.

gourmet /guʀmɛ/ *nm* gourmet.

gourmette /guʀmɛt/ *nf* chain bracelet.

gousse /gus/ *nf* **∼ d'ail** clove of garlic.

goût /gu/ *nm* taste; (gré) liking; **prendre ∼ à** develop a taste for; **avoir bon ∼** (*aliment*) taste nice; (*personne*) have good taste; **donner du ∼ à** give flavour.

goûter /gute/ [1] *vt* taste; (apprécier) enjoy; **∼ à** *ou* **de** taste. ● *vi* have tea. ● *nm* tea, snack.

goutte /gut/ *nf* drop; (Méd) gout. **goutte-à-goutte** *nm inv* drip. **goutter** [1] *vi* drip.

gouttière /gutjɛʀ/ *nf* gutter.

gouvernail /guvɛʀnaj/ *nm* rudder; (barre) helm.

gouvernement /guvɛʀnəmɑ̃/ *nm* government.

gouverner /guvɛʀne/ [1] *vt/i* govern; (dominer) control. **gouverneur** *nm* governor.

grâce /gʀɑs/ *nf* (charme) grace; (faveur) favour; (volonté) grace; (Jur) pardon; (Relig) grace; **∼ à** thanks to; **rendre ∼(s) à** give thanks to.

gracier /gʀasje/ [45] *vt* pardon.

gracieusement /gʀasjøzmɑ̃/ *adv* gracefully; (gratuitement) free (of charge).

gracieux, -ieuse /gʀasjø, -z/ *a* graceful.

grade /gʀad/ *nm* rank; **monter en ∼** be promoted.

gradin /gʀadɛ̃/ *nm* tier, step; **en ∼s** terraced; **les ∼s** terraces.

gradué, ∼e /gʀadɥe/ *a* graded, graduated; **verre ∼** measuring jug.

graffiti /gʀafiti/ *nmpl* graffiti.

grain /gʀɛ̃/ *nm* grain; (Naut) squall; **∼ de beauté** beauty spot; **∼ de café** coffee bean; **∼ de poivre** pepper corn; **∼ de raisin** grape.

graine /gʀɛn/ *nf* seed.

graisse /gʀɛs/ *nf* fat; (lubrifiant)

G

grease. **graisser** [1] *vt* grease. **graisseux, -euse** *a* greasy.

grammaire /gʀam(m)ɛʀ/ *nf* grammar.

gramme /gʀam/ *nm* gram.

grand, ~e /gʀɑ̃, -d/ *a* big, large; (haut) tall; (intense, fort) great; (brillant) great; (principal) main; (plus âgé) big, elder; (adulte) grown-up; **au ~ air** in the open air; **au ~ jour** in broad daylight; (fig) in the open; **en ~e partie** largely; **~e banlieue** outer suburbs; **~ ensemble** housing estate; **~es lignes** (Rail) main lines; **~ magasin** department store; **~e personne** grown-up; **~ public** general public; **~e surface** hypermarket; **~es vacances** summer holidays. ●*adv* (*ouvrir*) wide; **~ ouvert** wide open; **voir ~** think big. ●*nm, f* (adulte) grown-up; (enfant) big boy, big girl; (Scol) senior.

Grande-Bretagne /gʀɑ̃dbʀətaɲ/ *nf* Great Britain.

grand-chose /gʀɑ̃ʃoz/ *pron* **pas ~** not much, not a lot.

grandeur /gʀɑ̃dœʀ/ *nf* greatness; (dimension) size; **folie des ~s** delusions of grandeur.

grandir /gʀɑ̃diʀ/ [2] *vi* grow; (*bruit*) grow louder. ●*vt* (*talons*) make taller; (*loupe*) magnify.

grand-mère (*pl* **grands-mères**) /gʀɑ̃mɛʀ/ *nf* grandmother.

grand-père (*pl* **grands-pères**) /gʀɑ̃pɛʀ/ *nm* grandfather.

grands-parents /gʀɑ̃paʀɑ̃/ *nmpl* grandparents.

grange /gʀɑ̃ʒ/ *nf* barn.

granulé /gʀanyle/ *nm* granule.

graphique /gʀafik/ *a* graphic; (Ordinat) graphics; **informatique ~** computer graphics. ●*nm* graph.

graphologie /gʀafɔlɔʒi/ *nf* graphology.

grappe /gʀap/ *nf* cluster; **~ de raisin** bunch of grapes.

gras, ~se /gʀɑ, -s/ *a* (gros) fat; (*aliment*) fatty; (*surface, peau, cheveux*) greasy; (épais) thick; (*caractères*) bold; **faire la ~se matinée** sleep late. ●*nm* (Culin) fat.

gratifiant, ~e /gʀatifjɑ̃, -t/ *a* gratifying; (*travail*) rewarding.

gratifier /gʀatifje/ [45] *vt* favour, reward (**de** with).

gratin /gʀatɛ̃/ *nm* gratin (*baked dish with cheese topping*); (élite [!]) upper crust.

gratis /gʀatis/ *adv* free.

gratitude /gʀatityd/ *nf* gratitude.

gratte-ciel /gʀatsjɛl/ *nm inv* skyscraper.

gratter /gʀate/ [1] *vt/i* scratch; (avec un outil) scrape; **ça me gratte** [!] it itches. □ **se ~** *vpr* scratch oneself; **se ~ la tête** scratch one's head.

gratuiciel /gʀatɥisjɛl/ *nm* (Internet) freeware.

gratuit, ~e /gʀatɥi, -t/ *a* free; (*acte*) gratuitous. **gratuitement** *adv* free (of charge).

grave /gʀav/ *a* (*maladie, accident, problème*) serious; (solennel) grave; (*voix*) deep; (*accent*) grave. **gravement** *adv* seriously; gravely.

graver /gʀave/ [1] *vt* engrave; (sur bois) carve.

gravier /gʀavje/ *nm* **du ~** gravel.

gravité /gʀavite/ *nf* gravity.

graviter /gʀavite/ [1] *vi* revolve.

gravure /gʀavyʀ/ *nf* engraving; (de tableau, photo) print, plate.

gré /gʀe/ *nm* (volonté) will; (goût) taste; **à son ~** (*agir*) as one likes; **de bon ~** willingly; **bon ~ mal ~** like it or not; **je vous en saurais ~** I'd be grateful for that.

grec, ~que /gʀɛk/ *a* Greek. ●*nm* (Ling) Greek. **G~, ~que** *nm, f* Greek.

Grèce *nf* /gʀɛs/ Greece.

greffe /gʀɛf/ *nf* graft; (d'organe)

transplant. **greffer** [1] *vt* graft; transplant.

greffier, -ière /gʀefje, -jɛʀ/ *nm, f* clerk of the court.

grêle /gʀɛl/ *a* (maigre) spindly; (*voix*) shrill. ● *nf* hail.

grêler /gʀele/ [1] *vi* hail; **il grêle** it's hailing. **grêlon** *nm* hailstone.

grelot /gʀəlo/ *nm* (little) bell.

grelotter /gʀəlɔte/ [1] *vi* shiver.

grenade /gʀənad/ *nf* (fruit) pomegranate; (explosif) grenade.

grenat /gʀəna/ *a inv* dark red.

grenier /gʀənje/ *nm* attic; (pour grain) loft.

grenouille /gʀənuj/ *nf* frog.

grès /gʀɛ/ *nm* sandstone; (poterie) stoneware.

grésiller /gʀezije/ [1] *vi* sizzle; (*radio*) crackle.

grève /gʀɛv/ *nf* (rivage) shore; (cessation de travail) strike; **faire ~, être en ~** be on strike; **se mettre en ~** go on strike. **gréviste** *nmf* striker.

gribouiller /gʀibuje/ [1] *vt/i* scribble.

grief /gʀijɛf/ *nm* grievance.

grièvement /gʀijɛvmɑ̃/ *adv* seriously.

griffe /gʀif/ *nf* claw; (de couturier) label; **coup de ~** scratch.

griffé, ~e /gʀife/ *a* (*vêtement, article*) designer.

griffer /gʀife/ [1] *vt* scratch, claw.

grignoter /gʀiɲɔte/ [1] *vt/i* nibble.

gril /gʀil/ *nm* (de cuisinière) grill; (plaque) grill pan.

grillade /gʀijad/ *nf* (viande) grill.

grillage /gʀijaʒ/ *nm* wire netting.

grille /gʀij/ *nf* railings; (portail) (metal) gate; (de fenêtre) bars; (de cheminée) grate; (fig) grid. **grille-pain** *nm inv* toaster.

griller /gʀije/ [1] *vt* (*pain*) toast; (*viande*) grill; (*ampoule*) blow; (*feu rouge*) go through; (*appareil*) burn out. ● *vi* (*ampoule*) blow; (Culin) **faire ~** (*viande*) grill; (*pain*) toast.

grillon /gʀijɔ̃/ *nm* cricket.

grimace /gʀimas/ *nf* (funny) face; (de douleur, dégoût) grimace; **faire des ~s** make faces; **faire la ~** pull a face, grimace.

grimper /gʀɛ̃pe/ [1] *vt* climb. ● *vi* climb; **~ sur** *ou* **dans un arbre** climb a tree.

grincement /gʀɛ̃smɑ̃/ *nm* creak(ing).

grincer /gʀɛ̃se/ [10] *vi* creak; **~ des dents** grind one's teeth.

grincheux, -euse /gʀɛ̃ʃø, -z/ *a* grumpy.

grippe /gʀip/ *nf* influenza, flu.

grippé, ~e /gʀipe/ *a* **être ~** have (the) flu; (*mécanisme*) be seized up *ou* jammed.

gris, ~e /gʀi, -z/ *a* grey; (saoul) tipsy.

grivois, ~e /gʀivwa, -z/ *a* bawdy.

grog /gʀɔg/ *nm* hot toddy.

grogner /gʀɔɲe/ [1] *vi* (*animal*) growl; (*personne*) grumble.

grognon /gʀɔɲɔ̃/ *am* grumpy.

groin /gʀwɛ̃/ *nm* snout.

gronder /gʀɔ̃de/ [1] *vi* (*tonnerre, volcan*) rumble; (*chien*) growl; (*conflit*) be brewing. ● *vt* scold.

groom /gʀum/ *nm* bellboy.

gros, ~se /gʀo, -s/ *a* big, large; (gras) fat; (important) big; (épais) thick; (lourd) heavy; (*buveur, fumeur*) heavy; **~ bonnet** Ⓘ bigwig; **~ lot** jackpot; **~ mot** swear word; **~ plan** close-up; **~se caisse** bass drum; **~ titre** headline. ● *nm, f* fat man, fat woman. ● *adv* (*écrire*) big; (*risquer, gagner*) a lot. ● *nm* **le ~ de** the bulk of; **de ~** (Comm)

G

wholesale; **en ~** roughly; (Comm) wholesale.

groseille /gʀozɛj/ *nf* redcurrant; **~ à maquereau** gooseberry.

grossesse /gʀosɛs/ *nf* pregnancy.

grosseur /gʀosœʀ/ *nf* (volume) size; (enflure) lump.

grossier, -ière /gʀosje, -jɛʀ/ *a* (sans finesse) coarse, rough; (rudimentaire) crude; (vulgaire) coarse; (impoli) rude; (*erreur*) gross. **grossièrement** *adv* (sommairement) roughly; (vulgairement) coarsely. **grossièreté** *nf* coarseness; crudeness; rudeness; (mot) rude word.

grossir /gʀosiʀ/ [2] *vt* (faire augmenter) increase, boost; (agrandir) enlarge; (exagérer) exaggerate; **~ les rangs** *ou* **la foule** swell the ranks. ● *vi* (*personne*) put on weight; (augmenter) grow.

grossiste /gʀosist/ *nmf* wholesaler.

grosso modo /gʀosomodo/ *adv* roughly.

grotesque /gʀɔtɛsk/ *a* grotesque; (ridicule) ludicrous.

grotte /gʀɔt/ *nf* cave; grotto.

grouiller /gʀuje/ [1] *vi* swarm; **~ de** be swarming with.

groupe /gʀup/ *nm* group; (Mus) group, band; **~ électrogène** generating set; **~ scolaire** school; **~ de travail** working party.

groupement /gʀupmɑ̃/ *nm* grouping.

grouper /gʀupe/ [1] *vt* put together. □ **se ~** *vpr* group (together).

grue /gʀy/ *nf* (machine, oiseau) crane.

gruyère /gʀyjɛʀ/ *nm* gruyère (cheese).

gué /ge/ *nm* ford; **passer** *ou* **traverser à ~** ford.

guenon /gənɔ̃/ *nf* female monkey.

guépard /gepaʀ/ *nm* cheetah.

guêpe /gɛp/ *nf* wasp.

guère /gɛʀ/ *adv* **ne ~** hardly; **il n'y a ~ d'espoir** there is no hope; **elle n'a ~ dormi** she didn't sleep much, she hardly slept.

guérilla /geʀija/ *nf* guerrilla warfare; (groupe) guerillas.

guérir /geʀiʀ/ [2] *vt* (*personne, maladie, mal*) cure (**de** of); (*plaie, membre*) heal. ● *vi* get better; (*blessure*) heal; **~ de** recover from. **guérison** *nf* curing; healing; (de personne) recovery.

guerre /gɛʀ/ *nf* war; **en ~** at war; **faire la ~** wage war (**à** against); **~ civile** civil war; **~ mondiale** world war.

guerrier, -ière /gɛʀje, -jɛʀ/ *a* warlike. ● *nm, f* warrior.

guet /gɛ/ *nm* watch; **faire le ~** be on the watch. **guet-apens** (*pl* **guets-apens**) *nm* ambush.

guetter /gete/ [1] *vt* watch; (attendre) watch out for.

gueule /gœl/ *nf* mouth; (figure [!]) face; **ta ~!** [!!] shut up!; **~ de bois** [!] hangover.

gueuleton /gœltɔ̃/ *nm* [!] blow-out, slap-up meal.

gui /gi/ *nm* mistletoe.

guichet /giʃɛ/ *nm* window, counter; (de gare) ticket-office; (Théât) box-office; **jouer à ~s fermés** (*pièce*) be sold out; **~ automatique** cash dispenser.

guide /gid/ *nm* guide. ● *nf* (fille scout) girl guide.

guider /gide/ [1] *vt* guide.

guidon /gidɔ̃/ *nm* handlebars.

guignol /giɲɔl/ *nm* puppet; (personne) clown; (spectacle) puppet-show.

guillemets /gijmɛ/ *nmpl* quotation marks, inverted

commas; **entre ~** in inverted commas.

guillotine /gijɔtin/ *nf* guillotine.

guimauve /gimov/ *nf* marshmallow; **c'est de la ~** [!] it's slushy *ou* schmaltzy [!].

guindé, **~e** /gɛ̃de/ *a* stiff, formal; (*style*) stilted.

guirlande /giʀlɑ̃d/ *nf* garland; tinsel.

guitare /gitaʀ/ *nf* guitar.

gym /ʒim/ *nf* gymnastics; (Scol) physical education, PE.

gymnase /ʒimnɑz/ *nm* gym(nasium). **gymnastique** *nf* gymnastics.

gynécologie /ʒinekɔlɔʒi/ *nf* gynaecology.

habile /abil/ *a* skilful, clever.

habillé, **~e** /abije/ *a* (*vêtement*) smart; (*soirée*) formal.

habillement /abijmɑ̃/ *nm* clothing.

habiller /abije/ [1] *vt* dress (**de** in); (équiper) clothe; (recouvrir) cover (**de** with). ▫ **s'~** *vpr* get dressed; (élégamment) dress up.

habit /abi/ *nm* (de personnage) outfit; (de cérémonie) tails; **~s** clothes.

habitant, **~e** /abitɑ̃, -t/ *nm,f* (de maison, quartier) resident; (de pays) inhabitant.

habitat /abita/ *nm* (mode de peuplement) settlement; (conditions) housing.

habitation /abitasjɔ̃/ *nf* (logement) house.

habité, **~e** /abite/ *a* (*terre*) inhabited.

habiter /abite/ [1] *vi* live. ● *vt* live in.

habitude /abityd/ *nf* habit; **avoir l'~ de** be used to; **d'~** usually; **comme d'~** as usual.

habitué, **~e** /abitɥe/ *nm,f* (client) regular.

habituel, **~le** /abitɥɛl/ *a* usual. **habituellement** *adv* usually.

habituer /abitɥe/ [1] *vt* **~ qn à** get sb used to. ▫ **s'~ à** *vpr* get used to.

hache /'aʃ/ *nf* axe.

haché, **~e** /'aʃe/ *a* (viande) minced; (phrases) jerky.

hacher /'aʃe/ [1] *vt* mince; (au couteau) chop.

hachis /'aʃi/ *nm* minced meat; (US) ground meat; **~ Parmentier** ≈ *shepherd's pie*.

hachisch /'aʃiʃ/ *nm* hashish.

hachoir /'aʃwaʀ/ *nm* (appareil) mincer; (couteau) chopper; (planche) chopping board.

haie /'ɛ/ *nf* hedge; (de personnes) line; **course de ~s** hurdle race.

haillon /'ɑjɔ̃/ *nm* rag.

haine /'ɛn/ *nf* hatred.

haïr /'aiʀ/ [36] *vt* hate.

hâlé /'ɑle/ *a* (sun-)tanned.

haleine /alɛn/ *nf* breath; **travail de longue ~** long job.

haleter /'alte/ [6] *vi* pant.

hall /'ol/ *nm* hall; (de gare) concourse.

halle /'al/ *nf* market hall; **~s** covered market.

halte /'alt/ *nf* stop; **faire ~** stop. ● *interj* stop; (Mil) halt.

haltère /altɛʀ/ *nm* dumbbell; **faire des ~s** to do weightlifting.

hameau (*pl* **~x**) /'amo/ *nm* hamlet.

hameçon /amsɔ̃/ *nm* hook.

hanche /'ɑ̃ʃ/ *nf* hip.

handicap /'ɑ̃dikap/ *nm* handicap. **handicapé**, **~e** *a & nm,f* disabled (person).

hangar /'ɑ̃gaʀ/ *nm* shed; (pour avions) hangar.

hanter /'ɑ̃te/ [1] *vt* haunt.

hantise /'ɑ̃tiz/ *nf* dread; **avoir la ~ de** dread.

haras /'aʀɑ/ *nm* stud-farm.

harasser /'aʀase/ [1] *vt* exhaust.

harcèlement /'aʀsɛlmɑ̃/ *nm* **~ sexuel** sexual harassment.

harceler /'aʀsəle/ [6] *vt* harass.

hardi, **~e** /'aʀdi/ *a* bold.

hareng /'aʀɑ̃/ *nm* herring.

hargne /'aʀɲ/ *nf* (aggressive) bad temper.

haricot /'aʀiko/ *nm* bean; **~ vert** French bean; (US) green bean.

harmonie /aʀmɔni/ *nf* harmony. **harmonieux**, **-ieuse** *a* harmonious.

harmoniser /aʀmɔnize/ [1] *vt* harmonize. ▫ **s'~** *vpr* harmonize.

harnacher /'aʀnaʃe/ [1] *vt* harness.

harnais /'aʀnɛ/ *nm* harness.

harpe /'aʀp/ *nf* harp.

harpon /'aʀpɔ̃/ *nm* harpoon.

hasard /'azaʀ/ *nm* chance; (coïncidence) coincidence; **les ~s de** the fortunes of; **au ~** (choisir etc.) at random; (flâner) aimlessly. **hasardeux**, **-euse** *a* risky.

hasarder /'azaʀde/ [1] *vt* risk; (remarque) venture.

hâte /'ɑt/ *nf* haste; **à la ~**, **en ~** hurriedly; **avoir ~ de** look forward to.

hâter /'ɑte/ [1] *vt* hasten. ▫ **se ~** *vpr* hurry (**de** to).

hâtif, **-ive** /'ɑtif, -v/ *a* hasty; (précoce) early.

hausse /'os/ *nf* rise (**de** in); **~ des prix** price rise; **en ~** rising.

hausser /'ose/ [1] *vt* raise; (épaules) shrug.

haut, **~e** /'o, 'ot/ *a* high; (de taille) tall; **à voix ~e** aloud; **~ en couleur** colourful; **plus ~** higher up; (dans un texte) above; **en ~ lieu** in high places. ●*adv* high; **tout ~** out loud. ●*nm* top; **des ~s et des bas** ups and downs; **en ~** (regarder) up; (à l'étage) upstairs; **en ~** (**de**) at the top (of).

hautbois /'obwa/ *nm* oboe.

haut-de-forme /'odfɔʀm/ (*pl* **hauts-de-forme**) *nm* top hat.

hauteur /'otœʀ/ *nf* height; (colline) hill; (arrogance) haughtiness; **être à la ~** be up to it; **à la ~ de** (*ville*) near; **être à la ~ de la situation** be equal to the situation.

haut-le-cœur /'olkœʀ/ *nm inv* nausea.

haut-parleur (*pl* **~s**) /'opaʀlœʀ/ *nm* loudspeaker.

havre /'ɑvʀ/ *nm* haven (**de** of).

hayon /'ɑjɔ̃/ *nm* (Auto) hatchback.

hebdomadaire /ɛbdɔmadɛʀ/ *a & nm* weekly.

hébergement /ebɛʀʒəmɑ̃/ *nm* accommodation.

héberger /ebɛʀʒe/ [40] *vt* (*ami*) put up; (*réfugiés*) take in.

hébreu (*pl* **~x**) /ebʀø/ *am* Hebrew. ●*nm* (Ling) Hebrew; **c'est de l'~!** it's all Greek to me!

Hébreu (*pl* **~x**) /ebʀø/ *nm* Hebrew; **les ~x** the Hebrews.

hécatombe /ekatɔ̃b/ *nf* slaughter.

hectare /ɛktaʀ/ *nm* hectare (= 10,000 square metres).

hélas /'elɑs/ *interj* alas. ●*adv* sadly.

hélice /elis/ *nf* propeller.

hélicoptère /elikɔptɛʀ/ *nm* helicopter.

helvétique /ɛlvetik/ *a* Swiss.

hématome /ematom/ *nm* bruise.

hémorragie /emɔʀaʒi/ *nf* haemorrhage.

hémorroïdes /emɔʀɔid/ *nfpl* piles, haemorrhoids.
hennir /'eniʀ/ [2] *vi* neigh.
hépatite /epatit/ *nf* hepatitis.
herbe /ɛʀb/ *nf* grass; (Méd, Culin) herb; **en ~** in the blade; (fig) budding.
héréditaire /eʀeditɛʀ/ *a* hereditary.
hérédité /eʀedite/ *nf* heredity.
hérisser /'eʀise/ [1] *vt* bristle; **~ qn** (fig) ruffle sb. □ **se ~** *vpr* bristle.
hérisson /'eʀisɔ̃/ *nm* hedgehog.
héritage /eʀitaʒ/ *nm* inheritance; (spirituel) heritage.
hériter /eʀite/ [1] *vt/i* inherit (**de** from); **~ de qch** inherit sth. **héritier, -ière** *nm,f* heir, heiress.
hermétique /ɛʀmetik/ *a* airtight; (fig) unfathomable.
hernie /'ɛʀni/ *nf* hernia.
héroïne /eʀɔin/ *nf* (femme) heroine; (drogue) heroin.
héroïque /eʀɔik/ *a* heroic.
héros /'eʀo/ *nm* hero.
hésiter /ezite/ [1] *vi* hesitate (**à** to); **j'hésite** I'm not sure.
hétérogène /eteʀɔʒɛn/ *a* heterogeneous.
hétérosexuel, ~le /eteʀɔsek-sɥɛl/ *nm/f & a* heterosexual.
hêtre /'ɛtʀ/ *nm* beech.
heure /œʀ/ *nf* time; (soixante minutes) hour; **quelle ~ est-il?** what time is it?; **il est dix ~s** it is ten o'clock; **à l'~** (*venir, être*) on time; **d'~ en ~** by the hour; **toutes les deux ~s** every two hours; **~ de pointe** rush-hour; **~ de cours** (Scol) period; **~ indue** ungodly hour; **~s creuses** off-peak periods; **~s supplémentaires** overtime.
heureusement /œʀøzmɑ̃/ *adv* fortunately, luckily.
heureux, -euse /œʀø, -z/ *a* happy; (chanceux) lucky, fortunate.
heurt /'œʀ/ *nm* collision; (conflit) clash; **sans ~** smoothly.
heurter /'œʀte/ [1] *vt* (cogner) hit; (*mur*) bump into, hit; (choquer) offend. □ **se ~ à** *vpr* bump into, hit; (fig) come up against.
hexagone /ɛgzagon/ *nm* hexagon; **l'~** France.
hiberner /ibɛʀne/ [1] *vi* hibernate.
hibou (*pl* **~x**) /'ibu/ *nm* owl.
hier /jɛʀ/ *adv* yesterday; **~ soir** last night, yesterday evening.
hiérarchie /'jeʀaʀʃi/ *nf* hierarchy.
hilare /ilaʀ/ *a* (*visage*) merry; **être ~** be laughing.
hindou, ~e /ɛ̃du/ *a & nm,f* Hindu. **H~, ~e** *nm,f* Hindu.
hippique /ipik/ *a* equestrian; **le concours ~** showjumping.
hippodrome /ipɔdʀom/ *nm* racecourse.
hippopotame /ipɔpɔtam/ *nm* hippopotamus.
hirondelle /iʀɔ̃dɛl/ *nf* swallow.
hisser /'ise/ [1] *vt* hoist, haul. □ **se ~** *vpr* heave oneself up.
histoire /istwaʀ/ *nf* (récit) story; (étude) history; (affaire) business; **~(s)** (chichis) fuss; (ennuis) trouble. **historique** *a* historical.
hiver /ivɛʀ/ *nm* winter. **hivernal, ~e** (*mpl* **-aux**) *a* winter; (glacial) wintry.
H.L.M. *abbrév m ou f* (**habitation à loyer modéré**) block of council flats; (US) low-rent apartment building.
hocher /'ɔʃe/ [1] *vt* **~ la tête** (pour dire oui) nod; (pour dire non) shake one's head.
hochet /'ɔʃɛ/ *nm* rattle.
hockey /'ɔkɛ/ *nm* hockey; **~ sur glace** ice hockey.
hollandais, ~e /'ɔlɑ̃dɛ, -z/ *a* Dutch. ● *nm* (Ling) Dutch. **H~,**

~e *nm,f* Dutchman, Dutchwoman.

Hollande /'ɔlɑ̃d/ *nf* Holland.

homard /'ɔmaʀ/ *nm* lobster.

homéopathie /ɔmeɔpati/ *nf* homoeopathy.

homicide /ɔmisid/ *nm* homicide; **~ involontaire** manslaughter.

hommage /ɔmaʒ/ *nm* tribute; **~s** (salutations) respects; **rendre ~ à** pay tribute to.

homme /ɔm/ *nm* man; (espèce) man(kind); **~ d'affaires** businessman; **~ de la rue** man in the street; **~ d'État** statesman; **~ politique** politician.

homogène /ɔmɔʒɛn/ *a* homogeneous.

homonyme /ɔmɔnim/ *nm* (personne) namesake.

homosexualité /ɔmɔsɛksɥalite/ *nf* homosexuality.

homosexuel, ~le /ɔmɔsɛksɥɛl/ *a & nm,f* homosexual.

Hongrie /'ɔ̃gʀi/ *nf* Hungary.

hongrois, ~e /'ɔ̃gʀwa, -z/ *a* Hungarian. ● *nm* (Ling) Hungarian. **H~, ~e** *nm,f* Hungarian.

honnête /ɔnɛt/ *a* honest; (juste) fair. **honnêteté** *nf* honesty.

honneur /ɔnœʀ/ *nm* honour; (mérite) credit; **d'~** (*invité, place*) of honour; **en l'~ de** in honour of; **en quel ~?** 🅸 why?; **faire ~ à** (*équipe, famille*) bring credit to.

honorable /ɔnɔʀabl/ *a* honourable; (convenable) respectable.

honoraire /ɔnɔʀɛʀ/ *a* honorary. **honoraires** *nmpl* fees.

honorer /ɔnɔʀe/ [1] *vt* honour; (faire honneur à) do credit to.

honte /'ɔ̃t/ *nf* shame; **avoir ~** be ashamed (**de** of); **faire ~ à** make ashamed. **honteux, -euse** *a* (*personne*) ashamed (**de** of); (*action*) shameful.

hôpital (*pl* **-aux**) /ɔpital, -o/ *nm* hospital.

hoquet /'ɔkɛ/ *nm* **le ~** (the) hiccups.

horaire /ɔʀɛʀ/ *a* hourly. ● *nm* timetable; **~s libres** flexitime.

horizon /ɔʀizɔ̃/ *nm* horizon; (Fig) outlook.

horizontal, ~e (*mpl* **-aux**) /ɔʀizɔ̃tal, -o/ *a* horizontal.

horloge /ɔʀlɔʒ/ *nf* clock.

hormis /'ɔʀmi/ *prép* save.

hormonal, ~e (*mpl* **-aux**) /ɔʀmɔnal, -o/ *a* hormonal, hormone.

hormone /ɔʀmon/ *nf* hormone.

horreur /ɔʀœʀ/ *nf* horror; **avoir ~ de** hate.

horrible /ɔʀibl/ *a* horrible.

horrifier /ɔʀifje/ [45] *vt* horrify.

hors /'ɔʀ/ *prép* **~ de** outside, (avec mouvement) out of; **~ d'atteinte** out of reach; **~ d'haleine** out of breath; **~ de prix** extremely expensive; **~ pair** outstanding; **~ de soi** beside oneself. **hors-bord** *nm inv* speedboat. **hors-d'œuvre** *nm inv* hors-d'œuvre. **hors-jeu** *a inv* offside. **hors-la-loi** *nm inv* outlaw. **hors-piste** *nm* off-piste skiing. **hors-taxe** *a inv* duty-free.

horticulteur, -trice /ɔʀtikyltœʀ, -tʀis/ *nm,f* horticulturist.

hospice /ɔspis/ *nm* home.

hospitalier, -ière /ɔspitalje, -jɛʀ/ *a* hospitable; (Méd) hospital. **hospitaliser** [1] *vt* take to hospital. **hospitalité** *nf* hospitality.

hostile /ɔstil/ *a* hostile. **hostilité** *nf* hostility.

hôte /ot/ *nm* (maître) host; (invité) guest.

hôtel /otɛl/ *nm* hotel; **~ (particulier)** (private) mansion; **~ de ville** town hall.

hôtelier, -ière /otəlje, -jɛʀ/ *a*

hotel. ● *nm, f* hotel keeper. **hôtellerie** *nf* hotel business.

hôtesse /otɛs/ *nf* hostess; ~ **de l'air** stewardess.

hotte /'ɔt/ *nf* basket; ~ **aspirante** extractor (hood), (US) ventilator.

houblon /'ublɔ̃/ *nm* **le** ~ hops.

houille /'uj/ *nf* coal; ~ **blanche** hydroelectric power.

houle /'ul/ *nf* swell. **houleux, -euse** *a* (*mer*) rough; (*débat*) stormy.

housse /'us/ *nf* cover; ~ **de siège** seat cover.

houx /'u/ *nm* holly.

huées /'ɥe/ *nfpl* boos. **huer** [1] *vt* boo.

huile /ɥil/ *nf* oil; (personne 🄸) bigwig. **huiler** [1] *vt* oil. **huileux, -euse** *a* oily.

huis /'ɥi/ *nm* **à** ~ **clos** in camera.

huissier /ɥisje/ *nm* (Jur) bailiff; (portier) usher.

huit /'ɥi(t)/ *a* eight; ~ **jours** a week; **lundi en** ~ a week on Monday. ● *nm* eight. **huitième** *a & nmf* eighth.

huître /ɥitʀ/ *nf* oyster.

humain, ~e /ymɛ̃, -ɛn/ *a* human; (compatissant) humane. **humanitaire** *a* humanitarian. **humanité** *nf* humanity.

humble /œ̃bl/ *a* humble.

humeur /ymœʀ/ *nf* mood; (tempérament) temper; **de bonne/ mauvaise** ~ in a good/bad mood.

humide /ymid/ *a* damp; (*chaleur, climat*) humid; (*lèvres, yeux*) moist. **humidité** *nf* humidity.

humilier /ymilje/ [45] *vt* humiliate.

humoristique /ymɔʀistik/ *a* humorous.

humour /ymuʀ/ *nm* humour; **avoir de l'**~ have a sense of humour.

hurlement /'yʀləmɑ̃/ *nm* howl (ing). **hurler** [1] *vt/i* howl.

hutte /'yt/ *nf* hut.

hydratant, ~e /idʀatɑ̃, -t/ *a* (*lotion*) moisturizing.

hydravion /idʀavjɔ̃/ *nm* seaplane.

hydroélectrique /idʀɔelɛktʀik/ *a* hydroelectric.

hydrogène /idʀɔʒɛn/ *nm* hydrogen.

hygiène /iʒjɛn/ *nf* hygiene. **hygiénique** *a* hygienic.

hymne /imn/ *nm* hymn; ~ **national** national anthem.

hyperlien /ipɛʀlɛ̃/ *nm* (Internet) hyperlink.

hypermarché /ipɛʀmaʀʃe/ *nm* (supermarché) hypermarket.

hypertension /ipɛʀtɑ̃sjɔ̃/ *nf* high blood-pressure.

hypertexte /ipɛʀtɛkst/ *nm* (Internet) hypertext.

hypnotiser /ipnɔtize/ [1] *vt* hypnotize.

hypocrisie /ipɔkʀizi/ *nf* hypocrisy.

hypocrite /ipɔkʀit/ *a* hypocritical. ● *nmf* hypocrite.

hypothèque /ipɔtɛk/ *nf* mortgage.

hypothèse /ipɔtɛz/ *nf* hypothesis.

hystérie /isteʀi/ *nf* hysteria.

ici /isi/ *adv* (dans l'espace) here; (dans le temps) now; **d'~ demain** by tomorrow; **d'~ là** in the meantime; **d'~ peu** shortly; ~ **même** in this very place; **jusqu'~**

until now; (dans le passé) until then.

idéal, **~e** (*mpl* **-aux**) /ideal, -o/ *a* & *nm* ideal. **idéaliser** [1] *vt* idealize.

idée /ide/ *nf* idea; (esprit) mind; **avoir dans l'~ de faire** plan to do; **il ne me viendrait jamais à l'~ de faire** it would never occur to me to do; **~ fixe** obsession; **~ reçue** conventional opinion.

identification /idɑ̃tifikasjɔ̃/ *nf* identification. **identifier** [45] *vt*, **s'identifier** *vpr* identify (**à** with).

identique /idɑ̃tik/ *a* identical.

identité /idɑ̃tite/ *nf* identity.

idéologie /ideɔlɔʒi/ *nf* ideology.

idiome /idjom/ *nm* idiom.

idiot, **~e** /idjo, -ɔt/ *a* idiotic. ● *nm, f* idiot. **idiotie** *nf* idiocy; (acte, parole) idiotic thing.

idole /idɔl/ *nf* idol.

if /if/ *nm* yew.

ignare /iɲaʀ/ *a* ignorant. ● *nmf* ignoramus.

ignoble /iɲɔbl/ *a* vile.

ignorance /iɲɔʀɑ̃s/ *nf* ignorance.

ignorant, **~e** /iɲɔʀɑ̃, -t/ *a* ignorant. ● *nm, f* ignoramus.

ignorer /iɲɔʀe/ [1] *vt* not know; **je l'ignore** I don't know; (*personne*) ignore.

il /il/ *pron* (personne, animal familier) he; (chose, animal) it; (impersonnel) it; **~ est vrai que** it is true that; **~ neige/pleut** it is snowing/raining; **~ y a** there is; (pluriel) there are; (temps) ago; (durée) for; **~ y a 2 ans** 2 years ago; **~ y a plus d'une heure que j'attends** I've been waiting for over an hour.

île /il/ *nf* island; **~ déserte** desert island; **~s anglo-normandes** Channel Islands; **~s Britanniques** British Isles.

illégal, **~e** (*mpl* **~aux**) /ilegal, -o/ *a* illegal.

illégitime /ileʒitim/ *a* illegitimate.

illettré, **~e** /iletʀe/ *a* & *nm,f* illiterate.

illicite /ilisit/ *a* illicit; (Jur) unlawful.

illimité, **~e** /ilimite/ *a* unlimited.

illisible /ilizibl/ *a* illegible; (*livre*) unreadable.

illogique /ilɔʒik/ *a* illogical.

illuminé, **~e** /ilymine/ *a* lit up; (*monument*) floodlit.

illusion /ilyzjɔ̃/ *nf* illusion; **se faire des ~s** delude oneself. **illusoire** *a* illusory.

illustre /ilystʀ/ *a* illustrious.

illustré, **~e** /ilystʀe/ *a* illustrated. ● *nm* comic.

illustrer /ilystʀe/ [1] *vt* illustrate. □ **s'~** *vpr* become famous.

îlot /ilo/ *nm* islet; (de maisons) block.

ils /il/ *pron* they.

image /imaʒ/ *nf* picture; (métaphore) image; (reflet) reflection. **imagé**, **~e** *a* full of imagery.

imaginaire /imaʒinɛʀ/ *a* imaginary. **imaginatif**, **-ive** *a* imaginative. **imagination** *nf* imagination.

imaginer /imaʒine/ [1] *vt* imagine; (inventer) think up. □ **s'~** *vpr* (se représenter) imagine (**que** that); (croire) think (**que** that).

imbécile /ɛ̃besil/ *a* idiotic. ● *nmf* idiot.

imbiber /ɛ̃bibe/ [1] *vt* soak (**de** with). □ **s'~** *vpr* become soaked (**de** with).

imbriqué, **~e** /ɛ̃bʀike/ *a* (lié) interlinked, interlocking; (*tuiles*) overlapping.

imbu, **~e** /ɛ̃by/ *a* **~ de** full of.

imitateur, **-trice** /imitatœʀ, -tʀis/ *nm, f* imitator; (*comédien*) impersonator. **imiter** [1] *vt* imitate; (*personnage*) impersonate; (*signature*) forge; (faire comme) do the same as.

immatriculation /imatʀikylasjɔ̃/ *nf* registration.

immatriculer /imatʀikyle/ [1] *vt* register; **se faire ∼** register; **faire ∼ une voiture** have a car registered.

immédiat, **∼e** /imedja, -t/ *a* immediate. ● *nm* **dans l'∼** for the time being.

immense /imɑ̃s/ *a* huge, immense.

immerger /imɛʀʒe/ [40] *vt* immerse. □ **s'∼** *vpr* immerse oneself (**dans** in).

immeuble /imœbl/ *nm* block of flats, building; **∼ de bureaux** office building *ou* block.

immigrant, **∼e** /imigʀɑ̃, -t/ *a & nm,f* immigrant. **immigration** *nf* immigration. **immigré**, **∼e** *a & nm,f* immigrant. **immigrer** [1] *vi* immigrate.

imminent, **∼e** /iminɑ̃, -t/ *a* imminent.

immobile /imɔbil/ *a* still, motionless.

immobilier, **-ière** /imɔbilje, -jɛʀ/ *a* property; **agence immobilière** estate agent's office, (US) real estate office; **agent ∼** estate agent; (US) real estate agent. ● *nm* **l'∼** property; (US) real estate.

immobiliser /imɔbilize/ [1] *vt* immobilize; (stopper) stop. □ **s'∼** *vpr* stop.

immonde /imɔ̃d/ *a* filthy.

immoral, **∼e** (*mpl* **-aux**) /imɔʀal, -o/ *a* immoral.

immortel, **∼le** /imɔʀtɛl/ *a* immortal.

immuable /imɥabl/ *a* unchanging.

immuniser /imynize/ [1] *vt* immunize; **immunisé contre** (à l'abri de) immune to. **immunité** *nf* immunity.

impact /ɛ̃pakt/ *nm* impact.

impair, **∼e** /ɛ̃pɛʀ/ *a* (*numéro*) odd. ● *nm* blunder, faux pas.

imparfait, **∼e** /ɛ̃paʀfɛ, -t/ *a & nm* imperfect.

impasse /ɛ̃pɑs/ *nf* (rue) dead end; (situation) deadlock.

impatient, **∼e** /ɛ̃pasjɑ̃, -t/ *a* impatient.

impatienter /ɛ̃pasjɑ̃te/ [1] *vt* annoy. □ **s'∼** *vpr* get impatient (**contre qn** with sb).

impayé, **∼e** /ɛ̃peje/ *a* unpaid.

impeccable /ɛ̃pekabl/ *a* (propre) impeccable, spotless; (soigné) perfect.

impensable /ɛ̃pɑ̃sabl/ *a* unthinkable.

impératif, **-ive** /ɛ̃peʀatif, -v/ *a* imperative. ● *nm* (Gram) imperative; (contrainte) imperative; **∼s** (exigences) requirements, demands (**de** of).

impératrice /ɛ̃peʀatʀis/ *nf* empress.

impérial, **∼e** (*mpl* **-iaux**) /ɛ̃peʀjal, -jo/ *a* imperial.

impérieux, **-ieuse** /ɛ̃peʀjø, -z/ *a* imperious; (pressant) pressing.

imperméable /ɛ̃pɛʀmeabl/ *a* impervious (**à** to); (*manteau, tissu*) waterproof. ● *nm* raincoat.

impersonnel, **∼le** /ɛ̃pɛʀsɔnɛl/ *a* impersonal.

impertinent, **∼e** /ɛ̃pɛʀtinɑ̃, -t/ *a* impertinent.

imperturbable /ɛ̃pɛʀtyʀbabl/ *a* unshakeable, unruffled.

impétueux, **-euse** /ɛ̃petɥø, -z/ *a* impetuous.

impitoyable /ɛ̃pitwajabl/ *a* merciless.

implant /ɛ̃plɑ̃/ *nm* implant.

implanter /ɛ̃plɑ̃te/ [1] *vt* establish, set up. □ **s'∼** *vpr* become established.

I

implication /ɛ̃plikasjɔ̃/ *nf* (conséquence) implication; (participation) involvement.

impliquer /ɛ̃plike/ [1] *vt* (mêler) implicate (**dans** in); (signifier) imply, mean (**que** that); (nécessiter) involve (**de faire** doing).

implorer /ɛ̃plɔʀe/ [1] *vt* implore, beg for.

impoli, **∼e** /ɛ̃pɔli/ *a* impolite, rude.

importance /ɛ̃pɔʀtɑ̃s/ *nf* importance; (taille) size; (ampleur) extent; **sans ∼** unimportant.

important, **∼e** /ɛ̃pɔʀtɑ̃, -t/ *a* important; (en quantité) considerable, sizeable, big; (*air*) self-important. ● *nm* **l'∼** the important thing.

importateur, **-trice** /ɛ̃pɔʀtatœʀ, -tʀis/ *nm,f* importer. ● *a* importing. **importation** *nf* import.

importer /ɛ̃pɔʀte/ [1] *vt* (Comm) import. ● *vi* matter, be important (**à** to); **il importe que** it is important that; **n'importe, peu importe** it does not matter; **n'importe comment** anyhow; **n'importe où** anywhere; **n'importe qui** anybody; **n'importe quoi** anything.

importun, **∼e** /ɛ̃pɔʀtœ̃, -yn/ *a* troublesome. ● *nm,f* nuisance.

imposer /ɛ̃poze/ [1] *vt* impose (**à** on); (taxer) tax; **en ∼ à qn** impress sb. □ **s'∼** *vpr* (*action*) be essential; (se faire reconnaître) stand out; (s'astreindre à) **s'∼ de faire** force oneself to do.

imposition /ɛ̃pozisjɔ̃/ *nf* taxation; **∼ des mains** laying-on of hands.

impossible /ɛ̃posibl/ *a* impossible. ● *nm* **faire l'∼** do one's utmost.

impôt /ɛ̃po/ *nm* tax; **∼s** (contributions) tax(ation), taxes; **∼ sur le revenu** income tax.

impotent, **∼e** /ɛ̃pɔtɑ̃, -t/ *a* disabled.

imprécis, **∼e** /ɛ̃pʀesi, -z/ *a* imprecise.

imprégner /ɛ̃pʀeɲe/ [14] *vt* fill (**de** with); (imbiber) impregnate (**de** with). □ **s'∼ de** *vpr* (fig) immerse oneself in.

impression /ɛ̃pʀesjɔ̃/ *nf* impression; (de livre) printing. **impressionnant** *a* impressive; (choquant) disturbing. **impressionner** [1] *vt* impress; (choquer) disturb.

imprévisible /ɛ̃pʀevizibl/ *a* unpredictable.

imprévu, **∼e** /ɛ̃pʀevy/ *a* unexpected. ● *nm* unexpected incident; **sauf ∼** unless anything unexpected happens.

imprimante /ɛ̃pʀimɑ̃t/ *nf* (Ordinat) printer; **∼ à jet d'encre** ink-jet printer; **∼ (à) laser** laser printer.

imprimé, **∼e** /ɛ̃pʀime/ *a* printed. ● *nm* printed form.

imprimer /ɛ̃pʀime/ [1] *vt* print; (marquer) imprint. **imprimerie** *nf* (art) printing; (lieu) printing works. **imprimeur** *nm* printer.

improbable /ɛ̃pʀɔbabl/ *a* unlikely, improbable.

impropre /ɛ̃pʀɔpʀ/ *a* incorrect; **∼ à** unfit for.

improviste: **à l'∼** /alɛ̃pʀɔvist/ *loc* unexpectedly.

imprudence /ɛ̃pʀydɑ̃s/ *nf* carelessness; (acte) careless action.

imprudent, **∼e** /ɛ̃pʀydɑ̃, -t/ *a* careless; **il est ∼ de** it is unwise to.

impudent, **∼e** /ɛ̃pydɑ̃, -t/ *a* impudent.

impuissant, **∼e** /ɛ̃pɥisɑ̃, -t/ *a* helpless; (Méd) impotent; **∼ à faire** powerless to do.

impulsif, **-ive** /ɛ̃pylsif, -v/ *a* impulsive. **impulsion** *nf* (poussée,

influence) impetus; (instinct, mouvement) impulse.
impur, **~e** /ɛ̃pyʀ/ *a* impure.
imputer /ɛ̃pyte/ [1] *vt* **~ à** attribute to, impute to.
inabordable /inabɔʀdabl/ *a* (*prix*) prohibitive.
inacceptable /inaksɛptabl/ *a* unacceptable.
inactif, **-ive** /inaktif, -v/ *a* inactive.
inadapté, **~e** /inadapte/ *a* maladjusted. ● *nm,f* (Psych) maladjusted person.
inadmissible /inadmisibl/ *a* unacceptable.
inadvertance /inadvɛʀtɑ̃s/ *nf* **par ~** by mistake.
inanimé, **~e** /inanime/ *a* (évanoui) unconscious; (mort) lifeless; (*matière*) inanimate.
inaperçu, **~e** /inapɛʀsy/ *a* unnoticed.
inapte /inapt/ *a* unsuited (**à** to); **~ à faire** incapable of doing; **~ au service militaire** unfit for military service.
inattendu, **~e** /inatɑ̃dy/ *a* unexpected.
inaugurer /inogyʀe/ [1] *vt* inaugurate.
incapable /ɛ̃kapabl/ *a* incapable (**de qch** of sth); **~ de faire** unable to do, incapable of doing. ● *nmf* incompetent.
incapacité /ɛ̃kapasite/ *nf* inability, incapacity; **être dans l'~ de faire** be unable to do.
incarcérer /ɛ̃kaʀseʀe/ [14] *vt* imprison, incarcerate.
incarnation /ɛ̃kaʀnasjɔ̃/ *nf* embodiment, incarnation. **incarné**, **~e** *a* (*ongle*) ingrowing.
incassable /ɛ̃kɑsabl/ *a* unbreakable.
incendiaire /ɛ̃sɑ̃djɛʀ/ *a* incendiary; (*propos*) inflammatory. ● *nmf* arsonist.
incendie /ɛ̃sɑ̃di/ *nm* fire; **~ criminel** arson. **incendier** [45] *vt* set fire to.
incertain, **~e** /ɛ̃sɛʀtɛ̃, -ɛn/ *a* uncertain; (*contour*) vague; (*temps*) unsettled. **incertitude** *nf* uncertainty.
inceste /ɛ̃sɛst/ *nm* incest.
incidence /ɛ̃sidɑ̃s/ *nf* effect.
incident /ɛ̃sidɑ̃/ *nm* incident; **~ technique** technical hitch.
incinérer /ɛ̃sineʀe/ [14] *vt* incinerate; (*mort*) cremate.
inciser /ɛ̃size/ [1] *vt* make an incision in; (*abcès*) lance. **incisif**, **-ive** *a* incisive. **incision** *nf* incision; (d'abcès) lancing.
incitation /ɛ̃sitasjɔ̃/ *nf* (Jur) incitement (**à** to); (encouragement) incentive. **inciter** [1] *vt* incite (**à** to); (encourager) encourage.
inclinaison /ɛ̃klinɛzɔ̃/ *nf* incline; (de la tête) tilt.
inclination /ɛ̃klinasjɔ̃/ *nf* (penchant) inclination; (geste) (du buste) bow; (de la tête) nod.
incliner /ɛ̃kline/ [1] *vt* tilt, lean; (courber) bend; (inciter) encourage (**à** to); **~ la tête** (approuver) nod; (révérence) bow. ● *vi* **~ à** be inclined to. □ **s'~** *vpr* lean forward; (se courber) bow down (**devant** before); (céder) give in, yield (**devant** to); (*chemin*) slope.
inclure /ɛ̃klyʀ/ [16] *vt* include; (enfermer) enclose; **jusqu'au lundi inclus** up to and including Monday.
incohérence /ɛ̃kɔeʀɑ̃s/ *nf* incoherence; (contradiction) discrepancy. **incohérent**, **~e** *a* incoherent, inconsistent.
incolore /ɛ̃kɔlɔʀ/ *a* colourless; (*verre*) clear.
incommoder /ɛ̃kɔmɔde/ [1] *vt* inconvenience, bother.
incompatible /ɛ̃kɔ̃patibl/ *a* incompatible.

I

incompétent, **~e** /ɛ̃kɔ̃petɑ̃, -t/ *a* incompetent.

incomplet, **-ète** /ɛ̃kɔ̃plɛ, -t/ *a* incomplete.

incompréhension /ɛ̃kɔ̃pʀeɑ̃sjɔ̃/ *nf* lack of understanding.

incompris, **~e** /ɛ̃kɔ̃pʀi, -z/ *a* misunderstood.

inconcevable /ɛ̃kɔ̃svabl/ *a* inconceivable.

incongru, **~e** /ɛ̃kɔ̃gʀy/ *a* unseemly.

inconnu, **~e** /ɛ̃kɔny/ *a* unknown (**à** to). ● *nm, f* stranger. ● *nm* **l'~** the unknown.

inconscience /ɛ̃kɔ̃sjɑ̃s/ *nf* unconsciousness; (folie) madness.

inconscient, **~e** /ɛ̃kɔ̃sjɑ̃, -t/ *a* unconscious (**de** of); (fou) mad. ● *nm* (Psych) subconscious.

incontestable /ɛ̃kɔ̃tɛstabl/ *a* indisputable.

incontrôlable /ɛ̃kɔ̃tʀolabl/ *a* unverifiable; (non maîtrisé) uncontrollable.

inconvenant, **~e** /ɛ̃kɔ̃vnɑ̃, -t/ *a* improper.

inconvénient /ɛ̃kɔ̃venjɑ̃/ *nm* disadvantage, drawback; (objection) objection.

incorporer /ɛ̃kɔʀpɔʀe/ [1] *vt* incorporate; (Culin) blend (**à** into); (Mil) enlist.

incorrect, **~e** /ɛ̃kɔʀɛkt/ *a* (faux) incorrect; (malséant) improper; (impoli) impolite; (déloyal) unfair.

incrédule /ɛ̃kʀedyl/ *a* incredulous.

incriminer /ɛ̃kʀimine/ [1] *vt* (*personne*) incriminate; (*conduite, action*) attack.

incroyable /ɛ̃kʀwajabl/ *a* incredible.

incruster /ɛ̃kʀyste/ [1] *vt* inlay (**de** with).

incubateur /ɛ̃kybatœʀ/ *nm* incubator.

inculpation /ɛ̃kylpasjɔ̃/ *nf* charge (**de, pour** of). **inculpé**, **~e** *nm, f* accused. **inculper** [1] *vt* charge (**de** with).

inculquer /ɛ̃kylke/ [1] *vt* instil (**à** into).

inculte /ɛ̃kylt/ *a* uncultivated; (*personne*) uneducated.

incurver /ɛ̃kyʀve/ [1] *vt* curve, bend. □ **s'~** *vpr* curve, bend.

Inde /ɛ̃d/ *nf* India.

indécent, **~e** /ɛ̃desɑ̃, -t/ *a* indecent.

indécis, **~e** /ɛ̃desi, -z/ *a* (de nature) indecisive; (temporairement) undecided.

indéfini, **~e** /ɛ̃defini/ *a* (Gram) indefinite; (vague) undefined; (sans limites) indeterminate.

indemne /ɛ̃dɛmn/ *a* unharmed.

indemniser /ɛ̃dɛmnize/ [1] *vt* compensate (**de** for).

indemnité /ɛ̃dɛmnite/ *nf* indemnity, compensation; (allocation) allowance; **~s de licenciement** redundancy payment.

indépendance /ɛ̃depɑ̃dɑ̃s/ *nf* independence. **indépendant**, **~e** *a* independent.

indéterminé, **~e** /ɛ̃detɛʀmine/ *a* unspecified.

index /ɛ̃dɛks/ *nm* forefinger; (liste) index.

indicateur, **-trice** /ɛ̃dikatœʀ, -tʀis/ *nm, f* (police) informer. ● *nm* (livre) guide; (Tech) indicator.

indicatif, **-ve** /ɛ̃dikatif, -v/ *a* indicative (**de** of). ● *nm* (à la radio) signature tune; (téléphonique) dialling code; (Gram) indicative.

indication /ɛ̃dikasjɔ̃/ *nf* indication; (renseignement) information; (directive) instruction.

indice /ɛ̃dis/ *nm* sign; (dans une enquête) clue; (des prix) index; (évaluation) rating; **~ d'écoute** audience ratings.

indifférence /ɛ̃diferɑ̃s/ *nf* indifference.

indifférent, **~e** /ɛ̃diferɑ̃, -t/ *a* indifferent (**à** to); **ça m'est ~** it makes no difference to me.

indigène /ɛ̃diʒɛn/ *a & nmf* native, indigenous; (du pays) local. ● *nmf* native.

indigent, **~e** /ɛ̃diʒɑ̃, -t/ *a* destitute.

indigeste /ɛ̃diʒɛst/ *a* indigestible. **indigestion** *nf* indigestion.

indigne /ɛ̃diɲ/ *a* unworthy (**de** of); (*acte*) vile. **indigner (s')** [1] *vpr* become indignant (**de** at).

indiqué, **~e** /ɛ̃dike/ *a* (*heure*) appointed; (opportun) appropriate; (conseillé) recommended.

indiquer /ɛ̃dike/ [1] *vt* (montrer) show, indicate; (renseigner sur) point out, tell; (déterminer) give, state, appoint; **~ du doigt** point to *ou* out *ou* at.

indirect, **~e** /ɛ̃dirɛkt/ *a* indirect.

indiscipliné, **~e** /ɛ̃disipline/ *a* unruly.

indiscret, **-ète** /ɛ̃diskrɛ, -t/ *a* (*personne*) inquisitive; (*question*) indiscreet.

indiscutable /ɛ̃diskytabl/ *a* unquestionable.

indispensable /ɛ̃dispɑ̃sabl/ *a* indispensable; **il est ~ qu'il vienne** it is essential that he comes.

individu /ɛ̃dividy/ *nm* individual.

individuel, **~le** /ɛ̃dividɥɛl/ *a* (pour une personne) individual; (qui concerne l'individu) personal; **chambre ~le** single room; **maison ~le** detached house.

indolore /ɛ̃dɔlɔr/ *a* painless.

Indonésie /ɛ̃dɔnezi/ *nf* Indonesia.

indu, **~e** /ɛ̃dy/ *a* **à une heure ~e** at some ungodly hour.

induire /ɛ̃dɥir/ [17] *vt* infer (**de** from); (inciter) induce (**à faire** to do); **~ en erreur** mislead.

indulgence /ɛ̃dylʒɑ̃s/ *nf* indulgence; (de jury) leniency. **indulgent**, **~e** *a* indulgent; (clément) lenient.

industrialisé, **~e** /ɛ̃dystrijalize/ *a* industrialized.

industrie /ɛ̃dystri/ *nf* industry.

industriel, **~le** /ɛ̃dystrijɛl/ *a* industrial. ● *nm* industrialist.

inédit, **~e** /inedi, -t/ *a* unpublished; (fig) original.

inefficace /inefikas/ *a* (*remède, mesure*) ineffective; (*appareil, système*) inefficient.

inégal, **~e** (*mpl* **-aux**) /inegal, -o/ *a* unequal; (irrégulier) uneven. **inégalable** *a* matchless. **inégalité** *nf* (injustice) inequality; (irrégularité) unevenness; (disproportion) disparity.

inéluctable /inelyktabl/ *a* inescapable.

inepte /inɛpt/ *a* inept, absurd.

inerte /inɛrt/ *a* inert; (immobile) lifeless; (sans énergie) apathetic. **inertie** *nf* inertia; (fig) apathy.

inespéré, **~e** /inɛspere/ *a* unhoped for.

inestimable /inɛstimabl/ *a* priceless; (*aide*) invaluable.

inexact, **~e** /inɛgza(kt), -kt/ *a* (imprécis) inaccurate; (incorrect) incorrect.

in extremis /inɛkstremis/ *adv* (par nécessité) as a last resort; (au dernier moment) at the last minute. ● *a* last-minute.

infaillible /ɛ̃fajibl/ *a* infallible.

infâme /ɛ̃fɑm/ *a* vile.

infantile /ɛ̃fɑ̃til/ *a* (puéril) infantile; (*maladie*) childhood; (*mortalité*) infant.

infarctus /ɛ̃farktys/ *nm* coronary, heart attack.

infatigable /ɛ̃fatigabl/ *a* tireless.

infect, **~e** /ɛ̃fɛkt/ *a* revolting.

infecter /ɛ̃fɛkte/ [1] *vt* infect. □ **s'~** *vpr* become infected.

I

infectieux, -ieuse *a* infectious.
infection *nf* infection.

inférieur, ~e /ɛ̃feʀjœʀ/ *a* (plus bas) lower; (moins bon) inferior (**à** to); **~ à** (plus petit que) smaller than; (plus bas que) lower than. ● *nm, f* inferior. **infériorité** *nf* inferiority.

infernal, ~e (*mpl* **-aux**) /ɛ̃fɛʀnal, -o/ *a* infernal.

infester /ɛ̃fɛste/ [1] *vt* infest.

infidèle /ɛ̃fidɛl/ *a* unfaithful (**à** to). **infidélité** *nf* unfaithfulness; (acte) infidelity.

infiltrer (s') /sɛ̃filtʀe/ [1] *vpr* **s'~ (dans)** (*personnes, idées*) infiltrate; (*liquide*) seep through.

infime /ɛ̃fim/ *a* tiny, minute.

infini, ~e /ɛ̃fini/ *a* infinite. ● *nm* infinity; **à l'~** endlessly.

infinité /ɛ̃finite/ *nf* **l'~** infinity; **une ~ de** an endless number of.

infinitif /ɛ̃finitif/ *nm* infinitive.

infirme /ɛ̃fiʀm/ *a* disabled. ● *nmf* disabled person. **infirmerie** *nf* sickbay, infirmary. **infirmier** *nm* (male) nurse. **infirmière** *nf* nurse. **infirmité** *nf* disability.

inflammable /ɛ̃flamabl/ *a* inflammable.

inflation /ɛ̃flasjɔ̃/ *nf* inflation.

infliger /ɛ̃fliʒe/ [40] *vt* inflict; (*sanction*) impose.

influence /ɛ̃flyɑ̃s/ *nf* influence. **influencer** [10] *vt* influence. **influent, ~e** *a* influential.

influer /ɛ̃flye/ [1] *vi* **~ sur** influence.

informateur, -trice /ɛ̃fɔʀmatœʀ, -tʀis/ *nm, f* informant; (pour la police) informer.

informaticien, ~ne /ɛ̃fɔʀmatisjɛ̃, -ɛn/ *nm, f* computer scientist.

information /ɛ̃fɔʀmasjɔ̃/ *nf* information; (Jur) inquiry; **une ~** (some) information; (nouvelle) (some) news; **les ~s** the news.

informatique /ɛ̃fɔʀmatik/ *nf* computer science; (techniques) information technology. **informatiser** [1] *vt* computerize.

informer /ɛ̃fɔʀme/ [1] *vt* inform (**de** about, of). □ **s'~** *vpr* enquire (**de** about).

inforoute /ɛ̃fɔʀut/ *nf* (Ordinat) information highway.

infortune /ɛ̃fɔʀtyn/ *nf* misfortune.

infraction /ɛ̃fʀaksjɔ̃/ *nf* offence; **~ à** (*loi, règlement*) breach of.

infrastructure /ɛ̃fʀastʀyktyʀ/ *nf* infrastructure; (équipements) facilities.

infructueux, -euse /ɛ̃fʀyktɥø, -z/ *a* fruitless.

infuser /ɛ̃fyze/ [1] *vt/i* infuse, brew. **infusion** *nf* herbal tea, infusion.

ingénier (s') /(s)ɛ̃ʒenje/ [45] *vpr* **s'~ à** strive to.

ingénieur /ɛ̃ʒenjœʀ/ *nm* engineer.

ingénieux, -ieuse /ɛ̃ʒenjø, -z/ *a* ingenious. **ingéniosité** *nf* ingenuity.

ingénu, ~e /ɛ̃ʒeny/ *a* naïve.

ingérence /ɛ̃ʒeʀɑ̃s/ *nf* interference.

ingérer (s') /sɛ̃ʒeʀe/ [14] *vpr* **s'~ dans** interfere in.

ingrat, ~e /ɛ̃gʀa, -t/ *a* (*personne*) ungrateful; (*travail*) unrewarding, thankless; (*visage*) unattractive.

ingrédient /ɛ̃gʀedjɑ̃/ *nm* ingredient.

ingurgiter /ɛ̃gyʀʒite/ [1] *vt* swallow.

inhabité, ~e /inabite/ *a* uninhabited.

inhabituel, ~le /inabitɥɛl/ *a* unusual.

inhumain, ~e /inymɛ̃, -ɛn/ *a* inhuman.

inhumation /inymasjɔ̃/ *nf* burial.

initial, **~e** (*mpl* **-iaux**) /inisjal, -jo/ *a* initial. **initiale** *nf* initial.

initialisation /inisjalizasjɔ̃/ *nf* (Ordinat) formatting. **initialiser** [1] *vt* format.

initiation /inisjasjɔ̃/ *nf* initiation; (formation) introduction (**à** to); **cours d'~** introductory course.

initiative /inisjativ/ *nf* initiative.

initier /inisje/ [45] *vt* initiate (**à** into); (faire découvrir) introduce (**à** to). □ **s'~** *vpr* **s'~ à qch** learn sth.

injecter /ɛ̃ʒɛkte/ [1] *vt* inject; **injecté de sang** bloodshot. **injection** *nf* injection.

injure /ɛ̃ʒyʀ/ *nf* insult. **injurier** [45] *vt* insult. **injurieux**, **-ieuse** *a* insulting.

injuste /ɛ̃ʒyst/ *a* unjust, unfair. **injustice** *nf* injustice.

inné, **~e** /inne/ *a* innate, inborn.

innocence /inɔsɑ̃s/ *nf* innocence. **innocent**, **~e** *a & nm,f* innocent. **innocenter** [1] *vt* clear, prove innocent.

innombrable /inɔ̃bʀabl/ *a* countless.

innovateur, **-trice** /inɔvatœʀ, -tʀis/ *nm,f* innovator. **innovation** *nf* innovation. **innover** [1] *vi* innovate.

inodore /inɔdɔʀ/ *a* odourless.

inoffensif, **-ive** /inɔfɑ̃sif, -v/ *a* harmless.

inondation /inɔ̃dasjɔ̃/ *nf* flood; (action) flooding.

inonder /inɔ̃de/ [1] *vt* flood; (mouiller) soak; (envahir) inundate (**de** with); **inondé de soleil** bathed in sunlight.

inopiné, **~e** /inɔpine/ *a* unexpected; (*mort*) sudden.

inopportun, **~e** /inɔpɔʀtœ̃, -yn/ *a* inopportune, ill-timed.

inoubliable /inublijabl/ *a* unforgettable.

inouï, **~e** /inwi/ *a* incredible; (*événement*) unprecedented.

inox® /inɔks/ *nm* stainless steel.

inoxydable /inɔksidabl/ *a* **acier ~** stainless steel.

inqualifiable /ɛ̃kalifjabl/ *a* unspeakable.

inquiet, **-iète** /ɛ̃kjɛ, -t/ *a* worried. **inquiétant**, **~e** *a* worrying.

inquiéter /ɛ̃kjete/ [14] *vt* worry. □ **s'~** *vpr* worry (**de** about). **inquiétude** *nf* anxiety, worry.

insaisissable /ɛ̃sezisabl/ *a* (*personne*) elusive; (*nuance*) indefinable.

insalubre /ɛ̃salybʀ/ *a* unhealthy.

insatisfaisant, **~e** /ɛ̃satisfəzɑ̃, -t/ *a* unsatisfactory. **insatisfait**, **~e** *a* (mécontent) dissatisfied; (frustré) unfulfilled.

inscription /ɛ̃skʀipsjɔ̃/ *nf* inscription; (immatriculation) enrolment.

inscrire /ɛ̃skʀiʀ/ [30] *vt* write (down); (graver, tracer) inscribe; (*personne*) enrol; (sur une liste) put down. □ **s'~** *vpr* put one's name down; **s'~ à** (*école*) enrol at; (*club, parti*) join; (*examen*) enter for.

insecte /ɛ̃sɛkt/ *nm* insect.

insécurité /ɛ̃sekyʀite/ *nf* insecurity.

insensé, **~e** /ɛ̃sɑ̃se/ *a* mad.

insensibilité /ɛ̃sɑ̃sibilite/ *nf* insensitivity. **insensible** *a* insensitive (**à** to); (graduel) imperceptible.

insérer /ɛ̃seʀe/ [14] *vt* insert. □ **s'~** *vpr* be inserted; **s'~ dans** be part of.

insigne /ɛ̃siɲ/ *nm* badge; **~s** (d'une fonction) insignia.

insignifiant, **~e** /ɛ̃siɲifjɑ̃, -t/ *a* insignificant.

insinuation /ɛ̃sinɥasjɔ̃/ *nf* insinuation.

insinuer /ɛ̃sinɥe/ [1] *vt* insinuate. □ **s'~** *vpr* (socialement) ingratiate oneself (**auprès de qn** with sb);

I

s'~ dans (se glisser) slip into; (*idée, nuance*) creep into.

insipide /ɛ̃sipid/ *a* insipid.

insistance /ɛ̃sistɑ̃s/ *nf* insistence. **insistant, ~e** *a* insistent.

insister /ɛ̃siste/ [1] *vi* insist (**pour faire** on doing); **~ sur** stress.

insolation /ɛ̃sɔlasjɔ̃/ *nf* (Méd) sunstroke.

insolent, ~e /ɛ̃sɔlɑ̃, -t/ *a* insolent.

insolite /ɛ̃sɔlit/ *a* unusual.

insolvable /ɛ̃sɔlvabl/ *a* insolvent.

insomnie /ɛ̃sɔmni/ *nf* insomnia.

insonoriser /ɛ̃sɔnɔʀize/ [1] *vt* soundproof.

insouciance /ɛ̃susjɑ̃s/ *nf* lack of concern. **insouciant, ~e** *a* carefree.

insoutenable /ɛ̃sutnabl/ *a* unbearable; (*argument*) untenable.

inspecter /ɛ̃spɛkte/ [1] *vt* inspect. **inspecteur, -trice** *nm, f* inspector. **inspection** *nf* inspection.

inspiration /ɛ̃spiʀasjɔ̃/ *nf* inspiration; (respiration) breath.

inspirer /ɛ̃spiʀe/ [1] *vt* inspire; **~ la méfiance à qn** inspire distrust in sb. ● *vi* breathe in. □ **s'~ de** *vpr* be inspired by.

instabilité /ɛ̃stabilite/ *nf* instability; unsteadiness. **instable** *a* unstable; (*temps*) unsettled.

installation /ɛ̃stalasjɔ̃/ *nf* installation; (de local) fitting out; (de locataire) settling in. **installations** *nfpl* facilities.

installer /ɛ̃stale/ [1] *vt* install; (*meuble*) put in; (*étagère*) put up; (*gaz, téléphone*) connect; (équiper) fit out. □ **s'~** *vpr* settle (down); (emménager) settle in; **s'~ comme** set oneself up as.

instance /ɛ̃stɑ̃s/ *nf* authority; (prière) entreaty; **avec ~** with insistence; **en ~** pending; **en ~ de** in the course of, on the point of.

instant /ɛ̃stɑ̃/ *nm* moment, instant; **à l'~** this instant.

instantané, ~e /ɛ̃stɑ̃tane/ *a* instantaneous; (*café*) instant.

instar: **à l'~ de** /alɛ̃staʀdə/ *loc* like.

instaurer /ɛ̃stoʀe/ [1] *vt* institute.

instigateur, -trice /ɛ̃stigatœʀ, -tʀis/ *nm, f* instigator.

instinct /ɛ̃stɛ̃/ *nm* instinct; **d'~** instinctively. **instinctif, -ive** *a* instinctive.

instituer /ɛ̃stitɥe/ [1] *vt* establish.

institut /ɛ̃stity/ *nm* institute; **~ de beauté** beauty parlour.

instituteur, -trice /ɛ̃stitytœʀ, -tʀis/ *nm, f* primary-school teacher.

institution /ɛ̃stitysjɔ̃/ *nf* institution; (école) private school.

instructif, -ive /ɛ̃stʀyktif, -v/ *a* instructive.

instruction /ɛ̃stʀyksjɔ̃/ *nf* (formation) education; (Mil) training; (document) directive; **~s** (ordres, mode d'emploi) instructions; (Ordinat) (énoncé) instruction; (pas de séquence) statement.

instruire /ɛ̃stʀɥiʀ/ [17] *vt* teach, educate; **~ de** inform of. □ **s'~** *vpr* learn, educate oneself; **s'~ de** enquire about. **instruit, ~e** *a* educated.

instrument /ɛ̃stʀymɑ̃/ *nm* instrument; (outil) tool; (moyen: fig) instrument; **~ de gestion** management tool; **~s de bord** (Aviat) controls.

insu: **à l'~ de** /alɛ̃sydə/ *loc* without the knowledge of.

insuffisance /ɛ̃syfizɑ̃s/ *nf* (pénurie) shortage; (médiocrité) inadequacy. **insuffisant, ~e** *a*

inadequate; (en nombre) insufficient.
insulaire /ɛ̃sylɛʀ/ *a* island. ● *nmf* islander.
insuline /ɛ̃sylin/ *nf* insulin.
insulte /ɛ̃sylt/ *nf* insult. **insulter** [1] *vt* insult.
insupportable /ɛ̃sypɔʀtabl/ *a* unbearable.
insurger (s') /(s)ɛ̃syʀʒe/ [40] *vpr* rebel.
intact, ~e /ɛ̃takt/ *a* intact.
intangible /ɛ̃tɑ̃ʒibl/ *a* intangible; (*principe*) inviolable.
intarissable /ɛ̃taʀisabl/ *a* inexhaustible.
intégral, ~e (*mpl* **-aux**) /ɛ̃tegʀal, -o/ *a* complete; (*texte, édition*) unabridged; (*paiement*) full, in full. **intégralement** *adv* in full. **intégralité** *nf* whole.
intègre /ɛ̃tɛgʀ/ *a* upright.
intégrer /ɛ̃tegʀe/ [14] *vt* integrate. □ **s'~** *vpr* (*personne*) integrate; (*maison*) fit in.
intégriste /ɛ̃tegʀist/ *nmf* fundamentalist.
intégrité /ɛ̃tegʀite/ *nf* integrity.
intellect /ɛ̃telɛkt/ *nm* intellect.
intellectuel, ~le *a & nm,f* intellectual.
intelligence /ɛ̃teliʒɑ̃s/ *nf* intelligence; (compréhension) understanding; (complicité) agreement; **agir d'~ avec qn** act in agreement with sb. **intelligent, ~e** *a* intelligent.
intempéries /ɛ̃tɑ̃peʀi/ *nfpl* severe weather.
intempestif, -ive /ɛ̃tɑ̃pɛstif, -v/ *a* untimely.
intenable /ɛ̃tnabl/ *a* unbearable; (*enfant*) impossible.
intendance /ɛ̃tɑ̃dɑ̃s/ *nf* (Scol) bursar's office.
intendant, ~e /ɛ̃tɑ̃dɑ̃, -t/ *nm* (Mil) quartermaster. ● *nm,f* (Scol) bursar.
intense /ɛ̃tɑ̃s/ *a* intense; (*circulation*) heavy. **intensif, -ive** *a* intensive. **intensité** *nf* intensity.
intenter /ɛ̃tɑ̃te/ [1] *vt* **~ un procès** *ou* **une action** institute proceedings (**à, contre** against).
intention /ɛ̃tɑ̃sjɔ̃/ *nf* intention (**de faire** of doing); **à l'~ de qn** for sb. **intentionnel, ~le** *a* intentional.
interactif, -ive /ɛ̃tɛʀaktif, -v/ *a* (*TV, vidéo*) interactive.
interaction /ɛ̃tɛʀaksjɔ̃/ *nf* interaction.
intercaler /ɛ̃tɛʀkale/ [1] *vt* insert.
intercéder /ɛ̃tɛʀsede/ [14] *vi* intercede (**en faveur de** on behalf of).
intercepter /ɛ̃tɛʀsɛpte/ [1] *vt* intercept.
interdiction /ɛ̃tɛʀdiksjɔ̃/ *nf* ban; **~ de fumer** no smoking.
interdire /ɛ̃tɛʀdiʀ/ [37] *vt* forbid; (officiellement) ban, prohibit; **~ à qn de faire** forbid sb to do.
interdit, ~e /ɛ̃tɛʀdi, -t/ *a* prohibited, forbidden; (étonné) dumbfounded.
intéressant, ~e /ɛ̃teʀɛsɑ̃, -t/ *a* interesting; (avantageux) attractive.
intéressé, ~e /ɛ̃teʀese/ *a* (en cause) concerned; (pour profiter) self-interested. ● *nm,f* person concerned.
intéresser /ɛ̃teʀese/ [1] *vt* interest; (concerner) concern. □ **s'~ à** *vpr* be interested in.
intérêt /ɛ̃teʀɛ/ *nm* interest; (égoïsme) self-interest; **~(s)** (Comm) interest; **vous avez ~ à** it is in your interest to.
interface /ɛ̃tɛʀfas/ *nf* (Ordinat) interface.
intérieur, ~e /ɛ̃teʀjœʀ/ *a* inner, inside; (*mur, escalier*) internal; (*vol, politique*) domestic; (*vie, calme*) inner. ● *nm* interior; (de

I

boîte, tiroir) inside; **à l'~ (de)** inside; (fig) within. **intérieurement** *adv* inwardly.

intérim /ɛ̃teʀim/ *nm* interim; **assurer l'~** deputize (**de** for); **par ~** on an interim basis; **président par ~** acting president; **faire de l'~** temp.

intérimaire /ɛ̃teʀimɛʀ/ *a* temporary, interim. ● *nmf* (secrétaire) temp; (médecin) locum.

interjection /ɛ̃tɛʀʒɛksjɔ̃/ *nf* interjection.

interlocuteur, **-trice** /ɛ̃tɛʀlɔkytœʀ, -tʀis/ *nm, f* **son ~** the person one is speaking to.

interloqué, **~e** /ɛ̃tɛʀlɔke/ *a* **être ~** be taken aback.

intermède /ɛ̃tɛʀmɛd/ *nm* interlude.

intermédiaire /ɛ̃tɛʀmedjɛʀ/ *a* intermediate. ● *nmf* intermediary. ● *nm* **sans ~** without an intermediary, direct; **par l'~ de** through.

interminable /ɛ̃tɛʀminabl/ *a* endless.

intermittence /ɛ̃tɛʀmitɑ̃s/ *nf* **par ~** intermittently.

internat /ɛ̃tɛʀna/ *nm* boarding-school.

international, **~e** (*mpl* **-aux**) /ɛ̃tɛʀnasjɔnal, -o/ *a* international.

internaute /ɛ̃tɛʀnot/ *nmf* (Ordinat) Netsurfer, Internet user.

interne /ɛ̃tɛʀn/ *a* internal; (*cours, formation*) in-house. ● *nmf* (Scol) boarder; (Méd) house officer; (US) intern.

internement /ɛ̃tɛʀnəmɑ̃/ *nm* (Pol) internment. **interner** [1] *vt* (Pol) intern; (Méd) commit.

Internet /ɛ̃tɛʀnet/ *nm* Internet.

interpellation /ɛ̃tɛʀpelasjɔ̃/ *nf* (Pol) questioning. **interpeller** [1] *vt* shout to; (apostropher) shout at; (interroger) question.

interphone /ɛ̃tɛʀfɔn/ *nm* intercom; (d'immeuble) entry phone.

interposer (s') /(s)ɛ̃tɛʀpoze/ [1] *vpr* intervene.

interprétariat /ɛ̃tɛʀpʀetaʀja/ *nm* interpreting. **interprétation** *nf* interpretation; (d'artiste) performance. **interprète** *nmf* interpreter; (artiste) performer. **interpréter** [14] *vt* interpret; (jouer) play; (chanter) sing.

interrogateur, **-trice** /ɛ̃tɛʀɔgatœʀ, -tʀis/ *a* questioning. **interrogatif**, **-ive** *a* interrogative. **interrogation** *nf* question; (action) questioning; (épreuve) test. **Interrogatoire** *nm* interrogation. **interroger** [40] *vt* question; (*élève*) test.

interrompre /ɛ̃teʀɔ̃pʀ/ [3] *vt* break off, interrupt; (*personne*) interrupt. □ **s'~** *vpr* break off. **interrupteur** *nm* switch. **interruption** *nf* interruption; (arrêt) break.

interurbain, **~e** /ɛ̃tɛʀyʀbɛ̃, -ɛn/ *a* long-distance, trunk.

intervalle /ɛ̃tɛʀval/ *nm* space; (temps) interval; **dans l'~** in the meantime.

intervenir /ɛ̃tɛʀvəniʀ/ [58] *vi* (agir) intervene (**auprès de qn** with sb); (survenir) occur, take place; (Méd) operate. **intervention** *nf* intervention; (Méd) operation.

intervertir /ɛ̃tɛʀvɛʀtiʀ/ [2] *vt* invert; (*rôles*) reverse.

interview /ɛ̃tɛʀvju/ *nf* interview. **interviewer** [1] *vt* interview.

intestin /ɛ̃tɛstɛ̃/ *nm* intestine.

intime /ɛ̃tim/ *a* intimate; (*fête, vie*) private; (*dîner*) quiet. ● *nmf* intimate friend.

intimider /ɛ̃timide/ [1] *vt* intimidate.

intimité /ɛ̃timite/ *nf* intimacy; (vie privée) privacy.

intituler /ɛ̃tityle/ [1] *vt* call,

entitle. ▫ **s'~** *vpr* be called *ou* entitled.

intolérable /ɛ̃tɔleRabl/ *a* intolerable. **intolérance** *nf* intolerance. **intolérant, ~e** *a* intolerant.

intonation /ɛ̃tɔnasjɔ̃/ *nf* intonation.

intox /ɛ̃tɔks/ *nf* ▣ brainwashing.

intoxication /ɛ̃tɔksikasjɔ̃/ *nf* poisoning; (fig) brainwashing; **~ alimentaire** food poisoning. **intoxiquer** [1] *vt* poison; (fig) brainwash.

intraitable /ɛ̃tRɛtabl/ *a* inflexible.

Intranet /ɛ̃tRanɛt/ *nm* (Ordinat) Intranet.

intransigeant, ~e /ɛ̃tRɑ̃ziʒɑ̃, -t/ *a* intransigent.

intransitif, -ive /ɛ̃tRɑ̃zitif, -v/ *a* intransitive.

intraveineux, -euse /ɛ̃tRavɛnø, -z/ *a* intravenous.

intrépide /ɛ̃tRepid/ *a* fearless.

intrigue /ɛ̃tRig/ *nf* intrigue; (scénario) plot.

intrinsèque /ɛ̃tRɛ̃sɛk/ *a* intrinsic.

introduction /ɛ̃tRɔdyksjɔ̃/ *nf* introduction; (insertion) insertion.

introduire /ɛ̃tRɔdɥiR/ [17] *vt* introduce, bring in; (insérer) put in, insert; **~ qn** show sb in. ▫ **s'~** *vpr* get in; **s'~ dans** get into, enter.

introuvable /ɛ̃tRuvabl/ *a* that cannot be found.

introverti, ~e /ɛ̃tRɔvɛRti/ *nm, f* introvert. ● *a* introverted.

intrus, ~e /ɛ̃tRy, -z/ *nm, f* intruder. **intrusion** *nf* intrusion.

intuitif, -ive /ɛ̃tɥitif, -iv/ *a* intuitive. **intuition** *nf* intuition.

inusable /inyzabl/ *a* hard-wearing.

inusité, ~e /inyzite/ *a* little used.

inutile /inytil/ *a* useless; (vain) needless. **inutilement** *adv* needlessly. **inutilisable** *a* unusable.

invalide /ɛ̃valid/ *a & nmf* disabled (person).

invariable /ɛ̃vaRjabl/ *a* invariable.

invasion /ɛ̃vɑzjɔ̃/ *nf* invasion.

invectiver /ɛ̃vɛktive/ [1] *vt* abuse.

inventaire /ɛ̃vɑ̃tɛR/ *nm* inventory; (Comm) stocklist; **faire l'~** draw up an inventory; (Comm) do a stocktake.

inventer /ɛ̃vɑ̃te/ [1] *vt* invent. **inventeur, -trice** *nm, f* inventor. **inventif, -ive** *a* inventive. **invention** *nf* invention.

inverse /ɛ̃vɛRs/ *a* opposite; (*ordre*) reverse; **en sens ~** in *ou* from the opposite direction. ● *nm* reverse; **c'est l'~** it's the other way round. **inversement** *adv* conversely. **inverser** [1] *vt* reverse, invert.

investir /ɛ̃vɛstiR/ [2] *vt* invest. **investissement** *nm* investment.

investiture /ɛ̃vɛstityR/ *nf* (de candidat) nomination; (de président) investiture.

invétéré, ~e /ɛ̃veteRe/ *a* inveterate; (*menteur*) compulsive; (enraciné) deep-rooted.

invisible /ɛ̃vizibl/ *a* invisible.

invitation /ɛ̃vitasjɔ̃/ *nf* invitation. **invité, ~e** *nm, f* guest. **inviter** [1] *vt* invite (**à** to).

involontaire /ɛ̃vɔlɔ̃tɛR/ *a* involuntary; (*témoin, héros*) unwitting.

invoquer /ɛ̃vɔke/ [1] *vt* call upon, invoke.

invraisemblable /ɛ̃vRɛsɑ̃blabl/ *a* improbable, unlikely; (incroyable) incredible. **invraisemblance** *nf* improbability.

iode /jɔd/ *nm* iodine.

ira, irait /iRa, iRɛ/ ⇒ALLER [8].

Irak /iʀak/ *nm* Iraq.

Iran /iʀɑ̃/ *nm* Iran.

iris /iʀis/ *nm* iris.

irlandais, **~e** /iʀlɑ̃dɛ, -z/ *a* Irish. **I~**, **~e** *nm, f* Irishman, Irishwoman.

Irlande /iʀlɑ̃d/ *nf* Ireland.

ironie /iʀɔni/ *nf* irony. **ironique** *a* ironic.

irrationnel, **~le** /iʀasjɔnɛl/ *a* irrational.

irréalisable /iʀealizabl/ *a* (*idée, rêve*) unachievable; (*projet*) unworkable.

irrécupérable /iʀekypeʀabl/ *a* irretrievable; (*capital*) irrecoverable.

irréel, **~le** /iʀeɛl/ *a* unreal.

irréfléchi, **~e** /iʀefleʃi/ *a* thoughtless.

irrégulier, **-ière** /iʀegylje, -jɛʀ/ *a* irregular.

irrémédiable /iʀemedjabl/ *a* irreparable.

irremplaçable /iʀɑ̃plasabl/ *a* irreplaceable.

irréparable /iʀepaʀabl/ *a* (*objet*) beyond repair; (*tort, dégâts*) irreparable.

irréprochable /iʀepʀɔʃabl/ *a* flawless.

irrésistible /iʀezistibl/ *a* irresistible; (drôle) hilarious.

irrésolu, **~e** /iʀezɔly/ *a* indecisive; (*problème*) unsolved.

irrespirable /iʀɛspiʀabl/ *a* stifling.

irresponsable /iʀɛspɔ̃sabl/ *a* irresponsible.

irrigation /iʀigasjɔ̃/ *nf* irrigation. **irriguer** [1] *vt* irrigate.

irritable /iʀitabl/ *a* irritable.

irriter /iʀite/ [1] *vt* irritate. □ **s'~** *vpr* get annoyed (**de** at).

irruption /iʀypsjɔ̃/ *nf* **faire ~ dans** burst into.

Islam /islam/ *nm* Islam. **islamique** *a* Islamic.

islandais, **~e** /islɑ̃dɛ, -z/ *a* Icelandic. ● *nm* (Ling) Icelandic. **I~**, **~e** *nm, f* Icelander.

Islande /islɑ̃d/ *nf* Iceland.

isolant /izɔlɑ̃/ *nm* insulating material. **isolation** *nf* insulation.

isolé, **~e** /izɔle/ *a* isolated. **isolement** *nm* isolation.

isoler /izɔle/ [1] *vt* isolate; (Électr) insulate. □ **s'~** *vpr* isolate oneself.

isoloir /izɔlwaʀ/ *nm* polling booth.

Isorel® /izɔʀɛl/ *nm* hardboard.

Israël /isʀaɛl/ *nm* Israel. **israélien**, **~ne** *a* Israeli.

israélite /isʀaelit/ *a* Jewish. ● *nmf* Jew.

issu, **~e** /isy/ *a* **être ~ de** (*personne*) come from; (résulter de) result *ou* stem from.

issue /isy/ *nf* (sortie) exit; (résultat) outcome; (fig) solution; **à l'~ de** at the conclusion of; **~ de secours** emergency exit; **rue** *ou* **voie sans ~** dead end.

Italie /itali/ *nf* Italy.

italien, **~ne** /italjɛ̃, -ɛn/ *a* Italian. ● *nm* (Ling) Italian. **I~**, **~ne** *nm, f* Italian.

italique /italik/ *nm* italics.

itinéraire /itineʀɛʀ/ *nm* itinerary, route.

I.U.T. *abrév m* (**Institut universitaire de technologie**) university institute of technology.

I.V.G. *abrév f* (**interruption volontaire de grossesse**) abortion.

ivoire /ivwaʀ/ *nm* ivory.

ivre /ivʀ/ *a* drunk. **ivresse** *nf* drunkenness; (fig) exhilaration. **ivrogne** *nmf* drunk(ard).

j' /ʒ/ ⇨JE.

jacinthe /ʒasɛ̃t/ *nf* hyacinth.

jadis /ʒadis/ *adv* long ago.

jaillir /ʒajiʀ/ [2] *vi* (*liquide*) spurt (out); (*lumière*) stream out; (apparaître) burst forth, spring out.

jalonner /ʒalɔne/ [1] *vt* mark (out).

jalousie /ʒaluzi/ *nf* jealousy; (store) (venetian) blind. **jaloux, -ouse** *a* jealous.

jamais /ʒamɛ/ *adv* ever; **ne ~** never; **il ne boit ~** he never drinks; **à ~** for ever; **si ~** if ever.

jambe /ʒɑ̃b/ *nf* leg.

jambon /ʒɑ̃bɔ̃/ *nm* ham. **jambonneau** (*pl* **~x**) *nm* knuckle of ham.

janvier /ʒɑ̃vje/ *nm* January.

Japon /ʒapɔ̃/ *nm* Japan.

japonais, ~e /japɔnɛ, -z/ *a* Japanese. ●*nm* (Ling) Japanese. **J~, ~e** *nm, f* Japanese.

japper /ʒape/ [1] *vi* yap.

jaquette /ʒakɛt/ *nf* (de livre, femme) jacket; (d'homme) morning coat.

jardin /ʒaʀdɛ̃/ *nm* garden; **~ d'enfants** nursery (school); **~ public** public park. **jardinage** *nm* gardening. **jardiner** [1] *vi* do some gardening, garden. **jardinier, -ière** *nm, f* gardener.

jardinière /ʒaʀdinjɛʀ/ *nf* (meuble) plant-stand; **~ de légumes** mixed vegetables.

jarretelle /ʒaʀtɛl/ *nf* suspender; (US) garter.

jarretière /ʒaʀtjɛʀ/ *nf* garter.

jatte /ʒat/ *nf* bowl.

jauge /ʒoʒ/ *nf* capacity; (de navire) tonnage; (compteur) gauge; **~ d'huile** dipstick.

jaune /ʒon/ *a & nm* yellow; (péj) scab; **~ d'œuf** (egg) yolk; **rire ~** give a forced laugh. **jaunir** [2] *vt/i* turn yellow. **jaunisse** *nf* jaundice.

javelot /ʒavlo/ *nm* javelin.

jazz /dʒɑz/ *nm* jazz.

J.C. *abrév m* (**Jésus-Christ**) **500 avant/après ~** 500 B.C./A.D.

je, j' /ʒə, ʒ/ *pron* I.

jean /dʒin/ *nm* jeans; **un ~** a pair of jeans.

jet¹ /ʒɛ/ *nm* throw; (de liquide, vapeur) jet; **~ d'eau** fountain.

jet² /dʒɛt/ *nm* (avion) jet.

jetable /ʒətabl/ *a* disposable.

jetée /ʒəte/ *nf* pier.

jeter /ʒəte/ [38] *vt* throw; (au rebut) throw away; (*regard, ancre, lumière*) cast; (*cri*) utter; (*bases*) lay; **~ un coup d'œil** have *ou* take a look (à at). □ **se ~** *vpr* **se ~ contre** crash *ou* bash into; **se ~ dans** (*fleuve*) flow into; **se ~ sur** (se ruer sur) rush at.

jeton /ʒətɔ̃/ *nm* token; (pour compter) counter; (au casino) chip.

jeu (*pl* **~x**) /ʒø/ *nm* game; (amusement) play; (au casino) gambling; (Théât) acting; (série) set; (de lumière, ressort) play; **en ~** (*honneur*) at stake; (*forces*) at work; **~ de cartes** (paquet) pack of cards; **~ d'échecs** (boîte) chess set; **~ de mots** pun; **~ télévisé** television quiz; **~x de grattage** scratch cards.

jeudi /ʒødi/ *nm* Thursday.

jeun; à ~ /aʒœ̃/ *loc* on an empty stomach.

jeune /ʒœn/ *a* young; **~ fille** girl; **~s mariés** newlyweds. ●*nmf* young person; **les ~s** young people.

jeûne /ʒøn/ *nm* fast.

J

jeunesse /ʒœnɛs/ *nf* youth; (apparence) youthfulness; **la ~** (jeunes) the young.

joaillerie /ʒɔajʀi/ *nf* jewellery; (magasin) jeweller's shop.

joie /ʒwa/ *nf* joy.

joindre /ʒwɛ̃dʀ/ [22] *vt* join (**à** to); (*mains, pieds*) put together; (*efforts*) combine; (contacter) contact; (dans une enveloppe) enclose. □ **se ~ à** *vpr* join.

joint, **~e** /ʒwɛ̃, -t/ *a* (*efforts*) joint; (*pieds*) together. ● *nm* joint; (de robinet) washer.

joli, **~e** /ʒɔli/ *a* pretty, nice; (*somme, profit*) nice; **c'est du ~!** (ironique) charming! **c'est bien ~ mais** that is all very well but.

joncher /ʒɔ̃ʃe/ [1] *vt* litter, be strewn over; **jonché de** littered with.

jonction /ʒɔ̃ksjɔ̃/ *nf* junction.

jongleur, **-euse** /ʒɔ̃glœʀ, øz/ *nm,f* juggler.

jonquille /ʒɔ̃kij/ *nf* daffodil.

joue /ʒu/ *nf* cheek.

jouer /ʒwe/ [1] *vt/i* play; (Théât) act; (au casino) gamble; (fonctionner) work; (*film, pièce*) put on; (*cheval*) back; (être important) count; **~ à** (*jeu*, Sport) play; **~ de** (Mus) play; **~ la comédie** put on an act; **bien joué!** well done!

jouet /ʒwɛ/ *nm* toy; (personne: fig) plaything; (victime) victim.

joueur, **-euse** /ʒwœʀ, -øz/ *nm,f* player; (parieur) gambler.

joufflu, **~e** /ʒufly/ *a* chubby-cheeked; (*visage*) chubby.

jouir /ʒwiʀ/ [2] *vi* (sexe) come; **~ de** (*droit, avantage*) enjoy; (*bien, concession*) enjoy the use of. **jouissance** *nf* pleasure; (usage) use (**de qch** of sth).

joujou (*pl* **~x**) /ʒuʒu/ *nm* [!] toy.

jour /ʒuʀ/ *nm* day; (opposé à nuit) day(time); (lumière) daylight; (aspect) light; (ouverture) gap; **de nos ~s** nowadays; **du ~ au lendemain** overnight; **il fait ~** it is (day)light; **~ chômé** *ou* **férié** public holiday; **~ de fête** holiday; **~ ouvrable**, **~ de travail** working day; **mettre à ~** update; **mettre au ~** uncover; **au grand ~** in the open; **donner le ~** give birth; **voir le ~** be born; **vivre au ~ le jour** live from day to day.

journal (*pl* **-aux**) /ʒuʀnal, -o/ *nm* (news)paper; (spécialisé) journal; (intime) diary; (à la radio) news; **~ de bord** log-book.

journalier, **-ière** /ʒuʀnalje, -jɛʀ/ *a* daily.

journalisme /ʒuʀnalism/ *nm* journalism. **journaliste** *nmf* journalist.

journée /ʒuʀne/ *nf* day.

jovial, **~e** (*mpl* **-iaux**) /ʒɔvjal, -jo/ *a* jovial.

joyau (*pl* **~x**) /ʒwajo/ *nm* gem.

joyeux, **-euse** /ʒwajø, -z/ *a* merry, joyful; **~ anniversaire** happy birthday.

jubiler /ʒybile/ [1] *vi* be jubilant.

jucher /ʒyʃe/ [1] *vt* perch. □ **se ~** *vpr* perch.

judaïsme /ʒydaism/ *nm* Judaism.

judiciaire /ʒydisjɛʀ/ *a* judicial.

judicieux, **-ieuse** /ʒydisjø, -z/ *a* judicious.

judo /ʒydo/ *nm* judo.

juge /ʒyʒ/ *nm* judge; (arbitre) referee; **~ de paix** Justice of the Peace; **~ de touche** linesman.

jugé: **au ~** /oʒyʒe/ *loc* by guesswork.

jugement /ʒyʒmɑ̃/ *nm* judgement; (criminel) sentence.

juger /ʒyʒe/ [40] *vt/i* judge; (estimer) consider (**que** that); **~ de** judge.

juguler /ʒygyle/ [1] *vt* stamp out; curb.

juif, **-ive** /ʒɥif, -v/ *a* Jewish. ● *nm,f* Jew.

juillet /ʒɥijɛ/ *nm* July.

juin /ʒɥɛ̃/ *nm* June.
jumeau, -elle (*mpl* ~**x**) /ʒymo, -ɛl/ *a & nm,f* twin. **jumeler** [38] *vt* (*villes*) twin.
jumelles /ʒymɛl/ *nfpl* binoculars.
jument /ʒymɑ̃/ *nf* mare.
junior /ʒynjɔʀ/ *a & nmf* junior.
jupe /ʒyp/ *nf* skirt.
jupon /ʒypɔ̃/ *nm* slip, petticoat.
juré, ~e /ʒyʀe/ *nm,f* juror. ● *a* sworn.
jurer /ʒyʀe/ [1] *vt* swear (**que** that). ● *vi* (pester) swear; (contraster) clash (**avec** with).
jurldiction /ʒyʀidiksjɔ̃/ *nf* jurisdiction; (tribunal) court of law.
juridique /ʒyʀidik/ *a* legal.
juriste /ʒyʀist/ *nmf* legal expert.
juron /ʒyʀɔ̃/ *nm* swear-word.
jury /ʒyʀi/ *nm* (Jur) jury; (examinateurs) panel of judges.
jus /ʒy/ *nm* juice; (de viande) gravy; ~ **de fruit** fruit juice.
jusque /ʒysk(ə)/ *prép* **jusqu'à** (up) to, as far as; (temps) until, till; (limite) up to; (y compris) even; **jusqu'à ce que** until; **jusqu'à présent** until now; **jusqu'en** until; **jusqu'où?** how far?; ~ **dans,** ~ **sur** as far as.
juste /ʒyst/ *a* fair, just; (légitime) just; (correct, exact) right; (vrai) true; (*vêtement*) tight; (*quantité*) on the short side; **le** ~ **milieu** the happy medium. ● *adv* rightly, correctly; (*chanter*) in tune; (seulement, exactement) just; (**un peu**) ~ (*calculer, mesurer*) a bit fine *ou* close; **au** ~ exactly; **c'était** ~ (presque raté) it was a close thing. **justement** *adv* (précisément) precisely; (à l'instant) just; (avec justesse) correctly; (légitimement) justifiably.
justesse /ʒystɛs/ *nf* accuracy; **de** ~ just, narrowly.
justice /ʒystis/ *nf* justice; (autorités) law; (tribunal) court.
justifier /ʒystifje/ [45] *vt* justify. ● *vi* ~ **de** prove. □ **se** ~ *vpr* justify oneself.
juteux, -euse /ʒytø, -z/ *a* juicy.
juvénile /ʒyvenil/ *a* youthful; (*délinquance, mortalité*) juvenile.

kaki /kaki/ *a inv & nm* khaki.
kangourou /kɑ̃guʀu/ *nm* kangaroo.
karaté /kaʀate/ *nm* karate.
kart /kaʀt/ *nm* go-cart.
kascher /kaʃɛʀ/ *a inv* kosher.
kayak /kajak/ *nm* kayak.
képi /kepi/ *nm* kepi.
kermesse /kɛʀmɛs/ *nf* fête.
kidnapper /kidnape/ [1] *vt* kidnap.
kilo /kilo/ *nm* kilo.
kilogramme /kilɔgʀam/ *nm* kilogram.
kilométrage /kilɔmɛtʀaʒ/ *nm* ≈ mileage. **kilomètre** *nm* kilometre.
kinésithérapeute /kineziteʀapøt/ *nmf* physiotherapist. **kinésithérapie** *nf* physiotherapy.
kiosque /kjɔsk/ *nm* kiosk; ~ **à musique** bandstand.
kit /kit/ *nm* kit.
kiwi /kiwi/ *nm* kiwi.
klaxon® /klaksɔn/ *nm* (Auto) horn. **klaxonner** [1] *vi* sound one's horn.
Ko *abrév m* (**kilo-octet**) (Ordinat) KB.
KO *abrév m* (**knock-out**) KO [!].
K-way® /kawɛ/ *nm inv* windcheater.
kyste /kist/ *nm* cyst.

l', **la** /l, la/ ⇨LE.

là /la/

●*adverbe*

····➤ (dans ce lieu) there; (ici) here; (chez soi) in; **c'est ~ que** this is where; **~ où** where; **par ~** (dans cette direction) this way; (dans cette zone) around there; **de ~** hence.

····➤ (à ce moment) then; **c'est ~ que** that's when.

····➤ **cet homme-~** that man; **ces maisons-~** those houses.

●*interjection*

····➤ **~! c'est fini** there (now), it's all over!

là-bas /labɑ/ *adv* there; (à l'endroit que l'on indique) over there.

label /labɛl/ *nm* seal, label.

laboratoire /labɔʀatwaʀ/ *nm* laboratory.

laborieux, **-ieuse** /labɔʀjø, -z/ *a* laborious; (*personne*) industrious; **classes laborieuses** working classes.

labour /labuʀ/ *nm* ploughing; (US) plowing. **labourer** [1] *vt* plough; (US) plow; (déchirer) rip at.

labyrinthe /labiʀɛ̃t/ *nm* maze, labyrinth.

lac /lak/ *nm* lake.

lacer /lase/ [10] *vt* lace up.

lacet /lasɛ/ *nm* (de chaussure) (shoe-)lace; (de route) sharp bend.

lâche /lɑʃ/ *a* cowardly; (détendu) loose; (sans rigueur) lax. ● *nmf* coward.

lâcher /lɑʃe/ [1] *vt* let go of; (laisser tomber) drop; (abandonner) give up; (laisser) leave; (libérer) release; (*flèche, balle*) fire; (*juron, phrase*) come out with; (desserrer) loosen; **~ prise** let go. ● *vi* give way.

lâcheté /lɑʃte/ *nf* cowardice.

lacrymogène /lakʀimɔʒɛn/ *a* **gaz ~** tear gas.

lacune /lakyn/ *nf* gap.

là-dedans /lad(ə)dɑ̃/ *adv* (près) in here; (plus loin) in there.

là-dessous /lad(ə)su/ *adv* (près) under here; (plus loin) under there.

là-dessus /lad(ə)sy/ *adv* (sur une surface) on here; (plus loin) on there; (sur ce) with that; (quelque temps après) after that; **qu'avez-vous à dire ~?** what have you got to say about it?

ladite /ladit/ ⇨LEDIT.

lagune /lagyn/ *nf* lagoon.

là-haut /lao/ *adv* (en hauteur) up here; (plus loin) up there; (à l'étage) upstairs.

laïc /laik/ *nm* layman.

laid, **~e** /lɛ, lɛd/ *a* ugly; (*action*) vile. **laideur** *nf* ugliness.

lainage /lɛnaʒ/ *nm* woollen garment.

laine /lɛn/ *nf* wool; **de ~** woollen.

laïque /laik/ *a* (*état, loi*) secular; (*habit, personne*) lay; (*école*) nondenominational. ● *nmf* layman, laywoman.

laisse /lɛs/ *nf* lead, leash; **tenir en ~** keep on a lead.

laisser /lese/ [1] *vt* (déposer) leave, drop off; (confier) leave (**à qn** with sb); (abandonner) leave; (rendre) **~ qn perplexe/froid** leave sb puzzled/cold; **~ qch à qn** (céder, prêter) let sb have sth; (donner) (*choix, temps*) give sb sth. □ **se ~**

vpr **se ~ persuader/insulter** let oneself be persuaded/insulted; **elle ne se laisse pas faire** she won't be pushed around; **laisse-toi faire** leave it to me/him/her *etc.*; **se ~ aller** let oneself go. ● *v aux* **~ qn/qch faire** let sb/sth do; **laisse-moi faire** (ne m'aide pas) let me do it; (je m'en occupe) leave it to me; **laisse faire!** so what! **laisser-aller** *nm inv* carelessness; (dans la tenue) scruffiness. **laissez-passer** *nm inv* pass.

lait /lɛ/ *nm* milk; **~ longue conservation** long-life *ou* UHT milk; **frère/sœur de ~** foster-brother/-sister. **laitage** *nm* milk product. **laiterie** *nf* dairy. **laiteux, -euse** *a* milky.

laitier, -ière /letje, -jɛʀ/ *a* dairy. ● *nm, f* (livreur) milkman, milkwoman.

laiton /lɛtɔ̃/ *nm* brass.

laitue /lety/ *nf* lettuce.

lama /lama/ *nm* llama.

lambeau (*pl* **~x**) /lɑ̃bo/ *nm* shred; **en ~x** in shreds.

lame /lam/ *nf* blade; (lamelle) strip; (vague) wave; **~ de fond** ground swell; **~ de rasoir** razor blade.

lamentable /lamɑ̃tabl/ *a* deplorable. **lamenter (se)** [1] *vpr* moan (**sur** about, over).

lampadaire /lɑ̃padɛʀ/ *nm* standard lamp; (de rue) street lamp.

lampe /lɑ̃p/ *nf* lamp; (ampoule) bulb; (de radio) valve; **~ (de poche)** torch; (US) flashlight; **~ à souder** blowlamp; **~ de chevet** bedside lamp; **~ solaire, ~ à bronzer** sunlamp.

lance /lɑ̃s/ *nf* spear; (de tournoi) lance; (tuyau) hose; **~ d'incendie** fire hose.

lancement /lɑ̃smɑ̃/ *nm* throwing; (de navire, de missile, mise sur le marché) launch.

lance-missiles /lɑ̃smisil/ *nm inv* missile launcher.

lance-pierres /lɑ̃spjɛʀ/ *nm inv* catapult.

lancer /lɑ̃se/ [10] *vt* throw; (avec force) hurl; (*navire, idée, artiste*) launch; (émettre) give out; (*regard*) cast; (*moteur*) start. □ **se ~** *vpr* (Sport) gain momentum; (se précipiter) rush; **se ~ dans** (*explication*) launch into; (*passe-temps*) take up. ● *nm* throw; (action) throwing.

lancinant, ~e /lɑ̃sinɑ̃, -t/ *a* (*douleur*) shooting; (*problème*) nagging.

landau /lɑ̃do/ *nm* pram; (US) baby carriage.

lande /lɑ̃d/ *nf* heath, moor.

langage /lɑ̃gaʒ/ *nm* language; **~ machine/de programmation** machine/programming language.

langouste /lɑ̃gust/ *nf* spiny lobster. **langoustine** *nf* Dublin Bay prawn.

langue /lɑ̃g/ *nf* (Anat) tongue; (Ling) language; **il m'a tiré la ~** he stuck his tongue out at me; **de ~ anglaise** (*personne*) English-speaking; (*journal*) English-language; **~ maternelle** mother tongue; **~ vivante** modern language.

lanière /lanjɛʀ/ *nf* strap.

lanterne /lɑ̃tɛʀn/ *nf* lantern; (électrique) lamp; (de voiture) sidelight.

lapin /lapɛ̃/ *nm* rabbit; **poser un ~ à qn** [!] stand sb up; **le coup du ~** rabbit punch; (en voiture) whiplash injury.

lapsus /lapsys/ *nm* slip (of the tongue).

laque /lak/ *nf* lacquer; (pour cheveux) hairspray; (peinture) gloss paint.

laquelle /lakɛl/ ⇒LEQUEL.

lard /laʀ/ *nm* streaky bacon.

L

large /laʀʒ/ *a* wide, broad; (grand) large; (généreux) generous; **avoir les idées ~s** be broad-minded; **~ d'esprit** broad-minded. ● *adv* (*calculer, mesurer*) on the generous side; **voir ~** think big. ● *nm* **faire 10 cm de ~** be 10 cm wide; **le ~** (mer) the open sea; **au ~ de** (Naut) off. **largement** *adv* widely; (*ouvrir*) wide; (amplement) amply; (généreusement) generously; (au moins) easily.

largesse /laʀʒɛs/ *nf* generous gift.

largeur /laʀʒœʀ/ *nf* width, breadth; **~ d'esprit** broad-mindedness.

larguer /laʀge/ [1] *vt* drop; **~ les amarres** cast off.

larme /laʀm/ *nf* tear; (goutte 🅸) drop; **en ~s** in tears.

larmoyant, ~e /laʀmwajɑ̃, -t/ *a* full of tears. **larmoyer** [31] *vi* (*yeux*) water; (pleurnicher) whine.

larynx /laʀɛ̃ks/ *nm* larynx.

las, ~se /lɑ, lɑs/ *a* weary.

lasagnes /lazaɲ/ *nfpl* lasagna.

laser /lazɛʀ/ *nm* laser.

lasser /lɑse/ [1] *vt* weary. ▫ **se ~** *vpr* grow tired, get weary (**de** of).

latéral, ~e (*mpl* **-aux**) /lateʀal, -o/ *a* lateral.

latin, ~e /latɛ̃, -in/ *a* Latin. ● *nm* (Ling) Latin.

latte /lat/ *nf* lath; (de plancher) board; (de siège) slat; (de mur, plafond) lath.

lauréat, ~e /lɔʀea, -t/ *a* prize-winning. ● *nm, f* prize-winner.

laurier /lɔʀje/ *nm* (Bot) laurel; (Culin) bay-leaves.

lavable /lavabl/ *a* washable.

lavabo /lavabo/ *nm* wash-basin; **~s** toilet(s).

lavage /lavaʒ/ *nm* washing; **~ de cerveau** brainwashing.

lavande /lavɑ̃d/ *nf* lavender.

lave /lav/ *nf* lava.

lave-glace (*pl* **~s**) /lavglas/ *nm* windscreen washer.

lave-linge /lavlɛ̃ʒ/ *nm inv* washing machine.

laver /lave/ [1] *vt* wash; **~ qn de** (fig) clear sb of. ▫ **se ~** *vpr* wash (oneself); **se ~ les mains** wash one's hands.

laverie /lavʀi/ *nf* **~ (automatique)** launderette; (US) laundromat.

lave-vaisselle /lavvɛsɛl/ *nm inv* dishwasher.

laxatif, -ive /laksatif, -v/ *a & nm* laxative.

layette /lɛjɛt/ *nf* baby clothes.

---

le, la, l' (*pl* **les**) /lə, la, l, le/

l' before vowel or mute h.

● *déterminant*

····➤ the.

····➤ (notion générale) **aimer la musique** like music; **l'amour** love.

····➤ (possession) **avoir les yeux verts** have green eyes; **il s'est cassé la jambe** he broke his leg.

····➤ (prix) **10 francs ~ kilo** 10 francs a kilo.

····➤ (temps) **~ lundi** on Mondays; **tous les mardis** every Tuesday.

····➤ (avec nom propre) **les Dury** the Durys; **la reine Margot** Queen Margot; **la Belgique** Belgium.

····➤ (avec adjectif) the; **je veux la rouge** I want the red one; **les riches** the rich.

● *pronom*

····➤ (homme) him; (femme) her; (chose, animal) it; (au pluriel) them.

····➤ (remplaçant une phrase) **je te l'avais bien dit** I told you so; **je ~ croyais aussi** I thought so too.

---

lécher /leʃe/ [14] *vt* lick; (*flamme*) lick; (*mer*) lap.

lèche-vitrines /lɛʃvitʀin/ *nm inv* **faire du ~** go window-shopping.

leçon /ləsɔ̃/ *nf* lesson; **faire la ~ à** lecture; **~ particulière** private lesson; **~s de conduite** driving lessons.

lecteur, -trice /lɛktœʀ, -tʀis/ *nm, f* reader; (Univ) foreign language assistant; **~ de cassettes** cassette player; **~ de disquettes** (disk) drive; **~ laser** CD player; **~ optique** optical scanner.

lecture /lɛktyʀ/ *nf* reading.

ledit, ladite (*pl* **lesdit(e)s**) /lədi, ladit, ledi(t)/ *a* the aforementioned.

légal, ~e (*mpl* **-aux**) /legal, -o/ *a* legal. **légaliser** [1] *vt* legalize. **légalité** *nf* legality; (loi) law.

légendaire /leʒɑ̃dɛʀ/ *a* legendary. **légende** *nf* (histoire, inscription) legend; (de carte) key; (d'illustration) caption.

léger, -ère /leʒe, ɛʀ/ *a* light; (*bruit, faute, maladie*) slight; (*café, argument*) weak; (imprudent) thoughtless; (frivole) fickle; **à la légère** thoughtlessly. **légèrement** *adv* lightly; (*agir*) thoughtlessly; (un peu) slightly. **légèreté** *nf* lightness; thoughtlessness.

légion /leʒjɔ̃/ *nf* legion.

législatif, -ive /leʒislatif, -v/ *a* legislative; **élections législatives** general election.

legislature /leʒislatyʀ/ *nf* term of office.

légitime /leʒitim/ *a* (Jur) legitimate; (fig) rightful; **agir en état de ~ défense** act in self-defence. **légitimité** *nf* legitimacy.

legs /lɛg/ *nm* legacy; (d'effets personnels) bequest.

léguer /lege/ [14] *vt* bequeath.

légume /legym/ *nm* vegetable.

lendemain /lɑ̃dmɛ̃/ *nm* **le ~** the next day; (fig) the future; **le ~ de** the day after; **le ~ matin/soir** the next morning/evening; **du jour au ~** from one day to the next.

lent, ~e /lɑ̃, -t/ *a* slow. **lentement** *adv* slowly. **lenteur** *nf* slowness.

lentille /lɑ̃tij/ *nf* (Culin) lentil; (verre) lens; **~s de contact** contact lenses.

léopard /leɔpaʀ/ *nm* leopard.

lèpre /lɛpʀ/ *nf* leprosy.

---

lequel, laquelle (*pl* **les-quel(le)s**), **auquel** (*pl* **auxquel(le)s**), **duquel** (*pl* **desquel(le)s**) /ləkɛl, lakɛl, lekɛl, ɔkɛl, dykɛl, dekɛl/

à + lequel = auquel,
à + lesquel(le)s = auxquel(le)s;
de + lequel = duquel,
de + lesquel(le)s = desquel(le)s

● *pronom*

····➤ (relatif) (personne) who; (complément indirect) whom; (autres cas) which; **l'ami auquel tu as écrit** the friend to whom you wrote; **les voisins chez lesquels Sophie est allée** the neighbours whose house Sophie went to.

····➤ (interrogatif) which; **~ tu veux?** which one do you want?

● *adjectif*

····➤ **auquel cas** in which case.

---

les /le/ ⇒LE.

lesbienne /lɛsbjɛn/ *nf* lesbian.

léser /leze/ [14] *vt* wrong.

lésiner /lezine/ [1] *vi* **ne pas ~ sur** not stint on.

lesquels, lesquelles /lekɛl/ ⇒LEQUEL.

lessive /lesiv/ *nf* (poudre) washing-powder; (liquide) washing liquid; (linge, action) washing.

leste /lɛst/ *a* agile, nimble; (grivois) coarse.

Lettonie /letɔni/ *nf* Latvia.

lettre /lɛtʀ/ *nf* letter; **à la ~, au pied de la ~** literally; **en toutes ~s** in full; **les ~s** (Univ) (the) arts.

leucémie /løsemi/ *nf* leukaemia.

leur (*pl* **~s**) /lœʀ/

●*pronom personnel invariable*

····➤them; **donne-le ~** give it to them; **je ~ fais confiance** I trust them.

●*adjectif possessif*

····➤their; **~s enfants** their children; **à ~ arrivée** when they arrived.

●**le leur, la leur,** (*pl* **les leurs**) *pronom possessif*

····➤theirs; **chacun le ~** one each; **je suis des ~s** I am one of them.

levain /ləvɛ̃/ *nm* leaven.

levé, ~e /ləve/ *a* (debout) up.

levée /ləve/ *nf* (de peine, de sanctions) lifting; (de courrier) collection; (de troupes, d'impôts) levying.

lever /ləve/ [6] *vt* lift (up), raise; (*interdiction*) lift; (*séance*) close; (*armée, impôts*) levy. ●*vi* (*pâte*) rise. ▫ **se ~** *vpr* get up; (*soleil, rideau*) rise; (*jour*) break. ●*nm* **au ~** on getting up; **~ du jour** daybreak; **~ de rideau** (Théât) curtain (up); **~ du soleil** sunrise.

levier /ləvje/ *nm* lever; **~ de changement de vitesse** gear lever.

lèvre /lɛvʀ/ *nf* lip.

lévrier /levʀije/ *nm* greyhound.

levure /ləvyʀ/ *nf* yeast; **~ chimique** baking powder.

lexique /lɛksik/ *nm* vocabulary; (glossaire) lexicon.

lézard /lezaʀ/ *nm* lizard.

lézarde /lezaʀd/ *nf* crack.

liaison /ljɛzɔ̃/ *nf* connection; (transport, Ordinat) link; (contact) contact; (Gram, Mil) liaison; (amoureuse) affair; **être en ~ avec** be in contact with; **assurer la ~ entre** liaise between.

liane /ljan/ *nf* creeper.

Liban /libɑ̃/ *nm* Lebanon.

libeller /libele/ [1] *vt* (*chèque*) write; (contrat) draw up; **libellé à l'ordre de** made out to.

libellule /libelyl/ *nf* dragonfly.

libéral, ~e (*mpl* **-aux**) /libeʀal, -o/ *a* liberal; **les professions ~es** the professions.

libérateur, -trice /libeʀatœʀ, -tʀis/ *a* liberating. ●*nm, f* liberator. **libération** *nf* release; (de pays) liberation.

libérer /libeʀe/ [14] *vt* (*personne*) free, release; (*pays*) liberate, free; (*bureau, lieux*) vacate; (*gaz*) release. ▫ **se ~** *vpr* free oneself.

liberté /libɛʀte/ *nf* freedom, liberty; (loisir) free time; **être/mettre en ~** be/set free; **~ conditionnelle** parole; **~ provisoire** provisional release (*pending trial*); **~ surveillée** probation; **~s publiques** civil liberties.

Libertel /libɛʀtɛl/ *nm* (Internet) Freenet.

libraire /libʀɛʀ/ *nmf* bookseller. **librairie** *nf* bookshop.

libre /libʀ/ *a* free; (*place, pièce*) vacant, free; (*passage*) clear; (*école*) private (*usually religious*); **~ de qch/de faire** free from sth/to do. **libre-échange** *nm* free trade. **libre-service** (*pl* **libres-services**) *nm* (magasin) self-service shop; (restaurant) self-service restaurant.

licence /lisɑ̃s/ *nf* licence; (Univ) degree.

licencié, ~e /lisɑ̃sje/ *nm, f* graduate; **~ ès lettres/sciences** Bachelor of Arts/Science.

licenciements /lisɑ̃simɑ̃/ *nm* redundancy; (pour faute) dismissal.

licencier [45] *vt* make redundant; (pour faute) dismiss.
licorne /likɔʀn/ *nf* unicorn.
liège /ljɛʒ/ *nm* cork.
lien /ljɛ̃/ *nm* (rapport) link; (attache) bond, tie; (corde) rope; **~s affectifs/de parenté** emotional/family ties.
lier /lje/ [45] *vt* tie (up), bind; (relier) link; (engager, unir) bind; **~ conversation** strike up a conversation; **ils sont très liés** they are very close. □ **se ~ avec** *vpr* make friends with.
lierre /ljɛʀ/ *nm* ivy.
lieu (*pl* **~x**) /ljø/ *nm* place; **~x** (locaux) premises; (d'un accident) scene; **sur les ~x** at the scene; **au ~ de** instead of; **avoir ~** take place; **donner ~ à** give rise to; **tenir ~ de** serve as; **s'il y a ~** if necessary; **en premier ~** firstly; **en dernier ~** lastly; **~ commun** commonplace; **~ de rencontre** meeting place.
lièvre /ljɛvʀ/ *nm* hare.
lifting /liftiŋ/ *nm* face-lift.
ligne /liɲ/ *nf* line; (trajet) route; (de métro, train) line; (formes) lines; (de femme) figure; **en ~** (joueurs) lined up; (au téléphone) on the phone; (Ordinat) on line; **~ spécialisée** (Internet) dedicated line.
ligoter /ligɔte/ [1] *vt* tie up.
ligue /lig/ *nf* league. **liguer (se)** [1] *vpr* join forces (**contre** against).
lilas /lila/ *nm & a inv* lilac.
limace /limas/ *nf* slug.
limande /limɑ̃d/ *nf* (poisson) dab.
lime /lim/ *nf* file; **~ à ongles** nail file.
limitation /limitasjɔ̃/ *nf* limitation; **~ de vitesse** speed limit.
limite /limit/ *nf* limit; (de jardin, champ) boundary; **à la ~ de** (fig) verging on, bordering on; **à la ~** if it comes to it, at a pinch; **dans une certaine ~** up to a point; **dans la ~ du possible** as far as possible. ● *a* (*vitesse, âge*) maximum; **cas ~** borderline case; **date ~** deadline; **date ~ de vente** sell-by date.
limiter /limite/ [1] *vt* limit; (délimiter) form the border of. □ **se ~** *vpr* limit oneself (**à** to).
limonade /limɔnad/ *nf* lemonade.
limpide /lɛ̃pid/ *a* limpid, clear.
lin /lɛ̃/ *nm* (tissu) linen.
linge /lɛ̃ʒ/ *nm* linen; (lessive) washing; (torchon) cloth; **~ (de corps)** underwear. **lingerie** *nf* underwear. **lingette** *nf* wipe.
lingot /lɛ̃go/ *nm* ingot.
linguistique /lɛ̃gɥistik/ *a* linguistic. ● *nf* linguistics.
lion /ljɔ̃/ *nm* lion; **le L~** Leo.
lionceau (*pl* **~x**) *nm* lion cub.
lionne *nf* lioness.
liquidation /likidasjɔ̃/ *nf* liquidation; (vente) (clearance) sale; **entrer en ~** go into liquidation.
liquide /likid/ *a* liquid. ● *nm* (**argent**) **~** ready money; **payer en ~** pay cash; **~ de frein** brake fluid.
liquider /likide/ [1] *vt* liquidate; (vendre) sell.
lire /liʀ/ [39] *vt/i* read. ● *nf* lira.
lis[1] /li/ ⇒LIRE[39].
lis[2] /lis/ *nm* (fleur) lily.
lisible /lizibl/ *a* legible; (*roman*) readable.
lisière /lizjɛʀ/ *nf* edge.
lisse /lis/ *a* smooth.
liste /list/ *nf* list; **~ d'attente** waiting list; **~ électorale** register of voters; **être sur (la) ~ rouge** be ex-directory.
listing /listiŋ/ *nm* printout.
lit /li/ *nm* bed; **se mettre au ~** get into bed; **~ de camp** camp-bed;

L

~ d'enfant cot; **~ d'une personne** single bed; **~ de deux personnes, grand ~** double bed.

literie /litʀi/ *nf* bedding.

litière /litjɛʀ/ *nf* litter.

litige /litiʒ/ *nm* dispute.

litre /litʀ/ *nm* litre.

littéraire /liteʀɛʀ/ *a* literary; (*études, formation*) arts.

littéral, **~e** (*mpl* **-aux**) /liteʀal, -o/ *a* literal.

littérature /liteʀatyʀ/ *nf* literature.

littoral (*pl* **-aux**) /litɔʀal, -o/ *nm* coast.

Lituanie /litɥani/ *nf* Lithuania.

livide /livid/ *a* deathly pale.

livraison /livʀɛzɔ̃/ *nf* delivery.

livre /livʀ/ *nf* (monnaie, poids) pound. ● *nm* book; **~ de bord** log-book; **~ de compte** books; **~ de poche** paperback.

livrer /livʀe/ [1] *vt* (Comm) deliver; (abandonner) give over (**à** to); (remettre) (*coupable, document*) hand over (**à** to); **livré à soi-même** left to oneself. ▫ **se ~** *vpr* (se rendre) give oneself up (**à** to); **se ~ à** (*boisson, actes*) indulge in; (*ami*) confide in.

livret /livʀɛ/ *nm* book; (Mus) libretto; **~ de caisse d'épargne** savings book; **~ scolaire** school report (book).

livreur, **-euse** /livʀœʀ, -øz/ *nm,f* delivery man, delivery woman.

local¹, **~e** (*mpl* **-aux**) /lɔkal, -o/ *a* local.

local² (*pl* **-aux**) /lɔkal, -o/ *nm* premises; **locaux** premises.

localement /lɔkalmɑ̃/ *adv* locally.

localiser /lɔkalize/ [1] *vt* (repérer) locate; (circonscrire) localize.

locataire /lɔkatɛʀ/ *nmf* tenant; (de chambre) lodger.

location /lɔkasjɔ̃/ *nf* (de maison) renting; (de voiture, de matériel) hire, rental; (de place) booking, reservation; (par propriétaire) renting out; hiring out; **en ~** (*voiture*) on hire, rented; (*habiter*) in rented accommodation.

locomotive /lɔkɔmɔtiv/ *nf* engine, locomotive.

locution /lɔkysjɔ̃/ *nf* phrase.

loge /lɔʒ/ *nf* (de concierge, de franc-maçons) lodge; (d'acteur) dressing-room; (de spectateur) box.

logement /lɔʒmɑ̃/ *nm* accommodation; (appartement) flat; (habitat) housing.

loger /lɔʒe/ [40] *vt* (*réfugié, famille*) house; (*ami*) put up; (*client*) accommodate. ● *vi* live. ▫ **se ~** *vpr* live; **trouver à se ~** find accommodation; **se ~ dans** (*balle*) lodge itself in.

logiciel /lɔʒisjɛl/ *nm* software; **~ contributif** shareware; **~ d'application** application software; **~ de groupe** groupware; **~ de jeux** games software; **~ de navigation** browser; **~ public** freeware.

logique /lɔʒik/ *a* logical. ● *nf* logic.

logis /lɔʒi/ *nm* dwelling.

logistique /lɔʒistik/ *nf* logistics.

loi /lwa/ *nf* law.

loin /lwɛ̃/ *adv* far (away); **au ~** far away; **de ~** from far away; (de beaucoup) by far; **~ de là** far from it; **plus ~** further; **il revient de ~** (fig) he had a close shave.

lointain, **~e** /lwɛ̃tɛ̃, -ɛn/ *a* distant. ● *nm* distance; **dans le ~** in the distance.

loir /lwaʀ/ *nm* dormouse.

loisir /lwaziʀ/ *nm* (spare) time; **~s** (temps libre) leisure, spare time; (distractions) leisure activities; **à ~** at one's leisure; **avoir le ~ de faire** have time to do.

londonien, **~ne** /lɔ̃dɔnjɛ̃, -ɛn/ *a* London. **L~**, **~e** *nm,f* Londoner.

Londres /lɔ̃dʀ/ *npr* London.
long, longue /lɔ̃, lɔ̃g/ *a* long; **à ~ terme** long-term; **être ~ à faire** be a long time doing. ● *nm* **de ~** (mesure) long; **de ~ en large** back and forth; (**tout**) **le ~ de** (all) along. ● *adv* **en dire ~ sur qn/qch** say a lot about sb/sth; **en savoir plus ~ sur** know more about.
longer /lɔ̃ʒe/ [40] *vt* go along; (limiter) border.
longitude /lɔ̃ʒityd/ *nf* longitude.
longtemps /lɔ̃tɑ̃/ *adv* a long time; **avant ~** before long; **trop ~** too long; **ça prendra ~** it will take a long time; **prendre plus ~ que prévu** take longer than anticipated.
longuement /lɔ̃gmɑ̃/ *adv* (longtemps) for a long time; (en détail) at length.
longueur /lɔ̃gœʀ/ *nf* length; **~s** (de texte) over-long parts; **à ~ de journée** all day long, **en ~** lengthwise; **~ d'onde** wavelength.
lopin /lɔpɛ̃/ *nm* **~ de terre** patch of land.
loque /lɔk/ *nf* **~s** rags; **~** (**humaine**) (human) wreck.
loquet /lɔkɛ/ *nm* latch.
lors de /lɔʀdə/ *prép* (au moment de) at the time of; (pendant) during.
lorsque /lɔʀsk(ə)/ *conj* when.
losange /lɔzɑ̃ʒ/ *nm* diamond.
lot /lo/ *nm* (portion) share; (aux enchères) lot; (Ordinat) batch; (destin) lot; **gagner le gros ~** hit the jackpot.
loterie /lɔtʀi/ *nf* lottery.
lotion /losjɔ̃/ *nf* lotion.
lotissement /lɔtismɑ̃/ *nm* (à construire) building plot; (construit) (housing) development.
louable /luabl/ *a* praiseworthy.
louange *nf* praise.
louche /luʃ/ *a* shady, dubious. ● *nf* ladle.
loucher /luʃe/ [1] *vi* squint.
louer /lwe/ [1] *vt* (approuver) praise (**de** for); (prendre en location) (*maison*) rent; (*voiture, matériel*) hire, rent; (*place*) book, reserve; (donner en location) (*maison*) rent out; (*matériel*) rent out, hire out; **à ~** to let, for rent (US).
loufoque /lufɔk/ *a* 🅸 crazy.
loup /lu/ *nm* wolf.
loupe /lup/ *nf* magnifying glass.
louper /lupe/ [1] *vt* 🅸 miss; (*examen*) flunk 🅸.
lourd, ~e /luʀ, -d/ *a* heavy; (*faute*) serious; **~ de dangers** fraught with danger; **il fait ~** it's close *ou* muggy.
loutre /lutʀ/ *nf* otter.
louveteau (*pl* **~x**) /luvto/ *nm* wolf cub; (scout) Cub (Scout).
loyal, ~e (*mpl* **-aux**) /lwajal, -o/ *a* loyal, faithful; (honnête) fair. **loyauté** *nf* loyalty; fairness.
loyer /lwaje/ *nm* rent.
lu /ly/ ⇒LIRE [39].
lubrifiant /lybʀifjɑ̃/ *nm* lubricant.
lucide /lysid/ *a* lucid. **lucidité** *nf* lucidity.
lucratif, -ive /lykʀatif, -v/ *a* lucrative; **à but non ~** non-profit-making.
ludiciel /lydisjɛl/ *nm* (Ordinat) games software.
lueur /lɥœʀ/ *nf* (faint) light, glimmer; (fig) glimmer, gleam.
luge /lyʒ/ *nf* toboggan.
lugubre /lygybʀ/ *a* gloomy.

lui /lɥi/

● *pronom*

····➤ (masculin) (sujet) he; **~, il est à l'étranger** he's abroad; **c'est ~!** it's him!; (objet) him; (animal) it; **c'est à ~** it's his; **elle conduit mieux que ~** she's a better driver than he is.

····➤ (féminin) her; **je ~ ai annoncé** I told her.

····➤ (masculin/féminin) **donne-le-~** give it to him/her.

lui-même /lɥimɛm/ *pron* himself; (animal) itself.
luire /lɥiʀ/ [17] *vi* shine; (reflet humide) glisten; (reflet chaud, faible) glow.
lumière /lymjɛʀ/ *nf* light; **~s** (connaissances) knowledge; **faire (toute) la ~ sur une affaire** clear a matter up.
luminaire /lyminɛʀ/ *nm* lamp.
lumineux, **-euse** /lyminø, -z/ *a* luminous; (éclairé) illuminated; (*rayon*) of light; (radieux) radiant; **source lumineuse** light source.
lunaire /lynɛʀ/ *a* lunar.
lunatique /lynatik/ *a* temperamental.
lunch /lœnʃ/ *nm* buffet lunch.
lundi /lœ̃di/ *nm* Monday.
lune /lyn/ *nf* moon; **~ de miel** honeymoon.
lunettes /lynɛt/ *nfpl* glasses; (de protection) goggles; **~ de ski/natation** ski/swimming goggles; **~ noires** dark glasses; **~ de soleil** sun-glasses.
lustre /lystʀ/ *nm* (éclat) lustre; (objet) chandelier.
lutin /lytɛ̃/ *nm* goblin.
lutte /lyt/ *nf* fight, struggle; (Sport) wrestling. **lutter** [1] *vi* fight, struggle; (Sport) wrestle. **lutteur**, **-euse** *nm, f* fighter; (Sport) wrestler.
luxe /lyks/ *nm* luxury; **de ~** luxury; (*produit*) de luxe.
Luxembourg /lyksɑ̃buʀ/ *nm* Luxemburg.
luxer (se) /(sə)lykse/ [1] *vpr* **se ~ le genou** dislocate one's knee.
luxueux, **-euse** /lyksɥø, -z/ *a* luxurious.
lycée /lise/ *nm* (secondary) school. **lycéen**, **~ne** *nm, f* pupil (at secondary school).
lyophilisé, **~e** /ljɔfilize/ *a* freeze-dried.
lyrique /liʀik/ *a* (*poésie*) lyric; (passionné) lyrical; **artiste/théâtre ~** opera singer/house.
lys /lis/ *nm* lily.

m' /m/ ⇨ME.
ma /ma/ ⇨MON.
macabre /makabʀ/ *a* macabre.
macadam /makadam/ *nm* Tarmac®.
macaron /makaʀɔ̃/ *nm* (gâteau) macaroon; (insigne) badge.
macédoine /masedwan/ *nf* mixed diced vegetables; **~ de fruits** fruit salad.
macérer /maseʀe/ [14] *vt/i* soak; (dans du vinaigre) pickle.
mâcher /mɑʃe/ [1] *vt* chew; **ne pas ~ ses mots** not mince one's words.
machin /maʃɛ̃/ *nm* [!] (chose) thing; (dont on ne trouve pas le nom) whatsit [!].
machinal, **~e** (*mpl* **-aux**) /maʃinal, -o/ *a* automatic. **machinalement** *adv* mechanically, automatically.
machination /maʃinasjɔ̃/ *nf* plot; **des ~s** machinations.
machine /maʃin/ *nf* machine; (d'un train, navire) engine; **~ à écrire** typewriter; **~ à laver/coudre** washing-/sewing-machine; **~ à sous** fruit machine; (US) slot-machine. **machine-outil** (*pl* **machines-outils**) *nf* machine tool. **machinerie** *nf* machinery.

machiniste /maʃinist/ *nm* (Théât) stage-hand; (conducteur) driver.

mâchoire /mɑʃwaʀ/ *nf* jaw.

mâchonner /mɑʃɔne/ [1] *vt* chew.

maçon /masɔ̃/ *nm* (entrepreneur) builder; (poseur de briques) bricklayer; (qui construit en pierre) mason. **maçonnerie** *nf* (briques) brickwork; (pierres) stonework, masonry; (travaux) building.

madame (*pl* **mesdames**) /madam, medam/ *nf* (à une inconnue) (dans une lettre) **M~** Dear Madam; **bonjour, ~** good morning; **mesdames et messieurs** ladies and gentlemen; (à une femme dont on connaît le nom) (dans une lettre) **Chère M~** Dear Mrs *ou* Ms X; **bonjour, ~** good morning Mrs *ou* Ms X; **oui M~ le Ministre** yes Minister; (formule de respect) **oui M~** yes madam.

mademoiselle (*pl* **mesdemoiselles**) /madmwazɛl, medmwazɛl/ *nf* (à une inconnue) (dans une lettre) **M~** Dear Madam; **bonjour, ~** good morning; **entrez mesdemoiselles** come in (ladies); (à une jeune fille dont on connait le nom) (dans une lettre) **Chère M~** Dear Ms *ou* Miss X; **bonjour, ~** good morning Miss *ou* Ms X.

magasin /magazɛ̃/ *nm* shop, store; (entrepôt) warehouse; (d'une arme) magazine; **en ~** in stock.

magazine /magazin/ *nm* magazine; (émission) programme.

Maghreb /magʀɛb/ *nm* North Africa.

magicien, ~ne /maʒisjɛ̃, -ɛn/ *nm, f* magician.

magie /maʒi/ *nf* magic. **magique** *a* magic; (mystérieux) magical.

magistral, ~e (*mpl* **-aux**) /maʒistʀal, -o/ *a* masterly; (grand: hum) tremendous; **cours ~** lecture.

magistrat /maʒistʀa/ *nm* magistrate.

magistrature /maʒistʀatyʀ/ *nf* judiciary; (fonction) public office.

magner (se) /(sə)maɲe/ [1] *vpr* ▣ get a move on.

magnétique /maɲetik/ *a* magnetic. **magnétiser** [1] *vt* magnetize. **magnétisme** *nm* magnetism.

magnétophone /maɲetɔfɔn/ *nm* tape recorder; (à cassettes) cassette recorder.

magnétoscope /maɲetɔskɔp/ *nm* video recorder.

magnificence /maɲifisɑ̃s/ *nf* magnificence. **magnifique** *a* magnificent.

magot /mago/ *nm* ▣ hoard (of money).

magouille /maguj/ *nf* ▣ scheming, skulduggery.

magret /magʀɛ/ *nm* **~ de canard** duck breast.

mai /mɛ/ *nm* May.

maigre /mɛgʀ/ *a* thin; (*viande*) lean; (*yaourt*) low-fat; (fig) poor, meagre; **faire ~** abstain from meat. **maigreur** *nf* thinness; leanness; (fig) meagreness.

maigrir /megʀiʀ/ [2] *vi* get thin-(ner); (en suivant un régime) slim. ● *vt* make thin(ner).

maille /mɑj/ *nf* stitch; (de filet) mesh; **~ qui file** ladder, run; **avoir ~ à partir avec qn** have a brush with sb.

maillet /majɛ/ *nm* mallet.

maillon /mɑjɔ̃/ *nm* link.

maillot /majo/ *nm* (Sport) shirt, jersey; **~ (de corps)** vest; (US) undershirt; **~ (de bain)** (swimming) costume.

main /mɛ̃/ *nf* hand; **donner la ~ à qn** hold sb's hand; **se donner la ~** hold hands; **en ~s propres** in person; **en bonnes ~s** in good hands; **~ courante** handrail; **se**

M

faire la ~ get the hang of it; **perdre la ~** lose one's touch; **sous la ~** to hand; **vol à ~ armée** armed robbery; **fait (à la) ~** handmade; **haut les ~s!** hands up! **main-d'œuvre** (*pl* **mains-d'œuvre**) *nf* labour; (ouvriers) labour force.

main-forte /mɛ̃fɔʀt/ *nf inv* **prêter ~ à qn** come to sb's aid.

maint, ~e /mɛ̃, mɛ̃t/ *a* many a (+ *sg*); **~s** many; **à ~es reprises** many times.

maintenant /mɛ̃t(ə)nɑ̃/ *adv* now; (de nos jours) nowadays; (l'époque actuelle) today.

maintenir /mɛ̃t(ə)niʀ/ [58] *vt* keep, maintain; (soutenir) support, hold up; (affirmer) maintain; (*decision*) stand by. ▫ **se ~** *vpr* (*tendance*) persist; (*prix, malade*) remain stable.

maintien /mɛ̃tjɛ̃/ *nm* (attitude) bearing; (conservation) maintenance.

maire /mɛʀ/ *nm* mayor.

mairie /meʀi/ *nf* town hall; (administration) town council.

mais /mɛ/ *conj* but; **~ oui** of course; **~ non** of course not.

maïs /mais/ *nm* maize, corn; (Culin) sweetcorn.

maison /mɛzɔ̃/ *nf* house; (foyer) home; (immeuble) building; **~ (de commerce)** firm; **à la ~** at home; **rentrer** *ou* **aller à la ~** go home; **~ des jeunes (et de la culture)** youth club; **~ de repos** rest home; **~ de convalescence** convalescent home; **~ de retraite** old people's home; **~ mère** parent company. ● *a inv* (Culin) home-made.

maître, -esse /mɛtʀ, -ɛs/ *a* (qui contrôle) **être ~ de soi** be one's own master; **~ de la situation** in control of the situation; (principal) (*idée, qualité*) key, main. ● *nm, f* (Scol) teacher; (d'animal) owner, master. ● *nm* (expert, guide) master; (dirigeant) leader; **~ de conférences** senior lecturer; **~ d'hôtel** head waiter; (domestique) butler. **maître-assistant, ~e** (*pl* **maîtres-assistants**) *nm, f* lecturer. **maître-chanteur** (*pl* **maîtres-chanteurs**) *nm* blackmailer. **maître-nageur** (*pl* **maîtres-nageurs**) *nm* swimming instructor. **maîtresse** *nf* (amante) mistress.

maîtrise /mɛtʀiz/ *nf* mastery; (contrôle) control; (Mil) supremacy; (Univ) master's degree; **~ (de soi)** self-control.

maîtriser /mɛtʀize/ [1] *vt* (*sujet, technique*) master; (*incendie, sentiment, personne*) control. ▫ **se ~** *vpr* have self-control.

maïzena® /maizena / *nf* cornflour.

majesté /maʒɛste/ *nf* majesty.

majestueux, -euse /maʒɛstɥø, z/ *a* majestic.

majeur, ~e /maʒœʀ/ *a* major, main; (Jur) of age; **en ~e partie** mostly; **la ~e partie de** most of. ● *nm* middle finger.

majoration /maʒɔʀasjɔ̃/ *nf* increase (**de** in). **majorer** [1] *vt* increase.

majoritaire /maʒɔʀitɛʀ/ *a* majority; **être ~** be in the majority. **majorité** *nf* majority; **en ~** chiefly.

Majorque /majɔʀk/ *nf* Majorca.

majuscule /maʒyskyl/ *a* capital. ● *nf* capital letter.

mal[1] /mal/ *adv* badly; (incorrectement) wrong(ly); **aller ~** (*personne*) be unwell; (*affaires*) go badly; **~ entendre/comprendre** not hear/understand properly; **~ en point** in a bad state; **pas ~** quite a lot. ● *a inv* bad, wrong; **c'est ~ de** it is wrong *ou* bad to; **ce n'est pas ~** [!] it's not bad; **Nick**

n'est pas ~ ! Nick is not bad-looking.

mal² (*pl* **maux**) /mal, mo/ *nm* evil; (douleur) pain, ache; (maladie) disease; (effort) trouble; (dommage) harm; (malheur) misfortune; **avoir ~ à la tête/à la gorge** have a headache/a sore throat; **avoir le ~ de mer/du pays** be seasick/ homesick; **faire ~** hurt; **se faire ~** hurt oneself; **j'ai ~** it hurts; **faire du ~ à** hurt, harm; **se donner du ~ pour faire qch** go to a lot of trouble to do sth.

malade /malad/ *a* sick, ill; (*bras, œil*) bad; (*plante, poumons, côlon*) diseased; **tomber ~** fall ill; (*fou* !) mad. ● *nmf* sick person; (d'un médecin) patient; **~ mental** mentally ill person.

maladie /maladi/ *nf* illness, disease; (manie !) mania.

maladif, -ive /maladif, -v/ *a* sickly; (*jalousie, peur*) pathological.

maladresse /maladʀɛs/ *nf* clumsiness; (erreur) blunder.

maladroit, ~e /maladʀwa, -t/ *a* clumsy; (sans tact) tactless.

malaise /malɛz/ *nm* feeling of faintness; (gêne) uneasiness; (état de crise) unrest.

malaisé, ~e /maleze/ *a* difficult.

Malaisie /malɛzi/ *nf* Malaysia.

malaria /malaʀja/ *nf* malaria.

malaxer /malakse/ [1] *vt* (pétrir) knead; (mêler) mix.

malchance /malʃɑ̃s/ *nf* misfortune. **malchanceux, -euse** *a* unlucky.

mâle /mɑl/ *a* male; (viril) manly. ● *nm* male.

malédiction /malediksjɔ̃/ *nf* curse.

maléfice /malefis/ *nm* evil spell. **maléfique** *a* evil.

malentendant, ~e /malɑ̃tɑ̃dɑ̃, -t/ *a* hard of hearing.

malentendu /malɑ̃tɑ̃dy/ *nm* misunderstanding.

malfaçon /malfasɔ̃/ *nf* defect.

malfaisant, ~e /malfəzɑ̃, -t/ *a* harmful; (*personne*) evil.

malfaiteur /malfɛtœʀ/ *nm* criminal.

malformation /malfɔʀmasjɔ̃/ *nf* malformation.

malgré /malgʀe/ *prép* in spite of, despite; **~ tout** nevertheless.

malheur /malœʀ/ *nm* misfortune; (accident) accident; **par ~** unfortunately; **faire un ~** ! be a big hit; **porter ~** be *ou* bring bad luck.

malheureusement /malœʀøzmɑ̃/ *adv* unfortunately.

malheureux, -euse /malœʀø, -z/ *a* unhappy; (regrettable) unfortunate; (sans succès) unlucky; (insignifiant) paltry, pathetic. ● *nm, f* (poor) wretch.

malhonnête /malɔnɛt/ *a* dishonest. **malhonnêteté** *nf* dishonesty.

malice /malis/ *nf* mischief; **sans ~** harmless; **avec ~** mischievously. **malicieux, -ieuse** *a* mischievous.

malignité /maliɲite/ *nf* malignancy. **malin, -igne** *a* clever, smart; (méchant) malicious; (*tumeur*) malignant; (difficile !) difficult.

malingre /malɛ̃gʀ/ *a* puny.

malle /mal/ *nf* (valise) trunk; (Auto) boot; (US) trunk.

mallette /malɛt/ *nf* (small) suitcase; (pour le bureau) briefcase.

malmener /malməne/ [6] *vt* manhandle; (fig) give a rough ride to.

malnutrition /malnytʀisjɔ̃/ *nf* malnutrition.

malodorant, ~e /malɔdɔʀɑ̃, -t/ *a* smelly, foul-smelling.

M

malpoli, **~e** /malpɔli/ *a* rude, impolite.
malpropre /malpʀɔpʀ/ *a* dirty.
malsain, **~e** /malsɛ̃, -ɛn/ *a* unhealthy.
malt /malt/ *nm* malt.
Malte /malt/ *nf* Malta.
maltraiter /maltʀete/ [1] *vt* ill-treat.
malveillance /malvɛjɑ̃s/ *nf* malice. **malveillant**, **~e** *a* malicious.
maman /mamɑ̃/ *nf* mum(my), mother; (US) mom(my).
mamelle /mamɛl/ *nf* teat.
mamelon /mamlɔ̃/ *nm* (Anat) nipple; (colline) hillock.
mamie /mami/ *nf* 🅸 granny.
mammifère /mamifɛʀ/ *nm* mammal.
manche /mɑ̃ʃ/ *nf* sleeve; (Sport, Pol) round. ● *nm* (d'un instrument) handle; **~ à balai** broomstick; (Aviat) joystick. **M~** *nf* **la M~** the Channel; **le tunnel sous la M~** the Channel tunnel.
manchette /mɑ̃ʃɛt/ *nf* cuff; (de journal) headline.
manchot, **~te** /mɑ̃ʃo, -ɔt/ *nm,f* one-armed person; (sans bras) armless person. ● *nm* (oiseau) penguin.
mandarine /mɑ̃daʀin/ *nf* tangerine, mandarin (orange).
mandat /mɑ̃da/ *nm* (postal) money order; (Pol) mandate; (procuration) proxy; (de police) warrant; **~ d'arrêt** arrest warrant.
mandataire /mɑ̃datɛʀ/ *nm* representative; (Jul) proxy.
manège /manɛʒ/ *nm* riding school; (à la foire) merry-go-round; (manœuvre) trick, ploy.
manette /manɛt/ *nf* lever; (de jeu) joystick.
mangeable /mɑ̃ʒabl/ *a* edible.
mangeoire /mɑ̃ʒwaʀ/ *nf* trough; (pour oiseaux) feeder.
manger /mɑ̃ʒe/ [40] *vt* eat; (*fortune*) go through; (*profits*) eat away at; (*économies*) use up; (ronger) eat into. ● *vi* eat; **donner à ~ à** feed. ● *nm* food.
mangue /mɑ̃g/ *nf* mango.
maniable /manjabl/ *a* easy to handle.
maniaque /manjak/ *a* fussy. ● *nmf* fusspot; (fou) maniac; (fanatique) fanatic; **un ~ de l'ordre** a stickler for tidiness.
manie /mani/ *nf* habit; (marotte) obsession.
maniement /manimɑ̃/ *nm* handling. **manier** [45] *vt* handle.
manière /manjɛʀ/ *nf* way, manner; **~s** (politesse) manners; (chichis) fuss; **à la ~ de** in the style of; **de ~ à** so as to; **de toute ~** anyway, in any case.
maniéré, **~e** /manjeʀe/ *a* affected.
manif /manif/ *nf* 🅸 demo.
manifestant, **~e** /manifɛstɑ̃, -t/ *nm,f* demonstrator.
manifestation /manifɛstasjɔ̃/ *nf* expression, manifestation; (de maladie, phénomène) appearance; (Pol) demonstration; (événement) event; **~ culturelle** cultural event.
manifeste /manifɛst/ *a* obvious. ● *nm* manifesto.
manifester /manifɛste/ [1] *vt* show, manifest; (*désir, crainte*) express. ● *vi* (Pol) demonstrate. □ **se ~** *vpr* (*sentiment*) show itself; (apparaître) appear; (répondre à un appel) come forward.
manigance /manigɑ̃s/ *nf* little plot. **manigancer** [10] *vt* plot.
manipulation /manipylasjɔ̃/ *nf* handling; (péj) manipulation.
manivelle /manivɛl/ *nf* handle, crank.
mannequin /mankɛ̃/ *nm* (personne) model; (statue) dummy.
manœuvrer /manœvʀe/ [1] *vt*

manoeuvre; (*machine*) operate. ● *vi* manoeuvre.

manoir /manwaʀ/ *nm* manor.

manque /mɑ̃k/ *nm* lack (**de** of); (lacune) gap; **~ à gagner** loss of earnings; **en (état de) ~** having withdrawal symptoms.

manqué, ~e /mɑ̃ke/ *a* (*écrivain*) failed; **garçon ~** tomboy.

manquement /mɑ̃kmɑ̃/ *nm* **~ à** breach of.

manquer /mɑ̃ke/ [1] *vt* miss; (gâcher) spoil; **~ à** (*devoir*) fail in; **~ de** be short of, lack; **il/ça lui manque** he misses him/it; **~ (de) faire** (faillir) nearly do; **ne manquez pas de** be sure to; **~ à sa parole** break one's word. ● *vi* be short *ou* lacking; (être absent) be absent; (en moins, disparu) be missing; **il me manque 20 francs** I'm 20 francs short.

mansarde /mɑ̃saʀd/ *nf* attic (room).

manteau (*pl* **~x**) /mɑ̃to/ *nm* coat.

manucure /manykyʀ/ *nmf* manicurist. ● *nf* (soins) manicure.

manuel, ~le /manɥɛl/ *a* manual. ● *nm* (livre) manual; (Scol) textbook.

manufacture /manyfaktyʀ/ *nf* factory; (fabrication) manufacture. **manufacturer** [1] *vt* manufacture.

manuscrit, ~e /manyskʀi, -t/ *a* handwritten. ● *nm* manuscript.

mappemonde /mapmɔ̃d/ *nf* world map; (sphère) globe.

maquereau (*pl* **~x**) /makʀo/ *nm* (poisson) mackerel; 🅘 pimp.

maquette /makɛt/ *nf* (scale) model; **~ (de mise en page)** paste-up.

maquillage /makijaʒ/ *nm* make-up.

maquiller /makije/ [1] *vt* make up; (truquer) doctor, fake. □ **se ~** *vpr* make (oneself) up.

maquis /maki/ *nm* (paysage) scrub; (Mil) Maquis, underground.

maraîcher, -ère /maʀeʃe, -ɛʀ/ *nm, f* market gardener; (US) truck farmer.

marais /maʀɛ/ *nm* marsh.

marasme /maʀasm/ *nm* slump, stagnation; **dans le ~** in the doldrums.

marbre /maʀbʀ/ *nm* marble.

marc /maʀ/ *nm* (eau-de-vie) marc; **~ de café** coffee grounds.

marchand, ~e /maʀʃɑ̃, -d/ *a* (*valeur*) market. ● *nm, f* trader; (de charbon, vins) merchant; **~ de couleurs** ironmonger; (US) hardware merchant; **~ de journaux** newsagent; **~ de légumes** greengrocer; **~ de poissons** fishmonger.

marchander /maʀʃɑ̃de/ [1] *vt* haggle over. ● *vi* haggle.

marchandise /maʀʃɑ̃diz/ *nf* goods.

marche /maʀʃ/ *nf* (démarche, trajet) walk; (rythme) pace; (Mil, Mus, Pol) march; (d'escalier) step; (Sport) walking; (de machine) operation, working; (de véhicule) running; **en ~** (*train*) moving; (*moteur, machine*) running; **faire ~ arrière** (*véhicule*) reverse; **mettre en ~** start (up); **se mettre en ~** start moving.

marché /maʀʃe/ *nm* market; (contrat) deal; **faire son ~** do one's shopping; **~ aux puces** flea market; **~ noir** black market.

marchepied /maʀʃəpje/ *nm* (de train, camion) step.

marcher /maʀʃe/ [1] *vi* walk; (poser le pied) tread (**sur** on); (aller) go; (fonctionner) work, run; (prospérer) go well; (*film, livre*) do well; (consentir 🅘) agree; **faire ~ qn** 🅘 pull sb's leg.

M

mardi /maʀdi/ *nm* Tuesday; **M~ gras** Shrove Tuesday.

mare /maʀ/ *nf* (étang) pond; (flaque) pool.

marécage /maʀekaʒ/ *nm* marsh; (sous les tropiques) swamp.

maréchal (*pl* **-aux**) /maʀeʃal, -o/ *nm* field marshal.

maréchal-ferrant (*pl* **-aux-ferrants** /maʀeʃalfeʀɑ̃/ *nm* blacksmith.

marée /maʀe/ *nf* tide; (poissons) fresh fish; **~ haute/basse** high/ low tide; **~ noire** oil slick.

marelle /maʀɛl/ *nf* hopscotch.

margarine /maʀgaʀin/ *nf* margarine.

marge /maʀʒ/ *nf* margin; **en ~ de** (à l'écart de) on the fringe(s) of; **~ bénéficiaire** profit margin.

marginal, **~e** (*mpl* **-aux**) /maʀʒinal, -o/ *a* marginal. ● *nm, f* drop-out.

marguerite /maʀgəʀit/ *nf* daisy; (qui imprime) daisy-wheel.

mari /maʀi/ *nm* husband.

mariage /maʀjaʒ/ *nm* marriage; (cérémonie) wedding.

marié, **~e** /maʀje/ *a* married. ● *nm, f* (bride)groom, bride; **les ~s** the bride and groom.

marier /maʀje/ [45] *vt* marry. □ **se ~** *vpr* get married, marry; **se ~ avec** marry, get married to.

marin, **~e** /maʀɛ̃, -in/ *a* sea. ● *nm* sailor.

marine /maʀin/ *nf* navy; **~ marchande** merchant navy. ● *a inv* navy (blue).

marionnette /maʀjɔnɛt/ *nf* puppet; (à fils) marionette.

maritalement /maʀitalmɑ̃/ *adv* (*vivre*) as husband and wife.

maritime /maʀitim/ *a* maritime, coastal; (*agent, compagnie*) shipping.

marmaille /maʀmaj/ *nf* [!] brats.

marmelade /maʀməlad/ *nf* stewed fruit; **~ d'oranges** (orange) marmalade.

marmite /maʀmit/ *nf* (cooking-) pot.

marmonner /maʀmɔne/ [1] *vt* mumble.

marmot /maʀmo/ *nm* [!] kid.

Maroc /maʀɔk/ *nm* Morocco.

maroquinerie /maʀɔkinʀi/ *nf* (magasin) leather goods shop.

marquant, **~e** /maʀkɑ̃, -t/ *a* (remarquable) outstanding; (qu'on n'oublie pas) memorable.

marque /maʀk/ *nf* mark; (de produits) brand, make; (décompte) score; **à vos ~s!** (Sport) on your marks!; **de ~** (Comm) brand name; (fig) important; **~ de fabrique** trademark; **~ déposée** registered trademark.

marquer /maʀke/ [1] *vt* mark; (indiquer) show, say; (écrire) note down; (*point, but*) score; (*joueur*) mark; (influencer) leave its mark on; (exprimer) (*volonté, sentiment*) show. ● *vi* (laisser une trace) leave a mark; (*événement*) stand out; (Sport) score.

marquis, **~e** /maʀki, -z/ *nm, f* marquis, marchioness.

marraine /maʀɛn/ *nf* godmother.

marrant, **~e** /maʀɑ̃, -t/ *a* [!] funny.

marre /maʀ/ *adv* **en avoir ~** [!] be fed up (**de** with).

marrer (**se**) /(sə)maʀe/ [1] *vpr* [!] laugh, have a (good) laugh.

marron /maʀɔ̃/ *nm* chestnut; (couleur) brown; (coup [!]) thump; **~ d'Inde** horse chestnut. ● *a inv* brown.

mars /maʀs/ *nm* March.

marteau (*pl* **~x**) /maʀto/ *nm* hammer; **~ (de porte)** (door) knocker; **~ piqueur** *ou* **pneumatique** pneumatic drill; **être ~** [!] be mad.

marteler /maʀtəle/ [6] *vt*

hammer; (*poings, talons*) pound; (scander) rap out.

martial, **~e** (*mpl* **-iaux**) /maʀsjal, -jo/ *a* military; (*art*) martial.

martien, **~ne** /maʀsjɛ̃, -ɛn/ *a & nm, f* Martian.

martyr, **~e** /maʀtiʀ/ *nm, f* martyr. ● *a* martyred; (*enfant*) battered.

martyre /maʀtiʀ/ *nm* (Relig) martyrdom; (fig) agony, suffering.

martyriser /maʀtiʀize/ [1] *vt* (Relig) martyr; (torturer) torture; (*enfant*) batter.

marxisme /maʀksism/ *nm* Marxism. **marxiste** *a & nmf* Marxist.

masculin, **~e** /maskylɛ̃, -in/ *a* masculine; (*sexe*) male; (*mode, équipe*) men's. ● *nm* masculine.

masochisme /mazoʃism/ *nm* masochism.

masochiste /mazɔʃist/ *nmf* masochist. ● *a* masochistic.

masque /mask/ *nm* mask; **~ de beauté** face pack. **masquer** [1] *vt* (cacher) hide, conceal (**à** from); (*lumière*) block (off).

massacre /masakʀ/ *nm* massacre. **massacrer** [1] *vt* massacre; (abîmer ⊡) ruin.

massage /masaʒ/ *nm* massage.

masse /mas/ *nf* (volume) mass; (gros morceau) lump, mass; (outil) sledge-hammer; **en ~** (*vendre*) in bulk; (*venir*) in force; **produire en ~** mass-produce; **la ~** (foule) the masses; **une ~ de** ⊡ masses of; **la ~ de** the majority of.

masser /mase/ [1] *vt* (assembler) assemble; (pétrir) massage. □ **se ~** *vpr* (*gens, foule*) mass.

massif, **-ive** /masif, -v/ *a* massive; (*or, argent*) solid. ● *nm* (de fleurs) clump; (parterre) bed; (Géog) massif. **massivement** *adv* (en masse) in large numbers.

massue /masy/ *nf* club, bludgeon.

mastic /mastik/ *nm* putty; (pour trous) filler.

mastiquer /mastike/ [1] *vt* (mâcher) chew.

mat /mat/ *a* (*couleur*) matt; (*bruit*) dull; (*teint*) olive; **être ~** (aux échecs) be in checkmate.

mât /mɑ/ *nm* mast; (pylône) pole; **~ de drapeau** flagpole.

match /matʃ/ *nm* match; (US) game; **faire ~ nul** tie, draw; **~ aller** first leg; **~ retour** return match.

matelas /matla/ *nm* mattress; **~ pneumatique** air bed.

matelassé, **~e** /matlase/ *a* padded; (*tissu*) quilted.

matelot /matlo/ *nm* sailor.

mater /mate/ [1] *vt* (*révolte*) put down; (*personne*) bring into line.

matérialiser (se) /(sə)mateʀjalize/ [1] *vpr* materialize.

matérialiste /mateʀjalist/ *a* materialistic. ● *nmf* materialist.

matériau (*pl* **~x**) /mateʀjo/ *nm* material.

matériel, **~le** /mateʀjɛl/ *a* material. ● *nm* equipment, materials; **~ informatique** hardware.

maternel, **~le** /matɛʀnɛl/ *a* maternal; (comme d'une mère) motherly. **maternelle** *nf* nursery school.

maternité /matɛʀnite/ *nf* maternity hospital; (état de mère) motherhood; **de ~** maternity.

mathématicien, **~ne** /matematisjɛ̃, -ɛn/ *nm, f* mathematician.

mathématique /matematik/ *a* mathematical. **mathématiques** *nfpl* mathematics (+ *sg*).

maths /mat/ *nfpl* ⊡ maths (+ *sg*).

matière /matjɛʀ/ *nf* matter; (produit) material; (sujet) subject; **en**

M

~ de as regards; **~ plastique** plastic; **~s grasses** fat content; **~s premières** raw materials.

matin /matɛ̃/ *nm* morning; **de bon ~** early in the morning.

matinal, **~e** (*mpl* **-aux**) /matinal, -o/ *a* morning; (de bonne heure) early; **être ~** be up early; (d'habitude) be an early riser.

matinée /matine/ *nf* morning; (spectacle) matinée.

matou /matu/ *nm* tomcat.

matraque /matʀak/ *nf* (de police) truncheon; (US) billy (club). **matraquer** [1] *vt* club, beat; (*produit, chanson*) plug.

matrimonial, **~e** (*mpl* **-iaux**) /matʀimɔnjal, -jo/ *a* matrimonial; **agence ~e** marriage bureau.

maturité /matyʀite/ *nf* maturity.

maudire /modiʀ/ [41] *vt* curse.

maudit, **~e** /modi, -t/ *a* [!] blasted, damned.

maugréer /mogʀee/ [15] *vi* grumble.

mausolée /mozɔle/ *nm* mausoleum.

maussade /mosad/ *a* gloomy.

mauvais, **~e** /mɔvɛ, -z/ *a* bad; (erroné) wrong; (malveillant) evil; (désagréable) nasty, bad; (*mer*) rough; **le ~ moment** the wrong time; **~e herbe** weed; **~e langue** gossip; **~e passe** tight spot; **~ traitements** ill-treatment. ● *adv* (*sentir*) bad; **il fait ~** the weather is bad. ● *nm* **le bon et le ~** the good and the bad.

mauve /mov/ *a & nm* mauve.

mauviette /movjɛt/ *nf* weakling, wimp.

maux /mo/ ⇨ MAL**2**.

maximal, **~e** (*mpl* **-aux**) /maksimal, -o/ *a* maximum.

maxime /maksim/ *nf* maxim.

maximum /maksimɔm/ *a* maximum. ● *nm* maximum; **au ~** as much as possible; (tout au plus) at most; **faire le ~** do one's utmost.

mazout /mazut/ *nm* (fuel) oil.

me, **m'** /mə, m/ *pron* me; (indirect) (to) me; (réfléchi) myself.

méandre /meɑ̃dʀ/ *nm* meander.

mec /mek/ *nm* [!] bloke, guy.

mécanicien, **~ne** /mekanisjɛ̃, -jɛn/ *nm, f* mechanic. ● *nm* train driver.

mécanique /mekanik/ *a* mechanical; (*jouet*) clockwork; **problème ~** engine trouble. ● *nf* mechanics (+ *sg*); (mécanisme) mechanism. **mécaniser** [1] *vt* mechanize.

mécanisme /mekanism/ *nm* mechanism.

méchamment /meʃamɑ̃/ *adv* spitefully. **méchanceté** *nf* nastiness; (action) wicked action.

méchant, **~e** /meʃɑ̃, -t/ *a* (cruel) wicked; (désagréable, grave) nasty; (*enfant*) naughty; (*chien*) vicious; (sensationnel [!]) terrific. ● *nm, f* (enfant) naughty child.

mèche /mɛʃ/ *nf* (de cheveux) lock; (de bougie) wick; (d'explosif) fuse; (outil) drill bit; **de ~ avec** in league with.

méconnaissable /mekɔnɛsabl/ *a* unrecognizable.

méconnaître /mekɔnɛtʀ/ [18] *vt* misunderstand, misread; (mésestimer) underestimate.

méconnu, **~e** /mekɔny/ *a* unrecognized; (*artiste*) neglected.

mécontent, **~e** /mekɔ̃tɑ̃, -t/ *a* dissatisfied (**de** with); (irrité) annoyed (**de** at, with). **mécontentement** *nm* dissatisfaction; annoyance. **mécontenter** [1] *vt* dissatisfy; (irriter) annoy.

médaille /medaj/ *nf* medal; (insigne) badge; (bijou) medallion. **médaillé**, **~e** *nm, f* medallist.

médaillon /medajɔ̃/ *nm* medallion; (bijou) locket.

médecin /mɛdsɛ̃/ *nm* doctor.

médecine /mɛdsin/ *nf* medicine.

média /medja/ *nm* medium; **les ~s** the media.

médiateur, -trice /medjatœʀ, -tʀis/ *nm, f* mediator.

médiatique /medjatik/ *a* (*événement, personnalité*) media.

médical, ~e (*mpl* **-aux**) /medikal, -o/ *a* medical.

médicament /medikamɑ̃/ *nm* medicine, drug.

médico-légal, ~e (*mpl* **-aux**) /medikɔlegal, -o/ *a* forensic.

médiéval, ~e (*mpl* **-aux**) /medjeval, -o/ *a* medieval.

médiocre /medjɔkʀ/ *a* mediocre, poor. **médiocrité** *nf* mediocrity.

médire /mediʀ/ [37] *vi* **~ de** speak ill of, malign.

médisance /medizɑ̃s/ *nf* **~(s)** malicious gossip.

méditer /medite/ [1] *vi* meditate (**sur** on). ● *vt* contemplate; (*paroles, conseils*) mull over; **~ de** plan to.

Méditerranée /meditɛʀane/ *nf* **la ~** the Mediterranean.

méditerranéen, ~ne /meditɛʀaneɛ̃, -ɛn/ *a* Mediterranean.

médium /medjɔm/ *nm* (personne) medium.

méduse /medyz/ *nf* jellyfish.

meeting /mitiŋ/ *nm* meeting.

méfait /mefɛ/ *nm* misdeed; **les ~s de** (conséquences) the ravages of.

méfiance /mefjɑ̃s/ *nf* suspicion, distrust. **méfiant, ~e** *a* suspicious, distrustful.

méfier (se) /(sə)mefje/ [45] *vpr* be wary *ou* careful; **se ~ de** distrust, be wary of.

mégaoctet /megaɔktɛ/ *nm* (Ordinat) megabyte.

mégère /meʒɛʀ/ *nf* (femme) shrew.

mégot /mego/ *nm* cigarette end.

meilleur, ~e /mɛjœʀ/ *a* (comparatif) better (**que** than); (superlatif) best; **le ~ livre** the best book; **mon ~ ami** my best friend; **~ marché** cheaper. ● *nm, f* **le ~, la ~e** the best (one). ● *adv* (*sentir*) better; **il fait ~** the weather is better.

mél /mel/ *nm* e-mail; **envoyer un ~** send an e-mail.

mélancolie /melɑ̃kɔli/ *nf* melancholy.

mélange /melɑ̃ʒ/ *nm* mixture, blend.

mélanger /melɑ̃ʒe/ [40] *vt* mix; (*thés, parfums*) blend. ▫ **se ~** *vpr* mix; (*thés, parfums*) blend; (*idées*) get mixed up.

mélasse /melas/ *nf* black treacle; (US) molasses.

mêlée /mele/ *nf* free for all; (au rugby) scrum.

mêler /mele/ [1] *vt* mix (**à** with); (*qualités*) combine; (embrouiller) mix up; **~ qn à** (impliquer dans) involve sb in. ▫ **se ~** *vpr* mix; combine; **se ~ à** (se joindre à) mingle with; (participer à) join in; **se ~ de** meddle in; **mêle-toi de ce qui te regarde** mind your own business.

méli-mélo (*pl* **mélis-mélos**) /melimelo/ *nm* jumble.

mélo /melo/ ⓘ *nm* melodrama. ● *a inv* slushy, schmaltzy ⓘ.

mélodie /melɔdi/ *nf* melody. **mélodieux, -ieuse** *a* melodious. **mélodique** *a* melodic.

mélodramatique /melɔdʀamatik/ *a* melodramatic. **mélodrame** *nm* melodrama.

mélomane /melɔman/ *nmf* music lover.

melon /məlɔ̃/ *nm* melon; (**chapeau**) **~** bowler (hat).

M

membrane /mɑ̃bʀan/ *nf* membrane.

membre /mɑ̃bʀ/ *nm* (Anat) limb; (adhérent) member.

même /mɛm/ *a* same; **ce livre ~** this very book; **la bonté ~** kindness itself; **en ~ temps** at the same time. ● *pron* **le ~, la ~** the same (one). ● *adv* even; **à ~** (sur) directly on; **à ~ de** in a position to; **de ~** (aussi) too; (de la même façon) likewise; **de ~ que** just as; **~si** even if.

mémé /meme/ *nf* [!] granny.

mémo /memo/ *nm* note, memo.

mémoire /memwaʀ/ *nm* (rapport) memorandum; (Univ) dissertation; **~s** (souvenirs écrits) memoirs. ● *nf* memory; **à la ~ de** to the memory of; **de ~** from memory; **~ morte/ vive** (Ordinat) ROM/RAM.

mémorable /memɔʀabl/ *a* memorable.

menace /mənas/ *nf* threat. **menacer** [10] *vt* threaten (**de faire** to do).

ménage /menaʒ/ *nm* (couple) couple; (travail) housework; (famille) household; **se mettre en ~** set up house.

ménagement /menaʒmɑ̃/ *nm* **avec ~s** gently; **sans ~s** (*dire*) bluntly; (*jeter, pousser*) roughly.

ménager[1], **-ère** /menaʒe, -ɛʀ/ *a* household, domestic; **travaux ~s** housework.

ménager[2] /menaʒe/ [40] *vt* be gentle with, handle carefully; (utiliser) be careful with; (organiser) prepare (carefully); **ne pas ~ ses efforts** spare no effort.

ménagère /menaʒɛʀ/ *nf* housewife.

ménagerie /menaʒʀi/ *nf* menagerie.

mendiant, **~e** /mɑ̃djɑ̃, -t/ *nm,f* beggar.

mendier /mɑ̃dje/ [45] *vt* beg for. ● *vi* beg.

mener /məne/ [6] *vt* lead; (*entreprise, pays*) run; (*étude, enquête*) carry out; (*politique*) pursue; **~ à** (accompagner à) take to; (faire aboutir) lead to; **~ à bien** see through. ● *vi* lead.

méningite /menɛ̃ʒit/ *nf* meningitis.

menotte /mənɔt/ *nf* [!] hand; **~s** handcuffs.

mensonge /mɑ̃sɔ̃ʒ/ *nm* lie; (action) lying. **mensonger**, **-ère** *a* untrue, false.

mensualité /mɑ̃sɥalite/ *nf* monthly payment.

mensuel, **~le** /mɑ̃sɥɛl/ *a* monthly. ● *nm* monthly (magazine). **mensuellement** *adv* monthly.

mensurations /mɑ̃syʀasjɔ̃/ *nfpl* measurements.

mental, **~e** (*mpl* **-aux**) /mɑ̃tal, -o/ *a* mental; **malade ~** mentally ill person; **handicapé ~** mentally handicapped person.

mentalité /mɑ̃talite/ *nf* mentality.

menteur, **-euse** /mɑ̃tœʀ, -øz/ *nm,f* liar. ● *a* untruthful.

menthe /mɑ̃t/ *nf* mint.

mention /mɑ̃sjɔ̃/ *nf* mention; (annotation) note; (Scol) grade; **rayer la ~ inutile** delete as appropriate. **mentionner** [1] *vt* mention.

mentir /mɑ̃tiʀ/ [46] *vi* lie.

menton /mɑ̃tɔ̃/ *nm* chin.

menu, **~e** /məny/ *a* (petit) tiny; (fin) fine; (insignifiant) minor. ● *adv* (*couper*) fine. ● *nm* (carte) menu; (repas) meal; (Ordinat) menu; **~ déroulant** pull-down menu.

menuiserie /mənɥizʀi/ *nf* carpentry, joinery. **menuisier** *nm* carpenter, joiner.

méprendre (**se**) /(sə)mepʀɑ̃dʀ/

[50] *vpr* **se ~ sur** be mistaken about.
mépris /mepRi/ *nm* contempt, scorn (**de** for); **au ~ de** regardless of.
méprisable /mepRizabl/ *a* contemptible, despicable.
méprise /mepRiz/ *nf* mistake.
méprisant, **~e** /mepRizɑ̃, -t/ *a* scornful. **mépriser** [1] *vt* scorn, despise.
mer /mɛR/ *nf* sea; (marée) tide; **en pleine ~** out at sea.
mercenaire /mɛRsənɛR/ *nm & a* mercenary.
mercerie /mɛRs(ə)Ri/ *nf* haberdashery; (US) notions store. **mercier**, **-ière** *nm, f* haberdasher; (US) notions seller.
merci /mɛRsi/ *interj* thank you, thanks (**de, pour** for); **~ beaucoup**, **~ bien** thank you very much. ● *nm* thank you. ● *nf* mercy.
mercredi /mɛRkRədi/ *nm* Wednesday; **~ des Cendres** Ash Wednesday.
merde /mɛRd/ *nf* ⊠ shit ⊠.
mère /mɛR/ *nf* mother; **~ de famille** mother.
méridional, **~e** (*mpl* **-aux**) /meRidjɔnal, -o/ *a* southern. ● *nm, f* Southerner.
mérite /meRit/ *nm* merit; **avoir du ~ à faire** deserve credit for doing.
mériter /meRite/ [1] *vt* deserve; **~ d'être lu** be worth reading.
méritoire /meRitwaR/ *a* commendable.
merlan /mɛRlɑ̃/ *nm* whiting.
merle /mɛRl/ *nm* blackbird.
merveille /mɛRvɛj/ *nf* wonder, marvel; **à ~** wonderfully; **faire des ~s** work wonders.
merveilleux, **-euse** /mɛRvɛjø, -z/ *a* wonderful, marvellous.
mes /me/ ⇒MON.
mésange /mezɑ̃ʒ/ *nf* tit(mouse).
mésaventure /mezavɑ̃tyR/ *nf* misadventure; **par ~** by some misfortune.
mesdames /medam/ ⇒MADAME.
mesdemoiselles /medmwazɛl/ ⇒MADEMOISELLE.
mésentente /mezɑ̃tɑ̃t/ *nf* disagreement.
mesquin, **~e** /mɛskɛ̃, -in/ *a* mean-minded, petty; (chiche) mean. **mesquinerie** *nf* meanness.
mess /mɛs/ *nm* (Mil) mess.
message /mesaʒ/ *nm* message; **un ~ électronique** an e-mail.
messager, **-ère** /mesaʒe, -ɛR/ *nm, f* messenger. ● *nm* **~ de poche** pager.
messagerie /mesaʒRi/ *nf* (transports) freight forwarding; (télécommunications) messaging; **~ électronique** electronic mail; **~ vocale** voice mail.
messe /mɛs/ *nf* (Relig) mass.
messieurs /mesjø/ ⇒MONSIEUR.
mesure /məzyR/ *nf* measurement; (quantité, unité) measure; (disposition) measure, step; (cadence) time; **en ~** in time; (modération) moderation; **à ~ que** as; **dans la ~ où** in so far as; **dans une certaine ~** to some extent; **en ~ de** in a position to; **sans ~** to excess; (**fait**) **sur ~** made-to-measure.
mesuré, **~e** /məzyRe/ *a* measured; (atttitude) moderate.
mesurer /məzyRe/ [1] *vt* measure; (juger) assess; (*argent, temps*) ration. ● *vi* **~ 15 mètres de long** be 15 metres long. □ **se ~ avec** *vpr* pit oneself against.
met /mɛ/ ⇒METTRE [42].
métal (*pl* **-aux**) /metal, -o/ *nm* metal. **métallique** *a* (*objet*) metal; (*éclat*) metallic.
métallurgie /metalyRʒi/ *nf* (industrie) metalworking industry.
métamorphoser /metamɔRfoze/

M

[1] *vt* transform. ▫ **se ~** *vpr* be transformed; **se ~ en** metamorphose into.

métaphore /metafɔʀ/ *nf* metaphor.

météo /meteo/ *nf* (bulletin) weather forecast.

météore /meteɔʀ/ *nm* meteor.

météorologie /meteɔʀɔlɔʒi/ *nf* meteorology.

météorologique /meteɔʀɔlɔʒik/ *a* meteorological; **conditions ~s** weather conditions.

méthode /metɔd/ *nf* method; (ouvrage) course, manual. **méthodique** *a* methodical.

méticuleux, -euse /metikylø, -z/ *a* meticulous.

métier /metje/ *nm* job; (manuel) trade; (intellectuel) profession; (expérience) experience, skill; **~ (à tisser)** loom; **remettre qch sur le ~** rework sth.

métis, ~se /metis/ *a* mixed race. ● *nm, f* person of mixed race.

métrage /metʀaʒ/ *nm* length; **court ~** short (film); **long ~** feature-length film.

mètre /mɛtʀ/ *nm* metre; (règle) rule; **~ ruban** tape-measure.

métreur, -euse /metʀœʀ, -øz/ *nm, f* quantity surveyor.

métrique /metʀik/ *a* metric.

métro /metʀo/ *nm* underground; (US) subway.

métropole /metʀɔpɔl/ *nf* metropolis; (pays) mother country. **métropolitain, ~e** *a* metropolitan.

mets /mɛ/ *nm* dish. ● ⇒METTRE [42].

mettable /mɛtabl/ *a* wearable.

metteur /mɛtœʀ/ *nm* **~ en scène** director.

mettre /mɛtʀ/ [42] *vt* put; (*radio, chauffage*) put *ou* switch on; (*réveil*) set; (installer) put in; (revêtir) put on; (porter habituellement) (vêtement, lunettes) wear; (prendre) take; (investir, dépenser) put; (écrire) write, say; **elle a mis deux heures** it took her two hours; **~ la table** lay the table; **~ en question** question; **~ en valeur** highlight; (*terrain*) develop; **mettons que** let's suppose that. ● *vi* **~ bas** (*animal*) give birth. ▫ **se ~** *vpr* (*vêtement, maquillage*) put on; (se placer) (*objet*) go; (*personne*) (debout) stand; (assis) sit; (couché) lie; **se ~ en short** put shorts on; **se ~ debout** stand up; **se ~ au lit** go to bed; **se ~ à table** sit down at table; **se ~ en ligne** line up; **se ~ du sable dans les yeux** get sand in one's eyes; **se ~ au chinois/tennis** take up Chinese/tennis; **se ~ au travail** set to work; **se ~ à faire** start to do.

meuble /mœbl/ *nm* piece of furniture; **~s** furniture.

meublé /møble/ *nm* furnished flat.

meubler /møble/ [1] *vt* furnish; (fig) fill. ▫ **se ~** *vpr* buy furniture.

meugler /møgle/ [1] *vi* moo.

meule /møl/ *nf* millstone; **~ de foin** haystack.

meunier, -ière /mønje, -jɛʀ/ *nm, f* miller.

meurs, meurt /mœʀ/ ⇒MOURIR [43].

meurtre /mœʀtʀ/ *nm* murder.

meurtrier, -ière /mœʀtʀije, -jɛʀ/ *a* deadly. ● *nm, f* murderer, murderess.

meurtrir /mœʀtʀiʀ/ [2] *vt* bruise.

meute /møt/ *nf* pack of hounds.

Mexique /mɛksik/ *nm* Mexico.

mi- /mi/ *préf* mid-, half-; **à mi-chemin** half-way; **à mi-pente** half-way up the hill; **à la mi-juin** in mid-June.

miauler /mjole/ [1] *vi* miaow.

micro /mikʀo/ *nm* microphone, mike; (Ordinat) micro.

microbe /mikRɔb/ *nm* germ.

microfilm /mikRɔfilm/ *nm* microfilm.

micro-onde /mikRɔɔ̃d/ *nf* microwave; **un four à ~s** microwave (oven). **micro-ondes** *nm inv* microwave (oven).

micro-ordinateur (*pl* **~s**) /mikRɔɔRdinatœR/ *nm* personal computer.

microphone /mikRɔfɔn/ *nm* microphone.

microprocesseur /mikRɔpRɔsɛsœR/ *nm* microprocessor.

microscope /mikRɔskɔp/ *nm* microscope.

midi /midi/ *nm* twelve o'clock, midday, noon; (déjeuner) lunch-time; (sud) south. **Midi** *nm* **le M~** the South of France.

mie /mi/ *nf* soft part (of the loaf); **un pain de ~** a sandwich loaf.

miel /mjɛl/ *nm* honey.

mielleux, -euse /mjɛlø, -z/ *a* unctuous.

mien, ~ne /mjɛ̃, -ɛn/ *pron* **le ~, la ~ne, les ~(ne)s** mine.

miette /mjɛt/ *nf* crumb; (fig) scrap; **en ~s** in pieces.

mieux /mjø/ *a inv* better (**que** than); **le** *ou* **la** *ou* **les ~** (the) best. ● *nm* best; (progrès) improvement; **faire de son ~** do one's best; **le ~ serait de** the best thing would be to. ● *adv* better; **le** *ou* **la** *ou* **les ~** (de deux) the better; (de plusieurs) the best; **elle va ~** she is better; **j'aime ~ rester** I'd rather stay; **il vaudrait ~ partir** it would be best to leave; **tu ferais ~ de faire** you would be best to do.

mièvre /mjɛvR/ *a* insipid.

mignon, ~ne /miɲɔ̃, -ɔn/ *a* cute; (gentil) kind.

migraine /migRɛn/ *nf* headache; (plus fort) migraine.

migration /migRasjɔ̃/ *nf* migration.

mijoter /miʒɔte/ [1] *vt/i* simmer; (tramer Ⓘ) cook up.

mil /mil/ *nm* a thousand.

milice /milis/ *nf* militia.

milieu (*pl* **~x**) /miljø/ *nm* middle; (environnement) environment; (appartenance sociale) background; (groupe) circle; (voie) middle way; (criminel) underworld; **au ~ de** in the middle of; **en plein** *ou* **au beau ~ de** right in the middle (of).

militaire /militɛR/ *a* military. ● *nm* soldier, serviceman.

militant, ~e /militɑ̃, -t/ *nm,f* militant.

militer /milite/ [1] *vi* be a militant; **~ pour** militate in favour of.

mille[1] /mil/ *a & nm inv* a thousand; **deux ~** two thousand; **mettre dans le ~** (fig) hit the nail on the head.

mille[2] /mil/ *nm* **~** (**marin**) (nautical) mile.

millénaire /milenɛR/ *nm* millennium. ● *a* a thousand years old.

mille-pattes /milpat/ *nm inv* centipede.

millésime /milezim/ *nm* date; (de vin) vintage.

millet /mijɛ/ *nm* millet.

milliard /miljaR/ *nm* thousand million, billion. **milliardaire** *nmf* multimillionaire.

millième /miljɛm/ *a & nmf* thousandth.

millier /milje/ *nm* thousand; **un ~ (de)** about a thousand.

millimètre /milimɛtR/ *nm* millimetre.

million /miljɔ̃/ *nm* million; **deux ~s (de)** two million. **millionnaire** *nmf* millionaire.

mime /mim/ *nmf* mime-artist.

M

● *nm* (art) mime. **mimer** [1] *vt* mime; (imiter) mimic.
mimique /mimik/ *nf* expressions and gestures.
minable /minabl/ *a* ⓘ (*logement*) shabby; (médiocre) pathetic, crummy.
minauder /minode/ [1] *vi* simper.
mince /mɛ̃s/ *a* thin; (svelte) slim; (faible) (*espoir, majorité*) slim. ● *interj* ⓘ blast ⓘ, darn it ⓘ. **minceur** *nf* thinness; slimness.
mincir /mɛ̃siʀ/ [2] *vi* get slimmer; **ça te mincit** it makes you look slimmer.
mine /min/ *nf* expression; (allure) appearance; **avoir bonne ~** look well; **faire ~ de** make as if to; (exploitation, explosif) mine; (de crayon) lead; **~ de charbon** coal-mine.
miner /mine/ [1] *vt* (saper) undermine; (garnir d'explosifs) mine.
minerai /minʀɛ/ *nm* ore.
minéral, **~e** (*mpl* **-aux**) /mineʀal, -o/ *a* mineral. ● *nm* (*pl* **-aux**) mineral.
minéralogique /mineʀalɔʒik/ *a* **plaque ~** numberplate; (US) license plate.
minet, **~te** /minɛ, -t/ *nm, f* (chat ⓘ) pussy(cat).
mineur, **~e** /minœʀ/ *a* minor; (Jur) under age. ● *nm, f* (Jur) minor. ● *nm* (ouvrier) miner.
miniature /minjatyʀ/ *nf & a* miniature.
minier, **-ière** /minje, -jɛʀ/ *a* mining.
minimal, **~e** (*mpl* **-aux**) /minimal,o/ *a* minimal, minimum.
minime /minim/ *a* minimal, minor. ● *nmf* (Sport) junior.
minimum /minimɔm/ *a* minimum. ● *nm* minimum; **au ~** (pour le moins) at the very least; **en faire un ~** do as little as possible.
ministère /ministɛʀ/ *nm* ministry; (gouvernement) government; **~ public** public prosecutor's office. **ministériel**, **~le** *a* ministerial, government.
ministre /ministʀ/ *nm* minister; (au Royaume-Uni) Secretary of State; (US) Secretary.
Minitel® /minitɛl/ *nm* Minitel (*telephone videotext system*).
minorer /minɔʀe/ [1] *vt* reduce.
minoritaire /minɔʀitɛʀ/ *a* minority; **être ~** be in the minority. **minorité** *nf* minority.
minuit /minɥi/ *nm* midnight.
minuscule /minyskyl/ *a* minute. ● *nf* (lettre) **~** lower case.
minute /minyt/ *nf* minute; **'talons ~'** 'heels repaired while you wait'.
minuterie /minytʀi/ *nf* time-switch.
minutie /minysi/ *nf* meticulousness.
minutieux, **-ieuse** /minysjø, -z/ *a* meticulous.
mioche /mjɔʃ/ *nm, f* ⓘ kid.
mirabelle /miʀabɛl/ *nf* (mirabelle) plum.
miracle /miʀɑkl/ *nm* miracle; **par ~** miraculously.
miraculeux, **-euse** /miʀakylø, -z/ *a* miraculous.
mirage /miʀaʒ/ *nm* mirage.
mire /miʀ/ *nf* (fig) centre of attraction; (TV) test card.
mirobolant, **~e** /miʀɔbɔlɑ̃, -t/ *a* ⓘ marvellous.
miroir /miʀwaʀ/ *nm* mirror.
miroiter /miʀwate/ [1] *vi* shimmer, sparkle.
mis, **~e** /mi, miz/ *a* **bien ~** well-dressed. ● ⇒METTRE [42].
mise /miz/ *nf* (argent) stake; (tenue) attire; **~ à feu** blast-off; **~ au point** adjustment; (fig) clarification; **~ de fonds** capital

outlay; ~ **en garde** warning; ~ **en plis** set; ~ **en scène** direction.

miser /mize/ [1] *vt* (*argent*) bet, stake (**sur** on). ● *vi* ~ **sur** (parier) place a bet on; (compter sur) bank on.

misérable /mizeʀabl/ *a* miserable, wretched; (indigent) destitute; (minable) seedy, squalid.

misère /mizɛʀ/ *nf* destitution; (malheur) trouble, woe. **miséreux, -euse** *nm, f* destitute person.

miséricorde /mizeʀikɔʀd/ *nf* mercy.

missel /misɛl/ *nm* missal.

missile /misil/ *nm* missile.

mission /misjɔ̃/ *nm* mission. **missionnaire** *nmf* missionary.

missive /misiv/ *nf* missive.

mistral /mistʀal/ *nm* (vent) mistral.

mitaine /mitɛn/ *nf* fingerless mitt.

mite /mit/ *nf* (clothes-)moth.

mi-temps /mitɑ̃/ *nf inv* (arrêt) half-time; (période) half. ● *nm inv* part-time work; **à** ~ part time.

miteux, -euse /mitø, -z/ *a* shabby.

mitigé, ~e /mitiʒe/ *a* (modéré) lukewarm; (*succès*) qualified.

mitonner /mitɔne/ [1] *vt* cook slowly with care; (fig) cook up.

mitoyen, ~ne /mitwajɛ̃, -ɛn/ *a* **mur** ~ party wall.

mitrailler /mitʀɑje/ [1] *vt* machine-gun; (fig) bombard.

mitraillette /mitʀɑjɛt/ *nf* submachine gun. **mitrailleuse** *nf* machine gun.

mi-voix: à ~ /amivwa/ *loc* in a low voice.

mixeur /miksœʀ/ *nm* liquidizer, blender; (batteur) mixer.

mixte /mikst/ *a* mixed; (*commission*) joint; (*école*) coeducational; (*peau*) combination.

mobile /mɔbil/ *a* mobile; (*pièce*) moving; (*feuillet*) loose. ● *nm* (art) mobile; (raison) motive.

mobilier /mɔbilje/ *nm* furniture.

mobilisation /mɔbilizasjɔ̃/ *nf* mobilization. **mobiliser** [1] *vt* mobilize.

mobilité /mɔbilite/ *nf* mobility.

mobylette® /mɔbilɛt/ *nf* moped.

moche /mɔʃ/ *a* [I] (laid) ugly; (mauvais) lousy.

modalités /mɔdalite/ *nfpl* (conditions) terms; (façon de fonctionner) practical details.

mode /mɔd/ *nf* fashion; (coutume) custom; **à la** ~ fashionable. ● *nm* method, mode; (genre) way; ~ **d'emploi** directions (for use).

modèle /mɔdɛl/ *a* model. ● *nm* model; (exemple) example; (Comm) (type) model; (taille) size; (style) style; ~ **familial** family size; ~ **réduit** (small-scale) model.

modeler /mɔdle/ [6] *vt* model (**sur** on). □ **se** ~ **sur** *vpr* model oneself on.

modem /mɔdɛm/ *nm* modem.

modérateur, -trice /mɔdeʀatœʀ, -tʀis/ *a* moderating. **modération** *nf* moderation.

modéré, ~e /mɔdeʀe/ *a & nm, f* moderate.

modérer /mɔdeʀe/ [14] *vt* (*propos*) moderate; (*désirs, sentiments*) curb. □ **se** ~ *vpr* restrain oneself.

moderne /mɔdɛʀn/ *a* modern. **moderniser** [1] *vt* modernize.

modeste /mɔdɛst/ *a* modest. **modestie** *nf* modesty.

modification /mɔdifikasjɔ̃/ *nf* modification.

modifier /mɔdifje/ [45] *vt* change, modify. □ **se** ~ *vpr* change, alter.

modique /mɔdik/ *a* modest.

modiste /mɔdist/ *nf* milliner.

M

moduler /mɔdyle/ [1] *vt* modulate; (adapter) adjust.

moelle /mwal/ *nf* marrow; **~ épinière** spinal cord; **~ osseuse** bone marrow.

moelleux, **-euse** /mwalø, -z/ *a* soft; (onctueux) smooth.

mœurs /mœʀ(s)/ *nfpl* (morale) morals; (usages) customs; (manières) habits, ways.

moi /mwa/ *pron* me; (indirect) (to) me; (sujet) I. ● *nm* self.

moignon /mwaɲɔ̃/ *nm* stump.

moi-même /mwamɛm/ *pron* myself.

moindre /mwɛ̃dʀ/ *a* (moins grand) lesser; **le** *ou* **la ~, les ~s** the slightest, the least.

moine /mwan/ *nm* monk.

moineau (*pl* **~x**) /mwano/ *nm* sparrow.

moins /mwɛ̃/ *prép* minus; (pour dire l'heure) to; **une heure ~ dix** ten to one. ● *adv* less (**que** than); **le** *ou* **la** *ou* **les ~** the least; **le ~ grand/haut** the smallest/lowest; **~ de** (avec un nom non dénombrable) less (**que** than); **~ de dix francs** less than ten francs; **~ de livres** fewer books; **au ~, du ~** at least; **à ~ que** unless; **de ~** less; **de ~ en ~** less and less; **en ~** less; (manquant) missing.

mois /mwa/ *nm* month.

moisi, **~e** /mwazi/ *a* mouldy. ● *nm* mould; **de ~** (*odeur*) musty. **moisir** [2] *vi* go mouldy. **moisissure** *nf* mould.

moisson /mwasɔ̃/ *nf* harvest.

moissonner /mwasɔne/ [1] *vt* harvest, reap. **moissonneur**, **-euse** *nm, f* harvester.

moite /mwat/ *a* sticky, clammy.

moitié /mwatje/ *nf* half; (milieu) halfway mark; **s'arrêter à la ~** stop halfway through; **à ~ vide** half empty; **à ~ prix** (at) half-price; **la ~ de** half (of). **moitié-moitié** *adv* half-and-half.

mol /mɔl/ ⇒MOU.

molaire /mɔlɛʀ/ *nf* molar.

molécule /mɔlekyl/ *nf* molecule.

molester /mɔlɛste/ [1] *vt* manhandle, rough up.

molle /mɔl/ ⇒MOU.

mollement /mɔlmɑ̃/ *adv* softly; (faiblement) feebly. **mollesse** *nf* softness; (faiblesse) feebleness; (apathie) listlessness.

mollet /mɔlɛ/ *nm* (de jambe) calf.

mollir /mɔliʀ/ [2] *vi* soften; (céder) yield.

môme /mom/ *nmf* [!] kid.

moment /mɔmɑ̃/ *nm* moment; (période) time; (**petit**) **~** short while; **au ~ où** when; **par ~s** now and then; **du ~ où** *ou* **que** (pourvu que) as long as, provided that; (puisque) since; **en ce ~** at the moment.

momentané, **~e** /mɔmɑ̃tane/ *a* momentary. **momentanément** *adv* momentarily; (en ce moment) at present.

momie /mɔmi/ *nf* mummy.

mon, **ma** (**mon** *before vowel or mute h*) (*pl* **mes**) /mɔ̃, ma, mɔ̃n, me/ *a* my.

Monaco /mɔnako/ *npr* Monaco.

monarchie /mɔnaʀʃi/ *nf* monarchy.

monarque /mɔnaʀk/ *nm* monarch.

monastère /mɔnastɛʀ/ *nm* monastery.

monceau (*pl* **~x**) /mɔ̃so/ *nm* heap, pile.

mondain, **~e** /mɔ̃dɛ̃, -ɛn/ *a* society, social.

monde /mɔ̃d/ *nm* world; **du ~** (a lot of) people; (quelqu'un) somebody; **le** (**grand**) **~** (high) society; **se faire** (**tout**) **un ~ de qch** make a great deal of fuss about sth; **pas le moins du ~** not in the least.

mondial, ~e (*mpl* **-iaux**) /mɔ̃djal, -jo/ *a* world; (*influence*) worldwide. **mondialement** *adv* the world over.

monétaire /mɔnetɛʀ/ *a* monetary.

moniteur, -trice /mɔnitœʀ, -tʀis/ *nm, f* instructor; (de colonie de vacances) group leader; (US) (camp) counselor.

monnaie /mɔnɛ/ *nf* currency; (pièce) coin; (appoint) change; **faire la ~ de** get change for; **faire de la ~ à qn** give sb change; **menue** *ou* **petite ~** small change.

monnayer /mɔneje/ [31] *vt* convert into cash.

mono /mɔno/ *a inv* mono.

monologue /mɔnɔlɔg/ *nm* monologue.

monopole /mɔnɔpɔl/ *nm* monopoly. **monopoliser** [1] *vt* monopolize.

monospace /mɔnɔspas/ *nm* (Auto) people carrier.

monotone /mɔnɔtɔn/ *a* monotonous. **monotonie** *nf* monotony.

Monseigneur (*pl* **Messeigneurs**) /mɔ̃sɛɲœʀ/ *nm* (à un duc, archevêque) Your Grace; (à un prince) Your Highness.

monsieur (*pl* **messieurs**) /məsjø, mesjø/ *nm* (à un inconnu) (dans une lettre) **M~** Dear Sir; **bonjour, ~** good morning; **mesdames et messieurs** ladies and gentlemen; (à un homme dont on connaît le nom) (dans une lettre) **Cher M~** Dear Mr X; **bonjour, ~** good morning Mr X; **M~ le curé** Father X; **oui M~ le ministre** yes Minister; (homme) man; (formule de respect) sir.

monstre /mɔ̃stʀ/ *nm* monster. ● *a* Ⓘ colossal.

monstrueux, -euse /mɔ̃stʀyø, -z/ *a* monstrous. **monstruosité** *nf* monstrosity.

mont /mɔ̃/ *nm* mountain; **le ~ Everest** Mount Everest; **être toujours par ~s et par vaux** be always on the move.

montage /mɔ̃taʒ/ *nm* (assemblage) assembly; (au cinéma) editing.

montagne /mɔ̃taɲ/ *nf* mountain; (région) mountains; **~s russes** roller-coaster. **montagneux, -euse** *a* mountainous.

montant, ~e /mɔ̃tɑ̃, -t/ *a* rising; (*col*) high; (*chemin*) uphill. ● *nm* amount; (pièce de bois) upright.

mont-de-piété (*pl* **monts-de-piété**) /mɔ̃dpjete/ *nm* pawnshop.

monte-charge /mɔ̃tʃaʀʒ/ *nm inv* goods lift.

montée /mɔ̃te/ *nf* ascent, climb; (de prix) rise; (de coûts, risques) increase; (côte) hill.

monter /mɔ̃te/ [1] *vt* (*aux.* avoir) take up; (à l'étage) take upstairs; (*escalier, rue, pente*) go up; (assembler) assemble; (*tente, échafaudage*) put up; (*col, manche*) set in; (organiser) (*pièce*) stage; (*société*) set up, (*attaque, garde*) mount. ● *vi* (*aux.* être) go *ou* come up; (à l'étage) go *ou* come upstairs; (*avion*) climb; (*route*) go uphill, climb; (augmenter) rise; (*marée*) come up; **~ sur** (*trottoir, toit*) get up on; (*cheval, bicyclette*) get on; **~ à l'échelle/l'arbre** climb the ladder/tree; **~ dans** (*voiture*) get in; (*train, bus, avion*) get on; **~ à bord** climb on board; **~ (à cheval)** ride; **~ à bicyclette/moto** ride a bike/motorbike.

monteur, -euse /mɔ̃tœʀ, -øz/ *nm, f* (Tech) fitter; (au cinéma) editor.

montre /mɔ̃tʀ/ *nf* watch; **faire ~ de** show.

montrer /mɔ̃tʀe/ [1] *vt* show (**à** to); **~ du doigt** point to. □ **se ~**

vpr show oneself; (être) be; (s'avérer) prove to be.

monture /mɔ̃tyʀ/ *nf* (cheval) mount; (de lunettes) frames (+ *pl*); (de bijou) setting.

monument /mɔnymɑ̃/ *nm* monument; **~ aux morts** war memorial. **monumental** (*mpl* **-aux**) *a* monumental.

moquer (se) /(sə)mɔke/ [1] *vpr* **se ~ de** make fun of; **je m'en moque** [!] I couldn't care less. **moquerie** *nf* mockery. **moqueur, -euse** *a* mocking.

moquette /mɔkɛt/ *nf* fitted carpet; (US) wall-to-wall carpeting.

moral, ~e (*mpl* **-aux**) /mɔʀal, -o/ *a* moral. ● *nm* (*pl* **-aux**) morale; **ne pas avoir le ~** feel down; **avoir le ~** be in good spirits; **ça m'a remonté le ~** it gave me a boost.

morale /mɔʀal/ *nf* moral code; (mœurs) morals; (de fable) moral; **faire la ~ à** lecture. **moralité** *nf* (de personne) morals (+ *pl*); (d'action, œuvre) morality; (de fable) moral.

moralisateur, -trice /mɔʀalizatœʀ, -tʀis/ *a* moralizing.

morbide /mɔʀbid/ *a* morbid.

morceau (*pl* **~x**) /mɔʀso/ *nm* piece, bit; (de sucre) lump; (de viande) cut; (passage) passage; **manger un ~** [!] have a bite to eat; **mettre en ~x** smash *ou* tear to bits.

morceler /mɔʀsəle/ [6] *vt* divide up.

mordant, ~e /mɔʀdɑ̃, -t/ *a* scathing; (*froid*) biting. ● *nm* vigour, energy.

mordiller /mɔʀdije/ [1] *vt* nibble at.

mordre /mɔʀdʀ/ [3] *vi* bite (**dans** into); **~ sur** (*ligne*) go over; (*territoire*) encroach on; **~ à l'hameçon** bite. ● *vt* bite.

mordu, ~e /mɔʀdy/ [!] *nm, f* fan. ● *a* smitten; **~ de** crazy about.

morfondre (se) /(sə)mɔʀfɔ̃dʀ/ [3] *vpr* wait anxiously; (languir) mope.

morgue /mɔʀg/ *nf* morgue, mortuary; (attitude) arrogance.

moribond, ~e /mɔʀibɔ̃, -d/ *a* dying.

morne /mɔʀn/ *a* dull.

morphine /mɔʀfin/ *nf* morphine.

mors /mɔʀ/ *nm* (de cheval) bit.

morse /mɔʀs/ *nm* (animal) walrus; (code) Morse code.

morsure /mɔʀsyʀ/ *nf* bite.

mort¹ /mɔʀ/ *nf* death.

mort², ~e /mɔʀ, -t/ *a* dead; **~ de fatigue** dead tired. ● *nm, f* dead man, dead woman; **les ~s** the dead.

mortalité /mɔʀtalite/ *nf* mortality; (**taux de**) **~** death rate.

mortel, ~le /mɔʀtɛl/ *a* mortal; (*accident*) fatal; (*poison, silence*) deadly. ● *nm, f* mortal. **mortellement** *adv* mortally.

mortifié, ~e /mɔʀtifje/ *a* mortified.

mort-né, ~e /mɔʀne/ *a* stillborn.

mortuaire /mɔʀtɥɛʀ/ *a* (*cérémonie*) funeral.

morue /mɔʀy/ *nf* cod.

mosaïque /mɔzaik/ *nf* mosaic.

mosquée /mɔske/ *nf* mosque.

mot /mo/ *nm* word; (lettre, message) note; **~ d'ordre** watchword; **~ de passe** password; **~s croisés** crossword (puzzle).

motard /mɔtaʀ/ *nm* biker; (policier) police motorcyclist.

moteur, -trice /mɔtœʀ, -tʀis/ *a* (Méd) motor; (*force*) driving; **à 4 roues motrices** 4-wheel drive. ● *nm* engine, motor; **barque à ~** motor launch; **~ de recherche** (Internet) search engine.

motif /mɔtif/ *nm* (raisons) grounds

(+ *pl*); (cause) reason; (Jur) motive; (dessin) pattern.

motion /mosjɔ̃/ *nf* motion.

motivation /mɔtivasjɔ̃/ *nf* motivation. **motiver** [1] *vt* motivate.

moto /mɔto/ *nf* motor cycle. **motocycliste** *nmf* motorcyclist.

motorisé, **~e** /mɔtɔʀize/ *a* motorized.

motrice /mɔtʀis/ ⇒MOTEUR.

motte /mɔt/ *nf* lump; (de beurre) slab; (de terre) clod; **~ de gazon** turf.

mou (**mol** *before vowel or mute h*), **molle** /mu, mɔl/ *a* soft; (*ventre*) flabby; (sans conviction) feeble; (apathique) sluggish, listless. ●*nm* slack; **avoir du ~** be slack.

mouchard, **~e** /muʃaʀ, -d/ *nm,f* informer; (Scol) sneak.

mouche /muʃ/ *nf* fly; (de cible) bull's eye.

moucher (**se**) /(sə)muʃe/ [1] *vpr* blow one's nose.

moucheron /muʃʀɔ̃/ *nm* midge.

moucheté, **~e** /muʃte/ *a* speckled.

mouchoir /muʃwaʀ/ *nm* handkerchief, hanky; **~ en papier** tissue.

moue /mu/ *nf* pout; **faire la ~** pout.

mouette /mwɛt/ *nf* (sea)gull.

moufle /mufl/ *nf* (gant) mitten.

mouillé, **~e** /muje/ *a* wet.

mouiller /muje/ [1] *vt* wet, make wet; **~ l'ancre** drop anchor. □ **se ~** *vpr* get (oneself) wet.

moulage /mulaʒ/ *nm* cast.

moule /mul/ *nf* (coquillage) mussel. ●*nm* mould; **~ à gâteau** cake tin; **~ à tarte** flan dish. **mouler** [1] *vt* mould; (*statue*) cast.

moulin /mulɛ̃/ *nm* mill; **~ à café** coffee grinder; **~ à poivre** pepper mill; **~ à vent** windmill.

moulinet /mulinɛ/ *nm* (de canne à pêche) reel; **faire des ~s avec qch** twirl sth around.

moulinette® /mulinɛt/ *nf* vegetable mill.

moulu, **~e** /muly/ *a* ground; (fatigué ⓘ) worn out.

moulure /mulyʀ/ *nf* moulding.

mourant, **~e** /muʀɑ̃, -t/ *a* dying. ●*nm,f* dying person.

mourir /muʀiʀ/ [43] *vi* (*aux. être*) die; **~ d'envie de** be dying to; **~ de faim** be starving; **~ d'ennui** be dead bored.

mousquetaire /muskətɛʀ/ *nm* musketeer.

mousse /mus/ *nf* moss; (écume) froth, foam; (de savon) lather; (dessert) mousse; **~ à raser** shaving foam. ●*nm* ship's boy.

mousseline /muslin/ *nf* muslin; (de soie) chiffon.

mousser /muse/ [1] *vi* froth, foam; (*savon*) lather.

mousseux, **-euse** /musø, -z/ *a* frothy. ●*nm* sparkling wine.

mousson /musɔ̃/ *nf* monsoon.

moustache /mustaʃ/ *nf* moustache; **~s** (d'animal) whiskers.

moustique /mustik/ *nm* mosquito.

moutarde /mutaʀd/ *nf* mustard.

mouton /mutɔ̃/ *nm* sheep; (peau) sheepskin; (viande) mutton.

mouvant, **~e** /muvɑ̃, -t/ *a* changing; (*terrain*) shifting, unstable.

mouvement /muvmɑ̃/ *nm* movement; (agitation) bustle; (en gymnastique) exercise; (impulsion) impulse; (tendance) tend, tendency; **en ~** in motion.

mouvementé, **~e** /muvmɑ̃te/ *a* eventful.

moyen, **~ne** /mwajɛ̃, -ɛn/ *a* average; (médiocre) poor; **de taille moyenne** medium-sized. ●*nm* means, way; **~s** means; (dons)

M

ability; **au ~ de** by means of; **il n'y a pas ~ de** it is not possible to. **Moyen Âge** *nm* Middle Ages (+ *pl*).

moyennant /mwajɛnɑ̃/ *prép* (pour) for; (grâce à) with.

moyenne /mwajɛn/ *nf* average; (Scol) pass-mark; **en ~** on average; **~ d'âge** average age. **moyennement** *adv* moderately.

Moyen-Orient /mwajɛnɔʀjɑ̃/ *nm* Middle East.

moyeu (*pl* **~x**) /mwajø/ *nm* hub.

mû, **mue** /my/ *a* driven (**par** by).

mucoviscidose /mykɔvisidoz/ *nf* cystic fibrosis.

mue /my/ *nf* moulting; (de voix) breaking of the voice.

muer /mɥe/ [1] *vi* moult; (*voix*) break. ▫ **se ~ en** *vpr* change into.

muet, **~te** /mɥɛ, -t/ *a* (Méd) dumb; (fig) speechless (**de** with); (silencieux) silent. ● *nm, f* mute.

mufle /myfl/ *nm* nose, muzzle; (personne [!]) boor, lout.

mugir /myʒiʀ/ [2] *vi* (*vache*) moo; (*bœuf*) bellow; (fig) howl.

muguet /mygɛ/ *nm* lily of the valley.

mule /myl/ *nf* (female) mule; (pantoufle) mule.

mulet /mylɛ/ *nm* (male) mule.

multicolore /myltikɔlɔʀ/ *a* multicoloured.

multimédia /myltimedja/ *a & nm* multimedia.

multinational, **~e** (*mpl* **-aux**) /myltinasjɔnal, -o/ *a* multinational. **multinationale** *nf* multinational (company).

multiple /myltipl/ *nm* multiple. ● *a* numerous, many; (naissances) multiple.

multiplication /myltiplikasjɔ̃/ *nf* multiplication.

multiplicité /myltiplisite/ *nf* multiplicity.

multiplier /myltiplije/ [45] *vt* multiply; (*risques*) increase. ▫ **se ~** *vpr* multiply; (*accidents*) be on the increase; (*difficultés*) increase.

multitude /myltityd/ *nf* multitude, mass.

municipal, **~e** (*mpl* **-aux**) /mynisipal, -o/ *a* municipal; **conseil ~** town council. **municipalité** *nf* (ville) municipality; (conseil) town council.

munir /myniʀ/ [2] *vt* **~ de** provide with. ▫ **se ~ de** *vpr* (apporter) bring; (emporter) take.

munitions /mynisjɔ̃/ *nfpl* ammunition.

mur /myʀ/ *nm* wall; **~ du son** sound barrier.

mûr, **~e** /myʀ/ *a* ripe; (*personne*) mature.

muraille /myʀɑj/ *nf* (high) wall.

mural, **~e** (*mpl* **-aux**) /myʀal, -o/ *a* wall; **peinture ~e** mural.

mûre /myʀ/ *nf* blackberry.

mûrir /myʀiʀ/ [2] *vi* ripen; (*abcès*) come to a head; (*personne, projet*) mature. ● *vt* (*fruit*) ripen; (*personne*) mature.

murmure /myʀmyʀ/ *nm* murmur.

musc /mysk/ *nm* musk.

muscade /myskad/ *nf* **noix ~** nutmeg.

muscle /myskl/ *nm* muscle. **musclé**, **~e** *a* muscular. **musculaire** *a* muscular.

musculation /myskylasjɔ̃/ *nf* bodybuilding.

musculature /myskylatyʀ/ *nf* muscles (+ *pl*).

museau (*pl* **~x**) /myzo/ *nm* muzzle; (de porc) snout.

musée /myze/ *nm* museum; (de peinture) art gallery.

muselière /myzəljɛʀ/ *nf* muzzle.

musette /myzɛt/ *nf* haversack.

muséum /myzeɔm/ *nm* natural history museum.

musical, **~e** (*mpl* **-aux**) /myzikal, -o/ *a* musical.

musicien, **~ne** /myzisjɛ̃, -ɛn/ *a* musical. ● *nm, f* musician.

musique /myzik/ *nf* music; (orchestre) band.

musulman, **~e** /myzylmɑ̃, -an/ *a & nm,f* Muslim.

mutation /mytasjɔ̃/ *nf* change; (biologique) mutation; (d'un employé) transfer.

muter /myte/ [1] *vt* transfer. ● *vi* mutate.

mutilation /mytilasjɔ̃/ *nf* mutilation. **mutiler** [1] *vt* mutilate. **mutilé**, **~e** *nm, f* disabled person.

mutin, **~e** /mytɛ̃, -in/ *a* mischievous. ● *nm* mutineer; (prisonnier) rioter.

mutinerie /mytinʀi/ *nf* mutiny; (de prisonniers) riot.

mutisme /mytism/ *nm* silence.

mutuel, **~le** /mytɥɛl/ *a* mutual. **mutuelle** *nf* mutual insurance company. **mutuellement** *adv* mutually; (l'un l'autre) each other.

myope /mjɔp/ *a* short-sighted. **myopie** *nf* short-sightedness.

myosotis /mjozɔtis/ *nm* forget-me-not.

myrtille /miʀtij/ *nf* bilberry, blueberry.

mystère /mistɛʀ/ *nm* mystery.

mystérieux, **-ieuse** /misteʀjø, -z/ *a* mysterious.

mystification /mistifikasjɔ̃/ *nf* hoax.

mysticisme /mistisism/ *nm* mysticism.

mystique /mistik/ *a* mystic(al). ● *nmf* mystic. ● *nf* mystique.

mythe /mit/ *nm* myth. **mythique** *a* mythical.

mythologie /mitɔlɔʒi/ *nf* mythology.

n' /n/ ⇒NE.

nacre /nakʀ/ *nf* mother-of-pearl.

nage /naʒ/ *nf* swimming; (manière) stroke; **traverser à la ~** swim across; **en ~** sweating.

nageoire /naʒwaʀ/ *nf* fin; (de mammifère) flipper.

nager /naʒe/ [40] *vt/i* swim. **nageur**, **-euse** *nm, f* swimmer.

naguère /nagɛʀ/ *adv* (autrefois) formerly.

naïf, **-ive** /naif, -v/ *a* naïve.

nain, **~e** /nɛ̃, nɛn/ *nm,f & a* dwarf.

naissance /nɛsɑ̃s/ *nf* birth; **donner ~ à** give birth to; (fig) give rise to.

naître /nɛtʀ/ [44] *vi* be born; (résulter) arise (**de** from); **faire ~** (susciter) give rise to.

naïveté /naivte/ *nf* naïvety.

nappe /nap/ *nf* tablecloth; (de pétrole, gaz) layer; **~ phréatique** ground water.

napperon /napʀɔ̃/ *nm* (cloth) tablemat.

narco-dollars /naʀkodɔlaʀ/ *nmpl* drug money.

narcotique /naʀkɔtik/ *a & nm* narcotic. **narco(-)trafiquant**, **~e** (*pl* **~s**) *nm, f* drug trafficker.

narguer /naʀge/ [1] *vt* taunt; (*autorité*) flout.

narine /naʀin/ *nf* nostril.

nasal, **~e** (*mpl* **-aux**) /nazal, -o/ *a* nasal.

naseau (*pl* **~x**) /nazo/ *nm* nostril.

natal, **~e** (*mpl* **~s**) /natal/ *a* native.
natalité /natalite/ *nf* birth rate.
natation /natasjɔ̃/ *nf* swimming.
natif, **-ive** /natif, -v/ *a* native.
nation /nasjɔ̃/ *nf* nation.
national, **~e** (*mpl* **-aux**) /nasjɔnal, -o/ *a* national. **nationale** *nf* A road; (US) highway. **nationaliser** [1] *vt* nationalize.
nationalité /nasjɔnalite/ *nf* nationality.
natte /nat/ *nf* (de cheveux) plait; (US) braid; (tapis de paille) mat.
nature /natyʀ/ *nf* nature; **~ morte** still life; **de ~ à** likely to; **payer en ~** pay in kind. ● *a inv* plain; (*yaourt*) natural; (*thé*) black.
naturel, **~le** /natyʀɛl/ *a* natural. ● *nm* nature; (simplicité) naturalness; (Culin) **au ~** plain; (*thon*) in brine. **naturellement** *adv* naturally; (bien sûr) of course.
naufrage /nofʀaʒ/ *nm* shipwreck; **faire ~** be shipwrecked; (*bateau*) be wrecked.
nauséabond, **~e** /nozeabɔ̃, -d/ *a* nauseating.
nausée /noze/ *nf* nausea.
nautique /notik/ *a* nautical; **sports ~s** water sports.
naval, **~e** (*mpl* **~s**) /naval/ *a* naval; **chantier ~** shipyard.
navet /navɛ/ *nm* turnip; (film: péj) flop; (US) turkey.
navette /navɛt/ *nf* shuttle (service); **faire la ~** shuttle back and forth.
navigateur, **-trice** /navigatœʀ, -tʀis/ *nm, f* sailor; (qui guide) navigator; (Internet) browser. **navigation** *nf* navigation; (trafic) shipping; (Internet) browsing.
naviguer /navige/ [1] *vi* sail; (piloter) navigate; (Internet) browse; **~ dans l'Internet** surf the Internet.
navire /naviʀ/ *nm* ship.
navré, **~e** /navʀe/ *a* sorry (**de** to).

---

ne, **n'** /nə, n/

n' before vowel or mute h.

● *adverbe*

····> **je n'ai que 10 francs** I've only got 10 francs.

····> **tu n'avais qu'à le dire!** you only had to say so!

····> **je crains qu'il ~ parte** I am afraid he will leave.

! Pour les expressions comme **ne... guère**, **ne... jamais**, **ne... pas**, **ne... plus**, etc. ⇒**guère**, **jamais**, **pas**, **plus**, etc.

---

né, **~e** /ne/ *a* born; **~e Martin** née Martin; (dans composés) **dernier-~** last-born. ● ⇒NAÎTRE [44].
néanmoins /neɑ̃mwɛ̃/ *adv* nevertheless.
néant /neɑ̃/ *nm* nothingness; **réduire à ~** (*effet, efforts*) negate, nullify; (*espoir*) dash; **'revenus: ~'** 'income: nil'.
nécessaire /nesesɛʀ/ *a* necessary. ● *nm* (sac) bag; (trousse) kit; **le ~** (l'indispensable) the necessities *ou* essentials; **faire le ~** do what is necessary.
nécessité /nesesite/ *nf* necessity; **de première ~** vital.
nécessiter /nesesite/ [1] *vt* necessitate.
néerlandais, **~e** /neɛʀlɑ̃dɛ, -z/ *a* Dutch. ● *nm* (Ling) Dutch. **N~**, **~e** *nm, f* Dutchman, Dutchwoman.
néfaste /nefast/ *a* harmful (**à** to).
négatif, **-ive** /negatif, -v/ *a & nm* negative.
négligé, **~e** /negliʒe/ *a* (*travail*)

careless; (*tenue*) scruffy. ● *nm* (tenue) negligee.

négligent, **~e** /negliʒɑ̃, -t/ *a* careless, negligent.

négliger /negliʒe/ [40] *vt* neglect; (ne pas tenir compte de) ignore, disregard; **~ de faire** fail to do. □ **se ~** *vpr* neglect oneself.

négoce /negɔs/ *nm* business, trade. **négociant**, **~e** *nm, f* merchant.

négociation /negɔsjasjɔ̃/ *nf* negotiation. **négocier** [45] *vt/i* negotiate.

nègre /nɛgʀ/ *a* (*musique, art*) Negro. ● *nm* (écrivain) ghost writer.

neige /nɛʒ/ *nf* snow. **neiger** [40] *vi* snow.

nénuphar /nenyfaʀ/ *nm* waterlily.

nerf /nɛʀ/ *nm* nerve; (vigueur) stamina; **être sur les ~s** be on edge.

nerveux, **-euse** /nɛʀvø, -z/ *a* nervous; (irritable) nervy; (*centre, cellule*) nerve; (*voiture*) responsive. **nervosité** *nf* nervousness; (irritabilité) touchiness.

net, **~te** /nɛt/ *a* (clair, distinct) clear; (propre) clean; (notable) marked; (soigné) neat; (*prix, poids*) net. ● *adv* (*s'arrêter*) dead; (*refuser*) flatly; (*parler*) plainly; (*se casser*) cleanly; (*tuer*) outright. **nettement** *adv* (*expliquer*) clearly; (*augmenter, se détériorer*) markedly; (indiscutablement) distinctly, decidedly. **netteté** *nf* clearness.

nettoyage /nɛtwajaʒ/ *nm* cleaning; **~ à sec** dry-cleaning; **produit de ~** cleaner.

nettoyer /nɛtwaje/ [31] *vt* clean.

neuf¹ /nœf/ (/nœv/ *before vowels and mute h*) *a inv & nm* nine.

neuf², **-euve** /nœf, -v/ *a* new; **tout ~** brand new. ● *nm* new; **remettre à ~** brighten up; **du ~** a new development; **quoi de ~?** what's new?

neutre /nøtʀ/ *a* neutral; (Gram) neuter. ● *nm* (Gram) neuter.

neutron /nøtʀɔ̃/ *nm* neutron.

neuve /nœv/ ⇒NEUF².

neuvième /nœvjɛm/ *a & nm, f* ninth.

neveu (*pl* **~x**) /nəvø/ *nm* nephew.

névrose /nevʀoz/ *nf* neurosis. **névrosé**, **~e** *a & nm,f* neurotic.

nez /ne/ *nm* nose; **~ à ~** face to face; **~ retroussé** turned-up nose; **avoir du ~** have flair.

ni /ni/ *conj* neither, nor; **~ grand ~ petit** neither big nor small; **~ l'un ~ l'autre ne fument** neither (one nor the other) smokes; **sortir sans manteau ~ chapeau** go without a coat or hat; **elle n'a dit ~ oui ~ non** she didn't say either yes or no.

niais, **~e** /njɛ, -z/ *a* silly.

niche /niʃ/ *nf* (de chien) kennel; (cavité) niche.

nicher /niʃe/ [1] *vi* nest. □ **se ~** *vpr* nest; (se cacher) hide.

nicotine /nikɔtin/ *nf* nicotine.

nid /ni/ *nm* nest; **faire un ~** build a nest. **nid-de-poule** (*pl* **nids-de-poule**) *nm* pot-hole.

nièce /njɛs/ *nf* niece.

nier /nje/ [45] *vt* deny.

nigaud, **~e** /nigo, -d/ *nm, f* silly idiot.

nippon, **~ne** /nipɔ̃, -ɔn/ *a* Japanese. **N~**, **~ne** *nm, f* Japanese.

niveau (*pl* **~x**) /nivo/ *nm* level; (compétence) standard; (étage) storey; (US) story; **au ~** up to standard; **mettre à ~** (Ordinat) upgrade; **~ à bulle** (d'air) spirit-level; **~ de vie** standard of living.

niveler /nivle/ [6] *vt* level.

noble /nɔbl/ *a* noble. ● *nm, f* nobleman, noblewoman.

noblesse *nf* nobility.

noce /nɔs/ *nf* (fête ⊡) party; (invités) wedding guests; **~s** wedding; **faire la ~** ⊡ live it up, party.

nocif, **-ive** /nɔsif, -v/ *a* harmful.

noctambule /nɔktɑ̃byl/ *nmf* late-night reveller.

nocturne /nɔktyʀn/ *a* nocturnal. ● *nm* (Mus) nocturne. ● *nf* (Sport) evening fixture; (de magasin) late-night opening.

Noël /nɔɛl/ *nm* Christmas.

nœud /nø/ *nm* (Naut) knot; (pour lier) knot; (pour orner) bow; **~s** (fig) ties; **~ coulant** slipknot, noose; **~ papillon** bow-tie.

noir, **~e** /nwaʀ/ *a* black; (obscur, sombre) dark; (triste) gloomy. ● *nm* black; (obscurité) dark; **travail au ~** moonlighting. ● *nm, f* (personne) Black.

noircir /nwaʀsiʀ/ [2] *vt* blacken; **~ la situation** paint a black picture of the situation. ● *vi* (*banane*) go black; (*mur*) get dirty; (*métal*) tarnish. □ **se ~** *vpr* (*ciel*) darken.

noire /nwaʀ/ *nf* (Mus) crotchet.

noisette /nwazɛt/ *nf* hazelnut; (de beurre) knob.

noix /nwa/ *nf* nut; (du noyer) walnut; (de beurre) knob; **~ de cajou** cashew nut; **~ de coco** coconut; **à la ~** ⊡ useless.

nom /nɔ̃/ *nm* name; (Gram) noun; **au ~ de** on behalf of; **~ et prénom** full name; **~ déposé** registered trademark; **~ de famille** surname; **~ de jeune fille** maiden name; **~ de plume** pen name; **~ propre** proper noun.

nomade /nɔmad/ *a* nomadic. ● *nmf* nomad.

nombre /nɔ̃bʀ/ *nm* number; **au ~ de** (parmi) among; (l'un de) one of; **en** (**grand**) **~** in large numbers; **sans ~** countless.

nombreux, **-euse** /nɔ̃bʀø, -z/ *a* (en grand nombre) many, numerous; (important) large; **de ~ enfants** many children; **nous étions très ~** there were a great many of us.

nombril /nɔ̃bʀil/ *nm* navel.

nomination /nɔminasjɔ̃/ *nf* appointment.

nommer /nɔme/ [1] *vt* name; (élire) (à un poste) appoint; (à un lieu) post. □ **se ~** *vpr* (s'appeler) be called.

non /nɔ̃/ *adv* no; (pas) not; **~** (**pas**) **que** not that; **il vient, ~?** he is coming, isn't he?; **moi ~ plus** neither am/do/can/*etc.* I. ● *nm inv* no.

non- /nɔ̃/ *préf* non-; **~-fumeur** non-smoker.

nonante /nɔnɑ̃t/ *a & nm* ninety.

non-sens /nɔ̃sɑ̃s/ *nm inv* absurdity.

nord /nɔʀ/ *a inv* (*façade, côte*) north; (*frontière, zone*) northern. ● *nm* north; **le ~ de l'Europe** northern Europe; **vent de ~** northerly (wind); **aller vers le ~** go north; **le Nord** the North; **du Nord** northern. **nord-est** *nm* north-east.

nordique /nɔʀdik/ *a* Scandinavian.

nord-ouest /nɔʀwɛst/ *nm* north-west.

normal, **~e** (*mpl* **-aux**) /nɔʀmal, -o/ *a* normal. **normale** *nf* normality; (norme) norm; (moyenne) average.

normand, **~e** /nɔʀmɑ̃, -d/ *a* Norman. **N~**, **~e** *nm, f* Norman.

Normandie /nɔʀmɑ̃di/ *nf* Normandy.

norme /nɔʀm/ *nf* norm; (de production) standard; **~s de sécurité** safety standards.

Norvège /nɔʀvɛʒ/ *nf* Norway.

norvégien, **~ne** /nɔʀvɛʒjɛ̃, -ɛn/ *a* Norwegian. **N~**, **~ne** *nm, f* Norwegian.

nos /no/ ⇒NOTRE.

nostalgie /nɔstalʒi/ *nf* nostalgia; **avoir la ~ de son pays** be homesick. **nostalgique** *a* nostalgic.

notaire /nɔtɛʀ/ *nm* notary public.

notamment /nɔtamɑ̃/ *adv* notably.

note /nɔt/ *nf* (remarque) note; (chiffrée) mark, grade; (facture) bill; (Mus) note; **~ (de service)** memorandum; **prendre ~ de** take note of.

noter /nɔte/ [1] *vt* note, notice; (écrire) note (down); (*devoir*) mark; (US) grade; **bien/mal noté** (*employé*) highly/poorly rated.

notice /nɔtis/ *nf* note; (mode d'emploi) instructions, directions.

notifier /nɔtifje/ [45] *vt* notify (**à** to).

notion /nosjɔ̃/ *nf* notion; **avoir des ~s de** have a basic knowledge of.

notoire /nɔtwaʀ/ *a* well-known; (*criminel*) notorious.

notre (*pl* **nos**) /nɔtʀ, no/ *a* our.

nôtre /notʀ/ *pron* **le** *ou* **la ~**, **les ~s** ours.

nouer /nwe/ [1] *vt* tie, knot; (*relations*) strike up.

nouille /nuj/ *nf* (Culin) noodle; **des ~s** noodles, pasta; (idiot ⓘ) idiot.

nounours /nunuʀs/ *nm* ⓘ teddy bear.

nourri, **~e** /nuʀi/ *a* **être logé ~** have bed and board; **~ au sein** breastfed.

nourrice /nuʀis/ *nf* childminder.

nourrir /nuʀiʀ/ [2] *vt* feed; (*espoir, crainte*) harbour; (*projet*) nurture; (*passion*) fuel. ● *vi* be nourishing. □ **se ~** *vpr* eat; **se ~ de** feed on. **nourrissant**, **~e** *a* nourishing.

nourrisson /nuʀisɔ̃/ *nm* infant.

nourriture /nuʀityʀ/ *nf* food.

nous /nu/ *pron* (sujet) we; (complément) us; (indirect) (to) us; (réfléchi) ourselves; (l'un l'autre) each other; **la voiture est à ~** the car is ours. **nous-mêmes** *pron* ourselves.

nouveau (**nouvel** *before vowel or mute h*), **nouvelle** (*mpl* **~x**) /nuvo, nuvɛl/ *a* new; **nouvel an** new year; **~x mariés** newly-weds; **~ venu, nouvelle venue** newcomer. ● *nm, f* (élève) new boy, new girl. ● *nm* **du ~** (fait nouveau) a new development; **de ~**, **à ~** again. **nouveau-né** (*pl* **~s**) *nm* newborn baby.

nouveauté /nuvote/ *nf* novelty; (chose) new thing; (livre) new publication; (disque) new release.

nouvelle /nuvɛl/ *nf* (piece of) news; (récit) short story; **~s** news.

Nouvelle-Zélande /nuvɛlzelɑ̃d/ *nf* New Zealand.

novembre /nɔvɑ̃bʀ/ *nm* November.

noyade /nwajad/ *nf* drowning.

noyau (*pl* **~x**) /nwajo/ *nm* (de fruit) stone; (US) pit; (de cellule) nucleus; (groupe) group; (centre; fig) core.

noyer /nwaje/ [31] *vt* drown; (inonder) flood. □ **se ~** *vpr* drown; (volontairement) drown oneself; **se ~ dans un verre d'eau** make a mountain out of a molehill. ● *nm* walnut-tree.

nu, **~e** /ny/ *a* (*corps, personne*) naked; (*mains, mur, fil*) bare; **à l'œil ~** to the naked eye. ● *nm* nude; **mettre à ~** expose.

nuage /nyaʒ/ *nm* cloud.

nuance /nyɑ̃s/ *nf* shade; (de sens) nuance; (différence) difference. **nuancer** [10] *vt* (*opinion*) qualify.

nucléaire /nykleɛʀ/ *a* nuclear. ● *nm* **le ~** nuclear energy.

nudisme /nydism/ *nm* nudism.

N

nudité /nydite/ *nf* nudity; (de lieu) bareness.

nuée /nɥe/ *nf* swarm, host.

nues /ny/ *nfpl* **tomber des ~** be amazed; **porter qn aux ~** praise sb to the skies.

nuire /nɥiʀ/ [17] *vi* **~ à** harm.

nuisible /nɥizibl/ *a* harmful (**à** to).

nuit /nɥi/ *nf* night; **cette ~** tonight; (hier) last night; **il fait ~** it is dark; **~ blanche** sleepless night; **la ~, de ~** at night; **~ de noces** wedding night.

nul, ~le /nyl/ *a* (aucun) no; (zéro) nil; (qui ne vaut rien) useless; (non valable) null; (*contrat*) void; (*testament*) invalid; **match ~** draw; **~ en sciences** no good at science; **nulle part** nowhere; **~ autre** no one else. ● *pron* no one. **nullement** *adv* not at all. **nullité** *nf* uselessness; (personne) nonentity.

numérique /nymeʀik/ *a* numerical; (*montre, horloge*) digital.

numéro /nymeʀo/ *nm* number; (de journal) issue; (spectacle) act; **~ de téléphone** telephone number; **~ vert** freephone number. **numéroter** [1] *vt* number.

nuque /nyk/ *nf* nape (of the neck).

nurse /nœʀs/ *nf* nanny.

nutritif, -ive /nytʀitif, -v/ *a* nutritious; (*valeur*) nutritional.

oasis /ɔazis/ *nf* oasis.

obéir /ɔbeiʀ/ [2] *vt* **~ à** obey. ● *vi* obey. **obéissance** *nf* obedience. **obéissant, ~e** *a* obedient.

obèse /ɔbɛz/ *a* obese.

objecter /ɔbʒɛkte/ [1] *vt* object.

objectif, -ive /ɔbʒɛktif, -v/ *a* objective. ● *nm* objective; (Photo) lens.

objection /obʒɛksjɔ̃/ *nf* objection; **soulever des ~s** raise objections.

objet /ɔbʒɛ/ *nm* (chose) object; (sujet) subject; (but) purpose, object; **être** *ou* **faire l'~ de** be the subject of; **~ d'art** objet d'art; **~s trouvés** lost property; (US) lost and found.

obligation /ɔbligasjɔ̃/ *nf* obligation; (Comm) bond; **être dans l'~ de** be under obligation to.

obligatoire /ɔbligatwaʀ/ *a* compulsory. **obligatoirement** *adv* (par règlement) of necessity; (inévitablement) inevitably.

obligeance /ɔbliʒɑ̃s/ *nf* **avoir l'~ de faire** be kind enough to do.

obliger /ɔbliʒe/ [40] *vt* compel, force (**à faire** to do); (aider) oblige; **être obligé de** have to (**de** for).

oblique /ɔblik/ *a* oblique; **regard ~** sidelong glance; **en ~** at an angle.

oblitérer /ɔbliteʀe/ [14] *vt* (*timbre*) cancel.

obnubilé, ~e /ɔbnybile/ *a* obsessed.

obscène /ɔpsɛn/ *a* obscene.

obscur, ~e /ɔpskyʀ/ *a* dark;

(confus, humble) obscure; (vague) vague.

obscurcir /ɔpskyʀsiʀ/ [2] *vt* make dark; (fig) obscure. □ **s'~** *vpr* (*ciel*) darken.

obscurité /ɔpskyʀite/ *nf* dark-(ness); (de passage, situation) obscurity.

obsédant, ~e /ɔpsedɑ̃, -t/ *a* (*problème*) nagging; (*musique, souvenir*) haunting.

obsédé, ~e /ɔpsede/ *nm, f* **~** (**sexuel**) sex maniac; **~ du ski/jazz** ski/jazz freak.

obséder /ɔpsede/ [14] *vt* obsess.

obsèques /ɔpsɛk/ *nfpl* funeral.

observateur, -trice /ɔpsɛʀvatœʀ, -tʀis/ *a* observant. ● *nm, f* observer.

observation /ɔpsɛʀvasjɔ̃/ *nf* observation; (remarque) remark, comment; (reproche) criticism; (obéissance) observance; **en ~** under observation.

observer /ɔpsɛʀve/ [1] *vt* (regarder) observe; (surveiller) watch, observe; (remarquer) notice, observe; **faire ~ qch** point sth out (**à** to).

obsession /ɔpsesjɔ̃/ *nf* obsession.

obstacle /ɔpstakl/ *nm* obstacle; (pour cheval) fence, jump; (pour athlète) hurdle; **faire ~ à** stand in the way of, obstruct.

obstétrique /ɔpstetʀik/ *nf* obstetrics (+ *sg*).

obstiné, ~e /ɔpstine/ *a* stubborn, obstinate.

obstiner (s') /(s)ɔpstine/ [1] *vpr* persist (**à** in).

obstruction /ɔpstʀyksjɔ̃/ *nf* obstruction; (de conduit) blockage.

obstruer /ɔpstʀye/ [1] *vt* obstruct, block.

obtenir /ɔptəniʀ/ [58] *vt* get, obtain. **obtention** *nf* obtaining.

obus /ɔby/ *nm* shell.

occasion /ɔkazjɔ̃/ *nf* opportunity (**de faire** of doing); (circonstance) occasion; (achat) bargain; (article non neuf) second-hand buy; **à l'~** sometimes; **d'~** second-hand. **occasionnel, ~le** *a* occasional.

occasionner /ɔkazjɔne/ [1] *vt* cause.

occident /ɔksidɑ̃/ *nm* (direction) west; **l'O~** the West.

occidental, ~e (*mpl* **-aux**) /ɔksidɑ̃tal, -o/ *a* western. **O~, ~e** (*mpl* **-aux**) *nm, f* westerner.

occulte /ɔkylt/ *a* occult.

occupant, ~e /ɔkypɑ̃, -t/ *nm, f* occupant. ● *nm* (Mil) forces of occupation.

occupation /ɔkypasjɔ̃/ *nf* occupation.

occupé, ~e /ɔkype/ *a* busy; (*place, pays*) occupied; (*téléphone*) engaged, busy; (*toilettes*) engaged.

occuper /ɔkype/ [1] *vt* occupy; (*poste*) hold; (*espace, temps*) take up. □ **s'~** *vpr* (s'affairer) keep busy (**à faire** doing); **s'~ de** (*personne, problème*) take care of; (*bureau, firme*) be in charge of; (se mêler) **occupe-toi de tes affaires** mind your own business.

occurrence: **en l'~** /ɑ̃lɔkyʀɑ̃s/ *loc* in this case.

océan /ɔseɑ̃/ *nm* ocean.

Océanie /ɔseani/ *nf* Oceania.

ocre /ɔkʀ/ *a inv* ochre.

octante /ɔktɑ̃t/ *a* eighty.

octet /ɔktɛ/ *nm* byte.

octobre /ɔktɔbʀ/ *nm* October.

octogone /ɔktɔgɔn/ *nm* octagon.

octroyer /ɔktʀwaje/ [31] *vt* grant.

oculaire /ɔkylɛʀ/ *a* **témoin ~** eye-witness; **troubles ~s** eye trouble.

oculiste /ɔkylist/ *nmf* ophthalmologist.

odeur /ɔdœʀ/ *nf* smell.

odieux, -ieuse /ɔdjø, -z/ *a* odious.

odorant, ~e /ɔdɔRɑ̃, -t/ *a* sweet-smelling.

odorat /ɔdɔRa/ *nm* sense of smell.

œil (*pl* **yeux**) /œj, jø/ *nm* eye; **à l'~** 🅘 for free; **à mes yeux** in my view; **faire de l'~ à** make eyes at; **faire les gros yeux à** glare at; **ouvrir l'~** keep one's eyes open; **~ poché** black eye; **fermer les yeux** shut one's eyes; (fig) turn a blind eye.

œillères /œjɛR/ *nfpl* blinkers.

œillet /œjɛ/ *nm* (plante) carnation; (trou) eyelet.

œuf (*pl* **~s**) /œf, ø/ *nm* egg; **~ à la coque/dur/sur le plat** boiled/hard-boiled/fried egg.

œuvre /œvR/ *nf* (ouvrage, travail) work; **~ d'art** work of art; **~ (de bienfaisance)** charity; **être à l'~** be at work; **mettre en ~** (*réforme, moyens*) implement; **mise en ~** implementation. ● *nm* (ensemble spécifié) **l'~ sculpté de X** the sculptures of X; **l'~ entier de Beethoven** the complete works of Beethoven.

œuvrer /œvRe/ [1] *vi* work.

off /ɔf/ *a inv* **voix ~** voice-over.

offense /ɔfɑ̃s/ *nf* insult.

offenser /ɔfɑ̃se/ [1] *vt* offend. □ **s'~** *vpr* take offence (**de** at).

offensive /ɔfɑ̃siv/ *nf* offensive.

offert, ~e /ɔfɛR, -t/ ⇒OFFRIR [21].

office /ɔfis/ *nm* office; (Relig) service; (de cuisine) pantry; **faire ~ de** act as; **d'~** without consultation, automatically; **~ du tourisme** tourist information office.

officiel, ~le /ɔfisjɛl/ *a* official. ● *nm* official.

officier /ɔfisje/ [45] *vi* (Relig) officiate. ● *nm* officer.

officieux, -ieuse /ɔfisjø, -z/ *a* unofficial.

offre /ɔfR/ *nf* offer; (aux enchères) bid; **l'~ et la demande** supply and demand; **'~s d'emploi'** 'situations vacant'.

offrir /ɔfRiR/ [21] *vt* offer (**de faire** to do); (*cadeau*) give; (acheter) buy; **~ à boire à** (chez soi) give a drink to; (au café) buy a drink for. □ **s'~** *vpr* (se proposer) offer oneself (**comme** as); (*solution*) present itself; (s'acheter) treat oneself to.

ogive /ɔʒiv/ *nf* **~ nucléaire** nuclear warhead.

oie /wa/ *nf* goose.

oignon /ɔɲɔ̃/ *nm* (légume) onion; (de fleur) bulb.

oiseau (*pl* **~x**) /wazo/ *nm* bird.

oisif, -ive /wazif, -v/ *a* idle.

olive /ɔliv/ *nf & a inv* olive.
olivier *nm* olive tree.

olympique /ɔlɛ̃pik/ *a* Olympic.

ombrage /ɔ̃bRaʒ/ *nm* shade; **prendre ~ de** take offence at.
ombragé, ~e *a* shady.
ombrageux, -euse *a* easily offended.

ombre /ɔ̃bR/ *nf* (pénombre) shade; (contour) shadow; (soupçon: fig) hint, shadow; **dans l'~** (*agir, rester*) behind the scenes; **faire de l'~ à qn** be in sb's light.

ombrelle /ɔ̃bRɛl/ *nf* parasol.

omelette /ɔmlɛt/ *nf* omelette.

omettre /ɔmɛtR/ [42] *vt* omit, leave out.

omnibus /ɔmnibys/ *nm* stopping *ou* local train.

omoplate /ɔmɔplat/ *nf* shoulder blade.

on /ɔ̃/ *pron* (tu, vous) you; (nous) we; (ils, elles) they; (les gens) people, they; (quelqu'un) someone; (indéterminé) one, you; **~ dit** people say, they say, it is said; **~ m'a demandé mon avis** I was asked for my opinion.

oncle /ɔ̃kl/ *nm* uncle.

onctueux, -euse /ɔ̃ktɥø, -z/ *a* smooth.

onde /ɔ̃d/ *nf* wave; **~s courtes/longues** short/long wave; **sur les ~s** on the air.

on-dit /ɔ̃di/ *nm inv* **les ~** hearsay.

onduler /ɔ̃dyle/ [1] *vi* undulate; (*cheveux*) be wavy.

onéreux, -euse /ɔneʀø, -z/ *a* costly.

ongle /ɔ̃gl/ *nm* (finger)nail; **~ de pied** toenail; **se faire les ~s** do one's nails.

ont /ɔ̃/ ⇒AVOIR [5].

ONU *abrév f* (**Organisation des Nations unies**) UN.

onze /ɔ̃z/ *a & nm* eleven. **onzième** *a & nmf* eleventh.

OPA *abrév f* (**offre publique d'achat**) takeover bid.

opéra /ɔpeʀa/ *nm* opera; (édifice) opera house. **opéra-comique** (*pl* **opéras-comiques**) *nm* light opera.

opérateur, -trice /ɔpeʀatœʀ, -tʀis/ *nm, f* operator; **~ (de prise de vue)** cameraman.

opération /ɔpeʀasjɔ̃/ *nf* operation; (Comm) deal; (calcul) calculation.

opératoire /ɔpeʀatwaʀ/ *a* (Méd) surgical; **bloc ~** operating suite.

opérer /ɔpeʀe/ [14] *vt* (*personne*) operate on; (exécuter) carry out, make; **~ qn d'une tumeur** operate on sb to remove a tumour; **se faire ~** have surgery *ou* an operation. ● *vi* (Méd) operate; (faire effet) work. □ **s'~** *vpr* (se produire) occur.

opiniâtre /ɔpinjɑtʀ/ *a* tenacious.

opinion /ɔpinjɔ̃/ *nf* opinion

opportuniste /ɔpɔʀtynist/ *nmf* opportunist.

opposant, ~e /ɔpozɑ̃, -t/ *nm, f* opponent.

opposé, ~e /ɔpoze/ *a* (*sens, angle, avis*) opposite; (*factions*) opposing; (*intérêts*) conflicting; **être ~ à** be opposed to. ● *nm* opposite; **à l'~ de** (contrairement à) contrary to, unlike.

opposer /ɔpoze/ [1] *vt* (*objets*) place opposite each other; (*personnes*) match, oppose; (contraster) contrast; (*résistance, argument*) put up. □ **s'~** *vpr* (*personnes*) confront each other; (*styles*) contrast; **s'~ à** oppose.

opposition /ɔpozisjɔ̃/ *nf* opposition; **par ~ à** in contrast with; **entrer en ~ avec** come into conflict with; **faire ~ à un chèque** stop a cheque.

oppressant, ~e /ɔpʀesɑ̃, -t/ *a* oppressive.

opprimer /ɔpʀime/ [1] *vt* oppress.

opter /ɔpte/ [1] *vi* **~ pour** opt for.

opticien, ~ne /ɔptisjɛ̃, -ɛn/ *nm, f* optician.

optimisme /ɔptimism/ *nm* optimism.

optimiste /ɔptimist/ *nmf* optimist. ● *a* optimistic.

option /ɔpsjɔ̃/ *nf* option.

optique /ɔptik/ *a* (*verre*) optical. ● *nf* (science) optics (+ *sg*); (perspective) perspective.

or[1] /ɔʀ/ *nm* gold; **d'~** golden; **en ~** gold; (*occasion*) golden.

or[2] /ɔʀ/ *conj* now, well; (indiquant une opposition) and yet.

orage /ɔʀaʒ/ *nm* (thunder)storm. **orageux, -euse** *a* stormy.

oral, ~e (*mpl* **-aux**) /ɔʀal, -o/ *a* oral. ● *nm* (*pl* **-aux**) oral.

orange /ɔʀɑ̃ʒ/ *a inv* orange; (Aut) (*feu*) amber; (US) yellow. ● *nf* orange. **orangeade** *nf* orangeade. **oranger** *nm* orange tree.

orateur, -trice /ɔʀatœʀ, -tʀis/ *nm, f* speaker.

orbite /ɔʀbit/ *nf* orbit; (d'œil) socket.

orchestre /ɔʀkɛstʀ/ *nm* orchestra; (de jazz) band; (parterre) stalls.

ordinaire /ɔʀdinɛʀ/ *a* ordinary; (habituel) usual; (*qualité*) standard; (médiocre) very average. ● *nm* **l'~** the ordinary; (nourriture) the standard fare; **d'~**, **à l'~** usually. **ordinairement** *adv* usually.

ordinateur /ɔʀdinatœʀ/ *nm* computer; **~ personnel/de bureau** personal/desktop computer; **~ portable** laptop (computer); **~ hôte** (Internet) host.

ordonnance /ɔʀdɔnɑ̃s/ *nf* (ordre, décret) order; (de médecin) prescription.

ordonné, **~e** /ɔʀdɔne/ *a* tidy.

ordonner /ɔʀdɔne/ [1] *vt* order (**à qn de** sb to); (agencer) arrange; (Méd) prescribe; (*prêtre*) ordain.

ordre /ɔʀdʀ/ *nm* order; (propreté) tidiness; **aux ~s de qn** at sb's disposal; **avoir de l'~** be tidy; **en ~** tidy, in order; **de premier ~** first-rate; **d'~ officiel** of an official nature; **l'~ du jour** (programme) agenda; **mettre de l' ~ dans** tidy up; **jusqu'à nouvel ~** until further notice; **un ~ de grandeur** an approximate idea.

ordure /ɔʀdyʀ/ *nf* filth; **~s** (détritus) rubbish; (US) garbage; **~s ménagères** household refuse.

oreille /ɔʀɛj/ *nf* ear.

oreiller /ɔʀeje/ *nm* pillow.

oreillons /ɔʀɛjɔ̃/ *nmpl* mumps.

orfèvre /ɔʀfɛvʀ/ *nm* goldsmith.

organe /ɔʀgan/ *nm* organ.

organigramme /ɔʀganigʀam/ *nm* organization chart; (Ordinat) flowchart.

organique /ɔʀganik/ *a* organic.

organisateur, **-trice** /ɔʀganizatœʀ, -tʀis/ *nm, f* organizer.

organisation /ɔʀganizasjɔ̃/ *nf* organization.

organiser /ɔʀganize/ [1] *vt* organize. ◻ **s'~** *vpr* organize oneself, get organized.

organisme /ɔʀganism/ *nm* body, organism.

orge /ɔʀʒ/ *nf* barley.

orgelet /ɔʀʒəlɛ/ *nm* sty.

orgue /ɔʀg/ *nm* organ; **~ de Barbarie** barrel-organ. **orgues** *nfpl* organ.

orgueil /ɔʀgœj/ *nm* pride. **orgueilleux**, **-euse** *a* proud.

orient /ɔʀjɑ̃/ *nm* (direction) east; **l'O~** the Orient.

oriental, **~e** (*mpl* **-aux**) /ɔʀjɑ̃tal, -o/ *a* eastern; (de l'Orient) oriental. **O~**, **~e** (*mpl* **-aux**) *nm, f* Asian.

orientation /ɔʀjɑ̃tasjɔ̃/ *nf* direction; (tendance politique) leanings (+ *pl*); (de maison) aspect; (Sport) orienteering; **~ professionnelle** careers advice; **~ scolaire** curriculum counselling.

orienter /ɔʀjɑ̃te/ [1] *vt* position; (*personne*) direct. ◻ **s'~** *vpr* (se repérer) find one's bearings; **s'~ vers** turn towards.

origan /ɔʀigɑ̃/ *nm* oregano.

originaire /ɔʀiʒinɛʀ/ *a* **être ~ de** be a native of.

original, **~e** (*mpl* **-aux**) /ɔʀiʒinal, -o/ *a* original; (curieux) eccentric. ● *nm* (œuvre) original. ● *nm, f* eccentric. **originalité** *nf* originality; eccentricity.

origine /ɔʀiʒin/ *nf* origin; **à l'~** originally; **d'~** (*pièce, pneu*) original; **être d'~ noble** come from a noble background.

originel, **~le** /ɔʀiʒinɛl/ *a* original.

orme /ɔʀm/ *nm* elm.

ornement /ɔʀnəmɑ̃/ *nm* ornament.

orner /ɔʀne/ [1] *vt* decorate.

orphelin, **~e** /ɔʀfəlɛ̃, -in/ *nm, f* orphan. ● *a* orphaned. **orphelinat** *nm* orphanage.

orteil /ɔʀtɛj/ *nm* toe.

orthodoxe /ɔʀtɔdɔks/ *a* orthodox.

orthographe /ɔʀtɔgʀaf/ *nf* spelling.

ortie /ɔʀti/ *nf* nettle.

os /ɔs, o/ *nm inv* bone.

OS *abrév m* ⇒OUVRIER SPÉCIALISÉ.

osciller /ɔsile/ [1] *vi* sway; (Tech) oscillate; (hésiter) waver; (fluctuer) fluctuate.

osé, **~e** /oze/ *a* daring.

oseille /ozɛj/ *nf* (plante) sorrel.

oser /oze/ [1] *vi* dare.

osier /ozje/ *nm* wicker.

ossature /ɔsatyʀ/ *nf* skeleton, frame.

ossements /ɔsmɑ̃/ *nmpl* bones, remains.

osseux, **-euse** /ɔsø, -z/ *a* bony; (Méd) bone.

otage /ɔtaʒ/ *nm* hostage.

OTAN /ɔtɑ̃/ *abrév f* (**Organisation du traité de l'Atlantique Nord**) NATO.

otarie /ɔtaʀi/ *nf* eared seal.

ôter /ote/ [1] *vt* remove (**à qn** from sb); (déduire) take away.

otite /ɔtit/ *nf* ear infection.

ou /u/ *conj* or; **~ bien** or else; **~ (bien)... ~ (bien)...** either... or...; **vous ~ moi** either you or me.

où /u/ *pron* where; (dans lequel) in which; (sur lequel) on which; (auquel) at which; **d'~** from which; (pour cette raison) hence; **par ~** through which; **~ qu'il soit** wherever he may be; **juste au moment ~** just as; **le jour ~** the day when. ● *adv* where; **d'~?** where from?

ouate /wat/ *nf* cotton wool; (US) absorbent cotton.

oubli /ubli/ *nm* forgetfulness; (trou de mémoire) lapse of memory; (négligence) oversight; **tomber dans l'~** sink into oblivion.

oublier /ublije/ [45] *vt* forget; (omettre) leave out, forget. □ **s'~** *vpr* (*chose*) be forgotten.

ouest /wɛst/ *a inv* (*façade, côte*) west; (*frontière, zone*) western. ● *nm* west; **l'~ de l'Europe** western Europe; **vent d'~** westerly (wind); **aller vers l'~** go west; **l'O~** the West; **de l'O~** western.

oui /wi/ *adv & nm inv* yes.

ouï-dire: **par ~** /paʀwidiʀ/ *loc* by hearsay.

ouïe /wi/ *nf* hearing; (de poisson) gill.

ouragan /uʀagɑ̃/ *nm* hurricane.

ourlet /uʀlɛ/ *nm* hem.

ours /uʀs/ *nm* bear; **~ blanc** polar bear; **~ en peluche** teddy bear.

outil /uti/ *nm* tool. **outillage** *nm* tools (+ *pl*). **outiller** [1] *vt* equip.

outrage /utʀaʒ/ *nm* (grave) insult.

outrance /utʀɑ̃s/ *nf* **à ~** excessively. **outrancier**, **-ière** *a* extreme.

outre /utʀ/ *prép* besides. ● *adv* **passer ~** pay no heed; **~ mesure** unduly; **en ~** in addition. **outre-mer** *adv* overseas.

outrepasser /utʀəpɑse/ [1] *vt* exceed.

outrer /utʀe/ [1] *vt* exaggerate; (indigner) incense.

ouvert, **~e** /uvɛʀ, -t/ *a* open; (*gaz, radio*) on. ● ⇒OUVRIR [21].

ouverture /uvɛʀtyʀ/ *nf* opening; (Mus) overture; (Photo) aperture; **~s** (offres) overtures; **~ d'esprit** open-mindedness.

ouvrable /uvʀabl/ *a* **jour ~** working day; **aux heures ~s** during business hours.

ouvrage /uvʀaʒ/ *nm* (travail, livre) work; (couture) (piece of) needlework.

ouvre-boîtes /uvʀəbwat/ *nm inv* tin-opener.

O

ouvre-bouteilles /uvʀəbutɛj/ *nm inv* bottle-opener.

ouvreur, **-euse** /uvʀœʀ, -øz/ *nm,f* usherette.

ouvrier, **-ière** /uvʀije, -jɛʀ/ *nm,f* worker; **~ qualifié/spécialisé** skilled/unskilled worker. ● *a* working-class; (*conflit*) industrial; **syndicat ~** trade union.

ouvrir /uvʀiʀ/ [21] *vt* open (up); (*gaz, robinet*) turn *ou* switch on. ● *vi* open (up). □ **s'~** *vpr* open (up); **s'~ à qn** open one's heart to sb.

ovaire /ɔvɛʀ/ *nm* ovary.

ovale /ɔval/ *a & nm* oval.

ovni /ɔvni/ *abrév m* (**objet volant non-identifié**) UFO.

ovule /ɔvyl/ *nm* (à féconder) ovum; (gynécologique) pessary.

oxygène /ɔksiʒɛn/ *nm* oxygen.

oxygéner (s') /(s)ɔksiʒene/ [14] *vpr* get some fresh air.

ozone /ozon/ *nf* ozone; **la couche d'~** the ozone layer.

pacifique /pasifik/ *a* peaceful; (*personne*) peaceable; (Géog) Pacific. **P~** *nm* **le P~** the Pacific (Ocean).

pacotille /pakɔtij/ *nf* junk, rubbish.

pagaie /pagɛ/ *nf* paddle.

pagaille /pagaj/ *nf* 🅸 mess, shambles (+ *sg*).

page /paʒ/ *nf* page; **mise en ~** layout; **tourner la ~** turn over a new leaf; **être à la ~** be up to date; **~ d'accueil** (Internet) home page.

paie /pɛ/ *nf* pay.

paiement /pɛmɑ̃/ *nm* payment.

païen, **~ne** /pajɛ̃, -ɛn/ *a & nm,f* pagan.

paillasson /pajasɔ̃/ *nm* doormat.

paille /pɑj/ *nf* straw. ● *a* (*cheveux*) straw-coloured; **jaune ~** straw yellow.

paillette /pajɛt/ *nf* (sur robe) sequin; (de savon) flake; **robe à ~s** sequined dress.

pain /pɛ̃/ *nm* bread; (miche) loaf (of bread); (de savon, cire) bar; **~ d'épices** gingerbread; **~ grillé** toast.

pair, **~e** /pɛʀ/ *a* (*nombre*) even. ● *nm* (personne) peer; **aller de ~** go together (**avec** with); **au ~** (*jeune fille*) au pair. **paire** *nf* pair.

paisible /pezibl/ *a* peaceful.

paître /pɛtʀ/ [44] *vi* graze.

paix /pɛ/ *nf* peace; **fiche-moi la ~!** 🅸 leave me alone!

Pakistan /pakistɑ̃/ *nm* Pakistan.

palace /palas/ *nm* luxury hotel.

palais /palɛ/ *nm* palace; (Anat) palate; **~ de Justice** law courts; **~ des sports** sports stadium.

pâle /pɑl/ *a* pale.

Palestine /palɛstin/ *nf* Palestine.

palier /palje/ *nm* (d'escalier) landing; (étape) stage.

pâlir /pɑliʀ/ [2] *vt/i* (turn) pale.

palissade /palisad/ *nf* fence.

pallier /palje/ [45] *vt* compensate for.

palmarès /palmaʀɛs/ *nm* list of prize-winners.

palme /palm/ *nf* palm leaf; (de nageur) flipper. **palmé**, **~e** *a* (*patte*) webbed.

palmier /palmje/ *nm* palm (tree).

palper /palpe/ [1] *vt* feel.

palpiter /palpite/ [1] *vi* (battre) pound; (frémir) quiver.

paludisme /palydism/ *nm* malaria.

pamplemousse /pɑ̃pləmus/ *nm* grapefruit.

panaché, **~e** /panaʃe/ *a* (bariolé, mélangé) motley; **glace ~e** mixed-flavour ice cream. ● *nm* shandy.

pancarte /pɑ̃kaʀt/ *nf* sign; (de manifestant) placard.

pané, **~e** /pane/ *a* breaded.

panier /panje/ *nm* basket; (de basket-ball) basket; **mettre au ~** 🄸 throw out; **~ à salade** salad shaker; (fourgon 🄸) police van.

panique /panik/ *nf* panic. **paniquer** [1] *vi* panic.

panne /pan/ *nf* breakdown; **être en ~** have broken down; **être en ~ sèche** have run out of petrol; **~ d'électricité** *ou* **de courant** power failure.

panneau (*pl* **~x**) /pano/ *nm* sign; (publicitaire) hoarding; (de porte) panel; **~ (d'affichage)** notice board; **~ (de signalisation)** road sign.

panoplie /panɔpli/ *nf* (jouet) outfit; (gamme) range.

pansement /pɑ̃smɑ̃/ *nm* dressing; **~ adhésif** plaster. **panser** [1] *vt* (*plaie*) dress; (*personne*) dress the wound(s) of; (*cheval*) groom.

pantalon /pɑ̃talɔ̃/ *nm* trousers (+ *pl*).

panthère /pɑ̃tɛʀ/ *nf* panther.

pantin /pɑ̃tɛ̃/ *nm* puppet.

pantomime /pɑ̃tɔmim/ *nf* mime; (spectacle) mime show.

pantoufle /pɑ̃tufl/ *nf* slipper.

paon /pɑ̃/ *nm* peacock.

papa /papa/ *nm* dad(dy).

pape /pap/ *nm* pope.

paperasse /papʀas/ *nf* (péj) bumf.

papeterie /papetʀi/ *nf* (magasin) stationer's shop.

papier /papje/ *nm* paper; (formulaire) form; **~s (d'identité)** (identity) papers; **~ absorbant** kitchen paper; **~ aluminium** tin foil; **~ buvard** blotting paper; **~ cadeau** wrapping paper; **~ calque** tracing paper; **~ carbone** carbon paper; **~ collant** adhesive tape; **~ hygiénique** toilet paper; **~ journal** newspaper; **~ à lettres** writing paper; **~ mâché** papier mâché; **~ peint** wallpaper; **~ de verre** sandpaper.

papillon /papijɔ̃/ *nm* butterfly; (contravention 🄸) parking-ticket; **~ de nuit** moth.

papoter /papɔte/ [1] *vi* 🄸 chatter.

paquebot /pakbo/ *nm* liner.

pâquerette /pɑkʀɛt/ *nf* daisy.

Pâques /pɑk/ *nfpl & nm* Easter.

paquet /pakɛ/ *nm* packet; (de cartes) pack; (colis) parcel; **un ~ de** (beaucoup 🄸) a mass of.

par /paʀ/ *prép* by; (à travers) through; (motif) out of, from; (provenance) from; **commencer/finir ~ qch** begin/end with sth; **commencer/finir ~ faire** begin by/ end up (by) doing; **~ an/mois** a *ou* per year/month; **~ jour** a day; **~ personne** each, per person; **~ avion** (lettre) (by) airmail; **~-ci, ~-là** here and there; **~ contre** on the other hand; **~ ici/là** this/that way.

parachute /paʀaʃyt/ *nm* parachute. **parachutiste** *nmf* parachutist; (Mil) paratrooper.

parader /paʀade/ [1] *vi* show off.

paradis /paʀadi/ *nm* (Relig) heaven; (lieu idéal) paradise; **~ fiscal** tax haven.

paradoxal, **~e** (*mpl* **-aux**) /paʀadɔksal, -o/ *a* paradoxical.

paraffine /paʀafin/ *nf* paraffin wax.

parages /paʀaʒ/ *nmpl* **dans les ~** around.

P

paragraphe /paʀagʀaf/ *nm* paragraph.

paraître /paʀɛtʀ/ [18] *vi* (se montrer) appear; (sembler) seem, appear; (*ouvrage*) be published, come out; **faire ∼** (*ouvrage*) bring out; **il paraît qu'ils...** apparently they...; **oui, il paraît** so I hear.

parallèle /paʀalɛl/ *a* parallel; (illégal) unofficial. ● *nm* parallel; **faire le ∼** make a connection. ● *nf* parallel (line).

paralyser /paʀalize/ [1] *vt* paralyse. **paralysie** *nf* paralysis.

parapente /paʀapɑ̃t/ *nm* paraglider; (activité) paragliding.

parapher /paʀafe/ [1] *vi* initial; (signer) sign.

parapluie /paʀaplɥi/ *nm* umbrella.

parasite /paʀazit/ *nm* parasite; **∼s** (radio) interference (+ *sg*).

parasol /paʀasɔl/ *nm* sunshade.

paratonnerre /paʀatɔnɛʀ/ *nm* lightning conductor *ou* rod.

paravent /paʀavɑ̃/ *nm* screen.

parc /paʀk/ *nm* park; (de bétail) pen; (de bébé) play-pen; (entrepôt) depot; **∼ relais** park and ride; **∼ de stationnement** car park.

parce que /paʀsk(ə)/ *conj* because.

parchemin /paʀʃəmɛ̃/ *nm* parchment.

parcmètre /paʀkmɛtʀ/ *nm* parking meter.

parcourir /paʀkuʀiʀ/ [20] *vt* travel *ou* go through; (*distance*) travel; (des yeux) glance at *ou* over.

parcours /paʀkuʀ/ *nm* route; (voyage) journey.

par-delà /paʀdəla/ *prép* beyond.

par-derrière /paʀdɛʀjɛʀ/ *adv* (*attaquer*) from behind; (*critiquer*) behind sb's back.

par-dessous /paʀdəsu/ *prép & adv* under(neath).

pardessus /paʀdəsy/ *nm* overcoat.

par-dessus /paʀdəsy/ *prép & adv* over; **∼ bord** overboard; **∼ le marché** [!] into the bargain; **∼ tout** above all.

par-devant /paʀdəvɑ̃/ *adv* (*passer*) by the front.

pardon /paʀdɔ̃/ *nm* forgiveness; **(je vous demande) ∼!** (I am) sorry!; (pour demander qch) excuse me.

pardonner /paʀdɔne/ [1] *vt* forgive; **∼ qch à qn** forgive sb for sth.

pare-brise /paʀbʀiz/ *nm inv* windscreen.

pare-chocs /paʀʃɔk/ *nm inv* bumper.

pareil, ∼le /paʀɛj/ *a* similar **(à** to); (tel) such (a); **c'est ∼** it's the same; **ce n'est pas ∼** it's not the same thing. ● *nm, f* equal. ● *adv* [!] the same.

parent, ∼e /paʀɑ̃, -t/ *a* related **(de** to). ● *nm, f* relative, relation; **∼s** (père et mère) parents; **∼ isolé** single parent; **réunion de ∼s d'élèves** parents' evening.

parenté /paʀɑ̃te/ *nf* relationship.

parenthèse /paʀɑ̃tɛz/ *nf* bracket, parenthesis; (fig) digression.

parer /paʀe/ [1] *vt* (esquiver) parry; (orner) adorn. ● *vi* **∼ à** deal with; **∼ au plus pressé** tackle the most urgent things first.

paresse /paʀɛs/ *nf* laziness.

paresseux, -euse /paʀɛsø, -z/ *a* lazy. ● *nm, f* lazy person.

parfait, ∼e /paʀfɛ, -t/ *a* perfect. **parfaitement** *adv* perfectly; (bien sûr) absolutely.

parfois /paʀfwa/ *adv* sometimes.

parfum /paʀfœ̃/ *nm* (senteur) scent; (substance) perfume, scent; (goût) flavour. **parfumé, ∼e** *a* fragrant; (*savon*) scented; (*thé*) flavoured.

parfumer /paʀfyme/ [1] *vt* (embaumer) scent; (*gâteau*) flavour. □ **se ~** *vpr* put on one's perfume. **parfumerie** *nf* (produits) perfumes; (boutique) perfume shop.

pari /paʀi/ *nm* bet.

Paris /paʀi/ *npr* Paris.

parisien, **~ne** /paʀizjɛ̃, -ɛn/ *a* Parisian; (*banlieue*) Paris. **P~**, **~ne** *nm, f* Parisian.

parking /paʀkiŋ/ *nm* car park.

parlement /paʀləmɑ̃/ *nm* parliament.

parlementaire /paʀləmɑ̃tɛʀ/ *a* parliamentary. ● *nmf* Member of Parliament.

parlementer /paʀləmɑ̃te/ [1] *vi* negotiate.

parler /paʀle/ [1] *vi* talk (**à** to); **~ de** talk about; **tu parles d'un avantage!** call that a benefit!; **de quoi ça parle?** what is it about? ● *vt* (*langue*) speak; (*politique, affaires*) talk. □ **se ~** *vpr* (*personnes*) talk (to each other); (*langue*) be spoken. ● *nm* speech; (dialecte) dialect.

parmi /paʀmi/ *prép* among(st).

paroi /paʀwa/ *nf* wall; **~ rocheuse** rock face.

paroisse /paʀwas/ *nf* parish.

parole /paʀɔl/ *nf* (mot, promesse) word; (langage) speech; **demander la ~** ask to speak; **prendre la ~** (begin to) speak; **tenir ~** keep one's word; **croire qn sur ~** take sb's word for it.

parquet /paʀkɛ/ *nm* (parquet) floor; **lame de ~** floorboard; **le ~** (Jur) prosecution.

parrain /paʀɛ̃/ *nm* godfather; (fig) sponsor.

parsemer /paʀsəme/ [6] *vt* strew (**de** with).

part /paʀ/ *nf* share, part; **à ~** (de côté) aside; (séparément) separate; (excepté) apart from; **d'une ~** on the one hand; **d'autre ~** on the other hand; (de plus) moreover; **de la ~ de** from; **de toutes ~s** from all sides; **de ~ et d'autre** on both sides; **faire ~ à qn** inform sb (**de** of); **faire la ~ des choses** make allowances; **prendre ~ à** take part in; (*joie, douleur*) share; **pour ma ~** as for me.

partage /paʀtaʒ/ *nm* (division) dividing; (répartition) sharing out; **recevoir qch en ~** be left sth in a will.

partager /paʀtaʒe/ [40] *vt* divide; (distribuer) share out; (avoir en commun) share. □ **se ~ qch** *vpr* share sth.

partenaire /paʀtənɛʀ/ *nmf* partner.

parterre /paʀtɛʀ/ *nm* flower-bed; (Théât) stalls.

parti /paʀti/ *nm* (Pol) party; (décision) decision; (en mariage) match; **~ pris** bias; **prendre ~** get involved; **prendre ~ pour qn** side with sb; **j'en ai pris mon ~** I've come to terms with that.

partial, **~e** (*mpl* **-iaux**) /paʀsjal, -jo/ *a* biased.

participe /paʀtisip/ *nm* (Gram) participle.

participant, **~e** /paʀtisipɑ̃, -t/ *nm, f* participant (**à** in).

participation /paʀtisipasjɔ̃/ *nf* participation; (financière) contribution; (d'un artiste) appearance.

participer /paʀtisipe/ [1] *vi* **~ à** take part in, participate in; (*profits, frais*) share.

particule /paʀtikyl/ *nf* particle.

particulier, **-ière** /paʀtikylje, -jɛʀ/ *a* (spécifique) particular; (bizarre) unusual; (privé) private; **rien de ~** nothing special. ● *nm* private individual; **en ~** in particular, particularly. **particulièrement** *adv* particularly.

partie /paʀti/ *nf* part; (cartes, Sport)

P

game; (Jur) party; **une ~ de pêche** a fishing trip; **en ~** partly, in part; **en grande ~** largely; **faire ~ de** be part of; (adhérer à) be a member of; **faire ~ intégrante de** be an integral part of.

partiel, **~le** /paʀsjɛl/ *a* partial. ● *nm* (Univ) exam based on a module.

partir /paʀtiʀ/ [46] *vi* (*aux être*) go; (quitter un lieu) leave, go; (*tache*) come out; (*bouton*) come off; (*coup de feu*) go off; (commencer) start; **~ pour le Brésil** leave for Brazil; **~ du principe que** work on the assumption that; **à ~ de** from; **à ~ de maintenant** from now on.

partisan, **~e** /paʀtizɑ̃, -an/ *nm, f* supporter. ● *nm* (Mil) partisan; **être ~ de** be in favour of.

partition /paʀtisjɔ̃/ *nf* (Mus) score.

partout /paʀtu/ *adv* everywhere; **~ où** wherever.

paru /paʀy/ ⇒PARAÎTRE [18].

parure /paʀyʀ/ *nf* finery; (bijoux) set of jewels; (de draps) set.

parution /paʀysjɔ̃/ *nf* publication.

parvenir /paʀvəniʀ/ [58] *vi* (*aux être*) **~ à** reach; **~ à faire** manage to do; **faire ~** send.

parvenu, **~e** /paʀvəny/ *nm, f* upstart.

pas[1] /pɑ/

Pour les expressions comme **pas encore**, **pas mal**, etc. ⇒**encore**, **mal**, etc.

●*adverbe*

····➤ not; **ne ~** not; **je ne sais ~** I don't know; **je ne pense ~** I don't think so; **il a aimé, moi ~** he liked it, I didn't; **~ cher/poli** cheap/impolite.

····➤ **~ du tout** not at all; **~ de chance!** tough luck!

····➤ **on a bien ri, ~ vrai?** [!] we had a good laugh, didn't we?

! In spoken colloquial French **ne... pas** is often shortened to **pas**. You will often hear **j'ai pas compris** instead of **je n'ai pas compris** (*I didn't understand*). Note that this would not be correct in written French.

pas[2] /pɑ/ *nm* step; (bruit) footstep; (trace) footprint; (vitesse) pace; **à deux ~ (de)** a step away (from); **marcher au ~** march; **rouler au ~** move very slowly; **à ~ de loup** stealthily; **faire les cent ~** walk up and down; **faire le premier ~** make the first move; **~ de porte** doorstep; **~ de vis** (Tech) thread.

passage /pɑsaʒ/ *nm* (traversée) crossing; (visite) visit; (chemin) way, passage; (d'une œuvre) passage; **de ~** (*voyageur*) visiting; (*amant*) casual; **la tempête a tout emporté sur son ~** the storm swept everything away; **~ clouté** pedestrian crossing; **~ interdit** (panneau) no thoroughfare; **~ à niveau** level crossing; **~ souterrain** subway.

passager, **-ère** /pɑsaʒe, -ɛʀ/ *a* temporary. ● *nm, f* passenger; **~ clandestin** stowaway.

passant, **~e** /pɑsɑ̃, -t/ *a* (*rue*) busy. ● *nm, f* passer-by. ● *nm* (anneau) loop.

passe /pɑs/ *nf* pass; **bonne/mauvaise ~** good/bad patch; **en ~ de** on the road to.

passé, **~e** /pɑse/ *a* (révolu) past; (dernier) last; (fané) faded; **~ de mode** out of fashion. ● *nm* past. ● *prép* after.

passe-partout /pɑspaʀtu/ *nm*

inv master-key. ● *a inv* for all occasions.

passeport /paspɔʀ/ *nm* passport.

passer /pase/ [1] *vi* (*aux être ou avoir*) go past, pass; (aller) go; (venir) come; (*temps, douleur*) pass; (*film*) be on; (*couleur*) fade; **laisser ~** let through, (*occasion*) miss; **~ devant** (à pied) walk past; (en voiture) drive past; **~ par** go through; **où est-il passé?** where did he get to?; **~ outre** take no notice; **passons!** let's forget about it!; **passons aux choses sérieuses** let's turn to serious matters; **~ dans la classe supérieure** go up a year; **~ pour un idiot** look a fool. ● *vt* (*aux avoir*) (franchir) pass, cross; (donner) pass, hand; (*temps*) spend; (enfiler) slip on; (*vidéo, disque*) put on; (*examen*) take, sit; (*commande*) place; (faire) **~ le temps** while away the time; **~ l'aspirateur** hoover; **~ un coup de fil à qn** give sb a ring; **je vous passe Mme X** (par le standard) I'll put you through to Mrs X; (en donnant l'appareil) I'll pass you over to Mrs X; **~ qch en fraude** smuggle sth. □ **se ~** *vpr* happen, take place; (s'écouler) go by; **se ~ de** go *ou* do without.

passerelle /pasʀɛl/ *nf* footbridge; (de navire) gangway; (d'avion) (passenger) footbridge; (Internet) gateway.

passe-temps /pastɑ̃/ *nm inv* pastime.

passif, -ive /pasif, -v/ *a* passive. ● *nm* (Comm) liabilities.

passion /pasjɔ̃/ *nf* passion. **passionnant, ~e** *a* fascinating.

passionné, ~e /pasjɔne/ *a* passionate; **être ~ de** have a passion for.

passionner /pasjɔne/ [1] *vt* fascinate. □ **se ~ pour** *vpr* have a passion for.

passoire /paswaʀ/ *nf* (à thé) strainer; (à légumes) colander.

pastèque /pastɛk/ *nf* watermelon.

pasteur /pastœʀ/ *nm* (Relig) minister.

pastille /pastij/ *nf* (médicament) pastille, lozenge.

patate /patat/ *nf* 🅸 spud; **~ (douce)** sweet potato.

patauger /patoʒe/ [40] *vi* splash about.

pâte /pɑt/ *nf* paste; (à gâteau) dough; (à tarte) pastry; (à frire) batter; **~s (alimentaires)** pasta (+ *sg*); **~ à modeler** Plasticine®; **~ d'amandes** marzipan.

pâté /pɑte/ *nm* (Culin) pâté; (d'encre) blot; (de sable) sandpie; **~ en croûte** ≈ pie; **~ de maisons** block (of houses).

pâtée /pɑte/ *nf* feed, mash.

patente /patɑ̃t/ *nf* trade licence.

paternel, ~le /patɛʀnɛl/ *a* paternal. **paternité** *nf* paternity.

pathétique /patetik/ *a* moving.

patience /pasjɑ̃s/ *nf* patience. **patient, ~e** *a & nm,f* patient. **patienter** [1] *vi* wait.

patin /patɛ̃/ *nm* skate; **~ à roulettes** roller-skate.

patinage /patinaʒ/ *nm* skating. **patiner** [1] *vi* skate; (*roue*) spin. **patinoire** *nf* ice rink.

pâtisserie /pɑtisʀi/ *nf* cake shop; (gâteau) pastry; (secteur) cake making. **pâtissier, -ière** *nm,f* confectioner, pastry-cook.

patrie /patʀi/ *nf* homeland.

patrimoine /patʀimwan/ *nm* heritage.

patriote /patʀijɔt/ *a* patriotic. ● *nmf* patriot.

patron, ~ne /patʀɔ̃, -ɔn/ *nm,f* employer, boss; (propriétaire) owner, boss; (saint) patron saint. ● *nm* (couture) pattern. **patronal,**

P

~e (*mpl* **-aux**) *a* employers'. **patronat** *nm* employers (+ *pl*).

patrouille /patʀuj/ *nf* patrol.

patte /pat/ *nf* leg; (pied) foot; (de chat) paw; **~s** (favoris) sideburns; **marcher à quatre ~s** walk on all fours; (*bébé*) crawl; **~s de derrière** hind legs.

paume /pom/ *nf* (de main) palm.

paumé, **~e** /pome/ *nm, f* 🄸 misfit.

paupière /popjɛʀ/ *nf* eyelid.

pause /poz/ *nf* pause; (halte) break.

pauvre /povʀ/ *a* poor. ● *nmf* poor man, poor woman. **pauvreté** *nf* poverty.

pavé /pave/ *nm* cobblestone.

pavillon /pavijɔ̃/ *nm* (maison) house; (drapeau) flag.

payant, **~e** /pɛjɑ̃, -t/ *a* (*hôte*) paying; **c'est ~** you have to pay to get in.

payer /peje/ [31] *vt/i* pay; (*service, travail*) pay for; **~ qch à qn** buy sb sth; **faire ~ qn** charge sb; **il me le paiera!** he'll pay for this. □ **se ~** *vpr* **se ~ qch** buy oneself sth; **se ~ la tête de** make fun of.

pays /pei/ *nm* country; (région) region; **du ~** local.

paysage /peizaʒ/ *nm* landscape.

paysan, **~ne** /peizɑ̃, -an/ *nm, f* farmer, country person; (péj) peasant. ● *a* (agricole) farming; (rural) country.

Pays-Bas /peibɑ/ *nmpl* **les ~** the Netherlands.

PCV *abrév m* (**paiement contre vérification**) **téléphoner en ~** reverse the charges.

PDG *abrév m* (**président-directeur général**) chairman and managing director.

péage /peaʒ/ *nm* toll; (lieu) tollgate.

peau (*pl* **~x**) /po/ *nf* skin; (cuir) hide; **~ de chamois** shammy (leather); **~ de mouton** sheepskin; **être bien/mal dans sa ~** be/not be at ease with oneself.

pêche /pɛʃ/ *nf* (fruit) peach; (activité) fishing; (poissons) catch; **~ à la ligne** angling.

péché /peʃe/ *nm* sin.

pêcher /peʃe/ *vt* (*poisson*) catch; (dénicher 🄸) dig up. ● *vi* fish. **pêcheur** *nm* fisherman; (à la ligne) angler.

pécuniaire /pekynjɛʀ/ *a* financial.

pédagogie /pedagɔʒi/ *nf* education.

pédale /pedal/ *nf* pedal.

pédalo® /pedalo/ *nm* pedal boat.

pédant, **~e** /pedɑ̃, -t/ *a* pedantic.

pédestre /pedɛstʀ/ *a* **faire de la randonnée ~** go walking *ou* hiking.

pédiatre /pedjatʀ/ *nmf* paediatrician.

pédicure /pedikyʀ/ *nmf* chiropodist.

peigne /pɛɲ/ *nm* comb.

peigner /peɲe/ [1] *vt* comb; (*personne*) comb the hair of. □ **se ~** *vpr* comb one's hair.

peignoir /pɛɲwaʀ/ *nm* dressing-gown.

peindre /pɛ̃dʀ/ [22] *vt* paint.

peine /pɛn/ *nf* sadness, sorrow; (effort, difficulté) trouble; (Jur) sentence; **avoir de la ~** feel sad; **faire de la ~ à** hurt; **ce n'est pas la ~ de sonner** you don't need to ring the bell; **j'ai de la ~ à le croire** I find it hard to believe; **se donner** *ou* **prendre la ~ de faire** go to the trouble of doing; **~ de mort** death penalty. ● *adv* **à ~** hardly.

peiner /pene/ [1] *vi* struggle. ● *vt* sadden.

peintre /pɛ̃tʀ/ *nm* painter; **~ en bâtiment** house painter.

peinture /pɛ̃tyʀ/ *nf* painting;

(matière) paint; ~ **à l'huile** oil painting.

péjoratif, -ive /peʒɔʀatif, -v/ *a* pejorative.

pelage /pəlaʒ/ *nm* coat, fur.

pêle-mêle /pɛlmɛl/ *adv* in a jumble.

peler /pəle/ [6] *vt/i* peel.

pèlerinage /pɛlʀinaʒ/ *nm* pilgrimage.

pelle /pɛl/ *nf* shovel; (d'enfant) spade.

pellicule /pelikyl/ *nf* film; **~s** (cheveux) dandruff.

pelote /pəlɔt/ *nf* (of wool) ball.

peloton /p(ə)lɔtɔ̃/ *nm* platoon; (Sport) pack; ~ **d'exécution** firing squad.

pelotonner (se) /(sə)plɔtɔne/ [1] *vpr* curl up.

pelouse /p(ə)luz/ *nf* lawn.

peluche /p(ə)lyʃ/ *nf* (matière) plush; (jouet) cuddly toy; **en** ~ (*lapin, chien*) fluffy.

pénal, ~e (*mpl* **-aux**) /penal, -o/ *a* penal. **pénaliser** [1] *vt* penalize. **pénalité** *nf* penalty.

penchant /pɑ̃ʃɑ̃/ *nm* inclination; (goût) liking (**pour** for).

pencher /pɑ̃ʃe/ [1] *vt* tilt; ~ **pour** favour. ● *vi* lean (over), tilt. ▫ **se** ~ *vpr* lean (forward); **se** ~ **sur** (*problème*) examine.

pendaison /pɑ̃dɛzɔ̃/ *nf* hanging.

pendant¹ /pɑ̃dɑ̃/ *prép* (au cours de) during; (durée) for; ~ **que** while.

pendant², ~e /pɑ̃dɑ̃, -t/ *a* hanging; **jambes ~es** with one's legs dangling. ● *nm* (contrepartie) matching piece (**de** to); ~ **d'oreille** drop ear-ring.

pendentif /pɑ̃dɑ̃tif/ *nm* pendant.

penderie /pɑ̃dʀi/ *nf* wardrobe.

pendre /pɑ̃dʀ/ [3] *vt/i* hang. ▫ **se** ~ *vpr* hang (**à** from); (se tuer) hang oneself.

pendule /pɑ̃dyl/ *nf* clock. ● *nm* pendulum.

pénétrer /penetʀe/ [14] *vi* ~ (**dans**) enter; **faire** ~ **une crème** rub a cream in. ● *vt* penetrate.

pénible /penibl/ *a* (*travail*) hard; (*nouvelle*) painful; (*enfant*) tiresome.

péniche /peniʃ/ *nf* barge.

pénitence /penitɑ̃s/ *nf* (Relig) penance; (punition) punishment; **faire** ~ repent.

pénitentiaire /penitɑ̃sjɛʀ/ *a* (*établissement*) penal.

pénombre /penɔ̃bʀ/ *nf* half-light.

pensée /pɑ̃se/ *nf* (idée) thought; (fleur) pansy.

penser /pɑ̃se/ [1] *vt/i* think; ~ **à** (réfléchir à) think about; (se souvenir de, prévoir) think of; ~ **faire** think of doing; **faire** ~ **à** remind one of.

pensif, -ive /pɑ̃sif, -v/ *a* pensive.

pension /pɑ̃sjɔ̃/ *nf* (Scol) boarding school; (repas, somme) board; (allocation) pension; ~ (**de famille**) guest house; ~ **alimentaire** (Jur) alimony. **pensionnaire** *nmf* (Scol) boarder; (d'hôtel) guest. **pensionnat** *nm* boarding school.

pente /pɑ̃t/ *nf* slope; **en** ~ sloping.

Pentecôte /pɑ̃tkot/ *nf* **la** ~ Whitsun.

pénurie /penyʀi/ *nf* shortage.

pépin /pepɛ̃/ *nm* (graine) pip; (ennui 🅸) hitch.

pépinière /pepinjɛʀ/ *nf* (tree) nursery.

perçant, ~e /pɛʀsɑ̃, -t/ *a* (*cri*) shrill; (*regard*) piercing.

perce-neige /pɛʀsənɛʒ/ *nm or f inv* snowdrop.

percepteur /pɛʀsɛptœʀ/ *nm* tax inspector.

percer /pɛʀse/ [10] *vt* pierce; (avec perceuse) drill; (*mystère*) penetrate. ● *vi* break through; (*dent*) come through. **perceuse** *nf* drill.

P

percevoir /pɛʀsəvwaʀ/ [52] *vt* perceive; (*impôt*) collect.

perche /pɛʀʃ/ *nf* (bâton) pole.

percher (se) /(sə)pɛʀʃe/ [1] *vpr* perch.

percolateur /pɛʀkɔlatœʀ/ *nm* coffee machine.

percuter /pɛʀkyte/ [1] *vt* (*véhicule*) crash into.

perdant, **~e** /pɛʀdɑ̃, -t/ *a* losing. ● *nm, f* loser.

perdre /pɛʀdʀ/ [3] *vt/i* lose; (gaspiller) waste; **~ ses poils** (*chat*) moult. ▫ **se ~** *vpr* get lost; (rester inutilisé) go to waste.

perdrix /pɛʀdʀi/ *nf* partridge.

perdu, **~e** /pɛʀdy/ *a* lost; (*endroit*) isolated; (*balle*) stray; **c'est du temps ~** it's a waste of time.

père /pɛʀ/ *nm* father; **~ de famille** father, family man; **~ spirituel** father figure; **le ~ Noël** Santa Claus.

perfection /pɛʀfɛksjɔ̃/ *nf* perfection.

perfectionner /pɛʀfɛksjɔne/ [1] *vt* (*technique*) perfect; (*art*) refine. ▫ **se ~** *vpr* improve; **se ~ en anglais** improve one's English.

perforer /pɛʀfɔʀe/ [1] *vt* perforate; (*billet, bande*) punch.

performance /pɛʀfɔʀmɑ̃s/ *nf* performance.

perfusion /pɛʀfysjɔ̃/ *nf* drip; **sous ~** on a drip.

péridurale /peʀidyʀal/ *nf* epidural.

péril /peʀil/ *nm* peril; **à tes risques et ~s** at your own risk.

périlleux, **-euse** /peʀijø, -z/ *a* perilous.

périmé, **~e** /peʀime/ *a* (*produit*) past its use-by date; (désuet) outdated.

période /peʀjɔd/ *nf* period.

périodique /peʀjɔdik/ *a* periodic(al). ● *nm* (journal) periodical.

péripétie /peʀipesi/ *nf* (unexpected) event, adventure.

périphérique /peʀifeʀik/ *a* peripheral. ● *nm* (**boulevard**) **~** ring road.

périple /peʀipl/ *nm* journey.

périr /peʀiʀ/ [2] *vi* perish, die.

perle /pɛʀl/ *nf* (d'huître) pearl; (de verre) bead.

permanence /pɛʀmanɑ̃s/ *nf* permanence; (Scol) study room; **de ~** on duty; **en ~** permanently; **assurer une ~** keep the office open.

permanent, **~e** /pɛʀmanɑ̃, -t/ *a* permanent; (constant) constant; **formation ~e** continuous education. **permanente** *nf* (coiffure) perm.

permettre /pɛʀmɛtʀ/ [42] *vt* allow; **~ à qn de** allow sb to. ▫ **se ~** *vpr* (*achat*) afford; **se ~ de faire** take the liberty of doing.

permis, **~e** /pɛʀmi, -z/ *a* allowed. ● *nm* licence, permit; **~ (de conduire)** driving licence.

permission /pɛʀmisjɔ̃/ *nf* permission; **en ~** (Mil) on leave.

Pérou /peʀu/ *nm* Peru.

perpendiculaire /pɛʀpɑ̃dikylɛʀ/ *a & nf* perpendicular.

perpétuité /pɛʀpetɥite/ *nf* **à ~** for life.

perplexe /pɛʀplɛks/ *a* perplexed.

perquisition /pɛʀkizisjɔ̃/ *nf* (police) search.

perron /pɛʀɔ̃/ *nm* (front) steps.

perroquet /pɛʀɔkɛ/ *nm* parrot.

perruche /peʀyʃ/ *nf* budgerigar.

perruque /peʀyk/ *nf* wig.

persécuter /pɛʀsekyte/ [1] *vt* persecute.

persévérance /pɛʀseveʀɑ̃s/ *nf* perseverance. **persévérer** [14] *vi* persevere.

persienne /pɛʀsjɛn/ *nf* (outside) shutter.

persil /pɛʀsi/ *nm* parsley.

persistance /pɛʀsistɑ̃s/ *nf* persistence. **persistant, ~e** *a* persistent; (*feuillage*) evergreen.

persister /pɛʀsiste/ [1] *vi* persist (**à faire** in doing).

personnage /pɛʀsɔnaʒ/ *nm* character; (personne célèbre) personality.

personnalité /pɛʀsɔnalite/ *nf* personality.

personne /pɛʀsɔn/ *nf* person; **~s** people. ● *pron* nobody, no-one; **je n'ai vu ~** I didn't see anybody.

personnel, ~le /pɛʀsɔnɛl/ *a* personal; (égoïste) selfish. ● *nm* staff.

perspective /pɛʀspɛktiv/ *nf* (art, point de vue) perspective; (vue) view; (éventualité) prospect.

perspicace /pɛʀspikas/ *a* shrewd. **perspicacité** *nf* shrewdness.

persuader /pɛʀsɥade/ [1] *vt* persuade (**de faire** to do).

persuasif, -ive /pɛʀsɥazif, -v/ *a* persuasive.

perte /pɛʀt/ *nf* loss; (ruine) ruin; **à ~ de vue** as far as the eye can see; **~ de** (*temps, argent*) waste of; **~ sèche** total loss; **~s** (Méd) discharge.

pertinent, ~e /pɛʀtinɑ̃, -t/ *a* pertinent.

perturbateur, -trice /pɛʀtyʀbatœʀ, -tʀis/ *nm, f* disruptive element. **perturbation** *nf* disruption. **perturber** [1] *vt* disrupt; (*personne*) perturb.

pervers, ~e /pɛʀvɛʀ, -s/ *a* (dépravé) perverted; (méchant) wicked.

pervertir /pɛʀvɛʀtiʀ/ [2] *vt* pervert.

pesant, ~e /pəzɑ̃, -t/ *a* heavy.

pesanteur /pəzɑ̃tœʀ/ *nf* heaviness; **la ~** (force) gravity.

pesée /pəze/ *nf* weighing; (effort) pressure.

pèse-personne (*pl* **~s**) /pɛzpɛʀsɔn/ *nm* (bathroom) scales.

peser /pəze/ [6] *vt/i* weigh; **~ sur** bear upon

pessimiste /pesimist/ *a* pessimistic. ● *nmf* pessimist.

peste /pɛst/ *nf* plague; (personne 🄸) pest.

pet /pɛ/ *nm* 🄸 fart 🄸.

pétale /petal/ *nm* petal.

pétard /petaʀ/ *nm* banger.

péter /pete/ [14] *vi* 🄸 fart 🄸, go bang; (casser) snap.

pétillant, ~e /petijɑ̃, -t/ *a* (*boisson*) sparkling; (*personne*) bubbly.

pétiller /petije/ [1] *vi* (*feu*) crackle; (*champagne, yeux*) sparkle; **~ d'intelligence** sparkle with intelligence.

petit, ~e /p(ə)ti, -t/ *a* small; (avec nuance affective) little; (jeune) young, small; (*défaut*) minor; (mesquin) petty; **en ~** in miniature; **~ à ~** little by little; **un ~ peu** a little bit; **~ ami** boyfriend; **~e amie** girlfriend; **~es annonces** small ads; **~e cuillère** teaspoon; **~ déjeuner** breakfast; **~ pois** garden pea. ● *nm, f* little child; (Scol) junior; **~s** (de chat) kittens; (de chien) pups. **petite-fille** (*pl* **petites-filles**) *nf* granddaughter. **petit-fils** (*pl* **petits-fils**) *nm* grandson.

pétition /petisjɔ̃/ *nf* petition.

petits-enfants /pətizɑ̃fɑ̃/ *nmpl* grandchildren.

pétrin /petʀɛ̃/ *nm* **dans le ~** 🄸 in a fix 🄸.

pétrir /petʀiʀ/ [2] *vt* knead.

pétrole /petʀɔl/ *nm* oil; **~ brut** crude oil.

pétrolier, -ière /petʀɔlje, -jɛʀ/ *a* oil. ● *nm* (navire) oil-tanker.

peu /pø/ *adv* **~ (de)** (quantité) little, not much; (nombre) few, not many; **~ intéressant** not very interesting;

P

il mange ~ he doesn't eat very much. ● *pron* few. ● *nm* little; **un** ~ (**de**) a little; **à** ~ **près** more or less; **de** ~ only just; ~ **à** ~ gradually; ~ **après/avant** shortly after/before; ~ **de chose** not much; ~ **nombreux** few; ~ **souvent** seldom; **pour** ~ **que** if.

peuple /pœpl/ *nm* people. **peupler** [1] *vt* populate.

peuplier /pøplije/ *nm* poplar.

peur /pœʀ/ *nf* fear; **avoir** ~ be afraid (**de** of); **de** ~ **de** for fear of; **faire** ~ **à** frighten. **peureux, -euse** *a* fearful.

peut /pø/ ⇒POUVOIR [49].

peut-être /pøtɛtʀ/ *adv* perhaps, maybe; ~ **qu'il viendra** he might come.

peux /pø/ ⇒POUVOIR [49].

phare /faʀ/ *nm* (tour) lighthouse; (de véhicule) headlight; ~ **antibrouillard** fog lamp.

pharmacie /faʀmasi/ *nf* (magasin) chemist's (shop), pharmacy; (science) pharmacy; (armoire) medicine cabinet. **pharmacien, ~ne** *nm, f* chemist, pharmacist.

phénomène /fenɔmɛn/ *nm* phenomenon; (personne Ⓘ) eccentric.

philosophe /filɔzɔf/ *nmf* philosopher. ● *a* philosophical. **philosophie** *nf* philosophy. **philosophique** *a* philosophical.

phobie /fɔbi/ *nf* phobia.

phonétique /fɔnetik/ *a* phonetic. ● *nf* phonetics.

phoque /fɔk/ *nm* (animal) seal.

photo /fɔto/ *nf* photo; (art) photography; **prendre en** ~ take a photo of; ~ **d'identité** passport photograph.

photocopie /fɔtɔkɔpi/ *nf* photocopy. **photocopier** [45] *vt* photocopy.

photographe /fɔtɔgʀaf/ *nmf* photographer. **photographie** *nf* photograph; (art) photography. **photographier** [45] *vt* take a photo of.

phrase /fʀɑz/ *nf* sentence.

physicien, ~ne /fizisjɛ̃, -ɛn/ *nm, f* physicist.

physique /fizik/ *a* physical. ● *nm* physique; **au** ~ physically. ● *nf* physics (+ *sg*).

piano /pjano/ *nm* piano.

pianoter /pjanɔte/ [1] *vi* tinkle; ~ **sur** (*ordinateur*) tap at.

PIB *abrév m* (**produit intérieur brut**) GDP.

pic /pik/ *nm* (outil) pickaxe; (sommet) peak; (oiseau) woodpecker; **à** ~ (*falaise*) sheer; (*couler*) straight to the bottom; **tomber à** ~ Ⓘ come just at the right time.

pichet /piʃɛ/ *nm* jug.

picorer /pikɔʀe/ [1] *vt/i* peck.

picotement /pikɔtmɑ̃/ *nm* tingling. **picoter** [1] *vt* sting; (*yeux*) sting.

pie /pi/ *nf* magpie.

pièce /pjɛs/ *nf* (d'habitation) room; (de monnaie) coin; (Théât) play; (pour raccommoder) patch; (écrit) document; (morceau) piece; ~ (**de théâtre**) play; **dix francs (la)** ~ ten francs each; ~ **détachée** part; ~ **d'identité** identity paper; **~s jointes** enclosures; (courrier électronique) attachments; **~s justificatives** written proof; ~ **montée** tiered cake; ~ **de rechange** spare part; **un deux-~s** a two-room flat.

pied /pje/ *nm* foot; (de meuble) leg; (de lampe) base; (de verre) stem; (d'appareil photo) stand; **être ~s nus** be bare-foot; **à** ~ on foot; **au** ~ **de la lettre** literally; **avoir** ~ be able to touch the bottom; **jouer au tennis comme un** ~ Ⓘ be hopeless at tennis; **mettre sur** ~ set up; **sur un** ~ **d'égalité** on an equal footing; **mettre les ~s dans le plat** [!] put one's foot in it; **c'est le ~** [!] it's great. **pied-bot** (*pl* **pieds-bots**) *nm* club-foot.

piédestal /pjedɛstal/ *nm* pedestal.

piège /pjɛʒ/ *nm* trap.

piéger /pjeʒe/ [14] [40] *vt* trap; **lettre/voiture piégée** letter/car bomb.

pierre /pjɛʀ/ *nf* stone; **~ précieuse** precious stone; **~ tombale** tombstone.

piétiner /pjetine/ [1] *vi* (avancer lentement) shuffle along; (fig) make no headway; **~ d'impatience** hop up and down with impatience. ● *vt* trample (on).

piéton /pjetɔ̃/ *nm* pedestrian.

pieu (*pl* **~x**) /pjø/ *nm* post, stake.

pieuvre /pjœvʀ/ *nf* octopus.

pieux, -ieuse /pjø, -z/ *a* pious.

pigeon /piʒɔ̃/ *nm* pigeon.

piger /piʒe/ [40] *vt/i* [!] understand, get (it).

pile /pil/ *nf* (tas) pile; (Électr) battery; **~ ou face?** heads or tails? ● *adv* (*s'arrêter* [!]) dead; **à dix heures ~** [!] at ten on the dot.

pilier /pilje/ *nm* pillar.

pillage /pijaʒ/ *nm* looting. **pillard, ~e** *nm,f* looter. **piller** [1] *vt* loot.

pilote /pilɔt/ *nm* (Aviat, Naut) pilot; (Auto) driver. ● *a* pilot. **piloter** [1] *vt* (Aviat, Naut) pilot; (Auto) drive; (fig) guide.

pilule /pilyl/ *nf* pill; **la ~** the pill.

piment /pimɑ̃/ *nm* hot pepper; (fig) spice. **pimenté, ~e** *a* spicy.

pin /pɛ̃/ *nm* pine.

pinard /pinaʀ/ *nm* [!] plonk [!], cheap wine.

pince /pɛ̃s/ *nf* (outil) pliers (+ *pl*); (levier) crowbar; (de crabe) pincer; (à sucre) tongs (+ *pl*); **~ à épiler** tweezers (+ *pl*); **~ à linge** clothes peg.

pinceau (*pl* **~x**) /pɛ̃so/ *nm* paintbrush.

pincée /pɛ̃se/ *nf* pinch (**de** of).

pincer /pɛ̃se/ [10] *vt* pinch; (attraper [!]) catch. □ **se ~** *vpr* catch oneself; **se ~ le doigt** catch one's finger.

pince-sans-rire /pɛ̃ssɑ̃ʀiʀ/ *nmf inv* **c'est un ~** he has a deadpan sense of humour.

pingouin /pɛ̃gwɛ̃/ *nm* penguin.

pingre /pɛ̃gʀ/ *a* stingy.

pintade /pɛ̃tad/ *nf* guinea fowl.

piocher /pjɔʃe/ [1] *vt/i* dig; (étudier [!]) study hard, slog away (at).

pion /pjɔ̃/ *nm* (de jeu) counter; (aux échecs) pawn; (Scol [!]) supervisor.

pipe /pip/ *nf* pipe; **fumer la ~** smoke a pipe.

piquant, ~e /pikɑ̃, -t/ *a* (*barbe*) prickly; (*goût*) pungent; (*remarque*) cutting. ● *nm* prickle.

pique /pik/ *nm* (aux cartes) spades.

pique-nique (*pl* **~s**) /piknik/ *nm* picnic.

piquer /pike/ [1] *vt* (*épine*) prick; (*épice*) burn, sting; (*abeille, ortie*) sting; (*serpent, moustique*) bite; (enfoncer) stick; (coudre) (machine-) stitch; (*curiosité*) excite; (voler [!]) pinch. ● *vi* (*avion*) dive; (*goût*) be hot. □ **se ~** *vpr* prick oneself.

piquet /pikɛ/ *nm* stake; (de tente) peg; (de parasol) pole; **~ de grève** (strike) picket.

piqûre /pikyʀ/ *nf* prick; (d'abeille) sting; (de serpent) bite; (point) stitch; (Méd) injection, jab; **faire une ~ à qn** give sb an injection.

pirate /piʀat/ *nm* pirate; **~ informatique** computer hacker; **~ de l'air** hijacker.

pire /piʀ/ *a* worse (**que** than); **les ~s mensonges** the most wicked lies. ● *nm* **le ~** the worst; **au ~** at worst.

pis /pi/ *nm* (de vache) udder. ● *a*

inv & adv worse; **aller de mal en ~** go from bad to worse.

piscine /pisin/ *nf* swimming-pool; **~ couverte** indoor swimming-pool.

pissenlit /pisɑ̃li/ *nm* dandelion.

pistache /pistaʃ/ *nf* pistachio.

piste /pist/ *nf* track; (de personne, d'animal) track, trail; (Aviat) runway; (de cirque) ring; (de ski) slope; (de danse) floor; (Sport) racetrack; **~ cyclable** cycle lane.

pistolet /pistɔlɛ/ *nm* gun, pistol; (de peintre) spray-gun.

piteux, **-euse** /pitø, -z/ *a* pitiful.

pitié /pitje/ *nf* pity; **il me fait ~** I feel sorry for him.

piton /pitɔ̃/ *nm* (à crochet) hook; (sommet pointu) peak.

pitoyable /pitwajabl/ *a* pitiful.

pitre /pitʀ/ *nm* clown; **faire le ~** clown around.

pittoresque /pitɔʀɛsk/ *a* picturesque.

pivot /pivo/ *nm* pivot. **pivoter** [1] *vi* revolve; (*personne*) swing round.

placard /plakaʀ/ *nm* cupboard; (affiche) poster. **placarder** [1] *vt* (*affiche*) post up; (*mur*) cover with posters.

place /plas/ *nf* place; (espace libre) room, space; (siège) seat, place; (prix d'un trajet) fare; (esplanade) square; (emploi) position; (de parking) space; **à la ~ de** instead of; **en ~, à sa ~** in its place; **faire ~ à** give way to; **sur ~** on the spot; **remettre qn à sa ~** put sb in his place; **ça prend de la ~** it takes up a lot of room; **se mettre à la ~ de qn** put oneself in sb's shoes *ou* place.

placement /plasmɑ̃/ *nm* (d'argent) investment.

placer /plase/ [10] *vt* place; (*invité, spectateur*) seat; (*argent*) invest. ◻ **se ~** *vpr* (*personne*) take up a position.

plafond /plafɔ̃/ *nm* ceiling.

plage /plaʒ/ *nf* beach; **~ horaire** time slot.

plagiat /plaʒja/ *nm* plagiarism.

plaider /plede/ [1] *vt/i* plead. **plaidoirie** *nf* (defence) speech. **plaidoyer** *nm* plea.

plaie /plɛ/ *nf* wound; (personne ⓘ) nuisance.

plaignant, **~e** /plɛɲɑ̃, -t/ *nm,f* plaintiff.

plaindre /plɛ̃dʀ/ [22] *vt* pity. ◻ **se ~** *vpr* complain (**de** about); **se ~ de** (souffrir de) complain of.

plaine /plɛn/ *nf* plain.

plainte /plɛ̃t/ *nf* complaint; (gémissement) groan. **plaintif**, **-ive** *a* plaintive.

plaire /plɛʀ/ [47] *vi* **~ à** please; **ça lui plaît** he likes it; **elle lui plaît** he likes her; **ça me plaît de faire** I like *ou* enjoy doing; **s'il vous plaît** please. ◻ **se ~** *vpr* **il se plaît ici** he likes it here.

plaisance /plɛzɑ̃s/ *nf* **la (navigation de) ~** boating.

plaisant, **~e** /plɛzɑ̃, -t/ *a* pleasant; (drôle) amusing.

plaisanter /plɛzɑ̃te/ [1] *vi* joke. **plaisanterie** *nf* joke. **plaisantin** *nm* joker.

plaisir /pleziʀ/ *nm* pleasure; **faire ~ à** please; **pour le ~** for fun *ou* pleasure.

plan /plɑ̃/ *nm* plan; (de ville) map; (de livre) outline; **~ d'eau** artificial lake; **premier ~** foreground.

planche /plɑ̃ʃ/ *nf* board, plank; (gravure) plate; **~ à repasser** ironing-board; **~ à voile** windsurfing board; (Sport) windsurfing.

plancher /plɑ̃ʃe/ *nm* floor.

planer /plane/ [1] *vi* glide; **~ sur** (*mystère, danger*) hang over.

planète /planɛt/ *nf* planet.

planeur /planœʀ/ *nm* (avion) glider.

planifier /planifje/ [45] *vt* plan.

plant /plɑ̃/ *nm* seedling; (de légumes) patch.

plante /plɑ̃t/ *nf* plant; ~ **d'appartement** houseplant; ~ **des pieds** sole (of the foot).

planter /plɑ̃te/ [1] *vt* (*plante*) plant; (enfoncer) drive in; (*tente*) put up; **rester planté** Ⓘ stand still, remain standing.

plaque /plak/ *nf* plate; (de marbre) slab; (insigne) badge; ~ **chauffante** hotplate; ~ **commémorative** plaque; ~ **minéralogique** numberplate; ~ **de verglas** patch of ice.

plaquer /plake/ [1] *vt* (*bois*) veneer; (aplatir) flatten; (rugby) tackle; (abandonner Ⓘ) ditch Ⓘ; **tout** ~ chuck it all.

plastique /plastik/ *a & nm* plastic; **en** ~ plastic.

plastiquer /plastike/ [1] *vt* blow up.

plat, ~**e** /pla, -t/ *a* flat. ●*nm* (Culin) dish; (partie de repas) course; (de la main) flat. ● **à plat** *adv* (*poser*) flat; (*batterie, pneu*) flat; **à** ~ **ventre** flat on one's face.

platane /platan/ *nm* plane tree.

plateau (*pl* ~**x**) /plato/ *nm* tray; (de cinéma) set; (de balance) pan; (Géog) plateau; ~ **de fromages** cheeseboard; ~ **de fruits de mer** seafood platter. **plate-bande** (*pl* **plates-bandes**) *nf* flower-bed.

platine /platin/ *nm* platinum. ●*nf* (tourne-disque) turntable; ~ **laser** compact disc player.

plâtre /plɑtʀ/ *nm* plaster; (Méd) (plaster) cast.

plein, ~**e** /plɛ̃, -ɛn/ *a* full (**de** of); (total) complete. ●*nm* **faire le** ~ **(d'essence)** fill up (the tank); **à** ~ fully; **à** ~ **temps** full-time; **en** ~ **air** in the open air; **en** ~ **milieu/visage** right in the middle/the face; **en** ~**e nuit** in the middle of the night. ●*adv* **avoir des idées** ~ **la tête** be full of ideas.

pleinement *adv* fully.

pleurer /plœʀe/ [1] *vi* cry, weep (**sur** over); (*yeux*) water. ●*vt* mourn.

pleurnicher /plœʀniʃe/ [1] *vi* Ⓘ snivel.

pleurs /plœʀ/ *nmpl* tears; **en** ~ in tears.

pleuvoir /pløvwaʀ/ [48] *vi* rain; (fig) rain *ou* shower down; **il pleut** it is raining; **il pleut à verse** *ou* **des cordes** it is pouring.

pli /pli/ *nm* fold; (de jupe) pleat; (de pantalon) crease; (lettre) letter; (habitude) habit; (**faux**) ~ crease.

pliant, ~**e** /plijɑ̃, -t/ *a* folding. ●*nm* folding stool, camp-stool.

plier /plije/ [45] *vt* fold; (courber) bend; (soumettre) submit (**à** to). ●*vi* bend. □ **se** ~ *vpr* fold; **se** ~ **à** submit to.

plinthe /plɛ̃t/ *nf* skirting-board.

plissé, ~**e** /plise/ *a* (*jupe*) pleated.

plisser /plise/ [1] *vt* crease; (*yeux*) screw up.

plomb /plɔ̃/ *nm* lead; (fusible) fuse; ~**s** (de chasse) lead shot; **de** *ou* **en** ~ lead. **plombage** *nm* filling.

plomberie /plɔ̃bʀi/ *nf* plumbing.

plombier *nm* plumber.

plongée /plɔ̃ʒe/ *nf* diving; **en** ~ (*sous-marin*) submerged.

plongeoir /plɔ̃ʒwaʀ/ *nm* diving-board.

plonger /plɔ̃ʒe/ [40] *vi* dive; (*route*) plunge. ●*vt* plunge. □ **se** ~ *vpr* plunge into; **se** ~ **dans** (fig) (*lecture*) bury oneself in.

plongeur, **-euse** *nm, f* diver; (de restaurant) dishwasher.

plu /ply/ ⇒PLAIRE [47], PLEUVOIR [48].

pluie /plɥi/ *nf* rain; (averse)

P

shower; ~ **battante/diluvienne** driving/torrential rain.

plume /plym/ *nf* feather; (pointe) nib.

plumeau (*pl* ~**x**) /plymo/ *nm* feather duster.

plumier /plymje/ *nm* pencil box.

plupart: **la** ~ /laplypaʀ/ *loc* **la** ~ **des** (*gens, cas*) most; **la** ~ **du temps** most of the time; **pour la** ~ for the most part.

pluriel, ~**le** /plyʀjɛl/ *a & nm* plural.

plus /ply, plys, plyz/

●*adverbe de comparaison*

····➤ more (**que** than); ~ **âgé/tard** older/later; ~ **beau** more beautiful; ~ **j'y pense...** the more I think about it...; **deux fois** ~ twice as much; **deux fois** ~ **cher** twice as expensive.

····➤ **le** ~ the most; **le** ~ **grand** the biggest; (de deux) the bigger.

····➤ ~ **de** (*pain*) more; (*dix jours*) more than; **il est** ~ **de 8 heures** it is after 8 o'clock.

····➤ **de** ~ more (**que** than); (en outre) moreover; **les enfants de** ~ **de 10 ans** children over 10 years old; **de** ~ **en** ~ more and more.

····➤ **en** ~ on top of that; **c'est en** ~ it's extra; **en** ~ **de** in addition to.

····➤ ~ **ou moins** more or less.

····➤ **au** ~ **tard** at the latest.

●*adverbe de négation*

····➤ **ne** ~ (*temps*) no longer, not any more; **je n'y vais** ~ I don't go there any longer *ou* any more.

····➤ **ne** ~ **de** (quantité) no more; **il n'y a** ~ **de pain** there is no more bread.

····➤ ~ **que deux jours!** only two days left!

●*préposition & nom masculin*

····➤ (maths) plus.

plusieurs /plyzjœʀ/ *a & pron* several.

plus-value (*pl* ~**s**) /plyvaly/ *nf* (bénéfice) profit.

plutôt /plyto/ *adv* rather (**que** than).

pluvieux, -ieuse /plyvjø, -z/ *a* rainy.

PME *abrév f* (**petites et moyennes entreprises**) SME.

PNB *abrév m* (**produit national brut**) GNP.

pneu (*pl* ~**s**) /pnø/ *nm* tyre. **pneumatique** *a* inflatable.

poche /pɔʃ/ *nf* pocket; (sac) bag; ~**s** (sous les yeux) bags.

pocher /pɔʃe/ [1] *vt* (*œuf*) poach.

pochette /pɔʃɛt/ *nf* (de documents) folder; (sac) bag, pouch; (d'allumettes) book; (de disque) sleeve; (mouchoir) pocket handkerchief.

poêle /pwal/ *nf* ~ (**à frire**) frying-pan. ● *nm* stove.

poème /pɔɛm/ *nm* poem. **poésie** *nf* poetry; (poème) poem. **poète** *nm* poet. **poétique** *a* poetic.

poids /pwa/ *nm* weight; ~ **coq/lourd/plume** bantam weight/heavyweight/featherweight; ~ **lourd** (camion) lorry, juggernaut; (US) truck.

poignard /pwaɲaʀ/ *nm* dagger. **poignarder** [1] *vt* stab.

poigne /pwaɲ/ *nf* **avoir de la** ~ have a strong grip.

poignée /pwaɲe/ *nf* (de porte) handle; (quantité) handful; ~ **de main** handshake.

poignet /pwaɲɛ/ *nm* wrist; (de chemise) cuff.

poil /pwal/ *nm* hair; (pelage) fur; (de brosse) bristle; ~**s** (de tapis) pile; **à** ~ 🄸 naked; ~ **à gratter**

itching powder. **poilu, ~e** *a* hairy.

poinçon /pwɛ̃sɔ̃/ *nm* awl; (marque) hallmark. **poinçonner** [1] *vt* (*billet*) punch.

poing /pwɛ̃/ *nm* fist.

point /pwɛ̃/ *nm* (endroit, Sport) point; (marque visible) spot, dot; (de couture) stitch; (pour évaluer) mark; **enlever un ~ par faute** take a mark off for each mistake; **à ~** (Culin) medium; (*arriver*) at the right time; **faire le ~** take stock; **mettre au ~** (*photo*) focus; (*technique*) develop; **mettre les choses au ~** get things clear; **Camille n'est pas encore au ~ pour ses examens** Camille is not ready for her exams; **sur le ~ de** about to; **au ~ que** to the extent that; **~ (final)** full stop, period; **deux ~s** colon; **~ d'interrogation/d'exclamation** question/exclamation mark; **~s de suspension** suspension points; **~ virgule** semicolon; **~ culminant** peak; **~ du jour** daybreak; **~ mort** (Auto) neutral; **~ de repère** landmark; **~ de suture** (Méd) stitch; **~ de vente** point of sale; **~ de vue** point of view. ● *adv* **(ne) ~** not.

pointe /pwɛ̃t/ *nf* point, tip; (clou) tack; (de grille) spike; (fig) touch **(de** of); **de ~** (*industrie*) high-tech; **en ~** pointed; **heure de ~** peak hour; **sur la ~ des pieds** on tiptoe.

pointer /pwɛ̃te/ [1] *vt* (cocher) tick off; (diriger) point, aim. ● *vi* (*employé*) (en arrivant) clock in; (en sortant) clock out. ▫ **se ~** *vpr* 🄸 turn up.

pointillé /pwɛ̃tije/ *nm* dotted line.

pointilleux, -euse /pwɛ̃tijø, -z/ *a* fastidious, particular.

pointu, ~e /pwɛ̃ty/ *a* pointed; (aiguisé) sharp.

pointure /pwɛ̃tyʀ/ *nf* size.

poire /pwaʀ/ *nf* pear.

poireau (*pl* **~x**) /pwaʀo/ *nm* leek.

poirier /pwaʀje/ *nm* pear tree.

pois /pwa/ *nm* pea; (motif) dot; **robe à ~** polka dot dress.

poison /pwazɔ̃/ *nm* poison.

poisseux, -euse /pwasø, -z/ *a* sticky.

poisson /pwasɔ̃/ *nm* fish; **~ rouge** goldfish; **~ d'avril** April fool; **les P~s** Pisces. **poissonnerie** *nf* fish shop. **poissonnier, -ière** *nm,f* fishmonger.

poitrine /pwatʀin/ *nf* chest; (seins) bosom.

poivre /pwavʀ/ *nm* pepper. **poivré, ~e** *a* peppery. **poivrière** *nf* pepper-pot.

poivron /pwavʀɔ̃/ *nm* sweet pepper.

polaire /pɔlɛʀ/ *a* polar. ● *nf* (veste) fleece.

pôle /pol/ *nm* pole.

polémique /pɔlemik/ *nf* debate. ● *a* controversial.

poli, ~e /pɔli/ *a* (*personne*) polite.

police /pɔlis/ *nf* (force) police (+ *pl*); (discipline) (law and) order; (d'assurance) policy.

policier, -ière /pɔlisje, -jɛʀ/ *a* police; (*roman*) detective. ● *nm* policeman.

polir /pɔliʀ/ [2] *vt* polish.

politesse /pɔlitɛs/ *nf* politeness; (parole) polite remark.

politicien, ~ne /pɔlitisjɛ̃, -ɛn/ *nm,f* (péj) politician.

politique /pɔlitik/ *a* political; **homme ~** politician. ● *nf* politics; (ligne de conduite) policy.

pollen /pɔlɛn/ *nm* pollen.

polluant, ~e /pɔlɥɑ̃, -t/ *a* polluting. ● *nm* pollutant.

polluer /pɔlɥe/ [1] *vt* pollute. **pollution** *nf* pollution.

polo /pɔlo/ *nm* (Sport) polo; (vêtement) polo shirt.

Pologne /pɔlɔɲ/ *nf* Poland.

polonais, **~e** /pɔlɔnɛ, -z/ *a* Polish. ● *nm* (Ling) Polish. **P~**, **~e** *nm, f* Pole.

poltron, **~ne** /pɔltʀɔ̃, -ɔn/ *a* cowardly. ● *nm, f* coward.

polygame /pɔligam/ *nmf* polygamist.

polyvalent, **~e** /pɔlivalɑ̃, -t/ *a* varied; (*personne*) versatile.

pommade /pɔmad/ *nf* ointment.

pomme /pɔm/ *nf* apple; (d'arrosoir) rose; **~ d'Adam** Adam's apple; **~ de pin** pine cone; **~ de terre** potato; **~s frites** chips; (US) French fries; **tomber dans les ~s** ⓘ pass out.

pommette /pɔmɛt/ *nf* cheekbone.

pommier /pɔmje/ *nm* apple tree.

pompe /pɔ̃p/ *nf* pump; (splendeur) pomp; **~ à incendie** fire-engine; **~s funèbres** undertaker's (+ *sg*).

pomper /pɔ̃pe/ [1] *vt* pump; (copier ⓘ) copy, crib; **~ l'air à qn** ⓘ get on sb's nerves.

pompier /pɔ̃pje/ *nm* fireman.

pomponner (**se**) /(sə)pɔ̃pɔne/ [1] *vpr* get dolled up.

poncer /pɔ̃se/ [10] *vt* sand.

ponctuation /pɔ̃ktɥasjɔ̃/ *nf* punctuation.

ponctuel, **~le** /pɔ̃ktɥɛl/ *a* punctual.

pondre /pɔ̃dʀ/ [3] *vt/i* lay.

poney /pɔnɛ/ *nm* pony.

pont /pɔ̃/ *nm* bridge; (de navire) deck; (de graissage) ramp; **faire le ~** get an extended weekend; **~ aérien** airlift. **pont-levis** (*pl* **ponts-levis**) *nm* drawbridge.

populaire /pɔpylɛʀ/ *a* popular; (*expression*) colloquial; (*quartier, origine*) working-class. **popularité** *nf* popularity.

population /pɔpylasjɔ̃/ *nf* population.

porc /pɔʀ/ *nm* pig; (viande) pork.

porcelaine /pɔʀsəlɛn/ *nf* china, porcelain.

porc-épic (*pl* **porcs-épics**) /pɔʀkepik/ *nm* porcupine.

porcherie /pɔʀʃəʀi/ *nf* pigsty.

pornographie /pɔʀnɔgʀafi/ *nf* pornography.

port /pɔʀ/ *nm* port, harbour; **à bon ~** safely; **~ maritime** seaport; (transport) carriage; (d'armes) carrying; (de barbe) wearing.

portable /pɔʀtabl/ *nm* (Ordinat) laptop (computer); (telephone) mobile (phone).

portail /pɔʀtaj/ *nm* gate.

portatif, **-ive** /pɔʀtatif, -v/ *a* portable.

porte /pɔʀt/ *nf* door; (passage) doorway; (de jardin, d'embarquement) gate; **mettre à la ~** throw out; **~ d'entrée** front door.

porté, **~e** /pɔʀte/ *a* **~ à** inclined to; **~ sur** keen on.

porte-avions /pɔʀtavjɔ̃/ *nm inv* aircraft carrier.

porte-bagages /pɔʀtbagaʒ/ *nm inv* (de vélo) carrier.

porte-bonheur /pɔʀtbɔnœʀ/ *nm inv* lucky charm.

porte-clefs /pɔʀtəkle/ *nm inv* key ring.

porte-documents /pɔʀtdɔkymɑ̃/ *nm inv* briefcase.

portée /pɔʀte/ *nf* (d'une arme) range; (de voûte) span; (d'animaux) litter; (impact) significance; (Mus) stave; **à ~ de** (**la**) **main** within (arm's) reach; **hors de ~** (**de**) out of reach (of); **à la ~ de qn** at sb's level.

porte-fenêtre (*pl* **portes-fenêtres**) /pɔʀtfənɛtʀ/ *nf* French window.

portefeuille /pɔʀtəfœj/ *nm* wallet; (de ministre) portfolio.

porte-jarretelles /pɔRtʒaRtɛl/ *nm inv* suspender belt.

portemanteau (*pl* ~**x**) /pɔRtmɑ̃to/ *nm* coat *ou* hat stand.

porte-monnaie /pɔRtmɔnɛ/ *nm inv* purse.

porte-parole /pɔRtpaRɔl/ *nm inv* spokesperson.

porter /pɔRte/ [1] *vt* carry; (*vêtement, bague*) wear; (*fruits, responsabilité, nom*) bear; (*coup*) strike; (amener) bring; (inscrire) enter. ● *vi* (*bruit*) carry; (*coup*) hit home; ~ **sur** rest on; (concerner) be about. □ **se** ~ *vpr* **bien se** ~ be *ou* feel well; **se** ~ **candidat** stand as a candidate.

porteur, **-euse** /pɔRtœR, -øz/ *nm,f* (de nouvelles) bearer; (Méd) carrier. ● *nm* (Rail) porter.

portier /pɔRtje/ *nm* doorman.

portière /pɔRtjɛR/ *nf* door.

porto /pɔRto/ *nm* port (wine).

portrait /pɔRtRɛ/ *nm* portrait.

portrait-robot (*pl* **portraits-robots**) *nm* identikit®, photofit®.

portuaire /pɔRtɥɛR/ *a* port.

portugais, ~**e** /pɔRtygɛ, -z/ *a* Portuguese. ● *nm* (Ling) Portuguese. **P**~, ~**e** *nm,f* Portuguese.

Portugal /pɔRtygal/ *nm* Portugal.

pose /poz/ *nf* installation; (attitude) pose; (Photo) exposure.

posé, ~**e** /poze/ *a* calm, serious.

poser /poze/ [1] *vt* put (down); (installer) install, put in; (*fondations*) lay; (*question*) ask; (*problème*) pose; ~ **sa candidature** apply (**à** for). ● *vi* (*modèle*) pose. □ **se** ~ *vpr* (*avion, oiseau*) land; (*regard*) fall; (se présenter) arise.

positif, **-ive** /pozitif, -v/ *a* positive.

position /pozisjɔ̃/ *nf* position; **prendre** ~ take a stand.

posologie /pozɔlɔʒi/ *nf* dosage.

posséder /pɔsede/ [14] *vt* (*propriété*) own, possess; (*diplôme*) have.

possessif, **-ive** /pɔsesif, -v/ *a* possessive.

possession /pɔsesjɔ̃/ *nf* possession; **prendre** ~ **de** take possession of.

possibilité /pɔsibilite/ *nf* possibility.

possible /pɔsibl/ *a* possible; **dès que** ~ as soon as possible; **le plus tard** ~ as late as possible. ● *nm* **le** ~ what is possible; **faire son** ~ do one's utmost.

postal, ~**e** (*mpl* **-aux**) /pɔstal, -o/ *a* postal.

poste /pɔst/ *nf* (service) post; (bureau) post office; ~ **aérienne** airmail; **mettre à la** ~ post; ~ **restante** poste restante. ● *nm* (lieu, emploi) post; (de radio, télévision) set; (téléphone) extension (number); ~ **d'essence** petrol station; ~ **d'incendie** fire point; ~ **de pilotage** cockpit; ~ **de police** police station; ~ **de secours** first-aid post.

poster[1] /pɔste/ [1] *vt* (*lettre, personne*) post.

poster[2] /pɔstɛR/ *nm* poster.

postérieur, ~**e** /pɔsteRjœR/ *a* later; (*partie*) back; ~ **à** after. ● *nm* [!] posterior.

posthume /pɔstym/ *a* posthumous.

postiche /pɔstiʃ/ *a* false.

postier, **-ière** /pɔstje, -jɛR/ *nm,f* postal worker.

post-scriptum /pɔstskRiptɔm/ *nm inv* postscript.

postuler /pɔstyle/ [1] *vt/i* apply (**à** for); (*principe*) postulate.

pot /po/ *nm* pot; (en plastique) carton; (en verre) jar; (chance [!]) luck; (boisson [!]) drink; ~ **catalytique** catalytic converter; ~ **d'échappement** exhaust pipe.

P

potable /pɔtabl/ *a* **eau ~** drinking water.

potage /pɔtaʒ/ *nm* soup.

potager, **-ère** /pɔtaʒe, -ɛʀ/ *a* vegetable. ● *nm* vegetable garden.

pot-au-feu /pɔtofø/ *nm inv* (plat) stew.

pot-de-vin (*pl* **pots-de-vin**) /podvɛ̃/ *nm* bribe.

poteau (*pl* **~x**) /pɔto/ *nm* post; (télégraphique) pole; **~ indicateur** signpost.

potelé, **~e** /pɔtle/ *a* plump.

potentiel, **~le** /pɔtɑ̃sjɛl/ *a & nm* potential.

poterie /pɔtʀi/ *nf* pottery; (objet) piece of pottery. **potier** *nm* potter.

potins /pɔtɛ̃/ *nmpl* gossip (+ *sg*).

potiron /pɔtiʀɔ̃/ *nm* pumpkin.

pou (*pl* **~x**) /pu/ *nm* louse.

poubelle /pubɛl/ *nf* dustbin.

pouce /pus/ *nm* thumb; (de pied) big toe; (mesure) inch.

poudre /pudʀ/ *nf* powder; **~ (à canon)** gunpowder; **en ~** (*lait*) powdered; (*chocolat*) drinking.

poudrier /pudʀije/ *nm* (powder) compact.

pouf /puf/ *nm* pouffe.

poulailler /pulaje/ *nm* hen house.

poulain /pulɛ̃/ *nm* foal; (protégé) protégé.

poule /pul/ *nf* hen; (Culin) fowl; (femme ✖) tart.

poulet /pulɛ/ *nm* chicken.

pouliche /puliʃ/ *nf* filly.

poulie /puli/ *nf* pulley.

pouls /pu/ *nm* pulse.

poumon /pumɔ̃/ *nm* lung.

poupe /pup/ *nf* stern.

poupée /pupe/ *nf* doll.

pour /puʀ/ *prép* for; (envers) to; (à la place de) on behalf of; (comme) as; **~ cela** for that reason; **~ cent** per cent; **~ de bon** for good; **~ faire** (in order) to do; **~ que** so that; **~ moi** (à mon avis) as for me; **trop poli ~** too polite to; **~ ce qui est de** as for; **être ~** be in favour. ● *nm inv* **le ~ et le contre** the pros and cons.

pourboire /puʀbwaʀ/ *nm* tip.

pourcentage /puʀsɑ̃taʒ/ *nm* percentage.

pourparlers /puʀpaʀle/ *nmpl* talks.

pourpre /puʀpʀ/ *a & nm* crimson; (violet) purple.

pourquoi /puʀkwa/ *conj & adv* why. ● *nm inv* **le ~ et le comment** the why and the wherefore.

pourra, **pourrait** /puʀa, puʀɛ/ ⇨POUVOIR [49].

pourri, **~e** /puʀi/ *a* rotten. **pourrir** [2] *vt/i* rot. **pourriture** *nf* rot.

poursuite /puʀsɥit/ *nf* pursuit (**de** of); **~s** (Jur) legal action (+ *sg*).

poursuivre /puʀsɥivʀ/ [57] *vt* pursue; (continuer) continue (with); **~ (en justice)** take to court; (droit civil) sue. ● *vi* continue. □ **se ~** *vpr* continue.

pourtant /puʀtɑ̃/ *adv* yet.

pourvoir /puʀvwaʀ/ [63] *vi* **~ à** provide for; **pourvu de** supplied with.

pourvu que /puʀvyk(ə)/ *conj* (condition) provided (that); (souhait) let us hope (that).

pousse /pus/ *nf* growth; (bourgeon) shoot.

poussé, **~e** /puse/ *a* (*études*) advanced; (*enquête*) thorough.

poussée /puse/ *nf* pressure; (coup) push; (de prix) upsurge; (Méd) attack.

pousser /puse/ [1] *vt* push; (*cri*) let out; (*soupir*) heave; (continuer) continue; (exhorter) urge (**à** to); (forcer) drive (**à** to). ● *vi* push;

(grandir) grow; **faire ~** (*cheveux*) let grow; (*plante*) grow. □ **se ~** *vpr* move over *ou* up; **pousse-toi!** move over!

poussette /pusɛt/ *nf* pushchair.

poussière /pusjɛʀ/ *nf* dust. **poussiéreux, -euse** *a* dusty.

poussin /pusɛ̃/ *nm* chick.

poutre /putʀ/ *nf* beam; (en métal) girder.

pouvoir /puvwaʀ/ [49] *v aux* (possibilité) can, be able; (permission, éventualité) may, can; **il peut/pouvait/pourrait venir** he can/could/might come; **je n'ai pas pu** I couldn't; **j'ai pu faire** (réussi à) I managed to do; **je n'en peux plus** I am exhausted; **il se peut que** it may be that. ● *nm* power; (gouvernement) government; **au ~** in power; **~s publics** authorities.

prairie /pʀeʀi/ *nf* meadow.

praticien, ~ne /pʀatisjɛ̃, -ɛn/ *nm,f* practitioner.

pratiquant, ~e /pʀatikɑ̃, -t/ *a* practising. ● *nm,f* churchgoer.

pratique /pʀatik/ *a* practical. ● *nf* practice; (expérience) experience; **la ~ du golf/du cheval** golfing/riding. **pratiquement** *adv* (en pratique) in practice; (presque) practically.

pratiquer /pʀatike/ [1] *vt/i* practise; (Sport) play; (faire) make.

pré /pʀe/ *nm* meadow.

préalable /pʀealabl/ *a* preliminary, prior. ● *nm* precondition; **au ~** first.

préambule /pʀeɑ̃byl/ *nm* preamble.

préavis /pʀeavi/ *nm* notice.

précaire /pʀekɛʀ/ *a* precarious. **précarité** *nf* (d'emploi) insecurity.

précaution /pʀekosjɔ̃/ *nf* (mesure) precaution; (prudence) caution.

précédent, ~e /pʀesedɑ̃, -t/ *a* previous. ● *nm* precedent.

précéder /pʀesede/ [14] *vt/i* precede.

précepteur, -trice /pʀesɛptœʀ, -tʀis/ *nm,f* (private) tutor.

prêcher /pʀeʃe/ [1] *vt/i* preach.

précieux, -ieuse /pʀesjø, -z/ *a* precious.

précipitamment /pʀesipitamɑ̃/ *adv* hastily. **précipitation** *nf* haste.

précipiter /pʀesipite/ [1] *vt* throw, precipitate; (hâter) hasten. □ **se ~** *vpr* (se dépêcher) rush (**sur** at, on to); (se jeter) throw oneself; (s'accélérer) speed up.

précis, ~e /pʀesi, -z/ *a* precise, specific; (*mécanisme*) accurate; **dix heures ~es** ten o'clock sharp. ● *nm* summary.

préciser /pʀesize/ [1] *vt* specify; **précisez votre pensée** could you be more specific. □ **se ~** *vpr* become clear(er). **précision** *nf* precision; (détail) detail.

précoce /pʀekɔs/ *a* (*enfant*) precocious.

préconiser /pʀekɔnize/ [1] *vt* advocate.

précurseur /pʀekyʀsœʀ/ *nm* forerunner.

prédicateur /pʀedikatœʀ/ *nm* preacher.

prédilection /pʀedilɛksjɔ̃/ *nf* preference.

prédire /pʀediʀ/ [37] *vt* predict.

prédominer /pʀedɔmine/ [1] *vi* predominate.

préface /pʀefas/ *nf* preface.

préfecture /pʀefɛktyʀ/ *nf* prefecture; **~ de police** police headquarters.

préféré, ~e /pʀefeʀe/ *a & nm,f* favourite.

préférence /pʀefeʀɑ̃s/ *nf* preference; **de ~** preferably.

préférentiel, ~le /pʀefeʀɑ̃sjɛl/ *a* preferential.

préférer /pʀefeʀe/ [14] *vt* prefer

P

(à to); **~ faire** prefer to do; **je ne préfère pas** I'd rather not; **j'aurais préféré ne pas savoir** I wish I hadn't found out.

préfet /pʀefɛ/ *nm* prefect; **~ de police** prefect *ou* chief of police.

préfixe /pʀefiks/ *nm* prefix.

préhistorique /pʀeistɔʀik/ *a* prehistoric.

préjudice /pʀeʒydis/ *nm* harm, prejudice; **porter ~ à** harm.

préjugé /pʀeʒyʒe/ *nm* prejudice; **être plein de ~s** be very prejudiced.

prélasser (se) /(sə)pʀelɑse/ [1] *vpr* loll (about).

prélèvement /pʀelɛvmɑ̃/ *nm* deduction; (de sang) sample. **prélever** [6] *vt* deduct (**sur** from); (*sang*) take.

préliminaire /pʀeliminɛʀ/ *a & nm* preliminary; **~s** (sexuels) foreplay.

prématuré, ~e /pʀematyʀe/ *a* premature. ● *nm* premature baby.

premier, -ière /pʀəmje, -jɛʀ/ *a* first; (*rang*) front, first; (*enfance*) early; (*nécessité, souci*) prime; (*qualité*) top, prime; **de ~ ordre** first-rate; **~ ministre** Prime Minister. ● *nm, f* first (one). ● *nm* (date) first; (étage) first floor; **en ~** first. **première** *nf* (Rail) first class; (exploit jamais vu) first; (cinéma, Théât) première; (Aut) (vitesse) first (gear). **premièrement** *adv* firstly.

prémunir /pʀemyniʀ/ [2] *vt* protect (**contre** against).

prenant, ~e /pʀənɑ̃, -t/ *a* (*activité*) engrossing; (*enfant*) demanding.

prénatal, ~e (*mpl* **~s**) /pʀenatal/ *a* antenatal.

prendre /pʀɑ̃dʀ/ [50] *vt* take; (attraper) catch, get; (acheter) get; (*repas*) have; (engager, adopter) take on; (*poids*) put on; (chercher) pick up; **qu'est-ce qui te prend?** what's the matter with you? ● *vi* (*liquide*) set; (*feu*) catch; (*vaccin*) take. □ **se ~** *vpr* **se ~ pour** think one is; **s'en ~ à** attack; (rendre responsable) blame; **s'y ~** set about (it).

preneur, -euse /pʀənœʀ, -øz/ *nm, f* buyer; **être ~** be willing to buy; **trouver ~** find a buyer.

prénom /pʀenɔ̃/ *nm* first name.

prénommer /pʀenɔme/ [1] *vt* call. □ **se ~** *vpr* be called.

préoccupation /pʀeɔkypasjɔ̃/ *nf* (souci) worry; (idée fixe) preoccupation.

préoccuper /pʀeɔkype/ [1] *vt* worry; (absorber) preoccupy. □ **se ~ de** *vpr* think about.

préparation /pʀepaʀasjɔ̃/ *nf* preparation. **préparatoire** *a* preparatory.

préparer /pʀepaʀe/ [1] *vt* prepare; (*repas, café*) make; **plats préparés** ready-cooked meals. □ **se ~** *vpr* prepare oneself (**à** for); (s'apprêter) get ready; (être proche) be brewing.

préposé, ~e /pʀepoze/ *nm, f* employee; (des postes) postman, postwoman.

préposition /pʀepozisjɔ̃/ *nf* preposition.

préretraite /pʀeʀətʀɛt/ *nf* early retirement.

près /pʀɛ/ *adv* near, close; **~ de** near (to), close to; (presque) nearly; **à cela ~** except that; **de ~** closely.

présage /pʀezaʒ/ *nm* omen.

presbyte /pʀɛsbit/ *a* long-sighted, far-sighted.

prescrire /pʀɛskʀiʀ/ [30] *vt* prescribe.

préséance /pʀeseɑ̃s/ *nf* precedence.

présence /pʀezɑ̃s/ *nf* presence; (Scol) attendance.

présent, **~e** /pʀezɑ̃, -t/ *a* present. ● *nm* (temps, cadeau) present; **à ~** now.

présentateur, **-trice** /pʀesɑ̃tatœʀ, -tʀis/ *nm, f* presenter.

présentation /pʀezɑ̃tasjɔ̃/ *nf* (de personne) introduction; (exposé) presentation.

présenter /pʀezɑ̃te/ [1] *vt* present; (*personne*) introduce (**à** to); (montrer) show. ● *vi* **~ bien** have a pleasing appearance. □ **se ~** *vpr* introduce oneself (**à** to); (aller) go; (apparaître) appear; (*candidat*) come forward; (*occasion*) arise; **se ~ à** (*examen*) sit for; (*élection*) stand for; **se ~ bien** look good.

préservatif /pʀezɛʀvatif/ *nm* condom.

préserver /pʀezɛʀve/ [1] *vt* protect.

présidence /pʀezidɑ̃s/ *nf* (d'État) presidency; (de société) chairmanship.

président, **~e** /pʀezidɑ̃, -t/ *nm, f* president; (de société, comité) chairman, chairwoman; **~-directeur général** managing director.

présidentiel, **~le** /pʀezidɑ̃sjɛl/ *a* presidential.

présider /pʀezide/ [1] *vt* preside.

présomptueux, **-euse** /pʀezɔ̃ptɥø, -z/ *a* presumptuous.

presque /pʀɛsk(ə)/ *adv* almost, nearly; **~ jamais** hardly ever; **~ rien** hardly anything; **~ pas (de)** hardly any.

presqu'île /pʀɛskil/ *nf* peninsula.

pressant, **~e** /pʀɛsɑ̃, -t/ *a* pressing, urgent.

presse /pʀɛs/ *nf* (journaux, appareil) press.

pressentiment /pʀɛsɑ̃timɑ̃/ *nm* premonition. **pressentir** [46] *vt* have a premonition of.

pressé, **~e** /pʀese/ *a* in a hurry; (*orange, citron*) freshly squeezed.

presser /pʀese/ [1] *vt* squeeze, press; (appuyer sur, harceler) press; (hâter) hasten; (inciter) urge (**de** to). ● *vi* (*temps*) press; (*affaire*) be pressing. □ **se ~** *vpr* (se hâter) hurry; (se grouper) crowd.

pressing /pʀesiŋ/ *nm* (teinturerie) dry-cleaner's.

pression /pʀɛsjɔ̃/ *nf* pressure; (bouton) press-stud.

prestance /pʀɛstɑ̃s/ *nf* (imposing) presence.

prestation /pʀɛstasjɔ̃/ *nf* allowance; (d'artiste) performance.

prestidigitation /pʀɛstidiʒitasjɔ̃/ *nf* conjuring.

prestige /pʀɛstiʒ/ *nm* prestige. **prestigieux**, **-ieuse** *a* prestigious.

présumer /pʀezyme/ [1] *vt* presume; **~ que** assume that; **~ de** overrate.

prêt, **~e** /pʀɛ, -t/ *a* ready (**à qch** for sth, **à faire** to do). ● *nm* loan. **prêt-à-porter** *nm inv* ready-to-wear clothes.

prétendre /pʀetɑ̃dʀ/ [3] *vt* claim (**que** that); (vouloir) intend; **on le prétend riche** he is said to be very rich. **prétendu**, **~e** *a* so-called. **prétendument** *adv* supposedly, allegedly.

prétentieux, **-ieuse** /pʀetɑ̃sjø, -z/ *a* pretentious.

prêter /pʀete/ [1] *vt* lend (**à** to); (*attribuer*) attribute; **~ son aide à qn** give sb some help; **~ attention** pay attention; **~ serment** take an oath. ● *vi* **~ à** lead to.

prêteur, **-euse** /pʀɛtœʀ, -øz/ *nm, f* (money-)lender; **~ sur gages** pawnbroker.

prétexte /pʀetɛkst/ *nm* pretext, excuse.

prêtre /pʀɛtʀ/ *nm* priest.

preuve /pʀœv/ *nf* proof; **des ~s**

P

evidence (+ *sg*); **faire ~ de** show; **faire ses ~s** prove oneself.

prévaloir /pʀevalwaʀ/ [60] *vi* prevail.

prévenant, **~e** /pʀevnɑ̃, -t/ *a* thoughtful.

prévenir /pʀɛvniʀ/ [58] *vt* (menacer) warn; (informer) tell; (*médecin*) call; (éviter, anticiper) prevent.

préventif, **-ive** /pʀevɑ̃tif, -v/ *a* preventive.

prévention /pʀevɑ̃sjɔ̃/ *nf* prevention; **faire de la ~** take preventive action; **~ routière** road safety.

prévenu, **~e** /pʀɛvny/ *nm, f* defendant.

prévisible /pʀevizibl/ *a* predictable. **prévision** *nf* prediction; (météorologique) forecast.

prévoir /pʀevwaʀ/ [63] *vt* foresee; (*temps*) forecast; (organiser) plan (for), provide for; (envisager) allow (for); **prévu pour** (*jouet*) designed for; **comme prévu** as planned.

prévoyance /pʀevwajɑ̃s/ *nf* foresight. **prévoyant**, **~e** *a* far-sighted.

prier /pʀije/ [45] *vi* pray. ● *vt* pray to; (demander à) ask (**de** to); **je vous en prie** please; (il n'y a pas de quoi) don't mention it.

prière /pʀijɛʀ/ *nf* prayer; (demande) request; **~ de** (vous êtes prié de) will you please.

primaire /pʀimɛʀ/ *a* primary.

prime /pʀim/ *nf* free gift; (d'employé) bonus; (subvention) subsidy; (d'assurance) premium.

primé, **~e** /pʀime/ *a* prize-winning.

primeurs /pʀimœʀ/ *nfpl* early fruit and vegetables.

primevère /pʀimvɛʀ/ *nf* primrose.

primitif, **-ive** /pʀimitif, -v/ *a* primitive; (d'origine) original. ● *nm, f* primitive.

primordial, **~e** (*mpl* **-iaux**) /pʀimɔʀdjal, -jo/ *a* essential.

prince /pʀɛ̃s/ *nm* prince. **princesse** *nf* princess. **princier**, **-ière** *a* princely.

principal, **~e** (*mpl* **-aux**) /pʀɛ̃sipal, -o/ *a* main, principal. ● *nm* headmaster; (chose) main thing.

principe /pʀɛ̃sip/ *nm* principle; **en ~** in theory; (d'habitude) as a rule.

printanier, **-ière** /pʀɛ̃tanje, -jɛʀ/ *a* spring(-like).

printemps /pʀɛ̃tɑ̃/ *nm* spring.

prioritaire /pʀijɔʀitɛʀ/ *a* priority; **être ~** have priority. **priorité** *nf* priority; (Auto) right of way.

pris, **~e** /pʀi, -z/ *a* (*place*) taken; (*personne, journée*) busy; (*nez*) stuffed up; **~ de** (*peur, fièvre*) stricken with; **~ de panique** panic-stricken. ● ⇒PRENDRE [50].

prise /pʀiz/ *nf* hold, grip; (animal attrapé) catch; (Mil) capture; **~ (de courant)** (mâle) plug; (femelle) socket; **~ multiple** multiplug adapter; **avoir ~ sur qn** have a hold over sb; **aux ~s avec** to grips with; **~ de conscience** awareness; **~ de contact** first contact, initial meeting; **~ de position** stand; **~ de sang** blood test.

prisé, **~e** /pʀize/ *a* popular.

prison /pʀizɔ̃/ *nf* prison, jail; (réclusion) imprisonment. **prisonnier**, **-ière** *nm, f* prisoner.

privation /pʀivasjɔ̃/ *nf* deprivation; (sacrifice) hardship.

privatiser /pʀivatize/ [1] *vt* privatize.

privé /pʀive/ *a* private. ● *nm* (Comm) private sector; (Scol) private schools (+ *pl*); **en ~** in private.

priver /pRive/ [1] *vt* ~ **de** deprive of. ▫ **se** ~ (**de**) *vpr* go without.

privilège /pRivilɛʒ/ *nm* privilege. **privilégié**, ~**e** *nm, f* privileged person.

prix /pRi/ *nm* price; (récompense) prize; **à tout** ~ at all costs; **au** ~ **de** (fig) at the expense of; ~ **coûtant**, ~ **de revient** cost price; **à** ~ **fixe** set price.

probabilité /pRɔbabilite/ *nf* probability. **probable** *a* probable, likely. **probablement** *adv* probably.

probant, ~**e** /pRɔbɑ̃, -t/ *a* convincing, conclusive.

problème /pRɔblɛm/ *nm* problem.

procédé /pRɔsede/ *nm* process; (manière d'agir) practice.

procéder /pRɔsede/ [14] *vi* proceed; ~ **à** carry out.

procès /pRɔsɛ/ *nm* (criminel) trial; (civil) lawsuit, proceedings (+ *pl*).

processus /pRɔsesys/ *nm* process.

procès-verbal (*pl* **procès-verbaux**) /pRɔsɛvɛRbal, -o/ *nm* minutes (+ *pl*); (contravention) ticket.

prochain, ~**e** /pRɔʃɛ̃, -ɛn/ *a* (suivant) next; (proche) imminent; (*avenir*) near. ● *nm* fellow man. **prochainement** *adv* soon.

proche /pRɔʃ/ *a* near, close; (avoisinant) neighbouring; (*parent, ami*) close; ~ **de** close *ou* near to; **de** ~ **en** ~ gradually; **dans un** ~ **avenir** in the near future; **être** ~ (imminent) be approaching. ● *nm* close relative; (ami) close friend.

Proche-Orient /pRɔʃɔRjɑ̃/ *nm* Near East.

proclamation /pRɔklamasjɔ̃/ *nf* declaration, proclamation. **proclamer** [1] *vt* declare, proclaim.

procuration /pRɔkyRasjɔ̃/ *nf* proxy.

procurer /pRɔkyRe/ [1] *vt* bring (**à** to). ▫ **se** ~ *vpr* obtain.

procureur /pRɔkyRœR/ *nm* public prosecutor.

prodige /pRɔdiʒ/ *nm* (fait) marvel; (personne) prodigy; **enfant/musicien** ~ child/musical prodigy. **prodigieux**, **-ieuse** *a* tremendous, prodigious.

prodigue /pRɔdig/ *a* wasteful; **fils** ~ prodigal son.

producteur, **-trice** /pRɔdyktœR, -tRis/ *a* producing. ● *nm, f* producer. **productif**, **-ive** *a* productive. **production** *nf* production; (*produit*) product. **productivité** *nf* productivity.

produire /pRɔdɥiR/ [17] *vt* produce. ▫ **se** ~ *vpr* (survenir) happen; (*acteur*) perform.

produit /pRɔdɥi/ *nm* product; ~**s** (de la terre) produce (+ *sg*); ~ **chimique** chemical; ~**s alimentaires** foodstuffs; ~ **de consommation** consumer goods; ~ **intérieur brut** gross domestic product; ~ **national brut** gross national product.

proéminent, ~**e** /pRɔeminɑ̃, -t/ *a* prominent.

profane /pRɔfan/ *a* secular. ● *nmf* lay person.

proférer /pRɔfeRe/ [14] *vt* utter.

professeur /pRɔfɛsœR/ *nm* teacher; (Univ) lecturer; (avec chaire) professor.

profession /pRɔfɛsjɔ̃/ *nf* occupation; ~ **libérale** profession.

professionnel, ~**le** /pRɔfɛsjɔnɛl/ *a* professional; (*école*) vocational. ● *nm, f* professional.

profil /pRɔfil/ *nm* profile.

profit /pRɔfi/ *nm* profit; **au** ~ **de** in aid of. **profitable** *a* profitable.

profiter /pRɔfite/ [1] *vi* ~ **à** benefit; ~ **de** take advantage of.

profond, ~**e** /pRɔfɔ̃, -d/ *a* deep; (*sentiment, intérêt*) profound;

P

(*causes*) underlying; **au plus ~ de** in the depths of. **profondément** *adv* deeply; (*différent, triste*) profoundly; (*dormir*) soundly. **profondeur** *nf* depth.

progéniture /pʀɔʒenityʀ/ *nf* offspring.

progiciel /pʀɔʒisjɛl/ *nm* (Ordinat) package.

programmation /pʀɔgʀamasjɔ̃/ *nf* programming.

programme /pʀɔgʀam/ *nm* programme; (Scol) (d'une matière) syllabus; (général) curriculum; (Ordinat) program. **programmer** [1] *vt* (*ordinateur, appareil*) program; (*émission*) schedule. **programmeur, -euse** *nm, f* computer programmer.

progrès /pʀɔgʀɛ/ *nm & nmpl* progress; **faire des ~** make progress. **progresser** [1] *vi* progress. **progressif, -ive** *a* progressive. **progression** *nf* progression.

prohibitif, -ive /pʀɔibitif, -v/ *a* prohibitive.

proie /pʀwa/ *nf* prey; **en ~ à** tormented by.

projecteur /pʀɔʒɛktœʀ/ *nm* floodlight; (Mil) searchlight; (cinéma) projector.

projectile /pʀɔʒɛktil/ *nm* missile.

projection /pʀɔʒɛksjɔ̃/ *nf* projection; (séance) show.

projet /pʀɔʒɛ/ *nm* plan; (ébauche) draft; **~ de loi** bill.

projeter /pʀɔʒte/ [38] *vt* (prévoir) plan (**de** to); (*film*) project, show; (jeter) hurl, project.

prolétaire /pʀɔletɛʀ/ *nmf* proletarian.

prologue /pʀɔlɔg/ *nm* prologue.

prolongation /pʀɔlɔ̃gasjɔ̃/ *nf* extension; **~s** (football) extra time.

prolonger /pʀɔlɔ̃ʒe/ [40] *vt* extend. ▫ **se ~** *vpr* go on.

promenade /pʀɔmnad/ *nf* walk; (à bicyclette, à cheval) ride; (en auto) drive, ride; **faire une ~** go for a walk.

promener /pʀɔmne/ [6] *vt* take for a walk; **~ son regard sur** cast an eye over. ▫ **se ~** *vpr* walk; (**aller**) **se ~** go for a walk. **promeneur, -euse** *nm, f* walker.

promesse /pʀɔmɛs/ *nf* promise.

prometteur, -euse /pʀɔmɛtœʀ, -øz/ *a* promising.

promettre /pʀɔmɛtʀ/ [42] *vt/i* promise. ● *vi* be promising. ▫ **se ~ de** *vpr* resolve to.

promoteur /pʀɔmɔtœʀ/ *nm* (immobilier) property developer.

promotion /pʀɔmɔsjɔ̃/ *nf* promotion; (Univ) year; (Comm) special offer.

prompt, ~e /pʀɔ̃, -t/ *a* swift.

promu, ~e /pʀɔmy/ *a* **être ~** be promoted.

prôner /pʀone/ [1] *vt* extol.

pronom /pʀɔnɔ̃/ *nm* pronoun. **pronominal, ~e** (*mpl* **-aux**) *a* pronominal.

prononcé, ~e /pʀɔnɔ̃se/ *a* strong.

prononcer /pʀɔnɔ̃se/ [10] *vt* pronounce; (*discours*) make. ▫ **se ~** *vpr* (*mot*) be pronounced; (*personne*) make a decision (**pour** in favour of). **prononciation** *nf* pronunciation.

pronostic /pʀɔnɔstik/ *nm* forecast; (Méd) prognosis.

propagande /pʀɔpagɑ̃d/ *nf* propaganda.

propager /pʀɔpaʒe/ [40] *vt* spread. ▫ **se ~** *vpr* spread.

prophète /pʀɔfɛt/ *nm* prophet. **prophétie** *nf* prophecy.

propice /pʀɔpis/ *a* favourable.

proportion /pʀɔpɔʀsjɔ̃/ *nf* proportion; (en mathématiques) ratio; **toutes ~s gardées** relatively speaking. **proportionné, ~e** *a* proportionate (**à** to).

proportionnel, **~le** *a* proportional. **proportionnellement** *adv* proportionately.

propos /pRɔpo/ *nm* intention; (sujet) subject; **à ~** at the right time; (dans un dialogue) by the way; **à ~ de** about; **à tout ~** at every possible occasion. ● *nmpl* (paroles) remarks.

proposer /pRɔpoze/ [1] *vt* suggest, propose; (offrir) offer. □ **se ~** *vpr* volunteer (**pour** to). **proposition** *nf* proposal; (affirmation) proposition; (Gram) clause.

propre /pRɔpR/ *a* (non sali) clean; (soigné) neat; (honnête) decent; (à soi) own; (*sens*) literal; **~ à** (qui convient) suited to; (spécifique) particular to. ● *nm* **mettre au ~** write out again neatly; **c'est du ~!** (ironique) well done!

proprement /pRɔpRəmɑ̃/ *adv* (avec soin) neatly; (au sens strict) strictly; **le bureau ~ dit** the office itself.

propreté /pRɔpRəte/ *nf* cleanliness.

propriétaire /pRɔpRijetɛR/ *nmf* owner; (Comm) proprietor; (qui loue) landlord, landlady.

propriété /pRɔpRijete/ *nf* property; (droit) ownership.

propulser /pRɔpylse/ [1] *vt* propel.

proroger /pRɔRɔʒe/ [40] *vt* (*contrat*) defer; (*passeport*) extend.

proscrire /pRɔskRiR/ [30] *vt* proscribe.

proscrit, **~e** /pRɔskRi, -t/ *a* proscribed. ● *nm, f* (exilé) exile.

prose /pRoz/ *nf* prose.

prospectus /pRɔspɛktys/ *nm* leaflet.

prospère /pRɔspɛR/ *a* flourishing, thriving. **prospérer** [14] *vi* thrive, prosper. **prospérité** *nf* prosperity.

prosterner (**se**) /(sə)pRɔstɛRne/ [1] *vpr* prostrate oneself; **prosterné devant** prostrate before

prostituée /pRɔstitɥe/ *nf* prostitute. **prostitution** *nf* prostitution.

protecteur, **-trice** /pRɔtɛktœR, -tRis/ *nm, f* protector. ● *a* protective.

protection /pRɔtɛksjɔ̃/ *nf* protection.

protégé, **~e** /pRɔteʒe/ *nm, f* protégé.

protéger /pRɔteʒe/ [40] *vt* protect. □ **se ~** *vpr* protect oneself.

protéine /pRɔtein/ *nf* protein.

protestant, **~e** /pRɔtɛstɑ̃, -t/ *a & nm, f* Protestant.

protestation /pRɔtɛstasjɔ̃/ *nf* protest. **protester** [1] *vt/i* protest.

protocole /pRɔtɔkɔl/ *nm* protocol.

protubérant, **~e** /pRɔtybeRɑ̃/ *a* protruding.

proue /pRu/ *nf* bow, prow.

prouesse /pRuɛs/ *nf* feat, exploit.

prouver /pRuve/ [1] *vt* prove.

provenance /pRɔvnɑ̃s/ *nf* origin; **en ~ de** from.

provençal, **~e** (*mpl* **-aux**) /pRɔvɑ̃sal, -o/ *a & nm,f* Provençal.

provenir /pRɔvniR/ [58] *vi* **~ de** come from.

proverbe /pRɔvɛRb/ *nm* proverb.

province /pRɔvɛ̃s/ *nf* province; **de ~** provincial; **la ~** the provinces (+ *pl*). **provincial**, **~e** (*mpl* **-iaux**) *a & nm, f* provincial.

proviseur /pRɔvizœR/ *nm* headmaster, principal.

provision /pRɔvizjɔ̃/ *nf* supply, store; (sur un compte) credit (balance); (acompte) deposit; **~s** (vivres) food shopping.

P

provisoire /pRɔvizwaR/ *a* provisional.

provocant, **~e** /pRɔvɔkɑ̃, -t/ *a* provocative. **provocation** *nf* provocation. **provoquer** [1] *vt* cause; (sexuellement) arouse; (défier) provoke.

proxénète /pRɔksenɛt/ *nm* pimp, procurer.

proximité /pRɔksimite/ *nf* proximity; **à ~ de** close to.

prude /pRyd/ *a* prudish.

prudemment /pRydamɑ̃/ *adv* (*conduire*) carefully; (*attendre*) cautiously. **prudence** *nf* caution. **prudent**, **~e** *a* (au volant) careful; (à agir) cautious; (sage) wise.

prune /pRyn/ *nf* plum.

pruneau (*pl* **~x**) /pRyno/ *nm* prune.

prunelle /pRynɛl/ *nf* (pupille) pupil; (fruit) sloe.

prunier /pRynje/ *nm* plum tree.

psaume /psom/ *nm* psalm.

pseudonyme /psødɔnim/ *nm* pseudonym.

psychanalyse /psikanaliz/ *nf* psychoanalysis. **psychanalyste** *nmf* psychoanalyst.

psychiatre /psikjatR/ *nmf* psychiatrist. **psychiatrie** *nf* psychiatry. **psychiatrique** *a* psychiatric.

psychique /psiʃik/ *a* mental, psychological.

psychologie /psikɔlɔʒi/ *nf* psychology. **psychologique** *a* psychological. **psychologue** *nmf* psychologist.

pu /py/ ⇒POUVOIR [49].

puant, **~e** /pɥɑ̃, -t/ *a* stinking.

pub /pyb/ *nf* ! **la ~** advertising; **une ~** an advert.

puberté /pybɛRte/ *nf* puberty.

public, **-que** /pyblik/ *a* public. ● *nm* public; (assistance) audience; (Scol) state schools (+ *pl*); **en ~** in public.

publication /pyblikasjɔ̃/ *nf* publication.

publicitaire /pyblisitɛR/ *a* publicity. **publicité** *nf* publicity, advertising; (annonce) advertisement.

publier /pyblije/ [45] *vt* publish.

publiquement /pyblikmɑ̃/ *adv* publicly.

puce /pys/ *nf* flea; (électronique) chip; **marché aux ~s** flea market.

pudeur /pydœR/ *nf* modesty.

pudibond, **~e** /pydibɔ̃, -d/ *a* prudish.

pudique /pydik/ *a* modest.

puer /pɥe/ [1] *vi* stink. ● *vt* stink of.

puéricultrice /pɥeRikyltRis/ *nf* pediatric nurse.

puéril, **~e** /pɥeRil/ *a* puerile.

puis /pɥi/ *adv* then.

puiser /pɥize/ [1] *vt* draw (**dans** from). ● *vi* **~ dans qch** dip into sth.

puisque /pɥisk(ə)/ *conj* since, as.

puissance /pɥisɑ̃s/ *nf* power; **en ~** potential.

puissant, **~e** /pyisɑ̃, -t/ *a* powerful.

puits /pɥi/ *nm* well; (de mine) shaft.

pull(-over) /pyl(ɔvɛR)/ *nm* pullover, jumper.

pulpe /pylp/ *nf* pulp.

pulsation /pylsasjɔ̃/ *nf* (heart-) beat.

pulvériser /pylveRize/ [1] *vt* pulverize; (*liquide*) spray.

punaise /pynɛz/ *nf* (insecte) bug; (clou) drawing-pin.

punch¹ /pɔ̃ʃ/ *nm* (boisson) punch.

punch² /pœnʃ/ *nm* **avoir du ~** have drive.

punir /pyniR/ [2] *vt* punish. **punition** *nf* punishment.

pupille /pypij/ *nf* (de l'œil) pupil. ● *nmf* (enfant) ward.

pupitre /pypitʀ/ *nm* (Scol) desk; **~ à musique** music stand.

pur /pyʀ/ *a* pure; (*whisky*) neat.

purée /pyʀe/ *nf* purée; (de pommes de terre) mashed potatoes (+ *pl*).

pureté /pyʀte/ *nf* purity.

purgatoire /pyʀgatwaʀ/ *nm* purgatory.

purge /pyʀʒ/ *nf* purge. **purger** [40] *vt* (Pol, Méd) purge; (*peine*: Jur) serve.

purifier /pyʀifje/ [45] *vt* purify.

puritain, ~e /pyʀitɛ̃, -ɛn/ *nm,f* puritan. ● *a* puritanical.

pur-sang /pyʀsɑ̃/ *nm inv* (cheval) thoroughbred.

pus /py/ *nm* pus.

putain /pytɛ̃/ *nf* ☒ whore.

puzzle /pœzl/ *nm* jigsaw (puzzle).

P-V *abrév m* (**procès-verbal**) ticket, traffic fine.

pyjama /piʒama/ *nm* pyjamas (+ *pl*); **un ~** a pair of pyjamas.

pylône /pilon/ *nm* pylon.

Pyrénées /piʀene/ *nfpl* **les ~** the Pyrenees.

pyromane /piʀɔman/ *nmf* arsonist.

QG *abrév m* (**quartier général**) HQ.

QI *abrév m* (**quotient intellectuel**) IQ.

qu' /k/ ⇒QUE.

quadriller /kadʀije/ [1] *vt* (*armée*) take control of; (*police*) spread one's net over; **papier quadrillé** squared paper.

quadrupède /kadʀypɛd/ *nm* quadruped.

quadruple /kadʀypl/ *a* quadruple. ● *nm* **le ~ de** four times. **quadrupler** [1] *vt/i* quadruple.

quai /ke/ *nm* (de gare) platform; (de port) quay; (de rivière) bank.

qualification /kalifikasjɔ̃/ *nf* qualification; (compétence pratique) skills (+ *pl*).

qualifié, ~e /kalifje/ *a* (diplomé) qualified; (*main-d'œuvre*) skilled.

qualifier /kalifje/ [45] *vt* qualify; (décrire) describe (**de** as). □ **se ~** *vpr* qualify (**pour** for).

qualité /kalite/ *nf* quality; (titre) occupation; (fonction) position; **en sa ~ de** in his *ou* her capacity as.

quand /kɑ̃/ *adv* when; **~ même** all the same. ● *conj* when; (toutes les fois que) whenever; **~ bien même** even if.

quant à /kɑ̃ta/ *prép* as for.

quantité /kɑ̃tite/ *nf* quantity; **une ~ de** a lot of; **des ~s (de)** masses *ou* lots (*of*).

quarantaine /kaʀɑ̃tɛn/ *nf* (Méd) quarantine; **une ~ (de)** about forty; **avoir la ~** be in one's forties.

Q

quarante /kaʀɑ̃t/ *a & nm* forty.

quart /kaʀ/ *nm* quarter; (Naut) watch; **onze heures moins le ~** quarter to eleven; **~ (de litre)** quarter litre; **~ de finale** quarter-final; **~ d'heure** quarter of an hour; **~ de tour** ninety-degree turn.

quartier /kaʀtje/ *nm* area, district; (zone ethnique) quarter; (de lune, pomme, bœuf) quarter; (d'une orange) segment; **~s** (Mil) quarters; **de ~, du ~** local; **~ général** headquarters; **avoir ~ libre** be free.

quasiment /kazimɑ̃/ *adv* almost, practically.

quatorze /katɔʀz/ *a & nm* fourteen.

quatre /katʀ(ə)/ *a & nm* four. **quatre-vingt(s)** *a & nm* eighty. **quatre-vingt-dix** *a & nm* ninety.

quatrième /katʀijɛm/ *a & nmf* fourth. ● *nf* (Auto) fourth gear.

quatuor /kwatɥɔʀ/ *nm* quartet.

que, qu' /kə, k/

qu' before vowel or mute h.

●*conjonction*

····➤ that; **je crains ~**... I'm worried that...

····➤ (souhait, volonté) **je veux ~ tu viennes** I want you to come; **~ tu viennes ou non** whether you come or not; **qu'il entre** let him come in.

····➤ (comparaison) than; **plus grand ~ toi** taller than you.

●*pronom interrogatif*

····➤ what; **~ voulez-vous manger?** what would you like to eat?

●*pronom relatif*

····➤ (personne) whom, that; **l'homme ~ j'ai rencontré** the man (whom) I met.

····➤ (chose) that, which; **le cheval ~ Nick m'a offert** the horse (which) Nick gave me.

●*adverbe*

····➤ **~ c'est joli!** it's so pretty!; **~ de monde!** what a lot of people!

Québec /kebɛk/ *nm* Quebec.

quel, quelle (*pl* **quel(le)s**) /kɛl/

●*adjectif interrogatif*

····➤ which, what; **~ auteur a écrit...?** which writer wrote...?; **~ jour sommes-nous?** what day is it today?

●*adjectif exclamatif*

····➤ what; **~ idiot!** what an idiot!; **quelle horreur!** that's horrible!

●*adjectif relatif*

····➤ **~ que soit son âge** whatever his age; **quelles que soient tes raisons** whatever your reasons; **~ que soit le gagnant** whoever the winner is.

quelconque /kɛlkɔ̃k/ *a* any, some; (banal) ordinary; (médiocre) poor, second rate.

quelque /kɛlkə/ *a* some; **~s** a few, some. ● *adv* (environ) about, some; **et ~** [!] and a bit; **~ chose** something; (dans les phrases interrogatives) anything; **~ part** somewhere; **~ peu** somewhat.

quelquefois /kɛlkəfwa/ *adv* sometimes.

quelques-uns, -unes /kɛlkəzœ̃, -yn/ *pron* some, a few.

quelqu'un /kɛlkœ̃/ *pron* someone, somebody; (dans les phrases interrogatives) anyone, anybody.

querelle /kəʀɛl/ *nf* quarrel. **quereller (se)** [1] *vpr* quarrel. **querelleur, -euse** *a* quarrelsome.

question /kɛstjɔ̃/ *nf* question; (affaire) matter, question; **poser une ~** ask a question; **en ~** in question; **il est ~ de** (cela concerne) it is about; (on parle de) there is talk of; **il n'en est pas ~** it is out of the question; **pas ~!** no way!

questionnaire /kɛstjɔnɛʀ/ *nm* questionnaire.

questionner /kɛstjɔne/ [1] *vt* question.

quête /kɛt/ *nf* (Relig) collection; (recherche) search; **en ~ de** in search of.

queue /kø/ *nf* tail; (de poêle) handle; (de fruit) stalk; (de fleur) stem; (file) queue; (US) line; (de train) rear; **faire la ~** queue (up);

(US) line up; **~ de cheval** pony-tail; **faire une ~ de poisson à qn** (Auto) cut in front of sb.

qui /ki/

● *pronom interrogatif*

····➤ (sujet) who; **~ a fait ça?** who did that?

····➤ (complément) whom; **à ~ est ce livre?** whose book is this?

● *pronom relatif*

····➤ (personne sujet) who; **c'est Isabelle qui vient d'appeler** it's Isabelle who's just called.

····➤ (autres cas) that, which; **qu'est-ce ~ te prend?** what is the matter with you?; **invite ~ tu veux** invite whoever you want; **~ que ce soit** whoever it is, anybody.

quiche /kiʃ/ *nf* quiche.

quiconque /kikɔ̃k/ *pron* whoever; (n'importe qui) anyone.

quille /kij/ *nf* (de bateau) keel; (jouet) skittle.

quincaillerie /kɛ̃kɑjʀi/ *nf* hardware; (magasin) hardware shop. **quincaillier, -ière** *nm,f* hardware dealer.

quintal (*pl* **-aux**) /kɛ̃tal, -o/ *nm* quintal, one hundred kilos.

quinte /kɛ̃t/ *nf* **~ de toux** coughing fit.

quintuple /kɛ̃typl/ *a* quintuple. ● *nm* **le ~ de** five times. **quintupler** [1] *vt/i* quintuple, increase fivefold.

quinzaine /kɛ̃zɛn/ *nf* **une ~ (de)** about fifteen.

quinze /kɛ̃z/ *a & nm inv* fifteen; **~ jours** two weeks.

quiproquo /kipʀɔko/ *nm* misunderstanding.

quittance /kitɑ̃s/ *nf* receipt.

quitte /kit/ *a* quits (**envers** with); **~ à faire** even if it means doing.

quitter /kite/ [1] *vt* leave; (*vêtement*) take off; **ne quittez pas!** hold the line, please! □ **se ~** *vpr* part.

qui-vive /kiviv/ *nm inv* **être sur le ~** be alert.

quoi /kwa/ *pron* what; (après une préposition) which; **de ~ vivre** (assez) enough to live on; **de ~ écrire** something to write with; **~ qu'il dise** whatever he says; **~ que ce soit** anything; **il n'y a pas de ~** my pleasure; **il n'y a pas de ~ s'inquiéter** there's nothing to worry about.

quoique /kwak(ə)/ *conj* although, though.

quota /kɔta/ *nm* quota.

quote-part (*pl* **quotes-parts**) /kɔtpaʀ/ *nf* share.

quotidien, ~ne /kɔtidjɛ̃, -ɛn/ *a* daily; (banal) everyday. ● *nm* daily (paper); (vie quotidienne) everyday life. **quotidiennement** *adv* daily.

rabâcher /ʀabɑʃe/ [1] *vt* keep repeating.

rabais /ʀabɛ/ *nm* reduction, discount. **rabaisser** [1] *vt* (déprécier) belittle; (réduire) reduce.

rabat-joie /ʀabajwa/ *nm inv* killjoy.

rabattre /ʀabatʀ/ [11] *vt* (*chapeau, visière*) pull down; (refermer) shut; (diminuer) reduce; (déduire) take off; (*col, drap*) turn down. □ **se ~** *vpr* (*se refermer*) close; (*véhicule*) cut back in; **se ~ sur** make do with.

rabot /Rabo/ *nm* plane.

rabougri, **~e** /RabugRi/ *a* stunted.

racaille /Rakɑj/ *nf* rabble.

raccommoder /Rakɔmɔde/ [1] *vt* mend; (*personnes* [!]) reconcile.

raccompagner /Rakɔ̃paɲe/ [1] *vt* see *ou* take back (*home*).

raccord /RakɔR/ *nm* link; (de papier peint) join; (retouche) touch-up. **raccorder** [1] *vt* connect, join.

raccourci /RakuRsi/ *nm* short cut; **en ~** in short.

raccourcir /RakuRsiR/ [2] *vt* shorten. ● *vi* get shorter.

raccrocher /RakRɔʃe/ [1] *vt* hang back up; (*passant*) grab hold of; (relier) connect; **~ le combiné** *or* **le téléphone** hang up. ● *vi* hang up. ▫ **se ~ à** *vpr* cling to; (se relier à) be connected to *ou* with.

race /Ras/ *nf* race; (animale) breed; **de ~** (*chien*) pedigree; (*cheval*) thoroughbred.

racheter /Raʃte/ [6] *vt* buy (back); (acheter encore) buy more; (*nouvel objet*) buy another; (*société*) buy out; **~ des chaussettes** buy new socks. ▫ **se ~** *vpr* make amends.

racial, **~e** (*mpl* **-iaux**) /Rasjal, -o/ *a* racial.

racine /Rasin/ *nf* root; **~ carrée/cubique** square/cube root.

racisme /Rasism/ *nm* racism. **raciste** *a & nmf* racist.

racket /Rakɛt/ *nm* racketeering.

raclée /Rɑkle/ *nf* [!] thrashing.

racler /Rɑkle/ [1] *vt* scrape. ▫ **se ~** *vpr* **se ~ la gorge** clear one's throat.

racolage /Rakɔlaʒ/ *nm* soliciting.

raconter /Rakɔ̃te/ [1] *vt* (*histoire*) tell; (*vacances*) tell about; (*vie, épisode*) describe; **~ à qn que** tell sb that, say to sb that; **qu'est-ce que tu racontes?** what are you talking about?

radar /RadaR/ *nm* radar.

radeau (*pl* **~x**) /Rado/ *nm* raft.

radiateur /RadjatœR/ *nm* radiator; (électrique) heater.

radiation /Radjasjɔ̃/ *nf* radiation.

radical, **~e** (*mpl* **-aux**) /Radikal, -o/ *a* radical. ● *nm* (*pl* **-aux**) radical.

radieux, **-ieuse** /Radjø, -z/ *a* radiant.

radin, **~e** /Radɛ̃, -in/ *a* [!] stingy [!].

radio /Radjo/ *nf* radio; **à la ~** on the radio; (radiographie) X-ray.

radioactif, **-ive** /Radjɔaktif, -v/ *a* radioactive. **radioactivité** *nf* radioactivity.

radiocassette /Radjɔkasɛt/ *nf* radio cassette player.

radiodiffuser /Radjɔdifyze/ [1] *vt* broadcast.

radiographie /RadjɔgRafi/ *nf* (photographie) X-ray.

radiomessageur /Radjɔmesaʒœr/ *nm* pager.

radis /Radi/ *nm* radish; **ne pas avoir un ~** [!] be broke.

radoter /Radɔte/ [1] *vi* [!] talk drivel.

radoucir (se) /(sə)RadusiR/ [2] *vpr* (*humeur*) improve; (*temps*) become milder.

rafale /Rafal/ *nf* (de vent) gust; (de mitraillette) burst.

raffermir /RafɛRmiR/ [2] *vt* strengthen. ▫ **se ~** *vpr* become stronger.

raffiné, **~e** /Rafine/ *a* refined. **raffinement** *nm* refinement.

raffiner /Rafine/ [1] *vt* refine. **raffinerie** *nf* refinery.

raffoler /Rafɔle/ [1] *vt* [!] **~ de** be crazy about [!].

raffut /Rafy/ *nm* [!] din.

rafle /Rɑfl/ *nf* (police) raid.

rafraîchir /RafReʃiR/ [2] *vt* cool (down); (*mur*) give a fresh coat of paint to; (*personne, mémoire*) refresh. □ **se ~** *vpr* (boire) refresh oneself; (*temps*) get cooler. **rafraîchissant**, **~e** *a* refreshing.

rafraîchissement /RafReʃismɑ̃/ *nm* (boisson) cold drink; **~s** refreshments.

ragaillardir /RagajaRdiR/ [2] *vt* [!] cheer up.

rage /Raʒ/ *nf* rage; (maladie) rabies; **faire ~** (*bataille, incendie*) rage; (*maladie*) be rife; **~ de dents** raging toothache. **rageant**, **~e** *a* infuriating.

ragots /Rago/ *nmpl* [!] gossip.

ragoût /Ragu/ *nm* stew.

raid /Rɛd/ *nm* (Mil) raid; (Sport) trek.

raide /Rɛd/ *a* stiff; (*côte*) steep; (*corde*) tight; (*cheveux*) straight. ●*adv* (monter, descendre) steeply. **raideur** *nf* stiffness; steepness.

raidir /RediR/ [2] *vt* (*corps*) tense. □ **se ~** *vpr* tense up; (*position*) harden; (*corde*) tighten.

raie /Rɛ/ *nf* (ligne) line; (bande) strip; (de cheveux) parting; (poisson) skate.

raifort /Rɛfɔr/ *nm* horseradish.

rail /Rɑj/ *nm* rail, track; **le ~** (transport) rail.

raisin /Rɛzɛ̃/ *nm* **le ~** grapes; **~ sec** raisin; **un grain de ~** a grape.

raison /Rɛzɔ̃/ *nf* reason; **à ~ de** at the rate of; **avec ~** rightly; **avoir ~** be right (**de faire** to do); **avoir ~ de qn** get the better of sb; **donner ~ à** prove right; **en ~ de** because of; **~ de plus** all the more reason; **perdre la ~** lose one's mind

raisonnable /Rɛzɔnabl/ *a* reasonable, sensible.

raisonnement /Rɛzɔnmɑ̃/ *nm* reasoning; (propositions) argument.

raisonner /Rɛzɔne/ [1] *vi* think. ●*vt* (*personne*) reason with.

rajeunir /Raʒœnir/ [2] *vt* **~ qn** make sb (look) younger; (moderniser) modernize; (Méd) rejuvenate. ●*vi* (*personne*) look younger.

rajuster /Raʒyste/ [1] *vt* straighten; (*salaires*) (re)adjust.

ralenti, **~e** /Ralɑ̃ti/ *a* slow. ●*nm* (au cinéma) slow motion; **tourner au ~** tick over, idle.

ralentir /Ralɑ̃tiR/ [2] *vt/i* slow down. □ **se ~** *vpr* slow down.

ralentisseur /Ralɑ̃tisœR/ *nm* speed ramp.

râler /Rɑle/ [1] *vi* groan; (protester [!]) moan.

rallier /Ralje/ [45] *vt* rally; (rejoindre) rejoin. □ **se ~** *vpr* rally; **se ~ à** (*avis*) come round to; (*parti*) join.

rallonge /Ralɔ̃ʒ/ *nf* (de table) leaf; (de fil électrique) extension lead. **rallonger** [40] *vt* lengthen; (*séjour, fil, table*) extend.

rallumer /Ralyme/ [1] *vt* (*feu*) relight; (*lampe*) switch on again; (ranimer: fig) revive.

rallye /Rali/ *nm* rally.

ramassage /Ramasaʒ/ *nm* (cueillette) gathering; (d'ordures) collection; **~ scolaire** school bus service.

ramasser /Ramase/ [1] *vt* pick up; (récolter) gather; (recueillir, rassembler) collect. □ **se ~** *vpr* huddle up, curl up.

rame /Ram/ *nf* (aviron) oar; (train) train.

ramener /Ramne/ [1] *vt* (rapporter, faire revenir) bring back; (reconduire) take back; **~ à** (réduire à) reduce to. □ **se ~** *vpr* [!] turn up; **se ~ à** (*problème*) come down to.

ramer /Rame/ [1] *vi* row.

ramollir /RamɔliR/ [2] *vt* soften. □ **se ~** *vpr* become soft.

R

ramoneur /ʀamɔnœʀ/ *nm* (chimney) sweep.

rampe /ʀɑ̃p/ *nf* banisters; (pente) ramp; **~ d'accès** (Auto) slip road; **~ de lancement** launching pad.

ramper /ʀɑ̃pe/ [1] *vi* crawl.

rancard /ʀɑ̃kaʀ/ *nm* ⊡ date.

rancart /ʀɑ̃kaʀ/ *nm* **mettre** *ou* **jeter au ~** ⊡ scrap.

rance /ʀɑ̃s/ *a* rancid.

rancœur /ʀɑ̃kœʀ/ *nf* resentment.

rançon /ʀɑ̃sɔ̃/ *nf* ransom. **rançonner** [1] *vt* rob, extort money from.

rancune /ʀɑ̃kyn/ *nf* grudge; **sans ~!** no hard feelings! **rancunier, -ière** *a* vindictive.

randonnée /ʀɑ̃dɔne/ *nf* walk, ramble; **la ~ à cheval** pony trekking; **faire une ~** go walking *ou* rambling.

rang /ʀɑ̃/ *nm* row; (hiérarchie, condition) rank; **se mettre en ~** line up; **au premier ~** in the first row; (fig) at the forefront; **de second ~** (péj) second-rate.

rangée /ʀɑ̃ʒe/ *nf* row.

rangement /ʀɑ̃ʒmɑ̃/ *nm* (de pièce) tidying (up); (espace) storage space.

ranger /ʀɑʒe/ [40] *vt* put away; (*chambre*) tidy (up); (disposer) place. ▫ **se ~** *vpr* (*véhicule*) park; (s'écarter) stand aside; (*conducteur*) pull over; (s'assagir) settle down; **se ~ à** (*avis*) accept.

ranimer /ʀanime/ [1] *vt* revive; (Méd) resuscitate. ▫ **se ~** *vpr* come round.

rapace /ʀapas/ *nm* bird of prey. ● *a* grasping.

rapatriement /ʀapatʀimɑ̃/ *nm* repatriation. **rapatrier** [45] *vt* repatriate.

râpe /ʀɑp/ *nf* (Culin) grater; (lime) rasp.

râpé, ~e /ʀɑpe/ *a* (*vêtement*) threadbare; (*fromage*) grated.

râper /ʀɑpe/ [1] *vt* grate; (*bois*) rasp.

rapide /ʀapid/ *a* fast, rapid. ● *nm* (train) express (train); (cours d'eau) rapids (+ *pl*). **rapidement** *adv* fast, rapidly. **rapidité** *nf* speed.

rappel /ʀapɛl/ *nm* recall; (deuxième avis) reminder; (de salaire) back pay; (Méd) booster; (de diplomate) recall; (de réservistes) call-up; (Théât) curtain call.

rappeler /ʀaple/ [38] *vt* (par téléphone) call back; (*réserviste*) call up; (*diplomate*) recall; (évoquer) recall; **~ qch à qn** remind sb of sth. ▫ **se ~** *vpr* remember, recall.

rapport /ʀapɔʀ/ *nm* connection; (compte-rendu) report; (profit) yield; **~s** (relations) relations; **en ~ avec** (accord) in keeping with; **mettre/se mettre en ~ avec** put/get in touch with; **par ~ à** (comparé à) compared with; (vis-à-vis de) with regard to; **~s (sexuels)** intercourse.

rapporter /ʀapɔʀte/ [1] *vt* (ici) bring back; (là-bas) take back, return; (*profit*) bring in; (dire, répéter) report. ● *vi* (Comm) bring in a good return; (moucharder ⊡) tell tales. ▫ **se ~ à** *vpr* relate to; **s'en ~ à** rely on.

rapporteur, -euse /ʀapɔʀtœʀ, -øz/ *nm, f* (mouchard) tell-tale. ● *nm* protractor.

rapprochement /ʀapʀɔʃmɑ̃/ *nm* reconciliation; (Pol) rapprochement; (rapport) connection; (comparaison) parallel.

rapprocher /ʀapʀɔʃe/ *vt* move closer (**de** to); (réconcilier) bring together; (comparer) compare; (*date, rendez-vous*) bring forward. ▫ **se ~** *vpr* get *ou* come closer (**de** to); (*personnes, pays*) come together; (s'apparenter) be close (**de** to).

rapt /ʀapt/ *nm* abduction.

raquette /ʀakɛt/ *nf* (de tennis) racket; (de ping-pong) bat.

rare /ʀaʀ/ *a* rare; (insuffisant) scarce. **rarement** *adv* rarely, seldom. **rareté** *nf* rarity; scarcity; (objet) rarity.

ras, ~e /ʀɑ, ʀɑz/ *adv* **coupé ~** cut short. ● *a* (*herbe, poil*) short; **à ~ de terre** very close to the ground; **en avoir ~ le bol** [!] be really fed up; **~e campagne** open country; **à ~ bord** to the brim.

raser /ʀɑze/ [1] *vt* shave; (*cheveux, barbe*) shave off; (frôler) skim; (abattre) raze; (ennuyer [!]) bore. □ **se ~** *vpr* shave.

rasoir /ʀɑzwaʀ/ *nm* razor. ● *a inv* [!] boring.

rassasier /ʀasazje/ [45] *vt* satisfy, fill up; **être rassasié de** have had enough of.

rassemblement /ʀasɑ̃bləmɑ̃/ *nm* gathering; (manifestation) rally.

rassembler /ʀasɑ̃ble/ [1] *vt* gather; (*forces, courage*) summon up; (*idées*) collect. □ **se ~** *vpr* gather.

rassis, ~e /ʀasi, -z/ *a* (*pain*) stale.

rassurer /ʀasyʀe/ [1] *vt* reassure. □ **se ~** *vpr* reassure oneself; **rassure-toi** don't worry.

rat /ʀa/ *nm* rat.

rate /ʀat/ *nf* spleen.

raté, ~e /ʀate/ *nm, f* (personne) failure. ● *nm* **avoir des ~s** (*voiture*) backfire.

râteau (*pl* **~x**) /ʀɑto/ *nm* rake.

râtelier /ʀɑtəlje/ *nm* hayrack; (dentier [!]) dentures.

rater /ʀate/ [1] *vt* (*train, rendez-vous, cible*) miss; (gâcher) make a mess of, spoil; (*examen*) fail. ● *vi* fail.

ratio /ʀasjo/ *nm* ratio.

rationaliser /ʀasjɔnalize/ [1] *vt* rationalize.

rationnel, ~le /ʀasjɔnɛl/ *a* rational.

rationnement /ʀasjɔnmɑ̃/ *nm* rationing.

ratisser /ʀatise/ [1] *vt* rake, (fouiller) comb.

rattacher /ʀataʃe/ [1] *vt* (*lacets*) tie up again; (*ceinture de sécurité, collier*) refasten; (relier) link; (incorporer) join.

rattrapage /ʀatʀapaʒ/ *nm* (Comm) adjustment; **cours de ~** remedial lesson.

rattraper /ʀatʀape/ [1] *vt* catch; (rejoindre) catch up with; (*retard, erreur*) make up for. □ **se ~** *vpr* catch up; (se dédommager) make up for it; **se ~ à** catch hold of.

rature /ʀatyʀ/ *nf* deletion.

rauque /ʀok/ *a* raucous, harsh.

ravager /ʀavaʒe/ [40] *vt* devastate, ravage.

ravages /ʀavaʒ/ *nmpl* **faire des ~** wreak havoc.

ravaler /ʀavale/ [1] *vt* (*façade*) clean; (*colère*) swallow.

ravi, ~e /ʀavi/ *a* delighted (**que** that).

ravin /ʀavɛ̃/ *nm* ravine.

ravir /ʀaviʀ/ [2] *vt* delight; **~ qch à qn** rob sb of sth.

ravissant, ~e /ʀavisɑ̃, -t/ *a* beautiful.

ravisseur, -euse /ʀavisœʀ, -øz/ *nm, f* kidnapper.

ravitaillement /ʀavitajmɑ̃/ *nm* provision of supplies (**de** to); (denrées) supplies; **~ en essence** refuelling.

ravitailler /ʀavitɑje/ [1] *vt* provide with supplies; (*avion*) refuel. □ **se ~** *vpr* stock up.

raviver /ʀavive/ [1] *vt* revive; (*feu, colère*) rekindle.

rayé, ~e /ʀeje/ *a* striped.

rayer /ʀeje/ [31] *vt* scratch; (biffer) cross out; **'~ la mention inutile'** 'delete as appropriate'.

rayon /ʀɛjɔ̃/ *nm* ray; (étagère) shelf; (de magasin) department; (de roue) spoke; (de cercle) radius; **~ d'action** range; **~ de miel** honeycomb; **~ X** X-ray; **en connaître un ~** ⓘ know one's stuff ⓘ.

rayonnement /ʀɛjɔnmɑ̃/ *nm* (éclat) radiance; (influence) influence; (radiations) radiation. **rayonner** [1] *vi* radiate; (de joie) beam; (se déplacer) tour around (*from a central point*).

rayure /ʀɛjyʀ/ *nf* scratch; (dessin) stripe; **à ~s** striped.

raz-de-marée /ʀɑdmaʀe/ *nm inv* tidal wave; **~ électoral** electoral landslide.

réacteur /ʀeaktœʀ/ *nm* jet engine; (nucléaire) reactor.

réaction /ʀeaksjɔ̃/ *nf* reaction; **~ en chaîne** chain reaction; **moteur à ~** jet engine.

réagir /ʀeaʒiʀ/ [2] *vi* react; **~ sur** have an effect on.

réalisateur, **-trice** /ʀealizatœʀ, -tʀis/ *nm,f* (au cinéma) director; (TV) producer.

réalisation /ʀealizasjɔ̃/ *nf* (de rêve) fulfilment; (œuvre) achievement; (TV, cinéma) production; **projet en ~** project in progress.

réaliser /ʀealize/ [1] *vt* carry out; (*effort, bénéfice, achat*) make; (*rêve*) fulfil; (*film*) direct; (*capital*) realize; (se rendre compte de) realize. □ **se ~** *vpr* be fulfilled.

réalisme /ʀealism/ *nm* realism.

réaliste /ʀealist/ *a* realistic. ● *nmf* realist.

réalité /ʀealite/ *nf* reality.

réanimation /ʀeanimasjɔ̃/ *nf* resuscitation; **service de ~** intensive care. **réanimer** [1] *vt* resuscitate.

réarmement /ʀeaʀməmɑ̃/ *nm* rearmament.

rébarbatif, **-ive** /ʀebaʀbatif, -v/ *a* forbidding, off-putting.

rebelle /ʀəbɛl/ *a* rebellious; (*soldat*) rebel; **~ à** resistant to. ● *nmf* rebel.

rébellion /ʀebeljɔ̃/ *nf* rebellion.

rebondir /ʀəbɔ̃diʀ/ [2] *vi* bounce; rebound; (fig) get moving again.

rebondissement /ʀəbɔ̃dismɑ̃/ *nm* (new) development.

rebord /ʀəbɔʀ/ *nm* edge; **~ de la fenêtre** window ledge *ou* sill.

rebours: **à ~** /aʀəbuʀ/ *loc* (*compter, marcher*) backwards.

rebrousse-poil: **à ~** /aʀəbʀus-pwal/ *loc* the wrong way; (fig) **prendre qn à ~** rub sb up the wrong way.

rebrousser /ʀəbʀuse/ [1] *vt* **~ chemin** turn back.

rebut /ʀəby/ *nm* **mettre** *ou* **jeter au ~** scrap.

rebutant, **~e** /ʀəbytɑ̃, -t/ *a* off-putting.

recaler /ʀəkale/ [1] *vt* ⓘ fail; **se faire ~, être recalé** fail.

recel /ʀəsɛl/ *nm* receiving. **receler** [6] *vt* (*objet volé*) receive; (cacher) conceal.

récemment /ʀesamɑ̃/ *adv* recently.

recensement /ʀəsɑ̃smɑ̃/ *nm* census; (inventaire) inventory. **recenser** [1] *vt* (*population*) take a census of; (*objets*) list.

récent, **~e** /ʀesɑ̃, -t/ *a* recent.

récépissé /ʀesepise/ *nm* receipt.

récepteur /ʀesɛptœʀ/ *nm* receiver.

réception /ʀesɛpsjɔ̃/ *nf* reception; (de courrier) receipt. **réceptionniste** *nmf* receptionist.

récession /ʀesesjɔ̃/ *nf* recession.

recette /ʀəsɛt/ *nf* (Culin) recipe; (argent) takings; **~s** (Comm) receipts.

receveur, -euse /Rəs(ə)vœR, -øz/ *nm, f* (de bus) conductor; **~ des contributions** tax collector.

recevoir /Rəs(ə)vwaR/ [52] *vt* receive, get; (*client, malade*) see; (*invités*) welcome, receive; **être reçu à un examen** pass an exam.

rechange: **de ~** /dəRəʃɑ̃ʒ/ *loc* (*roue, vêtements*) spare; (*solution*) alternative.

réchapper /Reʃape/ [1] *vt/i* **~ de** come through, survive.

recharge /RəʃaRʒ/ *nf* (de stylo) refill.

réchaud /Reʃo/ *nm* stove.

réchauffement /Reʃofmɑ̃/ *nm* (de température) rise (**de** in); **le ~ de la planète** global warming.

réchauffer /Reʃofe/ [1] *vt* warm up. □ **se ~** *vpr* warm oneself up; (*temps*) get warmer.

rêche /Rɛʃ/ *a* rough.

recherche /RəʃɛRʃ/ *nf* search (**de** for); (raffinement) meticulousness; **~(s)** (Univ) research; **~s** (enquête) investigations; **~ d'emploi** job-hunting.

recherché, ~e /RəʃɛRʃe/ *a* in great demand; (*style*) original, recherché (péj); **~ pour meurtre** wanted for murder.

rechercher /RəʃɛRʃe/ [1] *vt* search for.

rechute /Rəʃyt/ *nf* (Méd) relapse; **faire une ~** have a relapse.

récidiver /Residive/ [1] *vi* commit a second offence.

récif /Resif/ *nm* reef.

récipient /Resipjɑ̃/ *nm* container.

réciproque /ResipRɔk/ *a* mutual, reciprocal.

réciproquement /ResipRɔkmɑ̃/ *adv* each other; **et ~** and vice versa.

récit /Resi/ *nm* (compte-rendu) account, story; (histoire) story.

réciter /Resite/ [1] *vt* recite.

réclamation /Reklamasjɔ̃/ *nf* complaint; (demande) claim.

réclame /Reklam/ *nf* advertisement; **faire de la ~** advertise; **en ~** on offer.

réclamer /Reklame/ [1] *vt* call for, demand. ● *vi* complain.

reclus, ~e /Rəkly, -z/ *nm, f* recluse. ● *a* reclusive.

réclusion /Reklyzjɔ̃/ *nf* imprisonment.

récolte /Rekɔlt/ *nf* (action) harvest; (produits) crop, harvest; (fig) crop. **récolter** [1] *vt* harvest, gather; (fig) collect, get.

recommandation /Rekɔmɑ̃da-sjɔ̃/ *nf* recommendation.

recommandé /Rəkɔmɑ̃de/ *nm* registered letter; **envoyer en ~** send by registered post.

recommander /Rəkɔmɑ̃de/ [1] *vt* recommend.

recommencer /Rəkɔmɑ̃se/ [10] *vt* (reprendre) begin *ou* start again; (refaire) repeat. ● *vi* start *ou* begin again; **ne recommence pas** don't do it again.

récompense /Rekɔ̃pɑ̃s/ *nf* reward; (prix) award. **récompenser** [1] *vt* reward (**de** for).

réconcilier /Rekɔ̃silje/ [45] *vt* reconcile. □ **se ~** *vpr* become reconciled (**avec** with).

reconduire /Rəkɔ̃dɥiR/ [17] *vt* see home; (à la porte) show out; (renouveler) renew.

réconfort /Rekɔ̃fɔR/ *nm* comfort.

reconnaissance /Rekɔnɛsɑ̃s/ *nf* gratitude; (fait de reconnaître) recognition; (Mil) reconnaissance. **reconnaissant, ~e** *a* grateful (**de** for).

reconnaître /RəkɔnɛtR/ [18] *vt* recognize; (admettre) admit (**que** that); (Mil) reconnoitre; (*enfant, tort*) acknowledge. □ **se ~** *vpr*

R

(s'orienter) know where one is; (l'un l'autre) recognize each other.

reconstituer /ʀəkɔ̃stitɥe/ [1] *vt* reconstitute; (*crime*) reconstruct; (*époque*) recreate.

reconversion /ʀəkɔ̃vɛʀsjɔ̃/ *nf* (de main-d'œuvre) redeployment.

recopier /ʀəkɔpje/ [45] *vt* copy out.

record /ʀəkɔʀ/ *nm & a inv* record.

recouper /ʀəkupe/ [1] *vt* confirm. □ **se ~** *vpr* check, tally, match up.

recourbé, ~e /ʀəkuʀbe/ *a* curved; (*nez*) hooked.

recourir /ʀəkuʀiʀ/ [20] *vi* **~ à** (*expédient, violence*) resort to; (*remède, méthode*) have recourse to.

recours /ʀəkuʀ/ *nm* resort; **avoir ~ à** have recourse to, resort to; **avoir ~ à qn** turn to sb.

recouvrer /ʀəkuvʀe/ [1] *vt* recover.

recouvrir /ʀəkuvʀiʀ/ [21] *vt* cover.

récréation /ʀekʀeasjɔ̃/ *nf* recreation; (Scol) break; (US) recess.

recroqueviller (se) /(sə)ʀəkʀɔkvije/ [1] *vpr* curl up.

recrudescence /ʀəkʀydesɑ̃s/ *nf* new outbreak.

recrue /ʀəkʀy/ *nf* recruit.

recrutement /ʀəkʀytmɑ̃/ *nm* recruitment. **recruter** [1] *vt* recruit.

rectangle /ʀɛktɑ̃gl/ *nm* rectangle. **rectangulaire** *a* rectangular.

rectifier /ʀɛktifje/ [45] *vt* correct, rectify.

recto /ʀɛkto/ *nm* **au ~** on the front of the page.

reçu, ~e /ʀəsy/ *a* accepted; (*candidat*) successful. ● *nm* receipt. ● ⇨RECEVOIR [52].

recueil /ʀəkœj/ *nm* collection.

recueillement /ʀəkœjmɑ̃/ *nm* meditation.

recueillir /ʀəkœjiʀ/ [25] *vt* collect; (prendre chez soi) take in. □ **se ~** *vpr* meditate.

recul /ʀəkyl/ *nm* retreat; (éloignement) distance; (déclin) decline; **avoir un mouvement de ~** recoil; **être en ~** be on the decline; **avec le ~** with hindsight.

reculé, ~e /ʀəkyle/ *a* (*région*) remote.

reculer /ʀəkyle/ [1] *vt* move back; (*véhicule*) reverse; (différer) postpone. ● *vi* move back; (*voiture*) reverse; (*armée*) retreat; (régresser) fall; (céder) back down; **~ devant** (fig) shrink from. □ **se ~** *vpr* move back.

récupération /ʀekypeʀasjɔ̃/ *nf* (de l'organisme, de dette) recovery; (d'objets) salvage.

récupérer /ʀekypeʀe/ [14] *vt* recover; (*vieux objets*) salvage. ● *vi* recover.

récurer /ʀekyʀe/ [1] *vt* scour; **poudre à ~** scouring powder.

récuser /ʀekyze/ [1] *vt* challenge. □ **se ~** *vpr* state that one is not qualified to judge.

recyclage /ʀəsiklaʒ/ *nm* (de personnel) retraining; (de matériau) recycling.

recycler /ʀəsikle/ [1] *vt* (*personne*) retrain; (*chose*) recycle. □ **se ~** *vpr* retrain.

rédacteur, -trice /ʀedaktœʀ, -tʀis/ *nm, f* author, writer; (de journal, magazine) editor.

rédaction /ʀedaksjɔ̃/ *nf* writing; (Scol) essay, composition; (personnel) editorial staff.

redevable /ʀədvabl/ *a* **être ~ à qn de** (*argent*) owe sb; (fig) be indebted to sb for.

redevance /ʀədvɑ̃s/ *nf* (de

télévision) licence fee; (de téléphone) rental charge.

rédiger /ʀediʒe/ [40] *vt* write; (*contrat*) draw up.

redire /ʀədiʀ/ [27] *vt* repeat; **avoir** *ou* **trouver à ~ à** find fault with.

redondant, **~e** /ʀədɔ̃dɑ̃, -t/ *a* superfluous.

redonner /ʀədɔne/ [1] *vt* (rendre) give back; (donner davantage) give more; (donner de nouveau) give again.

redoubler /ʀəduble/ [1] *vt* increase; (*classe*) repeat; **~ de prudence** be even more careful. ● *vi* (Scol) repeat a year; (s'intensifier) intensify.

redoutable /ʀədutabl/ *a* formidable.

redouter /ʀədute/ [1] *vt* dread.

redressement /ʀədʀɛsmɑ̃/ *nm* (reprise) recovery; **~ judiciaire** receivership.

redresser /ʀədʀese/ [1] *vt* straighten (out *ou* up); (*situation*) right, redress; (*économie, entreprise*) turn around. □ **se ~** *vpr* (*personne*) straighten (oneself) up; (se remettre debout) stand up; (*pays, économie*) recover.

réduction /ʀedyksjɔ̃/ *nf* reduction.

réduire /ʀedɥiʀ/ [17] *vt* reduce (**à** to). □ **se ~** *vpr* be reduced *ou* cut; **se ~ à** (revenir à) come down to.

réduit, **~e** /ʀedɥi, -t/ *a* (*objet*) small-scale; (limité) limited. ● *nm* cubbyhole.

rééducation /ʀeedykasjɔ̃/ *nf* (de handicapé) rehabilitation; (Méd) physiotherapy. **rééduquer** [1] *vt* (*personne*) rehabilitate; (*membre*) restore normal movement to.

réel, **~le** /ʀeɛl/ *a* real. ● *nm* reality. **réellement** *adv* really.

réexpédier /ʀeɛkspedje/ [45] *vt* forward; (retourner) send back.

refaire /ʀəfɛʀ/ [33] *vt* do again; (*erreur, voyage*) make again; (réparer) do up, redo.

réfectoire /ʀefɛktwaʀ/ *nm* refectory.

référence /ʀefeʀɑ̃s/ *nf* reference.

référendum /ʀefeʀɛ̃dɔm/ *nm* referendum.

référer /ʀefeʀe/ [14] *vi* **en ~ à** consult. □ **se ~ à** *vpr* refer to, consult.

refermer /ʀəfɛʀme/ [1] *vt* close (again). □ **se ~** *vpr* close (again).

réfléchi, **~e** /ʀefleʃi/ *a* (*personne*) thoughtful; (*verbe*) reflexive.

réfléchir /ʀefleʃiʀ/ [2] *vi* think (**à, sur** about). ● *vt* reflect. □ **se ~** *vpr* be reflected.

reflet /ʀəflɛ/ *nm* reflection; (nuance) sheen.

refléter /ʀəflete/ [14] *vt* reflect. □ **se ~** *vpr* be reflected.

réflexe /ʀeflɛks/ *a* reflex. ● *nm* reflex; (réaction) reaction.

réflexion /ʀeflɛksjɔ̃/ *nf* (pensée) thought, reflection; (remarque) remark, comment; **à la ~** on second thoughts.

refluer /ʀəflye/ [1] *vi* flow back; (*foule*) retreat; (*inflation*) go down.

reflux /ʀəfly/ *nm* (marée) ebb, tide.

réforme /ʀefɔʀm/ *nf* reform. **réformer** [1] *vt* reform; (*soldat*) invalid out.

refouler /ʀəfule/ [1] *vt* (*larmes*) hold back; (*désir*) repress; (*souvenir*) suppress.

refrain /ʀəfʀɛ̃/ *nm* chorus; **le même ~** the same old story.

refréner /ʀəfʀene/ [14] *vt* curb, check.

réfrigérateur /ʀefʀiʒeʀatœʀ/ *nm* refrigerator.

refroidir /ʀəfʀwadiʀ/ [2] *vt/i* cool

(down). ◻ **se** ~ *vpr* (*personne, temps*) get cold. **refroidissement** *nm* cooling; (rhume) chill.

refuge /Rəfyʒ/ *nm* refuge; (chalet) mountain hut.

réfugié, ~**e** /Refyʒje/ *nm, f* refugee. **réfugier** (**se**) [45] *vpr* take refuge.

refus /Rəfy/ *nm* refusal; **ce n'est pas de** ~ ⊡ I wouldn't say no.

refuser /Rəfyze/ [1] *vt* refuse (**de** to); (*client, spectateur*) turn away; (recaler) fail; (à un poste) turn down. ◻ **se** ~ **à** *vpr* (*évidence*) reject; **se** ~ **à faire** refuse to do.

regain /Rəgɛ̃/ *nm* ~ **de** renewal *ou* revival of; (Comm) rise.

régal (*pl* ~**s**) /Regal/ *nm* treat, delight.

régaler /Regale/ [1] *vt* ~ **qn de** treat sb to. ◻ **se** ~ *vpr* (de nourriture) **je me régale** it's delicious.

regard /RəgaR/ *nm* (expression, coup d'œil) look; (vue) eye; (yeux) eyes; ~ **fixe** stare; **au** ~ **de** with regard to; **en** ~ **de** compared with.

regardant, ~**e** /RəgaRdɑ̃, -t/ *a* ~ **avec son argent** careful with money; **peu** ~ (**sur**) not fussy (about).

regarder /RəgaRde/ [1] *vt* look at; (observer) watch; (considérer) consider; (concerner) concern; ~ **fixement** stare at; ~ **à** think about, pay attention to. ● *vi* look. ◻ **se** ~ *vpr* (*soi-même*) look at oneself; (*personnes*) look at each other.

régate /Regat/ *nf* regatta.

régie /Reʒi/ *nf* ~ **d'État** public corporation; (radio, TV) control room; (au cinéma) production; (Théât) stage management.

régime /Reʒim/ *nm* (organisation) system; (Pol) regime; (Méd) diet; (de moteur) speed; (de bananes) bunch; **se mettre au** ~ go on a diet; **à ce** ~ at this rate.

régiment /Reʒimɑ̃/ *nm* regiment.

région /Reʒjɔ̃/ *nf* region. **régional**, ~**e** (*mpl* **-aux**) *a* regional.

régir /ReʒiR/ [2] *vt* govern.

régisseur /ReʒisœR/ *nm* (Théât) stage manager; ~ **de plateau** (TV) floor manager; (au cinéma) studio manager.

registre /RəʒistR/ *nm* register.

réglage /Reglaʒ/ *nm* adjustment; (de moteur) tuning.

règle /Rɛgl/ *nf* rule; (instrument) ruler; ~**s** (de femme) period; **en** ~ in order.

réglé, ~**e** /Regle/ *a* (*vie*) ordered; (arrangé) settled; (*papier*) ruled.

règlement /Rɛgləmɑ̃/ *nm* (règles) regulations; (solution) settlement; (paiement) payment. **réglementaire** *a* (*uniforme*) regulation. **réglementation** *nf* regulation, rules. **réglementer** [1] *vt* regulate, control.

régler /Regle/ [14] *vt* settle; (*machine*) adjust; (programmer) set; (*facture*) settle; (*personne*) settle up with; ~ **son compte à** ⊡ settle a score with.

réglisse /Reglis/ *nf* liquorice.

règne /Rɛɲ/ *nm* reign; (végétal, animal, minéral) kingdom.

regret /RəgRɛ/ *nm* regret; **à** ~ with regret.

regretter /RəgRete/ [1] *vt* regret; (*personne*) miss; (pour s'excuser) be sorry.

regrouper /RəgRupe/ [1] *vt* group *ou* bring together. ◻ **se** ~ *vpr* gather *ou* group together.

régularité /RegylaRite/ *nf* regularity; (de rythme, progrès) steadiness; (de surface, écriture) evenness.

régulier, **-ière** /Regylje, -jɛR/ *a* regular; (*qualité, vitesse*) steady, even; (*ligne, paysage*) even; (légal) legal; (honnête) honest.

rehausser /ʀəose/ [1] *vt* raise; (faire valoir) enhance.

rein /ʀɛ̃/ *nm* kidney; **~s** (dos) small of the back.

reine /ʀɛn/ *nf* queen.

réinsertion /ʀeɛ̃sɛʀsjɔ̃/ *nf* reintegration.

réintégrer /ʀeɛ̃tegʀe/ [14] *vt* (*lieu*) return to; (Jur) reinstate; (*personne*) reintegrate.

réitérer /ʀeiteʀe/ [14] *vt* repeat.

rejaillir /ʀəʒajiʀ/ [2] *vi* **~ sur** splash back onto; **~ sur qn** (*succès*) reflect on sb.

rejet /ʀəʒɛ/ *nm* rejection; **~s** (déchets) waste.

rejeter /ʀəʒte/ [38] *vt* throw back; (refuser) reject; (déverser) discharge; **~ une faute sur qn** shift the blame for a mistake onto sb.

rejeton /ʀəʒtɔ̃/ *nm* (enfant 🅸) offspring (*inv*).

rejoindre /ʀəʒwɛ̃dʀ/ [22] *vt* go back to, rejoin; (rattraper) catch up with; (rencontrer) join, meet up with. □ **se ~** *vpr* (*personnes*) meet up; (*routes*) join, meet.

réjoui, **~e** /ʀeʒwi/ *a* joyful.

réjouir /ʀeʒwiʀ/ [2] *vt* delight. □ **se ~** *vpr* be delighted (**de** at).

réjouissances *nfpl* festivities.

réjouissant, **~e** *a* cheering.

relâche /ʀəlɑʃ/ *nm* (repos) break, rest; **faire ~** (Théât) be closed.

relâcher /ʀəlɑʃe/ [1] *vt* slacken; (*personne*) release; (*discipline*) relax. □ **se ~** *vpr* slacken.

relais /ʀəlɛ/ *nm* (Sport) relay; (hôtel) hotel; (intermédiaire) intermediary; **prendre le ~ de** take over from.

relancer /ʀəlɑ̃se/ [10] *vt* boost, revive; (renvoyer) throw back.

relatif, **-ive** /ʀəlatif, -v/ *a* relative; **~ à** relating to.

relation /ʀəlasjɔ̃/ *nf* relationship; (ami) acquaintance; (personne puissante) connection; **~s** relations; **~s extérieures** foreign affairs; **en ~ avec qn** in touch with sb.

relativement /ʀəlativmɑ̃/ *adv* relatively; **~ à** in relation to.

relativité /ʀəlativite/ *nf* relativity.

relax /ʀelaks/ *a inv* 🅸 laid-back.

relaxer (se) /(sə)ʀəlakse/ [1] *vpr* relax.

relayer /ʀəleje/ [31] *vt* relieve; (*émission*) relay. □ **se ~** *vpr* take over from one another.

reléguer /ʀəlege/ [14] *vt* relegate.

relent /ʀəlɑ̃/ *nm* stink; (fig) whiff.

relève /ʀəlɛv/ *nf* relief; **prendre** *ou* **assurer la ~** take over (**de** from).

relevé, **~e** /ʀəlve/ *a* spicy. ● *nm* (de compteur) reading; (facture) bill; **~ bancaire**, **~ de compte** bank statement; **faire le ~ de** list.

relever /ʀəlve/ [6] *vt* pick up; (*personne tombée*) help up; (remonter) raise; (*col*) turn up; (*compteur*) read; (*défi*) accept; (relayer) relieve; (remarquer, noter) note; (*plat*) spice up; (rebâtir) rebuild; **~ de** come within the competence of; (Méd) recover from. □ **se ~** *vpr* (*personne*) get up (again); (*pays, économie*) recover.

relief /ʀəljɛf/ *nm* relief; **mettre en ~** highlight.

relier /ʀəlje/ [45] *vt* link (up) (**à** to); (*livre*) bind.

religieux, **-ieuse** /ʀəliʒjø, -z/ *a* religious. ● *nm, f* monk, nun.

religion /ʀəliʒjɔ̃/ *nf* religion.

reliure /ʀəljyʀ/ *nf* binding.

reluire /ʀəlɥiʀ/ [17] *vi* shine.

remaniement /ʀəmanimɑ̃/ *nm* revision; **~ ministériel** cabinet reshuffle.

remarquable /ʀəmaʀkabl/ *a* remarkable.

R

remarque /ʀəmaʀk/ *nf* remark; (par écrit) comment.

remarquer /ʀəmaʀke/ [1] *vt* notice; (dire) say; **faire ~** point out (**à** to); **se faire ~** draw attention to oneself; **remarque(z)** mind you.

remblai /ʀɑ̃blɛ/ *nm* embankment.

remboursement /ʀɑ̃buʀsəmɑ̃/ *nm* (d'emprunt, dette) repayment; (Comm) refund.

rembourser /ʀɑ̃buʀse/ [1] *vt* (*dette, emprunt*) repay; (*billet, frais*) refund; (*client*) give a refund to; (*ami*) pay back.

remède /ʀəmɛd/ *nm* remedy; (médicament) medicine.

remédier /ʀəmedje/ [45] *vi* **~ à** remedy.

remerciements /ʀəmɛʀsimɑ̃/ *nmpl* thanks. **remercier** [45] *vt* thank (**de** for); (licencier) dismiss.

remettre /ʀəmɛtʀ/ [42] *vt* put back; (*vêtement*) put back on; (donner) hand over; (*devoir, démission*) hand in; (faire fonctionner) switch back on; (restituer) give back; (différer) put off; (ajouter) add; (se rappeler) remember; **~ en cause** *ou* **en question** call into question. □ **se ~** *vpr* (guérir) recover; **se ~ au tennis** take up tennis again; **se ~ au travail** get back to work; **se ~ à faire** start doing again; **s'en ~ à** leave it to.

remise /ʀəmiz/ *nf* (abri) shed; (rabais) discount; (transmission) handing over; (ajournement) postponement; **~ en cause** *ou* **en question** calling into question; **~ des prix** prizegiving; **~ des médailles** medals ceremony; **~ de peine** remission.

remontant /ʀəmɔ̃tɑ̃/ *nm* tonic.

remontée /ʀəmɔ̃te/ *nf* ascent; (d'eau, de prix) rise; **~ mécanique** ski lift.

remonte-pente (*pl* **~s**) /ʀəmɔ̃tpɑ̃t/ *nm* ski tow.

remonter /ʀəmɔ̃te/ [1] *vi* go *ou* come (back) up; (*prix, niveau*) rise (again); (revenir) go back (**à** to); **~ dans le temps** go back in time. ● *vt* (*rue, escalier*) go *ou* come (back) up; (relever) raise; (*montre*) wind up; (*objet démonté*) put together again; (*personne*) buck up.

remontoir /ʀəmɔ̃twaʀ/ *nm* winder.

remords /ʀəmɔʀ/ *nm* remorse; **avoir du** *or* **des ~** feel remorse.

remorque /ʀəmɔʀk/ *nf* trailer; **en ~** on tow. **remorquer** [1] *vt* tow.

remous /ʀəmu/ *nm* eddy; (de bateau) backwash; (fig) turmoil.

rempart /ʀɑ̃paʀ/ *nm* rampart.

remplaçant, ~e /ʀɑ̃plasɑ̃, -t/ *nm, f* replacement; (joueur) reserve, substitute.

remplacement /ʀɑ̃plasmɑ̃/ *nm* replacement; **faire des ~s** do supply teaching. **remplacer** [10] *vt* replace.

rempli, ~e /ʀɑ̃pli/ *a* full (**de** of); (*journée*) busy.

remplir /ʀɑ̃pliʀ/ [2] *vt* fill (up); (*formulaire*) fill in *ou* out; (*condition*) fulfil; (*devoir, tâche, rôle*) carry out. □ **se ~** *vpr* fill (up). **remplissage** *nm* filling; (de texte) padding.

remporter /ʀɑ̃pɔʀte/ [1] *vt* take back; (*victoire*) win.

remuant, ~e /ʀəmɥɑ̃, -t/ *a* boisterous.

remue-ménage /ʀəmymenaʒ/ *nm inv* commotion, bustle.

remuer /ʀəmɥe/ [1] *vt* move; (*thé, café*) stir; (*passé*) rake up. ● *vi* move; (gigoter) fidget. □ **se ~** *vpr* move.

rémunération /ʀemyneʀasjɔ̃/ *nf* payment.

renaissance /ʀənɛsɑ̃s/ *nf* rebirth.

renard /ʀənaʀ/ *nm* fox.

renchérir /ʀɑ̃ʃeʀiʀ/ [2] *vi* (dans une vente) raise the bidding; ~ **sur** go one better than. ● *vt* increase, put up.

rencontre /ʀɑ̃kɔ̃tʀ/ *nf* meeting; (de routes) junction; (Mil) encounter; (match) match; (US) game.

rencontrer /ʀɑ̃kɔ̃tʀe/ [1] *vt* meet; (heurter) hit; (trouver) find. □ **se** ~ *vpr* meet.

rendement /ʀɑ̃dmɑ̃/ *nm* yield; (travail) output.

rendez-vous /ʀɑ̃devu/ *nm* appointment; (d'amoureux) date; (lieu) meeting-place; **prendre** ~ (**avec**) make an appointment (with).

rendormir (se) /(sə)ʀɑ̃dɔʀmiʀ/ [46] *vpr* go back to sleep.

rendre /ʀɑ̃dʀ/ [3] *vt* give back, return; (donner en retour) return; (*monnaie*) give; (*justice*) dispense; (*jugement*) pronounce; ~ **heureux/possible** make happy/ possible; (vomir [!]) vomit; ~ **compte de** report on; ~ **service** (**à**) help; ~ **visite à** visit. ● *vi* (*terres*) yield; (*activité*) be profitable. □ **se** ~ *vpr* (capituler) surrender; (aller) go (**à** to); **se** ~ **utile** make oneself useful.

rêne /ʀɛn/ *nf* rein.

renfermé, ~**e** /ʀɑ̃fɛʀme/ *a* withdrawn. ● *nm* **sentir le** ~ smell musty.

renflé, ~**e** /ʀɑ̃fle/ *a* bulging.

renforcer /ʀɑ̃fɔʀse/ [10] *vt* reinforce.

renfort /ʀɑ̃fɔʀ/ *nm* reinforcement; **à grand** ~ **de** with a great deal of.

renier /ʀənje/ [45] *vt* (*personne, œuvre*) disown; (*foi*) renounce.

renifler /ʀənifle/ [1] *vt/i* sniff.

renne /ʀɛn/ *nm* reindeer.

renom /ʀənɔ̃/ *nm* renown; (réputation) reputation. **renommé**, ~**e** *a* famous. **renommée** *nf* (célébrité) fame; (réputation) reputation.

renoncement /ʀənɔ̃smɑ̃/ *nm* renunciation.

renoncer /ʀənɔ̃se/ [10] *vi* ~ **à** (*habitude, ami*) give up, renounce; (*projet*) abandon; ~ **à faire** abandon the idea of doing.

renouer /ʀənwe/ [1] *vt* tie up (again); (*amitié*) renew; ~ **avec qn** get back in touch with sb; (après une dispute) make up with sb.

renouveau (*pl* ~**x**) /ʀənuvo/ *nm* revival.

renouveler /ʀənuvle/ [38] *vt* renew; (réitérer) repeat; (remplacer) replace. □ **se** ~ *vpr* be renewed; (*incident*) recur, happen again.

renouvellement /ʀənuvɛlmɑ̃/ *nm* renewal.

rénovation /ʀenɔvasjɔ̃/ *nf* (d'édifice) renovation; (d'institution) reform.

renseignement /ʀɑ̃sɛɲ(ə)mɑ̃/ *nm* ~(**s**) information; (**bureau des**) ~**s** information desk; (**service des**) ~**s téléphoniques** directory enquiries.

renseigner /ʀɑ̃seɲe/ [1] *vt* inform, give information to. □ **se** ~ *vpr* enquire, make enquiries, find out.

rentabilité /ʀɑ̃tabilite/ *nf* profitability. **rentable** *a* profitable.

rente /ʀɑ̃t/ *nf* (private) income; (pension) annuity. **rentier**, **-ière** *nm, f* person of private means.

rentrée /ʀɑ̃tʀe/ *nf* return; (revenu) income; **la** ~ **parlementaire** the reopening of Parliament; **la** ~ (**des classes**) the start of the new school year; **faire sa** ~ make a comeback.

rentrer /ʀɑ̃tʀe/ [1] *vi* (*aux être*) go *ou* come back home, return home; (entrer) go *ou* come in;

R

(entrer à nouveau) go *ou* come back in; (*revenu*) come in; (*élèves*) go back (to school); ~ **dans** (heurter) smash into; **tout est rentré dans l'ordre** everything is back to normal; ~ **dans ses frais** break even. ● *vt* (*aux avoir*) bring in; (*griffes*) draw in; (*vêtement*) tuck in.

renverser /Rɑ̃vɛRse/ [1] *vt* knock over *ou* down; (*piéton*) knock down; (*liquide*) upset, spill; (mettre à l'envers) turn upside down; (*gouvernement*) overthrow; (inverser) reverse. □ **se** ~ *vpr* (*véhicule*) overturn; (*verre, vase*) fall over.

renvoi /Rɑ̃vwa/ *nm* return; (d'employé) dismissal; (d'élève) expulsion; (report) postponement; (dans un livre, fichier) cross-reference; (rot) burp.

renvoyer /Rɑ̃vwaje/ [32] *vt* send back, return; (*employé*) dismiss; (*élève*) expel; (ajourner) postpone; (référer) refer; (réfléchir) reflect.

repaire /RəpɛR/ *nm* den.

répandre /Repɑ̃dR/ [3] *vt* (liquide) spill; (étendre, diffuser) spread; (*odeur*) give off. □ **se** ~ *vpr* spread; (*liquide*) spill; **se** ~ **en injures** let out a stream of abuse.

répandu, ~**e** /Repɑ̃dy/ *a* widespread.

réparateur, -trice /RepaRatœR, -tRis/ *nm* engineer. **réparation** *nf* repair; (compensation) compensation. **réparer** [1] *vt* repair, mend; (*faute*) make amends for; (remédier à) put right.

repartie /RəpaRti/ *nf* retort; **avoir de la** ~ always have a ready reply.

repartir /RəpaRtiR/ [46] *vi* start again; (*voyageur*) set off again; (s'en retourner) go back; (*secteur économique*) pick up again.

répartir /RepaRtiR/ [2] *vt* distribute; (partager) share out; (étaler) spread. **répartition** *nf* distribution.

repas /Rəpɑ/ *nm* meal.

repassage /Rəpasaʒ/ *nm* ironing.

repasser /Rəpɑse/ [1] *vi* come *ou* go back; ~ **devant qch** go past sth again. ● *vt* (*linge*) iron; (*examen*) retake, resist; (*film*) show again.

repêcher /Rəpeʃe/ [1] *vt* recover, fish out; (*candidat*) allow to pass.

repentir[1] /Rəpɑ̃tiR/ *nm* repentance.

repentir[2] **(se)** /(sə)Rəpɑ̃tiR/ [2] *vpr* (Relig) repent (**de** of); **se** ~ **de** (regretter) regret.

répercuter /RepɛRkyte/ [1] *vt* (*bruit*) send back. □ **se** ~ *vpr* echo; **se** ~ **sur** have repercussions on.

repère /RəpɛR/ *nm* mark; (jalon) marker; (événement) landmark; (référence) reference point.

repérer /RəpeRe/ [14] *vt* locate, spot. □ **se** ~ *vpr* get one's bearings.

répertoire /RepɛRtwaR/ *nm* (artistique) repertoire; (liste) directory; ~ **téléphonique** telephone directory; (personnel) telephone book. **répertorier** [45] *vt* index.

répéter /Repete/ [14] *vt* repeat; (Théât) rehearse. ● *vi* rehearse. □ **se** ~ *vpr* be repeated; (*personne*) repeat oneself.

répétition /Repetisjɔ̃/ *nf* repetition; (Théât) rehearsal.

répit /Repi/ *nm* respite, break.

replier /Rəplije/ [45] *vt* fold (up); (*ailes, jambes*) tuck in. □ **se** ~ *vpr* withdraw (**sur soi-même** into oneself).

réplique /Replik/ *nf* reply; (riposte) retort; (objection) objection; (Théât) line; (copie) replica. **répliquer** [1] *vt/i* reply; (riposter) retort; (objecter) answer back.

répondeur /Repɔ̃dœR/ *nm* answering machine.

répondre /Repɔ̃dR/ [3] *vt* (*injure, bêtise*) reply with; ~ **que** answer *ou* reply that; ~ **à** (être conforme à) answer; (*affection, sourire*) return; (*avances, appel, critique*) respond to; ~ **de** answer for. ● *vi* answer, reply; (être insolent) answer back; (réagir) respond (**à** to)

réponse /Repɔ̃s/ *nf* answer, reply; (fig) response.

report /RəpɔR/ *nm* (transcription) transfer; (renvoi) postponement.

reportage /RəpɔRtaʒ/ *nm* report; (par écrit) article.

reporter[1] /RəpɔRte/ [1] *vt* take back; (ajourner) put off; (transcrire) transfer. □ **se ~ à** *vpr* refer to.

reporter[2] /RəpɔRtɛR/ *nm* reporter.

repos /Rəpo/ *nm* rest; (paix) peace. **reposant**, **~e** *a* restful.

reposer /Rəpoze/ [1] *vt* put down again; (délasser) rest. ● *vi* rest (**sur** on); **laisser ~** (*pâte*) leave to stand. □ **se ~** *vpr* rest; **se ~ sur** rely on.

repousser /Rəpuse/ [1] *vt* push back; (écarter) push away; (dégoûter) repel; (décliner) reject; (ajourner) postpone, put back. ● *vi* grow again.

reprendre /RəpRɑ̃dR/ [50] *vt* take back; (*confiance, conscience*) regain; (*souffle*) get back; (*évadé*) recapture; (recommencer) resume; (redire) repeat; (modifier) alter; (blâmer) reprimand; **~ du pain** take some more bread; **on ne m'y reprendra pas** I won't be caught out again. ● *vi* (recommencer) resume; (*affaires*) pick up. □ **se ~** *vpr* (se ressaisir) pull oneself together; (se corriger) correct oneself.

représailles /RəpRezɑj/ *nfpl* reprisals.

représentant, **~e** /RəpRezɑ̃tɑ̃, -t/ *nm, f* representative.

représentation /RəpRezɑ̃tasjɔ̃/ *nf* representation; (Théât) performance.

représenter /RəpRezɑ̃te/ [1] *vt* represent; (figures) depict, show; (*pièce de théâtre*) perform. □ **se ~** *vpr* (s'imaginer) imagine.

répression /RepResjɔ̃/ *nf* repression; (d'élan) suppression.

réprimande /RepRimɑ̃d/ *nf* reprimand.

réprimer /RepRime/ [1] *vt* (*peuple*) repress; (*sentiment*) suppress; (*fraude*) crack down on.

reprise /RəpRiz/ *nf* resumption; (Théât) revival; (TV) repeat; (de tissu) darn, mend; (essor) recovery; (Comm) part-exchange, trade-in; **à plusieurs ~s** on several occasions.

repriser /RəpRize/ [1] *vt* darn, mend.

reproche /RəpRɔʃ/ *nm* reproach; **faire des ~s à** find fault with.

reprocher /RəpRɔʃe/ [1] *vt* **~ qch à qn** reproach *ou* criticize sb for sth.

reproducteur, **-trice** /RepRɔdyktœR, -tRis/ *a* reproductive.

reproduire /RəpRɔdɥiR/ [17] *vt* reproduce; (répéter) repeat. □ **se ~** *vpr* reproduce; (se répéter) recur.

reptile /Rɛptil/ *nm* reptile.

repu, **~e** /Rəpy/ *a* satiated, replete.

républicain, **~e** /Repyblikɛ̃, -ɛn/ *a & nm, f* republican.

république /Repyblik/ *nf* republic; **~ populaire** people's republic.

répudier /Repydje/ [45] *vt* repudiate; (*droit*) renounce.

répugnance /Repyɲɑ̃s/ *nf* repugnance; (hésitation) reluctance; **avoir de la ~ pour** loathe. **répugnant**, **~e** *a* repulsive.

R

répugner /ʀepyɲe/ [1] *vt* be repugnant to, disgust; ~ **à** (*effort, violence*) be averse to; ~ **à faire** be reluctant to do.

répulsion /ʀepylsjɔ̃/ *nf* repulsion.

réputation /ʀepytasjɔ̃/ *nf* reputation.

réputé, ~**e** /ʀepyte/ *a* renowned (**pour** for); (*école, compagnie*) reputable; ~ **pour être** reputed to be.

requérir /ʀəkeʀiʀ/ [7] *vt* require, demand.

requête /ʀəkɛt/ *nf* request; (Jur) petition.

requin /ʀəkɛ̃/ *nm* shark.

requis, ~**e** /ʀəki, -z/ *a* (exigé) required; (nécessaire) necessary.

RER *abrév m* (**réseau express régional**) *Parisian rapid transit rail system.*

rescapé, ~**e** /ʀɛskape/ *nm,f* survivor. ● *a* surviving.

rescousse /ʀɛskus/ *nf* **à la** ~ to the rescue.

réseau (*pl* ~**x**) /ʀezo/ *nm* network; ~ **local** local area network, LAN; **le** ~ **des** ~**x** (Ordinat) Internet.

réservation /ʀezɛʀvasjɔ̃/ *nf* reservation, booking.

réserve /ʀezɛʀv/ *nf* reserve; (restriction) reservation, reserve; (indienne) reservation; (entrepôt) store-room; **en** ~ in reserve; **les** ~**s** (Mil) the reserves.

réserver /ʀezɛʀve/ [1] *vt* reserve; (*place*) book, reserve. □ **se** ~ *vpr* **se** ~ **qch** save sth for oneself; **se** ~ **pour** save oneself for; **se** ~ **le droit de** reserve the right to.

réservoir /ʀezɛʀvwaʀ/ *nm* tank; (lac) reservoir.

résidence /ʀezidɑ̃s/ *nf* residence; ~ **secondaire** second home; ~ **universitaire** hall of residence.

résident, ~**e** /ʀezidɑ̃, -t/ *nm,f* resident; (étranger) foreign resident.

résider /ʀezide/ [1] *vi* reside; ~ **dans qch** (*difficulté*) lie in.

résigner (se) /(sə)ʀeziɲe/ [1] *vpr* **se** ~ **à faire** resign oneself to doing.

résilier /ʀezilje/ [45] *vt* terminate.

résine /ʀezin/ *nf* resin.

résistance /ʀezistɑ̃s/ *nf* resistance; (fil électrique) element.

résistant, ~**e** *a* tough.

résister /ʀeziste/ [1] *vi* resist; ~ **à** (*agresseur, assaut, influence, tentation*) resist; (*corrosion, chaleur*) withstand.

résolu, ~**e** /ʀezɔly/ *a* resolute; ~ **à faire** determined to do. ● ⇒RÉSOUDRE [53].

résolution /ʀezɔlysjɔ̃/ *nf* (fermeté) resolution; (d'un problème) solving.

résonner /ʀezɔne/ [1] *vi* resound.

résorber /ʀezɔʀbe/ [1] *vt* reduce. □ **se** ~ *vpr* be reduced.

résoudre /ʀezudʀ/ [53] *vt* solve; (*crise, conflit*) resolve. □ **se** ~ **à** *vpr* (se décider) resolve to; (se résigner) resign oneself to.

respect /ʀɛspɛ/ *nm* respect.

respectabilité *nf* respectability.

respecter /ʀɛspɛkte/ [1] *vt* respect; **faire** ~ (*loi, décision*) enforce.

respectueux, **-euse** /ʀɛspɛktɥø, -z/ *a* respectful; ~ **de l'environnement** environmentally friendly.

respiration /ʀɛspiʀasjɔ̃/ *nf* breathing; (haleine) breath.

respiratoire *a* respiratory, breathing.

respirer /ʀɛspiʀe/ [1] *vi* breathe; (se reposer) catch one's breath. ● *vt* breathe (in); (exprimer) radiate.

resplendir /ʀɛsplɑ̃diʀ/ [2] *vi*

shine (**de** with). **resplendissant, ~e** *a* brilliant, radiant.

responsabilité /ʀɛspɔ̃sabilite/ *nf* responsibility; (légale) liability.

responsable /ʀɛspɔ̃sabl/ *a* responsible (**de** for); **~ de** (chargé de) in charge of. ● *nmf* person in charge; (coupable) person responsible.

resquiller /ʀɛskije/ [1] *vi* [!] (dans le train) fare-dodge; (au spectacle) get in without paying; (dans la queue) jump the queue.

ressaisir (se) /(sə)ʀəseziʀ/ [2] *vpr* pull oneself together; (*équipe sportive, valeurs boursières*) make a recovery.

ressemblance /ʀəsɑ̃blɑ̃s/ *nf* resemblance.

ressemblant, ~e /ʀəsɑ̃blɑ̃, -t/ *a* **être ~** (*portrait*) be a good likeness.

ressembler /ʀəsɑ̃ble/ [1] *vi* **~ à** resemble, look like. □ **se ~** *vpr* be alike; (physiquement) look alike.

ressentiment /ʀəsɑ̃timɑ̃/ *nm* resentment.

ressentir /ʀəsɑ̃tiʀ/ [46] *vt* feel. □ **se ~ de** *vpr* feel the effects of.

resserrer /ʀəseʀe/ [1] *vt* tighten; (contracter) compress; (*vêtement*) take in. □ **se ~** *vpr* tighten; (*route*) narrow; (se regrouper) move closer together.

ressort /ʀəsɔʀ/ *nm* (objet) spring; (fig) energy; **être du ~ de** be the province of; (Jur) be within the jurisdiction of; **en dernier ~** as a last resort.

ressortir /ʀəsɔʀtiʀ/ [46] *vi* go *ou* come back out; (se voir) stand out; (*film, disque*) be re-released; **faire ~** bring out; **il ressort que** it emerges that. ● *vt* take out again; (redire) come out with again; (*disque, film*) re-release.

ressortissant, ~e /ʀəsɔʀtisɑ̃, -t/ *nm, f* national.

ressource /ʀəsuʀs/ *nf* resource; **~s** resources; **à bout de ~** at one's wits' end.

ressusciter /ʀesysite/ [1] *vi* come back to life. ● *vt* bring back to life; (fig) revive.

restant, ~e /ʀɛstɑ̃, -t/ *a* remaining. ● *nm* remainder.

restaurant /ʀɛstɔʀɑ̃/ *nm* restaurant.

restauration /ʀɛstoʀasjɔ̃/ *nf* restoration; (hôtellerie) catering.

restaurer /ʀɛstɔʀe/ [1] *vt* restore. □ **se ~** *vpr* eat.

reste /ʀɛst/ *nm* rest; (d'une soustraction) remainder; **~s** remains (**de** of); (nourriture) leftovers; **un ~ de poulet** some left-over chicken; **au ~, du ~** moreover, besides.

rester /ʀɛste/ [1] *vi* (*aux être*) stay, remain; (subsister) be left, remain; **il reste du pain** there is some bread left (over); **il me reste du pain** I have some bread left (over); **il me reste à** it remains for me to; **en ~ à** go no further than; **en ~ là** stop there.

restituer /ʀɛstitɥe/ [1] *vt* (rendre) return; (recréer) reproduce; (rétablir) reconstruct.

restreindre /ʀɛstʀɛ̃dʀ/ [22] *vt* restrict. □ **se ~** *vpr* (dans les dépenses) cut back.

résultat /ʀezylta/ *nm* result.

résulter /ʀezylte/ [1] *vi* **~ de** result from, be the result of.

résumé /ʀezyme/ *nm* summary; **en ~** in short; (pour finir) to sum up. **résumer** [1] *vt* summarize.

résurrection /ʀezyʀɛksjɔ̃/ *nf* resurrection; (renouveau) revival.

rétablir /ʀetabliʀ/ [2] *vt* restore; (*personne*) restore to health. □ **se ~** *vpr* (*ordre, silence*) be restored; (guérir) recover.

rétablissement *nm* restoration; (de malade, monnaie) recovery.

R

retard /Rətar/ *nm* lateness; (sur un programme) delay; (infériorité) backwardness; **avoir du ~** be late; (*montre*) be slow; **en ~** late; (retardé) behind; **en ~ sur l'emploi du temps** behind schedule; **rattraper** *ou* **combler son ~** catch up; **prendre du ~** fall behind.

retardataire /RətaRdatɛR/ *nmf* latecomer. ● *a* late.

retarder /RətaRde/ [1] *vt* **~ qn/qch** delay sb/sth, hold sb/sth up; (par rapport à une heure convenue) make sb/sth late; (*montre*) put back. ● *vi* (*montre*) be slow; (*personne*) be out of touch.

retenir /RətniR/ [58] *vt* hold back; (*souffle, attention, prisonnier*) hold; (*eau, chaleur*) retain, hold; (*larmes*) hold back; (garder) keep; (retarder) detain, hold up; (réserver) book; (se rappeler) remember; (déduire) deduct; (accepter) accept. ▫ **se ~** *vpr* (se contenir) restrain oneself; **se ~ à** hold on to; **se ~ de faire** stop oneself from doing.

rétention /Retɑ̃sjɔ̃/ *nf* retention.

retentir /Rətɑ̃tiR/ [2] *vi* ring out, resound; **~ sur** have an impact on. **retentissant**, **~e** *a* resounding. **retentissement** *nm* (effet) effect.

retenue /Rətny/ *nf* restraint; (somme) deduction; (Scol) detention.

réticent, **~e** /Retisɑ̃, -t/ *a* (hésitant) hesitant; (qui rechigne) reluctant; (réservé) reticent.

rétine /Retin/ *nf* retina.

retiré, **~e** /RətiRe/ *a* (*vie*) secluded; (*lieu*) remote.

retirer /RətiRe/ [1] *vt* (sortir) take out; (ôter) take off; (*argent, offre, candidature*) withdraw; (écarter) (*main, pied*) withdraw; (*billet, bagages*) collect, pick up; (*avantage*) derive; **~ à qn** take away from sb. ▫ **se ~** *vpr* withdraw, retire.

retombées /Rətɔ̃be/ *nfpl* (conséquences) effects; **~ radioactives** nuclear fall-out.

retomber /Rətɔ̃be/ [1] *vi* (faire une chute) fall again; (retourner au sol) land, come down; **~ dans** (*erreur*) fall back into.

retouche /Rətuʃ/ *nf* alteration; (de photo, tableau) retouch.

retour /RətuR/ *nm* return; **être de ~** be back (**de** from); **~ en arrière** flashback; **par ~ du courrier** by return of post; **en ~** in return.

retourner /RətuRne/ [1] *vt* (*aux avoir*) turn over; (*vêtement*) turn inside out; (*maison*) turn upside down; (*lettre, compliment*) return; (émouvoir 🅸) shake, upset. ● *vi* (*aux être*) go back, return. ▫ **se ~** *vpr* turn round; (dans son lit) twist and turn; **s'en ~** go back; **se ~ contre** turn against.

retrait /RətRɛ/ *nm* withdrawal; (des eaux) receding; **être** (**situé**) **en ~** (**de**) be set back (from).

retraite /RətRɛt/ *nf* retirement; (pension) (retirement) pension; (fuite, refuge) retreat; **mettre à la ~** pension off; **prendre sa ~** retire.

retraité, **~e** /RətRete/ *a* retired. ● *nm, f* (old-age) pensioner.

retrancher /RətRɑ̃ʃe/ [1] *vt* remove; (soustraire) deduct, subtract. ▫ **se ~** *vpr* (Mil) entrench oneself; **se ~ derrière** take refuge behind.

retransmettre /RətRɑ̃smɛtR/ [42] *vt* broadcast.

rétrécir /RetResiR/ [2] *vt* make narrower; (*vêtement*) take in. ● *vi* (*tissu*) shrink. ▫ **se ~** *vpr* (*rue*) narrow.

rétribution /RetRibysjɔ̃/ *nf* payment.

rétroactif, **-ive** /RetRɔaktif, -v/ *a* retrospective; **augmentation à effet ~** backdated pay rise.

retrousser /Rətruse/ [1] *vt* pull up; (*manche*) roll up.

retrouvailles /Rətruvɑj/ *nfpl* reunion.

retrouver /Rətruve/ [1] *vt* find (again); (rejoindre) meet (again); (*forces, calme*) regain, (*lieu*) be back in; (se rappeler) remember. □ **se ~** *vpr* find oneself (back); (se réunir) meet (again); (être présent) be found; **s'y ~** (s'orienter, comprendre) find one's way; (rentrer dans ses frais ▣) break even.

rétroviseur /RetRɔvizœR/ *nm* (Auto) (rear-view) mirror.

réunion /Reynjɔ̃/ *nf* meeting; (rencontre) gathering; (après une séparation) réunion; (d'objets) collection.

réunir /ReyniR/ [2] *vt* gather, collect; (rapprocher) bring together; (convoquer) call together; (raccorder) join; (*qualités*) combine. □ **se ~** *vpr* meet.

réussi, ~e /Reysi/ *a* successful.

réussir /ReysiR/ [2] *vi* succeed, be successful; **~ à faire** succeed in doing, manage to do; **~ à un examen** pass an exam; **~ à qn** (*méthode*) work well for sb; (*climat, mode de vie*) agree with sb. ●*vt* (*vie*) make a success of.

réussite /Reysit/ *nf* success; (jeu) patience.

revaloir /RəvalwaR/ [60] *vt* **je vous revaudrai cela** (en mal) I'll pay you back for this; (en bien) I'll repay you some day.

revanche /Rəvɑ̃ʃ/ *nf* revenge; (Sport) return *ou* revenge match; **en ~** on the other hand.

rêvasser /Rɛvase/ [1] *vi* daydream.

rêve /Rɛv/ *nm* dream; **faire un ~** have a dream.

réveil /Revɛj/ *nm* waking up, (fig) awakening; (pendule) alarm clock.

réveillé, ~e /Reveje/ *a* awake.

réveille-matin /Revɛjmatɛ̃/ *nm inv* alarm clock.

réveiller /Reveje/ [1] *vt* wake (up); (*sentiment, souvenir*) awaken; (*curiosité*) arouse. □ **se ~** *vpr* wake up.

réveillon /Revɛjɔ̃/ *nm* (Noël) Christmas Eve; (nouvel an) New Year's Eve. **réveillonner** [1] *vi* see Christmas *ou* the New Year in.

révéler /Revele/ [14] *vt* reveal. □ **se ~** *vpr* be revealed; **se ~ facile** turn out to be easy, prove easy.

revendeur, -euse /Rəvɑ̃dœR, -øz/ *nm,f* dealer, stockist; **~ de drogue** drug dealer.

revendication /Rəvɑ̃dikasjɔ̃/ *nf* claim. **revendiquer** [1] *vt* claim.

revendre /Rəvɑ̃dR/ [3] *vt* sell (again); **avoir de l'énergie à ~** have energy to spare.

revenir /RəvniR/ [58] *vi* (*aux être*) come back, return (**à** to); **~ à** (*activité*) go back to; (se résumer à) come down to; (échoir à) fall to; **~ à 100 francs** cost 100 francs; **~ de** (*maladie, surprise*) get over; **~ sur ses pas** retrace one's steps; **faire ~** (Culin) brown; **ça me revient!** now I remember!; **je n'en reviens pas!** ▣ I can't get over it!

revenu /Rəvny/ *nm* income; (de l'État) revenue.

rêver /Reve/ [1] *vt/i* dream (**à** of; **de faire** of doing).

réverbère /RevɛRbɛR/ *nm* street lamp.

révérence /ReveRɑ̃s/ *nf* reverence; (salut d'homme) bow; (salut de femme) curtsy.

rêverie /RɛvRi/ *nf* daydream; (activité) daydreaming.

revers /RəvɛR/ *nm* reverse; (de main) back; (d'étoffe) wrong side; (de veste) lapel; (de pantalon) turn-up;

R

(de manche) cuff; (tennis) backhand; (fig) set-back.

revêtement /Rəvɛtmɑ̃/ *nm* covering; (de route) surface; ~ **de sol** floor covering. **revêtir** [61] *vt* cover; (*habit*) put on; (prendre, avoir) assume.

rêveur, -euse /RɛvœR, -øz/ *a* dreamy. ● *nm, f* dreamer.

réviser /Revize/ [1] *vt* revise; (*machine, véhicule*) service. **révision** *nf* revision; service.

revivre /RəvivR/ [62] *vi* come alive again. ● *vt* relive.

révocation /Revɔkasjɔ̃/ *nf* repeal; (d'un fonctionnaire) dismissal.

revoir[1] /RəvwaR/ [63] *vt* see (again); (réviser) revise.

revoir[2] /RəvwaR/ *nm* **au ~** goodbye.

révolte /Revɔlt/ *nf* revolt. **révolté, ~e** *nm, f* rebel.

révolter /Revɔlte/ [1] *vt* appal, revolt. □ **se ~** *vpr* revolt.

révolu, ~e /Revɔly/ *a* past; **avoir 21 ans ~s** be over 21 years of age.

révolution /Revɔlysjɔ̃/ *nf* revolution. **révolutionnaire** *a & nmf* revolutionary. **révolutionner** [1] *vt* revolutionize.

revolver /RevɔlvɛR/ *nm* revolver, gun.

révoquer /Revɔke/ [1] *vt* repeal; (*fonctionnaire*) dismiss.

revue /Rəvy/ *nf* (examen, défilé) review; (magazine) magazine; (spectacle) variety show.

rez-de-chaussée /Redʃose/ *nm inv* ground floor; (US) first floor.

RF *abrév f* (**République Française**) French Republic.

rhinocéros /RinɔseRɔs/ *nm* rhinoceros.

rhubarbe /RybaRb/ *nf* rhubarb.

rhum /Rɔm/ *nm* rum.

rhumatisme /Rymatism/ *nm* rheumatism.

rhume /Rym/ *nm* cold; ~ **des foins** hay fever.

ri /Ri/ ⇒RIRE [54].

ricaner /Rikane/ [1] *vi* snigger.

riche /Riʃ/ *a* rich (**en** in). ● *nmf* rich man, rich woman.

richesse /Riʃɛs/ *nf* wealth; (de sol, décor) richness; **~s** wealth; (ressources) resources.

ride /Rid/ *nf* wrinkle; (sur l'eau) ripple.

rideau (*pl* **~x**) /Rido/ *nm* curtain; (métallique) shutter; (fig) screen.

ridicule /Ridikyl/ *a* ridiculous. ● *nm* (d'une situation) absurdity; (le grotesque) **le ~** ridicule. **ridiculiser** [1] *vt* ridicule.

rien /Rjɛ̃/ *pron* nothing; (quoi que ce soit) anything; **de ~!** don't mention it!; ~ **de bon** nothing good; **elle n'a ~ dit** she didn't say anything; ~ **d'autre/de plus** nothing else/more; ~ **du tout** nothing at all; ~ **que** (seulement) just, only; **trois fois ~** next to nothing; **il n'y est pour ~** he has nothing to do with it; ~ **à faire!** (c'est impossible) it's no good!; (refus) no way! [!]. ● *nm* **un ~ de** a touch of; **être puni pour un ~** be punished for the slightest thing; **se disputer pour un ~** fight over nothing; **en un ~ de temps** in next to no time.

rieur, -euse /RijœR, -øz/ *a* cheerful; (*yeux*) laughing.

rigide /Riʒid/ *a* rigid.

rigolade /Rigɔlad/ *nf* fun.

rigoler /Rigɔle/ [1] *vi* laugh; (s'amuser) have some fun; (plaisanter) joke.

rigolo, ~te /Rigɔlo, -ɔt/ *a* [!] funny. ● *nm, f* [!] joker.

rigoureux, -euse /RiguRø, -z/ *a* rigorous; (*hiver*) harsh; (sévère) strict; (*travail, recherches*) meticulous.

rigueur /RigœR/ *nf* rigour; **à la ~**

at a pinch; **être de ~** be obligatory; **tenir ~ à qn de qch** bear sb a grudge for sth.

rime /ʀim/ *nf* rhyme.

rimer /ʀime/ [1] *vi* rhyme (**avec** with); **cela ne rime à rien** it makes no sense.

rinçage /ʀɛ̃saʒ/ *nm* rinse; (action) rinsing.

rincer /ʀɛ̃se/ [10] *vt* rinse.

riposte /ʀipɔst/ *nf* retort.

riposter /ʀipɔste/ [1] *vi* retaliate; **~ à** (*attaque*) counter; (*insulte*) reply to. ●*vt* retort (**que** that).

rire /ʀiʀ/ [54] *vi* laugh (**de** at); (plaisanter) joke; (s'amuser) have fun; **c'était pour ~** it was a joke. ●*nm* laugh; **des ~s** laughter.

risée /ʀize/ *nf* **la ~ de** the laughing-stock of.

risque /ʀisk/ *nm* risk. **risqué, ~e** *a* risky; (osé) daring.

risquer /ʀiske/ [1] *vt* risk (**de faire** of doing); (être passible de) face; **il risque de pleuvoir** it might rain; **tu risques de te faire mal** you might hurt yourself. ▫ **se ~ à/dans** *vpr* venture to/into.

ristourne /ʀistuʀn/ *nf* discount.

rite /ʀit/ *nm* rite; (habitude) ritual. **rituel, ~le** *a & nm* ritual.

rivage /ʀivaʒ/ *nm* shore.

rival, ~e (*mpl* **-aux**) /ʀival, -o/ *a & nm, f* rival. **rivaliser** [1] *vi* compete (**avec** with). **rivalité** *nf* rivalry.

rive /ʀiv/ *nf* (de fleuve) bank; (de lac) shore.

riverain, ~e /ʀivʀɛ̃, -ɛn/ *a* riverside. ●*nm, f* riverside resident; (d'une rue) resident.

rivière /ʀivjɛʀ/ *nf* river.

riz /ʀi/ *nm* rice. **rizière** *nf* paddy field.

robe /ʀɔb/ *nf* (de femme) dress; (de juge) robe; (de cheval) coat; **~ de chambre** dressing-gown.

robinet /ʀɔbinɛ/ *nm* tap; (US) faucet.

robot /ʀɔbo/ *nm* robot; **~ ménager** food processor.

robuste /ʀɔbyst/ *a* robust.

roche /ʀɔʃ/ *nf* rock.

rocher /ʀɔʃe/ *nm* rock.

rock /ʀɔk/ *nm* (Mus) rock.

rodage /ʀɔdaʒ/ *nm* **en ~** (Auto) running in.

roder /ʀɔde/ [1] *vt* (Auto) run in; **être rodé** (*personne*) have got the hang of things.

rôder /ʀode/ [1] *vi* roam; (*suspect*) prowl.

rogne /ʀɔɲ/ *nf* 🅸 anger; **en ~** in a temper.

rogner /ʀɔɲe/ [1] *vt* trim; **~ sur** cut down on.

rognon /ʀɔɲɔ̃/ *nm* (Culin) kidney.

roi /ʀwa/ *nm* king; **les R~ mages** the Magi; **la fête des R~** Twelfth Night.

rôle /ʀol/ *nm* role, part.

romain, ~e /ʀɔmɛ̃, -ɛn/ *a* Roman. **R~, ~e** *nm, f* Roman. **romaine** *nf* (laitue) cos.

roman /ʀɔmɑ̃/ *nm* novel; (genre) fiction.

romance /ʀɔmɑ̃s/ *nf* ballad.

romancier, -ière /ʀɔmɑ̃sje, -jɛʀ/ *nm, f* novelist.

romanesque /ʀɔmanɛsk/ *a* romantic; (fantastique) fantastic; (*récit*) fictional; **œuvres ~s** novels, fiction.

romantique /ʀɔmɑ̃tik/ *a & nmf* romantic. **romantisme** *nm* romanticism.

rompre /ʀɔ̃pʀ/ [3] *vt* break; (*relations*) break off. ●*vi* (se séparer) break up; **~ avec** (*fiancé*) break up with; (*parti*) break away from; (*tradition*) break with. ▫ **se ~** *vpr* break.

ronce /ʀɔ̃s/ *nf* bramble.

rond, ~e /ʀɔ̃, -d/ *a* round; (gras) plump; (ivre 🅸) drunk. ●*nm*

R

(cercle) ring; (tranche) slice; **en ~** in a circle; **il n'a pas un ~** [!] he hasn't got a penny.

ronde /Rɔ̃d/ *nf* (de policier) beat; (de soldat, gardien) watch; (Mus) semibreve.

rondelle /Rɔ̃dɛl/ *nf* (Tech) washer; (tranche) slice.

rondement /Rɔ̃dmɑ̃/ *adv* promptly; (franchement) frankly.

rondeur /Rɔ̃dœR/ *nf* roundness; (franchise) frankness; (embonpoint) plumpness.

rondin /Rɔ̃dɛ̃/ *nm* log.

rond-point (*pl* **ronds-points**) /Rɔ̃pwɛ̃/ *nm* roundabout; (US) traffic circle.

ronfler /Rɔ̃fle/ [1] *vi* snore; (*moteur*) purr.

ronger /Rɔ̃ʒe/ [40] *vt* gnaw (at); (*vers, acide*) eat into. ◻ **se ~** *vpr* **se ~ les ongles** bite one's nails.

rongeur /Rɔ̃ʒœR/ *nm* rodent.

ronronner /Rɔ̃Rɔne/ [1] *vi* purr.

rosbif /Rɔsbif/ *nm* roast beef.

rose /Roz/ *nf* rose. ● *a & nm* pink.

rosé, **~e** /Roze/ *a* pinkish. ● *nm* rosé.

roseau (*pl* **~x**) /Rozo/ *nm* reed.

rosée /Roze/ *nf* dew.

rosier /Rozje/ *nm* rose bush.

rossignol /Rɔsiɲɔl/ *nm* nightingale.

rotatif, **-ive** /Rɔtatif, -v/ *a* rotary.

roter /Rɔte/ [1] *vi* [!] burp.

rôti /Rɔti/ *nm* joint; (cuit) roast; **~ de porc** roast pork.

rotin /Rɔtɛ̃/ *nm* (rattan) cane.

rôtir /RɔtiR/ [2] *vt* roast.

rôtissoire /RɔtiswaR/ *nf* roasting spit.

rotule /Rɔtyl/ *nf* kneecap.

rouage /Rwaʒ/ *nm* (Tech) wheel; **les ~s** the works; (d'une organisation: fig) wheels.

roucouler /Rukule/ [1] *vi* coo.

roue /Ru/ *nf* wheel; **~ dentée** cog(wheel); **~ de secours** spare wheel.

rouer /Rwe/ [1] *vt* **~ de coups** thrash.

rouge /Ruʒ/ *a* red; (*fer*) red-hot. ● *nm* red; (vin) red wine; (fard) blusher; **~ à lèvres** lipstick. ● *nmf* (Pol) red. **rouge-gorge** (*pl* **rouges-gorges**) *nm* robin.

rougeole /Ruʒɔl/ *nf* measles (+ *sg*).

rouget /Ruʒɛ/ *nm* red mullet.

rougeur /RuʒœR/ *nf* redness; (tache) red blotch.

rougir /RuʒiR/ [2] *vi* turn red; (de honte) blush.

rouille /Ruj/ *nf* rust. **rouillé**, **~e** *a* rusty.

rouiller /Ruje/ [1] *vi* rust. ◻ **se ~** *vpr* get rusty.

rouleau (*pl* **~x**) /Rulo/ *nm* roll; (outil, vague) roller; **~ à pâtisserie** rolling pin; **~ compresseur** steamroller.

roulement /Rulmɑ̃/ *nm* rotation; (bruit) rumble; (alternance) rotation; (de tambour) roll; **~ à billes** ball-bearing; **travailler par ~** work in shifts.

rouler /Rule/ [1] *vt* roll; (*ficelle, manches*) roll up; (*pâte*) roll out; (duper [!]) cheat. ● *vi* (*véhicule, train*) go, travel; (*conducteur*) drive. ◻ **se ~ dans** *vpr* (*herbe*) roll in; (*couverture*) roll oneself up in.

roulette /Rulɛt/ *nf* (de meuble) castor; (de dentiste) drill; (jeu) roulette; **comme sur des ~s** very smoothly.

roulotte /Rulɔt/ *nf* caravan.

roumain, **~e** /Rumɛ̃, -ɛn/ *a* Romanian. **R~**, **~e** *nm,f* Romanian.

Roumanie /Rumani/ *nf* Romania.

rouquin, **~e** /Rukɛ̃, -in/ [!] *a* red-haired. ● *nm,f* redhead.

rouspéter /ʀuspete/ [14] *vi* ⓘ grumble, moan.

rousse /ʀus/ ⇒ROUX.

roussir /ʀusiʀ/ [2] *vt* scorch. ● *vi* turn brown.

route /ʀut/ *nf* road; (Naut, Aviat) route; (direction) way; (voyage) journey; (chemin: fig) path; **en ~** on the way; **en ~!** let's go!; **mettre en ~** start; **~ nationale** trunk road, main road; **se mettre en ~** set out; **il y a une heure de ~** it's an hour's journey.

routier, -ière /ʀutje, -jɛʀ/ *a* road. ● *nm* long-distance lorry *ou* truck driver; (restaurant) transport café; (US) truck stop.

routine /ʀutin/ *nf* routine.

roux, rousse /ʀu, ʀus/ *a* red, russet; (*personne*) red-haired; (*chat*) ginger. ● *nm, f* redhead.

royal, ~e (*mpl* **-aux**) /ʀwajal, -jo/ *a* royal; (*cadeau*) fit for a king.

royaume /ʀwajom/ *nm* kingdom.

Royaume-Uni /ʀwajomyni/ *nm* United Kingdom.

royauté /ʀwajote/ *nf* royalty.

ruban /ʀybɑ̃/ *nm* ribbon; (de chapeau) band; **~ adhésif** sticky tape; **~ magnétique** magnetic tape.

rubéole /ʀybeɔl/ *nf* German measles (+ *sg*).

rubis /ʀybi/ *nm* ruby; (de montre) jewel.

rubrique /ʀybʀik/ *nf* heading; (article) column.

ruche /ʀyʃ/ *nf* beehive.

rude /ʀyd/ *a* (au toucher) rough; (pénible) tough; (grossier) coarse; (fameux ⓘ) tremendous.

rudement /ʀydmɑ̃/ *adv* (*frapper*) hard; (*traiter*) harshly; (très ⓘ) really.

rudimentaire /ʀydimɑ̃tɛʀ/ *a* rudimentary.

rue /ʀy/ *nf* street.

ruée /ʀɥe/ *nf* rush.

ruer /ʀɥe/ [1] *vi* (*cheval*) buck. □ **se ~** *vpr* rush (**dans** into; **vers** towards); **se ~ sur** pounce on.

rugby /ʀygbi/ *nm* rugby.

rugir /ʀyʒiʀ/ [2] *vi* roar.

rugueux, -euse /ʀygø, -z/ *a* rough.

ruine /ʀɥin/ *nf* ruin; **en ~(s)** in ruins. **ruiner** [1] *vt* ruin.

ruisseau (*pl* **~x**) /ʀɥiso/ *nm* stream; (rigole) gutter.

rumeur /ʀymœʀ/ *nf* (nouvelle) rumour; (son) murmur, hum.

ruminer /ʀymine/ [1] *vi* (*animal*) ruminate; (méditer) meditate.

rupture /ʀyptyʀ/ *nf* break; (action) breaking; (de contrat) breach; (de pourparlers) breakdown; (de relations) breaking off; (de couple, coalition) break-up.

rural, ~e (*mpl* **-aux**) /ʀyʀal, -o/ *a* rural.

ruse /ʀyz/ *nf* cunning; **une ~** a trick, a ruse. **rusé, ~e** *a* cunning.

russe /ʀys/ *a* Russian. ● *nm* (Ling) Russian. **R~** *nmf* Russian.

Russie /ʀysi/ *nf* Russia.

rustique /ʀystik/ *a* rustic.

rythme /ʀitm/ *nm* rhythm; (vitesse) rate; (de la vie) pace. **rythmique** *a* rhythmical.

s' /s/ ⇒SE.

sa /sa/ ⇒SON[1].

SA *abrév f* (**société anonyme**) PLC.

sabbatique /sabatik/ *a* (*année*) sabbatical year.

sable /sɑbl/ *nm* sand; **~s**

mouvants quicksands. **sabler** *vt* [1] grit.

sablier /sablije/ *nm* (Culin) eggtimer.

sablonneux, -euse /sablɔnø, -z/ *a* sandy.

sabot /sabo/ *nm* (de cheval) hoof; (chaussure) clog; (de frein) shoe; **~ de Denver®** (wheel) clamp.

saboter /sabɔte/ [1] *vt* sabotage; (bâcler) botch.

sac /sak/ *nm* bag; (grand, en toile) sack; **mettre à ~** (*maison*) ransack; (*ville*) sack; **~ à dos** rucksack; **~ à main** handbag; **~ de couchage** sleeping-bag; **mettre dans le même ~** lump together.

saccadé, ~e /sakade/ *a* jerky.

saccager /sakaʒe/ [40] *vt* (abîmer) wreck; (*maison*) ransack; (*ville, pays*) sack.

saccharine /sakaʀin/ *nf* saccharin.

sachet /saʃɛ/ *nm* (small) bag; (d'aromates) sachet; **~ de thé** tea-bag.

sacoche /sakɔʃ/ *nf* bag; (de vélo) saddlebag.

sacre /sakʀ/ *nm* (de roi) coronation; (d'évêque) consecration. **sacré, ~e** *a* sacred; (maudit 🄸) damned. **sacrement** *nm* sacrament. **sacrer** [1] *vt* crown; consecrate.

sacrifice /sakʀifis/ *nm* sacrifice.

sacrifier /sakʀifje/ [45] *vt* sacrifice; **~ à** conform to. □ **se ~** *vpr* sacrifice oneself.

sacrilège /sakʀilɛʒ/ *nm* sacrilege. ● *a* sacrilegious.

sadique /sadik/ *a* sadistic. ● *nmf* sadist.

sage /saʒ/ *a* wise; (docile) good, well behaved. ● *nm* wise man.

sage-femme (*pl* **sages-femmes**) /saʒfam/ *nf* midwife.

sagesse /saʒɛs/ *nf* wisdom.

Sagittaire /saʒitɛʀ/ *nm* **le ~** Sagittarius.

saignant, ~e /sɛɲɑ̃, -t/ *a* (Culin) rare.

saigner /seɲe/ [1] *vt/i* bleed; **~ du nez** have a nosebleed.

saillant, ~e /sajɑ̃, -t/ *a* prominent.

sain, ~e /sɛ̃, sɛn/ *a* healthy; (*moralement*) sane; **~ et sauf** safe and sound.

saindoux /sɛ̃du/ *nm* lard.

saint, ~e /sɛ̃, -t/ *a* holy; (bon, juste) saintly. ● *nm, f* saint. **Saint-Esprit** *nm* Holy Spirit. **sainteté** *nf* holiness; (d'un lieu) sanctity. **Sainte Vierge** *nf* Blessed Virgin. **Saint-Sylvestre** *nf* New Year's Eve.

sais /sɛ/ ⇒SAVOIR [55].

saisie /sezi/ *nf* (Jur) seizure; (Comput) keyboarding; **~ de données** data capture.

saisir /seziʀ/ [2] *vt* grab (hold of); (*proie*) seize; (*occasion, biens*) seize; (comprendre) grasp; (frapper) strike; (Ordinat) keyboard, capture; **saisi de** (*peur*) stricken by, overcome by. □ **se ~ de** *vpr* seize. **saisissant, ~e** *a* (*spectacle*) gripping.

saison /sɛzɔ̃/ *nf* season; **la morte ~** the off season. **saisonnier, -ière** *a* seasonal.

sait /sɛ/ ⇒SAVOIR [55].

salade /salad/ *nf* (plat) salad; (plante) lettuce. **saladier** *nm* salad bowl.

salaire /salɛʀ/ *nm* wages (+ *pl*), salary.

salarié, ~e /salaʀje/ *a* wage-earning. ● *nm, f* wage earner.

sale /sal/ *a* dirty; (mauvais) nasty.

salé, ~e /sale/ *a* (*goût*) salty; (plat) salted; (opposé à sucré) savoury; (grivois 🄸) spicy; (excessif 🄸) steep. **saler** [1] *vt* salt.

saleté /salte/ *nf* dirtiness; (crasse)

dirt; (obscénité) obscenity; **~(s)** (camelote) rubbish; (détritus) mess.

salir /saliʀ/ [2] *vt* (make) dirty; (*réputation*) tarnish. □ **se ~** *vpr* get dirty. **salissant, ~e** *a* dirty; (*étoffe*) easily dirtied.

salive /saliv/ *nf* saliva.

salle /sal/ *nf* room; (grande, publique) hall; (de restaurant) dining room; (Théât, cinéma) auditorium; **cinéma à trois ~s** three-screen cinema; **~ à manger** dining room; **~ d'attente** waiting room; **~ de bains** bathroom; **~ de séjour** living room; **~ de classe** classroom; **~ d'embarquement** departure lounge; **~ d'opération** operating theatre; **~ des ventes** saleroom.

salon /salɔ̃/ *nm* lounge; (de coiffure, beauté) salon; (exposition) show; **~ de thé** tea-room.

salopette /salɔpɛt/ *nf* dungarees (+ *pl*); (d'ouvrier) overalls (+ *pl*).

saltimbanque /saltɛ̃bɑ̃k/ *nmf* (street) acrobat.

salubre /salybʀ/ *a* healthy.

saluer /salɥe/ [1] *vt* greet; (en partant) take one's leave of; (de la tête) nod to; (de la main) wave to; (Mil) salute; (accueillir favorablement) welcome.

salut /saly/ *nm* greeting; (de la tête) nod; (de la main) wave; (Mil) salute; (rachat) salvation. ●*interj* (bonjour Ⓘ) hello; (au revoir Ⓘ) bye.

salutation /salytasjɔ̃/ *nf* greeting.

samedi /samdi/ *nm* Saturday.

SAMU /samy/ *abrév m* (**Service d'assistance médicale d'urgence**) ≈ mobile accident unit.

sanction /sɑ̃ksjɔ̃/ *nf* sanction. **sanctionner** [1] *vt* sanction; (punir) punish.

sandale /sɑ̃dal/ *nf* sandal.

sang /sɑ̃/ *nm* blood; **se faire du mauvais ~** *ou* **un ~ d'encre** be worried stiff. **sang-froid** *nm inv* self-control. **sanglant, ~e** *a* bloody.

sangle /sɑ̃gl/ *nf* strap.

sanglier /sɑ̃glije/ *nm* wild boar.

sanglot /sɑ̃glo/ *nm* sob. **sangloter** [1] *vi* sob.

sanguin, ~e /sɑ̃gɛ̃, -in/ *a* (*groupe*) blood.

sanguinaire /sɑ̃ginɛʀ/ *a* bloodthirsty.

sanisette® /sanizɛt/ *nf* automatic public toilet.

sanitaire /sanitɛʀ/ *a* (*directives*) health; (*conditions*) sanitary; (*appareils, installations*) bathroom, sanitary. **sanitaires** *nmpl* bathroom.

sans /sɑ̃/ *prép* without; **~ ça, ~ quoi** otherwise; **~ arrêt** nonstop; **~ encombre/faute/tarder** without incident/fail/delay; **~ fin/goût/limite** endless/tasteless/limitless; **~ importance/pareil/précédent/travail** unimportant/unparalleled/unprecedented/unemployed; **j'ai aimé mais ~ plus** it was good, it wasn't great.

sans-abri /sɑ̃zabʀi/ *nmf inv* homeless person.

sans-gêne /sɑ̃ʒɛn/ *a inv* inconsiderate, thoughtless. ●*nm inv* thoughtlessness.

sans-papiers /sɑ̃papje/ *nm inv* illegal immigrant.

santé /sɑ̃te/ *nf* health; **à ta** *ou* **votre ~!** cheers!

saoul, ~e /su, sul/ ⇒SOÛL.

sapin /sapɛ̃/ *nm* fir(tree); **~ de Noël** Christmas tree.

sarcasme /saʀkasm/ *nm* sarcasm. **sarcastique** *a* sarcastic.

sardine /saʀdin/ *nf* sardine.

sas /sɑs/ *nm* (Naut, Aviat) airlock.

satané, ~e /satane/ *a* Ⓘ damned.

satellite /satelit/ *nm* satellite.

S

satin /satɛ̃/ *nm* satin.
satire /satiʀ/ *nf* satire.
satisfaction /satisfaksjɔ̃/ *nf* satisfaction.
satisfaire /satisfɛʀ/ [33] *vt* satisfy. ● *vi* ~ **à** fulfil. **satisfaisant**, ~**e** *a* (acceptable) satisfactory. **satisfait**, ~**e** *a* satisfied (**de** with).
saturer /satyʀe/ [1] *vt* saturate.
sauce /sos/ *nf* sauce; ~ **tartare** tartar sauce. **saucière** *nf* sauceboat.
saucisse /sosis/ *nf* sausage.
saucisson /sosisɔ̃/ *nm* (slicing) sausage.
sauf[1] /sof/ *prép* except; ~ **erreur** if I'm not mistaken; ~ **imprévu** unless anything unforeseen happens; ~ **avis contraire** unless otherwise stated.
sauf[2], **-ve** /sof, sov/ *a* safe, unharmed.
sauge /soʒ/ *nf* (Culin) sage.
saule /sol/ *nm* willow; ~ **pleureur** weeping willow.
saumon /somɔ̃/ *nm* salmon. ● *a inv* salmon-(pink).
sauna /sona/ *nm* sauna.
saupoudrer /sopudʀe/ [1] *vt* sprinkle (**de** with).
saut /so/ *nm* jump; **faire un** ~ **chez qn** pop round to sb's (place); **le** ~ (Sport) jumping; ~ **en hauteur/longueur** high/long jump; ~ **périlleux** somersault; **au** ~ **du lit** on getting up.
sauté, ~**e** /sote/ *a & nm* (Culin) sauté.
saute-mouton /sotmutɔ̃/ *nm inv* leap-frog.
sauter /sote/ [1] *vi* jump; (exploser) blow up; (*fusible*) blow; (se détacher) come off; **faire** ~ (détruire) blow up; (*fusible*) blow; (casser) break; ~ **à la corde** skip; ~ **aux yeux** be obvious; ~ **au cou de qn** fling one's arms round sb; ~ **sur une occasion** jump at an opportunity. ● *vt* jump (over); (page, classe) skip.
sauterelle /sotʀɛl/ *nf* grasshopper.
sautiller /sotije/ [1] *vi* hop.
sauvage /sovaʒ/ *a* wild; (primitif, cruel) savage; (farouche) unsociable; (illégal) unauthorized. ● *nmf* unsociable person; (brute) savage.
sauve /sov/ ⇒SAUF[2].
sauvegarder /sovgaʀde/ [1] *vt* safeguard; (Ordinat) back up.
sauver /sove/ [1] *vt* save; (d'un danger) rescue, save; (*matériel*) salvage. □ **se** ~ *vpr* (fuir) run away; (partir 🅸) be off. **sauvetage** *nm* rescue. **sauveteur** *nm* rescuer. **sauveur** *nm* saviour.
savant, ~**e** /savɑ̃, -t/ *a* learned; (habile) skilful. ● *nm* scientist.
saveur /savœʀ/ *nf* flavour; (fig) savour.
savoir /savwaʀ/ [55] *vt* know; **elle sait conduire/nager** she can drive/swim; **faire** ~ **à qn que** inform sb that; (**pas**) **que je sache** (not) as far as I know; **à** ~ namely. ● *nm* learning.
savon /savɔ̃/ *nm* soap; **passer un** ~ **à qn** 🅸 give sb a telling-off. **savonnette** *nf* bar of soap. **savonneux**, **-euse** *a* soapy.
savourer /savuʀe/ [1] *vt* savour. **savoureux**, **-euse** *a* tasty; (fig) spicy.
scandale /skɑ̃dal/ *nm* scandal; (tapage) uproar; (en public) noisy scene; **faire** ~ shock people; **faire un** ~ make a scene. **scandaleux**, **-euse** *a* scandalous. **scandaliser** [1] *vt* scandalize, shock.
scander /skɑ̃de/ [1] *vt* (*vers*) scan; (*slogan*) chant.
scandinave /skɑ̃dinav/ *a* Scandinavian. **S**~ *nmf* Scandinavian.

Scandinavie /skɑ̃dinavi/ *nf* Scandinavia.

scarabée /skaʀabe/ *nm* beetle.

sceau (*pl* ~**x**) /so/ *nm* seal.

scélérat /seleʀa/ *nm* scoundrel.

sceller /sele/ [1] *vt* seal; (fixer) cement.

scène /sɛn/ *nf* scene; (estrade, art dramatique) stage; **mettre en** ~ (*pièce*) stage; (*film*) direct; **mise en** ~ direction; ~ **de ménage** domestic dispute.

scepticisme /sɛptisism/ *nm* scepticism.

sceptique /sɛptik/ *a* sceptical. ● *nmf* sceptic.

schéma /ʃema/ *nm* diagram. **schématique** *a* schematic; (sommaire) sketchy. **schématiser** [1] *vt* simplify.

schizophrène /skizɔfʀɛn/ *a & nmf* schizophrenic.

sciatique /sjatik/ *a* (*nerf*) sciatic. ● *nf* sciatica.

scie /si/ *nf* saw.

sciemment /sjamɑ̃/ *adv* knowingly.

science /sjɑ̃s/ *nf* science; (savoir) knowledge.

science-fiction /sjɑ̃sfiksjɔ̃/ *nf* science fiction.

scientifique /sjɑ̃tifik/ *a* scientific. ● *nmf* scientist.

scier /sje/ [45] *vt* saw.

scintiller /sɛ̃tije/ [1] *vi* glitter; (*étoile*) twinkle.

scission /sisjɔ̃/ *nf* split.

sclérose /skleʀoz/ *nf* sclerosis; ~ **en plaques** multiple sclerosis.

scolaire /skɔlɛʀ/ *a* school. **scolarisé,** ~**e** *a* going to school. **scolarité** *nf* schooling.

score /skɔʀ/ *nm* score.

scorpion /skɔʀpjɔ̃/ *nm* scorpion; **le S**~ Scorpio.

scotch /skɔtʃ/ *nm* (boisson) Scotch (whisky); (ruban adhésif)® Sellotape®.

scout, ~**e** /skut/ *nm & a* scout.

scrupule /skʀypyl/ *nm* scruple. **scrupuleux, -euse** *a* scrupulous.

scruter /skʀyte/ [1] *vt* examine, scrutinize.

scrutin /skʀytɛ̃/ *nm* (vote) ballot; (élections) polls (+ *pl*).

sculpter /skylte/ [1] *vt* sculpt, carve. **sculpteur** *nm* sculptor. **sculpture** *nf* sculpture.

---

se, s' /sə, s/

s' before vowel or mute h.

● *pronom*

····➤ himself, (féminin) herself; (indéfini) oneself; (non humain) itself; (au pluriel) themselves; ~ **laver les mains** wash one's hands; (réciproque) each other, one another; **ils se détestent** they hate each other.

! The translation of **se** will vary according to which verb it is associated with. You should therefore refer to the verb to find it. For example, **se promener, se taire** will be treated respectively under **promener** and **taire**.

---

séance /seɑ̃s/ *nf* session; (Théât, cinéma) show; ~ **de pose** sitting; ~ **tenante** forthwith.

seau (*pl* ~**x**) /so/ *nm* bucket, pail.

sec, sèche /sɛk, sɛʃ/ *a* dry; (*fruits*) dried; (*coup, bruit*) sharp; (*cœur*) hard; (*whisky*) neat. ● *nm* **à** ~ (sans eau) dry; (sans argent) broke; **au** ~ in a dry place.

sèche-cheveux /sɛʃʃəvø/ *nm inv* hairdrier.

sèchement /sɛʃmɑ̃/ *adv* drily.

sécher /seʃe/ [14] *vt/i* dry; (*cours*: 🅸) skip; (ne pas savoir 🅸) be stumped. □ **se ~** *vpr* dry oneself. **sécheresse** *nf* (de climat) dryness; (temps sec) drought. **séchoir** *nm* drier.

second, ~e /səgɔ̃, -d/ *a & nm,f* second. ●*nm* (adjoint) second in command; (étage) second floor. **secondaire** *a* secondary. **seconde** *nf* (instant) second; (vitesse) second gear.

seconder /səgɔ̃de/ [1] *vt* assist.

secouer /səkwe/ [1] *vt* shake; (*poussière, torpeur*) shake off. □ **se ~** *vpr* [I] (se dépêcher) get a move on; (réagir) shake oneself up.

secourir /səkuʀiʀ/ [20] *vt* assist, help. **secouriste** *nmf* first-aid worker.

secours /səkuʀ/ *nm* assistance, help; **au ~!** help!; **de ~** (*sortie*) emergency; (*équipe, opération*) rescue. ●*nmpl* (Méd) first aid.

secousse /səkus/ *nf* jolt, jerk; (séisme) tremor.

secret, -ète /səkʀɛ, -t/ *a* secret. ●*nm* secret; (discrétion) secrecy; **le ~ professionnel** professional confidentiality; **~ de Polichinelle** open secret; **en ~** in secret, secretly.

secrétaire /səkʀetɛʀ/ *nmf* secretary; **~ de direction** personal assistant. ●*nm* (meuble) writing-desk; **~ d'État** junior minister.

secrétariat /səkʀetaʀja/ *nm* secretarial work; (bureau) secretariat.

sectaire /sɛktɛʀ/ *a* sectarian.

secte /sɛkt/ *nf* sect.

secteur /sɛktœʀ/ *nm* area; (Comm) sector; (circuit: Électr) mains (+ *pl*).

section /sɛksjɔ̃/ *nf* section; (Scol) stream; (Mil) platoon. **sectionner** [1] *vt* sever.

sécuriser /sekyʀize/ [1] *vt* reassure.

sécurité /sekyʀite/ *nf* security; (absence de danger) safety; **en ~** safe, secure. **Sécurité sociale** *nf* social services, social security services.

sédatif /sedatif/ *nm* sedative.

sédentaire /sedɑ̃tɛʀ/ *a* sedentary.

séducteur, -trice /sedyktœʀ, -tʀis/ *a* seductive. ●*nm,f* seducer. **séduction** *nf* seduction; (charme) charm.

séduire /sedɥiʀ/ [17] *vt* charm; (plaire à) appeal to; (sexuellement) seduce. **séduisant, ~e** *a* attractive.

ségrégation /segʀegasjɔ̃/ *nf* segregation.

seigle /sɛgl/ *nm* rye.

seigneur /sɛɲœʀ/ *nm* lord; **le S~** the Lord.

sein /sɛ̃/ *nm* breast; **au ~ de** within.

séisme /seism/ *nm* earthquake.

seize /sɛz/ *a & nm* sixteen.

séjour /seʒuʀ/ *nm* stay; (pièce) living room. **séjourner** [1] *vi* stay.

sel /sɛl/ *nm* salt; (piquant) spice.

sélectif, -ive /selɛktif, -v/ *a* selective.

sélection /selɛksjɔ̃/ *nf* selection. **sélectionner** [1] *vt* select.

selle /sɛl/ *nf* saddle; **aller à la ~** have a bowel movement; **~s** (Méd) stools.

sellette /sɛlɛt/ *nf* **sur la ~** (*personne*) in the hot seat.

selon /səlɔ̃/ *prép* according to; **~ que** depending on whether.

semaine /səmɛn/ *nf* week; **en ~** during the week.

sémantique /semɑ̃tik/ *a* semantic. ●*nf* semantics.

semblable /sɑ̃blabl/ *a* similar (**à** to). ●*nm* fellow (creature).

semblant /sɑ̃blɑ̃/ *nm* **faire ~ de**

pretend to; **un ~ de** a semblance of.

sembler /sɑ̃ble/ [1] *vi* seem (**à** to; **que** that); **il me semble que** it seems to me that.

semelle /səmɛl/ *nf* sole; **~ compensée** wedge heel.

semence /s(ə)mɑ̃s/ *nf* seed.

semer /s(ə)me/ [6] *vt* (*graine, doute*) sow; (jeter, parsemer) strew; (*personne* ①) lose; **~ la panique** spread panic.

semestre /səmɛstʀ/ *nm* half-year; (Univ) semester. **semestriel, ~le** *a* (revue) biannual; (examen) end-of-semester.

séminaire /seminɛʀ/ *nm* (Relig) seminary; (Univ) seminar.

semi-remorque /s(ə)miʀ(ə)mɔʀk/ *nm* articulated lorry.

semis /s(ə)mi/ *nm* (terrain) seedbed; (plant) seedling.

semoule /s(ə)mul/ *nf* semolina.

sénat /sena/ *nm* senate. **sénateur** *nm* senator.

sénile /senil/ *a* senile.

sens /sɑ̃s/ *nm* (Méd) sense; (signification) meaning, sense; (direction) direction; **à mon ~** to my mind; **à ~ unique** (*rue*) one-way; **ça n'a pas de ~** it doesn't make sense; **~ commun** common sense; **~ giratoire** roundabout; **~ interdit** no-entry sign; (rue) one-way street; **dans le ~ des aiguilles d'une montre** clockwise; **dans le ~ inverse des aiguilles d'une montre** anticlockwise; **~ dessus dessous** upside down; **~ devant derrière** back to front.

sensation /sɑ̃sasjɔ̃/ *nf* feeling, sensation; **faire ~** create a sensation. **sensationnel, ~le** *a* sensational.

sensé, ~e /sɑ̃se/ *a* sensible.

sensibiliser /sɑ̃sibilize/ [1] *vt* **~ l'opinion** increase people's awareness (**à qch** to sth).

sensibilité /sɑ̃sibilite/ *nf* sensitivity. **sensible** *a* sensitive (**à** to); (appréciable) noticeable. **sensiblement** *adv* noticeably; (à peu près) more or less.

sensoriel, ~le /sɑ̃sɔʀjɛl/ *a* sensory.

sensualité /sɑ̃sɥalite/ *nf* sensuousness; sensuality. **sensuel, ~le** *a* sensual.

sentence /sɑ̃tɑ̃s/ *nf* sentence.

senteur /sɑ̃tœʀ/ *nf* scent.

sentier /sɑ̃tje/ *nm* path.

sentiment /sɑ̃timɑ̃/ *nm* feeling; **faire du ~** sentimentalize; **j'ai le ~ que...** I get the feeling that... **sentimental, ~e** (*mpl* **-aux**) *a* sentimental.

sentir /sɑ̃tiʀ/ [46] *vt* feel; (*odeur*) smell; (pressentir) sense; **~ la lavande** smell of lavender; **je ne peux pas le ~** ① I can't stand him. ● *vi* smell. □ **se ~** *vpr* **se ~ fier/mieux** feel proud/better.

séparation /sepaʀasjɔ̃/ *nf* separation.

séparatiste /sepaʀatist/ *a & nmf* separatist.

séparé, ~e /sepaʀe/ *a* separate; (*conjoints*) separated.

séparer /sepaʀe/ [1] *vt* separate; (en deux) split. □ **se ~** *vpr* separate, part (**de** from); (se détacher) split; **se ~ de** (se défaire de) part with.

sept /sɛt/ *a & nm* seven.

septante /sɛptɑ̃t/ *a & nm* seventy.

septembre /sɛptɑ̃bʀ/ *nm* September.

septentrional, ~e (*mpl* **-aux**) /sɛptɑ̃tʀijɔnal, -o/ *a* northern.

septième /sɛtjɛm/ *a & nmf* seventh.

sépulture /sepyltyʀ/ *nf* burial; (lieu) burial place.

séquelles /sekɛl/ *nfpl* (maladie) aftereffects; (fig) aftermath (+ *sg*).

S

séquence /sekɑ̃s/ *nf* sequence.
séquestrer /sekɛstʀe/ [1] *vt* confine (illegally).
sera, serait /səʀa, səʀɛ/ ⇒ÊTRE [4].
serbe /sɛʀb/ *a* Serbian. **S~** *nmf* Serbian.
Serbie /sɛʀbi/ *nf* Serbia.
serein, ~e /səʀɛ̃, -ɛn/ *a* serene.
sérénité /seʀenite/ *nf* serenity.
sergent /sɛʀʒɑ̃/ *nm* sergeant.
série /seʀi/ *nf* series (+ *sg*); (d'objets) set; **de ~** (*véhicule etc.*) standard; **fabrication** *ou* **production en ~** mass production.
sérieusement /seʀjøzmɑ̃/ *adv* seriously.
sérieux, -ieuse /seʀjø, -z/ *a* serious; (digne de confiance) reliable; (*chances, raison*) good. ● *nm* seriousness; **garder son ~** keep a straight face; **prendre au ~** take seriously.
serin /səʀɛ̃/ *nm* canary.
seringue /səʀɛ̃g/ *nf* syringe.
serment /sɛʀmɑ̃/ *nm* oath; (promesse) vow.
sermon /sɛʀmɔ̃/ *nm* sermon. **sermonner** [1] *vt* lecture.
séropositif, -ive /seʀɔpɔsitif, -v/ *a* HIV positive.
serpent /sɛʀpɑ̃/ *nm* snake; **~ à sonnettes** rattlesnake.
serpillière /sɛʀpijɛʀ/ *nf* floorcloth.
serre /sɛʀ/ *nf* (de jardin) greenhouse; (griffe) claw.
serré, ~e /seʀe/ *a* (*habit, nœud, écrou*) tight; (*personnes*) packed, crowded; (*lutte, mailles*) close; (*écriture*) cramped; (*cœur*) heavy.
serrer /seʀe/ [1] *vt* (saisir) grip; (presser) squeeze; (*vis, corde, ceinture*) tighten; (*poing, dents*) clench; **~ qn dans ses bras** hug sb; **~ les rangs** close ranks; **~ qn** (vêtement) be tight on sb; **~ qn de près** follow sb closely; **~ la main à** shake hands with. ● *vi* **~ à droite** keep over to the right. □ **se ~** *vpr* (se rapprocher) squeeze (up) (**contre** against).
serrure /seʀyʀ/ *nf* lock. **serrurier** *nm* locksmith.
servante /sɛʀvɑ̃t/ *nf* (maid) servant.
serveur, -euse /sɛʀvœʀ, -øz/ *nm, f* (homme) waiter; (femme) waitress. ● *nm* (Ordinat) server.
serviable /sɛʀvjabl/ *a* helpful.
service /sɛʀvis/ *nm* service; (fonction, temps de travail) duty; (pourboire) service (charge); (dans une société) department; **~ (non) compris** service (not) included; **être de ~** be on duty; **pendant le ~** (when) on duty; **rendre ~ à qn** be a help to sb; **~ à thé** tea set; **~ d'ordre** stewards (+ *pl*); **~ après-vente** after-sales service; **~ militaire** military service; **les ~s secrets** the secret service (+ *sg*).
serviette /sɛʀvjɛt/ *nf* (de toilette) towel; (cartable) briefcase; **~ (de table**) serviette, napkin; **~ hygiénique** sanitary towel.
servir /sɛʀviʀ/ [46] *vt/i* serve; (être utile) be of use, serve; **~ qn** (**à table**) wait on sb; **ça sert à** (outil, récipient) it is used for; **ça me sert à/de** I use it to/as; **ça ne sert à rien** (*action*) it's pointless; **~ de** serve as, be used as; **~ à qn de guide** act as a guide for sb. □ **se ~** *vpr* (à table) help oneself (**de** to); **se ~ de** use. **serviteur** *nm* servant.
ses /se/ ⇒SON[1].
session /sesjɔ̃/ *nf* session.
seuil /sœj/ *nm* doorstep; (entrée) doorway; (fig) threshold.
seul, ~e /sœl/ *a* alone, on one's own; (unique) only; **un ~ exemple** only one example; **pas un ~ ami** not a single friend; **lui ~ le sait** only he knows; **dans le ~ but de** with the sole aim of; **parler tout ~**

talk to oneself; **faire qch tout ~** do sth on one's own. ● *nm,f* **le ~, la ~e** the only one. **seulement** *adv* only.

sève /sɛv/ *nf* sap.

sévère /sevɛʀ/ *a* severe. **sévérité** *nf* severity.

sévices /sevis/ *nmpl* physical abuse (+ *sg*).

sévir /seviʀ/ [2] *vi* (*fléau*) rage; **~ contre** punish.

sevrer /səvʀe/ [6] *vt* wean.

sexe /sɛks/ *nm* sex; (organes) genitals (+ *pl*). **sexiste** *a* sexist. **sexualité** *nf* sexuality. **sexuel, ~le** *a* sexual.

shampooing /ʃɑ̃pwɛ̃/ *nm* shampoo.

shérif /ʃeʀif/ *nm* sheriff.

short /ʃɔʀt/ *nm* shorts (+ *pl*).

si (**s'** *before il, ils*) /si, s/ *conj* if; (interrogation indirecte) if, whether; **~ on allait se promener?** what about a walk?; **s'il vous** *ou* **te plaît** please; **~ oui** if so; **~ seulement** if only. ● *adv* (tellement) so; (oui) yes; **un ~ bon repas** such a good meal; **~ habile qu'il soit** however skilful he may be; **~ bien que** with the result that.

sida /sida/ *nm* (Méd) Aids.

sidérurgie /sideʀyʀʒi/ *nf* steel industry.

siècle /sjɛkl/ *nm* century; (époque) age.

siège /sjɛʒ/ *nm* seat; (Mil) siege; **~ éjectable** ejector seat; **~ social** head office, headquarters (+ *pl*). **siéger** [14] [40] *vi* (assemblée) sit.

sien, ~ne /sjɛ̃, -ɛn/ *pron* **le ~, la ~ne, les ~(ne)s** (homme) his; (femme) hers; (chose) its; **les ~s** (famille) one's family.

sieste /sjɛst/ *nf* nap, siesta.

sifflement /sifləmɑ̃/ *nm* whistling; **un ~** a whistle.

siffler /sifle/ [1] *vi* whistle; (avec un sifflet) blow one's whistle; (*serpent, gaz*) hiss. ● *vt* (*air*) whistle; (*chien*) whistle to *ou* for; (*acteur*) hiss.

sifflet /siflɛ/ *nm* whistle; **~s** (huées) boos.

sigle /sigl/ *nm* acronym.

signal (*pl* **-aux**) /siɲal, -o/ *nm* signal; **~ sonore** (de répondeur) tone.

signalement /siɲalmɑ̃/ *nm* description.

signaler /siɲale/ [1] *vt* indicate; (par une sonnerie, un écriteau) signal; (dénoncer, mentionner) report; (faire remarquer) point out.

signalisation /siɲalizasjɔ̃/ *nf* signalling, signposting; (signaux) signals (+ *pl*).

signataire /siɲatɛʀ/ *nmf* signatory.

signature /siɲatyʀ/ *nf* signature; (action) signing.

signe /siɲ/ *nm* sign; (de ponctuation) mark; **faire ~ à qn** wave at sb; (contacter) contact; **faire ~ à qn de** beckon sb to; **faire ~ que non** shake one's head; **faire ~ que oui** nod.

signer /siɲe/ [1] *vt* sign. □ **se ~** *vpr* (Relig) cross oneself.

signet /siɲɛ/ *nm* (pour livre, Internet) bookmark; **~s favoris** (Internet) hotlist.

significatif, -ive /siɲifikatif, -v/ *a* significant.

signification /siɲifikasjɔ̃/ *nf* meaning. **signifier** [45] *vt* mean, signify; (faire connaître) make known (**à** to).

silence /silɑ̃s/ *nm* silence; (Mus) rest; **garder le ~** keep silent.

silencieux, -ieuse /silɑ̃sjø, -z/ *a* silent. ● *nm* silencer.

silex /silɛks/ *nm inv* flint.

silhouette /silwɛt/ *nf* outline, silhouette.

sillon /sijɔ̃/ *nm* furrow; (de disque) groove.

S

sillonner /sijɔne/ [1] *vt* crisscross.

similaire /similɛʀ/ *a* similar. **similitude** *nf* similarity.

simple /sɛ̃pl/ *a* simple; (non double) single. ● *nm* **~ dames/messieurs** ladies'/men's singles (+ *pl*). **simple d'esprit** *nmf* simpleton. **simplement** *adv* simply. **simplicité** *nf* simplicity; (naïveté) simpleness.

simplification /sɛ̃plifikasjɔ̃/ *nf* simplification. **simplifier** [45] *vt* simplify.

simpliste /sɛ̃plist/ *a* simplistic.

simulacre /simylakʀ/ *nm* pretence, sham.

simulation /simylasjɔ̃/ *nf* simulation. **simuler** [1] *vt* simulate.

simultané, ~e /simyltane/ *a* simultaneous.

sincère /sɛ̃sɛʀ/ *a* sincere. **sincérité** *nf* sincerity.

singe /sɛ̃ʒ/ *nm* monkey; (grand) ape. **singer** [40] *vt* mimic, ape.

singulier, -ière /sɛ̃gylje, -jɛʀ/ *a* peculiar, remarkable; (Gram) singular. ● *nm* (Gram) singular.

sinistre /sinistʀ/ *a* sinister. ● *nm* disaster; (incendie) blaze; (dommages) damage.

sinistré, ~e /sinistʀe/ *a* stricken. ● *nm, f* disaster victim.

sinon /sinɔ̃/ *conj* (autrement) otherwise; (sauf) except (**que** that); **difficile ~ impossible** difficult if not impossible.

sinueux, -euse /sinɥø, -z/ *a* winding; (fig) tortuous.

sirène /siʀɛn/ *nf* (appareil) siren; (femme) mermaid.

sirop /siʀo/ *nm* (de fruits, Méd) syrup; (boisson) cordial.

sis, ~e /si, siz/ *a* situated.

sismique /sismik/ *a* seismic.

site /sit/ *nm* site; **~ touristique** place of interest; **~ Internet** *or* **Web** Web site.

sitôt /sito/ *adv* **~ entré** immediately after coming in; **~ que** as soon as; **pas de ~** not for a while.

situation /sitɥasjɔ̃/ *nf* situation; (emploi) job, position; **~ de famille** marital status.

situé, ~e /sitɥe/ *a* situated.

situer /sitɥe/ [1] *vt* situate, locate. □ **se ~** *vpr* (se trouver) be situated.

six /sis/ (/si/ *before consonant,* /siz/ *before vowel*) *a & nm* six. **sixième** *a & nmf* sixth.

sketch (*pl* **~es**) /skɛtʃ/ *nm* (Théât) sketch.

ski /ski/ *nm* (matériel) ski; (Sport) skiing; **faire du ~** ski; **~ de fond** cross-country skiing; **~ nautique** water skiing. **skier** [45] *vi* ski.

slave /slav/ *a* Slav; (Ling) Slavonic.

slip /slip/ *nm* (d'homme) underpants (+ *pl*); (de femme) knickers (+ *pl*); **~ de bain** (swimming) trunks (+ *pl*); (du bikini) bikini bottom.

slogan /slɔgɑ̃/ *nm* slogan.

Slovaquie /slɔvaki/ *nf* Slovakia.

Slovénie /slɔveni/ *nf* Slovenia.

smoking /smɔkiŋ/ *nm* dinner jacket.

SNCF *abrév f* (**Société nationale des Chemins de fer français**) *French national railway company.*

snob /snɔb/ *nmf* snob. ● *a* snobbish. **snobisme** *nm* snobbery.

sobre /sɔbʀ/ *a* sober.

social, ~e (*mpl* **-iaux**) /sɔsjal, -jo/ *a* social.

socialisme /sɔsjalism/ *nm* socialism. **socialiste** *nmf & a* socialist.

société /sɔsjete/ *nf* society; (entreprise) company.

socle /sɔkl/ *nm* (de colonne, statue) plinth; (de lampe) base.
socquette /sɔkɛt/ *nf* ankle sock.
soda /sɔda/ *nm* fizzy drink.
sœur /sœʀ/ *nf* sister.
soi /swa/ *pron* oneself; **derrière ~** behind one; **en ~** in itself; **aller de ~** be obvious.
soi-disant /swadizɑ̃/ *a inv* so-called. ●*adv* supposedly.
soie /swa/ *nf* silk.
soif /swaf/ *nf* thirst; **avoir ~** be thirsty; **donner ~** make one thirsty.
soigné, **~e** /swaɲe/ *a* (apparence) tidy, neat; (travail) carefully done.
soigner /swaɲe/ [1] *vt* (s'occuper de) look after, take care of; (*tenue, style*) take care over; (*maladie*) treat. □ **se ~** *vpr* look after oneself.
soigneusement /swaɲøzmɑ̃/ *adv* carefully. **soigneux**, **-euse** *a* careful (**de** about); (ordonné) tidy.
soi-même /swamɛm/ *pron* oneself.
soin /swɛ̃/ *nm* care; (ordre) tidiness; **~s** care; (Méd) treatment; **avec ~** carefully; **avoir** *ou* **prendre ~ de qn/de faire** take care of sb/to do; **premiers ~s** first aid (+ *sg*).
soir /swaʀ/ *nm* evening; **à ce ~** see you tonight.
soirée /swaʀe/ *nf* evening; (réception) party.
soit /swa/ *conj* (à savoir) that is to say; **~ ... ~** either ... or. ●⇒ÊTRE [4].
soixante /swasɑ̃t/ *a & nm* sixty. **soixante-dix** *a & nm* seventy.
soja /sɔʒa/ *nm* (graines) soya beans (+ *pl*); (plante) soya.
sol /sɔl/ *nm* ground; (de maison) floor; (terrain agricole) soil.
solaire /sɔlɛʀ/ *a* solar; (*huile, filtre*) sun.
soldat /sɔlda/ *nm* soldier.
solde¹ /sɔld/ *nf* (salaire) pay.
solde² /sɔld/ *nm* (Comm) balance; **les ~s** the sales; **~s** (écrit en vitrine) sale; **en ~** (acheter) at sale price.
solder /sɔlde/ [1] *vt* sell off at sale price; (*compte*) settle. □ **se ~ par** *vpr* (aboutir à) end in.
sole /sɔl/ *nf* (poisson) sole.
soleil /sɔlɛj/ *nm* sun; (fleur) sunflower; **il y a du ~** it's sunny.
solennel, **~le** /sɔlanɛl/ *a* solemn.
solfège /sɔlfɛʒ/ *nm* musical theory.
solidaire /sɔlidɛʀ/ *a* (*mécanismes*) interdependent; (*collègues*) (mutually) supportive; **être ~ de qn** support sb. **solidarité** *nf* solidarity.
solide /sɔlid/ *a* solid; (*personne*) strong. ●*nm* solid.
solidifier /sɔlidifje/ [45] *vt* solidify. □ **se ~** *vpr* solidify.
solitaire /sɔlitɛʀ/ *a* solitary. ●*nmf* (*personne*) loner. **solitude** *nf* solitude.
solliciter /sɔlisite/ [1] *vt* seek; (faire appel à) call upon; **être très sollicité** be very much in demand.
sollicitude /sɔlisityd/ *nf* concern.
solo /sɔlo/ *nm & a inv* (Mus) solo.
solution /sɔlysjɔ̃/ *nf* solution.
solvable /sɔlvabl/ *a* solvent.
solvant /sɔlvɑ̃/ *nm* solvent.
sombre /sɔ̃bʀ/ *a* dark; (triste) sombre.
sombrer /sɔ̃bʀe/ [1] *vi* sink (**dans** into).
sommaire /sɔmɛʀ/ *a* (*exécution*) summary; (*description*) rough. ●*nm* contents (+ *pl*); **au ~** on the programme.
sommation /sɔmasjɔ̃/ *nf* (Mil) warning; (Jur) notice.
somme /sɔm/ *nf* sum; **en ~**, **~ toute** in short; **faire la ~ de** add (up), total (up). ●*nm* nap.
sommeil /sɔmɛj/ *nm* sleep; **avoir**

S

~ be *ou* feel sleepy; **en ~** (*projet*) put on ice. **sommeiller** [1] *vi* doze; (fig) lie dormant.

sommelier /sɔməlje/ *nm* wine steward.

sommer /sɔme/ [1] *vt* summon.

sommes /sɔm/ ⇒ÊTRE [4].

sommet /sɔmɛ/ *nm* top; (de montagne) summit; (de triangle) apex; (gloire) height.

sommier /sɔmje/ *nm* bed base.

somnambule /sɔmnɑ̃byl/ *nm* sleepwalker.

somnifère /sɔmnifɛʀ/ *nm* sleeping pill.

somnolent, ~e /sɔmnɔlɑ̃, -t/ *a* drowsy. **somnoler** [1] *vi* doze.

somptueux, -euse /sɔ̃ptɥø, -z/ *a* sumptuous.

son[1], sa (**son** *before vowel or mute h*) (*pl* **ses**) /sɔ̃, sa, sɔ̃n, se/ *a* (homme) his; (femme) her; (chose) its; (indéfini) one's.

son[2] /sɔ̃/ *nm* (bruit) sound; (de blé) bran; **baisser le ~** turn the volume down.

sondage /sɔ̃daʒ/ *nm* **~ (d'opinion)** (opinion) poll.

sonde /sɔ̃d/ *nf* (de forage) drill; (Méd) (d'évacuation) catheter; (d'examen) probe.

sonder /sɔ̃de/ [1] *vt* (*population*) poll; (explorer) sound; (*terrain*) drill; (*intentions*) sound out.

songe /sɔ̃ʒ/ *nm* dream.

songer /sɔʒe/ [40] *vt* **~ que** think that; **~ à** think about. **songeur, -euse** *a* pensive.

sonné, ~e /sɔne/ *a* (étourdi) groggy; 🅸 crazy.

sonner /sɔne/ [1] *vt/i* ring; (*clairon, glas*) sound; (*heure*) strike; (*domestique*) ring for; **midi sonné** well past noon; **~ de** (*clairon*) sound, blow.

sonnerie /sɔnʀi/ *nf* ringing; (de clairon) sounding; (sonnette) bell.

sonnet /sɔnɛ/ *nm* sonnet.

sonnette /sɔnɛt/ *nf* bell.

sonore /sɔnɔʀ/ *a* resonant; (*onde, effets*) sound; (*rire*) resounding.

sonorisation /sɔnɔʀizasjɔ̃/ *nf* (matériel) public address system.

sonorité /sɔnɔʀite/ *nf* resonance; (d'un instrument) tone.

sont /sɔ̃/ ⇒ÊTRE [4].

sophistiqué, ~e /sɔfistike/ *a* sophisticated.

sorcellerie /sɔʀsɛlʀi/ *nf* witchcraft. **sorcier** *nm* (guérisseur) witch doctor; (maléfique) sorcerer. **sorcière** *nf* witch.

sordide /sɔʀdid/ *a* sordid; (lieu) squalid.

sort /sɔʀ/ *nm* (destin, hasard) fate; (condition) lot; (maléfice) spell; **tirer (qch) au ~** draw lots (for sth).

sortant, ~e /sɔʀtɑ̃, -t/ *a* (*président etc.*) outgoing.

sorte /sɔʀt/ *nf* sort, kind; **de ~ que** so that; **en quelque ~** in a way; **de la ~** in this way; **faire en ~ que** make sure that.

sortie /sɔʀti/ *nf* exit; (promenade, dîner) outing; (*déclaration* 🅸) remark; (parution) publication; (de disque, film) release; (d'un ordinateur) output; **~s** (argent) outgoings.

sortilège /sɔʀtilɛʒ/ *nm* (magic) spell.

sortir /sɔʀtiʀ/ [46] *vi* (*aux être*) go out, leave; (venir) come out; (aller au spectacle) go out; (*livre, film*) come out; (*plante*) come up; **~ de** (*pièce*) leave; (*milieu social*) come from; (*limites*) go beyond; **~ du commun** *ou* **de l'ordinaire** be out of the ordinary. ● *vt* (*aux avoir*) take out; (*livre, modèle*) bring out; (dire 🅸) come out with; **~ qn de** get sb out of; **être sorti d'affaire** be in the clear. □ **s'en ~** *vpr* cope, manage.

sosie /sɔzi/ *nm* double.

sot, ~te /so, sɔt/ *a* silly.

sottise /sɔtiz/ *nf* silliness; (action,

remarque) foolish thing; **faire des ~s** be naughty.

sou /su/ *nm* ⓘ **~s** money; **sans le ~** without a penny; **près de ses ~s** tight-fisted.

soubresaut /subʀəso/ *nm* (sudden) start.

souche /suʃ/ *nf* (d'arbre) stump; (de famille) stock; (de carnet) counterfoil.

souci /susi/ *nm* (inquiétude) worry; (préoccupation) concern; (plante) marigold; **se faire du ~** worry.

soucier (se) /(sə)susje/ [45] *vpr* **se ~ de** care about. **soucieux, -ieuse** *a* concerned (**de** about).

soucoupe /sukup/ *nf* saucer; **~ volante** flying saucer.

soudain, ~e /sudɛ̃, -ɛn/ *a* sudden. ● *adv* suddenly.

soude /sud/ *nf* soda.

souder /sude/ [1] *vt* weld, solder; **famille très soudée** close-knit family. □ **se ~** *vpr* (os) knit (together).

soudoyer /sudwaje/ [31] *vt* bribe.

souffle /sufl/ *nm* (haleine) breath; (respiration) breathing; (explosion) blast; (vent) breath of air; **le ~ coupé** out of breath; **à couper le ~** breathtaking.

souffler /sufle/ [1] *vi* blow; (haleter) puff. ● *vt* (*bougie*) blow out; (*poussière, fumée*) blow; (*verre*) blow; (par explosion) destroy; (chuchoter) whisper; **~ la réplique à** prompt. **souffleur, -euse** *nm, f* (Théât) prompter.

souffrance /sufʀɑ̃s/ *nf* suffering; **en ~** (*affaire*) pending. **souffrant, ~e** *a* unwell.

souffrir /sufʀiʀ/ [21] *vi* suffer (**de** from). ● *vt* (endurer) suffer; **il ne peut pas le ~** he cannot stand *ou* bear him.

soufre /sufʀ/ *nm* sulphur.

souhait /swɛ/ *nm* wish; **à tes ~s!** bless you!; **paisible à ~** incredibly peaceful. **souhaitable** *a* desirable.

souhaiter /swete/ [1] *vt* **~ qch à qn** wish sb sth; **~ que/faire** hope that/to do; **~ la bienvenue à qn** welcome sb.

soûl, ~e /su, sul/ *a* drunk. ● *nm* **tout son ~** as much as one can.

soulagement /sulaʒmɑ̃/ *nm* relief. **soulager** [40] *vt* relieve.

soûler /sule/ [1] *vt* make drunk. □ **se ~** *vpr* get drunk.

soulèvement /sulɛvmɑ̃/ *nm* uprising.

soulever /sulve/ [6] *vt* lift, raise; (*question, poussière*) raise; (*enthousiasme*) arouse; (*foule*) stir up. □ **se ~** *vpr* lift *ou* raise oneself up; (se révolter) rise up.

soulier /sulje/ *nm* shoe.

souligner /suliɲe/ [1] *vt* underline; (*yeux*) outline; (taille) emphasize.

soumettre /sumɛtʀ/ [42] *vt* (assujettir) subject (**à** to); (présenter) submit (**à** to). □ **se ~** *vpr* submit (**à** to). **soumis, ~e** *a* submissive. **soumission** *nf* submission.

soupape /supap/ *nf* valve.

soupçon /supsɔ̃/ *nm* suspicion; **un ~ de** (un peu de) a touch of. **soupçonner** [1] *vt* suspect. **soupçonneux, -euse** *a* suspicious.

soupe /sup/ *nf* soup.

souper /supe/ [6] *vi* have supper. ● *nm* supper.

soupeser /supəze/ [1] *vt* judge the weight of; (fig) weigh up.

soupière /supjɛʀ/ *nf* (soup) tureen.

soupir /supiʀ/ *nm* sigh; **pousser un ~** heave a sigh.

soupirer /supiʀe/ [1] *vi* sigh.

souple /supl/ *a* supple; (*règlement, caractère*) flexible.

S

souplesse *nf* suppleness; (de règlement) flexibility.

source /suRs/ *nf* (de rivière, origine) source; (eau) spring; **prendre sa ~ à** rise in; **de ~ sûre** from a reliable source; **~ thermale** hot spring.

sourcil /suRsi/ *nm* eyebrow.

sourciller /suRsije/ [1] *vi* **sans ~** without batting an eyelid.

sourd, ~e /suR, -d/ *a* deaf; (*bruit, douleur*) dull; **faire la ~e oreille** turn a deaf ear. ●*nm, f* deaf person.

sourd-muet (*pl* **sourds-muets**), **sourde-muette** (*pl* **sourdes-muettes**) /suRmɥɛ, suRdmɥɛt/ *a* deaf and dumb. ●*nm, f* deaf-mute.

souricière /suRisjɛR/ *nf* mousetrap; (fig) trap.

sourire /suRiR/ [54] *vi* smile (**à** at); **~ à** (fortune) smile on. ●*nm* smile; **garder le ~** keep smiling.

souris /suRi/ *nf* mouse; **des ~** mice.

sournois, ~e /suRnwa, -z/ *a* sly, underhand.

sous /su/ *prép* under, beneath; **~ la main** handy; **~ la pluie** in the rain; **~ peu** shortly; **~ terre** underground.

sous-alimenté, ~e /suzalimɑ̃te/ *a* undernourished.

souscription /suskRipsjɔ̃/ *nf* subscription. **souscrire** [30] *vi* **~ à** subscribe to.

sous-entendre /suzɑ̃tɑ̃dR/ [3] *vt* imply. **sous-entendu** *nm* innuendo, insinuation.

sous-estimer /suzɛstime/ [1] *vt* underestimate.

sous-jacent, ~e /suʒasɑ̃, -t/ *a* underlying.

sous-marin, ~e /sumaRɛ̃, -in/ *a* underwater; (*plongée*) deep-sea. ●*nm* submarine.

soussigné, ~e /susiɲe/ *a & nm,f* undersigned.

sous-sol /susɔl/ *nm* (cave) basement.

sous-titre /sutitR/ *nm* subtitle.

soustraction /sustRaksjɔ̃/ *nf* (déduction) subtraction.

soustraire /sustRɛR/ [29] *vt* (déduire) subtract; (retirer) take away (**à** from). □ **se ~ à** *vpr* escape from.

sous-traitant /sutRɛtɑ̃/ *nm* subcontractor.

sous-verre /suvɛR/ *nm inv* glass mount.

sous-vêtement /suvɛtmɑ̃/ *nm* underwear.

soute /sut/ *nf* (de bateau) hold; **~ à charbon** coal-bunker.

soutenir /sutniR/ [59] *vt* support; (*effort, rythme*) sustain; (résister à) withstand; **~ que** maintain that.

soutenu, ~e /sutny/ *a* (constant) sustained; (style) formal.

souterrain, ~e /sutɛRɛ̃, -ɛn/ *a* underground. ●*nm* underground passage.

soutien /sutjɛ̃/ *nm* support.

soutien-gorge (*pl* **soutiens-gorge**) /sutjɛ̃gɔRʒ/ *nm* bra.

soutirer /sutiRe/ [1] *vt* **~ à qn** extract from sb.

souvenir[1] /suvniR/ *nm* memory, recollection; (objet) memento; (cadeau) souvenir; **en ~ de** in memory of.

souvenir[2] (se) /(sə)suvniR/ [59] *vpr* **se ~ de** remember; **se ~ que** remember that.

souvent /suvɑ̃/ *adv* often.

souverain, ~e /suvRɛ̃, -ɛn/ *a* sovereign. ●*nm, f* sovereign.

soviétique /sɔvjetik/ *a* Soviet.

soyeux, -euse /swajø, -z/ *a* silky.

spacieux, -ieuse /spasjø, -z/ *a* spacious.

sparadrap /spaRadRa/ *nm* (sticking) plaster.

spatial, **~e** (*mpl* **-iaux**) /spasjal, -jo/ *a* space.

speaker, **~ine** /spikœʀ, -kʀin/ *nm, f* announcer.

spécial, **~e** (*mpl* **-iaux**) /spesjal, -jo/ *a* special, (bizarre) odd. **spécialement** *adv* (exprès) specially; (très) especially.

spécialiser (se) /sɔspesjalize/ [1] *vpr* specialize (**dans** in). **spécialiste** *nmf* specialist. **spécialité** *nf* speciality; (US) specialty.

spécifier /spesifje/ [45] *vt* specify.

spécifique /spesifik/ *a* specific.

spécimen /spesimɛn/ *nm* specimen.

spectacle /spɛktakl/ *nm* show; (vue) sight, spectacle.

spectaculaire /spɛktakylɛʀ/ *a* spectacular.

spectateur, **-trice** /spɛktatœʀ, -tʀis/ *nm, f* (Sport) spectator; (témoin oculaire) onlooker; **les ~s** (Théât) the audience (+ *sg*).

spectre /spɛktʀ/ *nm* (revenant) spectre; (images) spectrum.

spéculateur, **-trice** /spekylatœʀ, -tʀis/ *nm, f* speculator. **spéculation** *nf* speculation. **spéculer** [1] *vi* speculate.

spéléologie /speleɔlɔʒi/ *nf* cave exploration, pot-holing.

spermatozoïde /spɛʀmatɔzɔid/ *nm* spermatozoon. **sperme** *nm* sperm.

sphère /sfɛʀ/ *nf* sphere.

spirale /spiʀal/ *nf* spiral.

spirituel, **~le** /spiʀitɥɛl/ *a* spiritual; (amusant) witty.

spiritueux /spiʀitɥø/ *nm* (alcool) spirit.

splendeur /splɑ̃dœʀ/ *nf* splendour. **splendide** *a* splendid.

sponsoriser /spɔ̃sɔʀize/ [1] *vt* sponsor.

spontané, **~e** /spɔ̃tane/ *a* spontaneous. **spontanéité** *nf* spontaneity.

sport /spɔʀ/ *a inv* (*vêtements*) casual. ● *nm* sport; **veste/voiture de ~** sports jacket/car.

sportif, **-ive** /spɔʀtif, -v/ *a* (*personne*) sporty; (*physique*) athletic; (*résultats*) sports. ● *nm, f* sportsman, sportswoman.

spot /spɔt/ *nm* spotlight; **~ (publicitaire)** ad.

square /skwaʀ/ *nm* small public garden.

squatter /skwate/ [1] *vt* squat in.

squelette /skəlɛt/ *nm* skeleton. **squelettique** *a* skeletal; (maigre) all skin and bone; (*rapport*) sketchy.

stabiliser /stabilize/ [1] *vt* stabilize. **stable** *a* stable.

stade /stad/ *nm* (Sport) stadium; (phase) stage.

stage /staʒ/ *nm* (cours) course; (professionnel) placement. **stagiaire** *nmf* course member; (apprenti) trainee.

stagner /stagne/ [1] *vi* stagnate.

stand /stɑ̃d/ *nm* stand; (de fête foraine) stall; **~ de tir** shooting range.

standard /stɑ̃daʀ/ *nm* switchboard. ● *a inv* standard. **standardiser** [1] *vt* standardize.

standardiste /stɑ̃daʀdist/ *nmf* switchboard operator.

standing /stɑ̃diŋ/ *nm* status, standing; **de ~** (*hôtel*) luxury.

starter /staʀtɛʀ/ *nm* (Auto) choke.

station /stasjɔ̃/ *nf* station; (halte) stop; **~ debout** standing position; **~ de taxis** taxi rank; **~ balnéaire/de ski** seaside/ski resort; **~ thermale** spa.

stationnaire /stasjɔnɛʀ/ *a* stationary.

stationnement /stasjɔnmɑ̃/ *nm* parking. **stationner** [1] *vi* park.

station-service (*pl* **stations-**

S

service) /stasjɔ̃sɛʀvis/ *nf* service station.
statique /statik/ *a* static.
statistique /statistik/ *nf* statistic; (science) statistics (+ *sg*). ● *a* statistical.
statue /staty/ *nf* statue.
statuer /statɥe/ [1] *vi* ~ **sur** give a ruling on.
statut /staty/ *nm* status. **statutaire** *a* statutory.
sténo /steno/ *nf* (sténographie) shorthand. **sténodactylo** *nf* shorthand typist. **sténographie** *nf* shorthand.
stéréo /steʀeo/ *nf & a inv* stereo.
stéréotype /steʀeɔtip/ *nm* stereotype.
stérile /steʀil/ *a* sterile.
stérilet /steʀilɛ/ *nm* coil, IUD.
stérilisation /steʀilizasjɔ̃/ *nf* sterilization. **stériliser** [1] *vt* sterilize.
stéroïde /steʀɔid/ *a & nm* steroid.
stimulant /stimylɑ̃/ *nm* stimulus; (médicament) stimulant.
stimulateur /stimylatœʀ/ *nm* ~ **cardiaque** (Méd) pacemaker.
stimuler /stimyle/ [1] *vt* stimulate.
stipuler /stipyle/ [1] *vt* stipulate.
stock /stɔk/ *nm* stock. **stocker** [1] *vt* stock.
stoïque /stɔik/ *a* stoical. ● *nmf* stoic.
stop /stɔp/ *interj* stop. ● *nm* stop sign; (feu arrière) brake light; **faire du** ~ ⊡ hitch-hike. **stopper** [1] *vt/i* stop.
store /stɔʀ/ *nm* blind; (de magasin) awning.
strapontin /stʀapɔ̃tɛ̃/ *nm* folding seat, jump seat.
stratégie /stʀateʒi/ *nf* strategy. **stratégique** *a* strategic.
stress /stʀɛs/ *nm* stress. **stressant**, ~**e** *a* stressful. **stressé**, ~**e** *a* stressed. **stresser** [1] *vt* put under stress.
strict /stʀikt/ *a* strict; (*tenue, vérité*) plain; **le** ~ **minimum** the bare minimum. **strictement** *adv* strictly.
strident, ~**e** /stʀidɑ̃, -t/ *a* shrill.
strophe /stʀɔf/ *nf* stanza, verse.
structure /stʀyktyʀ/ *nf* structure.
studieux, **-ieuse** /stydjø, -z/ *a* studious.
studio /stydjo/ *nm* (d'artiste, de télévision) studio; (logement) studio flat.
stupéfaction /stypefaksjɔ̃/ *nf* amazement. **stupéfait**, ~**e** *a* amazed.
stupéfiant, ~**e** /stypefjɑ̃, -t/ *a* astounding. ● *nm* drug, narcotic.
stupéfier /stypefje/ [45] *vt* amaze.
stupeur /stypœʀ/ *nf* amazement; (Méd) stupor.
stupide /stypid/ *a* stupid. **stupidité** *nf* stupidity.
style /stil/ *nm* style.
styliste /stilist/ *nmf* fashion designer.
stylo /stilo/ *nm* pen; ~ **(à) bille** ball-point pen; ~ **(à) encre** fountain pen.
su /sy/ ⇒SAVOIR [55].
suave /sɥav/ *a* sweet.
subalterne /sybaltɛʀn/ *a & nmf* subordinate.
subconscient /sypkɔ̃sjɑ̃/ *nm* subconscious.
subir /sybiʀ/ [2] *vt* be subjected to; (traitement, expériences) undergo.
subit, ~**e** /sybi, -t/ *a* sudden.
subjectif, **-ive** /sybʒɛktif, -v/ *a* subjective.
subjonctif /sybʒɔ̃ktif/ *nm* subjunctive.
subjuguer /sybʒyge/ [1] *vt* (charmer) captivate.
sublime /syblim/ *a* sublime.

submerger /sybmɛʀʒe/ [40] *vt* submerge; (fig) overwhelm.

subordonné, **~e** /sybɔʀdɔne/ *a & nm, f* subordinate.

subside /sybzid/ *nm* grant.

subsidiaire /sybzidjɛʀ/ *a* subsidiary; **question ~** tiebreaker.

subsistance /sybzistɑ̃s/ *nf* subsistence. **subsister** [1] *vi* subsist; (durer, persister) exist.

substance /sypstɑ̃s/ *nf* substance.

substantiel, **~le** /sypstɑ̃sjɛl/ *a* substantial.

substantif /sypstɑ̃tif/ *nm* noun.

substituer /sypstitɥe/ [1] *vt* substitute (**à** for). □ **se ~ à** *vpr* (remplacer) substitute for. **substitut** *nm* substitute; (Jur) deputy public prosecutor.

subtil, **~e** /syptil/ *a* subtle.

subtiliser /syptilize/ [1] *vt* **~ qch (à qn)** steal sth.

subvenir /sybvəniʀ/ [59] *vi* **~ à** provide for.

subvention /sybvɑ̃sjɔ̃/ *nf* subsidy. **subventionner** [1] *vt* subsidize.

subversif, **-ive** /sybvɛʀsif, -v/ *a* subversive.

suc /syk/ *nm* juice.

succédané /syksedane/ *nm* substitute (**de** for).

succéder /syksede/ [14] *vi* **~ à** succeed. □ **se ~** *vpr* succeed one another.

succès /syksɛ/ *nm* success; **à ~** (film, livre,) successful; **avoir du ~** be a success.

successeur /syksesœʀ/ *nm* successor. **successif**, **-ive** *a* successive. **succession** *nf* succession; (Jur) inheritance.

succinct, **~e** /syksɛ̃, -t/ *a* succinct.

succomber /sykɔ̃be/ [1] *vi* die; **~ à** succumb to.

succulent, **~e** /sykylɑ̃, -t/ *a* delicious.

succursale /sykyʀsal/ *nf* (Comm) branch.

sucer /syse/ [10] *vt* suck.

sucette /sysɛt/ *nf* (bonbon) lollipop; (tétine) dummy; (US) pacifier.

sucre /sykʀ/ *nm* sugar; **~ d'orge** barley sugar; **~ en poudre** caster sugar; **~ glace** icing sugar; **~ roux** brown sugar.

sucré /sykʀe/ *a* sweet; (additionné de sucre) sweetened. **sucrer** [1] *vt* sugar, sweeten. **sucreries** *nfpl* sweets.

sucrier, **-ière** /sykʀije, -jɛʀ/ *a* sugar. ● *nm* (récipient) sugar-bowl.

sud /syd/ *nm* south. ● *a inv* south; (*partie*) southern.

sud-est /sydɛst/ *nm* south-east.

sud-ouest /sydwɛst/ *nm* south-west.

Suède /sɥɛd/ *nf* Sweden.

suédois, **~e** /sɥedwa, -z/ *a* Swedish. ● *nm* (Ling) Swedish. **S~**, **~e** *nm, f* Swede.

suer /sɥe/ [1] *vt/i* sweat; **faire ~ qn** 🅘 get on sb's nerves.

sueur /sɥœʀ/ *nf* sweat; **en ~** covered in sweat.

suffire /syfiʀ/ [57] *vi* be enough (**à qn** for sb); **il suffit de compter** all you have to do is count; **une goutte suffit** a drop is enough; **~ à** (besoin) satisfy. □ **se ~** *vpr* **se ~ à soi-même** be self-sufficient.

suffisamment /syfizamɑ̃/ *adv* sufficiently; **~ de qch** enough of sth. **suffisance** *nf* (vanité) conceit. **suffisant**, **~e** *a* sufficient; (vaniteux) conceited.

suffixe /syfiks/ *nm* suffix.

suffoquer /syfɔke/ [1] *vt/i* choke, suffocate.

suffrage /syfʀaʒ/ *nm* (voix: Pol) vote; (système) suffrage.

suggérer /sygʒeʀe/ [14] *vt*

S

suggest. **suggestion** *nf* suggestion.

suicidaire /sɥisidɛʀ/ *a* suicidal. **suicide** *nm* suicide. **suicider** (**se**) [1] *vpr* commit suicide.

suinter /sɥɛ̃te/ [1] *vi* ooze.

suis /sɥi/ ⇒ÊTRE [4], SUIVRE [57].

Suisse /sɥis/ *nf* Switzerland. ●*nmf* Swiss. **suisse** *a* Swiss.

suite /sɥit/ *nf* continuation, rest; (d'un film) sequel; (série) series; (appartement, escorte) suite; (résultat) consequence; **à la ~, de ~** (successivement) in a row; **à la ~ de** (derrière) behind; **à la ~ de, par ~ de** (en conséquence) as a result of; **faire ~** (**à**) follow; **par la ~** afterwards; **~ à votre lettre du** further to your letter of the; **des ~s de** as a result of.

suivant[1], **~e** /sɥivɑ̃, -t/ *a* following, next. ●*nm, f* following *ou* next person.

suivant[2] /sɥivɑ̃/ *prép* (selon) according to.

suivi, **~e** /sɥivi/ *a* (*effort*) steady, sustained; (cohérent) consistent; **peu/très ~** (*cours*) poorly/well attended.

suivre /sɥivʀ/ [57] *vt/i* follow; (comprendre) follow; **faire ~** (courrier) forward. □ **se ~** *vpr* follow each other.

sujet, **~te** /syʒɛ, -t/ *a* **~ à** liable *ou* subject to. ●*nm* (d'un royaume) subject; (question) subject; (motif) cause; (Gram) subject; **au ~ de** about.

super /sypɛʀ/ *nm* (essence) four-star. ●*a inv* 🅸 (très) great. ●*adv* 🅸 ultra, really.

superbe /sypɛʀb/ *a* superb.

supérette /sypeʀɛt/ *nf* minimarket.

superficie /sypɛʀfisi/ *nf* area.

superficiel, **~le** /sypɛʀfisjɛl/ *a* superficial.

superflu /sypɛʀfly/ *a* superfluous. ●*nm* (excédent) surplus.

supérieur, **~e** /sypeʀjœʀ/ *a* (plus haut) upper; (*quantité, nombre*) greater (**à** than); (*études, principe*) higher (**à** than); (meilleur, hautain) superior (**à** to). ●*nm, f* superior. **supériorité** *nf* superiority.

superlatif, **-ive** /sypɛʀlatif, -v/ *a & nm* superlative.

supermarché /sypɛʀmaʀʃe/ *nm* supermarket.

superposer /sypɛʀpoze/ [1] *vt* superimpose; **lits superposés** bunk beds.

superproduction /sypɛʀpʀɔdyksjɔ̃/ *nf* (film) blockbuster.

superpuissance /sypɛʀpɥisɑ̃s/ *nf* superpower.

superstitieux, **-ieuse** /sypɛʀstisjø, -z/ *a* superstitious.

superviser /sypɛʀvize/ [1] *vt* supervise.

suppléant, **~e** /sypleɑ̃, -t/ *nmf & a* (**professeur**) **~** supply teacher; (**juge**) **~** deputy (judge).

suppléer /syplee/ [15] *vt* (remplacer) fill in for. ●*vi* **~ à** (compenser) make up for.

supplément /syplemɑ̃/ *nm* (argent) extra charge; (de frites, légumes) extra portion; **en ~** extra; **un ~ de** (travail) additional; **payer un ~** pay a supplement. **supplémentaire** *a* extra, additional.

supplice /syplis/ *nm* torture.

supplier /syplije/ [45] *vt* beg, beseech (**de** to).

support /sypɔʀ/ *nm* support; (Ordinat) medium.

supportable /sypɔʀtabl/ *a* bearable.

supporter[1] /sypɔʀtɛ/ [1] *vt* (*privations*) bear; (*personne*) put up with; (*structure*: Ordinat) support; **il ne supporte pas les enfants/de perdre** he can't stand children/losing.

supporter² /sypɔRtɛR/ *nm* (Sport) supporter.

supposer /sypoze/ [1] *vt* suppose; (impliquer) imply; **à ~ que** supposing that.

suppression /sypRɛsjɔ̃/ *nf* (de taxe) abolition; (de sanction) lifting; (de mot) deletion. **supprimer** [1] *vt* (*allocation*) withdraw; (*contrôle*) lift; (*train*) cancel; (*preuve*) suppress.

suprématie /sypRemasi/ *nf* supremacy.

suprême /sypRɛm/ *a* supreme.

sur /syR/ *prép* on, upon; (par-dessus) over; (au sujet de) about, on; (proportion) out of; (mesure) by; **~ la photo** in the photograph; **mettre/jeter ~** put/throw on to; **~ mesure** made to measure; **~ place** on the spot; **~ ce, je pars** with that, I must go; **~ le moment** at the time.

sûr /syR/ *a* certain, sure; (sans danger) safe; (digne de confiance) reliable; (*main*) steady; (*jugement*) sound; **être ~ de soi** be self-confident; **j'en étais ~!** I knew it!

surabondance /syRabɔ̃dɑ̃s/ *nf* overabundance.

surcharge /syRʃaRʒ/ *nf* overloading; (poids) excess load. **surcharger** [1] *vt* overload; (*texte*) alter.

surchauffer /syRʃofe/ [1] *vt* overheat.

surcroît /syRkRwa/ *nm* increase (**de** in); **de ~** in addition.

surdité /syRdite/ *nf* deafness.

surélever /syRɛlve/ [6] *vt* raise.

sûrement /syRmɑ̃/ *adv* certainly; (sans danger) safely; **il a ~ oublié** he must have forgotten.

surenchère /syRɑ̃ʃɛR/ *nf* higher bid. **surenchérir** [2] *vi* bid higher (**sur** than).

surestimer /syRɛstime/ [1] *vt* overestimate.

sûreté /syRte/ *nf* safety; (de pays) security; (d'un geste) steadiness; **être en ~** be safe; **S~ (nationale)** police (+ *pl*).

surexcité, **~e** /syRɛksite/ *a* very excited.

surf /sœRf/ *nm* surfing.

surface /syRfas/ *nf* surface; **faire ~** (*sous-marin*, fig) surface; **en ~** on the surface.

surfait, **~e** /syRfɛ, -t/ *a* overrated.

surfer /sœRfe/ [1] *vi* go surfing; **~ sur l'Internet** surf the Internet.

surgelé, **~e** /syRʒəle/ *a* (deep-) frozen; **aliments ~s** frozen food (+ *sg*).

surgir /syRʒiR/ [2] *vi* appear (suddenly); (*difficulté*) crop up.

sur-le-champ /syRləʃɑ̃/ *adv* right away.

surlendemain /syRlɑ̃dmɛ̃/ *nm* **le ~** two days later; **le ~ de** two days after.

surligneur /syRliɲœR/ *nm* highlighter (pen).

surmenage /syRmənaʒ/ *nm* overwork.

surmonter /syRmɔ̃te/ [1] *vt* (vaincre) overcome, surmount; (être au-dessus de) surmount, top.

surnaturel, **~le** /syRnatyRɛl/ *a* supernatural.

surnom /syRnɔ̃/ *nm* nickname. **surnommer** [1] *vt* nickname.

surpeuplé, **~e** /syRpœple/ *a* overpopulated.

surplomber /syRplɔ̃be/ [1] *vt/i* overhang.

surplus /syRply/ *nm* surplus.

suprenant, **~e** /syRpRənɑ̃, -t/ *a* surprising. **surprendre** [50] *vt* (étonner) surprise; (prendre au dépourvu) catch, surprise; (entendre) overhear. **surpris, ~e** *a* surprised (**de** at).

surprise /syʀpʀiz/ *nf* surprise.

surréaliste /syʀʀealist/ *a & nmf* surrealist.

sursaut /syʀso/ *nm* start, jump; **en ~** with a start; **~ de** (regain) burst of. **sursauter** [1] *vi* start, jump.

sursis /syʀsi/ *nm* reprieve; (Mil) deferment; **deux ans (de prison) avec ~** a two-year suspended sentence.

surtaxe /syʀtaks/ *nf* surcharge.

surtout /syʀtu/ *adv* especially; (avant tout) above all; **~ pas** certainly not.

surveillance /syʀvɛjɑ̃s/ *nf* watch; (d'examen) supervision; (de la police) surveillance. **surveillant, ~e** *nm,f* (de prison) warder; (au lycée) supervisor (in charge of discipline). **surveiller** [1] *vt* watch; (*travaux, élèves*) supervise.

survenir /syʀvəniʀ/ [58] *vi* occur, take place; (*personne*) turn up.

survêtement /syʀvɛtmɑ̃/ *nm* (Sport) tracksuit.

survie /syʀvi/ *nf* survival.

survivant, ~e /syʀvivɑ̃, -t/ *a* surviving. ● *nm,f* survivor.

survivre /syʀvivʀ/ [63] *vi* survive; **~ à** (*conflit*) survive; (*personne*) outlive.

survoler /syʀvɔle/ [1] *vt* fly over; (*livre*) skim through.

sus: **en ~** /ɑ̃sys/ *loc* in addition.

susceptible /sysɛptibl/ *a* touchy; **~ de faire** likely to do.

susciter /sysite/ [1] *vt* (éveiller) arouse; (occasionner) create.

suspect, ~e /syspɛ, -ɛkt/ *a* (*individu, faits*) suspicious; (*témoignage*) suspect; **~ de** suspected of. ● *nm,f* suspect. **suspecter** [1] *vt* suspect.

suspendre /syspɑ̃dʀ/ [3] *vt* (accrocher) hang (up); (interrompre, destituer) suspend; **suspendu à** hanging from. □ **se ~ à** *vpr* hang from.

suspens: **en ~** /ɑ̃syspɑ̃/ *loc* (*affaire*) outstanding; (dans l'indécision) in suspense.

suspense /syspɛns/ *nm* suspense.

suture /sytyʀ/ *nf* **point de ~** stitch.

svelte /svɛlt/ *a* slender.

S.V.P. *abrév* **(s'il vous plaît)** please.

syllabe /silab/ *nf* syllable.

symbole /sɛ̃bɔl/ *nm* symbol. **symboliser** [1] *vt* symbolize.

symétrie /simetʀi/ *nf* symmetry.

sympa /sɛ̃pa/ *a inv* 🅘 nice; **sois ~** be a pal.

sympathie /sɛ̃pati/ *nf* (goût) liking; (compassion) sympathy; **avoir de la ~ pour** like. **sympathique** *a* nice, pleasant. **sympathisant, ~e** *nm,f* sympathizer. **sympathiser** [1] *vi* get on well (**avec** with).

symphonie /sɛ̃fɔni/ *nf* symphony.

symptôme /sɛ̃ptom/ *nm* symptom.

synagogue /sinagɔg/ *nf* synagogue.

synchroniser /sɛ̃kʀɔnize/ [1] *vt* synchronize.

syncope /sɛ̃kɔp/ *nf* (Méd) blackout.

syndic /sɛ̃dik/ *nm* **~ (d'immeuble)** property manager.

syndicaliste /sɛ̃dikalist/ *nmf* (trade-)unionist. ● *a* (trade-) union.

syndicat /sɛ̃dika/ *nm* (trade) union; **~ d'initiative** tourist office.

syndiqué, ~e /sɛ̃dike/ *a* **être ~** be a (trade-)union member.

synonyme /sinɔnim/ *a* synonymous. ● *nm* synonym.

syntaxe /sɛ̃taks/ *nf* syntax.

synthèse /sɛ̃tɛz/ *nf* synthesis. **synthétique** *a* synthetic.

synthé(tiseur) /sɛ̃te(tizœʀ)/ *nm* synthesizer.

systématique /sistematik/ *a* systematic.

système /sistɛm/ *nm* system; **le ~ D** [!] resourcefulness.

t' /t/ ⇒TE.

ta /ta/ ⇒TON¹.

tabac /taba/ *nm* tobacco; (magasin) tobacconist's shop.

table /tabl/ *nf* table; **à ~!** dinner is ready!; **~ de nuit** bedside table; **~ des matières** table of contents; **~ à repasser** ironing board; **~ roulante** (tea-)trolley; (US) (serving) cart.

tableau (*pl* **~x**) /tablo/ *nm* picture; (peinture) painting; (panneau) board; (graphique) chart; (Scol) blackboard; **~ d'affichage** notice-board; **~ de bord** dashboard.

tablette /tablɛt/ *nf* shelf; **~ de chocolat** bar of chocolate.

tableur /tablœʀ/ *nm* spreadsheet.

tablier /tablije/ *nm* apron; (de pont) platform; (de magasin) shutter.

tabou /tabu/ *nm & a* taboo.

tabouret /tabuʀɛ/ *nm* stool.

tache /taʃ/ *nf* mark, spot, (salissure) stain; **faire ~ d'huile** spread; **~ de rousseur** freckle.

tâche /taʃ/ *nf* task, job.

tacher /taʃe/ [1] *vt* stain. □ **se ~** *vpr* (*personne*) get oneself dirty.

tâcher /taʃe/ [1] *vi* **~ de faire** try to do.

tacheté, ~e /taʃte/ *a* spotted.

tact /takt/ *nm* tact.

tactique /taktik/ *a* tactical. ● *nf* (Mil) tactics; **une ~** a tactic.

taie /tɛ/ *nf* **~ (d'oreiller)** pillowcase.

taille /tɑj/ *nf* (milieu du corps) waist; (hauteur) height; (grandeur) size; **de ~** sizeable; **être de ~ à faire** be up to doing.

taille-crayons /tajkʀɛjɔ̃/ *nm inv* pencil-sharpener.

tailler /taje/ [1] *vt* cut; (*arbre*) prune; (*crayon*) sharpen; (*vêtement*) cut out. □ **se ~** *vpr* [✱] clear off.

tailleur /tajœʀ/ *nm* (costume) woman's suit; (couturier) tailor; **en ~** cross-legged; **~ de pierre** stone-cutter.

taire /tɛʀ/ [47] *vt* not to reveal; **faire ~** silence. □ **se ~** *vpr* be silent *ou* quiet; (devenir silencieux) fall silent.

talc /talk/ *nm* talcum powder.

talent /talɑ̃/ *nm* talent. **talentueux, -euse** *a* talented, gifted.

talon /talɔ̃/ *nm* heel; (de chèque) stub.

tambour /tɑ̃buʀ/ *nm* drum; (d'église) vestibule.

Tamise /tamiz/ *nf* Thames.

tampon /tɑ̃pɔ̃/ *nm* (de bureau) stamp; (ouate) wad, pad; **~ (hygiénique)** tampon.

tamponner /tɑ̃pɔne/ [1] *vt* (*document*) stamp; (*véhicule*) crash into; (*plaie*) swab.

tandem /tɑ̃dɛm/ *nm* (vélo) tandem; (personnes: fig) duo.

tandis que /tɑ̃dik(ə)/ *conj* while.

tanière /tanjɛʀ/ *nf* den.

tant /tɑ̃/ *adv* (*travailler, manger*) so much; **~ de** (quantité) so much; (nombre) so many; **~ que** as long

T

as; **en ~ que** as; **~ mieux!** all the better!; **~ pis!** too bad!

tante /tɑ̃t/ *nf* aunt.

tantôt /tɑ̃to/ *adv* sometimes.

tapage /tapaʒ/ *nm* din.

tape /tap/ *nf* slap. **tape-à-l'œil** *a inv* flashy, tawdry.

taper /tape/ [1] *vt* hit; (prendre [!]) scrounge; **~ (à la machine)** type. ● *vi* (cogner) bang; (*soleil*) beat down; **~ dans** (puiser dans) dig into; **~ sur** hit; **~ sur l'épaule de qn** tap sb on the shoulder. ▫ **se ~** *vpr* (*corvée* [!]) get stuck with [!].

tapis /tapi/ *nm* carpet; (petit) rug; **~ de bain** bathmat; **~ roulant** (pour objets) conveyor belt; (pour piétons) moving walkway.

tapisser /tapise/ [1] *vt* (wall) paper; (fig) cover (**de** with). **tapisserie** *nf* tapestry; (papier peint) wallpaper.

taquin, ~e /takɛ̃, -in/ *a* fond of teasing. ● *nm,f* tease(r).

tard /taʀ/ *adv* late; **au plus ~** at the latest; **plus ~** later; **sur le ~** late in life.

tarder /taʀde/ [1] *vi* (être lent à venir) be a long time coming; **~ (à faire)** take a long time (doing), delay (doing); **sans (plus) ~** without (further) delay; **il me tarde de** I'm longing to.

tardif, -ive /taʀdif, -v/ *a* late.

tare /taʀ/ *nf* (défaut) defect.

tarif /taʀif/ *nm* rate; (de train, taxi) fare; **plein ~** full price.

tarir /taʀiʀ/ [2] *vt/i* dry up. ▫ **se ~** *vpr* dry up.

tarte /taʀt/ *nf* tart. ● *a inv* (ridicule [!]) ridiculous.

tartine /taʀtin/ *nf* slice of bread; **~ de beurre** slice of bread and butter. **tartiner** [1] *vt* spread.

tartre /taʀtʀ/ *nm* (de bouilloire) fur, scale; (sur les dents) tartar.

tas /tɑ/ *nm* pile, heap; **un** *ou* **des ~ de** [!] lots of.

tasse /tɑs/ *nf* cup; **~ à thé** teacup.

tasser /tɑse/ [1] *vt* pack, squeeze; (*terre*) pack (down). ▫ **se ~** *vpr* (*terrain*) sink; (se serrer) squeeze up.

tâter /tɑte/ [1] *vt* feel; (opinion: fig) sound out. ● *vi* **~ de** try out.

tatillon, ~ne /tatijɔ̃, -jɔn/ *a* finicky.

tâtonnements /tatɔnmɑ̃/ *nmpl* (essais) trial and error (+ *sg*).

tâtons: **à ~** /atatɔ̃/ *loc* **avancer à ~** grope one's way along.

tatouage /tatwaʒ/ *nm* (dessin) tattoo.

taupe /top/ *nf* mole.

taureau (*pl* **~x**) /tɔʀo/ *nm* bull; **le T~** Taurus.

taux /to/ *nm* rate.

taxe /taks/ *nf* tax.

taxi /taksi/ *nm* taxi(-cab); (personne [!]) taxi driver.

taxiphone® /taksifɔn/ *nm* pay phone.

Tchécoslovaquie /tʃekɔslɔvaki/ *nf* Czechoslovakia.

tchèque /tʃɛk/ *a* Czech; **République ~** Czech Republic. **T~** *nmf* Czech.

te, t' /tə, t/ *pron* you; (indirect) (to) you; (réfléchi) yourself.

technicien, ~ne /tɛknisjɛ̃, -ɛn/ *nm,f* technician.

technique /tɛknik/ *a* technical. ● *nf* technique.

techno /tɛkno/ *nf* (Mus) techno.

technologie /tɛknɔlɔʒi/ *nf* technology.

teindre /tɛ̃dʀ/ [22] *vt* dye. ▫ **se ~** *vpr* **se ~ les cheveux** dye one's hair.

teint /tɛ̃/ *nm* complexion.

teinte /tɛ̃t/ *nf* shade. **teinter** [1] *vt* (*verre*) tint; (*bois*) stain.

teinture /tɛ̃tyʀ/ *nf* (produit) dye.

teinturier, -ière /tɛ̃tyʀje, -jɛʀ/ *nm,f* dry-cleaner.

tel, **~le** /tɛl/ *a* such; **un ~ livre** such a book; **~ que** such as, like; (ainsi que) (just) as; **~ ou ~** such-and-such; **~ quel** (just) as it is.

télé /tele/ *nf* ▣ TV.

télécharger /teleʃaʀʒe/ [40] *vt* (Ordinat) download.

télécommande /telekɔmɑ̃d/ *nf* remote control.

télécommunications /telekɔmynikasjɔ̃/ *nfpl* telecommunications.

téléconférence /telekɔ̃feʀɑ̃s/ *nf* teleconferencing.

télécopie /telekɔpi/ *nf* fax. **télécopieur** *nm* fax machine.

téléfilm /telefilm/ *nm* TV film.

télégramme /telegʀam/ *nm* telegram.

télégraphier /telegʀafje/ [45] *vt/i* **~ (à)** cable.

téléguidé, **~e** /telegide/ *a* radio-controlled.

télématique /telematik/ *nf* telematics (+ *sg*).

téléphérique /telefeʀik/ *nm* cable car.

téléphone /telefɔn/ *nm* (tele-)phone; **~ à carte** cardphone. **téléphoner** [1] *vt/i* **~ (à)** (tele)phone. **téléphonique** *a* (tele)phone.

téléserveur /telesɛʀvœʀ/ *nm* (Internet) remote server.

télésiège /telesjɛʒ/ *nm* chairlift.

téléski /teleski/ *nm* ski tow.

téléspectateur, **-trice** /telespɛktatœʀ, -tʀis/ *nm,f* (television) viewer.

télévente /televɑ̃t/ *nf* telesales (+ *pl*).

télévisé, **~e** /televize/ *a* (*débat*) televised; **émission ~e** television programme. **télévision** *nf* television.

télex /telɛks/ *nm* telex.

tellement /tɛlmɑ̃/ *adv* (tant) so much; (si) so; **~ de** (quantité) so much; (nombre) so many.

téméraire /temeʀɛʀ/ *a* (*personne*) reckless.

témoignage /temwaɲaʒ/ *nm* testimony, evidence; (récit) account; **~ de** (marque) token of.

témoigner /temwaɲe/ [1] *vi* testify (**de** to). ●*vt* (montrer) show; **~ que** testify that.

témoin /temwɛ̃/ *nm* witness; (Sport) baton; **être ~ de** witness; **~ oculaire** eyewitness.

tempe /tɑ̃p/ *nf* (Anat) temple.

tempérament /tɑ̃peʀamɑ̃/ *nm* temperament, disposition.

température /tɑ̃peʀatyʀ/ *nf* temperature.

tempête /tɑ̃pɛt/ *nf* storm; **~ de neige** snowstorm.

temple /tɑ̃pl/ *nm* temple; (protestant) church.

temporaire /tɑ̃pɔʀɛʀ/ *a* temporary.

temps /tɑ̃/ *nm* (notion) time; (Gram) tense; (étape) stage; **à ~ partiel/plein** part-/full-time; **ces derniers ~** lately; **dans le ~** at one time; **dans quelque ~** in a while; **de ~ en ~** from time to time; **~ d'arrêt** pause; **avoir tout son ~** have plenty of time; (météo) weather; **~ de chien** filthy weather; **quel ~ fait-il?** what's the weather like?

tenace /tənas/ *a* stubborn.

tenaille /tənɑj/ *nf* pincers (+ *pl*).

tendance /tɑ̃dɑ̃s/ *nf* tendency; (évolution) trend; **avoir ~ à** tend to.

tendon /tɑ̃dɔ̃/ *nm* tendon.

tendre¹ /tɑ̃dʀ/ [3] *vt* stretch; (*piège*) set; (*bras*) stretch out; (*main*) hold out; (*cou*) crane; **~ qch à qn** hold sth out to sb; **~ l'oreille** prick up one's ears. ●*vi* **~ à** tend to.

tendre² /tɑ̃dʀ/ *a* tender; (couleur, bois) soft. **tendresse** *nf* tenderness.

T

tendu, **~e** /tɑ̃dy/ *a* (*corde*) tight; (*personne, situation*) tense.

ténèbres /tenɛbʀ/ *nfpl* darkness (+ *sg*).

teneur /tənœʀ/ *nf* content.

tenir /təniʀ/ [59] *vt* hold; (*pari, promesse, hôtel*) keep; (*place*) take up; (*propos*) utter; (*rôle*) play; **~ de** (avoir reçu de) have got from; **~ pour** regard as; **~ chaud** keep warm; **~ compte de** take into account; **~ le coup** hold out; **~ tête à** stand up to. ● *vi* hold; **~ à** be attached to; **~ à faire** be anxious to do; **~ bon** stand firm; **~ dans** fit into; **~ de qn** take after sb; **tiens!** (surprise) hey! ▫ **se ~** *vpr* (debout) stand; (avoir lieu) be held; **se ~ à** hold on to; **s'en ~ à** (se limiter à) confine oneself to.

tennis /tenis/ *nm* tennis; **~ de table** table tennis. ● *nmpl* (chaussures) sneakers.

ténor /tenɔʀ/ *nm* tenor.

tension /tɑ̃sjɔ̃/ *nf* tension; **avoir de la ~** have high blood-pressure.

tentation /tɑ̃tasjɔ̃/ *nf* temptation.

tentative /tɑ̃tativ/ *nf* attempt.

tente /tɑ̃t/ *nf* tent.

tenter /tɑ̃te/ [1] *vt* (allécher) tempt; (essayer) try (**de faire** to do).

tenture /tɑ̃tyʀ/ *nf* curtain; **~s** draperies.

tenu, **~e** /təny/ *a* **bien ~** well kept; **~ de** required. ● ⇒TENIR [58].

tenue /təny/ *nf* (habillement) dress; (de maison) upkeep; (conduite) (good) behaviour; (maintien) posture; **~ de soirée** evening dress.

Tergal® /tɛʀgal/ *nm* Terylene®.

terme /tɛʀm/ *nm* (mot) term; (date limite) time-limit; (fin) end; **né avant ~** premature; **à long/court ~** long-/short-term; **en bons ~s** on good terms (**avec** with).

terminaison /tɛʀminɛzɔ̃/ *nf* (Gram) ending.

terminal, **~e** (*mpl* **-aux**) /tɛʀminal, -o/ *a* terminal. ● *nm* terminal. **terminale** *nf* (Scol) ≈ sixth form; (US) twelfth grade.

terminer /tɛʀmine/ [1] *vt/i* finish; (*discours*) end, finish. ▫ **se ~** *vpr* end (**par** with).

terne /tɛʀn/ *a* dull, drab.

ternir /tɛʀniʀ/ [2] *vt/i* tarnish. ▫ **se ~** *vpr* tarnish.

terrain /tɛʀɛ̃/ *nm* ground; (parcelle) piece of land; (à bâtir) plot; **~ d'aviation** airfield; **~ de camping** campsite; **~ de golf** golf course; **~ de jeu** playground; **~ vague** waste ground.

terrasse /tɛʀas/ *nf* terrace; **à la ~** (d'un café) outside (a café).

terrasser /tɛʀase/ [1] *vt* (*adversaire*) knock down; (*maladie*) strike down.

terre /tɛʀ/ *nf* (planète, matière) earth; (étendue, pays) land; (sol) ground; **à ~** (Naut) ashore; **par ~** (dehors) on the ground; (dedans) on the floor; **~ (cuite)** terracotta; **la ~ ferme** dry land; **~ glaise** clay. **terreau** (*pl* **~x**) *nm* compost. **terre-plein** (*pl* **terres-pleins**) *nm* platform; (de route) central reservation.

terrestre /tɛʀɛstʀ/ *a* (*animaux*) land; (de notre planète) of the Earth.

terreur /tɛʀœʀ/ *nf* terror.

terrible /tɛʀibl/ *a* terrible; (formidable [!]) terrific.

terrier /tɛʀje/ *nm* (trou) burrow; (chien) terrier.

terrifier /tɛʀifje/ [45] *vt* terrify.

territoire /tɛʀitwaʀ/ *nm* territory.

terroir /tɛʀwaʀ/ *nm* land; **du ~** local.

terroriser /tɛʀɔʀize/ [1] *vt* terrorize.

terrorisme /tɛʀɔʀism/ *nm*

terrorism. **terroriste** *nmf* terrorist.

tertiaire /tɛRsjɛR/ *a* (*secteur*) service.

tes /te/ ⇒TON[1].

test /tɛst/ *nm* test.

testament /tɛstamɑ̃/ *nm* (Jur) will; (politique, artistique) testament; **Ancien/Nouveau T~** Old/New Testament.

tétanos /tetanos/ *nm* tetanus.

têtard /tɛtaR/ *nm* tadpole.

tête /tɛt/ *nf* head; (visage) face; (cheveux) hair; **à la ~ de** at the head of; **à ~ reposée** at one's leisure; **de ~** (*calculer*) in one's head; **faire la ~** sulk; **tenir ~ à qn** stand up to sb; **il n'en fait qu'à sa ~** he does just as he pleases; **en ~** (Sport) in the lead; **faire une ~** (au football) head the ball; **une forte ~** a rebel; **la ~ la première** head first; **de la ~ aux pieds** from head to toe.

tête-à-tête /tɛtatɛt/ *nm inv* tête-à-tête; **en ~** in private.

tétée /tete/ *nf* feed. **téter** [14] *vt*/*i* suck.

tétine /tetin/ *nf* (de biberon) teat; (sucette) dummy; (US) pacifier.

têtu, ~e /tety/ *a* stubborn.

texte /tɛkst/ *nm* text; (de leçon) subject; (morceau choisi) passage.

texteur /tɛkstœR/ *nm* (Ordinat) word-processor.

textile /tɛkstil/ *nm & a* textile.

TGV *abrév m* (**train à grande vitesse**) TGV, high-speed train.

thé /te/ *nm* tea.

théâtre /teɑtR/ *nm* theatre; (d'un crime) scene; **faire du ~** act.

théière /tejɛR/ *nf* teapot.

thème /tɛm/ *nm* theme; (traduction: Scol) prose.

théorie /teɔRi/ *nf* theory. **théorique** *a* theoretical.

thérapie /teRapi/ *nf* therapy.

thermique /tɛRmik/ *a* thermal.

thermomètre /tɛRmɔmɛtR/ *nm* thermometer.

thermos® /tɛRmos/ *nm ou f* Thermos® (flask).

thermostat /tɛRmɔsta/ *nm* thermostat.

thèse /tɛz/ *nf* thesis.

thon /tɔ̃/ *nm* tuna.

thym /tɛ̃/ *nm* thyme.

tibia /tibja/ *nm* shinbone.

tic /tik/ *nm* (contraction) tic, twitch; (manie) habit.

ticket /tikɛ/ *nm* ticket.

tiède /tjɛd/ *a* lukewarm; (*nuit*) warm.

tiédir /tjediR/ [2] *vt*/*i* (**faire**) **~** warm up.

tien, ~ne /tjɛ̃, -ɛn/ *pron* **le ~, la ~ne, les ~(ne)s** yours; **à la ~ne!** cheers!

tiens, tient /tjɛ̃/ ⇒TENIR [59].

tiercé /tjɛRse/ *nm* place-betting.

tiers, tierce /tjɛR, tjɛRs/ *a* third. ● *nm* (fraction) third; (personne) third party. **tiers-monde** *nm* Third World.

tige /tiʒ/ *nf* (Bot) stem, stalk; (en métal) shaft, rod.

tigre /tigR/ *nm* tiger.

tigresse /tigRɛs/ *nf* tigress.

tilleul /tijœl/ *nm* lime tree, linden tree; (infusion) linden tea.

timbre /tɛ̃bR/ *nm* stamp; (sonnette) bell; (de voix) tone. **~ poste** (*pl* **~s poste**) *nm* postage stamp. **timbrer** [1] *vt* stamp.

timide /timid/ *a* shy, timid. **timidité** *nf* shyness.

timoré, ~e /timɔRe/ *a* timorous.

tintement /tɛ̃tmɑ̃/ *nm* (de sonnette) ringing; (de clés) jingling.

tique /tik/ *nf* tick.

tir /tiR/ *nm* (Sport) shooting; (action de tirer) firing; (feu, rafale) fire; **~ à l'arc** archery; **~ au pigeon** clay pigeon shooting.

tirage /tiRaʒ/ *nm* (de photo)

T

printing; (de journal) circulation; (de livre) edition; (Ordinat) hard copy; (de cheminée) draught; ~ **au sort** draw.

tire-bouchon (*pl* ~**s**) /tiʀbuʃɔ̃/ *nm* corkscrew.

tirelire /tiʀliʀ/ *nf* piggy bank.

tirer /tiʀe/ [1] *vt* pull; (*langue*) stick out; (*conclusion, trait, rideaux*) draw; (*coup de feu*) fire; (*gibier*) shoot; (*photo*) print; ~ **de** (sortir) take *ou* get out of; (extraire) extract from; (*plaisir, nom*) derive from; ~ **parti de** take advantage of; ~ **profit de** profit from; **se faire** ~ **l'oreille** get told off. ● *vi* shoot, fire (**sur** at); ~ **sur** (*corde*) pull at; (*couleur*) verge on; ~ **à sa fin** be drawing to a close; ~ **au clair** clarify; ~ **au sort** draw lots (for). □ **se** ~ *vpr* [!] clear off; **se** ~ **de** get out of; **s'en** ~ (en réchapper) pull through; (réussir [!]) cope.

tiret /tiʀɛ/ *nm* dash.

tireur /tiʀœʀ/ *nm* gunman; ~ **d'élite** marksman; ~ **isolé** sniper.

tiroir /tiʀwaʀ/ *nm* drawer. **tiroir-caisse** (*pl* **tiroirs-caisses**) *nm* till, cash register.

tisane /tizan/ *nf* herbal tea.

tissage /tisaʒ/ *nm* weaving. **tisser** [1] *vt* weave. **tisserand** *nm* weaver.

tissu /tisy/ *nm* fabric, material; (biologique) tissue; **un** ~ **de mensonges** (fig) a pack of lies. **tissu-éponge** (*pl* **tissus-éponge**) *nm* towelling.

titre /titʀ/ *nm* title; (diplôme) qualification; (Comm) bond; ~**s** (droits) claims; (**gros**) ~**s** headlines; **à** ~ **d'exemple** as an example; **à juste** ~ rightly; **à** ~ **privé** in a private capacity; **à double** ~ on two accounts; ~ **de propriété** title deed.

tituber /titybe/ [1] *vi* stagger.

titulaire /titylɛʀ/ *a* **être** ~ be a permanent staff member; **être** ~ **de** hold. ● *nmf* (de permis) holder. **titulariser** [1] *vt* give permanent status to.

toast /tost/ *nm* (pain) piece of toast; (canapé, allocution) toast.

toboggan /tɔbɔgɑ̃/ *nm* (de jeu) slide; (Auto) flyover.

toi /twa/ *pron* you; (réfléchi) yourself; **dépêche-**~ hurry up.

toile /twal/ *nf* cloth; (tableau) canvas; ~ **d'araignée** cobweb; ~ **de fond** (fig) backdrop; **la** ~ (Internet) the Web.

toilette /twalɛt/ *nf* (habillement) outfit; ~**s** (cabinets) toilet(s); **de** ~ (articles, savon) toilet; **faire sa** ~ have a wash.

toi-même /twamɛm/ *pron* yourself.

toit /twa/ *nm* roof; ~ **ouvrant** (Auto) sunroof.

toiture /twatyʀ/ *nf* roof.

tôle /tol/ *nf* (plaque) iron sheet; ~ **ondulée** corrugated iron.

tolérant, ~**e** /tɔleʀɑ̃, -t/ *a* tolerant. **tolérer** [14] *vt* tolerate.

tomate /tɔmat/ *nf* tomato.

tombe /tɔ̃b/ *nf* grave; (pierre) gravestone.

tombeau (*pl* ~**x**) /tɔ̃bo/ *nm* tomb.

tomber /tɔ̃be/ [1] *vi* (*aux être*) fall; (*fièvre, vent*) drop; **faire** ~ knock over; (*gouvernement*) bring down; **laisser** ~ (*objet, amoureux*) drop; (*collègue*) let down; (*activité*) give up; **laisse** ~! [!] forget it!; ~ **à l'eau** (*projet*) fall through; ~ **bien** *ou* **à point** come at the right time; ~ **en panne** break down; ~ **en syncope** faint; ~ **sur** (trouver) run across.

tombola /tɔ̃bɔla/ *nf* tombola; (US) lottery.

tome /tɔm/ *nm* volume.

ton¹, **ta** (**ton** *before vowel or mute h*) (*pl* **tes**) /tɔ̃, ta, tɔ̃n, te/ *a* your.

ton² /tɔ̃/ *nm* (hauteur de voix) pitch; **d'un ~ sec** drily; **de bon ~** in good taste.

tonalité /tɔnalite/ *nf* (Mus) key; (de téléphone) dialling tone; (US) dial tone.

tondeuse /tɔ̃døz/ *nf* (à moutons) shears (+ *pl*); (à cheveux) clippers (+ *pl*); **~ à gazon** lawn-mower. **tondre** [3] *vt* (*herbe*) mow; (*mouton*) shear; (*cheveux*) clip.

tonne /tɔn/ *nf* tonne.

tonneau (*pl* **~x**) /tɔno/ *nm* barrel; (en voiture) somersault.

tonnerre /tɔnɛʀ/ *nm* thunder.

tonton /tɔ̃tɔ̃/ *nm* [!] uncle.

tonus /tɔnys/ *nm* energy.

torche /tɔʀʃ/ *nf* torch.

torchon /tɔʀʃɔ̃/ *nm* (pour la vaisselle) tea towel.

tordre /tɔʀdʀ/ [3] *vt* twist. □ **se ~** *vpr* **se ~ la cheville** twist one's ankle; **se ~ de douleur** writhe in pain; **se ~ (de rire)** split one's sides.

tordu, **~e** /tɔʀdy/ *a* twisted, bent; (*esprit*) warped, twisted.

torpille /tɔʀpij/ *nf* torpedo.

torrent /tɔʀɑ̃/ *nm* torrent.

torride /tɔʀid/ *a* torrid; (*chaleur*) scorching.

torse /tɔʀs/ *nm* chest; (Anat) torso.

tort /tɔʀ/ *nm* wrong; **avoir ~** be wrong (**de faire** to do); **donner ~ à** prove wrong; **être dans son ~** be in the wrong; **faire (du) ~ à** harm; **à ~** wrongly; **à ~ et à travers** without thinking.

torticolis /tɔʀtikɔli/ *nm* stiff neck.

tortiller /tɔʀtije/ [1] *vt* twist, twirl. □ **se ~** *vpr* wriggle.

tortionnaire /tɔʀsjɔnɛʀ/ *nm* torturer.

tortue /tɔʀty/ *nf* tortoise; (d'eau) turtle.

tortueux, **-euse** /tɔʀtɥø, -z/ *a* (*chemin*) twisting; (*explication*) tortuous.

torture /tɔʀtyʀ/ *nf* torture. **torturer** [1] *vt* torture.

tôt /to/ *adv* early; **au plus ~** at the earliest; **le plus ~ possible** as soon as possible; **~ ou tard** sooner or later; **ce n'est pas trop ~!** it's about time!

total, **~e** (*mpl* **-aux**) /tɔtal, -o/ *a* total. ● *nm* (*pl* **-aux**) total; **au ~** all in all. **totalement** *adv* totally. **totaliser** [1] *vt* total. **totalitaire** *a* totalitarian.

totalité /tɔtalite/ *nf* **la ~ de** all of.

touche /tuʃ/ *nf* (de piano) key; (de peinture) touch; (**ligne de**) **~** (Sport) touchline.

toucher /tuʃe/ [1] *vt* touch; (émouvoir) move, touch; (contacter) get in touch with; (*cible*) hit; (*argent*) draw; (*chèque*) cash; (concerner) affect. ● *vi* **~ à** touch; (*question*) touch on; (*fin, but*) approach; **je vais lui en ~ deux mots** I'll talk to him about it. □ **se ~** *vpr* (*lignes*) touch. ● *nm* (sens) touch.

touffe /tuf/ *nf* (de poils, d'herbe) tuft; (de plantes) clump.

toujours /tuʒuʀ/ *adv* always; (encore) still; (de toute façon) anyway; **pour ~** for ever; **~ est-il que** the fact remains that.

toupet /tupɛ/ *nm* (culot [!]) cheek, nerve.

tour /tuʀ/ *nf* tower; (immeuble) tower block; (échecs) rook; **~ de contrôle** control tower. ● *nm* (mouvement, succession, tournure) turn; (excursion) trip; (à pied) walk; (en auto) drive; (artifice) trick, (circonférence) circumference; (Tech) lathe; **~ (de piste)** lap; **à ~ de rôle** in turn; **à mon ~** when it is my turn; **c'est mon ~ de** it is my turn to; **faire le ~ de** go round; (*question*) survey; **~ d'horizon**

T

survey; ~ **de potier** potter's wheel; ~ **de taille** waist measurement; (ligne) waistline.
tourbillon /turbijɔ̃/ *nm* whirlwind; (d'eau) whirlpool; (fig) swirl.
tourisme /turism/ *nm* tourism; **faire du** ~ do some sightseeing.
touriste /turist/ *nmf* tourist. **touristique** *a* tourist; (*route*) scenic.
tourmenter /turmɑ̃te/ *vt* torment. □ **se** ~ *vpr* worry.
tournant, ~**e** /turnɑ̃, -t/ *a* (qui pivote) revolving. ● *nm* bend; (fig) turning-point.
tourne-disque (*pl* ~**s**) /turnədisk/ *nm* record-player.
tournée /turne/ *nf* (de facteur, au café) round; **c'est ma** ~ I'll buy this round; (d'artiste) tour.
tourner /turne/ [1] *vt* turn; (*film*) shoot, make; ~ **le dos à** turn one's back on; ~ **en dérision** mock. ● *vi* turn; (*toupie, tête*) spin; (*moteur, usine*) run; ~ **autour de** go round; (*personne, maison*) hang around; (*terre*) revolve round; (*question*) centre on; ~ **de l'œil** Ⓘ faint; **mal** ~ (*affaire*) turn out badly. □ **se** ~ *vpr* turn.
tournesol /turnəsɔl/ *nm* sunflower.
tournevis /turnəvis/ *nm* screwdriver.
tournoi /turnwa/ *nm* tournament.
tourte /turt/ *nf* pie.
tourterelle /turtərɛl/ *nf* turtle dove.
Toussaint /tusɛ̃/ *nf* **la** ~ All Saints' Day.
tousser /tuse/ [1] *vi* cough.
tout, ~**e** (*pl* **tous, toutes**) /tu, tut/ *nm* (ensemble) whole; **en** ~ in all; **pas du** ~! not at all! ● *a* all; (n'importe quel) any; ~ **le pays** the whole country, all the country; ~**e la nuit/journée** the whole night/day; ~ **un paquet** a whole pack; **tous les jours** every day; **tous les deux ans** every two years; ~ **le monde** everyone; **tous les deux, toutes les deux** both of them; **tous les trois** all three (of them). ● *pron* everything; all; anything; **tous** /tus/, **toutes** all; **tous ensemble** all together; **prends** ~ take everything; ~ **ce que tu veux** everything you want. ● *adv* (très) very; (entièrement) all; ~ **au bout/début** right at the end/ beginning; ~ **en marchant** while walking; ~ **à coup** all of a sudden; ~ **à fait** quite, completely; ~ **à l'heure** in a moment; (passé) a moment ago; ~ **au** *ou* **le long de** throughout; ~ **au plus/moins** at most/least; ~ **de même** all the same; ~ **de suite** straight away; ~ **entier** whole; ~ **neuf** brand new; ~ **nu** stark naked. **tout-à-l'égout** *nm inv* main drainage.
toutefois /tutfwa/ *adv* however.
tout(-)terrain /tuterɛ̃/ *a inv* all terrain.
toux /tu/ *nf* cough.
toxicomane /tɔksikɔman/ *nmf* drug addict.
toxique /tɔksik/ *a* toxic.
trac /trak/ *nm* **le** ~ nerves; (Théât) stage fright.
tracas /traka/ *nm* worry.
trace /tras/ *nf* (traînée, piste) trail; (d'animal, de pneu) tracks; ~**s de pas** footprints.
tracer /trase/ [10] *vt* draw; (écrire) write; (route) open up.
trachée-artère /traʃeartɛr/ *nf* windpipe.
tracteur /traktœr/ *nm* tractor.
tradition /tradisjɔ̃/ *nf* tradition. **traditionnel**, ~**le** *a* traditional.
traducteur, **-trice** /tradyktœr,

-tRis/ *nm, f* translator. **traduction** *nf* translation.

traduire /tRadɥiR/ [17] *vt* translate; ~ **en justice** take to court.

trafic /tRafik/ *nm* (commerce, circulation) traffic.

trafiquant, ~**e** /tRafikɑ̃, -t/ *nm, f* trafficker; (d'armes, de drogues) dealer.

trafiquer /tRafike/ [1] *vi* traffic. ● *vt* [!] (moteur) fiddle with.

tragédie /tRaʒedi/ *nf* tragedy. **tragique** *a* tragic.

trahir /tRaiR/ [2] *vt* betray. **trahison** *nf* betrayal; (Mil) treason.

train /tRɛ̃/ *nm* (Rail) train; (allure) pace; **aller bon** ~ walk briskly; **en** ~ **de faire** (busy) doing; ~ **d'atterrissage** undercarriage; ~ **électrique** (jouet) electric train set; ~ **de vie** lifestyle.

traîne /tRɛn/ *nf* (de robe) train; **à la** ~ lagging behind.

traîneau (*pl* ~**x**) /tRɛno/ *nm* sleigh.

traînée /tRɛne/ *nf* (trace) trail; (longue) streak; (femme: péj) slut.

traîner /tRɛne/ [1] *vt* drag (along); ~ **les pieds** drag one's feet. ● *vi* (pendre) trail; (rester en arrière) trail behind; (flâner) hang about; (*papiers, affaires*) lie around; ~ (**en longueur**) drag on; **ça n'a pas traîné!** that didn't take long! □ **se** ~ *vpr* (par terre) crawl.

traire /tRɛR/ [29] *vt* milk.

trait /tRɛ/ *nm* line; (en dessinant) stroke; (caractéristique) feature, trait; ~**s** (du visage) features; **avoir** ~ **à** relate to; **d'un** ~ (*boire*) in one gulp; ~ **d'union** hyphen; (fig) link

traite /tRɛt/ *nf* (de vache) milking; (Comm) draft; **d'une** (**seule**) ~ in one go, at a stretch.

traité /tRete/ *nm* (pacte) treaty; (ouvrage) treatise.

traitement /tRɛtmɑ̃/ *nm* treatment; (salaire) salary; ~ **de données** data processing; ~ **de texte** word processing.

traiter /tRete/ [1] *vt* treat; (*affaire*) deal with; (*données, produit*) process; ~ **qn de lâche** call sb a coward. ● *vi* deal (**avec** with); ~ **de** (*sujet*) deal with.

traiteur /tRɛtœR/ *nm* caterer; (boutique) delicatessen.

traître, **-esse** /tRɛtR, -ɛs/ *a* treacherous. ● *nm, f* traitor.

trajectoire /tRaʒɛktwaR/ *nf* path.

trajet /tRaʒɛ/ *nm* (voyage) journey; (itinéraire) route.

trame /tRam/ *nf* (de tissu) weft; (de récit) framework.

tramway /tRamwɛ/ *nm* tram; (US) streetcar.

tranchant, ~**e** /tRɑ̃ʃɑ̃, -t/ *a* sharp; (fig) cutting. ● *nm* cutting edge; **à double** ~ two-edged.

tranche /tRɑ̃ʃ/ *nf* (rondelle) slice; (bord) edge; (d'âge, de revenu) bracket.

tranchée /tRɑ̃ʃe/ *nf* trench.

trancher /tRɑ̃ʃe/ [1] *vt* cut; (*question*) decide; (contraster) contrast (**sur** with).

tranquille /tRɑ̃kil/ *a* quiet; (*esprit*) at rest; (*conscience*) clear; **être**/**laisser** ~ be/leave in peace; **tiens-toi** ~! be quiet! **tranquillisant** *nm* tranquillizer. **tranquilliser** [1] *vt* reassure. **tranquillité** *nf* (peace and) quiet; (d'esprit) peace of mind.

transcription /tRɑ̃skipsjɔ̃/ *nf* transcription; (copie) transcript. **transcrire** [30] *vt* transcribe.

transe /tRɑ̃s/ *nf* **en** ~ in a trance.

transférer /tRɑ̃sfeRe/ [14] *vt* transfer.

transfert /tRɑ̃sfɛR/ *nm* transfer; ~ **d'appel** (au téléphone) call diversion.

transformateur /tʀɑ̃sfɔʀmatœʀ/ *nm* transformer.

transformation /tʀɑ̃sfɔʀmasjɔ̃/ *nf* change; transformation.

transformer /tʀɑ̃sfɔʀme/ [1] *vt* change; (radicalement) transform; (*vêtement*) alter. □ **se ~** *vpr* change; (radicalement) be transformed; (**se**) **~ en** turn into.

transiger /tʀɑ̃siʒe/ [40] *vi* compromise.

transiter /tʀɑ̃zite/ [1] *vt/i* **~ par** pass through.

transitif, **-ive** /tʀɑ̃zitif, -v/ *a* transitive.

translucide /tʀɑ̃slysid/ *a* translucent.

transmettre /tʀɑ̃smɛtʀ/ [42] *vt* (*savoir, maladie*) pass on; (*ondes*) transmit; (à la radio) broadcast. **transmission** *nf* transmission; (*radio*) broadcasting.

transparence /tʀɑ̃spaʀɑ̃s/ *nf* transparency. **transparent**, **~e** *a* transparent.

transpercer /tʀɑ̃spɛʀse/ [10] *vt* pierce.

transpiration /tʀɑ̃spiʀasjɔ̃/ *nf* perspiration. **transpirer** [1] *vi* perspire.

transplanter /tʀɑ̃splɑ̃te/ [1] *vt* (Bot, Méd) transplant.

transport /tʀɑ̃spɔʀ/ *nm* transport (ation); **durant le ~** in transit; **les ~s** transport (+ *sg*); **les ~s en commun** public transport (+ *sg*).

transporter /tʀɑ̃spɔʀte/ [1] *vt* transport; (à la main) carry. **transporteur** *nm* haulier; (US) trucker.

transversal, **~e** (*mpl* **-aux**) /tʀɑ̃svɛʀsal, -o/ *a* cross, transverse.

trapu, **~e** /tʀapy/ *a* stocky.

traumatisant, **~e** /tʀɔmatizɑ̃, -t/ *a* traumatic. **traumatiser** *vt* [1] traumatize. **traumatisme** *nm* trauma.

travail (*pl* **-aux**) /tʀavaj, -o/ *nm* work; (emploi, tâche) job; (façonnage) working; **travaux** work (+ *sg*); (routiers) roadworks; **~ à la chaîne** production line work; **travaux dirigés** (Scol) practical; **travaux forcés** hard labour; **travaux manuels** handicrafts; **travaux ménagers** housework.

travailler /tʀavaje/ [1] *vi* work; (se déformer) warp. ● *vt* (façonner) work; (étudier) work at *ou* on.

travailleur, **-euse** /tʀavajœʀ, -øz/ *nm, f* worker. ● *a* hardworking.

travailliste /tʀavajist/ *a* Labour. ● *nmf* Labour party member.

travers /tʀavɛʀ/ *nm* (défaut) failing; **à ~** through; **au ~** (**de**) through; **de ~** (*chapeau, nez*) crooked; (*regarder*) askance; **j'ai avalé de ~** it went the wrong way; **en ~** (**de**) across.

traversée /tʀavɛʀse/ *nf* crossing.

traverser /tʀavɛʀse/ [1] *vt* cross; (transpercer) go (right) through; (*période, forêt*) go *ou* pass through.

traversin /tʀavɛʀsɛ̃/ *nm* bolster.

travesti /tʀavɛsti/ *nm* transvestite.

trébucher /tʀebyʃe/ [1] *vi* stumble, trip (over); **faire ~** trip (up).

trèfle /tʀɛfl/ *nm* (plante) clover; (cartes) clubs.

treillis /tʀeji/ *nm* trellis; (en métal) wire mesh; (tenue militaire) combat uniform.

treize /tʀɛz/ *a & nm* thirteen.

tréma /tʀema/ *nm* diaeresis.

tremblement /tʀɑ̃bləmɑ̃/ *nm* shaking; **~ de terre** earthquake. **trembler** [1] *vi* shake, tremble; (*lumière, voix*) quiver.

tremper /tʀɑ̃pe/ [1] *vt/i* soak; (plonger) dip; (*acier*) temper; **faire**

~ soak; **~ dans** (fig) be mixed up. □ **se ~** *vpr* (se baigner) have a dip.

tremplin /tʀɑ̃plɛ̃/ *nm* springboard.

trente /tʀɑ̃t/ *a & nm* thirty; **se mettre sur son ~ et un** dress up; **tous les ~-six du mois** once in a blue moon.

trépied /tʀepje/ *nm* tripod.

très /tʀɛ/ *adv* very; **~ aimé/estimé** much liked/esteemed.

trésor /tʀezɔʀ/ *nm* treasure; **le T~ public** the revenue department.

trésorerie /tʀezɔʀʀi/ *nf* (bureaux) accounts department; (du Trésor public) revenue office; (argent) funds (+ *pl*); (gestion) accounts (+ *pl*). **trésorier, -ière** *nm,f* treasurer.

tressaillement /tʀesajmɑ̃/ *nm* quiver; start.

tresse /tʀɛs/ *nf* braid, plait.

trêve /tʀɛv/ *nf* truce; (fig) respite; **~ de plaisanteries** that's enough joking.

tri /tʀi/ *nm* (classement) sorting; (sélection) selection; **faire le ~ de** (classer) sort; (choisir) select; **centre de ~** sorting office.

triangle /tʀijɑ̃gl/ *nm* triangle.

tribal, ~e (*mpl* **-aux**) /tʀibal, -o/ *a* tribal.

tribord /tʀibɔʀ/ *nm* starboard.

tribu /tʀiby/ *nf* tribe.

tribunal (*mpl* **-aux**) /tʀibynal, -o/ *nm* court.

tribune /tʀibyn/ *nf* (de stade) grandstand; (d'orateur) rostrum; (débat) forum; (d'église) gallery.

tribut /tʀiby/ *nm* tribute.

tributaire /tʀibytɛʀ/ *a* **~ de** dependent on.

tricher /tʀiʃe/ [1] *vi* cheat. **tricheur, -euse** *nm,f* cheat.

tricolore /tʀikɔlɔʀ/ *a* three-coloured; (*écharpe*) red, white and blue; (*équipe*) French.

tricot /tʀiko/ *nm* (activité) knitting; (pull) sweater; **en ~** knitted; **~ de corps** vest; (US) undershirt. **tricoter** [1] *vt/i* knit.

trier /tʀije/ [45] *vt* (classer) sort; (choisir) select.

trimestre /tʀimɛstʀ/ *nm* quarter; (Scol) term. **trimestriel, ~le** *a* quarterly; (*bulletin*) end-of term.

tringle /tʀɛ̃gl/ *nf* rail.

trinquer /tʀɛ̃ke/ [1] *vi* clink glasses.

triomphant, ~e /tʀijɔ̃fɑ̃, -t/ *a* triumphant. **triomphe** *nm* triumph. **triompher** [1] *vi* triumph (**de** over); (jubiler) be triumphant.

tripes /tʀip/ *nfpl* (mets) tripe (+ *sg*); (entrailles [!]) guts.

triple /tʀipl/ *a* triple, treble. ● *nm* **le ~** three times as much (**de** as). **triplés, -es** *nm, fpl* triplets.

tripot /tʀipo/ *nm* gambling den.

tripoter /tʀipɔte/ [1] *vt* [!] (*personne*) grope; (*objet*) fiddle with.

trisomique /tʀizɔmik/ *a* **être ~** have Down's syndrome.

triste /tʀist/ *a* sad; (*rue, temps, couleur*) dreary; (lamentable) dreadful. **tristesse** *nf* sadness; dreariness.

trivial, ~e (*mpl* **-iaux**) /tʀivjal, -jo/ *a* coarse.

troc /tʀɔk/ *nm* exchange; (Comm) barter.

trognon /tʀɔɲɔ̃/ *nm* (de fruit) core.

trois /tʀwɑ/ *a & nm* three; **hôtel ~ étoiles** three-star hotel. **troisième** *a & nmf* third.

trombone /tʀɔ̃bɔn/ *nm* (Mus) trombone; (agrafe) paperclip.

trompe /tʀɔ̃p/ *nf* (d'éléphant) trunk; (Mus) horn.

tromper /tʀɔ̃pe/ [1] *vt* deceive, mislead; (déjouer) elude. □ **se ~** *vpr* be mistaken; **se ~ de route/**

T

d'heure take the wrong road/get the time wrong.

trompette /tʀɔ̃pɛt/ *nf* trumpet.

trompeur, -euse /tʀɔ̃pœʀ, -øz/ *a* (*apparence*) deceptive.

tronc /tʀɔ̃/ *nm* trunk; (boîte) collection box.

tronçon /tʀɔ̃sɔ̃/ *nm* section.

tronçonneuse /tʀɔ̃sɔnøz/ *nf* chain saw.

trône /tʀon/ *nm* throne. **trôner** [1] *vi* (*vase*) have pride of place (**sur** on).

trop /tʀo/ *adv* (*grand, loin*) too; (*boire, marcher*) too much; **~ (de)** (quantité) too much; (nombre) too many; **ce serait ~ beau** one should be so lucky; **de ~, en ~** too much; too many; **il a bu un verre de ~** he's had one too many; **se sentir de ~** feel one is in the way.

trophée /tʀɔfe/ *nm* trophy.

tropical, ~e (*mpl* **-aux**) /tʀɔpikal, -o/ *a* tropical. **tropique** *nm* tropic.

trop-plein (*pl* **~s**) /tʀoplɛ̃/ *nm* excess; (dispositif) overflow.

troquer /tʀɔke/ [1] *vt* exchange; (Comm) barter (**contre** for).

trot /tʀo/ *nm* trot; **aller au ~** trot. **trotter** [1] *vi* trot.

trotteuse /tʀɔtøz/ *nf* (de montre) second hand.

trottoir /tʀɔtwaʀ/ *nm* pavement; (US) sidewalk; **~ roulant** moving walkway.

trou /tʀu/ *nm* hole; (moment) gap; (lieu: péj) dump; **~ (de mémoire)** memory lapse; **~ de serrure** keyhole; **faire son ~** carve one's niche.

trouble /tʀubl/ *a* (*eau, image*) unclear; (louche) shady. ● *nm* (émoi) emotion; **~s** (Pol) disturbances; (Méd) disorder (+ *sg*).

troubler /tʀuble/ [1] *vt* disturb; (*eau*) make cloudy; (inquiéter) trouble. □ **se ~** *vpr* (*personne*) become flustered.

trouer /tʀue/ [1] *vt* make a hole *ou* holes in; **mes chaussures sont trouées** my shoes have got holes in them.

troupe /tʀup/ *nf* troop; (d'acteurs) company.

troupeau (*pl* **~x**) /tʀupo/ *nm* herd; (de moutons) flock.

trousse /tʀus/ *nf* case, bag; **aux ~s de** hot on sb's heels; **~ de toilette** toilet bag.

trousseau (*pl* **~x**) /tʀuso/ *nm* (de clefs) bunch; (de mariée) trousseau.

trouver /tʀuve/ [1] *vt* find; (penser) think; **il est venu me ~** he came to see me. □ **se ~** *vpr* (être) be; (se sentir) feel; **il se trouve que** it happens that; **si ça se trouve** maybe; **se ~ mal** faint.

truand /tʀyɑ̃/ *nm* gangster.

truc /tʀyk/ *nm* (moyen) way; (artifice) trick; (chose [!]) thing. **trucage** *nm* (cinéma) special effect.

truffe /tʀyf/ *nf* (champignon, chocolat) truffle; (de chien) nose.

truffer /tʀyfe/ [1] *vt* (fig) fill, pack (**de** with).

truie /tʀɥi/ *nf* (animal) sow.

truite /tʀɥit/ *nf* trout.

truquer /tʀyke/ [1] *vt* fix, rig; (*photo*) fake; (*résultats*) fiddle.

tsar /tsaʀ/ *nm* tsar, czar.

tu /ty/ *pron* (parent, ami, enfant) you. ● ⇒TAIRE [47].

tuba /tyba/ *nm* (Mus) tuba; (Sport) snorkel.

tube /tyb/ *nm* tube.

tuberculose /tybɛʀkylɔz/ *nf* tuberculosis.

tuer /tɥe/ [1] *vt* kill; (d'une balle) shoot, kill; (épuiser) exhaust; **~ par balles** shoot dead. □ **se ~** *vpr* kill oneself; (accident) be killed.

tuerie /tyʀi/ *nf* killing.
tue-tête: **à ~** /atytɛt/ *loc* at the top of one's voice.
tuile /tɥil/ *nf* tile; (malchance 🄸) (stroke of) bad luck.
tulipe /tylip/ *nf* tulip.
tumeur /tymœʀ/ *nf* tumour.
tumulte /tymylt/ *nm* commotion; (désordre) turmoil.
tunique /tynik/ *nf* tunic.
Tunisie /tynizi/ *nf* Tunisia.
tunnel /tynɛl/ *nm* tunnel.
turbo /tyʀbɔ/ *a* turbo. ● *nf* (voiture) turbo.
turbulent, **~e** /tyʀbulɑ̃, -t/ *a* boisterous, turbulent.
turc, **-que** /tyʀk/ *a* Turkish. ● *nm* (Ling) Turkish. **T~**, **-que** Turk.
turfiste /tyʀfist/ *nmf* racegoer.
Turquie /tyʀki/ *nf* Turkey.
tutelle /tytɛl/ *nf* (Jur) guardianship; (fig) protection.
tuteur, **-trice** /tytœʀ, -tʀis/ *nm, f* (Jur) guardian. ● *nm* (bâton) stake.
tutoiement /tytwamɑ̃/ *nm* use of the 'tu' form. **tutoyer** [31] *vt* address using the 'tu' form.
tuyau (*pl* **~x**) /tɥijo/ *nm* pipe; (conseil 🄸) tip; **~ d'arrosage** hosepipe.
TVA *abrév f* (**taxe à la valeur ajoutée**) VAT.
tympan /tɛ̃pɑ̃/ *nm* ear-drum.
type /tip/ *nm* (genre, traits) type; (individu 🄸) bloke, guy; **le ~ même de** a classic example of. ● *a inv* typical.
typique /tipik/ *a* typical.
tyran /tiʀɑ̃/ *nm* tyrant. **tyrannie** *nf* tyranny. **tyranniser** [1] *vt* oppress, tyrannize.

UE *abrév f* (**Union européenne**) European Union.
Ukraine /ykʀɛn/ *nf* Ukraine.
ulcère /ylsɛʀ/ *nm* (Méd) ulcer.
ULM *abrév m* (**ultraléger motorisé**) microlight.
ultérieur, **~e** /ylteʀjœʀ/ *a* later. **ultérieurement** *adv* later.
ultime /yltim/ *a* final.

un, **une** /œ̃, yn/

● *déterminant*
···➤ a; (devant voyelle) an; **~ animal** an animal; **~ jour** one day; **pas ~ arbre** not a single tree; **il fait ~ froid!** it's so cold!

● *pronom*
···➤ one; **l'~ d'entre nous** one of us; **les ~s croient que...** some believe...
···➤ **la une** the front page.
···➤ **j'en veux une** I want one.

● *adjectif*
···➤ one, a, an; **j'ai ~ garçon et deux filles** I have a *ou* one boy and two girls; **il est une heure** it is one o'clock.

● *nom masculin & féminin*
···➤ **~ par ~** one by one.

unanime /ynanim/ *a* unanimous.
unanimité /ynanimite/ *nf* unanimity; **à l'~** unanimously.
uni, **~e** /yni/ *a* united; (*couple*) close; (*surface*) smooth; (*tissu*) plain.

unième /ynjɛm/ *a* -first; **vingt et ~** twenty-first; **cent ~** one hundred and first.

unifier /ynifje/ [45] *vt* unify.

uniforme /ynifɔʀm/ *nm* uniform. ● *a* uniform. **uniformiser** [1] *vt* standardize. **uniformité** *nf* uniformity.

unilatéral, **~e** (*mpl* **-aux**) /ynilateʀal, -o/ *a* unilateral.

union /ynjɔ̃/ *nf* union; **l'U~ européenne** the European Union.

unique /ynik/ *a* (seul) only; (*prix, voie*) one; (incomparable) unique; **enfant ~** only child; **sens ~** one-way street. **uniquement** *adv* only, solely.

unir /yniʀ/ [2] *vt* unite. ▫ **s'~** *vpr* unite, join.

unité /ynite/ *nf* unit; (harmonie) unity.

univers /ynivɛʀ/ *nm* universe.

universel, **~le** /ynivɛʀsɛl/ *a* universal.

universitaire /ynivɛʀsitɛʀ/ *a* (*résidence*) university; (*niveau*) academic. ● *nmf* academic.

université /ynivɛʀsite/ *nf* university.

uranium /yʀanjɔm/ *nm* uranium.

urbain, **~e** /yʀbɛ̃, -ɛn/ *a* urban. **urbanisme** *nm* town planning.

urgence /yʀʒɑ̃s/ *nf* (cas) emergency; (de situation, tâche) urgency; **d'~** (*mesure*) emergency; (*transporter*) urgently; **les ~s** casualty (+ *sg*). **urgent**, **~e** *a* urgent.

urine /yʀin/ *nf* urine. **urinoir** *nm* urinal.

urne /yʀn/ *nf* (*électorale*) ballot box; (vase) urn; **aller aux ~s** go to the polls.

urticaire /yʀtikɛʀ/ *nf* hives (+ *pl*), urticar.

us /ys/ *nmpl* **les ~ et coutumes** habits and customs.

usage /yzaʒ/ *nm* use; (coutume) custom; (de langage) usage; **à l'~ de** for; **d'~** (habituel) customary; **faire ~ de** make use of.

usagé, **~e** /yzaʒe/ *a* worn.

usager /yzaʒe/ *nm* user.

usé, **~e** /yze/ *a* worn (out); (banal) trite.

user /yze/ [1] *vt* wear (out). ● *vi* **~ de** use. ▫ **s'~** *vpr* (*tissu*) wear (out).

usine /yzin/ *nf* factory, plant; **~ sidérurgique** ironworks (+ *pl*).

usité, **~e** /yzite/ *a* common.

ustensile /ystɑ̃sil/ *nm* utensil.

usuel, **~le** /yzɥɛl/ *a* ordinary, everyday.

usure /yzyʀ/ *nf* (détérioration) wear (and tear).

utérus /yteʀys/ *nm* womb, uterus.

utile /ytil/ *a* useful.

utilisable /ytilizabl/ *a* usable. **utilisation** *nf* use. **utiliser** [1] *vt* use.

utopie /ytɔpi/ *nf* Utopia; (idée) Utopian idea. **utopique** *a* Utopian.

UV[1] *abrév f* (**unité de valeur**) course unit.

UV[2] *abrév mpl* (**ultraviolets**) ultraviolet rays; **faire des ~** use a sunbed.

va /va/ ⇒ALLER [8].

vacance /vakɑ̃s/ *nf* (poste) vacancy.

vacances /vakɑ̃s/ *nfpl* holiday (s); (US) vacation; **en ~** on holiday; **~ d'été, grandes ~**

summer holidays. **vacancier, -ière** *nm,f* holidaymaker; (US) vacationer.

vacant **~e** /vakɑ̃, -t/ *a* vacant.

vacarme /vakaʀm/ *nm* din.

vaccin /vaksɛ̃/ *nm* vaccine. **vacciner** [1] *vt* vaccinate.

vache /vaʃ/ *nf* cow. ● *a* (méchant 🄸) nasty.

vaciller /vasije/ [1] *vi* sway, wobble; (*lumière*) flicker; (hésiter) falter; (*santé, mémoire*) fail.

vadrouiller /vadʀuje/ [1] *vi* 🄸 wander about.

va-et-vient /vaevjɛ̃/ *nm inv* toing and froing; (de personnes) comings and goings; **faire le ~** go to and fro; (interrupteur) two-way switch.

vagabond, ~e /vagabɔ̃, -d/ *nm,f* vagrant.

vagin /vaʒɛ̃/ *nm* vagina.

vague /vag/ *a* vague. ● *nm* **regarder dans le ~** stare into space; **il est resté dans le ~** he was vague about it. ● *nf* wave; **~ de fond** ground swell; **~ de froid** cold spell; **~ de chaleur** heatwave.

vaillant, ~e /vajɑ̃, -t/ *a* brave; (vigoureux) strong.

vaille /vaj/ ⇒VALOIR [60].

vain, ~e /vɛ̃, vɛn/ *a* vain, futile; **en ~** in vain.

vaincre /vɛ̃kʀ/ [59] *vt* defeat; (surmonter) overcome. **vaincu, ~e** *nm,f* (Sport) loser. **vainqueur** *nm* victor; (Sport) winner.

vais /vɛ/ ⇒ALLER [8].

vaisseau (*pl* **~x**) /vɛso/ *nm* ship; (veine) vessel; **~ spatial** spaceship.

vaisselle /vɛsɛl/ *nf* crockery; (à laver) dishes; **faire la ~** do the washing-up, wash the dishes; **liquide ~** washing-up liquid.

valable /valabl/ *a* valid; (de qualité) worthwhile.

valet /valɛ/ *nm* (aux cartes) jack; **~ (de chambre)** manservant.

valeur /valœʀ/ *nf* value; (mérite) worth, value; **~s** (Comm) stocks and shares; **avoir de la ~** be valuable; **prendre/perdre de la ~** go up/down in value; **objets de ~** valuables; **sans ~** worthless.

valide /valid/ *a* (*personne*) fit; (*billet*) valid. **valider** [1] *vt* validate.

valise /valiz/ *nf* (suit)case; **faire ses ~s** pack (one's bags).

vallée /vale/ *nf* valley.

valoir /valwaʀ/ [60] *vi* (mériter) be worth; (égaler) be as good as; (être valable) (*règle*) apply; **faire ~** (*mérite, qualité*) emphasize; (*terrain*) cultivate; (*droit*) assert; **se faire ~** put oneself forward; **~ cher/100 francs** be worth a lot/100 francs; **que vaut ce vin?** what's this wine like?; **ne rien ~** be useless *ou* no good; **ça ne me dit rien qui vaille** I don't like the sound of that; **~ la peine** *or* **le coup** 🄸 be worth it; **il vaut/vaudrait mieux faire** it is/would be better to do. ● *vt* **~ qch à qn** (*éloges, critiques*) earn sb sth; (*admiration*) win sb sth. □ **se ~** *vpr* (être équivalents) be as good as each other; **ça se vaut** it's all the same.

valoriser /valɔʀize/ [1] *vt* add value to; (*produit*) promote; (*profession*) make attractive; (*région, ressources*) develop.

valse /vals/ *nf* waltz.

vandale /vɑ̃dal/ *nmf* vandal.

vanille /vanij/ *nf* vanilla.

vanité /vanite/ *nf* vanity. **vaniteux, -euse** *a* vain, conceited.

vanne /van/ *nf* (d'écluse) sluice-gate; (propos 🄸) dig 🄸.

vantard, ~e /vɑ̃taʀ, -d/ *a* boastful. ● *nm,f* boaster.

vanter /vɑ̃te/ [1] *vt* praise. □ **se ~** *vpr* boast (**de** about); **se ~ de faire** pride oneself on doing.

vapeur /vapœʀ/ *nf* (eau) steam; (brume, émanation) vapour; **~s** fumes; **à ~** (*bateau, locomotive*) steam; **faire cuire à la ~** steam.

vaporisateur /vapɔʀizatœʀ/ *nm* spray, atomizer. **vaporiser** [1] *vt* spray.

varappe /vaʀap/ *nf* rock-climbing.

variable /vaʀjabl/ *a* variable; (*temps*) changeable.

varicelle /vaʀisɛl/ *nf* chickenpox.

varié, ~e /vaʀje/ *a* (non monotone, étendu) varied; (divers) various; **sandwichs ~s** a selection of sandwiches.

varier /vaʀje/ [45] *vt/i* vary.

variété /vaʀjete/ *nf* variety; **spectacle de ~s** variety show.

vase /vɑz/ *nm* vase. ● *nf* silt, mud.

vaseux, -euse /vɑzø, -z/ *a* (confus 🄸) woolly, hazy.

vaste /vast/ *a* vast, huge.

vaurien, ~ne /voʀjɛ̃, -ɛn/ *nm,f* good-for-nothing.

vautour /votuʀ/ *nm* vulture.

vautrer (se) /(sə)votʀe/ [1] *vpr* sprawl; **se ~ dans** (*vice, boue*) wallow in.

veau (*pl* **~x**) /vo/ *nm* calf; (viande) veal; (cuir) calfskin.

vécu, ~e /veky/ *a* (réel) true, real. ● ⇒VIVRE [62].

vedette /vədɛt/ *nf* (artiste) star; **en ~** (*objet*) in a prominent position; (*personne*) in the limelight; **joueur ~** star player; (bateau) launch.

végétal (*mpl* **-aux**) /veʒetal, -o/ *a* plant. ● *nm* (*pl* **-aux**) plant.

végétalien, ~ne /veʒetaljɛ̃, -ɛn/ *a & nm,f* vegan.

végétarien, ~ne /veʒetaʀjɛ̃, -ɛn/ *a & nm,f* vegetarian.

végétation /veʒetasjɔ̃/ *nf* vegetation; **~s** (Méd) adenoids.

véhicule /veikyl/ *nm* vehicle.

veille /vɛj/ *nf* (état) wakefulness; (jour précédent) **la ~ (de)** the day before; **la ~ de Noël** Christmas Eve; **à la ~ de** on the eve of; **la ~ au soir** the previous evening.

veillée /veje/ *nf* evening (gathering).

veiller /veje/ [1] *vi* stay up; (monter la garde) be on watch. ● *vt* (*malade*) watch over; **~ à** attend to; **~ sur** watch over.

veilleur /vɛjœʀ/ *nm* **~ de nuit** night-watchman.

veilleuse /vɛjøz/ *nf* night light; (de véhicule) sidelight; (de réchaud) pilot light; **mettre qch en ~** put sth on the back burner.

veine /vɛn/ *nf* (Anat) vein; (nervure, filon) vein; (chance 🄸) luck; **avoir de la ~** 🄸 be lucky.

véliplanchiste /veliplɑ̃ʃist/ *nmf* windsurfer.

vélo /velo/ *nm* bike; (activité) cycling; **faire du ~** go cycling; **~ tout terrain** mountain bike.

vélomoteur /velɔmɔtœʀ/ *nm* moped.

velours /v(ə)luʀ/ *nm* velvet; **~ côtelé** corduroy.

velouté, ~e /vəlute/ *a* smooth. ● *nm* (Culin) **~ d'asperges** cream of asparagus soup.

vendanges /vɑ̃dɑ̃ʒ/ *nfpl* grape harvest.

vendeur, -euse /vɑ̃dœʀ, -øz/ *nm,f* shop assistant; (marchand) salesman, saleswoman; (Jur) vendor, seller.

vendre /vɑ̃dʀ/ [3] *vt* sell; **à ~** for sale. □ **se ~** *vpr* (être vendu) be sold; (trouver acquéreur) sell; **se ~ bien** sell well.

vendredi /vɑ̃dʀədi/ *nm* Friday; **V~ saint** Good Friday.

vénéneux, -euse /venenø, -z/ *a* poisonous.

vénérer /veneʀe/ [14] *vt* revere.

vénérien, ~ne /veneʀjɛ̃, -ɛn/ *a* **maladie ~ne** venereal disease.

vengeance /vɑ̃ʒɑ̃s/ *nf* revenge, vengeance.

venger /vɑ̃ʒe/ [40] *vt* avenge. □ **se ~** *vpr* take *ou* get one's revenge (**de qch** for sth; **de qn** on sb).

vengeur, -eresse /vɑ̃ʒœʀ, -əʀɛs/ *a* vengeful. ● *nm, f* avenger.

venimeux, -euse /vənimø, -z/ *a* poisonous, venomous.

venin /vənɛ̃/ *nm* venom.

venir /vəniʀ/ [58] *vi* (*aux être*) come (**de** from); **faire ~ qn** send for sb, call sb; **en ~ à** come to; **en ~ aux mains** come to blows; **où veut-elle en ~?** what is she driving at?; **il m'est venu à l'esprit** *or* **à l'idée que** it occurred to me that; **s'il venait à pleuvoir** if it should rain; **dans les jours à ~** in the next few days. ● *v aux* **~ de faire** have just done; **il vient/venait d'arriver** he has/had just arrived; **~ faire** come to do; **viens voir** come and see.

vent /vɑ̃/ *nm* wind; **il fait du ~** it is windy; **être dans le ~** Ⓘ be trendy.

vente /vɑ̃t/ *nf* sale; **~ (aux enchères)** auction; **en ~** on *ou* for sale; **mettre qch en ~** put sth up for sale; **~ de charité** (charity) bazaar; **~ au détail/en gros** retailing/wholesaling; **équipe de ~** sales team.

ventilateur /vɑ̃tilatœʀ/ *nm* fan, ventilator. **ventiler** [1] *vt* ventilate.

ventouse /vɑ̃tuz/ *nf* suction pad; (pour déboucher) plunger.

ventre /vɑ̃tʀ/ *nm* stomach; (d'animal) belly; (utérus) womb; **avoir du ~** have a paunch.

venu, ~e /vəny/ *a* **bien ~** (à propos) apt, timely; **mal ~** badly timed; **il serait mal ~ de faire** it wouldn't be a good idea to do. ● ⇒VENIR [59].

venue /vəny/ *nf* coming.

ver /vɛʀ/ *nm* worm; (dans la nourriture) maggot; (du bois) woodworm; **~ luisant** glow-worm; **~ à soie** silkworm; **~ solitaire** tapeworm; **~ de terre** earthworm.

verbal, ~e (*mpl* **-aux**) /vɛʀbal, -o/ *a* verbal.

verbe /vɛʀb/ *nm* verb.

verdir /vɛʀdiʀ/ [2] *vi* turn green.

véreux, -euse /veʀø, -z/ *a* wormy; (malhonnête) shady.

verger /vɛʀʒe/ *nm* orchard.

verglas /vɛʀgla/ *nm* black ice.

véridique /veʀidik/ *a* true.

vérification /veʀifikasjɔ̃/ *nf* check(ing), verification.

vérifier /veʀifje/ [45] *vt* check, verify; (confirmer) confirm.

véritable /veʀitabl/ *a* true, real; (authentique) real.

vérité /veʀite/ *nf* truth; (de tableau, roman) realism; **en ~** in fact, actually.

vermine /vɛʀmin/ *nf* vermin.

verni, ~e /vɛʀni/ *a* (*chaussures*) patent (leather); (chanceux Ⓘ) lucky.

vernir /vɛʀniʀ/ [2] *vt* varnish. □ **se ~** *vpr* **se ~ les ongles** apply nail polish.

vernis /vɛʀni/ *nm* varnish; (de poterie) glaze; **~ à ongles** nail polish.

verra, verrait /vɛʀa, vɛʀɛ/ ⇒VOIR [64].

verre /vɛʀ/ *nm* glass; (de lunettes) lens; **~ à vin** wine glass; **prendre** *ou* **boire un ~** have a drink; **~ de contact** contact lens; **~ dépoli** frosted glass.

verrière /vɛʀjɛʀ/ *nf* (toit) glass roof; (paroi) glass wall.

verrou /vɛʀu/ *nm* bolt; **sous les ~s** behind bars.

verrouillage /vɛʀujaʒ/ *nm* ~

central *or* **centralisé (des portes)** central locking.

verrue /vɛʀy/ *nf* wart; **~ plantaire** verruca.

vers[1] /vɛʀ/ *prép* towards; (aux environs de) (temps) about; (lieu) near, around; (période) towards; **~ le soir** towards evening.

vers[2] /vɛʀ/ *nm* (poésie) line of verse.

versatile /vɛʀsatil/ *a* unpredictable, volatile.

verse: **à ~** /avɛʀs/ *loc* in torrents.

Verseau /vɛʀso/ *nm* **le ~** Aquarius.

versement /vɛʀsəmɑ̃/ *nm* payment; (échelonné) instalment.

verser /vɛʀse/ [1] *vt/i* pour; (*larmes, sang*) shed; (payer) pay. ●*vi* pour; (*voiture*) overturn; **~ dans** (fig) lapse into.

version /vɛʀsjɔ̃/ *nf* version; (traduction) translation.

verso /vɛʀso/ *nm* back (of the page); **voir au ~** see overleaf.

vert, **~e** /vɛʀ, -t/ *a* green; (*vieillard*) sprightly. ●*nm* green; **les ~s** the Greens.

vertèbre /vɛʀtɛbʀ/ *nf* vertebra; **se déplacer une ~** slip a disc.

vertical, **~e** (*mpl* **-aux**) /vɛʀtikal, -o/ *a* vertical.

vertige /vɛʀtiʒ/ *nm* dizziness; **~s** dizzy spells; **avoir le ~** feel dizzy. **vertigineux**, **-euse** *a* dizzy; (très grand) staggering.

vertu /vɛʀty/ *nf* virtue; **en ~ de** in accordance with. **vertueux**, **-euse** *a* virtuous.

verveine /vɛʀvɛn/ *nf* verbena.

vessie /vesi/ *nf* bladder.

veste /vɛst/ *nf* jacket.

vestiaire /vɛstjɛʀ/ *nm* cloakroom; (Sport) changing-room; (US) locker-room.

vestibule /vɛstibyl/ *nm* hall; (Théât, d'hôtel) foyer.

vestige /vɛstiʒ/ *nm* (objet) relic; (trace) vestige.

veston /vɛstɔ̃/ *nm* jacket.

vêtement /vɛtmɑ̃/ *nm* article of clothing; **~s** clothes, clothing.

vétéran /veteʀɑ̃/ *nm* veteran.

vétérinaire /veteʀinɛʀ/ *nmf* vet, veterinary surgeon, (US) veterinarian.

vêtir /vetiʀ/ [61] *vt* dress. □ **se ~** *vpr* dress.

veto /veto/ *nm inv* veto.

vêtu, **~e** /vety/ *a* dressed (**de** in).

veuf, **veuve** /vœf, -v/ *a* widowed. ●*nm, f* widower, widow.

veuille /vœj/ ⇒VOULOIR [64].

veut, **veux** /vø/ ⇒VOULOIR [64].

vexation /vɛksasjɔ̃/ *nf* humiliation.

vexer /vɛkse/ [1] *vt* upset, hurt. □ **se ~** *vpr* be upset, be hurt.

viable /vjabl/ *a* viable; (*projet*) feasible.

viande /vjɑ̃d/ *nf* meat.

vibrer /vibʀe/ [1] *vi* vibrate; **faire ~** (*âme, foules*) stir.

vicaire /vikɛʀ/ *nm* curate.

vice /vis/ *nm* (moral) vice; (physique) defect.

vicier /visje/ [45] *vt* contaminate; (*air*) pollute.

vicieux, **-ieuse** /visjø, -z/ *a* depraved. ●*nm, f* pervert.

victime /viktim/ *nf* victim; (d'un accident) casualty.

victoire /viktwaʀ/ *nf* victory; (Sport) win. **victorieux**, **-ieuse** *a* victorious; (*équipe*) winning.

vidange /vidɑ̃ʒ/ *nf* emptying; (Auto) oil change; (tuyau) waste pipe *ou* outlet.

vide /vid/ *a* empty. ●*nm* (absence, manque) vacuum, void; (espace) space; (trou) gap; (sans air) vacuum; **à ~** empty; **emballé sous ~** vacuum packed; **suspendu dans le ~** dangling in space.

vidéo /video/ *a inv* video; **jeu ~**

video game. ● *nf* video. **vidéocassette** *nf* video(tape). **vidéoclip** *nm* music video. **vidéoconférence** *nf* videoconferencing; (séance) videoconference. **vidéodisque** *nm* videodisc.

vide-ordures /vidɔRdyR/ *nm inv* rubbish chute.

vidéothèque /videotɛk/ *nf* video library.

vider /vide/ [1] *vt* empty; (*poisson*) gut; (expulser Ⓘ) throw out; ~ **les lieux** leave. □ **se** ~ *vpr* empty.

vie /vi/ *nf* life; (durée) lifetime; **à** ~, **pour la** ~ for life; **donner la** ~ **à** give birth to; **en** ~ alive; **la** ~ **est chère** the cost of living is high.

vieil /vjɛj/ ⇒VIEUX.

vieillard /vjɛjaR/ *nm* old man.

vieille /vjɛj/ ⇒VIEUX.

vieillesse /vjɛjɛs/ *nf* old age.

vieillir /vjejiR/ [2] *vi* grow old, age; (*mot, idée*) become old-fashioned. ● *vt* age. **vieillissement** *nm* ageing.

viens, vient /vjɛ̃/ ⇒VENIR [59].

vierge /vjɛRʒ/ *nf* virgin; **la V**~ Virgo. ● *a* virgin; (*feuille, cassette*) blank; (*cahier, pellicule*) unused, new.

vieux (**vieil** *before vowel or mute h*), **vieille** (*mpl* **vieux**) /vjø, vjɛj/ *a* old. ● *nm, f* old man, old woman; **petit** ~ little old man; **les** ~ old people; **vieille fille** (péj) spinster; ~ **garçon** old bachelor. **vieux jeu** *a inv* old-fashioned.

vif, vive /vif, viv/ *a* (animé) lively; (*émotion, vent*) keen; (*froid*) biting; (*lumière*) bright; (*douleur, contraste, parole*) sharp; (*souvenir, style, teint*) vivid; (*succès, impatience*) great; **brûler/enterrer** ~ burn/bury alive; **de vive voix** personally. ● *nm* **à** ~ (*plaie*) open; **avoir les nerfs à** ~ be on edge; **blessé au** ~ cut to the quick.

vigie /viʒi/ *nf* lookout.

vigilant, ~e /viʒilɑ̃, -t/ *a* vigilant.

vigne /viɲ/ *nf* (plante) vine; (vignoble) vineyard. **vigneron, ~ne** *nm, f* wine-grower.

vignette /viɲɛt/ *nf* (étiquette) label; (Auto) road tax disc.

vignoble /viɲɔbl/ *nm* vineyard.

vigoureux, -euse /viguRø, -z/ *a* vigorous, sturdy.

vigueur /vigœR/ *nf* vigour; **être/entrer en** ~ (*loi*) be/come into force; **en** ~ current.

VIH *abrév m* (**virus immunodéficitaire humain**) HIV.

vilain, ~e /vilɛ̃, -ɛn/ *a* (mauvais) nasty; (laid) ugly. ● *nm, f* naughty boy, naughty girl.

villa /villa/ *nf* detached house.

village /vilaʒ/ *nm* village.

villageois, ~e /vilaʒwa, -z/ *a* village. ● *nm, f* villager.

ville /vil/ *nf* town; (importante) city; ~ **d'eaux** spa.

vin /vɛ̃/ *nm* wine; ~ **d'honneur** reception.

vinaigre /vinɛgR/ *nm* vinegar. **vinaigrette** *nf* oil and vinegar dressing, vinaigrette.

vingt /vɛ̃/ (/vɛ̃t/ *before vowel and in numbers 22-29*) *a & nm* twenty.

vingtaine /vɛ̃tɛn/ *nf* **une** ~ (**de**) about twenty.

vingtième /vɛ̃tjɛm/ *a & nmf* twentieth.

vinicole /vinikɔl/ *a* wine(-producing).

viol /vjɔl/ *nm* (de femme) rape; (de lieu, loi) violation.

violemment /vjɔlamɑ̃/ *adv* violently.

violence /vjɔlɑ̃s/ *nf* violence; (acte) act of violence. **violent, ~e** *a* violent.

violer /vjɔle/ [1] *vt* rape; (*lieu, loi*) violate.

violet, **~te** /vjɔlɛ, -t/ *a* purple. ● *nm* purple. **violette** *nf* violet.

violon /vjɔlɔ̃/ *nm* violin; **~ d'Ingres** hobby.

violoncelle /vjɔlɔ̃sɛl/ *nm* cello.

vipère /vipɛʀ/ *nf* viper, adder.

virage /viʀaʒ/ *nm* bend; (en ski) turn; (changement d'attitude: fig) change of course.

virée /viʀe/ *nf* [I] trip, tour; (en voiture) drive; (à vélo) ride.

virement /viʀmɑ̃/ *nm* (Comm) (credit) transfer; **~ automatique** standing order.

virer /viʀe/ [1] *vi* turn; **~ de bord** tack; (fig) do a U-turn; **~ au rouge** turn red. ● *vt* (*argent*) transfer; (expulser [I]) throw out; (*élève*) expel; (licencier [I]) fire.

virgule /viʀgyl/ *nf* comma; (dans un nombre) (decimal) point.

viril, **~e** /viʀil/ *a* virile.

virtuel, **~le** /viʀtɥɛl/ *a* (potentiel) potential; (*mémoire, réalité*) virtual.

virulent, **~e** /viʀylɑ̃, -t/ *a* virulent.

virus /viʀys/ *nm* virus.

vis[1] /vi/ ⇒VIVRE [62], VOIR [63].

vis[2] /vis/ *nf* screw.

visa /viza/ *nm* visa.

visage /vizaʒ/ *nm* face.

vis-à-vis /vizavi/ *prép* **~ de** (en face de) opposite; (à l'égard de) in relation to; (comparé à) compared to, beside. ● *nm inv* (personne) person opposite; **en ~** opposite each other.

visée /vize/ *nf* aim; **avoir des ~s sur** have designs on.

viser /vize/ [1] *vt* (*cible, centre*) aim at; (*poste, résultats*) aim for; (concerner) be aimed at; (*document*) stamp; **~ à** aim at; (*mesure, propos*) be aimed at; **~ à faire** aim to do. ● *vi* aim.

viseur /vizœʀ/ *nm* (d'arme) sights (+ *pl*); (Photo) viewfinder.

visière /vizjɛʀ/ *nf* (de casquette) peak; (de casque) visor.

vision /vizjɔ̃/ *nf* vision.

visite /vizit/ *nf* visit; (pour inspecter) inspection; (personne) visitor; **heures de ~** visiting hours; **~ guidée** guided tour; **~ médicale** medical; **rendre ~ à, faire une ~ à** pay a visit; **être en ~** (**chez qn**) be visiting (sb); **avoir de la ~** have visitors.

visiter /vizite/ [1] *vt* visit; (*appartement*) view. **visiteur**, **-euse** *nm, f* visitor.

visser /vise/ *vt* screw (on).

visuel, **~le** /vizɥɛl/ *a* visual. ● *nm* (Ordinat) visual display unit, VDU.

vit /vi/ ⇒VIVRE [62], VOIR [63].

vital, **~e** (*mpl* **-aux**) /vital, -o/ *a* vital.

vitamine /vitamin/ *nf* vitamin.

vite /vit/ *adv* fast, quickly; (tôt) soon; **~!** quick!; **faire ~** be quick; **au plus ~, le plus ~ possible** as quickly as possible.

vitesse /vitɛs/ *nf* speed; (régime: Auto) gear; **à toute ~** at top speed; **en ~** in a hurry, quickly; **boîte à cinq ~s** five-speed gearbox.

viticole /vitikɔl/ *a* (*industrie*) wine; (*région*) wine-producing. **viticulteur** *nm* wine-grower.

vitrage /vitʀaʒ/ *nm* (vitres) windows; **double ~** double glazing.

vitrail (*pl* **-aux**) /vitʀaj, -o/ *nm* stained-glass window.

vitre /vitʀ/ *nf* (window) pane; (de véhicule) window.

vitrine /vitʀin/ *nf* (shop) window; (meuble) display cabinet.

vivace /vivas/ *a* (*plante*) perennial; (durable) enduring.

vivacité /vivasite/ *nf* liveliness; (agilité) quickness; (d'émotion, d'intelligence) keenness; (de souvenir, style, teint) vividness.

vivant, **~e** /vivɑ̃, -t/ *a* (*example, symbole*) living; (en vie) alive, living; (actif, vif) lively. ● *nm* **un bon ~** a bon viveur; **de son ~** in his lifetime; **les ~s** the living.

vive¹ /viv/ ⇒VIF.

vive² /viv/ *interj* **~ le roi!** long live the king!

vivement /vivmɑ̃/ *adv* (fortement) strongly; (vite, sèchement) sharply; (avec éclat) vividly; (beaucoup) greatly; **~ la fin!** I'll be glad when it's the end!

vivier /vivje/ *nm* fish pond; (artificiel) fish tank.

vivifier /vivifje/ [45] *vt* invigorate.

vivre /vivʀ/ [62] *vi* live; **~ de** (*nourriture*) live on; **~ encore** be still alive; **faire ~** (*famille*) support. ● *vt* (*vie*) live; (*période, aventure*) live through.

vivres /vivʀ/ *nmpl* supplies.

VO *abrév f* (**version originale**) **en ~** in the original language.

vocabulaire /vɔkabylɛʀ/ *nm* vocabulary.

vocal, **~e** (*mpl* **-aux**) /vɔkal, -o/ *a* vocal.

vœu (*pl* **~x**) /vø/ *nm* (souhait) wish; (promesse) vow; **meilleurs ~x** best wishes.

vogue /vɔg/ *nf* fashion, vogue; **en ~** in fashion *ou* vogue.

voguer /vɔge/ [1] *vi* sail.

voici /vwasi/ *prép* here is, this is; (au pluriel) here are, these are; **me ~** here I am; **~ un an** (temps passé) a year ago; **~ un an que** it is a year since.

voie /vwa/ *nf* (route) road; (partie de route) lane; (chemin) way; (moyen) means, way; (rails) track; (quai) platform; **en ~ de** in the process of; **en ~ de développement** (*pays*) developing; **espèce en ~ de disparition** endangered species; **par la ~ des airs** by air; **par ~ orale** orally; **sur la bonne/mauvaise ~** (fig) on the right/wrong track; **montrer la ~** lead the way, **~ de dégagement** slip-road; **~ ferrée** railway; (US) railroad; **V~ lactée** Milky Way; **~ navigable** waterway; **~ publique** public highway; **~ sans issue** (sur panneau) no through road; (fig) dead end.

voilà /vwala/ *prép* there is, that is; (au pluriel) there are, those are; (voici) here is, here are; **le ~** there he is; **~!** right!; (en offrant qch) there you are!; **~ un an** (temps passé) a year ago; **~ un an que** it is a year since; **tu en veux? en ~** do you want some? here you are; **en ~ des histoires!** what a fuss!; **et ~ que** and then.

voilage /vwalaʒ/ *nm* net curtain.

voile /vwal/ *nf* (de bateau) sail; (Sport) sailing. ● *nm* veil; (tissu léger) net.

voilé, **~e** /vwale/ *a* (*allusion, femme*) veiled; (flou) hazy.

voiler /vwale/ [1] *vt* (dissimuler) veil; (déformer) buckle. □ **se ~** *vpr* (devenir flou) become hazy; (se déformer) (*roue*) buckle.

voilier /vwalje/ *nm* sailing ship.

voir /vwaʀ/ [63] *vt* see; **faire ~ qch à qn** show sth to sb; **laisser ~** show; **avoir quelque chose à ~ avec** have something to do with; **ça n'a rien à ~** that's got nothing to do with it; **je ne peux pas le ~** Ⓘ I can't stand him. ● *vi* **y ~** be able to see; **je n'y vois rien** I cannot see; **~ trouble** have blurred vision; **voyons** let's see now; **voyons, soyez sages!** come on now, behave yourselves! □ **se ~** *vpr* (dans la glace) see oneself; (être visible) show; (se produire) be seen; (se trouver) find oneself; (se

fréquenter, se rencontrer) see each other; (être vu) be seen.

voire /vwaʀ/ *adv* or even, not to say.

voirie /vwaʀi/ *nf* (service) highway maintenance.

voisin, ~e /vwazɛ̃, -in/ *a* (de voisinage) neighbouring; (proche) nearby; (adjacent) next (**de** to); (semblable) similar (**de** to). ● *nm, f* neighbour; **le ~** the man next door, the neighbour. **voisinage** *nm* neighbourhood; (proximité) proximity.

voiture /vwatyʀ/ *nf* (motor) car; (wagon) coach, carriage; **en ~!** all aboard!; **~ bélier** ramraiding car; **~ à cheval** horse-drawn carriage; **~ de course** racing car; **~ école** driving school car; **~ d'enfant** pram; (US) baby carriage; **~ de tourisme** saloon car.

voix /vwa/ *nf* voice; (suffrage) vote; **à ~ basse** in a whisper.

vol /vɔl/ *nm* (d'avion, d'oiseau) flight; (groupe d'oiseaux) flock, flight; (délit) theft; (hold-up) robbery; **~ à l'étalage** shoplifting; **~ à la tire** pickpocketing; **à ~ d'oiseau** as the crow flies; **de haut ~** high-ranking; **~ libre** hang-gliding; **~ à voile** gliding.

volaille /vɔlɑj/ *nf* **la ~** (poules) poultry; **une ~** a fowl.

volant /vɔlɑ̃/ *nm* (steering-) wheel; (de jupe) flounce; (de badminton) shuttlecock; **donner un coup de ~** turn the wheel sharply.

volcan /vɔlkɑ̃/ *nm* volcano.

volée /vɔle/ *nf* flight; (oiseaux) flight, flock; (de coups, d'obus, au tennis) volley; **à toute ~** hard; **à la ~** in flight, in mid-air.

voler /vɔle/ [1] *vi* (*oiseau*) fly; (dérober) steal (**à** from). ● *vt* steal; **~ qn** rob sb; **il ne l'a pas volé** he deserved it.

volet /vɔlɛ/ *nm* (de fenêtre) shutter; (de document) (folded *ou* tear-off) section; **trié sur le ~** hand-picked.

voleur, -euse /vɔlœʀ, -øz/ *nm, f* thief; **au ~!** stop thief! ● *a* thieving.

volley-ball /vɔlɛbol/ *nm* volleyball.

volontaire /vɔlɔ̃tɛʀ/ *a* (délibéré) voluntary; (opiniâtre) determined. ● *nmf* volunteer. **volontairement** *adv* voluntarily; (exprès) intentionally.

volonté /vɔlɔ̃te/ *nf* (faculté, intention) will; (souhait) wish; (énergie) willpower; **à ~** (comme on veut) as required; **du vin à ~** unlimited wine; **bonne ~** goodwill; **mauvaise ~** ill will.

volontiers /vɔlɔ̃tje/ *adv* (de bon gré) with pleasure, willingly, gladly; (*admettre*) readily.

volt /vɔlt/ *nm* volt.

volte-face /vɔltəfas/ *nf inv* (fig) U-turn; **faire ~** do a U-turn.

voltige /vɔltiʒ/ *nf* acrobatics (+ *pl*).

volume /vɔlym/ *nm* volume.

volumineux, -euse /vɔlyminø, -z/ *a* bulky; (*livre, dossier*) thick.

volupté /vɔlypte/ *nf* voluptuousness.

vomi /vɔmi/ *nm* vomit.

vomir /vɔmiʀ/ [2] *vt* vomit; (fig) belch out. ● *vi* be sick, vomit.

vomissement /vɔmismɑ̃/ *nm* vomiting; **~s du matin** morning sickness.

vont /vɔ̃/ ⇒ALLER [8].

vorace /vɔʀas/ *a* voracious.

vos /vo/ ⇒VOTRE.

votant, ~e /vɔtɑ̃, -t/ *nm, f* voter.

vote /vɔt/ *nm* (action) voting; (suffrage) vote; **~ d'une loi** passing of a bill; **~ par correspondance/procuration** postal/proxy vote.

voter /vɔte/ [1] *vi* vote. ● *vt* vote for; (adopter) pass; (*crédits*) vote.

votre (*pl* **vos**) /vɔtʀ, vo/ *a* your.

vôtre /votʀ/ *pron* **le** *ou* **la ~, les ~s** yours.

vouer /vwe/ [1] *vt* (*vie, temps*) dedicate (**à** to); **voué à l'échec** doomed to failure.

vouloir /vulwaʀ/ [64] *vt* (exiger) want (**faire** to do); (souhaiter) want; **que veux-tu boire?** what would you like to drink?; **je voudrais bien y aller** I'd really like to go; **je veux bien venir** I'm happy to come; **comme tu voudras** as you wish; (accepter) **veuillez vous asseoir** please sit down; **veuillez patienter** (au téléphone) please hold the line; (signifier) **~ dire** mean; **qu'est-ce que cela veut dire?** what does that mean?; **en ~ à qn** bear a grudge against sb. □ **s'en ~** *vpr* regret; **je m'en veux de lui avoir dit** I really regret having told her.

voulu, ~e /vuly/ *a* (délibéré) intentional; (requis) required.

vous /vu/ *pron* (sujet, complément) you; (indirect) (to) you; (réfléchi) yourself; (pluriel) yourselves; (l'un l'autre) each other. **vous-même** *pron* yourself. **vous-mêmes** *pron* yourselves.

voûte /vut/ *nf* (plafond) vault; (porche) archway.

vouvoiement /vuvwamɑ̃/ *nm* use of the 'vous' form. **vouvoyer** [31] *vt* address using the 'vous' form.

voyage /vwajaʒ/ *nm* trip; (déplacement) journey; (par mer) voyage; **~(s)** (action) travelling; **~ d'affaires** business trip; **~ d'études** study trip; **~ de noces** honeymoon; **~ organisé** (package) tour.

voyager /vwajaʒe/ [40] *vi* travel.

voyageur, -euse /vwajaʒœʀ, -øz/ *nm,f* traveller; (passager) passenger; **~ de commerce** travelling salesman.

voyant, ~e /vwajɑ̃, -t/ *a* gaudy. ● *nm* (signal) (warning) light.

voyelle /vwajɛl/ *nf* vowel.

voyou /vwaju/ *nm* hooligan.

vrac: **en ~** /ɑ̃vʀak/ *loc* (pêle-mêle) haphazardly; (sans emballage) loose; (en gros) in bulk.

vrai, ~e /vʀɛ/ *a* true; (authentique) real. ● *nm* truth; **à ~ dire** to tell the truth; **pour de ~** for real. **vraiment** *adv* really.

vraisemblable /vʀɛsɑ̃blabl/ *a* (probable) likely; (*excuse, histoire*) plausible. **vraisemblablement** *adv* probably. **vraisemblance** *nf* likelihood, plausibility.

vrombir /vʀɔ̃biʀ/ [2] *vi* roar.

VRP *abrév m* (**voyageur représentant placier**) rep, representative.

VTT *abrév m* (**vélo tout terrain**) mountain bike.

vu, ~e /vy/ *a* **bien ~** well thought of; **ce serait plutôt mal ~** it wouldn't go down well; **bien ~!** good point! ● *prép* in view of; **~ que** seeing that. ● ⇒VOIR [63].

vue /vy/ *nf* (spectacle) sight; (vision) (eye)sight; (panorama, idée, image, photo) view; **avoir en ~** have in mind; **à ~** (*tirer*) on sight; (*payable*) at sight; **de ~** by sight; **perdre de ~** lose sight of; **en ~** (proche) in sight; (célèbre) in the public eye; **en ~ de faire** with a view to doing; **à ~ d'œil** visibly; **avoir des ~s sur** have designs on.

vulgaire /vylgɛʀ/ *a* (grossier) vulgar; (ordinaire) common.

vulnérable /vylneʀabl/ *a* vulnerable.

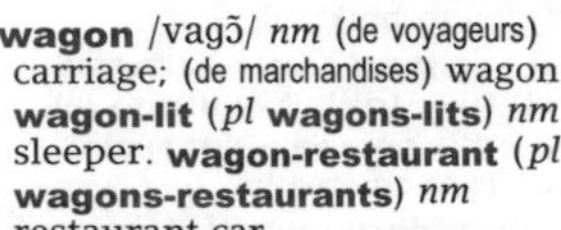

wagon /vagɔ̃/ *nm* (de voyageurs) carriage; (de marchandises) wagon. **wagon-lit** (*pl* **wagons-lits**) *nm* sleeper. **wagon-restaurant** (*pl* **wagons-restaurants**) *nm* restaurant car.

walkman® /wokman/ *nm* personal stereo, walkman®.

waters /watɛʀ/ *nmpl* toilets.

watt /wat/ *nm* watt.

wc /(dublə)vese/ *nmpl* toilet (+ *sg*).

Web /wɛb/ *nm* Web; **un site ~** a Web site.

week-end /wikɛnd/ *nm* weekend.

whisky (*pl* **-ies**) /wiski/ *nm* whisky.

xénophobe /gzenɔfɔb/ *a* xenophobic. ● *nmf* xenophobe.

xérès /gzeʀɛs/ *nm* sherry.

xylophone /ksilɔfɔn/ *nm* xylophone.

y /i/

● *adverbe*

....➤ there; (dessus) on it; (pluriel) on them; (dedans) in it; (pluriel) in them; **j'~ vais** I'm on my way; **n'~ va pas** don't go; **du lait? il n'~ en a pas** milk? there's none; **tu n'~ arriveras jamais** you'll never manage it.

● *pronom*

....➤ **s'~ habituer** get used to it.

....➤ **s'~ attendre** expect it.

....➤ **~ penser** think about it.

....➤ **~ être pour qch** have sth to do with it.

yaourt /ˈjauʀ(t)/ *nm* yoghurt. **yaourtière** *nf* yoghurt-maker.

yard /ˈjaʀd/ *nm* yard (= *91,44 cm*).

yen /ˈjɛn/ *nm* yen.

yeux /jø/ ⇒ŒIL.

yoga /ˈjɔga/ *nm* yoga.

yougoslave /ˈjugɔslav/ *a* Yugoslav. **Y~** *nmf* Yugoslav.

Yougoslavie /ˈjugɔslavi/ *nf* Yugoslavia.

yo-yo® /ˈjojo/ *nm inv* yo-yo®.

zèbre /zɛbʀ/ *nm* zebra.

zèle /zɛl/ *nm* zeal.

zéro /zeʀo/ *nm* nought, zero; (température) zero; (Sport) nil; (tennis) love; (personne) nonentity; **partir de ~** start from scratch; **repartir à ~** start all over again.

zeste /zɛst/ *nm* peel; **un ~ de** (fig) a touch of.

zézayer /zezeje/ [31] *vi* lisp.

zigzag /zigzag/ *nm* zigzag; **en ~** winding.

zinc /zɛ̃g/ *nm* (métal) zinc; (comptoir 🅸) bar.

zizanie /zizani/ *nf* discord; **semer la ~** put the cat among the pigeons.

zizi /zizi/ *nm* 🅸 willy.

zodiaque /zɔdjak/ *nm* zodiac.

zona /zona/ *nm* (Méd) shingles (+ *sg*).

zone /zon/ *nf* zone, area; (banlieue pauvre) slums; **~ bleue** restricted parking zone.

zoo /zo(o)/ *nm* zoo.

zoom /zum/ *nm* zoom lens.

zut /zyt/ *interj* 🅸 damn 🅸.

Test yourself with word games

This section contains a number of word games which will help you to use your dictionary more effectively and to build up your knowledge of French vocabulary and usage in an entertaining way. You will find answers to all puzzles and games at the end of the section.

1 Madame Irma

Madame Irma is very good at predicting the future, but she is not very good at conjugating French verbs in the future tense. Help her to replace all the verbs in brackets with the correct future form.

Lion 23 juillet–22 août

Cette semaine, les Lions (être) à la fête. **Travail**: Il ne (falloir) pas vous laisser démoraliser par les problèmes et les discussions qui (pouvoir) surgir en début de semaine. Les 19 et 20 avril vous (offrir) la possibilité d'un changement radical dans votre carrière. Pourquoi ne pas saisir votre chance? **Santé**: Le stress ne vous (épargner) pas, surtout le 18. Attention! Pour décompresser, faites un peu de sport et tout (aller) bien. **Amitié**: Vous êtes très sociable et cette semaine, vous vous (faire) encore de nouveaux amis. **Côté cœur**: Vénus (veiller) sur vous. Une nouvelle rencontre (survenir) peut-être. Si vous avez un partenaire, votre relation (être) au beau fixe.

2 Power cut

Unfortunately, there was a power cut while Jean was writing a computer manual for his office staff. He had just begun to label his diagram of a computer. Can you help Jean unscramble the letters and get on with his labelling?

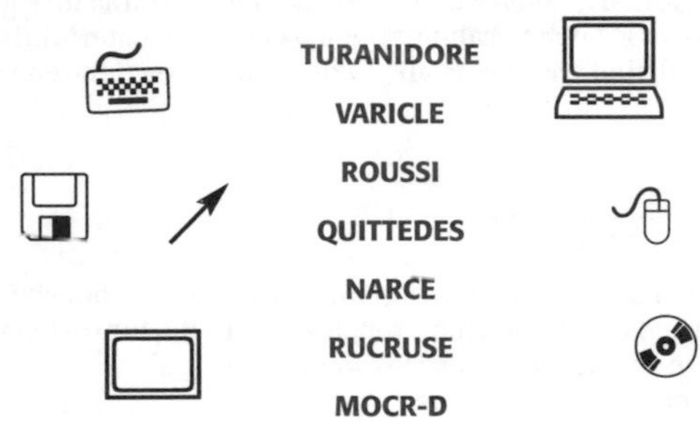

3 The odd meaning out

Watch out: one word can have different meanings. In the following exercise, only two of the suggested translations are correct. Use the dictionary to spot the odd one out, then find the correct French translation for it.

example:

blindé
- ❑ armoured
- ☑ blind
- ❑ immune

blind = aveugle

gauche
- ❑ left
- ❑ gauge
- ❑ awkward

lentille
- ❑ lentil
- ❑ lens
- ❑ lent

porte
- ❑ door
- ❑ carry
- ❑ port (wine)

duvet
- ❑ duvet
- ❑ down
- ❑ sleeping-bag

4 Word magnets

Antoine's brother took all his magnets off the fridge door to wipe it clean. He put them back the wrong way round. Can you help Antoine rewrite the correct sentences?

heure | hier | suis | me | levé | bonne | de | je

dit | pourtant | je | fois | lui | plusieurs | ai | le

sur | sortant | table | les | prends | clés | en | la

ira | Portugal | elle | prochaine | au | vacances | l'année | en

film | voir | un | allés | cinéma | sommes | nous | au

voisine | de | là | frère | pas | le | la | n'est

5 What are they like?

Here are two lists of adjectives you can use to describe people's characteristics. Each word in the second column is the opposite of one of the adjectives in the first column. Can you link them?

1.grand	A. intelligent
2. blond	B. méchant
3. bête	C. gros
4. énervé	D. petit
5. gentil	E. sympathique
6. timide	F. brun
7. patient	G. calme
8. désagréable	H. extraverti
9. poli	I. impatient
10. maigre	J. malpoli

example: 1.D. *grand* est le contraire de *petit*.

6 The odd one out

In each of the following series, all the words but one are related. Find the odd one out and explain why. If there are words you don't know, use your dictionary to find out what they mean.

example: stylo, agenda, livre, carnet scolaire, brosse à dents

The odd one out is 'brosse à dents', because you wouldn't find it in a schoolbag.

1. voiture, avion, moteur, train, autocar
2. casserole, poêle, cafetière, cendrier, saladier
3. télévision, cassette, chaîne-hifi, magnétoscope, baladeur
4. ski nautique, natation, plongée, varappe, planche à voile
5. redoubler, courir, sauter, glisser, descendre, monter
6. chou, sou, caillou, genou, hibou, bijou

7 The shopping list

Paul has prepared a shopping list. When his friend sees the list, he realises that he needs exactly the same things. He asks Paul whether he would mind buying two of everything. Help Paul rewrite his list.
Watch out: the plurals of compound nouns are irregular. If in doubt, look them up in your dictionary.

Acheter:	Acheter:
- un taille-crayons	deux taille-crayons
- un bloc-notes	....
- un timbre-poste	....
- un abat-jour	....
- un couvre-lit	....
- un cache-nez	....
- un tire-bouchon	....
- un ouvre-boîtes	....
- un réveille-matin	....
- un chou-fleur	....

8 The mystery word

To fill in the grid, find the French words for all the musical instruments illustrated below. Once you have completed the grid, you'll discover the name of a famous classical composer.

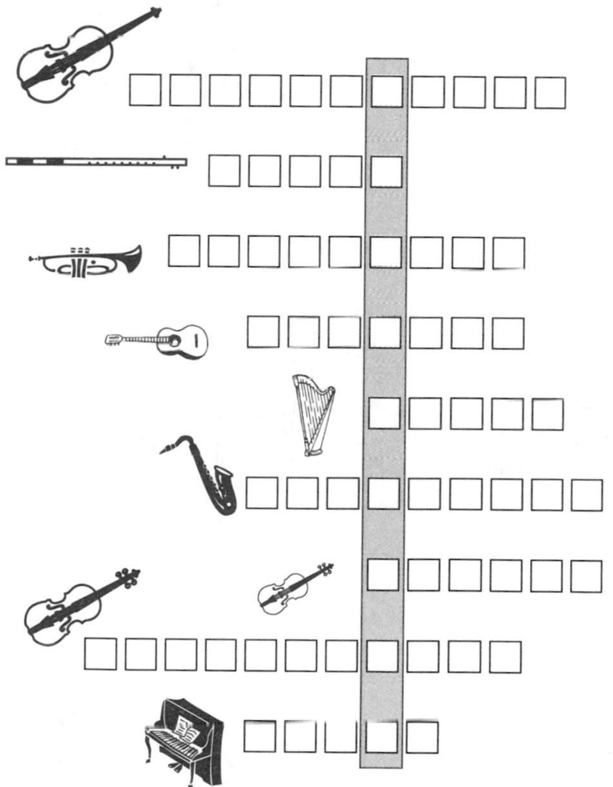

The composer is _ _ _ _ _ _ _ _ _.

9 Body parts

Can you put the right number in the boxes next to the French words in the list?

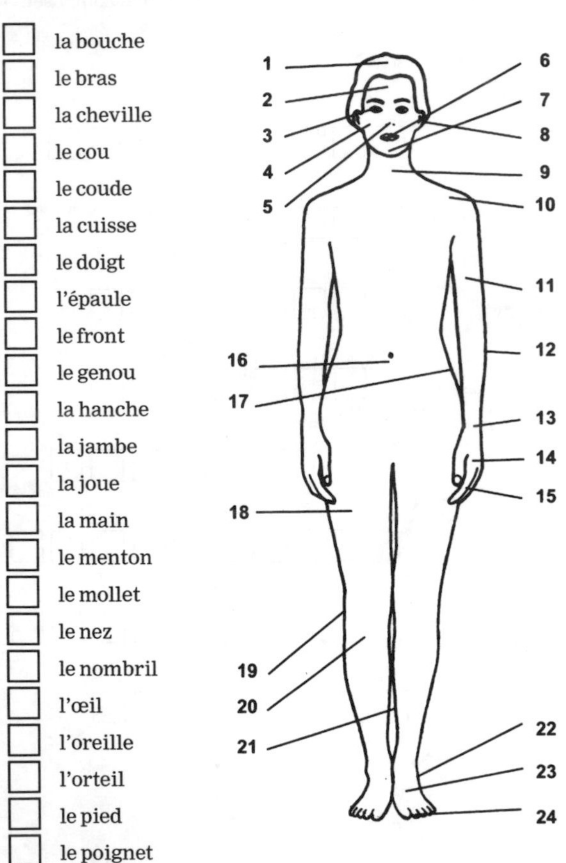

- ☐ la bouche
- ☐ le bras
- ☐ la cheville
- ☐ le cou
- ☐ le coude
- ☐ la cuisse
- ☐ le doigt
- ☐ l'épaule
- ☐ le front
- ☐ le genou
- ☐ la hanche
- ☐ la jambe
- ☐ la joue
- ☐ la main
- ☐ le menton
- ☐ le mollet
- ☐ le nez
- ☐ le nombril
- ☐ l'œil
- ☐ l'oreille
- ☐ l'orteil
- ☐ le pied
- ☐ le poignet
- ☐ la tête

10 Liar liar!

Today, Sabine had a day off. She tells her mother what she has been up to:

> “*Ce matin, je me suis levée juste après ton départ. J'ai bu du café au lait et j'ai mangé des tartines. Après avoir fait ma toilette et m'être habillée, je suis allée au parc. Il faisait très beau et j'avais envie de me promener. Je suis revenue à la maison pour chercher mon maillot de bain et je suis allée à la piscine découverte. J'y suis restée pendant deux heures. En sortant, j'avais très faim, alors je me suis installée dans un café. J'ai commandé un sandwich. Après ça, je suis allée au cinéma. Le film était super! Je suis rentrée à la maison un peu avant que tu arrives.*”

What she doesn't say is that her little brother, Adrien, skipped school to spend the day with her. Rewrite her statement.

> “*Ce matin, nous nous sommes levés juste après ton départ...*”

Answers

1

seronte
faudra
pourront
offriront
épargnera
ira
ferez
veillera
surviendra
sera

2

ordinateur
clavier
souris
disquette
écran
curseur
cd-rom

3

lent = prêté
port = porto
gauge = jauge
duvet = couette

4

Hier, je me suis levé de bonne heure.
Pourtant, je le lui ai dit plusieurs fois.
Prends les clés sur la table en sortant.
L'année prochaine, elle ira en vacances au Portugal.
Nous sommes allés voir un film au cinéma.
Le frère de la voisine n'est pas là.

5

1.D. *grand* est le contraire de *petit*.
2.F. *blond* est le contraire de *brun*.
3.A. *bête* est le contraire d'*intelligent*.
4.G. *énervé* est le contraire de *calme*.
5.B. *gentil* est le contraire de *méchant*.
6.H. *timide* est le contraire d'*extraverti*.
7.I. *patient* est le contraire d'*impatient*.
8.E. *désagréable* est le contraire de *sympathique*.
9.J. *poli* est le contraire de *malpoli*.
10.C. *maigre* est le contraire de *gros*.

6

1. moteur—because it isn't a vehicle
2. cendrier—because it is not used for cooking
3. cassette—because it isn't an electrical device
4. varappe—because it is the only sport in the list which isn't a water-sport
5. redoubler—because it is the only verb in the list which doesn't describe a movement
6. sou—because it ends in "-s" in the plural, not in "-x" like the other five

7

deux taille-crayons
deux blocs-notes
deux timbres-poste
deux abat-jour
deux couvre-lits
deux cache-nez
deux tire-bouchons
deux ouvre-boîtes
deux réveille-matin
deux choux-fleurs

8

```
  C O N T R E B A S S E
      F L U T E
    T R O M P E T T E
        G U I T A R E
              H A R P E
        S A X O P H O N E
              V I O L O N
V I O L O N C E L L E
        P I A N O
```

9

6. la bouche	15. le doigt	4. la joue	3. l'œil
11. le bras	10. l'épaule	14. la main	8. l'oreille
22. la cheville	2. le front	7. le menton	24. l'orteil
9. le cou	20. le genou	21. le mollet	23. le pied
12. le coude	17. la hanche	5. le nez	13. le poignet
18. la cuisse	19. la jambe	16. le nombril	1. la tête

10

"Ce matin, nous nous sommes levés, juste après ton départ. Nous avons bu du café au lait et nous avons mangé des tartines. Après avoir fait notre toilette et nous être habillés, nous sommes allés au parc. Il faisait très beau et nous avions envie de nous promener. Nous sommes revenus à la maison pour chercher nos maillots de bain et nous sommes allés à la piscine découverte. Nous y sommes restés pendant deux heures. En sortant, nous avions très faim, alors nous nous sommes installés dans un café. Nous avons commandé des sandwichs. Après ça, nous sommes allés au cinéma. Le film était super! Nous sommes rentrés à la maison un peu avant que tu arrives."

Calendar of French traditions, festivals, and holidays

January

1	8	15	22	29
2	9	16	23	30
3	10	17	24	31
4	11	18	25	
5	12	19	26	
6	13	20	27	
7	14	21	28	

February

1	8	15	22
2	9	16	23
3	10	17	24
4	11	18	25
5	12	19	26
6	13	20	27
7	**14**	21	28

March

1	8	15	22	29
2	9	16	23	30
3	10	17	24	31
4	11	18	25	
5	12	19	26	
6	13	20	27	
7	14	21	28	

April

1	8	15	22	29
2	9	16	23	30
3	10	17	24	31
4	11	18	25	
5	12	19	26	
6	13	20	27	
7	14	21	28	

May

1	**8**	15	22	29
2	9	16	23	30
3	10	17	24	31
4	11	18	25	
5	12	19	26	
6	13	20	27	
7	14	21	28	

June

1	8	15	22	29
2	9	16	23	30
3	10	17	**24**	
4	11	18	25	
5	12	19	26	
6	13	20	27	
7	14	21	28	

July

1	8	15	22	29
2	9	16	23	30
3	10	17	24	31
4	11	18	25	
5	12	19	26	
6	13	20	27	
7	**14**	21	28	

August

1	8	**15**	22	29
2	9	16	23	30
3	10	17	24	31
4	11	18	25	
5	12	19	26	
6	13	20	27	
7	14	21	28	

September

1	8	15	22	29
2	9	16	23	30
3	10	17	24	
4	11	18	25	
5	12	19	26	
6	13	20	27	
7	14	21	28	

October

1	8	15	22	29
2	9	16	23	30
3	10	17	24	31
4	11	18	25	
5	12	19	26	
6	13	20	27	
7	14	21	28	

November

1	8	15	22	29
2	9	16	23	30
3	10	17	24	
4	**11**	18	25	
5	12	19	26	
6	13	20	27	
7	14	21	28	

December

1	**8**	15	22	29
2	9	16	23	30
3	10	17	**24**	**31**
4	11	18	**25**	
5	12	19	**26**	
6	13	20	27	
7	14	21	28	

1 January

le jour de l'an (New Year's Day) is a public holiday and a day of family celebration, with a large lunch, traditionally featuring seafood of various kinds.

6 January

la Fête des Rois (Epiphany or Twelfth Night). Around this time, most families have a *galette des Rois*, a rich pastry cake filled with *frangipane* (almond paste). The cake contains a *fève*, literally a bean, as this is what was originally used. Nowadays the *fève* takes the form of a tiny plastic or ceramic figure. The person who gets the *fève* in their portion puts on the cardboard crown which comes with the cake.

2 February

la Chandeleur (Candlemas) is celebrated in the church but is not a public holiday. However, it is traditional to eat *crêpes* (pancakes) on this day.

14 February

la Saint Valentin (St Valentine's Day). As in many other countries, people celebrate a romantic relationship with gifts of flowers or chocolates.

1 April

le premier avril (April Fool's Day). The French also take advantage of this occasion to play tricks on one another, calling out *poisson d'avril!* (literally 'April fish').

1 May

La Fête du Travail (International Labour Day) is a public holiday.

8 May

le 8 mai or **la Fête de la Victoire** is a public holiday commemorating Victory in Europe on 8 May 1945.

24 June

la Saint-Jean (Midsummer's Day). In many areas, bonfires (*les feux de la Saint-Jean*) are lit on Midsummer's Night. People are supposed to jump over these, re-enacting a pagan custom intended to ward off the cold of winter.

14 July

la Fête Nationale or le 14 juillet is usually called Bastille Day in English and is a public holiday in France. It commemorates the taking of the Bastille prison in Paris and the liberation of its prisoners by the people of Paris in 1789, one of the first events of the Revolution. All over France there are parades on the day of the 14th and firework displays and *bals* (local dances) either on the night of the 13th or of the 14th.

15 August

l'Assomption (Feast of the Assumption) is a public holiday. Many people in France are either setting off on holiday around the 15th or else returning home, so this is traditionally a very busy time on the roads.

1 November

la Toussaint (All Saints' Day) is a public holiday and the day when people remember their dead relatives and friends, although properly speaking it is All Souls' Day the following day that is set aside for this in the church. People take flowers to the cemetery, particularly chrysanthemums, as these are in bloom at this time. Because of this association, it is best to avoid taking chrysanthemums as a gift for someone. Schoolchildren have a two-week holiday around this time.

11 November

le 11 novembre is a public holiday to commemorate the Armistice of 1918 and a day of remembrance for those who died in the two world wars and in subsequent conflicts. All towns and villages hold parades in which war veterans accompany local officials and a brass band to lay wreaths on the war memorial. In Paris, the President lays a wreath on the tomb of the unknown soldier beneath the *Arc de Triomphe* on the *Champs-Élysées*.

8 December

la fête de l'Immaculée Conception (Feast of the Immaculate Conception).
In the city of Lyons, this is celebrated as **la Fête de la Lumière** (Festival of Light) said to commemorate the Virgin's intervention to prevent the plague reaching Lyons in the Middle Ages. People put rows of candles in coloured glass jars on the outsides of their windowsills, so that all the buildings in the centre of the city are illuminated.

24 December

la veille de Noël (Christmas Eve) is the time when most people exchange presents. Many people go to *la messe de minuit* (midnight mass).

25 December

Noël (Christmas) is a public holiday and a day of eating and drinking. Lunch will often start with a variety of seafood, oysters being particularly popular. Turkey is often eaten as a main course, sometimes with chestnut stuffing. A variety of cheeses will be followed by *la bûche de Noël*, a rich chocolate cake in the form of a snow-covered log. French people do not usually send Christmas cards, the custom being to send wishes for the coming year to more distant friends and relatives during the month of January.

26 December

There is no particular name for the day after Christmas Day and it is not a public holiday.

31 December

la Saint-Sylvestre (New Year's Eve). Many people have parties to celebrate *le réveillon du Nouvel An* (New Year's Eve Party). Once again, food plays a major part and, as at Christmas, this is a time to splash out on luxury foods such as *foie gras*. There will often be dancing and the New Year will be welcomed in with champagne.

Movable feasts

Mardi gras
Shrove Tuesday, the last day of carnival before the beginning of Lent on Ash Wednesday. Traditionally, *crêpes* (pancakes) are eaten for supper. In many areas of France, sugared fritters called *bugnes* in and around Lyons and *oreillettes* farther south, are eaten between *la fête des Rois* and *mardi gras*.

le Vendredi saint
Good Friday is celebrated in the church, but is not a public holiday.

Pâques
Easter Sunday, *le dimanche de Pâques*, is for many people the occasion for a big family lunch Easter hunts are organised for children, with chocolate eggs, rabbits, hens, or fish traditionally hidden in the family garden. *Le lundi de Pâques* (Easter Monday) is a public holiday.

l'Ascension the Thursday forty days after Easter is a public holiday in France.

la Pentecôte (Whitsun) on the seventh Sunday after Easter represents for many people the first long weekend of the summer, as *le lundi de la Pentecôte* (Whit Monday) is a public holiday. Many families go to stay with friends or relatives in the country.

la Fête des mères (Mother's Day) is the Sunday after *Pentecôte*. This is another occasion for a big family meal, with presents for the mother. **La fête des pères** (Father's Day) is celebrated in similar fashion two weeks later.

A–Z of French life and culture

Académie française
A learned body whose main role nowadays is to monitor new developments in the French language and to make decisions as to what is acceptable and what is not, although these decisions are not always taken entirely seriously by the public at large. Its 40 members are elected for life on the basis of their contribution to scholarship or literature.

Alliance Française
A private organization which aims to spread awareness of French language and culture. It has centres in cities throughout the world, providing classes and a variety of cultural activities.

année scolaire
The French school year starts with the **RENTRÉE** des classes in early September and ends in early July. There is a week's holiday in late October/early November around *la Toussaint* (All Saints' Day, 1 November), two weeks around Christmas and New Year, two weeks in February, and two weeks in April.

Antenne 2 ▸ **FRANCE 2**

arrondissement
The three largest cities in France – Paris, Lyons, and Marseilles – are divided into numbered administrative areas called *arrondissements*. Each has its own mayor and council, and the number of the *arrondissement* is usually part of the postcode. The system makes for a convenient way for people to talk about which part of the city they live in e.g. '*le neuvième arrondissement*' or simply '*le neuvième*'. An *arrondissement* is also a sub-division of a **DÉPARTEMENT**.

ARTE
A television channel, run jointly by France and Germany, which provides a high standard of cultural programmes.

Assemblée Nationale
The lower house of the French parliament, also called the *Chambre des députés*. There are 577 **DÉPUTÉS**, elected for a five-year term, often after two rounds of voting as at least 50% of the vote must be obtained.

Astérix
A hugely popular comic-book character invented by cartoonists Goscinny and Uderzo. *Astérix* is a tiny but invincible village leader in the ancient province of Gaul, whose fictional adventures with his fellow-villagers often involve fighting and outwitting the occupying Romans and make for gentle mockery of cultures outside Gaul. The *Astérix* books have been translated into 40 languages.

autoroute
France has an extensive motorway system, which is largely financed by tolls calculated according to the distance travelled and the vehicle type. Tickets are obtained and tolls paid at *péages* (tollgates). There is a speed limit for standard vehicles of 130 km/h (approx. 80 mph) and 110 km/h (approx. 70 mph) in wet weather.

baccalauréat
The *baccalauréat*, generally known informally as the *Bac*, is the examination sat in the final year of the **LYCÉE** (la *terminale*), so usually at age 17 or 18. Students sit exams in a fairly broad range of subjects in a particular category: the *Bac S* places emphasis on the sciences, for example, whilst the *Bac L* has a literary bias. Some categories cater for students specializing in more directly job-based subjects such as agriculture. The final result is given as a single overall mark or grade out of 20, although the scores for individual subjects are also given. It is common to use the *Bac* as a point of reference in job advertisements, so that *Bac + 4* would mean a person who had completed 4 years of full-time study after the *Bac*, with appropriate diplomas to show for it.

bachelier
The holder of the **BACCALAURÉAT**, entitled to enrol for university courses.

bande dessinée (BD)
Comic books of all sorts and for a wide variety of age and interest groups are immensely popular in France and form an important part of French culture. Cartoon characters such as *Astérix*, *Lucky Luke*, and *Tintin* are household names and older comic books are often collectors' items.

Basque
The Basque country extends on both sides of the Pyrenees with about one quarter of a million Basques living in France and ten times that number in Spain. The French Basque region (*le Pays basque français*) does not have any autonomous status nor is

Basque recognized as an official language. It is, however, taught in some schools, and there are an estimated 40,000 Basque speakers in France.

boules

A type of bowls, also called **PÉTANQUE**, played all over France, using metal boules and a jack known as a *cochonnet*. Special areas (*terrains de boules*) are set aside for the game in towns and villages, although one of the obvious attractions of the game is that it can be played virtually anywhere. There are some regional variations, notably in the size and form of the playing area and the size of the bowls.

brasserie

The original meaning of *brasserie* is 'brewery', and although the word is still used in this sense, it has come also to mean a type of bar-restaurant, usually serving simple, traditional French food at reasonable prices. Most *brasseries* offer a fixed-price menu, especially at lunchtime.

Breton

The ancient Celtic language of Brittany (*Bretagne*). It is related to Welsh, Irish, Scottish Gaelic, and Cornish. Recent decades have seen a revival of interest in the language going hand in hand with the assertion of a regional cultural identity and a movement for independence from France. Breton is fairly widely spoken and is taught in secondary schools in the region, although it is not recognized as an official language in France.

Brevet d'études professionnelles (BEP)

A vocational qualification awarded at the end of a two-year, practically-based course in a **LYCÉE** specializing in providing teaching directly related to the workplace.

Brevet de technicien (BT)

A vocational qualification awarded at the end of a three-year course in a special section of a **LYCÉE**. There is considerable competition for entry to courses, and the standards required result in a high dropout rate.

Brevet de technicien supérieur (BTS)

A vocational qualification awarded at the end of a two-year course after the **BACCALAURÉAT** in a specific professional field.

Brevet des collèges

A general educational qualification taken in a range of subjects by students aged around 15 in the final year of **COLLÈGE**.

bureau de tabac
Tobacconists are either individual shops or else are to be found in a *bar-tabac* or *café-tabac*. They are also often combined with a newsagents (*marchand de journaux*). As well as being licensed to sell tobacco and cigarettes, they have a state licence to sell stamps, LOTO tickets, the *vignette* (road tax disc for motor vehicles), and certain other official documents.

Canal Plus (Canal+)
A privately-owned French television channel broadcasting mainly feature films. Viewers pay a subscription and access the channel using a decoder.

CAPES - certificat d'aptitude au professorat de l'enseignement du second degré
The qualification normally required in order to teach in a secondary school. Qualification is by means of a competitive examination (CONCOURS) usually at the end of a two-year course in a specialist teacher-training institute (*IUFM: Institut universitaire pour la formation des maîtres*).

Carte bleue
A credit card issued by French banks as part of the international Visa network.

Carte grise
The registration document for a motor vehicle. It is an offence not to carry it when driving the vehicle, and police checks are frequent. Vehicle registration numbers depend on the DÉPARTEMENT in which the owner lives and have to be changed if the owner moves to a different one.

Carte nationale d'identité
Although not obligatory, most French citizens possess a *carte nationale d'identité* (national identity card), obtained from their local MAIRIE, PREFECTUR, or *commissariat de police* (police station), as proof of identity is often required, for example when paying by cheque. It is also accepted as a travel document by all EC countries.

Catalan
The language spoken by 25 per cent of people in Spain and by some people in the Perpignan area of southwest France. It is taught in schools in the area but is not recognized as an official language in France.

CDI - Centre de documentation et d'information
A resource and information centre providing library and IT facilities in a school or college. The term has largely replaced *bibliothèque* (library) in this context.

CE - cycle élémentaire
Also called *cours élémentaire*, this is the programme for the two years of primary school for children aged 7 to 9 (*CE1* and *CE2*).

Césars
Prizes awarded annually for achievements in the film industry, so the French equivalent of the Oscars.

Chambre des députés ▸ **ASSEMBLÉE NATIONALE**

champignons
The French use the word *champignons* (mushrooms) to refer to any of the types of mushroom-like fungi that are to be found in the countryside, whether edible or not. Cultivated button mushrooms are called *champignons de Paris*. Hunting for edible *champignons* is almost a national leisure activity, and many varieties are highly prized. Advice on whether a *champignon* is edible or not can usually be obtained in a **PHARMACIE**.

Champs-Élysées
The world-famous avenue in central Paris, known for its luxury shops, hotels, and clubs. At one end is the *Arc de Triomphe*, the scene of the remembrance ceremony each year for the Armistice of 1918 and under which is the tomb of an unknown soldier, killed in World War I.

charcuterie
A shop or supermarket counter selling a wide variety of pork products. As well as cuts of pork, *charcutiers* usually sell chicken, both raw and ready-cooked, and there will be various types of raw and cooked ham, a variety of pâtés, often homemade in small shops, and a selection of *saucissons*. Most *charcuteries* also offer a variey of salads, various types of savoury pastries, and a number of dishes, different every day, which can be reheated at home or on the premises. Some also offer a catering service, in which case the shop will probably call itself a *charcutier-traiteur*. The word *charcuterie* is also used to mean pork products such as ham and *saucisson*.

chasse
La chasse (hunting) is a widely practised sport in France. Legislation as to the rights of hunters to hunt over privately-owned land varies according to the region and the amount of land concerned. During the hunting season, hunting is permitted on Thursdays, Saturdays, and Sundays. It is advisable not to stray from public footpaths when walking in the country-

side on these days. The hunters (*les chasseurs*) are a powerful political lobby and are represented in the **ASSEMBLÉE NATIONALE**.

Cinquième

La Cinquième is an educational television channel which broadcasts on the **ARTE** channel during the day.

Cinquième république

This is the present régime in France. The constitution was established in 1958 according to principles put forward by Charles de Gaulle.

classe de neige

A period, generally a week, which a school class, usually of under-twelves, spends in a mountain area. Ski tuition is integrated with normal school work.

classe préparatoire

An intensive two-year course, provided by some prestigious **LYCÉES**, which prepares students for the competitive examinations (**CONCOURS**) by means of which students are selected for the **GRANDES ÉCOLES**.

classes

In French schools, after CM, classes go in reverse order, starting at age 11-12 in *sixième* and progressing through *cinquième*, *quatrième*, *troisième*, *seconde*, *première*, and ending in *terminale* at age 17 or 18, the year in which the **BACCALAURÉAT** is taken. Education in France is compulsory up to the end of *seconde*.

CM - Cycle moyen

Also called *Cours moyen* this is the programme for the two years of primary school for children aged 9 to 11 (*CM1* and *CM2*).

collège

A state school for pupils between the ages of 11 and 15, between the **ÉCOLE PRIMAIRE** and the **LYCÉE**. The organisation of the school and the curriculum followed are laid down at national level.

colonie de vacances

A holiday village or summer camp for children. Originally set up as a means of giving poorer city children a means of getting out into the countryside, these are still largely state-subsidized. The informal word for them is *colo*.

commune

The *commune* is the smallest administrative unit of French local government. Each has its own **MAIRE** (mayor).

concours

Entry into many areas of the public services, including the teaching profession, as well as the most prestigious institutes of higher education,

depends on succeeding in a competitive examination or *concours*.
The number of candidates admitted depends on the number of posts or places available in a given year.

conduite accompagnée (CA)
A learner driver who has passed the theory part of the driving test (*code de la route*) in a state-approved driving school is allowed to practise driving a vehicle accompanied by a qualified driver over the age of 28. Such drivers are not allowed to drive on **AUTOROUTES** and are required to have a white sticker with a red 'A' displayed on the rear of their vehicle.

conseil de classe
A committee representing each class in a **COLLÈGE** or **LYCÉE** consisting of the class teachers, two elected parent members, and two elected class members. It is chaired by the head teacher. The *conseil de classe* meets regularly to discuss the progress of the class and any problems that have arisen.

CP - Cycle préparatoire
Also called *Cours préparatoire*, this is the first year of primary school, starting a child's formal education off at the statutory age of 6. Most children will have already attended an **ÉCOLE MATERNELLE.**

CRS – compagnies républicaines de sécurité
Special police units trained in public order techniques and riot control. They also police the **AUTOROUTES** and support mountain rescue and lifeguard work.

département
An administrative unit of government in France. Each *département* has a number and this appears as the first two digits in postcodes for addresses within the département and as the two-digit number at the end of registration numbers on motor vehicles.

député
An elected member of the **ASSEMBLÉE NATIONALE**.

droguerie
As a shop or supermarket section, there seems little connection between the name, which might be literally translated as 'drugstore', and the merchandise displayed. However, *drogue* can also mean the raw ingredients of dyes, and *droguistes* were originally dye merchants. Nowadays you will find not only dyes but household products and cleaning utensils, can-

dles, and a variey of other useful household items.

école libre
Private sector school education, provided predominantly by the Catholic Church.

école maternelle
A school providing free nursery education from age 2 to 6. Many children start at 2 and virtually all children attend between the ages of 4 and 6, which is the statutory school starting age and the time at which children move into the **ÉCOLE PRIMAIRE**.

école primaire
A primary school for children between the ages of 6, the statutory minimum age for starting school, and 11.

école secondaire
Secondary education in France consists of two phases: **COLLÈGE** (11–15 years) and **LYCÉE** (15/16 –17/18 years).

Élysée ▸ **PALAIS DE L' ÉLYSÉE**

Europe 1
A popular commercial French-language radio station, which broadcasts news, popular music, sport, and light entertainment from the Saarland in Germany.

Événement du jeudi - l'Événement du jeudi
A popular weekly news magazine.

Express - l'Express
A weekly news magazine offering in-depth coverage of political and cultural matters.

faculté
La faculté – and more usually and informally *la fac* – is the way that students refer to their university, particularly the location itself, so that *aller à la fac* would be the equivalent of 'to go into college'.

Figaro - le Figaro
A right-wing national daily newspaper with a wide circulation.

France 2
This is the main publicly-owned television channel and aims to provide a wide range of quality programmes.

France 3
A state-owned television channel which is regionally based and is required to promote regional diversity and to cover a wide range of beliefs and opinions.

France Culture
A 24-hour **RADIO FRANCE** radio station featuring serious talk programmes on a wide variety of cultural and social topics.

France Info
A 24-hour radio news station run by **RADIO FRANCE**.

France Inter
A **RADIO FRANCE** radio station broadcasting mainly light entertainment, including a considerable proportion of studio comedy shows, but also offering good news coverage.

France Musiques
A 24-hour **RADIO FRANCE** radio station. Its main focus is classical music but it also provides considerable coverage of jazz and world music.

Gendarmerie nationale
A section of the military which provides police services outside the major towns.

gîte rural
A farmhouse or other building in the country which has been turned into a holiday cottage. Houses displaying the official *gîte de France* sign must conform to certain standards.

grande école
A prestigious higher education establishment admitting students on the results of a **CONCOURS**. They have different areas of specialization and competition for entry is fierce, as they are widely believed to offer the highest level of education available and thus a guarantee of subsequent career success.

hôtel de ville ▸ **MAIRIE**

Humanité - l'Humanité
The communist national daily newspaper.

Internet
A wealth of useful information on French culture, society, and current affairs can be obtained on the Internet. All the main French newspapers have websites (e.g. http://www.lemonde.fr), as do the television channels (e.g. http://www.france3.fr and http://www.tf1.fr). The *Louvre* museum has an interesting site at http://web.culture.fr/louvre.

immatriculation ▸ **PLAQUE D'IMMATRICULATION**

Libération
A left-wing national daily newspaper published in Paris. A separate edition is published for Lyons.

licence
A university degree awarded after a year's study following the **DEUG**.

Loto
The French national lottery. People play the *Loto* using special machines which can be found in **BUREAUX DE TABAC** throughout France.

Luxembourg ▸ **PALAIS DU LUXEMBOURG**

lycée
A school providing the last

three years of secondary education after **COLLÈGE**. The first year is *seconde* at the age of 15/16, going through *première*, and ending with *terminale* at age 17/18. As well as those which provide a conventional academic education, there are a number of different types of *lycée* offering a more vocationally-based education.

M6

A popular, privately-owned, commercial television channel.

magasins

Opening and closing times of shops (*les magasins*) vary according to the type of shop and the location. Department stores (*les grands magasins*) are generally open all day from 9 a.m. to 7 p.m. In larger towns, most other shops, with the exception of small food shops, are also open all day. Privately-owned food shops such as butchers and fishmongers generally open at 8 a.m. and do not close in the evening until 7 or 7.30. Most, however, are closed between midday and 2 or 3 p.m. In small towns, all the shops, with the exception of bakers, generally close for 2 or 3 hours in the middle of the day. In both small and large towns, it is always possible to find all types of food shops open on Sunday mornings until midday. In smaller towns, however, many of the shops are closed on Mondays.

maire

The chief officer of a **COMMUNE**, he or she represents state authority locally, officiates at marriages, and supervises local elections.

mairie

The *mairie* (town hall) is the administrative headquarters of the **CONSEIL MUNICIPAL**. In larger towns the *mairie* is often called the **HÔTEL DE VILLE**.

marchés

All towns in France have a weekly market with stalls selling a variety of produce, and some areas in big cities have a market every day. Many stalls are held by local people selling their own produce. Despite supermarkets, many people do much of their food shopping *au marché*.

Marianne

The symbolic female figure often used to represent the French Republic. There are statues of her in public places all over France, and she also appears on the standard French stamp. She is always depicted wearing the Phrygian bonnet, a pointed cap which became one of the symbols of liberty as represented by the 1789 Revolution.

Marseillaise
The French national anthem, so called because it was the marching song of a group of republican volunteers from Marseilles a few years after the 1789 revolution.

Médecins du monde
A charitable organization which provides medical and humanitarian aid in areas stricken by war, famine, or natural disaster.

Médecins sans frontières
A charitable organisation which sends medical teams anywhere in the world where they are needed to cope with the effects on people of war and disaster.

Minitel
A computer terminal available in a variety of models to the subscribers of **FRANCE TÉLÉCOM**. It gives users access to the *Télétel* network, which has a huge variety of services, payable at different rates, including the telephone directory. It can now be accessed via the Internet.

MJC - Maison des jeunes et de la culture
A community youth centre offering a wide variety of services and activities.

Monde - le Monde
A national daily newspaper. Its political stance is left of centre, and it is entirely owned by its staff. It provides full coverage of national and international news and is known for its in-depth analysis of current issues. It is unusual in publishing virtually no photographs of current events.

Nouvel Observateur - le Nouvel Observateur
A left-wing weekly magazine providing in-depth articles on current political issues and good coverage of culture and the arts.

Palais Bourbon
A large eighteenth-century residence on the left bank of the Seine which is now the seat of the **ASSEMBLÉE NATIONALE**.

Palais de l'Élysée
The official residence and office of the French President, situated just off the **CHAMPS-ÉLYSÉES** in Paris.

Palais du Luxembourg
A seventeenth century palace in the jardin du Luxembourg in Paris. It is now the seat of the **SÉNAT**.

paysan
Since *paysan* can be used in French to mean both 'small farmer' and, more offensively, 'peasant', small farmers are

generally referred to as *agriculteurs*. However, many small farmers take pride in their identity as *paysans*, particularly in the more remote areas of the country, where small farms are still the usual form of cultivation. The difficulty of making a living with a limited amount of land has, however, led to many such farms being abandoned or amalgamated into larger units and a general movement of the traditional rural population towards the towns.

permis de conduire
A driving licence can be issued to a person over the age of 18 who has passed both parts of the driving test. The first part is the theory test (*code de la route*) and consists of forty questions based on the highway code. This can be sat from the age of 16 onwards and gives the right to **CONDUITE ACCOMPAGNÉE**. The practical driving test has to be taken within two years of the theory test. It is compulsory to carry your driving licence with you when you are driving a vehicle.

pétanque ▸ BOULES

pharmacie
Pharmacies in France generally sell only medicines and closely related products such as toiletries and some brands of make-up and perfume. The products of the major perfume houses are to be found in *parfumeries*. Pharmacists traditionally play an active paramedical role, and people will often consult them rather than a doctor in the case of minor ailments and accidents. Pharmacies are easily spotted by the green cross, which is lit up when the pharmacy is open. A *pharmacie de garde* (duty chemist) can dispense medicines outside normal opening hours as part of a local rota.

plaque d'immatriculation
A vehicle's registration plate. The last two figures indicate the number of the **DÉPARTEMENT** in which the owner lives. If you move into another *département*, you are obliged by law to change your registration plate accordingly.

Point – le Point
A centre-right weekly news magazine offering in-depth coverage of politics and economics.

police
There are three principal police forces: the *police municipale* who are responsible for routine local policing such as traffic offences, who are locally organized and are not armed, the *police nationale* who are nationally organized

and generally armed, and the *gendarmerie nationale* which is a branch of the military.

Poste – La Poste
The state monopoly postal service. Postboxes in France are yellow.

préfet
The most senior offical responsible for representing the state within the **DÉPARTEMENT**.

préfecture
The administrative headquarters of a DÉPARTEMENT.

Premier ministre
The chief minister of the government, appointed by the **PRÉSIDENT DE LA RÉPUBLIQUE** and responsible for the overall management of government affairs.

Président de la République
The president is the head of state and is elected for a term of 7 years. Under the constitution of the **CINQUIÈME RÉPUBLIQUE** the president plays a strong executive role in the governing of the country.

Quai d'Orsay
The *ministère des Affaires étrangères* (ministry of Foreign Affairs) is situated here, so *Quai d'Orsay* is often used by journalists to mean the ministry.

Radio France
The state-owned radio broadcasting company.

région
The largest administrative unit in France, consisting of a number of **DÉPARTEMENTS**. Each has its own *conseil régional* (regional council) which has responsibilities in education and economic planning.

rentrée
The week at the beginning of September when the new school year starts and around which much of French administrative life revolves. The preceding weeks see intensive advertising of associated merchandise, from books and stationery to clothes and sports equipment. *La rentrée littéraire* marks the start of the literary year and *la rentrée parlementaire* signals the reassembly of parliament after the recess.

repas
Traditionally the midday meal was the big meal of the day, and for people who live in country areas this is still largely the case. Even in big cities many people continue to eat a big meal in the middle of the day, though they are tending more and more to have a snack lunch and to eat their main meal in the

evening. In either case, the main meal virtually always consists of a number of courses, typically a starter such as pâté, *saucisson*, or salad, then meat or fish with a vegetable dish, followed by cheese and dessert. Cheese is virtually always eaten and is served before the dessert. In town and country alike, Sunday is the day for a big family meal in the middle of the day, and the **PÂTISSERIES** are usually crowded on Sunday mornings as people queue up to buy a large tart or cake for their hosts or guests.

restaurants

France is rightly famed for the quality of its restaurants. It is always possible to find restaurants and **BRASSERIES** offering fixed-price menus which are generally good value for money. A basket of bread is usually included in the price of the meal, and most restaurants will have several inexpensive house wines, available in *pichets* (jugs) of 1/4, 1/2, and 1 litre. Service is included in the bill, although many people do leave a tip if the meal and the service have been good.

route départementale

These are signalled on French road maps as 'D' followed by a number and are marked in yellow. They are roads maintained by the **DÉPARTEMENT** and are secondary roads, not intended to be used for fast travel from place to place. Many of them have stretches marked in green on maps to highlight areas or views of particular beauty.

route nationale

A *route nationale* forms part of the state-maintained road network, outside the **AUTOROUTES** but providing fast roads for travel between towns and cities. They are signalled by 'N' followed by the road number and are marked in red on French road maps.

SAMU – service d'aide médicale d'urgence

A 24 hour service coordinated by each **DÉPARTEMENT** to provide mobile medical services and staff, ambulances, and helicopters to accident scenes and emergencies.

Sénat

The upper house of parliament which meets in the **PALAIS DU LUXEMBOURG**. It consists of 321 elected *sénateurs*. It votes laws and the state budget.

SNCF – Société nationale des chemins de fer français

The state-owned railway company, which also has access to private finance.

tabac ▸ BUREAU DE TABAC

télécarte
A phone card for use in telephone kiosks, widely available from *France Télécom* (the state owned telephone company), *bureaux de poste*, *tabacs* and *marchands de journaux*.

TF1 - Télévision française 1
Originally a state-controlled television channel, now privately-owned, *TF1* has an obligation to ensure that 50% of its programmes are of French origin.

TGV - train à grande vitesse
The new-generation high-speed electric train. It runs on special tracks and can reach speeds of up to 300 km/h.

Tintin
A comic-book character invented by the Belgian cartoonist Hergé in 1929. Tintin's adventures with the irrepressible Capitaine Haddock are still bestsellers and have been translated into more than 40 languages.

Tour de France
Probably the most famous cycle race in the world, the *Tour de France* takes place over a different route each year but always ends around July 14 on the CHAMPS ÉLYSÉES. The overall winner after each section of the race is entitled to wear *le maillot jaune* (yellow jersey).

Letter-writing in French

Holiday postcard

■ Address. On an envelope Mr, Mrs, and Miss can be abbreviated to *M.*, *Mme*, *Mlle*, although the full forms are considered preferable in more formal letters. There is no direct equivalent for Ms. If you do not know a woman's marital status use *Madame* (*Mme*).

Road names such as *rue*, *avenue*, *place* are not generally given capital letters.

The name of the town comes after the postcode and on the same line.

■ Beginnings (informal): *Cher* is used for a man, *Chère* for a woman. A letter to two males or to a male and female begins with *Chers*. For two female correspondents *Chères Madeleine et Hélène*. For friends and relatives: *Chers amis*, *Chers cousins*, etc. For a family: *Chers tous*.

14.7.2000

Cher Alexandre,

Grosses bises d'Edimbourg! Cela fait trois jours que nous sommes ici et nous n'avons pas encore vu la pluie! Espérons que ça va durer. La vieille ville est très belle et du château on a une vue splendide jusqu'à l'estuaire. Et en Normandie, comment ça va?

A bientôt pour des retrouvailles parisiennes,

Marie et Dominique

M. A. Pilnard

38 rue Glacière

75013 Paris

■ Endings (informal): *Bien amicalement*, *Amitiés*; *A bientôt* = see you soon.

Christmas and New Year wishes (informal)

- On most personal letters French speakers do not put their address at the top of the letter. The date is given preceded by *le*. For the first day of the month le *1er* is used. Generally, the name of the town in which the letter is written is placed before the date.

  1 The tradition of Christmas cards is much less widespread in France than in Great Britain. While Christmas greetings may be sent, it is more customary to send best wishes for the New Year in January.

  2 In the year 2000/2001 etc. = *en l'an 2000/2001* etc., but *bonne année 2000/2001* etc.

le 18 décembre 2000 **1**

Chers Steve et Michelle,

Nous vous souhaitons un Joyeux Noël **1** et une très bonne année 2001 **2**! En espérant que ce nouveau millénaire vous apportera tout ce que vous désirez et que nous trouverons une occasion pour nous revoir!

Bises à vous deux,

Gérard

New Year wishes (formal)

le 5 janvier 2001

Je vous **1** présente mes meilleurs vœux pour l'année 2001. Que cette année vous apporte, à vous et à votre famille, bonheur et prospérité.

Pierre Carlier

1 Note the use of the formal form *vous*.

Invitation (informal)

Invitations to parties are usually by word of mouth, but for more formal events such as weddings, invitations are sent out.

1 Note the use of the informal form *tu* betweeen good friends.

Paris, le 28/04/01

Cher Denis,

Que fais-tu 1 cet été? Pascal et moi avons décidé d'inviter tous les copains d'Orléans à nous rejoindre dans notre maison de Dordogne pour le weekend du 14 juillet. Il y aura fête au village avec bal populaire et feu d'artifice. Le petit vin du pays n'est pas mal non plus!

Nous comptons sur toi pour venir trinquer avec nous,

Bises,

Martine

- Endings (informal): *Bises* (= lots of love) is very informal and is appropriate for very good friends and family. Alternatives for close friends and family include *Bien à toi, Bons baisers* or affectionately *Je t'embrasse*. If the letter is addressed to more than one person use *Bien à vous* or *Je vous embrasse*.

Invitation (formal)

Christine et Félix Prévost
81 rue Esque moise
59000 Lille

Lille, le 28 avril 2001

Chers amis,

Nous avons l'immense plaisir de vous annoncer le mariage de notre fils Victor et de mademoiselle Stéphanie Heusdens.

La cérémonie aura lieu à l'Hôtel de Ville à 15 heures le samedi 5 juin. Vous recevrez bientôt un faire-part et une invitation à dîner mais nous tenions à vous prévenir suffisamment tôt pour que vous puissiez arranger votre voyage. Nous espérons qu'il vous sera possible de vous joindre à nous.

Amicalement, **1**

Christine et Félix

- In a more formal letter, especially where a reply is generally required, the sender's address is written on the left-hand side of the page. An alternative is in the centre of the page, particularly on printed stationery.

1 Endings: Alternatives could be *Amitiés*, *Bien amicalement*.

Accepting an Invitation

Emilie Joly
2 rue de la Pompe
75016 Paris

le 16 mars 2001

Chère Madame Dubois,

Je vous **1** remercie de bien vouloir me recevoir pour les deux premières semaines de juillet. Je serai très heureuse de vous revoir ainsi que Natalie, bien entendu. Nous avons passé un si bon séjour linguistique à Manchester l'été dernier que nous avions très envie de nous retrouver. Mes parents ne pouvant m'envoyer en Angleterre cette année, c'est avec un immense plaisir que j'accepte votre invitation.

Je vous prie de bien vouloir accepter, Madame, l'expression de mes sentiments les meilleurs.

Emilie

- In a more formal social letter where the correspondent is known personally by name it can be used in the opening greeting.
- The title of the person receiving the letter must be repeated in the closing formula. These formulas are more elaborate than in English, with a number of possible variations. Some of these are shown in the following letters in this section.

1 Since the letter is from a young person to the mother of a friend, she uses the formal *vous* form and writes to her as Madame Dubois. Madame Dubois would address Emilie using *tu*.

Seeking a job as an au pair

Sally Paledra
5 Avon Crescent
Kenilworth
Warwickshire
CV8 2PQ

le 3 mars 2001

Madame,

Vos coordonnées m'ont été communiquées par l'agence 'Au Pair International', qui m'a demandé de vous écrire directement. Je suis en effet à la recherche d'un emploi au pair pour une période de neuf à dix mois à partir de septembre prochain.

J'aime beaucoup les enfants et ils apprécient également ma compagnie. J'ai une grande expérience du baby-sitting. J'ai aussi fait un stage d'un mois dans une crèche privée **1**.

Je suis enthousiaste, discrète et je sais prendre des initiatives. J'ai étudié le français au lycée pendant cinq ans et je connais un peu la France pour y avoir passé des vacances à plusieurs reprises. J'ai aussi mon permis de conduire.

Dans l'espoir d'une réponse positive de votre part, je vous prie d'agréer, Madame, l'expression de mes salutations respectueuses.

S. Paledra

P.J. :un CV avec photo

1 Or be more specific, e.g. *pour des enfants de 3 mois à 3 ans.*

■ To supply references: *Vous trouverez également ci-joint les adresses de personnes pouvant fournir une lettre de recommandation* or *pouvant me recommander.*

Enquiry to a tourist office

M. et Mme Baude
13 La Faverolle
45000 Orléans

Syndicat d'initiative
de St Gervais
74170 Saint-Gervais-les-Bains

Orléans, le 24 mars 2001

Monsieur,

Nous vous serions reconnaissants de bien vouloir nous faire parvenir toute la documentation dont vous disposez sur les villas de location à proximité de la station thermale. Nous désirons également recevoir des informations sur les activités de loisirs durant l'été.
Vous trouverez ci-joint une enveloppe timbrée **1** pour la réponse.

Dans l'attente de votre réponse, je vous prie d'agréer, Monsieur, l'expression de nos salutations distinguées.

J. Baude

1 *enveloppe timbrée* = stamped addressed envelope.

■ Note that, unlike in English, a reference or the purpose of a business letter is placed, where required, above the opening greeting. e.g. *Objet: commande 99/08/21* or *Réf: 000/23.*

Booking a hotel room

Miss Sylvia Daley
The Willows
49 North Terrace
Kings Barton
Nottinghamshire
NG8 4LQ
England

Hôtel Beauséjour
Chemin des Mimosas
06100 Grasse

le 8 avril 2001

Madame,

J'ai bien reçu le dépliant de votre hôtel et je vous en remercie.

Je souhaite réserver une chambre calme avec salle de bains, en pension complète **1** pour la période du 7 au 18 juin. Pour les arrhes, je vous prie de m'informer de leur montant et des modalités de paiement possibles depuis la Grande-Bretagne.

En vous remerciant d'avance, je vous prie de croire, Madame, en mes sentiments les meilleurs.

S. Daley

1 Or *une chambre avec douche en demi-pension* or *avec petit déjeuner*. The term en suite does not exist for bathroom facilities in French.

Booking a campsite

Frances Good
22 Daniel Avenue
Caldwood
Leeds LS8 7RR
tel. 0113 2998767

Camping 'Les Embruns'
18 allée des Capucins
22116 Moëlan-sur-Mer

le 25 avril 2001

Monsieur,

Nous souhaitons réserver dans votre camping, pour la période du 2 au 15 juillet, deux emplacements de tente côte à côte **1** et, si possible, pas trop loin de la plage **2**. Il s'agit de deux tentes de deux personnes. Nous aurons également deux motos de 1000cc chacune.

Dès que nous aurons confirmation de votre part, nous vous adresserons le montant de la réservation.

Pouvez-vous nous indiquer à cet effet, les possibilités de paiement depuis l'étranger.

Veuillez croire, Monsieur, en l'expression de nos sentiments les meilleurs.

F. Good

1 Or if you have a caravan *un emplacement de caravane*.
2 Other requirements might be *ombragé* (shady), or *abrité* (sheltered).

Cancelling a reservation

Mrs J. Warrington
Downlands
Steyning
West Sussex

Hôtel des Voyageurs
BN44 6LZ
9 cours Gambetta
91949 Les Ulis

le 15 février 2001

Monsieur,

Je suis au regret de devoir annuler la réservation de chambre pour deux personnes pour la nuit du 24 au 25 mars, que j'avais effectuée par téléphone le 18 janvier dernier. **1**

Je vous remercie de votre compréhension et vous prie d'agréer, Monsieur, l'expression de mes sentiments distingués.

J. Warrington

1 If reasons for the cancellation are specified these could include: *pour raisons de santé/de famille, en raison d'un décès dans la famille*, etc.

sending an email

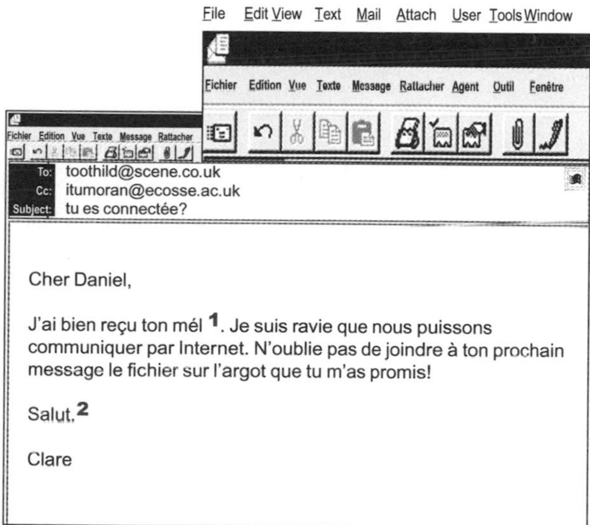

File Edit View Text Mail Attach User Tools Window
Fichier Edition Vue Texte Message Rattacher Agent Outil Fenêtre
Fichier Edition Vue Texte Message Rattacher
To: toothild@scene.co.uk
Cc: itumoran@ecosse.ac.uk
Subject: tu es connectée?
Cher Daniel,
J'ai bien reçu ton mél 1. Je suis ravie que nous puissons communiquer par Internet. N'oublie pas de joindre à ton prochain message le fichier sur l'argot que tu m'as promis!
Salut, 2
Clare

1 Note that *mél* is an abbreviated form of *message électronique*. To send an attachment = *joindre un fichier*.

2 Endings (informal): An alternative could be *A bientôt* or simply *Bises* to a close friend in an informal context.

a *determiner*

an avant voyelle ou h muet.

⇨ For expressions such as **make a noise, make a fortune** ⇒**noise, fortune**.

····▸ un/une; ~ **tree** un arbre; ~ **chair** une chaise.

····▸ (per) **ten francs ~ kilo** dix francs le kilo; **three times ~ day** trois fois par jour.

! When talking about what people do or are, **a** is not translated into French: **she's a teacher** *elle est professeur*, **he's a widower** *il est veuf*.

aback *adv* **taken ~** déconcerté.

abandon *vt* abandonner. ● *n* abandon *m*.

abate *vi* (*flood, fever*) baisser; (*storm*) se calmer. ● *vt* diminuer.

abbey *n* abbaye *f*.

abbot *n* abbé *m*.

abbreviate *vt* abréger. **abbreviation** *n* abréviation *f*.

abdicate *vt/i* abdiquer.

abdomen *n* abdomen *m*.

abduct *vt* enlever. **abductor** *n* ravisseur/-euse *m/f*.

abhor *vt* (*pt* **abhorred**) exécrer.

abide *vt* supporter; **~ by** respecter.

ability *n* capacité *f* (**to do** à faire); (talent) talent *m*.

abject *a* (*state*) misérable; (*coward*) abject.

ablaze *a* en feu.

able *a* (skilled) compétent; **be ~ to do** pouvoir faire; (know how to) savoir faire. **ably** *adv* avec compétence.

abnormal *a* anormal. **abnormality** *n* anomalie *f*.

aboard *adv* à bord. ● *prep* à bord de.

abode *n* demeure *f*; **of no fixed ~** sans domicile fixe.

abolish *vt* abolir.

Aborigine *n* aborigène *mf* (d'Australie).

abort *vt* faire avorter; (Comput) abandonner. ● *vi* avorter.

abortion *n* avortement *m*; **have an ~** se faire avorter.

abortive *a* (*attempt*) avorté; (*coup*) manqué.

about *adv* (approximately) environ; **~ the same** à peu près pareil; **there was no-one ~** il n'y avait personne. ● *prep* **it's ~ ...** il s'agit de ...; **what I like ~ her is** ce que j'aime chez elle c'est; **to wander ~ the streets** errer dans les rues; **how/what ~ some tea?** et si on prenait un thé?; **what ~ you?** et toi? ● *adj* **be ~ to do** être sur le point de faire; **be up and ~** être debout. **~-face, ~-turn** *n* (fig) volte-face *f inv*.

above *prep* au-dessus de; **he is not ~ lying** il n'est pas incapable de mentir; **~ all** surtout. ● *adv* **the apartment ~** l'appartement du dessus; **see ~** voir ci-dessus. **~-board** *a* honnête. **~-mentioned** *a* susmentionné.

abrasive *a* abrasif; (*manner*) mordant. ● *n* abrasif *m*.

abreast *adv* de front; **keep ~ of** se tenir au courant de.

abroad *adv* à l'étranger.

abrupt *a* (sudden, curt) brusque; (steep) abrupt. **abruptly** *adv* (suddenly) brusquement; (curtly) avec brusquerie.

abscess *n* abcès *m*.

abseil *vi* descendre en rappel.

absence *n* absence *f*; (lack) manque *m*; **in the ~ of** faute de.

absent *a* absent.

absentee *n* absent/-e *m*/*f*.

absent-minded *a* distrait.

absolute *a* (*monarch, majority*) absolu; (*chaos, idiot*) véritable. **absolutely** *adv* absolument.

absolve *vt* **~ sb of sth** décharger qn de qch.

absorb *vt* absorber.

abstain *vi* s'abstenir (**from** de).

abstract[1] *a* abstrait. ● *n* (summary) résumé *m*; **in the ~** dans l'abstrait.

abstract[2] *vt* tirer.

absurd *a* absurde.

abundance *n* abondance *f*. **abundant** *a* abondant. **abundantly** *adv* (entirely) tout à fait.

abuse[1] *vt* (*position*) abuser de; (*person*) maltraiter; (insult) injurier.

abuse[2] *n* (misuse) abus *m* (**of** de); (cruelty) mauvais traitement *m*; (insults) injures *fpl*.

abusive *a* (*person*) grossier; (*language*) injurieux.

abysmal *a* épouvantable.

abyss *n* abîme *m*.

academic *a* (*career*) universitaire; (*year*) académique; (scholarly) intellectuel; (theoretical) théorique. ● *n* universitaire *mf*.

academy *n* (school) école *f*; (society) académie *f*.

accelerate *vi* (speed up) s'accélérer; (Auto) accélérer. **accelerator** *n* accélérateur *m*.

accent[1] *n* accent *m*.

accent[2] *vt* accentuer.

accept *vt* accepter. **acceptable** *a* acceptable. **acceptance** *n* (of offer) acceptation *f*; (of proposal) approbation *f*.

access *n* accès *m*. **accessible** *a* accessible.

accessory *a* accessoire. ● *n* (Jur) complice *mf* (**to** de).

accident *n* accident *m*; (chance) hasard *m*; **by ~** par hasard. **accidental** *a* (*death*) accidentel; (*meeting*) fortuit. **accidentally** *adv* accidentellement; (by chance) par hasard.

acclaim *vt* applaudir. ● *n* louanges *fpl*.

acclimatize *vt*/*i* (s')acclimater (**to** à).

accommodate *vt* loger; (adapt to) s'adapter à; (satisfy) satisfaire. **accommodating** *a* accommodant. **accommodation** *n* logement *m*.

accompaniment *n* accompagnement *m*. **accompany** *vt* accompagner.

accomplice *n* complice *mf* (**in, to** de).

accomplish *vt* accomplir; (*objective*) réaliser. **accomplished** *a* très compétent. **accomplishment** *n* (feat) réussite *f*; (talent) talent *m*.

accord *vi* concorder (**with** avec). ● *vt* accorder (**sb sth** qch à qn). ● *n* accord *m*; **of my own ~** de moi-même.

accordance *n* **in ~ with** conformément à.

according *adv* **~ to** (*principle, law*) selon; (*person, book*) d'après. **accordingly** *adv* en conséquence.

accordion *n* accordéon *m*.

accost *vt* aborder.

account *n* (Comm) compte *m*; (description) compte-rendu *m*; **on ~**

of à cause de; **on no ~** en aucun cas; **take into ~** tenir compte de; **it's of no ~** peu importe. □ **~ for** (explain) expliquer; (represent) représenter. **accountability** *n* responsabilité *f*. **accountable** *a* responsable (**for** de, **to** envers).

accountancy *n* comptabilité *f*. **accountant** *n* comptable *mf*. **accounts** *npl* comptabilité *f*, comptes *mpl*.

accumulate *vt/i* (s')accumuler.

accuracy *n* (of figures) justesse *f*; (of aim) précision *f*; (of forecast) exactitude *f*. **accurate** *a* juste, précis. **accurately** *adv* exactement, précisément.

accusation *n* accusation *f*.

accuse *vt* accuser; **the ~d** l'accusé/-e *m/f*.

accustomed *a* accoutumé; **become ~ to** s'accoutumer à.

ace *n* (card, person) as *m*.

ache *n* douleur *f*. ● *vi* (*person*) avoir mal; **my leg ~s** ma jambe me fait mal.

achieve *vt* (*aim*) atteindre; (*result*) obtenir; (*ambition*) réaliser. **achievement** *n* (feat) réussite *f*; (fulfilment) réalisation *f* (**of** de).

acid *a & n* acide (*m*). **acidity** *n* acidité *f*. **~ rain** *n* pluies *fpl* acides.

acknowledge *vt* (*error, authority*) reconnaître; (*letter*) accuser réception de. **acknowledgement** *n* reconnaissance *f*.

acne *n* acné *f*.

acorn *n* (Bot) gland *m*.

acoustic *a* acoustique. **acoustics** *npl* acoustique *f*.

acquaint *vt* **~ sb with sth** mettre qn au courant de qch; **be ~ed with** (*person*) connaître; (*fact*) savoir. **acquaintance** *n* connaissance *f*.

acquire *vt* acquérir; (*habit*) prendre.

acquit *vt* (*pt* **acquitted**) (Jur) acquitter. **acquittal** *n* acquittement *m*.

acre *n* acre *f*, ≈ demi-hectare *m*.

acrid *a* âcre.

acrimonious *a* acrimonieux.

acrobat *n* acrobate *mf*. **acrobatics** *npl* acrobaties *fpl*.

acronym *n* acronyme *m*.

across *adv & prep* (side to side) d'un côté à l'autre (de); (on other side) de l'autre côté (**from** de); **go** *or* **walk ~** traverser; **lie ~ the bed** se coucher en travers du lit; **~ the world** partout dans le monde.

act *n* acte *m*; (Jur, Pol) loi *f*; **put on an ~** jouer la comédie. ● *vi* agir; (Theat) jouer; **~ as** servir de. ● *vt* (*part, role*) jouer.

acting *n* (Theat) jeu *m*. ● *a* (temporary) intérimaire.

action *n* action *f*; (Mil) combat *m*; **out of ~** hors service; **take ~** agir.

activate *vt* (*machine*) faire démarrer; (*alarm*) déclencher.

active *a* actif; (*volcano*) en activité; **take an ~ interest in** s'intéresser activement à. **activist** *n* activiste *mf*. **activity** *n* activité *f*.

actor *n* acteur *m*. **actress** *n* actrice *f*.

actual *a* réel; **the ~ words** les mots exacts; **in the ~ house** (the house itself) dans la maison elle-même. **actuality** *n* réalité *f*. **actually** *adv* (in fact) en fait; (really) vraiment.

acute *a* (*anxiety*) vif; (*illness*) aigu, (*shortage*) grave; (*mind*) pénétrant.

ad *n* (TV) pub *f* [!]; **small ~** petite annonce *f*.

AD *abbr* (**Anno Domini**) ap. J.-C.

adamant *a* catégorique.

adapt *vt/i* (s')adapter (**to** à). **adaptability** *n* adaptabilité *f*. **adaptable** *a* souple. **adaptation** *n* adaptation *f*. **adaptor** *n* (Electr) adaptateur *m*.

add *vt/i* ajouter (**to** à); (in maths) additionner. □ **~ up** (*facts, figures*) s'accorder; **~ sth up** additionner qch; **~ up to** s'élever à.

adder *n* vipère *f*.

addict *n* toxicomane *mf*; (fig) accro *mf* [!].

addicted *a* **be ~** avoir une dépendance (**to** à); (fig) être accro [!] (**to** à). **addiction** *n* (Med) dépendance *f* (**to** à); passion *f* (**to** pour). **addictive** *a* qui crée une dépendance.

addition *n* (item) ajout *m*; (in maths) addition *f*; **in ~** en plus. **additional** *a* supplémentaire.

additive *n* additif *m*.

address *n* adresse *f*; (speech) discours *m*. ● *vt* (*letter*) mettre l'adresse sur; (*crowd*) s'adresser à; **~ sth to** adresser qch à. **addressee** *n* destinataire *mf*.

adequate *a* suffisant; (satisfactory) satisfaisant.

adhere *vi* (lit, fig) adhérer (**to** à); **~ to** (*policy*) observer.

adjacent *a* contigu; **~ to** attenant à.

adjective *n* adjectif *m*.

adjoin *vt* être contigu à. **adjoining** *a* (*room*) voisin.

adjourn *vt* (*trial*) ajourner; **the session was ~ed** la séance a été levée. ● *vi* s'arrêter; (*Parliament*) lever la séance; **~ to** passer à.

adjust *vt* (*level, speed*) régler; (*price*) ajuster; (*clothes*) rajuster. ● *vt/i* **~ (oneself) to** s'adapter à. **adjustable** *a* réglable. **adjustment** *n* (of rates) rajustement *m*; (of control) réglage *m*; (of person) adaptation *f*.

ad lib *vt/i* (*pt* **ad libbed**) improviser.

administer *vt* administrer.

administration *n* administration *f*. **administrative** *a* administratif. **administrator** *n* administrateur/-trice *m/f*.

admiral *n* amiral *m*.

admiration *n* admiration *f*. **admire** *vt* admirer. **admirer** *n* admirateur/-trice *m/f*.

admission *n* (to a place) entrée *f*; (confession) aveu *m*.

admit *vt* (*pt* **admitted**) (acknowledge) reconnaître, admettre; (*crime*) avouer; (*new member*) admettre; **~ to** reconnaître. **admittance** *n* entrée *f*. **admittedly** *adv* il est vrai.

ado *n* **without more ~** sans plus de cérémonie.

adolescence *n* adolescence *f*. **adolescent** *n & a* adolescent/-e (*m/f*).

adopt *vt* adopter. **adopted** *a* (*child*) adoptif. **adoption** *n* adoption *f*. **adoptive** *a* adoptif.

adorable *a* adorable. **adoration** *n* adoration *f*. **adore** *vt* adorer.

adorn *vt* orner.

adrift *a & adv* à la dérive.

adult *a & n* adulte (*mf*).

adultery *n* adultère *m*.

adulthood *n* âge *m* adulte.

advance *vt* (*sum*) avancer; (*tape, career*) faire avancer; (*interests*) servir. ● *vi* (lit) avancer; (progress) progresser. ● *n* avance *f*; (progress) progrès *m*; **in ~** à l'avance. **advanced** *a* avancé; (*studies*) supérieur.

advantage *n* avantage *m*; **take ~ of** profiter de; (*person*) exploiter. **advantageous** *a* avantageux.

adventure *n* aventure *f*. **adventurer** *n* aventurier/-ière *m/f*. **adventurous** *a* aventureux.

A

adverb *n* adverbe *m*.
adverse *a* défavorable.
advert *n* annonce *f*; (TV) pub *f* [!].
advertise *vt* faire de la publicité pour; (*car, house, job*) mettre une annonce pour. ● *vi* faire de la publicité; (for staff) passer une annonce. **advertisement** *n* publicité *f*; (in newspaper) annonce *f*. **advertiser** *n* annonceur *m*. **advertising** *n* publicité *f*.
advice *n* conseils *mpl*; **some ~, a piece of ~** un conseil.
advise *vt* conseiller; (inform) aviser; **~ against** déconseiller. **adviser** *n* conseiller/-ère *m/f*. **advisory** *a* consultatif.
advocate¹ *n* (Jur) avocat *m*; (supporter) partisan *m*.
advocate² *vt* recommander.
aerial *a* aérien. ● *n* antenne *f*.
aerobics *n* aérobic *m*.
aeroplane *n* avion *m*.
aerosol *n* bombe *f* aérosol.
aesthetic *a* esthétique.
afar *adv* **from ~** de loin.
affair *n* (matter) affaire *f*; (romance) liaison *f*.
affect *vt* affecter.
affection *n* affection *f*. **affectionate** *a* affectueux.
affinity *n* affinité *f*.
afflict *vt* affliger. **affliction** *n* affection *f*.
affluence *n* richesse *f*.
afford *vt* avoir les moyens d'acheter; (provide) fournir; **can you ~ the time?** avez-vous le temps?
afloat *adj & adv* (*boat*) à flot.
afoot *adv* **sth is ~** il se prépare qch.
afraid *a* **be ~** (frightened) avoir peur (**of, to** de; **that** que); (worried) craindre (**that** que); **I'm ~ I can't come** je suis désolé mais je ne peux pas venir.
Africa *n* Afrique *f*.
African *n* Africain/-e *m/f*. ● *a* africain.
after *adv & prep* après; **soon ~** peu après; **be ~ sth** rechercher qch; **~ all** après tout. ● *conj* après que; **~ doing** après avoir fait.
aftermath *n* conséquences *fpl* (**of** de).
afternoon *n* après-midi *m or f inv*; **in the ~** (dans) l'après-midi.
after: **~shave** *n* après-rasage *m*. **~thought** *n* pensée *f* après coup.
afterwards *adv* après, par la suite.
again *adv* encore; **~ and ~** à plusieurs reprises; **start ~** recommencer; **she never saw him ~** elle ne l'a jamais revu.
against *prep* contre; **~ the law** illégal.
age *n* âge *m*; (era) ère *f*, époque *f*; **I've been waiting for ~s** j'attends depuis des heures. ● *vt/i* (*pres p* **ageing**) vieillir.
aged¹ *a* **~ six** âgé de six ans.
aged² *a* âgé.
agency *n* agence *f*.
agenda *n* ordre *m* du jour; (fig) programme *m*.
agent *n* agent *m*.
aggravate *vt* (make worse) aggraver; (annoy) exaspérer. **aggravation** *n* (worsening) aggravation *f*; (annoyance) ennuis *mpl*.
aggression *n* agression *f*. **aggressive** *a* agressif. **aggressiveness** *n* agressivité *f*. **aggressor** *n* agresseur *m*.
agitate *vt* agiter.
ago *adv* il y a; **a month ~** il y a un mois; **long ~** il y a longtemps; **how long ~?** il y a combien de temps?
agonize *vi* se tourmenter (**over** à

propos de). **agonized** *a* angoissé. **agonizing** *a* déchirant. **agony** *n* douleur *f* atroce; (mental) angoisse *f*.

agree *vi* être d'accord (**on** sur; **with** avec); ~ **to** consentir à; ~ **with** (approve of) approuver. ● *vt* être d'accord (**that** sur le fait que); (admit) convenir (**that** que); (*date, solution*) se mettre d'accord sur.

agreeable *a* agréable; **be** ~ (willing) être d'accord.

agreed *a* (*time, place*) convenu; **we're** ~ nous sommes d'accord.

agreement *n* accord *m*; **in** ~ d'accord.

agricultural *a* agricole. **agriculture** *n* agriculture *f*.

aground *adv* **run** ~ (*ship*) s'échouer.

ahead *adv* (in front) en avant, devant; (in advance) à l'avance; **be 10 points** ~ avoir 10 points d'avance; ~ **of time** en avance; **go** ~! allez-y!

aid *vt* aider. ● *n* aide *f*; **in** ~ **of** au profit de.

aide *n* aide *mf*.

Aids *n* (Med) sida *m*.

aim *vt* (*gun*) braquer (**at** sur); **be** ~**ed at sb** (*campaign, remark*) viser qn. ● *vi* ~ **for/at sth** viser qch; ~ **to do** avoir l'intention de faire. ● *n* but *m*; **take** ~ viser. **aimless** *a* sans but.

air *n* air *m*; **by** ~ par avion; **on the** ~ à l'antenne. ● *vt* aérer; (*views*) exprimer. ● *a* (*base, disaster*) aérien; (*pollution, pressure*) atmosphérique. ~**-bed** *n* matelas *m* pneumatique. ~**-conditioning** *n* climatisation *f*. ~**craft** *n inv* avion *m*. ~**craft carrier** *n* porte-avions *m inv*. ~**field** *n* terrain *m* d'aviation. ~ **force** *n* armée *f* de l'air. ~ **freshener** *n* désodorisant *m* d'atmosphère. ~ **hostess** *n* hôtesse *f* de l'air. ~**lift** *vt* transporter par pont aérien. ~**line** *n* compagnie *f* aérienne. ~**liner** *n* avion *m* de ligne. ~**lock** *n* (in pipe) bulle *f* d'air; (chamber) sas *m*. ~**mail** *n* (**by**) ~**mail** par avion. ~**plane** *n* (US) avion *m*. ~**port** *n* aéroport *m*. ~ **raid** *n* attaque *f* aérienne. ~**tight** *a* hermétique. ~ **traffic controller** *n* contrôleur/-euse *m*/*f* aérien/-ne. ~**waves** *npl* ondes *fpl*.

airy *a* (**-ier, -iest**) (*room*) clair et spacieux.

aisle *n* (of church) allée *f* centrale; (in train) couloir *m*.

ajar *adv & a* entrouvert.

akin *a* ~ **to** semblable à.

alarm *n* alarme *f*; (clock) réveil *m*; (feeling) frayeur *f*. ● *vt* inquiéter. ~**-clock** *n* réveil *m*.

alas *interj* hélas.

Albania *n* Albanie *f*.

album *n* album *m*.

alcohol *n* alcool *m*.

alcoholic *a* alcoolique; (*drink*) alcoolisé. ● *n* alcoolique *mf*.

ale *n* bière *f*.

alert *a* alerte; (watchful) vigilant. ● *n* alerte *f*; **on the** ~ sur le qui-vive. ● *vt* alerter; ~ **sb to** prévenir qn de. **alertness** *n* vivacité *f*; vigilance *f*.

A-level *n* ≈ baccalauréat *m*.

algebra *n* algèbre *f*.

Algeria *n* Algérie *f*.

alias *n* (*pl* ~**es**) faux nom *m*. ● *prep* alias.

alibi *n* alibi *m*.

alien *n & a* étranger/-ère (*m*/*f*) (**to** à).

alienate *vt* éloigner.

alight *a* en feu, allumé.

alike *a* semblable. ● *adv* de la même façon; **look** ~ se ressembler.

alive *a* vivant; **~ to** conscient de; **~ with** grouillant de.

all

● *pronoun*

····➤ (everything) tout; **is that ~?** c'est tout?; **that was ~ (that) he said** c'est tout ce qu'il a dit; **I ate it ~** j'ai tout mangé.

! Use the translation **tous** for a group of masculine or mixed gender people or objects and **toutes** for a group of feminine gender: **we were all delighted** *nous étions tous ravis*; **'where are the cups?'—'they're all in the kitchen'** *'où sont les tasses?'—'elles sont toutes dans la cuisine'*.

● *determiner*

····➤ tout/toute/tous/toutes; **~ the time** tout le temps; **~ his life** toute sa vie; **~ of us** nous tous; **~ (the) women** toutes les femmes.

● *adverb*

····➤ (completely) tout; **they were ~ alone** ils étaient tout seuls; **tell me ~ about it** raconte-moi tout; **~ for** tout à fait pour; **not ~ that well** pas si bien que ça; **~ too** bien trop.

! When the adjective that follows is in the feminine and begins with a consonant, the translation is *toute/toutes*: **she was all alone** *elle était toute seule.*

allege *vt* prétendre. **allegedly** *adv* prétendument.

allergic *a* allergique (**to** à). **allergy** *n* allergie *f*.

alleviate *vt* alléger.

alley *n* (street) ruelle *f*.

alliance *n* alliance *f*.

allied *a* allié.

alligator *n* alligator *m*.

allocate *vt* (*funds*) affecter; (*time*) accorder; (*task*) assigner.

allot *vt* (*pt* **allotted**) (*money*) attribuer; (*task*) assigner. **allotment** *n* attribution *f*; (land) parcelle *f* de terre.

all-out *a* (*effort*) acharné; (*strike*) total.

allow *vt* (authorize) autoriser à; (let) laisser; (enable) permettre; (concede) accorder; **~ for** tenir compte de.

allowance *n* allocation *f*; **make ~s for sth** tenir compte de qch; **make ~s for sb** essayer de comprendre qn.

alloy *n* alliage *m*.

all right *a* (not bad) pas mal; **are you ~?** ça va?; **is it ~ if ...?** est-ce que ça va si ...? ● *adv* (*see*) bien; (*function*) comme il faut. ● *interj* d'accord.

ally[1] *n* allié/-e *m*/*f*.

ally[2] *vt* allier; **~ oneself with** s'allier avec.

almighty *a* tout-puissant; (very great) formidable.

almond *n* amande *f*. **~ tree** *n* amandier *m*.

almost *adv* presque; **he ~ died** il a failli mourir.

alone *a & adv* seul.

along *prep* le long de; **walk ~ the beach** marcher sur la plage. ● *adv* **come ~** venir; **walk ~** marcher; **push/pull sth ~** pousser/tirer qch; **all ~** (time) depuis le début; **~ with** avec.

alongside *adv* à côté; **come ~** (Naut) accoster. ● *prep* (next to) à côté de; (all along) le long de.

aloof *a* distant.

aloud *adv* à haute voix.

alphabet *n* alphabet *m*. **alphabetical** *a* alphabétique.

alpine *a* (*landscape*) alpestre; (*climate*) alpin.

already *adv* déjà.

alright *a & adv* = ALL RIGHT.

Alsatian *n* (dog) berger *m* allemand.

also *adv* aussi.

altar *n* autel *m*.

alter *vt/i* changer; (*building*) transformer; (*garment*) retoucher. **alteration** *n* changement *m*; (to building) transformation *f*; (to garment) retouche *f*.

alternate[1] *vt/i* alterner.

alternate[2] *a* en alternance; **on ~ days** un jour sur deux. **alternately** *adv* alternativement.

alternative *a* autre; (*solution*) de rechange. ● *n* (specified option) alternative *f*; (possible option) choix *m*. **alternatively** *adv* sinon.

alternator *n* alternateur *m*.

although *conj* bien que.

altitude *n* altitude *f*.

altogether *adv* (completely) tout à fait; (on the whole) tout compte fait.

aluminium *n* aluminium *m*.

always *adv* toujours.

am ⇒BE.

a.m. *adv* du matin.

amalgamate *vt/i* (merge) fusionner; (*metals*) (s')amalgamer.

amateur *n & a* amateur (*m*).

amaze *vt* stupéfaire. **amazed** *a* stupéfait. **amazement** *n* stupéfaction *f*. **amazing** *a* stupéfiant; (great) exceptionnel.

ambassador *n* ambassadeur *m*.

amber *n* ambre *m*; (Auto) orange *m*.

ambiguity *n* ambiguïté *f*. **ambiguous** *a* ambigu.

ambition *n* ambition *f*. **ambitious** *a* ambitieux.

ambulance *n* ambulance *f*.

ambush *n* embuscade *f*. ● *vt* tendre une embuscade à.

amenable *a* obligeant; **~ to** (responsive) sensible à.

amend *vt* modifier. **amendment** *n* (to rule) amendement *m*.

amends *npl* **make ~** réparer son erreur.

amenities *npl* équipements *mpl*.

America *n* Amérique *f*.

American *n* Américain/-e *m/f*. ● *a* américain.

amiable *a* aimable.

amicable *a* amical.

amid(st) *prep* au milieu de.

amiss *a* **there is something ~** il y a quelque chose qui ne va pas.

ammonia *n* (gas) ammoniac *m*; (solution) ammoniaque *f*.

ammunition *n* munitions *fpl*.

amnesty *n* amnistie *f*.

among(st) *prep* parmi; (affecting a group) chez; **be ~ the poorest** être un des plus pauvres; **be ~ the first** être dans les premiers.

amorous *a* amoureux.

amount *n* quantité *f*; (total) montant *m*; (sum of money) somme *f*. ● *vi* **~ to** (add up to) s'élever à; (be equivalent to) revenir à.

amp *n* ampère *m*.

amphibian *n* amphibie *m*.

ample *a* (*resources*) largement suffisant; (*proportions*) généreux.

amplifier *n* amplificateur *m*.

amputate *vt* amputer.

amuse *vt* amuser.

amusement *n* (mirth) amusement *m*; (diversion) distraction *f*. **~ arcade** *n* salle *f* de jeux.

an ⇒A.

anaemia *n* anémie *f*.

anaesthetic *n* anesthésique *m*.

A

analyse *vt* analyser. **analysis** *n* (*pl* **-yses**) analyse *f*. **analyst** *n* analyste *mf*.

anarchist *n* anarchiste *mf*.

anatomical *a* anatomique. **anatomy** *n* anatomie *f*.

ancestor *n* ancêtre *m*.

anchor *n* ancre *f*. ● *vt* mettre à l'ancre. ● *vi* jeter l'ancre.

anchovy *n* anchois *m*.

ancient *a* ancien.

ancillary *a* auxiliaire.

and *conj* et; **two hundred ~ sixty** deux cent soixante; **go ~ see him** allez le voir; **richer ~ richer** de plus en plus riche.

anew *adv* (once more) encore, de nouveau; (in a new way) à nouveau.

angel *n* ange *m*.

anger *n* colère *f*. ● *vt* mettre en colère, fâcher.

angle *n* angle *m*. ● *vi* pêcher (à la ligne); **~ for** (fig) quêter. **angler** *n* pêcheur/-euse *m/f*.

Anglo-Saxon *a* anglo-saxon. ● *n* Anglo-Saxon/-ne *m/f*.

angry *a* (**-ier**, **-iest**) fâché, en colère; **get ~** se fâcher, se mettre en colère (**with** contre); **make sb ~** mettre qn en colère.

anguish *n* angoisse *f*.

animal *n & a* animal (*m*).

animate[1] *a* (*person*) vivant; (*object*) animé.

animate[2] *vt* animer.

aniseed *n* anis *m*.

ankle *n* cheville *f*. **~ sock** *n* socquette *f*.

annex *vt* annexer.

anniversary *n* anniversaire *m*.

announce *vt* annoncer (**that** que). **announcement** *n* (spoken) annonce *f*; (written) avis *m*. **announcer** *n* (radio, TV) speaker/-ine *m/f*.

annoy *vt* agacer, ennuyer. **annoyance** *n* contrariété *f*.

annoyed *a* fâché (**with** contre); **get ~ed** se fâcher. **annoying** *a* ennuyeux.

annual *a* annuel. ● *n* publication *f* annuelle. **annually** *adv* (*earn, produce*) par an; (*do, inspect*) tous les ans.

annul *vt* (*pt* **annulled**) annuler.

anonymity *n* anonymat *m*. **anonymous** *a* anonyme.

anorak *n* anorak *m*.

another *det & pron* un/-e autre; **~ coffee** (one more) encore un café; **~ ten minutes** encore dix minutes, dix minutes de plus; **can I have ~?** est-ce que je peux en avoir un autre?

answer *n* réponse *f*; (solution) solution *f*; (phone) **there's no ~** ça ne répond pas. ● *vt* répondre à; (*prayer*) exaucer; **~ the door** ouvrir la porte. ● *vi* répondre. □ **~ back** répondre; **~ for** répondre de; **~ to** (*superior*) dépendre de; (*description*) répondre à. **answerable** *a* responsable (**for** de; **to** devant). **answering machine** *n* répondeur *m*.

ant *n* fourmi *f*.

antagonism *n* antagonisme *m*. **antagonize** *vt* provoquer l'hostilité de.

Antarctic *n* **the ~** l'Antarctique *m*. ● *a* antarctique.

antenatal *a* prénatal.

antenna *n* (*pl* **-ae**) (of insect) antenne *f*; (*pl* **-as**; aerial: US) antenne *f*.

anthem *n* (Relig) motet *m*; (of country) hymne *m* national.

antibiotic *n & a* antibiotique (*m*).

antibody *n* anticorps *m*.

anticipate *vt* (foresee, expect) prévoir, s'attendre à; (forestall) devancer.

anticipation *n* attente *f*; **in ~ of** en prévision *or* attente de.

anticlimax *n* (let-down) déception *f*.
anticlockwise *adv & a* dans le sens inverse des aiguilles d'une montre.
antics *npl* pitreries *fpl*.
antifreeze *n* antigel *m*.
antiquated *a* (*idea*) archaïque; (*building*) vétuste.
antique *a* (old) ancien; (old-style) à l'ancienne. ● *n* objet *m* ancien, antiquité *f*. ~ **dealer** *n* antiquaire *mf*. ~ **shop** *n* magasin *m* d'antiquités.
anti-Semitic *a* antisémite.
antiseptic *a & n* antiseptique (*m*).
antisocial *a* asocial, antisocial; (reclusive) sauvage.
antlers *npl* bois *mpl*.
anxiety *n* (worry) anxiété *f*; (eagerness) impatience *f*.
anxious *a* (troubled) anxieux; (eager) impatient (**to** de).
any *det* (some) du, de l', de la, des; (after negative) de, d'; (every) tout; (no matter which) n'importe quel; **at** ~ **moment** à tout moment; **have you** ~ **water?** avez-vous de l'eau? ● *pron* (no matter which one) n'importe lequel; (any amount of it or them) en; **I do not have** ~ je n'en ai pas; **did you see** ~ **of them?** en avez-vous vu? ● *adv* (a little) un peu; **do you have** ~ **more?** en avez-vous encore?; **do you have** ~ **more tea?** avez-vous encore du thé?; **I don't do it** ~ **more** je ne le fais plus.
anybody *pron* (no matter who) n'importe qui; (somebody) quelqu'un; (after negative) personne; **he did not see** ~ il n'a vu personne.
anyhow *adv* (anyway) de toute façon; (carelessly) n'importe comment.
anyone *pron* = ANYBODY.
anything *pron* (no matter what) n'importe quoi; (something) quelque chose; (after negative) rien; **he did not see** ~ il n'a rien vu; ~ **but** nullement; ~ **you do** tout ce que tu fais.
anyway *adv* de toute façon.
anywhere *adv* (no matter where) n'importe où; (somewhere) quelque part; (after negative) nulle part; **he does not go** ~ il ne va nulle part; ~ **you go** partout où tu vas, où que tu ailles; ~ **else** partout ailleurs.
apart *adv* (on or to one side) à part; (separated) séparé; (into pieces) en pièces; ~ **from** à part, excepté; **ten metres** ~ à dix mètres l'un de l'autre; **come** ~ (break) tomber en morceaux; (*machine*) se démonter; **legs** ~ les jambes écartées; **keep** ~ séparer; **take** ~ démonter.
apartment *n* (US) appartement *m*.
ape *n* singe *m*. ● *vt* singer.
aperitif *n* apéritif *m*.
apex *n* sommet *m*.
apologetic *a* (*tone*) d'excuse; **be** ~ s'excuser. **apologetically** *adv* en s'excusant.
apologize *vi* s'excuser (**for** de; **to** auprès de).
apology *n* excuses *fpl*.
apostrophe *n* apostrophe *f*.
appal *vt* (*pt* **appalled**) horrifier. **appalling** *a* épouvantable.
apparatus *n* appareil *m*.
apparent *a* apparent. **apparently** *adv* apparemment.
appeal *n* appel *m*; (attractiveness) attrait *m*, charme *m*. ● *vi* (Jur) faire appel; ~ **to sb** (beg) faire appel à qn; (attract) plaire à qn; ~ **to sb for sth** demander qch à qn. **appealing** *a* (attractive) attirant.
appear *vi* apparaître; (arrive) se présenter; (seem, be published)

paraître; (Theat) jouer; ~ **on TV** passer à la télé. **appearance** *n* apparition *f*; (aspect) apparence *f*.

appease *vt* apaiser.

appendix *n* (*pl* **-ices**) appendice *m*.

appetite *n* appétit *m*.

appetizer *n* (snack) amuse-gueule *m inv*; (drink) apéritif *m*.

appetizing *a* appétissant.

applaud *vt/i* applaudir; (*decision*) applaudir à. **applause** *n* applaudissements *mpl*.

apple *n* pomme *f*. ~**-tree** *n* pommier *m*.

appliance *n* appareil *m*.

applicable *a* valable; **if** ~ le cas échéant.

applicant *n* candidat/-e *m/f* (**for** à).

application *n* application *f*; (request, form) demande *f*; (for job) candidature *f*.

apply *vt* appliquer. ● *vi* ~ **to** (refer) s'appliquer à; (ask) s'adresser à; ~ **for** (*job*) postuler pour; (*grant*) demander; ~ **oneself to** s'appliquer à.

appoint *vt* (to post) nommer; (fix) désigner; **well-~ed** bien équipé.

appointment *n* nomination *f*; (meeting) rendez-vous *m inv*; (job) poste *m*; **make an** ~ prendre rendez-vous (**with** avec).

appraisal *n* évaluation *f*. **appraise** *vt* évaluer.

appreciate *vt* (like) apprécier; (understand) comprendre; (be grateful for) être reconnaissant de. ● *vi* prendre de la valeur. **appreciation** *n* appréciation *f*; (gratitude) reconnaissance *f*; (rise) augmentation *f*. **appreciative** *a* reconnaissant; (*audience*) enthousiaste.

apprehend *vt* (arrest) appréhender; (understand) comprendre. **apprehension** *n* (arrest) appréhension *f*; (fear) crainte *f*.

apprehensive *a* inquiet; **be** ~ **of** craindre.

apprentice *n* apprenti *m*. ● *vt* mettre en apprentissage.

approach *vt* (s')approcher de; (accost) aborder; (with request) s'adresser à. ● *vi* (s')approcher. ● *n* approche *f*; **an** ~ **to** (*problem*) une façon d'aborder; (*person*) une démarche auprès de. **approachable** *a* abordable.

appropriate[1] *vt* s'approprier.

appropriate[2] *a* approprié, propre. **appropriately** *adv* à propos.

approval *n* approbation *f*; **on** ~ à *or* sous condition.

approve *vt* approuver. ● *vi* ~ **of** approuver. **approving** *a* approbateur.

approximate[1] *vi* ~ **to** se rapprocher de.

approximate[2] *a* approximatif. **approximately** *adv* environ. **approximation** *n* approximation *f*.

apricot *n* abricot *m*.

April *n* avril *m*. ~ **Fools Day** *n* le premier avril.

apron *n* tablier *m*.

apt *a* (suitable) approprié; **be** ~ **to** avoir tendance à.

aptitude *n* aptitude *f*.

aptly *adv* à propos.

Aquarius *n* Verseau *m*.

aquatic *a* aquatique; (Sport) nautique.

Arab *n* Arabe *mf*. ● *a* arabe.

Arabian *a* d'Arabie.

Arabic *a* & *n* (Ling) arabe (*m*).

arbitrary *a* arbitraire.

arbitrate *vi* arbitrer. **arbitration** *n* arbitrage *m*. **arbitrator** *n* médiateur/-trice *m/f*.

arcade *n* (shops) galerie *f*; (arches) arcades *fpl*.

arch *n* arche *f*; (of foot) voûte *f* plantaire. ●*vt/i* (s')arquer. ●*a* (playful) malicieux.

archaeological *a* archéologique. **archaeologist** *n* archéologue *mf*. **archaeology** *n* archéologie *f*.

archbishop *n* archevêque *m*.

archery *n* tir *m* à l'arc.

architect *n* architecte *mf*; (of plan) artisan *m*. **architectural** *a* architectural. **architecture** *n* architecture *f*.

archives *npl* archives *fpl*.

archway *n* voûte *f*.

Arctic *n* **the ~** l'Arctique *m*. ●*a* (*climate*) arctique; (*expedition*) polaire; (*conditions*) glacial.

ardent *a* ardent.

are ⇨BE.

area *n* (region) région *f*; (district) quartier *m*; (fig) domaine *m*; (in geometry) aire *f*; **parking/picnic ~** aire *f* de parking/de pique-nique.

arena *n* arène *f*.

aren't = ARE NOT.

Argentina *n* Argentine *f*.

arguable *a* discutable. **arguably** *adv* selon certains.

argue *vi* (quarrel) se disputer; (reason) argumenter. ●*vt* (debate) discuter; **~ that** alléguer que.

argument *n* dispute *f*; (reasoning) argument *m*; (discussion) débat *m*. **argumentative** *a* ergoteur.

Aries *n* Bélier *m*.

arise *vi* (*pt* **arose**; *pp* **arisen**) (*problem*) survenir; (*question*) se poser; **~ from** résulter de.

aristocrat *n* aristocrate *mf*.

arithmetic *n* arithmétique *f*.

ark *n* (Relig) arche *f*.

arm *n* bras *m*; **~ in arm** bras dessus bras dessous. ●*vt* armer; **~ed robbery** vol *m* à main armée.

armament *n* armement *m*.

arm: **~-band** *n* brassard *m*. **~chair** *n* fauteuil *m*.

armour *n* armure *f*. **armoured** *a* blindé. **armoury** *n* arsenal *m*.

armpit *n* aisselle *f*.

arms *npl* (weapons) armes *fpl*. **~ dealer** *n* trafiquant *m* d'armes.

army *n* armée *f*.

aroma *n* arôme *m*. **aromatic** *a* aromatique.

arose ⇨ARISE.

around *adv* (tout) autour; (here and there) çà et là. ●*prep* autour de; **~ here** par ici.

arouse *vt* (awaken, cause) éveiller; (excite) exciter.

arrange *vt* arranger; (*time, date*) fixer; **~ to** s'arranger pour.

arrangement *n* arrangement *m*; (agreement) entente *f*; **make ~s** prendre des dispositions.

array *n* **an ~ of** (display) un étalage impressionnant de.

arrears *npl* arriéré *m*; **in ~** (*rent*) arriéré; **he is in ~** il a des retards dans ses paiements.

arrest *vt* arrêter; (attention) retenir. ●*n* arrestation *f*; **under ~** en état d'arrestation.

arrival *n* arrivée *f*; **new ~** nouveau venu *m*, nouvelle venue *f*.

arrive *vi* arriver; **~ at** (*destination*) arriver à; (*decision*) parvenir à.

arrogance *n* arrogance *f*.

arrow *n* flèche *f*.

arse *n* ⊠ cul *m* ⊠.

arson *n* incendie *m* criminel. **arsonist** *n* incendiaire *mf*.

art *n* art *m*; (fine arts) beaux-arts *mpl*.

artery *n* artère *f*.

art gallery *n* (public) musée *m* (*d'art*); (private) galerie *f* (*d'art*).

arthritis *n* arthrite *f*.

artichoke *n* artichaut *m*.

article *n* article *m*; ~ **of clothing** vêtement *m*.

articulate *a* (*person*) capable de s'exprimer clairement; (*speech*) distinct.

articulated lorry *n* semi-remorque *m*.

artificial *a* artificiel.

artist *n* artiste *mf*.

arts *npl* **the** ~ les arts *mpl*; (Univ) lettres *fpl*.

artwork *n* (of book) illustrations *fpl*.

as *conj* comme; (while) pendant que; (over gradual period of time) au fur et à mesure que; ~ **she grew older** au fur et à mesure qu'elle vieillissait; **do ~ I say** fais ce que je dis; ~ **usual** comme d'habitude. ●*prep* ~ **a mother** en tant que mère; ~ **a gift** en cadeau; ~ **from Monday** à partir de lundi; ~ **for**, ~ **to** quant à; ~ **if** comme si; **you look ~ if you're tired** vous avez l'air (d'être) fatigué. ●*adv* ~ **tall** ~ aussi grand que; ~ **much** ~, ~ **many** ~ autant que; ~ **soon** ~ aussitôt que; ~ **well** ~ aussi bien que; ~ **wide** ~ **possible** aussi large que possible.

asbestos *n* amiante *f*.

ascend *vt* gravir. ●*vi* monter.

ascertain *vt* établir (**that** que).

ash *n* cendre *f*; ~(**-tree**) frêne *m*.

ashamed *a* **be** ~ avoir honte (**of** de).

ashore *adv* à terre.

ashtray *n* cendrier *m*.

Asia *n* Asie *f*.

Asian *n* Asiatique *mf*. ●*a* asiatique.

aside *adv* de côté; ~ **from** à part. ●*n* aparté *m*.

ask *vt/i* demander; (*a question*) poser; (invite) inviter; ~ **sb sth** demander qch à qn; ~ **sb to do** demander à qn de faire; ~ **about** (*thing*) se renseigner sur; (*person*) demander des nouvelles de; ~ **for** demander.

asleep *a* endormi; (numb) engourdi. ●*adv* **fall** ~ s'endormir.

asparagus *n* (plant) asperge *f*; (Culin) asperges *fpl*.

aspect *n* aspect *m*; (direction) orientation *f*.

asphyxiate *vt/i* (s')asphyxier.

aspire *vi* aspirer (**to** à; **to do** à faire).

aspirin *n* aspirine® *f*.

ass *n* âne *m*; (person Ⓘ) idiot/-e *m/f*.

assail *vt* attaquer. **assailant** *n* agresseur *m*.

assassin *n* assassin *m*. **assassinate** *vt* assassiner. **assassination** *n* assassinat *m*.

assault *n* (Mil) assaut *m*; (Jur) agression *f*. ●*vt* (*person*: Jur) agresser.

assemble *vt* (construct) assembler; (gather) rassembler. ●*vi* se rassembler.

assembly *n* assemblée *f*. ~ **line** *n* chaîne *f* de montage.

assent *n* assentiment *m*. ●*vi* consentir.

assert *vt* affirmer; (*rights*) revendiquer. **assertion** *n* affirmation *f*. **assertive** *a* assuré.

assess *vt* évaluer; (*payment*) déterminer le montant de. **assessment** *n* évaluation *f*. **assessor** *n* (valuer) expert *m*.

asset *n* (advantage) atout *m*; (financial) bien *m*; ~**s** (Comm) actif *m*.

assign *vt* (allot) assigner; ~ **sb to** (appoint) affecter qn à.

assignment *n* (task) mission *f*; (diplomatic) poste *m*; (academic) devoir *m*.

assist *vt/i* aider. **assistance** *n* aide *f*.

assistant *n* aide *mf*; (in shop) vendeur/-euse *m/f*. ● *a* (manager) adjoint.

associate[1] *n & a* associé/-e (*m/f*).

associate[2] *vt* associer. ● *vi* ~ **with** fréquenter. **association** *n* association *f*.

assorted *a* divers; (*foods*) assorti.

assortment *n* assortiment *m*; (of people) mélange *m*.

assume *vt* supposer; (*power, attitude*) prendre; (*role, burden*) assumer.

assurance *n* assurance *f*.

assure *vt* assurer.

asterisk *n* astérisque *m*.

asthma *n* asthme *m*.

astonish *vt* étonner.

astound *vt* stupéfier.

astray *adv* **go** ~ s'égarer; **lead** ~ égarer.

astride *adv & prep* à califourchon (sur).

astrologer *n* astrologue *mf*. **astrology** *n* astrologie *f*.

astronaut *n* astronaute *mf*.

astronomer *n* astronome *mf*.

asylum *n* asile *m*.

at *preposition*

⇨For expressions such as **laugh at, look at** ⇒**laugh, look**.

····➤ (in position or place) à; **he's ~ his desk** il est à son bureau; **she's ~ work/school** elle est au travail/à l'école.

····➤ (at someone's house or business) chez; ~ **Mary's/the dentist's** chez Mary/le dentiste.

····➤ (in times, ages) à; ~ **four o'clock** à quatre heures; ~ **two years of age** à l'âge de deux ans.

ate ⇒EAT.

atheist *n* athée *mf*.

athlete *n* athlète *mf*. **athletic** *a* athlétique. **athletics** *npl* athlétisme *m*; (US) sports *mpl*.

Atlantic *a* atlantique. ● *n* **the ~ (Ocean)** l'Atlantique *m*.

atlas *n* atlas *m*.

atmosphere *n* (air) atmosphère *f*; (mood) ambiance *f*. **atmospheric** *a* atmosphérique; d'ambiance.

atom *n* atome *m*.

atrocious *a* atroce.

atrocity *n* atrocité *f*.

attach *vt/i* (s')attacher; (*letter*) joindre (**to** à).

attaché *n* (Pol) attaché/-e *m/f*. ~ **case** *n* attaché-case *m*.

attached *a* **be ~ to** (like) être attaché à; **the ~ letter** la lettre ci-jointe.

attachment *n* (accessory) accessoire *m*; (affection) attachement *m*; (e-mail) pièces *fpl* jointes.

attack *n* attaque *f*; (Med) crise *f*. ● *vt* attaquer.

attain *vt* atteindre (à); (gain) acquérir.

attempt *vt* tenter. ● *n* tentative *f*; **an ~ on sb's life** un attentat contre qn.

attend *vt* assister à; (*class*) suivre; (*school, church*) aller à. ● *vi* assister; ~ (**to**) (look after) s'occuper de. **attendance** *n* présence *f*; (people) assistance *f*.

attendant *n* employé/-e *m/f*. ● *a* associé.

attention *n* attention *f*; **~!** (Mil) garde-à-vous!; **pay ~** faire *or* prêter attention (**to** à).

attentive *a* attentif; (considerate)

attentionné. **attentively** *adv* attentivement. **attentiveness** *n* attention *f*.

attest *vt/i* ~ (**to**) attester.

attic *n* grenier *m*.

attitude *n* attitude *f*.

attorney *n* (US) avocat/-e *m/f*.

attract *vt* attirer. **attraction** *n* attraction *f*; (charm) attrait *m*.

attractive *a* attrayant, séduisant. **attractively** *adv* agréablement. **attractiveness** *n* attrait *m*, beauté *f*.

attribute[1] *vt* ~ **to** attribuer à.

attribute[2] *n* attribut *m*.

aubergine *n* aubergine *f*.

auction *n* vente *f* aux enchères. ● *vt* vendre aux enchères. **auctioneer** *n* commissaire-priseur *m*.

audacious *a* audacieux.

audience *n* (theatre, radio) public *m*; (interview) audience *f*.

audiovisual *a* audiovisuel.

audit *n* vérification *f* des comptes. ● *vt* vérifier.

audition *n* audition *f*. ● *vt/i* auditionner (**for** pour).

auditor *n* commissaire *m* aux comptes.

August *n* août *m*.

aunt *n* tante *f*.

auspicious *a* favorable.

Australia *n* Australie *f*.

Australian *n* Australien/-ne *m/f*. ● *a* australien.

Austria *n* Autriche *f*.

Austrian *n* Autrichien/-ne *m/f*. ● *a* autrichien.

authentic *a* authentique.

author *n* auteur *m*.

authoritarian *a* autoritaire.

authoritative *a* (credible) qui fait autorité; (*manner*) autoritaire.

authority *n* autorité *f*; (permission) autorisation *f*.

authorization *n* autorisation *f*. **authorize** *vt* autoriser.

autistic *a* (*person*) autiste; (*response*) autistique.

autograph *n* autographe *m*. ● *vt* signer, dédicacer.

automate *vt* automatiser.

automatic *a* automatique. ● *n* (Auto) voiture *f* automatique.

automobile *n* (US) auto(mobile) *f*.

autonomous *a* autonome.

autumn *n* automne *m*.

auxiliary *a & n* auxiliaire (*mf*); ~ (**verb**) auxiliaire *m*.

avail *vt* ~ **oneself of** profiter de. ● *n* **of no** ~ inutile; **to no** ~ sans résultat.

availability *n* disponibilité *f*. **available** *a* disponible.

avenge *vt* venger; ~ **oneself** se venger (**on** de).

avenue *n* avenue *f*; (line of approach: fig) voie *f*.

average *n* moyenne *f*; **on** ~ en moyenne. ● *a* moyen. ● *vt* faire la moyenne de; (produce, do) faire en moyenne.

aviary *n* volière *f*.

avocado *n* avocat *m*.

avoid *vt* éviter. **avoidance** *n* (of injuries) prévention *f*; (of responsibility) refus *m*.

await *vt* attendre.

awake *vt/i* (*pt* **awoke**; *pp* **awoken**) (s')éveiller. ● *a* **be** ~ ne pas dormir, être (r)éveillé.

award *vt* (*grant*) attribuer; (*prize*) décerner; (*points*) accorder. ● *n* récompense *f*, prix *m*; (scholarship) bourse *f*; **pay** ~ augmentation *f* (de salaire).

aware *a* (well-informed) averti; **be** ~ **of** (*danger*) être conscient de; (*fact*) savoir; **become** ~ **of** prendre conscience de. **awareness** *n* conscience *f*.

away *adv* (far) (au) loin; (absent) absent, parti; ~ **from** loin de; **move** ~ s'écarter; (to new home) déménager; **six kilometres** ~ à six kilomètres (de distance); **take** ~ emporter; **he was snoring** ~ il ronflait. ● *a & n* ~ (**match**) match *m* à l'extérieur.

awe *n* crainte *f* (révérencielle).

awe-inspiring *a* impressionnant.

awesome *a* redoutable.

awful *a* affreux. **awfully** *adv* (badly) affreusement; (very ⊡) rudement.

awkward *a* difficile; (inconvenient) inopportun; (clumsy) maladroit; (embarrassing) gênant; (embarrassed) gêné. **awkwardly** *adv* maladroitement; avec gêne. **awkwardness** *n* maladresse *f*; (discomfort) gêne *f*.

awning *n* auvent *m*; (of shop) store *m*.

awoke, **awoken** ⇒AWAKE.

axe *n* hache *f*. ● *vt* (*pres p* **axing**) réduire; (eliminate) supprimer; (employee) renvoyer.

axis *n* (*pl* **axes**) axe *m*.

axle *n* essieu *m*.

BA *abbr* ⇒BACHELOR OF ARTS.

babble *vi* babiller; (*stream*) gazouiller. ● *n* babillage *m*.

baby *n* bébé *m*. ~ **carriage** *n* (US) voiture *f* d'enfant. ~**-sit** *vi* faire du babysitting, garder des enfants. ~**-sitter** *n* baby-sitter *mf*.

bachelor *n* célibataire *m*. **B**~ **of Arts** licencié/-e *m/f* ès lettres.

back *n* (of person, hand, page, etc.) dos *m*; (of house) derrière *m*; (of vehicle) arrière *m*; (of room) fond *m*; (of chair) dossier *m*; (in football) arrière *m*; **at the** ~ **of the book** à la fin du livre; **in** ~ **of** (US) derrière. ● *a* (*leg, wheel*) arrière *inv*; (*door, gate*) de derrière; (*taxes*) arriéré. ● *adv* en arrière; (returned) de retour, rentré; **come** ~ revenir; **give** ~ rendre; **take** ~ reprendre; **I want it** ~ je veux le récupérer. ● *vt* (support) appuyer; (bet on) miser sur; (*vehicle*) faire reculer. ● *vi* (of person, vehicle) reculer. □ ~ **down** céder; ~ **out** se désister; (Auto) sortir en marche arrière; ~ **up** (support) appuyer. ~**ache** *n* mal *m* de dos. ~**-bencher** *n* (Pol) député *m*. ~**bone** *n* colonne *f* vertébrale. ~**date** *vt* antidater. ~**fire** *vi* (Auto) pétarader; (fig) mal tourner. ~**gammon** *n* trictrac *m*.

background *n* fond *m*, arrière-plan *m*; (context) contexte *m*; (environment) milieu *m*; (experience) formation *f*. ● *a* (*music, noise*) de fond.

backhand *n* revers *m*. **backhander** *n* (bribe) pot-de-vin *m*.

backing *n* soutien *m*.

back: ~**lash** *n* retour *m* de bâton; réaction *f* violente (**against** contre). ~**log** *n* retard *m*. ~ **number** *n* vieux numéro *m*. ~**pack** *n* sac *m* à dos. ~**side** *n* (buttocks ⊡) derrière *m*. ~**stage** *a & adv* dans les coulisses. ~**stroke** *n* dos *m* crawlé. ~**track** *vi* rebrousser chemin; (change one's opinion) faire marche arrière.

back-up *n* soutien *m*; (Comput) sauvegarde *f*. ● *a* de secours; (Comput) de sauvegarde.

backward *a* (*step etc.*) en arrière; (retarded) arriéré.

B

backwards *adv* en arrière; (*walk*) à reculons; (*read*) à l'envers; **go ~ and forwards** aller et venir.
bacon *n* lard *m*; (in rashers) bacon *m*.
bacteria *npl* bactéries *fpl*.
bad *a* (**worse, worst**) mauvais; (wicked) méchant; (ill) malade; (*accident*) grave; (*food*) gâté; **feel ~** se sentir mal; **go ~** se gâter; **~ language** gros mots *mpl*; **too ~!** tant pis!; (I'm sorry) dommage!
badge *n* badge *m*; (coat of arms) insigne *m*.
badger *n* blaireau *m*. ● *vt* harceler.
badly *adv* mal; (*hurt*) gravement; **want ~** avoir grande envie de.
badminton *n* badminton *m*.
bad-tempered *a* irritable.
baffle *vt* déconcerter.
bag *n* sac *m*; **~s** (luggage) bagages *mpl*; (under eyes 🅘) valises *fpl*; **~s of** plein de.
baggage *n* bagages *mpl*; **~ reclaim** réception *f* des bagages.
baggy *a* large.
bagpipes *npl* cornemuse *f*.
bail *n* caution *f*; **on ~** sous caution; (cricket) bâtonnet *m*. ● *vt* mettre en liberté provisoire.
bailiff *n* huissier *m*.
bait *n* appât *m*. ● *vt* appâter; (fig) tourmenter.
bake *vt* faire cuire au four; **~ a cake** faire un gâteau. ● *vi* cuire; (*person*) faire du pain. **baked beans** *npl* haricots *mpl* blancs à la tomate. **baked potato** *n* pomme *f* de terre en robe des champs. **baker** *n* boulanger/-ère *m/f*. **bakery** *n* boulangerie *f*.
balance *n* équilibre *m*; (scales) balance *f*; (outstanding sum: Comm) solde *m*; (of payments, of trade) balance *f*; (remainder) restant *m*. ● *vt* mettre en équilibre; (weigh up *also* Comm) balancer; (*budget*) équilibrer; (to compensate) contrebalancer. ● *vi* être en équilibre.
balcony *n* balcon *m*.
bald *a* chauve; (*tyre*) lisse; (fig) simple.
balk *vt* contrecarrer. ● *vi* **~ at** reculer devant.
ball *n* (golf, tennis, etc.) balle *f*; (football) ballon *m*; (billiards) bille *f*; (of wool) pelote *f*; (sphere) boule *f*; (dance) bal *m*.
ballet *n* ballet *m*.
balloon *n* ballon *m*.
ballot *n* scrutin *m*. ● *vt* consulter par vote (**on** sur). **~-box** *n* urne *f*. **~-paper** *n* bulletin *m* de vote.
ballpoint pen *n* stylo *m* (à) bille.
ban *vt* (*pt* **banned**) interdire; **~ sb from** exclure qn de; **~ sb from doing** interdire à qn de faire. ● *n* interdiction *f* (**on** de).
banal *a* banal.
banana *n* banane *f*.
band *n* (strip, group of people) bande *f*; (pop group) groupe *m*; (brass band) fanfare *f*. ● *vi* **~ together** se réunir.
bandage *n* bandage *m*. ● *vt* bander.
B and B *abbr* ⇒BED AND BREAKFAST.
bandit *n* bandit *m*.
bandstand *n* kiosque *m* à musique.
bang *n* (blow, noise) coup *m*; (explosion) détonation *f*; (of door) claquement *m*. ● *vt/i* taper; (*door*) claquer; **~ one's head** se cogner la tête. ● *interj* vlan. ● *adv* 🅘 **~ in the middle** en plein milieu; **~ on time** à l'heure pile.
banger *n* (*firework*) pétard *m*; (Culin) saucisse *f*; (**old**) **~** (*car* 🅘) guimbarde *f*.
banish *vt* bannir.

banister *n* rampe *f* d'escalier.

bank *n* (Comm) banque *f*; (of river) rive *f*; (of sand) banc *m*. ● *vt* mettre en banque. ● *vi* (Aviat) virer; ~ **with** avoir un compte à; ~ **on** compter sur. ~ **account** *n* compte *m* en banque. ~ **card** *n* carte *f* bancaire. ~ **holiday** *n* jour *m* férié.

banking *n* opérations *fpl* bancaires; (as career) la banque.

banknote *n* billet *m* de banque.

bankrupt *a* **be** ~ être en faillite; **go** ~ faire faillite. ● *n* failli/-e *m/f*. ● *vt* mettre en faillite. **bankruptcy** *n* faillite *f*.

bank statement *n* relevé *m* de compte.

banner *n* bannière *f*.

baptism *n* baptême *m*. **baptize** *vt* baptiser.

bar *n* (of metal) barre *f*; (on window, cage) barreau *m*; (of chocolate) tablette *f*; (pub) bar *m*; (counter) comptoir *m*; (Mus) mesure *f*; (fig) obstacle *m*; ~ **of soap** savonnette *f*; **the** ~ (Jur) le barreau. ● *vt* (*pt* **barred**) (obstruct) barrer; (prohibit) interdire; (exclude) exclure. ● *prep* sauf.

barbecue *n* barbecue *m*. ● *vt* faire au barbecue.

barbed wire *n* fil *m* de fer barbelé.

barber *n* coiffeur *m* (*pour hommes*). ●

bar code *n* code *m* (à) barres.

bare *a* nu; (*cupboard*) vide. ● *vt* mettre à nu. ~**foot** *a* nu-pieds *inv*, pieds nus. **barely** *adv* à peine.

bargain *n* (deal) marché *m*; (cheap thing) occasion *f*. ● *vi* négocier; (haggle) marchander; **not** ~ **for** ne pas s'attendre à.

barge *n* péniche *f*. ● *vi* ~ **in** interrompre; (into room) faire irruption.

bark *n* (of tree) écorce *f*; (of dog) aboiement *m*. ● *vi* aboyer.

barley *n* orge *f*.

bar: ~**maid** *n* serveuse *f*. ~**man** *n* (*pl* **-men**) barman *m*.

barn *n* grange *f*.

barracks *npl* caserne *f*.

barrel *n* tonneau *m*; (of oil) baril *m*; (of gun) canon *m*.

barren *a* stérile.

barricade *n* barricade *f*. ● *vt* barricader.

barrier *n* barrière *f*; **ticket** ~ guichet *m*.

barrister *n* avocat *m*.

bartender *n* (US) barman *m*.

barter *n* troc *m*. ● *vt* troquer (**for** contre).

base *n* base *f*. ● *vt* baser (**on** sur; **in** à). ● *a* ignoble. **baseball** *n* base-ball *m*.

basement *n* sous-sol *m*.

bash ⊡ *vt* cogner; ~**ed in** enfoncé. ● *n* coup *m* violent; **have a** ~ **at** s'essayer à.

basic *a* fondamental, élémentaire; **the** ~**s** l'essentiel *m*. **basically** *adv* au fond.

basil *n* basilic *m*.

basin *n* (for liquids) cuvette *f*; (for food) bol *m*; (for washing) lavabo *m*; (of river) bassin *m*.

basis *n* (*pl* **bases**) base *f*.

bask *vi* se prélasser (**in** à).

basket *n* corbeille *f*; (with handle) panier *m*. **basketball** *n* basket(-ball) *m*.

Basque *n* (person) Basque *mf*; (Ling) basque *m*. ● *a* basque.

bass[1] *a* (*voice, part*) de basse; (*sound, note*) grave. ● *n* (*pl* **basses**) basse *f*.

bass[2] *n inv* (freshwater fish) perche *f*; (sea) bar *m*.

bassoon *n* basson *m*.

bastard *n* (illegitimate) bâtard/-e *m/f*; (insult ⊠) salaud *m* ⊠.

bat *n* (cricket etc.) batte *f*; (table tennis) raquette *f*; (animal) chauve-souris *f*. ● *vt* (*pt* **batted**) (ball) frapper; **not ~ an eyelid** ne pas sourciller.

batch *n* (of cakes, people) fournée *f*; (of goods, text *also* Comput) lot *m*.

bath *n* (*pl* **-s**) bain *m*; (tub) baignoire *f*; **have a ~** prendre un bain; (**swimming**) **~s** piscine *f*. ● *vt* donner un bain à.

bathe *vt* baigner. ● *vi* se baigner; (US) prendre un bain.

bathing *n* baignade *f*. **~-costume** *n* maillot *m* de bain.

bath: **~robe** *n* (US) robe *f* de chambre. **~room** *n* salle *f* de bains.

baton *n* (policeman's) matraque *f*; (Mus) baguette *f*.

batter *vt* battre. ● *n* (Culin) pâte *f* (à frire).

battery *n* (Mil, Auto) batterie *f*; (of torch, radio) pile *f*.

battle *n* bataille *f*; (fig) lutte *f*. ● *vi* se battre. **~field** *n* champ *m* de bataille.

baulk *vt/i* = BALK.

bay *n* (Bot) laurier *m*; (Geog, Archit) baie *f*; (area) aire *f*; (bark) aboiement *m*; **keep** *or* **hold at ~** tenir à distance. ● *vi* aboyer. **~-leaf** *n* feuille *f* de laurier. **~ window** *n* fenêtre *f* en saillie.

bazaar *n* (shop, market) bazar *m*; (sale) vente *f*.

BC *abbr* (**before Christ**) avant J.-C.

BBS *abbr* (**Bulletin Board System**) (Internet) babillard *m* électronique, BBS *m*.

---

be

present **am, is, are**; *past* **was, were**; *past participle* **been**.

● *intransitive verb*

····➤ être; **I am tired** je suis fatigué; **it's me** c'est moi.

····➤ (feelings) avoir; **I am hot** j'ai chaud; **he is hungry/thirsty** il a faim/soif; **her hands are cold** elle a froid aux mains.

····➤ (age) avoir; **I am 15** j'ai 15 ans.

····➤ (weather) faire; **it's warm** il fait chaud; **it's 25** il fait 25.

····➤ (health) aller; **how are you?** comment allez-vous *or* comment vas-tu?

····➤ (visit) aller; **I've never been to Italy** je ne suis jamais allé en Italie.

● *auxiliary verb*

····➤ (in tenses) **I am working** je travaille; **he was writing to his mother** il écrivait à sa mère; **she is to do it at once** (obligation) elle doit le faire tout de suite.

····➤ (in passives) **he was killed** il a été tué; **the window has been fixed** on a réparé la fenêtre.

····➤ (in tag questions) **their house is lovely, isn't it?** leur maison est très jolie, n'est-ce pas?

····➤ (in short answers) **'I am a painter'—'are you?'** 'je suis peintre'—'ah oui?'; **'are you a doctor?'—'yes, I am'** 'êtes-vous médecin?'—'oui'; **'you're not going out'—'yes I am'** 'tu ne sors pas'—'si'.

---

beach *n* plage *f*.

beacon *n* (lighthouse) phare *m*; (marker) balise *f*.

bead *n* perle *f*.

beak *n* bec *m*.

beaker *n* gobelet *m*

beam *n* (timber) poutre *f*; (of light) rayon *m*; (of torch) faisceau *m*. ● *vi* rayonner. ● *vt* (broadcast) transmettre.

bean *n* haricot *m*.

bear *n* ours *m*. ● *vt* (*pt* **bore**; *pp*

borne) (carry, show, feel) porter; (endure, sustain) supporter; (*child*) mettre au monde. ● *vi* ~ **left** (go) prendre à gauche; ~ **in mind** tenir compte de. □ ~ **out** confirmer; ~ **up** tenir le coup. **bearable** *a* supportable.

beard *n* barbe *f*.

bearer *n* porteur/-euse *m/f*.

bearing *n* (behaviour) maintien *m*; (relevance) rapport *m*; **get one's ~s** s'orienter.

beast *n* bête *f*; (*person*) brute *f*.

beat *vt/i* (*pt* **beat**; *pp* **beaten**) battre; ~ **a retreat** battre en retraite; ~ **it!** dégage! [!]; **it ~s me** [!] ça me dépasse. ● *n* (of drum, heart) battement *m*; (Mus) mesure *f*; (of policeman) ronde *f*. □ ~ **off** repousser; ~ **up** tabasser. **beating** *n* raclée *f*.

beautiful *a* beau.

beauty *n* beauté *f*. ~ **parlour** *n* institut *m* de beauté. ~ **spot** *n* grain *m* de beauté; (place) site *m* pittoresque.

beaver *n* castor *m*.

became ⇒BECOME.

because *conj* parce que; ~ **of** à cause de.

become *vt/i* (*pt* **became**; *pp* **become**) devenir; (befit) convenir à; **what has ~ of her?** qu'est-ce qu'elle est devenue?

bed *n* lit *m*; (layer) couche *f*; (of sea) fond *m*; (of flowers) parterre *m*; **go to ~** (aller) se coucher. ● *vi* (*pt* **bedded**) ~ **down** se coucher. **bed and breakfast** *n* chambre *f* avec petit déjeuner, chambre *f* d'hôte. **~bug** *n* punaise *f*. **~clothes** *npl* couvertures *fpl*.

bedding *n* literie *f*.

bed: **~ridden** *a* cloué au lit. **~room** *n* chambre *f* (à coucher). **~side** *n* chevet *m*. **~sit**, **~sitter** *n* chambre *f* meublée, studio *m*. **~spread** *n* dessus *m* de lit. **~time** *n* heure *f* du coucher.

bee *n* abeille *f*; **make a ~-line for** aller tout droit vers.

beech *n* hêtre *m*.

beef *n* bœuf *m*. **~burger** *n* hamburger *m*.

beehive *n* ruche *f*.

been ⇒BE.

beer *n* bière *f*.

beetle *n* scarabée *m*.

beetroot *n inv* betterave *f*.

before *prep* (time) avant; (place) devant; **the day ~ yesterday** avant-hier. ● *adv* avant; (already) déjà; **the day ~** la veille. ● *conj* ~ **leaving** avant de partir; ~ **I forget** avant que j'oublie. **beforehand** *adv* à l'avance.

beg *vt* (*pt* **begged**) (*food, money, favour*) demander (**from** à); ~ **sb to do** supplier qn de faire. ● *vi* mendier; **it is going ~ging** personne n'en veut.

began ⇒BEGIN.

beggar *n* mendiant/-e *m/f*.

begin *vt/i* (*pt* **began**, *pp* **begun**, *pres p* **beginning**) commencer (**to do** à faire). **beginner** *n* débutant/-e *m/f*. **beginning** *n* commencement *m*, début *m*.

begun ⇒BEGIN.

behalf *n* **on ~ of** (*act, speak, campaign*) pour; (*phone, write*) de la part de.

behave *vi* se conduire; ~ (**oneself**) se conduire bien.

behaviour, (US) **behavior** *n* comportement *m* (**towards** envers).

behead *vt* décapiter.

behind *prep* derrière; (in time) en retard sur. ● *adv* derrière; (late) en retard; **leave ~** oublier. ● *n* (buttocks [!]) derrière *m* [!].

beige *a* & *n* beige (*m*).

being *n* (person) être *m*.

belch *vi* avoir un renvoi. ●*vt* ~ **out** (*smoke*) s'échapper. ●*n* renvoi *m*.

Belgian *n* Belge *mf*. ●*a* belge. **Belgium** *n* Belgique *f*.

belief *n* conviction *f*; (trust) confiance *f*, (faith: Relig) foi *f*.

believe *vt/i* croire; ~ **in** croire à; (*deity*) croire en. **believer** *n* croyant/-e *m/f*.

bell *n* cloche *f*; (small) clochette *f*; (on door) sonnette *f*.

belly *n* ventre *m*. ~ **button** *n* nombril *m*.

belong *vi* ~ **to** appartenir à; (*club*) être membre de.

belongings *npl* affaires *fpl*.

beloved *a & n* bien-aimé/-e (*m/f*).

below *prep* sous, au-dessous de; (fig) indigne de. ●*adv* en dessous; (on page) ci-dessous.

belt *n* ceinture *f*; (Tech) courroie *f*; (fig) zone *f*. ●*vt* (hit ⊡) rosser. ●*vi* (rush ⊡) ~ **in/out** entrer/sortir à toute vitesse.

beltway *n* (US) périphérique *m*.

bemused *a* perplexe.

bench *n* banc *m*; **the** ~ (Jur) la magistrature (assise).

bend *vt* (*pt* **bent**) (*knee, arm, wire*) plier; (*head, back*) courber. ●*vi* (*road*) tourner; (*person*) ~ **down/over** se pencher. ●*n* courbe *f*; (in road) virage *m*; (of arm, knee) pli *m*.

beneath *prep* sous, au-dessous de; (fig) indigne de. ●*adv* en dessous.

benefactor *n* bienfaiteur/-trice *m/f*.

beneficial *a* bénéfique.

benefit *n* avantage *m*; (allowance) allocation *f*. ●*vt* (be useful to) profiter à; (do good to) faire du bien à. ●*vi* profiter; ~ **from** tirer profit de.

benign *a* (kindly) bienveillant; (Med) bénin.

bent ⇒BEND. ●*n* (talent) aptitude *f*; (inclination) penchant *m*. ●*a* tordu; ⊠ corrompu; ~ **on doing** décidé à faire.

bequest *n* legs *m*.

bereaved *a* endeuillé; **the** ~ la famille endeuillée. **bereavement** *n* deuil *m*.

berry *n* baie *f*.

berserk *a* fou furieux.

berth *n* (in train, ship) couchette *f*; (anchorage) mouillage *m*; **give a wide** ~ **to** éviter. ●*vi* mouiller.

beside *prep* à côté de; ~ **oneself** hors de soi; ~ **the point** sans rapport.

besides *prep* en plus de. ●*adv* en plus.

besiege *vt* assiéger.

best *a* meilleur; **the** ~ **book** le meilleur livre; **the** ~ **part of** la plus grande partie de; **the** ~ **thing is to** le mieux est de. ●*adv* (**the**) ~ (*behave, play*) le mieux. ●*n* **the** ~ le meilleur, la meilleure; **do one's** ~ faire de son mieux; **make the** ~ **of** s'accommoder de. ~ **man** *n* témoin. ~**-seller** *n* bestseller *m*, livre *m* à succès.

bet *n* pari *m*. ●*vt/i* (*pt* **bet** *or* **betted**, *pres p* **betting**) parier (**on** sur).

betray *vt* trahir.

better *a* meilleur; **the** ~ **part of** la plus grande partie de; **get** ~ s'améliorer; (recover) se remettre. ●*adv* mieux; **I had** ~ **go** je ferais mieux de partir. ●*vt* (improve) améliorer; (do better than) surpasser. ●*n* **get the** ~ **of** l'emporter sur; **so much the** ~ tant mieux. ~ **off** *a* (richer) plus riche; **he is/would be** ~ **off at home** il est/serait mieux chez lui.

betting-shop *n* bureau *m* du PMU.

B

between *prep* entre. ● *adv* **in ~** au milieu.

beverage *n* boisson *f*.

beware *vi* prendre garde (**of** à).

bewilder *vt* déconcerter.

beyond *prep* au-delà de; (*control, reach*) hors de; (besides) excepté. ● *adv* au-delà; **it is ~ me** ça me dépasse.

bias *n* (inclination) tendance *f*; (prejudice) parti *m* pris. ● *vt* (*pt* **biased**) influer sur. **biased** *a* partial.

bib *n* bavoir *m*.

Bible *n* Bible *f*.

biceps *n* biceps *m*.

bicycle *n* vélo *m*, bicyclette *f*. ● *a* (*bell, chain*) de vélo; (*pump, clip*) à vélo.

bid *n* (at auction) enchère *f*; (attempt) tentative *f*. ● *vt/i* (*pt* **bade**, *pp* **bidden** *or* **bid**, *pres p* **bidding**) (offer) offrir, mettre une enchère (de) (**for** pour); **~ sb good morning** dire bonjour à qn; **~ sb farewell** faire ses adieux à qn.

bidding *n* (at auction) enchères *fpl*; **he did my ~** il a fait ce que je lui ai dit.

bifocals *npl* verres *mpl* à double foyer.

big *a* (**bigger**, **biggest**) grand; (in bulk) gros.

bike *n* vélo *m*.

bikini *n* bikini *m*.

bilberry *n* myrtille *f*.

bilingual *a* bilingue.

bill *n* (invoice) facture *f*; (in hotel, for gas) note *f*; (in restaurant) addition *f*; (of sale) acte *m*; (Pol) projet *m* de loi; (banknote: US) billet *m* de banque; (Theat) **on the ~** à l'affiche; (of bird) bec *m*. ● *vt* (person: Comm) envoyer la facture à. **~board** *n* panneau *m* d'affichage.

billet *n* cantonnement *m*. ● *vt* (*pt* **billeted**) cantonner (**on** chez).

billiards *n* billard *m*.

billion *n* billion *m*; (US) milliard *m*.

bin *n* (for rubbish) poubelle *f*; (for storage) casier *m*.

bind *vt* (*pt* **bound**) attacher; (book) relier; **be bound by** être tenu par. ● *n* (bore) corvée *f*.

binding *n* reliure *f*. ● *a* (*agreement, contract*) qui lie.

binge *n* (drinking) beuverie *f*; (eating) gueuleton *m*.

binoculars *npl* jumelles *fpl*.

biochemistry *n* biochimie *f*.

biodegradable *a* biodégradable.

biographer *n* biographe *mf*. **biography** *n* biographie *f*.

biological *a* biologique.

biologist *n* biologiste *mf*.

biology *n* biologie *f*.

birch *n* (tree) bouleau *m*; (whip) fouet *m*.

bird *n* oiseau *m*; (girl ▣) nana *f*.

Biro® *n* stylo *m* à bille, bic® *m*.

birth *n* naissance *f*; **give ~** accoucher. **~ certificate** *n* acte *m* de naissance. **~-control** *n* contraception *f*. **~day** *n* anniversaire *m*. **~mark** *n* tache *f* de naissance. **~-rate** *n* taux *m* de natalité.

biscuit *n* biscuit *m*; (US) petit pain *m* (au lait).

bisect *vt* couper en deux.

bishop *n* évêque *m*.

bit ⇒BITE. ● *n* morceau *m*; (of horse) mors *m*; (of tool) mèche *f*; **a ~** (a little) un peu; (Comput) bit *m*.

bitch *n* chienne *f*; (woman ▣) garce *f* ▣. ● *vi* dire du mal (**about** de).

bite *vt/i* (*pt* **bit**; *pp* **bitten**) mordre; **~ one's nails** se ronger les ongles. ● *n* morsure *f*; (by insect) piqûre *f*; (mouthful) bouchée *f*; **have a ~** manger un morceau.

bitter *a* amer; (weather) glacial. ● *n* bière *f*. **bitterly** *adv* amèrement; **it is ~ly cold** il fait un temps glacial.

bizarre *a* bizarre.

black *a* noir; **~ and blue** couvert de bleus. ● *n* (colour) noir *m*; **B~** (person) Noir/-e *m/f*. ● *vt* noircir; (goods) boycotter. **~berry** *n* mûre *f*. **~bird** *n* merle *m*. **~board** *n* tableau *m* noir. **~currant** *n* cassis *m*.

blacken *vt/i* noircir.

black: **~ eye** *n* œil *m* poché. **~head** *n* point *m* noir. **~ ice** *n* verglas *m*. **~leg** *n* jaune *m*.

blacklist *n* liste *f* noire. ● *vt* mettre à l'index.

blackmail *n* chantage *m*. ● *vt* faire chanter. **blackmailer** *n* maître-chanteur *m*.

black: **~ market** *n* marché *m* noir. **~out** *n* panne *f* de courant; (Med) syncope *f*. **~ pudding** *n* boudin *m*. **~ sheep** *n* brebis *f* galeuse. **~smith** *n* forgeron *m*. **~ spot** *n* point *m* noir.

bladder *n* vessie *f*.

blade *n* (of knife) lame *f*; (of propeller, oar) pale *f*; **~ of grass** brin *m* d'herbe.

blame *vt* accuser; **~ sb for sth** reprocher qch à qn; **he is to ~** il est responsable (**for** de). ● *n* responsabilité *f* (**for** de).

bland *a* (insipid) fade.

blank *a* (*page*) blanc; (*screen*) vide; (*cheque*) en blanc; **to look ~** avoir l'air ébahi. ● *n* blanc *m*; **~ (cartridge)** cartouche *f* à blanc.

blanket *n* couverture *f*; (layer) couche *f*.

blasphemous *a* blasphématoire; (*person*) blasphémateur.

blast *n* explosion *f*; (wave of air) souffle *m*; (of wind) rafale *f*; (noise from siren etc.) coup *m*. ● *vt* (blow up) faire sauter. □ **~ off** décoller. **~ furnace** *n* haut-fourneau *m*. **~-off** *n* lancement *m*.

blatant *a* (obvious) flagrant; (shameless) éhonté.

blaze *n* feu *m*; (accident) incendie *m*. ● *vt* **~ a trail** faire œuvre de pionnier. ● *vi* (*fire*) brûler; (*sky, eyes*) flamboyer.

bleach *n* (for cleaning) eau *f* de Javel; (for hair, fabric) décolorant *m*. ● *vt/i* blanchir; (*hair*) décolorer.

bleak *a* (*landscape*) désolé; (*outlook, future*) sombre.

bleed *vt/i* (*pt* **bled**) saigner.

bleep *n* bip *m*.

blemish *n* imperfection *f*; (on fruit, reputation) tache *f*. ● *vt* entacher.

blend *vt* mélanger. ● *vi* se fondre ensemble; **to ~ with** se marier à. ● *n* mélange *m*. **blender** *n* mixeur *n*, mixer *n*.

bless *vt* bénir; **be ~ed with** jouir de; **~ you!** à vos souhaits! **blessed** *a* (holy) saint; (damned [!]) sacré. **blessing** *n* bénédiction *f*; (benefit) avantage *m*; (stroke of luck) chance *f*.

blew ⇨BLOW.

blight *n* (disease: Bot) rouille *f*; (fig) plaie *f*.

blind *a* aveugle (**to** à); (*corner, bend*) sans visibilité. ● *vt* aveugler. ● *n* (on window) store *m*; **the ~** les aveugles *mpl*.

blindfold *a* **be ~** avoir les yeux bandés. ● *adv* les yeux bandés. ● *n* bandeau *m*. ● *vt* bander les yeux à.

blindness *n* (Med) cécité *f*; (fig) aveuglement *m*.

blind spot *n* (Auto) angle *m* mort.

blink *vi* cligner des yeux; (*light*) clignoter.

bliss *n* délice *m*. **blissful** *a* délicieux.

blister *n* ampoule *f*; (on paint) cloque *f*. ● *vi* cloquer.

B

blitz *n* (Aviat) raid *m* éclair. ● *vt* bombarder.

blob *n* (drop) (grosse) goutte *f*; (stain) tache *f*.

block *n* bloc *m*; (buildings) pâté *m* de maisons; (in pipe) obstruction *f*; **~** (**of flats**) immeuble *m*; **~ letters** majuscules *fpl*. ● *vt* bloquer.

blockade *n* blocus *m*. ● *vt* bloquer.

blockage *n* obstruction *f*.

block-buster *n* gros succès *m*.

bloke *n* ⊡ type *m*.

blond *a & n* blond (*m*).

blonde *a & n* blonde (*f*).

blood *n* sang *m*. ● *a* (*donor, bath*) de sang; (*bank, poisoning*) du sang; (*group, vessel*) sanguin. **~-pressure** *n* tension *f* artérielle. **~shed** *n* effusion *f* de sang. **~shot** *a* injecté de sang. **~stream** *n* sang *m*. **~ test** *n* prise *f* de sang.

bloody *a* (**-ier, -iest**) sanglant; ⊠ sacré. ● *adv* ⊠ vachement ⊡. **~-minded** *a* ⊡ hargneux, obstiné.

bloom *n* fleur *f*. ● *vi* fleurir; (person) s'épanouir.

blossom *n* fleur(s) *f(pl)*. ● *vi* fleurir; (person) s'épanouir.

blot *n* tache *f*. ● *vt* (*pt* **blotted**) tacher; (dry) sécher; **~ out** effacer.

blotch *n* tache *f*.

blouse *n* chemisier *m*.

blow *vt/i* (*pt* **blew**; *pp* **blown**) souffler; (*fuse*) (faire) sauter; (squander ⊠) claquer; (*opportunity*) rater; **~ one's nose** se moucher; **~ a whistle** siffler. ● *n* coup *m*. □ **~ away** *or* **off** emporter; **~ out** souffler; **~ over** passer; **~ up** (faire) sauter; (*tyre*) gonfler; (Photo) agrandir.

blow-dry *n* brushing *m*. ● *vt* faire un brushing à.

blown ⇒BLOW.

bludgeon *n* matraque *f*. ● *vt* matraquer.

blue *a* bleu; (*movie*) porno. ● *n* bleu *m*; **come out of the ~** être inattendu; **have the ~s** avoir le cafard. **~bell** *n* jacinthe *f* des bois. **~print** *n* projet *m*.

bluff *vt/i* bluffer. ● *n* bluff *m*; **call sb's ~** dire chiche à qn. ● *a* (*person*) carré.

blunder *vi* faire une bourde; (move) avancer à tâtons. ● *n* gaffe *f*.

blunt *a* (*knife*) émoussé; (person) brusque. ● *vt* émousser. **bluntly** *adv* carrément.

blur *n* image *f* floue. ● *vt* (*pt* **blurred**) brouiller.

blurb *n* résumé *m* publicitaire.

blush *vi* rougir. ● *n* rougeur *f*. **blusher** *n* fard *m* à joues.

blustery *a* **~ wind** bourrasque *f*.

boar *n* sanglier *m*.

board *n* planche *f*; (for notices) tableau *m*; (food) pension *f*; **full ~** pension *f* complète; **half ~** demi-pension *f*; (committee) conseil *m*; **~ of directors** conseil *m* d'administration; **go by the ~** tomber à l'eau; **on ~** à bord. ● *vt/i* (*bus, train*) monter dans; (Naut) monter à bord (de); **~ with** être en pension chez.

boarding-school *n* école *f* privée avec internat.

boast *vi* se vanter (**about** de). ● *vt* s'enorgueillir de. ● *n* vantardise *f*.

boat *n* bateau *m*; (small) canot *m*; **in the same ~** logé à la même enseigne.

bode *vi* **~ well/ill** être de bon/mauvais augure.

bodily *a* (*need, well-being*) physique; (*injury*) corporel. ● *adv* physiquement; (in person) en personne.

body *n* corps *m*; (mass) masse *f*;

(organization) organisme *m*; **~(work)** (Auto) carrosserie *f*; **the main ~ of** le gros de. **~-building** *n* culturisme *m*. **~guard** *n* garde *m* du corps.

bog *n* marais *m*. ● *vt* (*pt* **bogged**) **get ~ged down** s'enliser dans.

bogus *a* faux.

boil *n* furoncle *m*; **bring to the ~** porter à ébullition. ● *vt/i* bouillir. □ **~ down to** se ramener à; **~ over** déborder. **boiled** *a* (*egg*) à la coque; (*potatoes*) à l'eau.

boiler *n* chaudière *f*; **~ suit** bleu *m* (de travail).

boisterous *a* tapageur; (*child*) turbulent.

bold *a* hardi; (cheeky) effronté; (*type*) gras.

Bolivia *n* Bolivie *f*.

bollard *n* (on road) balise *f*.

bolt *n* (on door) verrou *m*; (for nut) boulon *m*; (lightning) éclair *m*. ● *vt* (*door*) verrouiller; (*food*) engouffrer. ● *vi* s'emballer.

bomb *n* bombe *f*; **~ scare** alerte *f* à la bombe. ● *vt* bombarder.

bomber *n* (aircraft) bombardier *m*; (person) plastiqueur *m*.

bombshell *n* **be a ~** tomber comme une bombe.

bond *n* (agreement) engagement *m*; (link) lien *m*; (Comm) obligation *f*, bon *m*; **in ~** (entreposé) en douane.

bone *n* os *m*; (of fish) arête *f*. ● *vt* désosser. **~-dry** *a* tout à fait sec.

bonfire *n* feu *m*; (for celebration) feu *m* de joie.

bonnet *n* (hat) bonnet *m*; (of vehicle) capot *m*.

bonus *n* prime *f*.

bony *a* (**-ier**, **-iest**) (thin) osseux; (*fish*) plein d'arêtes.

boo *interj* hou. ● *vt/i* huer. ● *n* huée *f*.

booby-trap *n* mécanisme *m* piégé. ● *vt* (*pt* **-trapped**) piéger.

book *n* livre *m*; (*exercise*) cahier *m*; (of tickets etc.) carnet *m*; **~s** (Comm) comptes *mpl*. ● *vt* (reserve) réserver; (*driver*) dresser un PV à; (*player*) prendre le nom de; (write down) inscrire. ● *vi* retenir des places; (**fully**) **~ed** complet. **~case** *n* bibliothèque *f*. **booking-office** *n* guichet *m*. **~keeping** *n* comptabilité *f*. **booklet** *n* brochure *f*. **~maker** *n* bookmaker *m*. **~mark** *n* (for book, Internet) signet *m*. **~seller** *n* libraire *mf*. **~shop** *n* librairie *f*. **~stall** *n* kiosque *m* (à journaux).

boom *vi* (*gun, wind, etc.*) gronder; (*trade*) prospérer. ● *n* grondement *m*; (Comm) boom *m*, prospérité *f*.

boost *vt* stimuler; (*morale*) remonter; (*price*) augmenter; (publicize) faire de la réclame pour.

boot *n* (knee-length) botte *f*; (ankle-length) chaussure *f* (montante); (for walking) chaussure *f* de marche; (Sport) chaussure *f* de sport; (of vehicle) coffre *m*; **get the ~** ☒ se faire virer. ● *vt/i* **~ up** (Comput) amorcer.

booth *n* (for telephone) cabine *f*; (at fair) baraque *f*.

booze *vi* ⊡ boire (beaucoup). ● *n* ⊡ alcool *m*.

border *n* (edge) bord *m*; (frontier) frontière *f*; (in garden) bordure *f*. ● *vi* **~ on** être voisin de, avoisiner.

bore *vt* ennuyer; **be ~d** s'ennuyer; ⇒BEAR. ● *vi* (Tech) forer. ● *n* raseur/-euse *m/f*; (thing) ennui *m*. **boredom** *n* ennui *m*. **boring** *a* ennuyeux.

born *a* né; **be ~** naître.

borne ⇒BEAR.

borough *n* municipalité *f*.

borrow *vt* emprunter (**from** à).

Bosnia *n* Bosnie *f.*
Bosnian *a* bosniaque. ● *n* Bosniaque.
bosom *n* poitrine *f*; ~ **friend** ami/-e *m/f* intime.
boss *n* ⊡ patron/-ne *m/f.* ● *vt* ~ **(about)** ⊡ mener par le bout du nez.
bossy *a* autoritaire.
botch *vt* bâcler, saboter.
both *det* les deux; ~ **the books** les deux livres. ● *pron* tous/toutes (les) deux, l'un/-e et l'autre; **we ~ agree** nous sommes tous les deux d'accord; **I bought ~ (of them)** j'ai acheté les deux; **I saw ~ of you** je vous ai vus tous les deux; ~ **Paul and Anne** (et) Paul et Anne. ● *adv* à la fois.
bother *vt* (annoy, worry) ennuyer; (disturb) déranger. ● *vi* se déranger; **don't ~ (calling)** ce n'est pas la peine (d'appeler); **don't ~ about us** ne t'inquiète pas pour nous; **I can't be ~ed** j'ai la flemme ⊡. ● *n* ennui *m*; (effort) peine *f*; **it's no ~** ce n'est rien.
bottle *n* bouteille *f*; (for baby) biberon *m.* ● *vt* mettre en bouteille. □ ~ **up** contenir. ~ **bank** *n* collecteur *m* (*de verre usagé*). ~**neck** *n* (traffic jam) embouteillage *m.* ~**-opener** *n* ouvre-bouteilles *m inv.*
bottom *n* fond *m*; (of hill, page, etc.) bas *m*; (buttocks) derrière *m* ⊡. ● *a* inférieur, du bas.
bought ⇒BUY.
bounce *vi* rebondir; (*person*) faire des bonds, bondir; (*cheques* ⊠) être refusé. ● *vt* faire rebondir. ● *n* rebond *m.*
bound *vi* (leap) bondir; ~**ed by** limité par; ⇒BIND. ● *n* bond *m.* ● *a* **be ~ for** être en route pour, aller vers; ~ **to** (obliged) obligé de; (certain) sûr de.
boundary *n* limite *f.*
bounds *npl* limites *fpl*; **out of ~** être interdit d'accès.
bout *n* période *f*; (Med) accès *m*; (boxing) combat *m.*
bow[1] *n* (weapon) arc *m*; (of violin) archet *m*; (knot) nœud *m.*
bow[2] *n* salut *m*; (of ship) proue *f.* ● *vt/i* (s')incliner.
bowels *npl* intestins *mpl*; (fig) profondeurs *fpl.*
bowl *n* (for washing) cuvette *f*; (for food) bol *m*; (for soup) assiette *f* creuse. ● *vt/i* (cricket) lancer; ~ **over** bouleverser.
bowler *n* (cricket) lanceur *m*; ~ **(hat)** (chapeau) melon *m.*
bowling *n* (ten-pin) bowling *m*; (on grass) jeu *m* de boules. ~**-alley** *n* bowling *m.*
bow-tie *n* nœud *m* papillon.
box *n* boîte *f*; (*cardboard*) carton *m*; (Theat) loge *f*; **the ~** ⊡ la télé. ● *vt* mettre en boîte; (Sport) boxer; ~ **sb's ears** gifler qn; ~ **in** enfermer.
boxing *n* boxe *f.* ● *a* de boxe. **B~ Day** *n* le lendemain de Noël.
box office *n* guichet *m.*
boy *n* garçon *m.*
boycott *vt* boycotter. ● *n* boycottage *m.*
boyfriend *n* (petit) ami *m.*
bra *n* soutien-gorge *m.*
brace *n* (fastener) attache *f*; (dental) appareil *m*; (tool) vilbrequin *m*; ~**s** (for trousers) bretelles *fpl.* ● *vt* soutenir; ~ **oneself** rassembler ses forces.
bracket *n* (for shelf etc.) tasseau *m*, support *m*; (group) tranche *f*; **in ~s** entre parenthèses. ● *vt* mettre entre parenthèses *or* crochets.
braid *n* (trimming) galon *m*; (of hair) tresse *f.*
brain *n* cerveau *m*; ~**s** (fig) intelligence *f.* ● *vt* assommer. **brainless** *a* stupide. ~**wash** *vt*

faire subir un lavage de cerveau à. ~**wave** *n* idée *f* géniale, trouvaille *f*. **brainy** *a* (**-ier**, **-iest**) doué.

brake *n* (Auto *also* fig) frein *m*. ● *vt/i* freiner. ~ **light** *n* feu *m* stop.

bran *n* son *m*.

branch *n* (of tree) branche *f*; (of road) embranchement *m*; (Comm) succursale *f*; (of bank) agence *f*. ● *vi* ~ (**off**) bifurquer.

brand *n* marque *f*. ● *vt* ~ **sb as** désigner qn comme qch.

brand-new *a* tout neuf.

brandy *n* cognac *m*.

brass *n* cuivre *m*; **get down to** ~ **tacks** en venir aux choses sérieuses; **the** ~ (Mus) les cuivres *mpl*; **top** ~ ⊠ galonnés *mpl*.

brat *n* ⊡ môme *mf* ⊡.

brave *a* courageux; (*smile*) brave. ● *n* (American Indian) brave *m*. ● *vt* braver. **bravery** *n* courage *m*.

brawl *n* bagarre *f*. ● *vi* se bagarrer.

Brazil *n* Brésil *m*.

breach *n* (of copyright, privilege) violation *f*; (in relationship) rupture *f*; (gap) brèche *f*. ● *vt* ouvrir une brèche dans.

bread *n* pain *m*; ~ **and butter** tartine *f*. ~**-bin**, (US) ~**-box** *n* boîte *f* à pain. ~**crumbs** *npl* chapelure *f*.

breadth *n* largeur *f*.

bread-winner *n* soutien *m* de famille.

break *vt* (*pt* **broke**, *pp* **broken**) casser; (smash into pieces) briser; (*vow, silence, rank, etc.*) rompre; (*law*) violer; (*a record*) battre; (*news*) révéler; (*journey*) interrompre; (*heart, strike, ice*) briser; ~ **one's arm** se casser le bras. ● *vi* (se) casser; se briser. ● *n* cassure *f*, rupture *f*; (in relationship, continuity) rupture *f*; (interval) interruption *f*; (at school) récréation *f*, récré *f*; (for coffee) pause *f*; (luck ⊡) chance *f*. □ ~ **away from** se détacher; ~ **down** *vi* (collapse) s'effondrer; (*negotiations*) échouer; (machine) tomber en panne; *vt* (*door*) enfoncer; (analyse) analyser; ~ **even** rentrer dans ses frais; ~ **into** cambrioler; ~ **off** (se) détacher; (suspend) rompre; (stop talking) s'interrompre; ~ **out** (*fire, war, etc.*) éclater; ~ **up** (end) (faire) cesser; (*couple*) rompre; (*marriage*) (se) briser; (*crowd*) (se) disperser; (*schools*) être en vacances. **breakable** *a* fragile. **breakage** *n* casse *f*.

breakdown *n* (Tech) panne *f*; (Med) dépression *f*; (of figures) analyse *f*. ● *a* (Auto) de dépannage.

breakfast *n* petit déjeuner *m*.

break: ~**-in** *n* cambriolage *m*. ~**through** *n* percée *f*.

breast *n* sein *m*; (chest) poitrine *f*. ~**-feed** *vt* (*pt* **-fed**) allaiter. ~**-stroke** *n* brasse *f*.

breath *n* souffle *m*, haleine *f*; **out of** ~ à bout de souffle; **under one's** ~ tout bas.

breathalyser® *n* alcootest *m*.

breathe *vt/i* respirer. □ ~ **in** inspirer; ~ **out** expirer.

breathless *a* à bout de souffle.

breathtaking *a* à vous couper le souffle.

bred ⇒BREED.

breed *vt* (*pt* **bred**) élever; (give rise to) engendrer. ● *vi* se reproduire. ● *n* race *f*.

breeze *n* brise *f*.

brew *vt* (*beer*) brasser; (*tea*) faire infuser. ● *vi* (*beer*) fermenter; (*tea*) infuser; (fig) se préparer. ● *n* décoction *f*. **brewer** *n* brasseur *m*. **brewery** *n* brasserie *f*.

bribe *n* pot-de-vin *m*. ● *vt* soudoyer. **bribery** *n* corruption *f*.

brick *n* brique *f*. **~layer** *n* maçon *m*.

bridal *a* (*dress*) de mariée; (*car, chamber*) des mariés.

bride *n* mariée *f*. **~groom** *n* marié *m*. **~smaid** *n* demoiselle *f* d'honneur.

bridge *n* pont *m*; (Naut) passerelle *f*; (of nose) arête *f*; (card game) bridge *m*. ● *vt* **~ a gap** combler une lacune.

bridle *n* bride *f*. ● *vt* brider. **~-path** *n* piste *f* cavalière.

brief *a* bref. ● *n* instructions *fpl*; (Jur) dossier *m*. ● *vt* donner des instructions à.

briefcase *n* serviette *f*.

briefs *npl* slip *m*.

bright *a* brillant, vif; (*day, room*) clair; (cheerful) gai; (clever) intelligent.

brighten *vt* égayer. ● *vi* (*weather*) s'éclaircir; (*face*) s'éclairer.

brilliant *a* (*student, career*) brillant; (*light*) éclatant; (very good ⓘ) super.

brim *n* bord *m*. ● *vi* (*pt* **brimmed**); **~ over** déborder (**with** de).

bring *vt* (*pt* **brought**) (*thing*) apporter; (*person, vehicle*) amener; **~ to bear** (*pressure etc.*) exercer. □ **~ about** provoquer; **~ back** (return with) rapporter; (*colour, shine*) redonner; **~ down** faire tomber; (shoot down, knock down) abattre; **~ forward** avancer; **~ off** réussir; **~ out** (take out) sortir; (show) faire ressortir; (book) publier; **~ round** faire revenir à soi; **~ up** (*child*) élever; (Med) vomir; (*question*) aborder.

brink *n* bord *m*.

brisk *a* vif.

bristle *n* poil *m*. ● *vi* se hérisser; **bristling with** hérissé de.

Britain *n* Grande-Bretagne *f*.

British *a* britannique; **the ~** les Britanniques *mpl*.

Briton *n* Britannique *mf*.

Brittany *n* Bretagne *f*.

brittle *a* fragile.

broad *a* large; (*choice, range*) grand. **~ bean** *n* fève.

broadcast *vt/i* (*pt* **broadcast**) diffuser; (person) parler à la télévision *or* à la radio. ● *n* émission *f*.

broadly *adv* en gros.

broad-minded *a* large d'esprit.

broccoli *n inv* brocoli *m*.

brochure *n* brochure *f*.

broke ⇒BREAK. ● *a* (penniless ⊠) fauché.

broken ⇒BREAK. ● *a* **~ English** mauvais anglais *m*.

bronchitis *n* bronchite *f*.

bronze *n* bronze *m*. ● *vt/i* (se) bronzer.

brooch *n* broche *f*.

brood *n* nichée *f*, couvée *f*. ● *vi* (*bird*) couver; (fig) méditer tristement.

broom *n* balai *m*.

broth *n* bouillon *m*.

brothel *n* maison *f* close.

brother *n* frère *m*. **~hood** *n* fraternité *f*. **~-in-law** *n* (*pl* **~s-in-law**) beau-frère *m*.

brought ⇒BRING.

brow *n* front *m*; (of hill) sommet *m*.

brown *a* (*object*) marron; (*hair*) brun; **~ bread** pain *m* complet; **~ sugar** sucre *m* roux. ● *n* marron *m*; brun *m*. ● *vt/i* brunir; (Culin) (faire) dorer.

Brownie *n* jeannette *f*.

browse *vi* flâner; (*animal*) brouter. ● *vt* (Comput) naviguer. **browser** *n* (Comput) navigateur *m*.

bruise *n* bleu *m*. ● *vt* (*knee, arm*

etc.) faire un bleu à; (*fruit*) abîmer.

brush *n* brosse *f*; (skirmish) accrochage *m*; (bushes) broussailles *fpl*. ● *vt* brosser. □ ~ **against** frôler; ~ **aside** (dismiss) repousser; (move) écarter; ~ **up** (**on**) se remettre à.

Brussels *n* Bruxelles. ~ **sprouts** *npl* choux *mpl* de Bruxelles.

brutal *a* brutal.

brute *n* brute *f*; **by ~ force** par la force.

bubble *n* bulle *f*; **blow ~s** faire des bulles. ● *vi* bouillonner; ~ **over** déborder. ~ **bath** *n* bain *m* moussant.

buck *n* mâle *m*; (US, [*]) dollar *m*; **pass the ~** rejeter la responsabilité (**to** sur). ● *vi* (*horse*) ruer; ~ **up** [*] prendre courage; (hurry [*]) se grouiller [!].

bucket *n* seau *m* (**of** de).

buckle *n* boucle *f*. ● *vt/i* (fasten) (se) boucler; (bend) voiler. □ ~ **down to** s'atteler à.

bud *n* bourgeon *m*. ● *vi* (*pt* **budded**) bourgeonner.

Buddhism *n* bouddhisme *m*.

budding *a* (*talent*) naissant; (*athlete*) en herbe.

budge *vt/i* (faire) bouger.

budgerigar *n* perruche *f*.

budget *n* budget *m*. ● *vi* ~ **for** prévoir (dans son budget).

buff *n* (colour) chamois *m*; [!] fanatique *mf*.

buffalo *n* (*pl* **-oes** *or* **-o**) buffle *m*; (US) bison *m*.

buffer *n* tampon *m*; ~ **zone** zone *f* tampon.

buffet[1] *n* (meal, counter) buffet *m*; ~ **car** buffet *m*.

buffet[2] *n* (blow) soufflet *m*. ● *vt* (*pt* **buffeted**) souffleter.

bug *n* (bedbug) punaise *f*; (any small insect) bestiole *f*; (germ) microbe *m*; (stomachache [!]) ennuis *mpl* gastriques; (device) micro *m*; (defect) défaut *m*; (Comput) bogue *f*, bug *m*. ● *vt* (*pt* **bugged**) mettre des micros dans; [*] embêter.

buggy *n* poussette *f*

build *vt/i* (*pt* **built**) bâtir, construire. ● *n* carrure *f*. □ ~ **up** (increase) augmenter, monter; (accumulate) (s')accumuler. **builder** *n* entrepreneur *m* en bâtiment; (workman) ouvrier *m* du bâtiment.

building *n* (structure) bâtiment *m*; (dwelling) immeuble *m*. ~ **society** *n* caisse *f* d'épargne.

build-up *n* accumulation *f*; (fig) publicité *f*.

built ⇒BUILD.

built-in *a* encastré.

built-up area *a* agglomération *f*, zone *f* urbanisée.

bulb *n* (Bot) bulbe *m*; (Electr) ampoule *f*.

Bulgaria *n* Bulgarie *f*.

Bulgarian *n* (person) Bulgare *mf*; (Ling) bulgare *m*. ● *a* bulgare.

bulge *n* renflement *m*. ● *vi* se renfler, être renflé; **be bulging with** être gonflé *or* bourré de.

bulimia *n* boulimie *f*.

bulk *n* volume *f*; **in ~** (*buy, sell*) en gros; (transport) en vrac; **the ~ of** la majeure partie de.

bull *n* taureau *m*. **~dog** *n* bouledogue *m*. **~doze** *vt* raser au bulldozer.

bullet *n* balle *f*.

bulletin *n* bulletin *m*.

bullet-proof *a* (*vest*) pare-balles *inv*; (*vehicle*) blindé.

bullfight *n* corrida *f*.

bullion *n* or *m* or argent *m* en lingots.

bullring *n* arène *f*.

bull's-eye *n* mille *m*.

bully *n* (child) petite brute *f*; (adult) tyran *m*. ● *vt* maltraiter.

B

bum *n* ⊠ derrière *m* [!]; (US, ⊠) vagabond/-e *m/f*.

bumble-bee *n* bourdon *m*.

bump *n* (swelling) bosse *f*; (on road) bosse *f*. ● *vt/i* cogner, heurter. □ ~ **along** cahoter; ~ **into** (hit) rentrer dans; (meet) tomber sur.

bumper *n* pare-chocs *m inv*. ● *a* exceptionnel.

bumpy *a* (*road*) accidenté.

bun *n* (cake) petit pain *m*; (hair) chignon *m*.

bunch *n* (of flowers) bouquet *m*; (of keys) trousseau *m*; (of people) groupe *m*; (of bananas) régime *m*; ~ **of grapes** grappe *f* de raisin.

bundle *n* paquet *m*. ● *vt* mettre en paquet; (push) fourrer.

bung *n* bouchon *m*. ● *vt* (stop up) boucher; (throw ⊠) flanquer [!].

bunion *n* (Med) oignon *m*.

bunk *n* (on ship, train) couchette *f*. ~**-beds** *npl* lits *mpl* superposés.

buoy *n* bouée *f*. ● *vt* ~ **up** (hearten) soutenir, encourager.

buoyancy *n* (of floating object) flottabilité *f*; (cheerfulness) gaieté *f*.

burden *n* fardeau *m*. ● *vt* ennuyer (**with** de).

bureau *n* (*pl* **-eaux**) bureau *m*.

bureaucracy *n* bureaucratie *f*.

burglar *n* cambrioleur *m*; ~ **alarm** alarme *f*. **burglarize** *vt* (US) cambrioler. **burglary** *n* cambriolage *m*. **burgle** *vt* cambrioler.

Burgundy *n* (wine) bourgogne *m*.

burial *n* enterrement *m*.

burn *vt/i* (*pt* **burned** *or* **burnt**) brûler. ● *n* brûlure *f*. □ ~ **down** être réduit en cendres. **burning** *a* en flammes; (fig) brûlant.

burnt ⇒BURN.

burp *n* [!] rot *m*. ● *vi* [!] roter.

burrow *n* terrier *m*. ● *vt* creuser.

bursar *n* intendant/-e *m/f*. **bursary** *n* bourse *f*.

burst *vt/i* (*pt* **burst**) (*balloon, bubble*) crever; (*pipe*) (faire) éclater. ● *n* explosion *f*; (of laughter) éclat *m*; (surge) élan *m*. □ ~ **into** (*room*) faire interruption dans; ~ **into tears** fondre en larmes; ~ **out** ~ **out laughing** éclater de rire; ~ **with be** ~**ing with** déborder de.

bury *vt* (*person etc.*) enterrer; (hide, cover) enfouir; (engross, thrust) plonger.

bus *n* (*pl* **buses**) (auto)bus *m*. ● *vt* transporter en bus. ● *vi* (*pt* **bussed**) prendre l'autobus.

bush *n* (shrub) buisson *m*; (land) brousse *f*.

business *n* (task, concern) affaire *f*; (commerce) affaires *fpl*; (line of work) métier *m*; (shop) commerce *m*; **he has no** ~ **to** il n'a pas le droit de; **mean** ~ être sérieux; **that's none of your** ~! ça ne vous regarde pas! ~**like** *a* sérieux. ~**man** *n* homme *m* d'affaires.

busker *n* musicien/-ne *m/f* des rues.

bus-stop *n* arrêt *m* d'autobus.

bust *n* (statue) buste *m*; (bosom) poitrine *f*. ● *vt/i* (*pt* **busted** *or* **bust**) (burst ⊠) crever; (break ⊠) (se) casser. ● *a* (broken, finished ⊠) fichu; **go** ~ ⊠ faire faillite.

bustle *vi* s'affairer. ● *n* affairement *m*, remue-ménage *m*.

busy *a* (**-ier**, **-iest**) (*person*) occupé; (*street*) animé; (*day*) chargé. ● *vt* ~ **oneself with** s'occuper à.

but *conj* mais. ● *prep* sauf; ~ **for** sans; **nobody** ~ personne d'autre que; **nothing** ~ rien que. ● *adv* (only) seulement.

butcher *n* boucher *m*. ● *vt* massacrer.

butler *n* maître *m* d'hôtel.

butt *n* (of gun) crosse *f*; (of cigarette) mégot *m*; (of joke) cible *f*; (barrel) tonneau *m*; (US, ⊡) derrière *m* ⊡. ● *vi* ~ **in** interrompre.

butter *n* beurre *m*. ● *vt* beurrer. **~-bean** *n* haricot *m* blanc. **~cup** *n* bouton-d'or *m*.

butterfly *n* papillon *m*.

buttock *n* fesse *f*.

button *n* bouton *m*. ● *vt/i* ~ (**up**) (se) boutonner.

buttonhole *n* boutonnière *f*. ● *vt* accrocher.

buy *vt* (*pt* **bought**) acheter (**from** à); ~ **sth for sb** acheter qch à qn, prendre qch pour qn; (believe ⊠) croire, avaler.

buzz *n* bourdonnement *m*. ● *vi* bourdonner. **buzzer** *n* sonnerie *f*.

by *prep* par, de; (near) à côté de; (before) avant; (means) en, à, par; ~ **bike** à vélo; ~ **car** en auto; ~ **day** de jour; ~ **the kilo** au kilo; ~ **running** en courant; ~ **sea** par mer; ~ **that time** à ce moment-là; ~ **the way** à propos; ~ **oneself** tout seul. ● *adv* **close** ~ tout près; ~ **and large** dans l'ensemble.

bye(**-bye**) *interj* ⊡ au revoir, salut ⊡.

by-election *n* élection *f* partielle.

Byelorussia *n* Biélorussie *f*.

by-law *n* arrêté *m* municipal.

bypass *n* (Auto) rocade *f*; (Med) pontage *m*. ● *vt* contourner.

by-product *n* dérivé *m*; (fig) conséquence *f*.

byte *n* octet *m*.

cab *n* taxi *m*; (of lorry, train) cabine *f*.

cabbage *n* chou *m*.

cabin *n* (hut) cabane *f*; (in ship, aircraft) cabine *f*.

cabinet *n* petit placard *m*; (glass-fronted) vitrine *f*; (Pol) cabinet *m*.

cable *n* câble *m*. ● *vt* câbler. **~-car** *n* téléphérique *m*. ~ **television** *n* télévision *f* par câble.

cache *n* (hoard) cache *f*; (place) cachette *f*.

cackle *n* (of hen) caquet *m*; (laugh) ricanement *m*. ● *vi* caqueter; (laugh) ricaner.

cactus *n* (*pl* **-ti** *or* **~es**) cactus *m*.

cadet *n* élève *m* officier.

Caesarean *a* ~ (**section**) césarienne *f*.

café *n* café *m*, snack-bar *m*.

caffeine *n* caféine *f*.

cage *n* cage *f*. ● *vt* mettre en cage.

cagey *a* réticent.

cagoule *n* K-way® *m*.

cajole *vt* ~ **sb into doing sth** amener qn à faire qch par la cajolerie.

cake *n* gâteau *m*; (of soap) pain *m* ● *vi* former une croûte (**on** sur).

calculate *vt* calculer; (estimate) évaluer. **calculated** *a* délibéré; (*risk*) calculé. **calculating** *a* calculateur. **calculation** *n* calcul *m*. **calculator** *n* calculatrice *f*.

calculus *n* (*pl* **-li** *or* **~es**) calcul *m*.

calendar *n* calendrier *m*.

calf *n* (*pl* **calves**) (young cow or bull) veau *m*; (of leg) mollet *m*.

calibre *n* calibre *m*.

call *vt/i* appeler; (loudly) crier; **he's ~ed John** il s'appelle John; **~ sb stupid** traiter qn d'imbécile. ● *n* appel *m*; (of bird) cri *m*; (visit) visite *f*; **make/pay a ~ on** rendre visite à; **be on ~** être de garde; **~ box** cabine *f* téléphonique. □ **~ back** rappeler; (visit) repasser; **~ for** (*help*) appeler à; (demand) demander; (require) exiger; (collect) passer prendre; **~ in** passer; **~ off** annuler; **~ on** (visit) rendre visite à; (urge) demander à (**to do** de faire); **~ out** (**to**) appeler; **~ round** venir; **~ up** appeler.

calling *n* vocation *f*.

callous *a* inhumain.

calm *a* calme. ● *n* calme *m*. ● *vt/i* **~** (**down**) (se) calmer.

calorie *n* calorie *f*.

camcorder *n* caméscope® *m*.

came ⇒COME.

camel *n* chameau *m*.

camera *n* appareil(-photo) *m*; (TV, cinema) caméra *f*; **in ~** à huis clos. **~man** *n* (*pl* **-men**) cadreur *m*, cameraman *m*.

camouflage *n* camouflage *m*. ● *vt* camoufler.

camp *n* camp *m*. ● *vi* camper.

campaign *n* campagne *f*. ● *vi* faire campagne.

camper *n* campeur/-euse *m/f*. **~(-van)** *n* camping-car *m*.

camping *n* camping *m*; **go ~** faire du camping.

campsite *n* camping *m*.

campus *n* (*pl* **~es**) campus *m*.

can[1]

infinitive **be able to**; *present* **can**; *present negative* **can't**, **cannot** (*formal*); *past* **could**; *past participle* **been able to**

● *auxiliary verb*

- pouvoir; **where ~ I buy stamps?** où est-ce que je peux acheter des timbres?; **she can't come** elle ne peut pas venir.
- (be allowed to) pouvoir; **~ I smoke?** est-ce que je peux fumer?
- (know how to) savoir; **she ~ swim** elle sait nager; **he can't drive** il ne sait pas conduire.
- (with verbs of perception) **I ~ hear you** je t'entends; **~ they see us?** est-ce qu'ils nous voient?

can[2] *n* (for food) boîte *f*; (of petrol) bidon *m*. ● *vt* (*pt* **canned**) mettre en conserve.

Canada *n* Canada *m*.

Canadian *n* Canadien/-ne *m/f*. ● *a* canadien.

canal *n* canal *m*.

canary *n* canari *m*.

cancel *vt/i* (*pt* **cancelled**) (call off, revoke) annuler; (cross out) barrer; (a stamp) oblitérer; **~ out** (se) neutraliser. **cancellation** *n* annulation *f*.

cancer *n* cancer *m*; **have ~** avoir un cancer.

Cancer *n* Cancer *m*.

cancerous *a* cancéreux.

candid *a* franc.

candidate *n* candidat/-e *m/f*.

candle *n* bougie *f*; (in church) cierge *m*. **~stick** *n* bougeoir *m*.

candy *n* (US) bonbon(s) *m*(*pl*). **~-floss** *n* barbe *f* à papa.

cane *n* canne *f*; (for baskets) rotin

m; (for punishment) badine *f*. ● *vt* donner des coups de badine à.

canister *n* boîte *f*.

cannabis *n* cannabis *m*.

cannibal *n* cannibale *mf*.

cannon *n* (*pl* ~ *or* ~**s**) canon *m* ~**-ball** *n* boulet *m* de canon.

cannot = CAN NOT.

canoe *n* canoë *m*. ● *vi* faire du canoë. **canoeist** *n* canoéiste *mf*.

canon *n* (clergyman) chanoine *m*; (rule) canon *m*.

can-opener *n* ouvre-boîtes *m inv*.

canopy *n* dais *m*; (for bed) baldaquin *m*.

can't = CAN NOT.

canteen *n* (restaurant) cantine *f*; (flask) bidon *m*.

canter *n* petit galop *m*. ● *vi* aller au petit galop.

canvas *n* toile *f*.

canvass *vt*/*i* (Comm, Pol) faire du démarchage (auprès de); ~ **opinion** sonder l'opinion.

canyon *n* cañon *m*.

cap *n* (hat) casquette *f*; (of bottle, tube) bouchon *m*; (of beer or milk bottle) capsule *f*; (of pen) capuchon *m*; (for toy gun) amorce *f*. ● *vt* (*pt* **capped**) couronner.

capability *n* capacité *f*.

capable *a* (person) compétent; ~ **of doing** capable de faire.

capacity *n* capacité *f*; **in my** ~ **as a doctor** en ma qualité de médecin.

cape *n* (cloak) cape *f*; (Geog) cap *m*.

caper *vi* gambader. ● *n* (leap) cabriole *f*; (funny film) comédie *f*; (Culin) câpre *f*.

capital *a* (*letter*) majuscule; (*offence*) capital. ● *n* (town) capitale *f*; (money) capital *m*; ~ **(letter)** majuscule *f*.

capitalism *n* capitalisme *m*.

capitalize *vi* ~ **on** tirer parti de.

capitulate *vi* capituler.

Capricorn *n* Capricorne *m*.

capsize *vt*/*i* (faire) chavirer.

capsule *n* capsule *f*.

captain *n* capitaine *m*.

caption *n* (under photo) légende *f*; (subtitle) sous-titre *m*.

captivate *vt* captiver.

captive *a* & *n* captif/-ive (*m*/*f*). **captivity** *n* captivité *f*.

capture *vt* (*person, animal*) capturer; (*moment, likeness*) saisir. ● *n* capture *f*.

car *n* voiture *f*. ● *a* (*industry, insurance*) automobile; (*accident, phone*) de voiture; (*journey, chase*) en voiture.

caravan *n* caravane *f*.

carbohydrate *n* hydrate *m* de carbone.

carbon *n* carbone *m*.

carburettor *n* carburateur *m*.

card *n* carte *f*.

cardboard *n* carton *m*.

cardiac *a* cardiaque; ~ **arrest** arrêt *m* du cœur.

cardigan *n* cardigan *m*.

cardinal *a* (*sin*) capital; (*rule*) fondamental; (*number*) cardinal. ● *n* cardinal *m*.

card-index *n* fichier *m*.

care *n* (attention) soin *m*, attention *f*; (worry) souci *m*; (looking after) soins *mpl*; **take** ~ **of** (deal with) s'occuper de; (be careful with) prendre soin de; **take** ~ **to do sth** faire bien attention à faire qch. ● *vi* ~ **about** s'intéresser à; ~ **for** s'occuper de; (invalid) soigner; ~ **to do** vouloir faire; **I don't** ~ ça m'est égal.

career *n* carrière *f*. ● *vi* ~ **in/out** entrer/sortir à toute vitesse.

carefree *a* insouciant.

careful *a* prudent; (*research, study*) méticuleux; (**be**) ~**!** (fais) attention! **carefully** *adv* avec soin; (cautiously) prudemment.

careless *a* négligent; (work) bâclé.

caress *n* caresse *f*. ● *vt* caresser.

caretaker *n* concierge *mf*. ● *a* (*president*) par intérim.

car ferry *n* ferry *m*.

cargo *n* (*pl* ~**es**) chargement *m*; (Naut) cargaison *f*.

Caribbean *a* des Caraïbes, des Antilles. ● *n* **the** ~ (sea) la mer des Antilles; (islands) les Antilles *fpl*.

caring *a* affectueux. ● *n* affection *f*.

carnal *a* charnel.

carnation *n* œillet *m*.

carnival *n* carnaval *m*.

carol *n* chant *m* de Noël.

carp *n inv* carpe *f*. ● *vi* maugréer.

car-park *n* parc *m* de stationnement, parking *m*.

carpenter *n* (joiner) menuisier *m*; (builder) charpentier *m*. **carpentry** *n* menuiserie *f*; (structural) charpenterie *f*.

carpet *n* (fitted) moquette *f*; (loose) tapis *m*. ● *vt* (*pt* **carpeted**) mettre de la moquette dans.

carriage *n* (rail) wagon *m*; (ceremonial) carrosse *m*; (of goods) transport *m*; (cost) port *m*.

carriageway *n* chaussée *f*.

carrier *n* transporteur *m*; (Med) porteur/-euse *m/f*; ~ (**bag**) sac *m* en plastique.

carrot *n* carotte *f*.

carry *vt/i* porter; (*goods*) transporter; (*involve*) comporter; (*motion*) voter; **be carried away** s'emballer. □ ~ **off** emporter; (prize) remporter; ~ **on** (continue) continuer; (*business*) conduire; (*conversation*) mener; ~ **out** (*order, plan*) exécuter; (*duty*) remplir; (*experiment, operation, repair*) effectuer. ~**-cot** *n* porte-bébé *m*.

car sharing *n* covoiturage *m*.

cart *n* charrette *f*. ● *vt* (*heavy bag* ▯) trimballer ▯.

carton *n* (box) boîte *f*; (of yoghurt, cream) pot *m*; (of cigarettes) cartouche *f*.

cartoon *n* dessin *m* humoristique; (cinema) dessin *m* animé; (strip cartoon) bande *f* dessinée.

cartridge *n* cartouche *f*.

carve *vt* tailler; (meat) découper.

car-wash *n* lavage *m* automatique.

cascade *n* cascade *f*. ● *vi* tomber en cascade.

case *n* cas *m*; (Jur) affaire *f*; (suitcase) valise *f*; (crate) caisse *f*; (for spectacles) étui *m*; (**just**) **in** ~ au cas où; **in** ~ **he comes** au cas où il viendrait; **in** ~ **of fire** en cas d'incendie; **in any** ~ de toute façon; **the** ~ **for sth** les arguments *mpl* en faveur de qch; **the** ~ **for the defence** la défense.

cash *n* espèces *fpl*, argent *m*; **in** ~ en espèces. ● *a* (*price*) comptant. ● *vt* encaisser; ~ **in** (**on**) profiter (de). ~ **desk** *n* caisse *f*. ~ **dispenser** *n* distributeur *m* de billets.

cashew *n* cajou *m*.

cash-flow *n* marge *f* brute d'auto-financement.

cashier *n* caissier/-ière *m/f*.

cashmere *n* cachemire *m*.

cash: ~ **point** *n* distributeur *m* de billets. ~ **point card** *n* carte *f* de retrait. ~ **register** *n* caisse *f* enregistreuse.

casino *n* casino *m*.

casket *n* (box) coffret *m*; (coffin) cercueil *m*.

casserole *n* (pan) daubière *f*; (food) ragoût *m*.

cassette *n* cassette *f*.

cast *vt* (*pt* **cast**) (*object, glance*) jeter; (*shadow*) projeter; (*metal*) couler; ~ (**off**) (shed) se dépouiller de; ~ **one's vote** voter; ~ **iron** fonte *f*. ● *n* (cinema, Theat, TV) distribution *f*; (mould) moule *m*; (Med) plâtre *m*.

castaway *n* naufragé/-e *m/f*.

cast-iron *a* de fonte; (fig) en béton.

castle *n* château *m*; (chess) tour *f*.

cast-offs *npl* vieux vêtements *mpl*.

castor *n* (wheel) roulette *f*.

castrate *vt* châtrer.

casual *a* (informal) décontracté; (*remark*) désinvolte; (*acquaintance*) de passage; (*work*) temporaire. **casually** *adv* (*remark*) d'un air détaché; (*dress*) simplement.

casualty *n* victime *f*; (part of hospital) urgences *fpl*.

cat *n* chat *m*; (feline) félin *m*.

catalogue *n* catalogue *m*. ● *vt* dresser un catalogue de.

catalyst *n* catalyseur *m*.

catalytic *a* ~ **converter** pot *m* catalytique.

catapult *n* lance-pierres *m inv*. ● *vt* projeter.

cataract *n* (Med, Geog) cataracte *f*.

catarrh *n* catarrhe *m*.

catastrophe *n* catastrophe *f*.

catch *vt* (*pt* **caught**) attraper; (*bus, plane*) prendre; (understand) saisir; ~ **sb doing** surprendre qn en train de faire; ~ **fire** prendre feu; ~ **sight of** apercevoir; ~ **sb's attention/eye** attirer l'attention de qn. ● *vi* (get stuck) se prendre (**in** dans); (start to burn) prendre. ● *n* (fastening) fermeture *f*; (drawback) piège *m*; (in sport) prise *f*. □ ~ **on** devenir populaire; ~ **out** prendre de court; ~ **up** rattraper son retard; ~ **up with sb** rattraper qn.

catching *a* contagieux.

catchment *n* ~ **area** (School) secteur *m*.

catch-phrase *n* formule *f* favorite.

catchy *a* entraînant.

category *n* catégorie *f*.

cater *vi* organiser des réceptions; ~ **for/to** (*guests*) accueillir; (*needs*) pourvoir à; (*reader*) s'adresser à. **caterer** *n* traiteur *m*.

caterpillar *n* chenille *f*.

cathedral *n* cathédrale *f*.

catholic *a* éclectique. **Catholic** *a* & *n* catholique (*mf*). **Catholicism** *n* catholicisme *m*.

Catseye® *n* plot *m* rétroréfléchissant.

cattle *npl* bétail *m*.

catty *a* méchant.

caught ⇒CATCH.

cauliflower *n* chou-fleur *m*.

cause *n* cause *f*; (reason) raison *f*, motif *m*. ● *vt* causer; ~ **sth to grow/move** faire pousser/bouger qch.

causeway *n* chaussée *f*.

caution *n* prudence *f*; (warning) avertissement *m*. ● *vt* avertir. **cautious** *a* prudent. **cautiously** *adv* prudemment.

cave *n* grotte *f*. ● *vi* ~ **in** s'effondrer; (agree) céder. ~**man** *n* (*pl* **-men**) homme *m* des cavernes.

cavern *n* caverne *f*.

caviare *n* caviar *m*.

caving *n* spéléologie *f*.

CD *abbr* (**compact disc**) disque *m* compact, CD *m*.

CD-ROM *n* disque *m* optique compact, CD-ROM *m*.

cease *vt/i* cesser. ~**-fire** *n* cessez-le-feu *m inv*.

C

cedar *n* cèdre *m*.
cedilla *n* cédille *f*.
ceiling *n* plafond *m*.
celebrate *vt* (*occasion*) fêter; (*Easter, mass*) célébrer. ● *vi* faire la fête. **celebrated** *a* célèbre. **celebration** *n* fête *f*.
celebrity *n* célébrité *f*.
celery *n* céleri *m*.
cell *n* cellule *f*; (Electr) élément *m*.
cellar *n* cave *f*.
cellist *n* violoncelliste *mf*. **cello** *n* violoncelle *m*.
Celt *n* Celte *mf*.
cement *n* ciment *m*. ● *vt* cimenter. **~-mixer** *n* bétonnière *f*.
cemetery *n* cimetière *m*.
censor *n* censeur *m*. ● *vt* censurer.
censure *n* censure *f*. ● *vt* critiquer.
census *n* recensement *m*.
cent *n* (coin) cent *m*.
centenary *n* centenaire *m*.
centigrade *a* centigrade.
centilitre, (US) **centiliter** *n* centilitre *m*.
centimetre, (US) **centimeter** *n* centimètre *m*.
centipede *n* millepattes *m inv*.
central *a* central; **~ heating** chauffage *m* central; **~ locking** fermeture *f* centralisée des portes. **centralize** *vt* centraliser. **centrally** *adv* (situated) au centre.
centre, (US) **center** *n* centre *m*. ● *vt* (*pt* **centred**) centrer. ● *vi* **~ on** tourner autour de.
century *n* siècle *m*.
ceramic *a* (*art*) céramique; (*object*) en céramique.
cereal *n* céréale *f*.
ceremonial *a* (*dress*) de cérémonie. ● *n* cérémonial *m*. **ceremony** *n* cérémonie *f*.
certain *a* certain; **for ~** avec certitude; **make ~ of** s'assurer de. **certainly** *adv* certainement. **certainty** *n* certitude *f*.
certificate *n* certificat *m*.
certify *vt* certifier.
cesspit, **cesspool** *n* fosse *f* d'aisances.
chafe *vt/i* frotter (contre).
chagrin *n* dépit *m*.
chain *n* chaîne *f*; **~ reaction** réaction *f* en chaîne; **~ store** magasin *m* à succursales multiples. ● *vt* enchaîner. **~-smoke** *vi* fumer sans arrêt.
chair *n* chaise *f*; (armchair) fauteuil *m*; (Univ) chaire *f*; (chairperson) président/-e *m/f*. ● *vt* (preside over) présider. **~man** *n* (*pl* **-men**) président/-e *m/f*. **~woman** *n* (*pl* **-women**) présidente *f*.
chalk *n* craie *f*.
challenge *n* défi *m*; (opportunity) challenge *m*. ● *vt* (summon) défier (**to do** de faire); (question truth of) contester. **challenger** *n* (Sport) challenger *m*. **challenging** *a* stimulant.
chamber *n* (old use) chambre *f*. **~maid** *n* femme *f* de chambre. **~ music** *n* musique *f* de chambre. **~-pot** *n* pot *m* de chambre.
champagne *n* champagne *m*.
champion *n* champion/-ne *m/f*. ● *vt* défendre. **championship** *n* championnat *m*.
chance *n* (luck) hasard *m*; (opportunity) occasion *f*; (likelihood) chances *fpl*; (risk) risque *m*; **by ~** par hasard; **by any ~** par hasard; **~s are that** il est probable que. ● *a* fortuit. ● *vt* **~ doing** prendre le risque de faire; **~ it** tenter sa chance.
chancellor *n* chancelier *m*; **C~ of the Exchequer** Chancelier de l'Échiquier.
chandelier *n* lustre *m*.

change *vt* (alter) changer; (exchange) échanger (**for** contre); (*money*) changer; ~ **trains/one's dress** changer de train/de robe; ~ **one's mind** changer d'avis. ● *vi* changer; (change clothes) se changer; ~ **into** se transformer en; ~ **over** passer (**to** à). ● *n* changement *m*; (money) monnaie *f*; **a** ~ **for the better** une amélioration; **a** ~ **for the worse** un changement en pire; **a** ~ **of clothes** des vêtements de rechange; **for a** ~ pour changer. **changeable** *a* changeant. **changing room** *n* (in shop) cabine *f* d'essayage; (Sport) vestiaire *m*.

channel *n* (for liquid, information) canal *m*; (TV) chaîne *f*; (groove) rainure *f*. ● *vt* (*pt* **channelled**) canaliser. **C**~ *n* **the** (**English**) **C**~ la Manche; **the C**~ **tunnel** le tunnel sous la Manche; **the C**~ **Islands** les îles *fpl* Anglo-Normandes

chant *n* (Relig) mélopée *f*; (of demonstrators) chant *m* scandé. ● *vt/i* scander; (Relig) psalmodier.

chaos *n* chaos *m*.

chap *n* (man ⓘ) type *m* ⓘ.

chapel *n* chapelle *f*.

chaplain *n* aumônier *m*.

chapped *a* gercé.

chapter *n* chapitre *m*.

char *vt* (*pt* **charred**) carboniser.

character *n* caractère *m*; (in novel, play) personnage *m*; **of good** ~ de bonne réputation.

characteristic *a & n* caractéristique (*f*).

charcoal *n* charbon *m* de bois; (art) fusain *m*.

charge *n* (fee) frais *mpl*; (Mil) charge *f*; (Jur) inculpation *f*; (task, custody) charge *f*; **in** ~ **of** responsable de; **take** ~ **of** prendre en charge, se charger de. ● *vt* (*customer*) faire payer; (*enemy, gun*) charger; (Jur) inculper (**with** de); ~ **£20 an hour** prendre 20 livres de l'heure; ~ **card** carte *f* d'achat. ● *vi* faire payer; (*bull*) foncer; (*person*) se précipiter.

charisma *n* charisme *m*.

charismatic *a* charismatique.

charitable *a* charitable. **charity** *n* charité *f*; (organization) organisation *f* caritative.

charm *n* charme *m*; (trinket) amulette *f*. ● *vt* charmer. **charming** *a* charmant.

chart *n* (graph) graphique *m*; (table) tableau *m*; (map) carte *f*. ● *vt* (route) porter sur la carte.

charter *n* charte *f*; ~ (**flight**) charter *m*. ● *vt* affréter; ~**ed accountant** expert-comptable *m*.

chase *vt* poursuivre; ~ **away** *or* **off** chasser. ● *vi* courir (**after** après). ● *n* chasse *f*.

chassis *n* châssis *m*.

chastise *vt* châtier.

chastity *n* chasteté *f*.

chat *n* conversation *f*; **have a** ~ bavarder; ~ **show** talk-show *m*; ~ **mode** (Internet) mode *m* causerie. ● *vi* (*pt* **chatted**) bavarder. □ ~ **up** ⓘ draguer ⓘ.

chatter *n* bavardage *m*. ● *vi* bavarder; **his teeth are** ~**ing** il claque des dents. ~**box** *n* bavard/-e *m/f*.

chatty *a* bavard.

chauffeur *n* chauffeur *m*.

chauvinist *n* chauvin/-e *m/f*; macho *m*.

cheap *a* bon marché *inv*; (*fare, rate*) réduit; (*joke, gimmick*) facile; ~**er** meilleur marché *inv*. **cheapen** *vt* déprécier. **cheaply** *adv* à bas prix. **cheapness** *n* bas prix *m*.

cheat *vi* tricher. ● *vt* tromper. ● *n* tricheur/-euse *m/f*.

check *vt/i* vérifier; (*tickets, rises, inflation*) contrôler; (stop) arrêter;

(tick off: US) cocher. ● *n* contrôle *m*; (curb) frein *m*; (chess) échec *m*; (pattern) carreaux *mpl*; (bill: US) addition *f*; (cheque: US) chèque *m*. □ ~ **in** remplir la fiche; (at airport) enregistrer; ~ **out** partir; ~ **sth out** vérifier qch; ~ **up** vérifier; ~ **up on** (*story*) vérifier; (*person*) faire une enquête sur.

check: ~**-in** *n* enregistrement *m*. **checking account** *n* (US) compte *m* courant. ~**-list** *n* liste *f* de contrôle. ~**mate** *n* échec *m* et mat. ~**-out** *n* caisse *f*. ~**-point** *n* contrôle *m*. ~**-up** *n* examen *m* médical.

cheek *n* joue *f*; (impudence) culot *m* ⊡. **cheeky** *a* effronté.

cheer *n* gaieté *f*; ~**s** acclamations *fpl*; (when drinking) à la vôtre. ● *vt/i* applaudir; ~ **sb** (**up**) (gladden) remonter le moral à qn; ~ **up** prendre courage. **cheerful** *a* joyeux. **cheerfulness** *n* gaieté *f*.

cheerio *interj* ⊡ salut ⊡.

cheese *n* fromage *m*.

cheetah *n* guépard *m*.

chef *n* chef *m*.

chemical *a* chimique. ● *n* produit *m* chimique.

chemist *n* pharmacien/-ne *m/f*; (scientist) chimiste *mf*; ~**'s** (**shop**) pharmacie *f*. **chemistry** *n* chimie *f*.

cheque *n* chèque *m*. ~**-book** *n* chéquier *m*. ~ **card** *n* carte *f* bancaire.

chequered *a* (pattern) à damiers; (fig) en dents de scie.

cherish *vt* chérir; (hope) caresser.

cherry *n* cerise *f*; (tree, wood) cerisier *m*.

chess *n* échecs *mpl*. ~**-board** *n* échiquier *m*.

chest *n* (Anat) poitrine *f*; (box) coffre *m*; ~ **of drawers** commode *f*.

chestnut *n* (nut) marron *m*, châtaigne *f*; (tree) marronnier *m*; (sweet) châtaignier *m*.

chew *vt* mâcher.

chic *a* chic *inv*.

chick *n* poussin *m*.

chicken *n* poulet *m*. ● *a* ⊠ froussard. ● *vi* ~ **out** ⊠ se dégonfler. ~**-pox** *n* varicelle *f*.

chick-pea *n* pois *m* chiche.

chicory *n* (for salad) endive *f*; (in coffee) chicorée *f*.

chief *n* chef *m*. ● *a* principal. **chiefly** *adv* principalement.

chilblain *n* engelure *f*.

child *n* (*pl* **children**) enfant *mf*. ~**birth** *n* accouchement *m*. **childhood** *n* enfance *f*. **childish** *a* puéril. **childless** *a* sans enfants. **childlike** *a* enfantin. ~**-minder** *n* nourrice *f*.

Chile *n* Chili *m*.

chill *n* froid *m*; (Med) refroidissement *m*. ● *a* froid. ● *vt* (*person*) faire frissonner; (*wine*) rafraîchir; (*food*) mettre à refroidir.

chilli *n* (*pl* ~**es**) piment *m*.

chilly *a* froid; **it's** ~ il fait froid.

chime *n* carillon *m*. ● *vt/i* carillonner.

chimney *n* cheminée *f*. ~**-sweep** *n* ramoneur *m*.

chimpanzee *n* chimpanzé *m*.

chin *n* menton *m*.

china *n* porcelaine *f*.

China *n* Chine *f*.

Chinese *n* (person) Chinois/-e *m/f*; (Ling) chinois *m*. ● *a* chinois.

chip *n* (on plate) ébréchure *f*; (piece) éclat *m*; (of wood) copeau *m*; (Culin) frite *f*; (Comput) puce *f*; (**potato**) ~**s** (US) chips *fpl*. ● *vt/i* (*pt* **chipped**) (s')ébrécher; ~ **in** ⊡ dire son mot; (with money) contribuer.

chiropodist *n* pédicure *mf*.

chirp *n* pépiement *m*. ● *vi* pépier.

chirpy *a* gai.

chisel *n* ciseau *m*. ●*vt* (*pt* **chiselled**) ciseler.
chit *n* note *f*; (voucher) bon *m*.
chitchat *n* [!] bavardage *m*.
chivalrous *a* galant.
chives *npl* ciboulette *f*.
chlorine *n* chlore *m*.
choc-ice *n* esquimau *m*.
chock-a-block *a* plein à craquer.
chocolate *n* chocolat *m*.
choice *n* choix *m*. ●*a* de choix.
choir *n* chœur *m*. **~boy** *n* jeune choriste *m*.
choke *vt/i* (s')étrangler; **~ (up)** boucher. ●*n* starter *m*.
cholesterol *n* cholestérol *m*.
choose *vt/i* (*pt* **chose**; *pp* **chosen**) choisir; **~ to do** décider de faire. **choosy** *a* difficile.
chop *vt/i* (*pt* **chopped**) (*wood*) couper; (*food*) hacher; **chopping board** planche *f* à découper; **~ down** abattre. ●*n* (meat) côtelette *f*. **chopper** *n* hachoir *m*; [!] hélico *m* [!].
choppy *a* (*sea*) agité.
chopstick *n* baguette *f* (*chinoise*).
chord *n* (Mus) accord *m*.
chore *n* (routine) tâche *f*; (unpleasant) corvée *f*.
chortle *n* gloussement *m*. ●*vi* glousser.
chorus *n* chœur *m*; (of song) refrain *m*.
chose, chosen ⇨CHOOSE.
Christ *n* le Christ.
christen *vt* baptiser. **christening** *n* baptême *m*.
Christian *a* & *n* chrétien/-ne (*m*/*f*); **~ name** nom *m* de baptême. **Christianity** *n* christianisme *m*.
Christmas *n* Noël *m*; **~ Day/Eve** le jour/la veille de Noël. ●*a* (*card, tree*) de Noël.
chronic *a* (*situation, disease*) chronique; (bad [!]) nul.
chronicle *n* chronique *f*.
chronological *a* chronologique.
chrysanthemum *n* chrysanthème *m*.
chubby *a* (**-ier**, **-iest**) potelé.
chuck *vt* [!] lancer; **~ away** *or* **out** [!] balancer.
chuckle *n* gloussement *m*. ●*vi* glousser.
chuffed *a* [!] vachement content [!].
chunk *n* morceau *m*. **chunky** *a* (*sweater, jewellery*) gros; (*person*) costaud.
church *n* église *f*. **~goer** *n* pratiquant/-e *m*/*f*. **~yard** *n* cimetière *m*.
churn *n* baratte *f*; (milk-can) bidon *m*. ●*vt* baratter; **~ out** produire en série.
chute *n* toboggan *m*; (for rubbish) vide-ordures *m inv*.
chutney *n* condiment *m* aigre-doux.
cider *n* cidre *m*.
cigar *n* cigare *m*.
cigarette *n* cigarette *f*; **~ end** mégot *m*.
cinder *n* cendre *f*.
cinema *n* cinéma *m*.
cinnamon *n* cannelle *f*.
circle *n* cercle *m*; (Theat) balcon *m*. ●*vt* (go round) tourner autour de; (word, error) encercler. ●*vi* tourner en rond.
circuit *n* circuit *m*. **~ board** *n* carte *f* de circuit imprimé. **~-breaker** *n* disjoncteur *m*.
circuitous *a* indirect.
circular *a* & *n* circulaire (*f*).
circulate *vt/i* (faire) circuler. **circulation** *n* circulation *f*; (of newspaper) tirage *m*.
circumcise *vt* circoncire.

circumference *n* circonférence *f*.

circumflex *n* circonflexe *m*.

circumstance *n* circonstance *f*; **~s** (financial) situation *f*; **under no ~s** en aucun cas.

circus *n* cirque *m*.

cistern *n* réservoir *m*.

citation *n* citation *f*. **cite** *vt* citer.

citizen *n* citoyen/-ne *m*/*f*; (of town) habitant/-e *m*/*f*. **citizenship** *n* nationalité *f*.

citrus *a* **~ fruit**(**s**) agrumes *mpl*; **~ tree** citrus *m*.

city *n* (grande) ville *f*.

civic *a* (*official*) municipal; (*pride, duty*) civique.

civil *a* civil. **~ disobedience** *n* résistance *f* passive. **~ engineer** *n* ingénieur *m* des travaux publics.

civilian *a* & *n* civil/-e (*m*/*f*).

civilization *n* civilisation *f*. **civilize** *vt* civiliser.

civil: **~ law** *n* droit *m* civil. **~ liberties** *npl* libertés *fpl* individuelles. **~ rights** *npl* droits *mpl* civils. **~ servant** *n* fonctionnaire *mf*. **~ service** *n* fonction *f* publique. **~ war** *n* guerre *f* civile.

clad *a* **~ in** vêtu de.

claim *vt* (demand) revendiquer; (assert) prétendre. ● *n* revendication *f*; (assertion) affirmation *f*; (for insurance) réclamation *f*; (right) droit *m*. **claimant** *n* (of benefits) demandeur/-euse *m*/*f*.

clairvoyant *n* voyant/-e *m*/*f*.

clam *n* palourde *f*.

clamber *vi* grimper.

clammy *a* (**-ier**, **-iest**) moite.

clamour *n* clameur *f*. ● *vi* **~ for** réclamer.

clamp *n* valet *m*; (Med) pince *f*; (**wheel**) **~** sabot *m* de Denver. ● *vt* cramponner; (*jaw*) serrer; (*car*) mettre un sabot de Denver à; **~ down on** faire de la répression contre.

clan *n* clan *m*.

clang *n* son *m* métallique.

clap *vt*/*i* (*pt* **clapped**) applaudir; (put forcibly) mettre; **~ one's hands** frapper dans ses mains. ● *n* applaudissement *m*; (of thunder) coup *m*.

claret *n* bordeaux *m* rouge.

clarification *n* clarification *f*. **clarify** *vt*/*i* (se) clarifier.

clarinet *n* clarinette *f*.

clarity *n* clarté *f*.

clash *n* choc *m*; (fig) conflit *m*. ● *vi* (*metal objects*) s'entrechoquer; (*armies*) s'affronter; (*interests*) être incompatibles; (*meetings*) avoir lieu en même temps; (*colours*) jurer.

clasp *n* (fastener) fermoir *m*. ● *vt* serrer.

class *n* classe *f*. ● *vt* classer; **~ sb/sth as** assimiler qn/qch à.

classic *a* & *n* classique (*m*); **~s** (Univ) lettres *fpl* classiques. **classical** *a* classique.

classified *a* (*information*) secret; **~ (ad)** petite annonce *f*.

classroom *n* salle *f* de classe.

clatter *n* cliquetis *m*. ● *vi* cliqueter.

clause *n* clause *f*; (Gram) proposition *f*.

claw *n* (of animal, small bird) griffe *f*; (of bird of prey) serre *f*; (of lobster) pince *f*. ● *vt* griffer.

clay *n* argile *f*.

clean *a* propre; (shape, stroke) net. ● *adv* complètement. ● *vt* nettoyer; **~ one's teeth** se brosser les dents. ● *vi* **~ up** faire le nettoyage. **cleaner** *n* (at home) femme *f* de ménage; (industrial) agent *m* de nettoyage; (of clothes) teinturier/-ière *m/f*. **cleanliness** *n* propreté *f*. **cleanly** *adv* proprement; (sharply) nettement.

cleanse *vt* nettoyer; (fig) purifier.

clean-shaven *a* glabre.

clear *a* (*explanation*) clair; (*need, sign*) évident; (*glass*) transparent; (*profit*) net, (*road*) dégagé; **make sth ~** être très clair sur qch; **~ of** (away from) à l'écart de. ● *adv* complètement; **stand ~ of** s'éloigner de. ● *vt* (free) dégager (**of** de); (*table*) débarrasser; (*building*) évacuer; (*cheque*) compenser; (jump over) franchir; (*debt*) liquider; (Jur) disculper. ● *vi* (*fog*) se dissiper; (*cheque*) être compensé. □ **~ away** *or* **off** (remove) enlever; **~ off** *or* **out** 🄸 décamper; **~ out** (clean) nettoyer; **~ up** (tidy) ranger; (*mystery*) éclaircir; (*weather*) s'éclaircir.

clearance *n* (permission) autorisation *f*; (space) espace *m*; **~ sale** liquidation *f*.

clear-cut *a* net.

clearing *n* clairière *f*.

clearly *adv* clairement.

clef *n* (Mus) clé *f*.

cleft *n* fissure *f*.

clench *vt* serrer.

clergy *n* clergé *m*. **~man** *n* (*pl* **-men**) ecclésiastique *m*.

cleric *n* clerc *m*. **clerical** *a* (Relig) clérical; (*staff, work*) de bureau.

clerk *n* employé/-e *m/f* de bureau; (US) (**sales**) **~** vendeur/ -euse *m/f*.

clever *a* intelligent; (skilful) habile.

click *n* déclic *m*. ● *vi* faire un déclic; (people 🄸) sympathiser. ● *vt* (*heels, tongue*) faire claquer.

client *n* client/-e *m/f*.

clientele *n* clientèle *f*.

cliff *n* falaise *f*.

climate *n* climat *m*.

climax *n* (of story, contest) point *m* culminant; (sexual) orgasme *m*.

climb *vt* grimper; (*steps*) monter; (*tree, ladder*) grimper à; (*mountain*) faire l'ascension de. ● *vi* grimper; **~ into** (*car*) monter dans; **~ into bed** se mettre au lit. ● *n* (of mountain) escalade *f*; (steep hill, rise) montée *f*. □ **~ down** (fig) reculer. **climber** *n* (Sport) alpiniste *mf*.

clinch *vt* (*deal*) conclure; (*victory, order*) décrocher.

cling *vi* (*pt* **clung**) se cramponner (**to** à); (stick) coller. **~-film** *n* scellofrais® *m*.

clinic *n* centre *m* médical; (private) clinique *f*. **clinical** *a* clinique.

clink *n* tintement *m*. ● *vt/i* (faire) tinter.

clip *n* (for paper) trombone *m*; (for hair) barrette *f*; (for tube) collier *m*; (of film) extrait *m*. ● *vt* (*pt* **clipped**) (fasten) attacher (**to** à); (cut) couper.

clippers *npl* tondeuse *f*; (for nails) coupe-ongles *m inv*.

clipping *n* (from press) coupure *f* de presse.

cloak *n* cape *f*; (man's) houppelande *f*. **~room** *n* vestiaire *m*; (toilet) toilettes *fpl*.

clobber *n* 🄸 attirail *m*. ● *vt* (hit 🄸) tabasser 🄸.

clock *n* pendule *f*; (large) horloge *f*. ● *vi* **~ on/in** *or* **off/out** pointer; **~ up** (*miles*) faire. **~-tower** *n* beffroi *m*. **~wise** *a & adv* dans le sens des aiguilles d'une montre.

clockwork *n* mécanisme *m*. ● *a* mécanique.

clog *n* sabot *m*. ● *vt/i* (*pt* **clogged**) (se) boucher.

cloister *n* cloître *m*.

close[1] *a* (*friend, relative*) proche (**to** de); (*link, collaboration*) étroit; (*examination*) minutieux; (*result, match*) serré; (*weather*) lourd; **~**

C

together (crowded) serrés; ~ **by**, ~ **at hand** tout près; **have a ~ shave** l'échapper belle; **keep a ~ watch on** surveiller de près. ● *adv* près. ● *n* (street) impasse *f*.

close[2] *vt* fermer; (*meeting, case*) mettre fin à. ● *vi* se fermer; (*shop*) fermer; (*meeting, play*) prendre fin. ● *n* fin *f*.

closely *adv* (follow) de près. **closeness** *n* proximité *f*.

closet *n* (US) placard *m*.

close-up *n* gros plan *m*.

closure *n* fermeture *f*.

clot *n* (of blood) caillot *m*; (in sauce) grumeau *m*. ● *vt/i* (*pt* **clotted**) (se) coaguler.

cloth *n* (fabric) tissu *m*; (duster) chiffon *m*; (table-cloth) nappe *f*.

clothe *vt* vêtir.

clothes *npl* vêtements *mpl*. **~-hanger** *n* cintre *m*. **~-line** *n* corde *f* à linge.

clothing *n* vêtements *mpl*.

cloud *n* nuage *m*. ● *vi* ~ (**over**) se couvrir (de nuages); (*face*) s'assombrir. **cloudy** *a* (*sky*) couvert; (*liquid*) trouble.

clout *n* (blow) coup *m* de poing; (power) influence *f*. ● *vt* frapper.

clove *n* clou *m* de girofle; ~ **of garlic** gousse *f* d'ail.

clover *n* trèfle *m*.

clown *n* clown *m*. ● *vi* faire le clown.

club *n* (group) club *m*; (weapon) massue *f*; (**golf**) ~ club *m* (de golf); **~s** (cards) trèfle *m*. ● *vt/i* (*pt* **clubbed**) matraquer. □ ~ **together** cotiser.

cluck *vi* glousser.

clue *n* indice *m*; (in crossword) définition *f*; **I haven't a ~** 🄸 je n'en ai pas la moindre idée.

clump *n* massif *m*.

clumsy *a* (**-ier, -iest**) maladroit; (*tool*) peu commode.

clung ⇒CLING.

cluster *n* (of people, islands) groupe *m*; (of flowers, berries) grappe *f*. ● *vi* se grouper.

clutch *vt* (hold) serrer fort; (grasp) saisir. ● *vi* ~ **at** (try to grasp) essayer de saisir. ● *n* (Auto) embrayage *m*; (of eggs) couveé *f*; (of people) groupe *m*.

clutter *n* désordre *m*. ● *vt* ~ (**up**) encombrer.

coach *n* autocar *m*; (of train) wagon *m*; (horse-drawn) carrosse *m*; (Sport) entraîneur/-euse *m/f*. ● *vt* (*team*) entraîner; (*pupil*) donner des leçons particulières à.

coal *n* charbon *m*. **~field** *n* bassin *m* houiller. **~-mine** *n* mine *f* de charbon.

coarse *a* grossier.

coast *n* côte *f*. ● *vi* (car, bicycle) descendre en roue libre. **coastal** *a* côtier.

coast: **~guard** *n* (person) gardecôte *m*; (organization) gendarmerie *f* maritime. **~line** *n* littoral *m*.

coat *n* manteau *m*; (of animal) pelage *m*; (of paint) couche *f*; ~ **of arms** armoiries *fpl*. ● *vt* enduire, couvrir; (with chocolate) enrober (**with** de). **coating** *n* couche *f*.

coax *vt* cajoler.

cob *n* (of corn) épi *m*.

cobbler *n* cordonnier *m*.

cobblestones *npl* pavés *mpl*.

cobweb *n* toile *f* d'araignée.

cocaine *n* cocaïne *f*.

cock *n* (rooster) coq *m*; (oiseau) mâle *m*. ● *vt* (*gun*) armer; (*ears*) dresser.

cockerel *n* jeune coq *m*.

cockle *n* (Culin) coque *f*.

cock: **~pit** *n* poste *m* de pilotage. **~roach** *n* cafard *m*. **~tail** *n* cocktail *m*.

cocky *a* (**-ier**, **-iest**) trop sûr de soi.

cocoa *n* cacao *m*.

coconut *n* noix *f* de coco.

COD *abbr* (**cash on delivery**) envoi *m* contre remboursement.

cod *n inv* morue *f*; **~-liver oil** huile *f* de foie de morue.

code *n* code *m*. ●*vt* coder.

coerce *vt* contraindre.

coexist *vi* coexister.

coffee *n* café *m*. **~ bar** *n* café *m*. **~ bean** *n* grain *m* de café. **~-pot** *n* cafetière *f*. **~-table** *n* table *f* basse.

coffin *n* cercueil *m*.

cog *n* pignon *m*; (fig) rouage *m*.

cognac *n* cognac *m*.

coil *vt/i* (s')enrouler. ●*n* (of rope) rouleau *m*; (of snake) anneau *m*; (contraceptive) stérilet *m*.

coin *n* pièce *f* (*de monnaie*). ●*vt* (*word*) inventer.

coincide *vi* coïncider. **coincidence** *n* coïncidence *f*. **coincidental** *a* dû à une coïncidence.

colander *n* passoire *f*.

cold *a* froid; (*person*) **be** *or* **feel ~** avoir froid; **it is ~** il fait froid; **get ~ feet** avoir les jetons ⊡; **~-blooded** (lit) à sang froid; (fig) sans pitié. ●*n* froid *m*; (Med) rhume *m*; **~ sore** bouton *m* de fièvre. **coldness** *n* froideur *f*.

coleslaw *n* salade *f* de chou cru.

colic *n* coliques *fpl*.

collaborate *vi* collaborer.

collapse *vi* s'effondrer; (*person*) s'écrouler; (fold) se plier. ●*n* effondrement *m*.

collar *n* col *m*; (of dog) collier *m*. **~-bone** *n* clavicule *f*

collateral *n* nantissement *m*.

colleague *n* collègue *mf*.

collect *vt* rassembler; (pick up) ramasser; (call for) passer prendre; (*money, fare*) encaisser; (*taxes, rent*) percevoir; (as hobby) collectionner. ●*vi* se rassembler; (*dust*) s'amasser. ●*adv* **call ~** (US) appeler en PCV. **collection** *n* collection *f*; (of money) collecte *f*; (in church) quête *f*; (of mail) levée *f*.

collective *a* collectif.

collector *n* (as hobby) collectionneur/-euse *m/f*; (of taxes) percepteur *m*; (of rent, debt) encaisseur *m*.

college *n* (for higher education) établissement *m* d'enseignement supérieur; (within university) collège *m*; **be at ~** faire des études supérieures.

collide *vi* entrer en collision (**with** avec).

colliery *n* houillère *f*.

collision *n* collision *f*.

colloquial *a* familier. **colloquialism** *n* expression *f* familière.

Colombia *n* Colombie *f*.

colon *n* (Gram) deux-points *m inv*; (Anat) côlon *m*.

colonel *n* colonel *m*.

colonial *a* & *n* colonial/-e (*m/f*).

colour, (US) **color** *n* couleur *f*; **~-blind** daltonien. ●*a* (*photo*) en couleur; (*TV set*) couleur *inv*. ●*vt* colorer; (with crayon) colorier. **coloured** *a* de couleur. **colourful** *a* aux couleurs vives; (fig) haut en couleur. **colouring** *n* (of skin) teint *m*; (in food) colorant *m*.

colt *n* poulain *m*.

column *n* colonne *f*.

coma *n* coma *m*.

comb *n* peigne *m*. ●*vt* peigner; **~ one's hair** se peigner; **~ a place** passer un lieu au peigne fin.

combat *n* combat *m*. ●*vt* (*pt* **combated**) combattre.

combination *n* combinaison *f*.

combine¹ *vt/i* (se) combiner, (s')unir.

combine² *n* (Comm) groupe *m*; ~ (**harvester**) moissonneuse-batteuse *f*.

come *vi* (*pt* **came**; *pp* **come**) venir; (*bus, letter*) arriver; (*postman*) passer; ~ **and look!** viens voir!; ~ **in** (*size, colour*) exister en; **when it ~s to** lorsqu'il s'agit de. □ ~ **about** survenir; ~ **across** (*meaning*) passer; ~ **across sth** tomber sur qch; ~ **away** (leave) partir; (come off) se détacher; ~ **back** revenir; ~ **by** obtenir; ~ **down** descendre; (*price*) baisser; ~ **forward** se présenter; ~ **in** entrer; ~ **in useful** être utile; ~ **in for** recevoir; ~ **into** (money) hériter de; ~ **off** (succeed) réussir; (fare) s'en tirer; (detach) se détacher; ~ **on** (actor) entrer en scène; (light) s'allumer; (improve) faire des progrès; ~ **on!** allez!; ~ **out** sortir; ~ **round** reprendre connaissance; (change mind) changer d'avis; ~ **through** s'en tirer; ~ **to** reprendre connaissance; ~ **to sth** (*amount*) revenir à qch; (*decision, conclusion*) arriver à qch; ~ **up** (*problem*) être soulevé; (*opportunity*) se présenter; (*sun*) se lever; ~ **up against** se heurter à; ~ **up with** trouver.

comedian *n* comique *m*.

comedy *n* comédie *f*.

comfort *n* confort *m*; (consolation) réconfort *m*. ● *vt* consoler. **comfortable** *a* (*chair, car*) confortable; (*person*) à l'aise; (wealthy) aisé.

comfortably *adv* confortablement; ~ **off** aisé.

comfy *a* [I] = COMFORTABLE.

comic *a* comique. ● *n* (person) comique *m*; ~ (**book**), ~ **strip** bande *f* dessinée.

coming *n* arrivée *f*; **~s and goings** allées et venues *fpl*. ● *a* à venir.

comma *n* virgule *f*.

command *n* (authority) commandement *m*; (order) ordre *m*; (mastery) maîtrise *f*. ● *vt* ordonner à (**to do** de faire); (be able to use) disposer de; (*respect*) inspirer. **commandeer** *vt* réquisitionner. **commander** *n* commandant *m*. **commanding** *a* imposant. **commandment** *n* commandement *m*.

commando *n* commando *m*.

commemorate *vt* commémorer.

commence *vt/i* commencer.

commend *vt* (praise) louer; (entrust) confier.

commensurate *a* proportionné.

comment *n* commentaire *m*. ● *vi* faire des commentaires; ~ **on** commenter. **commentary** *n* commentaire *m*; (radio, TV) reportage *m*. **commentate** *vi* faire un reportage. **commentator** *n* commentateur/-trice *m/f*.

commerce *n* commerce *m*.

commercial *a* commercial; (*traveller*) de commerce. ● *n* publicité *f*.

commiserate *vi* compatir (**with** avec).

commission *n* commission *f*; (order for work) commande *f*; **out of ~** hors service. ● *vt* (order) commander; (Mil) nommer officier; ~ **to do** charger de faire. **commissioner** *n* préfet *m* (de police); (in EC) membre *m* de la Commission européenne.

commit *vt* (*pt* **committed**) commettre; (entrust) confier; ~ **oneself** s'engager; ~ **perjury** se parjurer; ~ **suicide** se suicider; ~

to memory apprendre par cœur. **commitment** *n* engagement *m*.

committee *n* comité *m*.

commodity *n* article *m*.

common *a* (shared by all) commun (**to** à); (usual) courant; (vulgar) vulgaire, commun; **in ~** en commun; **~ people** le peuple; **~ sense** bon sens *m*. ●*n* terrain *m* communal; **the C~s** Chambre *f* des Communes.

commoner *n* roturier/-ière *m/f*.

common law *n* droit *m* coutumier.

commonly *adv* communément.

commonplace *a* banal. ●*n* banalité *f*.

common-room *n* salle *f* de détente.

Commonwealth *n* **the ~** le Commonwealth *m*.

commotion *n* (noise) vacarme *m*; (disturbance) agitation *f*.

communal *a* (shared) commun; (*life*) collectif.

commune *n* (group) communauté *f*.

communicate *vt/i* communiquer. **communication** *n* communication *f*. **communicative** *a* communicatif.

communion *n* communion *f*.

Communism *n* communisme *m*. **Communist** *a & n* communiste (*mf*).

community *n* communauté *f*.

commute *vi* faire la navette. ●*vt* (Jur) commuer. **commuter** *n* navetteur/-euse *m/f*.

compact *a* compact; (lady's case) poudrier *m*.

compact disc *n* disque *m* compact. **~ player** *n* platine *f* laser.

companion *n* compagnon/-agne *m/f*. **companionship** *n* camaraderie *f*.

company *n* (companionship, firm) compagnie *f*; (guests) invités/-es *m/fpl*.

comparative *a* (*study, form*) comparatif; (*comfort*) relatif.

compare *vt* comparer (**with, to** à), **~d with** par rapport à. ●*vi* être comparable. **comparison** *n* comparaison *f*.

compartment *n* compartiment *m*.

compass *n* (for direction) boussole *f*; (scope) portée *f*; **a pair of ~es** compas *m*.

compassionate *a* compatissant.

compatible *a* compatible.

compel *vt* (*pt* **compelled**) contraindre. **compelling** *a* irrésistible.

compensate *vt/i* (financially) dédommager (**for** de); **~ for sth** compenser qch. **compensation** *n* compensation *f*; (financial) dédommagement *m*.

compete *vi* concourir; **~ with** rivaliser avec.

competent *a* compétent.

competition *n* (contest) concours *m*; (Sport) compétition *f*; (Comm) concurrence *f*.

competitive *a* (*prices*) compétitif; (*person*) qui a l'esprit de compétition.

competitor *n* concurrent/-e *m/f*.

compile *vt* (*list*) dresser; (*book*) rédiger.

complacency *n* suffisance *f*.

complain *vi* se plaindre (**about, of** de). **complaint** *n* plainte *f*; (official) réclamation *f*; (illness) maladie *f*.

complement *n* complément *m*. ●*vt* compléter. **complementary** *a* complémentaire.

complete *a* complet; (finished) achevé; (downright) parfait. ●*vt* achever; (*a form*) remplir. **completely** *adv* complètement. **completion** *n* achèvement *m*.

complex *a* complexe. ● *n* (Psych) complexe *m*.

complexion *n* (of face) teint *m*; (fig) caractère *m*.

compliance *n* (agreement) conformité *f*.

complicate *vt* compliquer. **complicated** *a* compliqué. **complication** *n* complication *f*.

compliment *n* compliment *m*. ● *vt* complimenter. **complimentary** *a* (offert) à titre gracieux; (praising) flatteur.

comply *vi* ~ **with** se conformer à, obéir à.

component *n* (of machine) pièce *f*; (chemical substance) composant *m*; (element: fig) composante *f*. ● *a* constituant.

compose *vt* composer; ~ **oneself** se calmer. **composed** *a* calme. **composer** *n* (Mus) compositeur *m*. **composition** *n* composition *f*.

composure *n* calme *m*.

compound *n* (substance, word) composé *m*; (enclosure) enclos *m*. ● *a* composé.

comprehend *vt* comprendre. **comprehension** *n* compréhension *f*.

comprehensive *a* étendu, complet; (*insurance*) tous risques *inv*. ~ **school** *n* collège *m* d'enseignement secondaire.

compress *vt* comprimer.

comprise *vt* comprendre, inclure.

compromise *n* compromis *m*. ● *vt* compromettre. ● *vi* transiger, arriver à un compromis.

compulsive *a* (Psych) compulsif; (*liar, smoker*) invétéré.

compulsory *a* obligatoire.

computer *n* ordinateur *m*; ~ **science** informatique *f*. **computerize** *vt* informatiser.

comrade *n* camarade *mf*.

con[1] *vt* (*pt* **conned**) ☒ rouler ☐, escroquer (**out of** de). ● *n* ☒ escroquerie *f*.

con[2] ⇒PRO.

conceal *vt* dissimuler (**from** à).

concede *vt* concéder. ● *vi* céder.

conceited *a* vaniteux.

conceive *vt/i* concevoir; ~ **of** concevoir.

concentrate *vt/i* (se) concentrer. **concentration** *n* concentration *f*.

concept *n* concept *m*.

conception *n* conception *f*.

concern *n* (interest, business) affaire *f*; (worry) inquiétude *f*; (firm: Comm) entreprise *f*, affaire *f*. ● *vt* concerner; ~ **oneself with, be ~ed with** s'occuper de. **concerned** *a* inquiet. **concerning** *prep* en ce qui concerne.

concert *n* concert *m*.

concession *n* concession *f*.

conciliation *n* conciliation *f*.

concise *a* concis.

conclude *vt* conclure. ● *vi* se terminer. **conclusion** *n* conclusion *f*. **conclusive** *a* concluant.

concoct *vt* confectionner; (invent: fig) fabriquer. **concoction** *n* mélange *m*.

concourse *n* (Rail) hall *m*.

concrete *n* béton *m*. ● *a* de béton; (fig) concret. ● *vt* bétonner.

concur *vi* (*pt* **concurred**) être d'accord.

concurrently *adv* simultanément.

concussion *n* commotion *f* (cérébrale).

condemn *vt* condamner.

condensation *n* (on walls) condensation *f*; (on windows) buée *f*. **condense** *vt/i* (se) condenser.

condition *n* condition *f*; **on ~ that** à condition que. ● *vt* conditionner. **conditional** *a* conditionnel.

conditioner *n* après-shampooing *m*.

condolences *npl* condoléances *fpl*.

condom *n* préservatif *m*.

condone *vt* pardonner, fermer les yeux sur.

conducive *a* ~ **to** favorable à.

conduct¹ *n* conduite *f*.

conduct² *vt* conduire; (*orchestra*) diriger. **conductor** *n* chef *m* d'orchestre; (of bus) receveur *m*; (on train: US) chef *m* de train; (Electr) conducteur *m*. **conductress** *n* receveuse *f*.

cone *n* cône *m*; (of ice-cream) cornet *m*.

confectioner *n* confiseur/-euse *m/f*. **confectionery** *n* confiserie *f*.

confer *vt/i* (*pt* **conferred**) conférer.

conference *n* conférence *f*.

confess *vt/i* avouer; (Relig) (se) confesser. **confession** *n* confession *f*; (of crime) aveu *m*.

confide *vt* confier. ● *vi* ~ **in** se confier à.

confidence *n* (trust) confiance *f*; (boldness) confiance *f* en soi; (secret) confidence *f*; **in** ~ en confidence. **confident** *a* sûr.

confidential *a* confidentiel.

confine *vt* enfermer; (limit) limiter; **~d space** espace *m* réduit; **~d to** limité à.

confirm *vt* confirmer. **confirmed** *a* (*bachelor*) endurci; (*smoker*) invétéré.

confiscate *vt* confisquer.

conflict¹ *n* conflit *m*.

conflict² *vi* (*statements, views*) être en contradiction (**with** avec); (*appointments*) tomber en même temps (**with** que). **conflicting** *a* contradictoire.

conform *vt/i* (se) conformer.

confound *vt* confondre.

confront *vt* affronter; ~ **with** confronter avec.

confuse *vt* (bewilder) troubler; (mistake, confound) confondre; **become ~d** s'embrouiller; **I am ~d** je m'y perds. **confusing** *a* déroutant. **confusion** *n* confusion *f*.

congeal *vt/i* (se) figer.

congested *a* (*road*) embouteillé; (*passage*) encombré; (Med) congestionné. **congestion** *n* (traffic) encombrement(s) *m*(*pl*); (Med) congestion *f*.

congratulate *vt* féliciter (**on** de). **congratulations** *npl* félicitations *fpl*.

congregate *vi* se rassembler. **congregation** *n* assemblée *f*.

congress *n* congrès *m*; **C~** (US) le Congrès.

conjugate *vt* conjuguer. **conjugation** *n* conjugaison *f*.

conjunction *n* (Ling) conjonction *f*; **in ~ with** conjointement avec.

conjunctivitis *n* conjonctivite *f*.

conjure *vi* faire des tours de passe-passe. ● *vt* ~ **up** faire apparaître. **conjuror** *n* prestidigitateur/-trice *m/f*.

con man *n* ⊠ escroc *m*.

connect *vt/i* (se) relier; (in mind) faire le rapport entre; (install, wire up to mains) brancher; ~ **with** (of train) assurer la correspondance avec; **~ed** (*idea, event*) lié; **be ~ed with** avoir rapport à.

connection *n* rapport *m*; (Rail) correspondance *f*; (phone call) communication *f*; (Electr) contact *m*; (joining piece) raccord *m*; **~s** (Comm) relations *fpl*.

connive *vi* ~ **at** se faire le complice de.

C

conquer *vt* vaincre; (country) conquérir. **conqueror** *n* conquérant *m*.

conquest *n* conquête *f*.

conscience *n* conscience *f*. **conscientious** *a* consciencieux.

conscious *a* conscient; (deliberate) voulu. **consciously** *adv* consciemment. **consciousness** *n* conscience *f*; (Med) connaissance *f*.

conscript *n* appelé *m*.

consecutive *a* consécutif.

consensus *n* consensus *m*.

consent *vi* consentir (**to** à). ● *n* consentement *m*.

consequence *n* conséquence *f*. **consequently** *adv* par conséquent.

conservation *n* préservation *f*; ~ **area** zone *f* protégée. **conservationist** *n* défenseur *m* de l'environnement.

conservative *a* conservateur; (*estimate*) minimal.

Conservative Party *n* parti *m* conservateur.

conservatory *n* (greenhouse) serre *f*; (room) véranda *f*.

conserve *vt* conserver; (*energy*) économiser.

consider *vt* considérer; (allow for) tenir compte de; (*possibility*) envisager (**doing** de faire).

considerable *a* considérable; (much) beaucoup de.

considerate *a* prévenant, attentionné. **consideration** *n* considération *f*; (respect) égard(s) *m*(*pl*).

considering *prep* compte tenu de.

consignment *n* envoi *m*.

consist *vi* consister (**of** en; **in doing** à faire).

consistency *n* (of liquids) consistance *f*; (of argument) cohérence *f*.

consistent *a* cohérent; ~ **with** conforme à.

consolation *n* consolation *f*.

consolidate *vt*/*i* (se) consolider.

consonant *n* consonne *f*.

conspicuous *a* (easily seen) en évidence; (showy) voyant; (noteworthy) remarquable.

conspiracy *n* conspiration *f*.

constable *n* agent *m* de police, gendarme *m*.

constant *a* (*questions*) incessant; (unchanging) constant; (*friend*) fidèle. ● *n* constante *f*. **constantly** *adv* constamment.

constellation *n* constellation *f*.

constipation *n* constipation *f*.

constituency *n* circonscription *f* électorale.

constituent *a* constitutif. ● *n* élément *m* constitutif; (Pol) électeur/-trice *m*/*f*.

constitution *n* constitution *f*.

constrain *vt* contraindre. **constraint** *n* contrainte *f*.

constrict *vt* (*flow*) comprimer; (*movement*) gêner.

construct *vt* construire. **construction** *n* construction *f*. **constructive** *a* constructif.

consulate *n* consulat *m*.

consult *vt* consulter. ● *vi* ~ **with** conférer avec. **consultant** *n* conseiller/-ère *m*/*f*; (Med) spécialiste *mf*. **consultation** *n* consultation *f*.

consume *vt* consommer; (destroy) consumer. **consumer** *n* consommateur/-trice *m*/*f*.

consummate *vt* consommer.

consumption *n* consommation *f*; (Med) phtisie *f*.

contact *n* contact *m*; (person) relation *f*. ● *vt* contacter. ~

lenses *npl* lentilles *fpl* (de contact).

contagious *a* contagieux.

contain *vt* contenir; **~ oneself** se contenir. **container** *n* récipient *m*; (for transport) container *m*.

contaminate *vt* contaminer.

contemplate *vt* (gaze at) contempler; (think about) envisager.

contemporary *a & n* contemporain/-e (*m/f*).

contempt *n* mépris *m*. **contemptible** *a* méprisable. **contemptuous** *a* méprisant.

contend *vt* soutenir. ● *vi* **~ with** (compete) rivaliser avec; (face) faire face à. **contender** *n* adversaire *mf*.

content¹ *n* (of letter) contenu *m*; (amount) teneur *f*; **~s** contenu *m*.

content² *a* satisfait. ● *vt* contenter. **contented** *a* satisfait. **contentment** *n* contentement *m*.

contest¹ *n* (competition) concours *m*; (struggle) lutte *f*.

contest² *vt* contester; (compete for or in) disputer. **contestant** *n* concurrent/-e *m/f*.

context *n* contexte *m*.

continent *n* continent *m*; **the C~** l'Europe *f* (continentale). **continental** *a* continental; européen. **continental quilt** *n* couette *f*.

contingency *n* éventualité *f*; **~ plan** plan *m* d'urgence.

continual *a* continuel.

continuation *n* continuation *f*; (after interruption) reprise *f*; (new episode) suite *f*.

continue *vt/i* continuer; (resume) reprendre. **continued** *a* continu.

continuous *a* continu. **continuously** *adv* (without a break) sans interruption; (repeatedly) continuellement.

contort *vt* tordre; **~ oneself** se contorsionner.

contour *n* contour *m*.

contraband *n* contrebande *f*.

contraception *n* contraception *f*. **contraceptive** *a & n* contraceptif (*m*).

contract¹ *n* contrat *m*.

contract² *vt/i* (se) contracter. **contraction** *n* contraction *f*.

contractor *n* entrepreneur/-euse *m/f*.

contradict *vt* contredire. **contradictory** *a* contradictoire.

contrary¹ *a* contraire (to à). ● *n* contraire *m*; **on the ~** au contraire. ● *adv* **~ to** contrairement à.

contrary² *a* entêté.

contrast¹ *n* contraste *m*.

contrast² *vt/i* contraster.

contravention *n* infraction *f*.

contribute *vt* donner. ● *vi* **~ to** contribuer à; (take part) participer à; (newspaper) collaborer à. **contribution** *n* contribution *f*. **contributor** *n* collaborateur/ -trice *m/f*.

contrive *vt* imaginer; **~ to do** trouver moyen de faire.

control *vt* (*pt* **controlled**) (*firm*) diriger; (check) contrôler; (restrain) maîtriser. ● *n* contrôle *m*; (mastery) maîtrise *f*; **~s** commandes *fpl*; (knobs) boutons *mpl*; **have under ~** (*event*) avoir en main; **in ~ of** maître de. **~ tower** *n* tour *f* de contrôle.

controversial *a* discutable, discuté. **controversy** *n* controverse *f*.

conurbation *n* agglomération *f*, conurbation *f*.

convalesce *vi* être en convalescence.

convene *vt* convoquer. ● *vi* se réunir.

convenience *n* commodité *f*; **∼s** toilettes *fpl*; **all modern ∼s** tout le confort moderne; **at your ∼** quand cela vous conviendra, à votre convenance. **∼ foods** *npl* plats *mpl* tout préparés.

convenient *a* commode, pratique; (*time*) bien choisi; **be ∼ for** convenir à.

convent *n* couvent *m*.

convention *n* (assembly, agreement) convention *f*; (custom) usage *m*. **conventional** *a* conventionnel.

conversation *n* conversation *f*. **conversational** *a* (*tone*) de la conversation; (*French*) de tous les jours.

converse[1] *vi* s'entretenir, converser (**with** avec).

converse[2] *a* & *n* inverse (*m*). **conversely** *adv* inversement.

conversion *n* conversion *f*.

convert[1] *vt* convertir; (*house*) aménager. ● *vi* **∼ into** se transformer en.

convert[2] *n* converti/-e *m*/*f*.

convertible *a* convertible. ● *n* (car) décapotable *f*.

convey *vt* (*wishes, order*) transmettre; (*goods, people*) transporter; (*idea, feeling*) communiquer. **conveyor belt** *n* tapis *m* roulant.

convict[1] *vt* déclarer coupable.

convict[2] *n* prisonnier/-ière *m*/*f*.

conviction *n* (Jur) condamnation *f*; (opinion) conviction *f*.

convince *vt* convaincre.

convoke *vt* convoquer.

convoy *n* convoi *m*.

convulse *vt* convulser; (fig) bouleverser; **be ∼d with laughter** se tordre de rire.

cook *vt*/*i* (faire) cuire; (of person) faire la cuisine; **∼ up** ⊡ fabriquer. ● *n* cuisinier/-ière *m*/*f*. **cooker** *n* (stove) cuisinière *f*. **cookery** *n* cuisine *f*.

cookie *n* (US) biscuit *m*.

cooking *n* cuisine *f*. ● *a* de cuisine.

cool *a* frais; (calm) calme; (unfriendly) froid. ● *n* fraîcheur *f*; (calmness ⊠) sang-froid *m*; **in the ∼** au frais. ● *vt*/*i* rafraîchir. **∼ box** *n* glacière *f*.

coolly *adv* calmement; froidement.

coop *n* poulailler *m*. ● *vt* **∼ up** enfermer.

co-operate *vi* coopérer. **co-operation** *n* coopération *f*.

co-operative *a* coopératif. ● *n* coopérative *f*.

co-ordinate *vt* coordonner.

cop *vt* (*pt* **copped**) ⊠ piquer. ● *n* (policeman ⊠) flic *m*. □ **∼ out** ⊠ se dérober.

cope *vi* s'en sortir ⊡, se débrouiller; **∼ with** (*problem*) faire face à.

copper *n* cuivre *m*; (coin) sou *m*; ⊠ flic *m*. ● *a* de cuivre.

copulate *vi* s'accoupler.

copy *n* copie *f*; (of book, newspaper) exemplaire *m*; (print: Photo) épreuve *f*. ● *vt*/*i* copier.

copyright *n* droit *m* d'auteur, copyright *m*.

copy-writer *n* rédacteur-concepteur *m*, rédactrice-conceptrice *f*.

cord *n* (petite) corde *f*; (of curtain, pyjamas) cordon *m*; (Electr) cordon *m* électrique; (fabric) velours *m* côtelé.

cordial *a* cordial. ● *n* (drink) sirop *m*.

corduroy *n* velours *m* côtelé.

core *n* (of apple) trognon *m*; (of problem) cœur *m*; (Tech) noyau *m*. ● *vt* (*apple*) évider.

cork *n* liège *m*; (for bottle) bouchon

m. ●*vt* boucher. **corkscrew** *n* tire-bouchon *m*.

corn *n* blé *m*; (maize: US) maïs *m*; (seed) grain *m*; (hard skin) cor *m*.

cornea *n* cornée *f*.

corner *n* coin *m*; (bend in road) virage *m*; (football) corner *m*. ●*vt* coincer, acculer; (*market*) accaparer. ●*vi* prendre un virage.

cornflour *n* farine *f* de maïs.

cornice *n* corniche *f*.

corny *a* (**-ier**, **-iest**) (*joke*) éculé.

corollary *n* corollaire *m*.

coronary *n* infarctus *m*.

coronation *n* couronnement *m*.

corporal *n* caporal *m*. ~ **punishment** *n* châtiment *m* corporel.

corporate *a* (*ownership*) en commun; (*body*) constitué.

corporation *n* (Comm) société *f*.

corpse *n* cadavre *m*.

corpuscle *n* globule *m*.

correct *a* (right) exact, juste, correct; (proper) correct; **you are** ~ vous avez raison. ●*vt* corriger.

correction *n* correction *f*.

correlate *vt*/*i* (faire) correspondre.

correspond *vi* correspondre. **correspondence** *n* correspondance *f*.

corridor *n* couloir *m*.

corrode *vt*/*i* (se) corroder.

corrugated *a* ondulé; ~ **iron** tôle *f* ondulée.

corrupt *a* corrompu. ●*vt* corrompre. **corruption** *n* corruption *f*.

Corsica *n* Corse *f*.

cosh *n* matraque *f*. ●*vt* matraquer.

cosmetic *n* produit *m* de beauté. ●*a* cosmétique; (fig, pej) superficiel. ~ **surgery** *n* chirurgie *f* esthétique

cosmopolitan *a* & *n* cosmopolite (*mf*).

cosmos *n* cosmos *m*.

cost *vt* (*pt* **cost**) coûter; (*pt* **costed**) établir le prix de. ●*n* coût *m*; ~**s** (Jur) dépens *mpl*; **at all** ~**s** à tout prix; **to one's** ~ à ses dépens. ~ **price** prix *m* de revient; ~ **of living** coût *m* de la vie. ~**-effective** *a* rentable.

costly *a* (**-ier**, **-iest**) coûteux; (valuable) précieux.

costume *n* costume *m*; (for swimming) maillot *m*. ~ **jewellery** *npl* bijoux *mpl* de fantaisie.

cosy *a* (**-ier**, **-iest**) confortable, intime.

cot *n* lit *m* d'enfant; (camp-bed: US) lit *m* de camp.

cottage *n* petite maison *f* de campagne; (thatched) chaumière *f*. ~ **pie** *n* hachis *m* Parmentier.

cotton *n* coton *m*; (for sewing) fil *m* (à coudre). ●*vi* ~ **on** ▣ piger. ~ **wool** *n* coton *m* hydrophile.

couch *n* canapé *m*. ●*vt* (express) formuler.

cough *vi* tousser. ●*n* toux *f*. □ ~ **up** ▣ cracher, payer.

could ⇨CAN[1].

couldn't = COULD NOT.

council *n* conseil *m*. ~ **house** *n* maison *f* louée par la municipalité, ≈ H.L.M. *m or f*.

councillor *n* conseiller/-ère *m*/*f* municipal/-e.

counsel *n* conseil *m*. ●*n inv* (Jur) avocat/-e *m*/*f*. **counsellor** *n* conseiller/-ère *m*/*f*.

count *vt*/*i* compter. ●*n* (numerical record) décompte *m*; (nobleman) comte *m*. □ ~ **on** compter sur.

counter *n* comptoir *m*; (in bank) guichet *m*; (token) jeton *m*. ●*adv* ~ **to** à l'encontre de. ●*a* opposé. ●*vt* opposer; (blow) parer. ●*vi* riposter.

counteract *vt* neutraliser.

C

counterbalance *n* contrepoids *m*. ●*vt* contrebalancer.

counterfeit *a & n* faux (*m*). ●*vt* contrefaire.

counterfoil *n* souche *f*.

counter-productive *a* qui produit l'effet contraire.

countess *n* comtesse *f*.

countless *a* innombrable.

country *n* (land, region) pays *m*; (homeland) patrie *f*; (countryside) campagne *f*.

countryman *n* (*pl* **-men**) campagnard *m*; (fellow citizen) compatriote *m*.

countryside *n* campagne *f*.

county *n* comté *m*.

coup *n* (achievement) joli coup *m*; (Pol) coup *m* d'état.

couple *n* (people, animals) couple *m*; **a ~ (of)** (two or three) deux ou trois. ●*vt/i* (s')accoupler.

coupon *n* coupon *m*; (for shopping) bon *m or* coupon *m* de réduction.

courage *n* courage *m*.

courgette *n* courgette *f*.

courier *n* messager/-ère *m/f*; (for tourists) guide *m*.

course *n* cours *m*; (for training) stage *m*; (series) série *f*; (Culin) plat *m*; (for golf) terrain *m*; (at sea) itinéraire *m*; **change ~** changer de cap; **~ (of action)** façon *f* de faire; **during the ~ of** pendant; **in due ~** en temps utile; **of ~** bien sûr.

court *n* cour *f*; (tennis) court *m*; **go to ~** aller devant les tribunaux. ●*vt* faire la cour à; (*danger*) rechercher.

courteous *a* courtois.

courtesy *n* courtoisie *f*; **by ~ of** avec la permission de.

court-house *n* (US) palais *m* de justice.

court-martial *vt* (*pt* **-martialled**) faire passer en conseil de guerre. ●*n* cour *f* martiale.

court: **~room** *n* salle *f* de tribunal. **~shoe** *n* escarpin *m*. **~yard** *n* cour *f*.

cousin *n* cousin/-e *m/f*; **first ~** cousin/-e *m/f* germain/-e.

cove *n* anse *f*, crique *f*.

covenant *n* convention *f*.

cover *vt* couvrir. ●*n* (for bed, book) couverture *f*; (lid) couvercle *m*; (for furniture) housse *f*; (shelter) abri *m*; **take ~** se mettre à l'abri. □ **~ up** cacher; (*crime*) couvrir; **~ up for** couvrir.

coverage *n* reportage *m*.

covering *n* enveloppe *f*; **~ letter** lettre *f* d'accompagnement.

covert *a* (*activity*) secret; (*threat*) voilé; (*look*) dérobé.

cover-up *n* opération *f* de camouflage.

cow *n* vache *f*.

coward *n* lâche *mf*.

cowboy *n* cow-boy *m*.

cowshed *n* étable *f*.

coy *a* (faussement) timide, qui fait le *or* la timide.

cozy US = COSY.

crab *n* crabe *m*. **~-apple** *n* pomme *f* sauvage.

crack *n* fente *f*; (in glass) fêlure *f*; (noise) craquement *m*; (joke ⊠) plaisanterie *f*. ●*a* ⊡ d'élite. ●*vt/i* (break partially) (se) fêler; (split) (se) fendre; (*nut*) casser; (*joke*) raconter; (*problem*) résoudre; **get ~ing** ⊡ s'y mettre. □ **~ down on** ⊡ sévir contre; **~ up** ⊡ craquer.

cracker *n* (Culin) biscuit *m* (salé); (for Christmas) diablotin *f*.

crackle *vi* crépiter. ●*n* crépitement *m*.

cradle *n* berceau *m*. ●*vt* bercer.

craft *n* métier *m* artisanal; (technique) art *m*; (boat) bateau *m*.

craftsman *n* (*pl* **-men**) artisan *m*. **craftsmanship** *n* art *m*.
crafty *a* (**-ier**, **-iest**) rusé.
crag *n* rocher *m* à pic.
cram *vt/i* (*pt* **crammed**); (for an exam) bachoter (**for** pour); **~ into** (pack) (s')entasser dans; **~ with** (fill) bourrer de.
cramp *n* crampe *f*.
cramped *a* à l'étroit.
cranberry *n* canneberge *f*.
crane *n* grue *f*. ● *vt* (*neck*) tendre.
crank *n* excentrique *mf*; (Tech) manivelle *f*.
crap *n* (nonsense ⊠) conneries *fpl* ⊠; (faeces ⊠) merde *f* ⊠.
crash *n* accident *m*; (noise) fracas *m*; (of thunder) coup *m*; (of firm) faillite *f*. ● *vt/i* avoir un accident (avec); (of plane) s'écraser; (two vehicles) se percuter; **~ into** rentrer dans. **~ course** *n* cours *m* intensif. **~-helmet** *n* casque *m* (anti-choc). **~-land** *vi* atterrir en catastrophe.
crate *n* cageot *m*.
cravat *n* foulard *m*.
crave *vt/i* **~ (for)** désirer ardemment. **craving** *n* envie *f* irrésistible.
crawl *vi* (*insect*) ramper; (*vehicle*) se traîner; **be ~ing with** grouiller de. ● *n* (pace) pas *m*; (swimming) crawl *m*.
crayfish *n inv* écrevisse *f*.
crayon *n* craie *f* grasse.
craze *n* engouement *m*.
crazy *a* (**-ier**, **-iest**) fou; **~ about** (person) fou de; (thing) fana *or* fou de.
creak *n* grincement *m*. ● *vi* grincer.
cream *n* crème *f*. ● *a* crème *inv*. ● *vt* écrémer.
crease *n* pli *m*. ● *vt/i* (se) froisser.
create *vt* créer. **creation** *n* création *f*. **creative** *a* (*person*) créatif; (*process*) créateur. **creator** *n* créateur/-trice *m/f*.
creature *n* créature *f*.
crèche *n* garderie *f*.
credentials *npl* (identity) pièces *fpl* d'identité; (competence) références *fpl*.
credibility *n* crédibilité *f*.
credit *n* (credence) crédit *m*; (honour) honneur *m*; **in ~** créditeur; **~s** (cinema) générique *m*. ● *a* (*balance*) créditeur. ● *vt* croire; (Comm) créditer; **~ sb with** attribuer à qn. **~ card** *n* carte *f* de crédit. **~ note** *n* avoir *m*.
creditor *n* créancier/-ière *m/f*.
credit-worthy *a* solvable.
creed *n* credo *m*.
creek *n* (US) ruisseau *m*; **up the ~** ⊠ dans le pétrin ⊡.
creep *vi* (*pt* **crept**) (*insect, cat*) ramper; (fig) se glisser. ● *n* (person ⊠) pauvre type *m* ⊡; **give sb the ~s** faire frissonner qn. **creeper** *n* liane *f*.
cremate *vt* incinérer. **cremation** *n* incinération *f*. **crematorium** *n* (*pl* **-ia**) crématorium *m*
crêpe *n* crêpe *m*. **~ paper** *n* papier *m* crêpon.
crept ⇒CREEP.
crescent *n* croissant *m*; (of houses) rue *f* en demi-lune.
cress *n* cresson *m*.
crest *n* crête *f*; (coat of arms) armoiries *fpl*.
cretin *n* crétin/-e *m/f*.
crevice *n* fente *f*.
crew *n* (of plane, ship) équipage *m*; (gang) équipe *f*. **~ cut** *n* coupe *f* en brosse. **~ neck** *n* (col) ras du cou *m*.
crib *n* lit *m* d'enfant. ● *vt/i* (*pt* **cribbed**) copier.
cricket *n* (Sport) cricket *m*; (insect) grillon *m*.

crime *n* crime *m*; (minor) délit *m*; (acts) criminalité *f*.

criminal *a & n* criminel/-le (*m/f*).

crimson *a & n* cramoisi (*m*).

cringe *vi* reculer; (fig) s'humilier.

crinkle *vt/i* (se) froisser. ●*n* pli *m*.

cripple *n* infirme *mf*. ●*vt* estropier; (fig) paralyser.

crisis *n* (*pl* **crises**) crise *f*.

crisp *a* (Culin) croquant; (air, reply) vif. **crisps** *npl* chips *fpl*.

criss-cross *a* entrecroisé. ●*vt/i* (s')entrecroiser.

criterion *n* (*pl* **-ia**) critère *m*.

critic *n* critique *m*. **critical** *a* critique. **critically** *adv* d'une manière critique; (*ill*) gravement.

criticism *n* critique *f*.

criticize *vt/i* critiquer.

croak *n* (*bird*) croassement *m*; (*frog*) coassement *m*. ●*vi* croasser; coasser.

Croatia *n* Croatie *f*.

Croatian *n* Croate *mf*. ●*a* Croate.

crochet *n* crochet *m*. ●*vt* faire du crochet.

crockery *n* vaisselle *f*.

crocodile *n* crocodile *m*.

crook *n* (criminal ▣) escroc *m*; (stick) houlette *f*.

crooked *a* tordu; (winding) tortueux; (askew) de travers; (dishonest: fig) malhonnête.

crop *n* récolte *f*; (fig) quantité *f*. ●*vt* (*pt* **cropped**) couper. ●*vi* **~ up** se présenter.

cross *n* croix *f*; (hybrid) hybride *m*. ●*vt/i* traverser; (*legs, animals*) croiser; (*cheque*) barrer; (*paths*) se croiser; **~ sb's mind** venir à l'esprit de qn. ●*a* en colère, fâché (**with** contre); **talk at ~ purposes** parler sans se comprendre. □ **~ off** *or* **out** rayer. **~-check** *vt* vérifier (pour confirmer). **~-country** (**running**) *n* cross *m*. **~-examine** *vt* faire subir un contre-interrogatoire à. **~-eyed** *a* **be ~-eyed** loucher. **~fire** *n* feux *mpl* croisés.

crossing *n* (by boat) traversée *f*; (on road) passage *m* clouté.

crossly *adv* avec colère.

cross: **~-reference** *n* renvoi *m*. **~roads** *n* carrefour *m*. **~word** *n* mots *mpl* croisés.

crotch *n* (of garment) entrejambes *m inv*.

crouch *vi* s'accroupir.

crow *n* corbeau *m*; **as the ~ flies** à vol d'oiseau. ●*vi* (of cock) chanter; (fig) jubiler. **~bar** *n* pied-de-biche *m*.

crowd *n* foule *f*. **crowded** *a* plein.

crown *n* couronne *f*; (top part) sommet *m*. ●*vt* couronner.

Crown Court *n* Cour *f* d'assises.

crucial *a* crucial.

crucifix *n* crucifix *m*.

crucify *vt* crucifier.

crude *a* (raw) brut; (rough, vulgar) grossier.

cruel *a* (**crueller**, **cruellest**) cruel.

cruise *n* croisière *f*. ●*vi* (*ship*) croiser; (*tourists*) faire une croisière; (*vehicle*) rouler; **cruising speed** vitesse *f* de croisière.

crumb *n* miette *f*.

crumble *vt/i* (s')effriter; (*bread*) (s')émietter; (collapse) s'écrouler.

crumple *vt/i* (se) froisser.

crunch *vt* croquer. ●*n* (event) moment *m* critique; **when it comes to the ~** quand ça devient sérieux.

crusade *n* croisade *f*. **crusader** *n* (knight) croisé *m*; (fig) militant/-e *m/f*.

crush *vt* écraser; (*clothes*) froisser. ●*n* (crowd) presse *f*; **a ~ on** ▣ le béguin pour.

crust *n* croûte *f*. **crusty** *a* croustillant.

crutch *n* béquille *f*; (crotch) entrejambes *m inv*.

crux *n* **the ~ of** (problem) le point crucial de.

cry *n* cri *m*. ● *vi* (weep) pleurer, (call out) crier. □ **~ off** se décommander.

crying *a* (*need*) urgent; **a ~ shame** une vraie honte. ● *n* pleurs *mpl*.

cryptic *a* énigmatique.

crystal *n* cristal *m*. **~-clear** *a* parfaitement clair.

cub *n* petit *m*; **Cub** (**Scout**) louveteau *m*.

Cuba *n* Cuba *f*.

cube *n* cube *m*. **cubic** *a* cubique; (*metre*) cube.

cubicle *n* (in room, hospital) box *m*; (at swimming-pool) cabine *f*.

cuckoo *n* coucou *m*.

cucumber *n* concombre *m*.

cuddle *vt* câliner. ● *vi* (**kiss and**) **~** s'embrasser. ● *n* caresse *f*. **cuddly** *a* câlin; **cuddly toy** peluche *f*.

cue *n* signal *m*; (Theat) réplique *f*; (billiards) queue *f*.

cuff *n* manchette *f*; (US: on trousers) revers *m*; **off the ~** impromptu. ● *vt* gifler. **~-link** *n* bouton *m* de manchette.

cul-de-sac *n* (*pl* **culs-de-sac**) impasse *f*.

cull *vt* (select) choisir; (kill) massacrer.

culminate *vi* **~ in** se terminer par. **culmination** *n* point *m* culminant.

culprit *n* coupable *mf*.

cult *n* culte *m*.

cultivate *vt* cultiver. **cultivation** *n* culture *f*.

cultural *a* culturel.

culture *n* culture *f*. **cultured** *a* cultivé.

cumbersome *a* encombrant.

cunning *a* rusé. ● *n* astuce *f*, ruse *f*.

cup *n* tasse *f*; (prize) coupe *f*; **Cup final** finale *f* de la coupe.

cupboard *n* placard *m*.

cup-tie *n* match *m* de coupe.

curate *n* vicaire *m*.

curator *n* (of museum) conservateur *m*.

curb *n* (restraint) frein *m*; (of path) (US) bord *m* du trottoir. ● *vt* (desires) refréner; (price increase) freiner.

cure *vt* guérir; (fig) éliminer; (Culin) fumer; (in brine) saler. ● *n* (recovery) guérison *f*; (remedy) remède *m*.

curfew *n* couvre-feu *m*.

curiosity *n* curiosité *f*. **curious** *a* curieux.

curl *vt/i* (*hair*) boucler. ● *n* boucle *f*. □ **~ up** se pelotonner; (shrivel) se racornir.

curler *n* bigoudi *m*.

curly *a* (**-ier, -iest**) bouclé.

currant *n* raisin *m* de Corinthe.

currency *n* (money) monnaie *f*; (of word) fréquence *f*; **foreign ~** devises *fpl* étrangères.

current *a* (*term, word*) usité; (topical) actuel; (*year*) en cours. ● *n* courant *m*. **~ account** *n* compte *m* courant. **~ events** *npl* l'actualité *f*.

currently *adv* actuellement.

curriculum *n* (*pl* **-la**) programme *m* scolaire. **~ vitae** *n* curriculum vitae *m*.

curry *n* curry *m*. ● *vt* **~ favour with** chercher les bonnes grâces de.

curse *n* (spell) malédiction *f*; (swearword) juron *m*. ● *vt* maudire. ● *vi* (swear) jurer.

cursor *n* curseur *m*.
curt *a* brusque.
curtain *n* rideau *m*.
curve *n* courbe *f*. ● *vi* (*line*) s'incurver; (*edge*) se recourber; (*road*) faire une courbe. ● *vt* courber.
cushion *n* coussin *m*. ● *vt* (a blow) amortir; (fig) protéger.
custard *n* crème *f* anglaise; (set) flan *m*.
custody *n* (of child) garde *f*; (Jur) détention *f* préventive.
custom *n* coutume *f*; (patronage: Comm) clientèle *f*. **customary** *a* habituel.
customer *n* client/-e *m*/*f*; (person 🅸) type *m*.
customize *vt* personnaliser.
custom-made *a* fait sur mesure.
customs *npl* douane *f*. ● *a* douanier. ~ **officer** *n* douanier *m*.
cut *vt*/*i* (*pt* **cut**; *pres p* **cutting**) *vt* couper; (*hedge*) tailler; (*prices*) réduire. ● *vi* couper. ● *n* (wound) coupure *f*; (of clothes) coupe *f*; (in surgery) incision *f*; (share) part *f*; (in prices) réduction *f*. □ ~ **back** *vi* faire des économies. *vt* réduire. ~ **down** (**on**) réduire; ~ **in** (in conversation) intervenir; ~ **off** couper; (*tide, army*) isoler; ~ **out** *vt* découper; (leave out) supprimer; *vi* (*engine*) s'arrêter. ~ **short** (visit) écourter; ~ **up** couper; (carve) découper.
cut-back *n* réduction *f*.
cute *a* 🅸 mignon.
cutlery *n* couverts *mpl*.
cutlet *n* côtelette *f*.
cut-price *a* à prix réduit.
cutting *a* cinglant. ● *n* (from newspaper) coupure *f*; (plant) bouture *f*.
CV *abbr* ⇨CURRICULUM VITAE.
cyanide *n* cyanure *m*.
cycle *n* cycle *m*; (bicycle) vélo *m*. ● *vi* aller à vélo.
cycling *n* cyclisme *m*. ~ **shorts** *npl* cycliste *m*.
cyclist *n* cycliste *mf*.
cylinder *n* cylindre *m*.
cymbal *n* cymbale *f*.
cynic *n* cynique *mf*. **cynical** *a* cynique. **cynicism** *n* cynisme *m*.
cypress *n* cyprès *m*.
Cypriot *n* Cypriote *mf*. ● *a* cypriote.
Cyprus *n* Chypre *f*.
cyst *n* kyste *m*.
czar *n* tsar *m*.
Czech *n* (person) Tchèque *mf*; (Ling) tchèque *m*. ~ **Republic** *n* République *f* tchèque.

dab *vt* (*pt* **dabbed**) tamponner; ~ **sth on** appliquer qch par petites touches. ● *n* touche *f*.
dabble *vi* ~ **in sth** faire qch en amateur.
dad *n* 🅸 papa *m*. **daddy** *n* 🅸 papa *m*.
daffodil *n* jonquille *f*.
daft *a* bête.
dagger *n* poignard *m*.
daily *a* quotidien. ● *adv* tous les jours. ● *n* (newspaper) quotidien *m*.
dainty *a* (**-ier**, **-iest**) (*lace, food*) délicat; (*shoe, hand*) mignon.
dairy *n* (on farm) laiterie *f*; (shop) crémerie *f*. ● *a* (*farm, cow, product*) laitier; (*butter*) fermier.
daisy *n* pâquerette *f*; (Comput) ~ **wheel** marguerite *f*.

dale *n* vallée *f*.

dam *n* barrage *m*.

damage *n* (to property) dégâts *mpl*; (Med) lésions *fpl*; **to do sth ~** (cause, trade) porter atteinte à; **~s** (Jur) dommages-intérêts *mpl*. ● *vt* (*property*) endommager; (*health*) nuire à; (*reputation*) porter atteinte à. **damaging** *a* (to health) nuisible; (to reputation) préjudiciable.

damn *vt* (Relig) damner; (condemn: fig) condamner. ● *interj* [I] zut [I], merde [X]. ● *n* **not give/care a ~ about** se ficher de [I]. ● *a* fichu [I]. ● *adv* franchement.

damp *n* humidité *f*. ● *a* humide. **dampen** *vt* (lit) humecter; (fig) refroidir. **dampness** *n* humidité *f*.

dance *vt/i* danser. ● *n* danse *f*; (gathering) bal *m*; **~ hall** dancing *m*. **dancer** *n* danseur/-euse *m/f*.

dandelion *n* pissenlit *m*.

dandruff *n* pellicules *fpl*.

Dane *n* Danois/-e *m/f*.

danger *n* danger *m*; (risk) risque *m*; **be in ~ of** risquer de. **dangerous** *a* dangereux.

dangle *vt* (*object*) balancer; (*legs*) laisser pendre. ● *vi* (*object*) se balancer (**from** à).

Danish *n* (Ling) danois *m*. ● *a* danois.

dare *vt* oser ((**to**) **do** faire); **~ sb to do** défier qn de faire. ● *n* défi *m*. **daring** *a* audacieux.

dark *a* (*day, colour, suit, mood, warning*) sombre; (*hair, eyes, skin*) brun; (*secret, thought*) noir. ● *n* noir *m*; (nightfall) tombée *f* de la nuit; **in the ~** (fig) dans le noir. **darken** *vt/i* (*sky*) (s')obscurcir; (*colour*) (se) foncer; (*mood*) (s')assombrir. **darkness** *n* obscurité *f*. **~-room** *n* chambre *f* noire.

darling *a* & *n* chéri/-e (*m/f*).

dart *n* fléchette *f*; **~s** (game) fléchettes *fpl*. ● *vi* **~ in/away** entrer/filer comme une flèche.

dash *vi* se précipiter; **~ off** se sauver. ● *vt* (*hope*) anéantir; **~ sth against** projeter qch contre. ● *n* course *f* folle; (of liquid) goutte *f*; (of colour) touche *f*; (in punctuation) tiret *m*.

dashboard *n* tableau *m* de bord.

data *npl* données *fpl*. **~base** *n* base *f* de données. **~ capture** *n* saisie *f* de données. **~ processing** *n* traitement *m* des données. **~ protection** *n* protection *f* de l'information.

date *n* date *f*; (meeting) rendez-vous *m*; (fruit) datte *f*; **out of ~** (old-fashioned) démodé; (*passport*) périmé; **to ~** à ce jour; **up to ~** (modern) moderne; (*list*) à jour. ● *vt/i* dater; (go out with) sortir avec; **~ from** dater de. **dated** *a* démodé.

daughter *n* fille *f*. **~-in-law** *n* (*pl* **~s-in-law**) belle-fille *f*.

daunt *vt* décourager.

dawdle *vi* flâner, traînasser [I].

dawn *n* aube *f*. ● *vi* (*day*) se lever; **it ~ed on me that** je me suis rendu compte que.

day *n* jour *m*; (whole day) journée *f*; (period) époque *f*; **the ~ before** la veille; **the following** *or* **next ~** le lendemain. **~break** *n* aube *f*.

daydream *n* rêves *mpl*. ● *vi* rêvasser (**about** de).

day: **~light** *n* jour *m*. **~time** *n* journée *f*.

daze *n* **in a ~** (from blow) étourdi; (from drug) hébété. **dazed** *a* (by blow) abasourdi; (by news) ahuri.

dazzle *vt* éblouir.

dead *a* mort; (numb) engourdi. ● *adv* complètement; **in ~ centre** au beau milieu; **stop ~** s'arrêter net. ● *n* **in the ~ of** au cœur de; **the ~** les morts. **deaden** *vt* (*sound, blow*) amortir; (*pain*) calmer. ~ **end** *n* impasse *f*. ~**line** *n* date *f* limite. ~**lock** *n* impasse *f*.

deadly *a* (**-ier**, **-iest**) mortel; (*weapon*) meurtrier.

deaf *a* sourd. **deafen** *vt* assourdir. **deafness** *n* surdité *f*.

deal *vt* (*pt* **dealt**) donner; (*blow*) porter. ● *vi* (trade) être en activité; ~ **in** être dans le commerce de. ● *n* affaire *f*; (cards) donne *f*; **a great** *or* **good** ~ beaucoup (**of** de). □ ~ **with** (handle, manage) s'occuper de; (be about) traiter de. **dealer** *n* marchand/-e *m/f*; (agent) concessionnaire *mf*. **dealings** *npl* relations *fpl*.

dear *a* cher; ~ **Sir/Madam** Monsieur/Madame. ● *n* (**my**) ~ mon chéri/ma chérie *m/f*. ● *adv* cher. ● *interj* **oh** ~! oh mon Dieu!

death *n* mort *f*; ~ **penalty** peine *f* de mort. **deathly** *a* de mort, mortel.

debase *vt* avilir.

debatable *a* discutable.

debate *n* (formal) débat *m*; (informal) discussion *f*. ● *vt* (formally) débattre de; (informally) discuter.

debit *n* débit *m*. ● *a* (*balance*) débiteur. ● *vt* (*pt* **debited**) débiter.

debris *n* débris *mpl*; (rubbish) déchets *mpl*.

debt *n* dette *f*; **be in** ~ avoir des dettes.

debug *vt* (Comput) déboguer.

decade *n* décennie *f*.

decadent *a* décadent.

decaffeinated *a* décaféiné.

decay *vi* (*vegetation*) pourrir; (*tooth*) se carier; (fig) décliner. ● *n* pourriture *f*; (of tooth) carie *f*; (fig) déclin *m*.

deceased *a* décédé. ● *n* défunt/-e *m/f*.

deceit *n* tromperie *f*. **deceitful** *a* trompeur. **deceitfully** *adv* d'une manière trompeuse.

deceive *vt* tromper.

December *n* décembre *m*.

decent *a* (respectable) comme il faut; (adequate) convenable; (good) bon; (kind) gentil; (not indecent) décent. **decently** *adv* convenablement.

deception *n* tromperie *f*. **deceptive** *a* trompeur.

decide *vt/i* décider (**to do** de faire); (question) régler; ~ **on** se décider pour. **decided** *a* (firm) résolu; (clear) net. **decidedly** *adv* nettement.

decimal *a* décimal. ● *n* décimale *f*; ~ **point** virgule *f*.

decipher *vt* déchiffrer.

decision *n* décision *f*.

decisive *a* (conclusive) décisif; (firm) décidé.

deck *n* pont *m*; (of cards: US) jeu *m*; (of bus) étage *m*. ~**-chair** *n* chaise *f* longue.

declaration *n* déclaration *f*. **declare** *vt* déclarer.

decline *vt/i* refuser; (fall) baisser. ● *n* (waning) déclin *m*; (drop) baisse *f*; **in** ~ sur le déclin.

decode *vt* décoder.

decompose *vt/i* (se) décomposer.

decor *n* décor *m*.

decorate *vt* décorer; (*room*) refaire, peindre. **decoration** *n* décoration *f*. **decorative** *a* décoratif.

decorator *n* peintre *m*; (**interior**) ~ décorateur/-trice *m/f*.

decoy *n* (person, vehicle) leurre *m*; (for hunting) appeau *m*.

decrease[1] *vt/i* diminuer.

decrease[2] *n* diminution *f*.

decree *n* (Pol, Relig) décret *m*; (Jur) jugement *m*. ● *vt* (*pt* **decreed**) décréter.

decrepit *a* (building) délabré; (person) décrépit.

dedicate *vt* dédier; **~ oneself to** se consacrer à.

dedicated *a* dévoué; **~ line** (Internet) ligne *f* spécialisée.

dedication *n* dévouement *m*; (in book) dédicace *f*.

deduce *vt* déduire.

deduct *vt* déduire; (from wages) retenir.

deed *n* acte *m*.

deem *vt* considérer.

deep *a* profond; (*mud, carpet*) épais. ● *adv* profondément; **~ in thought** absorbé dans ses pensées. **deepen** *vt/i* (*admiration, concern*) augmenter; (*colour*) foncer.

deep-freeze *n* congélateur *m*. ● *vt* congeler.

deer *n inv* cerf *m*; (doe) biche *f*.

deface *vt* dégrader.

default *vi* (Jur) **~ (on payments)** ne pas régler ses échéances. ● *n* (on payments) non-remboursement *m*; **by ~** par défaut; **win by ~** gagner par forfait. ● *a* (Comput) par défaut.

defeat *vt* vaincre; (thwart) faire échouer. ● *n* défaite *f*; (of plan) échec *m*.

defect[1] *n* défaut *m*.

defect[2] *vi* faire défection; **~ to** passer à.

defective *a* défectueux.

defector *n* transfuge *mf*.

defence *n* défense *f*.

defend *vt* défendre. **defendant** *n* (Jur) accusé/-e *m/f*. **defender** défenseur *m*.

defensive *a* défensif. ● *n* défensive *f*.

defer *vt* (*pt* **deferred**) (postpone) reporter; (*judgement*) suspendre; (*payment*) différer.

deference *n* déférence *f*. **deferential** *a* déférent.

defiance *n* défi *m*; **in ~ of** contre. **defiant** *a* rebelle. **defiantly** *adv* avec défi.

deficiency *n* insuffisance *f*; (fault) défaut *m*.

deficient *a* insuffisant; **be ~ in** manquer de.

deficit *n* déficit *m*.

define *vt* définir.

definite *a* (exact) précis; (obvious) net; (firm) ferme; (certain) certain. **definitely** *adv* certainement; (clearly) nettement.

definition *n* définition *f*.

deflate *vt* dégonfler.

deflect *vt* (*missile*) dévier; (*criticism*) détourner.

deforestation *n* déforestation *f*.

deform *vt* déformer.

defraud *vt* (*client, employer*) escroquer; (*state, customs*) frauder; **~ sb of sth** escroquer qch à qn.

defrost *vt* dégivrer.

deft *a* adroit.

defunct *a* défunt.

defuse *vt* désamorcer.

defy *vt* défier; (*attempts*) résister à.

degenerate[1] *vi* dégénérer (**into** en).

degenerate[2] *a & n* dégénéré/-e (*m/f*).

degrade *vt* (humiliate) humilier; (damage) dégrader.

degree *n* degré *m*; (Univ) diplôme *m* universitaire; (Bachelor's degree) licence *f*; **to such a ~ that** à tel point que.

dehydrate *vt/i* (se) déshydrater.

deign *vt* **~ to do** daigner faire.

dejected *a* découragé.

delay *vt* (*flight*) retarder; (*decision*) différer; **~ doing**

attendre pour faire. ● *n* (of plane, post) retard *m*; (time lapse) délai *m*.
delegate[1] *n* délégué/-e *m/f*.
delegate[2] *vt* déléguer. **delegation** *n* délégation *f*.
delete *vt* supprimer; (Comput) effacer; (with pen) barrer. **deletion** *n* suppression *f*; (with line) rature *f*.
deliberate[1] *vi* délibérer.
deliberate[2] *a* délibéré; (*steps, manner*) mesuré. **deliberately** *adv* (*do, say*) exprès; (*sarcastically, provocatively*) délibérément.
delicacy *n* délicatesse *f*; (food) mets *m* raffiné.
delicate *a* délicat.
delicatessen *n* épicerie *f* fine.
delicious *a* délicieux.
delight *n* joie *f*, plaisir *m*. ● *vt* ravir. ● *vi* ~ **in** prendre plaisir à. **delighted** *a* ravi. **delightful** *a* charmant/-e.
delinquent *a* & *n* délinquant/-e (*m/f*).
delirious *a* délirant.
deliver *vt* (*message*) remettre; (*goods*) livrer; (*speech*) faire; (*baby*) mettre au monde; (rescue) délivrer. **delivery** *n* (of goods) livraison *f*; (of mail) distribution *f*; (of baby) accouchement *m*.
delude *vt* tromper; ~ **oneself** se faire des illusions.
deluge *n* déluge *m*. ● *vt* submerger (**with** de).
delusion *n* illusion *f*.
delve *vi* fouiller.
demand *vt* (request, require) demander; (forcefully) exiger. ● *n* (request) demande *f*; (pressure) exigence *f*; **in** ~ très demandé; **on** ~ à la demande. **demanding** *a* exigeant.
demean *vt* ~ **oneself** s'abaisser.
demeanour, (US) **demeanor** *n* comportement *m*.
demented *a* fou.
demise *n* disparition *f*.
demo *n* (demonstration [!]) manif *f* [!].
democracy *n* démocratie *f*.
democrat *n* démocrate *mf*. **democratic** *a* démocratique.
demolish *vt* démolir.
demon *n* démon *m*.
demonstrate *vt* démontrer; (*concern, skill*) manifester. ● *vi* (Pol) manifester. **demonstration** *n* démonstration *f*; (Pol) manifestation *f*. **demonstrative** *a* démonstratif. **demonstrator** *n* manifestant/-e *m/f*.
demoralize *vt* démoraliser.
demote *vt* rétrograder.
den *n* (of lion) antre *m*; (room) tanière *f*.
denial *n* (of rumour) démenti *m*; (of rights) négation *f*; (of request) rejet *m*.
denim *n* jean *m*; ~**s** (jeans) jean *m*.
Denmark *n* Danemark *m*.
denomination *n* (Relig) confession *f*; (money) valeur *f*.
denounce *vt* dénoncer.
dense *a* dense. **densely** *adv* (*packed*) très. **density** *n* densité *f*.
dent *n* bosse *f*. ● *vt* cabosser.
dental *a* dentaire; ~ **floss** fil *m* dentaire; ~ **surgeon** chirurgien-dentiste *m*.
dentist *n* dentiste *mf*. **dentistry** *n* médecine *f* dentaire.
dentures *npl* dentier *m*.
deny *vt* nier (**that** que); (*rumour*) démentir; ~ **sb sth** refuser qch à qn.
deodorant *n* déodorant *m*.
depart *vi* partir; ~ **from** (deviate) s'éloigner de.
department *n* (in shop) rayon *m*; (in hospital, office) service *m*; (Univ) département *m*; **D~ of Health**

ministère *m* de la santé; ~ **store** grand magasin *m*.

departure *n* départ *m*; **a ~ from** (*custom, truth*) une entorse à.

depend *vi* dépendre (**on** de); ~ **on** (rely on) compter sur; **it (all) ~s** ça dépend; **~ing on the season** suivant la saison. **dependable** *a* (*person*) digne de confiance. **dependant** *n* personne *f* à charge. **dependence** *n* dépendance *f*.

dependent *a* dépendant; **be ~ on** dépendre de.

depict *vt* (describe) dépeindre; (in picture) représenter.

deplete *vt* réduire.

deport *vt* expulser.

depose *vt* déposer.

deposit *vt* (*pt* **deposited**) déposer. ● *n* (in bank) dépôt *m*; (on house) versement *m* initial; (on holiday) acompte *m*; (against damage) caution *f*; (on bottle) consigne *f*; (of mineral) gisement *m*; ~ **account** compte *m* de dépôt. **depositor** *n* (Comm) déposant/-e *m/f*.

depot *n* dépôt *m*; (US) gare *f*.

depreciate *vt/i* (se) déprécier.

depress *vt* déprimer. **depressing** *a* déprimant. **depression** *n* dépression *f*; (Econ) récession *f*.

deprivation *n* privation *f*.

deprive *vt* ~ **of** priver de. **deprived** *a* démuni.

depth *n* profondeur *f*; (of knowledge, ignorance) étendue *f*; (of colour, emotion) intensité *f*.

deputize *vi* ~ **for** remplacer.

deputy *n* adjoint/-e *m/f*. ● *a* adjoint; ~ **chairman** vice-président *m*.

derail *vt* faire dérailler. **derailment** *n* déraillement *m*.

deranged *a* dérangé.

derelict *a* abandonné.

deride *vt* ridiculiser. **derision** *n* moqueries *fpl*. **derisory** *a* dérisoire.

derivative *a & n* dérivé (*m*).

derive *vt* ~ **sth from** tirer qch de. ● *vi* ~ **from** découler de.

derogatory *a* (*word*) péjoratif; (*remark*) désobligeant.

descend *vt/i* descendre; **be ~ed from** descendre de. **descendant** *n* descendant/-e *m/f*. **descent** *n* descente *f*; (lineage) origine *f*.

describe *vt* décrire; ~ **sb as sth** qualifier qn de qch. **description** *n* description *f*. **descriptive** *a* descriptif.

desert[1] *n* désert *m*.

desert[2] *vt/i* abandonner; (*cause*) déserter. **deserted** *a* désert. **deserter** *n* déserteur *m*.

deserts *npl* **get one's ~** avoir ce qu'on mérite.

deserve *vt* mériter (**to** de). **deservedly** *adv* à juste titre. **deserving** *a* (*person*) méritant; (*action*) louable.

design *n* (sketch) plan *m*; (idea) conception *f*; (pattern) motif *m*; (art of designing) design *m*; (aim) dessein *m*. ● *vt* (sketch) dessiner; (devise, intend) concevoir.

designate *vt* désigner.

designer *n* concepteur/-trice *m/f*; (of fashion, furniture) créateur/-trice *m/f*. ● *a* (*clothes*) de haute couture; (*sunglasses, drink*) de dernière mode.

desirable *a* (*outcome*) souhaitable; (*person*) désirable.

desire *n* désir *m*. ● *vt* désirer.

desk *n* bureau *m*; (of pupil) pupitre *m*; (in hotel) réception *f*; (in bank) caisse *f*.

desolate *a* (place) désolé; (*person*) affligé.

despair *n* désespoir *m*. ● *vi* désespérer (**of** de).

desperate *a* désespéré; (criminal) prêt à tout; **be ~ for** avoir désespérément besoin de. **desperately** *adv* désespérément; (*worried*) terriblement; (*ill*) gravement.

desperation *n* désespoir *m*; **in ~** en désespoir de cause.

despicable *a* méprisable.

despise *vt* mépriser.

despite *prep* malgré.

despondent *a* découragé.

dessert *n* dessert *m*. **~spoon** *n* cuillère *f* à dessert.

destination *n* destination *f*.

destiny *n* destin *m*.

destitute *a* sans ressources.

destroy *vt* détruire; (*animal*) abattre. **destroyer** *n* (warship) contre-torpilleur *m*.

destruction *n* destruction *f*. **destructive** *a* destructeur.

detach *vt* détacher; **~ed house** maison *f* (individuelle).

detail *n* détail *m*; **go into ~** entrer dans les détails. ● *vt* (*plans*) exposer en détail.

detain *vt* retenir; (in prison) placer en détention. **detainee** *n* détenu/-e *m*/*f*.

detect *vt* (*error, trace*) déceler; (*crime, mine, sound*) détecter. **detection** *n* détection *f*. **detective** *n* inspecteur/-trice *m*/*f*; (private) détective *m*.

detention *n* détention *f*; (School) retenue *f*.

deter *vt* (*pt* **deterred**) dissuader (**from** de).

detergent *a* & *n* détergent (*m*).

deteriorate *vi* se détériorer.

determine *vt* déterminer; **~ to do** résoudre de faire. **determined** *a* (*person*) décidé; (*air*) résolu.

deterrent *n* moyen *m* de dissuasion. ● *a* (*effect*) dissuasif.

detest *vt* détester.

detonate *vt*/*i* (faire) détoner.

detonation *n* détonation *f*. **detonator** *n* détonateur *m*.

detour *n* détour *m*.

detract *vi* **~ from** (*success, value*) porter atteinte à; (*pleasure*) diminuer.

detriment *n* **to the ~ of** au détriment de. **detrimental** *a* nuisible (**to** à).

devalue *vt* dévaluer.

devastate *vt* (*place*) ravager; (*person*) accabler.

develop *vt* (*plan*) élaborer; (*mind, body*) développer; (*land*) mettre en valeur; (*illness*) attraper; (*habit*) prendre. ● *vi* (*child, country, plot, business*) se développer; (*hole, crack*) se former.

development *n* développement *m*; (**housing**) **~** lotissement *m*; (**new**) **~** fait *m* nouveau.

deviate *vi* dévier; **~ from** (*norm*) s'écarter de.

device *n* appareil *m*; (means) moyen *m*; (bomb) engin *m* explosif.

devil *n* diable *m*.

devious *a* (*person*) retors.

devise *vt* (*scheme*) concevoir; (*product*) inventer.

devoid *a* **~ of** dépourvu de.

devolution *n* (Pol) régionalisation *f*.

devote *vt* consacrer (**to** à). **devoted** *a* dévoué. **devotion** *n* dévouement *m*; (Relig) dévotion *f*.

devour *vt* dévorer.

devout *a* fervent.

dew *n* rosée *f*.

diabetes *n* diabète *m*.

diabolical *a* diabolique; (bad 🅸) atroce.

diagnose *vt* diagnostiquer. **diagnosis** *n* (*pl* **-oses**) diagnostic *m*.

diagonal *a* diagonal. ●*n* diagonale *f*.
diagram *n* schéma *m*.
dial *n* cadran *m*. ●*vt* (*pt* **dialled**) (*number*) faire; (*person*) appeler; **dialling code** indicatif *m*; **dialling tone** tonalité *f*.
dialect *n* dialecte *m*.
dialogue *n* dialogue *m*.
diameter *n* diamètre *m*.
diamond *n* diamant *m*; (shape) losange *m*; (baseball) terrain *m*; **~s** (cards) carreau *m*.
diaper *n* (US) couche *f*.
diaphragm *n* diaphragme *m*.
diarrhoea, (US) **diarrhea** *n* diarrhée *f*.
diary *n* (for appointments) agenda *m*; (journal) journal *m* intime.
dice *n inv* dé *m*. ●*vt* (*food*) couper en dés.
dictate *vt/i* dicter.
dictation *n* dictée *f*.
dictator *n* dictateur *m*. **dictatorship** *n* dictature *f*.
dictionary *n* dictionnaire *m*.
did ⇒DO.
didn't = DID NOT.
die *vi* (*pres p* **dying**) mourir; (*plant*) crever; **be dying to do** mourir d'envie de faire. □ **~ down** diminuer; **~ out** disparaître.
diesel *n* gazole *m*; **~ engine** moteur *m* diesel.
diet *n* (usual food) alimentation *f*; (restricted) régime *m*. ●*vi* être au régime. **dietary** *a* alimentaire. **dietician** *n* diététicien/-ne *m/f*.
differ *vi* différer (**from** de).
difference *n* différence *f*; (disagreement) différend *m*. **different** *a* différent (**from, to** de).
differentiate *vt* différencier. ●*vi* faire la différence (**between** entre).
differently *adv* différemment (**from** de).
difficult *a* difficile. **difficulty** *n* difficulté *f*.
diffuse¹ *a* diffus.
diffuse² *vt* diffuser.
dig *vt/i* (*pt* **dug**; *pres p* **digging**) (excavate) creuser; (in garden) bêcher. ●*n* (poke) coup *m* de coude; (remark) pique *f* ⊡; (Archeol) fouilles *fpl*. □ **~ up** déterrer.
digest *vt/i* digérer. **digestible** *a* digestible. **digestion** *n* digestion *f*.
digger *n* excavateur *m*.
digit *n* chiffre *m*.
digital *a* (*clock*) à affichage numérique; (*display, recording*) numérique. **~ audio tape** *n* cassette *f* audionumérique.
dignified *a* digne.
dignitary *n* dignitaire *m*.
dignity *n* dignité *f*.
digress *vi* faire une digression.
dilapidated *a* délabré.
dilate *vt/i* (se) dilater.
dilemma *n* dilemme *m*.
diligent *a* appliqué.
dilute *vt* diluer.
dim *a* (**dimmer, dimmest**) (weak) faible; (dark) sombre; (indistinct) vague; ⊡ stupide. ●*vt/i* (*pt* **dimmed**) (*light*) baisser.
dime *n* (US) (pièce *f* de) dix cents.
dimension *n* dimension *f*.
diminish *vt/i* diminuer.
dimple *n* fossette *f*.
din *n* vacarme *m*.
dine *vi* dîner. **diner** *n* dîneur/-euse *m/f*; (Rail) wagon-restaurant *m*; (US) restaurant *m* à service rapide.
dinghy *n* dériveur *m*.
dingy *a* (**-ier, -iest**) miteux, minable.
dining room *n* salle *f* à manger.
dinner *n* (evening meal) dîner *m*;

(lunch) déjeuner *m*; **have ~** dîner. **~-jacket** *n* smoking *m*. **~ party** *n* dîner *m*.

dinosaur *n* dinosaure *m*.

dip *vt*/*i* (*pt* **dipped**) plonger; **~ into** (*book*) feuilleter; (*savings*) puiser dans; **~ one's headlights** se mettre en code. ● *n* (slope) déclivité *f*; (in sea) bain *m* rapide.

diploma *n* diplôme *m* (**in** en).

diplomacy *n* diplomatie *f*. **diplomat** *n* diplomate *mf*. **diplomatic** *a* (Pol) diplomatique; (tactful) diplomate.

dire *a* affreux; (*need, poverty*) extrême.

direct *a* direct. ● *adv* directement. ● *vt* diriger; (*letter, remark*) adresser; (*a play*) mettre en scène; **~ sb to** indiquer à qn le chemin de; (order) signifier à qn de. **direction** *n* direction *f*; (Theat) mise *f* en scène; **~s** indications *fpl*; **ask ~s** demander le chemin; **~s for use** mode *m* d'emploi. **directly** *adv* directement; (at once) tout de suite. ● *conj* dès que. **director** *n* directeur/-trice *m*/*f*; (Theat) metteur *m* en scène. **directory** *n* (phone book) annuaire *m*. **~ enquiries** *npl* renseignements *mpl* téléphoniques.

dirt *n* saleté *f*; (earth) terre *f*; **~ cheap** ⊠ très bon marché *inv*. **~-track** *n* (Sport) cendrée *f*. **dirty** *a* (**-ier**, **-iest**) sale; (word) grossier; **get ~** se salir. ● *vt*/*i* (se) salir.

disability *n* handicap *m*. **disable** *vt* rendre infirme. **disabled** *a* handicapé.

disadvantage *n* désavantage *m*. **disadvantaged** *a* défavorisé.

disagree *vi* ne pas être d'accord (**with** avec); **~ with sb** (*food, climate*) ne pas convenir à qn. **disagreement** *n* désaccord *m*; (quarrel) différend *m*.

disappear *vi* disparaître. **disappearance** *n* disparition *f* (**of** de).

disappoint *vt* décevoir. **disappointment** *n* déception *f*.

disapproval *n* désapprobation *f* (**of** de).

disapprove *vi* **~ (of)** désapprouver.

disarm *vt*/*i* désarmer. **disarmament** *n* désarmement *m*.

disarray *n* désordre *m*.

disaster *n* désastre *m*. **disastrous** *a* désastreux.

disband *vi* disperser. ● *vt* dissoudre.

disbelief *n* incrédulité *f*.

disc *n* disque *m*; (Comput) = DISK.

discard *vt* se débarrasser de; (*beliefs*) abandonner.

discharge *vt* (unload) décharger; (*liquid*) déverser; (*duty*) remplir; (dismiss) renvoyer; (*prisoner*) libérer. ● *vi* (of pus) s'écouler.

disciple *n* disciple *m*.

disciplinary *a* disciplinaire.

discipline *n* discipline *f*. ● *vt* discipliner; (punish) punir.

disc jockey *n* disc-jockey *m*, animateur *m*.

disclaimer *n* démenti *m*.

disclose *vt* révéler. **disclosure** *n* révélation *f* (**of** de).

disco *n* (club ⊡) discothèque *f*; (event) soirée *f* disco.

discolour *vt*/*i* (se) décolorer.

discomfort *n* gêne *f*.

disconcert *vt* déconcerter.

disconnect *vt* détacher; (unplug) débrancher; (cut off) couper.

discontent *n* mécontentement *m*.

discontinue *vt* (*service*) supprimer; (*production*) arrêter.

discord *n* discorde *f*; (Mus) discordance *f*.
discount¹ *n* remise *f*; (on minor purchase) rabais *m*.
discount² *vt* (*advice*) ne pas tenir compte de; (*possibility*) écarter.
discourage *vt* décourager.
discourse *n* discours *m*.
discourteous *a* peu courtois.
discover *vt* découvrir. **discovery** *n* découverte *f*.
discreet *a* discret.
discrepancy *n* divergence *f*.
discretion *n* discrétion *f*.
discriminate *vt/i* distinguer; ~ **against** faire de la discrimination contre. **discriminating** *a* qui a du discernement. **discrimination** *n* discernement *m*; (bias) discrimination *f*.
discus *n* disque *m*.
discuss *vt* (talk about) discuter de; (in writing) examiner. **discussion** *n* discussion *f*.
disdain *n* dédain *m*.
disease *n* maladie *f*.
disembark *vt/i* débarquer.
disenchanted *a* désabusé.
disentangle *vt* démêler.
disfigure *vt* défigurer.
disgrace *n* (shame) honte *f*; (disfavour) disgrâce *f*. ● *vt* déshonorer. **disgraced** *a* (in disfavour) disgracié. **disgraceful** *a* honteux.
disgruntled *a* mécontent.
disguise *vt* déguiser. ● *n* déguisement *m*; **in** ~ déguisé.
disgust *n* dégoût *m*. ● *vt* dégoûter.
dish *n* plat *m*; **the** ~**es** (crockery) la vaisselle. ● *vt* ~ **out** 🅸 distribuer; ~ **up** servir.
dishcloth *n* lavette *f*; (for drying) torchon *m*.
dishearten *vt* décourager.
dishevelled *a* échevelé.
dishonest *a* malhonnête.
dishonour, (US) **dishonor** *n* déshonneur *m*.
dishwasher *n* lave-vaisselle *m inv*.
disillusion *vt* désabuser. **disillusionment** *n* désillusion *f*.

disincentive *n* **be a** ~ **to** décourager.
disinclined *a* ~ **to** peu disposé à.
disinfect *vt* désinfecter. **disinfectant** *n* désinfectant *m*.
disintegrate *vt/i* (se) désintégrer.
disinterested *a* désintéressé.
disjointed *a* (talk) décousu.
disk *n* (US) = DISC; (Comput) disque *m*. ~ **drive** *n* drive *m*, lecteur *m* de disquettes.
diskette *n* disquette *f*.
dislike *n* aversion *f*. ● *vt* ne pas aimer.
dislocate *vt* (limb) disloquer.
dislodge *vt* (move) déplacer; (drive out) déloger.
disloyal *a* déloyal (**to** envers).
dismal *a* morne, triste.
dismantle *vt* démonter, défaire.
dismay *n* consternation *f* (**at** devant). ● *vt* consterner.
dismiss *vt* renvoyer; (*appeal*) rejeter; (from mind) écarter. **dismissal** *n* renvoi *m*.
dismount *vi* descendre, mettre pied à terre.
disobedient *a* désobéissant.
disobey *vt* désobéir à. ● *vi* désobéir.
disorder *n* désordre *m*; (ailment) trouble(s) *m*(*pl*). **disorderly** *a* désordonné.
disorganized *a* désorganisé.
disown *vt* renier.
disparaging *a* désobligeant.
dispassionate *a* impartial; (unemotional) calme.
dispatch *vt* (send, complete)

expédier; (troops) envoyer. ● *n* expédition *f*; envoi *m*; (report) dépêche *f*.

dispel *vt* (*pt* **dispelled**) dissiper.

dispensary *n* (in hospital) pharmacie *f*, (in chemist's) officine *f*.

dispense *vt* distribuer; (*medicine*) préparer. ● *vi* ~ **with** se passer de. **dispenser** *n* (container) distributeur *m*.

disperse *vt/i* (se) disperser.

display *vt* montrer, exposer; (*feelings*) manifester. ● *n* exposition *f*; manifestation *f*; (Comm) étalage *m*; (of computer) visuel *m*.

displeased *a* mécontent (**with** de).

disposable *a* jetable.

disposal *n* (of waste) évacuation *f*; **at sb's** ~ à la disposition de qn.

dispose *vt* disposer. ● *vi* ~ **of** se débarrasser de; **well** ~**d to** bien disposé envers.

disposition *n* disposition *f*; (character) naturel *m*.

disprove *vt* réfuter.

dispute *vt* contester. ● *n* discussion *f*; (Pol) conflit *m*; **in** ~ contesté.

disqualify *vt* rendre inapte; (Sport) disqualifier; ~ **from driving** retirer le permis à.

disquiet *n* inquiétude *f*. **disquieting** *a* inquiétant.

disregard *vt* ne pas tenir compte de. ● *n* indifférence *f* (**for** à).

disrepair *n* délabrement *m*.

disreputable *a* peu recommendable.

disrepute *n* discrédit *m*.

disrespect *n* manque *m* de respect. **disrespectful** *a* irrespectueux.

disrupt *vt* (disturb, break up) perturber; (*plans*) déranger. **disruption** *n* perturbation *f*. **disruptive** *a* perturbateur.

dissatisfied *a* mécontent.

dissect *vt* disséquer.

disseminate *vt* diffuser.

dissent *vi* différer (**from** de). ● *n* dissentiment *m*.

dissertation *n* mémoire *m*.

disservice *n* **do a** ~ **to sb** rendre un mauvais service à qn.

dissident *a* & *n* dissident/-e (*m*/*f*).

dissimilar *a* dissemblable, différent.

dissipate *vt/i* (se) dissiper. **dissipated** *a* (person) dissolu.

dissolve *vt/i* (se) dissoudre.

dissuade *vt* dissuader.

distance *n* distance *f*; **from a** ~ de loin; **in the** ~ au loin. **distant** *a* éloigné, lointain; (*relative*) éloigné; (aloof) distant.

distaste *n* dégoût *m*. **distasteful** *a* désagréable.

distil *vt* (*pt* **distilled**) distiller.

distinct *a* distinct; (definite) net; **as** ~ **from** par opposition à. **distinction** *n* distinction *f*; (in exam) mention *f* très bien. **distinctive** *a* distinctif.

distinguish *vt/i* distinguer.

distort *vt* déformer. **distortion** *n* distorsion *f*; (of facts) déformation *f*.

distract *vt* distraire. **distracted** *a* (distraught) éperdu. **distracting** *a* gênant. **distraction** *n* (lack of attention, entertainment) distraction *f*.

distraught *a* éperdu.

distress *n* douleur *f*; (poverty, danger) détresse *f*. ● *vt* peiner. **distressing** *a* pénible.

distribute *vt* distribuer.

district *n* région *f*; (of town) quartier *m*.

distrust *n* méfiance *f*. ● *vt* se méfier de.

disturb *vt* déranger; (alarm, worry) troubler. **disturbance** *n* dérangement *m* (**of** de); (noise) tapage *m*. **disturbances** *npl* (Pol) troubles *mpl*. **disturbed** *a* troublé; (psychologically) perturbé. **disturbing** *a* troublant.

disused *a* désaffecté.

ditch *n* fossé *m*. ● *vt* ☒ abandonner.

ditto *adv* idem.

dive *vi* plonger; (rush) se précipiter. ● *n* plongeon *m*; (of plane) piqué *m*; (place ☒) bouge *m*. **diver** *n* plongeur/-euse *m/f*.

diverge *vi* diverger. **divergent** *a* divergent.

diverse *a* divers.

diversion *n* détournement *m*; (distraction) diversion *f*; (of traffic) déviation *f*. **divert** *vt* détourner; (*traffic*) dévier.

divide *vt/i* (se) diviser.

dividend *n* dividende *m*.

divine *a* divin.

diving: **~-board** *n* plongeoir *m*. **~-suit** *n* scaphandre *m*.

division *n* division *f*.

divorce *n* divorce *m* (**from** avec). ● *vt/i* divorcer (d'avec).

divulge *vt* divulguer.

DIY *abbr* →DO-IT-YOURSELF.

dizziness *n* vertige *m*.

dizzy *a* (**-ier**, **-iest**) vertigineux; **be** *or* **feel ~** avoir le vertige.

---

do

present **do**, **does**; *present negative* **don't**, **do not**; *past* **did**; *past participle* **done**

● *transitive and intransitive verb*

····➤ faire; **she is doing her homework** elle fait ses devoirs.

····➤ (progress, be suitable) aller; **how are you doing?** comment ça va?

····➤ (be enough) suffire; **will five dollars ~?** cinq dollars, ça suffira?

● *auxiliary verb*

····➤ (in questions) **~ you like Mozart?** aimes-tu Mozart?, est-ce que tu aimes Mozart?; **did your sister phone?** est-ce que ta sœur a téléphoné?, ta sœur a-t-elle téléphoné?

····➤ (in negatives) **I don't like Mozart** je n'aime pas Mozart.

····➤ (emphatic uses) **I ~ like your dress** j'aime beaucoup ta robe; **I ~ think you should go** je pense vraiment que tu devrais y aller.

····➤ (referring back to another verb) **I live in Oxford and so does Lily** j'habite à Oxford et Lily aussi; **she gets paid more than I ~** elle est payée plus que moi; **'I don't like carrots'—'neither ~ I'** 'je n'aime pas les carottes'—'moi non plus'.

····➤ (imperatives) **don't shut the door** ne ferme pas la porte; **~ be quiet** tais-toi!

····➤ (short questions and answers) **you like fish, don't you?** tu aimes le poisson, n'est-ce pas?; **Lola didn't phone, did she?** Lola n'a pas téléphoné par hasard?; **'does he play tennis?'—'no he doesn't/yes he does'** 'est-ce qu'il joue au tennis?'—'non/oui'; **'Marion didn't say that'—'yes she did'** 'Marion n'a pas dit ça'—'si'.

□ **do away with** supprimer;

do up (fasten) fermer; (*house*) refaire;

do with **it's to ~ with** c'est à propos de; **it's nothing to ~ with** ça n'a rien à voir avec;

do without se passer de.

---

docile *a* docile.

dock *n* (Jur) banc *m* des accusés; dock *m*. ● *vi* arriver au port. ● *vt* mettre à quai; (*wages*) faire une retenue sur.

doctor *n* médecin *m*, docteur *m*; (Univ) docteur *m*. ● *vt* (*cat*) châtrer; (fig) altérer.

doctorate *n* doctorat *m*.

document *n* document *m*. **documentary** *a & n* documentaire (*m*). **documentation** *n* documentation *f*.

dodge *vt* esquiver. ● *vi* faire un saut de côté. ● *n* mouvement *m* de côté.

dodgems *npl* autos *fpl* tamponneuses.

dodgy *a* (**-ier**, **-iest**) ([!]: difficult) épineux, délicat; (untrustworthy) louche [!].

doe *n* (deer) biche *f*.

does ⇒DO.

doesn't = DOES NOT.

dog *n* chien *m*. ● *vt* (*pt* **dogged**) poursuivre. **~-collar** *n* col *m* romain. **~-eared** *a* écorné.

dogged *a* obstiné.

dogma *n* dogme *m*. **dogmatic** *a* dogmatique.

dogsbody *n* bonne *f* à tout faire.

do-it-yourself *n* bricolage *m*.

doldrums *npl* **be in the ~** (person) avoir le cafard.

dole *vt* **~ out** distribuer. ● *n* [!] indemnité *f* de chômage; **on the ~** [!] au chômage.

doll *n* poupée *f*. ● *vt* **~ up** [!] bichonner.

dollar *n* dollar *m*.

dollop *n* (of food [!]) gros morceau *m*.

dolphin *n* dauphin *m*.

domain *n* domaine *m*.

dome *n* dôme *m*.

domestic *a* familial; (*trade, flights*) intérieur; (*animal*) domestique. **domesticated** *a* (*animal*) domestiqué.

domesticity *n* vie *f* de famille.

domestic science *n* arts *mpl* ménagers.

dominant *a* dominant.

dominate *vt/i* dominer. **domination** *n* domination *f*.

domineering *a* dominateur.

domino *n* (*pl* **~es**) domino *m*; **~es** (game) dominos *mpl*.

donate *vt* faire don de. **donation** *n* don *m*.

done ⇒DO.

donkey *n* âne *m*. **~ work** *n* travail *m* pénible.

donor *n* donateur/-trice *m/f*; (of blood) donneur/-euse *m/f*.

don't = DO NOT.

doodle *vi* griffonner.

doom *n* (ruin) ruine *f*; (fate) destin *m*. ● *vt* **be ~ed to** être destiné *or* condamné à; **~ed (to failure)** voué à l'échec.

door *n* porte *f*; (of vehicle) portière *f*, porte *f*. **~bell** *n* sonnette *f*. **~man** *n* (*pl* **-men**) portier *m*. **~mat** *n* paillasson *m*. **~step** *n* pas *m* de (la) porte, seuil *m*. **~way** *n* porte *f*.

dope *n* [!] cannabis *m*; (idiot [✱]) imbécile *mf*. ● *vt* doper. **dopey** *a* (foolish [✱]) imbécile.

dormant *a* en sommeil.

dormitory *n* dortoir *m*; (Univ, US) résidence *f*.

dosage *n* dose *f*; (on label) posologie *f*.

dose *n* dose *f*.

doss *vi* [✱] roupiller.

dot *n* point *m*; **on the ~** [!] à l'heure pile. **~-com** *n* société *f* en ligne *or* point com.

dote *vi* **~ on** adorer.

dotted *a* (*fabric*) à pois; **~ line** pointillé *m*; **~ with** parsemé de.

double *a* double; (*room, bed*) pour deux personnes; **~ the size** deux fois plus grand. ● *adv* deux fois; **pay ~** payer le double. ● *n* double *m*; (stuntman) doublure *f*; **~s** (tennis) double *m*; **at** or **on the ~** au pas de course. ● *vt/i* doubler; (fold) plier en deux. **~-bass** *n* (Mus) contrebasse *f*. **~-check** *vt* revérifier. **~ chin** *n* double menton *m*. **~-cross** *vt* tromper. **~-decker** *n* autobus *m* à impériale. **~ Dutch** *n* de l'hébreu *m*.

doubt *n* doute *m*. ● *vt* douter de; **~ if** *or* **that** douter que. **doubtful** *a* incertain, douteux; (*person*) qui a des doutes. **doubtless** *adv* sans doute.

dough *n* pâte *f*; (money ⊠) fric *m* ⊡.

doughnut *n* beignet *m*.

douse *vt* arroser; (*light, fire*) éteindre.

dove *n* colombe *f*.

Dover *n* Douvres.

dowdy *a* (**-ier, -iest**) (*clothes*) sans chic, monotone; (*person*) sans élégance.

down *adv* en bas; (of sun) couché; (lower) plus bas; **come** *or* **go ~** descendre; **go ~ to the post office** aller à la poste; **~ under** aux antipodes; **~ with** à bas. ● *prep* en bas de; (along) le long de. ● *vt* (knock down, shoot down) abattre; (drink) vider. ● *n* (fluff) duvet *m*.

down: **~-and-out** *n* clochard/-e *m/f*. **~cast** *a* démoralisé. **~fall** *n* chute *f*. **~grade** *vt* déclasser. **~-hearted** *a* découragé.

downhill *adv* **go ~** descendre; (pej) baisser.

down: **~load** *n* (Comput) télécharger. **~-market** *a* bas de gamme. **~ payment** *n* acompte *m*. **~pour** *n* grosse averse *f*.

downright *a* (utter) véritable; (honest) franc. ● *adv* carrément.

downstairs *adv* en bas. ● *a* d'en bas.

down: **~stream** *adv* en aval. **~-to-earth** *a* pratique.

downtown *a* (US) du centre-ville; **~ Boston** le centre de Boston.

downtrodden *a* tyrannisé.

downward *a & adv*, **downwards** *adv* vers le bas.

doze *vi* somnoler; **~ off** s'assoupir. ● *n* somme *m*.

dozen *n* douzaine *f*; **a ~ eggs** une douzaine d'œufs; **~s of** ⊡ des dizaines de.

Dr *abbr* (**Doctor**) Docteur.

drab *a* terne.

draft *n* (outline) brouillon *m*; (Comm) traite *f*; **the ~** (Mil, US) la conscription; **a ~ treaty** un projet de traité; (US) = DRAUGHT. ● *vt* faire le brouillon de; (draw up) rédiger.

drag *vt/i* (*pt* **dragged**) traîner; (*river*) draguer; (pull away) arracher; **~ on** s'éterniser. ● *n* (task ⊡) corvée *f*; (person ⊡) raseur/-euse *m/f*; **in ~** en travesti.

dragon *n* dragon *m*.

drain *vt* (*land*) drainer; (*vegetables*) égoutter; (*tank, glass*) vider; (use up) épuiser. **~ (off)** (*liquid*) faire écouler. ● *vi* **~ (off)** (of liquid) s'écouler. ● *n* (sewer) égout *m*; **~(-pipe)** tuyau *m* d'écoulement; **a ~ on** une ponction sur. **draining-board** *n* égouttoir *m*.

drama *n* art *m* dramatique, théâtre *m*; (play, event) drame *m*. **dramatic** *a* (situation) dramatique; (increase) spectaculaire. **dramatist** *n* dramaturge *m*. **dramatize** *vt* adapter pour la scène; (fig) dramatiser.

drank ⇒DRINK.

drape *vt* draper. **drapes** *npl* (US) rideaux *mpl*.

drastic *a* sévère.

draught *n* courant *m* d'air; **~s**

(game) dames *fpl*. ~ **beer** *n* bière *f* pression.

draughty *a* plein de courants d'air.

draw *vt* (*pt* **drew**; *pp* **drawn**) (*picture*) dessiner; (*line*) tracer; (pull) tirer; (attract) attirer. ● *vi* dessiner; (Sport) faire match nul; (come, move) venir. ● *n* (Sport) match *m* nul; (in lottery) tirage *m* au sort. □ ~ **back** reculer; ~ **near** (s')approcher (**to** de); ~ **out** (*money*) retirer; ~ **up** *vi* (stop) s'arrêter; *vt* (*document*) dresser; (*chair*) approcher.

drawback *n* inconvénient *m*.

drawbridge *n* pont-levis *m*.

drawer *n* tiroir *m*.

drawing *n* dessin *m*. ~**-board** *n* planche *f* à dessin. ~**-pin** *n* punaise *f*. ~**-room** *n* salon *m*.

drawl *n* voix *f* traînante.

drawn ⇒DRAW. ● *a* (*features*) tiré; (*match*) nul.

dread *n* terreur *f*, crainte *f*. ● *vt* redouter. **dreadful** *a* épouvantable, affreux. **dreadfully** *adv* terriblement.

dream *n* rêve *m*. ● *vt*/*i* (*pt* **dreamed** *or* **dreamt**) rêver; ~ **up** imaginer. ● *a* (ideal) de ses rêves.

dreary *a* (**-ier**, **-iest**) triste; (boring) monotone.

dredge *vt* (*river*) draguer; ~ **sth up** (fig) exhumer.

dregs *npl* lie *f*.

drench *vt* tremper.

dress *n* robe *f*; (clothing) tenue *f*. ● *vt*/*i* (s')habiller; (*food*) assaisonner; (*wound*) panser; ~ **up as** se déguiser en; **get** ~**ed** s'habiller. ~ **circle** *n* premier balcon *m*.

dresser *n* (furniture) buffet *m*; **be a stylish** ~ s'habiller avec chic.

dressing *n* (sauce) assaisonnement *m*; (bandage) pansement *m*. ~**-gown** *n* robe *f* de chambre. ~**-room** *n* (Sport) vestiaire *m*; (Theat) loge *f*. ~**-table** *n* coiffeuse *f*.

dressmaker *n* couturière *f*. **dressmaking** *n* couture *f*.

dress rehearsal *n* répétition *f* générale.

dressy *a* (**-ier**, **-iest**) chic *inv*.

drew ⇒DRAW.

dribble *vi* (*liquid*) dégouliner; (*person*) baver; (football) dribbler.

dried *a* (fruit) sec.

drier *n* séchoir *m*.

drift *vi* aller à la dérive; (pile up) s'amonceler; ~ **towards** glisser vers. ● *n* dérive *f*; amoncellement *m*; (of events) tournure *f*; (meaning) sens *m*; **snow** ~ congère *f*. **driftwood** *n* bois *m* flotté.

drill *n* (tool) perceuse *f*; (for teeth) roulette *f*; (training) exercice *m*; (procedure ⊡) marche *f* à suivre; (**pneumatic**) ~ marteau *m* piqueur. ● *vt* percer; (train) entraîner. ● *vi* être à l'exercice.

drink *vt*/*i* (*pt* **drank**; *pp* **drunk**) boire. ● *n* (liquid) boisson *f*; (glass of alcohol) verre *m*; **a** ~ **of water** un verre d'eau. **drinking water** *n* eau *f* potable.

drip *vi* (*pt* **dripped**) (é)goutter; (washing) s'égoutter. ● *n* goutte *f*; (person ⊠) lavette *f*.

drip-dry *vt* laisser égoutter. ● *a* sans essorage.

drive *vt* (*pt* **drove**; *pp* **driven**) (*vehicle*) conduire; (sb somewhere) chasser, pousser; (*machine*) actionner; ~ **mad** rendre fou. ● *vi* conduire. ● *n* promenade *f* en voiture; (private road) allée *f*; (fig) énergie *f*; (Psych) instinct *m*; (Pol) campagne *f*; (Auto) traction *f*; (golf, Comput) drive *m*; **it's a two-hour** ~ il y a deux heures de route; **left-hand** ~ conduite *f* à gauche. □ ~ **at** en venir à.

drivel *n* bêtises *fpl*.

driver *n* conducteur/-trice *m/f*, chauffeur *m*. **~'s license** *n* (US) permis *m* de conduire.

driving *n* conduite *f*; **take one's ~ test** passer son permis. ● *a* (*rain*) battant; (*wind*) cinglant. **~ licence** *n* permis *m* de conduire. **~ school** *n* auto-école *f*.

drizzle *n* bruine *f*. ● *vi* bruiner.

drone *n* (of engine) ronronnement *m*; (of insects) bourdonnement *m*. ● *vi* ronronner; bourdonner.

drool *vi* baver (**over** sur).

droop *vi* pencher, tomber.

drop *n* goutte *f*; (fall, lowering) chute *f*. ● *vt/i* (*pt* **dropped**) (laisser) tomber; (decrease, lower) baisser; **~** (**off**) (*person from car*) déposer; **~ a line** écrire un mot (**to** à). □ **~ in** passer (**on** chez); **~ off** (doze) s'assoupir; **~ out** se retirer (**of** de); (of student) abandonner.

drop-out *n* marginal/-e *m/f*, raté/-e *m/f*.

droppings *npl* crottes *fpl*.

drought *n* sécheresse *f*.

drove ⇒DRIVE.

droves *npl* foules *fpl*.

drown *vt/i* (se) noyer.

drowsy *a* somnolent; **be** *or* **feel ~** avoir envie de dormir.

drug *n* drogue *f*; (Med) médicament *m*. ● *vt* (*pt* **drugged**) droguer. **~ addict** *n* drogué/-e *m/f*. **drugstore** *n* (US) drugstore *m*.

drum *n* tambour *m*; (for oil) bidon *m*; **~s** batterie *f*. ● *vi* (*pt* **drummed**) tambouriner. ● *vt* **~ into sb** répéter sans cesse à qn; **~ up** (*support*) susciter; (*business*) créer. **drummer** *n* tambour *m*; (in pop group) batteur *m*.

drumstick *n* baguette *f* de tambour; (of chicken) pilon *m*.

drunk ⇒DRINK. ● *a* ivre; **get ~** s'enivrer. ● *n* ivrogne/-esse *m/f*. **drunkard** *n* ivrogne/-esse *m/f*.

drunken *a* ivre; (habitually) ivrogne. **drunkenness** *n* ivresse *f*.

dry *a* (**drier, driest**) sec; (*day*) sans pluie; **be** *or* **feel ~** avoir soif. ● *vt/i* (faire) sécher; **~ up** (dry dishes) essuyer la vaisselle; (of supplies) (se) tarir; (be silent ⊡) se taire. **~-clean** *vt* nettoyer à sec. **~-cleaner** *n* teinturier *m*. **~ run** *n* galop *m* d'essai.

dual *a* double. **~ carriageway** *n* route *f* à quatre voies. **~-purpose** *a* qui fait double emploi.

dub *vt* (*pt* **dubbed**) (film) doubler (**into** en); (nickname) surnommer.

dubious *a* (pej) douteux; **be ~ about sth** (*person*) avoir des doutes sur qch.

duck *n* canard *m*. ● *vi* se baisser subitement. ● *vt* (*head*) baisser; (*person*) plonger dans l'eau.

duct *n* conduit *m*.

dud *a* (*tool* ⊠) mal fichu; (*coin* ⊠) faux; (*cheque* ⊠) sans provision. ● *n* **be a ~** (not work ⊠) ne pas marcher.

due *a* (owing) dû; (expected) attendu; (proper) qui convient; **~ to** à cause de; (caused by) dû à; **she's ~ to leave now** il est prévu qu'elle parte maintenant; **in ~ course** (at the right time) en temps voulu; (later) plus tard. ● *adv* **~ east** droit vers l'est. ● *n* dû *m*; **~s** droits *mpl*; (of club) cotisation *f*.

duel *n* duel *m*.

duet *n* duo *m*.

dug ⇒DIG.

duke *n* duc *m*.

dull *a* ennuyeux; (*colour*) terne; (*weather*) maussade; (*sound*) sourd. ● *vt* (*pain*) atténuer; (*shine*) ternir.

duly *adv* comme il convient; (as expected) comme prévu.

dumb *a* muet; (stupid ⊡) bête.

dumbfound *vt* sidérer, ahurir.

dummy *n* (of tailor) mannequin *m*; (of baby) sucette *f*. ● *a* factice. **~ run** *n* galop *m* d'essai.

dump *vt* déposer; (get rid of ⓘ) se débarrasser de. ● *n* tas *m* d'ordures; (refuse tip) décharge *f*; (Mil) dépôt *m*; (dull place ⓘ) trou *m* ⓘ; **be in the ~s** ⓘ avoir le cafard.

dune *n* dune *f*.

dung *n* (excrement) bouse *f*, crotte *f*; (manure) fumier *m*.

dungarees *npl* salopette *f*.

dungeon *n* cachot *m*.

duplicate[1] *n* double *m*. ● *a* identique.

duplicate[2] *vt* faire un double de; (on machine) polycopier.

durable *a* (tough) résistant; (enduring) durable.

duration *n* durée *f*.

during *prep* pendant.

dusk *n* crépuscule *m*.

dusky *a* (**-ier**, **-iest**) foncé.

dust *n* poussière *f*. ● *vt/i* épousseter; (sprinkle) saupoudrer (**with** de). **~bin** *n* poubelle *f*.

duster *n* chiffon *m*.

dust: **~man** *n* (*pl* **-men**) éboueur *m*. **~pan** *n* pelle *f* (à poussière).

dusty *a* (**-ier**, **-iest**) poussiéreux.

Dutch *a* néerlandais; **go ~** partager les frais. ● *n* (Ling) néerlandais *m*. **~man** *n* Néerlandais *m*. **~woman** *n* Néerlandaise *f*.

dutiful *a* obéissant.

duty *n* devoir *m*; (tax) droit *m*; (of official) fonction *f*; **on ~** de service. **~-free** *a* hors-taxe.

duvet *n* couette *f*.

dwarf *n* nain/-e *m/f*. ● *vt* rapetisser.

dwell *vi* (*pt* **dwelt**) demeurer; **~ on** s'étendre sur. **dweller** *n* habitant/-e *m/f*. **dwelling** *n* habitation *f*.

dwindle *vi* diminuer.

dye *vt* teindre. ● *n* teinture *f*.

dying *a* mourant; (*art*) qui se perd.

dynamic *a* dynamique.

dynamite *n* dynamite *f*.

dysentery *n* dysenterie *f*.

dyslexia *n* dyslexie *f*. **dyslexic** *a & n* dyslexique (*mf*).

each *det* chaque *inv*; **~ one** chacun/-e *m/f*. ● *pron* chacun/-e *m/f*; **oranges at 30p ~** des oranges à 30 pence pièce.

each other *pron* l'un/l'une l'autre, les uns/les unes les autres; **know ~** se connaître; **love ~** s'aimer.

eager *a* impatient (**to** de); (*person, acceptance*) enthousiaste; **~ for** avide de.

eagle *n* aigle *m*.

ear *n* oreille *f*; (of corn) épi *m*. **~ache** *n* mal *m* à l'oreille. **~-drum** *n* tympan *m*.

earl *n* comte *m*.

early (**-ier**, **-iest**) *adv* tôt, de bonne heure; (ahead of time) en avance; **as I said earlier** comme je l'ai déjà dit. ● *a* (*attempt, years*) premier; (*hour*) matinal; (*fruit*) précoce; (*retirement*) anticipé; **have an ~ dinner** dîner tôt; **in ~ summer** au début de l'été; **at the earliest** au plus tôt.

earmark *vt* désigner (**for** pour).

earn *vt* gagner; (interest: Comm) rapporter.

earnest *a* sérieux; **in ~** sérieusement.
earnings *npl* salaire *m*; (profits) gains *mpl*.
ear: **~phones** *npl* casque *m*. **~-ring** *n* boucle *f* d'oreille. **~shot** *n* **within/in ~shot** à portée de voix.
earth *n* terre *f*; **why/how/where on ~...?** pourquoi/comment/où diable...? ● *vt* (Electr) mettre à la terre. **earthenware** *n* faïence *f*. **~quake** *n* tremblement *m* de terre.
ease *n* facilité *f*; (comfort) bien-être *m*; **at ~** à l'aise; (Mil) au repos; **with ~** facilement. ● *vt* (*pain, pressure*) atténuer; (*congestion*) réduire; (*transition*) faciliter. ● *vi* (*pain, pressure*) s'atténuer; (*congestion, rain*) diminuer.
easel *n* chevalet *m*.
east *n* est *m*; **the E~** (Orient) l'Orient *m*. ● *a* (*side, coast*) est; (*wind*) d'est. ● *adv* à l'est.
Easter *n* Pâques *m*; **~ egg** œuf *m* de Pâques.
easterly *a* (*wind*) d'est; (*direction*) de l'est.
eastern de l'est; **~ France** l'est de la France.
eastward *a* (*side*) est *inv*; (*journey*) vers l'est.
easy *a* (**-ier, -iest**) facile; **go ~ with** 🄸 y aller doucement avec; **take it ~** ne te fatigue pas. **~going** *a* accommodant.
eat *vt/i* (*pt* **ate**; *pp* **eaten**) manger; **~ into** ronger.
eavesdrop *vi* (*pt* **-dropped**) écouter aux portes.
ebb *n* reflux *m*. ● *vi* descendre; (fig) décliner.
ebony *n* ébène *f*.
EC *abbr* (**European Community**) CE *f*.
eccentric *a* & *n* excentrique (*mf*).
echo *n* (*pl* **-oes**) écho *m*. ● *vt* répercuter; (*idea, opinion*) reprendre. ● *vi* retentir, résonner (**to, with** de).
eclipse *n* éclipse *f*. ● *vt* éclipser.
ecological *a* écologique.
ecology *n* écologie *f*.
economic *a* économique; (profitable) rentable. **economical** *a* économique; (person) économe. **economics** *n* économie *f*, sciences *fpl* économiques. **economist** *n* économiste *mf*.
economize *vi* **~** (**on**) économiser.
economy *n* économie *f*.
ecosystem *n* écosystème *m*.
ecstasy *n* extase *f*; (drug) ecstasy *m*.
ECU *n* écu *m*.
eczema *n* eczéma *m*.
edge *n* bord *m*; (of town) abords *mpl*; (of knife) tranchant *m*; **have the ~ on** 🄸 l'emporter sur; **on ~** énervé. ● *vt* (trim) border. ● *vi* **~ forward** avancer doucement.
edgeways *adv* **I can't get a word in ~** je n'arrive pas à placer un mot.
edgy *a* énervé.
edible *a* comestible; (pleasant) mangeable.
edit *vt* (*pt* **edited**) (*newspaper, page*) être le rédacteur/la rédactrice de; (check) réviser; (cut) couper; (TV, cinema) monter.
edition *n* édition *f*.
editor *n* (writer) rédacteur/-trice *m/f*; (of works, anthology) éditeur/-trice *m/f*; (TV, cinema) monteur/-teuse *m/f*; **the ~** (**in chief**) le rédacteur en chef.
editorial *a* de la rédaction. ● *n* éditorial *m*.
educate *vt* instruire; (mind, public) éduquer. **educated** *a* instruit. **education** *n* éducation *f*; (schooling) études *fpl*. **educational**

E

a éducatif; (*establishment, method*) d'enseignement.

eel *n* anguille *f*.

eerie *a* (**-ier**, **-iest**) sinistre.

effect *n* effet *m*; **come into ~** entrer en vigueur; **in ~** effectivement; **take ~** agir. ● *vt* effectuer.

effective *a* efficace; (actual) effectif. **effectively** *adv* efficacement; (in effect) en réalité. **effectiveness** *n* efficacité *f*.

effeminate *a* efféminé.

effervescent *a* effervescent.

efficiency *n* efficacité *f*; (of machine) rendement *m*. **efficient** *a* efficace. **efficiently** *adv* efficacement.

effort *n* efforts *mpl*; **make an ~** faire un effort; **be worth the ~** en valoir la peine. **effortless** *a* facile.

effusive *a* expansif.

e.g. *abbr* par ex.

egg *n* œuf *m*. ● *vt* **~ on** pousser. **~-cup** *n* coquetier *m*. **~-plant** *n* (US) aubergine *f*. **~shell** *n* coquille *f* d'œuf.

ego *n* amour-propre *m*; (Psych) moi *m*. **egotism** *n* égotisme *m*. **egotist** *n* égotiste *mf*.

Egypt *n* Égypte *f*.

eiderdown *n* édredon *m*.

eight *a & n* huit (*m*). **eighteen** *a & n* dix-huit (*m*). **eighth** *a & n* huitième (*mf*). **eighty** *a & n* quatre-vingts (*m*).

either *det & pron* l'un/une ou l'autre; (with negative) ni l'un/une ni l'autre; **you can take ~** tu peux prendre n'importe lequel/laquelle. ● *adv* non plus. ● *conj* **~...or** ou (bien)...ou (bien); (with negative) ni...ni.

eject *vt* (*troublemaker*) expulser; (*waste*) rejeter.

elaborate[1] *a* compliqué.

elaborate[2] *vt* élaborer. ● *vi* préciser; **~ on** s'étendre sur.

elastic *a & n* élastique (*m*); **~ band** élastique *m*. **elasticity** *n* élasticité *f*.

elated *a* transporté de joie.

elbow *n* coude *m*; **~ room** espace *m* vital.

elder *a & n* aîné/-e (*m/f*); (tree) sureau *m*.

elderly *a* âgé; **the ~** les personnes *fpl* âgées.

eldest *a & n* aîné/-e (*m/f*).

elect *vt* élire; **~ to do** choisir de faire. ● *a* (president etc.) futur. **election** *n* élection *f*. **elector** *n* électeur/-trice *m/f*. **electoral** *a* électoral. **electorate** *n* électorat *m*.

electric *a* électrique; **~ blanket** couverture *f* chauffante. **electrical** *a* électrique. **electrician** *n* électricien/-ne *m/f*. **electricity** *n* électricité *f*. **electrify** *vt* électrifier; (excite) électriser. **electrocute** *vt* électrocuter.

electronic *a* électronique. **~ publishing** *n* éditique *f*. **electronics** *n* électronique *f*.

elegance *n* élégance *f*.

element *n* élément *m*; (of heater etc.) résistance *f*. **elementary** *a* élémentaire.

elephant *n* éléphant *m*.

elevate *vt* élever. **elevation** *n* élévation *f*. **elevator** *n* (US) ascenseur *m*.

eleven *a & n* onze (*m*). **eleventh** *a & n* onzième (*mf*).

elicit *vt* obtenir (**from** de).

eligible *a* admissible (**for** à); **be ~ for** (entitled to) avoir droit à.

eliminate *vt* éliminer.

elm *n* orme *m*.

elongate *vt* allonger.

elope *vi* s'enfuir (**with** avec).

elopement *n* fugue *f* (amoureuse).

eloquence *n* éloquence *f*.

else *adv* d'autre; **somebody/nothing ~** quelqu'un/rien d'autre; **everybody ~** tous les autres; **somewhere/something ~** autre part/chose; **or ~** ou bien. **elsewhere** *adv* ailleurs.

elude *vt* échapper à.

elusive *a* insaisissable.

emaciated *a* émacié.

e-mail *n* e-mail *m*, mél *m*.

emancipate *vt* émanciper.

embankment *n* (of river) quai *m*; (of railway) remblai *m*.

embark *vt* embarquer. ● *vi* (Naut) embarquer; **~ on** (*journey*) entreprendre; (*campaign, career*) se lancer dans.

embarrass *vt* plonger dans l'embarras; **be/feel ~ed** être/se sentir gêné. **embarrassment** *n* confusion *f*, gêne *f*.

embassy *n* ambassade *f*.

embed *vt* (*pt* **embedded**) enfoncer (**in** dans).

embellish *vt* embellir.

embers *npl* braises *fpl*.

embezzle *vt* détourner (**from** de). **embezzlement** *n* détournement *m* de fonds. **embezzler** *n* escroc *m*.

embitter *vt* aigrir; **become ~ed** s'aigrir.

emblem *n* emblème *m*.

embodiment *n* incarnation *f*. **embody** *vt* incarner; (legally) incorporer.

emboss *vt* (metal) repousser; (paper) gaufrer.

embrace *vt* (*person*) étreindre; (*religion*) embrasser; (include) comprendre. ● *n* étreinte *f*.

embroider *vt* broder. **embroidery** *n* broderie *f*.

embryo *n* embryon *m*.

emerald *n* émeraude *f*.

emerge *vi* (*person*) sortir (**from** de); **it ~d that** il est apparu que. **emergence** *n* apparition *f*.

emergency *n* (crisis) crise *f*; (urgent case: Med) urgence *f*; **in an ~** en cas d'urgence. ● *a* d'urgence; **~ exit** sortie *f* de secours; **~ landing** atterrissage *m* forcé.

emigrant *n* émigrant/-e *m/f*. **emigrate** *vi* émigrer.

eminence *n* éminence *f*. **eminent** *a* éminent.

emission *n* émission *f*.

emit *vt* (*pt* **emitted**) émettre.

emotion *n* émotion *f*. **emotional** *a* (*development*) émotif; (*reaction*) émotionel; (*film, scene*) émouvant.

emotive *a* qui soulève les passions.

emperor *n* empereur *m*.

emphasis *n* accent *m*; **lay ~ on** mettre l'accent sur. **emphasize** *vt* mettre l'accent sur. **emphatic** *a* catégorique; (manner) énergique.

empire *n* empire *m*.

employ *vt* employer. **employee** *n* employé/-e *m/f*. **employer** *n* employeur/-euse *m/f*.

employment *n* emploi *m*; **find ~** trouver du travail.

empower *vt* autoriser (**to do** à faire).

empty *a* (**-ier, -iest**) vide; (*street*) désert; (promise) vain; **on an ~ stomach** à jeun. ● *vt/i* (se) vider. **~-handed** *a* les mains vides.

emulate *vt* imiter.

enable *vt* **~ sb to** permettre à qn de.

enamel *n* émail *m*. ● *vt* (*pt* **enamelled**) émailler.

encampment *n* campement *m*.

encase *vt* revêtir, recouvrir (**in** de).

enchant *vt* enchanter.

E

enclose *vt* entourer; (land) clôturer; (with letter) joindre. **enclosed** *a* (space) clos; (with letter) ci-joint. **enclosure** *n* enceinte *f*; (with letter) pièce *f* jointe.

encompass *vt* inclure.

encore *interj & n* bis (*m*).

encounter *vt* rencontrer. ● *n* rencontre *f*.

encourage *vt* encourager.

encroach *vi* ~ **upon** empiéter sur.

encyclopaedia *n* encyclopédie *f*. **encyclopaedic** *a* encyclopédique.

end *n* fin *f*; (farthest part) bout *m*; **come to an** ~ prendre fin; **~-product** produit *m* fini; **in the** ~ finalement; **no** ~ **of** [!] énormément de; **on** ~ (upright) debout; (in a row) de suite; **put an** ~ **to** mettre fin à. ● *vt* (*marriage*) mettre fin à; ~ **one's days** finir ses jours. ● *vi* se terminer; ~ **up doing** finir par faire.

endanger *vt* mettre en danger.

endearing *a* attachant.

endeavour, (US) **endeavor** *n* (attempt) tentative *f*; (hard work) effort *m*. ● *vi* faire tout son possible (**to do** pour faire).

ending *n* fin *f*.

endive *n* chicorée *f*.

endless *a* interminable; (*supply*) inépuisable; (*patience*) infini.

endorse *vt* (*candidate, decision*) appuyer; (*product, claim*) approuver; (*cheque*) endosser.

endurance *n* endurance *f*.

endure *vt* supporter. ● *vi* durer. **enduring** *a* durable.

enemy *n & a* ennemi/-e (*m/f*).

energetic *a* énergique. **energy** *n* énergie *f*.

enforce *vt* (*rule, law*) appliquer, faire respecter; (*silence, discipline*) imposer (**on** à); **~d** forcé.

engage *vt* (*staff*) engager; (*attention*) retenir; **be ~d in** se livrer à. ● *vi* ~ **in** se livrer à. **engaged** *a* fiancé; (busy) occupé; **get ~d** se fiancer. **engagement** *n* fiançailles *fpl*; (meeting) rendez-vous *m*; (undertaking) engagement *m*.

engaging *a* attachant, engageant.

engine *n* moteur *m*; (of train) locomotive *f*; (of ship) machines *fpl*. **~-driver** *n* mécanicien *m*.

engineer *n* ingénieur *m*; (repairman) technicien *m*; (on ship) mécanicien *m*. ● *vt* (contrive) manigancer.

engineering *n* ingénierie *f*; (industry) mécanique *f*; **civil** ~ génie *m* civil.

England *n* Angleterre *f*.

English *a* anglais. ● *n* (Ling) anglais *m*; **the** ~ les Anglais *mpl*. **~man** *n* Anglais *m*. **~-speaking** *a* anglophone. **~woman** *n* Anglaise *f*.

engrave *vt* graver.

engrossed *a* absorbé (**in** dans).

engulf *vt* engouffrer.

enhance *vt* (*prospects, status*) améliorer; (*price, value*) augmenter.

enjoy *vt* aimer (**doing** faire); (benefit from) jouir de; ~ **oneself** s'amuser; ~ **your meal!** bon appétit! **enjoyable** *a* agréable. **enjoyment** *n* plaisir *m*.

enlarge *vt* agrandir. ● *vi* s'agrandir; (*pupil*) se dilater; ~ **on** s'étendre sur. **enlargement** *n* agrandissement *m*.

enlighten *vt* éclairer (**on** sur). **enlightenment** *n* instruction *f*; (information) éclaircissement *m*.

enlist *vt* (*person*) recruter; (fig) obtenir. ● *vi* s'engager.

enmity *n* inimitié *f*.

enormous *a* énorme.
enormously *adv* énormément.

enough *adv & n* assez; **have ~ of** en avoir assez de. ● *det* assez de; **~ glasses/time** assez de verres/de temps.

enquire ⇒INQUIRE. **enquiry** ⇒INQUIRY.

enrage *vt* mettre en rage, rendre furieux.

enrol *vt/i* (*pt* **enrolled**) (s')inscrire. **enrolment** *n* inscription *f*.

ensure *vt* garantir; **~ that** (ascertain) s'assurer que.

entail *vt* entraîner.

entangle *vt* emmêler.

enter *vt* (*room, club, phase*) entrer dans; (note down, register) inscrire; (data) entrer, saisir. ● *vi* entrer (**into** dans); **~ for** s'inscrire à.

enterprise *n* entreprise *f*; (boldness) initiative *f*. **enterprising** *a* entreprenant.

entertain *vt* amuser, divertir; (guests) recevoir; (ideas) considérer. **entertainer** *n* artiste *mf*. **entertaining** *a* divertissant. **entertainment** *n* divertissement *m*; (performance) spectacle *m*.

enthral *vt* (*pt* **enthralled**) captiver.

enthusiasm *n* enthousiasme *m* (**for** pour).

enthusiast *n* passionné/-e *m/f* (**for** de). **enthusiastic** *a* (supporter) enthousiaste; **be ~ic about** être enthusiasmé par. **enthusiastically** *adv* avec enthousiasme.

entice *vt* attirer; **~ to do** entraîner à faire.

entire *a* entier. **entirely** *adv* entièrement. **entirety** *n* **in its ~ty** en entier.

entitle *vt* donner droit à (**to sth** à qch; **to do** de faire); **~d** (book) intitulé; **be ~d to sth** avoir droit à qch.

entrance[1] *n* (entering, way in) entrée *f* (**to** de); (right to enter) admission *f*. ● *a* (charge, exam) d'entrée.

entrance[2] *vt* transporter.

entrant *n* (Sport) concurrent/-e *m/f*; (in exam) candidat/-e *m/f*.

entrenched *a* (*opinion*) inébranlable; (Mil) retranché.

entrepreneur *n* entrepreneur/-euse *m/f*.

entrust *vt* confier; **~ sb with sth** confier qch à qn.

entry *n* entrée *f*; **~ form** fiche *f* d'inscription.

envelop *vt* (*pt* **enveloped**) envelopper.

envelope *n* enveloppe *f*.

envious *a* envieux (**of** de).

environment *n* (ecological) environnement *m*; (social) milieu *m*. **environmental** *a* du milieu; de l'environnement. **environmentalist** *n* écologiste *mf*.

envisage *vt* prévoir (**doing** de faire).

envoy *n* envoyé/-e *m/f*.

envy *n* envie *f*. ● *vt* envier; **~ sb sth** envier qch à qn.

epic *n* épopée *f*. ● *a* épique.

epidemic *n* épidémie *f*.

epilepsy *n* épilepsie *f*.

episode *n* épisode *m*.

epitome *n* modèle *m*. **epitomize** *vt* incarner.

equal *a & n* égal/-e (*m/f*); **~ opportunities/rights** égalité *f* des chances/droits; **~ to** (*task*) à la hauteur de. ● *vt* (*pt* **equalled**) égaler. **equality** *n* égalité *f*. **equalize** *vt/i* égaliser. **equalizer** *n* (goal) but *m* égalisateur. **equally** *adv* (*divide*) en parts égales; (just as) tout aussi.

E

equanimity *n* sérénité *f*.
equate *vt* assimiler (**with** à). **equation** *n* équation *f*.
equator *n* équateur *m*.
equilibrium *n* équilibre *m*.
equip *vt* (*pt* **equipped**) équiper (**with** de). **equipment** *n* équipement *m*.
equity *n* équité *f*.
equivalence *n* équivalence *f*.
era *n* ère *f*, époque *f*.
eradicate *vt* éliminer; (*disease*) éradiquer.
erase *vt* effacer. **eraser** *n* (rubber) gomme *f*.
erect *a* droit. ●*vt* ériger. **erection** *n* érection *f*.
erode *vt* éroder; (fig) saper. **erosion** *n* érosion *f*.
erotic *a* érotique.
errand *n* commission *f*, course *f*.
erratic *a* (*behaviour, person*) imprévisible; (*performance*) inégal.
error *n* erreur *f*.
erupt *vi* (volcano) entrer en éruption; (fig) éclater.
escalate *vt* intensifier. ●*vi* (*conflict*) s'intensifier; (*prices*) monter en flèche. **escalation** *n* intensification *f*. **escalator** *n* escalier *m* mécanique, escalator® *m*.
escapade *n* frasque *f*.
escape *vt* échapper à. ●*vi* s'enfuir, s'évader; (*gas*) fuir. ●*n* fuite *f*, évasion *f*; (of gas etc.) fuite *f*; **have a lucky** *or* **narrow ~** l'échapper belle.
escapism *n* évasion *f* (*du réel*).
escort[1] *n* (guard) escorte *f*; (companion) compagnon/compagne *m*/*f*.
escort[2] *vt* escorter.
Eskimo *n* Esquimau/-de *m*/*f*.
especially *adv* en particulier.
espionage *n* espionnage *m*.
espresso *n* (café) express *m*.
essay *n* (in literature) essai *m*; (School) rédaction *f*; (Univ) dissertation *f*.
essence *n* essence *f*.
essential *a* essentiel; **the ~s** l'essentiel *m*. **essentially** *adv* essentiellement.
establish *vt* établir; (business) fonder.
establishment *n* (process) instauration *f*; (institution) établissement *m*; **the E~** l'ordre *m* établi.
estate *n* (house and land) domaine *m*; (possessions) biens *mpl*; (housing estate) cité *f*. **~ agent** *n* agent *m* immobilier. **~ car** *n* break *m*.
esteem *n* estime *f*.
esthetic *a* (US) = AESTHETIC.
estimate[1] *n* (calculation) estimation *f*; (Comm) devis *m*.
estimate[2] *vt* évaluer; **~ that** estimer que. **estimation** *n* (esteem) estime *f*; (judgment) opinion *f*.
Estonia *n* Estonie *f*.
estuary *n* estuaire *m*.
etc. *adv* etc.
eternal *a* éternel.
eternity *n* éternité *f*.
ethic *n* éthique *f*; **~s** moralité *f*. **ethical** *a* éthique.
ethnic *a* ethnique.
ethos *n* philosophie *f*.
etymology *n* étymologie *f*.
EU *abbr* (**European Union**) UE *f*, Union *f* européenne.
euphoria *n* euphorie *f*.
Euro *n* euro *m*.
Europe *n* Europe *f*.
European *a & n* européen/-ne (*m*/*f*); **~ Community** Communauté *f* Européenne.
euthanasia *n* euthanasie *f*.
evacuate *vt* évacuer.

evade *vt* (*blow*) esquiver; (*question*) éluder.

evaporate *vi* s'évaporer; **~d milk** lait *m* condensé.

evasion *n* fuite *f* (**of** devant); (excuse) faux-fuyant *m*; **tax ~** évasion *f* fiscale. **evasive** *a* évasif.

eve *n* veille *f* (**of** de).

even *a* (*surface, voice, contest*) égal; (*teeth, hem*) régulier; (number) pair; **get ~ with** se venger de. ● *adv* même; **~ better**/*etc.* (still) encore mieux/*etc.*; **~ so** quand même. □ **~ out** (*differences*) s'atténuer; **~ sth out** (*inequalities*) réduire qch; **~ up** équilibrer.

evening *n* soir *m*; (whole evening, event) soirée *f*.

evenly *adv* (*spread, apply*) uniformément; (*breathe*) régulièrement; (equally) en parts égales.

event *n* événement *m*; (Sport) épreuve *f*; **in the ~ of** en cas de. **eventful** *a* mouvementé.

eventual *a* (*outcome, decision*) final; (*aim*) à long terme. **eventuality** *n* éventualité *f*. **eventually** *adv* finalement; (in future) un jour ou l'autre.

ever *adv* jamais; (at all times) toujours.

evergreen *n* arbre *m* à feuilles persistantes.

everlasting *a* éternel.

ever since *prep & adv* depuis.

every *a* **~ house/window** toutes les maisons/les fenêtres; **~ time/minute** chaque fois/minute; **~ day** tous les jours; **~ other day** tous les deux jours. **everybody** *pron* tout le monde. **everyday** *a* quotidien. **everyone** *pron* tout le monde. **everything** *pron* tout. **everywhere** *adv* partout; **~where he goes** partout où il va.

evict *vt* expulser (**from** de).

evidence *n* (proof) preuves *fpl* (**that** que; **of, for** de); (testimony) témoignage *m*; (traces) trace *f* (**of** de); **give ~** témoigner; **be in ~** être visible. **evident** *a* manifeste. **evidently** *adv* (apparently) apparemment; (obviously) manifestement.

evil *a* malfaisant. ● *n* mal *m*.

evoke *vt* évoquer.

evolution *n* évolution *f*.

evolve *vi* évoluer. ● *vt* élaborer.

ewe *n* brebis *f*.

ex- *pref* ex-, ancien.

exact *a* exact; **the ~ opposite** exactement le contraire. ● *vt* exiger (**from** de). **exactly** *adv* exactement.

exaggerate *vt/i* exagérer.

exalted *a* élevé.

exam *n* 🄸 examen *m*.

examination *n* examen *m*.

examine *vt* examiner; (witness) interroger. **examiner** *n* examinateur/-trice *m/f*.

example *n* exemple *m*; **for ~** par exemple; **make an ~ of** punir pour l'exemple.

exasperate *vt* exaspérer.

excavate *vt* fouiller. **excavations** *npl* fouilles *fpl*.

exceed *vt* dépasser. **exceedingly** *adv* extrêmement.

excel *vi* (*pt* **excelled**) exceller (**at, in** en; **at doing** à faire). ● *vt* surpasser.

excellence *n* excellence *f*. **excellent** *a* excellent.

except *prep* sauf, excepté; **~ for** à part. ● *vt* excepter. **excepting** *prep* sauf, excepté.

exception *n* exception *f*; **take ~ to** s'offusquer. **exceptional** *a* exceptionnel.

excerpt *n* extrait *m*.

excess[1] *n* excès *m*.

E

excess² *a* ~ **weight** excès *m* de poids; ~ **baggage** excédent *m* de bagages.

excessive *a* excessif.

exchange *vt* échanger (**for** contre). ● *n* échange *m*; (between currencies) change *m*; ~ **rate** taux *m* de change; **telephone** ~ central *m* téléphonique.

Exchequer *n* (Pol) ministère *m* britannique des finances.

excise *n* excise *f*, taxe *f*.

excite *vt* exciter; (enthuse) enthousiasmer. **excited** *a* excité; **get ~d** s'exciter. **excitement** *n* excitation *f*. **exciting** *a* passionnant.

exclaim *vt* s'exclamer.

exclamation *n* exclamation *f*; ~ **mark** *or* **point** (US) point *m* d'exclamation.

exclude *vt* exclure.

exclusive *a* (*club*) fermé; (*rights*) exclusif; (*news item*) en exclusivité; ~ **of meals** repas non compris. **exclusively** *adv* exclusivement.

excruciating *a* atroce.

excursion *n* excursion *f*.

excuse¹ *vt* excuser; ~ **from** (exempt) dispenser de; ~ **me!** excusez-moi!, pardon!

excuse² *n* (reason) excuse *f*; (pretext) prétexte *m* (**for sth** à qch; **for doing** pour faire).

ex-directory *a* sur liste rouge.

execute *vt* exécuter. **executioner** *n* bourreau *m*.

executive *n* (person) cadre *m*; (committee) exécutif *m*. ● *a* exécutif.

exemplary *a* exemplaire.

exemplify *vt* illustrer.

exempt *a* exempt (**from** de). ● *vt* exempter.

exercise *n* exercice *m*; ~ **book** cahier *m*. ● *vt* exercer; (*restraint, patience*) faire preuve de. ● *vi* faire de l'exercice.

exert *vt* exercer; ~ **oneself** se fatiguer. **exertion** *n* effort *m*.

exhaust *vt* épuiser. ● *n* (Auto) pot *m* d'échappement.

exhaustive *a* exhaustif.

exhibit *vt* exposer; (fig) manifester. ● *n* objet *m* exposé.

exhibition *n* exposition *f*; (of skill) démonstration *f*. **exhibitionist** *n* exhibitionniste *mf*.

exhibitor *n* exposant/-e *m*/*f*.

exhilarate *vt* griser.

exile *n* exil *m*; (person) exilé/-e *m*/*f*. ● *vt* exiler.

exist *vi* exister. **existence** *n* existence *f*; **be in ~ence** exister. **existing** *a* actuel.

exit *n* sortie *f*. ● *vt*/*i* (*also* Comput) sortir (de).

exodus *n* exode *m*.

exonerate *vt* disculper.

exotic *a* exotique.

expand *vt* développer; (*workforce*) accroître. ● *vi* se développer; (*population*) s'accroître; (*metal*) se dilater.

expanse *n* étendue *f*.

expansion *n* développement *m*; (Pol, Comm) expansion *f*.

expatriate *a* & *n* expatrié/-e (*m*/*f*).

expect *vt* s'attendre à; (suppose) supposer; (demand) exiger; (*baby*) attendre.

expectancy *n* attente *f*.

expectant *a* ~ **mother** future maman *f*.

expectation *n* (assumption) prévision *f*; (hope) aspiration *f*; (demand) exigence *f*.

expedient *a* opportun. ● *n* expédient *m*.

expedition *n* expédition *f*.

expel *vt* (*pt* **expelled**) expulser; (*pupil*) renvoyer.

expend *vt* consacrer.

expenditure *n* dépenses *fpl*.

expense *n* frais *mpl*; **at sb's ~** aux frais de qn; **~ account** frais *mpl* de représentation. **expensive** *a* cher; (*tastes*) de luxe. **expensively** *adv* luxueusement.

experience *n* expérience *f*. ● *vt* (undergo) connaître; (feel) éprouver; **~d** expérimenté.

experiment *n* expérience *f*. ● *vi* expérimenter, faire des essais.

expert *n* spécialiste *mf*. ● *a* spécialisé, expert. **expertise** *n* compétence *f*. **expertly** *adv* de manière experte.

expire *vi* expirer; **~d** périmé. **expiry** *n* expiration *f*.

explain *vt* expliquer. **explanation** *n* explication *f*. **explanatory** *a* explicatif.

explicit *a* explicite.

explode *vt/i* (faire) exploser.

exploit¹ *n* exploit *m*.

exploit² *vt* exploiter.

exploration *n* exploration *f*. **exploratory** *a* (*talks*) exploratoire. **explore** *vt* explorer; (fig) étudier. **explorer** *n* explorateur/-trice *m/f*.

explosion *n* explosion *f*. **explosive** *a & n* explosif (*m*).

exponent *n* avocat/-e *m/f* (**of** de).

export¹ *vt* exporter.

export² *n* (process) exportation *f*; (product) produit *m* d'exportation.

expose *vt* exposer; (disclose) révéler.

exposure *n* révélation *f*; (Photo) pose *f*; **die of ~** mourir de froid.

express *vt* exprimer. ● *a* exprès. ● *adv* **send sth ~** envoyer qch en exprès. ● *n* (train) rapide *m*. **expression** *n* expression *f*. **expressive** *a* expressif. **expressly** *adv* expressément.

exquisite *a* exquis.

extend *vt* (visit) prolonger; (*house*) agrandir; (*range*) élargir; (*arm, leg*) étendre. ● *vi* (stretch) s'étendre; (in time) se prolonger. **extension** *n* (of line, road) prolongement *m*; (of visa, loan) prorogation *f*; (building) addition *f*; (phone number) poste *m*; (cable) rallonge *f*.

extensive *a* vaste; (study) approfondi; (damage) considérable. **extensively** *adv* (much) beaucoup; (very) très.

extent *n* (size, scope) étendue *f*; (degree) mesure *f*; **to some ~** dans une certaine mesure; **to such an ~ that** à tel point que.

extenuating *a* atténuant.

exterior *a & n* extérieur (*m*).

exterminate *vt* exterminer.

external *a* extérieur; (cause, medical use) externe.

extinct *a* (species) disparu; (volcano, passion) éteint.

extinguish *vt* éteindre. **extinguisher** *n* extincteur *m*.

extol *vt* (*pt* **extolled**) louer, chanter les louanges de.

extort *vt* extorquer (**from** à). **extortion** *n* (Jur) extorsion *f*. **extortionate** *a* exorbitant.

extra *a* supplémentaire; **~ charge** supplément *m*; **~ time** (football) prolongation *f*; **~ strong** extra-fort. ● *adv* encore; plus. ● *n* supplément *m*; (cinema) figurant/-e *m/f*.

extract¹ *vt* sortir (**from** de); (*tooth*) extraire; (*promise*) arracher.

extract² *n* extrait *m*.

extra-curricular *a* parascolaire.

extradite *vt* extrader.

extramarital *a* extraconjugal.

extramural *a* (Univ) hors faculté.

extraordinary *a* extraordinaire.

E

extravagance *n* prodigalité *f*. **extravagant** *a* (*person*) dépensier; (*claim*) extravagant.

extreme *a & n* extrême (*m*). **extremely** *adv* extrêmement. **extremist** *n* extrémiste *mf*. **extremity** *n* extrémité *f*.

extricate *vt* dégager.

extrovert *n* extraverti/-e *m/f*.

exuberance *n* exubérance *f*.

exude *vt* (*charm*) respirer; (*smell*) exhaler.

eye *n* œil *m* (*pl* yeux); **keep an ~ on** surveiller. ● *vt* (*pt* **eyed**; *pres p* **eyeing**) regarder. **~ball** *n* globe *m* oculaire. **~brow** *n* sourcil *m*. **~-catching** *a* attrayant. **~lash** *n* cil *m*. **~lid** *n* paupière *f*. **~-opener** *n* révélation *f*. **~-shadow** *n* ombre *f* à paupières. **~sight** *n* vue *f*. **~sore** *n* horreur *f*. **~witness** *n* témoin *m* oculaire.

fable *n* fable *f*.

fabric *n* (cloth) tissu *m*.

fabulous *a* fabuleux; (marvellous ⓘ) formidable.

face *n* visage *m*, figure *f*; (expression) air *m*; (appearance, dignity) face *f*; (of clock) cadran *m*; (Geol) face *f*; (of rock) paroi *f*; **in the ~ of** face à; **make a (funny) ~** faire la grimace; **~ to ~** face à face. ● *vt* être en face de; (*risk*) devoir affronter; (confront) faire face à; (deal with) **I can't ~ him** je n'ai pas le courage de le voir. ● *vi* (*person*) regarder; (*chair*) être tourné vers; (*window*) donner sur; **~ up to** faire face à; **~d with** face à.

face-lift *n* lifting *m*; **give a ~ to** donner un coup de neuf à.

face value *n* valeur *f* nominale; **take sth at ~** prendre qch au pied de la lettre.

facial *a* (*hair*) du visage; (*injury*) au visage. ● *n* soin *m* du visage.

facility *n* (building) complexe *m*; (feature) fonction *f*; **facilities** (equipment) équipements *mpl*.

facsimile *n* fac-similé *m*.

fact *n* fait *m*; **as a matter of ~, in ~** en fait; **know for a ~ that** savoir de source sûre que; **owing/due to the ~ that** étant donné que.

factor *n* facteur *m*.

factory *n* usine *f*.

factual *a* (*account, description*) basé sur les faits; (*evidence*) factuel.

faculty *n* faculté *f*.

fade *vi* (*sound*) s'affaiblir; (*memory*) s'effacer; (*flower*) se faner; (*material*) se décolorer; (*colour*) passer.

fail *vi* échouer; (grow weak) (s'af) faiblir; (run short) manquer; (*engine*) tomber en panne. ● *vt* (*exam*) échouer à; **~ to do** (not do) ne pas faire; (not be able) ne pas réussir à faire; **without ~** à coup sûr.

failing *n* défaut *m*; **~ that/this** sinon.

failure *n* échec *m*; (person) raté/-e *m/f*; (breakdown) panne *f*; **~ to do** (inability) incapacité *f* de faire.

faint *a* léger, faible; **feel ~** (ill) se sentir mal; **I haven't the ~est idea** je n'en ai pas la moindre idée. ● *vi* s'évanouir. ● *n* évanouissement *m*. **~-hearted** *a* timide.

fair *n* foire *f*. ● *a* (*hair, person*) blond; (*skin*) clair; (*weather*) beau; (*amount, quality*) raisonnable; (just) juste, équitable. ● *adv* (*play*) loyalement.

fair-ground *n* champ *m* de foire.

fairly *adv* (justly) équitablement; (rather) assez.

fairness *n* justice *f*.

fairy *n* fée *f*. ~ **story**, ~**-tale** *n* conte *m* de fées.

faith *n* (belief) foi *f*; (confidence) confiance *f*.

faithful *a* fidèle.

fake *n* (forgery) faux *m*; (person) imposteur *m*; **it is a** ~ c'est un faux. ● *a* faux. ● *vt* (*signature*) contrefaire; (*results*) falsifier; (*illness*) feindre.

falcon *n* faucon *m*.

fall *vi* (*pt* **fell**; *pp* **fallen**) tomber; ~ **short** être insuffisant. ● *n* chute *f*; (autumn: US) automne *m*; **Niagara F~s** chutes *fpl* du Niagara. □ ~ **back on** se rabattre sur; ~ **behind** prendre du retard; ~ **down** *or* **off** tomber; ~ **for** (*person* ⓘ) tomber amoureux de; (*a trick* ⓘ) se laisser prendre à; ~ **in** (Mil) se mettre en rangs; ~ **off** (decrease) diminuer; ~ **out** se brouiller (**with** avec); ~ **over** tomber (par terre); ~ **through** (*plans*) tomber à l'eau.

fallacy *n* erreur *f*.

false *a* faux. ~ **teeth** *npl* dentier *m*.

falter *vi* (*economy*) fléchir; (*courage*) faiblir; (when speaking) bafouiller ⓘ.

fame *n* renommée *f*. **famed** *a* célèbre (**for** pour).

familiar *a* familier; **be** ~ **with** connaître.

family *n* famille *f*. ● *a* de famille, familial.

famine *n* famine *f*.

famished *a* affamé.

famous *a* célèbre (**for** pour).

fan *n* (mechanical) ventilateur *m*; (hand-held) éventail *m*; (of person) fan *mf* ⓘ, admirateur/-trice *m/f*; (enthusiast) fervent/-e *m/f*, passionné/-e *m/f*. ● *vt* (*pt* **fanned**) (*face*) éventer; (fig) attiser. ● *vi* ~ **out** se déployer en éventail.

fanatic *n* fanatique *mf*.

fan belt *n* courroie *f* de ventilateur.

fancy *n* (whim, fantasy) fantaisie *f*; **take a** ~ **to sb** se prendre d'affection pour qn; **it took my** ~ ça m'a plu. ● *a* (*buttons etc.*) fantaisie *inv*; (*prices*) extravagant; (impressive) impressionnant. ● *vt* s'imaginer; (want ⓘ) avoir envie de; (like ⓘ) aimer. ~ **dress** *n* déguisement *m*.

fang *n* (of dog) croc *m*; (of snake) crochet *m*.

fantasize *vi* fantasmer.

fantastic *a* fantastique.

fantasy *n* fantaisie *f*; (daydream) fantasme *m*.

FAQ *abbr* (**Frequently Asked Questions**) (Internet) FAQ *f*, foire *f* aux questions.

far *adv* loin; (much) beaucoup; (very) très; ~ **away**, ~ **off** au loin; **as** ~ **as** (up to) jusqu'à; **as** ~ **as I know** autant que je sache; **by** ~ de loin; ~ **from** loin de. ● *a* lointain; (end, side) autre. ~**away** *a* lointain.

farce *n* farce *f*.

fare *n* (prix du) billet *m*; (food) nourriture *f*. ● *vi* (progress) aller; (manage) se débrouiller.

Far East *n* Extrême-Orient *m*.

farewell *interj* & *n* adieu (*m*).

farm *n* ferme *f*. ● *vt* cultiver; ~ **out** céder en sous-traitance. ● *vi* être fermier. **farmer** *n* fermier *m*. ~**house** *n* ferme *f*. **farming** *n* agriculture *f*. **~yard** *n* basse-cour *f*.

fart [!] *vi* péter [!]. ● *n* pet *m* [!].

farther *adv* plus loin. ● *a* plus éloigné.

farthest *adv* le plus loin. ● *a* le plus éloigné.

fascinate *vt* fasciner.

Fascism *n* fascisme *m*.

fashion *n* (current style) mode *f*; (manner) façon *f*; **in ~** à la mode; **out of ~** démodé. ● *vt* façonner. **fashionable** *a* à la mode.

fast *a* rapide; (colour) grand teint *inv*; (firm) fixe, solide; **be ~** (of a clock) avancer. ● *adv* vite; (firmly) ferme; **be ~ asleep** dormir d'un sommeil profond. ● *vi* jeûner. ● *n* jeûne *m*.

fasten *vt/i* (s')attacher. **fastener**, **fastening** *n* attache *f*, fermeture *f*.

fast food *n* fast-food *m*; restauration *f* rapide.

fat *n* graisse *f*; (on meat) gras *m*. ● *a* (**fatter**, **fattest**) gros, gras; (*meat*) gras; (*profit*) gros; **a ~ lot** [!] bien peu (**of** de).

fatal *a* mortel; (fateful, disastrous) fatal. **fatality** *n* mort *m*. **fatally** *adv* mortellement.

fate *n* sort *m*. **fateful** *a* fatidique.

father *n* père *m*. **~hood** *n* paternité *f*. **~-in-law** *n* (*pl* **~s-in-law**) beau-père *m*.

fathom *n* brasse *f* (=*1.8 m*). ● *vt* **~** (**out**) comprendre.

fatigue *n* épuisement *m*; (Tech) fatigue *f*. ● *vt* fatiguer.

fatten *vt/i* engraisser. **fattening** *a* qui fait grossir.

fatty *a* (*food*) gras; (*tissue*) adipeux.

faucet *n* (US) robinet *m*.

fault *n* (defect, failing) défaut *m*; (blame) faute *f*; (Geol) faille *f*; **at ~** fautif; **find ~ with** critiquer. ● *vt* **~ sth/sb** prendre en défaut qn/qch. **faulty** *a* défectueux.

favour, (US) **favor** *n* faveur *f*; **do sb a ~** rendre service à qn; **in ~ of** pour. ● *vt* favoriser; (support) être en faveur de; (prefer) préférer. **favourable** *a* favorable.

favourite *a* & *n* favori/-te (*m/f*).

fawn *n* (animal) faon *m*; (colour) beige *m* foncé. ● *vi* **~ on** flagorner.

fax *n* fax *m*, télécopie *f*. ● *vt* faxer, envoyer par télécopie. **~ machine** *n* fax *m*; télécopieur *m*; (for public use) Publifax® *m*.

FBI *abbr* (**Federal Bureau of Investigation**) (US) Police *f* judiciaire fédérale.

fear *n* crainte *f*, peur *f*; (fig) risque *m*; **for ~ of/that** de peur de/que. ● *vt* craindre.

feasible *a* faisable; (likely) plausible.

feast *n* festin *m*; (Relig) fête *f*. ● *vi* festoyer. ● *vt* régaler (**on** de).

feat *n* exploit *m*.

feather *n* plume *f*. ● *vt* **~ one's nest** s'enrichir.

feature *n* caractéristique *f*; (of person, face) trait *m*; (film) long métrage *m*; (article) article *m* de fond. ● *vt* (*advert*) représenter; (give prominence to) mettre en vedette. ● *vi* figurer (**in** dans).

February *n* février *m*.

fed ⇒FEED. ● *a* **be ~ up** [!] en avoir marre [!] (**with** de).

federal *a* fédéral.

fee *n* (for entrance) prix *m*; **~(s)** (of doctor) honoraires *mpl*; (of actor, artist) cachet *m*; (for tuition) frais *mpl*; (for enrolment) droits *mpl*.

feeble *a* faible.

feed *vt* (*pt* **fed**) nourrir, donner à manger à; (suckle) allaiter; (supply) alimenter. ● *vi* se nourrir (**on** de); **~ in information** rentrer des données. ● *n* nourriture *f*; (of baby) tétée *f*.

feedback *n* réaction(s) *f*(*pl*); (Med, Tech) feed-back *m*.

feel *vt* (*pt* **felt**) (touch) tâter; (be conscious of) sentir; (*emotion*) ressentir; (experience) éprouver; (think) estimer. ● *vi* (*tired, lonely*) se sentir; ~ **hot/thirsty** avoir chaud/soif; ~ **as if** avoir l'impression que; ~ **awful** (ill) se sentir malade; ~ **like** (want ⊡) avoir envie de.

feeler *n* antenne *f*; **put out ~s** tâter le terrain.

feeling *n* (emotion) sentiment *m*; (physical) sensation *f*; (impression) impression *f*.

feet ⇒FOOT.

feign *vt* feindre.

fell ⇒FALL. ● *vt* (cut down) abattre.

fellow *n* compagnon *m*, camarade *m*; (of society) membre *m*; (man ⊡) type *m* ⊡. **~-countryman** *n* compatriote *m*. **~-passenger** *n* compagnon *m* de voyage.

fellowship *n* camaraderie *f*; (group) association *f*.

felony *n* crime *m*.

felt ⇒FEEL. ● *n* feutre *m*. **~-tip** *n* feutre *m*.

female *a* (*animal*) femelle; (*voice, sex*) féminin. ● *n* femme *f*; (animal) femelle *f*.

feminine *a & n* féminin (*m*). **femininity** *n* féminité *f*. **feminist** *n* féministe *mf*.

fence *n* barrière *f*; **sit on the ~** ne pas prendre position. ● *vt* ~ **(in)** clôturer. ● *vi* (Sport) faire de l'escrime. **fencing** *n* escrime *f*.

fend *vi* ~ **for oneself** se débrouiller tout seul. ● *vt* ~ **off** (blow, attack) parer.

fender *n* (for fireplace) garde-cendre *m*; (mudguard: US) garde-boue *m inv*.

ferment[1] *n* ferment *m*; (excitement: fig) agitation *f*.

ferment[2] *vt*/*i* (faire) fermenter.

fern *n* fougère *f*.

ferocious *a* féroce.

ferret *n* (animal) furet *m*. ● *vi* ~ **about** fureter. ● *vt* ~ **out** dénicher.

ferry *n* (long-distance) ferry *m*; (short-distance) bac *m*. ● *vt* transporter.

fertile *a* fertile; (*person, animal*) fécond. **fertilizer** *n* engrais *m*.

festival *n* festival *m*; (Relig) fête *f*.

festive *a* de fête, gai; ~ **season** période *f* des fêtes. **festivity** *n* réjouissances *fpl*.

fetch *vt* (go for) aller chercher; (bring person) amener; (bring thing) apporter; (be sold for) rapporter.

fête *n* fête *f*; (church) kermesse *f*. ● *vt* fêter.

fetish *n* (object) fétiche *m*; (Psych) obsession *f*.

feud *n* querelle *f*.

fever *n* fièvre *f*. **feverish** *a* fiévreux.

few *det* peu de; **a ~ houses** quelques maisons; **quite a ~ people** un bon nombre de personnes. ● *pron* quelques-uns/quelques-unes.

fewer *det* moins de; **be ~** être moins nombreux (**than** que). **fewest** *det* le moins de.

fiancé *n* fiancé *m*. **fiancée** *n* fiancée *f*.

fibre, (US) **fiber** *n* fibre *f*. **~glass** *n* fibre *f* de verre.

fiction *n* fiction *f*; (**works of**) ~ romans *mpl*. **fictional** *a* fictif.

fiddle *n* ⊡ violon *m*; (swindle ⊡) combine *f*. ● *vi* ⊠ frauder. ● *vt* ⊡ falsifier; ~ **with** ⊡ tripoter ⊡.

fidget *vi* gigoter sans cesse.

field *n* champ *m*; (Sport) terrain *m*; (fig) domaine *m*. ● *vt* (*ball*: cricket) bloquer.

F

fierce *a* féroce; (*storm, attack*) violent.

fiery *a* (**-ier, -iest**) (hot) ardent; (spirited) fougueux.

fifteen *a & n* quinze (*m*).

fifth *a & n* cinquième (*mf*).

fifty *a & n* cinquante (*m*).

fig *n* figue *f*.

fight *vi* (*pt* **fought**) se battre; (struggle: fig) lutter; (quarrel) se disputer. ● *vt* se battre avec; (*evil*: fig) lutter contre. ● *n* (struggle) lutte *f*; (quarrel) dispute *f*; (brawl) bagarre *f*; (Mil) combat *m*. □ ~ **back** se défendre (**against** contre); ~ **off** surmonter; ~ **over** se disputer qch. **fighter** *n* (determined person) lutteur/-euse *m/f*; (plane) avion *m* de chasse. **fighting** *n* combats *mpl*.

figment *n* **a ~ of the imagination** un produit de l'imagination.

figure *n* (number) chiffre *m*; (diagram) figure *f*; (shape) forme *f*; (body) ligne *f*; **~s** arithmétique *f*. ● *vt* s'imaginer. ● *vi* (appear) figurer; **that ~s** (US, ⊡) c'est logique; **~ out** comprendre. **~ of speech** *n* façon *f* de parler.

file *n* (tool) lime *f*; dossier *m*, classeur *m*; (Comput) fichier *m*; (row) file *f*. ● *vt* limer; (*papers*) classer; (Jur) déposer. □ ~ **in** entrer en file; ~ **past** défiler devant.

filing cabinet *n* classeur *m*.

fill *vt/i* (se) remplir. ● *n* **have had one's ~** en avoir assez. □ ~ **in** (*form*) remplir; ~ **out** prendre du poids; ~ **up** (Auto) faire le plein (de carburant); (*bath, theatre*) (se) remplir.

fillet *n* filet *m*. ● *vt* découper en filets.

filling *n* (of tooth) plombage *m*; (of sandwich) garniture *f*. ~ **station** *n* station-service *f*.

film *n* film *m*; (Photo) pellicule *f*. ● *vt* filmer. **~-goer** *n* cinéphile *mf*. ~ **star** *n* vedette *f* de cinéma.

filter *n* filtre *m*; (traffic signal) flèche *f*. ● *vt/i* filtrer; (of traffic) suivre la flèche. ~ **coffee** *n* café *m* filtre.

filth *n* crasse *f*. **filthy** *a* crasseux.

fin *n* (of fish, seal) nageoire *f*; (of shark) aileron *m*.

final *a* dernier; (conclusive) définitif. ● *n* (Sport) finale *f*.

finale *n* (Mus) finale *m*.

finalize *vt* mettre au point, fixer.

finally *adv* (lastly, at last) enfin, finalement; (once and for all) définitivement.

finance *n* finance *f*. ● *a* financier. ● *vt* financer. **financial** *a* financier.

find *vt* (*pt* **found**) trouver; (*sth lost*) retrouver. ● *n* trouvaille *f*. ~ **out** *vt* découvrir; *vi* se renseigner (**about** sur). **findings** *npl* conclusions *fpl*.

fine *a* fin; (excellent) beau; ~ **arts** beaux-arts *mpl*. ● *n* amende *f*. ● *vt* condamner à une amende.

finger *n* doigt *m*. ● *vt* palper. **~-nail** *n* ongle *m*. **~print** *n* empreinte *f* digitale. **~tip** *n* bout *m* du doigt.

finish *vt/i* finir; ~ **doing** finir de faire; ~ **up doing** finir par faire; ~ **up in** se retrouver à. ● *n* fin *f*; (of race) arrivée *f*; (appearance) finition *f*.

finite *a* fini.

Finland *n* Finlande *f*. **Finn** *n* Finlandais/-e *m/f*.

Finnish *a* finlandais. ● *n* (Ling) finnois *m*.

fir *n* sapin *m*.

fire *n* (element) feu *m*; (blaze) incendie *m*; (heater) radiateur *m*; **set ~ to** mettre le feu à. ● *vt* (bullet) tirer; (dismiss) renvoyer; (fig) enflammer. ● *vi* tirer (**at** sur); **~ a gun** tirer un coup de revolver/de fusil. ~ **alarm** *n* alarme *f* incendie. **~arm** *n* arme *f* à feu. **~ brigade** *n* pompiers *mpl*. **~ engine** *n* voiture *f* de pompiers. **~ escape** *n* escalier *m* de secours. **~ extinguisher** *n* extincteur *m*. **~man** *n* (*pl* **-men**) pompier *m*. **~place** *n* cheminée *f*. **~ station** *n* caserne *f* de pompiers. **~wall** *n* mur *m* coupe-feu; (Internet) pare-feu *m inv*. **~wood** *n* bois *m* de chauffage. **~work** *n* feu *m* d'artifice.

firing-squad *n* peloton *m* d'exécution.

firm *n* entreprise *f*, société *f*. ● *a* ferme; (*belief*) solide.

first *a* premier; **at ~ hand** de première main; **at ~ sight** à première vue; **~ of all** tout d'abord. ● *n* premier/-ière *m/f*. ● *adv* d'abord, premièrement; (arrive) le premier, la première; **at ~** d'abord. **~ aid** *n* premiers soins *mpl*. **~-class** *a* de première classe. **~ floor** *n* premier étage *m*; (US) rez-de-chaussée *m inv*. **~ gear** *n* première (vitesse) *f*. **F~ Lady** *n* (US) épouse *f* du Président.

firstly *adv* premièrement.

first name *n* prénom *m*.

fish *n* poisson *m*; **~ shop** poissonnerie *f*. ● *vi* pêcher; **~ for** (*cod*) pêcher; **~ out** (from water) repêcher; (take out ▣) sortir. **fisherman** *n* (*pl* **-men**) *n* pêcheur *m*.

fishing *n* pêche *f*; **go ~** aller à la pêche. **~ rod** *n* canne *f* à pêche.

fishmonger *n* poissonnier/-ière *m/f*.

fist *n* poing *m*.

fit *n* accès *m*, crise *f*; **be a good ~** (*dress*) être à la bonne taille. ● *a* (**fitter, fittest**) en bonne santé; (proper) convenable; (good enough) bon; (able) capable; **in no ~ state to do** pas en état de faire. ● *vt/i* (*pt* **fitted**) (into space) aller; (install) poser. □ **~ in** *vt* caser; *vi* (*newcomer*) s'intégrer; **~ out**, **~ up** équiper.

fitness *n* forme *f*; (of remark) justesse *f*.

fitted *a* (*wardrobe*) encastré. **~ carpet** *n* moquette *f*.

fitting *a* approprié. ● *n* essayage *m*. **~ room** *n* cabine *f* d'essayage.

five *a* & *n* cinq (*m*).

fix *vt* (make firm, attach, decide) fixer; (mend) réparer; (deal with) arranger; **~ sb up with sth** trouver qch à qn.

fixture *n* (Sport) match *m*; **~s** (in house) installations *fpl*.

fizz *vi* pétiller. ● *n* pétillement *m*. **fizzy** *a* gazeux.

flabbergast *vt* sidérer.

flabby *a* flasque.

flag *n* drapeau *m*; (Naut) pavillon *m*. ● *vt* (*pt* **flagged**) **~ (down)** faire signe de s'arrêter à. ● *vi* (weaken) faiblir; (*sick person*) s'affaiblir. **~-pole** *n* mât *m*. **~stone** *n* dalle *f*.

flake *n* flocon *m*; (of paint, metal) écaille *f*. ● *vi* s'écailler.

flamboyant *a* (*colour*) éclatant; (*manner*) extravagant.

flame *n* flamme *f*; **burst into ~s** exploser; **go up in ~s** brûler. ● *vi* flamber.

flamingo *n* flamant *m* (rose).

flammable *a* inflammable.

flan *n* tarte *f*; (custard tart) flan *m*.

flank *n* flanc *m*. ● *vt* flanquer.

flannel *n* (material) flannelle *f*; (for face) gant *m* de toilette.

flap *vi* (*pt* **flapped**) battre. ● *vt* **~ its wings** battre des ailes. ● *n* (of pocket) rabat *m*; (of table) abattant *m*.

flare *vi* **~ up** (fighting) éclater. ● *n* flamboiement *m*; (Mil) fusée *f*

F

éclairante; (in skirt) évasement *m*. **flared** *a* évasé.

flash *vi* briller; (on and off) clignoter; ~ **past** passer à toute vitesse. ● *vt* faire briller; (aim torch) diriger (**at** sur); (flaunt) étaler; ~ **one's headlights** faire un appel de phares. ● *n* (of news, camera) flash *m*; **in a** ~ en un éclair. ~**back** *n* retour *m* en arrière. ~**light** *n* lampe *f* de poche.

flask *n* (for chemicals) flacon *m*; (for drinks) thermos® *m or f inv*.

flat *a* (**flatter**, **flattest**) plat; (*tyre*) à plat; (*refusal*) catégorique; (*fare, rate*) fixe. ● *adv* (*say*) carrément. ● *n* (rooms) appartement *m*; (tyre ⓘ) crevaison *f*; (Mus) bémol *m*.

flat out *adv* (*drive*) à toute vitesse; (*work*) d'arrache-pied.

flatten *vt/i* (s')aplatir.

flatter *vt* flatter.

flaunt *vt* étaler, afficher.

flavour, (US) **flavor** *n* goût *m*; (of ice-cream) parfum *m*. ● *vt* parfumer (**with** à), assaisonner (**with** de). **flavouring** *n* arôme *m* artificiel.

flaw *n* défaut *m*.

flea *n* puce *f*. ~ **market** *n* marché *m* aux puces.

fleck *n* petite tache *f*.

fled ⇒FLEE.

flee *vt/i* (*pt* **fled**) fuir.

fleece *n* toison *f*; (garment) polaire *f*. ● *vt* plumer.

fleet *n* (Naut, Aviat) flotte *f*; **a** ~ **of vehicles** (in reserve) parc *m*; (on road) convoi *m*.

fleeting *a* très bref.

Flemish *a* flamand. ● *n* (Ling) flamand *m*.

flesh *n* chair *f*; **one's (own)** ~ **and blood** la chair de sa chair.

flew ⇒FLY.

flex *vt* (*knee*) fléchir; (*muscle*) faire jouer. ● *n* (Electr) fil *m*.

flexible *a* flexible.

flexitime *n* horaire *m* variable.

flick *n* petit coup *m*. ● *vt* donner un petit coup à; ~ **through** feuilleter.

flight *n* (of bird, plane) vol *m*; ~ **of stairs** escalier *m*; (fleeing) fuite *f*; **take** ~ prendre la fuite. ~**-deck** *n* poste *m* de pilotage.

flimsy *a* (**-ier**, **-iest**) (pej) mince, peu solide.

flinch *vi* (wince) broncher; (draw back) reculer.

fling *vt* (*pt* **flung**) jeter.

flint *n* (rock) silex *m*.

flip *vt* (*pt* **flipped**) donner un petit coup à; ~ **through** feuilleter. ● *n* chiquenaude *f*.

flippant *a* désinvolte.

flipper *n* (of seal) nageoire *f*; (of swimmer) palme *f*.

flirt *vi* flirter. ● *n* flirteur/-euse *m*/*f*.

float *vt/i* (faire) flotter. ● *n* flotteur *m*; (cart) char *m*.

flock *n* (of sheep) troupeau *m*; (of people) foule *f*. ● *vi* affluer.

flog *vt* (*pt* **flogged**) (beat) fouetter; (sell ⓘ) vendre.

flood *n* inondation *f*; (fig) flot *m*. ● *vt* inonder. ● *vi* (*building*) être inondé; (*river*) déborder; (*people*: fig) affluer.

floodlight *n* projecteur *m*. ● *vt* (*pt* **floodlit**) illuminer.

floor *n* sol *m*, plancher *m*; (for dancing) piste *f*; (storey) étage *m*. ● *vt* (knock down) terrasser; (baffle) stupéfier. ~**-board** *n* planche *f*.

flop *vi* (*pt* **flopped**) (drop) s'affaler; (fail ⊠) échouer; (*head*) tomber. ● *n* ⓘ échec *m*, fiasco *m*.

floppy *a* lâche, flasque. ~ (**disk**) *n* disquette *f*.

florist *n* fleuriste *mf*.

flounder *vi* (*animal, person*) se débattre (**in** dans); (*economy*) stagner. ● *n* flet *m*; (US) poisson *m* plat.

flour *n* farine *f*.

flourish *vi* prospérer. ● *vt* brandir. ● *n* geste *m* élégant; (curve) fioriture *f*.

flout *vt* se moquer de.

flow *vi* couler; (circulate) circuler; (*traffic*) s'écouler; (hang loosely) flotter; ~ **in** affluer; ~ **into** (of river) se jeter dans. ● *n* (of liquid, traffic) écoulement *m*; (of tide) flux *m*; (of orders, words: fig) flot *m*. ~ **chart** *n* organigramme *m*.

flower *n* fleur *f*. ● *vi* fleurir.

flown ⇒FLY.

flu *n* grippe *f*.

fluctuate *vi* varier.

fluent *a* (*style*) aisé; **be ~ (in a language)** parler (une langue) couramment.

fluff *n* peluche(s) *f(pl)*; (down) duvet *m*.

fluid *a* & *n* fluide (*m*).

fluke *n* coup *m* de chance.

flung ⇒FLING.

fluoride *n* fluor *m*.

flush *vi* rougir. ● *vt* nettoyer à grande eau; ~ **the toilet** tirer la chasse d'eau. ● *n* (blush) rougeur *f*; (fig) excitation *f*. ● *a* ~ **with** (level with) au ras de. □ ~ **out** chasser.

fluster *vt* énerver.

flute *n* flûte *f*.

flutter *vi* voleter; (of wings) battre. ● *n* (*wings*) battement *m*; (fig) agitation *f*; (bet ⊡) pari *m*.

flux *n* changement *m* continuel.

fly *n* mouche *f*; (of trousers) braguette *f*. ● *vi* (*pt* **flew**; *pp* **flown**) voler; (*passengers*) voyager en avion; (*flag*) flotter; (rush) filer. ● *vt* (*aircraft*) piloter; (*passengers, goods*) transporter par avion; (*flag*) arborer. □ ~ **off** s'envoler.

flyer *n* (person) aviateur *m*; (circular) prospectus *m*.

flying *a* (*saucer*) volant; **with ~ colours** haut la main; ~ **start** excellent départ *m*; ~ **visit** visite *f* éclair (*a inv*). ● *n* (activity) aviation *f*.

flyover *n* pont *m* (routier).

foal *n* poulain *m*.

foam *n* écume *f*, mousse *f*; ~ **(rubber)** caoutchouc *m* mousse. ● *vi* écumer, mousser.

focus *n* (*pl* **~es** *or* **-ci**) foyer *m*; (fig) centre *m*; **be in/out of ~** être/ne pas être au point. ● *vt/i* (faire) converger; (*instrument*) mettre au point; (with camera) faire la mise au point (**on** sur); (fig) (se) concentrer.

fodder *n* fourrage *m*.

foe *n* ennemi/-e *m/f*.

foetus *n* fœtus *m*.

fog *n* brouillard *m*. ● *vt/i* (*pt* **fogged**) (*window*) (s')embuer.

foggy *a* brumeux; **it is ~** il fait du brouillard.

foil *n* (tin foil) papier *m* d'aluminium; (deterrent) repoussoir *m*. ● *vt* (thwart) déjouer.

fold *vt/i* (*paper, clothes*) (se) plier; (*arms*) croiser; (fail) s'effondrer. ● *n* pli *m*; (for sheep) parc *m* à moutons; (Relig) bercail *m*. **folder** *n* (file) chemise *f*; (leaflet) dépliant *m*. **folding** *a* pliant.

foliage *n* feuillage *m*.

folk *n* gens *mpl*; **~s** parents *mpl*. ● *a* (*dance*) folklorique; (*music*) folk.

folklore *n* folklore *m*.

follow *vt/i* suivre; **it ~s that** il s'ensuit que; ~ **suit** en faire autant; ~ **up** (*letter*) donner suite à. **follower** *n* partisan *m*.

following *n* partisans *mpl*. ● *a* suivant; ~ **day** lendemain. ● *prep* à la suite de.

F

fond *a* (loving) affectueux; (*hope*) cher; **be ~ of** aimer.

fondle *vt* caresser.

fondness *n* affection *f*; (for things) attachement *m*.

food *n* nourriture *f*; **French ~** la cuisine française. ● *a* alimentaire. **~ processor** *n* robot *m* (ménager).

fool *n* idiot/-e *m/f*. ● *vt* duper. ● *vi* **~ around** faire l'idiot. **foolish** *a* idiot.

foot *n* (*pl* **feet**) pied *m*; (measure) pied *m* (=30.48 cm); (*of stairs, page*) bas *m*; **on ~** à pied; **on** *or* **to one's feet** debout; **under sb's feet** dans les jambes de qn. ● *vt* (*bill*) payer.

footage *n* (of film) métrage *m*.

football *n* (ball) ballon *m*; (game) football *m*. **footballer** *n* footballeur *m*.

foot: **~-bridge** *n* passerelle *f*. **~hold** *n* prise *f*.

footing *n* **on an equal ~** sur un pied d'égalité; **be on a friendly ~ with sb** avoir des rapports amicaux avec qn; **lose one's ~** perdre pied.

foot: **~note** *n* note *f* (*en bas de la page*). **~path** *n* (in countryside) sentier *m*; (in town) chemin *m*. **~print** *n* empreinte *f* (*de pied*). **~step** *n* pas *m*. **~wear** *n* chaussures *fpl*.

for

● *preposition*

····➤ pour; **~ me** pour moi; **music ~ dancing** de la musique pour danser; **what is it ~?** ça sert à quoi?

····➤ (with a time period that is still continuing) depuis; **I've been waiting ~ two hours** j'attends depuis deux heures; **I haven't seen him ~ ten years** je ne l'ai pas vu depuis dix ans.

····➤ (with a time period that has ended) pendant; **I waited ~ two hours** j'ai attendu pendant deux heures.

····➤ (with a future time period) pour; **I'm going to Paris ~ six weeks** je vais à Paris pour six semaines.

····➤ (with distances) pendant; **I drove ~ 50 kilometres** j'ai roulé pendant 50 kilomètres.

forbade ⇒FORBID.

forbid *vt* (*pt* **forbade**; *pp* **forbidden**) interdire, défendre (**sb to do** à qn de faire); **~ sb sth** interdire *or* défendre qch à qn; **you are forbidden to leave** il vous est interdit de partir. **forbidding** *a* menaçant.

force *n* force *f*; **come into ~** entrer en vigueur; **the ~s** les forces *fpl* armées. ● *vt* forcer. □ **~ into** faire entrer de force; **~ on** imposer à. **forced** *a* forcé.

force-feed *vt* (*pt* **-fed**) (*person*) nourrir de force; (*animal*) gaver.

forceful *a* énergique.

ford *n* gué *m*. ● *vt* passer à gué.

forearm *n* avant-bras *m inv*.

forecast *vt* (*pt* **forecast**) prévoir. ● *n* **weather ~** météo *f*.

forecourt *n* (of garage) devant *m*; (of station) cour *f*.

forefinger *n* index *m*.

forefront *n* **at/in the ~ of** à la pointe de.

foregone *a* **it's a ~ conclusion** c'est couru d'avance.

foreground *n* premier plan *m*.

forehead *n* front *m*.

foreign *a* étranger; (*trade*) extérieur; (*travel*) à l'étranger. **foreigner** *n* étranger/-ère *m/f*.

foreman *n* (*pl* **-men**) contremaître *m*.

foremost *a* le plus éminent. ● *adv* **first and ~** tout d'abord.

forensic *a* médico-légal; **~ medicine** médecine *f* légale.

foresee *vt* (*pt* **-saw**; *pp* **-seen**) prévoir.

forest *n* forêt *f*. **forestry** *n* sylviculture *f*.

foretaste *n* avant-goût *m*.

forever *adv* toujours.

foreword *n* avant-propos *m inv*.

forfeit *n* (penalty) peine *f*; (in game) gage *m*. ● *vt* perdre.

forgave ⇒FORGIVE.

forge *n* forge *f*. ● *vt* (*metal, friendship*) forger; (copy) contrefaire, falsifier. ● *vi* **~ ahead** aller de l'avant, avancer. **forger** *n* faussaire *m*. **forgery** *n* faux *m*, contrefaçon *f*.

forget *vt/i* (*pt* **forgot**; *pp* **forgotten**) oublier; **~ oneself** s'oublier. **forgetful** *a* distrait. **~-me-not** *n* myosotis *m*.

forgive *vt* (*pt* **forgave**; *pp* **forgiven**) pardonner (**sb for sth** qch à qn).

fork *n* fourchette *f*; (for digging) fourche *f*; (in road) bifurcation *f*. ● *vi* (*road*) bifurquer; **~ out** 🅸 payer. **forked** *a* fourchu. **~-lift truck** *n* chariot *m* élévateur.

form *n* forme *f*; (document) formulaire *m*; (School) classe *f*; **on ~** en forme. ● *vt/i* (se) former.

formal *a* officiel, en bonne et due forme; (*person*) compassé, cérémonieux; (*dress*) de cérémonie; (*denial, grammar*) formel; (*language*) soutenu. **formality** *n* cérémonial *m*; (requirement) formalité *f*.

format *n* format *m*. ● *vt* (*pt* **formatted**) (*disk*) formater.

former *a* ancien; (first of two) premier. ● *n* **the ~** celui-là, celle-là. **formerly** *adv* autrefois.

formula *n* (*pl* **-ae** *or* **-as**) formule *f*. **formulate** *vt* formuler.

fort *n* (Mil) fort *m*; **to hold the ~** s'occuper de tout.

forth *adv* **from this day ~** à partir d'aujourd'hui; **and so ~** et ainsi de suite; **go back and ~** aller et venir.

forthcoming *a* à venir, prochain; (sociable 🅸) communicatif.

forthright *a* direct.

forthwith *adv* sur-le-champ.

fortnight *n* quinze jours *mpl*, quinzaine *f*.

fortnightly *a* bimensuel. ● *adv* tous les quinze jours.

fortunate *a* heureux; **be ~** avoir de la chance. **fortunately** *adv* heureusement.

fortune *n* fortune *f*; **make a ~** faire fortune; **have the good ~ to** avoir la chance de. **~-teller** *n* diseur/-euse *m/f* de bonne aventure.

forty *a & n* quarante (*m*); **~ winks** un petit somme.

forward *a* en avant; (advanced) précoce; (bold) effronté. ● *n* (Sport) avant *m*. ● *adv* en avant; **come ~** se présenter; **go ~** avancer. ● *vt* (*letter, e-mail*) faire suivre; (*goods*) expédier; (fig) favoriser. **forwardness** *n* précocité *f*. **forwards** *adv* en avant.

fossil *n & a* fossile (*m*).

foster *vt* (promote) encourager; (*child*) élever. ● *a* (*child, parent*) adoptif; (*family, home*) de placement.

fought ⇒FIGHT.

foul *a* (*smell, weather*) infect; (*place, action*) immonde; (*language*) ordurier. ● *n* (*football*) faute *f*. ● *vt* souiller, encrasser; **~ up** 🅸 gâcher. **~-mouthed** *a* grossier.

found ⇒FIND. ● *vt* fonder. **foundation** *n* fondation *f*; (basis)

F

fondement *m*; (make-up) fond *m* de teint. **founder** *n* fondateur/-trice *m/f*.

fountain *n* fontaine *f*. **~-pen** *n* stylo *m* à encre.

four *a & n* quatre (*m*).

fourteen *a & n* quatorze (*m*).

fourth *a & n* quatrième (*mf*).

four-wheel drive *n* (car) quatre-quatre *m*.

fowl *n* (one bird) poulet *m*; (group) volaille *f*.

fox *n* renard *m*. ● *vt* (baffle) mystifier; (deceive) tromper.

fraction *n* fraction *f*.

fracture *n* fracture *f*. ● *vt/i* (se) fracturer.

fragile *a* fragile.

fragment *n* fragment *m*.

fragrance *n* parfum *m*.

frail *a* frêle.

frame *n* (of building, boat) charpente *f*; (of picture) cadre *m*; (of window) châssis *m*; (of spectacles) monture *f*; **~ of mind** humeur *f*. ● *vt* encadrer; (fig) formuler; (Jur, ⊡) monter un coup contre. **~work** *n* structure *f*; (context) cadre *m*.

France *n* France *f*.

franchise *n* (Pol) droit *m* de vote; (Comm) franchise *f*.

frank *a* franc. ● *vt* affranchir. **frankly** *adv* franchement.

frantic *a* frénétique; **~ with** fou de.

fraternity *n* (bond) fraternité *f*; (group, club) confrérie *f*.

fraud *n* (deception) fraude *f*; (person) imposteur *m*. **fraudulent** *a* frauduleux.

fray *n* **the ~** la bataille. ● *vt/i* (s')effilocher.

freckle *n* tache *f* de rousseur.

free *a* libre; (gratis) gratuit; (lavish) généreux; **~ (of charge)** gratuit (ement); **a ~ hand** carte *f* blanche. ● *vt* (*pt* **freed**) libérer; (clear) dégager.

freedom *n* liberté *f*.

free: **~ enterprise** *n* la libre entreprise. **~ kick** *n* coup *m* franc. **~lance** *a & n* free-lance (*mf*), indépendant/-e (*m/f*).

freely *adv* librement.

Freemason *n* franc-maçon *m*.

Freenet *n* (Comput) Libertel *m*.

free: **~ phone**, **~ number** *n* numéro *m* vert. **~-range** *a* (*eggs*) de ferme.

Freeware *n* (Comput) Gratuiciel *m*.

freeway *n* (US) autoroute *f*.

freeze *vt/i* (*pt* **froze**; *pp* **frozen**) geler; (Culin) (se) congeler; (*wages*) bloquer. ● *n* gel *m*; blocage *m*. **~-dried** *a* lyophilisé.

freezer *n* congélateur *m*.

freezing *a* glacial; **below ~** au-dessous de zéro.

freight *n* fret *m*.

French *a* français. ● *n* (Ling) français *m*; **the ~** les Français *mpl*. **~ bean** *n* haricot *m* vert. **~ fries** *npl* frites *fpl*. **~man** *n* Français *m*. **~-speaking** *a* francophone. **~ window** *n* porte-fenêtre *f*. **~woman** *n* Française *f*.

frenzied *a* frénétique. **frenzy** *n* frénésie *f*.

frequent¹ *a* fréquent.

frequent² *vt* fréquenter.

fresco *n* fresque *f*.

fresh *a* frais; (different, additional) nouveau; (cheeky ⊡) culotté.

freshen *vi* (*weather*) fraîchir; **~ up** (*person*) se rafraîchir.

freshly *adv* nouvellement.

freshness *n* fraîcheur *f*.

freshwater *a* d'eau douce.

friction *n* friction *f*.

Friday *n* vendredi *m*.

fridge *n* frigo *m*.

fried ⇨FRY. ● *a* frit; ~ **eggs** œufs *mpl* sur le plat.

friend *n* ami/-e *m/f*. **friendly** *a* (**-ier**, **-iest**) amical, gentil. **friendship** *n* amitié *f*.

frieze *n* frise *f*.

fright *n* peur *f*; (person, thing) horreur *f*.

frighten *vt* effrayer; ~ **off** faire fuir; **frightened** *a* effrayé; **be ~ed** avoir peur (**of** de). **frightening** *a* effrayant.

frill *n* (trimming) fanfreluche *f*; **with no ~s** très simple.

fringe *n* (edging, hair) frange *f*; (of area) bordure *f*; (of society) marge *f*. ~ **benefits** *npl* avantages *mpl* sociaux.

frisk *vt* (search) fouiller.

fritter *n* beignet *m*. ● *vt* ~ **away** gaspiller.

frivolity *n* frivolité *f*.

frizzy *a* crépu.

fro ⇨TO AND FRO.

frog *n* grenouille *f*; **a ~ in one's throat** un chat dans la gorge.

frolic *vi* (*pt* **frolicked**) s'ébattre. ● *n* ébats *mpl*.

from *prep* de; (with time, prices) à partir de, de; (*habit, conviction*) par; (according to) d'après; **take ~ sb** prendre à qn; **take ~ one's pocket** prendre dans sa poche.

front *n* (of car, train) avant *m*; (of garment, building) devant *m*; (Mil, Pol) front *m*; (of book, pamphlet) début *m*; (appearance: fig) façade *f*. ● *a* de devant, avant *inv*; (first) premier; ~ **door** porte *f* d'entrée; **in ~ (of)** devant. **frontage** *n* façade *f*.

frontier *n* frontière *f*.

frost *n* gel *m*, gelée *f*; (on glass) givre *m*. ● *vt/i* (se) givrer. **~-bite** *n* gelure *f*.

frosty *a* (*weather, welcome*) glacial; (*window*) givré.

froth *n* (on beer) mousse *f*; (on water) écume *f*. ● *vi* mousser, écumer.

frown *vi* froncer les sourcils; ~ **on** désapprouver. ● *n* froncement *m* de sourcils.

froze ⇨FREEZE.

frozen ⇨FREEZE. ● *a* congelé.

fruit *n* fruit *m*; (collectively) fruits *mpl*. **fruitful** *a* (*discussions*) fructueux. ~ **machine** *n* machine *f* à sous.

frustrate *vt* (*plan*) faire échouer; (*person*: Psych) frustrer; (upset ⓘ) exaspérer. **frustration** *n* (Psych) frustration *f*; (disappointment) déception *f*.

fry *vt/i* (*pt* **fried**) (faire) frire. **frying-pan** *n* poêle *f* (à frire).

FTP *abbr* (**File Transfer Protocol**) (Internet) protocole *m* FTP.

fudge *n* caramel *m* mou. ● *vt* (*issue*) esquiver.

fuel *n* combustible *m*; (for car engine) carburant *m*. ● *vt* (*pt* **fuelled**) alimenter en combustible.

fugitive *n* & *a* fugitif/-ive (*m/f*).

fulfil *vt* (*pt* **fulfilled**) accomplir, réaliser; (*condition*) remplir; ~ **oneself** s'épanouir. **fulfilling** *a* satisfaisant. **fulfilment** *n* réalisation *f*; épanouissement *m*.

full *a* plein (**of** de); (*bus, hotel*) complet; (*programme*) chargé; (*skirt*) ample; **be ~ (up)** n'avoir plus faim; **at ~ speed** à toute vitesse. ● *n* **in ~** intégralement; **to the ~** complètement. ~ **back** *n* (Sport) arrière *m*. ~ **moon** *n* pleine lune *f*. ~ **name** *n* nom *m* et prénom *m*. **~-scale** *a* (*drawing etc.*) grandeur nature *inv*; (fig) de grande envergure. ~ **stop** *n* point *m*. **~-time** *a* & *adv* à plein temps.

fully *adv* complètement; ~ **fledged** (*member, citizen*) à part entière.

F

fume *vi* rager. **fumes** *npl* émanations *fpl*, vapeurs *fpl*.

fun *n* amusement *m*; **be ~** être chouette; **for ~** pour rire; **make ~ of** se moquer de.

function *n* (purpose, duty) fonction *f*; (event) réception *f*. ● *vi* fonctionner.

fund *n* fonds *m*. ● *vt* fournir les fonds pour.

fundamental *a* fondamental. **fundamentalist** *n* intégriste *mf*.

funeral *n* enterrement *m*. ● *a* funèbre.

fun-fair *n* fête *f* foraine.

fungus *n* (*pl* **-gi**) (plant) champignon *m*; (mould) moisissure *f*.

funnel *n* (for pouring) entonnoir *m*; (of ship) cheminée *f*.

funny *a* (**-ier**, **-iest**) drôle; (odd) bizarre.

fur *n* (for garment) fourrure *f*; (on animal) poils *mpl*; (in kettle) tartre *m*.

furious *a* furieux.

furnace *n* fourneau *m*.

furnish *vt* (*room*) meubler; (supply) fournir. **furnishings** *npl* ameublement *m*.

furniture *n* meubles *mpl*, mobilier *m*.

furry *a* (*animal*) à fourrure; (*toy*) en peluche.

further *a* plus éloigné; (additional) supplémentaire. ● *adv* plus loin; (more) davantage. ● *vt* avancer. **~ education** *n* formation *f* continue.

furthermore *adv* en outre, de plus.

furthest *a* le plus éloigné. ● *adv* le plus loin.

fury *n* fureur *f*.

fuse *vt/i* (melt) fondre; (unite: fig) fusionner; **~ the lights** faire sauter les plombs. ● *n* (of plug) fusible *m*; (of bomb) amorce *f*.

fuss *n* (when upset) histoire(s) *f(pl)*; (when excited) agitation *f*; **make a ~** faire des histoires; s'agiter; (about food) faire des chichis; **make a ~ of** faire grand cas de. ● *vi* s'agiter. **fussy** *a* (finicky) tatillon; (hard to please) difficile.

future *a* futur. ● *n* avenir *m*; (Gram) futur *m*; **in ~** à l'avenir.

fuzzy *a* (*hair*) crépu; (*photograph*) flou; (*person* [!]) à l'esprit confus.

Gaelic *n* gaélique *m*.

gag *n* (on mouth) bâillon *m*; (joke) blague *f*. ● *vt* (*pt* **gagged**) bâillonner.

gain *vt* (*respect, support*) gagner; (*speed, weight*) prendre. ● *vi* (of clock) avancer. ● *n* (increase) augmentation *f* (**in** de); (profit) gain *m*.

galaxy *n* galaxie *f*.

gale *n* tempête *f*.

gallery *n* galerie *f*; (**art**) **~** musée *m*.

Gallic *a* français.

gallon *n* gallon *m* (*imperial = 4.546 litres; Amer. = 3.785 litres*).

gallop *n* galop *m*. ● *vi* (*pt* **galloped**) galoper.

galore *adv* (*prizes, bargains*) en abondance; (*drinks, sandwiches*) à gogo [!].

gamble *vt/i* jouer; **~ on** miser sur. ● *n* (venture) entreprise *f* risquée; (bet) pari *m*; (risk) risque *m*. **gambling** *n* jeu *m*.

game *n* jeu *m*; (football) match *m*; (tennis) partie *f*; (animals, birds) gibier *m*. ● *a* (brave) courageux; ~ **for** prêt à. ~**keeper** *n* garde-chasse *m*.

gammon *n* jambon *m*.

gang *n* (of youths) bande *f*; (of workmen) équipe *f*. ● *vi* ~ **up** se liguer (**on, against** contre)

gangway *n* passage *m*; (aisle) allée *f*; (of ship) passerelle *f*.

gaol *n & vt* = JAIL.

gap *n* trou *m*, vide *m*; (in time) intervalle *m*; (in education) lacune *f*; (difference) écart *m*.

gape *vi* rester bouche bée. **gaping** *a* béant.

garage *n* garage *m*. ● *vt* mettre au garage.

garbage *n* (US) ordures *fpl*.

garden *n* jardin *m*. ● *vi* jardiner. **gardener** *n* jardinier/-ière *m/f*. **gardening** *n* jardinage *m*.

gargle *vi* se gargariser.

garish *a* (*clothes*) tape-à-l'œil; (*light*) cru.

garland *n* guirlande *f*.

garlic *n* ail *m*.

garment *n* vêtement *m*.

garnish *vt* garnir (**with** de). ● *n* garniture *f*.

garter *n* jarretière *f*.

gas *n* (*pl* ~**es**) gaz *m*; (Med) anesthésie *m*; (petrol: US) essence *f*. ● *a* (*mask, pipe*) à gaz. ● *vt* asphyxier; (Mil) gazer. ● *vi* 🄸 bavarder.

gash *n* entaille *f*. ● *vt* entailler.

gasoline *n* (petrol: US) essence *f*.

gasp *vi* haleter; (in surprise: fig) avoir le souffle coupé. ● *n* halètement *m*.

gate *n* (in garden, airport) porte *f*; (of field, level crossing) barrière *f*. ~**way** *n* porte *f*; (Internet) passerelle *f*.

gather *vt* (*people, objects*) rassembler; (pick up) ramasser; (*flowers*) cueillir; (fig) comprendre; ~ **speed** prendre de la vitesse; (sewing) froncer. ● *vi* (*people*) se rassembler; (pile up) s'accumuler. **gathering** *n* réunion *m*.

gauge *n* jauge *f*, indicateur *m*. ● *vt* (*speed, distance*) jauger; (*reaction, mood*) évaluer.

gaunt *a* décharné.

gauze *n* gaze *f*.

gave ⇒GIVE.

gay *a* (joyful) gai; (homosexual) gay *inv*. ● *n* gay *mf*.

gaze *vi* ~ (**at**) regarder (fixement). ● *n* regard *m* (fixe).

gazette *n* journal *m* (officiel).

GB *abbr* ⇒GREAT BRITAIN.

gear *n* (equipment) matériel *m*; (Tech) engrenage *m*; (Auto) vitesse *f*; **in** ~ en prise; **out of** ~ au point mort. ● *vt* **to be geared to** s'adresser à. ~**box** *n* (Auto) boîte *f* de vitesses. ~**-lever**, (US) ~**-shift** *n* levier *m* de vitesse.

geese ⇒GOOSE.

gel *n* (for hair) gel *m*.

gem *n* pierre *f* précieuse.

Gemini *n* Gémeaux *mpl*.

gender *n* (Ling) genre *m*; (of person) sexe *m*.

gene *n* gène *m*. ~ **library** *n* génothèque *f*.

general *a* général. ● *n* général *m*; **in** ~ en général.

general election *n* élections *fpl* législatives.

generalization *n* généralisation *f*. **generalize** *vt/i* généraliser.

general practitioner *n* (Med) généraliste *m*.

generate *vt* produire.

generation *n* génération *f*.

generator *n* (Electr) groupe *m* électrogène.

generosity *n* générosité *f*. **generous** *a* généreux; (plentiful) copieux.

genetics *n* génétique *f*.

Geneva *n* Genève.
genial *a* affable, sympathique.
genitals *npl* organes *mpl* génitaux.
genius *n* (*pl* **~es**) génie *m*.
gentle *a* (mild, kind) doux; (*pressure, breeze*) léger; (*reminder, hint*) discret.
gentleman *n* (*pl* **-men**) (man) monsieur *m*; (well-bred) gentleman *m*.
gently *adv* doucement.
gents *npl* (toilets) toilettes *fpl*; (on sign) 'Messieurs'.
genuine *a* (*reason, motive*) vrai; (*jewel, substance*) véritable; (*person, belief*) sincère.
geography *n* géographie *f*.
geology *n* géologie *f* .
geometry *n* géométrie *f*.
geriatric *a* gériatrique.
germ *n* (Med) microbe *m*.
German *n* (person) Allemand/-e *m/f*; (Ling) allemand *m*. ● *a* allemand. **Germanic** *a* germanique.
German measles *n* rubéole *f*.
Germany *n* Allemagne *f*.
gesture *n* geste *m*.

get

past **got**; *past participle* **got, gotten** (US); *present participle* **getting**

● *transitive verb*

····➤ recevoir; **we got a letter** nous avons reçu une lettre.

····➤ (obtain) **I got a job in Paris** j'ai trouvé un travail à Paris; **I'll ~ sth to eat at the airport** je mangerai qch à l'aéroport.

····➤ (buy) acheter; **~ sb a present** acheter un cadeau à qn.

····➤ (achieve) obtenir; **he got it right** il a obtenu le bon résultat; **~ good grades** avoir de bonnes notes.

····➤ (fetch) chercher; **go and ~ a chair** va chercher une chaise.

····➤ (transport) prendre; **we can ~ the bus** on peut prendre le bus.

····➤ (understand Ⓘ) comprendre; **now let me ~ this right** alors si je comprends bien...

····➤ (experience) **~ a surprise** être surpris; **~ a shock** avoir un choc.

····➤ (illness) **~ measles** attraper la rougeole; **~ a cold** s'enrhumer.

····➤ (ask or persuade) **~ him to call me** dis-lui de m'appeler; **I'll ~ her to help me** je lui demanderai de m'aider.

····➤ (cause to be done) **~ a TV repaired** faire réparer une télévision; **~ one's hair cut** se faire couper les cheveux.

● *intransitive verb*

····➤ devenir; **he's getting old** il vieillit; **it's getting late** il se fait tard.

····➤ (in passives) **~ married** se marier; **~ hurt** être blessé.

····➤ (arrive) arriver; **~ to the airport** arriver à l'aéroport.

□ **get about** (*person*) se déplacer.
get along (manage) se débrouiller; (progress) avancer.
get along with s'entendre avec.
get at (reach) atteindre; (imply) vouloir dire.
get away partir; (escape) s'échapper.
get back *vi* revenir. *vt* récupérer.
get by *vi* (manage) se débrouiller. *vt* (pass) passer.
get down *vt/i* déscendre. *vt* (depress) déprimer.
get in entrer.
get into (*car*) monter dans; (*dress*) mettre.

get off *vt* (*bus*) descendre; (remove) enlever. *vi* (from bus) descendre; (leave) partir; (Jur) être acquitté.
get on *vi* (to bus) monter; (succeed) réussir. *vt* (*bus*) monter.
get on with (*person*) s'entendre avec; (*job*) attaquer.
get out sortir.
get out of (fig) se soustraire.
get over (*illness*) se remettre de.
get round (*rule*) contourner; (*person*) entortiller.
get through *vi* passer; (on phone) **~ through to sb** avoir qn. *vt* traverser.
get up se lever.
get up to faire.

getaway *n* fuite *f*.
ghastly *a* (**-ier, -iest**) affreux.
gherkin *n* cornichon *m*.
ghetto *n* ghetto *m*.
ghost *n* fantôme *m*.
giant *n & a* géant (*m*).
gibberish *n* baragouin *m*, charabia *m*.
giblets *npl* abats *mpl*.
giddy *a* (**-ier, -iest**) vertigineux; **be** *or* **feel ~** avoir le vertige.
gift *n* (present) cadeau *m*; (ability) don *m*.
gifted *a* doué.
gift-wrap *n* paquet-cadeau *m*.
gigantic *a* gigantesque.
giggle *vi* ricaner (sottement), glousser. ● *n* ricanement *m*; **the ~s** le fou rire.
gimmick *n* truc *m*.
gin *n* gin *m*.
ginger *n* gingembre *m*. ● *a* (*hair*) roux. **~ beer** *n* boisson *f* gazeuse au gingembre. **~bread** *n* pain *m* d'épices.
gingerly *adv* avec précaution.
giraffe *n* girafe *f*.
girl *n* (child) (petite) fille *f*; (young woman) (jeune) fille *f*. **~friend** *n* amie *f*; (of boy) petite amie *f*.
giro *n* virement *m* bancaire; (cheque) mandat *m*.
gist *n* essentiel *m*.
give *vt* (*pt* **gave**; *pp* **given**) donner; (*gesture*) faire; (*laugh, sigh*) pousser; **~ sb sth** donner qch à qn. ● *vi* donner; (yield) céder; (stretch) se détendre. ● *n* élasticité *f*. □ **~ away** donner; (*secret*) trahir; **~ back** rendre; **~ in** (yield) céder (**to** à); **~ off** (*heat, fumes*) dégager, (*signal, scent*) émettre; **~ out** *vt* distribuer; **~ over** (devote) consacrer; (stop 🅸) cesser; **~ up** *vt*/*i* (renounce) renoncer (à); (yield) céder; **~ oneself up** se rendre; **~ way** céder; (collapse) s'effondrer.
given ⇨GIVE. ● *a* donné. **~ name** *n* prénom *m*.
glad *a* content. **gladly** *adv* avec plaisir.
glamorous *a* séduisant, ensorcelant.
glamour, (US) **glamor** *n* enchantement *m*, séduction *f*.
glance *n* coup *m* d'œil. ● *vi* **~ at** jeter un coup d'œil à.
gland *n* glande *f*.
glare *vi* briller très fort; **~ at** regarder d'un air furieux. ● *n* (of lights) éclat *m* (aveuglant); (stare: fig) regard *m* furieux. **glaring** *a* (dazzling) éblouissant; (obvious) flagrant.
glass *n* verre *m*. **glasses** *npl* (spectacles) lunettes *fpl*.
glaze *vt* (door) vitrer; (pottery) vernisser. ● *n* vernis *m*.
gleam *n* lueur *f*. ● *vi* luire.
glide *vi* glisser; (of plane) planer. **glider** *n* planeur *m*.
glimpse *n* (insight) aperçu *m*; **catch a ~ of** entrevoir.

G

glitter *vi* scintiller. ● *n* scintillement *m*.

global *a* (world-wide) mondial; (all-embracing) global. ~ **warming** *n* réchauffement *m* de la planète.

globe *n* globe *m*.

gloom *n* obscurité *f*; (sadness: fig) tristesse *f*. **gloomy** *a* triste; (pessimistic) pessimiste.

glorious *a* splendide; (*deed, hero*) glorieux.

glory *n* gloire *f*; (beauty) splendeur *f*. ● *vi* ~ **in** être très fier de.

gloss *n* lustre *m*, brillant *m*. ● *a* brillant. ● *vi* ~ **over** (make light of) glisser sur; (cover up) dissimuler.

glossary *n* glossaire *m*.

glossy *a* brillant.

glove *n* gant *m*. ~ **compartment** *n* (Auto) boîte *f* à gants.

glow *vi* (*fire*) rougeoyer; (*person, eyes*) rayonner. ● *n* rougeoiement *m*, éclat *m*. **glowing** *a* (*report*) enthousiaste.

glucose *n* glucose *m*.

glue *n* colle *f*. ● *vt* (*pres p* **gluing**) coller.

glutton *n* glouton/-ne *m/f*.

gnaw *vt/i* ronger.

GNP *abbr* (**Gross National Product**) produit *m* national brut, PNB *m*.

---

go

⇨ *present* **go, goes**; *past* **went**; *past participle* **gone**

● *intransitive verb*

····➤ aller; ~ **to school/town/market** aller à l'école/en ville/au marché; ~ **for a swim/walk/coffee** aller nager/se promener/ prendre un café.

····➤ (leave) s'en aller; **I must be ~ing** il faut que je m'en aille.

····➤ (vanish) **the money's gone** il n'y a plus d'argent; **my bike's gone** mon vélo n'est plus là.

····➤ (work, function) marcher; **is the car ~ing?** est-ce que la voiture marche?

····➤ (become) devenir; ~ **blind** devenir aveugle; ~ **pale/red** pâlir/rougir.

····➤ (turn out, progress) aller; **how's it going?** comment ça va?; **how did the exam ~?** comment s'est passé l'examen?

····➤ (in future tenses) **be ~ing to do** aller faire.

● *noun*

····➤ (turn) tour *m*; (try) essai *m*; **have a ~!** essaie!; **full of ~** [!] dynamique.

□ **go across** traverser.

go after poursuivre.

go away partir; ~ **away!** va-t'en!, allez-vous-en!

go back retourner; ~ **back in** rentrer; ~ **back to work** reprendre le travail.

go down (*quality, price*) baisser; (*person*) descendre; (*sun*) se coucher.

go in entrer.

go in for (*exam*) se présenter à.

go off (leave) partir; (*bomb*) exploser; (*alarm clock*) sonner; (*milk*) tourner; (*light*) s'éteindre.

go on (continue) continuer; (*light*) s'allumer; ~ **on doing** continuer à faire; **what's ~ing on?** qu'est-ce qui se passe?

go out sortir; (*light, fire*) s'éteindre.

go over vérifier.

go round (be enough) être assez; ~ **round to see sb** passer voir qn.

go through (check) examiner; (search) fouiller; ~ **through a difficult time** traverser une période difficile.

go together aller ensemble.
go under (sink) couler; (fail) échouer.
go up (*person*) monter; (*price, salary*) augmenter.
go without se passer de.

go-ahead *n* feu *m* vert. ● *a* dynamique.
goal *n* but *m*. **~keeper** *n* gardien *m* de but. **~-post** *n* poteau *m* de but.
goat *n* chèvre *f*.
gobble *vt* engouffrer.
go-between *n* intermédiaire *mf*.
god *n* dieu *m*. **~child** *n* (*pl* **-children**) filleul/-e *m/f*. **~daughter** *n* filleule *f*.
goddess *n* déesse *f*.
god: **~father** *n* parrain *m*. **~mother** *n* marraine *f*. **~send** *n* aubaine *f*. **~son** *n* filleul *m*.
goggles *npl* lunettes *fpl* (protectrices).
going *n* **it is slow/hard ~** c'est lent/difficile. ● *a* (*price, rate*) actuel.
go-kart *n* kart *m*.
gold *n* or *m*. ● *a* en or, d'or.
golden *a* en or, d'or; (in colour) doré; (opportunity) unique.
gold: **~fish** *n* poisson *m* rouge. **~-plated** *a* plaqué or. **~smith** *n* orfèvre *m*.
golf *n* golf *m*. **~-course** *n* terrain *m* de golf.
gone ⇒GO. ● *a* parti; **~ six o'clock** six heures passées; **the butter's all ~** il n'y a plus de beurre.
good *a* (**better**, **best**) bon; (weather) beau; (well-behaved) sage; **as ~ as** (almost) pratiquement; **that's ~ of you** c'est gentil (de ta part); **be ~ with** savoir s'y prendre avec; **feel ~** se sentir bien; **it is ~ for you** ça vous fait du bien. ● *n* bien *m*; **do ~** faire du bien; **is it any ~?** est-ce que c'est bien?; **it's no ~** ça ne vaut rien; **it is no ~ shouting** ça ne sert à rien de crier; **for ~** pour toujours. **~ afternoon** *interj* bonjour. **~bye** *interj & n* au revoir (*m inv*). **~ evening** *interj* bonsoir. **G~ Friday** *n* Vendredi *m* saint. **~-looking** *a* beau. **~ morning** *interj* bonjour. **~-natured** *a* gentil.
goodness *n* bonté *f*; **my ~!** mon Dieu!
good-night *interj* bonsoir, bonne nuit.
goods *npl* marchandises *fpl*.
goodwill *n* bonne volonté *f*.
goose *n* (*pl* **geese**) oie *f*. **gooseberry** *n* groseille *f* à maquereau. **~-pimples** *npl* chair *f* de poule.
gorge *n* (Geog) gorge *f*. ● *vt* **~ oneself** se gaver (**on** de).
gorgeous *a* magnifique, splendide, formidable.
gorilla *n* gorille *m*.
gory *a* (**-ier**, **-iest**) sanglant; (horrific: fig) horrible.
gospel *n* évangile *m*; **the G~** l'Évangile *m*.
gossip *n* bavardages *mpl*, commérages *mpl*; (person) bavard/-e *m/f*. ● *vi* bavarder.
got ⇒GET. ● **have ~** avoir; **have ~ to do** devoir faire.
govern *vt/i* gouverner. **governess** *n* gouvernante *f*. **government** *n* gouvernement *m*. **governor** *n* gouverneur *m*.
gown *n* robe *f*; (of judge, teacher) toge *f*.
GP *abbr* ⇒GENERAL PRACTITIONER.
grab *vt* (*pt* **grabbed**) saisir.
grace *n* grâce *f*. ● *vt* (honour) honorer; (adorn) orner. **graceful** *a* gracieux.
gracious *a* (kind) bienveillant; (elegant) élégant.

G

grade *n* catégorie *f*; (of goods) qualité *f*; (on scale) grade *m*; (school mark) note *f*; (class: US) classe *f*. ● *vt* classer; (school work) noter. ~ **school** *n* (US) école *f* primaire.

gradual *a* progressif, graduel. **gradually** *adv* progressivement, peu à peu.

graduate¹ *n* (Univ) diplômé/-e *m/f*.

graduate² *vi* obtenir son diplôme. ● *vt* graduer. **graduation** *n* remise *f* des diplômes.

graffiti *npl* graffiti *mpl*.

graft *n* (Med, Bot) greffe *f*; (work) boulot *m*. ● *vt* greffer (**on to** sur); (work) trimer.

grain *n* (seed, quantity, texture) grain *m*; (in wood) fibre *f*.

gram *n* gramme *m*.

grammar *n* grammaire *f*.

grand *a* magnifique; (*duke, chorus*) grand.

grandad *n* [!] papy *m*.

grand: ~**child** *n* (girl) petite-fille *f*; (boy) petit-fils *m*; **her ~children** ses petits-enfants *mpl*. ~**daughter** *n* petite-fille *f*. ~**father** *n* grand-père *m*. ~**ma** *n* = GRANNY. ~**mother** *n* grand-mère *f*. ~**parents** *npl* grands-parents *mpl*. ~ **piano** *n* piano *m* à queue. ~**son** *n* petit-fils *m*. ~**stand** *n* tribune *f*.

granny *n* [!] mémé *f*, mamie *f*.

grant *vt* (*permission*) accorder; (*request*) accéder à; (admit) admettre (**that** que); **take sth for ~ed** considérer qch comme une chose acquise. ● *n* subvention *f*; (Univ) bourse *f*.

granule *n* (*of sugar, salt*) grain *m*; (*of coffee*) granulé *m*.

grape *n* grain *m* de raisin; ~**s** raisin(s) *m*(*pl*).

grapefruit *n inv* pamplemousse *m*.

graph *n* graphique *m*.

graphic *a* (*arts*) graphique; (fig) vivant, explicite. **graphics** *npl* (Comput) graphiques *mpl*.

grasp *vt* saisir. ● *n* (hold) prise *f*; (strength of hand) poigne *f*; (reach) portée *f*; (fig) compréhension *f*.

grass *n* herbe *f*. ~**hopper** *n* sauterelle *f*. ~**land** *n* prairie *f*.

grass roots *npl* peuple *m*. ● *a* (*movement*) populaire; (*support*) de base.

grate *n* (hearth) âtre *m*; (fire basket) grille *f*. ● *vt* râper. ● *vi* grincer.

grateful *a* reconnaissant.

grater *n* râpe *f*.

gratified *a* très heureux. **gratify** *vt* faire plaisir à.

grating *n* (bars) grille *f*; (noise) grincement *m*.

gratitude *n* reconnaissance *f*.

gratuity *n* (tip) pourboire *m*; (bounty: Mil) prime *f*.

grave¹ *n* tombe *f*. ● *a* (serious) grave.

grave² *a* ~ **accent** accent *m* grave.

gravel *n* graviers *mpl*.

grave: ~**stone** *n* pierre *f* tombale. ~**yard** *n* cimetière *m*.

gravity *n* (seriousness) gravité *f*; (force) pesanteur *f*.

gravy *n* jus *m* (de viande).

gray (US) *a & n* = GREY.

graze *vi* (eat) paître. ● *vt* (touch) frôler; (scrape) écorcher. ● *n* écorchure *f*.

grease *n* graisse *f*. ● *vt* graisser. **greasy** *a* graisseux.

great *a* grand; (very good [!]) génial [!], formidable [!], (*grandfather, grandmother*) arrière.

Great Britain *n* Grande-Bretagne *f*.

greatly *adv* (very) très; (much) beaucoup.

Greece *n* Grèce *f*.

greed *n* avidité *f*; (for food) gourmandise *f*. **greedy** *a* avide; gourmand.

Greek *n* (person) Grec/-que *m/f*; (Ling) grec *m*. ● *a* grec.

green *a* vert; (fig) naïf. ● *n* vert *m*; (grass) pelouse *f*; (golf) green *m*; **~s** légumes *mpl* verts. **~grocer** *n* marchand/-e *m/f* de fruits et légumes.

green house *n* serre *f*; **~ effect** effet *m* de serre.

greet *vt* (welcome) accueillir; (address politely) saluer. **greeting** *n* accueil *m*.

greetings *interj* salutations! ● *npl* (*Christmas*) vœux *mpl*. **~ card** *n* carte *f* de vœux.

grew ⇨GROW.

grey *a* gris; (fig) triste; **go ~** (*hair, person*) grisonner. ● *n* gris *m*. **~hound** *n* lévrier *m*.

grid *n* grille *f*; (network: Electr) réseau *m*.

grief *n* chagrin *m*; **come to ~** (*person*) avoir un malheur; (fail) tourner mal.

grievance *n* griefs *mpl*.

grieve *vt/i* (s')affliger; **~ for** pleurer.

grill *n* (cooking device) gril *m*; (food) grillade *f*; (Auto) calandre *f*. ● *vt/i* (faire) griller; (interrogate) mettre sur la sellette.

grim *a* sinistre.

grimace *n* grimace *f*. ● *vi* grimacer.

grime *n* crasse *f*.

grin *vi* (*pt* **grinned**) sourire. ● *n* (large) sourire *m*.

grind *vt* (*pt* **ground**) (*grain*) écraser; (*coffee*) moudre; (sharpen) aiguiser; **~ one's teeth** grincer des dents. ● *vi* **~ to a halt** s'immobiliser. ● *n* corvée *f*.

grip *vt* (*pt* **gripped**) saisir; (interest) passionner. ● *n* prise *f*; (strength of hand) poigne *f*; **come to ~s with** en venir aux prises avec.

grisly *a* (**-ier, -iest**) (*remains*) macabre; (*sight*) horrible.

gristle *n* cartilage *m*.

grit *n* (for roads) sable *m*; (fig) courage *m*. ● *vt* (*pt* **gritted**) (*road*) sabler; (*teeth*) serrer.

groan *vi* gémir. ● *n* gémissement *m*.

grocer *n* (person) épicier/-ière *m/f*; (shop) épicerie *f*. **groceries** *npl* (shopping) courses *fpl*; (goods) épicerie *f*. **grocery** *n* (shop) épicerie *f*.

groin *n* aine *f*.

groom *n* marié *m*; (for horses) palefrenier/-ière *m/f*. ● *vt* (*horse*) panser; (fig) préparer.

groove *n* (for door etc.) rainure *f*; (in record) sillon *m*.

grope *vi* tâtonner; **~ for** chercher à tâtons.

gross *a* (*behaviour*) vulgaire; (Comm) brut. ● *n inv* grosse *f*.

grotto *n* (*pl* **~es**) grotte *f*.

grouch *vi* (grumble 🄸) rouspéter, râler.

ground[1] *n* terre *f*, sol *m*; (area) terrain *m*; (reason) raison *f*; (Electr, US) masse *f*; **~s** terres *fpl*, parc *m*; (of coffee) marc *m*; **on the ~** par terre; **lose ~** perdre du terrain. ● *vt/i* (Naut) échouer; (aircraft) retenir au sol.

ground[2] ⇨GRIND. ● *a* **~ beef** (US) bifteck *m* haché.

ground: **~ floor** *n* rez-de-chaussée *m inv*. **~work** *n* travail *m* préparatoire.

group *n* groupe *m*. ● *vt/i* (se) grouper. **~ware** *n* (Comput) logiciel *m* de groupe.

grovel *vi* (*pt* **grovelled**) ramper.

grow *vi* (*pt* **grew**; *pp* **grown**) (*person*) grandir; (*plant*) pousser; (become) devenir; (*crime*) augmenter. ● *vt* cultiver; **~ up**

G

devenir adulte, grandir. **grower** *n* cultivateur/-trice *m/f*.

growl *vi* (*dog*) gronder; (*person*) grogner. ● *n* grognement *m*.

grown ⇒GROW. ● *a* adulte. **~-up** *a & n* adulte (*mf*).

growth *n* (of person, plant) croissance *f*; (in numbers) accroissement *m*; (of hair, tooth) pousse *f*; (Med) grosseur *f*, tumeur *f*.

grudge *vt* **~ doing** faire à contrecœur; **~ sb sth** (*success, wealth*) en vouloir à qn de qch. ● *n* rancune *f*; **have a ~ against** en vouloir à.

grumble *vi* ronchonner, grogner (**at** après).

grumpy *a* (**-ier**, **-iest**) grincheux, grognon.

grunt *vi* grogner. ● *n* grognement *m*.

guarantee *n* garantie *f*. ● *vt* garantir.

guard *vt* protéger; (watch) surveiller. ● *vi* **~ against** se protéger contre. ● *n* (Mil) garde *f*; (person) garde *m*; (on train) chef *m* de train.

guardian *n* gardien/-ne *m/f*; (of orphan) tuteur/-trice *m/f*.

guess *vt/i* deviner; (suppose) penser. ● *n* conjecture *f*.

guest *n* invité/-e *m/f*; (in hotel) client/-e *m/f*. **~-house** *n* pension *f*. **~-room** *n* chambre *f* d'amis.

guidance *n* (advice) conseils *mpl*; (information) information *f*.

guide *n* (person, book) guide *m*; (girl) guide *f*. ● *vt* guider. **~book** *n* guide *m*. **~-dog** *n* chien *m* d'aveugle. **~line** *n* indication *f*; (advice) conseils *mpl*.

guillotine *n* (for execution) guillotine *f*; (for paper) massicot *m*.

guilt *n* culpabilité *f*. **guilty** *a* coupable.

guinea-pig *n* (animal) cochon *m* d'Inde; (fig) cobaye *m*.

guitar *n* guitare *f*.

gulf *n* (part of sea) golfe *m*; (hollow) gouffre *m*.

gull *n* mouette *f*, (larger) goéland *m*.

gullible *a* crédule.

gully *n* (ravine) ravin *m*; (drain) rigole *f*.

gulp *vt* **~** (**down**) avaler en vitesse. ● *vi* (from fear etc.) avoir la gorge serrée. ● *n* gorgée *f*.

gum *n* (Anat) gencive *f*; (glue) colle *f*; (for chewing) chewing-gum *m*. ● *vt* (*pt* **gummed**) gommer.

gun *n* (pistol) revolver *m*; (rifle) fusil *m*; (large) canon *m*. ● *vt* (*pt* **gunned**) **~ down** abattre. **~fire** *n* fusillade *f*. **~powder** *n* poudre *f* à canon. **~shot** *n* coup *m* de feu.

gurgle *n* (of water) gargouillement *m*; (of baby) gazouillis *m*. ● *vi* (*water*) gargouiller; (*baby*) gazouiller.

gush *vi* **~** (**out**) jaillir. ● *n* jaillissement *m*.

gust *n* rafale *f*; (of smoke) bouffée *f*.

gut *n* (belly ▯) ventre *m*. ● *vt* (*pt* **gutted**) (*fish*) vider; (of fire) dévaster.

guts *npl* ▯ (insides of human) tripes *fpl* ▯; (insides of animal, building) entrailles *fpl*; (courage) cran *m* ▯.

gutter *n* (on roof) gouttière *f*; (in street) caniveau *m*.

guy *n* (man ▯) type *m*.

gym *n* (place) gymnase *m*; (activity) gym(nastique) *f*.

gymnasium *n* gymnase *m*.

gymnastics *npl* gymnastique *f*.

gynaecologist *n* gynécologue *mf*.

gypsy *n* bohémien/-ne *m/f*.

habit *n* habitude *f*; (costume: Relig) habit *m*; **be in/get into the ~ of** avoir/prendre l'habitude de.

habitual *a* (usual) habituel; (*smoker, liar*) invétéré.

hack *n* (writer) écrivaillon *m*. ●*vi* (Comput) pirater; **~ into** s'introduire dans. ●*vt* tailler. **hacker** *n* (Comput) pirate *m* informatique.

hackneyed *a* rebattu.

had ⇒HAVE.

haddock *n inv* églefin *m*.

haemorrhage *n* hémorragie *f*.

haggard *a* (*person*) exténué; (*face, look*) défait.

haggle *vi* marchander; **~ over sth** discuter du prix de qch.

hail *n* grêle *f*. ●*vt* (greet) saluer; (*taxi*) héler. ●*vi* grêler; **~ from** venir de. **~stone** *n* grêlon *m*.

hair *n* (on head) cheveux *mpl*; (on body, of animal) poils *mpl*; (single strand on head) cheveu *m*; (on body) poil *m*. **~brush** *n* brosse *f* à cheveux. **~cut** *n* coupe *f* de cheveux. **~-do** *n* ! coiffure *f*. **~dresser** *n* coiffeur/-euse *m/f*. **~-drier** *n* séchoir *m* (à cheveux). **~pin** *n* épingle *f* à cheveux. **~ remover** *n* dépilatoire *m*. **~-style** *n* coiffure *f*.

hairy *a* (**-ier, -iest**) poilu; (terrifying !) horrifiant.

half *n* (*pl* **halves**) (part) moitié *f*; (fraction) demi *m*; **~ a dozen** une demi-douzaine; **~ an hour** une demi-heure; **four and a ~** quatre et demi; **an hour and a ~** une heure et demie; **~ and half** moitié moitié; **in ~** en deux. ●*a* demi; **~ price** à moitié prix. ●*adv* à moitié. **~-back** *n* (Sport) demi *m*. **~-hearted** *a* tiède. **~-mast** *n* **at ~-mast** en berne. **~-term** *n* vacances *fpl* de demi-trimestre. **~-time** *n* mi-temps *f*. **~-way** *adv* à mi-chemin. **~-wit** *n* imbécile *mf*.

hall *n* (in house) entrée *f*; (corridor) couloir *m*; (in airport) hall *m*; (for events) salle *f*; **~ of residence** résidence *f* universitaire.

hallmark *n* (on gold) poinçon *m*; (fig) caractéristique *f*.

hallo = HELLO.

Hallowe'en *n* la veille de la Toussaint.

halt *n* arrêt *m*; (temporary) suspension *f*; (Mil) halte *f*. ●*vt* (*proceedings*) interrompre; (*arms sales, experiments*) mettre fin à. ●*vi* (*vehicle*) s'arrêter; (*army*) faire halte.

halve *vt* (*time*) réduire de moitié; (*fruit*) couper en deux.

ham *n* jambon *m*.

hamburger *n* hamburger *m*.

hammer *n* marteau *m*. ●*vt/i* marteler; **~ sth into sth** enfoncer qch dans qch; **~ sth out** (*agreement*) parvenir à qch.

hammock *n* hamac *m*.

hamper *n* panier *m*. ●*vt* gêner.

hamster *n* hamster *m*.

hand *n* main *f*; (of clock) aiguille *f*; (writing) écriture *f*; (worker) ouvrier/-ière *m/f*; (cards) jeu *m*; **give sb a ~** donner un coup de main à qn; **at ~** proche; **on ~** disponible; **on the one ~...on the other ~** d'une part...d'autre part; **to ~** à portée de la main. ●*vt* **~ sb sth, ~ sth to sb** donner qch à qn. □ **~ in** *or* **over** remettre; **~ out** distribuer. **~bag** *n* sac *m* à main. **~-baggage** *n* bagages *mpl* à

H

main. **~book** *n* manuel *m*. **~brake** *n* frein *m* à main. **~cuffs** *npl* menottes *fpl*.

handicap *n* handicap *m*. ● *vt* (*pt* **handicapped**) handicaper.

handkerchief *n* (*pl* **~s**) mouchoir *m*.

handle *n* (of door, bag) poignée *f*; (of implement) manche *m*; (of cup, bucket) anse *f*; (of frying pan) queue *f*. ● *vt* (manage) manier; (deal with) traiter; (touch) manipuler.

hand: **~-out** *n* document *m*; (leaflet) prospectus *m*; (money) aumône *f*. **~shake** *n* poignée *f* de main.

handsome *a* (good looking) beau; (generous) généreux.

handwriting *n* écriture *f*.

handy *a* (**-ier**, **-iest**) (*book, skill*) utile; (*size, shape, tool*) pratique; (*person*) doué. **~man** *n* (*pl* **-men**) bricoleur *m*, homme *m* à tout faire.

hang *vt* (*pt* **hung**) (from hook, hanger) accrocher; (from rope) suspendre; (*pt* **hanged**) (*person*) pendre. ● *vi* (from hook) être accroché; (from rope) être suspendu; (*person*) être pendu. ● *n* **get the ~ of doing** ▣ piger comment faire ▣. □ **~about** traîner; **~ on** ▣ (hold out) tenir; (wait) attendre; **~ on to sth** s'agripper à qch; **~ out** *vi* ▣ (live) crécher ▣; (spend time) passer son temps; *vt* (*washing*) étendre; **~ up** (telephone) raccrocher.

hanger *n* (for clothes) cintre *m*.

hang-gliding *n* vol *m* libre.

hangover *n* gueule *f* de bois ▣.

hang-up *n* ▣ complexe *m*.

hankering *n* envie *f*.

haphazard *a* peu méthodique.

happen *vi* arriver, se passer; **~ to sb** arriver à qn; **it so ~s that** il se trouve que.

happily *adv* joyeusement; (fortunately) heureusement.

happiness *n* bonheur *m*.

happy *a* (**-ier**, **-iest**) heureux; **I'm not ~ about it** je ne suis pas content; **~ with sth** satisfait de qch; **~ medium** juste milieu *m*.

harass *vt* harceler. **harassment** *n* harcèlement *m*.

harbour, (US) **harbor** *n* port *m*. ● *vt* (shelter) héberger.

hard *a* dur; (difficult) difficile, dur; (*evidence, fact*) solide; **find it ~ to do** avoir du mal à faire; **~ on sb** dur envers qn. ● *adv* (work) dur; (pull, hit, cry) fort; (think, study) sérieusement. **~board** *n* aggloméré *m*. **~ copy** *n* (Comput) tirage *m*. **~ disk** *n* disque *m* dur.

hardly *adv* à peine; (*expect, hope*) difficilement; **~ ever** presque jamais.

hardship *n* (poverty) privations *fpl*; (ordeal) épreuve *f*.

hard: **~ shoulder** *n* bande *f* d'arrêt d'urgence. **~ up** *a* ▣ fauché ▣. **~ware** *n* (Comput) matériel *m*, hardware *m*; (goods) quincaillerie *f*. **~-working** *a* travailleur.

hardy *a* (**-ier**, **-iest**) résistant.

hare *n* lièvre *m*. ● *vi* **~ around** courir partout.

harm *n* mal *m*; **there is no ~ in** il n'y a pas de mal à. ● *vt* (*person*) faire du mal à; (*object*) endommager. **harmful** *a* nuisible. **harmless** *a* inoffensif.

harmony *n* harmonie *f*.

harness *n* harnais *m*. ● *vt* (*horse*) harnacher; (use) exploiter.

harp *n* harpe *f*. ● *vi* **~ on** (**about**) rabâcher.

harrowing *a* (*experience*) atroce; (*story*) déchirant.

harsh *a* (*punishment*) sévère; (*person*) dur; (*light*) cru; (*voice*) rude; (*chemical*) corrosif. **harshness** *n* dureté *f*.

harvest *n* récolte *f*; **the wine ~** les vendanges *fpl*. ●*vt* (*corn*) moissonner; (*vegetables*) récolter.

has ⇒HAVE.

hassle *n* complications *fpl*. ●*vt* 🄸 talonner (**about** à propos de); (worry) stresser.

haste *n* hâte *f*; **in ~** à la hâte; **make ~** se dépêcher.

hasty *a* (**-ier**, **-iest**) précipité.

hat *n* chapeau *m*.

hatch *n* (Aviat) panneau *m* mobile; (Naut) écoutille *f*; (for food) passe-plats *m inv*. ●*vt/i* (*eggs*) (faire) éclore.

hate *n* haine *f*. ●*vt* détester; (violently) haïr; (*sport, food*) avoir horreur de.

hatred *n* haine *f*.

haughty *a* (**-ier**, **-iest**) hautain.

haul *vt* tirer. ●*n* (by thieves) butin *m*; (by customs) saisie *f*; **it will be a long ~** l'étape sera longue; **long/short ~** (*transport*) long/court courrier *m*. **haulage** *n* transport *m* routier. **haulier** *n* (firm) société *f* de transports routiers.

haunt *vt* hanter. ●*n* lieu *m* de prédilection.

have

present **have**, **has**; *past* **had**; *past participle* **had**

●*transitive verb*

····➤ (possess) avoir; **I ~ (got) a car** j'ai une voiture; **they ~ (got) problems** ils ont des problèmes.

····➤ (do sth) **~ a try** essayer; **~ a bath** prendre un bain.

····➤ **~ sth done** faire faire qch; **~ your hair cut** se faire couper les cheveux.

●*auxiliary verb*

····➤ (in perfect tenses) avoir; être; **I ~ seen him** je l'ai vu; **she had fallen** elle était tombée.

····➤ (in tag questions) **you've seen her, haven't you?** tu l'as vue, n'est-ce pas?; **you haven't seen her, ~ you?** tu ne l'as pas vue, par hasard?

····➤ (in short answers) **'you've never met him'—'yes I ~'** 'tu ne l'as jamais rencontré'—'mais si!'

····➤ (must) **~ to** devoir; **I ~ to go** je dois partir; **you don't ~ to do it** tu n'es pas obligé de le faire.

⇨For expressions such as **have a walk, have dinner** ⇒**walk, dinner**.

haven *n* refuge *m*; (fig) havre *m*.

havoc *n* dévastation *f*.

hawk *n* faucon *m*.

hay *n* foin *m*; **~ fever** rhume *m* des foins.

haywire *a* **go ~** (*plans*) dérailler; (*machine*) se détraquer.

hazard *n* risque *m*; **~ (warning) lights** feux *mpl* de détresse. ●*vt* hasarder.

haze *n* brume *f*.

hazel *n* (bush) noisetier *m*. **~nut** *n* noisette *f*.

hazy *a* (**-ier**, **-iest**) (misty) brumeux; (fig) vague.

he *pron* il; (emphatic) lui; **here ~ is** le voici.

head *n* tête *f*; (leader) chef *m*; (of beer) mousse *f*; **~s or tails?** pile ou face? ●*vt* (*list*) être en tête de; (*team*) être à la tête de; (*chapter*) intituler; **~ the ball** faire une tête. ●*vi* **~ for** se diriger vers.

headache *n* mal *m* de tête; **have a ~** avoir mal à la tête.

heading *n* titre *m*; (subject category) rubrique *f*.

head: **~lamp**, **~light** *n* phare *m*. **~line** *n* gros titre *m*. **~master** *n*

H

directeur *m*. **~mistress** *n* directrice *f*. **~ office** *n* siège *m* social. **~-on** *a & adv* de front. **~phones** *npl* casque *m*. **~quarters** *npl* siège *m* social; (Mil) quartier *m* général. **~ rest** *n* (Auto) repose-tête *m inv*. **~strong** *a* têtu.

heal *vt/i* guérir.

health *n* santé *f*. **~ centre** *n* centre *m* médico-social. **~ food** *n* produits *mpl* diététiques. **~ insurance** *n* assurance *f* maladie.

healthy *a* (*person, plant, skin, diet*) sain; (*air*) salutaire.

heap *n* tas *m*; **~s of** ⓘ un tas de. ● *vt* **~** (**up**) entasser.

hear *vt* (*pt* **heard**) entendre; (*news, rumour*) apprendre; (*lecture, broadcast*) écouter. ● *vi* entendre; **~ from** recevoir des nouvelles de; **~ of** *or* **about** entendre parler de.

hearing *n* ouïe *f*; (of case) audience *f*; **give sb a ~** écouter qn. **~-aid** *n* prothèse *f* auditive.

hearse *n* corbillard *m*.

heart *n* cœur *m*; **~s** (cards) cœur *m*; **at ~** au fond; **by ~** par cœur; **be ~-broken** avoir le cœur brisé; **lose ~** perdre courage. **~ attack** *n* crise *f* cardiaque. **~burn** *n* brûlures *fpl* d'estomac. **~felt** *a* sincère.

hearth *n* foyer *m*.

heartily *adv* (*greet*) chaleureusement; (*laugh, eat*) de bon cœur.

hearty *a* (**-ier**, **-iest**) (sincere) chaleureux; (*meal*) solide.

heat *n* chaleur *f*; (contest) épreuve *f* éliminatoire. ● *vt* (*house*) chauffer; **~** (**up**) (*food*) faire chauffer; (reheat) réchauffer. **heated** *a* (fig) passionné; (lit) (*pool*) chauffé. **heater** *n* appareil *m* de chauffage.

heather *n* bruyère *f*.

heating *n* chauffage *m*.

heave *vt* (lift) hisser; (pull) traîner péniblement; **~ a sigh** pousser un soupir. ● *vi* (pull) tirer de toutes ses forces; (retch) avoir un haut-le-cœur.

heaven *n* ciel *m*.

heavily *adv* lourdement; (smoke, drink) beaucoup.

heavy *a* (**-ier**, **-iest**) lourd; (*cold, work*) gros; (*traffic*) dense. **~ goods vehicle** *n* poids *m* lourd. **~-handed** *a* maladroit. **~weight** *n* poids *m* lourd.

Hebrew *n* (person) Hébreu *m*; (Ling) hébreu *m*. ● *a* hébreu; (Ling) hébraïque.

hectic *a* (*activity*) intense; (*period, day*) mouvementé.

hedge *n* haie *f*. ● *vi* (in answering) se dérober.

hedgehog *n* hérisson *m*.

heel *n* talon *m*.

hefty *a* (**-ier**, **-iest**) (*person*) costaud ⓘ; (*object*) pesant.

height *n* hauteur *f*; (of person) taille *f*; (of plane, mountain) altitude *f*; (of fame, glory) apogée *m*; (of joy, folly, pain) comble *m*.

heir *n* héritier/-ière *m/f*. **heiress** *n* héritière *f*. **heirloom** *n* objet *m* de famille.

held ⇒HOLD.

helicopter *n* hélicoptère *m*.

hell *n* enfer *m*.

hello *interj* bonjour!; (on phone) allô!

helmet *n* casque *m*.

help *vt/i* aider (**to do** à faire); **~** (**sb**) **with a bag/the housework** aider qn à porter un sac/à faire le ménage; **~ oneself** se servir; **he can't ~ it** ce n'est pas de sa faute. ● *n* aide *f*. ● *interj* au secours! **helper** *n* aide *mf*. **helpful** *a* utile; (*person*) serviable. **helping** *n* portion *f*. **helpless** *a* impuissant.

hem *n* ourlet *m*. ●*vt* (*pt* **hemmed**) faire un ourlet à; ~ **in** cerner.

hen *n* poule *f*.

hence *adv* (for this reason) d'où; (from now) d'ici. **henceforth** *adv* désormais.

hepatitis *n* hépatite *f*.

her *pron* la, l'; (indirect object) lui; **it's** ~ c'est elle; **for** ~ pour elle. ●*a* son, sa; *pl* ses.

herb *n* herbe *f*; ~**s** (Culin) fines herbes *fpl*.

herd *n* troupeau *m*.

here *adv* ici; ~**!** (take this) tiens!; tenez!; ~ **is**, ~ **are** voici; **I'm** ~ je suis là. **hereabouts** *adv* par ici. **hereafter** *adv* après; (in book) ci-après. **hereby** *adv* par le présent acte; (in letter) par la présente.

herewith *adv* ci-joint.

heritage *n* patrimoine *m*.

hernia *n* hernie *f*.

hero *n* (*pl* ~**es**) héros *m*.

heroic *a* héroïque.

heroin *n* héroïne *f*.

heroine *n* héroïne *f*.

heron *n* héron *m*.

herring *n* hareng *m*.

hers *pron* le sien, la sienne, les sien(ne)s; **it is** ~ c'est à elle *or* le sien *or* la sienne.

herself *pron* (emphatic) elle-même; (reflexive) se; **proud of** ~ fière d'elle; **by** ~ toute seule.

hesitate *vi* hésiter. **hesitation** *n* hésitation *f*.

heterosexual *a* & *n* hétérosexuel/-le (*m*/*f*).

hexagon *n* hexagone *m*.

heyday *n* apogée *m*.

HGV *abbr* →HEAVY GOODS VEHICLE.

hi *interj* [!] salut! [!].

hiccup *n* hoquet *m*; **(the)** ~**s** le hoquet. ●*vi* hoqueter.

hide *vt* (*pt* **hid**; *pp* **hidden**) cacher (**from** à). ●*vi* se cacher (**from** de); **go into hiding** se cacher. ●*n* (skin) peau *f*.

hideous *a* (*monster, object*) hideux; (*noise*) affreux.

hiding *n* **go into** ~ se cacher; **give sb a** ~ administrer une correction à qn.

hierarchy *n* hiérarchie *f*.

hi-fi *n* (chaîne *f*) hi-fi *f inv*.

high *a* haut; (*price, number*) élevé; (*priest, speed*) grand; (*voice*) aigu; **in the** ~ **season** en pleine saison. ●*n* **a (new)** ~ un niveau record. ●*adv* haut. ~**brow** *a* & *n* intellectuel/-le (*m*/*f*). ~ **chair** *n* chaise *f* haute. ~ **court** *n* cour *f* suprême. **higher education** *n* enseignement *m* supérieur. ~**-jump** *n* saut *m* en hauteur. ~**-level** *a* à haut niveau.

highlight *n* (best moment) point *m* fort; ~**s** (in hair) reflet *m*; (artificial) mèches *fpl*; (Sport) résumé *m*. ●*vt* (emphasize) souligner.

highly *adv* extrêmement; (paid) très bien; **speak/think** ~ **of** dire/penser beaucoup de bien de.

Highness *n* Altesse *f*.

high: ~**-rise (building)** *n* tour *f*. ~ **school** *n* lycée *m*. ~**-speed** *a* (*train*) à grande vitesse; (*film*) ultrarapide. ~ **street** *n* rue *f* principale. ~**-tech** *a* de pointe.

highway *n* route *f* nationale; (US) autoroute *f*; ~ **code** code *m* de la route.

hijack *vt* détourner. ●*n* détournement *m*. **hijacker** *n* pirate *m* (de l'air).

hike *n* randonnée *f*; **price** ~ hausse *f* de prix. ●*vi* faire de la randonnée.

hilarious *a* désopilant.

hill *n* colline *f*; (slope) côte *f*. **hilly** *a* vallonné.

H

him *pron* le, l'; (indirect object) lui; **it's ~** c'est lui; **for ~** pour lui.

himself *pron* (emphatic) lui-même; (reflexive) se; **proud of ~** fier de lui; **by ~** tout seul.

hind *a* de derrière.

hinder *vt* (hamper) gêner; (prevent) empêcher. **hindrance** *n* obstacle *m*, gêne *f*.

hindsight *n* **with ~** rétrospectivement.

Hindu *n* Hindou/-e *m/f*. ● *a* hindou.

hinge *n* charnière *f*. ● *vi* **~ on** dépendre de.

hint *n* allusion *f*; (of spice, accent) pointe *f*; (of colour) touche *f*; (advice) conseil *m*. ● *vt* laisser entendre. ● *vi* **~ at** faire allusion à.

hip *n* hanche *f*.

hippopotamus *n* (*pl* **~es**) hippopotame *m*.

hire *vt* (*thing*) louer; (*person*) engager. ● *n* location *f*. **~-car** *n* voiture *f* de location. **~-purchase** *n* achat *m* à crédit.

his *a* son, sa, *pl* ses. ● *pron* le sien, la sienne, les sien(ne)s; **it is ~** c'est à lui *or* le sien *or* la sienne.

hiss *n* sifflement *m*. ● *vt/i* siffler.

history *n* histoire *f*; **make ~** entrer dans l'histoire.

hit *vt* (*pt* **hit**; *pres p* **hitting**) frapper; (collide with) heurter; (find) trouver; (affect, reach) toucher. ● *vi* **~ on** (find) tomber sur; **~ it off** s'entendre bien (**with** avec). ● *n* (blow) coup *m*; (fig) succès *m*; (song) tube *m* [!].

hitch *vt* (fasten) accrocher; **~ up** remonter. ● *n* (snag) anicroche *f*. **~-hike** *vi* faire du stop [!]. **~-hiker** *n* auto-stoppeur/-euse *m/f*.

hi-tech *a & n* = HIGH-TECH.

hitherto *adv* jusqu'ici.

HIV *abbr* (**human immunodeficiency virus**) VIH *m*.

hive *n* ruche *f*. ● *vt* **~ off** séparer; (*industry*) céder.

HIV-positive *a* séropositif.

hoard *vt* amasser; (*supplies*) stocker. ● *n* trésor *m*; (of provisions) provisions *fpl*.

hoarse *a* enroué.

hoax *n* canular *m*.

hobby *n* passe-temps *m inv*. **~-horse** *n* (fig) dada *m*.

hockey *n* hockey *m*.

hog *n* cochon *m*. ● *vt* (*pt* **hogged**) [!] monopoliser.

hold *vt* (*pt* **held**) tenir; (contain) contenir; (*conversation, opinion*) avoir; (*shares, record, person*) détenir; **~ (the line), please** ne quittez pas. ● *vi* (*rope, weather*) tenir. ● *n* prise *f*; **get ~ of** attraper; (*ticket*) se procurer; (*person*) (by phone) joindre; **on ~** en attente. □ **~ back** (contain) retenir; (hide) cacher; **~ down** (*job*) garder; (*person*) tenir; (*costs*) limiter; **~ on** (stand firm) tenir bon; (wait) attendre; **~ on to** (keep) garder; (cling to) se cramponner à; **~ out** *vt* (offer) offrir; *vi* (resist) tenir le coup; **~ up** (support) soutenir; (delay) retarder; (rob) attaquer.

holder *n* détenteur/-trice *m/f*; (of passport, post) titulaire *mf*; (for object) support *m*.

hold-up *n* retard *m*; (of traffic) embouteillage *m*; (robbery) hold-up *m inv*.

hole *n* trou *m*.

holiday *n* vacances *fpl*; (public) jour *m* férié; (time off) congé *m*. ● *vi* passer ses vacances. ● *a* de vacances. **~-maker** *n* vacancier/-ière *m/f*.

Holland *n* Hollande *f*.

hollow *a* creux; (fig) faux. ● *n* creux *m*. ● *vt* creuser.

holly *n* houx *m*.

holy *a* (**-ier**, **-iest**) saint; (water) bénit; **H~ Ghost**, **H~ Spirit** Saint-Esprit *m*.

homage *n* hommage *m*.

home *n* (place to live) logement *m*; maison *f*; (institution) maison *f*; (family base) foyer *m*; (country) pays *m*. ● *a* de la maison, du foyer; (of family) de famille; (Pol) intérieur; (*match, visit*) à domicile. ● *adv* (**at**) **~** à la maison, chez soi; **come** *or* **go ~** rentrer; (from abroad) rentrer dans son pays; **feel at ~ with** être à l'aise avec. **~ computer** *n* ordinateur *m*, PC *m*.

homeless *a* sans abri. ● *n* **the ~** les sans-abri *mpl*.

homely *a* (**-ier**, **-iest**) (cosy) accueillant; (simple) sans prétention; (person: US) sans attraits.

home: **~-made** *a* (fait) maison. **H~ Office** *n* ministère *m* de l'Intérieur. **~ page** *n* (Internet) page *f* d'accueil. **H~ Secretary** *n* Ministre *m* de l'Intérieur. **~sick** *a* **be ~sick** avoir le mal du pays. **~work** *n* devoirs *mpl*.

homosexual *a* & *n* homosexuel/-le (*m*/*f*).

honest *a* (truthful) intègre; (trustworthy) honnête; (sincere) franc. **honestly** *adv* honnêtement; franchement. **honesty** *n* honnêteté *f*.

honey *n* miel *m*; (person ⓘ) chéri/-e *m*/*f*. **~moon** *n* voyage *m* de noces; (fig) lune *f* de miel.

honk *vi* klaxonner.

honorary *a* (*person*) honoraire; (*degree*) honorifique.

honour, (US) **honor** *n* honneur *m*. ● *vt* honorer.

hood *n* capuchon *m*; (on car, pram) capote *f*; (car engine cover: US) capot *m*.

hoof *n* (*pl* **~s**) sabot *m*.

hook *n* crochet *m*; (on garment) agrafe *f*; (for fishing) hameçon *m*; **off the ~** tiré d'affaire; (phone) décroché. ● *vt* accrocher.

hoot *n* (of owl) (h)ululement *m*; (of car) coup *m* de klaxon. ● *vi* (*owl*) (h)ululer; (*car*) klaxonner; (jeer) huer.

hoover *vt* **~ a room** passer l'aspirateur dans une pièce.

Hoover® *n* aspirateur *m*.

hop *vi* (*pt* **hopped**) sauter (à cloche-pied); **~ in!** ⓘ vas-y, monte! ● *n* bond *m*; **~s** houblon *m*.

hope *n* espoir *m*. ● *vt*/*i* espérer; **~ for** espérer avoir; **I ~ so** je l'espère.

hopeful *a* (*news, sign*) encourageant; (*person*) plein d'espoir; (*mood*) optimiste. **hopefully** *adv* (with luck) avec un peu de chance; (with hope) avec optimisme.

hopeless *a* désespéré; (useless: fig) nul ⓘ.

horizon *n* horizon *m*.

horizontal *a* horizontal.

hormone *n* hormone *f*.

horn *n* corne *f*; (of car) klaxon® *m*; (Mus) cor *m*.

horoscope *n* horoscope *m*.

horrible *a* horrible.

horrid *a* horrible.

horrific *a* horrifiant.

horrify *vt* horrifier.

horror *n* horreur *f*. ● *a* (*film, story*) d'épouvante.

horse *n* cheval *m*. **~back** *n* **on ~back** à cheval. **~-chestnut** *n* marron *m* (d'Inde). **~man** *n* (*pl* **-men**) cavalier *m*. **~power** *n* puissance *f* (en chevaux). **~-race** *n* course *f* de chevaux. **~-radish** *n* raifort *m*. **~shoe** *n* fer *m* à cheval. **~show** *n* concours *m* hippique.

hose *n* tuyau *m*. ● *vt* arroser. **~-pipe** *n* tuyau *m*.

hospitable *a* hospitalier.

hospital *n* hôpital *m*.

host *n* (to guests) hôte *m*; (on TV) animateur *m*; (Internet) ordinateur *m* hôte; **a ~ of** une foule de; (Relig) hostie *f*.

hostage *n* otage *m*; **hold sb ~** garder qn en otage.

hostel *n* foyer *m*; (**youth**) **~** auberge *f* (de jeunesse).

hostess *n* hôtesse *f*.

hostile *a* hostile.

hot *a* (**hotter**, **hottest**) chaud; (Culin) épicé; **be** *or* **feel ~** avoir chaud; **it is ~** il fait chaud; **in ~ water** ⊡ dans le pétrin. ● *vt/i* (*pt* **hotted**) **~ up** ⊡ chauffer. **~ air balloon** *n* montgolfière *f*. **~ dog** *n* hot-dog *m*.

hotel *n* hôtel *m*.

hot: **~headed** *a* impétueux. **~ list** *n* (Internet) signets *mpl* favoris. **~plate** *n* plaque *f* chauffante. **~ water bottle** *n* bouillotte *f*.

hound *n* chien *m* de chasse. ● *vt* poursuivre.

hour *n* heure *f*.

hourly *a* horaire; **on an ~ basis** à l'heure. ● *adv* toutes les heures.

house[1] *n* maison *f*; (Pol) Chambre *f*; **on the ~** aux frais de la maison.

house[2] *vt* loger; (of building) abriter.

household *n* (house, family) ménage *m*. ● *a* ménager.

house: **~keeper** *n* gouvernante *f*. **~-proud** *a* méticuleux. **~-warming** *n* pendaison *f* de crémaillère. **~wife** *n* (*pl* **-wives**) ménagère *f*. **~work** *n* travaux *mpl* ménagers.

housing *n* logement *m*; **~ association** service *m* de logement; **~ development** cité *f*; (smaller) lotissement *m*.

hover *vi* (*bird*) voleter; (vacillate) vaciller. **hovercraft** *n* aéroglisseur *m*.

how *adv* comment; **~ are you?** comment allez-vous?; **~ long/tall is...?** quelle est la longueur/hauteur de...?; **~ many?**, **~ much?** combien?; **~ pretty!** comme *or* que c'est joli!; **~ about a walk?** si on faisait une promenade?; **~ do you do?** (greeting) enchanté.

however *adv* (nevertheless) cependant; **~ hard I try** j'ai beau essayer; **~ much it costs** quel que soit le prix; **~ young/poor he is** si jeune/pauvre soit-il; **~ you like** comme tu veux.

howl *n* hurlement *m*. ● *vi* hurler.

HP *abbr* ⇒HIRE-PURCHASE.

hp *abbr* ⇒HORSEPOWER.

HQ *abbr* ⇒HEADQUARTERS.

hub *n* moyeu *m*; (fig) centre *m*.

hug *vt* (*pt* **hugged**) serrer dans ses bras. ● *n* étreinte *f*; **give sb a ~** serrer qn dans ses bras.

huge *a* énorme.

hull *n* (of ship) coque *f*.

hum *vt/i* (*pt* **hummed**) (*person*) fredonner; (*insect*) bourdonner; (*engine*) ronronner. ● *n* bourdonnement *m*; ronronnement *m*.

human *a* humain. ● *n* humain *m*. **~ being** *n* être *m* humain.

humane *a* (*person*) humain; (*act*) d'humanité; (*killing*) sans cruauté.

humanitarian *a* humanitaire.

humanity *n* humanité *f*.

humble *a* humble.

humid *a* humide.

humiliate *vt* humilier.

humorous *a* humoristique; (*person*) plein d'humour.

humour, (US) **humor** *n* humour

m; (mood) humeur *f*. ● *vt* amadouer.

hump *n* bosse *f*. ● *vt* 🅸 porter.

hunchback *n* bossu/-e *m/f*.

hundred *a & n* cent (*m*); **two ~ and one** deux cent un; **~s of** des centaines de. **hundredth** *a & n* centième (*mf*).

hung ⇒HANG.

Hungarian *n* (person) Hongrois/-e *m/f*; (Ling) hongrois *m*. ● *a* hongrois. **Hungary** *n* Hongrie *f*.

hunger *n* faim *f*. ● *vi* **~ for** avoir faim de.

hungry *a* (**-ier**, **-iest**) affamé; **be ~** avoir faim.

hunt *vt/i* chasser; **~ for** chercher. ● *n* chasse *f*. **hunter** *n* chasseur *m*. **hunting** *n* chasse *f*.

hurdle *n* (Sport) haie *f*; (fig) obstacle *m*.

hurricane *n* ouragan *m*.

hurry *vi* se dépêcher; **~ out** sortir précipitamment. ● *vt* (*work*) terminer à la hâte; (*person*) bousculer. ● *n* hâte *f*; **in a ~** pressé.

hurt *vt/i* (*pt* **hurt**) faire mal (à); (injure, offend) blesser. ● *a* blessé. ● *n* blessure *f*.

hurtle *vi* **~ down** dévaler; **~ along a road** foncer sur une route.

husband *n* mari *m*.

hush *vt* faire taire; **~ up** (*news*) étouffer. ● *n* silence *m*. ● *interj* chut!

husky *a* (**-ier**, **-iest**) enroué. ● *n* husky *m*.

hustle *vt* (push, rush) bousculer. ● *vi* (hurry) se dépêcher; (work: US) se démener. ● *n* **~ and bustle** agitation *f*.

hut *n* cabane *f*

hyacinth *n* jacinthe *f*.

hydrant *n* (fire) **~** bouche *f* d'incendie.

hydraulic *a* hydraulique.

hydroelectric *a* hydroélectrique.

hydrogen *n* hydrogène *m*; **~ bomb** bombe *f* à hydrogène.

hyena *n* hyène *f*.

hygiene *n* hygiène *f*. **hygienic** *a* hygiénique.

hymn *n* cantique *m*; (fig) hymne *m*.

hype *n* 🅸 battage *m* publicitaire. ● *vt* **~ (up)** (*film, book*) faire du battage pour.

hyperactive *a* hyperactif.

hyperlink *n* hyperlien *m*.

hypermarket *n* hypermarché *m*.

hypertext *n* hypertexte *m*.

hyphen *n* trait *m* d'union.

hypnosis *n* hypnose *f*.

hypocrisy *n* hypocrisie *f*. **hypocrite** *n* hypocrite *mf*. **hypocritical** *a* hypocrite.

hypothesis *n* (*pl* **-ses**) hypothèse *f*.

hysteria *n* hystérie *f*. **hysterical** *a* hystérique.

hysterics *npl* crise *f* de nerfs; **be in ~** rire aux larmes.

I *pron* je, j'; (stressed) moi.

ice *n* glace *f*; (on road) verglas *m*. ● *vt* (*cake*) glacer. ● *vi* **~ (up)** (*window*) se givrer; (*river*) geler. **~box** *n* (US) réfrigérateur *m*. **~-cream** *n* glace *f*. **~-cube** *n* glaçon *m*. **~ hockey** *n* hockey *m* sur glace.

Iceland *n* Islande *f*. **Icelander** *n* Islandais/-e *m/f*. **Icelandic** *a & n* islandais (*m*).

ice: **~ lolly** *n* glace *f* (*sur*

bâtonnet). ~ **rink** *n* patinoire *f*. ~ **skate** *n* patin *m* à glace.

icicle *n* stalactite *f* (de glace).

icing *n* (sugar) glaçage *m*.

icy *a* (**-ier**, **-iest**) (*hands, wind*) glacé; (*road*) verglacé; (*manner, welcome*) glacial.

ID *n* pièce *f* d'identité; ~ **card** carte *f* d'identité.

idea *n* idée *f*.

ideal *a* idéal. ● *n* idéal *m*.

identical *a* identique.

identification *n* identification *f*; (papers) pièce *f* d'identité.

identify *vt* identifier. ● *vi* ~ **with** s'identifier à.

identikit *n* ~ **picture** portrait-robot *m*.

identity *n* identité *f*.

ideological *a* idéologique.

idiom *n* (phrase) idiome *m*; (language) parler *m*, langue *f*. **idiomatic** *a* idiomatique.

idiosyncrasy *n* particularité *f*.

idiot *n* idiot/-e *m/f*. **idiotic** *a* idiot.

idle *a* (lazy) paresseux; (doing nothing) oisif; (*boast, threat*) vain. ● *vi* (*engine*) tourner au ralenti. ● *vt* ~ **away** gaspiller.

idol *n* idole *f*. **idolize** *vt* idolâtrer.

idyllic *a* idyllique.

i.e. *abbr* c-à-d, c'est-à-dire.

if *conj* si.

ignite *vt/i* (s')enflammer.

ignition *n* (Auto) allumage *m*; ~ (**switch**) contact *m*; ~ **key** clé *f* de contact.

ignorance *n* ignorance *f*. **ignorant** *a* ignorant (**of** de). **ignorantly** *adv* par ignorance.

ignore *vt* (*person*) ignorer; (*mistake, remark*) ne pas relever; (*feeling, fact*) ne pas tenir compte de.

ill *a* malade. ● *adv* mal. ● *n* mal *m*. ~**-advised** *a* malavisé. ~ **at ease** *a* mal à l'aise. ~**-bred** *a* mal élevé.

illegal *a* illégal.

illegible *a* illisible.

illegitimate *a* illégitime.

ill: ~**-fated** *a* malheureux. ~ **feeling** *n* ressentiment *m*.

illiterate *a & n* analphabète (*mf*).

illness *n* maladie *f*.

ill-treat *vt* maltraiter.

illuminate *vt* éclairer; (decorate with lights) illuminer. **illumination** *n* éclairage *m*; illumination *f*.

illusion *n* illusion *f*.

illustrate *vt* illustrer. **illustration** *n* illustration *f*. **illustrative** *a* qui illustre.

image *n* image *f*; (of firm, person) image *f* de marque. **imagery** *n* images *fpl*.

imaginable *a* imaginable. **imaginary** *a* imaginaire. **imagination** *n* imagination *f*. **imaginative** *a* plein d'imagination.

imagine *vt* (s')imaginer (**that** que); ~ **being rich** s'imaginer riche.

imbalance *n* déséquilibre *m*.

imitate *vt* imiter.

immaculate *a* impeccable.

immaterial *a* sans importance (**to** pour; **that** que).

immature *a* (*person*) immature; (*plant*) qui n'est pas arrivé à maturité.

immediate *a* immédiat.

immediately *adv* immédiatement. ● *conj* dès que.

immense *a* immense. **immensely** *adv* extrêmement, immensément. **immensity** *n* immensité *f*.

immerse *vt* plonger (**in** dans). **immersion** *n* immersion *f*; **immersion heater** chauffe-eau *m inv* électrique.

immigrant *n & a* immigré/-e (*m/f*); (newly-arrived) immigrant/-e (*m/f*). **immigrate** *vi* immigrer. **immigration** *n* immigration *f*.

imminent *a* imminent.

immoral *a* immoral.

immortal *a* immortel.

immune *a* immunisé (**from, to** contre); (*reaction, system*) immunitaire. **immunity** *n* immunité *f*. **immunization** *n* immunisation *f*. **immunize** *vt* immuniser.

impact *n* impact *m*.

impair *vt* (*performance*) affecter; (*ability*) affaiblir.

impart *vt* communiquer, transmettre.

impartial *a* impartial.

impassable *a* (*barrier*) infranchissable; (*road*) impraticable.

impassive *a* impassible.

impatience *n* impatience *f*. **impatient** *a* impatient; **get impatient** s'impatienter. **impatiently** *adv* impatiemment.

impeccable *a* impeccable.

impede *vt* entraver.

impediment *n* entrave *f*; **speech ~** défaut *m* d'élocution.

impending *a* imminent.

imperative *a* urgent. ● *n* impératif *m*.

imperfect *a* incomplet; (faulty) défectueux. ● *n* (Gram) imparfait *m*. **imperfection** *n* imperfection *f*.

imperial *a* impérial; (measure) conforme aux normes britanniques. **imperialism** *n* impérialisme *m*.

impersonal *a* impersonnel.

impersonate *vt* se faire passer pour; (mimic) imiter.

impertinent *a* impertinent.

impervious *a* imperméable (**to** à).

impetuous *a* impétueux.

impetus *n* impulsion *f*.

impinge *vi* ~ **on** affecter; (encroach) empiéter sur.

implement *n* instrument *m*; (tool) outil *m*. ● *vt* exécuter, mettre en application; (*software*) implanter.

implicit *a* (implied) implicite (**in** dans); (unquestioning) absolu.

imply *vt* (assume, mean) impliquer; (insinuate) laisser entendre.

impolite *a* impoli.

import[1] *vt* importer.

import[2] *n* (*article*) importation *f*; (*meaning*) signification *f*.

importance *n* importance *f*. **important** *a* important.

impose *vt* imposer (**on sb** à qn; **on sth** sur qch). ● *vi* s'imposer; ~ **on sb** abuser de la bienveillance de qn. **imposing** *a* imposant. **imposition** *n* dérangement *m*; (tax) imposition *f*.

impossible *a* impossible. ● *n* **the ~** l'impossible *m*.

impotent *a* impuissant.

impound *vt* confisquer, saisir.

impoverish *vt* appauvrir.

impractical *a* peu réaliste.

impregnable *a* imprenable.

impress *vt* impressionner; ~ **sth on sb** faire bien comprendre qch à qn. **impression** *n* impression *f*. **impressionable** *a* impressionnable. **impressive** *a* impressionnant.

imprint[1] *n* empreinte *f*.

imprint[2] *vt* (fix) graver (**on** dans); (print) imprimer.

imprison *vt* emprisonner.

improbable *a* (not likely) improbable; (incredible) invraisemblable.

improper *a* (unseemly) malséant; (dishonest) irrégulier.

I

improve *vt/i* (s')améliorer. **improvement** *n* amélioration *f*.
improvise *vt/i* improviser.
impudent *a* impudent.
impulse *n* impulsion *f*; **on ~** sur un coup de tête. **impulsive** *a* impulsif. **impulsively** *adv* par impulsion.
impurity *n* impureté *f*.
in *prep* (inside, within) dans; (expressing place, position) à, en; (expressing time) en, dans; **~ the box/garden** dans la boîte/le jardin; **~ Paris/school** à Paris/ l'école; **~ town** en ville; **~ the country** à la campagne; **~ English** en anglais; **~ India** en Inde; **~ Japan** au Japon; **~ winter** en hiver; **~ spring** au printemps; **~ an hour** (at end of) au bout d'une heure; **~ an hour('s time**) dans une heure; **~ (the space of) an hour** en une heure; **~ doing** en faisant; **~ the evening** le soir; **one ~ ten** un sur dix; **~ between** entre les deux; (time) entretemps; **~ a firm voice** d'une voix ferme; **~ blue** en bleu; **~ ink** à l'encre; **~ uniform** en uniforme; **~ a skirt** en jupe; **~ a whisper** en chuchotant; **~ a loud voice** d'une voix forte; **the best ~** le meilleur de; **we are ~ for** on va avoir; **have it ~ for sb** 🄸 avoir qn dans le collimateur. ● *adv* (inside) dedans; (at home) là, à la maison; (in fashion) à la mode; **come ~** entrer; **run ~** entrer en courant.
inability *n* incapacité *f* (**to do** de faire).
inaccessible *a* inaccessible.
inaccurate *a* inexact.
inactive *a* inactif. **inactivity** *n* inaction *f*.
inadequate *a* insuffisant.
inadvertently *adv* par mégarde.
inadvisable *a* inopportun, à déconseiller.
inane *a* idiot, débile.
inanimate *a* inanimé.
inappropriate *a* inopportun; (*term*) inapproprié.
inarticulate *a* qui a du mal à s'exprimer.
inasmuch as *adv* dans la mesure où; (because) vu que.
inaugurate *vt* (open, begin) inaugurer; (*person*) investir.
inborn *a* inné.
inbred *a* (inborn) inné.
Inc. *abbr* (**incorporated**) S.A.
incapable *a* incapable (**of doing** de faire).
incapacitate *vt* immobiliser.
incense¹ *n* encens *m*.
incense² *vt* mettre en fureur.
incentive *n* motivation *f*; (payment) prime *f*.
incessant *a* incessant. **incessantly** *adv* sans cesse.
incest *n* inceste *m*. **incestuous** *a* incestueux.
inch *n* pouce *m* (*=2.54 cm.*). ● *vi* **~ towards** se diriger petit à petit vers.
incidence *n* fréquence *f*.
incident *n* incident *m*. **incidental** *a* secondaire. **incidentally** *adv* à propos; (by chance) par la même occasion.
incinerate *vt* incinérer. **incinerator** *n* incinérateur *m*.
incite *vt* inciter, pousser.
inclination *n* (tendency) tendance *f*; (desire) envie *f*.
incline¹ *vt/i* (s')incliner; **be ~d to** avoir tendance à.
incline² *n* pente *f*.
include *vt* comprendre, inclure. **including** *prep* (y) compris. **inclusion** *n* inclusion *f*.
inclusive *a & adv* inclus; **~ of delivery** livraison comprise.
income *n* revenus *mpl*; **~ tax** impôt *m* sur le revenu.

incoming *a* (*tide*) montant; (*tenant, government*) nouveau; (*call*) qui vient de l'extérieur.

incompatible *a* incompatible.

incompetent *a* incompétent.

incomplete *a* incomplet.

incomprehensible *a* incompréhensible.

inconceivable *a* inconcevable.

inconclusive *a* peu concluant.

incongruous *a* déconcertant, surprenant.

inconsiderate *a* (*person*) peu attentif à autrui; (*act*) maladroit.

inconsistent *a* (*argument*) incohérent; (*performance*) inégal; (*behaviour*) changeant; **~ with** en contradiction avec.

inconspicuous *a* qui passe inaperçu.

incontinent *a* incontinent.

inconvenience *n* dérangement *m*; (drawback) inconvénient *m*. ● *vt* déranger. **inconvenient** *a* incommode; **if it's not inconvenient for you** si cela ne vous dérange pas.

incorporate *vt* incorporer (**into** dans); (contain) comporter.

incorrect *a* incorrect.

increase[1] *n* augmentation *f* (**in, of** de); **be on the ~** être en progression.

increase[2] *vt/i* augmenter. **increasing** *a* croissant. **increasingly** *adv* de plus en plus.

incredible *a* incroyable.

incriminate *vt* incriminer. **incriminating** *a* compromettant.

incubate *vt* (eggs) couver. **incubation** *n* incubation *f*. **incubator** *n* couveuse *f*.

incur *vt* (*pt* **incurred**) (*penalty, anger*) encourir; (*debts*) contracter.

indebted *a* **~ to sb** redevable à qn (**for** de); (grateful) reconnaissant à qn.

indecent *a* indécent.

indecisive *a* indécis; (ending) peu concluant.

indeed *adv* en effet, (emphatic) vraiment.

indefinite *a* vague; (period, delay) illimité. **indefinitely** *adv* indéfiniment.

indelible *a* indélébile.

indemnity *n* (protection) assurance *f*; (payment) indemnité *f*.

indent *vt* (text) renfoncer. **indentation** *n* (dent) marque *f*.

independence *n* indépendance *f*. **independent** *a* indépendant. **independently** *adv* de façon indépendante; **independently of** indépendamment de.

index *n* (*pl* **~es**) (in book) index *m*; (in library) catalogue *m*; (in economy) indice *m*; **~ card** fiche *f*; **~** (**finger**) index *m*. ● *vt* classer. **~-linked** *a* indexé.

India *n* Inde *f*.

Indian *n* Indien/-ne *m/f*. ● *a* indien.

indicate *vt* indiquer. **indication** *n* indication *f*.

indicative *a & n* indicatif (*m*).

indicator *n* (pointer) aiguille *f*; (on vehicle) clignotant *m*; (board) tableau *m*.

indict *vt* inculper. **indictment** *n* accusation *f*.

indifferent *a* indifférent; (not good) médiocre.

indigenous *a* indigène.

indigestible *a* indigeste. **indigestion** *n* indigestion *f*.

indignant *a* indigné.

indirect *a* indirect. **indirectly** *adv* indirectement.

indiscreet *a* indiscret. **indiscretion** *n* indiscrétion *f*.

indiscriminate *a* sans

distinction. **indiscriminately** *adv* sans distinction.

indisputable *a* indiscutable.

individual *a* individuel; (*tuition*) particulier. ● *n* individu *m*. **individualist** *n* individualiste *mf*. **individuality** *n* individualité *f*. **individually** *adv* individuellement.

indoctrinate *vt* endoctriner. **indoctrination** *n* endoctrinement *m*.

indolent *a* indolent.

Indonesia *n* Indonésie *f*.

indoor *a* (*clothes*) d'intérieur; (pool, court) couvert. **indoors** *adv* à l'intérieur.

induce *vt* (influence) persuader; (stronger) inciter (**to do** à faire). **inducement** *n* (financial) récompense *f*; (incentive) motivation *f*.

induction *n* (Electr) induction *f*; (inauguration) installation *f*.

indulge *vt* (*person, whim*) céder à; (*child*) gâter. ● *vi* ~ **in** se livrer à. **indulgence** *n* indulgence *f*; (treat) plaisir *m*. **indulgent** *a* indulgent.

industrial *a* industriel; (accident) du travail; ~ **action** grève *f*; ~ **dispute** conflit *m* social. **industrialist** *n* industriel/-le *m*/*f*. **industrialized** *a* industrialisé.

industrious *a* diligent.

industry *n* industrie *f*; (zeal) zèle *m*.

inebriated *a* ivre.

inedible *a* immangeable.

ineffective *a* inefficace.

inefficient *a* inefficace; (person) incompétent.

ineligible *a* inéligible; **be ~ for** ne pas avoir droit à.

inept *a* incompétent; (tactless) maladroit.

inequality *n* inégalité *f*.

inescapable *a* indéniable.

inevitable *a* inévitable.

inexcusable *a* inexcusable.

inexhaustible *a* inépuisable.

inexpensive *a* pas cher.

inexperience *n* inexpérience *f*. **inexperienced** *a* inexpérimenté.

infallible *a* infaillible.

infamous *a* (*person*) tristement célèbre; (*deed*) infâme.

infancy *n* petite enfance *f*; **in its ~** (fig) à ses débuts *mpl*. **infant** *n* (baby) bébé *m*; (at school) enfant *m*. **infantile** *a* infantile.

infatuated *a* ~ **with** entiché de. **infatuation** *n* engouement *m*.

infect *vt* contaminer; ~ **sb with sth** transmettre qch à qn. **infection** *n* infection *f*. **infectious** *a* contagieux.

infer *vt* (*pt* **inferred**) (deduce) déduire.

inferior *a* inférieur (**to** à); (*work, product*) de qualité inférieure. ● *n* inférieur/-e *m*/*f*. **inferiority** *n* infériorité *f*.

inferno *n* (hell) enfer *m*; (blaze) brasier *m*.

infertile *a* infertile.

infest *vt* infester (**with** de).

infidelity *n* infidélité *f*.

infighting *n* conflits *mpl* internes.

infinite *a* infini. **infinitely** *adv* infiniment. **infinitive** *n* infinitif *m*. **infinity** *n* infinité *f*.

infirm *a* infirme. **infirmary** *n* hôpital *m*; (sick-bay) infirmerie *f*. **infirmity** *n* infirmité *f*.

inflame *vt* enflammer. **inflammable** *a* inflammable. **inflammation** *n* inflammation *f*. **inflammatory** *a* incendiaire.

inflatable *a* gonflable. **inflate** *vt* (lit, fig) gonfler.

inflation *n* inflation *f*.

inflection *n* (of word root) flexion *f*; (of vowel, voice) inflexion *f*.

inflict *vt* infliger (**on** à).

influence *n* influence *f*; **under the ~** (drunk [!]) éméché. ● *vt* (*person*) influencer; (*choice*) influer sur. **influential** *a* (powerful) influent; (*theory, artist*) très suivi.

influenza *n* grippe *f*.

influx *n* afflux *m*.

inform *vt* informer (**of** de); **keep ~ed** tenir au courant.

informal *a* (simple) simple, sans façons; (unofficial) officieux; (colloquial) familier. **informality** *n* simplicité *f*. **informally** *adv* (*dress*) en tenue décontractée; (*speak*) en toute simplicité.

informant *n* indicateur/-trice *m/f*.

information *n* renseignements *mpl*, informations *fpl*; **some ~** un renseignement. **~ superhighway** *n* autoroute *f* de l'information. **~ technology** *n* informatique *f*.

informative *a* (*book*) riche en renseignements; (*visit*) instructif.

informer *n* indicateur/-trice *m/f*.

infrequent *a* rare.

infringe *vt* (*rule*) enfreindre; (*rights*) ne pas respecter. **infringement** *n* infraction *f*.

infuriate *vt* exaspérer.

ingenuity *n* ingéniosité *f*.

ingot *n* lingot *m*.

ingrained *a* (*hatred*) enraciné; (*dirt*) bien incrusté.

ingratiate *vt* **~ oneself with** se faire bien voir de.

ingredient *n* ingrédient *m*.

inhabit *vt* habiter. **inhabitable** *a* habitable. **inhabitant** *n* habitant/-e *m/f*.

inhale *vt* inhaler; (smoke) avaler. **inhaler** *n* inhalateur *m*.

inherent *a* inhérent (**in** à). **inherently** *adv* en soi, par sa nature.

inherit *vt* hériter de; **~ sth from sb** hériter qch de qn. **inheritance** *n* héritage *m*.

inhibit *vt* (restrain) inhiber; (prevent) entraver.

inhospitable *a* inhospitalier.

inhuman *a* inhumain.

initial *n* initiale *f*. ● *vt* (*pt* **initialled**) parapher. ● *a* initial.

initiate *vt* (*project*) mettre en œuvre; (*talks*) amorcer; (*person*) initier (**into** à). **initiation** *n* initiation *f*; (start) amorce *f*.

initiative *n* initiative *f*.

inject *vt* injecter (**into** dans); (*new element*: fig) insuffler (**into** à). **injection** *n* injection *f*, piqûre *f*.

injure *vt* blesser; (damage) nuire à. **injury** *n* blessure *f*.

injustice *n* injustice *f*.

ink *n* encre *f*.

inkling *n* petite idée *f*.

inland *a* intérieur; **I~ Revenue** service *m* des impôts britannique.

in-laws *npl* (parents) beaux-parents *mpl*; (family) belle-famille *f*.

inlay[1] *vt* (*pt* **inlaid**) incruster (**with** de); (on wood) marqueter.

inlay[2] *n* incrustation *f*; (on wood) marqueterie *f*.

inlet *n* bras *m* de mer; (Tech) arrivée *f*.

inmate *n* (of asylum) interné/-e *m/f*; (of prison) détenu/-e *m/f*.

inn *n* auberge *f*.

innate *a* inné.

inner *a* intérieur; **~ city** quartiers *mpl* déshérités; **~ tube** chambre *f* à air.

innocent *a* & *n* innocent/-e (*m/f*).

innocuous *a* inoffensif.

innovate *vi* innover.

innuendo *n* (*pl* **~es**)

I

insinuations *fpl*; (sexual) allusions *fpl* grivoises.

innumerable *a* innombrable.

inoculate *vt* vacciner (**against** contre).

inopportune *a* inopportun.

in-patient *n* malade *mf* hospitalisé/-e.

input *n* (of energy) alimentation *f* (**of** en); (contribution) contribution *f*; (data) données *fpl*; (computer process) saisie *f* des données. ●*vt* (*data*) saisir.

inquest *n* enquête *f*.

inquire *vi* se renseigner (**about, into** sur). ●*vt* demander.

inquiry *n* demande *f* de renseignements; (inquest) enquête *f*.

inquisitive *a* curieux.

inroad *n* **make ~s into** faire une avancée sur.

insane *a* fou; (Jur) aliéné. **insanity** *n* folie *f*; (Jur) aliénation *f* mentale.

inscribe *vt* inscrire. **inscription** *n* inscription *f*.

inscrutable *a* énigmatique.

insect *n* insecte *m*. **insecticide** *n* insecticide *m*.

insecure *a* (*person*) qui manque d'assurance; (job) précaire; (*lock, property*) peu sûr. **insecurity** *n* (of person) manque *m* d'assurance; (of situation) insécurité *f*.

insensitive *a* insensible; (*remark*) indélicat.

inseparable *a* inséparable (**from** de).

insert *vt* insérer (**in** dans).

in-service *a* (training) continu.

inshore *a* côtier.

inside *n* intérieur *m*; **~s** [I] entrailles *fpl*. ●*a* intérieur. ●*adv* à l'intérieur; **go ~** entrer. ●*prep* à l'intérieur de; (of time) en moins de; **~ out** à l'envers; (thoroughly) à fond.

insight *n* (perception) perspicacité *f*; (idea) aperçu *m*.

insignia *npl* insigne *m*.

insignificant *a* (*cost, difference*) négligeable; (*person*) insignifiant.

insincere *a* peu sincère.

insinuate *vt* insinuer.

insist *vt/i* insister (**that** pour que); **~ on** exiger; **~ on doing** vouloir à tout prix faire. **insistence** *n* insistance *f*. **insistent** *a* insistant. **insistently** *adv* avec insistance.

insofar as *adv* dans la mesure où.

insolent *a* insolent.

insolvent *a* insolvable.

insomnia *n* insomnie *f*. **insomniac** *n* insomniaque *mf*.

inspect *vt* (*school, machinery*) inspecter; (*tickets*) contrôler. **inspection** *n* inspection *f*; (of passport, ticket) contrôle *m*. **inspector** *n* inspecteur/-trice *m*/*f*; (on bus) contrôleur/-euse *m*/*f*.

inspiration *n* inspiration *f*. **inspire** *vt* inspirer.

install *vt* installer.

instalment *n* (payment) versement *m*; (of serial) épisode *m*.

instance *n* exemple *m*; (case) cas *m*; **for ~** par exemple; **in the first ~** en premier lieu.

instant *a* immédiat; (*food*) instantané. ●*n* instant *m*. **instantaneous** *a* instantané. **instantly** *adv* immédiatement.

instead *adv* plutôt; **~ of doing** au lieu de faire; **~ of sb** à la place de qn.

instep *n* cou-de-pied *m*.

instigate *vt* (*attack*) lancer; (*proceedings*) engager.

instil *vt* (*pt* **instilled**) inculquer; (*fear*) insuffler.

instinct *n* instinct *m*. **instinctive** *a* instinctif.

institute *n* institut *m*. ● *vt* instituer; (*proceedings*) engager. **institution** *n* institution *f*; (school, hospital) établissement *m*.

instruct *vt* (teach) instruire; (order) ordonner; ~ **sb in sth** enseigner qch à qn; ~ **sb to do** donner l'ordre à qn de faire. **instruction** *n* instruction *f*. **instructions** *npl* (for use) mode *m* d'emploi. **instructive** *a* instructif. **instructor** *n* (skiing, driving) moniteur/-trice *m/f*.

instrument *n* instrument *m*.

instrumental *a* instrumental; **be ~ in** contribuer à. **instrumentalist** *n* instrumentaliste *mf*.

insubordinate *a* insubordonné.

insufficient *a* insuffisant.

insular *a* (Geog) insulaire; (mind, person: fig) borné.

insulate *vt* (room, wire) isoler.

insulin *n* insuline *f*.

insult[1] *vt* insulter.

insult[2] *n* insulte *f*.

insurance *n* assurance *f* (**against** contre).

insure *vt* assurer; ~ **that** (US) s'assurer que.

intact *a* intact.

intake *n* (of food) consommation *f*; (School, Univ) admissions *fpl*.

integral *a* intégral (**to** à).

integrate *vt/i* (s')intégrer (**with** à; **into** dans).

integrity *n* intégrité *f*.

intellect *n* intelligence *f*. **intellectual** *a & n* intellectuel/-le (*m/f*).

intelligence *n* intelligence *f*; (Mil) renseignements *mpl*. **intelligent** *a* intelligent. **intelligently** *adv* intelligemment.

intend *vt* (*outcome*) vouloir; ~ **to do** avoir l'intention de faire. **intended** *a* (*result*) voulu; (*visit*) projeté.

intense *a* intense; (person) sérieux. **intensely** *adv* (very) extrêmement.

intensify *vt/i* (s')intensifier.

intensive *a* intensif; **in ~ care** en réanimation.

intent *n* intention *f*. ● *a* absorbé; **~ on doing** résolu à faire.

intention *n* intention *f*. **intentional** *a* intentionnel.

intently *adv* attentivement.

interact *vi* (*factors*) agir l'un sur l'autre; (*people*) communiquer. **interactive** *a* (*TV, video*) interactif.

intercept *vt* intercepter.

interchange *n* (road junction) échangeur *m*; (exchange) échange *m*.

interchangeable *a* interchangeable.

intercom *n* interphone® *m*.

interconnected *a* (*parts*) raccordé; (*problems*) lié.

intercourse *n* rapports *mpl*.

interest *n* intérêt *m*; **~ rate** taux *m* d'intérêt. ● *vt* intéresser (**in** à). **interested** *a* intéressé; **be ~ed in** s'intéresser à. **interesting** *a* intéressant.

interfere *vi* se mêler des affaires des autres; **~ in** se mêler de; **~ with** (*freedom*) empiéter sur; (tamper with) toucher. **interference** *n* ingérence *f*; (sound, light waves) brouillage *m*; (radio) parasites *mpl*.

interim *n* **in the ~** entre-temps. ● *a* (*government*) provisoire; (*payment*) intermédiaire.

interior *n* intérieur *m*. ● *a* intérieur.

interjection *n* interjection *f*.

interlock *vt/i* (Tech) (s')emboîter, (s')enclencher.

I

interlude *n* intervalle *m*; (Theat, Mus) intermède *m*.

intermediary *a & n* intermédiaire (*mf*).

intermediate *a* intermédiaire; (*exam, level*) moyen.

intermission *n* (Theat) entracte *m*.

intermittent *a* intermittent.

intern[1] *vt* interner.

intern[2] *n* (US) stagiaire *mf*; (Med) interne *mf*.

internal *a* interne; (domestic: Pol) intérieur; **I~ Revenue** (US) service *m* des impôts américain.

international *a* international.

Internet *n* Internet *m*; **on the ~** sur l'Internet; **~ service provider** fournisseur *m* d'accès à l'Internet.

interpret *vt* interpréter (**as** comme). ● *vi* faire l'interprète. **interpretation** *n* interprétation *f*. **interpreter** *n* interprète *mf*.

interrelated *a* interdépendant, lié.

interrogate *vt* interroger. **interrogative** *a & n* (Ling) interrogatif (*m*).

interrupt *vt/i* interrompre. **interruption** *n* interruption *f*.

intersect *vt/i* (lines, roads) (se) croiser. **intersection** *n* intersection *f*.

interspersed *a* parsemé (**with** de).

intertwine *vt/i* (s')entrelacer.

interval *n* intervalle *m*; (Theat) entracte *m*.

intervene *vi* intervenir; (of time) s'écouler (**between** entre); (happen) arriver.

interview *n* (for job) entretien *m*; (by a journalist) interview *f*. ● *vt* (*candidate*) faire passer un entretien à; (*celebrity*) interviewer.

intestine *n* intestin *m*.

intimacy *n* intimité *f*.

intimate[1] *vt* (state) annoncer; (hint) laisser entendre.

intimate[2] *a* intime. **intimately** *adv* intimement.

intimidate *vt* intimider.

into *prep* (put, go, fall) dans; (divide, translate, change) en; **be ~ jazz** être fana du jazz ⓘ; **8 ~ 24 is 3** 24 divisé par 8 égale 3.

intolerant *a* intolérant.

intonation *n* intonation *f*.

intoxicate *vt* enivrer. **intoxicated** *a* ivre. **intoxication** *n* ivresse *f*.

intractable *a* (*person*) intraitable; (*problem*) rebelle.

Intranet *n* (Comput) Intranet *m*.

intransitive *a* intransitif.

intravenous *a* (Med) intraveineux.

intricate *a* complexe.

intrigue *vt* intriguer. ● *n* intrigue *f*. **intriguing** *a* fascinant; (curious) curieux.

intrinsic *a* intrinsèque (**to** à).

introduce *vt* (*person, idea, programme*) présenter; (*object, law*) introduire (**into** dans). **introduction** *n* introduction *f*; (of person) présentation *f*. **introductory** *a* (words) préliminaire.

introvert *n* introverti/-e *m/f*.

intrude *vi* (person) s'imposer (**on sb** à qn), déranger. **intruder** *n* intrus/-e *m/f*. **intrusion** *n* intrusion *f*.

intuition *n* intuition *f*. **intuitive** *a* intuitif.

inundate *vt* inonder (**with** de).

invade *vt* envahir.

invalid[1] *n* malade *mf*; (disabled) infirme *mf*.

invalid[2] *a* (*passport*) pas valable; (*claim*) sans fondement.

invalidate *vt* (*argument*) infirmer; (*claim*) annuler.

invaluable *a* inestimable.

invariable *a* invariable. **invariably** *adv* invariablement.

invasion *n* invasion *f*.

invent *vt* inventer. **invention** *n* invention *f*. **inventive** *a* inventif. **inventor** *n* inventeur/-trice *m/f*.

inventory *n* inventaire *m*.

invert *vt* (*order*) intervertir; (*image, values*) renverser; **~ed commas** guillemets *mpl*.

invest *vt* investir; (time, effort) consacrer. ● *vi* faire un investissement; **~ in** (buy) s'acheter.

investigate *vt* examiner; (*crime*) enquêter sur. **investigation** *n* investigation *f*. **investigator** *n* (police) enquêteur/-euse *m/f*.

investment *n* investissement *m*; **emotional ~** engagement *m* personnel. **investor** *n* investisseur/-euse *m/f*; (in shares) actionnaire *mf*.

invigilate *vi* (*exam*) surveiller. **invigilator** *n* surveillant/-e *m/f*.

invigorate *vt* revigorer.

invisible *a* invisible.

invitation *n* invitation *f*. **invite** *vt* inviter; (ask for) demander. **inviting** *a* engageant.

invoice *n* facture *f*. ● *vt* facturer.

involuntary *a* involontaire.

involve *vt* impliquer; (*person*) faire participer (**in** à). **involved** *a* (complex) compliqué; (at stake) en jeu; **be ~d in** (*work*) participer à; (*crime*) être mêlé à. **involvement** *n* participation *f* (**in** à).

inward *a* (*feeling*) intérieur. **inwardly** *adv* intérieurement. **inwards** *adv* vers l'intérieur.

iodine *n* iode *m*; (antiseptic) teinture *f* d'iode.

iota *n* iota *m*; **not one ~ of** pas un grain de.

IOU *abbr* (**I owe you**) reconnaissance *f* de dette.

IQ *abbr* (**intelligence quotient**) QI *m*.

Iran *n* Iran *m*.

Iraq *n* Irak *m*.

irate *a* furieux.

IRC *abbrev* (**Internet Relay Chat**) (Internet) conversation *f* IRC.

Ireland *n* Irlande *f*.

Irish *n & a* irlandais (*m*). **~man** *n* Irlandais *m*. **~woman** *n* Irlandaise *f*.

iron *n* fer *m*; (appliance) fer *m* (à repasser). ● *a* (*will*) de fer; (*bar*) en fer. ● *vt* repasser; **~ out** (fig) aplanir.

ironic(al) *a* ironique.

iron: **ironing-board** *n* planche *f* à repasser. **~monger** *n* quincaillier *m*.

irony *n* ironie *f*.

irrational *a* irrationnel; (person) pas raisonnable.

irregular *a* irrégulier.

irrelevant *a* hors de propos.

irreplaceable *a* irremplaçable.

irresistible *a* irrésistible.

irrespective *a* **~ of** sans tenir compte de.

irresponsible *a* irresponsable.

irreverent *a* irrévérencieux.

irreversible *a* irréversible.

irrigate *vt* irriguer.

irritable *a* irritable.

irritate *vt* irriter. **irritating** *a* irritant.

is ⇒BE.

Islam *n* (faith) islam *m*; (Muslims) Islam *m*. **Islamic** *a* islamique.

island *n* île *f*. **islander** *n* insulaire *mf*.

isle *n* île *f*.

isolate *vt* isoler. **isolation** *n* isolement *m*.

Israel *n* Israël *m*.

Israeli *n* Israélien/-ne *m/f*. ● *a* israélien.

issue *n* question *f*; (outcome) résultat *m*; (of magazine) numéro *m*; (of stamps) émission *f*; (offspring) descendance *f*; **at ~** en cause. ● *vt* distribuer; (stamps) émettre; (*book*) publier; (*order*) délivrer. ● *vi* **~ from** provenir de.

it

● *pronoun*

- (subject) il, elle; **'where's the book/chair?'—'~'s in the kitchen'** 'où est le livre/la chaise?'—'il/elle est dans la cuisine'.
- (object) le, la, l'; **~'s my book and I want ~** c'est mon livre et je le veux; **I liked his shirt, did you notice ~?** sa chemise m'a plu, l'as-tu remarquée?; **give ~ to me** donne-le-moi.
- (with preposition) **we talked a lot about ~** on en a beaucoup parlé; **Elliott went to ~** Elliott y est allé.
- (impersonal) il; **~'s raining** il pleut; **~ will snow** il va neiger.

IT *abbr* ⇒INFORMATION TECHNOLOGY.

Italian *n* (person) Italien/-ne *m/f*; (Ling) italien *m*. ● *a* italien.

italics *npl* italique *m*.

Italy *n* Italie *f*.

itch *n* démangeaison *f*. ● *vi* démanger; **my arm ~es** j'ai le bras qui me démange; **be ~ing to do** mourir d'envie de faire.

item *n* article *m*; (on agenda) point *m*.

itemize *vt* détailler; **~d bill** facture *f* détaillée.

itinerary *n* itinéraire *m*.

its *det* son, sa; *pl* ses.

it's = IT IS, IT HAS.

itself *pron* lui-même, elle-même; (reflexive) se.

ivory *n* ivoire *m*; **~ tower** tour *f* d'ivoire.

ivy *n* lierre *m*.

jab *vt* (*pt* **jabbed**) **~ sth into sth** planter qch dans qch. ● *n* coup *m*; (injection) piqûre *f*.

jack *n* (Auto) cric *m*; (cards) valet *m*; (Electr) jack *m*. ● *vt* **~ up** soulever avec un cric.

jackal *n* chacal *m*.

jacket *n* veste *f*, veston *m*; (of book) jaquette *f*.

jack-knife *n* couteau *m* pliant. ● *vi* (lorry) se mettre en portefeuille.

jackpot *n* gros lot *m*; **hit the ~** gagner le gros lot.

jade *n* (stone) jade *m*.

jaded *a* (tired) fatigué; (bored) blasé.

jagged *a* (*rock*) déchiqueté; (*knife*) dentelé.

jail *n* prison *f*. ● *vt* mettre en prison.

jam *n* confiture *f*; (**traffic**) **~** embouteillage *m*. ● *vt/i* (*pt* **jammed**) (wedge) (se) coincer; (cram) (s')entasser; (*street*) encombrer; (*radio*) brouiller.

Jamaica *n* Jamaïque *f*.

jam-packed *a* [I] bondé; **~ with** bourré de.

jangle *n* tintement *m*. ● *vt/i* (faire) tinter.

janitor *n* (US) gardien *m*.

January *n* janvier *m*.

Japan *n* Japon *m*.
Japanese *n* (person) Japonais/-e *m/f*; (Ling) japonais *m*. ● *a* japonais.
jar *n* pot *m*, bocal *m*. ● *vi* (*pt* **jarred**) rendre un son discordant; (*colours*) détonner. ● *vt* ébranler.
jargon *n* jargon *m*.
jaundice *n* jaunisse *f*.
javelin *n* javelot *m*.
jaw *n* mâchoire *f*.
jay *n* geai *m*.
jazz *n* jazz *m*. ● *vt* ~ **up** (*dress*) rajeunir; (*event*) ranimer.
jealous *a* jaloux. **jealousy** *n* jalousie *f*.
jeans *npl* jean *m*.
jeer *vt/i* ~ (at) huer. ● *n* huée *f*.
jelly *n* gelée *f*. **~fish** *n* méduse *f*.
jeopardize *vt* (*career, chance*) compromettre; (*lives*) mettre en péril.
jerk *n* secousse *f*; (fool ⊠) crétin *m* ⊡. ● *vt* tirer brusquement. ● *vi* tressaillir. **jerky** *a* saccadé.
jersey *n* (garment) pull-over *m*; (fabric) jersey *m*.
jet *n* (plane, stream) jet *m*; (mineral) jais *m*; ~ **lag** décalage *m* horaire.
jettison *vt* jeter par-dessus bord; (Aviat) larguer; (fig) rejeter.
jetty *n* jetée *f*.
Jew *n* juif/juive *m/f*.
jewel *n* bijou *m*. **jeweller** *n* bijoutier/-ière *m/f*. **jeweller('s)** *n* (shop) bijouterie *f*. **jewellery** *n* bijoux *mpl*.
Jewish *a* juif.
jibe *n* moquerie *f*.
jigsaw *n* puzzle *m*.
jingle *vt/i* (faire) tinter. ● *n* tintement *m*; (advertising) refrain *m* publicitaire, sonal *m*.
jinx *n* (person) porte-malheur *m* *inv*; (curse) sort *m*.
jitters *npl* **have the** ~ ⊡ être nerveux. **jittery** *a* nerveux.
job *n* emploi *m*; (post) poste *m*; **out of a** ~ sans emploi; **it is a good** ~ **that** heureusement que; **just the** ~ tout à fait ce qu'il faut. ~ **centre** *n* bureau *m* des services nationaux de l'emploi. **jobless** *a* sans emploi.
jockey *n* jockey *m*.
jog *n* **go for a** ~ aller faire un jogging. ● *vt* (*pt* **jogged**) heurter; (*memory*) rafraîchir. ● *vi* faire du jogging. **jogging** *n* jogging *m*.
join *vt* (attach) réunir, joindre; (*club*) devenir membre de; (*company*) entrer dans; (*army*) s'engager dans; (*queue*) se mettre dans; ~ **sb** (in activity) se joindre à qn; (meet) rejoindre qn. ● *vi* (become member) adhérer; (*pieces*) se joindre; (*roads*) se rejoindre. ● *n* raccord *m*. □ ~ **in** participer; ~ **in sth** participer à qch; ~ **up** (Mil) s'engager; ~ **sth up** relier qch. **joiner** *n* menuisier/-ière *m/f*.
joint *a* (*action*) collectif; (*measures, venture*) commun; (*winner*) ex aequo *inv*; (*account*) joint; ~ **author** coauteur *m*. ● *n* (join) joint *m*; (Anat) articulation *f*; (Culin) rôti *m*; **out of** ~ déboîté.
joke *n* plaisanterie *f*; (trick) farce *f*; **it's no** ~ ce n'est pas drôle. ● *vi* plaisanter. **joker** *n* blagueur/-euse *m/f*; (cards) joker *m*.
jolly *a* (**-ier**, **-iest**) (*person*) enjoué; (*tune*) joyeux. ● *adv* ⊡ drôlement.
jolt *vt* secouer. ● *vi* cahoter. ● *n* secousse *f*; (shock) choc *m*.
jostle *vt/i* (se) bousculer.
jot *vt* (*pt* **jotted**) ~ (**down**) noter.
journal *n* journal *m*. **journalism** *n* journalisme *m*. **journalist** *n* journaliste *mf*.
journey *n* (trip) voyage *m*; (short or habitual) trajet *m*. ● *vi* voyager.
joy *n* joie *f*. **joyful** *a* joyeux.

J

joy: **~riding** *n* rodéo *m* à la voiture volée. **~stick** *n* (Comput) manette *f*; (Aviat) manche *m* à balai.

jubilant *a* (*person*) exultant; (*mood*) réjoui.

Judaism *n* judaïsme *m*.

judge *n* juge *m*. ● *vt* juger; (*distance*) estimer; **judging by/from** à en juger par. **judg(e)ment** *n* jugement *m*.

judicial *a* judiciaire. **judiciary** *n* magistrature *f*.

judo *n* judo *m*.

jug *n* (glass) carafe *f*; (pottery) pichet *m*.

juggernaut *n* (lorry) poids *m* lourd.

juggle *vt/i* jongler (avec). **juggler** *n* jongleur/-euse *m/f*.

juice *n* jus *m*. **juicy** *a* juteux; (*details* ▣) croustillant.

jukebox *n* juke-box *m*.

July *n* juillet *m*.

jumble *vt* mélanger. ● *n* (of objects) tas *m*; (of ideas) fouillis *m*; **~ sale** vente *f* de charité.

jumbo *n* (also **~ jet**) gros-porteur *m*.

jump *vt* sauter; **~ the lights** passer au feu rouge; **~ the queue** passer devant tout le monde. ● *vi* sauter; (in surprise) sursauter; (*price*) monter en flèche; **~ at** (*opportunity*) sauter sur. ● *n* saut *m*, bond *m*; (increase) bond *m*.

jumper *n* pull(-over) *m*; (dress: US) robe *f* chasuble.

jump-leads *npl* câbles *mpl* de démarrage.

jumpy *a* nerveux.

junction *n* (of roads) carrefour *m*; (on motorway) échangeur *m*.

June *n* juin *m*.

jungle *n* jungle *f*.

junior *a* (young) jeune; (in rank) subalterne; (school) primaire. ● *n* cadet/-te *m/f*; (School) élève *mf* du primaire.

junk *n* bric-à-brac *m inv*; (poor quality) camelote *f*; **~ food** nourriture *f* industrielle.

junkie *n* ▣ drogué/-e *m/f*.

junk: **~ mail** *n* prospectus *mpl*. **~-shop** *n* boutique *f* de bric-à-brac.

jurisdiction *n* compétence *f*; (Jur) juridiction *f*.

juror *n* juré *m*.

jury *n* jury *m*.

just *a* (fair) juste. ● *adv* (immediately, slightly) juste; (simply) tout simplement; (exactly) exactement; **he has/had ~ left** il vient/venait de partir; **have ~ missed** avoir manqué de peu; **I'm ~ leaving** je suis sur le point de partir; **it's ~ a cold** ce n'est qu'un rhume; **~ as tall/well as** tout aussi grand/bien que; **~ listen!** écoutez donc!; **it's ~ ridiculous** c'est vraiment ridicule.

justice *n* justice *f*; **J~ of the Peace** juge *m* de paix.

justification *n* justification *f*. **justify** *vt* justifier.

jut *vi* (*pt* **jutted**) **~ (out)** s'avancer en saillie.

juvenile *a* (childish) puéril; (*offender*) mineur; (*delinquent*) jeune. ● *n* jeune *mf*; (Jur) mineur/-e *m/f*.

juxtapose *vt* juxtaposer.

kangaroo *n* kangourou *m*.

karate *n* karaté *m*.

kebab *n* brochette *f*.

keel *n* (of ship) quille *f*. ● *vi* ~ **over** (*bateau*) chavirer; (*person*) s'écrouler.

keen *a* (*interest, wind, feeling*) vif; (*mind, analysis*) pénétrant; (*edge, appetite*) aiguisé; (eager) enthousiaste; **be ~ on** être passionné de; **be ~ to do** *or* **on doing** tenir beaucoup à faire. **keenly** *adv* vivement. **keenness** *n* enthousiasme *m*.

keep *vt* (*pt* **kept**) garder; (*promise, shop, diary*) tenir; (*family*) faire vivre; (*animals*) élever; (*rule*) respecter; (celebrate) célébrer; (delay) retenir; **~ sth clean/warm** garder qch propre/au chaud; **~ sb in/out** empêcher qn de sortir/d'entrer; **~ sb from doing** empêcher qn de faire. ● *vi* (*food*) se conserver; **~** (**on**) continuer (**doing** à faire). ● *n* pension *f*; (of castle) donjon *m*. □ **~ down** rester allongé; **~ sth down** limiter qch; **~ your voice down!** baisse la voix!; **~ to** (*road*) ne pas s'écarter de; (*rules*) respecter; **~ up** (*car, runner*) suivre; (*rain*) continuer; **~ up with sb** (in speed) aller aussi vite que; (*class, inflation, fashion, news*) suivre.

keeper *n* gardien/-ne *m/f*.

keepsake *n* souvenir *m*.

kennel *n* niche *f*.

kept ⇒KEEP.

kerb *n* bord *m* du trottoir.

kernel *n* amande *f*; **~ of truth** fond *m* de vérité.

kettle *n* bouilloire *f*.

key *n* clé *f*; (of computer, piano) touche *f*. ● *a* (*industry, figure*) clé (*inv*). ● *vt* ~ (**in**) saisir. **~board** *n* clavier *m*. **~hole** *n* trou *m* de serrure. **~-pad** *n* (of telephone) clavier *m* numérique. **~-ring** *n* porte-clés *m inv*. **~stroke** *n* (Comput) frappe *f*.

khaki *a* kaki *inv*.

kick *vt/i* donner un coup de pied (à); (*horse*) botter. ● *n* coup *m* de pied; (of gun) recul *m*; **get a ~ out of doing** [!] prendre plaisir à faire. □ **~ out** [!] virer [!].

kick-off *n* coup *m* d'envoi.

kid *n* (*goat, leather*) chevreau *m*; (child [!]) gosse *mf* [!]. ● *vt/i* (*pt* **kidded**) blaguer.

kidnap *vt* (*pt* **kidnapped**) enlever. **kidnapping** *n* enlèvement *m*.

kidney *n* rein *m*; (Culin) rognon *m*.

kill *vt* tuer; (*rumour*: fig) arrêter. ● *n* mise *f* à mort. **killer** *n* tueur/-euse *m/f*. **killing** *n* meurtre *m*.

kiln *n* four *m*.

kilo *n* kilo *m*.

kilobyte *n* kilo-octet *m*.

kilogram *n* kilogramme *m*.

kilometre, (US) **kilometer** *n* kilomètre *m*.

kilowatt *n* kilowatt *m*.

kin *n* parents *mpl*.

kind *n* genre *m*, sorte *f*; **in ~** en nature; **~ of** (somewhat [!]) assez. ● *a* gentil, bon

kindergarten *n* jardin *m* d'enfants.

kindle *vt/i* (s')allumer.

kindly *a* (**-ier, -iest**) (*person*) gentil; (*interest*) bienveillant. ● *adv* avec gentillesse; **would you**

~ **do** auriez-vous l'amabilité de faire.

kindness *n* bonté *f*.

king *n* roi *m*. **kingdom** *n* royaume *m*; (Bot) règne *m*. ~**fisher** *n* martin-pêcheur *m*. ~**-size**(**d**) *a* géant.

kiosk *n* kiosque *m*; **telephone** ~ cabine *f* téléphonique; (Internet) borne *f* interactive, kiosque *m*.

kiss *n* baiser *m*. ● *vt*/*i* (s')embrasser.

kit *n* (clothing) affaires *fpl*; (set of tools) trousse *f*; (for assembly) kit *m*. ● *vt* (*pt* **kitted**) ~ **out** équiper.

kitchen *n* cuisine *f*.

kite *n* (toy) cerf-volant *m*; (bird) milan *m*.

kitten *n* chaton *m*.

kitty *n* (fund) cagnotte *f*.

knack *n* tour *m* de main (**of doing** pour faire).

knead *vt* pétrir.

knee *n* genou *m*. ~**cap** *n* rotule *f*.

kneel *vi* (*pt* **knelt**) ~ (**down**) se mettre à genoux; (in prayer) s'agenouiller.

knew ⇨KNOW.

knickers *npl* petite culotte *f*, slip *m*.

knife *n* (*pl* **knives**) couteau *m*. ● *vt* poignarder.

knight *n* chevalier *m*; (chess) cavalier *m*. ● *vt* anoblir. ~**hood** *n* titre *m* de chevalier.

knit *vt*/*i* (*pt* **knitted** *or* **knit**) tricoter; (*bones*) (se) souder. **knitting** *n* tricot *m*. **knitwear** *n* tricots *mpl*.

knob *n* bouton *m*.

knock *vt*/*i* cogner; (criticize [!]) critiquer; ~ **sth off**/**out** faire tomber qch. ● *n* coup *m*. □ ~ **down** (*chair, pedestrian*) renverser; (demolish) abattre; (reduce) baisser; ~ **off** (stop work [!]) arrêter de travailler; ~ **£10 off** faire une réduction de 10 livres; ~ **it off!** [!] ça suffit!; ~ **out** assommer; ~ **over** renverser; ~ **up** (*meal*) préparer en vitesse.

knock-out *n* (boxing) knock-out *m*.

knot *n* nœud *m*. ● *vt* (*pt* **knotted**) nouer.

know *vt*/*i* (*pt* **knew**; *pp* **known**) (*answer, reason, language*) savoir (**that** que); (*person, place, name, rule, situation*) connaître; (recognize) reconnaître; ~ **how to do** savoir faire; ~ **about** (*event*) être au courant de; (*subject*) s'y connaître en; ~ **of** (from experience) connaître; (from information) avoir entendu parler de. ~**-how** *n* savoir-faire *m inv*.

knowingly *adv* (intentionally) délibérément; (meaningfully) d'un air entendu.

knowledge *n* connaissance *f*; (learning) connaissances *fpl*. **knowledgeable** *a* savant.

knuckle *n* jointure *f*, articulation *f*.

Koran *n* Coran *m*.

Korea *n* Corée *f*.

kosher *a* casher *inv*.

lab *n* [!] labo *m*.

label *n* étiquette *f*. ● *vt* (*pt* **labelled**) étiqueter.

laboratory *n* laboratoire *m*.

laborious *a* laborieux.

labour, (US) **labor** *n* travail *m*; (workers) main-d'œuvre *f*; **in** ~ en train d'accoucher. ● *vi* peiner (**to do** à faire). ● *vt* trop insister sur.

Labour *n* le parti travailliste. ● *a* travailliste.

laboured *a* laborieux.

labourer *n* ouvrier/-ière *m/f*; (on farm) ouvrier/-ière *m/f* agricole.

lace *n* dentelle *f*; (of shoe) lacet *m*. ● *vt* (*shoe*) lacer; (*drink*) arroser.

lacerate *vt* lacérer.

lack *n* manque *m*; **for ~ of** faute de. ● *vt* manquer de; **be ~ing** manquer (**in** de).

lad *n* garçon *m*, gars *m*.

ladder *n* échelle *f*; (in stocking) maille *f* filée. ● *vt/i* (*stocking*) filer.

laden *a* chargé (**with** de).

ladle *n* louche *f*.

lady *n* (*pl* **ladies**) dame *f*; **ladies and gentlemen** mesdames et messieurs; **young ~** jeune femme *or* fille *f*. **~bird** *n* coccinelle *f*.

ladylike *a* distingué.

lag *vi* (*pt* **lagged**) traîner. ● *vt* (*pipes*) calorifuger. ● *n* (interval) décalage *m*.

lager *n* bière *f* blonde.

lagoon *n* lagune *f*.

laid ⇒LAY[1]. **~ back** *a* décontracté.

lain ⇒LIE[2].

lake *n* lac *m*.

lamb *n* agneau *m*; **leg of ~** gigot *m* d'agneau.

lame *a* boiteux.

lament *n* lamentation *f*. ● *vt/i* se lamenter (sur).

laminated *a* laminé.

lamp *n* lampe *f*. **~post** *n* réverbère *m*. **~shade** *n* abat-jour *m inv*.

lance *vt* (Med) inciser.

land *n* terre *f*; (plot) terrain *m*; (country) pays *m*. ● *a* terrestre; (*policy, reform*) agraire. ● *vt/i* débarquer; (*aircraft*) (se) poser, (faire) atterrir; (fall) tomber; (obtain) décrocher; (*a blow*) porter; **~ up** se retrouver.

landing *n* débarquement *m*; (Aviat) atterrissage *m*; (top of stairs) palier *m*. **~-stage** *n* débarcadère *m*.

land: **~lady** *n* propriétaire *f*; (of pub) patronne *f*. **~lord** *n* propriétaire *m*; (of pub) patron *m*. **~mark** *n* (point de) repère *m*. **~mine** *n* mine *f* terrestre.

landscape *n* paysage *m*. ● *vt* aménager.

landslide *n* glissement *m* de terrain; (Pol) raz-de-marée *m inv* (électoral).

lane *n* (path, road) chemin *m*; (strip of road) voie *f*; (of traffic) file *f*; (Aviat) couloir *m*.

language *n* langue *f*; (speech, style) langage *m*. **~ engineering** *n* ingénierie *f* des langues. **~ laboratory** *n* laboratoire *m* de langue.

lank *a* (*hair*) plat.

lanky *a* (**-ier**, **-iest**) grand et maigre.

lantern *n* lanterne *f*.

lap *n* genoux *mpl*; (Sport) tour *m* (de piste). ● *vi* (*pt* **lapped**) (*waves*) clapoter. □ **~ up** laper.

lapel *n* revers *m*.

lapse *vi* (decline) se dégrader; (expire) se périmer; **~ into** retomber dans. ● *n* défaillance *f*, erreur *f*; (of time) intervalle *m*.

laptop *n* (Comput) portable *m*.

lard *n* saindoux *m*.

larder *n* garde-manger *m inv*.

large *a* grand, gros; **at ~** en liberté; **by and ~** en général. **largely** *adv* en grande mesure.

lark *n* (bird) alouette *f*; (bit of fun Ⓘ) rigolade *f*. ● *vi* Ⓘ rigoler.

larva *n* (*pl* **-vae**) larve *f*.

laryngitis *n* laryngite *f*.

laser *n* laser *m*. **~ printer** *n*

L

imprimante *f* laser. ~ **treatment** *n* (Med) laserothérapie *f*.

lash *vt* fouetter. ● *n* coup *m* de fouet; (eyelash) cil *m*. □ ~ **out** (spend) dépenser follement; ~ **out against** attaquer.

lass *n* jeune fille *f*.

lasso *n* lasso *m*.

last *a* dernier; **the ~ straw** le comble; **the ~ word** le mot de la fin; **on its ~ legs** sur le point de rendre l'âme; ~ **night** hier soir. ● *adv* en dernier; (most recently) la dernière fois. ● *n* dernier/-ière *m/f*; (remainder) reste *m*; **at (long) ~** enfin. ● *vi* durer. **~-ditch** *a* ultime. **lasting** *a* durable. **lastly** *adv* en dernier lieu. **~-minute** *a* de dernière minute.

latch *n* loquet *m*.

late *a* (not on time) en retard; (former) ancien; (*hour, fruit*) tardif; **the ~ Mrs X** feu Mme X. ● *adv* (not early) tard; (not on time) en retard; **in ~ July** fin juillet; **of ~** dernièrement. **lately** *adv* dernièrement. **latest** *a* ⇒LATE; (last) dernier.

lathe *n* tour *m*.

lather *n* mousse *f*. ● *vt* savonner. ● *vi* mousser.

Latin *n* (Ling) latin *m*. ● *a* latin. ~ **America** *n* Amérique *f* latine.

latitude *n* latitude *f*.

latter *a* dernier. ● *n* **the ~** celui-ci, celle-ci.

Latvia *n* Lettonie *f*.

laudable *a* louable.

laugh *vi* rire (**at** de). ● *n* rire *m*. **laughable** *a* ridicule.

laughing stock *n* risée *f*.

laughter *n* (act) rire *m*; (sound of laughs) rires *mpl*.

launch *vt* (*rocket*) lancer; (*boat*) mettre à l'eau; ~ **(out) into** se lancer dans. ● *n* lancement *m*; (boat) vedette *f*. **launching pad** *n* aire *f* de lancement.

launderette *n* laverie *f* automatique.

laundry *n* (place) blanchisserie *f*; (clothes) linge *m*.

laurel *n* laurier *m*.

lava *n* lave *f*.

lavatory *n* toilettes *fpl*.

lavender *n* lavande *f*.

lavish *a* (*person*) généreux; (lush) somptueux. ● *vt* prodiguer (**on** à). **lavishly** *adv* luxueusement.

law *n* loi *f*; (profession, subject of study) droit *m*; ~ **and order** l'ordre public. **~-abiding** *a* respectueux des lois. **~court** *n* tribunal *m*.

lawful *a* légal.

lawn *n* pelouse *f*, gazon *m*. **~-mower** *n* tondeuse *f* à gazon.

lawsuit *n* procès *m*.

lawyer *n* avocat *m*.

lax *a* (*government*) laxiste; (*security*) relâché.

laxative *n* laxatif *m*.

lay[1] *a* (non-clerical) laïque; (*worker*) non-initié. ● *vt* (*pt* **laid**) poser, mettre; (*trap*) tendre; (*table*) mettre; (*plan*) former; (*eggs*) pondre. ● *vi* pondre; ~ **waste** ravager. □ ~ **aside** mettre de côté; ~ **down** (dé)poser; (condition) (im-)poser; ~ **off** *vt* (*worker*) licencier; *vi* ▣ arrêter; ~ **on** (provide) fournir; ~ **out** (design) dessiner; (display) disposer; (*money*) dépenser.

lay[2] ⇒LIE[2].

lay-by *n* (*pl* **~s**) aire *f* de repos.

layer *n* couche *f*.

layman *n* (*pl* **-men**) profane *m*.

layout *n* disposition *f*.

laze *vi* paresser. **laziness** *n* paresse *f*. **lazy** *a* (**-ier, -iest**) paresseux.

lead[1] *vt/i* (*pt* **led**) mener; (*team*) diriger; (*life*) mener; (induce) amener; ~ **to** conduire à, mener à. ● *n* avance *f*; (clue) indice *m*;

(leash) laisse *f*; (Theat) premier rôle *m*; (wire) fil *m*; **in the ~** en tête. □ **~ away** emmener; **~ up to** (come to) en venir à; (precede) précéder.

lead² *n* plomb *m*; (of pencil) mine *f*.

leader *n* chef *m*; (of country, club) dirigeant/-e *m/f*; (leading article) éditorial *m*. **leadership** *n* direction *f*.

lead-free *a* (*petrol*) sans plomb.

leading *a* principal.

leaf *n* (*pl* **leaves**) feuille *f*; (of table) rallonge *f*. ● *vi* **~ through** feuilleter.

leaflet *n* prospectus *m*.

leafy *a* feuillu.

league *n* ligue *f*; (Sport) championnat *m*; **in ~ with** de mèche avec.

leak *n* fuite *f*. ● *vi* fuir; (news: fig) s'ébruiter. ● *vt* répandre; (fig) divulguer.

lean¹ *a* maigre. ● *n* (of meat) maigre *m*.

lean² *vt/i* (*pt* **leaned** *or* **leant**) (rest) (s')appuyer; (slope) pencher. □ **~ out** se pencher à l'extérieur; **~ over** (of person) se pencher.

leaning *a* penché. ● *n* tendance *f*.

leap *vi* (*pt* **leaped** *or* **leapt**) bondir. ● *n* bond *m*. **~ year** *n* année *f* bissextile.

learn *vt/i* (*pt* **learned** *or* **learnt**) apprendre (**to do** à faire). **learned** *a* érudit. **learner** *n* débutant/-e *m/f*.

lease *n* bail *m*. ● *vt* louer à bail.

leash *n* laisse *f*.

least *a* **the ~** (smallest amount of) le moins de; (slightest) le *or* la moindre. ● *n* le moins. ● *adv* le moins; (with adjective) le *or* la moins; **at ~** au moins.

leather *n* cuir *m*.

leave *vt* (*pt* **left**) laisser; (depart from) quitter; (*person*) laisser tranquille; **be left** (**over**) rester. ● *n* (holiday) congé *m*; (consent) permission *f*; **take one's ~** prendre congé (**of** de); **on ~** (Mil) en permission. □ **~ alone** (*thing*) ne pas toucher; (*person*) laisser tranquille; **~ behind** laisser; **~ out** omettre.

Lebanon *n* Liban *m*.

lecture *n* cours *m*, conférence *f*; (rebuke) réprimande *f*. ● *vt/i* faire un cours *or* une conférence (à); (rebuke) réprimander. **lecturer** *n* conférencier/-ière *m/f*; (Univ) enseignant/-e *m/f*.

led ⇒LEAD¹.

ledge *n* (window) rebord *m*; (rock) saillie *f*.

ledger *n* grand livre *m*.

leech *n* sangsue *f*.

leek *n* poireau *m*.

leer *vi* **~** (**at**) lorgner. ● *n* regard *m* sournois.

leeway *n* (fig) liberté *f* d'action; (Naut) dérive *f*.

left ⇒LEAVE. ● *a* gauche. ● *adv* à gauche. ● *n* gauche *f*. **~-hand** *a* à *or* de gauche. **~-handed** *a* gaucher.

left luggage (**office**) *n* consigne *f*.

left-overs *npl* restes *mpl*.

left-wing *a* de gauche.

leg *n* jambe *f*; (of animal) patte *f*; (of table) pied *m*; (of chicken) cuisse *f*; (of lamb) gigot *m*; (of journey) étape *f*.

legacy *n* legs *m*.

legal *a* légal; (affairs) juridique.

legend *n* légende *f*.

leggings *npl* (for woman) caleçon *m*.

legible *a* lisible.

legionnaire *n* légionnaire *m*.

legislation *n* (body of laws) législation *f*; (law) loi *f*. **legislature** *n* corps *m* législatif.

L

legitimate *a* légitime.

leisure *n* loisirs *mpl*; **at one's ~** à tête reposée. ● *a* (*centre*) de loisirs.

leisurely *a* lent. ● *adv* sans se presser.

lemon *n* citron *m*.

lemonade *n* (fizzy) limonade *f*; (still) citronnade *f*.

lend *vt* (*pt* **lent**) prêter; (*credibility*) conférer; **~ itself to** se prêter à.

length *n* longueur *f*; (in time) durée *f*; (section) morceau *m*; **at ~** (at last) enfin; **at (great) ~** longuement.

lengthen *vt/i* (s')allonger.

lengthways *adv* dans le sens de la longueur.

lengthy *a* long.

lenient *a* indulgent.

lens *n* lentille *f*; (of spectacles) verre *m*; (Photo) objectif *m*.

lent ⇒LEND.

Lent *n* Carême *m*.

lentil *n* lentille *f*.

Leo *n* Lion *m*.

leopard *n* léopard *m*.

leotard *n* body *m*.

leprosy *n* lèpre *f*.

lesbian *n* lesbienne *f*. ● *a* lesbien.

less *a* (in quantity) moins de (**than** que). ● *adv, n & prep* moins; **~ than** (with numbers) moins de; **work ~ than** travailler moins que; **ten pounds ~** dix livres de moins; **~ and ~** de moins en moins. **lessen** *vt/i* diminuer. **lesser** *a* moindre.

lesson *n* leçon *f*.

let *vt* (*pt* **let**; *pres p* **letting**) laisser; (lease) louer. ● *v aux* **~ us do, ~'s do** faisons; **~ him do** qu'il fasse; **~ me know the results** informe-moi des résultats. ● *n* location *f*. □ **~ down** baisser; (deflate) dégonfler; (fig) décevoir; **~ go** *vt* lâcher; *vi* lâcher prise; **~ sb in/out** laisser *or* faire entrer/sortir qn; **~ a dress out** élargir une robe; **~ oneself in for** (*task*) s'engager à; (*trouble*) s'attirer; **~ off** (explode, fire) faire éclater *or* partir; (excuse) dispenser; (not punish) ne pas punir; **~ up** [!] s'arrêter.

let-down *n* déception *f*.

lethal *a* mortel; (weapon) meurtrier.

letter *n* lettre *f*. **~-bomb** *n* lettre *f* piégée. **~-box** *n* boîte *f* à *or* aux lettres.

lettering *n* (letters) caractères *mpl*.

lettuce *n* laitue *f*, salade *f*.

let-up *n* répit *m*.

leukaemia *n* leucémie *f*.

level *a* plat, uni; (on surface) horizontal; (in height) au même niveau (**with** que); (in score) à égalité. ● *n* niveau *m*; (**spirit**) **~** niveau *m* à bulle; **be on the ~** [!] être franc. ● *vt* (*pt* **levelled**) niveler; (aim) diriger. **~ crossing** *n* passage *m* à niveau. **~-headed** *a* équilibré.

lever *n* levier *m*. ● *vt* soulever au moyen d'un levier.

leverage *n* influence *f*.

levy *vt* (*tax*) prélever. ● *n* impôt *m*.

lexicon *n* lexique *m*.

liability *n* responsabilité *f*; [!] handicap *m*; **liabilities** (debts) dettes *fpl*.

liable *a* **be ~ to do** avoir tendance à faire, pouvoir faire; **~ to** (illness) sujet à; (fine) passible de; **~ for** responsable de.

liaise *vi* [!] faire la liaison. **liaison** *n* liaison *f*.

liar *n* menteur/-euse *m/f*.

libel *n* diffamation *f*. ● *vt* (*pt* **libelled**) diffamer.

liberal *a* libéral; (generous) généreux, libéral.
Liberal *a & n* (Pol) libéral/-e (*m*/*f*).
liberate *vt* libérer.
liberty *n* liberté *f*; **at ~ to** libre de; **take liberties** prendre des libertés.
Libra *n* Balance *f*.
librarian *n* bibliothécaire *mf*.
library *n* bibliothèque *f*.
libretto *n* livret *m*.
lice ⇒LOUSE.
licence, (US) **license** *n* permis *m*; (for television) redevance *f*; (Comm) licence *f*; (liberty: fig) licence *f*. **~ plate** *n* plaque *f* minéralogique.
license *vt* accorder un permis à, autoriser.
lick *vt* lécher; (defeat ▯) rosser; (fig) **a ~ of paint** un petit coup de peinture. ● *n* coup *m* de langue.
lid *n* couvercle *m*.
lie[1] *n* mensonge *m*. ● *vi* (*pt* **lied**; *pres p* **lying**) (tell lies) mentir.
lie[2] *vi* (*pt* **lay**; *pp* **lain**; *pres p* **lying**) s'allonger; (remain) rester; (be) se trouver, être; (in grave) reposer; **be lying** être allongé. □ **~ down** s'allonger; **~ in** faire la grasse matinée; **~ low** se cacher.
lieutenant *n* lieutenant *m*.
life *n* (*pl* **lives**) vie *f*. **~belt** *n* bouée *f* de sauvetage. **~boat** *n* canot *m* de sauvetage. **~buoy** *n* bouée *f* de sauvetage. **~ cycle** *n* cycle *m* de vie. **~-guard** *n* sauveteur *m*. **~ insurance** *n* assurance-vie *f*. **~-jacket** *n* gilet *m* de sauvetage.
lifeless *a* inanimé.
lifelike *a* très ressemblant.
life: **~long** *a* de toute la vie. **~ sentence** *n* condamnation *f* à perpétuité. **~-size(d)** *a* grandeur nature *inv*. **~ story** *n* vie *f*. **~-style** *n* style *m* de vie. **~ support machine** *n* appareil *m* de respiration artificielle.
lifetime *n* vie *f*; **in one's ~** de son vivant.
lift *vt* lever; (steal ▯) voler. ● *vi* (of fog) se lever. ● *n* (in building) ascenseur *m*; **give a ~ to** emmener (en voiture). **~-off** *n* (Aviat) décollage *m*.
light *n* lumière *f*; (lamp) lampe *f*; (for fire, on vehicle) feu *m*; (headlight) phare *m*; **bring to ~** révéler; **come to ~** être révélé; **have you got a ~?** vous avez du feu? ● *a* (not dark) clair; (not heavy) léger. ● *vt* (*pt* **lit** *or* **lighted**) allumer; (*room*) éclairer; (*match*) frotter. □ **~ up** *vi* s'allumer; *vt* (*room*) éclairer. **~ bulb** *n* ampoule *f*.
lighten *vt* (give light to) éclairer; (make brighter) éclaircir; (make less heavy) alléger.
lighter *n* briquet *m*; (for stove) allume-gaz *m inv*.
light: **~-headed** *a* (dizzy) qui a un vertige; (frivolous) étourdi. **~-hearted** *a* gai. **~house** *n* phare *m*.
lighting *n* éclairage *m*.
lightly *adv* légèrement.
lightning *n* éclair *m*, foudre *f*. ● *a* (*visit*) éclair *inv*.
lightweight *a* léger. ● *n* (boxing) poids *m* léger.
light-year *n* année *f* lumière.
like[1] *a* semblable, pareil; **be ~-minded** avoir les mêmes sentiments. ● *prep* comme. ● *conj* ▯ comme. ● *n* pareil *m*; **the ~s of you** les gens comme vous.
like[2] *vt* aimer (bien); **I should ~** je voudrais, j'aimerais; **would you ~?** voudriez-vous?, voudrais-tu?; **~s** goûts *mpl*. **likeable** *a* sympathique.
likelihood *n* probabilité *f*.

L

likely *a* (**-ier**, **-iest**) probable. ● *adv* probablement; **he is ~ to do** il fera probablement; **not ~!** 🅸 pas question!
likeness *n* ressemblance *f*.
likewise *adv* également.
liking *n* (for thing) penchant *m*; (for person) affection *f*.
lilac *n* lilas *m*. ● *a* lilas *inv*.
Lilo® *n* matelas *m* pneumatique.
lily *n* lis *m*, lys *m*. **~ of the valley** *n* muguet *m*.
limb *n* membre *m*.
limber *vi* **~ up** faire des exercices d'assouplissement.
limbo *n* **be in ~** (forgotten) être tombé dans l'oubli.
lime *n* (fruit) citron *m* vert; **~(-tree)** tilleul *m*.
limelight *n* **in the ~** en vedette.
limestone *n* calcaire *m*.
limit *n* limite *f*. ● *vt* limiter.
limited company *n* société *f* anonyme.
limp *vi* boiter. ● *n* **have a ~** boiter. ● *a* mou.
line *n* ligne *f*; (track) voie *f*; (wrinkle) ride *f*; (row) rangée *f*, file *f*; (of poem) vers *m*; (rope) corde *f*; (of goods) gamme *f*; (queue: US) queue *f*; **be in ~ for** avoir de bonnes chances de; **hold the ~** ne quittez pas; **in ~ with** en accord avec; **stand in ~** faire la queue. ● *vt* (*paper*) régler; (*streets*) border; (*garment*) doubler; (fill) remplir, garnir. □ **~ up** (s')aligner; (in queue) faire la queue; **~ sth up** prévoir qch.
linen *n* (sheets) linge *m*; (material) lin *m*.
liner *n* paquebot *m*.
linesman *n* (football) juge *m* de touche; (tennis) juge *m* de ligne.
linger *vi* s'attarder; (smells) persister.
linguist *n* linguiste *mf*. **linguistics** *n* linguistique *f*.
lining *n* doublure *f*.
link *n* lien *m*; (of chain) maillon *m*. ● *vt* relier; (relate) (re)lier; **~ up** (of roads) se rejoindre. **linkage** *n* lien *m*. **links** *n inv* terrain *m* de golf. **~-up** *n* liaison *f*.
lino *n* lino *m*.
lion *n* lion *m*. **lioness** *n* lionne *f*.
lip *n* lèvre *f*; (edge) rebord *m*; **pay ~-service to** n'approuver que pour la forme. **~-read** *vt/i* lire sur les lèvres. **~salve** *n* baume *m* pour les lèvres. **~stick** *n* rouge *m* (à lèvres).
liquid *n & a* liquide (*m*).
liquidation *n* liquidation *f*; **go into ~** déposer son bilan.
liquidize *vt* passer au mixeur. **liquidizer** *n* mixeur *m*.
liquor *n* alcool *m*.
liquorice *n* réglisse *f*.
lisp *n* zézaiement *m*; **with a ~** en zézayant. ● *vi* zézayer.
list *n* liste *f*. ● *vt* dresser la liste de. ● *vi* (*ship*) gîter.
listen *vi* écouter; **~ to**, **~ in (to)** écouter. **listener** *n* auditeur/-trice *m/f*.
listless *a* apathique.
lit ⇨LIGHT.
liter ⇨LITRE.
literal *a* (*meaning*) littéral; (*translation*) mot à mot. **literally** *adv* littéralement; mot à mot.
literary *a* littéraire.
literate *a* qui sait lire et écrire.
literature *n* littérature *f*; (brochures) documentation *f*.
Lithuania *n* Lituanie *f*.
litigation *n* litiges *mpl*.
litre, (US) **liter** *n* litre *m*.
litter *n* (rubbish) détritus *mpl*, papiers *mpl*; (animals) portée *f*. ● *vt* éparpiller; (make untidy) laisser

des détritus dans; **~ed with** jonché de. **~-bin** *n* poubelle *f*.

little *a* petit; (not much) peu de. ● *n* peu *m*; **a ~** un peu (de). ● *adv* peu.

live[1] *a* vivant; (*wire*) sous tension; (*broadcast*) en direct; **be a ~ wire** être très dynamique.

live[2] *vt/i* vivre; (reside) habiter, vivre; **~ it up** mener la belle vie. □ **~ down** faire oublier; **~ on** (feed oneself on) vivre de; (continue) survivre; **~ up to** se montrer à la hauteur de.

livelihood *n* moyens *mpl* d'existence.

lively *a* (**-ier, -iest**) vif, vivant.

liven *vt/i* **~ up** (s')animer; (cheer up) (s')égayer.

liver *n* foie *m*.

livestock *n* bétail *m*.

livid *a* livide; (angry) furieux.

living *a* vivant. ● *n* vie *f*; **make a ~** gagner sa vie; **~ conditions** conditions *fpl* de vie. **~-room** *n* salle *f* de séjour.

lizard *n* lézard *m*.

load *n* charge *f*; (loaded goods) chargement *m*, charge *f*; (weight, strain) poids *m*; **~s of** ⊡ des tas de ⊡. ● *vt* charger.

loaf *n* (*pl* **loaves**) pain *m*. ● *vi* **~** (**about**) fainéanter.

loan *n* prêt *m*; (money borrowed) emprunt *m*. ● *vt* prêter.

loathe *vt* détester (**doing** faire). **loathing** *n* dégoût *m*.

lobby *n* entrée *f*, vestibule *m*; (Pol) lobby *m*, groupe *m* de pression. ● *vt* faire pression sur.

lobster *n* homard *m*.

local *a* local; (*shops*) du quartier; **~ government** administration *f* locale. ● *n* personne *f* du coin; (pub ⊡) pub *m* du coin.

locally *adv* localement; (nearby) dans les environs.

locate *vt* (situate) situer; (find) repérer.

location *n* emplacement *m*; **on ~** (cinema) en extérieur.

lock *n* (of door) serrure *f*; (on canal) écluse *f*; (of hair) mèche *f*. ● *vt/i* fermer à clef; (wheels: Auto) (se) bloquer. □ **~ in** *or* **up** (*person*) enfermer; **~ out** (by mistake) enfermer dehors.

locker *n* casier *m*.

locket *n* médaillon *m*.

locksmith *n* serrurier *m*.

locum *n* (doctor) remplaçant/-e *m/f*.

lodge *n* (house) pavillon *m* (de gardien *or* de chasse); (of porter) loge *f*. ● *vt* (accommodate) loger; (*money, complaint*) déposer. ● *vi* être logé (**with** chez); (become fixed) se loger. **lodger** *n* locataire *mf*, pensionnaire *mf*. **lodgings** *n* logement *m*.

loft *n* grenier *m*.

lofty *a* (**-ier, -iest**) (tall, noble) élevé; (haughty) hautain.

log *n* (of wood) bûche *f*; **~(-book)** (Naut) journal *m* de bord; (Auto) ≈ carte *f* grise. ● *vt* (*pt* **logged**) noter; (distance) parcourir. □ **~ on** (Comput) se connecter; **~ off** (Comput) se déconnecter.

logic *a* logique. **logical** *a* logique.

logistics *n* logistique *f*.

loin *n* (Culin) filet *m*; **~s** reins *mpl*.

loiter *vi* traîner.

loll *vi* se prélasser.

lollipop *n* sucette *f*.

London *n* Londres. **Londoner** *n* Londonien/-ne *m/f*.

lone *a* solitaire.

lonely (**-ier, -iest**) solitaire; (person) seul, solitaire.

long *a* long; **how ~ is?** quelle est la longueur de?; (in time) quelle est la durée de?; **how ~?** combien de temps?; **a ~ time**

L

longtemps. ● *adv* longtemps; **he will not be ~** il n'en a pas pour longtemps; **as** *or* **so ~ as** pourvu que; **before ~** avant peu; **I no ~er do** je ne fais plus. ● *vi* avoir bien *or* très envie (**for, to** de); **~ for sb** (pine for) se languir de qn. **~-distance** *a* (*flight*) sur long parcours; (*phone call*) interurbain; (*runner*) de fond. **~ face** *n* grimace *f*. **~hand** *n* écriture *f* courante.

longing *n* envie *f* (**for** de); (nostalgia) nostalgie *f* (**for** de).

longitude *n* longitude *f*.

long: **~ jump** *n* saut *m* en longueur. **~-range** *a* (*missile*) à longue portée; (*forecast*) à long terme. **~-sighted** *a* presbyte. **~-standing** *a* de longue date. **~-term** *a* à long terme. **~ wave** *n* grandes ondes *fpl*. **~-winded** *a* verbeux.

loo *n* 🅸 toilettes *fpl*.

look *vi* regarder; (seem) avoir l'air; **~ like** ressembler à, avoir l'air de. ● *n* regard *m*; (appearance) air *m*, aspect *m*; (**good**) **~s** beauté *f*. □ **~ after** s'occuper de, soigner; **~ at** regarder; **~ back on** repenser à; **~ down on** mépriser; **~ for** chercher; **~ forward to** attendre avec impatience; **~ in on** passer voir; **~ into** examiner; **~ out** faire attention; **~ out for** (*person*) guetter; (*symptoms*) guetter l'apparition de; **~ round** se retourner; **~ up** (*word*) chercher; (visit) passer voir; **~ up to** respecter.

look-out *n* (Mil) poste *m* de guet; (person) guetteur *m*; **be on the ~ for** rechercher.

loom *vi* surgir; (*war*) menacer; (*interview*) être imminent. ● *n* métier *m* à tisser.

loony *n* & *a* 🅸 fou, folle (*mf*).

loop *n* boucle *f*. ● *vt* boucler. **~hole** *n* lacune *f*.

loose *a* (*knot*) desserré; (*page*) détaché; (*clothes*) ample, lâche; (*tooth*) qui bouge; (lax) relâché; (not packed) en vrac; (inexact) vague; (pej) immoral; **at a ~ end** désœuvré; **come ~** bouger. **loosely** *adv* sans serrer; (roughly) vaguement. **loosen** *vt* (slacken) desserrer; (untie) défaire.

loot *n* butin *m*. ● *vt* piller.

lord *n* seigneur *m*; (British title) lord *m*; **the L~** le Seigneur; (**good**) **L~!** mon Dieu!

lorry *n* camion *m*.

lose *vt/i* (*pt* **lost**) perdre; **get lost** se perdre. **loser** *n* perdant/-e *m/f*.

loss *n* perte *f*; **be at a ~** être perplexe; **be at a ~ to** être incapable de; **heat ~** déperdition *f* de chaleur.

lost ⇒LOSE. ● *a* perdu. **~ property** *n* objets *mpl* trouvés.

lot *n* **the ~** (le) tout *m*; (people) tous *mpl*, toutes *fpl*; **a ~** (**of**), **~s** (**of**) 🅸 beaucoup (de); **quite a ~** (**of**) 🅸 pas mal (de); (fate) sort *m*; (at auction) lot *m*; (land) lotissement *m*.

lotion *n* lotion *f*.

lottery *n* loterie *f*.

loud *a* bruyant, fort. ● *adv* fort; **out ~** tout haut. **loudly** *adv* fort. **~speaker** *n* haut-parleur *m*.

lounge *vi* paresser. ● *n* salon *m*.

louse *n* (*pl* **lice**) pou *m*.

lousy *a* (**-ier, -iest**) 🅸 infect.

lout *n* rustre *m*.

lovable *a* adorable.

love *n* amour *m*; (tennis) zéro *m*; **in ~** amoureux (**with** de); **make ~** faire l'amour. ● *vt* (*person*) aimer; (like greatly) aimer (beaucoup) (**to do** faire). **~ affair** *n* liaison *f* amoureuse. **~ life** *n* vie *f* amoureuse.

lovely *a* (**-ier**, **-iest**) joli; (delightful [!]) très agréable.

lover *n* (male) amant *m*; (female) maîtresse *f*; (devotee) amateur *m* (**of** de).

loving *a* affectueux.

low *a & adv* bas; **~ in sth** à faible teneur en qch. ● *n* (low pressure) dépression *f*; **reach a (new) ~** atteindre son niveau le plus bas. ● *vi* meugler. **~-calorie** *a* basses calories. **~-cut** *a* décolleté.

lower *a & adv* ⇒LOW. ● *vt* baisser; **~ oneself** s'abaisser.

low: **~-fat** *a* (*diet*) sans matières grasses; (*cheese*) allégé. **~-key** *a* modéré; (discreet) discret. **~lands** *npl* plaine(s) *f(pl)*. **~-lying** *a* à faible altitude.

loyal *a* loyal (**to** envers).

lozenge *n* (shape) losange *m*; (tablet) pastille *f*.

LP *n* (disque *m*) 33 tours *m*.

Ltd. *abbr* (**Limited**) SA.

lubricant *n* lubrifiant *m*. **lubricate** *vt* lubrifier.

luck *n* chance *f*; **bad ~** malchance *f*; **good ~!** bonne chance!

luckily *adv* heureusement.

lucky *a* (**-ier**, **-iest**) qui a de la chance, heureux; (event) heureux; (number) qui porte bonheur; **it's ~ that** heureusement que.

ludicrous *a* ridicule.

lug *vt* (*pt* **lugged**) traîner.

luggage *n* bagages *mpl*. **~-rack** *n* porte-bagages *m inv*.

lukewarm *a* tiède.

lull *vt* **he ~ed them into thinking that** il leur a fait croire que. ● *n* accalmie *f*.

lullaby *n* berceuse *f*.

lumber *n* bois *m* de charpente. ● *vt* [!] **~ sb with** (*chore*) coller à qn [!]. **~jack** *n* bûcheron *m*.

luminous *a* lumineux.

lump *n* morceau *m*; (swelling on body) grosseur *f*; (in liquid) grumeau *m*. ● *vt* **~ together** réunir. **~ sum** *n* somme *f* globale.

lunacy *n* folie *f*.

lunar *a* lunaire.

lunatic *n* fou/ folle *m/f*.

lunch *n* déjeuner *m*. ● *vi* déjeuner.

luncheon *n* déjeuner *m*. **~ voucher** *n* chèque-repas *m*.

lung *n* poumon *m*.

lunge *vi* bondir (**at** sur; **forward** en avant).

lurch *n* **leave in the ~** planter là, laisser en plan. ● *vi* (*person*) tituber.

lure *vt* appâter, attirer. ● *n* (attraction) attrait *m*, appât *m*.

lurid *a* choquant, affreux; (gaudy) voyant.

lurk *vi* se cacher; (in ambush) s'embusquer; (prowl) rôder; (*suspicion, danger*) menacer.

luscious *a* appétissant.

lush *a* luxuriant. ● *n* (US, [!]) ivrogne/-esse *m/f*.

lust *n* luxure *f*. ● *vi* **~ after** convoiter.

Luxemburg *n* Luxembourg *m*.

luxurious *a* luxueux.

luxury *n* luxe *m*. ● *a* de luxe.

lying ⇒LIE¹, LIE². ● *n* mensonges *mpl*.

lyric *a* lyrique. **lyrical** *a* lyrique. **lyrics** *npl* paroles *fpl*.

MA *abbr* ⇒MASTER OF ARTS.
mac *n* 🅸 imper *m*.
machine *n* machine *f*. ● *vt* (sew) coudre à la machine; (Tech) usiner. **~-gun** *n* mitrailleuse *f*.
mackerel *n inv* maquereau *m*.
mackintosh *n* imperméable *m*.
mad *a* (**madder**, **maddest**) fou; (foolish) insensé; (*dog*) enragé; (angry 🅸) furieux; **be ~ about** se passionner pour; (*person*) être fou de; **drive sb ~** exaspérer qn; **like ~** comme un fou.
madam *n* madame *f*; (unmarried) mademoiselle *f*.
made ⇒MAKE.
madly *adv* (*interested, in love*) follement; (frantically) comme un fou.
madman *n* (*pl* **-men**) fou *m*.
madness *n* folie *f*.
magazine *n* revue *f*, magazine *m*; (of gun) magasin *m*.
maggot *n* (in fruit) ver *m*, (for fishing) asticot *m*.
magic *n* magie *f*. ● *a* magique.
magician *n* magicien/-ne *m*/*f*.
magistrate *n* magistrat *m*.
magnet *n* aimant *m*. **magnetic** *a* magnétique.
magnificent *a* magnifique.
magnify *vt* grossir; (*sound*) amplifier; (fig) exagérer. **magnifying glass** *n* loupe *f*.
magpie *n* pie *f*.
mahogany *n* acajou *m*.
maid *n* (servant) bonne *f*; (in hotel) femme *f* de chambre.
maiden *n* (old use) jeune fille *f*. ● *a* (*aunt*) célibataire; (*voyage*) premier. **~ name** *n* nom *m* de jeune fille.
mail *n* (postal service) poste *f*; (letters) courrier *m*; (armour) cotte *f* de mailles. ● *a* (*bag, van*) postal. ● *vt* envoyer par la poste. **~ box** *n* boîte *f* aux lettres; (Comput) boîte *f* aux lettres électronique. **mailing list** *n* liste *f* d'adresses. **~man** *n* (*pl* **-men**) (US) facteur *m*. **~ order** *n* vente *f* par correspondance. **~ shot** *n* publipostage *m*.
main *a* principal; **a ~ road** une grande route. ● *n* (**water/gas**) **~** conduite *f* d'eau/de gaz; **the ~s** (Electr) le secteur; **in the ~** en général. **~frame** *n* unité *f* centrale. **~land** *n* continent *m*. **~stream** *n* tendance *f* principale, ligne *f*.
maintain *vt* (continue, keep, assert) maintenir; (*house, machine, family*) entretenir; (*rights*) soutenir.
maintenance *n* (care) entretien *m*; (continuation) maintien *m*; (allowance) pension *f* alimentaire.
maisonette *n* duplex *m*.
maize *n* maïs *m*.
majestic *a* majestueux.
majesty *n* majesté *f*.
major *a* majeur. ● *n* commandant *m*. ● *vi* **~ in** (Univ, US) se spécialiser en.
majority *n* majorité *f*; **the ~ of people** la plupart des gens. ● *a* majoritaire.
make *vt*/*i* (*pt* **made**) faire; (manufacture) fabriquer; (*friends*) se faire; (*money*) gagner; (*decision*) prendre; (*place, position*) arriver à; (cause to be) rendre; **~ sb do sth** faire faire qch à qn; (force) obliger qn à faire qch; **be made of** être fait de; **~ oneself at home** se

mettre à l'aise; **~ sb happy** rendre qn heureux; **~ it** arriver; (succeed) réussir; **I ~ it two o'clock** j'ai deux heures; **I ~ it 150** d'après moi, ça fait 150; **I cannot ~ anything of it** je n'y comprends rien; **can you ~ Friday?** vendredi, c'est possible?; **~ as if to** faire mine de. ● *n* (brand) marque *f*. □ **~ do** (manage) se débrouiller (**with** avec); **~ for** se diriger vers; (cause) tendre à créer; **~ good** *vi* réussir; *vt* compenser; (repair) réparer; **~ off** filer (**with** avec); **~ out** distinguer; (understand) comprendre; (draw up) faire; (assert) prétendre; **~ up** *vt* faire, former; (*story*) inventer; (*deficit*) combler; *vi* se réconcilier; **~ up** (**one's face**) se maquiller; **~ up for** compenser; (*time*) rattraper; **~ up one's mind** se décider; **~ up to** se concilier les bonnes grâces de.

make-believe *a* feint, illusoire. ● *n* fantaisie *f*.

maker *n* fabricant *m*.

makeshift *a* improvisé.

make-up *n* maquillage *m*; (of object) constitution *f*; (Psych) caractère *m*.

malaria *n* paludisme *m*.

Malaysia *n* Malaisie *f*.

male *a* (*voice, sex*) masculin; (Bot, Tech) mâle. ● *n* mâle *m*.

malfunction *n* mauvais fonctionnement *m*. ● *vi* mal fonctionner.

malice *n* méchanceté *f*. **malicious** *a* méchant.

malignant *a* malveillant; (*tumour*) malin.

mall *n* (**shopping**) **~** (in suburbs) centre *m* commercial; (in town) galerie *f* marchande.

malnutrition *n* sous-alimentation *f*.

Malta *n* Malte *f*.

mammal *n* mammifère *m*.

mammoth *n* mammouth *m*. ● *a* (*task*) gigantesque; (*organization*) géant.

man *n* (*pl* **men**) homme *m*; (in sports team) joueur *m*; (chess) pièce *f*; **~ to man** d'homme à homme. ● *vt* (*pt* **manned**) (*desk*) tenir; (*ship*) armer; (*guns*) servir; (be on duty at) être de service à.

manage *vt* (*project, organization*) diriger; (*shop, affairs*) gérer; (handle) manier; **I could ~ another drink** ⊡ je prendrais bien encore un verre; **can you ~ Friday?** vendredi, c'est possible? ● *vi* se débrouiller; **~ to do** réussir à faire. **manageable** *a* (*tool, size, person*) maniable; (*job*) faisable.

management *n* (managers) direction *f*; (of shop) gestion *f*.

manager *n* directeur/-trice *m/f*; (of shop) gérant/-e *m/f*; (of actor) impresario *m*.

mandate *n* mandat *m*.

mandatory *a* obligatoire.

mane *n* crinière *f*.

mango *n* (*pl* **~es**) mangue *f*.

manhandle *vt* maltraiter, malmener.

man: **~hole** *n* regard *m*. **~hood** *n* âge *m* d'homme; (quality) virilité *f*.

maniac *n* maniaque *mf*, fou *m*, folle *f*.

manicure *n* manucure *f*. ● *vt* soigner, manucurer.

manifest *a* manifeste. ● *vt* manifester.

manipulate *vt* (*tool, person*) manipuler.

mankind *n* genre *m* humain.

manly *a* viril.

man-made *a* (*fibre*) synthétique; (*pond*) artificiel; (*disaster*) d'origine humaine.

manned *a* (*spacecraft*) habité.

manner *n* manière *f*; (attitude)

attitude *f*; (kind) sorte *f*; **~s** (social behaviour) manières *fpl*.
mannerism *n* particularité *f*; (quirk) manie *f*.
manoeuvre *n* manœuvre *f*. ● *vt/i* manœuvrer.
manor *n* manoir *m*.
manpower *n* main-d'œuvre *f*.
mansion *n* (in countryside) demeure *f*; (in town) hôtel *m* particulier.
manslaughter *n* homicide *m* involontaire.
mantelpiece *n* (manteau *m* de) cheminée.
manual *a* (*labour*) manuel; (*typewriter*) mécanique. ● *n* (handbook) manuel *m*.
manufacture *vt* fabriquer. ● *n* fabrication *f*.
manure *n* fumier *m*.
many *a & n* beaucoup (de); **a great** *or* **good ~** un grand nombre (de); **~ a** bien des.
map *n* carte *f*; (of streets) plan *m*. ● *vt* (*pt* **mapped**) faire la carte de; **~ out** (*route*) tracer; (arrange) organiser.
mar *vt* (*pt* **marred**) gâcher.
marble *n* marbre *m*; (for game) bille *f*.
March *n* mars *m*.
march *vi* (Mil) marcher (au pas). ● *vt* **~ off** (lead away) emmener. ● *n* marche *f*.
margin *n* marge *f*.
marginal *a* marginal; (*increase*) léger, faible; (*seat*: Pol) disputé.
marinate *vt* faire mariner (**in** dans).
marine *a* marin. ● *n* (shipping) marine *f*; (sailor) fusilier *m* marin.
marital *a* conjugal. **~ status** *n* situation *f* de famille.
mark *n* (currency) mark *m*; (stain) tache *f*; (trace) marque *f*; (School) note *f*; (target) but *m*. ● *vt* marquer; (*exam*) corriger; **~ out** délimiter; (*person*) désigner; **~ time** marquer le pas.
marker *n* (pen) marqueur *m*; (tag) repère *m*; (School, Univ) examinateur/-trice *m/f*.
market *n* marché *m*; **on the ~** en vente. ● *vt* (sell) vendre; (launch) commercialiser. **~ research** *n* étude *f* de marché.
marmalade *n* confiture *f* d'oranges.
maroon *n* bordeaux *m inv*. ● *a* bordeaux *inv*.
marooned *a* abandonné; (snow-bound) bloqué.
marquee *n* grande tente *f*; (of circus) chapiteau *m*; (awning: US) auvent *m*.
marriage *n* mariage *m* (**to** avec).
married *a* marié (**to** à); (life) conjugal; **get ~** se marier (**to** avec).
marrow *n* (of bone) moelle *f*; (vegetable) courge *f*.
marry *vt* épouser; (give or unite in marriage) marier. ● *vi* se marier.
marsh *n* marais *m*.
marshal *n* maréchal *m*; (at event) membre *m* du service d'ordre. ● *vt* (*pt* **marshalled**) rassembler.
martyr *n* martyr/-e *m/f*. ● *vt* martyriser.
marvel *n* merveille *f*. ● *vi* (*pt* **marvelled**) s'émerveiller (**at** de).
marvellous *a* merveilleux.
marzipan *n* pâte *f* d'amandes.
masculine *a & n* masculin (*m*).
mash *n* (potatoes [!]) purée *f*. ● *vt* écraser. **mashed potatoes** *npl* purée *f* (de pommes de terre).
mask *n* masque *m*. ● *vt* masquer.
Mason *n* franc-maçon *m*.
masonry *n* maçonnerie *f*.
mass *n* (Relig) messe *f*; masse *f*; **the ~es** les masses *fpl*. ● *vt/i* (se) masser.

massacre *n* massacre *m*. ● *vt* massacrer.

massage *n* massage *m*. ● *vt* masser.

massive *a* (large) énorme; (heavy) massif.

mass media *n* médias *mpl*.

mass-produce *vt* fabriquer en série.

mast *n* (on ship) mât *m*; (for radio, TV) pylône *m*.

master *n* maître *m*; (in secondary school) professeur *m*; **M~ of Arts** titulaire *mf* d'une maîtrise ès lettres. ● *vt* maîtriser.

masterpiece *n* chef-d'œuvre *m*.

mastery *n* maîtrise *f*.

mat *n* (petit) tapis *m*; (at door) paillasson *m*.

match *n* (for lighting fire) allumette *f*; (Sport) match *m*; (equal) égal/-e *m*/*f*; (marriage) mariage *m*; (sb to marry) parti *m*; **be a ~ for** pouvoir tenir tête à. ● *vt* opposer; (go with) aller avec; (*cups*) assortir; (equal) égaler. ● *vi* (be alike) être assorti. **matchbox** *n* boîte *f* à allumettes.

matching *a* assorti.

mate *n* camarade *mf*; (of animal) compagnon *m*, compagne *f*; (assistant) aide *mf*; (chess) mat *m*. ● *vt*/*i* (s')accoupler (**with** avec).

material *n* matière *f*; (fabric) tissu *m*; (documents, for building) matériau (x) *m*(*pl*); **~s** (equipment) matériel *m*. ● *a* matériel; (fig) important. **materialistic** *a* matérialiste.

materialize *vi* se matérialiser, se réaliser.

maternal *a* maternel.

maternity *n* maternité *f*. ● *a* (*clothes*) de grossesse. **~ hospital** *n* maternité *f*. **~ leave** *n* congé *m* maternité.

mathematics *n* & *npl* mathématiques *fpl*.

maths, (US) **math** *n* maths *fpl*.

mating *n* accouplement *m*.

matrimony *n* mariage *m*.

matron *n* (married, elderly) dame *f* âgée; (in hospital) infirmière *f* en chef.

matt *a* mat.

matter *n* (substance) matière *f*; (affair) affaire *f*; **as a ~ of fact** en fait; **what is the ~?** qu'est-ce qu'il y a? ● *vi* importer; **it does not ~** ça ne fait rien; **no ~ what happens** quoi qu'il arrive.

mattress *n* matelas *m*.

mature *a* (psychologically) mûr; (*plant*) adulte. ● *vt*/*i* (se) mûrir. **maturity** *n* maturité *f*.

mauve *a* & *n* mauve (*m*).

maverick *n* non-conformiste *mf*.

maximize *vt* porter au maximum.

maximum *a* & *n* (*pl* **-ima**) maximum (*m*).

may

past **might**

● *auxiliary verb*

····➤ (possibility) **they ~ be able to come** ils pourront peut-être venir; **she ~ not have seen him** elle ne l'a peut-être pas vu; **it ~ rain** il risque de pleuvoir; **'will you come?'—'I might'** 'tu viendras?'—'peut-être'.

····➤ (permission) **you ~ leave** vous pouvez partir; **~ I smoke?** puis-je fumer?

····➤ (wish) **~ he be happy** qu'il soit heureux.

May *n* mai *m*.

maybe *adv* peut-être.

mayhem *n* (havoc) ravages *mpl*.

mayonnaise *n* mayonnaise *f*.

mayor *n* maire *m*.

maze *n* labyrinthe *m*.

Mb *abbr* (**megabyte**) (Comput) Mo.

me *pron* me, m'; (after prep.) moi; (indirect object) me, m'; **he knows ~** il me connaît.

meadow *n* pré *m*.

meagre *a* maigre.

meal *n* repas *m*; (grain) farine *f*.

mean *a* (poor) misérable; (miserly) avare; (unkind) méchant; (average) moyen. ● *n* milieu *m*; (average) moyenne *f*; **in the ~ time** en attendant. ● *vt* (*pt* **meant**) vouloir dire, signifier; (involve) entraîner; **I ~ that!** je suis sérieux; **be meant for** être destiné à; **~ to do** avoir l'intention de faire.

meaning *n* sens *m*, signification *f*. **meaningful** *a* significatif. **meaningless** *a* dénué de sens.

means *n* moyen(s) *m(pl)*; **by ~ of sth** au moyen de qch. ● *npl* (wealth) moyens *mpl* financiers; **by all ~** certainement; **by no ~** nullement.

meant ⇒MEAN.

meantime, **meanwhile** *adv* en attendant.

measles *n* rougeole *f*.

measure *n* mesure *f*; (ruler) règle *f*. ● *vt/i* mesurer; **~ up to** être à la hauteur de.

meat *n* viande *f*. **meaty** *a* de viande; (fig) substantiel.

mechanic *n* mécanicien/-ne *m/f*.

mechanical *a* mécanique.

mechanism *n* mécanisme *m*.

medal *n* médaille *f*.

meddle *vi* (interfere) se mêler (**in** de); (tinker) toucher (**with** à).

media *n* ⇒MEDIUM. ● *npl* **the ~** les média *mpl*; **talk to the ~** parler à la presse.

median *a* médian. ● *n* médiane *f*.

mediate *vi* servir d'intermédiaire.

medical *a* médical; (student) en médecine. ● *n* visite *f* médicale.

medication *n* médicaments *mpl*.

medicine *n* (science) médecine *f*; (substance) médicament *m*.

medieval *a* médiéval.

mediocre *a* médiocre.

meditate *vt/i* méditer.

Mediterranean *a* méditerranéen. ● *n* **the ~** la Méditerranée *f*.

medium *n* (*pl* **media**) (mid-point) milieu *m*; (for transmitting data) support *m*; (*pl* **mediums**) (person) médium *m*. ● *a* moyen.

medley *n* mélange *m*; (Mus) pot-pourri *m*.

meet *vt* (*pt* **met**) rencontrer; (see again) retrouver; (be introduced to) faire la connaissance de; (face) faire face à; (*requirement*) satisfaire. ● *vi* se rencontrer; (see each other again) se retrouver; (in session) se réunir.

meeting *n* réunion *f*; (between two people) rencontre *f*.

megabyte *n* (Comput) mégaoctet *m*.

melancholy *n* mélancolie *f*. ● *a* mélancolique.

mellow *a* (*fruit*) mûr; (*sound, colour*) moelleux, doux; (*person*) mûri. ● *vt/i* (mature) mûrir; (soften) (s')adoucir.

melody *n* mélodie *f*.

melon *n* melon *m*.

melt *vt/i* (faire) fondre.

member *n* membre *m*. **M~ of Parliament** *n* député *m*. **membership** *n* adhésion *f*; (members) membres *mpl*; (fee) cotisation *f*.

memento *n* (*pl* **~es**) (object) souvenir *m*.

memo *n* note *f*.

memoir *n* (record, essay) mémoire *m*.

memorandum *n* note *f*.

memorial *n* monument *m*. ● *a* commémoratif.

memorize *vt* apprendre par cœur.

memory *n* (mind, in computer) mémoire *f*; (thing remembered) souvenir *m*; **from ~** de mémoire; **in ~ of** à la mémoire de.

men ⇒MAN.

menace *n* menace *f*; (nuisance) peste *f*. ● *vt* menacer.

mend *vt* réparer; (darn) raccommoder; **~ one's ways** s'amender. ● *n* raccommodage *m*; **on the ~** en voie de guérison.

meningitis *n* méningite *f*.

menopause *n* ménopause *f*.

mental *a* mental; (*hospital*) psychiatrique.

mentality *n* mentalité *f*.

mention *vt* mentionner; **don't ~ it!** il n'y a pas de quoi!, je vous en prie! ● *n* mention *f*.

menu *n* (food, on computer) menu *m*; (list) carte *f*.

MEP *abbr* (**Member of the European Parliament**) député *m* au Parlement européen.

mercenary *a* & *n* mercenaire (*m*).

merchandise *n* marchandises *fpl*.

merchant *n* marchand *m*. ● *a* (*ship, navy*) marchand. **~ bank** *n* banque *f* de commerce.

merciful *a* miséricordieux.

mercury *n* mercure *m*.

mercy *n* pitié *f*; **at the ~ of** à la merci de.

mere *a* simple. **merest** *a* moindre.

merge *vt/i* (se) mêler (**with** à); (*companies*: Comm) fusionner. **merger** *n* fusion *f*.

mermaid *n* sirène *f*.

merrily *adv* (happily) joyeusement; (unconcernedly) avec insouciance.

merry *a* (**-ier**, **-iest**) gai; **make ~** faire la fête. **~-go-round** *n* manège *m*.

mesh *n* maille *f*; (fabric) tissu *m* à mailles; (network) réseau *m*.

mesmerize *vt* hypnotiser.

mess *n* désordre *m*, gâchis *m*; (dirt) saleté *f*; (Mil) mess *m*; **make a ~ of** gâcher. ● *vt* **~ up** gâcher. ● *vi* **~ about** s'amuser; (dawdle) traîner; **~ with** (tinker with) tripoter.

message *n* message *m*.

messenger *n* messager/-ère *m/f*.

messy *a* (**-ier**, **-iest**) en désordre; (dirty) sale.

met ⇒MEET.

metal *n* métal *m*. ● *a* de métal. **metallic** *a* métallique; (paint, colour) métallisé.

metallurgy *n* métallurgie *f*.

metaphor *n* métaphore *f*.

meteor *n* météore *m*.

meteorite *n* météorite *m*.

meteorology *n* météorologie *f*.

meter *n* compteur *m*; (US) = METRE.

method *n* méthode *f*.

methylated spirit(**s**) *n* alcool *m* à brûler.

meticulous *a* méticuleux.

metre, (US) **meter** *n* mètre *m*.

metric *a* métrique.

metropolis *n* métropole *f*. **metropolitan** *a* métropolitain.

mew *n* miaulement *m*. ● *vi* miauler.

mews *npl* appartements *mpl* chic aménagés dans d'anciennes écuries.

Mexico *n* Mexique *m*.

miaow *n* & *vi* = MEW.

mice ⇒MOUSE.

mickey *n* **take the ~ out of** [!] se moquer de.

M

microchip *n* puce *f*; circuit *m* intégré.

microlight *n* ULM *m*.

microprocessor *n* microprocesseur *m*.

microscope *n* microscope *m*.

microwave *n* micro-onde *f*; ~ (oven) four *m* à micro-ondes. ● *vt* passer au four à micro-ondes.

mid *a* **in ~ air** en plein ciel; **in ~ March** à la mi-mars; **~ afternoon** milieu *m* de l'après-midi; **he's in his ~ twenties** il a environ vingt-cinq ans.

midday *n* midi *m*.

middle *a* (*door, shelf*) du milieu; (*size*) moyen. ● *n* milieu *m*; **in the ~ of** au milieu de. **~-aged** *a* d'âge mûr. **M~ Ages** *n* Moyen Âge *m*. **~ class** *n* classe *f* moyenne. **M~ East** *n* Moyen-Orient *m*.

midge *n* moucheron *m*.

midget *n* nain/-e *m*/*f*. ● *a* minuscule.

midnight *n* minuit *f*; **it's ~** il est minuit.

midst *n* **in the ~ of** au beau milieu de; **in our ~** parmi nous.

midsummer *n* milieu *m* de l'été; (solstice) solstice *m* d'été.

midway *adv* **~ between/along** à mi-chemin entre/le long de.

midwife *n* (*pl* **-wives**) sage-femme *f*.

might[1] *v aux* **I ~ have been killed!** j'aurais pu être tué; **you ~ try doing sth** vous pourriez faire qch; ⇒MAY.

might[2] *n* puissance *f*.

mighty *a* puissant; (huge [!]) énorme. ● *adv* [!] vachement [!].

migrant *a* & *n* (*bird*) migrateur (*m*); (*worker*) migrant/-e (*m*/*f*).

migrate *vi* émigrer. **migration** *n* migration *f*.

mild *a* (*surprise, taste, tobacco, attack*) léger; (*weather, cheese, soap, person*) doux; (*case, infection*) bénin.

mile *n* mile *m* (= *1.6 km*); **walk for ~s** marcher pendant des kilomètres; **~s better** [!] bien meilleur. **mileage** *n* nombre *m* de miles, kilométrage *m*.

milestone *n* (lit) borne *f*; (fig) étape *f* importante.

military *a* militaire.

militia *n* milice *f*.

milk *n* lait *m*. ● *vt* (*cow*) traire; (fig) pomper.

milkman *n* (*pl* **-men**) laitier *m*.

milky *a* (*skin, colour*) laiteux; (*tea*) au lait; **M~ Way** Voie *f* lactée.

mill *n* moulin *m*; (factory) usine *f*. ● *vt* moudre. ● *vi* **~ around** grouiller.

millennium *n* (*pl* **~s**) millénaire *m*.

millimetre, (US) **millimeter** *n* millimètre *m*.

million *n* million *m*; **a ~ pounds** un million de livres. **millionaire** *n* millionnaire *m*.

millstone *n* meule *f*; (fig) boulet *m*.

mime *n* (actor) mime *mf*; (art) mime *m*. ● *vt*/*i* mimer.

mimic *vt* (*pt* **mimicked**) imiter. ● *n* imitateur/-trice *m*/*f*.

mince *vt* hacher; **not to ~ matters** ne pas mâcher ses mots. ● *n* viande *f* hachée.

mind *n* esprit *m*; (sanity) raison *f*; (opinion) avis *m*; **be on sb's ~** préoccuper qn; **bear that in ~** ne l'oubliez pas; **change one's ~** changer d'avis; **make up one's ~** se décider (**to** à). ● *vt* (have charge of) s'occuper de; (heed) faire attention à; **I do not ~ the noise** le bruit ne me dérange pas; **I don't ~** ça m'est égal; **would you ~**

checking? je peux vous demander de vérifier?

minder *n* (bodyguard) garde *m* de corps; (**child**) ~ nourrice *f*.

mindless *a* (*programme*) bête; (*work*) abrutissant; (*vandalism*) gratuit.

mine *n* mine *f*. ● *vt* extraire; (Mil) miner. ● *pron* le mien, la mienne, les mien(ne)s; **the blue car is** ~ la voiture bleue est la mienne *or* à moi.

minefield *n* (lit) champ *m* de mines; (fig) terrain *m* miné.

miner *n* mineur *m*.

mineral *n* & *a* minéral (*m*); ~ **water** eau *f* minérale.

minesweeper *n* (ship) dragueur *m* de mines.

mingle *vt/i* (se) mêler (**with** à).

minibus *n* minibus *m*.

minicab *n* taxi *m* (*non agréé*).

minimal *a* minimal.

minimize *vt* minimiser; (Comput) réduire.

minimum *a* & *n* (*pl* **-ima**) minimum (*m*).

minister *n* ministre *m*. **ministerial** *a* ministériel. **ministry** *n* ministère *m*.

mink *n* vison *m*.

minor *a* (*change, surgery*) mineur; (*injury, burn*) léger; (*road*) secondaire. ● *n* (Jur) mineur/-e *m/f*.

minority *n* minorité *f*; **in the** ~ en minorité. ● *a* minoritaire.

mint *n* (Bot, Culin) menthe *f*; (sweet) bonbon *m* à la menthe; (fortune 🗉) fortune *f*. ● *vt* frapper; **in** ~ **condition** à l'état neuf.

minus *prep* moins; (without 🗉) sans. ● *n* moins *m*; (drawback) inconvénient *m*.

minute¹ *n* minute *f*; ~**s** (of meeting) compte-rendu *m*.

minute² *a* (*object*) minuscule; (*risk, variation*) minime.

miracle *n* miracle *m*.

mirror *n* miroir *m*, glace *f*; (Auto) rétroviseur. ● *vt* refléter.

misbehave *vi* se conduire mal.

miscalculation *n* (lit) erreur *f* de calcul; (fig) mauvais calcul *m*.

miscarriage *n* fausse couche *f*; ~ **of justice** erreur *f* judiciaire.

miscellaneous *a* divers.

mischief *n* (playfulness) espièglerie *f*; (by children) bêtises *fpl*. **mischievous** *a* espiègle; (malicious) méchant.

misconduct *n* mauvaise conduite *f*.

misconstrue *vt* mal interpréter.

misdemeanour, (US) **misdemeanor** *n* (Jur) délit *m*.

miser *n* avare *mf*.

miserable *a* (sad) malheureux; (wretched) misérable; (*performance, result*) lamentable.

misery *n* (unhappiness) souffrance *f*; (misfortune) misère *f*; (person 🗉) rabat-joie *mf inv*.

misfit *n* inadapté/-e *m/f*.

misfortune *n* malheur *m*.

misgiving *n* (doubt) doute *m*; (apprehension) crainte *f*.

misguided *a* (foolish) imprudent; (mistaken) erroné; **be** ~ (*person*) se tromper.

mishap *n* incident *m*.

misjudge *vt* (*distance, speed*) mal évaluer; (*person*) mal juger.

mislay *vt* (*pt* **mislaid**) égarer.

mislead *vt* (*pt* **misled**) tromper. **misleading** *a* trompeur.

misplace *vt* mal ranger; (lose) égarer. **misplaced** *a* (*fear, criticism*) déplacé.

misprint *n* coquille *f*, faute *f* typographique.

misread *vt* (*pt* **misread**) mal lire; (*intentions*) mal interpréter.

M

miss *vt/i* manquer; (*bus*) rater; **he ~es her/Paris** elle/Paris lui manque; **you're ~ing the point** tu n'as rien compris; **~ sth out** omettre qch; **~ out on sth** laisser passer qch. ● *n* coup *m* manqué; **it was a near ~** on l'a échappé belle.

Miss *n* Mademoiselle *f*; **~ Smith** (written) Mlle Smith.

misshapen *a* difforme.

missile *n* (Mil) missile *m*; (thrown) projectile *m*.

mission *n* mission *f*. **missionary** *n* missionnaire *mf*.

misspell *vt* (*pt* **misspelt** *or* **misspelled**) mal écrire.

mist *n* brume *f*; (on window) buée *f*. ● *vt/i* (s')embuer.

mistake *n* erreur *f*; **by ~** par erreur; **make a ~** faire une erreur. ● *vt* (*pt* **mistook**; *pp* **mistaken**) (*meaning*) mal interpréter; **~ for** prendre pour.

mistaken *a* (*enthusiasm*) mal placé; **be ~** avoir tort.

mistletoe *n* gui *m*.

mistreat *vt* maltraiter.

mistress *n* maîtresse *f*.

misty *a* (**-ier**, **-iest**) brumeux; (*window*) embué.

misunderstanding *n* malentendu *m*.

misuse *vt* (*word*) mal employer; (*power*) abuser de; (*equipment*) faire mauvais usage de.

mitten *n* moufle *f*.

mix *n* mélange *m*. ● *vt* mélanger; (*drink*) préparer; (*cement*) malaxer. ● *vi* se mélanger (**with** avec, à); (socially) être sociable; **~ with sb** fréquenter qn. □ **~ up** (confuse) confondre; (jumble up) mélanger; **get ~ed up in** se trouver mêlé à.

mixed *a* (*school*) mixte; (*collection, diet*) varié; (*nuts, sweets*) assorti.

mixer *n* (Culin) batteur *m* électrique; **be a good ~** être sociable; **~ tap** mélangeur *m*.

mixture *n* mélange *m*.

mix-up *n* confusion *f* (**over** sur).

moan *n* gémissement *m*. ● *vi* gémir; (complain ⓘ) râler ⓘ.

mob *n* (crowd) foule *f*; (gang) gang *m*; **the M~** la Mafia. ● *vt* (*pt* **mobbed**) assaillir.

mobile *a* mobile; **~ phone** téléphone *m* portable. ● *n* mobile *m*.

mobilize *vt/i* mobiliser.

mock *vt/i* se moquer (de). ● *a* faux.

mockery *n* moquerie *f*; **a ~ of** une parodie de.

mock-up *n* maquette *f*.

mode *n* mode *m*.

model *n* (Comput, Auto) modèle *m*; (scale representation) maquette *f*; (person showing clothes) mannequin *m*. ● *a* modèle; (*car*) modèle réduit *inv*; (*railway*) miniature. ● *vt* (*pt* **modelled**) modeler; (*clothes*) présenter. ● *vi* être mannequin; (pose) poser. **modelling** *n* métier *m* de mannequin.

modem *n* modem *m*.

moderate *a* & *n* modéré/-e (*m*/*f*).

moderation *n* modération *f*; **in ~** avec modération.

modern *a* moderne; **~ languages** langues *fpl* vivantes. **modernize** *vt* moderniser.

modest *a* modeste. **modesty** *n* modestie *f*.

modification *n* modification *f*.

modify *vt* modifier.

module *n* module *m*.

moist *a* (*soil*) humide; (*skin, palms*) moite; (*cake*) moelleux. **moisten** *vt* humecter. **moisture** *n* humidité *f*. **moisturizer** *n* crème *f* hydratante.

molar *n* molaire *f*.
mold (US) = MOULD.
mole *n* grain *m* de beauté; (animal) taupe *f*.
molecule *n* molécule *f*.
molest *vt* (pester) importuner; (sexually) agresser sexuellement.
moment *n* (short time) instant *m*; (point in time) moment *m*. **momentarily** *adv* momentanément; (soon: US) très bientôt. **momentary** *a* momentané.
momentum *n* élan *m*.
monarch *n* monarque *m*. **monarchy** *n* monarchie *f*.
Monday *n* lundi *m*.
monetary *a* monétaire.
money *n* argent *m*; **make ~** (*person*) gagner de l'argent; (*business*) rapporter de l'argent. **~-box** *n* tirelire *f*. **~ order** *n* mandat *m* postal.
monitor *n* dispositif *m* de surveillance; (Comput) moniteur *m*. ● *vt* surveiller; (*broadcast*) être à l'écoute de.
monk *n* moine *m*.
monkey *n* singe *m*.
monopolize *vt* monopoliser. **monopoly** *n* monopole *m*.
monotonous *a* monotone. **monotony** *n* monotonie *f*.
monsoon *n* mousson *f*.
monster *n* monstre *m*. **monstrous** *a* monstrueux.
month *n* mois *m*.
monthly *a* mensuel. ● *adv* (*pay*) au mois; (*publish*) tous les mois. ● *n* (periodical) mensuel *m*.
monument *n* monument *m*.
moo *vi* meugler.
mood *n* humeur *f*; **in a good/bad ~** de bonne/mauvaise humeur. **moody** *a* d'humeur changeante.
moon *n* lune *f*.
moonlight *n* clair *m* de lune.
moonlighting *n* 🄸 travail *m* au noir.
moor *n* lande *f*. ● *vt* amarrer.
mop *n* balai *m* à franges; **~ of hair** crinière *f* 🄸. ● *vt* (*pt* **mopped**) **~** (**up**) éponger.
moped *n* vélomoteur *m*.
moral *a* moral. ● *n* morale *f*; **~s** moralité *f*.
morale *n* moral *m*.
morbid *a* morbide.
more *adv* plus; **~ serious** plus sérieux; **work ~** travailler plus; **sleep ~ and ~** dormir de plus en plus; **once ~** une fois de plus; **I don't go there any ~** je n'y vais plus; **~ or less** plus ou moins. ● *det* plus de; **a little ~ wine** un peu plus de vin; **~ bread** encore un peu de pain; **there's no ~ bread** il n'y a plus de pain; **nothing ~** rien de plus. ● *pron* plus; **cost ~ than** coûter plus cher que; **I need ~ of it** il m'en faut davantage.
moreover *adv* de plus.
morning *n* matin *m*; (whole morning) matinée *f*.
Morocco *n* Maroc *m*.
morsel *n* morceau *m*.
mortal *a & n* mortel/-le (*m/f*).
mortgage *n* emprunt-logement *m*. ● *vt* hypothéquer.
mortuary *n* morgue *f*.
mosaic *n* mosaïque *f*.
mosque *n* mosquée *f*.
mosquito *n* (*pl* **~es**) moustique *m*.
moss *n* mousse *f*.
most *det* (nearly all) la plupart de; **~ people** la plupart des gens; **the ~ votes/money** le plus de voix/ d'argent. ● *n* le plus. ● *pron* la plupart; **~ of us** la plupart d'entre nous; **~ of the money** la plus grande partie de l'argent; **the ~ I can do is ...** tout ce que je

peux faire c'est ... ● *adv* **the ~ beautiful house/hotel in Oxford** la maison la plus belle/l'hôtel le plus beau d'Oxford; **~ interesting** très intéressant; **what I like ~** (**of all**) **is** ce que j'aime le plus c'est. **mostly** *adv* surtout.

moth *n* papillon *m* de nuit; (in cloth) mite *f*.

mother *n* mère *f*. ● *vt* (lit) materner; (fig) dorloter. **motherhood** *n* maternité *f*. **~-in-law** *n* (*pl* **~s-in-law**) belle-mère *f*. **~-of-pearl** *n* nacre *f*. **M~'s Day** *n* la fête des mères. **~-to-be** *n* future maman *f*. **~ tongue** *n* langue *f* maternelle.

motion *n* mouvement *m*; (proposal) motion *f*; **~ picture** (US) film *m*. ● *vt/i* **~** (**to**) **sb to** faire signe à qn de. **motionless** *a* immobile.

motivate *vt* motiver.

motive *n* motif *m*; (Jur) mobile *m*.

motor *n* moteur *m*; (car) auto *f*. ● *a* (*industry, insurance, vehicle*) automobile; (*activity, disorder*: Med) moteur. **~bike** *n* moto *f*. **~ car** *n* auto *f*. **~-cyclist** *n* motocycliste *mf*. **~ home** *n* auto-caravane *f*.

motorist *n* automobiliste *mf*.

motorway *n* autoroute *f*.

mottled *a* tacheté.

motto *n* (*pl* **~es**) devise *f*.

mould *n* (shape) moule *m*; (fungus) moisissure *f*. ● *vt* mouler; (influence) former. **moulding** *n* moulure *f*. **mouldy** *a* moisi.

mount *n* (hill) mont *m*; (horse) monture *f*. ● *vt* (*stairs*) gravir; (*platform, horse, bike*) monter sur; (*jewel, picture, campaign, exhibit*) monter. ● *vi* monter; (*number, toll*) augmenter; (*concern*) grandir.

mountain *n* montagne *f*; **~ bike** (vélo) tout terrain *m*, VTT *m*. **mountaineer** *n* alpiniste *mf*.

mourn *vt/i* **~** (**for**) pleurer. **mournful** *a* mélancolique. **mourning** *n* deuil *m*.

mouse *n* (*pl* **mice**) souris *f*. **~trap** *n* souricière *f*.

mouth *n* bouche *f*; (of dog, cat) gueule *f*; (of cave, tunnel) entrée *f*. **mouthful** *n* bouchée *f*. **~wash** *n* eau *f* dentifrice. **~watering** *a* appétissant.

move *vt* (*object*) déplacer; (*limb, head*) bouger; (emotionally) émouvoir; **~ house** déménager. ● *vi* bouger; (*vehicle*) rouler; (change address) déménager; (act) agir. ● *n* mouvement *m*; (in game) coup *m*; (player's turn) tour *m*; (step, act) manœuvre *f*; (house change) déménagement *m*; **on the ~** en mouvement. □ **~ back** reculer; **~ in** emménager; **~ in with** s'installer avec; **~ on** (*person*) se mettre en route; (*vehicle*) repartir; (*time*) passer; **~ sth on** faire avancer qch; **~ sb on** faire circuler qn; **~ over** *or* **up** se pousser.

movement *n* mouvement *m*.

movie *n* (US) film *m*; **the ~s** le cinéma.

moving *a* (*vehicle*) en marche; (*part, target*) mobile; (*staircase*) roulant; (touching) émouvant.

mow *vt* (*pp* **mowed** *or* **mown**) (*lawn*) tondre; (*hay*) couper; **~ down** faucher. **mower** *n* tondeuse *f*.

MP *abbr* ⇒MEMBER OF PARLIAMENT.

Mr *n* (*pl* **Messrs**) **~ Smith** Monsieur *or* M. Smith; **~ President** Monsieur le Président.

Mrs *n* (*pl* **Mrs**) **~ Smith** Madame *or* Mme Smith.

Ms *n* Mme.

much *adv* beaucoup; **too ~** trop; **very ~** beaucoup; **I like them as ~ as you** (**do**) je les aime autant que toi. ● *pron* beaucoup; **not ~** pas grand-chose; **he didn't say ~** il n'a pas dit grand-chose; **I ate so ~ that** j'ai tellement mangé que. ● *det* beaucoup de; **too ~ money** trop d'argent; **how ~ time is left?** combien de temps reste-t-il?

muck *n* saletés *fpl*; (manure) fumier *m*. □ **~ about** ⊡ faire l'imbécile. **mucky** *a* sale.

mud *n* boue *f*.

muddle *n* (mix-up) malentendu *m*; (mess) pagaille *f* ⊡; **get into a ~** s'embrouiller. □ **~ through** se débrouiller; **~ up** embrouiller.

muddy *a* couvert de boue.

muffle *vt* emmitoufler; (*bell*) assourdir; (*voice*) étouffer.

mug *n* grande tasse *f*; (for beer) chope *f*; (face ⊡) gueule *f* ⊠; (fool ⊡) poire *f* ⊡. ● *vt* (*pt* **mugged**) agresser. **mugger** *n* agresseur *m*.

muggy *a* lourd.

mule *n* mulet *m*.

multicoloured *a* multicolore.

multiple *a & n* multiple (*m*); **~ sclerosis** sclérose *f* en plaques.

multiplication *n* multiplication *f*. **multiply** *vt/i* (se) multiplier.

multistorey *a* (*car park*) à niveaux multiples.

mum *n* ⊡ maman *f*.

mumble *vt/i* marmonner.

mummy *n* (mother ⊡) maman *f*; (embalmed body) momie *f*.

mumps *n* oreillons *mpl*.

munch *vt* mâcher.

mundane *a* terre-à-terre.

municipal *a* municipal.

mural *a* mural. ● *n* peinture *f* murale.

murder *n* meurtre *m*. ● *vt* assassiner. **murderer** *n* meurtrier *m*, assassin *m*.

murky *a* (**-ier, -iest**) (*water*) glauque; (*past*) trouble.

murmur *n* murmure *m*. ● *vt/i* murmurer.

muscle *n* muscle *m*. ● *vi* **~ in** ⊡ s'imposer (**on** dans).

muscular *a* (*tissue, disease*) musculaire; (*body, person*) musclé.

museum *n* musée *m*.

mushroom *n* champignon *m*. ● *vi* (*town*) proliférer; (*demand*) s'accroître rapidement.

music *n* musique *f*.

musical *a* (*person*) musicien; (*voice*) mélodieux; (*accompaniment*) musical; (*instrument*) de musique. ● *n* comédie *f* musicale.

musician *n* musicien/-ne *m/f*.

Muslim *n* Musulman/-e *m/f*. ● *a* musulman.

mussel *n* moule *f*.

must *v aux* devoir; **you ~ go** vous devez partir, il faut que vous partiez; **she ~ be consulted** il faut la consulter; **he ~ be old** il doit être vieux; **I ~ have done it** j'ai dû le faire. ● *n* **be a ~** ⊡ être indispensable.

mustard *n* moutarde *f*.

musty *a* (**-ier, -iest**) (*room*) qui sent le renfermé; (*smell*) de moisi.

mute *a & n* muet/-te (*m/f*). **muted** *a* (*colour*) sourd; (*response*) tiède; (*celebration*) mitigé.

mutilate *vt* mutiler.

mutter *vt/i* marmonner.

mutton *n* mouton *m*.

mutual *a* (reciprocal) réciproque; (common) commun; (*consent*) mutuel. **mutually** *adv* mutuellement.

muzzle *n* (snout) museau *m*; (device) muselière *f*; (of gun) canon *m*. ● *vt* museler.

my *a* mon, ma, *pl* mes.

myself *pron* (reflexive) me, m'; **I've hurt ~** je me suis fait mal; (emphatic) moi-même; **I did it ~** je l'ai fait moi-même; (after preposition) moi, moi-même; **I am proud of ~** je suis fier de moi.

mysterious *a* mystérieux.

mystery *n* mystère *m*.

mystic *a & n* mystique (*mf*). **mystical** *a* mystique.

myth *n* mythe *m*. **mythical** *a* mythique. **mythology** *n* mythologie *f*.

nag *vt/i* (*pt* **nagged**) critiquer; (pester) harceler. **nagging** *a* persistant.

nail *n* clou *m*; (of finger, toe) ongle *m*; **on the ~** sans tarder, tout de suite. ● *vt* clouer. **~ polish** *n* vernis *m* à ongles.

naïve *a* naïf.

naked *a* nu; **to the ~ eye** à l'œil nu.

name *n* nom *m*; (fig) réputation *f*. ● *vt* nommer; (*terms*) fixer; **be ~d after** porter le nom de.

namely *adv* à savoir.

nanny *n* nurse *f*.

nap *n* somme *m*.

nape *n* nuque *f*.

napkin *n* serviette *f*.

nappy *n* couche *f*.

narcotic *a & n* narcotique (*m*).

narrative *n* récit *m*. **narrator** *n* narrateur/-trice *m/f*.

narrow *a* étroit. ● *vt/i* (se) rétrécir; (limit) (se) limiter; **~ down the choices** limiter les choix. **~-minded** *a* à l'esprit étroit; (*ideas*) étroit.

nasal *a* nasal.

nasty *a* (**-ier**, **-iest**) mauvais, désagréable; (malicious) méchant.

nation *n* nation *f*.

national *a* national. ● *n* ressortissant/-e *m/f*.

nationality *n* nationalité *f*.

nationalize *vt* nationaliser.

nationally *adv* à l'échelle nationale.

native *n* (local inhabitant) autochtone *mf*; (non-European) indigène *mf*; **be a ~ of** être originaire de. ● *a* indigène; (*country*) natal; (inborn) inné; **~ language** langue *f* maternelle; **~ speaker of French** personne *f* de langue maternelle française.

natural *a* naturel.

naturally *adv* (normally, of course) naturellement; (by nature) de nature.

nature *n* nature *f*.

naughty *a* (**-ier**, **-iest**) vilain, méchant; (indecent) grivois.

nausea *n* nausée *f*. **nauseous** *a* (*smell*) écœurant.

nautical *a* nautique.

naval *a* (*battle*) naval; (*officer*) de marine.

navel *n* nombril *m*.

navigate *vt* (*sea*) naviguer sur; (*ship*) piloter. ● *vi* naviguer. **navigation** *n* navigation *f*.

navy *n* marine *f*. ● *a* **~ (blue)** bleu *inv* marine.

near *adv* près; **draw ~** (s')approcher (**to** de). ● *prep* près de. ● *a* proche; **~ to** près de. ● *vt* approcher de.

nearby *a* proche. ● *adv* à proximité.

nearly *adv* presque; **I ~ forgot** j'ai failli oublier; **not ~ as pretty as** loin d'être aussi joli que.

nearness *n* proximité *f*.

nearside *a* (Auto) du côté du passager.

neat *a* soigné, net; (*room*) bien rangé; (clever) habile; (*drink*) sec. **neatly** *adv* avec soin; habilement. **neatness** *n* netteté *f*.

necessarily *adv* nécessairement.

necessary *a* nécessaire.

necessitate *vt* nécessiter.

necessity *n* nécessité *f*; (thing) chose *f* indispensable.

neck *n* cou *m*; (of dress) encolure *f*. **~ and neck** *a* à égalité. **~lace** *n* collier *m*. **~line** *n* encolure *f*. **~tie** *n* cravate *f*.

nectarine *n* brugnon *m*, nectarine *f*.

need *n* besoin *m*. ● *vt* avoir besoin de; (demand) demander; **you ~ not come** vous n'êtes pas obligé de venir.

needle *n* aiguille *f*.

needless *a* inutile.

needlework *n* couture *f*; (object) ouvrage *m* (à l'aiguille).

needy *a* (**-ier**, **-iest**) nécessiteux. ● *n* **the ~** les indigents.

negative *a* négatif. ● *n* (of photograph) négatif *m*; (word: Gram) négation *f*; **in the ~** (answer) par la négative; (Gram) à la forme négative.

neglect *vt* négliger, laisser à l'abandon; **~ to do** négliger de faire. ● *n* manque *m* de soins; (**state of**) **~** abandon *m*.

negligent *a* négligent.

negotiate *vt*/*i* négocier. **negotiation** *n* négociation *f*.

neigh *n* hennissement *m*. ● *vi* hennir.

neighbour, (US) **neighbor** *n* voisin/-e *m*/*f*. **neighbourhood** *n* voisinage *m*, quartier *m*; **in the ~hood of** aux alentours de. **neighbouring** *a* voisin. **neighbourly** *a* amical.

neither *a & pron* aucun/-e des deux, ni l'un/-e ni l'autre. ● *adv* ni; **~ big nor small** ni grand ni petit. ● *conj* (ne) non plus; **~ am I coming** je ne viendrai pas non plus.

nephew *n* neveu *m*.

nerve *n* nerf *m*; (courage) courage *m*; (calm) sang-froid *m*; (impudence 🄸) culot *m*; **~s** (before exams) trac *m*. **~-racking** *a* éprouvant.

nervous *a* nerveux; **be** *or* **feel ~** (afraid) avoir peur; **~ breakdown** dépression *f* nerveuse. **nervousness** *n* nervosité *f*; (fear) crainte *f*.

nest *n* nid *m*. ● *vi* nicher. **~-egg** *n* pécule *m*.

nestle *vi* se blottir.

net *n* filet *m*; (Comput) net *m*, Internet *m*. ● *vt* (*pt* **netted**) prendre au filet. ● *a* (weight) net. **~ball** *n* netball *m*.

Netherlands *n* **the ~** les Pays-Bas *mpl*.

Netsurfer *n* Internaute *mf*.

nettle *n* ortie *f*.

network *n* réseau *m*.

neurotic *a & n* névrosé/-e (*m*/*f*).

neuter *a & n* neutre (*m*). ● *vt* (castrate) castrer.

neutral *a* neutre; **~** (**gear**) (Auto) point *m* mort.

never *adv* (ne) jamais; **he ~ refuses** il ne refuse jamais; **I ~ saw him** 🄸 je ne l'ai pas vu; **~ again** plus jamais; **~ mind** (don't worry) ne vous en faites pas; (it doesn't matter) peu importe.

nevertheless *adv* néanmoins, toutefois.

new *a* nouveau; (brand-new) neuf. **~-born** *a* nouveau-né. **~comer** *n* nouveau venu *m*, nouvelle venue *f*.

N

newly *adv* nouvellement. **~-weds** *npl* jeunes mariés *mpl*.

news *n* nouvelle(s) *f(pl)*; (radio, press) informations *fpl*; (TV) actualités *fpl*, informations *fpl*. **~ agency** *n* agence *f* de presse. **~agent** *n* marchand/-e *m/f* de journaux. **~caster** *n* présentateur/-trice *m/f*. **~group** *n* (Internet) forum *m* de discussion. **~letter** *n* bulletin *m*. **~paper** *n* journal *m*.

new year *n* nouvel an *m*. **New Year's Day** *n* le jour de l'an. **New Year's Eve** *n* la Saint-Sylvestre.

New Zealand *n* Nouvelle-Zélande *f*.

next *a* prochain; (adjoining) voisin; (following) suivant; **~ to** à côté de; **~ door** à côté (**to** de). ● *adv* la prochaine fois; (afterwards) ensuite. ● *n* suivant/-e *m/f*; (*e-mail*) message *m* suivant. **~-door** *a* d'à côté. **~ of kin** *n* parent *m* le plus proche.

nib *n* plume *f*.

nibble *vt/i* grignoter.

nice *a* agréable, bon; (kind) gentil; (pretty) joli; (respectable) bien *inv*; (subtle) délicat. **nicely** *adv* agréablement; gentiment; (well) bien.

nicety *n* subtilité *f*.

niche *n* (recess) niche *f*; (fig) place *f*, situation *f*.

nick *n* petite entaille *f*; **be in good/bad ~** être en bon/mauvais état. ● *vt* (steal, arrest ⓘ) piquer.

nickel *n* (metal) nickel *m*; (US) pièce *f* de cinq cents.

nickname *n* surnom *m*. ● *vt* surnommer.

nicotine *n* nicotine *f*.

niece *n* nièce *f*.

niggling *a* (*person*) tatillon; (*detail*) insignifiant.

night *n* nuit *f*; (evening) soir *m*. ● *a* de nuit. **~-cap** *n* boisson *f* (*avant d'aller se coucher*). **~-club** *n* boîte *f* de nuit. **~-dress** *n* chemise *f* de nuit. **~fall** *n* tombée *f* de la nuit. **nightie** *n* chemise *f* de nuit.

nightingale *n* rossignol *m*.

nightly *a & adv* (de) chaque nuit *or* soir.

night: **~mare** *n* cauchemar *m*. **~-time** *n* nuit *f*.

nil *n* (Sport) zéro *m*. ● *a* (*chances, risk*) nul.

nimble *a* agile.

nine *a & n* neuf (*m*).

nineteen *a & n* dix-neuf (*m*).

ninety *a & n* quatre-vingt-dix (*m*).

ninth *a & n* neuvième (*mf*).

nip *vt/i* (*pt* **nipped**) (pinch) pincer; (rush ⓘ) courir; **~ out/back** sortir/rentrer rapidement. ● *n* pincement *m*.

nipple *n* mamelon *m*; (of baby's bottle) tétine *f*.

nippy *a* (**-ier, -iest**) (*air*) piquant; (*car*) rapide.

nitrogen *n* azote *m*.

no *det* aucun/-e; pas de; **~ man** aucun homme; **~ money/time** pas d'argent/de temps; **~ one** = NOBODY; **~ smoking/entry** défense de fumer/d'entrer; **~ way!** ⓘ pas question! ● *adv* non. ● *n*(*pl* **noes**) non *m inv*.

nobility *n* noblesse *f*.

noble *a* noble. **~ man** *n* (*pl* **-men**) noble *m*.

nobody *pron* (ne) personne; **he knows ~** il ne connaît personne. ● *n* nullité *f*.

nocturnal *a* nocturne.

nod *vt/i* (*pt* **nodded**); **~ (one's head)** faire un signe de tête; **~ off** s'endormir. ● *n* signe *m* de tête.

noise *n* bruit *m*; **make a ~** faire du bruit. **noisily** *adv*.

bruyamment. **noisy** *a* (**-ier**, **-iest**) bruyant.

no man's land *n* no man's land *m*.

nominal *a* symbolique, nominal; (*value*) nominal.

nominate *vt* nommer; (put forward) proposer.

none *pron* aucun/-e; ~ **of us** aucun/-e de nous; **I have** ~ je n'en ai pas.

non-existent *a* inexistant.

nonplussed *a* perplexe.

nonsense *n* absurdités *fpl*.

non-smoker *n* non-fumeur *m*.

non-stick *a* antiadhésif.

non-stop *a* (*train, flight*) direct. ● *adv* sans arrêt.

noodles *npl* nouilles *fpl*.

noon *n* midi *m*.

nor *adv* ni. ● *conj* (ne) non plus; ~ **shall I come** je ne viendrai pas non plus.

norm *n* norme *f*.

normal *a* normal.

Norman *n* Normand/-e *m/f*. ● *a* (*village*) normand; (*arch*) roman.

north *n* nord *m*. ● *a* nord *inv*, du nord. ● *adv* vers le nord.

North America *n* Amérique *f* du Nord.

north-east *n* nord-est *m*.

northerly *a* (*wind, area*) du nord; (*point*) au nord.

northern *a* (*accent*) du nord; (*coast*) nord. **northerner** *n* habitant/-e *m/f* du nord.

northward *a* (*side*) nord *inv*; (*journey*) vers le nord.

north-west *n* nord-ouest *m*.

Norway *n* Norvège *f*.

Norwegian *n* (*person*) Norvégien/-ne *m/f*; (*language*) norvégien *m*. ● *a* norvégien.

nose *n* nez *m*. ● *vi* ~ **about** fouiner.

nosedive *n* piqué *m*. ● *vi* descendre en piqué.

nostalgia *n* nostalgie *f*.

nostril *n* narine *f*; (of horse) naseau *m*.

nosy *a* (**-ier**, **-iest**) [!] curieux, indiscret.

not *adv* (ne) pas; **I do** ~ **know** je ne sais pas; ~ **at all** pas du tout; ~ **yet** pas encore; **I suppose** ~ je suppose que non.

notably *adv* notamment.

notch *n* entaille *f*. ● *vt* ~ **up** (score) marquer.

note *n* note *f*; (banknote) billet *m*; (short letter) mot *m*. ● *vt* noter; (notice) remarquer. ~**book** *n* carnet *m*.

nothing *pron* (ne) rien; **he eats** ~ il ne mange rien; ~ **else** rien d'autre; ~ **much** pas grand-chose; **for** ~ pour rien, gratis. ● *n* rien *m*; (person) nullité *f*. ● *adv* nullement.

notice *n* avis *m*, annonce *f*; (poster) affiche *f*; (**advance**) ~ préavis *m*; **at short** ~ dans des délais très brefs; **give in one's** ~ donner sa démission; **take** ~ faire attention (**of** à). ● *vt* remarquer, observer. **noticeable** *a* visible. ~**-board** *n* tableau *m* d'affichage.

notify *vt* (inform) aviser; (make known) notifier.

notion *n* idée *f*, notion *f*.

notorious *a* (*criminal*) notoire; (*district*) mal famé; (*case*) tristement célèbre.

notwithstanding *prep* malgré. ● *adv* néanmoins.

nought *n* zéro *m*.

noun *n* nom *m*.

nourish *vt* nourrir. **nourishing** *a* nourrissant. **nourishment** *n* nourriture *f*.

novel *n* roman *m*. ● *a* nouveau. **novelist** *n* romancier/-ière *m/f*. **novelty** *n* nouveauté *f*.

November *n* novembre *m*.

now *adv* maintenant. ● *conj* maintenant que; **just ~** maintenant; (a moment ago) tout à l'heure; **~ and again, ~ and then** de temps à autre.

nowadays *adv* de nos jours.

nowhere *adv* nulle part.

nozzle *n* (tip) embout *m*; (of hose) jet *m*.

nuclear *a* nucléaire.

nude *a* nu. ● *n* nu/-e *m/f*; **in the ~** tout nu.

nudge *vt* pousser du coude. ● *n* coup *m* de coude.

nudism *n* nudisme *m*. **nudity** *n* nudité *f*.

nuisance *n* (thing, event) ennui *m*; (person) peste *f*; **be a ~** être embêtant.

null *a* nul.

numb *a* engourdi (**with** par). ● *vt* engourdir.

number *n* nombre *m*; (of ticket, house, page) numéro *m*; (written figure) chiffre *m*; **a ~ of people** plusieurs personnes. ● *vt* numéroter; (count, include) compter. **~-plate** *n* plaque *f* d'immatriculation.

numeral *n* chiffre *m*.

numerate *a* qui sait compter.

numerical *a* numérique.

numerous *a* nombreux.

nun *n* religieuse *f*.

nurse *n* infirmier/-ière *m/f*; (nanny) nurse *f*. ● *vt* soigner; (*hope*) nourrir.

nursery *n* (room) chambre *f* d'enfants; (for plants) pépinière *f*; (**day**) **~** crèche *f*. **~ rhyme** *n* comptine *f*. **~ school** *n* (école) maternelle *f*.

nursing home *n* maison *f* de retraite.

nut *n* (walnut, Brazil nut) noix *f*; (hazelnut) noisette *f*; (peanut) cacahuète *f*; (Tech) écrou *m*. **~crackers** *npl* casse-noix *m inv*.

nutmeg *n* muscade *f*.

nutrient *n* substance *f* nutritive.

nutritious *a* nutritif.

nuts *a* (crazy ⓘ) cinglé.

nutshell *n* coquille *f* de noix; **in a ~** en un mot.

nylon *n* nylon *m*.

oak *n* chêne *m*.

OAP *abbr* (**old-age pensioner**) retraité/-e *m/f*.

oar *n* rame *f*.

oath *n* (promise) serment *m*; (swear-word) juron *m*.

oats *npl* avoine *f*.

obedience *n* obéissance *f*. **obedient** *a* obéissant. **obediently** *adv* docilement.

obese *a* obèse.

obey *vt/i* obéir (à).

object[1] *n* (thing) objet *m*; (aim) but *m*; (Gram) complément *m* d'objet; **money is no ~** l'argent n'est pas un problème.

object[2] *vi* protester. ● *vt* **~ that** objecter que; **~ to** (*behaviour*) désapprouver; (*plan*) protester contre. **objection** *n* objection *f*; (drawback) inconvénient *m*.

objective *a & n* objectif (*m*).

obligation *n* devoir *m*.

obligatory *a* obligatoire.

oblige *vt* obliger (**to do** à faire).

oblivion *n* oubli *m*. **oblivious** *a* inconscient (**to, of** de).

oblong *a* oblong. ● *n* rectangle *m*.

obnoxious *a* odieux.

oboe *n* hautbois *m*.

obscene *a* obscène.

obscure *a* obscur. ● *vt* obscurcir; (conceal) cacher.

observance *n* (of law) respect *m*; (of sabbath) observance *f*. **observant** *a* observateur.

observation *n* observation *f*.

observe *vt* observer; (remark) remarquer.

obsess *vt* obséder. **obsession** *n* obsession *f*. **obsessive** *a* (*person*) maniaque; (*thought*) obsédant; (*illness*) obsessionnel.

obsolete *a* dépassé.

obstacle *n* obstacle *m*.

obstinate *a* obstiné.

obstruct *vt* (*road*) bloquer; (*view*) cacher; (*progress*) gêner. **obstruction** *n* (act) obstruction *f*; (thing) obstacle *m*; (in traffic) encombrement *m*.

obtain *vt* obtenir. ● *vi* avoir cours. **obtainable** *a* disponible.

obvious *a* évident. **obviously** *adv* manifestement.

occasion *n* occasion *f*; (big event) événement *m*; **on ~** à l'occasion.

occasional *a* (*event*) qui a lieu de temps en temps; **the ~ letter** une lettre de temps en temps. **occasionally** *adv* de temps à autre.

occupation *n* (activity) occupation *f*; (job) métier *m*, profession *f*. **occupational therapy** *n* ergothérapie *f*.

occupier *n* occupant/-e *m/f*.

occupy *vi* occuper.

occur *vi* (*pt* **occurred**) se produire; (arise) se présenter; **~ to sb** venir à l'esprit de qn.

occurrence *n* (event) fait *m*; (instance) occurrence *f*.

ocean *n* océan *m*.

Oceania *n* Océanie *f*.

o'clock *adv* **it is six ~** il est six heures; **at one ~** à une heure.

October *n* octobre *m*.

octopus *n* (*pl* **~es**) pieuvre *f*.

odd *a* bizarre; (*number*) impair; (left over) qui reste; (*sock*) dépareillé; **write the ~ article** écrire un article de temps en temps; **~ jobs** menus travaux *mpl*; **twenty ~** vingt et quelques. **oddity** *n* bizarrerie *f*.

odds *npl* chances *fpl*; (in betting) cote *f* (**on** de); **at ~** en désaccord; **it makes no ~** ça ne fait rien; **~ and ends** des petites choses.

odour, (US) **odor** *n* odeur *f*. **odourless** *a* inodore.

of

⇨ For expressions such as **of course, consist of** ⇨**course, consist.**

● *preposition*

····➤ de; **a photo ~ the dog** une photo du chien; **the king ~ the beasts** le roi des animaux; (**made**) **~ gold** en or; **it's kind ~ you** c'est très gentil de votre part; **some ~ us** quelques-uns d'entre nous; **~ it/them** en; **have you heard ~ it?** est-ce que tu en as entendu parler?

off *adv* **be ~** partir, s'en aller; **I'm ~** je m'en vais; **30 metres ~** à 30 mètres; **a month ~** dans un mois. ● *a* (*gas, water*) coupé; (*tap*) fermé; (*light, TV*) éteint; (*party, match*) annulé; (bad) (*food*) avarié; (*milk*) tourné; **Friday is my day ~** je ne travaille pas le vendredi; **25% ~** 25% de remise. ● *prep* **3 metres ~ the ground** 3 mètres (au-dessus) du sol; **just ~ the kitchen** juste à côté de la cuisine; **that is ~ the point** là n'est pas la question.

O

offal *n* abats *mpl*.

offence *n* (Jur) infraction *f*; **give ~ to** offenser; **take ~** s'offenser (**at** de).

offend *vt* offenser; **be ~ed** s'offenser (**at** de). ● *vi* (Jur) commettre une infraction. **offender** *n* délinquant/-e *m/f*.

offensive *a* (*remark*) injurieux; (*language*) grossier; (*smell*) repoussant; (*weapon*) offensif. ● *n* offensive *f*.

offer *vt* (*pt* **offered**) offrir. ● *n* offre *f*; **on ~** en promotion.

offhand *a* désinvolte. ● *adv* à l'improviste.

office *n* bureau *m*; (duty) fonction *f*; **in ~** au pouvoir. ● *a* de bureau.

officer *n* (army) officier *m*; (**police**) **~** policier *m*; (**government**) **~** fonctionnaire *mf*.

official *a* officiel. ● *n* (civil servant) fonctionnaire *mf*; (of party, union) officiel/-le *m/f*; (of police, customs) agent *m*.

off: **~-licence** *n* magasin *m* de vins et spiritueux. **~-line** *a* autonome; (switched off) déconnecté. **~-load** *vt* (*stock*) écouler; (Comput) décharger. **~-peak** *a* (*call*) au tarif réduit; (*travel*) en période creuse. **~-putting** *a* rebutant. **~set** *vt* (*pt* **-set**; *pres p* **-setting**) compenser. **~shore** *a* (*waters*) du large; (*funds*) hors-lieu *inv*. **~side** *a* (Sport) hors jeu *inv*; (Auto) du côté du conducteur. **~spring** *n inv* progéniture *f*. **~-white** *a* blanc cassé *inv*.

often *adv* souvent; **how ~ do you meet?** vous vous voyez tous les combien?; **every so ~** de temps en temps.

oil *n* (for lubrication, cooking) huile *f*; (for fuel) pétrole *m*; (for heating) mazout *m*. ● *vt* huiler. **~field** *n* gisement *m* pétrolifère. **~-painting** *n* peinture *f* à l'huile. **~skins** *npl* ciré *m*. **~-tanker** *n* pétrolier *m*.

oily *a* graisseux.

ointment *n* pommade *f*.

OK, okay *a* d'accord; **is it ~ if...?** ça va si...?; **feel ~** aller bien.

old *a* vieux; (*person*) vieux, âgé; (former) ancien; **how ~ is he?** quel âge a-t-il?; **he is eight years ~** il a huit ans; **~er, ~est** aîné. **~ age** *n* vieillesse *f*. **~-age pensioner** *n* retraité/-e *m/f*. **~-fashioned** *a* démodé; (person) vieux jeu *inv*. **~ man** *n* vieillard *m*, vieux *m*. **~ woman** *n* vieille *f*.

olive *n* olive *f*; **~ oil** huile *f* d'olive. ● *a* olive *inv*.

Olympic *a* olympique. **~ Games** *npl* Jeux *mpl* olympiques.

omelette *n* omelette *f*.

omen *n* augure *m*.

ominous *a* (*presence, cloud*) menaçant; (*sign*) de mauvais augure.

omission *n* omission *f*. **omit** *vt* (*pt* **omitted**) omettre.

on *prep* sur; **~ the table** sur la table; **put the key ~ it** mets la clé dessus; **~ 22 March** le 22 mars; **~ Monday** lundi; **~ TV** à la télé; **~ video** en vidéo; **be ~ steroids** prendre des stéroïdes; **~ arriving** en arrivant. ● *a* (*TV, oven, light*) allumé; (*dishwasher, radio*) en marche; (*tap*) ouvert; (*lid*) mis; **the match is still ~** le match aura lieu quand même; **the news is ~ in 10 minutes** les informations sont dans 10 minutes. ● *adv* **have sth ~** porter qch; **20 years ~** 20 ans plus tard; **from that day ~** à partir de ce jour-là; **further ~** plus loin; **~ and off** (occasionally) de temps en temps; **go ~ and ~** (*person*) parler pendant des heures.

once *adv* une fois; (formerly)

autrefois. ● *conj* une fois que; **all at ~** tout d'un coup.

oncoming *a* (*vehicle*) qui approche.

one *det & n* un/-e (*m/f*). ● *pron* un/-e *m/f*; (impersonal) on; **~ (and only)** seul (et unique); **a big ~** un grand/une grande; **this/that ~** celui-ci/-là, celle-ci/-là; **~ another** l'un/-e l'autre. **~-off** *a* ▣ unique, exceptionnel. **~self** *pron* soi-même; (reflexive) se. **~-way** *a* (*street*) à sens unique; (*ticket*) simple.

ongoing *a* (*process*) continu; **be ~** être en cours.

onion *n* oignon *m*.

onlooker *n* spectateur/-trice *m/f*.

only *a* seul; **~ son** fils unique. ● *adv & conj* seulement; **he is ~ six** il n'a que six ans; **~ too** extrêmement.

onset *n* début *m*.

onward(s) *adv* en avant.

open *a* ouvert; (*view*) dégagé; (free to all) public; (undisguised) manifeste; (*question*) en attente; **in the ~ air** en plein air. ● *vt/i* (*door*) (s')ouvrir; (*shop, play*) ouvrir; **~ out** *or* **up** (s')ouvrir. **~-ended** *a* (*stay*) de durée indéterminée; (*debate, question*) ouvert. **~-heart** *a* (*surgery*) à cœur ouvert.

opening *n* (of book) début *m*; (of exhibition, shop) ouverture *f*; (of film) première *f*; (in market) débouché *m*; (job) poste *m* (disponible).

open: **~-minded** *a* **be ~-minded** avoir l'esprit ouvert. **~-plan** *a* paysagé.

opera *n* opéra *m*.

operate *vt/i* opérer; (Tech) (faire) fonctionner; **~ on** (Med) opérer; **operating theatre** salle *f* d'opération.

operation *n* opération *f*; **have an ~** se faire opérer; **in ~** (*plan*) en vigueur; (*mine*) en service.

operative *n* employé/-e *m/f*. ● *a* (*law*) en vigueur.

operator *n* opérateur/-trice *m/f*; (telephonist) standardiste *mf*.

opinion *n* opinion *f*, avis *m*. **opinionated** *a* qui a des avis sur tout.

opponent *n* adversaire *mf*.

opportunity *n* occasion *f* (**to do** de faire).

oppose *vt* s'opposer à; **as ~d to** par opposition à. **opposing** *a* opposé.

opposite *a* (*direction, side*) opposé; (*building*) d'en face. ● *n* contraire *m*. ● *adv* en face. ● *prep* **~ (to)** en face de.

opposition *n* opposition *f*.

oppress *vt* opprimer. **oppressive** *a* (cruel) oppressif; (*heat*) oppressant.

opt *vi* **~ for** opter pour; **~ out** refuser de participer (**of** à); **~ to do** choisir de faire.

optical *a* optique. **~ illusion** *n* illusion *f* d'optique. **~ scanner** *n* lecteur *m* optique.

optician *n* opticien/-ne *m/f*.

optimism *n* optimisme *m*. **optimist** *n* optimiste *mf*. **optimistic** *a* optimiste.

option *n* option *f*; (choice) choix *m*.

optional *a* facultatif; **~ extras** accessoires *mpl* en option.

or *conj* ou; (with negative) ni.

oral *n & a* oral (*m*).

orange *n* (fruit) orange *f*; (*colour*) orange *m*. ● *a* (colour) orange *inv*.

orbit *n* orbite *f*. ● *vt* décrire une orbite autour de.

orchard *n* verger *m*.

orchestra *n* orchestre *m*.

orchid *n* orchidée *f*.

ordeal *n* épreuve *f*.

order *n* ordre *m*; (Comm)

O

commande *f*; **in ~** (tidy) en ordre; (*document*) en règle; **in ~ that** pour que; **in ~ to** pour. ● *vt* ordonner; (*goods*) commander; **~ sb to** ordonner à qn de.

orderly *a* (tidy) ordonné; (not unruly) discipliné. ● *n* (Mil) planton *m*; (Med) aide-soignant/-e *m/f*.

ordinary *a* (usual) ordinaire; (average) moyen.

ore *n* minerai *m*.

organ *n* organe *m*; (Mus) orgue *m*.

organic *a* organique; (*produce*) biologique.

organization *n* organisation *f*.

organize *vt* organiser.

organizer *n* organisateur/-trice *m/f*; **electronic ~** agenda *m* électronique.

orgasm *n* orgasme *m*.

Orient *n* **the ~** l'Orient *m*. **oriental** *a* oriental.

origin *n* origine *f*.

original *a* original; (*inhabitant*) premier; (*member*) originaire. **originality** *n* originalité *f*. **originally** *adv* (at the outset) à l'origine.

originate *vi* (plan) prendre naissance; **~ from** provenir de; (person) venir de. ● *vt* être l'auteur de. **originator** *n* (of idea) auteur *m*; (of invention) créateur/-trice *m/f*.

ornament *n* (decoration) ornement *m*; (object) objet *m* décoratif.

orphan *n* orphelin/-e *m/f*. ● *vt* rendre orphelin. **orphanage** *n* orphelinat *m*.

orthopaedic *a* orthopédique.

ostentatious *a* tape-à-l'œil *inv*.

osteopath *n* ostéopathe *mf*.

ostrich *n* autruche *f*.

other *a* autre; **the ~ one** l'autre *mf*. ● *n & pron* autre *mf*; (**some**) **~s** d'autres. ● *adv* **~ than** (apart from) à part; (otherwise than) autrement que. **otherwise** *adv* autrement.

otter *n* loutre *f*.

ouch *interj* aïe!

ought *v aux* devoir; **you ~ to stay** vous devriez rester; **he ~ to succeed** il devrait réussir; **I ~ to have done it** j'aurais dû le faire.

ounce *n* once *f* (= *28.35 g*).

our *a* notre, *pl* nos.

ours *poss* le *or* la nôtre, les nôtres.

ourselves *pron* (reflexive) nous; (emphatic) nous-mêmes; (after preposition) **for ~** pour nous, pour nous-mêmes.

out *adv* dehors; **he's ~** il est sorti; **further ~** plus loin; **be ~** (*book*) être publié; (*light*) être éteint; (*sun*) briller; (*flower*) être épanoui; (*tide*) être bas; (*player*) être éliminé; **~ of** hors de; **go/walk/get ~ of** sortir de; **~ of pity** par pitié; **made ~ of** fait de; **5 ~ of 6** 5 sur 6. **~break** *n* (of war) déclenchement *m*; (of violence, boils) éruption *f*. **~burst** *n* explosion *f*. **~cast** *n* paria *m*. **~class** *vt* surclasser. **~come** *n* résultat *m*. **~cry** *n* tollé *m*. **~dated** *a* démodé. **~door** *a* (*activity*) de plein air; (*pool*) en plein air. **~doors** *adv* dehors.

outer *a* extérieur; **~ space** espace *m* extra-atmosphérique.

outfit *n* (clothes) tenue *f*.

outgoing *a* (*minister, tenant*) sortant; (sociable) ouvert. **outgoings** *npl* dépenses *fpl*.

outgrow *vt* (*pt* **-grew**; *pp* **-grown**) (*clothes*) devenir trop grand pour; (*habit*) dépasser.

outing *n* sortie *f*.

outlaw *n* hors-la-loi *m inv*. ● *vt* déclarer illégal.

outlet *n* (for water, gas) tuyau *m* de sortie; (for goods) débouché *m*; (for feelings) exutoire *m*.

outline *n* contour *m*; (of plan) grandes lignes *fpl*; (of essay) plan *m*. ● *vt* tracer le contour de; (summarize) exposer brièvement.

out: **~live** *vt* survivre à. **~look** *n* perspective *f*. **~number** *vt* surpasser en nombre. **~ of date** *a* démodé; (expired) périmé. **~ of hand** *a* incontrôlable. **~ of order** *a* en panne. **~ of work** *a* sans travail. **~patient** *n* malade *mf* externe.

output *n* rendement *m*; (Comput) sortie *f*. ● *vt/i* (Comput) sortir.

outrage *n* (anger) indignation *f*; (atrocity) attentat *m*; (scandal) outrage *m*. ● *vt* (*morals*) outrager; (*person*) scandaliser. **outrageous** *a* scandaleux.

outright *adv* (completely) catégoriquement; (killed) sur le coup. ● *a* (*majority*) absolu; (*ban*) catégorique; (*hostility*) pur et simple.

outset *n* début *m*.

outside *n* extérieur *m*. ● *adv* dehors. ● *prep* en dehors de; (in front of) devant. ● *a* extérieur. **outsider** *n* étranger/-ère *m/f*; (Sport) outsider *m*.

out: **~skirts** *npl* périphérie *f*. **~spoken** *a* franc. **~standing** *a* exceptionnel; (not settled) en suspens.

outward *a & adv* vers l'extérieur; (*sign*) extérieur; (*journey*) d'aller. **outwards** *adv* vers l'extérieur.

oval *n & a* ovale (*m*).

ovary *n* ovaire *m*.

oven *n* four *m*.

over *prep* (across) par-dessus; (above) au-dessus de; (covering) sur; (more than) plus de; **it's ~ the road** c'est de l'autre côté de la rue; **~ here/there** par ici/là; **children ~ six** les enfants de plus de six ans; **~ the weekend** pendant le week-end; **all ~ the house** partout dans la maison. ● *a, adv* (*term*) terminé; (*war*) fini; **get sth ~ with** en finir avec qch; **ask sb ~** inviter qn; **~ and ~** (**again**) à plusieurs reprises; **five times ~** cinq fois de suite.

overall *a* global, d'ensemble; (*length*) total. ● *adv* globalement.

overalls *npl* combinaison *f*.

over: **~board** *adv* par-dessus bord. **~cast** *a* couvert. **~charge** *vt* faire payer trop cher à. **~coat** *n* pardessus *m*.

overcome *vt* (*pt* **-came**; *pp* **-come**) (*enemy*) vaincre; (*difficulty, fear*) surmonter; **~ by** accablé de.

overcrowded *a* bondé; (*country*) surpeuplé.

overdo *vt* (*pt* **-did**; *pp* **-done**) (Culin) trop cuire; **~ it** (overwork) en faire trop.

over: **~dose** *n* surdose *f*, overdose *f*. **~draft** *n* découvert *m*. **~draw** *vt* (*pt* **-drew**; *pp* **-drawn**) faire un découvert sur. **~due** *a* en retard; (*bill*) impayé.

overflow[1] *vi* déborder.

overflow[2] *n* (outlet) trop-plein *m*.

overhaul *vt* réviser.

overhead[1] *adv* au-dessus; (in sky) dans le ciel.

overhead[2] *a* aérien; **~ projector** rétroprojecteur *m*. **overheads** *npl* frais *mpl* généraux.

over: **~hear** *vt* (*pt* **-heard**) entendre par hasard. **~lap** *vt/i* (*pt* **-lapped**) (se) chevaucher. **~leaf** *adv* au verso. **~load** *vt* surcharger. **~look** *vt* (*window*) donner sur; (miss) ne pas voir.

overnight[1] *adv* dans la nuit; (instantly: fig) du jour au lendemain.

overnight[2] *a* (*train*) de nuit; (*stay*) d'une nuit; (fig) soudain.

over: **~power** *vt* (*thief*) maîtriser; (*army*) vaincre; (fig) accabler. **~priced** *a* trop cher.

~rate *vt* surestimer. **~react** *vi* réagir de façon excessive. **~riding** *a* (*consideration*) numéro un; (*importance*) primordial. **~rule** *vt* (*decision*) annuler.

overrun *vt* (*pt* **-ran**; *pp* **-run**; *pres p* **-running**) (*country*) envahir; (*budget*) dépasser. ● *vi* (meeting) durer plus longtemps que prévu.

overseas *a* étranger. ● *adv* outre-mer, à l'étranger.

over: **~see** *vt* (*pt* **-saw**; *pp* **-seen**) surveiller. **~sight** *n* omission *f*. **~sleep** *vi* (*pt* **-slept**) se réveiller trop tard. **~take** *vt/i* (*pt* **-took**; *pp* **-taken**) dépasser; (fig) frapper. **~time** *n* heures *fpl* supplémentaires. **~turn** *vt/i* (se) renverser. **~weight** *a* trop gros.

overwhelm *vt* (*enemy*) écraser; (*shame*) accabler. **overwhelmed** *a* (with offers, calls) submergé (**with, by** de); (with shame, work) accablé; (by sight) ébloui. **overwhelming** *a* (*heat, grief*) accablant; (*defeat, victory*) écrasant; (*urge*) irrésistible.

overwork *vt/i* (se) surmener. ● *n* surmenage *m*.

owe *vt* devoir. **owing** *a* dû; **owing to** en raison de.

owl *n* hibou *m*.

own *a* propre. ● *pron* **my ~** le mien, la mienne; **a house of one's ~** sa propre maison; **on one's ~** tout seul. ● *vt* posséder; **~ up** (**to**) [!] avouer. **owner** *n* propriétaire *mf*. **ownership** *n* propriété *f*; (of land) possession *f*.

oxygen *n* oxygène *m*.

oyster *n* huître *f*.

ozone *n* ozone *m*; **~ layer** couche *f* d'ozone.

PA *abbr* ⇒PERSONAL ASSISTANT.

pace *n* pas *m*; (speed) allure *f*; **keep ~ with** suivre. ● *vt* (*room*) arpenter. ● *vi* **~** (**up and down**) faire les cent pas.

Pacific *n* **~** (**Ocean**) océan *m* Pacifique.

pack *n* paquet *m*; (Mil) sac *m*; (of hounds) meute *f*; (of thieves) bande *f*; (of lies) tissu *m*. ● *vt* (into case) mettre dans une valise; (into box, crate) emballer; (for sale) conditionner; (*crowd*) remplir complètement; **~ one's suitcase** faire sa valise. ● *vi* faire ses valises; **~ into** (cram) s'entasser dans; **~ off** expédier; **send ~ing** envoyer promener.

package *n* paquet *m*; (Comput) progiciel *m*; **~ deal** offre *f* globale; **~ holiday** voyage *m* organisé. ● *vt* empaqueter.

packed *a* (crowded) bondé; **~ lunch** repas *m* froid.

packet *n* paquet *m*.

packing *n* (action, material) emballage *m*.

pad *n* (of paper) bloc *m*; (to protect) protection *f*; (for ink) tampon *m*; (**launch**) **~** rampe *f* de lancement. ● *vt* (*pt* **padded**) rembourrer; (text: fig) délayer. ● *vi* (*pt* **padded**) (walk) marcher à pas feutrés. **padding** *n* rembourrage *m*.

paddle *n* pagaie *f*. ● *vt* **~ a canoe** pagayer. ● *vi* patauger.

padlock *n* cadenas *m*. ● *vt* cadenasser.

paediatrician *n* pédiatre *mf*.

pagan *a & n* païen/-ne (*m/f*).

page *n* (of book) page *f*. ● *vt* (on pager) rechercher; (over speaker) faire appeler. **pager** *n* radiomessageur *m*.

pain *n* douleur *f*; **~s** efforts *mpl*; **be in ~** souffrir; **take ~s to** se donner du mal pour. ● *vt* (grieve) peiner. **painful** *a* douloureux; (laborious) pénible. **~-killer** *n* analgésique *m*. **painless** *a* (*operation*) indolore; (*death*) sans souffrance; (trouble-free) sans peine. **painstaking** *a* minutieux.

paint *n* peinture *f*; **~s** (in tube, box) couleurs *fpl*. ● *vt/i* peindre. **~brush** *n* pinceau *m*. **painter** *n* peintre *m*. **painting** *n* peinture *f*. **~work** *n* peintures *fpl*.

pair *n* paire *f*; (of people) couple *m*; **a ~ of trousers** un pantalon. ● *vi* **~ off** former un couple.

pajamas *npl* (US) = PYJAMAS.

Pakistan *n* Pakistan *m*.

palace *n* palais *m*.

palatable *a* (*food*) savoureux; (*solution*) acceptable. **palate** *n* palais *m*.

pale *a* pâle. ● *vi* pâlir.

Palestine *n* Palestine *f*.

pallid *a* pâle.

palm *n* (of hand) paume *f*; (tree) palmier *m*; (symbol) palme *f*. □ **~ off** 🅸 **~ sth off as** faire passer qch pour; **~ sth off on sb** refiler qch à qn 🅸.

palpitate *vi* palpiter.

paltry *a* (**-ier, -iest**) dérisoire, piètre.

pamper *vt* choyer.

pamphlet *n* brochure *f*.

pan *n* casserole *f*; (for frying) poêle *f*.

pancake *n* crêpe *f*.

pandemonium *n* tohu-bohu *m*.

pander *vi* **~ to** (*person, taste*) flatter bassement.

pane *n* carreau *m*, vitre *f*.

panel *n* (of door) panneau *m*; (of experts, judges) commission *f*; (on discussion programme) invités *mpl*; (**instrument**) **~** tableau *m* de bord.

pang *n* serrement *m* au cœur; **~s of conscience** remords *mpl*.

panic *n* panique *f*. ● *vt/i* (*pt* **panicked**) (s')affoler. **~-stricken** *a* pris de panique, affolé.

pansy *n* (Bot) pensée *f*.

pant *vi* haleter.

panther *n* panthère *f*.

pantomime *n* (show) spectacle *m* de Noël; (mime) mime *m*.

pantry *n* garde-manger *m inv*.

pants *npl* (underwear) slip *m*; (trousers: US) pantalon *m*.

paper *n* papier *m*; (newspaper) journal *m*; (exam) épreuve *f*; (essay) exposé *m*; (wallpaper) papier *m* peint; (identity) **~s** papiers *mpl* (d'identité); **on ~** par écrit. ● *vt* (*room*) tapisser. **~back** *n* livre *m* de poche. **~-clip** *n* trombone *m*. **~ feed tray** *n* (Comput) bac *m* d'alimentation en papier. **~work** *n* (work) travail *m* administratif; (documentation) documents *mpl*.

par *n* **be below ~** ne pas être en forme; **on a ~ with** (*performance*) comparable à; (*person*) l'égal de; (golf) par *m*.

parachute *n* parachute *m*. ● *vi* descendre en parachute.

parade *n* (procession) parade *f*; (Mil) défilé *m*. ● *vi* défiler. ● *vt* faire étalage de.

paradise *n* paradis *m*.

paradox *n* paradoxe *m*.

paraffin *n* pétrole *m* (*lampant*); (wax) paraffine *f*.

paragliding *n* parapente *m*.

paragon *n* modèle *m*.

paragraph *n* paragraphe *m*.

P

parallel *a* parallèle. ● *n* parallèle *m*; (maths) parallèle *f*.

paralyse *vt* paralyser. **paralysis** *n* paralysie *f*.

paramedic *n* auxiliaire *mf* médical/-e.

paramount *a* suprême.

paranoia *n* paranoïa *f*. **paranoid** *a* paranoïaque; (Psych) paranoïde.

paraphernalia *n* attirail *m*.

parasol *n* ombrelle *f*; (on table, at beach) parasol *m*.

paratrooper *n* (Mil) parachutiste *mf*.

parcel *n* paquet *m*.

parchment *n* parchemin *m*.

pardon *n* pardon *m*; (Jur) grâce *f*; **I beg your ~** je vous demande pardon. ● *vt* (*pt* **pardoned**) pardonner (**sb for sth** qch à qn); (Jur) gracier.

parent *n* parent *m*.

parenthesis *n* (*pl* **-theses**) parenthèse *f*.

parenthood *n* (fatherhood) paternité *f*; (motherhood) maternité *f*.

Paris *n* Paris.

parish *n* (Relig) paroisse *f*; (municipal) commune *f*.

park *n* parc *m*. ● *vt/i* (se) garer; (remain parked) stationner. **~ and ride** *n* parc *m* relais.

parking *n* stationnement *m*; **no ~** stationnement interdit. **~-lot** *n* (US) parking *m*. **~-meter** *n* parcmètre *m*. **~ ticket** *n* (fine) contravention *f*, PV *m* [!].

parliament *n* parlement *m*. **parliamentary** *a* parlementaire.

parlour, (US) **parlor** *n* salon *m*.

parody *n* parodie *f*. ● *vt* parodier.

parole *n* **on ~** en liberté conditionnelle.

parrot *n* perroquet *m*.

parry *vt* (Sport) parer; (*question*) éluder. ● *n* parade *f*.

parsley *n* persil *m*.

parsnip *n* panais *m*.

part *n* partie *f*; (of serial) épisode *m*; (of machine) pièce *f*; (Theat) rôle *m*; (side in dispute) parti *m*; **in ~** en partie; **on the ~ of** de la part de; **take ~ in** participer à. ● *a* partiel. ● *adv* en partie. ● *vt/i* (separate) (se) séparer; **~ with** se séparer de.

part-exchange *n* reprise *f*; **take sth in ~** reprendre qch.

partial *a* partiel; (biased) partial; **be ~ to** avoir un faible pour.

participant *n* participant/-e *m/f*. **participate** *vi* participer (**in** à). **participation** *n* participation *f*.

participle *n* participe *m*.

particular *n* détail *m*; **~s** détails *mpl*; **in ~** en particulier. ● *a* particulier; (fussy) difficile; (careful) méticuleux; **that ~ man** cet homme-là. **particularly** *adv* particulièrement.

parting *n* séparation *f*; (in hair) raie *f*. ● *a* d'adieu.

partition *n* (of room) cloison *f*; (Pol) partition *f*. ● *vt* (*room*) cloisonner; (*country*) partager.

partly *adv* en partie.

partner *n* (professional) associé/-e *m/f*; (economic, sporting) partenaire *mf*; (spouse) époux/-se *m/f*; (unmarried) partenaire *mf*. **partnership** *n* association *f*.

partridge *n* perdrix *f*.

part-time *a & adv* à temps partiel.

party *n* fête *f*; (formal) réception *f*; (group) groupe *m*; (Pol) parti *m*; (Jur) partie *f*.

pass *vt/i* (*pt* **passed**) passer; (overtake) dépasser; (in exam) réussir; (approve) (*candidate*) admettre; (*invoice*) approuver; (*remark*) faire; (*judgement*) prononcer; (*law, bill*) adopter; **~ (by)** (*building*) passer devant;

(*person*) croiser. ● *n* (permit) laisser-passer *m inv*; (ticket) carte *f* d'abonnement; (Geog) col *m*; (Sport) passe *f*; ~ (**mark**) (in exam) moyenne *f*. □ ~ **away** mourir; ~ **out** (faint) s'évanouir; ~ **sth out** distribuer qch; ~ **over** (overlook) délaisser; ~ **up** (forego) laisser passer.

passage *n* (way through, text) passage *m*; (voyage) traversée *f*; (corridor) couloir *m*.

passenger *n* (in car, plane, ship) passager/-ère *m/f*; (in train, bus, tube) voyageur/-euse *m/f*.

passer-by *n* (*pl* **passers-by**) passant/-e *m/f*.

passing *a* (*motorist*) qui passe; (*whim*) passager; (*reference*) en passant.

passion *n* passion *f*. **passionate** *a* passionné.

passive *a* passif.

passport *n* passeport *m*.

password *n* mot *m* de passe.

past *a* (*times, problems*) passé; (*president*) ancien; **the ~ months** ces derniers mois. ● *n* passé *m*. ● *prep* (beyond) après; **walk/go ~ sth** passer devant qch; **10 ~ 6** six heures dix; **it's ~ 11** il est 11 heures passées. ● *adv* **go/walk ~** passer.

pasta *n* pâtes *fpl* (alimentaires).

paste *n* (glue) colle *f*; (dough) pâte *f*; (of fish, meat) pâté *m*; (jewellery) strass *m*. ● *vt* coller.

pasteurize *vt* pasteuriser.

pastime *n* passe-temps *m inv*.

pastry *n* (dough) pâte *f*; (tart) pâtisserie *f*.

pat *vt* (*pt* **patted**) tapoter. ● *n* petite tape *f*.

patch *n* pièce *f*; (over eye) bandeau *m*; (spot) tache *f*; (of snow, ice) plaque *f*; (of vegetables) carré *m*; **bad ~** période *f* difficile. □ ~ **up** (*trousers*) rapiécer; (*quarrel*) résoudre.

patent *a* (obvious) manifeste; (patented) breveté; ~ **leather** cuir *m* verni. ● *n* brevet *m*. ● *vt* faire breveter.

path *n* (*pl* **-s**) sentier *m*, chemin *m*; (in park) allée *f*; (of rocket) trajectoire *f*.

pathetic *a* misérable; (bad [!]) lamentable.

patience *n* patience *f*.

patient *a* patient. ● *n* patient/-e *m/f*. **patiently** *adv* patiemment.

patriotic *a* patriotique; (*person*) patriote.

patrol *n* patrouille *f*; ~ **car** voiture *f* de police. ● *vt/i* patrouiller (dans).

patron *n* (of the arts) mécène *m*; (customer) client/-e *m/f*. **patronage** *n* clientèle *f*; (support) patronage *m*. **patronize** *vt* (*person*) traiter avec condescendance; (*establishment*) fréquenter.

patter *n* (of steps) bruit *m*; (of rain) crépitement *m*.

pattern *n* motif *m*, dessin *m*; (for sewing) patron *m*; (for knitting) modèle *m*.

paunch *n* ventre *m*.

pause *n* pause *f*. ● *vi* faire une pause; (hesitate) hésiter.

pave *vt* paver; ~ **the way** ouvrir la voie (**for** à).

pavement *n* trottoir *m*; (US) chaussée *f*.

paving stone *n* pavé *m*.

paw *n* patte *f*. ● *vt* (*animal*) donner des coups de patte à; (touch [!]) peloter [!].

pawn *n* pion *m*. ● *vt* mettre en gage. ~**broker** *n* prêteur/-euse *m/f* sur gages. ~**-shop** *n* mont-de-piété *m*.

pay *vt* (*pt* **paid**) payer; (*interest*) rapporter; (*compliment, attention*)

P

faire; (*visit, homage*) rendre. ● *vi* payer; (*business*) rapporter; ~ **for sth** payer qch. ● *n* salaire *m*; ~ **rise** augmentation *f* (*de salaire*). □ ~ **back** rembourser; ~ **in** déposer; ~ **off** (*loan*) rembourser; (*worker*) congédier; (succeed) être payant; ~ **out** payer, débourser.

payable *a* payable; ~ **to** (*cheque*) à l'ordre de.

payment *n* paiement *m*; (regular) versement *m*; (reward) récompense *f*.

payroll *n* fichier *m* des salaires; **be on the ~ of** être employé par.

PC *abbr* ⇒PERSONAL COMPUTER.

PE *abbr* (**physical education**) éducation *f* physique, EPS *f*.

pea *n* (petit) pois *m*.

peace *n* paix *f*; ~ **of mind** tranquillité *f* d'esprit. **peaceful** *a* (tranquil) paisible; (peaceable) pacifique.

peach *n* pêche *f*.

peacock *n* paon *m*.

peak *n* (of mountain) pic *m*; (of cap) visière *f*; (maximum) maximum *m*; (on graph) sommet *m*; (of career) apogée *m*; (of fitness) meilleur *m*; ~ **hours** heures *fpl* de pointe.

peal *n* (of bells) carillon *m*; (of laughter) éclat *m*.

peanut *n* cacahuète *f*; ~**s** (money ⊠) clopinettes *fpl* ⊡.

pear *n* poire *f*.

pearl *n* perle *f*.

peasant *n* paysan/-ne *m*/*f*.

peat *n* tourbe *f*.

pebble *n* caillou *m*; (on beach) galet *m*.

peck *vt*/*i* (*food*) picorer; (attack) donner des coups de bec (à). ● *n* coup *m* de bec; **a ~ on the cheek** une bise.

peckish *a* **be ~** ⊡ avoir faim.

peculiar *a* (odd) bizarre; (special) particulier (**to** à). **peculiarity** *n* bizarrerie *f*.

pedal *n* pédale *f*. ● *vi* pédaler.

pedantic *a* pédant.

peddle *vt* colporter; (*drugs*) faire du trafic de.

pedestrian *n* piéton *m*. ● *a* (*precinct, street*) piétonnier; (fig) prosaïque; ~ **crossing** passage *m* pour piétons.

pedigree *n* (of animal) pedigree *m*; (of person) ascendance *f*. ● *a* (*dog*) de pure race.

pee *vi* ⊡ faire pipi ⊡.

peek *vi* & *n* = PEEP.

peel *n* (on fruit) peau *m*; (removed) épluchures *fpl*. ● *vt* (*fruit, vegetables*) éplucher; (*prawn*) décortiquer. ● *vi* (of skin) peler; (of paint) s'écailler.

peep *vi* jeter un coup d'œil (furtif) (**at** à). ● *n* coup *m* d'œil (furtif). ~**hole** *n* judas *m*.

peer *vi* ~ (**at**) regarder fixement. ● *n* (equal, noble) pair *m*; (contemporary) personne *f* de la même génération. **peerage** *n* pairie *f*.

peg *n* (for clothes) pince *f* à linge; (to hang coats) patère *f*; (for tent) piquet *m*. ● *vt* (*pt* **pegged**) (*clothes*) accrocher avec des pinces; (*prices*) indexer.

pejorative *a* péjoratif.

pelican *n* pélican *m*; ~ **crossing** passage *m* pour piétons.

pellet *n* (round mass) boulette *f*; (for gun) plomb *m*.

pelt *vt* bombarder (**with** de). ● *n* (skin) peau *f*.

pelvis *n* (Anat) bassin *m*.

pen *n* stylo *m*; (for sheep) enclos *m*; (for baby, cattle) parc *m*.

penal *a* pénal. **penalize** *vt* pénaliser.

penalty *n* peine *f*; (fine) amende *f*; (in football) penalty *m*.

penance *n* pénitence *f*.

pence ⇒PENNY.

pencil *n* crayon *m*. ● *vt* (*pt* **pencilled**) crayonner; **~ in** noter provisoirement. **~-sharpener** *n* taille-crayons *m inv*.

pending *a* (*matter*) en souffrance; (Jur) en instance. ● *prep* (until) en attendant.

penetrate *vt* pénetrer; (*silence, defences*) percer; (*organization*) infiltrer. ● *vi* pénétrer. **penetrating** *a* pénétrant.

pen-friend *n* correspondant/-e *m/f*.

penguin *n* manchot *m*, pingouin *m*.

pen: **~knife** *n* (*pl* **-knives**) canif *m*. **~-name** *n* pseudonyme *m*.

penniless *a* sans le sou.

penny *n* (*pl* **pennies** *or* **pence**) (unit of currency) penny *m*; (small amount) centime *m*.

pension *n* (from state) pension *f*; (from employer) retraite *f*; **~ scheme** plan *m* de retraite. ● *vt* **~ off** mettre à la retraite. **pensioner** *n* retraité/-e *m/f*.

pensive *a* songeur.

penthouse *n* appartement *m* de luxe (*au dernier étage*).

penultimate *a* avant-dernier.

people *npl* gens *mpl*, personnes *fpl*; **English ~** les Anglais *mpl*; **~ say** on dit. ● *n* peuple *m*. ● *vt* peupler. **~ carrier** *n* monospace *m*.

pepper *n* poivre *m*; (vegetable) poivron *m*. ● *vt* (Culin) poivrer.

peppermint *n* (plant) menthe *f* poivrée; (sweet) bonbon *m* à la menthe.

per *prep* par; **~ annum** par an; **~ cent** pour cent; **~ kilo** le kilo; **ten km ~ hour** dix km à l'heure.

percentage *n* pourcentage *m*.

perception *n* perception *f*. **perceptive** *a* perspicace.

perch *n* (of bird) perchoir *m*. ● *vi* (se) percher.

perennial *a* perpétuel; (*plant*) vivace.

perfect[1] *vt* perfectionner.

perfect[2] *a* parfait. ● *n* (Ling) parfait *m*. **perfectly** *adv* parfaitement.

perfection *n* perfection *f*; **to ~** à la perfection.

perforate *vt* perforer.

perform *vt* (*task*) exécuter; (*function*) remplir; (*operation*) procéder à; (*play*) jouer; (*song*) chanter. ● *vi* (*actor, musician, team*) jouer; **~ well/badly** (*candidate, business*) avoir de bons/de mauvais résultats. **performance** *n* interprétation *f*; (of car, team) performance *f*; (show) représentation *f*; (fuss) histoire *f*. **performer** *n* artiste *mf*.

perfume *n* parfum *m*.

perhaps *adv* peut-être.

peril *n* péril *m*. **perilous** *a* périlleux.

perimeter *n* périmètre *m*.

period *n* période *f*; (era) époque *f*; (lesson) cours *m*; (Gram) point *m*; (Med) règles *fpl*. ● *a* d'époque. **periodical** *n* périodique *m*.

peripheral *a* (*vision, suburb*) périphérique; (*issue*) annexe. ● *n* (Comput) périphérique *m*.

perish *vi* périr; (*rubber*) se détériorer.

perjury *n* faux témoignage *m*.

perk *n* 🄸 avantage *m*. ● *vt/i* **~ up** 🄸 (se) remonter. **perky** *a* 🄸 gai.

perm *n* permanente *f*. ● *vt* **have one's hair ~ed** se faire faire une permanente.

permanent *a* permanent. **permanently** *adv* (*happy*) en permanence; (*employed*) de façon permanente.

P

permissible *a* permis.
permission *n* permission *f*.
permissive *a* libéral; (pej) permissif.
permit[1] *vt* (*pt* **permitted**) permettre (**sb to** à qn de), autoriser (**sb to** qn à).
permit[2] *n* permis *m*.
perpendicular *a* perpendiculaire.
perpetrator *n* auteur *m*.
perpetuate *vt* perpétuer.
perplexed *a* perplexe.
persecute *vt* persécuter.
perseverance *n* persévérance *f*.
persevere *vi* persévérer.
persist *vi* persister (**in doing** à faire). **persistence** *n* persistance *f*. **persistent** *a* (*cough, snow*) persistant; (obstinate) obstiné; (*noise, pressure*) continuel.
person *n* personne *f*; **in ~** en personne.
personal *a* (*life, problem, opinion*) personnel; (*safety, freedom, insurance*) individuel. **~ ad** *n* petite annonce *f*. **~ assistant** *n* secrétaire *mf* de direction. **~ computer** *n* ordinateur *m* (personnel), micro-ordinateur *m*.
personality *n* personnalité *f*; (star) vedette *f*.
personal: **~ organizer** *n* agenda *m*. **~ stereo** *n* baladeur *m*.
personnel *n* personnel *m*.
perspiration *n* (sweat) sueur *f*; (sweating) transpiration *f*. **perspire** *vi* transpirer.
persuade *vt* persuader (**to** de). **persuasion** *n* persuasion *f*. **persuasive** *a* persuasif.
pertinent *a* pertinent.
perturb *vt* troubler.
Peru *n* Pérou *m*.
pervasive *a* (*smell*) pénétrant; (*feeling*) envahissant.
perverse *a* (*desire*) pervers; (*refusal, attitude*) illogique. **perversion** *n* perversion *f*.
pervert[1] *vt* (*truth*) travestir; (*values*) fausser; (*justice*) entraver.
pervert[2] *n* pervers/-e *m/f*.
pessimist *n* pessimiste *mf*. **pessimistic** *a* pessimiste.
pest *n* (insect) insecte *m* nuisible; (animal) animal *m* nuisible; (person [!]) enquiquineur/-euse *m/f* [!].
pester *vt* harceler.
pet *n* animal *m* de compagnie; (favourite) chouchou/-te *m/f*. ● *a* (*theory, charity*) favori; **~ hate** bête *f* noire; **~ name** petit nom *m*. ● *vt* (*pt* **petted**) caresser; (spoil) chouchouter [!].
petal *n* pétale *m*.
peter *vi* **~ out** (*conversation*) tarir; (*supplies*) s'épuiser.
petite *a* (*woman*) menue.
petition *n* pétition *f*. ● *vt* adresser une pétition à.
petrol *n* essence *f*. **~ bomb** *n* cocktail *m* molotov. **~ station** *n* station-service *f*. **~ tank** *n* réservoir *m* d'essence.
petticoat *n* jupon *m*.
petty *a* (**-ier, -iest**) (minor) petit; (mean) mesquin; **~ cash** petite caisse *f*.
pew *n* banc *m* (d'église).
pharmacist *n* pharmacien/-ne *m/f*. **pharmacy** *n* pharmacie *f*.
phase *n* phase *f*. ● *vt* **~ in/out** introduire/supprimer peu à peu.
PhD *abbr* (**Doctor of Philosophy**) doctorat *m*.
pheasant *n* faisan/-e *m/f*.
phenomenon *n* (*pl* **-ena**) phénomène *m*.
phew *interj* ouf.
philosopher *n* philosophe *mf*. **philosophical** *a* philosophique;

(resigned) philosophe. **philosophy** *n* philosophie *f*.

phlegm *n* (Med) mucosité *f*.

phobia *n* phobie *f*.

phone *n* téléphone *m*; **on the ~** au téléphone. ●*vt* (person) téléphoner à; **~ England** téléphoner en Angleterre. ●*vi* téléphoner; **~ back** rappeler. **~ book** *n* annuaire *m*. **~ booth, ~ box** *n* cabine *f* téléphonique. **~ call** *n* coup *m* de fil [I]. **~card** *n* télécarte *f*. **~-in** *n* émission *f* à ligne ouverte. **~ number** *n* numéro *m* de téléphone.

phonetic *a* phonétique.

phoney *a* (**-ier, -iest**) [I] faux. ●*n* [I] (person) charlatan *m*; **it's a ~** c'est un faux.

photocopier *n* photocopieuse *f*.

photocopy *n* photocopie *f*. ●*vt* photocopier.

photograph *n* photographie *f*. ●*vt* photographier. **photographer** *n* photographe *mf*.

phrase *n* expression *f*; (idiom) locution *f*. ●*vt* exprimer, formuler. **~-book** *n* guide *m* de conversation.

physical *a* physique.

physicist *n* physicien/-ne *m/f*.

physics *n* physique *f*.

physiotherapist *n* kinésithérapeute *mf*. **physiotherapy** *n* kinésithérapie *f*.

physique *n* physique *m*.

piano *n* piano *m*.

pick *n* choix *m*; (best) meilleur/-e *m/f*; (tool) pioche *f*. ●*vt* choisir; (*flower*) cueillir; (*lock*) crocheter; **~ a quarrel with** chercher querelle à; **~ one's nose** se curer le nez. □ **~ on** harceler; **~ out** choisir; (identify) distinguer; **~ up** *vt* ramasser; (*sth fallen*) relever; (*weight*) soulever; (*habit, passenger, speed*) prendre; (learn) apprendre; *vi* s'améliorer.

pickaxe *n* pioche *f*.

picket *n* (striker) gréviste *mf*; (stake) piquet *m*; **~ (line)** piquet *m* de grève. ●*vt* (*pt* **picketed**) installer un piquet de grève devant.

pickle *n* conserves *fpl* au vinaigre; (gherkin) cornichon *m*. ●*vt* conserver dans du vinaigre.

pick-up *n* (stylus-holder) lecteur *m*; (on guitar) capteur *m*; (collection) ramassage *m*; (improvement) reprise *f*.

picnic *n* pique-nique *m*. ●*vi* (*pt* **picnicked**) pique-niquer.

pictorial *a* (*magazine*) illustré; (*record*) graphique.

picture *n* image *f*; (painting) tableau *m*; (photograph) photo *f*; (drawing) dessin *m*; (film) film *m*; (fig) description *f*; **the ~s** le cinéma. ●*vt* s'imaginer; **be ~d** (shown) être représenté.

picturesque *a* pittoresque.

pie *n* (sweet) tarte *f*; (savoury) tourte *f*.

piece *n* morceau *m*; (of string, ribbon) bout *m*; (of currency, machine) pièce *f*; **a ~ of advice/furniture** un conseil/meuble; **go to ~s** (fig) s'effondrer; **take to ~s** démonter.

pier *n* jetée *f*.

pierce *vt* percer.

pig *n* porc *m*, cochon *m*.

pigeon *n* pigeon *m*. **~-hole** *n* casier *m*.

pig-headed *a* entêté.

pigsty *n* porcherie *f*.

pigtail *n* natte *f*.

pike *n inv* (fish) brochet *m*.

pile *n* (heap) tas *m*; (stack) pile *f*; (of carpet) poil *m*; **~s of** [I] un tas de [I]. ●*vt* **~ (up)** entasser. ●*vi* **~ into** s'engouffrer dans; **~ up** (*snow, leaves*) s'entasser; (*debts,* *work*) s'accumuler. **~-up** *n* (Auto) carambolage *m*.

pilgrim *n* pèlerin *m*. **pilgrimage** *n* pèlerinage *m*.

pill *n* pilule *f*.

pillar *n* pilier *m*. **~-box** *n* boîte *f* aux lettres.

pillion *n* siège *m* de passager; **ride ~** monter en croupe.

pillow *n* oreiller *m*. **~case** *n* taie *f* d'oreiller.

pilot *n* pilote *m*. ● *a* pilote. ● *vt* (*pt* **piloted**) piloter. **~-light** *n* veilleuse *f*.

pimple *n* bouton *m*.

pin *n* épingle *f*; (of plug) fiche *f*; (for wood, metal) goujon *m*; (in surgery) broche *f*; **have ~s and needles** avoir des fourmis. ● *vt* (*pt* **pinned**) épingler, attacher; (trap) coincer; **~ sb down** (fig) forcer qn à se décider; **~ up** accrocher.

pinafore *n* tablier *m*.

pincers *npl* tenailles *fpl*.

pinch *vt* pincer; (steal 🅸) piquer. ● *vi* (be too tight) serrer. ● *n* (mark) pinçon *m*; (of salt) pincée *f*; **at a ~** à la rigueur.

pine *n* (tree) pin *m*. ● *vi* **~** (**away**) dépérir; **~ for** languir après.

pineapple *n* ananas *m*.

pinecone *n* pomme *f* de pin.

pink *a* & *n* rose (*m*).

pinpoint *vt* (*problem, cause, location*) indiquer; (*time*) déterminer.

pint *n* pinte *f* (GB = *0.57 litre*; US = *0.47 litre*).

pin-up *n* 🅸 pin-up *f inv* 🅸.

pioneer *n* pionnier *m*. ● *vt* **~ the use of** être le premier à utiliser.

pious *a* pieux.

pip *n* (seed) pépin *m*; (sound) top *m*.

pipe *n* tuyau *m*; (to smoke) pipe *f*; (Mus) chalumeau *m*; **~s** cornemuse *f*. ● *vt* transporter par tuyau. □ **~ down** se taire.

pipeline *n* oléoduc *m*; **in the ~** en cours.

piping *n* tuyauterie *f*; **~ hot** fumant.

pique *n* dépit *m*.

pirate *n* pirate *m*. ● *vt* pirater.

Pisces *n* Poissons *mpl*.

pistol *n* pistolet *m*.

pit *n* fosse *f*; (mine) puits *m*; (quarry) carrière *f*; (for orchestra) fosse *f*; (of stomach) creux *m*; (of cherry: US) noyau *m*. ● *vt* (*pt* **pitted**) marquer; (fig) opposer; **~ oneself against** se mesurer à.

pitch *n* (Sport) terrain *m*; (of voice, note) hauteur *f*; (degree) degré *m*; (Mus) ton *m*; (tar) brai *m*. ● *vt* jeter; (*tent*) planter. ● *vi* (*ship*) tanguer. □ **~ in** 🅸 contribuer.

pitfall *n* écueil *m*.

pitiful *a* pitoyable. **pitiless** *a* impitoyable.

pittance *n* **earn a ~** gagner trois fois rien.

pity *n* pitié *f*; (regrettable fact) dommage *m*; **take ~ on** avoir pitié de; **what a ~!** quel dommage! ● *vt* avoir pitié de.

pivot *n* pivot *m*. ● *vi* (*pt* **pivoted**) pivoter.

placard *n* affiche *f*.

place *n* endroit *m*, lieu *m*; (house) maison *f*; (seat, rank) place *f*; **at** *or* **to my ~** chez moi; **change ~s** changer de place; **in the first ~** d'abord; **out of ~** déplacé; **take ~** avoir lieu. ● *vt* placer; (*order*) passer; (remember) situer; **be ~d** (in race) se placer. **~-mat** *n* set *m*.

placid *a* placide.

plagiarism *n* plagiat *m*. **plagiarize** *vt*/*i* plagier.

plague *n* (bubonic) peste *f*; (epidemic) épidémie *f*; (of ants, locusts) invasion *f*. ● *vt* harceler.

plaice *n inv* carrelet *m*.

plain *a* (obvious) clair; (candid)

franc; (simple) simple; (not pretty) sans beauté; (not patterned) uni; ~ **chocolate** chocolat *m* noir; **in ~ clothes** en civil. ● *adv* franchement. ● *n* plaine *f*. **plainly** *adv* clairement; franchement; simplement.

plaintiff *n* plaignant/-e *m/f*.

plaintive *a* plaintif.

plait *vt* tresser. ● *n* natte *f*.

plan *n* projet *m*, plan *m*; (diagram) plan *m*. ● *vt* (*pt* **planned**) projeter (**to do** de faire); (*timetable, day*) organiser; (*economy, work*) planifier. ● *vi* prévoir; ~ **on** s'attendre à.

plane *n* (level) plan *m*; (aeroplane) avion *m*; (tool) rabot *m*. ● *a* plan. ● *vt* raboter.

planet *n* planète *f*.

plank *n* planche *f*.

planning *n* (of economy, work) planification *f*; (of holiday, party) organisation *f*; (of town) urbanisme *m*; **family ~** planning *m* familial; ~ **permission** permis *m* de construire.

plant *n* plante *f*; (Tech) matériel *m*; (factory) usine *f*. ● *vt* planter; (*bomb*) placer.

plaster *n* plâtre *m*; (adhesive) sparadrap *m*. ● *vt* plâtrer; (cover) couvrir (**with** de).

plastic *a* en plastique; (*art, substance*) plastique; ~ **surgery** chirurgie *f* esthétique. ● *n* plastique *m*.

plate *n* assiette *f*; (of metal) plaque *f*; (silverware) argenterie *f*; (in book) gravure *f*. ● *vt* (*metal*) plaquer.

plateau *n* (*pl* ~**x**) plateau *m*; (fig) palier *m*.

platform *n* (stage) estrade *f*; (for speaking) tribune *f*; (Rail) quai *m*; (Pol) plate-forme *f*.

platoon *n* (Mil) section *f*.

play *vt/i* jouer; (*instrument*) jouer de; (*record*) mettre; (*game*) jouer à; (*opponent*) jouer contre; (*match*) disputer; ~ **safe** ne pas prendre de risques. ● *n* jeu *m*; (Theat) pièce *f*. □ ~ **down** minimiser; ~ **on** (*fears*) exploiter; ~ **up** 🗈 commencer à faire des siennes 🗈; ~ **up sth** mettre l'accent sur qch.

playful *a* (*remark*) taquin; (*child*) joueur.

play: ~**ground** *n* cour *f* de récréation. ~**-group**, ~**-school** *n* garderie *f*.

playing *n* (Sport) jeu *m*; (Theat) interprétation *f*. ~**-card** *n* carte *f* à jouer. ~**-field** *n* terrain *m* de sport.

play: ~**-pen** *n* parc *m* (pour bébé). ~**wright** *n* auteur *m* dramatique.

plc *abbr* (**public limited company**) SA.

plea *n* (for mercy, tolerance) appel *m*; (for food, money) demande *f*; (reason) excuse *f*; **make a ~ of guilty** plaider coupable.

plead *vt/i* supplier; (Jur) plaider.

pleasant *a* agréable.

please *vt/i* plaire (à), faire plaisir (à); ~ **oneself, do as one ~s** faire ce qu'on veut. ● *adv* s'il vous *or* te plaît. **pleased** *a* content (**with** de). **pleasing** *a* agréable.

pleasure *n* plaisir *m*; **with ~** avec plaisir; **my ~** je vous en prie.

pleat *n* pli *m*. ● *vt* plisser.

pledge *n* (token) gage *m*; (promise) promesse *f*. ● *vt* promettre; (pawn) mettre en gage.

plentiful *a* abondant.

plenty *n* abondance *f*; ~ (**of**) (a great deal) beaucoup (de); (enough) assez (de).

pliers *npl* pinces *fpl*.

plight *n* détresse *f*.

plinth *n* socle *m*.

plod *vi* (*pt* **plodded**) avancer péniblement.

P

plonk *n* [!] pinard *m* [!].

plot *n* (*conspiracy*) complot *m*; (of novel) intrigue *f*; ~ **(of land)** terrain *m*. ● *vt/i* (*pt* **plotted**) (plan) comploter; (mark out) tracer.

plough *n* charrue *f*. ● *vt/i* labourer. □ ~ **back** réinvestir; ~ **through** avancer péniblement dans.

plow *n & vt/i* (US) = PLOUGH.

ploy *n* stratagème *m*.

pluck *vt* (*flower, fruit*) cueillir; (*bird*) plumer; (*eyebrows*) épiler; (*strings*: Mus) pincer; ~ **up courage** prendre son courage à deux mains. **plucky** *a* courageux.

plug *n* (for sink) bonde *f*; (Electr) fiche *f*, prise *f*. ● *vt* (*pt* **plugged**) (*hole*) boucher; (publicize [!]) faire du battage autour de. □ ~ **in** brancher. ~**-hole** *n* bonde *f*.

plum *n* prune *f*; ~ **pudding** (plum-)pudding *m*.

plumber *n* plombier *m*.

plume *n* (of feathers) panache *m*.

plummet *vi* tomber, plonger.

plump *a* potelé, dodu.

plunge *vt/i* (dive, thrust) plonger; (fall) tomber. ● *n* plongeon *m*; (fall) chute *f*; **take the** ~ se jeter à l'eau. **plunger** *n* (for sink) ventouse *f*.

plural *a* pluriel; (*noun*) au pluriel; (*ending*) du pluriel. ● *n* pluriel *m*.

plus *prep* plus; **ten** ~ plus de dix. ● *a* (Electr & fig) positif. ● *n* signe *m* plus; (fig) atout *m*.

ply *vt* (*tool*) manier; (*trade*) exercer. ● *vi* faire la navette; ~ **sb with drink** offrir continuellement à boire à qn.

plywood *n* contreplaqué *m*.

p.m. *adv* de l'après-midi *or* du soir.

pneumatic drill *n* marteau-piqueur *m*.

pneumonia *n* pneumonie *f*.

PO *abbr* ⇒POST OFFICE.

poach *vt/i* (*game*) braconner; (*staff*) débaucher; (Culin) pocher.

PO Box *n* boîte *f* postale.

pocket *n* poche *f*; **be out of** ~ avoir perdu de l'argent. ● *a* de poche. ● *vt* empocher. ~**-book** *n* (notebook) carnet *m*; (wallet: US) portefeuille *m*; (handbag: US) sac *m* à main. ~**-money** *n* argent *m* de poche.

pod *n* (peas) cosse *f*; (vanilla) gousse *f*.

podgy *a* (**-ier**, **-iest**) dodu.

poem *n* poème *m*. **poet** *n* poète *m*. **poetic** *a* poétique. **poetry** *n* poésie *f*.

point *n* (position) point *m*; (tip) pointe *f*; (decimal point) virgule *f*; (remark) remarque *f*; **good** ~**s** qualités *fpl*; **on the** ~ **of** sur le point de; ~ **in time** moment *m*; ~ **of view** point *m* de vue; **to the** ~ pertinent; **what is the** ~**?** à quoi bon? ● *vt* (aim) braquer; (show) indiquer; ~ **out** signaler. ● *vi* indiquer du doigt; ~ **out that, make the** ~ **that** faire remarquer que. ~**-blank** *a & adv* à bout portant.

pointed *a* (sharp) pointu; (window) en pointe; (*remark*) lourd de sens.

pointless *a* inutile.

poise *n* (confidence) assurance *f*; (physical elegance) aisance *f*.

poison *n* poison *m*. ● *vt* empoisonner. **poisonous** *a* (*substance*) toxique; (*plant*) vénéneux; (*snake*) venimeux.

poke *vt/i* (push) pousser; (*fire*) tisonner; (thrust) fourrer; ~ **fun at** se moquer de. ● *n* (petit) coup *m*. □ ~ **out** (*head*) sortir.

poker *n* (for fire) tisonnier *m*; (cards) poker *m*.

Poland *n* Pologne *f*.

polar *a* polaire.

pole *n* (stick) perche *f*; (for flag) mât *m*; (Geog) pôle *m*.

Pole *n* Polonais/-e *m/f*.

pole-vault *n* saut *m* à la perche.

police *n* police *f*. ●*vt* faire la police dans. ~ **constable** *n* agent *m* de police. ~**man** *n* (*pl* **-men**) agent *m* de police. ~ **station** *n* commissariat *m* de police. ~**woman** *n* (*pl* **-women**) femme-agent *f*.

policy *n* politique *f*; (*insurance*) police *f* (d'assurance).

polish *vt* polir; (*shoes, floor*) cirer. ●*n* (for shoes) cirage *m*; (for floor) encaustique *f*; (for nails) vernis *m*; (shine) poli *m*; (fig) raffinement *m*. □ ~ **off** finir en vitesse; ~ **up** (*language*) perfectionner.

Polish *a* polonais. ●*n* (Ling) polonais *m*.

polished *a* raffiné.

polite *a* poli.

political *a* politique.

politician *n* homme *m* politique, femme *f* politique.

politics *n* politique *f*.

poll *n* (vote casting) scrutin *m*; (survey) sondage *m*; **go to the ~s** aller aux urnes. ●*vt* (*votes*) obtenir.

pollen *n* pollen *m*.

polling booth *n* isoloir *m*.

polling station *n* bureau *m* de vote.

pollution *n* pollution *f*.

polo *n* polo *m*. ~ **neck** *n* col *m* roulé.

pomegranate *n* grenade *f*.

pomp *n* pompe *f*.

pompous *a* pompeux.

pond *n* étang *m*; (artificial) bassin *m*; (stagnant) mare *f*.

ponder *vt/i* réfléchir (à), méditer (sur).

pong *n* (stink ⓘ) puanteur *f*. ●*vi* ⓘ puer.

pony *n* poney *m*. ~**tail** *n* queue *f* de cheval.

poodle *n* caniche *m*.

pool *n* (puddle) flaque *f*; (pond) étang *m*; (of blood) mare *f*; (for swimming) piscine *f*; (fund) fonds *m* commun; (of ideas) réservoir *m*; (snooker) billard *m* américain; ~**s** pari *m* mutuel sur le football. ●*vt* mettre en commun.

poor *a* (not wealthy) pauvre; (not good) médiocre, mauvais.

poorly *a* malade. ●*adv* mal.

pop *n* (noise) pan *m*; (music) pop *m*. ●*a* pop *inv*. ●*vt/i* (*pt* **popped**) (burst) crever; (put) mettre; ~ **in/out/off** entrer/sortir/partir. □ ~ **up** surgir.

pope *n* pape *m*.

poppy *n* pavot *m*; (wild) coquelicot *m*.

popular *a* populaire; (in fashion) en vogue; **be ~ with** plaire à.

population *n* population *f*.

porcelain *n* porcelaine *f*.

porcupine *n* porc-épic *m*.

pork *n* porc *m*.

pornography *n* pornographie *f*.

port *n* (harbour) port *m*; (left: Naut) bâbord *m*; ~ **of call** escale *f*; (wine) porto *m*.

portable *a* portable.

porter *n* (carrier) porteur *m*; (door-keeper) portier *m*.

portfolio *n* (Pol, Comm) portefeuille *m*.

portion *n* (at meal) portion *f*; (part) partie *f*.

portrait *n* portrait *m*.

portray *vt* représenter.

Portugal *n* Portugal *m*.

Portuguese *n* (Ling) portugais *m*; (*person*) Portugais/-e *m/f*. ●*a* portugais.

pose *vt/i* poser; ~ **as** (*expert*) se poser en. ● *n* pose *f*.

poser *n* (person) frimeur/-euse *m/f*; (puzzle) colle *f*.

posh *a* ⊡ chic *inv*.

position *n* position *f*; (job, state) situation *f*. ● *vt* placer.

positive *a* positif; (sure) sûr, certain; (real) réel, vrai.

possess *vt* posséder.

possession *n* possession *f*; **take ~ of** prendre possession de.

possessive *a* possessif.

possible *a* possible.

possibly *adv* peut-être; **if I ~ can** si cela m'est possible; **I cannot ~ leave** il m'est impossible de partir.

post *n* (pole) poteau *m*; (station, job) poste *m*; (mail service) poste *f*; (letters) courrier *m*. ● *a* postal. ● *vt* (*letter*) poster; **keep ~ed** tenir au courant; ~ (**up**) (a notice) afficher; (appoint) affecter.

postage *n* affranchissement *m*; tarif *m* postal.

postal *a* postal. ~ **order** *n* mandat *m*.

post: ~**box** *n* boîte *f* aux lettres. ~**card** *n* carte *f* postale. ~ **code** *n* code *m* postal.

poster *n* (for information) affiche *f*; (for decoration) poster *m*.

postgraduate *n* étudiant/-e *m/f* de troisième cycle.

posthumous *a* posthume.

post: ~**man** *n* (*pl* **-men**) facteur *m*. ~**mark** *n* cachet *m* de la poste.

post-mortem *n* autopsie *f*.

post office *n* poste *f*.

postpone *vt* remettre.

postscript *n* (to letter) post-scriptum *m inv*.

posture *n* posture *f*. ● *vi* prendre des poses.

pot *n* pot *m*; (drug ⊡) hasch *m*; **go to ~** ⊡ aller à la ruine; **take ~ luck** tenter sa chance. ● *vt* (*plants*) mettre en pot.

potato *n* (*pl* ~**es**) pomme *f* de terre.

pot-belly *n* bedaine *f*.

potential *a* & *n* potentiel (*m*).

pot-hole *n* (in rock) caverne *f*; (in road) nid *m* de poule. **pot-holing** *n* spéléologie *f*.

potter *n* potier *m*. ● *vi* bricoler.

pottery *n* (art) poterie *f*; (objects) poteries *fpl*.

potty *a* (**-ier**, **-iest**) (crazy ⊠) toqué. ● *n* pot *m*.

pouch *n* poche *f*; (for tobacco) blague *f*.

poultry *n* volailles *fpl*.

pounce *vi* bondir (**on** sur). ● *n* bond *m*.

pound *n* (weight) livre *f* (= *454 g*); (money) livre *f*; (for dogs, cars) fourrière *f*. ● *vt* (crush) piler; (bombard) pilonner. ● *vi* frapper fort; (of heart) battre fort; (walk) marcher à pas lourds.

pour *vt* verser. ● *vi* couler, ruisseler (**from** de); (rain) pleuvoir à torrents. □ ~ **in/out** (*people*) arriver/sortir en masse; ~ **off** *or* **out** vider. **pouring rain** *n* pluie *f* torrentielle.

pout *vi* faire la moue.

poverty *n* misère *f*, pauvreté *f*.

powder *n* poudre *f*. ● *vt* poudrer.

power *n* (strength) puissance *f*; (control) pouvoir *m*; (energy) énergie *f*; (Electr) courant *m*. ● *vt* (*engine*) faire marcher; (*plane*) propulser; ~**ed by** (*engine*) propulsé par; (*generator*) alimenté par. ~ **cut** *n* coupure *f* de courant.

powerful *a* puissant.

powerless *a* impuissant.

power: ~ **point** *n* prise *f* de courant. ~**-station** *n* centrale *f* électrique.

practical *a* pratique. ~ **joke** *n* farce *f*.

practice *n* (procedure) pratique *f*; (of profession) exercice *m*; (Sport) entraînement *m*; **in ~** (in fact) en pratique; (well-trained) en forme; **out of ~** rouillé; **put into ~** mettre en pratique.

practise *vt*/*i* (*musician, typist*) s'exercer (à); (Sport) s'entraîner (à); (put into practice) pratiquer; (*profession*) exercer.

praise *vt* faire l'éloge de; (*God*) louer. ● *n* éloges *mpl*, louanges *fpl*.

pram *n* landau *m*.

prance *vi* caracoler.

prawn *n* crevette *f* rose.

pray *vi* prier. **prayer** *n* prière *f*.

preach *vt*/*i* prêcher; ~ **at** *or* **to** prêcher.

precarious *a* précaire.

precaution *n* précaution *f*

precede *vt* précéder.

precedence *n* (in importance) priorité *f*; (In rank) préséance *f*.

precedent *n* précédent *m*.

precinct *n* quartier *m* commerçant; (pedestrian area) zone *f* piétonne; (district: US) circonscription *f*.

precious *a* précieux.

precipitate *vt* (*person, event, chemical*) précipiter.

précis *n* résumé *m*.

precise *a* précis; (careful) méticuleux. **precision** *n* précision *f*.

precocious *a* précoce.

preconceived *a* préconçu.

predator *n* prédateur *m*.

predicament *n* situation *f* difficile.

predict *vt* prédire. **predictable** *a* prévisible. **prediction** *n* prédiction *f*.

predispose *vt* prédisposer (**to do** à faire).

predominant *a* prédominant.

pre-empt *vt* (anticipate) anticiper; (*person*) devancer.

preface *n* (to book) préface *f*; (to speech) préambule *m*.

prefect *n* (pupil) élève *m*/*f* chargé/-e de la discipline; (official) préfet *m*.

prefer *vt* (*pt* **preferred**) préférer (**to do** faire). **preferably** *adv* de préférence. **preference** *n* préférence *f*. **preferential** *a* préférentiel.

prefix *n* préfixe *m*.

pregnancy *n* grossesse *f*. **pregnant** *a* (*woman*) enceinte; (*animal*) pleine; (*pause*) éloquent.

prehistoric *a* préhistorique.

prejudge *vt* (*issue*) préjuger de; (*person*) juger d'avance.

prejudice *n* préjugé(s) *m*(*pl*); (harm) préjudice *m*. ● *vt* (*claim*) porter préjudice à; (*person*) léser. **prejudiced** *a* partial; (person) qui a des préjugés.

premature *a* prématuré.

premeditated *a* prémédité.

premises *npl* locaux *mpl*; **on the ~** sur les lieux.

premium *n* (*insurance*) prime *f*; **be at a ~** être précieux.

preoccupied *a* préoccupé.

preparation *n* préparation *f*; **~s** préparatifs *mpl*.

preparatory *a* préparatoire. **~ school** *n* école *f* primaire privée; (US) école *f* secondaire privée.

prepare *vt*/*i* (se) préparer (**for** à); **be ~d for** (expect) s'attendre à; **~d to** prêt à.

preposition *n* préposition *f*.

preposterous *a* absurde, ridicule.

P

prep school *n* = PREPARATORY SCHOOL.

prerequisite *n* condition *f* préalable.

prescribe *vt* prescrire.

prescription *n* (Med) ordonnance *f*.

presence *n* présence *f*; **~ of mind** présence *f* d'esprit.

present[1] *a* présent. ● *n* présent *m*; (gift) cadeau *m*; **at ~** à présent; **for the ~** pour le moment.

present[2] *vt* présenter; (*film, concert*) donner; **~ sb with** offrir à qn. **presentation** *n* présentation *f*. **presenter** *n* présentateur/-trice *m/f*.

preservation *n* (of food) conservation *f*; (of wildlife) préservation *f*.

preservative *n* (Culin) agent *m* de conservation.

preserve *vt* préserver; (Culin) conserver. ● *n* réserve *f*; (fig) domaine *m*; (jam) confiture *f*.

presidency *n* présidence *f*.

president *n* président/-e *m/f*.

press *vt/i* (*button*) appuyer (sur); (squeeze) presser; (iron) repasser; (pursue) poursuivre; **be ~ed for** (*time*) manquer de; **~ for sth** faire pression pour avoir qch; **~ sb to do sth** pousser qn à faire qch; **~ on** continuer (**with sth** qch). ● *n* (newspapers, machine) presse *f*; (for wine) pressoir *m*. **~ cutting** *n* coupure *f* de presse.

pressing *a* pressant.

press: **~ release** *n* communiqué *m* de presse. **~-stud** *n* bouton-pression *m*. **~-up** *n* pompe *f*.

pressure *n* pression *f*. ● *vt* faire pression sur. **~-cooker** *n* cocotte-minute *f*. **~ group** *n* groupe *m* de pression.

pressurize *vt* (*cabin*) pressuriser; (*person*) faire pression sur.

prestige *n* prestige *m*.

presumably *adv* vraisemblablement.

presume *vt* (suppose) présumer.

pretence, (US) **pretense** *n* feinte *f*, simulation *f*; (claim) prétention *f*; (pretext) prétexte *m*.

pretend *vt/i* faire semblant (**to do** de faire); **~ to** (lay claim to) prétendre à.

pretentious *a* prétentieux.

pretext *n* prétexte *m*.

pretty *a* (**-ier**, **-iest**) joli. ● *adv* assez; **~ much** presque.

prevail *vi* (be usual) prédominer; (win) prévaloir; **~ on** persuader (**to do** de faire). **prevailing** *a* actuel; (*wind*) dominant.

prevalent *a* répandu.

prevent *vt* empêcher (**from doing** de faire). **prevention** *n* prévention *f*. **preventive** *a* préventif.

preview *n* avant-première *f*; (fig) aperçu *m*.

previous *a* précédent, antérieur; **~ to** avant. **previously** *adv* auparavant.

prey *n* proie *f*; **bird of ~** rapace *m*. ● *vi* **~ on** faire sa proie de; (worry) préoccuper.

price *n* prix *m*. ● *vt* fixer le prix de. **priceless** *a* inestimable; (amusing [!]) impayable [!].

prick *vt* (with pin) piquer; **~ up one's ears** dresser l'oreille. ● *n* piqûre *f*.

prickle *n* piquant *m*.

pride *n* orgueil *m*; (satisfaction) fierté *f*; **~ of place** place *f* d'honneur. ● *vpr* **~ oneself on** s'enorgueillir de.

priest *n* prêtre *m*.

prim *a* (**primmer**, **primmest**) guindé, méticuleux.

primarily *adv* essentiellement.

primary *a* (*school, elections*) primaire; (chief, basic) premier, fondamental. ● *n* (Pol: US) primaire *f*.

prime *a* principal, premier; (first-rate) excellent. ● *vt* (*pump, gun*) amorcer; (*surface*) apprêter. **P~ Minister** *n* Premier Ministre *m*.

primitive *a* primitif.

primrose *n* primevère *f* (*jaune*).

prince *n* prince *m*. **princess** *n* princesse *f*.

principal *a* principal. ● *n* (of school) directeur/-trice *m/f*.

principle *n* principe *m*; **in/on ~** en/par principe.

print *vt* imprimer; (write in capitals) écrire en majuscules; **~ed matter** imprimés *mpl*. ● *n* (of foot) empreinte *f*; (letters) caractères *mpl*; (photograph) épreuve *f*; (engraving) gravure *f*; **in ~** disponible; **out of ~** épuisé. **printer** *n* (person) imprimeur *m*; (Comput) imprimante *f*.

prior *a* précédent. ● *n* (Relig) prieur *m*. **~ to** *prep* avant (de).

priority *n* priorité *f*; **take ~** avoir la priorité (**over** sur).

prise *vt* forcer; **~ open** ouvrir en forçant.

prison *n* prison *f*. **prisoner** *n* prisonnier/-ière *m/f*. **~ officer** *n* gardien/-ne *m/f* de prison.

pristine *a* **be in ~ condition** être comme neuf.

privacy *n* intimité *f*, solitude *f*.

private *a* privé; (confidential) personnel; (*lessons, house*) particulier; (*ceremony*) intime; **in ~** en privé; (of ceremony) dans l'intimité. ● *n* (soldier) simple soldat *m*. **privately** *adv* en privé; dans l'intimité; (inwardly) intérieurement.

privilege *n* privilège *m*. **privileged** *a* privilégié; **be ~d to** avoir le privilège de.

prize *n* prix *m*. ● *a* (*entry*) primé; (*fool*) parfait. ● *vt* (value) priser.

pro *n* **the ~s and cons** le pour et le contre.

probable *a* probable. **probably** *adv* probablement.

probation *n* (testing) essai *m*; (Jur) liberté *f* surveillée.

probe *n* (device) sonde *f*; (fig) enquête *f*. ● *vt* sonder. ● *vi* **~ into** sonder.

problem *n* problème *m*. ● *a* difficile. **problematic** *a* problématique.

procedure *n* procédure *f*; (way of doing sth) démarche *f* à suivre.

proceed *vi* (go) aller, avancer; (pass) passer (**to** à); (act) procéder; **~ (with)** continuer; **~ to do** se mettre à faire.

proceedings *npl* (discussions) débats *mpl*; (meeting) réunion *f*; (report) actes *mpl*; (Jur) poursuites *fpl*.

proceeds *npl* (profits) produit *m*, bénéfices *mpl*.

process *n* processus *m*; (method) procédé *m*; **in ~** en cours; **in the ~ of doing** en train de faire. ● *vt* (*material, data*) traiter.

procession *n* défilé *m*.

procrastinate *vi* différer, tergiverser.

procure *vt* obtenir.

prod *vt/i* (*pt* **prodded**) pousser doucement. ● *n* petit coup *m*.

prodigy *n* prodige *m*.

produce[1] *n* produits *mpl*.

produce[2] *vt/i* produire; (bring out) sortir; (show) présenter; (cause) provoquer; (Theat, TV) mettre en scène; (radio) réaliser; (cinema) produire. **producer** *n* metteur *m* en scène, réalisateur *m*; producteur *m*.

product *n* produit *m*.

production *n* production *f*; (Theat, TV) mise *f* en scène; (radio) réalisation *f*.

P

productive *a* productif. **productivity** *n* productivité *f.*

profession *n* profession *f.*

professional *a* professionnel; (of high quality) de professionnel; (*person*) qui exerce une profession libérale. ● *n* professionnel/-le *m/f.*

professor *n* professeur *m* (*titulaire d'une chaire*).

proficient *a* compétent.

profile *n* (of face) profil *m*; (of body, mountain) silhouette *f*; (by journalist) portrait *m.*

profit *n* profit *m*, bénéfice *m.* ● *vi* ~ **by** tirer profit de. **profitable** *a* rentable.

profound *a* profond.

profusely *adv* (*bleed*) abondamment; (*apologize*) avec effusion. **profusion** *n* profusion *f.*

program *n* (US) = PROGRAMME; (**computer**) ~ programme *m.* ● *vt* (*pt* **programmed**) programmer.

programme *n* programme *m*; (broadcast) émission *f.*

programmer *n* programmeur/ -euse *m/f.*

programming *n* (Comput) programmation *f.*

progress[1] *n* progrès *m*(*pl*); **in** ~ en cours; **make** ~ faire des progrès; ~ **report** compte-rendu *m.*

progress[2] *vi* (advance, improve) progresser.

progressive *a* progressif; (reforming) progressiste.

prohibit *vt* interdire (**sb from doing** à qn de faire).

project[1] *vt* projeter. ● *vi* (jut out) être en saillie.

project[2] *n* (plan) projet *m*; (undertaking) entreprise *f*; (School) dossier *m.*

projection *n* projection *f*; saillie *f*; (estimate) prévision *f.*

projector *n* projecteur *m.*

proliferate *vi* proliférer.

prolong *vt* prolonger.

prominent *a* (projecting) proéminent; (conspicuous) bien en vue; (fig) important.

promiscuous *a* de mœurs faciles.

promise *n* promesse *f.* ● *vt/i* promettre. **promising** *a* prometteur; (*person*) qui promet.

promote *vt* promouvoir; (advertise) faire la promotion de. **promotion** *n* promotion *f.*

prompt *a* rapide; (punctual) à l'heure, ponctuel. ● *adv* (on the dot) pile. ● *vt* inciter; (cause) provoquer; (Theat) souffler à. ● *n* (Comput) message *m* guide-opérateur. **prompter** *n* souffleur/ -euse *m/f.* **promptly** *adv* rapidement; ponctuellement.

prone *a* ~ **to** sujet à.

pronoun *n* pronom *m.*

pronounce *vt* prononcer. **pronunciation** *n* prononciation *f.*

proof *n* (evidence) preuve *f*; (test, trial copy) épreuve *f*; (of alcohol) teneur *f* en alcool. ● *a* ~ **against** à l'épreuve de.

prop *n* support *m*; (Theat) accessoire *m.* ● *vt* (*pt* **propped**) ~ (**up**) (support) étayer; (lean) appuyer.

propaganda *n* propagande *f.*

propel *vt* (*pt* **propelled**) (*vehicle, ship*) propulser; (*person*) pousser.

propeller *n* hélice *f.*

proper *a* correct, bon; (adequate) convenable; (real) vrai; (thorough [!]) parfait. **properly** *adv* correctement, comme il faut; (adequately) convenablement.

proper noun *n* nom *m* propre.

property *n* (house) propriété *f*; (things owned) biens *mpl*, propriété *f.* ● *a* immobilier, foncier.

prophecy *n* prophétie *f*.
prophet *n* prophète *m*.
proportion *n* (ratio, dimension) proportion *f*; (amount) partie *f*.
proposal *n* proposition *f*; (of marriage) demande *f* en mariage.
propose *vt* proposer. ● *vi* faire une demande en mariage; ~ **to do** se proposer de faire.
proposition *n* proposition *f*; (matter ⓘ) affaire *f*. ● *vt* ⓘ faire des propositions malhonnêtes à.
proprietor *n* propriétaire *mf*.
propriety *n* (correct behaviour) bienséance *f*.
prose *n* prose *f*; (translation) thème *m*.
prosecute *vt* poursuivre en justice. **prosecution** *n* poursuites *fpl*. **prosecutor** *n* procureur *m*.
prospect¹ *n* (outlook) perspective *f*; (chance) espoir *m*.
prospect² *vt/i* prospecter.
prospective *a* (future) futur; (possible) éventuel.
prospectus *n* brochure *f*; (Univ) livret *m* de l'étudiant.
prosperity *n* prospérité *f*. **prosperous** *a* prospère.
prostitute *n* prostituée *f*.
prostrate *a* (prone) à plat ventre; (exhausted) prostré.
protect *vt* protéger. **protection** *n* protection *f*. **protective** *a* protecteur; (*clothes*) de protection.
protein *n* protéine *f*.
protest¹ *n* protestation *f*; **under ~** en protestant.
protest² *vt/i* protester.
Protestant *a & n* protestant/-e (*m/f*).
protester *n* manifestant/-e *m/f*.
protocol *n* protocole *m*.
protrude *vi* dépasser.
proud *a* fier, orgueilleux.
prove *vt* prouver. ● *vi* ~ **(to be) easy** se révéler facile; ~ **oneself** faire ses preuves. **proven** *a* éprouvé.
proverb *n* proverbe *m*.
provide *vt* fournir (**sb with sth** qch à qn). ● *vi* ~ **for** (allow for) prévoir; (guard against) parer à; (*person*) pourvoir aux besoins de.
provided *conj* ~ **that** à condition que.
providing *conj* = PROVIDED.
province *n* province *f*; (fig) compétence *f*.
provision *n* (stock) provision *f*; (supplying) fourniture *f*; (stipulation) dispositions *fpl*; **~s** (food) provisions *fpl*.
provisional *a* provisoire.
provocative *a* provocant.
provoke *vt* provoquer.
prow *n* proue *f*.
prowess *n* prouesses *fpl*.
prowl *vi* rôder.
proxy *n* **by ~** par procuration.
prudish *a* pudibond, prude.
prune *n* pruneau *m*. ● *vt* (cut) tailler.
pry *vi* ~ **into** mettre son nez dans.
psalm *n* psaume *m*.
pseudonym *n* pseudonyme *m*.
psychiatric *a* psychiatrique. **psychiatrist** *n* psychiatre *mf*. **psychiatry** *n* psychiatrie *f*.
psychic *a* (*phenomenon*) métapsychique; (*person*) doué de télépathie.
psychoanalyse *vt* psychanalyser.
psychological *a* psychologique. **psychologist** *n* psychologue *mf*. **psychology** *n* psychologie *f*.
PTO *abbr* (**please turn over**) TSVP.
pub *n* pub *m*.
puberty *n* puberté *f*.

P

public *a* public; (*library*) municipal; **in ~** en public.
publican *n* patron/-ne *m/f* de pub.
publication *n* publication *f*.
public house *n* pub *m*.
publicity *n* publicité *f*.
publicize *vt* faire connaître au public.
public: **~ relations** *n* relations *fpl* publiques. **~ school** *n* école *f* privée; (US) école *f* publique. **~ transport** *n* transports *mpl* en commun.
publish *vt* publier. **publisher** *n* éditeur *m*. **publishing** *n* édition *f*.
pudding *n* dessert *m*; (steamed) pudding *m*.
puddle *n* flaque *f* d'eau.
puff *n* (of smoke) bouffée *f*; (of breath) souffle *m*. ● *vt/i* souffler. □ **~ at** (*cigar*) tirer sur. **~ out** (swell) (se) gonfler.
pull *vt/i* tirer; (*muscle*) se froisser; **~ a face** faire une grimace; **~ one's weight** faire sa part du travail; **~ sb's leg** faire marcher qn. ● *n* traction *f*; (fig) attraction *f*; (influence) influence *f*; **give a ~** tirer. □ **~ away** (Auto) démarrer; **~ back** *or* **out** (withdraw) (se) retirer; **~ down** (*building*) démolir; **~ in** (enter) entrer; (stop) s'arrêter; **~ off** enlever; (fig) réussir; **~ out** (from bag) sortir; (extract) arracher; (Auto) déboîter; **~ over** (Auto) se ranger (sur le côté); **~ through** s'en tirer; **~ oneself together** se ressaisir.
pull-down menu *n* (Comput) menu *m* déroulant.
pulley *n* poulie *f*.
pullover *n* pull(-over) *m*.
pulp *n* (of fruit) pulpe *f*; (for paper) pâte *f* à papier.
pulpit *n* chaire *f*.
pulsate *vi* battre.
pulse *n* (Med) pouls *m*.
pump *n* pompe *f*; (plimsoll) chaussure *f* de sport. ● *vt/i* pomper; (*person*) soutirer des renseignements à; **~ up** gonfler.
pumpkin *n* citrouille *f*.
pun *n* jeu *m* de mots.
punch *vt* donner un coup de poing à; (*ticket*) poinçonner. ● *n* coup *m* de poing; (vigour ⊡) punch *m*; (device) poinçonneuse *f*; (drink) punch *m*. **~-line** *n* chute *f*.
punctual *a* à l'heure; (habitually) ponctuel.
punctuation *n* ponctuation *f*.
puncture *n* crevaison *f*. ● *vt/i* crever.
pungent *a* âcre.
punish *vt* punir (**for sth** de qch). **punishment** *n* punition *f*.
punk *n* (music, fan) punk *m*; (US: ⊡) voyou *m*.
punt *n* (boat) barque *f*; (Irish pound) livre *f* irlandaise.
puny *a* (**-ier**, **-iest**) chétif.
pupil *n* (person) élève *mf*; (of eye) pupille *f*.
puppet *n* marionnette *f*.
puppy *n* chiot *m*.
purchase *vt* acheter (**from sb** à qn). ● *n* achat *m*.
pure *a* pur.
purgatory *n* purgatoire *m*.
purge *vt* purger (**of** de). ● *n* purge *f*.
purification *n* (of water, air) épuration *f*; (Relig) purification *f*. **purify** *vt* épurer; purifier.
puritan *n* puritain/-e *m/f*.
purity *n* pureté *f*.
purple *a* & *n* violet (*m*).
purpose *n* but *m*; (determination) résolution *f*; **on ~** exprès; **to no ~** sans résultat.
purr *n* ronronnement *m*. ● *vi* ronronner.
purse *n* porte-monnaie *m inv*;

(handbag: US) sac *m* à main. ● *vt* (*lips*) pincer.

pursue *vt* poursuivre.

pursuit *n* poursuite *f*; (hobby) activité *f*, occupation *f*.

pus *n* pus *m*

push *vt/i* pousser; (*button*) appuyer sur; (thrust) enfoncer; (recommend 🄸) proposer avec insistance; **be ~ed for** (*time*) manquer de; **be ~ing thirty** 🄸 friser la trentaine; **~ sb around** bousculer qn. ● *n* poussée *f*; (effort) gros effort *m*; (drive) dynamisme *m*; **give the ~ to** 🄸 flanquer à la porte 🄸. □ **~ in** resquiller; **~ on** continuer; **~ up** (lift) relever; (*prices*) faire monter.

pushchair *n* poussette *f*.

pusher *n* revendeur/-euse *m/f* (de drogue).

push-up *n* pompe *f*.

put *vt/i* (*pt* **put**; *pres p* **putting**) mettre, placer, poser; (*question*) poser; **~ the damage at a million** estimer les dégâts à un million; **~ sth tactfully** dire qch avec tact. □ **~ across** communiquer; **~ away** ranger; (in hospital, prison) enfermer; **~ back** (postpone) remettre; (delay) retarder; **~ down** (dé)poser; (write) inscrire; (pay) verser; (suppress) réprimer; **~ forward** (*plan*) soumettre; **~ in** (insert) introduire; (fix) installer; (submit) soumettre; **~ in for** faire une demande de; **~ off** (postpone) renvoyer à plus tard; (disconcert) déconcerter; (displease) rebuter; **~ sb off sth** dégoûter qn de qch; **~ on** (*clothes, radio*) mettre; (*light*) allumer; (*accent, weight*) prendre; **~ out** sortir; (stretch) (é)tendre; (extinguish) éteindre; (disconcert) déconcerter; (inconvenience) déranger; **~ up** lever, remonter; (*building*) construire; (*notice*) mettre; (*price*) augmenter; (*guest*) héberger; (*offer*) offrir; **~ up with** supporter.

putty *n* mastic *m*.

puzzle *n* énigme *f*; (game) casse-tête *m inv*, (jigsaw) puzzle *m*. ● *vt* rendre perplexe. ● *vi* se creuser la tête.

pyjamas *npl* pyjama *m*.

pylon *n* pylône *m*.

quack *n* (of duck) coin-coin *m inv*; (doctor) charlatan *m*.

quadrangle (of college) *n* cour *f*.

quadruple *a & n* quadruple (*m*). ● *vt/i* quadrupler.

quail *n* (bird) caille *f*.

quaint *a* pittoresque; (old) vieillot, (odd) bizarre.

qualification *n* diplôme *m*; (ability) compétence *f*; (fig) réserve *f*, restriction *f*.

qualified *a* diplômé; (able) qualifié (**to do** pour faire); (fig) conditionnel.

qualify *vt* qualifier; (modify) mettre des réserves à; (*statement*) nuancer. ● *vi* obtenir son diplôme (**as** de); (Sport) se qualifier; **~ for** remplir les conditions requises pour.

quality *n* qualité *f*.

qualm *n* scrupule *m*.

quantity *n* quantité *f*.

quarantine *n* quarantaine *f*.

quarrel *n* dispute *f*, querelle *f*. ● *vi* (*pt* **quarrelled**) se disputer.

quarry *n* (excavation) carrière *f*; (prey) proie *f*. ● *vt* extraire.

quart *n* ≈ litre *m*.

quarter *n* quart *m*; (of year) trimestre *m*; (25 cents: US) quart *m* de dollar; (district) quartier *m*; **~s** logement *m*; **from all ~s** de toutes parts. ● *vt* diviser en quatre; (*troops*) cantonner.

quarterly *a* trimestriel. ● *adv* tous les trois mois.

quartet *n* quatuor *m*.

quartz *n* quartz *m*. ● *a* (*watch*) à quartz.

quash *vt* (suppress) étouffer; (Jur) annuler.

quaver *vi* trembler, chevroter. ● *n* (Mus) croche *f*.

quay *n* (Naut) quai *m*.

queasy *a* **feel ~** avoir mal au cœur.

queen *n* reine *f*; (cards) dame *f*.

queer *a* étrange; (dubious) louche; ⊠ homosexuel.

quench *vt* éteindre; (*thirst*) étancher; (*desire*) étouffer.

query *n* question *f*. ● *vt* mettre en question.

quest *n* recherche *f*.

question *n* question *f*; **in ~** en question; **out of the ~** hors de question. ● *vt* interroger; (doubt) mettre en question, douter de. **~ mark** *n* point *m* d'interrogation.

questionnaire *n* questionnaire *m*.

queue *n* queue *f*. ● *vi* (*pres p* **queuing**) faire la queue.

quibble *vi* ergoter.

quick *a* rapide; (clever) vif/vive; **be ~** (hurry) se dépêcher. ● *adv* vite. ● *n* **cut to the ~** piquer au vif. **quicken** *vt/i* (s')accélérer. **quickly** *adv* rapidement, vite. **~sand** *n* sables *mpl* mouvants.

quid *n inv* ⊡ livre *f* sterling.

quiet *a* (calm, still) tranquille; (silent) silencieux; (gentle) doux; (discreet) discret; **keep ~** se taire. ● *n* tranquillité *f*; **on the ~** en cachette. **quieten** *vt/i* (se) calmer. **quietly** *adv* (*speak*) doucement; (*sit*) en silence.

quilt *n* édredon *m*; (**continental**) **~** couette *f*.

quirk *n* bizarrerie *f*.

quit *vt* (*pt* **quitted**) quitter; (*smoking*) arrêter de. ● *vi* abandonner; (resign) démissionner; **~ doing** (US) cesser de faire.

quite *adv* tout à fait, vraiment; (rather) assez; **~ a few** un bon nombre (de).

quits *a* quitte (**with** envers); **call it ~** en rester là.

quiver *vi* trembler.

quiz *n* (*pl* **quizzes**) test *m*; (game) jeu-concours *m*. ● *vt* (*pt* **quizzed**) questionner.

quotation *n* citation *f*; (price) devis *m*; (stock exchange) cotation *f*; **~ marks** guillemets *mpl*.

quote *vt* citer; (*reference, number*) rappeler; (*price*) indiquer; (*share price*) coter. ● *vi* **~ for** faire un devis pour; **~ from** citer. ● *n* (quotation) citation *f*; (estimate) devis *m*; **in ~s** ⊡ entre guillemets.

rabbi *n* rabbin *m*.

rabbit *n* lapin *m*.

rabies *n* (disease) rage *f*.

race *n* (contest) course *f*; (group) race *f*. ● *a* racial; **~ relations**

relations *fpl* inter-raciales. ● *vt* (compete with) faire la course avec; (*horse*) faire courir. ● *vi* courir; (*pulse*) battre précipitamment; (*engine*) s'emballer. **~course** *n* champ *m* de courses. **~horse** *n* cheval *m* de course. **~-track** *n* piste *f*; (for horses) champ *m* de courses.

racing *n* courses *fpl*; **~ car** voiture *f* de course.

racism *n* racisme *m*. **racist** *a* & *n* raciste (*mf*).

rack *n* (shelf) étagère *f*; (for clothes) portant *m*; (for luggage) compartiment *m* à bagages; (for dishes) égouttoir *m*. ● *vt* **~ one's brains** se creuser la cervelle.

racket *n* (Sport) raquette *f*; (noise) vacarme *m*; (swindle) escroquerie *f*; (crime) trafic *m*.

radar *n* & *a* radar (*m*).

radial *n* **~ (tyre)** pneu *m* radial.

radiate *vt* (*happiness*) rayonner de; (*heat*) émettre. ● *vi* rayonner (**from** de). **radiation** *n* (radioactivity) radiation *f*. **radiator** *n* radiateur *m*.

radical *n* & *a* radical/-e (*m*/*f*).

radio *n* radio *f*; **on the ~** à la radio. ● *vt* (*message*) envoyer par radio; (*person*) appeler par radio.

radioactive *a* radioactif.

radiographer *n* manipulateur/-trice *m*/*f* radiographe.

radish *n* radis *m*.

radius *n* (*pl* **-dii**) rayon *m*.

raffle *n* tombola *f*.

rag *n* chiffon *m*; **~s** loques *fpl*.

rage *n* rage *f*, colère *f*; **be all the ~** faire fureur. ● *vi* (*person*) tempêter; (*storm, battle*) faire rage.

ragged *a* (*clothes*) en loques; (*person*) dépenaillé.

raid *n* (Mil, on stock market) raid *m*; (by police) rafle *f*; (by criminals) hold-up *m inv*. ● *vt* faire un raid *or* une rafle *or* un hold-up dans. **raider** *n* (thief) pillard *m*; (Mil) commando *m*; (corporate) raider *m*.

rail *n* (on balcony) balustrade *f*; (stairs) rampe *f*; (for train) rail *m*; (for curtain) tringle *f*; **by ~** par chemin de fer.

railing *n* (*also* **~s**) grille *f*.

railway, (US) **railroad** *n* chemin *m* de fer. **~ line** *n* voie *f* ferrée. **~ station** *n* gare *f*.

rain *n* pluie *f*. ● *vi* pleuvoir. **~bow** *n* arc-en-ciel *m*. **~coat** *n* imperméable *m*. **~fall** *n* précipitation *f*. **~ forest** *n* forêt *f* tropicale.

rainy *a* (**-ier**, **-iest**) pluvieux; (*season*) des pluies.

raise *vt* (*barrier, curtain*) lever; (*child, cattle*) élever; (*question*) soulever; (*price, salary*) augmenter. ● *n* (US) augmentation *f*.

raisin *n* raisin *m* sec.

rake *n* râteau *m*. ● *vt* (*garden*) ratisser; (search) fouiller dans. □ **~ in** (*money*) amasser; **~ up** (*past*) remuer.

rally *vt*/*i* (sc) rallier; (*strength*) reprendre; (after illness) aller mieux; **~ round** venir en aide. ● *n* rassemblement *m*; (Auto) rallye *m*; (tennis) échange *m*.

ram *n* bélier *m*. ● *vt* (*pt* **rammed**) (thrust) enfoncer; (crash into) rentrer dans.

RAM *abbr* (**random access memory**) RAM *f*.

ramble *n* randonnée *f*. ● *vi* faire une randonnée. □ **~ on** discourir.

ramp *n* (slope) rampe *f*; (in garage) pont *m* de graissage.

rampage[1] *vi* se déchaîner (**through** dans).

rampage[2] *n* **go on the ~** tout saccager.

ran ⇨RUN.

R

rancid *a* rance.

random *a* (fait) au hasard. ● *n* **at ~** au hasard.

rang ⇒RING².

range *n* (of prices, products) gamme *f*; (of people, beliefs) variété *f*; (of radar, weapon) portée *f*; (of aircraft) autonomie *f*; (of mountains) chaîne *f*. ● *vi* aller; (vary) varier.

rank *n* rang *m*; (Mil) grade *m*. ● *vt/i* **~ among** (se) classer parmi.

ransack *vt* (search) fouiller; (pillage) mettre à sac.

ransom *n* rançon *f*.

rap *n* coup *m* sec; (Mus) rap *m*. ● *vi* (*pt* **rapped**) donner des coups secs (**on** sur).

rape *vt* violer. ● *n* viol *m*.

rapid *a* rapide.

rapist *n* violeur *m*.

rapturous *a* (*delight*) extasié; (*welcome*) enthousiaste.

rare *a* rare; (Culin) saignant. **rarely** *adv* rarement.

rascal *n* coquin/-e *m/f*.

rash *n* (Med) rougeurs *fpl*. ● *a* irréfléchi.

raspberry *n* framboise *f*.

rat *n* rat *m*. ● *vi* (*pt* **ratted**) **~ on** (desert) lâcher; (inform on) dénoncer.

rate *n* (ratio, level) taux *m*; (speed) rythme *m*; (price) tarif *m*; (of exchange) taux *m*; **at any ~** en tout cas. ● *vt* (value) estimer; (deserve) mériter; **~ sth highly** admirer beaucoup qch. ● *vi* **~ as** être considéré comme.

rather *adv* (by preference) plutôt; (fairly) assez, plutôt; (a little) un peu; **I would ~ go** j'aimerais mieux partir; **~ than go** plutôt que de partir.

rating *n* (score, value) cote *f*; **the ~s** (TV) l'indice *m* d'écoute, l'audimat® *m*.

ratio *n* proportion *f*.

ration *n* ration *f*. ● *vt* rationner.

rational *a* rationnel; (*person*) sensé.

rationalize *vt* justifier; (organize) rationaliser.

rattle *vi* (*bottles, chains*) s'entrechoquer; (*window*) vibrer. ● *vt* (*bottles, chains*) faire s'entrechoquer; (fig, 🅸) énerver. ● *n* cliquetis *m*; (toy) hochet *m*. **~snake** *n* serpent *m* à sonnette, crotale *m*.

rave *vi* (enthuse) s'emballer; (in fever) délirer; (in anger) tempêter.

raven *n* corbeau *m*.

ravenous *a* **be ~** avoir une faim de loup.

ravine *n* ravin *m*.

raving *a* **~ lunatic** fou *m* furieux, folle *f* furieuse.

ravishing *a* ravissant.

raw *a* cru; (not processed) brut; (*wound*) à vif; (immature) inexpérimenté; **get a ~ deal** être mal traité; **~ material** matière *f* première.

ray *n* (of light) rayon *m*; **~ of hope** lueur *f* d'espoir.

razor *n* rasoir *m*. **~-blade** *n* lame *f* de rasoir.

re *prep* au sujet de; (at top of letter) objet.

reach *vt* (*place, level*) atteindre; (*decision*) arriver à; (contact) joindre; (*audience, market*) toucher. ● *vi* **~ up/down** lever/baisser le bras; **~ across** étendre le bras. ● *n* portée *f*; **within ~ of** à portée de; (close to) à proximité de.

react *vi* réagir. **reaction** *n* réaction *f*. **reactor** *n* réacteur *m*.

read *vt/i* (*pt* **read**) lire; (study) étudier; (*instrument*) indiquer; **~ about sb** lire quelque chose sur qn; **~ out** lire à haute voix. **reader** *n* lecteur/-trice *m/f*. **reading** *n* lecture *f*; (measurement) indication *f*; (interpretation) interprétation *f*.

readjust *vt* rajuster. ● *vi* se réadapter (**to** à).

read-only memory, ROM *n* mémoire *f* morte.

ready *a* (**-ier, -iest**) prêt; (quick) prompt. **~-made** *a* tout fait. **~-to-wear** *a* prêt-à-porter.

real *a* (not imaginary) véritable, réel; (not artificial) vrai; **it's a ~ shame** c'est vraiment dommage. **~ estate** *n* biens *mpl* immobiliers.

realism *n* réalisme *m*. **realistic** *a* réaliste.

reality *n* réalité *f*.

realize *vt* se rendre compte de, comprendre; (fulfil, turn into cash) réaliser; (*price*) atteindre.

really *adv* vraiment.

reap *vt* (*crop*) recueillir; (*benefits*) récolter.

reappear *vi* reparaître.

rear *n* arrière *m*; (of person) derrière *m* ▣. ● *a* (*seat*) arrière *inv*; (*entrance*) de derrière. ● *vt* élever. ● *vi* (*horse*) se cabrer. **~-view mirror** *n* rétroviseur *m*.

reason *n* raison *f* (**to do, for doing** de faire); **within ~** dans la limite du raisonnable. ● *vi* **~ with sb** raisonner qn.

reasonable *a* raisonnable.

reassurance *n* réconfort *m*. **reassure** *vt* rassurer.

rebate *n* (refund) remboursement *m*; (discount) remise *f*.

rebel[1] *n & a* rebelle (*mf*).

rebel[2] *vi* (*pt* **rebelled**) se rebeller. **rebellion** *n* rébellion *f*.

rebound[1] *vi* rebondir; **~ on** (backfire) se retourner contre.

rebound[2] *n n* rebond *m*.

rebuke *vt* réprimander. ● *n* réprimande *f*.

recall *vt* (remember) se souvenir de; (call back) rappeler. ● *n* (memory) mémoire *f*; (Comput, Mil) rappel *m*.

recap *vt/i* (*pt* **recapped**) récapituler. ● *n* récapitulation *f*.

recede *vi* s'éloigner; **his hair is receding** son front se dégarnit.

receipt *n* (written) reçu *m*; (of letter) réception *f*; **~s** (Comm) recettes *fpl*.

receive *vt* recevoir; (*stolen goods*) receler. **receiver** *n* (telephone) combiné *m*; (TV) récepteur *m*.

recent *a* récent. **recently** *adv* récemment.

receptacle *n* récipient *m*.

reception *n* réception *f*; **give sb a warm ~** donner un accueil chaleureux à qn.

recess *n* (alcove) alcôve *m*; (for door) embrasure *f*; (Jur, Pol) vacances *fpl*; (School, US) récréation *f*.

recession *n* récession *f*.

recharge *vt* recharger.

recipe *n* recette *f*.

recipient *n* (of honour) récipiendaire *mf*; (of letter) destinataire *mf*.

reciprocate *vt* (*compliment*) retourner; (*kindness*) payer de retour. ● *vi* en faire autant.

recite *vi* réciter.

reckless *a* imprudent.

reckon *vt/i* calculer; (judge) considérer; (think) penser; **~ on/with** compter sur/avec. **reckoning** *n* (guess) estimation *f*; (calculation) calculs *mpl*.

reclaim *vt* récupérer; (*flooded land*) assécher.

recline *vi* s'allonger; (*seat*) s'incliner.

recluse *n* reclus/-e *m/f*.

recognition *n* reconnaissance *f*; **beyond ~** méconnaissable; **gain ~** être reconnu.

recognize *vt* reconnaître.

R

recollect *vt* se souvenir de, se rappeler. **recollection** *n* souvenir *m*.

recommend *vt* recommander. **recommendation** *n* recommandation *f*.

reconcile *vt* (*people*) réconcilier; (*facts*) concilier; ~ **oneself to** se résigner à.

recondition *vt* remettre à neuf.

reconsider *vt* réexaminer. ● *vi* réfléchir.

reconstruct *vt* reconstruire; (*crime*) faire une reconstitution de.

record[1] *vt/i* (in register, on tape) enregistrer; (in diary) noter; ~ **that** rapporter que.

record[2] *n* (of events) compte-rendu *m*; (official) procès-verbal *m*; (personal, administrative) dossier *m*; (historical) archives *fpl*; (past history) réputation *f*; (Mus) disque *m*; (Sport) record *m*; (**criminal**) ~ casier *m* judiciaire; **off the** ~ officieusement. ● *a* record *inv*.

recorder *n* (Mus) flûte *f* à bec.

recording *n* enregistrement *m*.

record-player *n* tourne-disque *m*.

recover *vt* récupérer. ● *vi* se remettre; (*economy*) se redresser. **recovery** *n* (Med) rétablissement *m*; (of economy) relance *f*.

recreation *n* récréation *f*.

recruit *n* recrue *f*. ● *vt* recruter. **recruitment** *n* recrutement *m*.

rectangle *n* rectangle *m*.

rectify *vt* rectifier.

recuperate *vt* récupérer. ● *vi* se rétablir.

recur *vi* (*pt* **recurred**) se reproduire.

recycle *vt* recycler.

red *a* (**redder**, **reddest**) rouge; (*hair*) roux. ● *n* rouge *m*; **in the** ~ en déficit. **R~ Cross** *n* Croix-Rouge *f*. **~currant** *n* groseille *f*.

redecorate *vt* repeindre, refaire.

redeploy *vt* réorganiser; (*troops*) répartir.

red: **~-handed** *a* en flagrant délit. **~-hot** *a* brûlant.

redirect *vt* (*traffic*) dévier; (*letter*) faire suivre.

redness *n* rougeur *f*.

redo *vt* (*pt* **-did**; *pp* **-done**) refaire.

redress *vt* (*wrong*) redresser; (*balance*) rétablir. ● *n* réparation *f*.

reduce *vt* réduire; (*temperature*) faire baisser. **reduction** *n* réduction *f*.

redundancy *n* licenciement *m*.

redundant *a* superflu; (*worker*) licencié; **make** ~ licencier.

reed *n* (plant) roseau *m*.

reef *n* récif *m*, écueil *m*.

reel *n* (of thread) bobine *f*; (of film) bande *f*; (winding device) dévidoir *m*. ● *vi* chanceler. ● *vt* ~ **off** réciter.

refectory *n* réfectoire *m*.

refer *vt/i* (*pt* **referred**) ~ **to** (allude to) faire allusion à; (concern) s'appliquer à; (consult) consulter; (direct) renvoyer à.

referee *n* (Sport) arbitre *m*. ● *vt* (*pt* **refereed**) arbitrer.

reference *n* référence *f*; (mention) allusion *f*; (person) personne *f* pouvant fournir des références; **in** *or* **with** ~ **to** en ce qui concerne; (Comm) suite à.

referendum *n* (*pl* **~s**) référendum *m*.

refill[1] *vt* (*glass*) remplir à nouveau; (*pen*) recharger.

refill[2] *n* recharge *f*.

refine *vt* raffiner.

reflect *vt* refléter; (*heat, light*) renvoyer. ● *vi* réfléchir (**on** à); ~

well/badly on sb faire honneur/du tort à qn.

reflection *n* réflexion *f*; (image) reflet *m*; **on ~** à la réflexion.

reflective *a* (*surface*) réfléchissant; (*person*) réfléchi

reflector *n* (on car) catadioptre *m*.

reflex *a & n* réflexe (*m*).

reflexive *a* (Gram) réfléchi.

reform *vt* réformer. ● *vi* (*person*) s'amender. ● *n* réforme *f*.

refrain *n* refrain *m*. ● *vi* s'abstenir (**from** de).

refresh *vt* (*drink*) rafraîchir; (*rest*) reposer. **refreshments** *npl* rafraîchissements *mpl*.

refrigerate *vt* réfrigérer. **refrigerator** *n* réfrigérateur *m*.

refuel *vt/i* (*pt* **refuelled**) (se) ravitailler.

refuge *n* refuge *m*; **take ~** se réfugier. **refugee** *n* réfugié/-e *m/f*.

refund¹ *vt* rembourser.

refund² *n* remboursement *m*.

refurbish *vt* remettre à neuf.

refuse¹ *vt/i* refuser.

refuse² *n* ordures *fpl*.

regain *vt* retrouver; (*lost ground*) regagner.

regard *vt* considérer; **as ~s** en ce qui concerne. ● *n* égard *m*, estime *f*; **in this ~** à cet égard; **~s** amitiés *fpl*. **regarding** *prep* en ce qui concerne.

regardless *adv* malgré tout; **~ of** sans tenir compte de.

regime *n* régime *m*.

regiment *n* régiment *m*.

region *n* région *f*; **in the ~ of** environ.

register *n* registre *m*. ● *vt* (record) enregistrer; (*vehicle*) faire immatriculer; (*birth*) déclarer; (*letter*) recommander; (indicate) indiquer; (express) exprimer. ● *vi* (enrol) s'inscrire; (at hotel) se présenter; (fig) être compris.

registrar *n* officier *m* de l'état civil; (Univ) responsable *m* du bureau de la scolarité.

registration *n* (of voter, student) inscription *f*; (of birth) déclaration *f*; **~ (number)** (Auto) numéro *m* d'immatriculation.

registry office *n* bureau *m* de l'état civil.

regret *n* regret *m*. ● *vt* (*pt* **regretted**) regretter (**to do** de faire). **regretfully** *adv* à regret.

regular *a* régulier; (usual) habituel. ● *n* habitué/-e *m/f*. **regularity** *n* régularité *f*. **regularly** *adv* régulièrement.

regulate *vt* régler. **regulation** *n* (rule) règlement *m*; (process) réglementation *f*.

rehabilitate *vt* (in public esteem) réhabiliter; (prisoner) réinsérer.

rehearsal *n* répétition *f*. **rehearse** *vt/i* répéter.

reign *n* règne *m*. ● *vi* régner (**over** sur).

reimburse *vt* rembourser.

reindeer *n inv* renne *m*.

reinforce *vt* renforcer. **reinforcement** *n* renforcement *m*; **~s** renforts *mpl*.

reinstate *vt* (*person*) réintégrer; (*law*) rétablir.

reject¹ *n* marchandise *f* de deuxième choix.

reject² *vt* (*offer, plea*) rejeter; (*goods*) refuser. **rejection** *n* (personal) rejet *m*; (of candidate, work) refus *m*.

rejoice *vi* se réjouir.

relapse *n* rechute *f*. ● *vi* rechuter; **~ into** retomber dans.

relate *vt* raconter; (associate) associer. ● *vi* **~ to** se rapporter à; (get on with) s'entendre avec. **related** *a* (*ideas*) lié; **we are ~d** nous sommes parents.

R

relation *n* rapport *m*; (person) parent/-e *m/f*. **relationship** *n* relations *fpl*; (link) rapport *m*.

relative *n* parent/-e *m/f*. ●*a* relatif; (respective) respectif.

relax *vt* (*grip*) relâcher; (*muscle*) décontracter; (*discipline*) assouplir. ●*vi* (*person*) se détendre; (*grip*) se relâcher. **relaxation** *n* détente *f*. **relaxing** *a* délassant.

relay[1] *n* (also ~ **race**) course *f* de relais.

relay[2] *vt* relayer.

release *vt* (*prisoner*) libérer; (*fastening*) faire jouer; (*object, hand*) lâcher; (*film*) faire sortir; (*news*) publier. ●*n* libération *f*; (of film) sortie *f*; (new record, film) nouveauté *f*.

relevance *n* pertinence *f*, intérêt *m*.

relevant *a* pertinent; **be ~ to** avoir rapport à.

reliability *n* (of firm) sérieux *m*; (of car) fiabilité *f*; (of person) honnêteté *f*. **reliable** *a* (*firm*) sérieux; (*person, machine*) fiable.

reliance *n* dépendance *f*.

relic *n* vestige *m*; (object) relique *f*.

relief *n* soulagement *m* (**from** à); (assistance) secours *m*; (outline) relief *m*; ~ **road** route *f* de délestage.

relieve *vt* soulager; (help) secourir; (take over from) relayer.

religion *n* religion *f*. **religious** *a* religieux.

relish *n* plaisir *m*; (Culin) condiment *m*. ●*vt* (*food*) savourer; (*idea*) se réjouir de.

relocate *vt* muter. ●*vi* (*company*) déménager; (*worker*) être muté.

reluctance *n* répugnance *f*.

reluctant *a* (*person*) peu enthousiaste; (*consent*) accordé à contrecœur; ~ **to** peu disposé à. **reluctantly** *adv* à contrecœur.

rely *vi* ~ **on** (count) compter sur; (be dependent) dépendre de.

remain *vi* rester. **remainder** *n* reste *m*.

remand *vt* mettre en détention provisoire. ●*n* **on ~** en détention provisoire.

remark *n* remarque *f*. ●*vt* remarquer. ●*vi* ~ **on** faire des remarques sur. **remarkable** *a* remarquable.

remedy *n* remède *m*. ●*vt* remédier à.

remember *vt* se souvenir de, se rappeler; ~ **to do** ne pas oublier de faire. **remembrance** *n* souvenir *m*.

remind *vt* rappeler (**sb of sth** qch à qn); ~ **sb to do** rappeler à qn de faire. **reminder** *n* rappel *m*.

reminisce *vi* évoquer ses souvenirs.

remission *n* (Med) rémission *f*; (Jur) remise *f*.

remnant *n* reste *m*; (trace) vestige *m*; (of cloth) coupon *m*.

remodel *vt* (*pt* **remodelled**) remodeler.

remorse *n* remords *m*.

remote *a* (*place, time*) lointain; (*person*) distant; (slight) vague; ~ **control** télécommande *f*.

removable *a* amovible.

removal *n* (of employee) renvoi *m*; (of threat) suppression *f*; (of troops) retrait *m*; (of stain) détachage *m*; (from house) déménagement *m*; ~ **men** déménageurs *mpl*.

remove *vt* enlever; (dismiss) renvoyer; (do away with) supprimer; (Comput) effacer.

remunerate *vt* rémunérer. **remuneration** *n* rémunération *f*.

render *vt* rendre.

renegade *n* renégat/-e *m/f*.

renew *vt* renouveler; (resume) reprendre. **renewable** *a* renouvelable.

renounce *vt* renoncer à; (disown) renier.

renovate *vt* rénover.

renown *n* renommée *f*.

rent *n* loyer *m*. ● *vt* louer; **for ~** à louer. **rental** *n* prix *m* de location.

reopen *vt/i* rouvrir.

reorganize *vt* réorganiser.

rep *n* (Comm) représentant/-e *m/f*.

repair *vt* réparer. ● *n* réparation *f*; **in good/bad ~** en bon/mauvais état.

repatriate *vt* rapatrier. **repatriation** *n* rapatriement *m*.

repay *vt* (*pt* **repaid**) rembourser; (reward) récompenser. **repayment** *n* remboursement *m*.

repeal *vt* abroger. ● *n* abrogation *f*.

repeat *vt/i* répéter; (renew) renouveler; **~ itself, ~ oneself** se répéter. ● *n* répétition *f*; (broadcast) reprise *f*.

repel *vt* (*pt* **repelled**) repousser.

repent *vi* se repentir (**of** de).

repercussion *n* répercussion *f*.

repetition *n* répétition *f*.

replace *vt* (put back) remettre; (take the place of) remplacer. **replacement** *n* remplacement *m* (**of** de); (person) remplaçant/-e *m/f*; (new part) pièce *f* de rechange.

replay *n* (Sport) match *m* rejoué; (recording) répétition *f* immédiate.

replenish *vt* (refill) remplir; (renew) renouveler.

replica *n* copie *f* exacte.

reply *vt/i* répondre. ● *n* réponse *f*.

report *vt* rapporter, annoncer (**that** que); (notify) signaler; (denounce) dénoncer. ● *vi* faire un rapport; **~ (on)** (*news item*) faire un reportage sur; **~ to** (go) se présenter chez. ● *n* rapport *m*; (in press) reportage *m*; (School) bulletin *m*. **reporter** *n* reporter *m*.

repossess *vt* reprendre.

represent *vt* représenter.

representation *n* représentation *f*; **make ~s to** protester auprès de.

representative *a* représentatif, typique (**of** de). ● *n* représentant/-e *m/f*.

repress *vt* réprimer.

reprieve *n* (delay) sursis *m*; (pardon) grâce *f*. ● *vt* accorder un sursis à; gracier.

reprimand *vt* réprimander. ● *n* réprimande *f*.

reprisals *npl* représailles *fpl*.

reproach *vt* reprocher (**sb for sth** qch à qn). ● *n* reproche *m*.

reproduce *vt/i* (se) reproduire. **reproduction** *n* reproduction *f*. **reproductive** *a* reproducteur.

reptile *n* reptile *m*.

republic *n* république *f*. **republican** *a & n* républicain/-e (*m/f*).

repudiate *vt* répudier; (*contract*) refuser d'honorer.

reputable *a* honorable, de bonne réputation.

reputation *n* réputation *f*.

repute *n* réputation *f*.

request *n* demande *f*. ● *vt* demander (**of, from** à).

require *vt* (of thing) demander; (of person) avoir besoin de; (demand, order) exiger. **required** *a* requis. **requirement** *n* exigence *f*; (condition) condition *f* (requise).

rescue *vt* sauver. ● *n* sauvetage *m* (**of** de); (help) secours *m*.

research *n* recherche(s) *f(pl)*. ● *vt/i* faire des recherches (sur). **researcher** *n* chercheur/-euse *m/f*.

resemblance *n* ressemblance *f*. **resemble** *vt* ressembler à.

resent *vt* être indigné de, s'offenser de. **resentment** *n* ressentiment *m*.

reservation *n* (doubt) réserve *f*; (booking) réservation *f*; (US) réserve *f* (indienne); **make a ~** réserver.

reserve *vt* réserver. ● *n* (*stock, land*) réserve *f*; (Sport) remplaçant/-e *m*/*f*; **in ~** en réserve; **the ~s** (Mil) les réserves *fpl*. **reserved** *a* (*person, room*) réservé.

reshuffle *vt* (Pol) remanier. ● *n* (Pol) remaniement *m* (ministériel).

residence *n* résidence *f*; (of students) foyer *m*; **in ~** (*doctor*) résidant.

resident *a* résidant; **be ~** résider. ● *n* habitant/-e *m*/*f*; (foreigner) résident/-e *m*/*f*; (in hotel) pensionnaire *mf*. **residential** *a* résidentiel.

resign *vt* abandonner; (*job*) démissionner de. ● *vi* démissionner; **~ oneself to** se résigner à. **resignation** *n* résignation *f*; (from job) démission *f*. **resigned** *a* résigné.

resilience *n* élasticité *f*; ressort *m*.

resin *n* résine *f*.

resist *vt*/*i* résister (à). **resistance** *n* résistance *f*. **resistant** *a* (Med) rebelle; (*metal*) résistant.

resolution *n* résolution *f*.

resolve *vt* résoudre (**to do** de faire). ● *n* résolution *f*.

resort *vi* **~ to** avoir recours à. ● *n* (recourse) recours *m*; (place) station *f*; **in the last ~** en dernier ressort.

resource *n* ressource *f*; **~s** (wealth) ressources *fpl*. **resourceful** *a* ingénieux.

respect *n* respect *m*; (aspect) égard *m*; **with ~ to** à l'égard de, relativement à. ● *vt* respecter.

respectability *n* respectabilité *f*. **respectable** *a* respectable.

respectful *a* respectueux.

respective *a* respectif.

respite *n* répit *m*.

respond *vi* répondre (**to** à); **~ to** (react to) réagir à. **response** *n* réponse *f*.

responsibility *n* responsabilité *f*. **responsible** *a* responsable; (*job*) qui comporte des responsabilités.

responsive *a* réceptif.

rest *vt*/*i* (se) reposer; (lean) (s')appuyer (**on** sur); (be buried, lie) reposer; (remain) demeurer. ● *n* repos *m*; (support) support *m*; **have a ~** se reposer; **the ~** (remainder) le reste (**of** de); (other people) les autres.

restaurant *n* restaurant *m*.

restless *a* agité.

restoration *n* rétablissement *m*; restauration *f*.

restore *vt* rétablir; (*building*) restaurer; **~ sth to sb** restituer qch à qn.

restrain *vt* contenir; **~ sb from** retenir qn de. **restrained** *a* (moderate) mesuré; (in control of self) maître de soi.

restrict *vt* restreindre.

rest room *n* (US) toilettes *fpl*.

result *n* résultat *m*. ● *vi* résulter; **~ in** aboutir à.

resume *vt*/*i* reprendre.

résumé *n* résumé *m*; (of career: US) CV *m*, curriculum vitae *m*.

resurrect *vt* ressusciter.

resuscitate *vt* réanimer.

retail *n* détail *m*. ● *a & adv* au détail. ● *vt*/*i* (se) vendre (au détail). **retailer** *n* détaillant/-e *m*/*f*.

retain *vt* (hold back, remember) retenir; (keep) conserver.

retaliate *vi* riposter. **retaliation** *n* représailles *fpl*.

retch *vi* avoir un haut-le-cœur.

retire *vi* (from work) prendre sa retraite; (withdraw) se retirer; (go to bed) se coucher. **retired** *a* retraité. **retirement** *n* retraite *f*.

retort *vt/i* répliquer. ● *n* réplique *f*.

retrace *vt* ~ **one's steps** revenir sur ses pas.

retract *vt/i* (se) rétracter.

retrain *vt/i* (se) recycler.

retreat *vi* (Mil) battre en retraite. ● *n* retraite *f*.

retrieval *n* (Comput) extraction *f*. **retrieve** *vt* (*object*) récupérer; (*situation*) redresser; (*data*) extraire.

retrospect *n* **in** ~ rétrospectivement.

return *vi* (come back) revenir; (go back) retourner; (go home) rentrer. ● *vt* (give back) rendre; (bring back) rapporter; (send back) renvoyer; (put back) remettre. ● *n* retour *m*; (yield) rapport *m*; **~s** (Comm) bénéfices *mpl*; **in ~ for** en échange de. **~ ticket** *n* aller-retour *m*.

reunion *n* réunion *f*.

reunite *vt* réunir.

rev *n* (Auto 🅘) tour *m*. ● *vt/i* (*pt* **revved**) **~ (up)** (engine 🅘) (s')emballer.

reveal *vt* révéler; (allow to appear) laisser voir.

revelation *n* révélation *f*.

revenge *n* vengeance *f*. ● *vt* venger.

revenue *n* revenu *m*.

reverberate *vi* (*sound, light*) se répercuter.

reverend *a* révérend.

reversal *n* renversement *m*; (of view) revirement *m*.

reverse *a* contraire, inverse. ● *n* contraire *m*; (back) revers *m*, envers *m*; (gear) marche *f* arrière. ● *vt* (*situation, bracket*) renverser; (*order*) inverser; (*decision*) annuler; **~ the charges** appeler en PCV. ● *vi* (Auto) faire marche arrière.

review *n* (inspection, magazine) revue *f*; (of book) critique *f*. ● *vt* passer en revue; (situation) réexaminer; faire la critique de. **reviewer** *n* critique *m*.

revise *vt* réviser; (*text*) revoir. **revision** *n* révision *f*.

revival *n* (of economy) reprise *f*; (of interest) regain *m*.

revive *vt* (person, hopes) ranimer; (custom) rétablir. ● *vi* se ranimer.

revoke *vt* révoquer.

revolt *vt/i* (se) révolter. ● *n* révolte *f*. **revolting** *a* dégoûtant.

revolution *n* révolution *f*.

revolve *vi* tourner.

revolver *n* revolver *m*.

revolving door *n* porte *f* à tambour.

reward *n* récompense *f*. ● *vt* récompenser (**for** de). **rewarding** *a* rémunérateur; (worthwhile) qui (en) vaut la peine.

rewind *vt* (*pt* **rewound**) rembobiner.

rewire *vt* refaire l'installation électrique de.

rhetorical *a* (de) rhétorique; (*question*) de pure forme.

rheumatism *n* rhumatisme *m*.

rhinoceros *n* (*pl* **~es**) rhinocéros *m*.

rhubarb *n* rhubarbe *f*.

rhyme *n* rime *f*; (poem) vers *mpl*. ● *vt/i* (faire) rimer.

rhythm *n* rythme *m*. **rhythmic(al)** *a* rythmique.

rib *n* côte *f*.

ribbon *n* ruban *m*; **in ~s** en lambeaux.

rice *n* riz *m*. **~ pudding** *n* riz *m* au lait.

rich *a* riche.

rid *vt* (*pt* **rid**; *pres p* **ridding**) débarrasser (**of** de); **get ~ of** se débarrasser de.

ridden ⇒RIDE.

riddle *n* énigme *f*. ● *vt* **~ with** (*bullets*) cribler de; (*mistakes*) bourrer de.

ride *vi* (*pt* **rode**; *pp* **ridden**) aller (à bicyclette, à cheval); (in car) rouler; (on a horse as sport) monter à cheval. ● *vt* (a particular horse) monter; (distance) parcourir. ● *n* promenade *f*, tour *m*; (distance) trajet *m*; **give sb a ~** (US) prendre qn en voiture; **go for a ~** aller faire un tour (à bicyclette, à cheval). **rider** *n* cavalier/-ière *m*/*f*; (in horse race) jockey *m*; (cyclist) cycliste *mf*; (motorcyclist) motocycliste *mf*.

ridge *n* arête *f*, crête *f*.

ridiculous *a* ridicule.

riding *n* équitation *f*.

rifle *n* fusil *m*. ● *vt* (rob) dévaliser.

rift *n* (crack) fissure *f*; (between people) désaccord *m*.

rig *vt* (*pt* **rigged**) (equip) équiper; (*election, match*) truquer. ● *n* (for oil) derrick *m*. □ **~ out** habiller; **~ up** (arrange) arranger.

right *a* (morally) bon; (fair) juste; (best) bon, qu'il faut; (not left) droit; **be ~** (person) avoir raison (**to** de); (calculation, watch) être exact; **put ~** arranger, rectifier. ● *n* (entitlement) droit *m*; (not left) droite *f*; (not evil) le bien; **be in the ~** avoir raison; **on the ~** à droite. ● *vt* (a wrong, sth fallen) redresser. ● *adv* (not left) à droite; (directly) tout droit; (exactly) bien, juste; (completely) tout (à fait); **~ away** tout de suite; **~ now** (at once) tout de suite; (at present) en ce moment.

righteous *a* vertueux.

rightful *a* légitime.

right-handed *a* droitier.

rightly *adv* correctement; (with reason) à juste titre.

right of way *n* (Auto) priorité *f*.

right wing *a* de droite.

rigid *a* rigide.

rigorous *a* rigoureux.

rim *n* bord *m*.

rind *n* (on cheese) croûte *f*; (on bacon) couenne *f*; (on fruit) écorce *f*.

ring[1] *n* (hoop) anneau *m*; (jewellery) bague *f*; (circle) cercle *m*; (boxing) ring *m*; (**wedding**) **~** alliance *f*. ● *vt* entourer; (word in text) entourer d'un cercle.

ring[2] *vt*/*i* (*pt* **rang**; *pp* **rung**) sonner; (of words) retentir; **~ the bell** sonner. ● *n* sonnerie *f*; **give sb a ~** donner un coup de fil à qn. □ **~ back** rappeler; **~ off** raccrocher; **~ up** téléphoner (à).

ring road *n* périphérique *m*.

rink *n* patinoire *f*.

rinse *vt* rincer; **~ out** rincer. ● *n* rinçage *m*.

riot *n* émeute *f*; (of colours) profusion *f*; **run ~** se déchaîner. ● *vi* faire une émeute.

rip *vt*/*i* (*pt* **ripped**) (se) déchirer; **let ~** (not check) laisser courir; **~ off** ⊠ rouler. ● *n* déchirure *f*.

ripe *a* mûr. **ripen** *vt*/*i* mûrir.

rip-off *n* [!] vol *m*; arnaque *f* [!].

ripple *n* ride *f*, ondulation *f*. ● *vt*/*i* (*water*) (se) rider.

rise *vi* (*pt* **rose**; *pp* **risen**) (go upwards, increase) monter, s'élever; (stand up, get up from bed) se lever; (rebel) se soulever; (*sun*) se lever; (*water*) monter; **~ up** se soulever. ● *n* (slope) pente *f*; (increase) hausse *f*; (in pay) augmentation *f*;

(progress, boom) essor *m*; **give ~ to** donner lieu à.

risk *n* risque *m*; **at ~** menacé. ● *vt* risquer; **~ doing** (venture) se risquer à faire. **risky** *a* risqué.

rite *n* rite *m*; **last ~s** derniers sacrements *mpl*.

rival *n* rival/-e *m/f*. ● *a* rival; (*claim*) opposé. ● *vt* (*pt* **rivalled**) rivaliser avec.

river *n* rivière *f*; (flowing into sea) fleuve *m*. ● *a* (*fishing, traffic*) fluvial.

rivet *n* (bolt) rivet *m*. ● *vt* (*pt* **riveted**) river, riveter.

Riviera *n* **the** (**French**) **~** la Côte d'Azur.

road *n* route *f*; (in town) rue *f*; (small) chemin *m*; **the ~ to** (*glory*: fig) le chemin de. ● *a* (*sign, safety*) routier. **~-map** *n* carte *f* routière. **~ rage** *n* violence *f* au volant. **~worthy** *a* en état de marche.

roam *vi* errer. ● *vt* (*streets, seas*) parcourir.

roar *n* hurlement *m*; (of lion, wind) rugissement *m*; (of lorry, thunder) grondement *m*. ● *vt/i* hurler; (*lion, wind*) rugir; (*lorry, thunder*) gronder; **~ with laughter** rire aux éclats.

roast *vt/i* rôtir. ● *n* (meat) rôti *m*. ● *a* rôti. **~ beef** *n* rôti *m* de bœuf.

rob *vt* (*pt* **robbed**) voler (**sb of sth** qch à qn); (*bank, house*) dévaliser; (deprive) priver (**of** de). **robber** *n* voleur/-euse *m/f*. **robbery** *n* vol *m*.

robe *n* (of judge) robe *f*; (dressing-gown) peignoir *m*.

robin *n* rouge-gorge *m*.

robot *n* robot *m*.

robust *a* robuste.

rock *n* roche *f*; (rock face, boulder) rocher *m*; (hurled stone) pierre *f*; (sweet) sucre *m* d'orge; (Mus) rock *m*; **on the ~s** (*drink*) avec des glaçons; (*marriage*) en crise. ● *vt/i* (se) balancer; (shake) (faire) trembler; (*child*) bercer. **~-climbing** *n* varappe *f*.

rocket *n* fusée *f*.

rocking-chair *n* fauteuil *m* à bascule.

rocky *a* (**-ier, -iest**) (*ground*) rocailleux; (*hill*) rocheux; (shaky: fig) branlant.

rod *n* (metal) tige *f*; (wooden) baguette *f*; (for fishing) canne *f* à pêche.

rode ⇒RIDE.

roe *n* œufs *mpl* de poisson.

rogue *n* (dishonest) bandit *m*, voleur/-euse *m/f*; (mischievous) coquin/-e *m/f*.

role *n* rôle *m*.

roll *vt/i* rouler; **~** (**about**) (*child, dog*) se rouler; **be ~ing** (**in money**) ⊡ rouler sur l'or. ● *n* rouleau *m*; (list) liste *f*; (bread) petit pain *m*; (of drum, thunder) roulement *m*; (of ship) roulis *m*. □ **~ out** étendre; **~over** se retourner; **~ up** (*sleeves*) retrousser.

roll-call *n* appel *m*.

roller *n* rouleau *m*. **~-coaster** *n* montagnes *fpl* russes. **~-skate** *n* patin *m* à roulettes.

ROM (*abbr*) (**read-only memory**) mémoire *f* morte.

Roman *a* & *n* romain/-e (*m/f*). **~ Catholic** *a* & *n* catholique (*mf*).

romance *n* (novel) roman *m* d'amour; (love) amour *m*; (affair) idylle *f*; (fig) poésie *f*.

Romania *n* Roumanie *f*.

Romanian *a* roumain. ● *n* (person) Roumain/-e *m/f*; (language) roumain *m*.

romantic *a* (*love*) romantique; (of the imagination) romanesque.

roof *n* toit *m*; (of mouth) palais *m*. ● *vt* recouvrir. **~-rack** *n* galerie *f*. **~-top** *n* toit *m*.

room *n* pièce *f*; (bedroom) chambre *f*; (large hall) salle *f*; (space) place *f*; **~ for manoeuvre** marge *f* de manœuvre. **~-mate** *n* camarade *mf* de chambre.

roomy *a* spacieux; (*clothes*) ample.

root *n* racine *f*; (source) origine *f*; **take ~** prendre racine. ● *vt/i* (s')enraciner. □ **~ about** fouiller; **~ for** (US [!]) encourager; **~ out** extirper.

rope *n* corde *f*; **know the ~s** être au courant. ● *vt* attacher; **~ in** (*person*) enrôler.

rose *n* rose *f*. ● ⇒RISE.

rosé *n* rosé *m*.

rosy *a* (**-ier**, **-iest**) rose; (hopeful) plein d'espoir.

rot *vt/i* (*pt* **rotted**) pourrir. ● *n* pourriture *f*.

rota *n* liste *f* (de service).

rotary *a* rotatif.

rotate *vt/i* (faire) tourner; (change round) alterner.

rotten *a* pourri; (*tooth*) gâté; (bad [!]) mauvais, sale.

rough *a* (*manners*) rude; (to touch) rugueux; (*ground*) accidenté; (violent) brutal; (bad) mauvais; (*estimate*) approximatif. ● *adv* (*live*) à la dure; (*play*) brutalement.

roughage *n* fibres *fpl* (alimentaires).

roughly *adv* rudement; (approximately) à peu près.

round *a* rond. ● *n* (circle) rond *m*; (slice) tranche *f*; (of visits, drinks) tournée *f*; (competition) partie *f*, manche *f*; (boxing) round *m*; (of talks) série *f*; **~ of applause** applaudissements *mpl*; **go the ~s** circuler. ● *prep* autour de; **she lives ~ here** elle habite par ici; **~ the clock** vingt-quatre heures sur vingt-quatre. ● *adv* autour; **~ about** (nearby) par ici; (fig) à peu près; **go** *or* **come ~ to** (*a friend*) passer chez; **enough to go ~** assez pour tout le monde. ● *vt* (*object*) arrondir; (*corner*) tourner. □ **~ off** terminer; **~ up** rassembler

roundabout *n* (in fairground) manège *m*; (for traffic) rond-point *m* (*à sens giratoire*). ● *a* indirect.

round trip *n* voyage *m* aller-retour.

round-up *n* rassemblement *m*; (of suspects) rafle *f*.

route *n* itinéraire *m*, parcours *m*; (Naut, Aviat) route *f*.

routine *n* routine *f*. ● *a* de routine.

row[1] *n* rangée *f*, rang *m*; **in a ~** (consecutive) consécutif. ● *vi* ramer; (Sport) faire de l'aviron. ● *vt* **~ a boat up the river** remonter la rivière à la rame.

row[2] *n* (noise [!]) tapage *m*; (quarrel [!]) dispute *f*. ● *vi* [!] se disputer.

rowdy *a* (**-ier**, **-iest**) tapageur.

rowing *n* aviron *m*. **~-boat** *n* bateau *m* à rames.

royal *a* royal. **royalty** *n* famille *f* royale; **royalties** droits *mpl* d'auteur.

rub *vt/i* (*pt* **rubbed**) frotter; **~ it in** insister, en rajouter. ● *n* friction *f*. □ **~ out** (s')effacer.

rubber *n* caoutchouc *m*; (eraser) gomme *f*. **~ band** *n* élastique *m*. **~ stamp** *n* tampon *m*.

rubbish *n* (refuse) ordures *fpl*; (junk) saletés *fpl*; (fig) bêtises *fpl*.

rubble *n* décombres *mpl*.

ruby *n* rubis *m*.

rucksack *n* sac *m* à dos.

rude *a* impoli, grossier; (improper) indécent; (*blow*) brutal.

ruffle *vt* (*hair*) ébouriffer; (*clothes*) froisser; (*person*) contrarier. ● *n* (frill) ruche *f*.

rug *n* petit tapis *m*.

rugby *n* rugby *m*.

rugged *a* (*surface*) rude, rugueux; (*ground*) accidenté; (*character, features*) rude.

ruin *n* ruine *f*. ● *vt* (destroy) ruiner; (damage) abîmer; (spoil) gâter.

rule *n* règle *f*; (regulation) règlement *m*; (Pol) gouvernement *m*; **as a ~** en règle générale. ● *vt* gouverner; (master) dominer; (decide) décider; **~ out** exclure. ● *vi* régner. **ruler** *n* dirigeant/-e *m/f*, gouvernant *m*; (measure) règle *f*.

ruling *a* (*class*) dirigeant; (*party*) au pouvoir. ● *n* décision *f*.

rum *n* rhum *m*.

rumble *vi* gronder; (*stomach*) gargouiller. ● *n* grondement *m*; gargouillement *m*.

rumour, (US) **rumor** *n* bruit *m*, rumeur *f*; **there's a ~ that** le bruit court que.

rump *n* (of animal) croupe *f*; (of bird) croupion *m*; (steak) romsteck *m*.

run *vi* (*pt* **ran**; *pp* **run**; *pres p* **running**) courir; (flow) couler; (pass) passer; (function) marcher; (melt) fondre; (extend) s'étendre; (of bus) circuler; (of play) se jouer; (last) durer; (of colour in washing) déteindre; (in election) être candidat. ● *vt* (manage) diriger; (*event*) organiser; (*risk, race*) courir; (*house*) tenir; (*temperature, errand*) faire; (Comput) exécuter. ● *n* course *f*; (journey) parcours *m*; (outing) promenade *f*; (rush) ruée *f*; (series) série *f*; (for chickens) enclos *m*; (in cricket) point *m*; **in the long ~** avec le temps; **on the ~** en fuite. □ **~ across** rencontrer par hasard; **~ away** s'enfuir; **~ down** descendre en courant; (of vehicle) renverser; (*production*) réduire progressivement; (belittle) dénigrer; **~ into** (hit) heurter; **~ off** (*copies*) tirer; **~ out** (be used up) s'épuiser; (of lease) expirer; **~ out of** manquer de; **~ over** (of vehicle) écraser; (*details*) revoir; **~ through** regarder qch rapidement; **~ sth through sth** passer qch à travers qch; **~ up** (*bill*) accumuler.

runaway *n* fugitif/-ive *m/f*. ● *a* fugitif; (*horse, vehicle*) fou; (*inflation*) galopant.

rung ⇒RING². ● *n* (of ladder) barreau *m*.

runner *n* coureur/-euse *m/f*. **~ bean** *n* haricot *m* d'Espagne. **~-up** *n* second/-e *m/f*.

running *n* course *f* à pied; (of business) gestion *f*; (of machine) marche *f*; **be in the ~ for** être sur les rangs pour. ● *a* (*commentary*) suivi; (*water*) courant; **four days ~** quatre jours de suite.

runway *n* piste *f*.

rural *a* rural.

rush *vi* (move) se précipiter; (be in a hurry) se dépêcher. ● *vt* (*person*) bousculer; (Mil) prendre d'assaut; **~ to** envoyer d'urgence à. ● *n* ruée *f*; (haste) bousculade *f*; (plant) jonc *m*; **in a ~** pressé. **~-hour** *n* heure *f* de pointe.

Russia *n* Russie *f*.

Russian *a* russe. ● *n* (person) Russe *mf*; (language) russe.

rust *n* rouille *f*. ● *vt/i* rouiller.

rustle *vt/i* (*papers*) froisser.

rusty *a* rouillé.

ruthless *a* impitoyable.

rye *n* seigle *m*.

R

sabbath *n* (Jewish) sabbat *m*; (Christian) jour *m* du seigneur.

sabbatical *a* (Univ) sabbatique.

sabotage *n* sabotage *m*. ● *vt* saboter.

saccharin *n* saccharine *f*.

sack *n* (bag) sac *m*; **get the ~** 🄸 être renvoyé. ● *vt* 🄸 renvoyer; (plunder) saccager. **sacking** *n* (cloth) toile *f* à sac; (dismissal 🄸) renvoi *m*.

sacrament *n* sacrement *m*.

sacred *a* sacré.

sacrifice *n* sacrifice *m*. ● *vt* sacrifier.

sad *a* (**sadder**, **saddest**) triste.

saddle *n* selle *f*. ● *vt* (*horse*) seller.

sadist *n* sadique *mf*. **sadistic** *a* sadique.

sadly *adv* tristement; (unfortunately) malheureusement.

sadness *n* tristesse *f*.

safe *a* (not dangerous) sans danger; (reliable) sûr; (out of danger) en sécurité; (after accident) sain et sauf; **~ from** à l'abri de. ● *n* coffre-fort *m*.

safeguard *n* sauvegarde *f*. ● *vt* sauvegarder.

safely *adv* sans danger; (in safe place) en sûreté.

safety *n* sécurité *f*. **~-belt** *n* ceinture *f* de sécurité. **~-pin** *n* épingle *f* de sûreté. **~-valve** *n* soupape *f* de sûreté.

saffron *n* safran *m*.

sag *vi* (*pt* **sagged**) (*beam, mattress*) s'affaisser; (*flesh*) être flasque.

sage *n* (herb) sauge *f*.

Sagittarius *n* Sagittaire *m*.

said ⇒SAY.

sail *n* voile *f*; (journey) tour *m* en bateau. ● *vi* (*person*) voyager en bateau; (as sport) faire de la voile; (set off) prendre la mer; **~ across** traverser. ● *vt* (*boat*) piloter; (*sea*) traverser. **sailing-boat**, **sailing-ship** *n* voilier *m*.

sailor *n* marin *m*.

saint *n* saint/-e *m*/*f*.

sake *n* **for the ~ of** pour.

salad *n* salade *f*.

salaried *a* salarié.

salary *n* salaire *m*.

sale *n* vente *f*; **for ~** à vendre; **on ~** en vente; (reduced) en solde; **~s** (reductions) soldes *mpl*; **~s assistant**, (US) **~s clerk** vendeur/-euse *m*/*f*.

salesman *n* (*pl* **-men**) (in shop) vendeur *m*; (traveller) représentant *m*.

saline *a* salin. ● *n* sérum *m* physiologique.

saliva *n* salive *f*.

salmon *n inv* saumon *m*.

salon *n* salon *m*.

saloon *n* (on ship) salon *m*; **~** (**car**) berline *f*.

salt *n* sel *m*. ● *vt* saler. **salty** *a* salé.

salutary *a* salutaire.

salute *n* salut *m*. ● *vt* saluer. ● *vi* faire un salut.

salvage *n* sauvetage *m*; (of waste) récupération *f*. ● *vt* sauver; (for re-use) récupérer.

same *a* même (**as** que). ● *pron* **the ~** le même, la même, les mêmes; **at the ~ time** en même temps; **the ~** (**thing**) la même chose.

sample *n* échantillon *m*; (of blood)

prélèvement *m*. ● *vt* essayer; (*food*) goûter.
sanctimonious *a* (pej) supérieur.
sanction *n* sanction *f*. ● *vt* sanctionner.
sanctity *n* sainteté *f*.
sanctuary *n* (safe place) refuge *m*; (Relig) sanctuaire *m*; (for animals) réserve *f*.
sand *n* sable *m*; **~s** (beach) plage *f*.
sandal *n* sandale *f*.
sandpaper *n* papier *m* de verre. ● *vt* poncer.
sandpit *n* bac *m* à sable.
sandwich *n* sandwich *m*; **~ course** cours *m* avec stage pratique.
sandy *a* (*beach*) de sable; (*soil*) sablonneux; (hair) blond roux *inv*.
sane *a* (*view*) sensé; (*person*) sain d'esprit.
sang ⇒SING.
sanitary *a* (clean) hygiénique; (*system*) sanitaire; **~ towel** serviette *f* hygiénique.
sanitation *n* installations *fpl* sanitaires.
sanity *n* équilibre *m* mental; (sense) bon sens *m*.
sank ⇒SINK.
Santa (**Claus**) *n* le père Noël.
sapphire *n* saphir *m*.
sarcasm *n* sarcasme *m*. **sarcastic** *a* sarcastique.
sash *n* (on uniform) écharpe *f*; (on dress) ceinture *f*.
sat ⇒SIT.
satchel *n* cartable *m*.
satellite *n & a* satellite (*m*); **~ dish** antenne *f* parabolique.
satire *n* satire *f*. **satirical** *a* satirique.
satisfaction *n* satisfaction *f*.
satisfactory *a* satisfaisant.
satisfy *vt* satisfaire; (convince) convaincre.
saturate *vt* saturer. **saturated** *a* (wet) trempé.
Saturday *n* samedi *m*.
sauce *n* sauce *f*.
saucepan *n* casserole *f*.
saucer *n* soucoupe *f*.
Saudi Arabia *n* Arabie *f* saoudite.
sausage *n* (for cooking) saucisse *f*; (ready to eat) saucisson *m*.
savage *a* (*blow, temper*) violent; (*attack*) sauvage. ● *n* sauvage *mf*. ● *vt* attaquer sauvagement.
save *vt* sauver; (*money*) économiser; (*time*) gagner; (keep) garder; **~ (sb) doing sth** éviter (à qn) de faire qch. ● *n* (football) arrêt *m*. **saver** *n* épargnant/-e *m/f*. **saving** *n* économie *f*. **savings** *npl* économies *fpl*.
saviour, (US) **savior** *n* sauveur *m*.
savour, (US) **savor** *n* saveur *f*. ● *vt* savourer. **savoury** *a* (tasty) savoureux; (Culin) salé.
saw ⇒SEE. ● *n* scie *f*. ● *vt* (*pt* **sawed**; *pp* **sawn** *or* **sawed**) scier.
sawdust *n* sciure *f*.
saxophone *n* saxophone *m*.
say *vt/i* (*pt* **said**) dire; (*prayer*) faire. ● *n* **have a ~** dire son mot; (in decision) avoir voix au chapitre. **saying** *n* proverbe *m*.
scab *n* croûte *f*.
scaffolding *n* échafaudage *m*.
scald *vt* (injure, cleanse) ébouillanter. ● *n* brûlure *f*.
scale *n* (for measuring) échelle *f*; (extent) étendue *f*; (Mus) gamme *f*; (on fish) écaille *f*; **on a small ~** sur une petite échelle; **~ model** maquette *f*. ● *vt* (climb) escalader; **~ down** réduire. **scales** *npl* (for weighing) balance *f*.
scallop *n* coquille *f* Saint-Jacques.
scalp *n* cuir *m* chevelu.

S

scampi *npl* (fresh) langoustines *fpl*; (breaded) scampi *mpl*.

scan *vt* (*pt* **scanned**) scruter; (quickly) parcourir. ● *n* (ultrasound) échographie *f*; (CAT) scanner *m*.

scandal *n* scandale *m*; (gossip) potins *mpl* ⊡.

Scandinavia *n* Scandinavie *f*.

scanty *a* (**-ier**, **-iest**) maigre; (*clothing*) minuscule.

scapegoat *n* bouc *m* émissaire.

scar *n* cicatrice *f*. ● *vt* (*pt* **scarred**) marquer.

scarce *a* rare. **scarcely** *adv* à peine.

scare *vt* faire peur à; **be ~d** avoir peur. ● *n* peur *f*; **bomb ~** alerte *f* à la bombe. **scarecrow** *n* épouvantail *m*.

scarf *n* (*pl* **scarves**) écharpe *f*; (over head) foulard *m*.

scarlet *a* écarlate; **~ fever** scarlatine *f*.

scary *a* (**-ier**, **-iest**) ⊡ qui fait peur.

scathing *a* cinglant.

scatter *vt* (throw) éparpiller, répandre; (disperse) disperser. ● *vi* se disperser.

scavenge *vi* fouiller (dans les ordures). **scavenger** *n* (animal) charognard *m*.

scene *n* scène *f*; (of accident, crime) lieu *m*; (sight) spectacle *m*; **behind the ~s** en coulisse. **scenery** *n* paysage *m*; (Theat) décors *mpl*. **scenic** *a* panoramique.

scent *n* (perfume) parfum *m*; (trail) piste *f*. ● *vt* flairer; (make fragrant) parfumer.

sceptic *n* sceptique *mf*. **sceptical** *a* sceptique. **scepticism** *n* scepticisme *m*.

schedule *n* horaire *m*; (for job) planning *m*; **behind ~** en retard; **on ~** dans les temps. ● *vt* prévoir; **~d flight** vol *m* régulier.

scheme *n* projet *m*; (dishonest) combine *f*; **pension ~** plan *m* de retraite. ● *vi* comploter.

schizophrenic *a & n* schizophrène (*mf*).

scholar *n* érudit/-e *m/f*.

school *n* école *f*; **go to ~** aller à l'école. ● *a* (*age, year, holidays*) scolaire. **~boy** *n* élève *m*. **~girl** *n* élève *f*. **schooling** *n* scolarité *f*. **~teacher** *n* (primary) instituteur/-trice *m/f*; (secondary) professeur *m*.

science *n* science *f*; **teach ~** enseigner les sciences. **scientific** *a* scientifique. **scientist** *n* scientifique *mf*.

scissors *npl* ciseaux *mpl*.

scold *vt* gronder.

scoop *n* (shovel) pelle *f*; (measure) mesure *f*; (for ice cream) cuillère *f* à glace; (news) exclusivité *f*.

scooter *n* (child's) trottinette *f*; (motor cycle) scooter *m*.

scope *n* étendue *f*; (competence) compétence *f*; (opportunity) possibilité *f*.

scorch *vt* brûler; (*iron*) roussir.

score *n* score *m*; (Mus) partition *f*; **on that ~** à cet égard. ● *vt* marquer; (*success*) remporter. ● *vi* marquer un point; (football) marquer un but; (keep score) marquer les points. **scorer** *n* (Sport) marqueur *m*.

scorn *n* mépris *m*. ● *vt* mépriser.

Scorpio *n* Scorpion *m*.

Scot *n* Écossais/-e *m/f*.

Scotland *n* Écosse *f*.

Scottish *a* écossais.

scoundrel *n* gredin *m*.

scour *vt* (*pan*) récurer; (search) parcourir. **scourer** *n* tampon *m* à récurer.

scourge *n* fléau *m*.

scout *n* éclaireur *m*. ● *vi* **~ around for** rechercher.

scowl *n* air *m* renfrogné. ● *vi* prendre un air renfrogné.

scramble *vi* (clamber) grimper. ● *vt* (*eggs*) brouiller. ● *n* (rush) course *f*.

scrap *n* petit morceau *m*; **~s** (of metal, fabric) déchets *mpl*; (of food) restes *mpl*; (fight [!]) bagarre *f*. ● *vt* (*pt* **scrapped**) abandonner; (*car*) détruire.

scrape *vt* gratter; (damage) érafler. ● *vi* **~ against** érafler. ● *n* raclement *m*. □ **~ through** réussir de justesse.

scrap: **~-paper** *n* papier *m* brouillon. **~ yard** *n* casse *f*.

scratch *vt/i* (se) gratter; (with claw, nail) griffer; (graze) érafler; (mark) rayer. ● *n* (on body) égratignure *f*; (on surface) éraflure *f*; **start from ~** partir de zéro; **up to ~** à la hauteur. **~ card** *n* jeu *m* de grattage.

scrawl *n* gribouillage *m*. ● *vt/i* gribouiller.

scrawny *a* (**-ier**, **-iest**) décharné.

scream *vt/i* crier. ● *n* cri *m* (perçant).

screech *vi* (scream) hurler; (*tyres*) crisser. ● *n* cri *m* strident; (of tyres) crissement *m*.

screen *n* écran *m*; (folding) paravent *m*. ● *vt* masquer; (protect) protéger; (*film*) projeter; (*candidates*) filtrer; (Med) faire subir un test de dépistage. **screening** *n* (cinema) projection *f*; (Med) dépistage *m*.

screen: **~play** *n* scénario *m*. **~ saver** *n* protecteur *m* d'écran.

screw *n* vis *f*. ● *vt* visser; **~ up** (*eyes*) plisser; (ruin [!]) cafouiller [!]. **~driver** *n* tournevis *m*.

scribble *vt/i* griffonner. ● *n* griffonnage *m*.

script *n* script *m*; (of play) texte *m*.

scroll *n* rouleau *m*. ● *vt/i* (Comput) (faire) défiler.

scrounge [!] *vt* (*favour*) quémander; (*cigarette*) piquer [!]; **~ money from sb** taper de l'argent à qn. ● *vi* **~ off sb** vivre sur le dos de qn.

scrub *n* (land) broussailles *fpl*. ● *vt/i* (*pt* **scrubbed**) nettoyer (à la brosse), frotter.

scruffy *a* (**-ier**, **-iest**) [!] dépenaillé.

scrum *n* (rugby) mêlée *f*.

scruple *n* scrupule *m*.

scrutinize *vt* scruter. **scrutiny** *n* examen *m* minutieux.

scuba-diving *n* plongée *f* sous-marine.

scuffle *n* bagarre *f*.

sculpt *vt/i* sculpter. **sculptor** *n* sculpteur *m*.

sculpture *n* sculpture *f*.

scum *n* (on liquid) mousse *f*; (people: pej) racaille *f*.

scurry *vi* se précipiter, courir (**for** pour chercher); **~ off** se sauver.

sea *n* mer *f*; **at ~** en mer; **by ~** par mer. ● *a* (*air*) marin; (*bird*) de mer; (*voyage*) par mer. **~food** *n* fruits *mpl* de mer. **~gull** *n* mouette *f*.

seal *n* (animal) phoque *m*; (insignia) sceau *m*; (with wax) cachet *m*. ● *vt* sceller; cacheter; (stick down) coller. □ **~ off** (*area*) boucler.

seam *n* (in cloth) couture *f*; (of coal) veine *f*.

search *vt/i* (examine) fouiller; (seek) chercher; (study) examiner; (Comput) rechercher. ● *n* fouille *f*; (quest) recherches *fpl*; (Comput) recherche *f*; **in ~ of** à la recherche de. **~ engine** *n* (Internet) moteur *m* de recherche. **~light** *n* projecteur *m*. **~-warrant** *n* mandat *m* de perquisition.

sea: **~shell** *n* coquillage *m*. **~shore** *n* (coast) littoral *m*; (beach) plage *f*.

S

seasick *a* **be ~** avoir le mal de mer.

seaside *n* bord *m* de la mer.

season *n* saison *f*; **~ ticket** carte *f* d'abonnement. ● *vt* assaisonner. **seasonal** *a* saisonnier. **seasoning** *n* assaisonnement *m*.

seat *n* siège *m*; (place) place *f*; (of trousers) fond *m*; **take a ~** asseyez-vous. ● *vt* (put) placer; **the room ~s 30** la salle peut accueillir 30 personnes. **~-belt** *n* ceinture *f* (*de sécurité*).

seaweed *n* algue *f* marine.

secluded *a* retiré.

seclusion *n* isolement *m*.

second[1] *a* deuxième, second; **a ~ chance** une nouvelle chance; **have ~ thoughts** avoir des doutes. ● *n* deuxième *mf*, second/-e *m*/*f*; (unit of time) seconde *f*; **~s** (food) rab *m* [!]. ● *adv* (in race) deuxième; (secondly) deuxièmement. ● *vt* (*proposal*) appuyer.

second[2] *vt* (transfer) détacher (**to** à).

secondary *a* secondaire; **~ school** lycée *m*, école *f* secondaire.

second-best *n* pis-aller *m*.

second-class *a* (Rail) de deuxième classe; (*post*) au tarif lent.

second hand *n* (on clock) trotteuse *f*.

second-hand *a & adv* (*article*) d'occasion; (*information*) de seconde main.

secondly *adv* deuxièmement.

second-rate *a* médiocre.

secrecy *n* secret *m*.

secret *a* secret. ● *n* secret *m*; **in ~** en secret.

secretarial *a* (*work*) de secrétaire.

secretary *n* secrétaire *mf*; **S~ of State** ministre *m*; (US) ministre *m* des Affaires étrangères.

secrete *vt* (Med) sécréter; (hide) cacher.

secretive *a* secret. **secretly** *adv* secrètement.

sect *n* secte *f*. **sectarian** *a* sectaire.

section *n* partie *f*; (in store) rayon *m*; (of newspaper) rubrique *f*; (of book) passage *m*.

sector *n* secteur *m*.

secular *a* (*school*) laïque; (*art, music*) profane.

secure *a* (safe) sûr; (*job, marriage*) stable; (*knot, lock*) solide; (*window*) bien fermé; (*feeling*) de sécurité; (*person*) sécurisé. ● *vt* attacher; (obtain) s'assurer; (ensure) assurer.

security *n* (safety) sécurité *f*; (for loan) caution *f*; **~ guard** vigile *m*.

sedate *a* calme. ● *vt* donner un sédatif à. **sedative** *n* sédatif *m*.

seduce *vt* séduire. **seducer** *n* séducteur/-trice *m*/*f*. **seduction** *n* séduction *f*. **seductive** *a* séduisant.

see *vt*/*i* (*pt* **saw**; *pp* **seen**) voir; **see you (soon)!** à bientôt!; **~ing that** vu que. □ **~ out** (*person*) raccompagner à la porte; **~ through** (*deception*) déceler; (*person*) percer à jour; **~ sth through** mener qch à bonne fin; **~ to** s'occuper de; **~ to it that** veiller à ce que.

seed *n* graine *f*; (collectively) graines *fpl*; (origin: fig) germe *m*; (tennis) tête *f* de série. **seedling** *n* plant *m*.

seek *vt* (*pt* **sought**) chercher.

seem *vi* sembler; **he ~s to think** il a l'air de croire.

seen ⇒SEE.

seep *vi* suinter; **~ into** s'infiltrer dans.

see-saw *n* tapecul *m*. ●*vt* osciller.

seethe *vi* ~ **with** (*anger*) bouillir de; (*people*) grouiller de.

segment *n* segment *m*; (of orange) quartier *m*.

segregate *vt* séparer.

seize *vt* saisir; (*territory, prisoner*) s'emparer de. ●*vi* ~ **on** (*chance*) saisir; ~ **up** (*engine*) se gripper.

seizure *n* (Med) crise *f*.

seldom *adv* rarement.

select *vt* sélectionner. ●*a* privilégié. **selection** *n* sélection *f*. **selective** *a* sélectif.

self *n* (*pl* **selves**) moi *m*; (on cheque) moi-même. **~-assured** *a* plein d'assurance. **~-catering** *a* (*holiday*) en location. **~-centred**, (US) **~-centered** *a* égocentrique. **~-confident** *a* sûr de soi. **~-conscious** *a* timide. **~-contained** *a* (*flat*) indépendant. **~-control** *n* sang-froid *m*. **~-defence** *n* autodéfense *f*; (Jur) légitime défense *f*. **~-employed** *a* qui travaille à son compte. **~-esteem** *n* amour-propre *m*. **~-governing** *a* autonome. **~-indulgent** *a* complaisant. **~-interest** *n* intérêt *m* personnel.

selfish *a* égoïste.

selfless *a* désintéressé.

self: **~-portrait** *n* autoportrait *m*. **~-reliant** *a* autosuffisant. **~-respect** *n* respect *m* de soi. **~-righteous** *a* satisfait de soi. **~-sacrifice** *n* abnégation *f*. **~-satisfied** *a* satisfait de soi. **~-seeking** *a* égoïste. **~-service** *n & a* libre-service (*m*).

sell *vt/i* (*pt* **sold**) vendre; ~ **well** se vendre bien. □ ~ **off** liquider; ~ **out** (*items*) se vendre; **have sold out** avoir tout vendu.

Sellotape® *n* scotch® *m*.

sell-out *n* (betrayal) [!] revirement *m*; **be a** ~ (*show*) afficher complet.

semester *n* (Univ) semestre *m*.

semicircle *n* demi-cercle *m*.

semicolon *n* point-virgule *m*.

semi-detached *a* ~ **house** maison *f* jumelée.

semifinal *n* demi-finale *f*.

seminar *n* séminaire *m*.

semolina *n* semoule *f*.

senate *n* sénat *m*. **senator** *n* sénateur *m*.

send *vt/i* (*pt* **sent**) envoyer. □ ~ **away** (dismiss) renvoyer; ~ (**away** *or* **off**) **for** commander (par la poste); ~ **back** renvoyer; ~ **for** (*person, help*) envoyer chercher; ~ **up** [!] parodier.

senile *a* sénile.

senior *a* plus âgé (**to** que); (in rank) haut placé; **be** ~ **to sb** être le supérieur de qn. ●*n* aîné/-e *m/f*. ~ **citizen** *n* personne *f* âgée. ~ **school** *n* lycée *m*.

sensation *n* sensation *f*. **sensational** *a* sensationnel.

sense *n* sens *m*; (mental impression) sentiment *m*; (common sense) bon sens *m*; **~s** (mind) raison *f*; **there's no** ~ **in doing** cela ne sert à rien de faire; **make** ~ avoir un sens; **make** ~ **of** comprendre. ●*vt* (pres)sentir. **senseless** *a* insensé; (Med) sans connaissance.

sensible *a* raisonnable; (*clothing*) pratique.

sensitive *a* sensible (**to** à); (*issue*) difficile.

sensory *a* sensoriel.

sensual *a* sensuel. **sensuality** *n* sensualité *f*.

sensuous *a* sensuel.

sent ⇒SEND.

sentence *n* phrase *f*; (punishment:

S

Jur) peine *f*. ● *vt* ~ **to** condamner à.

sentiment *n* sentiment *m*. **sentimental** *a* sentimental.

sentry *n* sentinelle *f*.

separate[1] *a* (*piece*) à part; (*issue*) autre; (*sections*) différent; (*organizations*) distinct.

separate[2] *vt*/*i* (se) séparer.

separately *adv* séparément.

separation *n* séparation *f*.

September *n* septembre *m*.

septic *a* (*wound*) infecté; ~ **tank** fosse *f* septique.

sequel *n* suite *f*.

sequence *n* (order) ordre *m*; (series) suite *f*; (in film) séquence *f*.

Serb *a* serbe. ● *n* (person) Serbe *mf*; (Ling) serbe *m*.

Serbia *n* Serbie *f*.

sergeant *n* (Mil) sergent *m*; (policeman) brigadier *m*.

serial *n* feuilleton *m*. ● *a* (Comput) série *inv*.

series *n inv* série *f*.

serious *a* sérieux; (*accident, crime*) grave.

seriously *adv* sérieusement; (*ill*) gravement; **take** ~ prendre au sérieux.

sermon *n* sermon *m*.

serpent *n* serpent *m*.

serrated *a* dentelé.

serum *n* sérum *m*.

servant *n* domestique *mf*.

serve *vt*/*i* servir; faire; (*transport, hospital*) desservir; ~ **as**/**to** servir de/à; ~ **a purpose** être utile; ~ **a sentence** (Jur) purger une peine. ● *n* (tennis) service *m*.

server *n* serveur *m*; **remote** ~ téléserveur *m*.

service *n* service *m*; (maintenance) révision *f*; (Relig) office *m*; ~**s** (Mil) forces *fpl* armées. ● *vt* (*car*) réviser. ~ **area** *n* (Auto) aire *f* de services. ~ **charge** *n* service *m*. ~ **station** *n* station-service *f*.

session *n* séance *f*; **be in** ~ (Jur) tenir séance.

set *vt* (*pt* **set**; *pres p* **setting**) placer; (*table*) mettre; (*limit*) fixer; (*clock*) mettre à l'heure; (*example, task*) donner; (TV, cinema) situer; ~ **fire to** mettre le feu à; ~ **free** libérer; ~ **to music** mettre en musique. ● *vi* (*sun*) se coucher; (*jelly*) prendre; ~ **sail** partir. ● *n* (of chairs, stamps) série *f*; (of knives, keys) jeu *m*; (of people) groupe *m*; (TV, radio) poste *m*; (Theat) décor *m*; (tennis) set *m*; (mathematics) ensemble *m*. ● *a* (*time, price*) fixe; (*procedure*) bien determiné; (*meal*) à prix fixe; (*book*) au programme; ~ **against sth** opposé à; **be** ~ **on doing** tenir absolument à faire. □ ~ **about** se mettre à; ~ **back** (delay) retarder; (cost 🅸) coûter; ~ **in** (take hold) s'installer, commencer; ~ **off** *or* **out** partir; ~ **off** (*panic, riot*) déclencher; (*bomb*) faire exploser; ~ **out** (state) présenter; (arrange) disposer; ~ **out to do sth** chercher à faire qch; ~ **up** (*stall*) monter; (*equipment*) assembler; (*experiment*) préparer; (*company*) créer; (*meeting*) organiser. ~**-back** *n* revers *m*.

settee *n* canapé *m*.

setting *n* cadre *m*; (on dial) position *f*.

settle *vt* (arrange, pay) régler; (*date*) fixer; (*nerves*) calmer. ● *vi* (come to rest) (*bird*) se poser; (*dust*) se déposer; (live) s'installer. □ ~ **down** se calmer; (marry etc.) se ranger; ~ **for** accepter; ~ **in** s'installer; ~ **up** (**with**) régler.

settlement *n* règlement *m* (**of** de); (agreement) accord *m*; (place) colonie *f*.

settler *n* colon *m*.

seven *a & n* sept (*m*).

seventeen *a & n* dix-sept (*m*).

seventh *a & n* septième (*mf*).

seventy *a & n* soixante-dix (*m*).

sever *vt* (cut) couper; (*relations*) rompre.

several *a & pron* plusieurs; **~ of us** plusieurs d'entre nous.

severe *a* (harsh) sévère; (serious) grave.

sew *vt/i* (*pt* **sewed**; *pp* **sewn** *or* **sewed**) coudre.

sewage *n* eaux *fpl* usées.

sewer *n* égout *m*.

sewing *n* couture *f*. **~-machine** *n* machine *f* à coudre.

sewn ⇒SEW.

sex *n* sexe *m*; **have ~** avoir des rapports (sexuels). ● *a* sexuel. **sexist** *a & n* sexiste (*mf*). **sexual** *a* sexuel.

shabby *a* (**-ier**, **-iest**) (*place, object*) miteux; (*person*) habillé de façon miteuse; (*treatment*) mesquin.

shack *n* cabane *f*.

shade *n* ombre *f*; (of colour, opinion) nuance *f*; (for lamp) abat-jour *m inv*; **a ~ bigger** légèrement plus grand. ● *vt* (*tree*) ombrager; (*hat*) projeter une ombre sur.

shadow *n* ombre *f*. ● *vt* (follow) filer. **S~ Cabinet** *n* cabinet *m* fantôme.

shady *a* (**-ier**, **-iest**) ombragé; (dubious) véreux.

shaft *n* (of tool) manche *m*; (of arrow) tige *f*; (in machine) axe *m*; (of mine) puits *m*; (of light) rayon *m*.

shake *vt* (*pt* **shook**; *pp* **shaken**) secouer; (*bottle*) agiter; (*belief*) ébranler; **~ hands with** serrer la main à; **~ one's head** dire non de la tête. ● *vi* trembler. ● *n* secousse *f*; **give sth a ~** secouer qch. □ **~ off** se débarrasser de. **~-up** *n* (Pol) remaniement *m*.

shaky *a* (**-ier**, **-iest**) (*hand, voice*) tremblant; (*ladder*) branlant; (weak: fig) instable.

shall *v aux* **I ~ do** je ferai; **we ~ see** nous verrons; **~ we go...?** si on allait...?

shallow *a* peu profond; (fig) superficiel.

shame *n* honte *f*; **it's a ~** c'est dommage. ● *vt* faire honte à.

shampoo *n* shampooing *m*. ● *vt* faire un shampooing à.

shandy *n* panaché *m*.

shan't = SHALL NOT.

shanty *n* (shack) baraque *f*; **~ town** bidonville *m*.

shape *n* forme *f*. ● *vt* (*clay*) modeler; (*rock*) façonner; (*future*: fig) déterminer; **~ sth into balls** faire des boules avec qch. ● *vi* **~ up** (*plan*) prendre tournure; (*person*) faire des progrès.

share *n* part *f*; (Comm) action *f*. ● *vt/i* partager; (*feature*) avoir en commun. **~holder** *n* actionnaire *mf*. **~ware** *n* (Comput) logiciel *m* contributif.

shark *n* requin *m*.

sharp *a* (*knife*) tranchant; (*pin*) pointu; (*point, angle, cry*) aigu; (*person, mind*) vif; (*tone*) acerbe. ● *adv* (*stop*) net; (*sing, play*) trop haut; **six o'clock ~** six heures pile. ● *n* (Mus) dièse *m*.

sharpen *vt* aiguiser; (*pencil*) tailler.

shatter *vt* (*glass*) fracasser; (*hope*) briser. ● *vi* (*glass*) voler en éclats.

shave *vt/i* (se) raser. ● *n* **have a ~** se raser. **shaver** *n* rasoir *m* électrique.

shaving *n* (of wood) copeau *m*. ● *a* (*cream, foam, gel*) à raser.

shawl *n* châle *m*.

she *pron* elle. ● *n* (animal) femelle *f*.

S

shear *vt* (*pp* **shorn** *or* **sheared**) (*sheep*) tondre; ~ **off** se détacher.

shears *npl* cisaille *f*.

shed *n* remise *f*. ● *vt* (*pt* **shed**; *pres p* **shedding**) perdre; (*light, tears*) répandre.

sheen *n* lustre *m*.

sheep *n inv* mouton *m*. **~-dog** *n* chien *m* de berger.

sheepish *a* penaud.

sheepskin *n* peau *f* de mouton.

sheer *a* pur; (steep) à pic; (*fabric*) très fin. ● *adv* à pic.

sheet *n* drap *m*; (of paper) feuille *f*; (of glass, ice) plaque *f*.

shelf *n* (*pl* **shelves**) étagère *f*; (in shop, fridge) rayon *m*; (in oven) plaque *f*.

shell *n* coquille *f*; (on beach) coquillage *m*; (of building) carcasse *f*; (explosive) obus *m*. ● *vt* (*nut*) décortiquer; (*peas*) écosser; (Mil) bombarder.

shellfish *npl* (lobster etc.) crustacés *mpl*; (mollusc) coquillages *mpl*.

shelter *n* abri *m*. ● *vt/i* (s')abriter; (give lodging to) donner asile à.

shelve *vt* (*plan*) mettre en suspens.

shepherd *n* berger *m*; **~'s pie** hachis *m* Parmentier. ● *vt* (*people*) guider.

sherry *n* xérès *m*.

shield *n* bouclier *m*; (screen) écran *m*. ● *vt* protéger.

shift *vt/i* (se) déplacer, bouger; (exchange, alter) changer de. ● *n* changement *m*; (workers) équipe *f*; (work) poste *m*; ~ **work** travail *m* posté, travail *m* par roulement.

shifty *a* (**-ier**, **-iest**) louche.

shimmer *vi* chatoyer. ● *n* chatoiement *m*.

shin *n* tibia *m*.

shine *vt* (*pt* **shone**) (*torch*) braquer (**on** sur). ● *vi* (*light, sun, hair*) briller; (*brass*) reluire. ● *n* lustre *m*.

shingle *n* (pebbles) galets *mpl*; (on roof) bardeau *m*.

shingles *npl* (Med) zona *m*.

shiny *a* (**-ier**, **-iest**) brillant.

ship *n* bateau *m*, navire *m*. ● *vt* (*pt* **shipped**) transporter. **shipment** *n* (by sea) cargaison *f*; (by air, land) chargement *m*. **shipping** *n* (ships) navigation *f*. **~wreck** *n* épave *f*; (event) naufrage *m*.

shirt *n* chemise *f*; (woman's) chemisier *m*.

shiver *vi* frissonner. ● *n* frisson *m*.

shock *n* choc *m*; (Electr) décharge *f*; **in** ~ en état de choc; ~ **absorber** amortisseur *m*. ● *a* (*result*) choc *inv*; (*tactics*) de choc. ● *vt* choquer.

shoddy *a* (**-ier**, **-iest**) mal fait; (*behaviour*) mesquin.

shoe *n* chaussure *f*; (of horse) fer *m*; (**brake**) ~ sabot *m* (*de frein*). ● *vt* (*pt* **shod** ; *pres p* **shoeing**) (*horse*) ferrer. **~lace** *n* lacet *m*. ~ **size** *n* pointure *f*.

shone ⇒SHINE.

shook ⇒SHAKE.

shoot *vt* (*pt* **shot**) (*gun*) tirer un coup de; (*bullet*) tirer; (*missile, glance*) lancer; (*person*) tirer sur; (kill) abattre; (execute) fusiller; (*film*) tourner. ● *vi* tirer (**at** sur). ● *n* (Bot) pousse *f*. □ ~ **down** abattre; ~ **out** (rush) sortir en vitesse; ~ **up** (spurt) jaillir; (grow) pousser vite.

shooting *n* (killing) meurtre *m* (*par arme à feu*); **hear** ~ entendre des coups de feu.

shop *n* magasin *m*; (small) boutique *f*; (workshop) atelier *m*. ● *vi* (*pt* **shopped**) faire ses courses; ~ **around** comparer les prix. ~ **assistant** *n* vendeur/

-euse *m/f*. **~-floor** *n* (workers) ouvriers *mpl*. **~keeper** *n* commerçant/-e *m/f*. **~lifter** *n* voleur/-euse *m/f* à l'étalage.

shopper *n* acheteur/-euse *m/f*.

shopping *n* (goods) achats *mpl*; **go ~** (for food) faire les courses; (for clothes etc.) faire les magasins. **~ bag** *n* sac *m* à provisions. **~ centre**, (US) **~ center** *n* centre *m* commercial.

shop window *n* vitrine *f*.

shore *n* côte *f*, rivage *m*; **on ~** à terre.

short *a* court; (*person*) petit; (brief) court, bref; (curt) brusque; **be ~ (of)** manquer (de); **everything ~ of** tout sauf; **nothing ~ of** rien de moins que; **cut ~** écourter; **cut sb ~** interrompre qn; **fall ~ of** ne pas arriver à; **he is called Tom for ~** son diminutif est Tom; **in ~** en bref. ● *adv* (*stop*) net. ● *n* (Electr) court-circuit *m*; (film) court-métrage *m*; **~s** (trousers) short *m*.

shortage *n* manque *m*.

short: **~bread** *n* sablé *m*. **~-change** *vt* (cheat) rouler ⓘ. **~ circuit** *n* court-circuit *m*. **~coming** *n* défaut *m*. **~ cut** *n* raccourci *m*.

shorten *vt* raccourcir.

shortfall *n* déficit *m*.

shorthand *n* sténographie *f*; **~ typist** sténodactylo *f*.

short: **~ list** *n* liste *f* des candidats choisis. **~-lived** *a* de courte durée.

shortly *adv* bientôt.

short: **~-sighted** *a* myope. **~-staffed** *a* à court de personnel; **~ story** *n* nouvelle *f* **~-term** *a* à court terme.

shot ⇒SHOOT. ● *n* (firing, attempt) coup *m* de feu; (person) tireur *m*; (bullet) balle *f*; (photograph) photo *f*; (injection) piqûre *f*; **like a ~** sans hésiter. **~-gun** *n* fusil *m* de chasse.

should *v aux* devoir; **you ~ help me** vous devriez m'aider; **I ~ have stayed** j'aurais dû rester; **I ~ like to** j'aimerais bien; **if he ~ come** s'il venait.

shoulder *n* épaule *f*. ● *vt* (*responsibility*) endosser; (*burden*) se charger de. **~-bag** *n* sac *m* à bandoulière. **~-blade** *n* omoplate *f*

shout *n* cri *m*. ● *vt/i* crier (**at** après); **~ sth out** lancer qch à haute voix.

shove *n* **give sth a ~** pousser qch. ● *vt/i* pousser; **~ off!** ⓘ tire-toi! ⓘ.

shovel *n* pelle *f*. ● *vt* (*pt* **shovelled**) pelleter.

show *vt* (*pt* **showed**; *pp* **shown**) montrer; (*dial, needle*) indiquer; (put on display) exposer; (*film*) donner; (conduct) conduire; **~ sb in/out** faire entrer/sortir qn. ● *vi* (be visible) se voir. ● *n* (exhibition) exposition *f*, salon *m*; (Theat) spectacle *m*; (cinema) séance *f*; (of strength) démonstration *f*; **for ~** pour l'effet; **on ~** exposé. □ **~ off** faire le fier/la fière; **~ sth/sb off** exhiber qch/qn; **~ up** se voir; (appear) se montrer; **~ sb up** ⓘ faire honte à qn.

shower *n* douche *f*; (of rain) averse *f*. ● *vt* **~ with** couvrir de. ● *vi* se doucher.

showing *n* performance *f*; (cinema) séance *f*.

show-jumping *n* concours *m* hippique.

shown ⇒SHOW.

show: **~-off** *n* m'as-tu-vu *mf inv* ⓘ. **~room** *n* salle *f* d'exposition.

shrank ⇒SHRINK.

shrapnel *n* éclats *mpl* d'obus.

shred *n* lambeau *m*; (least amount:

S

fig) parcelle *f*. ● *vt* (*pt* **shredded**) déchiqueter; (Culin) râper.

shrewd *a* (*person*) habile; (*move*) astucieux.

shriek *n* hurlement *m*. ● *vt/i* hurler.

shrill *a* (*voice*) perçant; (*tone*) strident.

shrimp *n* crevette *f*.

shrine *n* (place) lieu *m* de pèlerinage.

shrink *vt/i* (*pt* **shrank**; *pp* **shrunk**) rétrécir; (lessen) diminuer; ~ **from** reculer devant.

shrivel *vt/i* (*pt* **shrivelled**) (se) ratatiner.

shroud *n* linceul *m*. ● *vt* (veil) envelopper.

Shrove Tuesday *n* mardi *m* gras.

shrub *n* arbuste *m*.

shrug *vt* (*pt* **shrugged**) ~ **one's shoulders** hausser les épaules; ~ **sth off** ignorer qch.

shrunk ⇒SHRINK.

shudder *vi* frémir. ● *n* frémissement *m*.

shuffle *vt* (*feet*) traîner; (*cards*) battre. ● *vi* traîner les pieds.

shun *vt* (*pt* **shunned**) fuir.

shut *vt* (*pt* **shut**; *pres p* **shutting**) fermer. ● *vi* (*door*) se fermer; (*shop*) fermer. □ ~ **in** *or* **up** enfermer; ~ **up** ⓘ se taire; ~ **sb up** faire taire qn.

shutter *n* volet *m*; (Photo) obturateur *m*.

shuttle *n* (bus) navette *f*; ~ **service** navette *f*. ● *vi* faire la navette. ● *vt* transporter.

shuttlecock *n* (badminton) volant *m*.

shy *a* timide. ● *vi* ~ **away from** se tenir à l'écart de.

sibling *n* frère/sœur *m/f*.

sick *a* malade; (*humour*) macabre; (*mind*) malsain; **be** ~ (vomit) vomir; **be** ~ **of** ⓘ en avoir assez *or* marre de ⓘ; **feel** ~ avoir mal au cœur. **~-leave** *n* congé *m* de maladie.

sickly *a* (**-ier**, **-iest**) (*person*) maladif; (*taste, smell*) écœurant.

sickness *n* maladie *f*.

sick-pay *n* indemnité *f* de maladie.

side *n* côté *m*; (of road, river) bord *m*; (of hill, body) flanc *m*; (Sport) équipe *f*; (TV ⓘ) chaîne *f*; ~ **by** ~ côte à côte. ● *a* latéral. ● *vi* ~ **with** se ranger du côté de. **~board** *n* buffet *m*. **~-effect** *n* effet *m* secondaire. **~light** *n* (Auto) feu *m* de position. **~line** *n* activité *f* secondaire. **~-show** *n* attraction *f*. **~-step** *vt* (*pt* **-stepped**) éviter. **~-street** *n* rue *f* latérale. **~-track** *vt* fourvoyer. **~walk** *n* (US) trottoir *m*.

sideways *a* (*look*) de travers. ● *adv* (*move*) latéralement; (*look at*) de travers.

siding *n* voie *f* de garage.

sidle *vi* s'avancer furtivement (**up to** vers).

siege *n* siège *m*.

siesta *n* sieste *f*.

sieve *n* tamis *m*; (for liquids) passoire *f*. ● *vt* tamiser.

sift *vt* tamiser. ● *vi* ~ **through** examiner.

sigh *n* soupir *m*. ● *vt/i* soupirer.

sight *n* vue *f*; (scene) spectacle *m*; (on gun) mire *f*; **at** *or* **on** ~ à vue; **catch** ~ **of** apercevoir; **in** ~ visible; **lose** ~ **of** perdre de vue. ● *vt* apercevoir.

sightseeing *n* tourisme *m*.

sign *n* signe *m*; (notice) panneau *m*. ● *vt/i* signer. □ ~ **on** (as unemployed) pointer au chômage; ~ **up** (s')engager.

signal *n* signal *m*. ● *vt* (*pt* **signalled**) (gesture) faire signe (**that** que); (indicate) indiquer.

signatory *n* signataire *mf*.

signature *n* signature *f*; ~ **tune** indicatif *m*.

significance *n* importance *f*; (meaning) signification *f*. **significant** *a* important; (meaningful) significatif. **significantly** *adv* (much) sensiblement.

signify *vt* signifier.

signpost *n* panneau *m* indicateur.

silence *n* silence *m*. ● *vt* faire taire.

silent *a* silencieux; (*film*) muet. **silently** *adv* silencieusement.

silhouette *n* silhouette *f*. ● *vt* **be ~d against** se profiler contre.

silicon *n* silicium *m*; ~ **chip** puce *f* électronique.

silk *n* soie *f*.

silly *a* (**-ier**, **-iest**) bête, idiot.

silver *n* argent *m*; (silverware) argenterie *f*. ● *a* en argent.

similar *a* semblable (**to** à). **similarity** *n* ressemblance *f*. **similarly** *adv* de même.

simile *n* comparaison *f*.

simmer *vt*/*i* (*soup*) mijoter; (*water*) (laisser) frémir.

simple *a* simple.

simplicity *n* simplicité *f*.

simplify *vt* simplifier.

simplistic *a* simpliste.

simply *adv* simplement; (absolutely) absolument.

simulate *vt* simuler.

simultaneous *a* simultané.

sin *n* péché *m*. ● *vi* (*pt* **sinned**) pécher.

since

● *preposition*

····➤ depuis; **I haven't seen him ~ Monday** je ne l'ai pas vu depuis lundi; **I've been waiting ~ yesterday** j'attends depuis hier; **she had been living in Paris ~ 1985** elle habitait Paris depuis 1985.

● *conjunction*

····➤ (in time expressions) depuis que; **~ she's been working here** depuis qu'elle travaille ici; **~ she left** depuis qu'elle est partie *or* depuis son départ.

····➤ (because) comme; **~ he was ill, he couldn't go** comme il était malade, il ne pouvait pas y aller.

● *adverb*

····➤ depuis; **he hasn't been seen ~** on ne l'a pas vu depuis.

sincere *a* sincère. **sincerely** *adv* sincèrement. **sincerity** *n* sincérité *f*.

sinful *a* immoral; ~ **man** pécheur *m*.

sing *vt*/*i* (*pt* **sang**; *pp* **sung**) chanter.

singe *vt* (*pres p* **singeing**) brûler légèrement; (with iron) roussir.

singer *n* chanteur/-euse *m*/*f*.

single *a* seul; (not double) simple; (unmarried) célibataire; (*room, bed*) pour une personne; (*ticket*) simple; **in ~ file** en file indienne. ● *n* (ticket) aller simple *m*; (record) 45 tours *m inv*; **~s** (tennis) simple *m*. ● *vt* **~ out** choisir. **~-handed** *a* tout seul. **~-minded** *a* tenace. **~ parent** *n* parent *m* isolé.

singular *n* singulier *m*. ● *a* (strange) singulier; (*noun*) au singulier.

sinister *a* sinistre.

sink *vt* (*pt* **sank**; *pp* **sunk**) (*boat*) couler; (*well*) forer; (*post*) enfoncer. ● *vi* (*boat*) couler; (*sun, level*) baisser; (*wall*) s'effondrer. ● *n* (in kitchen) évier *m*; (wash-basin)

S

lavabo *m.* □ ~ **in** (*news*) faire son chemin.

sinner *n* pécheur/-eresse *m/f.*

sip *n* petite gorgée *f.* ● *vt* (*pt* **sipped**) boire à petites gorgées.

siphon *n* siphon *m.* ● *vt* ~ **off** siphonner.

sir *n* Monsieur *m*; **Sir** (title) Sir *m.*

siren *n* sirène *f.*

sirloin *n* aloyau *m.*

sister *n* sœur *f*; (nurse) infirmière *f* en chef. **~-in-law** *n* (*pl* **~s-in-law**) belle-sœur *f.*

sit *vt/i* (*pt* **sat**; *pres p* **sitting**) (s')asseoir; (*committee*) siéger; ~ (**for**) (exam) se présenter à; **be ~ting** être assis. □ ~ **around** ne rien faire; ~ **down** s'asseoir.

site *n* emplacement *m*; (**building**) ~ chantier *m.* ● *vt* construire.

sitting *n* séance *f*; (in restaurant) service *m.* **~-room** *n* salon *m.*

situate *vt* situer; **be ~d** être situé. **situation** *n* situation *f.*

six *a & n* six (*m*).

sixteen *a & n* seize (*m*).

sixth *a & n* sixième (*mf*).

sixty *a & n* soixante (*m*).

size *n* dimension *f*; (of person, garment) taille *f*; (of shoes) pointure *f*; (of sum, salary) montant *m*; (extent) ampleur *f.* □ ~ **up** (*person*) se faire une opinion de; (*situation*) évaluer. **sizeable** *a* assez grand.

skate *n* patin *m*; (fish) raie *f.* ● *vi* patiner.

skating *n* patinage *m.*

skeletal *a* squelettique.

skeleton *n* squelette *m*; ~ **staff** effectifs *mpl* minimums.

sketch *n* esquisse *f*; (hasty) croquis *m*; (Theat) sketch *m.* ● *vt* faire une esquisse *or* un croquis de. ● *vi* faire des esquisses.

sketchy *a* (**-ier**, **-iest**) (*details*) insuffisant; (*memory*) vague.

skewer *n* brochette *f.*

ski *n* ski *m.* ● *a* de ski. ● *vi* (*pt* **ski'd** *or* **skied**; *pres p* **skiing**) skier; (go skiing) faire du ski.

skid *vi* (*pt* **skidded**) déraper. ● *n* dérapage *m.*

skier *n* skieur/-euse *m/f.*

skiing *n* ski *m.*

ski jump *n* saut *m* à ski.

skilful *a* habile.

ski lift *n* remontée *f* mécanique.

skill *n* habileté *f*; (craft) compétence *f*; **~s** connaissances *fpl.* **skilled** *a* (*worker*) qualifié; (talented) consommé.

skim *vt* (*pt* **skimmed**) écumer; (*milk*) écrémer; (pass over) effleurer. ● *vi* ~ **through** parcourir.

skimpy *a* (*clothes*) étriqué; (*meal*) chiche.

skin *n* peau *f.* ● *vt* (*pt* **skinned**) (*animal*) écorcher; (*fruit*) éplucher.

skinny *a* (**-ier**, **-iest**) [!] maigre.

skip *vi* (*pt* **skipped**) sautiller; (with rope) sauter à la corde. ● *vt* (*page, class*) sauter. ● *n* petit saut *m*; (container) benne *f.*

skipper *n* capitaine *m.*

skirmish *n* escarmouche *f*, accrochage *m.*

skirt *n* jupe *f.* ● *vt* contourner. **skirting-board** *n* plinthe *f.*

skittle *n* quille *f.*

skull *n* crâne *m.*

sky *n* ciel *m.* **~-blue** *a & n* bleu ciel *m inv.* **~scraper** *n* gratte-ciel *m inv.*

slab *n* (of stone) dalle *f.*

slack *a* (not tight) détendu; (*person*) négligent; (*period*) creux. ● *n* (in rope) mou *m.* ● *vi* se relâcher.

slacken *vt* (*rope*) donner du mou à; (*grip*) relâcher; (*pace*) réduire. ● *vi* (*grip, rope*) se relâcher;

(*activity*) ralentir; (*rain*) se calmer.

slam *vt/i* (*pt* **slammed**) (*door*) claquer; (throw) flanquer; (criticize [!]) critiquer. ● *n* (noise) claquement *m*

slander *n* (offence) diffamation *f*; (statement) calomnie *f*. ● *vt* calomnier; (Jur) diffamer. **slanderous** *a* diffamatoire.

slang *n* argot *m*.

slant *vt/i* (faire) pencher; (*news*) présenter sous un certain jour. ● *n* inclinaison *f*; (bias) angle *m*. **slanted** *a* (biased) orienté; (sloping) en pente.

slap *vt* (*pt* **slapped**) (strike) donner une tape à; (*face*) gifler; (put) flanquer [!]. ● *n* claque *f*; (on face) gifle *f*. ● *adv* tout droit.

slapdash *a* (*person*) brouillon [!]; (*work*) baclé [!].

slash *vt* (*picture, tyre*) taillader; (*face*) balafrer; (*throat*) couper; (fig) réduire (radicalement). ● *n* lacération *f*.

slat *n* (in blind) lamelle *f*; (on bed) latte *f*.

slate *n* ardoise *f*. ● *vt* [!] taper sur [!].

slaughter *vt* massacrer; (*animal*) abattre. ● *n* massacre *m*; abattage *m*.

slave *n* esclave *mf*. ● *vi* trimer [!]. **slavery** *n* esclavage *m*.

sleazy *a* (**-ier**, **-iest**) [!] (*story*) scabreux; (*club*) louche.

sledge *n* luge *f*; (horse-drawn) traîneau *m*.

sleek *a* (*hair*) lisse, brillant; (*shape*) élégant.

sleep *n* sommeil *m*; **go to ~** s'endormir. ● *vi* (*pt* **slept**) dormir; (spend the night) coucher; **~ in** faire la grasse matinée. ● *vt* loger.

sleeper *n* (Rail) (berth) couchette *f*; (on track) traverse *f*.

sleeping-bag *n* sac *m* de couchage.

sleeping-pill *n* somnifère *m*.

sleep-walker *n* somnambule *mf*.

sleepy *a* (**-ier**, **-iest**) somnolent; **be ~** avoir sommeil.

sleet *n* neige *f* fondue.

sleeve *n* manche *f*; (of record) pochette *f*; **up one's ~** en réserve.

sleigh *n* traîneau *m*.

slender *a* (*person*) mince; (*majority*) faible.

slept ⇒SLEEP.

slice *n* tranche *f*. ● *vt* couper (en tranches).

slick *a* (adept) habile; (insincere) roublard [!]. ● *n* (**oil**) **~** marée *f* noire.

slide *vt/i* (*pt* **slid**) glisser; **~ into** (go silently) se glisser dans. ● *n* glissade *f*; (fall: fig) baisse *f*; (in playground) toboggan *m*; (for hair) barrette *f*; (Photo) diapositive *f*.

sliding *a* (*door*) coulissant; **~ scale** échelle *f* mobile.

slight *a* petit, léger; (slender) mince; (frail) frêle. ● *vt* (insult) offenser. ● *n* affront *m*. **slightest** *a* moindre. **slightly** *adv* légèrement, un peu.

slim *a* (**slimmer**, **slimmest**) mince. ● *vi* (*pt* **slimmed**) maigrir.

slime *n* dépôt *m* gluant; (on river-bed) vase *f*. **slimy** *a* visqueux; (fig) servile.

sling *n* (weapon, toy) fronde *f*; (bandage) écharpe *f*. ● *vt* (*pt* **slung**) jeter, lancer.

slip *vt/i* (*pt* **slipped**) glisser; **~ped disc** hernie *f* discale; **~ sb's mind** échapper à qn. ● *n* (mistake) erreur *f*; (petticoat) combinaison *f*; (paper) bout *m* de papier; **~ of the tongue** lapsus *m*. □ **~ away** s'esquiver; **~ into** (go) se glisser dans; (*clothes*) mettre; **~ up** [!] faire une gaffe [!].

S

slipper *n* pantoufle *f*.

slippery *a* glissant.

slip road *n* bretelle *f*.

slit *n* fente *f*. ● *vt* (*pt* **slit**; *pres p* **slitting**) déchirer; ~ **sth open** ouvrir qch; ~ **sb's throat** égorger qn.

slither *vi* glisser.

sliver *n* (of glass) éclat *m*; (of soap) reste *m*.

slobber *vi* [!] baver.

slog [!] *vt* (*pt* **slogged**) (hit) frapper dur. ● *vi* (work) bosser [!]. ● *n* (work) travail *m* dur.

slogan *n* slogan *m*.

slope *vi* être en pente; (*handwriting*) pencher. ● *n* pente *f*; (of mountain) flanc *m*.

sloppy *a* (**-ier**, **-iest**) (*food*) liquide; (*work*) négligé; (*person*) négligent.

slosh *vt* [!] répandre; (hit [!]) frapper. ● *vi* clapoter.

slot *n* fente *f*. ● *vt*/*i* (*pt* **slotted**) (s')insérer.

sloth *n* paresse *f*.

slot-machine *n* distributeur *m* automatique; (for gambling) machine *f* à sous.

slouch *vi* être avachi.

Slovakia *n* Slovaquie *f*.

Slovenia *n* Slovénie *f*.

slovenly *a* débraillé.

slow *a* lent; **be** ~ (*clock*) retarder; **in** ~ **motion** au ralenti. ● *adv* lentement. ● *vt*/*i* ralentir. **slowly** *adv* lentement. **slowness** *n* lenteur *f*.

sludge *n* vase *f*.

slug *n* (mollusc) limace *f*; (bullet [!]) balle *f*; (blow [!]) coup *m*.

sluggish *a* (*person*) léthargique; (*circulation*) lent.

slum *n* taudis *m*.

slump *n* (Econ) effondrement *m*; (in support) baisse *f*. ● *vi* (*demand*, *trade*) chuter; (*economy*) s'effondrer; (*person*) s'affaler.

slung ⇒SLING.

slur *vt*/*i* (*pt* **slurred**) (*words*) mal articuler. ● *n* calomnie *f* (**on** sur).

slush *n* (snow) neige *f* fondue. ~ **fund** *n* caisse *f* noire.

sly *a* (crafty) rusé; (secretive) sournois. ● *n* **on the** ~ en cachette.

smack *n* tape *f*; (on face) gifle *f*. ● *vt* donner une tape à; gifler. ● *vi* ~ **of sth** sentir qch. ● *adv* [!] tout droit.

small *a* petit. ● *n* ~ **of the back** creux *m* des reins. ● *adv* (*cut*) menu. ~ **ad** *n* petite annonce *f*. ~ **business** *n* petite entreprise *f*. ~ **change** *n* petite monnaie *f*. ~ **pox** *n* variole *f*. ~ **print** *n* petits caractères *mpl*. ~ **talk** *n* banalités *fpl*.

smart *a* élégant; (clever [!]) malin, habile; (*restaurant*) chic *inv*; (Comput) intelligent. ● *vi* (*wound*) brûler.

smarten *vt*/*i* ~ (**up**) embellir; ~ (**oneself**) **up** s'arranger.

smash *vt*/*i* (se) briser, (se) fracasser; (*opponent*, *record*) pulvériser. ● *n* (noise) fracas *m*; (blow) coup *m*; (car crash) collision *f*; (hit record [!]) tube *m* [!].

smashing *a* [!] épatant.

SME *abbr* (**small and medium enterprises**) PME.

smear *vt* (stain) tacher; (coat) enduire; (discredit: fig) diffamer. ● *n* tache *f*; (effort to discredit) propos *m* diffamatoire; ~ (**test**) frottis *m*.

smell *n* odeur *f*; (sense) odorat *m*. ● *vt*/*i* (*pt* **smelt** *or* **smelled**) sentir; ~ **of** sentir. **smelly** *a* qui sent mauvais.

smelt ⇒SMELL.

smile *n* sourire *m*. ● *vi* sourire.

smiley *n* (Internet) binette *f*.

smirk *n* petit sourire *m* satisfait.

smitten *a* (in love) fou d'amour.

smog *n* smog *m*.

smoke *n* fumée *f*; **have a ~** fumer. ● *vt/i* fumer. **smoked** *a* fumé. **smokeless** *a* (*fuel*) non polluant. **smoker** *n* fumeur/-euse *m/f*. **smoky** *a* (*air*) enfumé.

smooth *a* lisse; (*movement*) aisé; (*manners*) onctueux; (*flight*) sans heurts. ● *vt* lisser; (*process*) faciliter.

smoothly *adv* (*move, flow*) doucement; (*brake, start*) en douceur; **go ~** marcher bien.

smother *vt* (stifle) étouffer; (cover) couvrir.

smoulder *vi* (lit) se consumer; (fig) couver.

smudge *n* trace *f*. ● *vt/i* (*ink*) (s')étaler.

smug *a* (**smugger, smuggest**) suffisant.

smuggle *vt* passer (en contrebande). **smuggler** *n* contrebandier/-ière *m/f*. **smuggling** *n* contrebande *f*.

smutty *a* grivois.

snack *n* casse-croûte *m inv*.

snag *n* inconvénient *m*; (in cloth) accroc *m*.

snail *n* escargot *m*.

snake *n* serpent *m*.

snap *vt/i* (*pt* **snapped**) (*whip, fingers*) (faire) claquer; (break) (se) casser net; (say) dire sèchement. ● *n* claquement *m*; (Photo) photo *f*. ● *a* soudain. □ **~ up** (buy) sauter sur.

snapshot *n* photo *f*.

snare *n* piège *m*.

snarl *vi* gronder (en montrant les dents). ● *n* grondement *m*. **~-up** *n* embouteillage *m*.

snatch *vt* (grab) attraper; (steal) voler; (*opportunity*) saisir; **~ sth from sb** arracher qch à qn. ● *n* (theft) vol *m*; (short part) fragment *m*.

sneak *vi* aller furtivement. ● *n* ! rapporteur/-euse *m/f*.

sneer *n* sourire *m* méprisant. ● *vi* sourire avec mépris.

sneeze *n* éternuement *m*. ● *vi* éternuer.

snide *a* narquois.

sniff *vt/i* renifler. ● *n* reniflement *m*.

snigger *n* ricanement *m*. ● *vi* ricaner.

snip *vt* (*pt* **snipped**) couper.

sniper *n* tireur *m* embusqué.

snippet *n* bribe *f*.

snivel *vi* (*pt* **snivelled**) pleurnicher.

snob *n* snob *mf*.

snooker *n* snooker *m*.

snoop *vi* ! fourrer son nez partout.

snooty *a* (**-ier, -iest**) ! snob *inv*, hautain.

snooze *n* petit somme *m*. ● *vi* sommeiller.

snore *n* ronflement *m*. ● *vi* ronfler.

snorkel *n* tuba *m*.

snort *n* grognement *m*. ● *vi* (*person*) grogner; (*horse*) s'ébrouer.

snout *n* museau *m*.

snow *n* neige *f*. ● *vi* neiger; **be ~ed under with** être submergé de.

snowball *n* boule *f* de neige. ● *vi* faire boule de neige.

snow: **~boarding** *n* surf *m* des neiges. **~-bound** *a* bloqué par la neige. **~-drift** *n* congère *f*. **~drop** *n* perce-neige *m or f inv*. **~flake** *n* flocon *m* de neige. **~man** *n* (*pl* **-men**) bonhomme *m* de neige. **~-plough** *n* chasse-neige *m inv*.

snub *vt* (*pt* **snubbed**) rembarrer. ● *n* rebuffade *f*.

snuffle *vi* renifler.

snug *a* (**snugger**, **snuggest**) (cosy) confortable; (tight) bien ajusté.

snuggle *vi* se pelotonner.

so *adv* si, tellement; (thus) ainsi; ~ **am I** moi aussi; ~ **good as** aussi bon que; **that is** ~ c'est ça; **I think** ~ je pense que oui; **five or** ~ environ cinq; ~ **as to** de manière à; ~ **far** jusqu'ici; ~ **long!** ☐ à bientôt!; ~ **many**, ~ **much** tant (de); ~ **that** pour que. ● *conj* donc, alors.

soak *vt/i* (faire) tremper (**in** dans). □ ~ **in** pénétrer; ~ **up** absorber. **soaking** *a* trempé.

soap *n* savon *m*. ● *vt* savonner. ~ **opera** *n* feuilleton *m*. ~ **powder** *n* lessive *f*.

soar *vi* monter (en flèche).

sob *n* sanglot *m*. ● *vi* (*pt* **sobbed**) sangloter.

sober *a* qui n'a pas bu d'alcool; (serious) sérieux. ● *vi* ~ **up** dessoûler.

soccer *n* football *m*.

sociable *a* sociable.

social *a* social. ● *n* réunion *f* (amicale), fête *f*.

socialism *n* socialisme *m*. **socialist** *a & n* socialiste (*mf*).

socialize *vi* se mêler aux autres; ~ **with** fréquenter.

socially *adv* socialement; (*meet*) en société.

social: ~ **security** *n* aide *f* sociale. ~ **worker** *n* travailleur/-euse *m/f* social/-e.

society *n* société *f*.

sociological *a* sociologique. **sociologist** *n* sociologue *mf*. **sociology** *n* sociologie *f*.

sock *n* chaussette *f*. ● *vt* (hit ☐) flanquer un coup (de poing) à.

socket *n* (for lamp) douille *f*; (Electr) prise *f* (de courant); (of eye) orbite *f*.

soda *n* soude *f*; ~(**-water**) eau *f* de Seltz.

sodden *a* détrempé.

sofa *n* canapé *m*. ~ **bed** *n* canapé-lit *m*.

soft *a* (gentle, lenient) doux; (not hard) doux, mou; (*heart, wood*) tendre; (silly) ramolli. ~ **drink** *n* boisson *f* non alcoolisée.

soften *vt/i* (se) ramollir; (tone down, lessen) (s')adoucir.

soft spot *n* **to have a** ~ **for sb** avoir un faible pour qn.

software *n* logiciel *m*.

soggy *a* (**-ier**, **-iest**) (*ground*) détrempé; (*food*) ramolli.

soil *n* sol *m*, terre *f*. ● *vt/i* (se) salir.

sold ⇒SELL. ● *a* ~ **out** épuisé.

solder *n* soudure *f*. ● *vt* souder.

soldier *n* soldat *m*. ● *vi* ~ **on** ☐ persévérer.

sole *n* (of foot) plante *f*; (of shoe) semelle *f*; (fish) sole *f*. ● *a* unique, seul. **solely** *adv* uniquement.

solemn *a* solennel.

solicitor *n* notaire *m*; (for court and police work) ≈ avocat/-e *m/f*.

solid *a* solide; (not hollow) plein; (*gold*) massif; (*mass*) compact; (*meal*) substantiel. ● *n* solide *m*; ~**s** (food) aliments *mpl* solides.

solidarity *n* solidarité *f*.

solidify *vt/i* (se) solidifier.

solitary *a* (alone) solitaire; (only) seul.

solo *n* solo *m*. ● *a* (Mus) solo *inv*; (*flight*) en solitaire.

soluble *a* soluble.

solution *n* solution *f*.

solve *vt* résoudre.

solvent *a* (Comm) solvable. ● *n* (dis)solvant *m*.

some

● *determiner*

····➤ (unspecified amount) du/de l'/de la/des; **I have to buy ~ bread** je dois acheter du pain; **have ~ water** prenez de l'eau; **~ sweets** des bonbons.

····➤ (certain) certains/certaines; **~ people say that** certains disent que.

····➤ (unknown) un/une; **~ man came to the house** un homme est venu à la maison.

····➤ (considerable amount) **we stayed there for ~ time** nous sommes restés là assez longtemps; **it will take ~ doing** ça ne va pas être facile à faire.

! In front of a plural adjective *des* changes to *de*: **some pretty dresses** *de jolies robes*.

● *pronoun*

····➤ en; **he wants ~** il en veut; **have ~ more** reprenez-en.

····➤ (certain) certains/certaines; **~ are expensive** certains sont chers.

● *adverb*

····➤ environ; **~ 20 people** environ 20 personnes.

somebody *pron* quelqu'un. ● *n* **be a ~** être quelqu'un.

somehow *adv* d'une manière ou d'une autre; (for some reason) je ne sais pas pourquoi.

someone *pron & n* = SOMEBODY.

someplace *adv* (US) = SOMEWHERE.

somersault *n* roulade *f*. ● *vi* faire une roulade.

something *pron & n* quelque chose (*m*); **~ good** quelque chose de bon; **~ like** un peu comme.

sometime *adv* un jour; **~ in June** en juin. ● *a* (former) ancien.

sometimes *adv* quelquefois, parfois.

somewhat *adv* quelque peu, un peu.

somewhere *adv* quelque part.

son *n* fils *m*.

song *n* chanson *f*; (of bird) chant *m*.

son-in-law *n* (*pl* **sons-in-law**) gendre *m*.

soon *adv* bientôt; (early) tôt; **I would ~er stay** j'aimerais mieux rester; **~ after** peu après; **~er or later** tôt ou tard.

soot *n* suie *f*.

soothe *vt* calmer.

sophisticated *a* raffiné; (*machine*) sophistiqué.

sopping *a* trempé.

soppy *a* (**-ier**, **-iest**) 🄸 sentimental.

sorcerer *n* sorcier *m*.

sordid *a* sordide.

sore *a* douloureux; (vexed) en rogne (**at**, **with** contre). ● *n* plaie *f*.

sorely *adv* fortement.

sorrow *n* chagrin *m*.

sorry *a* (**-ier**, **-iest**) (regretful) désolé (**to** de; **that** que); (wretched) triste; **feel ~ for** plaindre; **~!** pardon!

sort *n* genre *m*, sorte *f*, espèce *f*; (person 🄸) type *m*; **what ~ of?** quel genre de?; **be out of ~s** ne pas être dans son assiette. ● *vt* **~ (out)** (classify) trier; **~ out** (tidy) ranger; (arrange) arranger; (*problem*) régler.

so-so *a & adv* comme ci comme ça.

sought ⇒SEEK.

soul *n* âme *f*

sound *n* son *m*, bruit *m*. ● *a* solide; (healthy) sain; (sensible) sensé. ● *vt/i* sonner; (seem) sembler (**as if** que); (test) sonder; **~ out** sonder; **~ a horn** klaxonner; **~ like** sembler être. **~**

asleep *a* profondément endormi. ~ **barrier** *n* mur *m* du son.
soundly *adv* (*sleep*) à poings fermés; (*built*) solidement.
sound-proof *a* insonorisé. ● *vt* insonoriser.
sound-track *n* bande *f* sonore.
soup *n* soupe *f*, potage *m*.
sour *a* aigre. ● *vt/i* (s')aigrir.
source *n* source *f*.
south *n* sud *m*. ● *a* sud *inv*, du sud. ● *adv* vers le sud.
South Africa *n* Afrique *f* du Sud.
South America *n* Amérique *f* du Sud.
south-east *n* sud-est *m*.
southern *a* du sud. **southerner** *n* habitant/-e *m*/*f* du sud.
southward *a* (*side*) sud *inv*; (*journey*) vers le sud.
south-west *n* sud-ouest *m*.
souvenir *n* souvenir *m*.
sovereign *n* & *a* souverain/-e (*m*/*f*).
sow[1] *vt* (*pt* **sowed**; *pp* **sowed** *or* **sown**) (*seed*) semer; (*land*) ensemencer.
sow[2] *n* (pig) truie *f*.
soya *n* soja *m*. ~ **sauce** *n* sauce *f* soja.
spa *n* station *f* thermale.
space *n* espace *m*; (room) place *f*; (period) période *f*. ● *a* (*research*) spatial. ● *vt* ~ (**out**) espacer. ~**craft** *n inv*, ~**ship** *n* engin *m* spatial. ~**suit** *n* combinaison *f* spatiale.
spacious *a* spacieux.
spade *n* (for garden) bêche *f*; (child's) pelle *f*; (cards) pique *m*. ~**work** *n* (fig) travail *m* préparatoire.
spaghetti *n* spaghetti *mpl*.
Spain *n* Espagne *f*.
span *n* (of arch) portée *f*; (of wings) envergure *f*; (of time) durée *f*. ● *vt* (*pt* **spanned**) enjamber; (in time) embrasser.
Spaniard *n* Espagnol/-e *m*/*f*.
spaniel *n* épagneul *m*.
Spanish *a* espagnol. ● *n* espagnol *m*.
spank *vt* donner une fessée à.
spanner *n* (tool) clé *f* (plate); (adjustable) clé *f* à molette.
spare *vt* (treat leniently) épargner; (do without) se passer de; (afford to give) donner, accorder. ● *a* en réserve; (surplus) de trop; (*tyre, shoes*) de rechange; (*room, bed*) d'ami; **are there any ~ tickets?** y a-t-il encore des places? ● *n* ~ (**part**) pièce *f* de rechange. ~ **time** *n* loisirs *mpl*.
sparing *a* frugal. **sparingly** *adv* en petite quantité.
spark *n* étincelle *f*. ● *vt* ~ **off** (initiate) provoquer.
sparkle *vi* étinceler. ● *n* étincellement *m*. **sparkling** *a* (*wine*) mousseux, pétillant; (*eyes*) brillant.
spark-plug *n* bougie *f*.
sparrow *n* moineau *m*.
sparse *a* clairsemé. **sparsely** *adv* (*furnished*) peu.
spasm *n* (of muscle) spasme *m*; (of coughing, anger) accès *m*.
spasmodic *a* intermittent.
spat ⇒SPIT.
spate *n* **a ~ of** (*letters*) une avalanche de.
spatter *vt* éclabousser (**with** de).
spawn *n* frai *m*, œufs *mpl*. ● *vt* pondre. ● *vi* frayer.
speak *vi* (*pt* **spoke**; *pp* **spoken**) parler. ● *vt* (say) dire; (*language*) parler. □ ~ **up** parler plus fort.
speaker *n* (in public) orateur *m*; (Pol) président *m*; (loudspeaker) baffle *m*; **be a French/a good ~** parler français/bien.
spear *n* lance *f*.
spearmint *n* menthe *f* verte.

special *a* spécial; (exceptional) exceptionnel.

specialist *n* spécialiste *mf*.

speciality, (US) **specialty** *n* spécialité *f*.

specialize *vi* se spécialiser (**in** en).

specially *adv* spécialement.

species *n inv* espèce *f*.

specific *a* précis, explicite.

specification *n* (of design) spécification *f*; (of car equipment) caractéristiques *fpl*. **specify** *vt* spécifier.

specimen *n* spécimen *m*, échantillon *m*.

speck *n* (stain) (petite) tache *f*; (particle) grain *m*.

specs *npl* ▣ lunettes *fpl*.

spectacle *n* spectacle *m*. **spectacles** *n* lunettes *fpl*. **spectacular** *a* spectaculaire.

spectator *n* spectateur/-trice *m*/*f*.

spectrum *n* (*pl* **-tra**) spectre *m*; (of ideas) gamme *f*.

speculate *vi* s'interroger (**about** sur); (Comm) spéculer. **speculation** *n* conjectures *fpl*; (Comm) spéculation *f*. **speculator** *n* spéculateur/-trice *m*/*f*.

speech *n* (faculty) parole *f*; (diction) élocution *f*; (dialect) langage *m*; (address) discours *m*. **speechless** *a* muet (**with** de).

speed *n* (of movement) vitesse *f*; (swiftness) rapidité *f*. ● *vi* (*pt* **sped**) aller vite; (*pt* **speeded**) (drive too fast) aller trop vite. □ **~ up** accélérer; (of pace) s'accélérer.

speedboat *n* vedette *f*.

speeding *n* excès *m* de vitesse.

speed limit *n* limitation *f* de vitesse.

speedometer *n* compteur *m* (de vitesse).

spell *n* (magic) charme *m*, sortilège *m*; (curse) sort *m*; (of time) (courte) période *f*. ● *vt/i* (*pt* **spelled** *or* **spelt**) écrire; (mean) signifier; **~ out** épeler; (explain) expliquer. **~checker** *n* correcteur *m* orthographique.

spelling *n* orthographe *f*. ● *a* (*mistake*) d'orthographe.

spend *vt* (*pt* **spent**) (*money*) dépenser (**on** pour); (*time, holiday*) passer; (*energy*) consacrer (**on** à). ● *vi* dépenser.

spent ⇒SPEND. ● *a* (used) utilisé; (*person*) épuisé.

sperm *n* (*pl* **sperms** *or* **sperm**) sperme *m*.

sphere *n* sphère *f*.

spice *n* épice *f*; (fig) piquant *m*.

spick-and-span *a* impeccable.

spicy *a* épicé; piquant.

spider *n* araignée *f*.

spike *n* pointe *f*.

spill *vt* (*pt* **spilled** *or* **spilt**) renverser, répandre. ● *vi* se répandre; **~ over** déborder.

spin *vt/i* (*pt* **spun**; *pres p* **spinning**) (*wool, web*) filer; (turn) (faire) tourner; (*story*) débiter; **~ out** faire durer. ● *n* (movement, excursion) tour *m*.

spinach *n* épinards *mpl*.

spinal *a* vertébral. **~ cord** *n* moelle *f* épinière.

spin-drier *n* essoreuse *f*.

spine *n* colonne *f* vertébrale; (prickle) piquant *m*.

spin-off *n* avantage *m* accessoire; (by-product) dérivé *m*.

spinster *n* célibataire *f*; (pej) vieille fille *f*.

spiral *a* en spirale; (*staircase*) en colimaçon. ● *n* spirale *f*. ● *vi* (*pt* **spiralled**) (*prices*) monter (en flèche).

spire *n* flèche *f*.

spirit *n* esprit *m*; (boldness) courage *m*; **~s** (morale) moral *m*;

S

(drink) spiritueux *mpl*. ● *vt* ~ **away** faire disparaître. **spirited** *a* fougueux. ~**-level** *n* niveau *m* à bulle.

spiritual *a* spirituel.

spit *vt/i* (*pt* **spat** *or* **spit**; *pres p* **spitting**) cracher; (of rain) crachiner; ~ **out** cracher; **the** ~**ting image of** le portrait craché *or* vivant de. ● *n* crachat(s) *m(pl)*; (for meat) broche *f*.

spite *n* rancune *f*; **in** ~ **of** malgré. ● *vt* contrarier.

splash *vt* éclabousser. ● *vi* faire des éclaboussures; ~ (**about**) patauger. ● *n* (act, mark) éclaboussure *f*; (sound) plouf *m*; (of colour) tache *f*.

spleen *n* (Anat) rate *f*.

splendid *a* magnifique, splendide.

splint *n* (Med) attelle *f*.

splinter *n* éclat *m*; (in finger) écharde *f*. ~ **group** *n* groupe *m* dissident.

split *vt/i* (*pt* **split**; *pres p* **splitting**) (se) fendre; (tear) (se) déchirer; (divide) (se) diviser; (share) partager; ~ **one's sides** se tordre (de rire). ● *n* fente *f*; déchirure *f*; (share ⊡) part *f*, partage *m*; (quarrel) rupture *f*; (Pol) scission *f*. □ ~ **up** (*couple*) rompre. ~ **second** *n* fraction *f* de seconde.

splutter *vi* crachoter; (stammer) bafouiller; (*engine*) tousser.

spoil *vt* (*pt* **spoilt** *or* **spoiled**) (pamper) gâter; (ruin) abîmer; (mar) gâcher, gâter. ● *n* ~(**s**) butin *m*. ~**-sport** *n* trouble-fête *mf inv*.

spoke[1] *n* rayon *m*.

spoke[2], **spoken** ⇒SPEAK.

spokesman *n* (*pl* **-men**) porte-parole *m inv*.

sponge *n* éponge *f*. ● *vt* éponger. ● *vi* ~ **on** vivre aux crochets de. ~**-bag** *n* trousse *f* de toilette. ~**-cake** *n* génoise *f*.

sponsor *n* (of concert) parrain *m*, sponsor *m*; (surety) garant *m*; (for membership) parrain *m*, marraine *f*. ● *vt* parrainer, sponsoriser; (*member*) parrainer. **sponsorship** *n* patronage *m*; parrainage *m*.

spontaneous *a* spontané.

spoof *n* ⊡ parodie *f*.

spoon *n* cuiller *f*, cuillère *f*.

spoonful *n* (*pl* ~**s**) cuillerée *f*.

sport *n* sport *m*; (**good**) ~ (person ⊡) chic type *m*; ~**s car/coat** voiture/veste *f* de sport. ● *vt* (display) exhiber, arborer.

sporting *a* sportif; **a** ~ **chance** une assez bonne chance.

sportsman *n* (*pl* **-men**) sportif *m*.

sporty *a* ⊡ sportif.

spot *n* (mark, stain) tache *f*; (dot) point *m*; (in pattern) pois *m*; (drop) goutte *f*; (place) endroit *m*; (pimple) bouton *m*; **a** ~ **of** ⊡ un peu de; **on the** ~ sur place; (without delay) sur le coup. ● *vt* (*pt* **spotted**) ⊡ apercevoir. ~ **check** *n* contrôle *m* surprise.

spotless *a* impeccable.

spotlight *n* (lamp) projecteur *m*, spot *m*.

spotty *a* (*skin*) boutonneux.

spouse *n* époux *m*, épouse *f*.

spout *n* (of teapot) bec *m*; (of liquid) jet *m*; **up the** ~ (ruined ⊡) fichu. ● *vi* jaillir.

sprain *n* entorse *f*, foulure *f*. ● *vt* ~ **one's wrist** se fouler le poignet.

sprang ⇒SPRING.

sprawl *vi* (*town, person*) s'étaler. ● *n* étalement *m*.

spray *n* (of flowers) gerbe *f*; (water) gerbe *f* d'eau; (from sea) embruns *mpl*; (device) bombe *f*, atomiseur *m*. ● *vt* (*surface, insecticide, plant*) vaporiser; (*person*) asperger; (*crops*) traiter.

spread *vt/i* (*pt* **spread**) (stretch, extend) (s')étendre; (*news, fear*) (se) répandre; (*illness*) (se) propager; (*butter*) (s')étaler. ● *n* propagation *f*; (of population) distribution *f*; (paste) pâte *f* à tartiner; (food) belle table *f*. **~-eagled** *a* bras et jambes écartés. **~sheet** *n* tableur *m*.

spree *n* **go on a ~** (have fun Ⓘ) faire la noce.

sprig *n* petite branche *f*.

sprightly *a* (**-ier, -iest**) alerte, vif.

spring *vi* (*pt* **sprang**; *pp* **sprung**) bondir. ● *vt* **~ sth on sb** annoncer qch de but en blanc à qn. ● *n* bond *m*; (device) ressort *m*; (season) printemps *m*; (of water) source *f*. □ **~ from** provenir de; **~ up** surgir. **~board** *n* tremplin *m*. **~ onion** *n* oignon *m* blanc.

springy *a* (**-ier, -iest**) élastique.

sprinkle *vt* (with liquid) arroser (**with** de); (with salt, flour) saupoudrer (**with** de); (*sand*) répandre. **sprinkler** *n* (in garden) arroseur *m*; (for fires) extincteur *m* (à déclenchement) automatique.

sprint *vi* (Sport) sprinter. ● *n* sprint *m*.

sprout *vt/i* pousser. ● *n* (on plant) pousse *f*; (**Brussels**) **~s** choux *mpl* de Bruxelles.

spruce *a* pimpant. ● *vt* **~ oneself up** se faire beau. ● *n* (tree) épicéa *m*.

sprung ⇒SPRING.

spud *n* Ⓘ patate *f*.

spun ⇒SPIN.

spur *n* (of rider) éperon *m*; (stimulus) aiguillon *m*; **on the ~ of the moment** sous l'impulsion du moment. ● *vt* (*pt* **spurred**) éperonner.

spurious *a* faux.

spurn *vt* repousser.

spurt *vi* jaillir; (fig) accélérer. ● *n* jet *m*; (of energy) sursaut *m*.

spy *n* espion/-ne *m/f*. ● *vi* espionner. ● *vt* apercevoir.

squabble *vi* se chamailler. ● *n* chamaillerie *f*.

squad *n* (of soldiers) escouade *f*; (Sport) équipe *f*.

squadron *n* (Mil) escadron *m*; (Aviat) escadrille *f*.

squalid *a* sordide.

squander *vt* (*money, time*) gaspiller.

square *n* carré *m*; (open space in town) place *f*. ● *a* carré; (honest) honnête; (*meal*) solide; (boring Ⓘ) ringard; (**all**) **~** (quits) quitte; **~ metre** mètre *m* carré. ● *vt* (settle) régler; **~ up to** faire face à.

squash *vt* écraser; (crowd) serrer. ● *n* (game) squash *m*; (marrow: US) courge *f*; **lemon ~** citronnade *f*; **orange ~** orangeade *f*.

squat *vi* (*pt* **squatted**) s'accroupir; **~ in a house** squatteriser une maison. ● *a* (dumpy) trapu. **squatter** *n* squatter *m*.

squawk *n* cri *m* rauque. ● *vi* pousser un cri rauque.

squeak *n* petit cri *m*; (of door) grincement *m*. ● *vi* crier; grincer.

squeal *n* cri *m* aigu. ● *vi* pousser un cri aigu; **~ on** (inform on Ⓘ) dénoncer.

squeamish *a* (trop) délicat.

squeeze *vt* presser; (*hand, arm*) serrer; (extract) exprimer (**from** de); (extort) soutirer (**from** à). ● *vi* (force one's way) se glisser. ● *n* pression *f*; (Comm) restrictions *fpl* de crédit.

squid *n* calmar *m*.

squint *vi* loucher; (with half-shut eyes) plisser les yeux. ● *n* (Med) strabisme *m*.

squirm *vi* se tortiller.

squirrel *n* écureuil *m*.

squirt *vt/i* (faire) jaillir. ● *n* jet *m*.

stab *vt* (*pt* **stabbed**) (with knife) poignarder. ● *n* coup *m* (de couteau); **have a ~ at sth** essayer de faire qch.

stability *n* stabilité *f*. **stabilize** *vt* stabiliser.

stable *a* stable. ● *n* écurie *f*. **~-boy** *n* lad *m*.

stack *n* tas *m*. ● *vt* **~ (up)** entasser, empiler.

stadium *n* stade *m*.

staff *n* personnel *m*; (in school) professeurs *mpl*; (Mil) état-major *m*; (stick) bâton *m*. ● *vt* pourvoir en personnel.

stag *n* cerf *m*.

stage *n* (Theat) scène *f*; (phase) stade *m*, étape *f*; (platform in hall) estrade *f*; **go on the ~** faire du théâtre. ● *vt* mettre en scène; (fig) organiser. **~ door** *n* entrée *f* des artistes. **~ fright** *n* trac *m*.

stagger *vi* chanceler. ● *vt* (shock) stupéfier; (*payments*) échelonner. **staggering** *a* stupéfiant.

stagnate *vi* stagner.

stag night *n* soirée *f* pour enterrer une vie de garçon.

staid *a* sérieux.

stain *vt* tacher; (*wood*) colorer. ● *n* tache *f*; (colouring) colorant *m*. **stained glass window** *n* vitrail *m*.

stainless steel *n* acier *m* inoxydable.

stain remover *n* détachant *m*.

stair *n* marche *f*; **the ~s** l'escalier *m*. **~case**, **~way** *n* escalier *m*.

stake *n* (post) pieu *m*; (wager) enjeu *m*; **at ~** en jeu. ● *vt* (*area*) jalonner; (*wager*) jouer; **~ a claim to** revendiquer.

stale *a* pas frais; (*bread*) rassis; (*smell*) de renfermé.

stalk *n* (of plant) tige *f*. ● *vi* marcher de façon guindée. ● *vt* (*hunter*) chasser; (*murderer*) suivre.

stall *n* (in stable) stalle *f*; (in market) éventaire *m*; **~s** (Theat) orchestre *m*. ● *vt/i* (Auto) caler; **~ (for time)** temporiser.

stallion *n* étalon *m*.

stamina *n* résistance *f*.

stammer *vt/i* bégayer. ● *n* bégaiement *m*.

stamp *vt/i* **~ (one's foot)** taper du pied. ● *vt* (*letter*) timbrer. ● *n* (for postage, marking) timbre *m*; (mark: fig) sceau *m*. □ **~ out** supprimer. **~-collecting** *n* philatélie *f*.

stampede *n* fuite *f* désordonnée; (rush: fig) ruée *f*. ● *vi* s'enfuir en désordre; se ruer.

stand *vi* (*pt* **stood**) être *or* se tenir (debout); (rise) se lever; (be situated) se trouver; (Pol) être candidat (**for** à); **~ in line** (US) faire la queue; **~ to reason** être logique. ● *vt* mettre (debout); (tolerate) supporter; **~ a chance** avoir une chance. ● *n* (stance) position *f*; (Mil) résistance *f*; (for lamp) support *m*; (at fair) stand *m*; (in street) kiosque *m*; (for spectators) tribune *f*; (Jur, US) barre *f*; **make a ~** prendre position. □ **~ back** reculer; **~ by** *or* **around** ne rien faire; **~ by** (be ready) se tenir prêt; (*promise, person*) rester fidèle à; **~ down** se désister; **~ for** représenter; ▣ supporter; **~ in for** remplacer; **~ out** ressortir; **~ up** se lever; **~ up for** défendre; **~ up to** résister à.

standard *n* norme *f*; (level) niveau *m* (voulu); (flag) étendard *m*; **~ of living** niveau *m* de vie; **~s** (morals) principes *mpl*. ● *a* ordinaire.

standard of living *n* niveau *m* de vie.

stand-by *a* de réserve. ● *n* **be a ~** être de réserve.

stand-in *n* remplaçant/-e *m/f*.

standing *a* debout *inv.* ● *n* réputation *f*; (duration) durée *f.* ~ **order** *n* prélèvement *m* bancaire.

standpoint *n* point *m* de vue.

standstill *n* **at a** ~ immobile; **bring/come to a** ~ (s')immobiliser.

stank ⇒STINK.

staple *n* agrafe *f.* ● *vt* agrafer. ● *a* principal, de base. **stapler** *n* agrafeuse *f.*

star *n* étoile *f*; (person) vedette *f.* ● *vt* (*pt* **starred**) (*film*) avoir pour vedette. ● *vi* ~ **in** être la vedette de.

starch *n* amidon *m*; (in food) fécule *f.* ● *vt* amidonner.

stardom *n* célébrité *f.*

stare *vi* ~ **at** regarder fixement. ● *n* regard *m* fixe.

starfish *n* étoile *f* de mer.

stark *a* (desolate) désolé; (severe) austère; (utter) complet; (*fact*) brutal. ● *adv* complètement.

starling *n* étourneau *m.*

start *vt/i* commencer; (*machine*) (se) mettre en marche; (*fashion*) lancer; (cause) provoquer; (jump) sursauter; (of vehicle) démarrer; ~ **to do** commencer *or* se mettre à faire; ~**ing tomorrow** à partir de demain. ● *n* commencement *m*, début *m*; (of race) départ *m*; (lead) avance *f*; (jump) sursaut *m.* □ ~ **off** commencer (**doing** par faire); ~ **out** partir; ~ **up** (*business*) lancer. **starter** *n* (Auto) démarreur *m*; (runner) partant *m*; (Culin) entrée *f.*

starting point *n* point *m* de départ.

startle *vt* (make jump) faire tressaillir; (shock) alarmer.

starvation *n* faim *f.*

starve *vi* mourir de faim. ● *vt* affamer; (deprive) priver.

stash *vt* cacher.

state *n* état *m*; (pomp) apparat *m*; **S**~ État *m*; **the S~s** les États-Unis; **get into a** ~ s'affoler. ● *a* d'État, de l'État; (*school*) public. ● *vt* affirmer (**that** que); (*views*) exprimer; (fix) fixer.

stately *a* (**-ier**, **-iest**) majestueux. ~ **home** *n* château *m.*

statement *n* déclaration *f*; (of account) relevé *m.*

statesman *n* (*pl* **-men**) homme *m* d'État.

static *a* statique. ● *n* (radio, TV) parasites *mpl.*

station *n* (Rail) gare *f*; (TV) chaîne *f*; (Mil) poste *m*; (rank) condition *f.* ● *vt* poster, placer; ~**ed at** *or* **in** (Mil) en garnison à.

stationary *a* immobile, stationnaire; (*vehicle*) à l'arrêt.

stationery *n* papeterie *f.*

station wagon *n* (US) break *m.*

statistic *n* statistique *f*; ~**s** statistique *f.*

statue *n* statue *f.*

status *n* (*pl* ~**es**) situation *f*, statut *m*; (prestige) standing *m.*

statute *n* loi *f*; ~**s** (rules) statuts *mpl.* **statutory** *a* statutaire; (*holiday*) légal.

staunch *a* (*friend*) loyal, fidèle.

stave *n* (Mus) portée *f.* ● *vt* ~ **off** éviter, conjurer.

stay *vi* rester; (spend time) séjourner; (reside) loger. ● *vt* (*hunger*) tromper. ● *n* séjour *m.* □ ~ **away from** (*school*) ne pas aller à; ~ **behind** *or* ~ **on** rester; ~ **in** rester à la maison; ~ **up** veiller, se coucher tard.

stead *n* **stand sb in good** ~ être utile à qn.

steadfast *a* ferme.

steady *a* (**-ier**, **-iest**) stable; (*hand, voice*) ferme; (regular) régulier; (staid) sérieux. ● *vt* maintenir, assurer; (calm) calmer.

steak *n* steak *m*, bifteck *m*; (of fish) darne *f.*

S

steal *vt/i* (*pt* **stole**; *pp* **stolen**) voler (**from sb** à qn).

steam *n* vapeur *f*; (on glass) buée *f*. ● *vt* (cook) cuire à la vapeur. ● *vi* fumer. **~-engine** *n* locomotive *f* à vapeur

steamer *n* (Culin) cuit-vapeur *m*; (boat) (bateau à) vapeur *m*.

steel *n* acier *m*; **~ industry** sidérurgie *f*. ● *vpr* **~ oneself** s'endurcir, se cuirasser.

steep *a* raide, rapide; (*price*: [!]) excessif. ● *vt* (soak) tremper; **~ed in** (fig) imprégné de.

steeple *n* clocher *m*.

steer *vt* diriger; (*ship*) gouverner; (fig) guider. ● *vi* (in ship) gouverner; **~ clear of** éviter.

steering-wheel *n* volant *m*.

stem *n* tige *f*; (of glass) pied *m*. ● *vi* (*pt* **stemmed**) **~ from** provenir de. ● *vt* (*pt* **stemmed**) (check, stop) endiguer, contenir.

stench *n* puanteur *f*.

stencil *n* pochoir *m*. ● *vt* (*pt* **stencilled**) décorer au pochoir.

step *vi* (*pt* **stepped**) marcher, aller. ● *n* pas *m*; (stair) marche *f*; (of train) marchepied *m*; (action) mesure *f*; **~s** (ladder) escabeau *m*; **in ~** au pas; (fig) conforme (**with** à). □ **~ down** (resign) démissionner; (from ladder) descendre; **~ forward** faire un pas en avant; **~ in** (intervene) intervenir; **~ up** (pressure) augmenter. **~brother** *n* demi-frère *m*. **~daughter** *n* belle-fille *f*. **~father** *n* beau-père *m*. **~-ladder** *n* escabeau *m*. **~mother** *n* belle-mère *f*. **stepping-stone** *n* (fig) tremplin *m*. **~sister** *n* demi-sœur *f*. **~son** *n* beau-fils *m*.

stereo *n* stéréo *f*; (record-player) chaîne *f* stéréo. ● *a* stéréo *inv*.

stereotype *n* stéréotype *m*. **stereotyped** *a* stéréotypé.

sterile *a* stérile. **sterility** *n* stérilité *f*.

sterilize *vt* stériliser.

sterling *n* livre(s) *f*(*pl*) sterling. ● *a* sterling *inv*; (*silver*) fin; (fig) excellent.

stern *a* sévère. ● *n* (of ship) arrière *m*.

steroid *n* stéroïde *m*.

stew *vt/i* cuire à la casserole; **~ed fruit** compote *f*; **~ed tea** thé *m* trop infusé. ● *n* ragoût *m*.

steward *n* (of club) intendant *m*; (on ship) steward *m*. **stewardess** *n* hôtesse *f*.

stick *vt* (*pt* **stuck**) (glue) coller; (put [!]) mettre; (endure [!]) supporter. ● *vi* (adhere) coller, adhérer; (to pan) attacher; (remain [!]) rester; (be jammed) être coincé; **be stuck with sb** [!] se farcir qn. ● *n* bâton *m*; (for walking) canne *f*. □ **~ at** persévérer dans; **~ out** *vt* (*head*) sortir; (*tongue*) tirer; *vi* (protrude) dépasser; **~ to** (*promise*) rester fidèle à; **~ up for** [!] défendre.

sticker *n* autocollant *m*.

sticky *a* (**-ier, -iest**) poisseux; (*label, tape*) adhésif.

stiff *a* raide; (*limb, joint*) ankylosé; (tough) dur; (*drink*) fort; (*price*) élevé; (*manner*) guindé; **~ neck** torticolis *m*.

stifle *vt/i* étouffer.

stiletto *a* & *n* **~s**, **~ heels** talons *mpl* aiguille.

still *a* immobile; (quiet) calme, tranquille; **keep ~!** arrête de bouger! ● *n* silence *m*. ● *adv* encore, toujours; (even) encore; (nevertheless) tout de même.

stillborn *a* mort-né.

still life *n* nature *f* morte.

stimulate *vt* stimuler. **stimulation** *n* stimulation *f*.

stimulus *n* (*pl* **-li**) (spur) stimulant *m*.

sting *n* piqûre *f*; (of insect) aiguillon *m*. ● *vt/i* (*pt* **stung**) piquer.

stingy *a* (**-ier**, **-iest**) avare (**with** de).

stink *n* puanteur *f*. ● *vi* (*pt* **stank** *or* **stunk**; *pp* **stunk**) ~ (**of**) puer.

stipulate *vt* stipuler.

stir *vt/i* (*pt* **stirred**) (move) remuer; (excite) exciter; ~ **up** (*trouble*) provoquer. ● *n* agitation *f*.

stirrup *n* étrier *m*.

stitch *n* point *m*; (in knitting) maille *f*; (Med) point *m* de suture; (muscle pain) point *m* de côté; **be in ~es** ⊡ avoir le fou rire. ● *vt* coudre.

stock *n* réserve *f*; (Comm) stock *m*; (financial) valeurs *fpl*; (family) souche *f*; (soup) bouillon *m*; **we're out of** ~ il n'y en a plus; **take** ~ (fig) faire le point; **in** ~ en stock. ● *a* (goods) courant. ● *vt* (*shop*) approvisionner; (sell) vendre. ● *vi* ~ **up** s'approvisionner (**with** de). ~ **broker** *n* agent *m* de change. ~ **cube** *n* bouillon-cube *m*. **S~ Exchange** *n* Bourse *f*.

stocking *n* bas *m*.

stock market *n* Bourse *f*.

stockpile *n* stock *m*. ● *vt* stocker; (*arms*) amasser.

stock-taking *n* (Comm) inventaire *m*.

stocky *a* (**-ier**, **-iest**) trapu.

stodgy *a* lourd.

stole, stolen ⇒STEAL.

stomach *n* estomac *m*; (abdomen) ventre *m*. ● *vt* (put up with) supporter. **~-ache** *n* mal *m* à l'estomac *or* au ventre.

stone *n* pierre *f*; (pebble) caillou *m*; (in fruit) noyau *m*; (weight) 6,350 kg. ● *a* de pierre; **~-cold/-deaf** complètement froid/sourd. ● *vt* (throw stones) lapider; (*fruit*) dénoyauter.

stony *a* pierreux.

stood ⇒STAND.

stool *n* tabouret *m*.

stoop *vi* (bend) se baisser; (condescend) s'abaisser. ● *n* **have a** ~ être voûté.

stop *vt/i* (*pt* **stopped**) arrêter (**doing** de faire); (*moving, talking*) s'arrêter; (prevent) empêcher (**from** de); (*hole, leak*) boucher; (*pain, noise*) cesser; (stay ⊡) rester. ● *n* arrêt *m*; (full stop) point *m*; **~(-over)** halte *f*; (port of call) escale *f*. □ ~ **off** s'arrêter; ~ **up** boucher.

stopgap *n* bouche-trou *m*. ● *a* intérimaire.

stoppage *n* arrêt *m*; (of work) arrêt *m* de travail; (of pay) retenue *f*.

stopper *n* bouchon *m*.

stop-watch *n* chronomètre *m*.

storage *n* (of goods, food) emmagasinage *m*. ~ **heater** *n* radiateur *m* électrique à accumulation.

store *n* réserve *f*; (warehouse) entrepôt *m*; (shop) grand magasin *m*; (US) magasin *m*; **have in ~ for** réserver à; **set ~ by** attacher du prix à. ● *vt* (for future) mettre en réserve; (in warehouse, mind) emmagasiner. **~-room** *n* réserve *f*.

storey *n* étage *m*.

stork *n* cigogne *f*.

storm *n* tempête *f*, orage *m*. ● *vt* prendre d'assaut. ● *vi* (rage) tempêter.

story *n* histoire *f*; (in press) article *m*; (storey: US) étage *m*. **~-teller** *n* conteur/-euse *m/f*.

stout *a* corpulent; (strong) solide. ● *n* bière *f* brune.

stove *n* cuisinière *f*.

stow *vt* ~ **away** (put away) ranger; (hide) cacher. ● *vi* voyager clandestinement.

straddle *vt* être à cheval sur, enjamber.

straggler *n* traînard/-e *m/f*.

S

straight *a* droit; (tidy) en ordre; (frank) franc; ~ **face** visage *m* sérieux; **get sth** ~ mettre qch au clair. ● *adv* (in straight line) droit; (direct) tout droit; ~ **ahead** *or* **on** tout droit; ~ **away** tout de suite; ~ **off** 🅸 sans hésiter. ● *n* (Sport) ligne *f* droite.

straighten *vt* (*nail, situation*) redresser; (tidy) arranger.

straightforward *a* honnête; (easy) simple.

straight off *a* 🅸 sans hésiter.

strain *vt* (*rope, ears*) tendre; (*limb*) fouler; (*eyes*) fatiguer; (*muscle*) froisser; (filter) passer; (*vegetables*) égoutter; (fig) mettre à l'épreuve. ● *vi* fournir des efforts. ● *n* tension *f*; (fig) effort *m*; (breed) race *f*; (of virus) variété *f*; ~**s** (tune: Mus) accents *mpl*. **strained** *a* forcé; (*relations*) tendu. **strainer** *n* passoire *f*.

strait *n* détroit *m*; ~**s** détroit *m*; **be in dire** ~**s** être aux abois. ~**-jacket** *n* camisole *f* de force.

strand *n* (thread) fil *m*, brin *m*; (of hair) mèche *f*.

stranded *a* (*person*) en rade; (*ship*) échoué.

strange *a* étrange; (unknown) inconnu. **stranger** *n* inconnu/-e *m/f*.

strangle *vt* étrangler.

stranglehold *n* **have a** ~ **on** tenir à la gorge.

strap *n* (of leather) courroie *f*; (of dress) bretelle *f*; (of watch) bracelet *m*. ● *vt* (*pt* **strapped**) attacher.

strategic *a* stratégique. **strategy** *n* stratégie *f*.

straw *n* paille *f*; **the last** ~ le comble.

strawberry *n* fraise *f*.

stray *vi* s'égarer; (deviate) s'écarter. ● *a* perdu; (isolated) isolé. ● *n* animal *m* perdu.

streak *n* raie *f*, bande *f*; (trace) trace *f*; (period) période *f*; (tendency) tendance *f*. ● *vt* (mark) strier. ● *vi* filer à toute allure.

stream *n* ruisseau *m*; (current) courant *m*; (flow) flot *m*; (in school) classe *f* (de niveau). ● *vi* ruisseler (**with** de); (*eyes, nose*) couler.

streamline *vt* rationaliser. **streamlined** *a* (*shape*) aérodynamique.

street *n* rue *f*. ~**car** *n* (US) tramway *m*. ~ **lamp** *n* réverbère *m*. ~ **map** *n* indicateur *m* des rues.

strength *n* force *f*; (of wall, fabric) solidité *f*; **on the** ~ **of** en vertu de. **strengthen** *vt* renforcer, fortifier.

strenuous *a* (*exercise*) énergique; (*work*) ardu.

stress *n* (emphasis) accent *m*; (pressure) pression *f*; (Med) stress *m*. ● *vt* souligner, insister sur.

stretch *vt* (pull taut) tendre; (*arm, leg*) étendre; (*neck*) tendre; (*clothes*) étirer; (*truth*) forcer; ~ **one's legs** se dégourdir les jambes. ● *vi* s'étendre; (*person*) s'étirer; (*clothes*) se déformer. ● *n* étendue *f*; (period) période *f*; (of road) tronçon *m*; **at a** ~ d'affilée. ● *a* (*fabric*) extensible.

stretcher *n* brancard *m*.

strew *vt* (*pt* **strewed**; *pp* **strewed** *or* **strewn**) (scatter) répandre; (cover) joncher.

strict *a* strict.

stride *vi* (*pt* **strode**; *pp* **stridden**) faire de grands pas. ● *n* grand pas *m*.

strife *n* conflit(s) *m*(*pl*).

strike *vt* (*pt* **struck**) frapper; (*blow*) donner; (*match*) frotter; (*gold*) trouver. ● *vi* faire grève; (attack) attaquer; (*clock*) sonner. ● *n* (of workers) grève *f*; (Mil) attaque *f*; (find) découverte *f*; **on** ~ en grève. □ ~ **off** *or* **out** rayer; ~ **up** (*a friendship*) lier amitié (**with**

avec). **striker** *n* gréviste *mf*; (football) attaquant/-e *m/f*. **striking** *a* frappant.

string *n* ficelle *f*; (of violin, racket) corde *f*; (of pearls) collier *m*; (of lies) chapelet *m*; **the ~s** (Mus) les cordes; **pull ~s** faire jouer ses relations. ● *vt* (*pt* **strung**) (thread) enfiler. **stringed** *a* (*instrument*) à cordes.

stringent *a* rigoureux, strict.

stringy *a* filandreux.

strip *vt/i* (*pt* **stripped**) (undress) (se) déshabiller; (deprive) dépouiller. ● *n* bande *f*.

stripe *n* rayure *f*, raie *f*. **striped** *a* rayé.

strip light *n* néon *m*.

stripper *n* strip-teaseur/-euse *m/f*; (solvent) décapant.

strip-tease *n* strip-tease *m*.

strive *vi* (*pt* **strove**; *pp* **striven**) s'efforcer (**to** de).

strode ⇒STRIDE.

stroke *vt* (with hand) caresser. ● *n* coup *m*; (of pen) trait *m*; (swimming) nage *f*; (Med) attaque *f*, congestion *f*; **at a ~** d'un seul coup.

stroll *vi* flâner; **~ in** entrer tranquillement. ● *n* petit tour *m*. **stroller** *n* (US) poussette *f*.

strong *a* fort; (*shoes, fabric*) solide; **be fifty ~** être fort de cinquante personnes. **~hold** *n* bastion *m*.

strongly *adv* (greatly) fortement; (with energy) avec force; (deeply) profondément.

strove ⇒STRIVE.

struck ⇒STRIKE.

structure *n* (of cell, poem) structure *f*; (building) construction *f*.

struggle *vi* lutter, se battre. ● *n* lutte *f*; (effort) effort *m*; **have a ~ to** avoir du mal à.

strum *vt* (*pt* **strummed**) gratter de.

strung ⇒STRING. ● *a* **~ up** (tense) nerveux.

strut *n* (support) étai *m*. ● *vi* (*pt* **strutted**) se pavaner.

stub *n* bout *m*; (counterfoil) talon *m*. ● *vt* (*pt* **stubbed**) **~ one's toe** se cogner le doigt de pied. □ **~ out** écraser.

stubble *n* (on chin) barbe *f* de plusieurs jours; (remains of wheat) chaume *m*.

stubborn *a* obstiné.

stuck ⇒STICK. ● *a* (jammed) coincé; **I'm ~** (for answer) je sèche. **~-up** *a* 🄸 prétentieux.

stud *n* (on jacket) clou *m*; (for collar) bouton *m*; (stallion) étalon *m*; (horse farm) haras *m*. ● *vt* (*pt* **studded**) clouter.

student *n* (Univ) étudiant/-e *m/f*; (School) élève *mf*. ● *a* (*restaurant, life*) universitaire.

studio *n* studio *m*.

studious *a* (*person*) studieux; (deliberate) étudié.

study *n* étude *f*; (office) bureau *m*. ● *vt/i* étudier.

stuff *n* substance *f*; 🄸 chose(s) *f(pl)*. ● *vt* rembourrer; (*animal*) empailler; (cram) bourrer; (Culin) farcir; (block up) boucher; (put) fourrer. **stuffing** *n* bourre *f*; (Culin) farce *f*.

stuffy *a* (**-ier**, **-iest**) mal aéré; (dull 🄸) vieux jeu *inv*.

stumble *vi* trébucher; **~ across** *or* **on** tomber sur. **stumbling-block** *n* obstacle *m*.

stump *n* (of tree) souche *f*; (of limb) moignon *m*; (of pencil) bout *m*.

stumped *a* embarrassé.

stun *vt* (*pt* **stunned**) étourdir; (bewilder) stupéfier.

stung ⇒STING.

stunk ⇒STINK.

stunning *a* (delightful 🄸) sensationnel.

stunt *vt* (*growth*) retarder. ● *n* (feat [!]) tour *m* de force; (trick [!]) truc *m*; (dangerous) cascade *f*.

stupid *a* stupide, bête. **stupidity** *n* stupidité *f*.

sturdy *a* (**-ier**, **-iest**) robuste.

stutter *vi* bégayer. ● *n* bégaiement *m*.

sty *n* (pigsty) porcherie *f*; (on eye) orgelet *m*.

style *n* style *m*; (fashion) mode *f*; (sort) genre *m*; (pattern) modèle *m*; **do sth in ~** faire qch avec classe. ● *vt* (design) créer; **~ sb's hair** coiffer qn.

stylish *a* élégant.

stylist *n* (of hair) coiffeur/-euse *m/f*.

suave *a* (urbane) courtois; (smooth: pej) doucereux.

subconscious *a & n* inconscient (*m*), subconscient (*m*).

subcontract *vt* sous-traiter.

subdue *vt* (*feeling*) maîtriser; (*country*) subjuguer. **subdued** *a* (*person, mood*) morose; (*light*) tamisé; (*criticism*) contenu.

subject[1] *a* (*state*) soumis; **~ to** soumis à; (liable to, dependent on) sujet à. ● *n* sujet *m*; (focus) objet *m*; (School, Univ) matière *f*; (citizen) ressortissant/-e *m/f*, sujet/-te *m/f*.

subject[2] *vt* soumettre.

subjective *a* subjectif.

subject-matter *n* contenu *m*.

subjunctive *a & n* subjonctif (*m*).

sublet *vt* sous-louer.

submarine *n* sousmarin *m*.

submerge *vt* submerger. ● *vi* plonger.

submissive *a* soumis.

submit *vt/i* (*pt* **submitted**) (se) soumettre (**to** à).

subordinate *a* subalterne; (Gram) subordonné. ● *n* subordonné/-e *m/f*.

subpoena *n* (Jur) citation *f*, assignation *f*.

subscribe *vt/i* verser (de l'argent) (**to** à); **~ to** (*loan, theory*) souscrire à; (*newspaper*) s'abonner à, être abonné à. **subscriber** *n* abonné/-e *m/f*. **subscription** *n* abonnement *m*; (membership dues) cotisation *f*.

subsequent *a* (later) ultérieur; (next) suivant. **subsequently** *adv* par la suite.

subside *vi* (*land*) s'affaisser; (*flood, wind*) baisser.

subsidiary *a* accessoire. ● *n* (Comm) filiale *f*.

subsidize *vt* subventionner. **subsidy** *n* subvention *f*.

substance *n* substance *f*.

substandard *a* de qualité inférieure.

substantial *a* considérable; (*meal*) substantiel.

substitute *n* succédané *m*; (person) remplaçant/-e *m/f*. ● *vt* substituer (**for** à).

subtitle *n* sous-titre *m*.

subtle *a* subtil.

subtract *vt* soustraire.

suburb *n* faubourg *m*, banlieue *f*; **~s** banlieue *f*. **suburban** *a* de banlieue. **suburbia** *n* la banlieue.

subway *n* passage *m* souterrain; (US) métro *m*.

succeed *vi* réussir (**in doing** à faire). ● *vt* (follow) succéder à.

success *n* succès *m*, réussite *f*.

successful *a* réussi, couronné de succès; (favourable) heureux; (in exam) reçu; **be ~ in doing** réussir à faire.

succession *n* succession *f*; **in ~** de suite.

successive *a* successif; **six ~ days** six jours consécutifs.

successor *n* successeur *m*.

such *det & pron* tel(le), tel(le)s;

(so much) tant (de). ● *adv* si; ~ **a book** un tel livre; ~ **books** de tels livres; ~ **courage** tant de courage; ~ **a big house** une si grande maison; ~ **as** comme, tel que; **as** ~ en tant que tel; **there's no** ~ **thing** ça n'existe pas. ~**-and-**~ *a* tel ou tel.

suck *vt* sucer. □ ~ **in** *or* **up** aspirer. **sucker** *n* (rubber pad) ventouse *f*; (person ⊡) dupe *f*.

suction *n* succion *f*.

sudden *a* soudain, subit; **all of a** ~ tout à coup. **suddenly** *adv* subitement, brusquement.

sue *vt* (*pres p* **suing**) poursuivre (en justice).

suede *n* daim *m*.

suffer *vt/i* souffrir; (*loss, attack*) subir. **sufferer** *n* victime *f*, malade *mf*. **suffering** *n* souffrance(s) *f(pl)*.

sufficient *a* (enough) suffisamment de; (big enough) suffisant.

suffix *n* suffixe *m*.

suffocate *vt/i* suffoquer.

sugar *n* sucre *m*. ● *vt* sucrer.

suggest *vt* suggérer. **suggestion** *n* suggestion *f*.

suicidal *a* suicidaire.

suicide *n* suicide *m*; **commit** ~ se suicider.

suit *n* (man's) costume *m*; (woman's) tailleur *m*; (cards) couleur *f*. ● *vt* convenir à; (*garment, style*) aller à; (adapt) adapter.

suitable *a* qui convient (**for** à), convenable. **suitably** *adv* convenablement.

suitcase *n* valise *f*.

suite *n* (rooms) suite *f*; (furniture) mobilier *m*.

suited *a* (**well**) ~ (matched) bien assorti; ~ **to** fait pour, apte à.

sulk *vi* bouder.

sullen *a* maussade.

sultana *n* raisin *m* de Smyrne, raisin *m* sec.

sultry *a* (**-ier, -iest**) étouffant, lourd; (fig) sensuel.

sum *n* somme *f*; (in arithmetic) calcul *m*. ● *vt/i* (*pt* **summed**) ~ **up** résumer, récapituler; (assess) évaluer.

summarize *vt* résumer.

summary *n* résumé *m*. ● *a* sommaire.

summer *n* été *m*. ● *a* d'été. ~**time** *n* (season) été *m*.

summery *a* estival.

summit *n* sommet *m*; ~ (**conference**) (Pol) (conférence *f* au) sommet *m*.

summon *vt* appeler; ~ **sb to a meeting** convoquer qn à une réunion; ~ **up** (*strength, courage*) rassembler.

summons *n* (Jur) assignation *f*. ● *vt* assigner.

sun *n* soleil *m*. ● *vt* (*pt* **sunned**) ~ **oneself** se chauffer au soleil. ~**burn** *n* coup *m* de soleil.

Sunday *n* dimanche *m*. ~ **school** *n* catéchisme *m*.

sundry *a* divers; **sundries** articles *mpl* divers; **all and** ~ tout le monde.

sunflower *n* tournesol *m*.

sung ⇒SING.

sun-glasses *npl* lunettes *fpl* de soleil.

sunk ⇒SINK.

sunken *a* (*ship*) submergé; (*eyes*) creux.

sunlight *n* soleil *m*.

sunny *a* (**-ier, -iest**) ensoleillé.

sun: ~**rise** *n* lever *m* du soleil. ~**-roof** *n* toit *m* ouvrant. ~ **screen** *n* filtre *m* solaire. ~**set** *n* coucher *m* du soleil. ~**shine** *n* soleil *m*. ~**stroke** *n* insolation *f*.

sun-tan *n* bronzage *m*. ~ **lotion**

n lotion *f* solaire. ~ **oil** *n* huile *f* solaire.

super *a* [!] formidable.

superb *a* superbe.

superficial *a* superficiel.

superfluous *a* superflu.

superimpose *vt* superposer (**on** à).

superintendent *n* directeur/ -trice *m/f*; (of police) commissaire *m*.

superior *a & n* supérieur/-e (*m/ f*).

superlative *a* suprême. ● *n* (Gram) superlatif *m*.

supermarket *n* supermarché *m*.

supersede *vt* remplacer, supplanter.

superstition *n* superstition *f*. **superstitious** *a* superstitieux.

superstore *n* hypermarché *m*.

supervise *vt* surveiller, diriger. **supervision** *n* surveillance *f*. **supervisor** *n* surveillant/-e *m/f*; (shop) chef *m* de rayon; (firm) chef *m* de service.

supper *n* dîner *m*; (late at night) souper *m*.

supple *a* souple.

supplement[1] *n* supplément *m*. **supplementary** *a* supplémentaire.

supplement[2] *vt* compléter.

supplier *n* fournisseur *m*.

supply *vt* fournir; (equip) pourvoir; (feed) alimenter (**with** en). ● *n* provision *f*; (of gas) alimentation *f*; **supplies** (food) vivres *mpl*; (material) fournitures *fpl*.

support *vt* soutenir; (*family*) assurer la subsistance de. ● *n* soutien *m*, appui *m*; (Tech) support *m*. **supporter** *n* partisan/ -e *m/f*; (Sport) supporter *m*. **supportive** *a* qui soutient et encourage.

suppose *vt/i* supposer; **be ~d to do** être censé faire, devoir faire; **supposing he comes** supposons qu'il vienne. **supposedly** *adv* soi-disant, prétendument.

suppress *vt* (put an end to) supprimer; (restrain) réprimer; (stifle) étouffer.

supreme *a* suprême.

surcharge *n* supplément *m*; (tax) surtaxe *f*.

sure *a* sûr; **make ~ of** s'assurer de; **make ~ that** vérifier que. ● *adv* (US [!]) pour sûr. **surely** *adv* sûrement.

surf *n* ressac *m*. ● *vi* faire du surf; (*Internet*) surfer.

surface *n* surface *f*. ● *a* superficiel. ● *vt* revêtir. ● *vi* faire surface; (fig) réapparaître.

surfer *n* surfeur/-euse *m/f*; (*Internet*) internaute *mf*.

surge *vi* (*waves, crowd*) déferler; (increase) monter. ● *n* (wave) vague *f*; (rise) montée *f*.

surgeon *n* chirurgien *m*.

surgery *n* chirurgie *f*; (office) cabinet *m*; (session) consultation *f*; **need ~** devoir être opéré.

surgical *a* chirurgical. ~ **spirit** *n* alcool *m* à 90 degrés.

surly *a* (**-ier, -iest**) bourru.

surname *n* nom *m* de famille.

surplus *n* surplus *m*. ● *a* en surplus.

surprise *n* surprise *f*. ● *vt* surprendre. **surprised** *a* surpris (**at** de). **surprising** *a* surprenant.

surrender *vi* se rendre. ● *vt* (hand over) remettre; (Mil) rendre. ● *n* (Mil) reddition *f*; (of passport) remise *f*.

surround *vt* entourer; (Mil) encercler. **surrounding** *a* environnant. **surroundings** *npl* environs *mpl*; (setting) cadre *m*.

surveillance *n* surveillance *f*.

survey[1] *vt* (review) passer en

revue; (inquire into) enquêter sur; (*building*) inspecter.

survey² *n* (inquiry) enquête *f*; inspection *f*; (general view) vue *f* d'ensemble.

surveyor *n* expert *m* (géomètre).

survival *n* survie *f*.

survive *vt/i* survivre (à). **survivor** *n* survivant/-e *m/f*.

susceptible *a* sensible (**to** à); ~ **to** (prone to) prédisposé à.

suspect¹ *vt* soupçonner; (doubt) douter de.

suspect² *n & a* suspect/-e (*m/f*).

suspend *vt* (hang, stop) suspendre; (*licence*) retirer provisoirement. **suspended sentence** *n* condamnation *f* avec sursis.

suspender *n* jarretelle *f*; ~**s** (braces: US) bretelles *fpl*. ~ **belt** *n* porte-jarretelles *m*.

suspension *n* suspension *f*; retrait *m* provisoire.

suspicion *n* soupçon *m*; (distrust) méfiance *f*.

suspicious *a* soupçonneux; (causing suspicion) suspect; **be ~ of** se méfier de. **suspiciously** *adv* de façon suspecte.

sustain *vt* supporter; (*effort*) soutenir; (suffer) subir.

sustenance *n* (food) nourriture *f*; (nourishment) valeur *f* nutritive.

swallow *vt/i* avaler; ~ **up** (absorb, engulf) engloutir. ● *n* hirondelle *f*.

swam ⇒SWIM.

swamp *n* marais *m*. ● *vt* (flood, overwhelm) submerger.

swan *n* cygne *m*.

swap *vt/i* (*pt* **swapped**) ⊡ échanger. ● *n* ⊡ échange *m*.

swarm *n* essaim *m*. ● *vi* fourmiller; ~ **into** *or* **round** (*crowd*) envahir.

swat *vt* (*pt* **swatted**) (*fly*) écraser.

sway *vt/i* (se) balancer; (influence) influencer. ● *n* balancement *m*; (rule) empire *m*.

swear *vt/i* (*pt* **swore**; *pp* **sworn**) jurer (**to sth** de qch); ~ **at** injurier; ~ **by sth** ⊡ ne jurer que par qch. ~**-word** *n* juron *m*.

sweat *n* sueur *f*. ● *vi* suer.

sweater *n* pull-over *m*.

sweat-shirt *n* sweat-shirt *m*.

swede *n* rutabaga *m*.

Swede *n* Suédois/-e *m/f*. **Sweden** *n* Suède *f*.

Swedish *a* suédois. ● *n* (Ling) suédois *m*.

sweep *vt/i* (*pt* **swept**) (*floor*) balayer; (carry away) emporter, entraîner; (*chimney*) ramoner. ● *n* coup *m* de balai; (curve) courbe *f*; (mouvement) geste *m*, mouvement *m*; (for chimneys) ramoneur *m*. □ ~ **by** passer rapidement *or* majestueusement. **sweeper** *n* (for carpet) balai *m* mécanique; (football) libero *m*.

sweet *a* (not sour, pleasant) doux; (not savoury) sucré; (charming ⊡) gentil; **have a ~ tooth** aimer les sucreries. ● *n* bonbon *m*; (dish) dessert *m*. ~**corn** *n* maïs *m*.

sweeten *vt* sucrer; (fig) adoucir. **sweetener** *n* édulcorant *m*.

sweetheart *n* petit/-e ami/-e *m/f*; (term of endearment) chéri/-e *m/f*.

sweetly *adv* gentiment.

sweetness *n* douceur *f*; goût *m* sucré.

sweet pea *n* pois *m* de senteur.

swell *vt/i* (*pt* **swelled**; *pp* **swollen** *or* **swelled**) (increase) grossir; (expand) (se) gonfler; (*hand, face*) enfler. ● *n* (of sea) houle *f*. **swelling** *n* (Med) enflure *f*.

sweltering *a* étouffant.

swept ⇒SWEEP.

swerve *vi* faire un écart.

S

swift *a* rapide. ● *n* (bird) martinet *m*.

swim *vi* (*pt* **swam**; *pp* **swum**; *pres p* **swimming**) nager; (be dizzy) tourner. ● *vt* traverser à la nage; (*distance*) nager. ● *n* baignade *f*; **go for a ~** aller se baigner. **swimmer** *n* nageur/-euse *m/f*. **swimming** *n* natation *f*.

swimming-pool *n* piscine *f*.

swim-suit *n* maillot *m* (de bain).

swindle *vt* escroquer. ● *n* escroquerie *f*.

swine *npl* (pigs) pourceaux *mpl*. ● *n inv* (person [!]) salaud *m*.

swing *vt/i* (*pt* **swung**) (se) balancer; (turn round) tourner; (*pendulum*) osciller. ● *n* balancement *m*; (seat) balançoire *f*; (of opinion) revirement *m* (**towards** en faveur de); (Mus) rythme *m*; **be in full ~** battre son plein. □ **~ round** (*person*) se retourner.

swipe *vt* (hit [!]) frapper; (steal [!]) piquer.

swirl *vi* tourbillonner. ● *n* tourbillon *m*.

Swiss *a* suisse. ● *n inv* Suisse *mf*.

switch *n* bouton *m* (électrique), interrupteur *m*; (shift) changement *m*, revirement *m*. ● *vt* (transfer) transférer; (exchange) échanger (**for** contre); (reverse positions of) changer de place; **~ trains** (change) changer de train. ● *vi* changer. □ **~ off** éteindre; **~ on** mettre, allumer.

switchboard *n* standard *m*.

Switzerland *n* Suisse *f*.

swivel *vt/i* (*pt* **swivelled**) (faire) pivoter.

swollen ⇒SWELL.

swoop *vi* (*bird*) fondre; (*police*) faire une descente, foncer. ● *n* (police raid) descente *f*.

sword *n* épée *f*.

swore ⇒SWEAR.

sworn ⇒SWEAR. ● *a* (*enemy*) juré; (*ally*) dévoué.

swot *vt/i* (*pt* **swotted**) (study [!]) bûcher [!]. ● *n* [!] bûcheur/-euse *m/f* [!].

swum ⇒SWIM.

swung ⇒SWING.

syllabus *n* (*pl* **~es**) (School, Univ) programme *m*.

symbol *n* symbole *m*. **symbolic(al)** *a* symbolique. **symbolize** *vt* symboliser.

symmetrical *a* symétrique.

sympathetic *a* compatissant; (fig) compréhensif.

sympathize *vi* **~ with** (pity) plaindre; (fig) comprendre les sentiments de. **sympathizer** *n* sympathisant/-e *m/f*.

sympathy *n* (pity) compassion *f*; (fig) compréhension *f*; (solidarity) solidarité *f*; (condolences) condoléances *fpl*; (affinity) affinité *f*; **be in ~ with** comprendre, être en accord avec.

symptom *n* symptôme *m*.

synagogue *n* synagogue *f*.

synonym *n* synonyme *m*.

synopsis *n* (*pl* **-opses**) résumé *m*.

syntax *n* syntaxe *f*.

synthesis *n* (*pl* **-theses**) synthèse *f*.

synthetic *a* synthétique.

syringe *n* seringue *f*.

syrup *n* (liquid) sirop *m*; (treacle) mélasse *f* raffinée.

system *n* système *m*; (body) organisme *m*; (order) méthode *f*. **systematic** *a* systématique.

systems analyst *n* analyste-programmeur/-euse *m/f*.

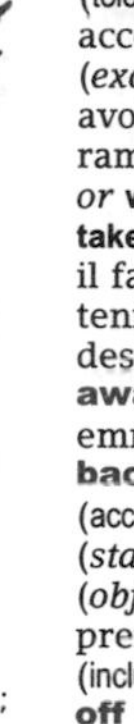

tab *n* (on can) languette *f*; (on garment) patte *f*; (label) étiquette *f*; (US ☐) addition *f*; (Comput) tabulatrice *f*; (setting) tabulation *f*.

table *n* table *f*. **at (the) ~** à table; **lay** *or* **set the ~** mettre la table. ● *vt* (*motion*) présenter. **~-cloth** *n* nappe *f*. **~-mat** *n* set *m* de table. **~spoon** *n* cuillère *f* de service.

tablet *n* (of stone) plaque *f*; (drug) comprimé *m*.

table tennis *n* tennis *m* de table; ping-pong® *m*.

taboo *n & a* tabou (*m*).

tacit *a* tacite.

tack *n* (nail) clou *m*; (stitch) point *m* de bâti; (course of action) voie *f*. ● *vt* (nail) clouer; (stitch) bâtir; (add) ajouter. ● *vi* (Naut) louvoyer.

tackle *n* équipement *m*; (in soccer) tacle *m*; (in rugby) plaquage *m*. ● *vt* (*problem*) s'attaquer à; (*player*) tacler, plaquer.

tact *n* tact *m*. **tactful** *a* plein de tact.

tactics *npl* tactique *f*.

tadpole *n* têtard *m*.

tag *n* (label) étiquette *f*. ● *vt* (*pt* **tagged**) (label) étiqueter. ● *vi* **~ along** ☐ suivre.

tail *n* queue *f*; **~s** (coat) habit *m*; **~s!** (on coin) pile! ● *vt* (follow) filer. ● *vi* **~ away** *or* **off** diminuer. **~-back** *n* bouchon *m*. **~-gate** *n* hayon *m*.

tailor *n* tailleur *m*. ● *vt* (*garment*) façonner; (fig) adapter. **~-made** *a* fait sur mesure.

take *vt/i* (*pt* **took**; *pp* **taken**) prendre (**from sb** à qn); (carry) emporter, porter (**to** à); (escort) emmener; (contain) contenir; (tolerate) supporter; (accept) accepter; (*prize*) remporter; (*exam*) passer; (*precedence*) avoir; (*view*) adopter; **~ sb home** ramener qn chez lui; **be taken by** *or* **with** être impressionné par; **be taken ill** tomber malade; **it ~s time** il faut du temps pour. ☐ **~ after** tenir de; **~ apart** démonter; (fig) descendre en flammes ☐; **~ away** (*object*) enlever; (*person*) emmener; (*pain*) supprimer; **~ back** reprendre; (return) rendre; (accompany) raccompagner; (*statement*) retirer; **~ down** (*object*) descendre; (*notes*) prendre; **~ in** (*object*) rentrer; (include) inclure; (cheat) tromper; **~ off** (Aviat) décoller; **~ sth off** enlever qch; **~ sb off** imiter qn; **~ on** (*task, staff, passenger*) prendre; (*challenger*) relever le défi de; **~ out** sortir; (*stain*) enlever; **~ over** *vt* (*country, firm*) prendre le contrôle de; *vi* prendre le pouvoir; **~ over from** remplacer; **~ part** participer (**in** à); **~ place** avoir lieu; **~ to** se prendre d'amitié pour; (*activity*) prendre goût à; **~ to doing** se mettre à faire; **~ up** (*object*) monter; (*hobby*) se mettre à; (occupy) prendre; (resume) reprendre; **~ up with** se lier avec. **~-away** *n* (meal) repas *m* à emporter. **~-off** *n* (Aviat) décollage *m*. **~over** *n* (Pol) prise *f* de pouvoir; (Comm) rachat *m*.

tale *n* conte *m*; (report) récit *m*; (lie) histoire *f*.

talent *n* talent *m*. **talented** *a* doué.

talk *vt/i* parler; (chat) bavarder; **~ sb into doing** persuader qn de faire; **~ sth over** discuter de qch.

T

● *n* (talking) propos *mpl*; (conversation) conversation *f*; (lecture) exposé *m*.

talkative *a* bavard.

tall *a* (high) haut; (*person*) grand.

tame *a* apprivoisé; (dull) insipide. ● *vt* apprivoiser; (*lion*) dompter.

tamper *vi* ~ **with** (*lock, machine*) tripoter; (*accounts, evidence*) trafiquer.

tan *vt/i* (*pt* **tanned**) bronzer; (*hide*) tanner. ● *n* bronzage *m*.

tangerine *n* mandarine *f*.

tangle *vt/i* ~ (**up**) s'emmêler. ● *n* enchevêtrement *m*.

tank *n* réservoir *m*; (vat) cuve *f*; (for fish) aquarium *m*; (Mil) char *m* (de combat).

tanker *n* (lorry) camion-citerne *m*; (ship) navire-citerne *m*; **oil/petrol** ~ pétrolier *m*.

tantrum *n* crise *f* (de colère).

tap *n* (for water) robinet *m*; (knock) petit coup *m*; **on** ~ disponible. ● *vt* (*pt* **tapped**) (knock) taper (doucement); (*resources*) exploiter; (*phone*) mettre sur écoute.

tape *n* bande *f* (magnétique); (cassette) cassette *f*; (video) cassette *f* vidéo; (fabric) ruban *m*; (sticky) scotch® *m*. ● *vt* (record) enregistrer; ~ **sth to sth** coller qch à qch. ~**-measure** *n* mètre *m* ruban. ~ **recorder** *n* magnétophone *m*.

tapestry *n* tapisserie *f*.

tar *n* goudron *m*. ● *vt* (*pt* **tarred**) goudronner.

target *n* cible *f*; (objective) objectif *m*. ● *vt* (*city*) prendre pour cible; (*weapon*) diriger; (in marketing) viser.

tariff *n* (price list) tarif *m*; (on imports) droit *m* de douane.

tarmac, **Tarmac®** *n* macadam *m*; (runway) piste *f*.

tarpaulin *n* bâche *f*.

tarragon *n* estragon *m*.

tart *n* tarte *f*. ● *a* aigrelet.

task *n* tâche *f*.

taste *n* goût *m*; (experience) aperçu *m*. ● *vt* (eat, enjoy) goûter à; (try) goûter; (perceive taste of) sentir (le goût de). ● *vi* ~ **of** *or* **like** avoir un goût de. **tasteful** *a* de bon goût.

tattoo *vt* tatouer. ● *n* tatouage *m*.

tatty *a* (**-ier**, **-iest**) [I] miteux.

taught ⇒TEACH.

taunt *vt* railler. ● *n* raillerie *f*.

Taurus *n* Taureau *m*.

tax *n* (on goods, services) taxe *f*; (on income) impôt *m*. ● *vt* imposer; (put to test: fig) mettre à l'épreuve. **taxable** *a* imposable. **taxation** *n* imposition *f*; (taxes) impôts *mpl*.

tax: ~**-collector** *n* percepteur *m*. ~**-deductible** *a* déductible des impôts. ~ **disc** *n* vignette *f*. ~**-free** *a* exempt d'impôts. ~ **haven** *n* paradis *m* fiscal.

taxi *n* taxi *m*. ~ **rank** *n* station *f* de taxi.

tax: ~**payer** *n* contribuable *mf*. ~ **relief** *n* dégrèvement *m* fiscal. ~ **return** *n* déclaration *f* d'impôts.

tea *n* (drink, meal) thé *m*; (children's snack) goûter *m*; ~ **bag** sachet *m* de thé.

teach *vt* (*pt* **taught**) apprendre (**sb sth** qch à qn); (in school) enseigner (**sb sth** qch à qn). ● *vi* enseigner. **teacher** *n* enseignant/-e *m/f*; (secondary) professeur *m*; (primary) instituteur/-trice *m/f*.

team *n* équipe *f*; (of animals) attelage *m*. ● *vi* ~ **up** faire équipe (**with** avec).

teapot *n* théière *f*.

tear[1] *vt/i* (*pt* **tore**; *pp* **torn**) (se) déchirer; (snatch) arracher (**from** à); (rush) aller à toute vitesse. ● *n* déchirure *f*.

tear[2] *n* larme *f*; **in** ~**s** en larmes. ~**-gas** *n* gaz *m* lacrymogène.

tease *vt* taquiner. ● *n* taquin/-e *m/f*.

tea: **~-shop** *n* salon *m* de thé. **~spoon** *n* petite cuillère *f*.

teat *n* tétine *f*.

tea-towel *n* torchon *m*.

technical *a* technique.

technician *n* technicien/-ne *m/f*.

technique *n* technique *f*.

techno *n* (Mus) techno *f*.

technology *n* technologie *f*.

teddy *a* **~ bear** ours *m* en peluche.

tedious *a* ennuyeux.

tee *n* (golf) tee *m*.

teenage *a* (*girl, boy*) adolescent; (*fashion*) des adolescents. **teenager** *n* jeune *mf*, adolescent/-e *m/f*.

teens *npl* **in one's ~** adolescent.

teeth ⇒TOOTH.

teethe *vi* faire ses dents.

teetotaller *n* personne *f* qui ne boit pas d'alcool.

telecommunications *npl* télécommunications *fpl*.

telecommuting *n* télétravail *m*.

teleconferencing *n* téléconférence *f*.

telegram *n* télégramme *m*.

telegraph *n* télégraphe *m*. ● *a* télégraphique.

telephone *n* téléphone *m*. ● *vt* (*person*) téléphoner à; (*message*) téléphoner. ● *vi* téléphoner. **~ book** annuaire *m*. **~ booth**, **~-box** *n* cabine *f* téléphonique. **~ call** *n* coup *m* de téléphone. **~ number** *n* numéro *m* de téléphone.

telephoto *a* **~ lens** téléobjectif *m*.

telescope *n* télescope *m*. ● *vt/i* (se) télescoper.

teletext *n* télétexte *m*.

televise *vt* téléviser.

television *n* télévision *f*; **~ set** poste *m* de télévision, téléviseur *m*.

telex *n* télex *m*. ● *vt* envoyer par télex.

tell *vt* (*pt* **told**) dire (**sb sth** qch à qn); (*story*) raconter; (distinguish) distinguer; **~ sb to do sth** dire à qn de faire qch; **~ sth from sth** voir la différence entre qch et qch. ● *vi* (show) avoir un effet; (know) savoir. □ **~ off** 🄸 gronder.

temp *n* intérimaire *mf*. ● *vi* faire de l'intérim.

temper *n* humeur *f*; (anger) colère *f*; **lose one's ~** se mettre en colère.

temperament *n* tempérament *m*. **temperamental** *a* capricieux.

temperature *n* température *f*; **have a ~** avoir de la fièvre *or* de la température.

temple *n* temple *m*; (of head) tempe *f*.

temporary *a* temporaire, provisoire.

tempt *vt* tenter; **~ sb to do** donner envie à qn de faire.

ten *a & n* dix (*m*).

tenacious *a* tenace.

tenancy *n* location *f*. **tenant** *n* locataire *mf*.

tend *vt* s'occuper de. ● *vi* **~ to** (be apt to) avoir tendance à; (look after) s'occuper de. **tendency** *n* tendance *f*.

tender *a* tendre; (sore, painful) sensible. ● *vt* offrir, donner. ● *vi* faire une soumission. ● *n* (Comm) soumission *f*; **be legal ~** (money) avoir cours.

tendon *n* tendon *m*.

tennis *n* tennis *m*. ● *a* (*court, match*) de tennis; **~ shoes** tennis *mpl*.

tenor *n* (meaning) sens *m* général; (Mus) ténor *m*.

tense *n* (Gram) temps *m*. ● *a*

tendu. ● *vt* (*muscles*) tendre, raidir. ● *vi* (*face*) se crisper.
tension *n* tension *f*.
tent *n* tente *f*.
tentative *a* provisoire; (hesitant) timide.
tenth *a* & *n* dixième (*mf*).
tepid *a* tiède.
term *n* (word, limit) terme *m*; (of imprisonment) temps *m*; (School) trimestre *m*; **~s** conditions *fpl*; **on good/bad ~s** en bons/mauvais termes; **in the short/long ~** à court/long terme; **come to ~s with sth** accepter qch; **~ of office** (Pol) mandat *m*. ● *vt* appeler.
terminal *a* (*point*) terminal; (*illness*) incurable. ● *n* (oil, computer) terminal *m*; (Rail) terminus *m*; (Electr) borne *f*; (**air**) **~** aérogare *f*.
terminate *vt* mettre fin à. ● *vi* prendre fin.
terminus *n* (*pl* **-ni**) (station) terminus *m*.
terrace *n* terrasse *f*; (houses) rangée *f* de maisons contiguës; **the ~s** (Sport) les gradins *mpl*.
terracotta *n* terre *f* cuite.
terrible *a* affreux, atroce.
terrific *a* (huge) énorme; (great [!]) formidable.
terrify *vt* terrifier; **be terrified of** avoir très peur de.
territory *n* territoire *m*.
terror *n* terreur *f*.
terrorism *n* terrorisme *m*. **terrorist** *n* terroriste *mf*.
test *n* épreuve *f*; (written exam) contrôle *m*; (of machine, product) essai *m*; (of sample) analyse *f*; **driving ~** examen *m* du permis de conduire. ● *vt* évaluer; (School) contrôler; (*machine, product*) essayer; (*sample*) analyser; (*patience, strength*) mettre à l'épreuve. ● *vi* **~ for** faire une recherche de.
testament *n* testament *m*; **Old/New T~** Ancien/Nouveau Testament *m*.
testicle *n* testicule *m*.
testify *vt/i* témoigner (**to** de; **that** que).
testimony *n* témoignage *m*.
test tube *n* éprouvette *f*.
tetanus *n* tétanos *m*.
text *n* texte *m*. **~book** *n* manuel *m*.
texture *n* (of paper) grain *m*; (of fabric) texture *f*.
Thames *n* **the ~** la Tamise.
than *conj* que, qu'; (with numbers) de; **more/less ~ ten** plus/moins de dix.
thank *vt* remercier; **~ you!**, **~s!** merci! **thankful** *a* reconnaissant (**for** de). **thanks** *npl* remerciements *mpl*; **~s to** grâce à. **Thanksgiving** (**Day**) *n* (US) jour *m* d'Action de Grâces (*fête nationale*).

that *pl* **those**

●*determiner*

····➤ ce, cet, cette, ces; **~ dog** ce chien; **~ man** cet homme; **~ woman** cette femme; **those books** ces livres; **at ~ moment** à ce moment-là.

! To distinguish from **this** and **these**, you need to add *-là* after the noun: **I prefer that car** *je préfère cette voiture-là.*

●*pronoun*

····➤ cela, ça, ce; **what's ~?, what are those?** qu'est-ce que c'est (que ça)?; **who's ~?** qui est-ce?; **~ is my brother** c'est *or* voilà mon frère; **those are my parents** ce sont mes parents.

····➤ (emphatic) celui-là, celle-là, ceux-là, celles-là; **all the dresses**

are nice but I like ~/those best toutes les robes sont jolies mais je préfère celle-là/celles-là.

● *relative pronoun*

····➤ (for subject) qui; **the man ~ stole the car** l'homme qui a volé la voiture.

····➤ (for object) que; **the girl ~ I met** la fille que j'ai rencontrée.

! With a preposition, use *lequel/laquelle/lesquels/lesquelles*: **the chair ~ I was sitting on** *la chaise sur laquelle j'étais assis.*

! With a preposition that translates as *à*, use *auquel/à laquelle/auxquels/auxquelles*: **the girls ~ I was talking to** *les filles auxquelles je parlais.*

! With a preposition that translates as *de*, use *dont*: **the people ~ I've talked about** *les personnes dont j'ai parlé.*

● *conjunction* que; **she said ~ she would do it** elle a dit qu'elle le ferait.

thatched *a* de chaume; **~ cottage** chaumière *f.*

thaw *vt/i* (faire) dégeler; (*snow*) (faire) fondre. ● *n* dégel *m.*

the *determiner*

····➤ le, l', la, les; **~ dog** le chien; **~ tree** l'arbre; **~ chair** la chaise; **to ~ shops** aux magasins.

! With a preposition that translates as *à*: *à + le = au* and *à + les = aux.*

theatre *n* théâtre *m.*

theft *n* vol *m.*

their *a* leur, *pl* leurs.

theirs *pron* le *or* la leur, les leurs.

them *pron* les; (after preposition) eux, elles; (**to**) **~** leur; **phone ~!** téléphone-leur!; **I know ~** je les connais; **both of ~** tous/toutes les deux.

themselves *pron* eux-mêmes, elles-mêmes; (reflexive) se; (after preposition) eux, elles.

then *adv* alors; (next) ensuite, puis; (therefore) alors, donc. ● *a* d'alors; **from ~ on** dès lors.

theology *n* théologie *f.*

theory *n* théorie *f.*

therapy *n* thérapie *f.*

there *adv* là; (with verb) y; (over there) là-bas; **he goes ~** il y va; **on ~** là-dessus; **~ is, ~ are** il y a; (pointing) voilà. ● *interj*; **~, ~!** allons, allons!

therefore *adv* donc.

thermal *a* thermique.

thermometer *n* thermomètre *m.*

Thermos® *n* thermos® *m or f inv.*

thermostat *n* thermostat *m.*

thesaurus *n* (*pl* **-ri**) dictionnaire *m* de synonymes.

these ⇒THIS.

thesis *n* (*pl* **theses**) thèse *f.*

they *pron* ils, elles; (emphatic) eux, elles; (people in general) on.

thick *a* épais; (stupid) bête; **be 6 cm ~** avoir 6 cm d'épaisseur.

thief *n* (*pl* **thieves**) voleur/-euse *m/f.*

thigh *n* cuisse *f.*

thin *a* (**thinner, thinnest**) mince; (*person*) maigre, mince; (sparse) clairsemé; (fine) fin. ● *vt/i* (*pt* **thinned**) **~** (**down**) (*paint*) diluer; (*soup*) allonger.

thing *n* chose *f*; **~s** (belongings) affaires *fpl*; **the best ~ is to** le mieux est de; **the** (**right**) **~** ce qu'il faut (**for sb** à qn).

think *vt/i* (*pt* **thought**) penser

T

(**about**, **of** à); (carefully) réfléchir (**about**, **of** à); (believe) croire; **I ~ so** je crois que oui; **~ of doing** envisager de faire. □ **~ over** bien réfléchir à; **~ up** inventer.

third *a* troisième. ● *n* troisième *mf*; (fraction) tiers *m*. **T~ World** *n* tiers-monde *m*.

thirst *n* soif *f*.

thirsty *a* **be ~** avoir soif; **make ~** donner soif à.

thirteen *a & n* treize (*m*).

thirty *a & n* trente (*m*).

this *pl* **these**

● *determiner*

····➤ ce/cet/cette/ces; **~ dog** ce chien; **~ man** cet homme; **~ woman** cette femme; **these books** ces livres.

> **!** To distinguish from **that** and **those**, you need to add *-ci* after the noun: **I prefer this car** *je préfère cette voiture-ci*.

● *pronoun*

····➤ ce; **what's ~?, what are these?** qu'est-ce que c'est?; **who is ~?** qui est-ce?; **~ is the kitchen** voici la cuisine; **~ is Sophie** je te *or* vous présente Sophie; **these are your things** ce sont tes affaires.

····➤ (emphatic) celui-ci/celle-ci/ceux-ci/celles-ci; **all the dresses are nice but I like ~/these best** toutes les robes sont jolies mais je préfère celle-ci/celles-ci.

thistle *n* chardon *m*.

thorn *n* épine *f*.

thorough *a* (detailed) approfondi; (meticulous) minutieux. **thoroughly** *adv* (*clean, study*) à fond; (very) tout à fait.

those ⇒THAT.

though *conj* bien que. ● *adv* quand même.

thought ⇒THINK. ● *n* pensée *f*, idée *f*. **thoughtful** *a* pensif; (kind) prévenant.

thousand *a & n* mille (*m inv*); **~s of** des milliers de. **thousandth** *a & n* millième (*mf*).

thread *n* (yarn & fig) fil *m*; (of screw) pas *m*. ● *vt* enfiler; **~ one's way** se faufiler.

threat *n* menace *f*. **threaten** *vt/i* menacer (**with** de).

three *a & n* trois (*m*).

threw ⇒THROW.

thrill *n* frisson *m*; (pleasure) plaisir *m*. ● *vt* transporter (de joie); **be ~ed** être ravi. ● *vi* frissonner (de joie).

thrive *vi* (*pt* **thrived** *or* **throve**; *pp* **thrived** *or* **thriven**) prospérer; **he ~s on it** cela lui réussit.

throat *n* gorge *f*; **have a sore ~** avoir mal à la gorge.

throb *vi* (*pt* **throbbed**) (*heart*) battre; (*engine*) vibrer. ● *n* (pain) élancement *m*; (of engine) vibration *f*. **throbbing** *a* (*pain*) lancinant.

throne *n* trône *m*.

through *prep* à travers; (during) pendant; (by means or way of, out of) par; (by reason of) grâce à, à cause de. ● *adv* à travers; (entirely) jusqu'au bout. ● *a* (*train*) direct; **be ~** (finished) avoir fini; **come** *or* **go ~** (cross, pierce) traverser; **I'm putting you ~** je vous passe votre correspondant.

throughout *prep* **~ the country** dans tout le pays; **~ the day** pendant toute la journée. ● *adv* (place) partout; (time) tout le temps.

throw *vt* (*pt* **threw**; *pp* **thrown**) jeter, lancer; (baffle) déconcerter; **~ a party** faire une fête. ● *n* jet *m*; (of dice) coup *m*. □ **~ away** jeter; **~ off** (get rid of) se débarrasser de; ~ **out** jeter; (*person*) expulser; (reject) rejeter; ~ **up** (*arms*) lever; (vomit [!]) vomir.

thrust *vt* (*pt* **thrust**) pousser. ● *n* poussée *f*.

thud *n* bruit *m* sourd.

thug *n* voyou *m*.

thumb *n* pouce *m*. ● *vt* (*book*) feuilleter; ~ **a lift** faire de l'auto-stop. ~**-index** *n* répertoire *m* à onglets.

thump *vt/i* cogner (sur); (*heart*) battre fort. ● *n* coup *m*.

thunder *n* tonnerre *m*. ● *vi* (*weather, person*) tonner. ~**storm** *n* orage *m*.

Thursday *n* jeudi *m*.

thus *adv* ainsi.

thwart *vt* contrecarrer.

thyme *n* thym *m*.

tick *n* (sound) tic-tac *m*; (mark) coche *f*; (moment [!]) instant *m*; (insect) tique *f*. ● *vi* faire tic-tac. ● *vt* ~ (**off**) cocher. □ ~ **over** tourner au ralenti.

ticket *n* billet *m*; (for bus, cloakroom) ticket *m*; (label) étiquette *f*. ~**-collector** *n* contrôleur/-euse *m/f*. ~**-office** *n* guichet *m*.

tickle *vt* chatouiller; (amuse: fig) amuser. ● *n* chatouillement *m*.

tidal *a* (*river*) à marées; ~ **wave** raz-de-marée *m inv*.

tide *n* marée *f*; (of events) cours *m*.

tidy *a* (**-ier, -iest**) (*room*) bien rangé; (*appearance, work*) soigné; (methodical) ordonné; (amount [!]) joli. ● *vt/i* ~ (**up**) faire du rangement; ~ **sth** (**up**) ranger qch; ~ **oneself up** s'arranger.

tie *vt* (*pres p* **tying**) attacher; (*knot*) faire; (*scarf*) nouer; (link) lier. ● *vi* (in football) faire match nul; (in race) être ex aequo. ● *n* (necktie) cravate *f*; (fastener) attache *f*; (link) lien *m*; (draw) match *m* nul. □ ~ **down** attacher; ~ **in with** être lié à; ~ **up** attacher; (*money*) immobiliser; (occupy) occuper.

tier *n* étage *m*, niveau *m*; (in stadium) gradin *m*.

tiger *n* tigre *m*.

tight *a* (*clothes, budget*) serré; (*grip*) ferme; (*rope*) tendu; (*security*) strict; (*angle*) aigu. ● *adv* (*hold, sleep*) bien; (*squeeze*) fort.

tighten *vt/i* (se) tendre; (*bolt*) (se) resserrer; (*control*) renforcer.

tights *npl* collant *m*.

tile *n* (on wall, floor) carreau *m*; (on roof) tuile *f*. ● *vt* carreler; couvrir de tuiles.

till *n* caisse *f* (enregistreuse). ● *vt* (*land*) cultiver. ● *prep & conj* = UNTIL.

timber *n* bois *m* (de construction); (trees) arbres *mpl*.

time *n* temps *m*; (moment) moment *m*; (epoch) époque *f*; (by clock) heure *f*; (occasion) fois *f*; (rhythm) mesure *f*. ~**s** (multiplying) fois *fpl*; **any** ~ n'importe quand; **for the** ~ **being** pour le moment; **from** ~ **to** ~ de temps en temps; **have a good** ~ s'amuser; **in no** ~ en un rien de temps; **in** ~ à temps; (eventually) avec le temps; **a long** ~ longtemps; **on** ~ à l'heure; **what's the** ~? quelle heure est-il?; ~ **off** du temps libre. ● *vt* choisir le moment de; (measure) minuter; (Sport) chronométrer. ~**-limit** *n* délai *m*.

timer *n* minuterie *f*; (for cooker) minuteur *m*.

time: ~**-scale** *n* délais *mpl*. ~**table** *n* horaire *m*. ~ **zone** *n* fuseau *m* horaire.

timid *a* timide; (fearful) peureux.

tin *n* étain *m*; (container) boîte *f*; ~(**plate**) fer-blanc *m*. ● *vt* (*pt* **tinned**) mettre en boîte. ~ **foil** *n* papier *m* d'aluminium.

T

tingle *vi* picoter. ● *n* picotement *m*.

tin-opener *n* ouvre-boîtes *m inv*.

tint *n* teinte *f*; (for hair) shampooing *m* colorant. ● *vt* teinter.

tiny *a* (**-ier**, **-iest**) tout petit.

tip *n* (of stick, pen, shoe, ski) pointe *f*; (of nose, finger, wing) bout *m*; (gratuity) pourboire *m*; (advice) tuyau *m*; (for rubbish) décharge *f*. ● *vt/i* (*pt* **tipped**) (tilt) pencher; (overturn) (faire) basculer; (pour) verser; (empty) déverser; (give money) donner un pourboire à. □ ~ **off** prévenir.

tiptoe *n* **on** ~ sur la pointe des pieds.

tire *vt/i* (se) fatiguer; ~ **of** se lasser de. ● *n* (US) pneu *m*.

tired *a* fatigué; **be** ~ **of** en avoir assez de.

tiring *a* fatigant.

tissue *n* tissu *m*; (handkerchief) mouchoir *m* en papier; ~ (**paper**) papier *m* de soie.

tit *n* (bird) mésange *f*; **give** ~ **for tat** rendre coup pour coup.

title *n* titre *m*. ~ **deed** *n* titre *m* de propriété.

---

to

● *preposition*

····➤ à; ~ **Paris** à Paris; **give the book** ~ **Jane** donne le livre à Jane; ~ **the office** au bureau; ~ **the shops** aux magasins.

····➤ (with feminine countries) en; ~ **France** en France.

····➤ (to + personal pronoun) me/te/lui/nous/vous/leur; **she gave it** ~ **them** elle le leur a donné; **I'll say it** ~ **her** je vais le lui dire.

! *à + le = au*
à + les = aux.

● *in infinitive*

to is not normally translated (**to go** *aller*, **to sing** *chanter*)

····➤ (in order to) pour; **he's gone into town** ~ **buy a shirt** il est parti en ville pour acheter une chemise.

····➤ (after adjectives) à; de; **be easy/difficult** ~ **read** être facile/difficile à lire; **it's easy/difficult to read her writing** c'est facile/difficile de lire son écriture.

⇨ For verbal expressions using the infinitive 'to' such as **tell sb to do sth, help sb to do sth** ⇒**tell**, **help**.

---

toad *n* crapaud *m*.

toast *n* pain *m* grillé, toast *m*; (drink) toast *m*. ● *vt* (*bread*) faire griller; (drink to) porter un toast à. **toaster** *n* grille-pain *m inv*.

tobacco *n* tabac *m*.

tobacconist *n* marchand/-e *m/f* de tabac; ~**'s** (**shop**) tabac *m*.

toboggan *n* toboggan *m*, luge *f*.

today *n & adv* aujourd'hui (*m*).

toddler *n* bébé *m* (*qui fait ses premiers pas*).

toe *n* orteil *m*; (of shoe) bout *m*; **on one's** ~**s** vigilant. ● *vt* ~ **the line** se conformer.

together *adv* ensemble; (at same time) à la fois; ~ **with** avec.

toilet *n* toilettes *fpl*.

toiletries *npl* articles *mpl* de toilette.

token *n* (symbol) témoignage *m*; (voucher) bon *m*; (coin) jeton *m*. ● *a* symbolique.

told ⇒TELL.

tolerance *n* tolérance *f*.

tolerate *vt* tolérer.

toll *n* péage *m*; **death** ~ nombre *m* de morts; **take its** ~ faire des ravages. ● *vi* (*bell*) sonner.

tomato *n* (*pl* ~**es**) tomate *f*.

tomb *n* tombeau *m*.

tomorrow *n & adv* demain (*m*); ~ **morning/night** demain matin/ soir; **the day after** ~ après-demain.

ton *n* tonne *f* (= *1016 kg*); (**metric**) ~ tonne *f* (= *1000 kg*); ~**s of** [I] des masses de.

tone *n* ton *m*; (of radio, telephone) tonalité *f*. ● *vt* ~ **down** atténuer. ● *vi* ~ (**in**) s'harmoniser (**with** avec).

tongs *npl* (for coal) pincettes *fpl*; (for sugar) pince *f*; (for hair) fer *m*.

tongue *n* langue *f*.

tonic *n* (Med) tonique *m*. ● *a* (*effect, accent*) tonique; ~ (**water**) tonic *m*, Schweppes® *m*.

tonight *n & adv* (evening) ce soir; (night) cette nuit.

tonsil *n* amygdale *f*.

too *adv* trop; (also) aussi; ~ **many people** trop de gens; **I've got** ~ **much/many** j'en ai trop; **me** ~ moi aussi.

took ⇒TAKE.

tool *n* outil *m*. ~**-box** *n* boîte *f* à outils.

toot *n* coup *m* de klaxon®. ● *vt/i* ~ (**the horn**) klaxonner.

tooth *n* (*pl* **teeth**) dent *f*. ~**ache** *n* mal *m* de dents. ~**brush** *n* brosse *f* à dents. ~**paste** *n* dentifrice *m*. ~**pick** *n* cure-dents *m inv*.

top *n* (highest point) sommet *m*; (upper part) haut *m*; (upper surface) dessus *m*; (lid) couvercle *m*; (of bottle, tube) bouchon *m*; (of beer bottle) capsule *f*; (of list) tête *f*; **on** ~ **of** sur; (fig) en plus de. ● *a* (*shelf*) du haut; (*step, floor*) dernier; (in rank) premier; (best) meilleur; (distinguished) éminent; (maximum) maximum. ● *vt* (*pt* **topped**) (exceed) dépasser; (list) venir en tête de; ~ **up** remplir; ~**ped with** (*dome*) surmonté de; (*cream*) recouvert de.

topic *n* sujet *m*.

topless *a* aux seins nus.

torch *n* (electric) lampe *f* de poche; (flaming) torche *f*.

tore ⇒TEAR[1]

torment *vt* tourmenter; (annoy) agacer.

torn ⇒TEAR[1].

torrent *n* torrent *m*.

tortoise *n* tortue *f*. ~**shell** *n* écaille *f*.

torture *n* torture *f*; (fig) supplice *m*. ● *vt* torturer.

Tory *n & a* tory (*mf*), conservateur/-trice (*m/f*).

toss *vt* lancer; (*salad*) tourner; (*pancake*) faire sauter. ● *vi* se retourner; ~ **a coin**, ~ **up** tirer à pile ou face (**for** pour).

tot *n* petit/-e enfant *m/f*; (drink) petit verre *m*.

total *n & a* total (*m*). ● *vt* (*pt* **totalled**) (add up) additionner; (amount to) se monter à.

touch *vt* toucher; (tamper with) toucher à. ● *vi* se toucher. ● *n* (sense) toucher *m*; (contact) contact *m*; (of artist, writer) touche *f*; **a** ~ **of** (small amount) un petit peu de; **get in** ~ **with** se mettre en contact avec; **out of** ~ **with** déconnecté de. □ ~ **down** (Aviat) atterrir; ~ **up** retoucher. ~**down** *n* atterrissage *m*; (Sport) essai *m*. ~**-line** *n* ligne *f* de touche. ~**-tone** *a* (*phone*) à touches.

tough *a* (*negotiator*) coriace; (*law*) sévère; (*time*) difficile; (robust) robuste.

tour *n* voyage *m*; (visit) visite *f*; (by team) tournée *f*; **on** ~ en tournée. ● *vt* visiter.

tourist *n* touriste *mf*. ● *a* touristique. ~ **office** *n* syndicat *m* d'initiative.

tournament *n* tournoi *m*.

tout *vi* ~ (**for**) racoler [I]. ● *vt* (sell)

T

revendre. ● *n* racoleur/-euse *m/f*; revendeur/-euse *m/f*.

tow *vt* remorquer. ● *n* remorque *f*; **on ~** en remorque.

toward(s) *prep* vers; (of attitude) envers.

towel *n* serviette *f*.

tower *n* tour *f*. ● *vi* **~ above** dominer.

town *n* ville *f*; **in ~** en ville. **~ council** *n* conseil *m* municipal. **~ hall** *n* mairie *f*.

tow: **~-path** *n* chemin *m* de halage. **~ truck** *n* dépanneuse *f*.

toxic *a* toxique.

toy *n* jouet *m*. ● *vi* **~ with** (object) jouer avec; (idea) caresser.

trace *n* trace *f*. ● *vt* (*person*) retrouver; (*cause*) déterminer; (*life*) retracer; (draw) tracer; (with tracing paper) décalquer.

track *n* (of person, car) traces *fpl*; (of missile) trajectoire *f*; (path) sentier *m*; (Sport) piste *f*; (Rail) voie *f*; (on disc) morceau *m*; **keep ~ of** suivre. ● *vt* suivre la trace *or* la trajectoire de. □ **~ down** retrouver. **~ suit** *n* survêtement *m*.

tractor *n* tracteur *m*.

trade *n* commerce *m*; (job) métier *m*; (swap) échange *m*. ● *vi* faire du commerce; **~ on** exploiter. ● *vt* échanger. ● *a* (*route, deficit*) commercial. **~-in** *n* reprise *f*. **~ mark** *n* marque *f* (de fabrique); (registered) marque *f* déposée.

trader *n* commerçant/-e *m/f*; (on stockmarket) opérateur/-trice *m/f*.

trade union *n* syndicat *m*.

trading *n* commerce *m*; (on stockmarket) transactions *fpl* (boursières).

tradition *n* tradition *f*.

traffic *n* trafic *m*; (on road) circulation *f*. ● *vi* (*pt* **trafficked**) faire du trafic (in de). **~ jam** *n* embouteillage *m*. **~-lights** *npl* feux *mpl* (de circulation). **~ warden** contractuel/-le *m/f*.

trail *vt/i* traîner; (*plant*) ramper; (track) suivre; **~ behind** traîner. ● *n* (of powder) traînée *f*; (track) piste *f*; (path) sentier *m*.

trailer *n* remorque *f*; (caravan) caravane *f*; (film) bande-annonce *f*.

train *n* (Rail) train *m*; (underground) rame *f*; (procession) file *f*; (of dress) traîne *f*. ● *vt* (instruct, develop) former; (*sportsman*) entraîner; (*animal*) dresser; (*ear*) exercer; (*aim*) braquer. ● *vi* être formé, étudier; (Sport) s'entraîner. **trained** *a* (skilled) qualifié; (*doctor*) diplômé. **trainee** *n* stagiaire *mf*. **trainer** *n* (Sport) entraîneur/-euse *m/f*. **trainers** *npl* (shoes) chaussures *fpl* de sport. **training** *n* formation *f*; (Sport) entraînement *m*.

tram *n* tram(way) *m*.

tramp *vi* marcher (d'un pas lourd). ● *vt* parcourir. ● *n* (vagrant) clochard/-e *m/f*; (sound) bruit *m*.

trample *vt/i* **~ (on)** piétiner; (fig) fouler aux pieds.

tranquil *a* tranquille. **tranquillizer** *n* tranquillisant *m*.

transact *vt* négocier. **transaction** *n* transaction *f*.

transcript *n* transcription *f*.

transfer[1] *vt* (*pt* **transferred**) transférer; (*power*) céder; (*employee*) muter. ● *vi* être transféré; (*employee*) être muté.

transfer[2] *n* transfert *m*; (of employee) mutation *f*; (image) décalcomanie *f*.

transform *vt* transformer.

transitive *a* transitif.

translate *vt* traduire. **translation** *n* traduction *f*. **translator** *n* traducteur/-trice *m/f*.

transmit *vt* (*pt* **transmitted**)

transmettre. **transmitter** *n* émetteur *m*.

transparency *n* transparence *f*; (Photo) diapositive *f*.

transplant *n* transplantation *f*; (Med) greffe *f*.

transport¹ *vt* transporter.

transport² *n* transport *m*.

trap *n* piège *m*. ● *vt* (*pt* **trapped**) (jam, pin down) coincer; (cut off) bloquer; (snare) prendre au piège.

trash *n* (refuse) ordures *fpl*; (nonsense) idioties *fpl*. **~-can** *n* (US) poubelle *f*.

trauma *n* traumatisme *m*. **traumatic** *a* traumatisant.

travel *vi* (*pt* **travelled**, US **traveled**) voyager; (*vehicle, bullet*) aller. ● *vt* parcourir. ● *n* voyages *mpl*. **~ agency** *n* agence *f* de voyages.

traveller, (US) **traveler** *n* voyageur/-euse *m/f*; **~'s cheque** chèque *m* de voyage.

trawler *n* chalutier *m*.

tray *n* plateau *m*; (on office desk) corbeille *f*.

treacle *n* mélasse *f*.

tread *vi* (*pt* **trod**; *pp* **trodden**) marcher (**on** sur). ● *vt* fouler. ● *n* (sound) pas *m*; (of tyre) chape *f*.

treasure *n* trésor *m*. ● *vt* (*gift, memory*) chérir; (*friendship, possession*) tenir beaucoup à.

treasury *n* trésorerie *f*; **the T~** le ministère des Finances.

treat *vt* traiter; **~ sb to sth** offrir qch à qn. ● *n* (pleasure) plaisir *m*; (food) gâterie *f*. **treatment** *n* traitement *m*.

treaty *n* traité *m*.

treble *a* triple; **~ clef** clé *f* de sol. ● *vt/i* tripler. ● *n* (voice) soprano *m*.

tree *n* arbre *m*.

trek *n* randonnée *f*. ● *vi* (*pt* **trekked**) **~ across/through** traverser péniblement; **go ~king** faire de la randonnée.

tremble *vi* trembler.

tremendous *a* énorme; (excellent) formidable.

tremor *n* tremblement *m*; **(earth) ~** secousse *f*.

trench *n* tranchée *f*.

trend *n* tendance *f*; (fashion) mode *f*. **trendy** *a* ▣ branché ▣.

trespass *vi* s'introduire illégalement (**on** dans). **trespasser** *n* intrus/-e *m/f*.

trial *n* (Jur) procès *m*; (test) essai *m*; (ordeal) épreuve *f*; **go on ~** passer en jugement; **by ~ and error** par expérience.

triangle *n* triangle *m*.

tribe *n* tribu *f*.

tribunal *n* tribunal *m*.

tributary *n* affluent *m*.

tribute *n* tribut *m*; **pay ~ to** rendre hommage à.

trick *n* tour *m*; (dishonest) combine *f*; (knack) astuce *f*; **do the ~** ▣ faire l'affaire. ● *vt* tromper. **trickery** *n* ruse *f*.

trickle *vi* dégouliner; **~ in/out** arriver *or* partir en petit nombre. ● *n* filet *m*; (fig) petit nombre *m*.

tricky *a* (*task*) difficile; (*question*) épineux; (*person*) malin.

trifle *n* bagatelle *f*; (cake) diplomate *m*; **a ~** (small amount) un peu. ● *vi* **~ with** jouer avec.

trigger *n* (of gun) gâchette *f*; (of machine) manette *f*. ● *vt* **~ (off)** (initiate) déclencher.

trim *a* (**trimmer, trimmest**) soigné; (figure) svelte. ● *vt* (*pt* **trimmed**) (*hair, grass*) couper; (*budget*) réduire; (decorate) décorer. ● *n* (cut) coupe *f* d'entretien; (decoration) garniture *f*; **in ~** en forme.

trinket *n* babiole *f*.

trip *vt/i* (*pt* **tripped**) (faire)

T

trébucher. ● *n* (journey) voyage *m*; (outing) excursion *f*.

triple *a* triple. ● *vt/i* tripler. **triplets** *npl* triplés/-es *m/fpl*.

tripod *n* trépied *m*.

trite *a* banal.

triumph *n* triomphe *m*. ● *vi* triompher (**over** de).

trivial *a* insignifiant.

trod, trodden ⇒TREAD.

trolley *n* chariot *m*.

trombone *n* (Mus) trombone *m*.

troop *n* bande *f*; **~s** (Mil) troupes *fpl*. ● *vi* **~ in/out** entrer/sortir en bande.

trophy *n* trophée *m*.

tropic *n* tropique *m*; **~s** tropiques *mpl*.

trot *n* trot *m*; **on the ~** [!] coup sur coup. ● *vi* (*pt* **trotted**) trotter.

trouble *n* problèmes *mpl*; ennuis *mpl*; (pains, effort) peine *f*; **be in ~** avoir des ennuis; **go to a lot of ~** se donner du mal; **what's the ~?** quel est le problème? ● *vt* (bother) déranger; (worry) tracasser. ● *vi* **~ (oneself) to do** se donner la peine de faire. **~maker** *n* provocateur/-trice *m/f*. **~shooter** *n* conciliateur/-trice *m/f*; (Tech) expert *m*.

troublesome *a* ennuyeux.

trousers *npl* pantalon *m*; **short ~** short *m*.

trout *n inv* truite *f*.

trowel *n* (garden) déplantoir *m*; (for mortar) truelle *f*.

truant *n* (School) élève *mf* qui fait l'école buissonnière; **play ~** sécher les cours.

truce *n* trève *f*.

truck *n* (lorry) camion *m*; (cart) chariot *m*; (Rail) wagon *m* de marchandises. **~-driver** *n* routier *m*.

true *a* vrai; (accurate) exact; (faithful) fidèle.

truffle *n* truffe *f*.

truly *adv* vraiment; (faithfully) fidèlement; (truthfully) sincèrement.

trumpet *n* trompette *f*.

trunk *n* (of tree, body) tronc *m*; (of elephant) trompe *f*; (box) malle *f*; (Auto, US) coffre *m*; **~s** (for swimming) slip *m* de bain.

trust *n* confiance *f*; (association) trust *m*; **in ~** en dépôt. ● *vt* avoir confiance en; **~ sb with** confier à qn. ● *vi* **~ in** *or* **to** s'en remettre à. **trustee** *n* administrateur/-trice *m/f*. **trustworthy** *a* digne de confiance.

truth *n* (*pl* **-s**) vérité *f*. **truthful** *a* (*account*) véridique; (*person*) qui dit la vérité.

try *vt/i* (*pt* **tried**) essayer; (be a strain on) éprouver; (Jur) juger; **~ on** *or* **out** essayer; **~ to do** essayer de faire. ● *n* (attempt) essai *m*; (rugby) essai *m*.

T-shirt *n* tee-shirt *m*.

tub *n* (for flowers) bac *m*; (of ice cream) pot *m*; (bath) baignoire *f*.

tube *n* tube *m*; **the ~** [!] le métro.

tuberculosis *n* tuberculose *f*.

tuck *n* pli *m*. ● *vt* (put away, place) ranger; (hide) cacher. ● *vi* **~ in** *or* **into** [!] attaquer; **~ in** (shirt) rentrer; (blanket, person) border.

Tuesday *n* mardi *m*.

tug *vt* (*pt* **tugged**) tirer. ● *vi* **~ at/on** tirer sur. ● *n* (boat) remorqueur *m*.

tuition *n* cours *mpl*; (fee) frais *mpl* pédagogiques.

tulip *n* tulipe *f*.

tumble *vi* (fall) dégringoler. ● *n* chute *f*. **~-drier** *n* sèche-linge *m inv*.

tumbler *n* verre *m* droit.

tummy *n* [!] ventre *m*.

tumour *n* tumeur *f*.

tuna *n inv* thon *m*.

tune *n* air *m*; **be in ~/out of ~**

(instrument) être/ne pas être en accord; (singer) chanter juste/faux. ● *vt* (*engine*) régler; (Mus) accorder. ● *vi* ~ **in** (**to**) (radio, TV) écouter. □ ~ **up** s'accorder.

Tunisia *n* Tunisie *f*.

tunnel *n* tunnel *m*; (in mine) galerie *f*. ● *vi* (*pt* **tunnelled**) creuser un tunnel (**into** dans).

turf *n* (*pl* **turf** *or* **turves**) gazon *m*; **the** ~ (racing) le turf. ● *vt* ~ **out** ⓘ jeter dehors.

Turk *n* Turc *m*, Turque *f*. **Turkey** *n* Turquie *f*.

turkey *n* dinde *f*.

Turkish *a* turc. ● *n* (Ling) turc *m*.

turn *vt*/*i* tourner; (*person*) se tourner; (to other side) retourner; (change) (se) transformer (**into** en); (become) devenir; (deflect) détourner; (milk) tourner. ● *n* tour *m*; (in road) tournant *m*; (of mind, events) tournure *f*; **do a good** ~ rendre service; **in** ~ à tour de rôle; **take** ~**s** se relayer. □ ~ **against** se retourner contre; ~ **away** *vi* se détourner; *vt* (avert) détourner; (refuse) refuser; (send back) renvoyer; ~ **back** *vi* (return) retourner; (*vehicle*) faire demi-tour; *vt* (fold) rabattre; ~ **down** refuser; (fold) rabattre; (reduce) baisser; ~ **off** (*light*) éteindre; (*engine*) arrêter; (*tap*) fermer; (of driver) tourner; ~ **on** (*light*) allumer; (*engine*) allumer; (*tap*) ouvrir; ~ **out** *vt* (*light*) éteindre; (empty) vider; (produce) produire; *vi* **it** ~**s out that** il se trouve que; ~ **out well/badly** bien/mal se terminer; ~ **over** (se) retourner; ~ **round** (person) se retourner; ~ **up** *vi* arriver; (be found) se retrouver; *vt* (find) déterrer; (collar) remonter.

turning *n* rue *f*; (bend) virage *m*.

turnip *n* navet *m*.

turn: ~**-out** *n* assistance *f*. ~**over** *n* (pie) chausson *m*; (money) chiffre *m* d'affaires. ~**table** *n* (for record) platine *f*.

turquoise *a* turquoise *inv*.

turtle *n* tortue *f* (de mer). ~**-neck** *n* col *m* montant.

tutor *n* (private) professeur *m* particulier; (Univ) (GB) chargé/-e *m*/*f* de travaux dirigés.

tutorial *n* (Univ) classe *f* de travaux dirigés.

tuxedo *n* (US) smoking *m*.

TV *n* télé *f*.

tweezers *npl* pince *f* (à épiler).

twelfth *a* & *n* douzième (*mf*).

twelve *a* & *n* douze (*m*); ~ (**o'clock**) midi *m* *or* minuit *m*.

twentieth *a* & *n* vingtième (*mf*).

twenty *a* & *n* vingt (*m*).

twice *adv* deux fois.

twig *n* brindille *f*.

twilight *n* crépuscule *m*. ● *a* crépusculaire.

twin *n* & *a* jumeau/-elle (*m*/*f*). ● *vt* (*pt* **twinned**) jumeler.

twinge *n* (of pain) élancement *m*; (of conscience, doubt) accès *m*.

twinkle *vi* (*star*) scintiller; (*eye*) pétiller. ● *n* scintillement *m*; pétillement *m*.

twinning *n* jumelage *m*.

twist *vt* tordre; (weave together) entortiller; (roll) enrouler; (distort) déformer. ● *vi* (*rope*) s'entortiller; (*road*) zigzaguer. ● *n* torsion *f*; (in rope) tortillon *m*; (in road) tournant *m*; (in play, story) coup *m* de théâtre.

twitch *vi* (*person*) trembloter; (*mouth*) trembler; (*string*) vibrer. ● *n* (tic) tic *m*, (jerk) secousse *f*.

two *a* & *n* deux (*m*); **in** ~**s** par deux; **break in** ~ casser en deux.

tycoon *n* magnat *m*.

type *n* type *m*, genre *m*; (print) caractères *mpl*. ● *vt*/*i* (write) taper (à la machine). ~**face** *n* police *f*

(de caractères). **~writer** *n* machine *f* à écrire.
typical *a* typique.
typist *n* dactylo *mf*.
tyrant *n* tyran *m*.
tyre *n* pneu *m*.

udder *n* pis *m*, mamelle *f*.
UFO *n* OVNI *m inv*.
UHT *abbr* (**ultra heat treated**) **~ milk** lait *m* longue conservation.
ugly *a* (**-ier**, **-iest**) laid.
UK *abbr* ⇒UNITED KINGDOM.
Ukraine *n* Ukraine *f*.
ulcer *n* ulcère *m*.
ulterior *a* ultérieur; **~ motive** arrière-pensée *f*.
ultimate *a* dernier, ultime; (definitive) définitif; (basic) fondamental.
ultrasound *n* ultrason *m*.
umbilical cord *n* cordon *m* ombilical.
umbrella *n* parapluie *m*.
umpire *n* arbitre *m*. ● *vt* arbitrer.
umpteenth *a* [!] énième.
UN *abbr* (**United Nations**) ONU *f*.
unable *a* incapable; (through circumstances) dans l'impossibilité (**to do** de faire).
unacceptable *a* (*suggestion*) inacceptable; (*behaviour*) inadmissible.
unanimous *a* unanime.
unanimously *adv* à l'unanimité.
unattended *a* sans surveillance.
unattractive *a* (*idea*) peu attrayant; (*person*) peu attirant.
unauthorized *a* non autorisé.
unavoidable *a* inévitable.
unbearable *a* insupportable.
unbelievable *a* incroyable.
unbiased *a* impartial.
unblock *vt* déboucher.
unborn *a* (*child*) à naître; (*generation*) à venir.
uncalled-for *a* injustifié, déplacé.
uncanny *a* (**-ier**, **-iest**) étrange, troublant.
uncivilized *a* barbare.
uncle *n* oncle *m*.
uncomfortable *a* (*chair*) inconfortable; (*feeling*) pénible; **feel** *or* **be ~** (person) être mal à l'aise.
uncommon *a* rare.
unconscious *a* sans connaissance, inanimé; (not aware) inconscient (**of** de). ● *n* inconscient *m*.
unconventional *a* peu conventionnel.
uncouth *a* grossier.
uncover *vt* découvrir.
undecided *a* indécis.
under *prep* sous; (less than) moins de; (according to) selon. ● *adv* au-dessous; **~ it/there** là-dessous. **~ age** *a* mineur. **~cover** *a* secret. **~cut** *vt* (*pt* **-cut**; *pres p* **-cutting**) (Comm) vendre moins cher que. **~dog** *n* (Pol) opprimé/-e *m/f*; (socially) déshérité/-e *m/f*. **~done** *a* pas assez cuit. **~estimate** *vt* sous-estimer. **~fed** *a* sous-alimenté. **~go** *vt* (*pt* **-went**; *pp* **-gone**) subir. **~graduate** *n* étudiant/-e *m/f* (*qui prépare la licence*).
underground *a* souterrain; (secret) clandestin. ● *adv* sous terre. ● *n* (rail) métro *m*.

under: **~line** *vt* souligner. **~mine** *vt* saper.

underneath *prep* sous. ● *adv* (en) dessous.

under: **~pants** *npl* slip *m*. **~rate** *vt* sous-estimer.

understand *vt/i* (*pt* **-stood**) comprendre.

understanding *a* compréhensif. ● *n* compréhension *f*; (agreement) entente *f*.

undertake *vt* (*pt* **-took**; *pp* **-taken**) entreprendre. **~taker** *n* entrepreneur *m* de pompes funèbres. **~taking** *n* (task) entreprise *f*; (promise) promesse *f*.

underwater *a* sous-marin. ● *adv* sous l'eau.

under: **~wear** *n* sous-vêtements *mpl*. **~world** *n* (of crime) milieu *m*, pègre *f*.

undo *vt* (*pt* **-did**; *pp* **-done**) défaire, détacher; (*wrong*) réparer; (Comput) annuler.

undress *vt/i* (se) déshabiller; **get ~ed** se déshabiller.

undue *a* excessif.

unearth *vt* déterrer.

uneasy *a* (ill at ease) mal à l'aise; (worried) inquiet; (*situation*) difficile.

uneducated *a* (*person*) inculte; (*speech*) populaire.

unemployed *a* en chômage. ● *npl* **the ~** les chômeurs *mpl*.

unemployment *n* chômage *m*; **~ benefit** allocations *fpl* de chômage.

uneven *a* inégal.

unexpected *a* inattendu, imprévu. **unexpectedly** *adv* (*arrive*) à l'improviste; (*small, fast*) étonnamment.

unfair *a* injuste.

unfaithful *a* infidèle.

unfit *a* (Med) pas en forme; (ill) malade; (unsuitable) impropre (**for** à); **~ to** (unable) pas en état de.

unfold *vt* déplier; (expose) exposer. ● *vi* se dérouler.

unforeseen *a* imprévu.

unforgettable *a* inoubliable.

unfortunate *a* malheureux; (*event*) fâcheux.

ungrateful *a* ingrat.

unhappy *a* (**-ier, -iest**) (*person*) malheureux; (*face*) triste; (not pleased) mécontent (**with** de).

unharmed *a* indemne, sain et sauf.

unhealthy *a* (**-ier, -iest**) (*climate*) malsain; (*person*) en mauvaise santé.

unheard-of *a* inouï.

unhurt *a* indemne.

uniform *n* uniforme *m*. ● *a* uniforme.

unify *vt* unifier.

unintentional *a* involontaire.

uninterested *a* indifférent (**in** à).

union *n* union *f*; (trade union) syndicat *m*; **U~ Jack** drapeau *m* du Royaume-Uni.

unique *a* unique.

unit *n* unité *f*; (of furniture) élément *m*; **~ trust** ≈ SICAV *f*.

unite *vt/i* (s')unir.

United Kingdom *n* Royaume-Uni *m*.

United Nations *npl* Nations *fpl* Unies.

United States (**of America**) *npl* États-Unis *mpl* (d'Amérique).

unity *n* unité *f*.

universal *a* universel.

universe *n* univers *m*.

university *n* université *f*. ● *a* universitaire; (*student, teacher*) d'université.

unkind *a* pas gentil, méchant.

unknown *a* inconnu. ● *n* **the ~** l'inconnu *m*.

unleaded *a* sans plomb.

U

unless *conj* à moins que.
unlike *a* différent. ● *prep* contrairement à; (different from) différent de.
unlikely *a* improbable.
unload *vt* décharger.
unlock *vt* ouvrir.
unlucky *a* (**-ier**, **-iest**) malheureux; (*number*) qui porte malheur.
unmarried *a* célibataire.
unnatural *a* pas naturel, anormal.
unnecessary *a* inutile.
unnoticed *a* inaperçu.
unofficial *a* officieux.
unpack *vt* (*suitcase*) défaire; (*contents*) déballer. ● *vi* défaire sa valise.
unpleasant *a* désagréable (**to** avec).
unplug *vt* débrancher.
unpopular *a* impopulaire; **~ with** mal vu de.
unprofessional *a* peu professionnel.
unqualified *a* non diplômé; (*success*) total; **be ~ to** ne pas être qualifié pour.
unravel *vt* (*pt* **unravelled**) démêler.
unreasonable *a* irréaliste.
unrelated *a* sans rapport (**to** avec).
unreliable *a* peu sérieux; (*machine*) peu fiable.
unrest *n* troubles *mpl*.
unroll *vt* dérouler.
unruly *a* indiscipliné.
unsafe *a* (dangerous) dangereux; (*person*) en danger.
unscheduled *a* pas prévu.
unscrupulous *a* sans scrupules, malhonnête.
unsettled *a* instable.
unsightly *a* laid.
unskilled *a* (worker) non qualifié.
unsound *a* (*roof*) en mauvais état; (*investment*) douteux.
unsteady *a* (*step*) chancelant; (*ladder*) instable; (*hand*) mal assuré.
unsuccessful *a* (*result, candidate*) malheureux; (*attempt*) infructueux; **be ~** ne pas réussir (**in doing** à faire).
unsuitable *a* inapproprié; **be ~** ne pas convenir.
unsure *a* incertain.
untidy *a* (**-ier**, **-iest**) (*person*) désordonné; (*room*) en désordre; (*work*) mal soigné.
untie *vt* (*knot, parcel*) défaire; (*person*) détacher.
until *prep* jusqu'à; **not ~** pas avant. ● *conj* jusqu'à ce que; **not ~** pas avant que.
untrue *a* faux.
unused *a* (new) neuf; (not in use) inutilisé.
unusual *a* exceptionnel; (strange) insolite, étrange.
unwanted *a* (useless) superflu; (*child*) non désiré.
unwelcome *a* fâcheux; (*guest*) importun.
unwell *a* souffrant.
unwilling *a* peu disposé (**to** à); (*accomplice*) malgré soi.
unwind *vt/i* (*pt* **unwound**) (se) dérouler; (relax 🅸) se détendre.
unwise *a* imprudent.
unwrap *vt* déballer.
up *adv* en haut, en l'air; (*sun, curtain*) levé; (out of bed) levé, debout; (finished) fini; **be ~** (*level, price*) avoir monté. ● *prep* (a hill) en haut de; (a tree) dans; (a ladder) sur; **come** *or* **go ~** monter; **~ in the bedroom** là-haut dans la chambre; **~ there** là-haut; **~ to** jusqu'à; (*task*) à la hauteur de; **it is ~ to you** ça dépend de vous (**to**

de); **be ~ to sth** (able) être capable de qch; (plot) préparer qch; **be ~ to** (in book) en être à; **be ~ against** faire face à; **~ to date** moderne; (*news*) récent. ● *n* **~s and downs** les hauts et les bas *mpl*.

up-and-coming *a* prometteur.

upbringing *n* éducation *f*.

update *vt* mettre à jour.

upgrade *vt* améliorer; (*person*) promouvoir.

upheaval *n* bouleversement *m*.

uphill *a* qui monte; (fig) difficile. ● *adv* **go ~** monter.

upholstery *n* rembourrage *m*; (in vehicle) garniture *f*.

upkeep *n* entretien *m*.

up-market *a* haut-de-gamme.

upon *prep* sur.

upper *a* supérieur; **have the ~ hand** avoir le dessus. ● *n* (of shoe) empeigne *f*. **~ class** *n* aristocratie *f*. **~most** *a* (highest) le plus haut.

upright *a* droit. ● *n* (post) montant *m*.

uprising *n* soulèvement *m*.

uproar *n* tumulte *m*.

uproot *vt* déraciner.

upset[1] *vt* (*pt* **upset**; *pres p* **upsetting**) (overturn) renverser; (*plan, stomach*) déranger; (*person*) contrarier, affliger. ● *a* peiné.

upset[2] *n* dérangement *m*; (distress) chagrin *m*.

upside-down *adv* (lit) à l'envers; (fig) sens dessus dessous.

upstairs *adv* en haut. ● *a* (*flat*) du haut.

uptight *a* 🅸 tendu, coincé 🅸.

up-to-date *a* à la mode; (*records*) à jour.

upward *a & adv*, **upwards** *adv* vers le haut.

urban *a* urbain.

urge *vt* conseiller vivement (**to do** de faire); **~ on** encourager. ● *n* forte envie *f*.

urgency *n* urgence *f*; (of request, tone) insistance *f*. **urgent** *a* urgent; (*request*) pressant.

urinal *n* urinoir *m*.

urine *n* urine *f*.

us *pron* nous; (**to**) **~** nous; **both of ~** tous/toutes les deux.

US *abbr* ⇒UNITED STATES.

USA *abbr* ⇒UNITED STATES OF AMERICA.

use[1] *vt* se servir de, utiliser; (consume) consommer; **~ up** épuiser.

use[2] *n* usage *m*, emploi *m*; **in ~** en usage; **it is no ~ doing** ça ne sert à rien de faire; **make ~ of** se servir de; **of ~** utile.

used[1] *a* (*car*) d'occasion.

used[2] *v aux* **he ~ to smoke** il fumait (autrefois). ● *a* **~ to** habitué à.

useful *a* utile.

useless *a* inutile; (*person*) incompétent.

user *n* (of road, service) usager *m*; (of product) utilisateur/-trice *m/f*. **~-friendly** *a* facile d'emploi; (Comput) convivial.

usual *a* habituel, normal; **as ~** comme d'habitude. **usually** *adv* d'habitude.

utility *n* utilité *f*; (**public**) **~** service *m* public.

utmost *a* (furthest, most intense) extrême; **the ~ care** le plus grand soin. ● *n* **do one's ~** faire tout son possible.

utter *a* complet, absolu. ● *vt* prononcer.

U-turn *n* demi-tour *m*; (fig) volte-face *f inv*.

vacancy *n* (post) poste *m* vacant; (room) chambre *f* disponible.

vacant *a* (*post*) vacant; (*seat*) libre; (*look*) vague.

vacate *vt* quitter.

vacation *n* vacances *fpl*.

vaccinate *vt* vacciner.

vacuum *n* vide *m*. ~ **cleaner** *n* aspirateur *m*. **~-packed** *a* emballé sous vide.

vagina *n* vagin *m*.

vagrant *n* vagabond/-e *m*/*f*.

vague *a* vague; (*outline*) flou; **be ~ about** ne pas préciser.

vain *a* (conceited) vaniteux, (useless) vain; **in ~** en vain.

valentine *n* ~ (**card**) carte *f* de la Saint-Valentin.

valid *a* (*argument, ticket*) valable; (*passport*) valide.

valley *n* vallée *f*.

valuable *a* (object) de valeur; (*help*) précieux. **valuables** *npl* objets *mpl* de valeur.

valuation *n* (of painting) expertise *f*; (of house) évaluation *f*.

value *n* valeur *f*; ~ **added tax** taxe *f* à la valeur ajoutée, TVA *f*. ● *vt* (appraise) évaluer; (cherish) attacher de la valeur à.

valve *n* (Tech) soupape *f*; (of tyre) valve *f*; (Med) valvule *f*.

van *n* camionnette *f*.

vandal *n* vandale *mf*.

vanguard *n* **in the ~ of** à l'avant-garde *f* de.

vanilla *n* vanille *f*.

vanish *vi* disparaître.

vapour *n* vapeur *f*.

variable *a* variable.

varicose *a* ~ **veins** varices *fpl*.

varied *a* varié.

variety *n* variété *f*; (entertainment) variétés *fpl*.

various *a* divers.

varnish *n* vernis *m*. ● *vt* vernir.

vary *vt*/*i* varier.

vase *n* vase *m*.

vast *a* (*space*) vaste; (in quantity) énorme.

vat *n* cuve *f*.

VAT *abbr* (**value added tax**) TVA *f*.

vault *n* (roof) voûte *f*; (in bank) chambre *f* forte; (tomb) caveau *m*; (jump) saut *m*. ● *vt*/*i* sauter.

VCR *abbr* ⇒VIDEO CASSETTE RECORDER.

VDU *abbr* ⇒VISUAL DISPLAY UNIT.

veal *n* veau *m*.

vegan *a* & *n* végétalien/-ne (*m*/*f*).

vegetable *n* légume *m*. ● *a* végétal.

vegetarian *a* & *n* végétarien/-ne (*m*/*f*).

vehicle *n* véhicule *m*.

veil *n* voile *m*.

vein *n* (in body, rock) veine *f*; (on leaf) nervure *f*.

velvet *n* velours *m*.

vending-machine *n* distributeur *m* automatique.

veneer *n* (on wood) placage *m*; (fig) vernis *m*.

venereal *a* vénérien.

venetian *a* ~ **blind** jalousie *f*.

vengeance *n* vengeance *f*; **with a ~** de plus belle.

venison *n* venaison *f*.

venom *n* venin *m*.

vent *n* bouche *f*, conduit *m*; (in coat) fente *f*. ● *vt* (*anger*) décharger (**on** sur).

ventilate *vt* ventiler. **ventilator** *n* ventilateur *m*.
venture *n* entreprise *f*. ●*vt/i* (se) risquer.
venue *n* lieu *m*.
verb *n* verbe *m*.
verbal *a* verbal.
verbatim *a & adv* mot pour mot.
verdict *n* verdict *m*.
verge *n* bord *m*; **on the ~ of doing** sur le point de faire. ●*vi* **~ on** friser, frôler.
verify *vt* vérifier.
vermin *n* vermine *f*.
versatile *a* (*person*) aux talents variés; (*mind*) souple.
verse *n* strophe *f*; (of Bible) verset *m*; (poetry) vers *mpl*.
version *n* version *f*.
versus *prep* contre.
vertebra *n* (*pl* **-brae**) vertèbre *f*.
vertical *a* vertical.
vertigo *n* vertige *m*.
very *adv* très. ●*a* (actual) même; **the ~ day** le jour même; **at the ~ end** tout à la fin; **the ~ first** le tout premier; **~ much** beaucoup.
vessel *n* vaisseau *m*.
vest *n* maillot *m* de corps; (waistcoat: US) gilet *m*.
vet *n* vétérinaire *mf*. ●*vt* (*pt* **vetted**) (*candidate*) examiner (de près).
veteran *n* vétéran *m*; (**war**) **~** ancien combattant *m*.
veterinary *a* vétérinaire; **~ surgeon** vétérinaire *mf*.
veto *n* (*pl* **~es**) veto *m*; (right) droit *m* de veto. ●*vt* mettre son veto à.
via *prep* via, par.
vibrate *vt/i* (faire) vibrer.
vicar *n* pasteur *m*.
vice *n* (depravity) vice *m*; (Tech) étau *m*.
vicinity *n* environs *mpl*; **in the ~ of** à proximité de.
vicious *a* (spiteful) méchant; (violent) brutal; **~ circle** cercle *m* vicieux.
victim *n* victime *f*.
victor *n* vainqueur *m*. **victory** *n* victoire *f*.
video *a* (*game, camera*) vidéo *inv*. ●*n* (recorder) magnétoscope *m*; (film) vidéo *f*; **~** (**cassette**) cassette *f* vidéo. ●*vt* enregistrer.
videotape *n* bande *f* vidéo. ●*vt* (*programme*) enregistrer; (*wedding*) filmer avec une caméra vidéo.
view *n* vue *f*; **in my ~** à mon avis; **in ~ of** compte tenu de; **on ~** exposé; **with a ~ to** dans le but de. ●*vt* (watch) regarder; (consider) considérer (**as** comme); (*house*) visiter. **viewer** *n* (TV) téléspectateur/-trice *m/f*.
view: **~finder** *n* viseur *m*. **~point** *n* point *m* de vue.
vigilant *a* vigilant.
vigour, (US) **vigor** *n* vigueur *f*.
vile *a* (base) vil; (bad) abominable.
villa *n* pavillon *m*; (for holiday) villa *f*.
village *n* village *m*.
villain *n* scélérat *m*, bandit *m*; (in story) méchant *m*.
vindictive *a* vindicatif.
vine *n* vigne *f*.
vinegar *n* vinaigre *m*.
vineyard *n* vignoble *m*.
vintage *n* (year) année *f*, millésime *m*. ●*a* (*wine*) de grand cru; (*car*) d'époque.
viola *n* (Mus) alto *m*.

violate *vt* violer.
violence *n* violence *f*. **violent** *a* violent.
violet *n* (Bot) violette *f*; (colour) violet *m*.
violin *n* violon *m*.
VIP *abbr* (**very important person**) personnalité *f*, VIP *m*.

virgin *n* (woman) vierge *f*.
Virgo *n* Vierge *f*.
virtual *a* quasi-total; (Comput) virtuel. **virtually** *adv* pratiquement.
virtue *n* vertu *f*; (advantage) mérite *m*; **by ~ of** en raison de.
virus *n* virus *m*.
visa *n* visa *m*.
visibility *n* visibilité *f*. **visible** *a* visible.
vision *n* vision *f*.
visit *vt* (*pt* **visited**) (*person*) rendre visite à; (*place*) visiter. ● *vi* être en visite. ● *n* (tour, call) visite *f*; (stay) séjour *m*. **visitor** *n* visiteur/-euse *m/f*; (guest) invité/-e *m/f*.
visual *a* visuel. **~ display unit** *n* visuel *m*, console *f* de visualisation.
visualize *vt* se représenter; (foresee) envisager.
vital *a* vital.
vitamin *n* vitamine *f*.
vivacious *a* plein de vivacité.
vivid *a* (*colour, imagination*) vif; (*description, dream*) frappant.
vivisection *n* vivisection *f*.
vocabulary *n* vocabulaire *m*.
vocal *a* vocal; (*person*) qui s'exprime franchement. **~ cords** *npl* cordes *fpl* vocales.
vocation *n* vocation *f*. **vocational** *a* professionnel.
voice *n* voix *f*. ● *vt* (express) formuler. **~ mail** *n* messagerie *f* vocale.
void *a* vide (**of** de); (not valid) nul. ● *n* vide *m*.
volatile *a* (*person*) versatile; (*situation*) explosif.
volcano *n* (*pl* **~es**) volcan *m*.
volley *n* (of blows, in tennis) volée *f*; (of gunfire) salve *f*.
volt *n* (Electr) volt *m*. **voltage** *n* tension *f*.
volume *n* volume *m*.
voluntary *a* volontaire; (unpaid) bénévole.
volunteer *n* volontaire *mf*. ● *vi* s'offrir (**to do** pour faire); (Mil) s'engager comme volontaire. ● *vt* offrir.
vomit *vt/i* (*pt* **vomited**) vomir. ● *n* vomi *m*.
vote *n* vote *m*; (right) droit *m* de vote. ● *vt/i* voter; **~ sb in** élire qn. **voter** *n* électeur/-trice *m/f*. **voting** *n* vote *m* (**of** de); (poll) scrutin *m*.
vouch *vi* **~ for** se porter garant de.
voucher *n* bon *m*.
vowel *n* voyelle *f*.
voyage *n* voyage *m* (en mer).
vulgar *a* vulgaire.
vulnerable *a* vulnérable.

wad *n* (pad) tampon *m*; (bundle) liasse *f*.
wade *vi* **~ through** (*mud*) patauger dans; (*book*: fig) avancer péniblement dans.
wafer *n* (biscuit) gaufrette *f*.
waffle *n* (talk 🅸) verbiage *m*; (cake) gaufre *f*. ● *vi* 🅸 divaguer.
wag *vt/i* (*pt* **wagged**) (tail) remuer.
wage *vt* (campaign) mener; **~ war** faire la guerre. ● *n* (weekly, daily) salaire *m*; **~s** salaire *m*. **~-earner** *n* salarié/-e *m/f*.
wagon *n* (horse-drawn) chariot *m*; (Rail) wagon *m* (de marchandises).

wail *vi* gémir. ● *n* gémissement *m*.

waist *n* taille *f*. **~coat** *n* gilet *m*.

wait *vt/i* attendre; **I can't ~ to start** j'ai hâte de commencer; **let's ~ and see** attendons voir; **~ for** attendre; **~ on** servir. ● *n* attente *f*.

waiter *n* garçon *m*, serveur *m*.

waiting-list *n* liste *f* d'attente.

waiting-room *n* salle *f* d'attente.

waitress *n* serveuse *f*.

waive *vt* renoncer à.

wake *vt/i* (*pt* **woke**; *pp* **woken**) **~** (**up**) (se) réveiller. ● *n* (track) sillage *m*; **in the ~ of** (after) à la suite de. **~ up call** *n* réveil *m* téléphoné.

Wales *n* pays *m* de Galles.

walk *vi* marcher; (not ride) aller à pied; (stroll) se promener. ● *vt* (*streets*) parcourir; (distance) faire à pied; (*dog*) promener. ● *n* promenade *f*, tour *m*; (gait) démarche *f*; (pace) marche *f*, pas *m*; (path) allée *f*; **have a ~** faire une promenade. □ **~ out** (go away) partir; (worker) faire grève; **~ out on** abandonner.

walkie-talkie *n* talkie-walkie *m*.

walking *n* marche *f* (à pied). ● *a* (*corpse, dictionary*: fig) ambulant.

walkman® *n* walkman® *m*, baladeur *m*.

walk: **~-out** *n* grève *f* surprise. **~-over** *n* victoire *f* facile.

wall *n* mur *m*; (of tunnel, stomach) paroi *f*. ● *a* mural. **walled** *a* (*city*) fortifié.

wallet *n* portefeuille *m*.

wallpaper *n* papier *m* peint. ● *vt* tapisser.

walnut *n* (nut) noix *f*; (tree) noyer *m*.

waltz *n* valse *f*. ● *vi* valser.

wander *vi* errer; (stroll) flâner; (digress) s'écarter du sujet; (in mind) divaguer.

wane *vi* décroître.

want *vt* vouloir (**to do** faire); (need) avoir besoin de (**doing** d'être fait); (ask for) demander; **I ~ you to do it** je veux que vous le fassiez. ● *vi* **~ for** manquer de. ● *n* (need, poverty) besoin *m*; (desire) désir *m*; (lack) manque *m*; **for ~ of** faute de. **wanted** *a* (*criminal*) recherché par la police.

war *n* guerre *f*; **at ~** en guerre; **on the ~path** sur le sentier de la guerre.

ward *n* (in hospital) salle *f*; (minor: Jur) pupille *mf*; (Pol) division *f* électorale. ● *vt* **~ off** (*danger*) prévenir.

warden *n* directeur/-trice *m/f*; (of park) gardien/-ne *m/f*; (**traffic**) **~** contractuel/-le *m/f*.

wardrobe *n* (furniture) armoire *f*; (clothes) garde-robe *f*.

warehouse *n* entrepôt *m*.

wares *npl* marchandises *fpl*.

warfare *n* guerre *f*.

warm *a* chaud; (hearty) chaleureux; **be** *or* **feel ~** avoir chaud; **it is ~** il fait chaud. ● *vt/i* **~** (**up**) (se) réchauffer; (*food*) chauffer; (liven up) (s')animer; (exercise) s'échauffer.

warmth *n* chaleur *f*.

warn *vt* avertir, prévenir; **~ sb off sth** (advise against) mettre qn en garde contre qch; (forbid) interdire qch à qn.

warning *n* avertissement *m*; (notice) avis *m*; **without ~** sans prévenir. **~ light** *n* voyant *m*. **~ triangle** *n* triangle *m* de sécurité.

warp *vt/i* (*wood*) (se) voiler; (pervert) pervertir; (*judgment*) fausser.

warrant *n* (for arrest) mandat *m* (d'arrêt); (Comm) autorisation *f*. ● *vt* justifier.

W

warranty *n* garantie *f*.

wart *n* verrue *f*.

wartime *n* **in ~** en temps de guerre.

wary *a* (**-ier**, **-iest**) prudent.

was ⇒BE.

wash *vt/i* (se) laver; (flow over) baigner; **~ one's hands of** se laver les mains de. ● *n* lavage *m*; (clothes) lessive *f*; **have a ~** se laver. □ **~ up** faire la vaisselle; (US) se laver. **~-basin** *n* lavabo *m*.

washer *n* rondelle *f*.

washing *n* lessive *f*. **~-machine** *n* machine *f* à laver. **~-powder** *n* lessive *f*.

washing-up *n* vaisselle *f*. **~ liquid** *n* liquide *m* vaisselle.

wash: **~-out** *n* ⊡ fiasco *m*. **~-room** *n* (US) toilettes *fpl*.

wasp *n* guêpe *f*.

wastage *n* gaspillage *m*.

waste *vt* gaspiller; (*time*) perdre. ● *vi* **~ away** dépérir. ● *a* superflu; **~ products** *or* **matter** déchets *mpl*. ● *n* gaspillage *m*, (of time) perte *f*; (rubbish) déchets *mpl*; **lay ~** dévaster. **wasteful** *a* peu économique; (*person*) gaspilleur.

waste: **~ land** *n* (desolate) terre *f* désolée; (unused) terre *f* inculte; (in town) terrain *m* vague. **~ paper** *n* vieux papiers *mpl*. **~-paper basket** *n* corbeille *f* (à papier).

watch *vt/i* (*television*) regarder; (observe) observer; (guard, spy on) surveiller; (be careful about) faire attention à. ● *n* (for telling time) montre *f*; (Naut) quart *m*; **be on the ~** guetter; **keep ~ on** surveiller. □ **~ out** (take care) faire attention (**for** à); **~ out for** (keep watch) guetter.

water *n* eau *f*; **by ~** en bateau. ● *vt* arroser. ● *vi* (*eyes*) larmoyer; **my/his mouth ~s** l'eau me/lui vient à la bouche. □ **~ down** couper (d'eau); (tone down) édulcorer. **~-colour** *n* (painting) aquarelle *f*. **~cress** *n* cresson *m* (de fontaine). **~fall** *n* chute *f* d'eau, cascade *f*. **~ heater** *n* chauffe-eau *m*. **watering-can** *n* arrosoir *m*. **~-lily** *n* nénuphar *m*. **~-melon** *n* pastèque *f*. **~proof** *a* (*material*) imperméable. **~shed** *n* (in affairs) tournant *m* décisif. **~-skiing** *n* ski *m* nautique. **~tight** *a* étanche. **~way** *n* voie *f* navigable.

watery *a* (*colour*) délavé; (*eyes*) humide; (*soup*) trop liquide.

wave *n* vague *f*; (in hair) ondulation *f*; (radio) onde *f*; (sign) signe *m*. ● *vt* agiter. ● *vi* faire signe (de la main); (move in wind) flotter.

waver *vi* vaciller.

wavy *a* (*line*) onduleux; (*hair*) ondulé.

wax *n* cire *f*; (for skis) fart *m*. ● *vt* cirer; farter; (*car*) lustrer.

way *n* (road, path) chemin *m* (**to** de); (distance) distance *f*; (direction) direction *f*; (manner) façon *f*; (means) moyen *m*; **~s** (habits) habitudes *fpl*; **be in the ~** bloquer le passage; (hindrance: fig) gêner (qn); **be on one's** *or* **the ~** être sur son *or* le chemin; **by the ~** à propos; **by the ~side** au bord de la route; **by ~ of** comme; (via) par; **go out of one's ~** se donner du mal; **in a ~** dans un sens; **make one's ~ somewhere** se rendre quelque part; **push one's ~ through** se frayer un passage; **that ~** par là; **this ~** par ici; **~ in** entrée *f*; **~ out** sortie *f*. ● *adv* ⊡ loin.

we *pron* nous.

weak *a* faible; (delicate) fragile.

weakness *n* faiblesse *f*; (fault) point *m* faible; **a ~ for** (liking) un faible pour.

wealth *n* richesse *f*; (riches, resources) richesses *fpl*; (quantity) profusion *f*.

wealthy *a* (**-ier, -iest**) riche. ● *n* **the ~** les riches *mpl*.

wean *vt* (*baby*) sevrer.

weapon *n* arme *f*.

wear *vt* (*pt* **wore**; *pp* **worn**) porter; (put on) mettre; (*expression*) avoir. ● *vi* (last) durer; **~ (out)** (s')user. ● *n* (use) usage *m*; (damage) usure *f*. □ **~ down** user; **~ off** (*colour, pain*) passer; **~ out** (exhaust) épuiser.

weary *a* (**-ier, -iest**) fatigué, las. ● *vi* **~ of** se lasser de.

weather *n* temps *m*; **under the ~** patraque. ● *a* météorologique. ● *vt* (survive) réchapper de *or* à. **~ forecast** *n* météo *f*.

weave *vt/i* (*pt* **wove**; *pp* **woven**) tisser; (*basket*) tresser; (move) se faufiler. ● *n* (style) tissage *m*.

web *n* (of spider) toile *f*; (on foot) palmure *f*.

Web *n* (Comput) Web *m*. **~master** *n* administrateur *m* de site Internet. **~ site** *n* site *m* Internet.

wedding *n* mariage *m*. **~-ring** *n* alliance *f*.

wedge *n* (of wood) coin *m*; (under wheel) cale *f*. ● *vt* caler; (push) enfoncer; (crowd) coincer.

Wednesday *n* mercredi *m*.

weed *n* mauvaise herbe *f*. ● *vt/i* désherber; **~ out** extirper.

week *n* semaine *f*; **a ~ today/tomorrow** aujourd'hui/demain en huit. **~day** *n* jour *m* de semaine. **~end** *n* week-end *m*, fin *f* de semaine.

weekly *adv* toutes les semaines. ● *a & n* (periodical) hebdomadaire (*m*).

weep *vt/i* (*pt* **wept**) pleurer (**for sb** qn).

weigh *vt/i* peser; **~ anchor** lever l'ancre. □ **~ down** lester (avec un poids); (bend) faire plier; (fig) accabler; **~ up** (examine 🅸) calculer.

weight *n* poids *m*; **lose/put on ~** perdre/prendre du poids. **~-lifting** *n* haltérophilie *f*. **~ training** *n* musculation *f* en salle.

weird *a* mystérieux; (strange) bizarre.

welcome *a* agréable; (timely) opportun; **be ~** être le *or* la bienvenu(e), être les bienvenu(e)s; **you're ~!** il n'y a pas de quoi!; **~ to do** libre de faire. ● *interj* soyez le *or* la bienvenu(e), soyez les bienvenu(e)s. ● *n* accueil *m*. ● *vt* accueillir; (as greeting) souhaiter la bienvenue à; (fig) se réjouir de.

weld *vt* souder. ● *n* soudure *f*.

welfare *n* bien-être *m*; (aid) aide *f* sociale. **W~ State** *n* État-providence *m*.

well[1] *n* puits *m*.

well[2] *adv* (**better, best**) bien; **do ~** (succeed) réussir; **~ done!** bravo! ● *a* bien *inv*; **as ~** aussi; **be ~** (healthy) aller bien. ● *interj* eh bien; (surprise) tiens.

well: **~-behaved** *a* sage. **~-being** *n* bien-être *m inv*.

wellington *n* (boot) botte *f* de caoutchouc.

well: **~-known** *a* (bien) connu. **~-meaning** *a* bien intentionné. **~ off** aisé, riche. **~-read** *a* instruit. **~-to-do** *a* riche. **~-wisher** *n* admirateur/-trice *m/f*.

Welsh *a* gallois. ● *n* (Ling) gallois *m*.

went ⇒GO.

wept ⇒WEEP.

were ⇒BE.

west *n* ouest *m*; **the W~** (Pol) l'Occident *m*. ● *a* d'ouest. ● *adv* vers l'ouest.

western *a* de l'ouest; (Pol) occidental. ● *n* (film) western *m*. **westerner** *n* occidental/-e *m/f*.

West Indies *n* Antilles *fpl*.

westward *a* (*side*) ouest *inv*; (*journey*) vers l'ouest.

wet *a* (**wetter, wettest**) mouillé; (damp, rainy) humide; (*paint*) frais; **get ~** se mouiller. ● *vt* (*pt* **wetted**) mouiller. ● *n* **the ~** l'humidité *f*; (rain) la pluie *f*. **~ suit** *n* combinaison *f* de plongée.

whale *n* baleine *f*.

wharf *n* quai *m*.

what

●*pronoun*

····➤ (in questions as object pronoun) qu'est-ce que?; **~ are we going to do?** qu'est-ce que nous allons faire?

····➤ (in questions as subject pronoun) qu'est-ce qui?; **~ happened?** qu'est-ce qui s'est passé?

····➤ (introducing clause as object) ce que; **I don't know ~ he wants** je ne sais pas ce qu'il veut.

····➤ (introducing clause as subject) ce qui; **tell me ~ happened** raconte-moi ce qui s'est passé.

····➤ (with prepositions) quoi; **~ are you thinking about?** à quoi penses-tu?

●*determiner*

····➤ quel/quelle/quels/quelles; **~ train did you catch?** quel train as-tu pris?; **~ time is it?** quelle heure est-il?

whatever *a* **~ book** quel que soit le livre. ● *pron* (no matter what) quoi que, quoi qu'; (anything that) tout ce qui; (object) tout ce que *or* qu'; **~ happens** quoi qu'il arrive; **~ happened?** qu'est-ce qui est arrivé?; **~ the problems** quels que soient les problèmes; **~ you want** tout ce que vous voulez; **nothing ~** rien du tout.

whatsoever *a & pron* = WHATEVER.

wheat *n* blé *m*, froment *m*.

wheel *n* roue *f*; **at the ~** (of vehicle) au volant; (helm) au gouvernail. ● *vt* pousser. ● *vi* tourner; **~ and deal** faire des combines. **~barrow** *n* brouette *f*. **~chair** *n* fauteuil *m* roulant.

when *adv & pron* quand. ● *conj* quand, lorsque; **the day/moment ~** le jour/moment où.

whenever *conj & adv* (at whatever time) quand; (every time that) chaque fois que.

where *adv, conj & pron* où; (whereas) alors que; (the place that) là où.

whereabouts *adv* (à peu près) où. ● *n* **sb's ~** l'endroit où se trouve qn.

whereas *conj* alors que.

wherever *conj & adv* où que; (everywhere) partout où; (anywhere) (là) où; (emphatic where) où donc.

whether *conj* si; **not know ~** ne pas savoir si; **~ I go or not** que j'aille ou non.

which

●*pronoun*

····➤ (in questions) lequel/laquelle/lesquels/lesquelles; **there are three peaches, ~ do you want?** il y a trois pêches, laquelle veux-tu?

····➤ (in questions with superlative adjective) quel/quelle/quels/quelles; **~ (apple) is the biggest?** quelle est la plus grosse?

····➤ (in relative clauses as subject) qui; **the book ~ is on the table** le livre qui est sur la table.

····➤ (in relative clauses as object) que; **the book ~ Tina is reading** le livre que lit Tina.

● *determiner*

····➤ quel/quelle/quels/quelles; **~ car did you choose?** quelle voiture as-tu choisie?

whichever *a* **~ book** quel que soit le livre que *or* qui; **take ~ book you wish** prenez le livre que vous voulez. ● *pron* celui/celle/ceux/celles qui *or* que.

while *n* moment *m*. ● *conj* (when) pendant que; (although) bien que; (as long as) tant que. ● *vt* **~ away** (*time*) passer.

whilst *conj* = WHILE.

whim *n* caprice *m*.

whine *vi* gémir, se plaindre. ● *n* gémissement *m*.

whip *n* fouet *m*. ● *vt* (*pt* **whipped**) fouetter; (Culin) fouetter, battre, (seize) enlever brusquement. ● *vi* (move) aller en vitesse. □ **~ up** exciter; (cause) provoquer; (*meal* 🅸) préparer.

whirl *vt/i* (faire) tourbillonner. ● *n* tourbillon *m*. **~pool** *n* tourbillon *m*. **~wind** *n* tourbillon *m* (de vent).

whisk *vt* (snatch) enlever *or* emmener brusquement; (Culin) fouetter. ● *n* (Culin) fouet *m*.

whiskers *npl* (of animal) moustaches *fpl*; (of man) favoris *mpl*.

whisper *vt/i* chuchoter. ● *n* chuchotement *m*; (rumour: fig) rumeur *f*, bruit *m*.

whistle *n* sifflement *m*; (instrument) sifflet *m*. ● *vt/i* siffler; **~ at** *or* **for** siffler.

white *a* blanc. ● *n* blanc *m*; (person) blanc/-che *m/f*. **~ coffee** *n* café *m* au lait. **~-collar worker** *n* employé/-e *m/f* de bureau. **~ elephant** *n* projet *m* coûteux et peu rentable. **~ lie** *n* pieux mensonge *m*. **W~ Paper** *n* livre *m* blanc.

whitewash *n* blanc *m* de chaux. ● *vt* blanchir à la chaux; (*person*: fig) blanchir.

Whitsun *n* la Pentecôte.

whiz *vi* (*pt* **whizzed**) (through air) fendre l'air; (hiss) siffler; (rush) aller à toute vitesse. **~-kid** *n* jeune prodige *m*.

who *pron* qui.

whoever *pron* (no matter who) qui que ce soit qui *or* que; (the one who) quiconque; **tell ~ you want** dites-le à qui vous voulez.

whole *a* entier; (intact) intact; **the ~ house** toute la maison. ● *n* totalité *f*; (unit) tout *m*; **on the ~** dans l'ensemble. **~foods** *npl* aliments *mpl* naturels et diététiques. **~-hearted** *a* sans réserve. **~meal** *a* complet.

wholesale *a* (*firm*) de gros; (fig) systématique. ● *adv* (in large quantities) en gros; (fig) en masse.

wholesome *a* sain.

wholly *adv* entièrement.

whom *pron* (that) que, qu'; (after prepositions & in questions) qui; **of ~** dont; **with ~** avec qui.

whooping cough *n* coqueluche *f*.

whose *pron & a* à qui, de qui; **~ hat is this?, ~ is this hat?** à qui est ce chapeau?; **~ son are you?** de qui êtes-vous le fils?; **the man ~ hat I see** l'homme dont je vois le chapeau.

why *adv* pourquoi; **the reason ~** la raison pour laquelle.

wicked *a* méchant, mauvais, vilain.

wide *a* large; (*ocean*) vaste. ● *adv* (*fall*) loin du but; **open ~** ouvrir tout grand; **~ open** grand ouvert; **~ awake** éveillé. **widely** *adv* (*spread, space*) largement;

(*travel*) beaucoup; (generally) généralement; (extremely) extrêmement.

widespread *a* très répandu.

widow *n* veuve *f*. **widowed** *a* (*man*) veuf; (*woman*) veuve. **widower** *n* veuf *m*.

width *n* largeur *f*.

wield *vt* (*axe*) manier; (*power*: fig) exercer.

wife *n* (*pl* **wives**) femme *f*, épouse *f*.

wig *n* perruque *f*.

wiggle *vt*/*i* remuer; (*hips*) tortiller; (*worm*) se tortiller.

wild *a* sauvage; (*sea, enthusiasm*) déchaîné; (mad) fou; (angry) furieux. ●*adv* (*grow*) à l'état sauvage; **run ~** (free) courir en liberté.

wildlife *n* faune *f*.

will[1]

present **will**; *present negative* **won't, will not**; *past* **would**

●*auxiliary verb*

····➤ (in future tense) **he'll come** il viendra; **it ~ be sunny tomorrow** il va faire du soleil demain.

····➤ (inviting and requesting) **~ you have some coffee?** est-ce que vous voulez du café?

····➤ (making assumptions) **they won't know what's happened** ils ne doivent pas savoir ce qui s'est passé.

····➤ (in short questions and answers) **you'll come again, won't you?** tu reviendras, n'est-ce pas?; **'they won't forget'—'yes they ~'** 'ils n'oublieront pas'—'si'.

····➤ (capacity) **the lift ~ hold 12** l'ascenseur peut transporter 12 personnes.

····➤ (ability) **the car won't start** la voiture ne veut pas démarrer.

●*transitive verb*

····➤ **~ sb's death** souhaiter ardemment la mort de qn.

will[2] *n* volonté *f*; (document) testament *m*; **at ~** quand *or* comme on veut.

willing *a* (*help, offer*) spontané; (*helper*) bien disposé; **~ to** disposé à. **willingly** *adv* (with pleasure) volontiers; (not forced) volontairement. **willingness** *n* empressement *m* (**to do** à faire).

willow *n* saule *m*.

will-power *n* volonté *f*.

win *vt*/*i* (*pt* **won**; *pres p* **winning**) gagner; (*victory, prize*) remporter; (*fame, fortune*) acquérir, trouver; **~ round** convaincre. ●*n* victoire *f*.

winch *n* treuil *m*. ●*vt* hisser au treuil.

wind[1] *n* vent *m*; (breath) souffle *m*; **get ~ of** avoir vent de; **in the ~** dans l'air. ●*vt* essouffler.

wind[2] *vt*/*i* (*pt* **wound**) (s')enrouler; (of path, river) serpenter; **~ (up)** (*clock*) remonter; **~ up** (end) (se) terminer; **~ up in hospital** finir à l'hôpital.

windmill *n* moulin *m* à vent.

window *n* fenêtre *f*; (glass pane) vitre *f*; (in vehicle, train) vitre *f*; (in shop) vitrine *f*; (counter) guichet *m*; (Comput) fenêtre *f*. **~-box** *n* jardinière *f*. **~-cleaner** *n* laveur *m* de carreaux. **~-dresser** *n* étalagiste *mf*. **~-ledge** *n* rebord *m* de (la) fenêtre. **~-shopping** *n* lèche-vitrines *m*. **~-sill** *n* (inside) appui *m* de (la) fenêtre; (outside) rebord *m* de (la) fenêtre.

windscreen *n* pare-brise *m inv*. **~ wiper** *n* essuie-glace *m*.

windshield *n* (US) = WINDSCREEN.

windsurfing *n* planche *f* à voile.

windy *a* (**-ier, -iest**) venteux; **it is ~** il y a du vent.

wine *n* vin *m*. ~**-cellar** *n* cave *f* (*à vin*). ~**glass** *n* verre *m* à vin. ~**-grower** *n* viticulteur *m*. ~ **list** *n* carte *f* des vins. ~**-tasting** *n* dégustation *f* de vins.

wing *n* aile *f*; ~**s** (Theat) coulisses *fpl*; **under one's** ~ sous son aile. ~ **mirror** *n* rétroviseur *m* extérieur.

wink *vi* faire un clin d'œil; (*light, star*) clignoter. ● *n* clin *m* d'œil; clignotement *m*.

winner *n* (of game) gagnant/-e *m/f*; (of fight) vainqueur *m*.

winning ⇒WIN. ● *a* (*number, horse*) gagnant; (*team*) victorieux; (*smile*) engageant. **winnings** *npl* gains *mpl*.

winter *n* hiver *m*.

wipe *vt* essuyer. ● *vi* ~ **up** essuyer la vaisselle. ● *n* coup *m* de torchon *or* d'éponge. □ ~ **out** (destroy) anéantir; (remove) effacer.

wire *n* fil *m*; (US) télégramme *m*.

wiring *n* (Electr) installation *f* électrique.

wisdom *n* sagesse *f*.

wise *a* prudent, sage; (*look*) averti.

wish *n* (specific) souhait *m*, vœu *m*; (general) désir *m*; **best** ~**es** (in letter) amitiés *fpl*; (on greeting card) meilleurs vœux *mpl*. ● *vt* souhaiter, vouloir, désirer (**to do** faire); (bid) souhaiter. ● *vi* ~ **for** souhaiter; **I** ~ **he'd leave** je voudrais bien qu'il parte.

wishful *a* **it's** ~ **thinking** c'est prendre ses désirs pour des réalités.

wistful *a* mélancolique.

wit *n* intelligence *f*; (humour) esprit *m*; (person) homme *m* d'esprit, femme *f* d'esprit.

witch *n* sorcière *f*.

with *prep* avec; (having) à; (because of) de; (at house of) chez; **the man** ~ **the beard** l'homme à la barbe; **fill** ~ remplir de; **pleased/shaking** ~ content/frémissant de.

withdraw *vt/i* (*pt* **withdrew**; *pp* **withdrawn**) (se) retirer. **withdrawal** *n* retrait *m*.

wither *vt/i* (se) flétrir.

withhold *vt* (*pt* **withheld**) refuser (de donner); (retain) retenir; (conceal) cacher (**from** à).

within *prep & adv* à l'intérieur (de); (in distances) à moins de; ~ **a month** (before) avant un mois; ~ **sight** en vue.

without *prep* sans; ~ **my knowing** sans que je sache.

withstand *vt* (*pt* **withstood**) résister à.

witness *n* témoin *m*; (evidence) témoignage *m*; **bear** ~ **to** témoigner de. ● *vt* être le témoin de, voir. ~ **box**, ~ **stand** *n* barre *f* des témoins.

witty *a* (**-ier**, **-iest**) spirituel.

wives ⇒WIFE.

wizard *n* magicien *m*; (genius: fig) génie *m*.

woke, **woken** ⇒WAKE.

wolf *n* (*pl* **wolves**) loup *m*. ● *vt* (*food*) engloutir.

woman *n* (*pl* **women**) femme *f*; ~ **doctor** femme *f* médecin; ~ **driver** femme *f* au volant.

women ⇒WOMAN.

won ⇒WIN.

wonder *n* émerveillement *m*; (thing) merveille *f*; **it is no** ~ ce *or* il n'est pas étonnant (**that** que). ● *vt* se demander (**if** si). ● *vi* s'étonner (**at** de); (reflect) songer (**about** à).

wonderful *a* merveilleux.

won't = WILL NOT.

wood *n* bois *m*.

wooden *a* en *or* de bois; (stiff: fig) raide, comme du bois.

wood: ~**wind** *n* (Mus) bois *mpl*.

~work *n* (craft, objects) menuiserie *f*.

wool *n* laine *f*. **woollen** *a* de laine. **woollens** *npl* lainages *mpl*.

woolly *a* laineux; (vague) nébuleux. ● *n* (garment ▣) lainage *m*.

word *n* mot *m*; (spoken) parole *f*, mot *m*; (promise) parole *f*; (news) nouvelles *fpl*; **by ~ of mouth** de vive voix; **give/keep one's ~** donner/tenir sa parole; **have a ~ with** parler à; **in other ~s** autrement dit. ● *vt* rédiger. **wording** *n* termes *mpl*.

word processing *n* traitement *m* de texte. **word processor** *n* machine *f* à traitement de texte.

wore ⇒WEAR.

work *n* travail *m*; (product, book) œuvre *f*, ouvrage *m*; (building work) travaux *mpl*; **~s** (Tech) mécanisme *m*; (factory) usine *f*. ● *vi* (*person*) travailler; (*drug*) agir; (Tech) fonctionner, marcher. ● *vt* (Tech) faire fonctionner, faire marcher; (*land, mine*) exploiter; (shape, hammer) travailler; **~ sb** (make work) faire travailler qn. □ **~ out** *vt* (solve) résoudre; (calculate) calculer; (elaborate) élaborer; *vi* (succeed) marcher; (Sport) s'entraîner; **~ up** *vt* développer; *vi* (to climax) monter vers; **~ed up** (*person*) énervé.

workaholic *n* ▣ bourreau *m* de travail.

worker *n* travailleur/-euse *m/f*; (manual) ouvrier/-ière *m/f*.

work-force *n* main-d'œuvre *f*.

working *a* (*day, lunch*) de travail; **~s** mécanisme *m*; **in ~ order** en état de marche.

working class *n* classe *f* ouvrière. ● *a* ouvrier.

workman *n* (*pl* **-men**) ouvrier *m*.

work: **~ out** *n* séance *f* de mise en forme. **~shop** *n* atelier *m*. **~-station** *n* poste *m* de travail.

world *n* monde *m*; **best in the ~** meilleur au monde. ● *a* (*power*) mondial; (*record*) du monde.

world-wide *a* universel.

World Wide Web, WWW *n* World Wide Web *m*, réseau *m* des réseaux.

worm *n* ver *m*. ● *vt* **~ one's way into** s'insinuer dans.

worn ⇒WEAR. ● *a* usé. **~-out** *a* (*thing*) complètement usé; (*person*) épuisé.

worried *a* inquiet.

worry *vt/i* (s')inquiéter. ● *n* souci *m*.

worse *a* pire, plus mauvais; **be ~ off** perdre. ● *adv* plus mal. ● *n* pire *m*. **worsen** *vt/i* empirer.

worship *n* (adoration) culte *m*. ● *vt* (*pt* **worshipped**) adorer. ● *vi* faire ses dévotions.

worst *a* pire, plus mauvais. ● *adv* (**the**) **~** (*sing*) le plus mal. ● *n* **the ~** (**one**) (person, object) le *or* la pire; **the ~** (**thing**) le pire.

worth *a* **be ~** valoir; **it is ~ waiting** ça vaut la peine d'attendre; **it is ~** (**one's**) **while** ça (en) vaut la peine. ● *n* valeur *f*; **ten pence ~ of** (pour) dix pence de. **worthless** *a* qui ne vaut rien. **worthwhile** *a* qui (en) vaut la peine.

worthy *a* (**-ier, -iest**) digne (**of** de); (laudable) louable.

would *v aux* **he ~ do/you ~ sing** (conditional tense) il ferait/tu chanterais; **he ~ have done** il aurait fait; **I ~ come every day** (used to) je venais chaque jour; **I ~ like some tea** je voudrais du thé; **~ you come here?** voulez-vous venir ici?; **he wouldn't come** il a refusé de venir. **~-be** *a* soi-disant.

wound¹ *n* blessure *f*. ● *vt* blesser; **the ~ed** les blessés *mpl*.

wound² ⇒WIND².

wove, woven ⇒WEAVE.

wrap *vt* (*pt* **wrapped**) ~ **(up)** envelopper. ● *vi* ~ **up** (dress warmly) se couvrir; **~ped up in** (engrossed) absorbé dans.

wrapping *n* emballage *m*.

wreak *vt* ~ **havoc** faire des ravages.

wreath *n* (of flowers, leaves) couronne *f*.

wreck *n* (sinking) naufrage *m*; (ship, remains, person) épave *f*; (vehicle) voiture *f* accidentée *or* délabrée. ● *vt* détruire; (*ship*) provoquer le naufrage de. **wreckage** *n* (pieces) débris *mpl*; (wrecked building) décombres *mpl*.

wrestle *vi* lutter, se débattre (**with** contre).

wrestling *n* lutte *f*; (**all-in**) ~ catch *m*.

wriggle *vt*/*i* (se) tortiller.

wring *vt* (*pt* **wrung**) (twist) tordre; (*clothes*) essorer; ~ **out of** (obtain from) arracher à.

wrinkle *n* (crease) pli *m*; (on skin) ride *f*. ● *vt*/*i* (se) rider.

wrist *n* poignet *m*.

write *vt*/*i* (*pt* **wrote**; *pp* **written**) écrire. □ ~ **back** répondre; ~ **down** noter; ~ **off** (*debt*) passer aux profits et pertes; (*vehicle*) considérer bon pour la casse; ~ **up** (from notes) rédiger.

write-off *n* perte *f* totale.

writer *n* auteur *m*, écrivain *m*; ~ **of** auteur de.

write-up *n* compte-rendu *m*.

writing *n* écriture *f*; **~(s)** (works) écrits *mpl*; **in** ~ par écrit. **~-paper** *n* papier *m* à lettres.

written ⇒WRITE.

wrong *a* (incorrect, mistaken) faux, mauvais; (unfair) injuste; (amiss) qui ne va pas; (*clock*) pas à l'heure; **be** ~ (*person*) avoir tort (**to** de); (be mistaken) se tromper; **go** ~ (err) se tromper; (turn out badly) mal tourner; **it is** ~ **to** (morally) c'est mal de; **what's ~?** qu'est-ce qui ne va pas?; **what is ~ with you?** qu'est-ce que vous avez? ● *adv* mal. ● *n* injustice *f*; (evil) mal *m*; **be in the** ~ avoir tort. ● *vt* faire (du) tort à. **wrongful** *a* injustifié, injuste. **wrongfully** *adv* à tort. **wrongly** *adv* mal; (*blame*) à tort.

wrote ⇒WRITE.

wrought iron *n* fer *m* forgé.

wrung ⇒WRING.

Xmas *n* Noël *m*.

X-ray *n* rayon *m* X; (photograph) radio(graphie) *f*. ● *vt* radiographier.

yank *vt* tirer brusquement. ● *n* coup *m* brusque.

yard *n* (measure) yard *m* (= *0.9144 metre*); (of house) cour *f*; (garden: US) jardin *m*; (for storage) chantier *m*, dépôt *m*. **~stick** *n* mesure *f*.

yawn *vi* bâiller. ● *n* bâillement *m*.

year *n* an *m*, année *f*; **school/tax**

~ année scolaire/fiscale; **be ten ~s old** avoir dix ans.

yearly *a* annuel. ● *adv* annuellement.

yearn *vi* avoir bien *or* très envie (**for, to** de).

yeast *n* levure *f*.

yell *vt/i* hurler. ● *n* hurlement *m*.

yellow *a* jaune; (cowardly ⓘ) froussard. ● *n* jaune *m*.

yes *adv* oui; (as answer to negative question) si. ● *n* oui *m inv*.

yesterday *n & adv* hier (*m*).

yet *adv* encore; (already) déjà. ● *conj* pourtant, néanmoins.

yew *n* if *m*.

yield *vt* (produce) produire, rendre; (*profit*) rapporter; (surrender) céder. ● *n* rendement *m*.

yoga *n* yoga *m*.

yoghurt *n* yaourt *m*.

yolk *n* jaune *m* (d'œuf).

you *pron* (familiar form) tu, *pl* vous; (polite form) vous; (object) te, t', *pl* vous; (polite) vous; (after prep.) toi, *pl* vous; (polite) vous; (indefinite) on; (object) vous; (**to**) ~ te, t', *pl* vous; (polite) vous; **I gave ~ a pen** je vous ai donné un stylo; **I know ~** je te connais *or* je vous connais.

young *a* jeune. ● *n* (people) jeunes *mpl*; (of animals) petits *mpl*.

your *a* (familiar form) ton, ta, *pl* tes; (polite form, & familiar form pl.) votre, *pl* vos.

yours *pron* (familiar form) le tien, la tienne, les tien(ne)s; (polite form, & familiar form pl.) le *or* la vôtre, les vôtres; **~ faithfully/sincerely** je vous prie d'agréer mes salutations les meilleures.

yourself *pron* (familiar form) toi-même; (polite form) vous-même; (reflexive & after prepositions) te, t'; vous; **proud of ~** fier de toi. **yourselves** *pron* vous-mêmes; (reflexive) vous.

youth *n* jeunesse *f*; (young man) jeune *m*. **~ hostel** *n* auberge *f* de jeunesse.

Yugoslav *a* yougoslave. ● *n* Yougoslave *mf*.

Yugoslavia *n* Yougoslavie *f*.

zap *vt* ⓘ (kill) descendre; (Comput) enlever.

zeal *n* zèle *m*.

zebra *n* zèbre *m*. **~ crossing** *n* passage *m* pour piétons.

zero *n* zéro *m*.

zest *n* (gusto) entrain *m*; (spice: fig) piment *m*; (of orange or lemon peel) zeste *m*.

zip *n* (vigour) allant *m*; **~(-fastener)** fermeture *f* éclair®. ● *vt* (*pt* **zipped**) fermer avec une fermeture éclair®; (Comput) compresser. **Zip code** (US) *n* code *m* postal.

zodiac *n* zodiaque *m*.

zone *n* zone *f*.

zoo *n* zoo *m*.

zoom *vi* (rush) se précipiter. □ **~ off** *or* **past** filer (comme une flèche). **~ lens** *n* zoom *m*.

zucchini *n inv* (US) courgette *f*.

Summary of French grammar

Grammar provides a useful description of the patterns which make up a language. The following pages offer a summary for reference.

1 NOUNS and GENDER

- All nouns are either *masculine* or *feminine* in French
- The gender is an important feature of each noun
- The gender is shown by the article (*definite* or *indefinite*)

1.1 The definite article (= THE)

	Singular	Plural
Masculine	***le***	***les***
Feminine	***la***	***les***

- ***le*** and ***la*** are reduced to ***l'*** before:
  a singular noun starting with a vowel (***école*** → ***l'école***)
  a singular noun starting with a silent h (***hôtel*** → ***l'hôtel***)
- ***les*** is the plural in all cases

1.2 The indefinite article (= A or AN; plural = SOME)

	Singular	Plural
Masculine	***un***	***des***
Feminine	***une***	***des***

- ***un*** and ***une*** also indicate the number 1 in counting:
  e.g. ***une pomme*** = one apple [*see* NUMBERS *section 9.1*]
- ***des*** is the plural in all cases

⚠ *Note:* Articles are rarely omitted:
e.g. ***les enfants aiment les bonbons*** = children like sweets
BUT when specifying someone's occupation, the article is dropped:
e.g. ***il est boucher*** = he is a butcher,
ma soeur est avocat = my sister is a lawyer

2 NOUNS and NUMBER

- number means *singular* or *plural*
- nouns in most cases add an ending in the plural

2.1 Typical nouns:

Most nouns add *-s* in the plural:
e.g. ***chaise*** → ***chaises*** (= chairs) ***chien*** → ***chiens*** (= dogs)

2.2 Nouns ending in -eu or -eau:

These nouns usually add *-x* in the plural:
e.g. ***jeu*** → ***jeux*** (= games) ***bureau*** → ***bureaux*** (= desks)

2.3 Nouns ending in -ou:

These nouns usually add *-s* in the plural.
BUT there are 6 common exceptions which add *-x*:

bijou → ***bijoux*** (= jewels) ***genou*** → ***genoux*** (= knees)
caillou → ***cailloux*** (= pebbles) ***hibou***→ ***hiboux*** (= owls)
chou → ***choux*** (= cabbages) ***joujou*** → ***joujoux*** (= toys)

2.4 Nouns ending in -al:

These nouns usually change from ***-al*** to ***-aux***:
e.g. ***rival*** → ***rivaux*** (= rivals); ***cheval*** → ***chevaux*** (= horses)
BUT there are exceptions: e.g. ***bal*** → ***bals*** (= dances)

2.5 Nouns ending in -ail:

These nouns usually add *-s*:
e.g. ***détail*** → ***détails*** (= details)
BUT there are exceptions:
e.g. ***travail*** → ***travaux*** (= works)

2.6 Some nouns have unusual plurals:

These plurals need to be learnt individually:
e.g. ***ciel*** → ***cieux*** (= skies) ***oeil*** → ***yeux*** (= eyes)

⚠ *Note*: the group: monsieur ‡ messieurs; madame ‡ mesdames; mademoiselle ‡ mesdemoiselles; mon-, ma- in these words meant 'my' originally (as in 'my lord', 'my lady')
[*See* POSSESSIVE ADJECTIVES *section 6*]

2.7 Hyphenated nouns

- The plurals of this group of nouns vary and depend on how the word is formed (*adjective* + *noun*, *verb* + *noun*, etc.)
- In cases where there is an ADJECTIVE + NOUN, it is normal for both words in the compound to change: e.g. ***beau-père*** → ***beaux-pères*** (= fathers-in-law)
- It is often helpful to translate the compound and find which word will logically become plural: e.g. ***arc-en-ciel*** (= rainbow) → ***arcs-en-ciel*** (= rainbows) (literally 'arc in the sky' → 'arcs in the sky')

⚠ *Note:* sometimes it is logical to leave the word unchanged in the plural because no noun is present in the make-up of the compound: e.g. ***un passe-partout*** = skeleton key ‡ ***des passe-partout*** = skeleton keys (literally 'a go-everywhere' : VERB + ADVERB)

2.8 Nouns showing no change between singular and plural

Nouns already ending in -*s*: e.g. ***bois*** → ***bois*** (= woods)
Nouns already ending in -*x*: e.g. ***voix*** → ***voix*** (= voices)
Nouns already ending in -*z*: e.g. ***nez*** → ***nez*** (= noses)

3 NOUNS and QUANTITY

- There are many nouns which indicate quantity e.g. ***un kilo de*** = a kilo of...; ***une livre de*** = a pound of...; ***une bouteille de*** = a bottle of...
- The word ***de*** is important in quantity expressions
- Sometimes ***de*** combines with ***le*** / ***la*** / ***l'*** / ***les*** to mean 'some'

3.1 The partitive article (= SOME)

de + NOUNS	
de + le → du	e.g. ***le pain*** → ***du pain*** = some bread
de + la → de la	e.g. ***la crème*** → ***de la crème*** = some cream
de + l' → de l'	e.g. ***l'huile*** → ***de l'huile*** = some oil
de + les → des	e.g. ***les oranges*** → ***des oranges*** = some oranges

⚠ *Note:* After a negative (*not, no more*, etc.: *see* NEGATIVES *section 12*), only use ***de*** or ***d'***: e.g. ***je n'ai plus de pain*** = I haven't got any more bread; ***il ne prend pas d'huile*** = he's not buying any oil
After a quantity expression such as ***un kilo de***, do not change ***de*** to ***des***: e.g. ***un kilo de pommes*** = a kilo of apples

4 NOUNS replaced by PRONOUNS

4.1 Subject pronouns

- Subject pronouns (*I, we, they*, etc.) replace nouns
- They refer to people or things
- They govern verbs (e.g. ***je chante*** = I sing) [*see* VERBS *section 10.1*]

Singular	Plural
je = I	***nous*** = we
tu = you	***vous*** = you
il = he /it	***ils*** = they [*masculine*]
elle = she / it	***elles*** = they [*feminine*]
on = one*	

• ***on*** is used as a less specific subject pronoun to mean 'one', 'you', 'people', 'we', 'they':
e.g. ***on mange ici?*** = shall we eat here?
on n'aime pas refuser = one doesn't like to refuse
on parle français là? = do they speak French there?

4.2 Object pronouns

4.2.a Direct object pronouns

- Direct object pronouns (*it, him, us*, etc.) replace nouns
- They refer to people or things
- They are the object (= affected by the action) of verbs: e.g. hit the ball; go on, hit it! = ***frappe la balle; allez, frappe-la!***

French	English
me / m'	me
te / t'	you [*singular*]
le / l'	him / it
la / l'	her / it
se / s'	himself/ herself/ itself
nous	us
vous	you [*plural*]
les	them
se / s'	themselves

- ***m' / t' / l' / s'*** are used if the word that follows starts with a vowel or a silent h:
  e.g. ***ils l'aiment*** = they love her
  elles l'ont humidifié = they sprayed it with water
- object pronouns affect the ending of a past participle [*see* VERBS *section 10.1.f*] if the object is feminine or plural:
  e.g. ***elle a poli la table → elle l'a polie*** (she polished it)

4.2.b Indirect object pronouns

- Indirect object pronouns (*to it, to him, to us*, etc.) replace nouns
- They refer to people or things
- They are the indirect object (= *indirectly* affected by the action) of verbs:
  e.g. ***donnez-lui la balle!*** = give the ball to him (or to her)!
  il m'a montré la photo = he showed me the photo

French	English
me / m'	(to) me
te / t'	(to) you [*singular*]
lui	(to) him or it
lui	(to) her or it
nous	(to) us
vous	(to) you [*plural*]
leur	(to) them

- (to) shows that the word 'to' is understood in the sentence even though it may not actually be said:
  e.g. give them that! = give that to them! = ***donne-le***-leur!

4.2.c Indirect object pronouns: places and quantities

- The indirect object pronoun referring to a place is:
  y (= there) e.g. ***j'y vais*** = I'm going there
- The indirect object pronoun referring to a quantity is:
  en (= of it, of them, some) e.g. ***j'en voudrais 3*** = I'd like 3 (of them); ***offrez-leur-en*** = offer them some

4.3 Order of object pronouns in the sentence

- Object pronouns come before most verb parts:
  e.g. ***elle leur rend les livres*** = she returns the books to them
- Object pronouns come before an infinitive:
  e.g. ***elle va leur rendre les livres*** = she is going to return the books to them
- Object pronouns come before the first part of a compound tense (= conjugated with ***avoir*** or ***être***: *see* VERBS *section 10.1.f*)
  e.g. ***elle leur a rendu les livres*** = she returned the books to them
- Object pronouns follow the imperative form of the verb and are linked to it by a hyphen:
  e.g. ***rends-leur les livres!*** = return the books to them!
- Object pronouns return to normal order even with an imperative if it is negative:
  e.g. ***ne les rendez pas!*** = don't return them!
- When they occur in multiples in a sentence, object pronouns have a fixed order

OBJECT PRONOUN ORDER (see above tables for meanings):

me				
te	***le***	***lui***	***y***	***en***
se*	***la***	***leur***		
nous	***les***			
vous				
se*				

- the first column (me, te, se) is also used with reflexive verbs [*see* VERBS *section 10.1*]
- ***se*** means: (to) himself, (to) herself, (to) oneself, (to) themselves

⚠ *Note:* any combination of object pronouns will fall in this order:
e.g. ***ils y en ont mis 6*** = they put 6 of them there
il le lui a payé = he bought it for her
ils le leur y ont expliqué = they explained it to them there

4.4 Disjunctive or emphatic pronouns

■ Pronouns are sometimes used for emphasis:

Disjunctive Pronouns	
moi	***nous***
toi	***vous***
lui	***eux***
elle	***elles***

■ They take on these spellings:
* after prepositions:
e.g. ***avec moi*** = with me
* after ***que*** or ***qu'*** in comparative sentences [*see* COMPARISON *section 8.1*]:
e.g. ***plus petit que lui*** = smaller than him
* to emphasize the subject:
e.g. ***lui, il n'aime pas le vin rouge mais elle, elle l'adore***
= he doesn't like red wine but she loves it
* with ***même*** meaning 'self' (*myself, yourself*, etc.):
e.g. ***toi-même*** = yourself
vous-mêmes = yourselves

 ***Note:*** that ***-s*** is added to ***même*** in the plural

Note: moi and ***toi*** are also used as 'emphatics' in imperatives when pronouns follow the verb: e.g. ***donnez-le-moi***! = give it to me! ***mettez-toi là***! = sit yourself there!

5 ADJECTIVES

- Adjectives qualify nouns
- They usually follow the noun in French
- They reflect the noun in both gender and number
- Many determiners (*this, my, all, three*, etc.) are adjectival
- Some adjectives are used alone as nouns
  e.g. ***il est intelligent, le petit*** = the little one (= boy) is bright

5.1 Common adjectival endings:

- The masculine form is that given in the dictionary
- Add ***-e*** to form the feminine:
  e.g. ***une jupe courte*** = a short skirt
- Add ***-s*** to the masculine to form the masculine plural:
  e.g. ***des voyages intéressants*** = interesting journeys
- Add ***-s*** to the feminine to form the feminine plural
  e.g. ***des histoires amusantes*** = funny stories

5. 2 Adjectives ending in -e

These stay the same in the feminine:
e.g. ***aimable*** → feminine ***aimable***

Note: unless the ***-e*** has an acute accent:
e.g. ***aimé*** → feminine ***aimée***

-s is added in the normal way in the plural:
e.g. ***aimable*** → plural ***aimables***

Note: this is true of all adjectives:
unless the ending is ***-x*** (e.g. ***curieux*** → masculine plural ***curieux***)
unless there is already a final ***-s*** (***bas*** → masculine plural ***bas***)

5.3 Table of adjectives showing typical endings and their feminines:

Typical ending	Adjective	Feminine	English
The following double the last letter and add an *-e*			
-as	***bas***	***basse***	low
-eil	***pareil***	***pareille***	similar
-el	***mortel***	***mortelle***	fatal
-en	***ancien***	***ancienne***	ancient
-et	***muet***	***muette***	mute
! sometimes !	***inquiet***	***inquiète***	anxious
-on	***bon***	***bonne***	good
-ul	***nul***	***nulle***	no good
The following add a final -e and lengthen the syllable by adding an accent or changing a consonant or consonant group			
-er	***premier***	***première***	first
-ef	***bref***	***brève***	brief
-if	***actif***	***active***	active
-eux	***fameux***	***fameuse***	infamous
-eur	***menteur***	***menteuse***	untruthful
-nc	***blanc***	***blanche***	white
-ic	***public***	***publique***	public
-gu	***aigu***	***aiguë***	acute

The following are examples of irregular adjectives which show additional variations

doux* → *douce (= sweet); ***faux* → *fausse*** (= false)
favori* → *favorite (= favourite); ***frais* → *fraîche*** (= fresh)
gentil* → *gentille (= kind); ***jaloux* → *jalouse*** (= jealous)
malin* → *maligne (= cunning); ***roux* → *rousse*** (= red)
sot* → *sotte (=silly)

5.4 Position of adjectives

- Most adjectives follow the noun; this is because an adjective distinguishes the noun in some way (colour, shape, etc.) and this position gives more emphasis in French: e.g. ***un chocolat chaud*** (= a hot chocolate)
- Some adjectives go before the noun: these are usually common adjectives where a distinguishing feature is less pronounced:
  e.g. ***un vieil ami de la famille*** (= an old family friend)

These may almost become part of the noun as a compound:
e.g. ***un jeune homme*** (= a young man)
les petits enfants (= the little children; the grandchildren)

- Some adjectives change meaning if they go before the noun: e.g. ***la pauvre fille*** (= the poor girl!)
  la fille pauvre (= the girl with little money)
  la mauvaise clé (= the wrong key)
  un animal mauvais (= a vicious animal)
  un seul président (= only one president)
  elle, seule, le sait (= she alone knows that)

5.4.a beau, nouveau, vieux

- These 3 adjectives go before the noun
- They form a group because they have an extra spelling:

Masculine	Masculine with vowel*	Masculine Plural	Feminine	Feminine Plural	English
beau	***bel***	***beaux***	***belle***	***belles***	beautiful
nouveau	***nouvel***	***nouveaux***	***nouvelle***	***nouvelles***	new
vieux	***vieil***	***vieux***	***vieille***	***vieilles***	old

- The extra spelling is used if the noun is masculine and starts with a vowel:

e.g. ***arbre → un bel arbre*** (= a lovely tree)

Examples: ***une belle femme*** (= a beautiful woman)
de nouveaux livres (= new books)
de vieilles histoires (= old stories)

 *Note:* ***des*** changes to ***de*** in front of a plural adjective

6 POSSESSION

- Possession is commonly expressed by using ***de***
- The style used is:
  'the dog of Paul' = ***le chien de Paul*** = Paul's dog
  'the clothes of Sophie' = ***les vêtements de Sophie*** = Sophie's clothes

- Possession is also shown by possessive adjectives (*my*, *your*, etc.):

POSSESSIVE ADJECTIVES

Masculine	Feminine	Plural	English
mon	***ma***	***mes***	my
ton	***ta***	***tes***	your
son	***sa***	***ses***	his/her/its/one's
notre	***notre***	***nos***	our
votre	***votre***	***vos***	your
leur	***leur***	***leurs***	their

- The word matches the gender and number of the 'thing' possessed NOT the speaker:
  e.g. ***ma soeur*** = my sister (the speaker may be male)
- ***ma***, ***ta***, and ***sa*** end in vowels; therefore they are not used before a vowel:
  e.g. NOT ***sa amie*** BUT ***son amie*** = his girlfriend

6.1 mine, yours, etc.

- These are expressed by possessive pronouns
- They reflect the gender and number of the 'thing' possessed:

POSSESSIVE PRONOUNS

Masculine	Feminine	Masculine Plural	Feminine Plural	English
le mien	***la mienne***	***les miens***	***les miennes***	mine
le tien	***la tienne***	***les tiens***	***les tiennes***	yours
le sien	***la sienne***	***les siens***	***les siennes***	his/hers/its
le nôtre	***la nôtre***	***les nôtres***	***les nôtres***	ours
le vôtre	***la vôtre***	***les vôtres***	***les vôtres***	yours
le leur	***la leur***	***les leurs***	***les leurs***	theirs

- The word matches the gender and number of the 'thing' possessed NOT the speaker:
  e.g. ***cette chaise est la mienne*** = this chair is mine (*the speaker may be male*)

7 ADVERBS

- Adverbs usually give additional information about a verb's action: i.e. they say 'how' (= in what way or manner), 'when', 'where' something happens
- Most adverbs are formed from the feminine adjective by adding *-**ment***
  e.g. ***heureux*** → ***heureuse*** → ***heureusement*** (= happily, fortunately)

Exceptions include:

7.1 masculine adjectives ending in a vowel

The feminine *-**e*** is dropped:
e.g. ***hardi*** → ***hardiment*** (= robustly)
résolu→ ***résolument*** (= resolutely)

7.2 adjectives ending in -ant or -ent

The *-**nt*** is dropped and the *-**m**-* is doubled:
e.g. ***constant*** → ***constamment*** (= constantly)
intelligent → ***intelligemment*** (= intelligently)
Note however ***lent*** → ***lentement*** (= slowly)

8 COMPARISON

8.1 Comparative of adjectives and adverbs

- The comparative in English is usually expressed by:
  'more...' (e.g. *more interesting*)
  'as...' (e.g. *as big*)
  'less...' (e.g. *less intelligent*)
  or the suffix '-er' (e.g. *bigger*)
- The comparative in French is expressed in most cases by: 'plus...' (e.g. ***plus intéressant***)
  'aussi...' (e.g. ***aussi grand***)
  'moins...' (e.g. ***moins intelligent***)
- The word for 'than' in French is ***que*** (or ***qu'***)
- The adjective reflects the gender and number of the noun described. Examples:
  il est plus grand que toi = he is taller than you
  cette rue est moins longue que celui-là = this road is shorter than that one

SOME IRREGULAR COMPARATIVES

Adjective	Comparative	English
bon = good	***meilleur***	better
mauvais = bad	***pire***	worse
petit = small	***moindre***	lesser, less great,
! *sometimes* !	***plus petit***	smaller
bien = well	***mieux***	better
mal = badly	***pis***	worse
! *sometimes* !	***plus mal***	
peu = little	***moins***	less

8.2 Superlative of adjectives and adverbs

- The superlative in English is usually expressed by 'most...' (e.g. *most interesting*)
  or the suffix '-est' (e.g. *biggest*)
- The superlative in French is expressed in most cases by: '***le/la/les plus***...' (e.g. ***le plus intéressant***)
- The article is repeated reflecting the gender and number of the noun described:
  e.g. ***la ville la plus belle*** = the most beautiful city
- The superlative is often followed by 'in' which is translated by ***de***...:
  e.g. ***la ville la plus belle du monde*** = the most beautiful city in the world

9 TIMES

- Time phrases begin with ***il est***... (= it is...)
- The French equivalent of 'o' clock' is ***heures***
  BUT 1 o' clock = ***une heure*** (i.e. no -***s*** required in the singular)
- The 24 hour clock is often used to make a.m. and p.m. clear
- The number of hours is stated first before any minutes are detailed:

  minutes 'past' the hour are simply added to the end of the phrase: e.g. ***il est sept heures dix***

'quarter past' is expressed by ***et quart***:
e.g. ***il est sept heures et quart***
minutes 'to' the hour follow the word ***moins*** (= minus):
e.g. ***il est quatre heures moins cinq*** (= five to four)
'quarter to' is expressed by ***moins le quart***:
e.g. ***il est quatre heures moins le quart***
'half past' is expressed by ***et demie***:
e.g. ***il est trois heures et demie***

⚠ *Note:* ***midi*** (= midday) and ***minuit*** (= midnight) are masculine; therefore ***et demie*** changes to ***et demi***: e.g. ***il est midi et demi***

9.1 The cardinal numbers 1-24
[*see* ORDINAL NUMBERS *section 9.5*]

1 un/e	**7** sept	**13** treize	**19** dix-neuf
2 deux	**8** huit	**14** quatorze	**20** vingt
3 trois	**9** neuf	**15** quinze	**21** vingt et un/e
4 quatre	**10** dix	**16** seize	**22** vingt-deux
5 cinq	**11** onze	**17** dix-sept	**23** vingt-trois
6 six	**12** douze	**18** dix-huit	**24** vingt-quatre

Examples:
1.00 = ***il est une heure***
2.00 = ***il est deux heures***
2.10 = ***il est deux heures dix***
2.15 = ***il est deux heures et quart***
[also ***il est deux heures quinze***]
2.30 = ***il est deux heures et demie***
[also ***il est deux heures trente***]
2.35 = ***il est trois heures moins vingt-cinq***
[also ***il est deux heures trente-cinq***]

9.2 The numbers 30-100 (in 10s)

30 trente	**70** soixante-dix
40 quarante	**80** quatre-vingts
50 cinquante	**90** quatre-vingt-dix
60 soixante	**100** cent

9.3 Numbers: norms and exceptions

- Numbers normally count up by linking each digit to 20, 30, etc. by a hyphen: e.g. ***vingt-deux, vingt-trois...***

Exceptions worthy of note include:

- Numbers ending in 1 (*31, 41*, etc.) add ***et un*** (= and one) to the main number: e.g. 61 = ***soixante et un*** EXCEPT for:
  81 (***quatre-vingt-un***); 91 (***quatre-vingt-onze***); 101 (***cent un***):
- Numbers 70-79 are unusual in that they count literally as:
  sixty-ten (***soixante-dix***) = 70
  sixty-eleven (***soixante et onze***) = 71
  sixty-twelve (***soixante-douze***) = 72 etc.
- Numbers 80-100 are unusual in that they count literally as:
  four-twenties (***quatre-vingts***) = 80
  four-twenties-one (***quatre-vingt-un***) = 81
  four-twenties-two (***quatre-vingt-deux***) = 82 etc.
  and over 90...
  four-twenties-seventeen (***quatre-vingt-dix-sept***) = 97 etc.

 *Note:* the final ***-s*** of ***vingts*** is dropped if any digit follows

- Over 100, there is no hyphen linking the 100, 200, etc. with following digits: e.g. ***trois cent dix-huit*** = 318

 *Note:* the final ***-s*** of ***cents*** is dropped if any digit follows

9.4 1000 and year dates

The number 1000 = ***mille***. However, in written dates, ***mille*** changes to ***mil***:
e.g. 1914 = ***mil neuf cent quatorze***

 *Note:* the word ***cent*** is not omitted

9.4.a Other dates

- The article ***le*** is used to specify the day of the month: e.g. ***c'est aujourd'hui le six septembre*** = today is the 6th of September
- The cardinal numbers (***un, deux***, ...) are used (NOT the ordinal numbers as in English style: *1st, 2nd*, etc.)

- sometimes the article ***le*** goes before the day :
  e.g. ***c'est le mardi deux juillet*** = it's Tuesday 2 July

9.5 Ordinal numbers

- The ordinal numbers count focusing on sequence or priority (*first, second, third,* etc.)
- Ordinal numbers in French are usually formed by adding ***-ième*** to the cardinal number:
  e.g. ***deuxième*** (= 2nd), ***troisième*** (= 3rd), etc.
  BUT there are exceptions:
  e.g. ***premier*** = 1st

⚠ *Note:* numbers like 21st do not follow this change:
e.g. 31st = ***trente-et-unième***

- There is sometimes a spelling change:
  e.g. ***neuvième*** = 9th (*-f-* changes to *-v-*)
  onzième = 11th (***onze*** drops the final *-e*)

10 VERBS

- Verbs add action to a phrase (***he kicks the ball***) or they describe a state (***she is lazy***)
- A sentence needs a verb for it to make sense (*he... the dog → he strokes the dog*)
- An infinitive is a verb preceded by 'to' (*I want to go*)
- A finite verb indicates tense (*will go; went*)
- Tense is the time at which something happens, exists, etc.

10.1 Regular verbs

- Some verbs belong to 'regular' groups where they follow the same pattern
- Regular patterns are identified by the endings ***-er, -ir***, and ***-re***
- Some regular verbs are REFLEXIVE which means the action involves *oneself*:
  e.g. ***je me lave*** = I wash myself [*see* PRONOUNS *section 4.3*]

10.1.a Regular verbs in the present tense

The present tense describes what is happening now (*it is raining*) or what regularly happens (*he plays football on Tuesdays*) or a current truth (*she does love chips*)

parler 'to speak' AN EXAMPLE OF AN -ER VERB

je parle = I speak	***nous parlons*** = we speak
tu parles = you speak	***vous parlez*** = you speak
il parle = he speaks	***ils (masc) parlent*** = they speak
elle parle = she speaks	***elles (fem) parlent*** = they speak

- ***tu*** is used to speak to a child or someone known well
- ***vous*** is used in polite speech or to more than one person
- ***ils*** also means 'they' referring to a mixed male and female group
- the translation *I speak*, etc., may also be *I am speaking* and *I do speak*

finir 'to finish' AN EXAMPLE OF AN -IR VERB

je finis = I finish	***nous finissons*** = we finish
tu finis = you finish	***vous finissez*** = you finish
il finit = he finishes	***ils (masc) finissent*** = they finish
elle finit = she finishes	***elles (fem) finissent*** = they finish

- note the lengthened stem -***iss***- in the plural

vendre 'to sell' AN EXAMPLE OF AN -RE VERB

je vends = I sell	***nous vendons*** = we sell
tu vends = you sell	***vous vendez*** = you sell
il vend = he sells	***ils (masc) vendent*** = they sell
elle vend = she sells	***elles (fem) vendent*** = they sell

- note the dropped verb ending with ***il*** and ***elle***

Other present tense patterns are individual to each verb or to a small number of verbs; these are known as 'irregular' verbs. [*see* VERB TABLES]

10.1.b Regular verbs in the imperative

- The imperative is a way of ordering, suggesting strongly
- 3 parts of the present tense are used: ***tu, nous, vous***

- The *-s* is dropped from the ***tu*** part of the verb:
  e.g. ***parle!*** (= talk!); ***parlons!*** (= let's talk!); ***parlez!*** (= talk!)

BUT there are exceptions [*see* VERB TABLES]:
  e.g. ***aie!*** (= have!); ***ayons!*** (= let's have!); ***ayez!*** (= have!)
  sois! (= be!); ***soyons!*** (= let's be!); ***soyez!*** (= be!)
  sache! (= know!); ***sachons!*** (= let's know!); ***sachez!*** (= know!)

10.1.c Regular verbs in the imperfect tense

The imperfect tense describes what was happening in the past (*it was raining*) or what used to be a fact or occurrence (*he used to like chocolate*; *he used to go to classes*); in French it also expresses what happened regularly (***il jouait au football tous les jeudis*** = he played football every Tuesday)

Imperfect tense endings	
-ais	***-ions***
-ais	***-iez***
-ait	***-aient***
-ait	***-aient***

- these endings apply to all verbs
- they are added to a stem
- the stem is taken from the *nous* part of the present tense
  e.g. ***nous finissons → finiss- → je finissais***
- the only irregular stem is ***ét-*** from ***être***:
  e.g. ***j'étais*** (= I was), ***tu étais*** (= you were)...etc.

10.1.d Regular verbs in the future tense

The future tense describes what will happen (*it will rain*) or what is expected to be a fact (*it will be easy*)

Future tense endings	
-ai	***-ons***
-as	***-ez***
-a	***-ont***
-a	***-ont***

- these endings apply to all verbs
- they are added to a stem: the stem is the infinitive
  e.g. ***finir*** → ***je finirai*** (= I shall finish)

BUT ***-re*** verbs drop the final ***-e***:
  e.g. ***vendre*** → ***je vendrai*** (= I shall sell)

- some irregular stems have to be learnt
- the future may also be expressed by:
  the verb ALLER + INFINITIVE = ***je vais finir***...
  (I am going to finish...)

TABLE of irregular future stems: [*see* VERB TABLES]

Infinitive	Future Stem	Infinitive	Future Stem
avoir	***j'aurai*** = I shall have	tenir	***je tiendrai*** = I shall hold
être	***je serai*** = I shall be	vouloir	***je voudrai*** = I shall want
faire	***je ferai*** = I shall make	pouvoir	***je pourrai*** = I shall be able
savoir	***je saurai*** = I shall know	recevoir	***je recevrai*** = I shall get
voir	***je verrai*** = I shall see	devoir	***je devrai*** = I shall have to
envoyer	***j'enverrai*** = I shall send	courir	***je courrai*** = I shall run
venir	***je viendrai*** = I shall come	mourir	***je mourrai*** = I shall die

- compounds of the above have the same stem:
  e.g. ***retenir*** (= to hold back) → ***je retiendrai***

10.1.e Regular verbs in the conditional tense

The conditional tense describes what would happen (*it would make him angry*) or what would be a fact (*it would be easy*)

Formation: = FUTURE STEM + CONDITIONAL ENDINGS

Conditional tense endings	
-ais	***-ions***
-ais	***-iez***
-ait	***-aient***
-ait	***-aient***

- these endings apply to all verbs
  e.g. ***il commencerait*** (= he would begin)
  tu devrais (= you ought to)
- the word ***si*** (= if) is often present or understood in the meaning: e.g. ***il le ferait si tu le lui demandais*** (= he'd do it if you asked him)

10.1.f Regular verbs in the perfect tense

The perfect tense describes what has happened (*it has snowed; they have written*). In French it is also used for what happened and remained the case until a specific point in time (***ils y sont restés jusqu'à mardi*** = they stayed there until Tuesday) or to state an action as part of a series, each action being complete in itself (***je me suis approché de la maison, j'ai sonné à la porte***... = I went up to the house, rang the doorbell...)

Formation of the perfect tense:

- Two common verbs are important in the formation of this tense: AVOIR and ÊTRE

avoir = to have	
j'ai	***nous avons***
tu as	***vous avez***
il a	***ils ont***
elle a	***elles ont***

être = to be	
je suis	***nous sommes***
tu es	***vous êtes***
il est	***ils sont***
elle est	***elles sont***

- 3 parts are needed to make the perfect tense:
  SUBJECT + AVOIR/ÊTRE + PAST PARTICIPLE
- The past participle of regular verbs is made by removing the last syllable of the infinitive (***regarder, choisir,***

rendre) and by replacing it with ***é, -i, -u*** respectively: e.g. ***regarder → regardé → j'ai regardé*** (= I have watched)
choisir → choisi → tu as choisi (= you have chosen)
rendre → rendu → il a rendu (= he has given back)
BUT some past participles have to be learnt [*see* VERB TABLES].

TABLE giving common irregular past participles following the auxiliary (= 'helper') verb *avoir*:

Infinitive	Past Participle	Infinitive	Past Participle
avoir	***j'ai eu*** = I have had	croire	***j'ai cru*** = I have believed
être	***j'ai été*** = I have been	savoir	***j'ai su*** = I have known
faire	***j'ai fait*** = I have made	voir	***j'ai vu*** = I have seen
boire	***j'ai bu*** = I have drunk	pleuvoir	***il a plu*** = it has rained
pouvoir	***j'ai pu*** = I have been able	dire	***j'ai dit*** = I have said
devoir	***j'ai dû*** = I have had to	écrire	***j'ai écrit*** = I have written
lire	***j'ai lu*** = I have read	mettre	***j'ai mis*** = I have put
vouloir	***j'ai voulu*** = I have wanted	prendre	***j'ai pris*** = I have taken

- the past participle does not change its spelling after ***avoir*** unless there is a direct object preceding it: e.g. ***j'ai vendu la table*** (= I sold the table)
BUT ***où est la table que tu as vendue***? (= where is the table you've sold?

■ Most verbs make their perfect tense with ***avoir*** but the exceptions are: 1 reflexive verbs and 2 a small group of verbs of 'motion'. These take ***être*** and the past participle behaves like an adjective.

1 ***se laver*** = to get washed / to wash oneself

je me suis lavé(e) = I got washed
tu t'es lavé(e) = you got washed
il s'est lavé = he got washed
elle s'est lavée = she got washed
nous nous sommes lavé(e)s = we got washed
vous vous êtes lavé(e)(s) = you got washed
ils se sont lavés = they got washed
elles se sont lavées = they got washed

- The alternatives in brackets depend on gender (masculine or feminine) and number (singular or plural)

2 VERBS OF MOTION WHICH TAKE ÊTRE

arriver	***je suis arrivé(e)*** = I arrived
partir	***je suis parti(e)*** = I left
retourner	***je suis retourné(e)*** = I returned
rester	***je suis resté(e)*** = I stayed
tomber	***je suis tombé(e)***= I fell
mourir	***je suis mort(e)*** = I died
naître	***je suis né(e)*** = I was born
monter	***je suis monté(e)*** = I went up
descendre	***je suis descendu(e)*** = I went down
entrer	***je suis entré(e)*** = I entered
aller	***je suis allé(e)*** = I went
sortir	***je suis sorti(e)*** = I went out
venir	***je suis venu(e)*** = I came
revenir	***je suis revenu(e)*** = I came back

- compounds of the above also take ***être*** e.g. ***devenir*** (= to become) → ***je suis devenu(e)***

10.1.g Regular verbs in the pluperfect tense

The pluperfect tense describes what had happened (*it had snowed; they had written*) or what had been the case (*it had been easy*).
Formation: = IMPERFECT TENSE OF AVOIR OR ÊTRE + PAST PARTICIPLE [*see* VERB TABLES]

Examples:
j'avais fini = I had finished
nous avions vendu l'appartement = we had sold the flat
elle s'était réveillée = she had woken up
nous étions partis = we had left

⚠ *Note:* past participles after ***être*** behave in the same way as they do for the perfect tense: i.e. they look like adjectives reflecting the gender and number of the subject

10.1.h Regular verbs in the future perfect tense

The future perfect tense describes what will have happened (*he will have arrived*) or what will have been the case (*it will not have been easy*)

Formation: = FUTURE TENSE OF AVOIR OR ÊTRE + PAST PARTICIPLE [*see* VERB TABLES]

Examples:
j'aurai fini = I shall have finished
nous aurons vendu la voiture= we shall have sold the car
nous serons descendus = we shall have gone down

⚠ *Note:* past participles after ***être*** behave in the same way as they do for the perfect tense: i.e. they look like adjectives reflecting the gender and number of the subject

10.2 Irregular verbs [*see* VERB TABLES]

11 NEGATIVES

- The negative expresses *not, never, no-one*, etc.
- In French the negative usually has 2 parts:
  e.g. ***ne... pas*** (= not), ***ne... jamais*** (= never), ***ne...personne*** (= nobody), etc.
- If the negative is the SUBJECT (*nobody knows*), then the negative reverses:
  i.e. ***ne...personne*** → ***personne ne...***
  e.g. ***personne ne sait***!
- Usually however with verbs, the 2 parts 'sandwich' the finite verb: e.g. ***il ne mange pas*** = he is not eating

BUT if an infinitive is present, they exclude the infinitive from the 'sandwich':

e.g. ***il ne veut pas manger*** = he doesn't want to eat

AND in a compound tense (e.g. *perfect, pluperfect*), they only sandwich the first verb:

e.g. ***il n'est pas allé*** = he didn't go

ALSO if object pronouns are present, these 'cling' to the verb within the 'sandwich':

e.g. ***elle l'a acheté*** → ***elle ne l'a pas acheté***
(= she didn't buy it)

- If no verb is present, as in a short response, then the ***ne***... is omitted:
  e.g. '***Qui a frappé***?' - '***Personne!***' (= 'Who knocked ?' 'Nobody!')

French verbs

1 chanter

Present indicative

je	chante
tu	chantes
il	chante
nous	chantons
vous	chantez
ils	chantent

Future indicative

je	chanterai
tu	chanteras
il	chantera
nous	chanterons
vous	chanterez
ils	chanteront

Imperfect indicative

je	chantais
tu	chantais
il	chantait
nous	chantions
vous	chantiez
ils	chantaient

Perfect indicative

j'	ai	chanté
tu	as	chanté
il	a	chanté
elle	a	chanté
nous	avons	chanté
vous	avez	chanté
ils	ont	chanté
elles	ont	chanté

Present subjunctive

(que)	je	chante
(que)	tu	chantes
(qu')	il	chante
(que)	nous	chantions
(que)	vous	chantiez
(qu')	ils	chantent

Present conditional

je	chanterais
tu	chanterais
il	chanterait
nous	chanterions
vous	chanteriez
ils	chanteraient

Past participle

chanté/chantée

Pluperfect indicative

j'	avais	chanté
tu	avais	chanté
il	avait	chanté
elle	avait	chanté
nous	avions	chanté
vous	aviez	chanté
ils	avaient	chanté
elles	avaient	chanté

2 finir

Present indicative

je	finis
tu	finis
il	finit
nous	finissons
vous	finissez
ils	finissent

Future indicative

je	finirai
tu	finiras
il	finira
nous	finirons
vous	finirez
ils	finiront

Imperfect indicative

je	finissais
tu	finissais
il	finissait
nous	finissions
vous	finissiez
ils	finissaient

Perfect indicative

j'	ai	fini
tu	as	fini
il	a	fini
elle	a	fini
nous	avons	fini
vous	avez	fini
ils	ont	fini
elles	ont	fini

Present subjunctive

(que)	je	finisse
(que)	tu	finisses
(qu')	il	finisse
(que)	nous	finissions
(que)	vous	finissiez
(qu')	ils	finissent

Present conditional

je	finirais
tu	finirais
il	finirait
nous	finirions
vous	finiriez
ils	finiraient

Past participle

fini/finie

Pluperfect indicative

j'	avais	fini
tu	avais	fini
il	avait	fini
elle	avait	fini
nous	avions	fini
vous	aviez	fini
ils	avaient	fini
elles	avaient	fini

3 attendre

Present indicative

j'	attends
tu	attends
il	attend
nous	attendons
vous	attendez
ils	attendent

Future indicative

j'	attendrai
tu	attendras
il	attendra
nous	attendrons
vous	attendrez
ils	attendront

Imperfect indicative

j'	attendais
tu	attendais
il	attendait
nous	attendions
vous	attendiez
ils	attendaient

Perfect indicative

j'	ai	attendu
tu	as	attendu
il	a	attendu
elle	a	attendu
nous	avons	attendu
vous	avez	attendu
ils	ont	attendu
elles	ont	attendu

Present subjunctive

(que)	j'	attende
(que)	tu	attendes
(qu')	il	attende
(que)	nous	attendions
(que)	vous	attendiez
(qu')	ils	attendent

Present conditional

j'	attendrais
tu	attendrais
il	attendrait
nous	attendrions
vous	attendriez
ils	attendraient

Past participle

attendu/attendue

Pluperfect indicative

j'	avais	attendu
tu	avais	attendu
il	avait	attendu
elle	avait	attendu
nous	avions	attendu
vous	aviez	attendu
ils	avaient	attendu
elles	avaient	attendu

4 être

Present indicative

je	suis
tu	es
il	est
nous	sommes
vous	êtes
ils	sont

Future indicative

je	serai
tu	seras
il	sera
nous	serons
vous	serez
ils	seront

Imperfect indicative

j'	étais
tu	étais
il	était
nous	étions
vous	étiez
ils	étaient

Perfect indicative

j'	ai	été
tu	as	été
il	a	été
elle	a	été
nous	avons	été
vous	avez	été
ils	ont	été
elles	ont	été

Present subjunctive

(que)	je	sois
(que)	tu	sois
(qu')	il	soit
(que)	nous	soyons
(que)	vous	soyez
(qu')	ils	soient

Present conditional

je	serais
tu	serais
il	serait
nous	serions
vous	seriez
ils	seraient

Past participle

été (*invariable*)

Pluperfect indicative

j'	avais	été
tu	avais	été
il	avait	été
elle	avait	été
nous	avions	été
vous	aviez	été
ils	avaient	été
elles	avaient	été

5 avoir

Present indicative

j'	ai
tu	as
il	a
nous	avons
vous	avez
ils	ont

Future indicative

j'	aurai
tu	auras
il	aura
nous	aurons
vous	aurez
ils	auront

Imperfect indicative

j'	avais
tu	avais
Il	avait
nous	avions
vous	aviez
ils	avaient

Perfect indicative

j'	ai	eu
tu	as	eu
il	a	eu
elle	a	eu
nous	avons	eu
vous	avez	eu
ils	ont	eu
elles	ont	eu

Present subjunotive

(que)	j'	aie
(que)	tu	aies
(qu')	il	ait
(que)	nous	ayons
(que)	vous	ayez
(qu')	ils	aient

Present conditional

j'	aurais
tu	aurais
il	aurait
nous	aurions
vous	auriez
ils	auraient

Past participle

eu/eue

Pluperfect indicative

j'	avais	eu
tu	avais	eu
il	avait	eu
elle	avait	eu
nous	avions	eu
vous	aviez	eu
ils	avaient	eu
elles	avaient	eu

[6] acheter
1 j'achète **2** j'achèterai **3** j'achetais **4** que j'achète **5** acheté

[7] acquérir
1 j'acquiers, nous acquérons, ils acquièrent **2** j'acquerrai **3** j'acquérais **4** que j'acquière **5** acquis

[8] aller
1 je vais, tu vas, il va, nous allons, vous allez, ils vont **2** j'irai **3** j'allais **4** que j'aille, que nous allions, qu'ils aillent **5** allé

[9] asseoir
1 j'assois, tu assois, il assoit, nous assoyons, vous assoyez, ils assoient **2** j'assoirai **3** j'assoyais **4** que j'assoie, que nous assoyions, qu'ils assoient **5** assis

[10] avancer
1 nous avançons **3** j'avançais

[11] battre
1 je bats, il bat, nous battons **2** je battrai **3** je battais **4** que je batte **5** battu

[12] boire
1 je bois, il boit, nous buvons, ils boivent **2** je boirai **3** je buvais **4** que je boive **5** bu

[13] bouillir
1 je bous, il bout, nous bouillons, ils bouillent **2** je bouillirai **3** je bouillais **4** que je bouille **5** bouilli

[14] céder
1 je cède, nous cédons, ils cèdent **2** je céderai **3** je cédais **4** que je cède **5** cédé

[15] créer
1 je crée, nous créons **2** je créerai **3** je créais **4** que je crée **5** créé

[16] conclure
1 je conclus, il conclut, nous concluons, ils concluent **2** je conclurai **3** je concluais **4** que je conclue **5** conclu (*but* inclus)

[17] conduire
1 je conduis, nous conduisons **2** je conduirai **3** je conduisais **4** que je conduise **5** conduit (*but* lui, nui)

[18] connaître
1 je connais, il connaît, nous connaissons **2** je connaîtrai **3** je connaissais **4** que je connaisse **5** connu

[19] coudre
1 je couds, il coud, nous cousons, ils cousent **2** je coudrai **3** je cousais **4** que je couse **5** cousu

[20] courir
1 je cours, il court, nous courons, ils courent **2** je courrai **3** je courais **4** que je coure **5** couru

[21] couvrir
1 je couvre **2** je couvrirai

3 je couvrais **4** que je couvre **5** couvert

[22] craindre
1 je crains, il craint, nous craignons, ils craignent **2** je craindrai **3** je craignais **4** que je craigne **5** craint

[23] croire
1 je crois, il croit, nous croyons, ils croient **2** je croirai **3** je croyais, nous croyions **4** que je croie, que nous croyions **5** cru

[24] croître
1 je croîs, il croît, nous croissons **2** je croîtrai **3** je croissais **4** que je croisse **5** crû/crue (*but* accru, décru)

[25] cueillir
1 je cueille **2** je cueillerai **3** je cueillais **4** que je cueille **5** cueilli

[26] devoir
1 je dois, il doit, nous devons, ils doivent **2** je devrai **3** je devais **4** que je doive, que nous devions **5** dû/due

[27] dire
1 je dis, il dit, nous disons, vous dites, ils disent **2** je dirai **3** je disais **4** que je dise **5** dit

[28] dissoudre
1 je dissous, il dissout, nous dissolvons, ils dissolvent **2** je dissoudrai **3** je dissolvais **4** que je dissolve **5** dissous/dissoute

[29] distraire
1 je distrais, il distrait, nous distrayons **2** je distrairai **3** je distrayais **4** que je distraie **5** distrait

[30] écrire
1 j'écris, il écrit, nous écrivons **2** j'écrirai **3** j'écrivais **4** que j'écrive **5** écrit

[31] employer
1 j'emploie, nous employons, ils emploient **2** j'emploierai **3** j'employais, nous employions **4** que j'emploie, que nous employions **5** employé

[32] envoyer
1 j'envoie, nous envoyons, ils envoient **2** j'enverrai **3** j'envoyais, nous envoyions **4** que j'envoie, que nous envoyions **5** envoyé

[33] faire
1 je fais, nous faisons (*say* /fəzɔ̃/), vous faites, ils font **2** je ferai **3** je faisais (*say* /fəzɛ/) **4** que je fasse, que nous fassions **5** fait

[34] falloir (*impersonal*)
1 il faut **2** il faudra **3** il fallait **4** qu'il faille **5** fallu

[35] fuir
1 je fuis, nous fuyons **2** je fuirai **3** je fuyais, nous fuyions **4** que je fuie, que nous fuyions **5** fui

[**36**] **haïr**
1 je hais, il hait, nous haïssons, ils haïssent **2** je haïrai **3** je haïssais **4** que je haïsse **5** haï

[**37**] **interdire**
1 j'interdis, vous interdisez **2** j'interdirai **3** j'interdisais **4** que j'interdise **5** interdit

[**38**] **jeter**
1 je jette, nous jetons, ils jettent **2** je jetterai **3** je jetais **4** que je jette **5** jeté

[**39**] **lire**
1 je lis, il lit, nous lisons **2** je lirai **3** je lisais **4** que je lise **5** lu

[**40**] **manger**
1 je mange, nous mangeons **2** je mangerai **3** je mangeais **4** que je mange, que nous mangions **5** mangé

[**41**] **maudire**
1 je maudis, il maudit, nous maudissons **2** je maudirai **3** je maudissais **4** que je maudisse **5** maudit

[**42**] **mettre**
1 je mets, tu mets, nous mettons **2** je mettrai **3** je mettais **4** que je mette **5** mis

[**43**] **mourir**
1 je meurs, il meurt, nous mourons **2** je mourrai **3** je mourais **4** que je meure **5** mort

[**44**] **naître**
1 je nais, il naît, nous naissons **2** je naîtrai **3** je naissais **4** que je naisse **5** né

[**45**] **oublier**
1 j'oublie, nous oublions, ils oublient **2** j'oublierai **3** j'oubliais, nous oubliions, vous oubliiez **4** que nous oubliions, que vous oubliiez **5** oublié

[**46**] **partir**
1 je pars, nous partons **2** je partirai **3** je partais **4** que je parte **5** parti

[**47**] **plaire**
1 je plais, il plaît (*but* il tait), nous plaisons **2** je plairai **3** je plaisais **4** que je plaise **5** plu

[**48**] **pleuvoir** (*impersonal*)
1 il pleut **2** il pleuvra **3** il pleuvait **4** qu'il pleuve **5** plu

[**49**] **pouvoir**
1 je peux, il peut, nous pouvons, ils peuvent **2** je pourrai **3** je pouvais **4** que je puisse, que nous puissions **5** pu

[**50**] **prendre**
1 je prends, il prend, nous prenons **2** je prendrai **3** je prenais **4** que je prenne **5** pris

[**51**] **prévoir**
1 je prévois, il prévoit, nous prévoyons, ils prévoient **2** je prévoirai **3** je prévoyais,

nous prévoyions **4** que je prévoie, que nous prévoyions **5** prévu

[52] recevoir
1 je reçois, il reçoit, nous recevons, ils reçoivent **2** je recevrai **3** je recevais **4** que je reçoive, que nous recevions **5** reçu

[53] résoudre
1 je résous, il résout, nous résolvons, ils résolvent **2** je résoudrai **3** je résolvais **4** que je résolve **5** résolu

[54] rire
1 je ris, nous rions, ils rient **2** je rirai **3** je riais, nous riions **4** que je rie, que nous riions **5** ri

[55] savoir
1 je sais, il sait, nous savons, ils savent **2** je saurai **3** je savais **4** que je sache, que nous sachions **5** su

[56] suffire
1 il suffit, ils suffisent **2** il suffira **3** il suffisait **4** qu'il suffise **5** suffi (*but* frit)

[57] suivre
1 je suis, il suit, nous suivons **2** je suivrai **3** je suivais **4** que je suive **5** suivi

[58] tenir
1 je tiens, il tient, nous tenons, ils tiennent **2** je tiendrai **3** je tenais **4** que je tienne, que nous tenions **5** tenu

[59] vaincre
1 je vaincs, il vainc, nous vainquons, ils vainquent **2** je vaincrai **3** je vainquais **4** que je vainque **5** vaincu

[60] valoir
1 je vaux, il vaut, nous valons **2** je vaudrai **3** je valais **4** que je vaille, que nous valions **5** valu

[61] vêtir
1 je vêts, il vêt, nous vêtons **2** je vêtirai **3** je vêtais **4** que je vête **5** vêtu

[62] vivre
1 je vis, il vit, nous vivons, ils vivent **2** je vivrai **3** je vivais **4** que je vive **5** vécu

[63] voir
1 je vois, nous voyons, ils voient **2** je verrai **3** je voyais, nous voyions **4** que je voie, que nous voyions **5** vu

[64] vouloir
1 je veux, il veut, nous voulons, ils veulent **2** je voudrai **3** je voulais **4** que je veuille, que nous voulions **5** voulu

What are the equivalent tenses in English

Present indicative
je chante = *I sing, I'm singing*

Future indicative
je chanterai = *I will sing*

Imperfect indicative
je chantais = *I was singing*

Perfect indicative
j'ai chanté
= *I sang, I have sung*

Pluperfect indicative
j'avais chanté = *I had sung*

Present subjunctive
bien que je chante
= *although I sing*

Present conditional
si je pouvais, je chanterais
= *if I could, I would sing*

Past participle
chanté/chantée = *sung*

How to conjugate a reflexive verb

Present indicative and other simple tenses

je me lave
tu te laves
il se lave
elle se lave
nous nous lavons
vous vous lavez
ils se lavent
elles se lavent

in the negative form

je ne me lave pas
tu ne te laves pas
il ne se lave pas
elle ne se lave pas
nous ne nous lavons pas
vous ne vous lavez pas
ils ne se lavent pas
elles ne se lavent pas

Perfect indicative and other compound tenses
(always with auxiliary ***être****)*

je me suis lavé
tu t'es lavé
il s'est lavé
elle s'est lavée
nous nous sommes lavés
vous vous êtes lavés
ils se sont lavés
elles se sont lavées

in the negative form

je ne me suis pas lavé
tu ne t'es pas lavé
il ne s'est pas lavé
elle ne s'est pas lavée
nous ne nous sommes pas lavés
vous ne vous êtes pas lavés
ils ne se sont pas lavés
elles ne se sont pas lavées